THE WEEKLY
LAW REPORTS
1978

VOLUME 3

London
THE INCORPORATED COUNCIL OF LAW REPORTING
FOR ENGLAND AND WALES
3 STONE BUILDINGS, LINCOLN'S INN, LONDON, WC2A 3XN

*Published by the Incorporated
Council of Law Reporting for
England and Wales · 3 Stone
Buildings, Lincoln's Inn, London,
WC2A 3XN, and printed by The
Eastern Press Ltd., London and
Reading*

THE INCORPORATED COUNCIL OF LAW REPORTING FOR ENGLAND AND WALES

EDITORS AND REPORTERS

*

Editor—C. J. Ellis, *Barrister-at-Law*

Assistant Editor—H. Jellie, *Barrister-at-Law*

*

REPORTERS

House of Lords
F. H. Cowper   J. A. Griffiths

Privy Council
T. J. Moeran

Court of Appeal, Queen's Bench Division and Courts-Martial Appeal Court

M. M. Hill   E. M. Wellwood   A. H. Bray
L. Norman Williams   M. Gardner   H. Jellie
C. Noon   J. Winch   L. G. Stott

Chancery Division
Akhtar Razi   T. C. C. Barkworth   K. N. Busfield

Family Division
M. Bryn Davies

Employment Appeal Tribunal
J. Winch

Barristers-at-Law

HOUSE OF LORDS

Lord Chancellor: LORD ELWYN-JONES

LORDS OF APPEAL IN ORDINARY

LORD WILBERFORCE
LORD DIPLOCK
VISCOUNT DILHORNE
LORD SALMON
LORD EDMUND-DAVIES

LORD FRASER OF TULLYBELTON
LORD RUSSELL OF KILLOWEN
LORD KEITH OF KINKEL
LORD SCARMAN

COURT OF APPEAL

Lord Chancellor: LORD ELWYN-JONES

Lord Chief Justice of England: LORD WIDGERY

Master of the Rolls: LORD DENNING

President of the Family Division: Sir GEORGE GILLESPIE BAKER

Sir JOHN MEGAW
Sir DENYS BURTON BUCKLEY
Sir EDWARD BLANSHARD STAMP
   (retired November 10, 1978)
Sir JOHN FREDERICK EUSTACE STEPHENSON
Sir ALAN STEWART ORR
Sir EUSTACE WENTWORTH ROSKILL
Sir FREDERICK HORACE LAWTON
Sir ROGER FRAY GREENWOOD ORMROD
Sir PATRICK REGINALD EVELYN BROWNE
Sir GEOFFREY DAWSON LANE

Sir REGINALD WILLIAM GOFF
Sir NIGEL CYPRIAN BRIDGE
Sir SEBAG SHAW
Sir GEORGE STANLEY WALLER
The Hon. Sir JAMES ROUALEYN-HOVELL-
   THURLOW CUMMING-BRUCE
Sir EDWARD WALTER EVELEIGH
Sir HENRY VIVIAN BRANDON, M.C.
   (appointed September 29, 1978)
Sir SYDNEY WILLIAM TEMPLEMAN
   (appointed November 13, 1978)

CHANCERY DIVISION

Lord Chancellor: LORD ELWYN-JONES

Vice-Chancellor: Sir ROBERT EDGAR MEGARRY

Sir JOHN PATRICK GRAHAM
Sir PETER HARRY BATSON WOODROFFE
  FOSTER
Sir JOHN NORMAN KEATES WHITFORD
Sir JOHN ANSON BRIGHTMAN
Sir ERNEST IRVINE GOULDING
Sir SYDNEY WILLIAM TEMPLEMAN
Sir RAYMOND HENRY WALTON

Sir PETER RAYMOND OLIVER
Sir MICHAEL JOHN FOX
Sir CHRISTOPHER JOHN SLADE
Sir NICOLAS CHRISTOPHER HENRY
  BROWNE-WILKINSON
Sir JOHN EVELYN VINELOTT
   (appointed December 4, 1978)

QUEEN'S BENCH DIVISION

Lord Chief Justice of England: LORD WIDGERY

Sir AUBREY MELFORD STEED STEVENSON
Sir GERALD ALFRED THESIGER
Sir BASIL NIELD (retired May 7, 1978)
Sir ALAN ABRAHAM MOCATTA
Sir JOHN THOMPSON
Sir HELENUS PATRICK JOSEPH MILMO
Sir JOSEPH DONALDSON CANTLEY
Sir HUGH EAMES PARK
Sir RALPH VINCENT CUSACK
        (died March 11, 1978)
Sir STEPHEN CHAPMAN
Sir JOHN RAMSAY WILLIS
Sir GRAHAM RUSSELL SWANWICK
Sir PATRICK MCCARTHY O'CONNOR
Sir JOHN FRANCIS DONALDSON
Sir SAMUEL BURGESS RIDGWAY COOKE
        (died April 12, 1978)
Sir BERNARD CAULFIELD
Sir HILARY GWYNNE TALBOT
Sir WILLIAM LLOYD MARS-JONES
Sir RALPH KILNER BROWN
Sir PHILLIP WIEN
Sir PETER HENRY ROWLEY BRISTOW
Sir HUGH HARRY VALENTINE FORBES
Sir DESMOND JAMES CONRAD ACKNER
Sir WILLIAM HUGH GRIFFITHS
Sir TASKER WATKINS, V.C.
Sir ROBERT HUGH MAIS
Sir NEIL LAWSON
Sir DAVID POWELL CROOM-JOHNSON

Sir JOHN RAYMOND PHILLIPS
Sir LESLIE KENNETH EDWARD BOREHAM
Sir JOHN DOUGLAS MAY
Sir MICHAEL ROBERT EMANUEL KERR
Sir ALFRED WILLIAM MICHAEL DAVIES
Sir JOHN DEXTER STOCKER
Sir KENNETH GEORGE ILLTYD JONES
Sir HAYDN TUDOR EVANS
        (transferred from Family Division,
                June 6, 1978)
Sir PETER RICHARD PAIN
Sir STEPHEN BROWN
Sir KENNETH GRAHAM JUPP
Sir ROBERT LIONEL ARCHIBALD GOFF
Sir GORDON SLYNN
Sir ROGER JOCELYN PARKER
Sir RALPH BRIAN GIBSON
Sir WALTER DEREK THORNLEY HODGSON
Sir ANTHONY JOHN LESLIE LLOYD
        (appointed January 9, 1978)
Sir FREDERICK MAURICE DRAKE, D.F.C.
        (appointed March 3, 1978)
Sir BRIAN THOMAS NEILL
        (appointed April 3, 1978)
Sir RODERICK PHILIP SMITH
        (appointed April 10, 1978)
Sir MICHAEL JOHN MUSTILL
        (appointed June 19, 1978)
Sir BARRY CROSS SHEEN
        (appointed September 29, 1978)

FAMILY DIVISION

President: Sir GEORGE GILLESPIE BAKER

Sir REGINALD WITHERS PAYNE
Sir JOHN BRINSMEAD LATEY
Dame ELIZABETH KATHLEEN LANE
Sir HENRY VIVIAN BRANDON, M.C.
Sir ROBIN HORACE WALFORD DUNN, M.C.
Sir ALFRED KENNETH HOLLINGS
Sir JOHN LEWIS ARNOLD
Sir CHARLES TREVOR REEVE
Sir FRANCIS BROOKS PURCHAS
Sir HAYDN TUDOR EVANS
Dame ROSE HEILBRON

Sir BRIAN DREX BUSH
Sir ALFRED JOHN BALCOMBE
Sir JOHN KEMBER WOOD
Sir JAMES PETER COMYN
        (appointed January 9, 1978)
Sir RONALD GOUGH WATERHOUSE
        (appointed January 9, 1978)
Sir JOHN GERVASSE KENSINGTON SHELDON
        (appointed March 3, 1978)
Sir THOMAS MICHAEL EASTHAM
        (appointed May 8, 1978)

ATTORNEY-GENERAL

SAM SILKIN, ESQ., Q.C.

SOLICITOR-GENERAL

PETER ARCHER, ESQ., Q.C.

CASES REPORTED

(Vol. 3)

SUBJECT MATTER

(Vol. 3)

HABEAS CORPUS
Commonwealth immigrant
Validity of return
    Detention order erroneously stating detention for further examination of immigrant
        —Examination completed—Whether order valid—Court's jurisdiction—Immigra-
        tion Act 1971, Sch. 2, para. 16 (1) (2)—Habeas Corpus Act 1816, ss. 3, 4
                                                    In re **Shahid Iqbal**, D.C. 884

HOUSING
Repairs
Local authority notice
    Works required to bring property to reasonable standard—Cost of required works
        exceeding value of house with sitting tenant after repair—Value of house—
        Appeal against notices—Discretion of judge—Financial implications for owners—
        Relevance—Housing Act 1957, ss. 9 (1A) (inserted by Housing Act 1969, s. 72),
        11 (1) (3), 39 (1)
                Hillbank Properties Ltd. v. Hackney London Borough Council, C.A. 260

HUSBAND AND WIFE
Divorce
Ancillary relief
    Court's jurisdiction
        Wife's application for ancillary relief for children—Wife's remarriage—Whether
            amendment of application to enable wife to apply for lump sum order
            permissible—Matrimonial Causes Act 1973, s. 28 (3)
                                    Nixon v. Fox (formerly Nixon), Dunn J. 565

Financial provision
Agreement
    Order of Court
        Undefended suit—Certificate of approval granted by registrar—Wife seeking to
            resile from agreement before hearing—Jurisdiction to review agreement—
            Matrimonial Causes Act 1973, s. 25   **Dean v. Dean**, Bush J. 288

Injunction
Injunction against abortion
    Paternal rights
        Husband seeking to restrain wife from having abortion—Whether husband
            having statutory or other right to prevent abortion—Abortion Act 1967, s. 1
                        Paton v. British Pregnancy Advisory Service Trustees,
                                                        Sir George Baker P. 687
Practice
Discovery
    Company documents *see* COMPANY: **Director**

INDUSTRIAL RELATIONS
Industrial tribunals
Procedure
    Discovery and inspection of documents—Complaint of discrimination on grounds
        of sex and trade unionism—Complaint of racial discrimination—Discovery of
        documents concerning other employees requested in both cases—Discretion of
        tribunal chairman or judge in county court to inspect documents and rule on
        disclosure—County Court Rules, Ord. 14, rr. 1, 2—Industrial Tribunals (Labour
        Relations) Regulations 1974, Sch., r. 4 (2) (*a*) (*b*)
                                        Science Research Council v. Nassé, C.A. 754
                                        Leyland Cars Ltd. v. Vyas, C.A. 754

INJUNCTION
Domestic violence
Exclusion from " matrimonial " home
    Man and woman living together—Joint tenants of council house—Breakdown of
        relationship—No serious physical violence—Need to provide home for children
        —Whether county court having jurisdiction to order man's exclusion from
        house—Domestic Violence and Matrimonial Proceedings Act 1976, ss. 1 (1)
        (*a*) (*b*) (*c*), 2 (1)   **Spindlow v. Spindlow**, C.A. 777

A

The Weekly Law Reports

B

Volume 3

Containing those cases which are intended to be included in
The Law Reports

C

[COURT OF APPEAL]

FIRMAN v. ELLIS

D

INCE AND OTHERS v. ROGERS

DOWN v. HARVEY AND OTHERS

PHEASANT AND OTHERS v. S. T. H. SMITH (TYRES) LTD. AND ANOTHER

E

[1977 F. No. 545; 1977 I. No. 4376; 1976 D. No. 40; 1977 D. No. 115; 1976 P. No. 1493]

1978 Jan. 11, 12;　　　　　　　　　　　Lord Denning M.R., Ormrod and
　　　Feb. 6　　　　　　　　　　　　　　　　Geoffrey Lane L.JJ.

F

Limitation of Action—Personal injuries—Time limit—Court's power
to override time limit—Writs issued but not served during
negotiations—Failure by Plaintiffs' solicitors to serve or renew
writs within limitation period—New writs issued—Court's dis-
cretion to " disapply " normal three-year limitation period—
Whether plaintiffs' possible remedy against own solicitors
relevant circumstance to be taken into account in exercising
discretion—Practice—Application to judge—Limitation Act
1939 (2 & 3 Geo. 6, c. 21) (as amended by Limitation Act 1975
G　*(c. 54), s. 1), s. 2D—Limitation Act 1975, s. 3*

After the Limitation Act 1975 came into operation plaintiffs in four actions, who had been injured in road collisions
on various dates, three of the accidents being in 1973 and the
fourth in 1970, applied to a judge of the High Court to be
allowed to proceed with their claims which were otherwise
statute-barred. In the first three cases, the claims had been
H　made soon after the accidents and the writs issued in time;
liability was not disputed; and negotiations for a settlement
were being carried on with the defendants' insurers, while
further delays were caused by medical examinations and reports.
In each case, by an oversight of plaintiffs' solicitors, the writs
issued were not served on the defendants or renewed within
the year provided under the Rules of the Supreme Court, and
applications to renew them out of time were opposed by the
defendants, who relied on the defence that the actions were
statute-barred under the Limitation Act 1939, though none was

1

Firman v. Ellis (C.A.)   [1978]

prejudiced thereby since they were well informed of the plain- A
tiffs' claims. In each case the registrar or master and the
judge on appeal had refused leave to renew the writs and held
that the actions were statute-barred.

In the fourth case, the defendant car driver had joined as
third parties a tyre company whose negligent repair of his
tyres was alleged by him to have caused the accident; the
plaintiffs therefore sought to amend their writ to join the tyre
company as defendants and the company agreed to an applica- B
tion for the joinder on a date within the limitation period; but
by a clerical error in the plaintiffs' solicitors' office, the application was made one day out of time; and though the registrar
granted leave to amend the writ to join the company as
defendants, that order was made in the absence of the company. The company thereupon applied to another registrar to
set the joinder order aside; the registrar did so, and Rees J. on
appeal set it aside on the ground, inter alia, that there was no C
power to add a defendant after the limitation period had
expired.

On the plaintiffs issuing new writs and subsequent applications, four judges of the High Court exercised their discretion
to allow the actions to proceed under section 2D (1) of the Act
of 1939 [1]; in the third case Lawson J., while granting the
application to proceed on a new writ, rejected an application
by the plaintiffs for leave to proceed by renewing the original D
writ under R.S.C., Ord. 6, r. 8.

In the fourth case, the defendants claimed on the trial of
preliminary issues before Cusack J. that the plaintiffs' action
could not be allowed to proceed and that they could not rely
on the retrospective provisions of section 3 of the Act of
1975 [2] because the order of Rees J. setting aside the amended
writ and joinder of the company was "a final order or judgment" within section 3 (2); that that disposed of the cause of E
action so far as the tyre company was concerned; that the
plaintiffs were estopped from reopening it; and that the issue
of limitation decided by Rees J. was res judicata. Cusack J.

[1] Limitation Act 1939, as amended, s. 2D: " (1) If it appears to the court that
it would be equitable to allow an action to proceed having regard to the degree to
which—(a) the provisions of section 2A or 2B of this Act prejudice the plaintiff
or any person whom he represents, and (b) any decision of the court under this F
subsection would prejudice the defendant or any person whom he represents, the
court may direct that those provisions shall not apply to the action, or shall not
apply to any specified cause of action to which the action relates. . . . (3) In acting
under this section the court shall have regard to all the circumstances of the case
and in particular to—(a) the length of, and the reasons for, the delay on the part
of the plaintiff; (b) the extent to which, having regard to the delay, the evidence
adduced or likely to be adduced by the plaintiff or the defendant is or is likely to
be less cogent than if the action had been brought within the time allowed by
section 2A or as the case may be 2B; (c) the conduct of the defendant after the G
cause of action arose, including the extent if any to which he responded to requests
reasonably made by the plaintiff for information or inspection for the purpose of
ascertaining facts which were or might be relevant to the plaintiff's cause of action
against the defendant; (d) the duration of any disability of the plaintiff arising after
the date of the accrual of the cause of action; (e) the extent to which the plaintiff
acted promptly and reasonably once he knew whether or not the act or omission
of the defendant, to which the injury was attributable, might be capable at that time
of giving rise to an action for damages; (f) the steps, if any, taken by the plaintiff
to obtain medical, legal or other expert advice and the nature of any such advice he H
may have received."

[2] Limitation Act 1975, s. 3: " (1) The provisions of this Act shall have effect in
relation to causes of action which accrued before, as well as causes of action which
accrue after, the commencement of this Act, and shall have effect in relation to any
cause of action which accrued before the commencement of this Act notwithstanding
that an action in respect thereof has been commenced and is pending at the commencement of this Act. (2) For the purposes of this section an action shall not be
taken to be pending at any time if a final order or judgment has been made or
given therein, notwithstanding that an appeal is pending or that the time for
appealing has not expired. . . ."

A   ordered that the plaintiffs' action against the company could proceed.

On appeal by the defendants in all four cases and a cross-appeal by the plaintiffs in the third action against Lawson J.'s refusal to give them leave to renew their original writ: —

Held, dismissing the defendants' appeals and the cross-appeal, (1) that Parliament had by clear words in section 2D conferred on the court a virtually unfettered discretion to

B   allow any action for damages for personal injuries to proceed after the normal three-year limitation had expired if it appeared to the court "equitable" to do so; that the case for exercising that discretion in favour of the plaintiffs in the cases under appeal was overwhelming, since it would prejudice them greatly to hold that their actions were statute-barred by reason of minor slips by their solicitors, whereas to allow the actions to proceed would not in the least prejudice defendants who had

C   been fully apprised of the claims soon after the cause of action accrued and who now sought to take advantage of the limitation defence, and thereby to transfer liability for damages from their own insurers to those of the plaintiffs' solicitors, a fortiori (*per* Ormrod L.J.) where, in the first three cases, the relevant circumstances to which the court had to have regard in acting under section 2D, set out in subsection (3) (*a*) to (*f*), were satisfied by those plaintiffs.

D   *Per curiam.* The grant by Parliament of the wide discretion to the courts by section 2D is a revolutionary and valuable change which will enable justice to be done even at the expense of some certainty; and the relevant words of the statute are so clear that they cannot be construed restrictively as applying only to exceptional cases.

Per Lord Denning M.R. In construing the new provisions

E   the court can and should consider the Law Reform Committee's Report to Parliament in 1974 as part of the background to the Act (post, p. 11A).

Per Ormrod and Geoffrey Lane L.JJ. Where the words of a statute are capable of having only one meaning, no further inquiry from reports of committees is proper or permissible (post, pp. 17G—18A, 21G, H).

F   (2) That the plaintiffs in the fourth action should also be allowed to proceed by issuing a fresh writ joining the tyre company as defendants, for (*per* Ormrod and Geoffrey Lane L.JJ.) though the registrar's order allowing them to join the company was not a nullity it became void when successfully challenged before Rees J. (*per* Lord Denning M.R.) the registrar's order allowing the joinder was void ab initio since it was made in the company's absence and everything that followed on it was equally void; that, accordingly, the plaintiffs could

G   not be said to have "commenced an action" concluded by "a final order" and they were therefore within the provisions of section 3 of the Act of 1975 and could commence an action by issuing a fresh writ joining the company as defendants, since there was no res which could found an estoppel and they were not estopped by res judicata.

(3) That applications under section 2D should be made by

H   the issue of a fresh writ and not by seeking the renewal of the original writ; and, in view of the wide range of matters to be considered in exercising the discretion under section 2D such applications should be made to a judge, and not to a master or a registrar, for decision.

Heaven v. *Road and Rail Wagons Ltd.* [1965] 2 Q.B. 355 considered.

(4) That as the court exercising the new discretion under section 2D had under subsection (3) to have regard to "all the circumstances of the case," the existence or non-existence of a

Firman v. Ellis (C.A.)   [1978]

remedy against the plaintiffs' solicitors was one of those cir- A
cumstances.
   Dicta in *Birkett* v. *James* [1978] A.C. 297, H.L.(E.) distinguished.
   Orders of Kerr, Talbot, Lawson and Cusack JJ. affirmed.

The following cases are referred to in the judgments:

Anisminic Ltd. v. *Foreign Compensation Commission* [1969] 2 A.C. 147;
 [1969] 2 W.L.R. 163; [1969] 1 All E.R. 208, H.L.(E.).   B
Bickel v. *Duke of Westminster* [1977] Q.B. 517; [1976] 3 W.L.R. 805;
 [1975] 3 All E.R. 801, C.A.
Birkett v. *James* [1978] A.C. 297; [1977] 3 W.L.R. 38; [1977] 2 All
 E.R. 801, C.A. and H.L.(E.).
Black-Clawson International Ltd. v. *Papierwerke Waldhof-Aschaffenburg*
 A.G. [1975] A.C. 591; [1975] 2 W.L.R. 513; [1975] 1 All E.R. 810,
 H.L.(E.).   C
Cartledge v. *E. Jopling & Sons Ltd.* [1963] A.C. 758; [1963] 2 W.L.R.
 210; [1963] 1 All E.R. 341, H.L.(E.).
Craig v. *Kanssen* [1943] K.B. 256; [1943] 1 All E.R. 108, C.A.
Dryden v. *Dryden* [1973] Fam. 217; [1973] 3 W.L.R. 524; [1973] 3 All
 E.R. 526.
Easy v. *Universal Anchorage Co. Ltd.* [1974] 1 W.L.R. 899; [1974] 2
 All E.R. 1105, C.A.   D
F. (Infants) (Adoption Order: Validity), In re [1977] Fam. 165; [1977]
 2 W.L.R. 488; [1977] 2 All E.R. 777, C.A.
Finch v. *Francis* (unreported), July 21, 1977, Griffiths J.
Heaven v. *Road and Rail Wagons Ltd.* [1965] 2 Q.B. 355; [1965] 2
 W.L.R. 1249; [1965] 2 All E.R. 409.
O'Connor v. *Isaacs* [1956] 2 Q.B. 288; [1956] 2 W.L.R. 585 & 3 W.L.R.
 172; [1956] 1 All E.R. 513 & 2 All E.R. 417, C.A.   E
Smith v. *Central Asbestos Co. Ltd.* [1973] A.C. 518; [1972] 3 W.L.R.
 333; [1972] 2 All E.R. 1135, H.L.(E.).
Wachtel v. *Wachtel* [1973] Fam. 72; [1973] 2 W.L.R. 366; [1973] 1
 All E.R. 829, C.A.
Ward v. *James* [1966] 1 Q.B. 273; [1965] 2 W.L.R. 455; [1965] 1 All
 E.R. 568, C.A.
                              F
The following additional cases were cited in argument:
Buck v. *English Electric Co. Ltd.* [1977] 1 W.L.R. 806; [1977] I.C.R.
 629.
Hilton v. *Sutton Steam Laundry (A Firm)* [1946] K.B. 65; [1945] 2 All
 E.R. 425, C.A.
Hoystead v. *Taxation Commissioner* [1926] A.C. 155, P.C.
Jones v. *Jones* [1970] 2 Q.B. 576; [1970] 3 W.L.R. 20; [1970] 3 All G
 E.R. 47, C.A.
McCafferty v. *Metropolitan Police District Receiver* [1977] 1 W.L.R.
 1073; [1977] I.C.R. 799; [1977] 2 All E.R. 756, C.A.
Mitchell v. *Harris Engineering Co. Ltd.* [1967] 2 Q.B. 703; [1967] 3
 W.L.R. 447; [1967] 2 All E.R. 682, C.A.
Seabridge v. *H. Cox & Sons (Plant Hire) Ltd.* [1968] 2 Q.B. 46; [1968]
 2 W.L.R. 629; [1968] 1 All E.R. 570, C.A.   H

FIRMAN v. ELLIS

INTERLOCUTORY APPEAL from Kerr J.
 The plaintiff, Michael Firman, was injured in a road accident on May
23, 1973, and claimed damages for personal injuries against the defendant,
Diane Ellis, by writ 1974 F. No. 112. The writ was not served within
the time limit and the action became statute-barred. On March 21, 1977,

A the plaintiff issued a new writ 1977 F. No. 545 and by order of July 4, 1977, Kerr J. granted the plaintiff leave to proceed with his action. The defendant appealed on the grounds that (1) the judge misdirected himself or erred in law in holding that it was equitable to allow the action to proceed; (2) he failed adequately to consider or to give proper weight to the evidence that the plaintiff on July 26, 1974, had issued a writ out of the Eastbourne District Registry of the High Court of Justice Queen's Bench
B Division in Action No. 1974 F. 112 but had failed to serve or renew the same in accordance with the provisions of R.S.C., Ord. 6, r. 8; (3) he was wrong in law and misdirected himself in holding that it was equitable to allow the action to proceed when the sole reason for the plaintiff having failed to issue and serve a writ within the time limits prescribed by section 2A of the Limitation Act 1939 (as amended by the Limitation Act 1975) was
C the breach of duty of the solicitor acting for him; (4) his decision was unjust in that its effect was to deprive the defendant of the benefit of a limitation period which had accrued; and (5) in the premises the judge wrongly exercised his discretion.

INCE AND OTHERS v. ROGERS

D INTERLOCUTORY APPEAL from Talbot J.

The plaintiffs, Pamela Mary Ince and her children, were injured in a motor accident on February 22, 1977. They began an action by writ 1975 I. No. 5015. The writ was not served within the time limit and an application for renewal of the writ was refused. A writ 1977 I. No. 4376 was issued on July 8, 1977, and the plaintiffs successfully applied to Talbot J. for leave to proceed with the action.

E The defendant, Michael Frank Stewart Rogers, appealed from the order of Talbot J. made on October 17, 1977, asking that the provisions of section 2A of the Limitation Act 1939 should not apply to the causes of action referred to in the writ 1977 I. No. 4376 and that the plaintiffs should not have leave to proceed notwithstanding the expiry of three years from the date on which the causes of action arose. The grounds of his appeal were
F that (1) the judge misdirected himself or erred in law in holding that it was equitable to allow the action to proceed; (2) he failed adequately to consider or to give proper weight to the evidence that the plaintiffs on June 24, 1975, had issued against the defendant a writ 1975 I. No. 5015 in respect of the cause of action pleaded by the writ in the present action but had failed to serve or renew the same in accordance with the provisions of R.S.C., Ord. 6, r. 8; (3) he was wrong in law and misdirected himself in holding that it
G was equitable to allow the action to proceed when the sole reason for the plaintiffs having failed to issue and serve a writ within the time limits prescribed by section 2A of the Limitation Act 1939 (as amended by the Limitation Act 1975) was the breach of duty of the solicitor acting for him in failing to serve the writ within the prescribed time; (4) his decision was unjust in that its effect was to deprive the defendant of the benefit of a
H limitation period which had accrued; and (5) in the premises the judge wrongly exercised his discretion.

DOWN v. HARVEY AND OTHERS

INTERLOCUTORY APPEALS from Lawson J.

The plaintiff, Frederick Henry Down, was injured in a road accident on February 16, 1973. He issued a writ 1976 D. No. 40 and, on February 8, 1977, the registrar renewed the writ but, on application by the defen-

dants, the registrar set aside the order and that decision was affirmed by A
a judge. The plaintiff issued a new writ 1977 D. No. 115 and successfully
applied to Talbot J. for leave to proceed with the action.

The defendants, Laurence George Harvey and O. Nicklin & Sons Ltd.
appealed from that order of Lawson J. made on July 27, 1977, who had
held that the statutory time limit for proceeding with the plaintiff's action
for damages for personal injuries against the defendants should not apply,
pursuant to section 2D of the Limitation Act 1939. They asked that the B
judge's order be set aside and that it might be ordered that the statutory
time limit for proceeding with the plaintiff's action for damages for personal
injuries should apply. The grounds of the first defendant's appeal were
that (1) the judge misdirected himself in holding that it would be equitable
to allow the action to proceed; (2) in considering whether, or the degree
to which, the plaintiff was prejudiced, the judge failed, or failed adequately, C
to take into account the fact that the plaintiff would have an alternative
remedy against his solicitors; and (3) that the judge's order was wrong and
ought to be set aside. The grounds of the second defendant's appeal
were that (1) the judge was wrong in law in overriding the limitation
period of three years; (2) the judge's interpretation of section 2D of the
Limitation Act 1939 was wrong in law because: (i) the delay on the part
of the plaintiff and/or his solicitors was inordinate and inexcusable and D
the plaintiff had not satisfactorily explained that delay; (ii) the evidence
to be adduced or likely to be adduced by the second defendant was or was
likely to be less cogent; (iii) the second defendant had every reason to
believe that the action was dead because it was not notified that any
steps had been or were to be taken against it following a meeting on
June 21, 1973, between a representative of the second defendant's insurers E
and the plaintiff's solicitors until April, 1977, when the second defendant
first became aware that the first writ (dated February 9, 1976) had been
issued; (3) the judge's decision to disapply section 2A of the Limitation
Act 1939 was against the weight of the evidence; (4) the judge was wrong
in law in holding that an acceptable reason for the plaintiff's delay was
due to the fact that the plaintiff's medical condition had not been resolved
by February 1977, notwithstanding that the accident happened and the F
cause of action (if any) of which the plaintiff was aware arose on February
16, 1973; (5) the judge attached no or alternatively insufficient weight to
the fact that if the plaintiff's application to override the limitation period
of three years was dismissed the plaintiff would have a cause of action for
damages and consequential loss against his solicitors; (6) the judge's decision was unjust in that its practical effect was to deprive the second defen- G
dant of its defence that the plaintiff's cause of action (if any) was
statute-barred; (7) alternatively, the judge exercised his discretion under
section 2D of the Limitation Act 1939 on the wrong principles; and (8)
in the premises, the judge should not have made the order.

The plaintiff, by a cross appeal, asked that the order of Lawson J. made
on October 20, 1977, dismissing the plaintiff's appeal from the order of a H
district registrar refusing to renew the original writ of summons and ordering that service thereof should not stand, be set aside. The grounds of
his cross appeal were that (1) the judge wrongly failed to disapply the
provisions of the Limitation Acts 1939 to 1975 pursuant to the provisions
of section 2D of the Act of 1975; (2) the judge in the action 1977 D. No.
115 between the same parties had ordered that the provisions of the Limitation Acts 1939 to 1975 should not apply thereto on one or more of the

A grounds set out in section 2D of the Limitation Act 1975 but was not prepared so to order in the present action when the effect of so doing would have had the practical result of making any second action between the parties unnecessary and thereby would have led to the saving of costs; (3) if the judge had disapplied the provisions of the Limitation Acts 1939 to 1975 the plaintiff's claim against both defendants would not have been statute-barred and the rule in *Heaven* v. *Road and Rail Wagons Ltd.*

B [1965] 2 Q.B. 355 would no longer have applied; (4) when it would other-wise have been a proper exercise of discretion to disapply the provisions of the Limitation Acts 1939 to 1975 the judge wrongly held that section 2D of the Limitation Act 1975 did not overrule or permit him to overrule *Heaven* v. *Road and Rail Wagons Ltd.*

C PHEASANT AND OTHERS *v.* S. T. H. SMITH (TYRES) LTD. AND ANOTHER

INTERLOCUTORY APPEAL from Cusack J.

The plaintiffs, Robert Henry Pheasant, his wife, Nellie Pheasant and their two children, were injured in a motor accident on July 10, 1970. The original writ 1972 P. No. 0038 claimed damages for personal injuries against Mr. Carver. Mr. Carver claimed that the accident was caused

D by a faulty tyre fitted to his car by S. T. H. Smith (Tyres) Ltd. and joined that company and its owner Terence Smith as third parties. The plaintiffs sought to join the third parties as defendants but as a result of an error in the plaintiffs' solicitors' office the application was made after the three-year limitation period had expired. The registrar ordered that the third parties be joined as defendants. The plaintiffs issued a new writ 1976 P. No. 1493, against the company and Mr. Smith. They applied

E for leave to proceed with that action. Cusack J. granted leave by order dated July 29, 1977.

The defendants, the company and Mr. Smith, appealed from Cusack J.'s judgment by which he had held (1) that the plaintiffs' causes of action were not res judicata; (2) that the plaintiffs were not estopped, from con-tending that their causes of action were not statute-barred; (3) ordered

F pursuant to section 2D of the Limitation Act 1939, that the provisions of section 2A of that Act should not apply to the action; and (4) ordered that the defendants should pay the costs of the trial of the preliminary issues. They asked for an order that the judge's judgment and order be set aside, and that there be judgment for the defendants. The grounds of the appeal were that (1) the judge was wrong in law in concluding that the causes of action were not res judicata; (2) he was wrong in law in concluding that

G the plaintiffs were not estopped from contending that their causes of action were not statute-barred; (3) he was wrong in law, having regard to all the circumstances of the case, in making the order pursuant to section 2D of the Limitation Act 1939.

The facts in all four appeals are stated in the judgment of Lord Denning M.R.

H *John Loyd* for the defendant Ellis.

Anthony Hacking for the plaintiff Firman.

John Loyd for the defendant Rogers.

Barry Green for the plaintiffs Ince and Others.

Michael Turner Q.C. and *Hugh Lewis* for the first defendant Harvey.

John Loyd for the second defendants, O. Nicklin & Sons Ltd.

Peter Fallon Q.C. and *John Royce* for the plaintiff Down.

Michael Hutchison Q.C. and *David Blunt* for the defendant company A
and the defendant Smith.

Ben Hytner Q.C. and *David Berkson* for the plaintiffs.

Cur. adv. vult.

February 6. The following judgments were read.
B

LORD DENNING M.R. On May 23, 1973, Michael Firman, aged 17,
was injured in a motor accident. He was a passenger in a car driven by
Miss Ellis. They were going from their homes in Seaford to Brighton.
She drove too fast and collided with an oncoming lorry. She afterwards
pleaded guilty to driving without due care and attention.

Michael Firman's injuries were to his head, neck and spine. It was C
difficult for the doctors to forecast his future state of health, and for him to
decide on his future career. Within three months his solicitors made a
claim on his behalf, which was passed to the insurers of the driver of the car.
Thenceforward, for the next three years, there were negotiations for a
settlement, medical examinations, advice on career prospects, and so
forth. There was no undue delay on the part of the plaintiff's advisers D
at all.

Pending the discussions, his solicitors issued a writ so as to protect his
interests: but they made a mistake in that they failed to renew it, as they
should have done. On that account the insurers say that Michael Firman's
claim is statute-barred. The dates are as follows: May 23, 1973: the
accident. August 17, 1973: plaintiff's solicitors write letter of claim.
July 26, 1974: protective writ issued and insurers notified of it. July 26, E
1975: writ ceased to be valid unless renewed: see R.S.C., Ord. 6, r. 8.
September 8, 1975: plaintiff's solicitors reminded insurers that writ had
been issued but not served because they hoped for a satisfactory negotiated
settlement. May 23, 1976: three years elapsed since the accident.
August to October 1976: Insurers ask for further medical examination and
pay expenses to travel to it. October 25, 1976: insurers ask for evidence F
that the writ had been renewed. Plaintiff's solicitors reply that it had not
been renewed. November 2, 1976: insurers say " snap." They say that
they had no proposal to make in settlement and they considered the
plaintiff's claim to be out of time. December 30, 1976: plaintiff's solicitors
apply to renew the writ and give history of negotiations in full detail.
March 10, 1977: registrar refuses leave to renew. July 4, 1977: judge G
affirms decision of registrar.

Apart from the Limitation Act 1975, it is clear that the plaintiff's claim
was statute-barred. His solicitors had failed in their duty to him because
they had not served the writ in time. The fact that negotiations for a
settlement were in progress did not afford any excuse for failing to do so:
see *Easy* v. *Universal Anchorage Co. Ltd.* [1974] 1 W.L.R. 899. The H
plaintiff's only remedy was to sue his solicitors for negligence.

On March 21, 1977 (after the registrar had refused to renew), the plaintiff issued a new writ against the defendant: and on July 4, 1977, applied
to the judge in chambers after the Limitation Act 1975 had come into
force for an order under section 2D of the amended Act of 1939 that the
plaintiff should not be barred by the three-year limitation. Kerr J. granted
the application. The defendant appeals to this court.

A   *Ince* v. *Rogers*

On February 22, 1973, Mrs. Ince was driving a car, taking two of her children to school, along a road in Buckinghamshire, on her proper side of the road. A car came up fast from the opposite direction on its wrong side of the road, overtaking a number of other vehicles. It collided head-on with Mrs. Ince's car and she was badly injured. On October 17,

B   1973, the driver of the other car was convicted of careless driving and other offences. Within two months Mrs. Ince's solicitor made a claim on her behalf, which was passed on to the insurers of the driver. Thenceforward for the next three years there were negotiations for a settlement, medical examinations, and so forth. There was no undue delay at all on behalf of the plaintiff's solicitors. They had to wait because it was very difficult to forecast to the future of Mrs. Ince.

C   The dates are as follows: February 22, 1973: accident. April 26, 1973: plaintiff's solicitors' letter of claim. June 24, 1975: plaintiff's solicitors issued protective writ. July 7, 1975: plaintiff's solicitors tell insurers that they have isued a writ, but did not intend to serve it for the time being. September 25, 1975: insurers pay £640 towards medical expenses of Mrs. Ince. February 22, 1976: three years elapsed since the accident.

D   March 25, 1976: copy writ sent to insurers at their request. June 24, 1976: writ ceased to be valid unless renewed. July 26, 1976: insurers pay £250 for dental fees for Mrs. Ince. September 10, 1976: plaintiff's solicitors apply ex parte to renew the writ. September 15, 1976: master renews writ. September 27, 1976: writ served. October 6, 1976: defendant enters conditional appearance and applies to set aside service. February 2, 1977: master refuses to set aside service. May 30, 1977: judge

E   allows appeal and sets aside service. July 22, 1977: Court of Appeal affirms judge.

Apart from the Limitation Act 1975, it is clear that the claim was statute-barred. Mrs. Ince's solicitors had failed in their duty to her to renew the writ in time. Her only remedy was to sue the solicitors for damages.

F   On July 8, 1977 (after the judge had refused to allow the renewal), the plaintiff issued a writ against the defendant: and applied to the judge in chambers for an order under section 2D that the plaintiff should not be barred by the three-year limitation. On October 13, 1977, Talbot J. granted the application. The defendant appeals to this court.

Down v. *Harvey and O. Nicklin & Sons Ltd.*

G   Mr. Down is in the employ of Nicklin & Sons Ltd. They sent him with a van to deliver a piano to Mr. Harvey. The van got stuck in a muddy track. Mr. Harvey got a Land-Rover to pull it out. While helping, Mr. Down's leg was caught in a rope and he was badly injured. He had many operations and eventually his left foot was amputated.

The dates are as follows: February 16, 1973: accident. March 1973: H   claim made and matter passed to insurers. May 1973–October 1974: medical examinations and negotiations. There was delay then until the plaintiff's condition could be better assessed. February 9, 1976: writ isued but not served. February 16, 1976: the three years elapsed since accident. February 8, 1977: application made to registrar ex parte for renewal: renewal granted. (Note: The writ might have been validly served on that day, but the plaintiff's solicitors chose instead to apply to renew it). April 7, 1977: writ served. June 9, 1977: conditional appear-

10

Lord Denning M.R.   **Firman v. Ellis (C.A.)**   **[1978]**

ance and application to set aside renewal of writ. June 30, 1977: registrar A
sets aside renewal of writ. October 20, 1977: judge in chambers affirms
registrar. Apart from the Limitation Act 1975, it is clear that action was
statute-barred. July 19, 1977: plaintiff issued new writ and applied to
judge in chambers for an order under section 2D that plaintiff was not
barred by the three-year limitation. July 27, 1977: Lawson J. granted
the application. The defendant appeals to this court.

B

Summarising those three cases, they have these features in common.
In each case the plaintiff had suffered personal injury. He instructed
solicitors at once. His solicitors made a claim against the defendant, who
passed it on to the insurers. The insurers did not dispute liability. There
were negotiations for a settlement. But the extent of the plaintiff's injuries
could not be ascertained for some time. So the plaintiff's solicitors issued C
a protective writ and told the insurers they had done so. This was all
during the negotiations. But unfortunately, by a slip, they forgot to serve
it within the one year allowed by the rules. And when they applied to
renew it, they were out of time. The three years had expired. On that
account the renewal was not allowed. So the action was, under the old
law, statute-barred. Now that old law has gone. We have the new Limitation Act 1975. The plaintiff in each case sought to take advantage of it. D
In each case the plaintiff's solicitors issued a new writ and sought to override the time limit. They asked the judge in chambers to exercise his
discretion under the new Limitation Act 1975. The judge in each case
allowed the extension. The defendant appeals to this court.

A short history   E

The common law laid down no time limit. In 1623 the statute of that
year prescribed six years for actions founded on simple contract or tort.
That stood for over 300 years until the subject was considered by the
Law Revision Committee (Cmnd. 5334), who recommended no change.
So six years was retained by the comprehensive statute, the Limitation Act
1939: see section 2 (1). Always it was six years from the date on which F
the cause of action accrued. Following a report by Lord Tucker's Committee in 1949 (Cmnd. 7740) this was reduced in 1954 to three years for
claims for personal injuries: see the Law Reform (Limitation of Actions)
Act 1954. The time ran from the date when the loss or damage was
suffered by the plaintiff, irrespective of his knowledge of such loss or
damage. The injustice of this rule was brought into prominence by the
decision of the House of Lords in *Cartledge* v. *E. Jopling & Sons Ltd.* G
[1963] A.C. 758, about insidious diseases, like pneumoconiosis. It was
held that a man was statute-barred before he even knew that he had
contracted the disease. This led to the report by the Edmund Davies
Committee in 1962 (Cmnd. 1829). It recommended that an injured
person should not be defeated by the three-year limitation if he could not
reasonably have been expected to know of his injury during that period: H
and started an action within 12 months of getting to know. This report
was followed by the Limitation Act 1963. But that Act was very obscure
and difficult to construe. Lord Reid said that it had " a strong claim to
the distinction of being the worst drafted Act on the statute book." There
was a clash of opinion among the judges about it. Some thought that time
did not run against a man until he knew that he had " a worthwhile cause
of action." Others thought that time ran against him as soon as he knew

A   all the material facts, even though he did not know that he had a cause
of action. The differing views were expressed in the House of Lords in
Smith v. *Central Asbestos Co. Ltd.* [1973] A.C. 518. They were examined
by Orr L.J.'s Committee in their interim report in May 1974 (Cmnd. 5630).
It contained a draft clause which was, in substance, included in the Limitation Act 1975. In my opinion this court can and should consider the
report as part of the background to the Act: see *Black-Clawson Inter-*
B   *national Ltd.* v. *Papierwerke Waldhof-Aschaffenburg A.G.* [1975] A.C.
591.

The proposal for a general discretion

Throughout that history there has been a strong body of opinion in
favour of giving the court a general discretion to override the statutory
C   time-limit. The proposal was that the three-year limitation should be
retained, but that the court should have an unfettered discretion to extend
it. This proposal was put before each of the committees, but rejected by
them. It was considered by the Law Revision Committee in 1936 and
rejected by them: see Cmnd. 5334, para. 7. It was considered by the
Edmund-Davies Committee and rejected by them: see Report of the
D   Committee on Limitation of Actions in Cases of Personal Injury: (1962)
(Cmnd. 1829), paras. 30 to 33. It was considered by Orr L.J. and his
committee and rejected by them: see Cmnd. 5630, paras. 34 and 35. The
reason for rejection was that if an unfettered discretion were given to
judges, it would lead to too much uncertainty. The proposal was condemned by Orr L.J.'s committee in the interim report (Cmnd. 5630) in
these words:

E
"To make the plaintiff entirely dependent on the court's discretion
would, in our view, be a retrograde step and we do not recommend
it": see paragraph 35.

Nevertheless, Orr L.J.'s committee did recommend that the court
should have a discretion in some "exceptional cases" to extend the time.
They described these cases as a "residual class of case" and the discretion
F   as a "residual discretionary power." This residual class was not defined
by the committee: but, so far as I can gather, they had in mind cases where
the plaintiff knew the facts—for instance, that he had suffered an injury
or contracted a disease which was due to his work—but he did not know
his legal rights. He did not know that he had a cause of action against
his employers on account of it. If the court were given a discretion—in
G   that exceptional class of case—to extend the time, it would enable the
court to do justice in them: see paras. 38, 56 and 87.

Apart from those exceptional cases, the committee thought that
the three years' limitation should continue. This view was echoed by
Griffiths J. in *Finch* v. *Francis* (unreported), July 21, 1977. He was a
member of Orr L.J.'s committee, and so his views are of special weight.
H   He said:

". . . the object of the discretion [to override the time limit] was
to provide for the occasional hard case. I cannot believe that it was
the intention of Parliament that section 2D should be applied to a
case such as this, where a person in the hands of a solicitor allows
time to run out in a straightforward running-down action. If the
court were to exercise its powers in a case such as this the value to
the defendant of the three-year time limit in personal injury cases

would be completely swept aside. Furthermore, the court would be   A
flooded with applications. In my view the court should be circum-
spect in its approach to the application of section 2D and it should
be reserved for cases of an unusual nature. I do not think that this
was a case of an unusual nature. It was a straightforward running-
down case in which time should never have been allowed to expire.
I can see no reason to extend it."
                                                                     B

The statute itself

Although those committees did not accept the proposal for a general
discretion, nevertheless, when Parliament passed the Act of 1975, it did
give the court a general discretion. Section 2D, as I read it, gives a wide
discretion to the court which is not limited to a " residual class of case "
at all. It is not limited to "exceptional cases." It gives the court a   C
discretion to extend the time in all cases where the three-year limitation
has expired before the issue of the writ. It retains three years as the
normal period of limitation (being three years from the date on which the
cause of action accrued, or the date, if later, of the plaintiff's knowledge
of the facts) but it confers on the court an unfettered discretion to extend
the three-year period in any case in which it considers it equitable to do so.   D
    The granting of this discretion is a revolutionary step. It alters our
whole approach to time bars. I do not regard it as a retrograde step.
In former times it was thought that judges should not be given discretionary
powers. It would lead to too much uncertainty. The law should define
with precision the circumstances in which judges should do this or that.
Those days are now passed. In statute after statute, Parliament has
given powers to the judges and entrusted them with a discretion as to the   E
manner in which those powers should be exercised. In many of these
statutes, Parliament sets out " guide lines " indicating some of the considerations to which judges should have regard. A notable example is
the Matrimonial Proceedings and Property Act 1970, section 5, regarding
the division of matrimonial property: see *Wachtel* v. *Wachtel* [1973] Fam.
72. A recent exception is the Unfair Contract Terms Act 1977, which sets   F
out " guide lines " for application of the reasonableness test. Sometimes
Parliament has entrusted the judge with a discretion without setting out
any guide lines, as in trial by jury under the Administration of Justice
(Miscellaneous Provisions) Act 1933: and then the judges themselves set
out the guide lines: see *Ward* v. *James* [1966] 1 Q.B. 273. In all such
cases the judges in making their decisions set a pattern from which the profession can forecast the likely result in any given set of circumstances: see   G
Bickel v. *Duke of Westminster* [1977] Q.B. 517, 524. So a sufficient
degree of certainty is achieved—as much certainty as is possible consistently
with justice.
    The value of this wide discretion is well shown by the present series of
cases. They all arise out of circumstances which the various committees
never had in mind at all. In each of the three cases there were negotiations   H
for a settlement, but the plaintiff's solicitors, by the merest slip, allowed time
to run out. They failed to renew the writ in time. This slip did not
prejudice the defendant or his insurers in the least. Yet as soon as the
defendant's insurers discovered it, they cried " snap " and broke off the
negotiations. They said to the plaintiff: " You are statute-barred. We
are not liable. You sue your own solicitors for negligence. Make their
insurers pay. And not us." All of the judges rejected this submission.

A   Each of the judges exercised his discretion in favour of the plaintiff. I think they were quite right. As a matter of simple justice, it is the defendant's insurers who should pay the plaintiff's claim. They have received the premiums to cover the risk of these accidents. They should not be allowed to foist their liability on to the plaintiff's solicitors or their insurers by calling " snap " as if it were a game of cards.

B *Pheasant* v. *Smith*

    On July 10, 1970, Mr. Pheasant was driving his wife and two young children in a Singer car along the M.5 motorway in Gloucestershire. A car driven by a Mr. Carver overtaking him came right across his path. There was a collision, in which Mr. and Mrs. Pheasant and their children were all injured.

C   On January 4, 1972, a writ was issued on their behalf against Mr. Carver: and a statement of claim on April 14, 1972. On June 23, 1972, Mr. Carver delivered a defence alleging that the collision was caused by a sudden deflation of one of the tyres of the car. He said that this was because the tyres had been negligently repaired by a repairer, Mr. Smith and his company, S. T. H. Smith (Tyres) Ltd. Mr. Carver joined Mr.

D Smith and his company as third parties. That was on September 21, 1972. In these circumstances it was clearly advisable for Mr. Pheasant to add Mr. Smith and his company as defendants: because if Mr. Carver was not negligent, it was essential for Mr. Pheasant to have the Smiths as defendants.

    So on April 30, 1973, Mr. Pheasant's solicitor applied by summons to add the Smiths as defendants. The summons was returnable on June 6,

E 1973. Now here is the point. The accident was on July 10, 1970. So three years would elapse on July 10, 1973. So the plaintiffs ought to add the Smiths before or on July 10, 1973.

    Now if the summons had been heard on June 6, 1973, and granted on that day, the Smiths could have been joined as defendants within the three years. The Smiths' solicitors wrote a letter, saying:

F   " . . . We give consent to your application before the district registrar on June 6, and we would be obliged if you would inform him of our consent."

    But, by a clerk's mistake, Mr. Pheasant's solicitor did not attend the summons on June 6, 1973. We are told that a lady clerk made too long a stroke with her pen so that it appeared in the diary as if that appointment

G was cancelled. Whereas it had not been. At any rate, as the solicitor did not attend on that day, the registrar did not make any order on that day joining the Smiths as defendants.

    Five weeks later, on July 11, 1973, Mr. Pheasant's solicitor discovered the mistake. He immediately asked the registrar for another appointment. The registrar gave it to him at once on July 11, 1973. So on July 11, 1973, Mr. Pheasant's solicitor attended before the registrar—he produced

H the letter from the Smiths' solicitors saying they would not oppose the joinder. Thereupon Mr. Registrar Morris Jones allowed the joinder and the order was drawn up as follows:

        " Upon hearing the solicitors for all parties it is ordered that the plaintiffs be granted leave to amend the writ and statement of claim to join in the third parties as co-defendants in this action. Dated this 11th day of July, 1973."

Now that order was inaccurate in this respect: the Smiths' solicitors   **A**
had not been heard. No notice had been given to the Smiths' solicitors
of the summons on July 11, 1973. Mr. Pheasant's solicitor, having missed
the appointment for June 6, 1973, simply went along to the next appointment on July 11, 1973, and produced the letter—which was really only a
consent for June 6, 1973, and not for July 11, 1973. Leave to amend
having been given, the Smiths were joined on August 3, 1973, and served
on August 24, 1973. Thereupon they entered a conditional appearance   **B**
and took out a summons to set aside the joinder as it had not been made
within the three years. On January 4, 1974, Mr. Registrar Verity set aside
the amendment and joinder. Mr. Pheasant's solicitor appealed to the
judge. On February 11, 1974, Rees J. set aside the order of Mr. Registrar
Morris Jones of July 11, 1973 (granting leave to join), and affirmed the
order of Mr. Registrar Verity of January 4, 1974 (setting aside the joinder).   **C**
The judge gave a reasoned judgment, citing many cases, and concluded:

"... On the present state of the authorities, I am not satisfied that
power exists to add a defendant after a limitation period has expired
... even if the power did exist, I am not satisfied that it should be
exercised otherwise than in exceptional circumstances, and I can find
no such circumstances in the present case."   **D**

Rees J. gave leave to appeal, but Mr. Pheasant's solicitor did not appeal.
He accepted the judge's decision, with the result that the Smiths were not
added as defendants to the action, because the claim against them was
statute-barred at the time of the leave given and of the amendment made.

That was February 11, 1974. No one would have thought at that
time that the decision would be reversed. But on September 1, 1975, the   **E**
Limitation Act 1975 came into operation. Mr. Pheasant's solicitors decided
to take advantage of it. On March 24, 1976, they issued a fresh writ
against the Smiths, claiming damages for the negligent repair of tyres
causing the accident on July 10, 1970. Pleadings were delivered in which
the Smiths pleaded the Statute of Limitations (three years) and also res
judicata and issue estoppel. Mr. Pheasant delivered a reply asking that
under the Limitation Act 1975 an order be made that the claim be not   **F**
statute-barred. This was set down as a preliminary issue. It was tried
by Cusack J. on July 29, 1977. He overrode the time-bar. The Smiths
appeal to this court.

Retrospective operation of the Act of 1975

This case raises a point on section 3 of the Limitation Act 1975. That   **G**
section makes the Act retrospective. It applies in relation to causes of
action which accrued before, as well as those which accrue after, the
commencement of the Act. It applies also to actions that have been
commenced before the Act, and are still pending at its commencement,
namely, on September 1, 1975. But it does not apply once "a final order
or judgment has been made or given therein."   **H**

It was submitted before us that the order of Rees J. on February 11,
1974, was a "final order or judgment" within section 3. Under the law
as it then stood, it finally disposed of the plaintiffs' cause of action against
the Smiths. But it is submitted by the plaintiffs that no action had been
"commenced" by them against the Smiths. They had tried to "commence" an action against the Smiths—by getting leave to join them as
defendants—but had failed. But the defendants say that the plaintiffs had

A " commenced " an action against the Smiths and it had been dismissed
by a " final " order: and the matter was res judicata or there was an issue
estoppel.

Void or voidable

This raises a nice question as to the status of the order of Mr. Registrar
B Morris Jones on July 11, 1973, when he gave leave to amend and join the
Smiths as defendants. Was it a nullity and void ab initio? For in that
case everything that followed from it was also a nullity and void: and no
action had been " commenced " against the Smiths. Or was it good when
it was made and only voidable? For in that case everything that followed
was good until it was set aside: and an action would have been " commenced " against the Smiths and then dismissed by Rees J. in a " final "
C order.

I think that the order of July 11, 1973, was a nullity and void ab initio
for two reasons: (i) it was made under a fundamental mistake in that the
registrar was told and believed that the Smiths agreed to it, when they
had not: and (ii) it was made contrary to the rules of natural justice,
because no notice of appointment had been given to the Smiths' solicitor.
D Such failures make the order a nullity and void ab initio: see *Anisminic
Ltd.* v. *Foreign Compensation Commission* [1969] 2 A.C. 147, 171 by
Lord Reid, and at p. 195 by Lord Pearce. It is true, of course, that the
Smiths might have waived their right to complain of it. They might have
entered an unconditional appearance. But they did not waive it. They
entered a conditional appearance and got it set aside. On being set aside,
it is thereupon shown to have been a nullity from the beginning and void.
E So, after some vacillation, I would adopt the meanings of " void " and
" voidable " given by Professor Wade in his *Administrative Law,* 4th ed.
(1977), pp. 300, 450. Seeing that it was a nullity, it follows that in point
of law no action had been " commenced " against the Smiths. So section
3 applies. The Act of 1975 operates retrospectively so as to enable Mr.
Pheasant to bring an action against the Smiths—provided always that he can
F persuade the court to exercise its discretion so as to override the time
limit.

Discretion

Once it comes to discretion, it is clear that it should be exercised in
favour of the Pheasants. It was a most unfortunate slip—an extended
stroke in a diary which led to the solicitor missing the appointment for
G June 6, 1973. It was just bad luck that it was not discovered until July 11,
1973—just one day too late. The insurers then called " snap " and invoked
the Statute of Limitations. That was all very well before the Act of 1975.
But now that the court has a discretion, it is a very proper case in which
to exercise it.

H *Remedy against solicitor*

The question was much discussed whether, in exercising discretion, the
court should have regard to the plaintiff's remedy against his own solicitor.
In *Birkett* v. *James* [1978] A.C. 297, 324, Lord Diplock said that, in
cases of dismissal for want of prosecution, it was not a relevant consideration: but Lord Salmon, at p. 330, said that it might have some weight.
But those cases are different. In cases under the Limitation Act 1975, I
think that the negligence of the plaintiff's solicitor—and a remedy against

him—is an admissible consideration. It is one of "the circumstances of A
the case" and one of "the reasons for the delay." It may tip the scale
where the defendant has been substantially prejudiced by the delay.

It was also suggested that, in section 2D (3) the words "the plaintiff"
refer only to the plaintiff personally, and do not include his solicitor or
agent. That depends on the context. In sub-paragraph (d) it refers to the
plaintiff personally. But in sub-paragraphs (a), (b) and (c) it includes his
solicitor. I think "the plaintiff" includes his solicitor or agent except B
where the context confines it to the plaintiff personally.

The court

A question also arose about the procedure under section 2D. To whom
is the application to be made? "The court" means "the court in which
the action has been brought": see section 2D (2). Some people have C
thought that "the court" there means the court which tries the case. But
it is not so limited. I think it means a judge of the High Court or in the
county court, as the case may be. It includes a judge in chambers: or a
judge hearing an application as a preliminary issue. I do not think it
includes a master in the High Court, or a registrar in the country court.
It should be dealt with separately from any application to renew it. D

Conclusion

These four cases show that the Limitation Act 1975 has made a great
change in our law of limitation. It means that in personal injury cases a
plaintiff is not absolutely barred by the three-year time limit. The judges
have a discretion to override the time limit where it is fair and just to do
so. I would, therefore, dismiss all these appeals. E

ORMROD L.J. Anyone looking for the kinds of mischief against which
the Limitation Act 1975 is directed would find these four appeals of
considerable interest. In all four, the defendants are appealing against
orders made under the new section 2D "disapplying" the provision in
section 2 under which an action for personal injuries becomes statute- F
barred after three years. In other words, the defendants are inviting this
court to hold, in the exercise of its discretion, that the plaintiffs' claims
should be statute-barred.

Section 1 of the Act of 1975 introduced a number of new sections into
the Limitation Act 1939 in respect of actions for damages for personal
injury, which have radically changed this branch of the law. Under section
2D the court can now extend the period of limitation if it considers it G
"equitable" to do so. The appellants, therefore, have to show that the
judge below was wrong in concluding that it was equitable to give the
plaintiffs leave to proceed with their actions notwithstanding the lapse of
time. If they succeed, it is difficult to imagine any set of circumstances in
which it would be proper to exercise this new discretionary power in favour
of a plaintiff. The appellants, as counsel frankly and inevitably conceded, H
have no merits at all; they are simply attempting to take advantage of
formal procedural mistakes by the plaintiffs' solicitors (which have caused
them no inconvenience, let alone any prejudice) to transfer liability for the
plaintiffs' claims from the defendants' insurers to the plaintiffs' solicitors'
insurers. Mr. Loyd and Mr. Fallon for the appellants in the first three
cases made no attempt to hide the nakedness of the point of law on which
they sought to rely; Mr. Hutchinson, in the fourth appeal, managed to find

A   an exiguous garment in which to wrap his case, but it proved on inspection
to be diaphanous in the extreme. He also relied on a plea of res judicata
which will be dealt with later.

The Act of 1975 is the third attempt to reform this branch of the
law since 1939. This time, Parliament has firmly grasped the nettle and
has decided that it cannot be made to work fairly and justly as between
plaintiffs and defendants, without introducing into it an element of judicial
B   discretion from which it has, hitherto, been immune. There appears to be
no other way of preventing what is in some cases a necessary protection
for defendants, from being exploited in others.

The scheme adopted by the Act of 1975, so far as it is relevant to these
appeals, is to prescribe two what might be called " normal " periods of
limitation, namely, three years from the date on which the cause of action
C   accrued and three years from the date of the plaintiffs' knowledge (section
2A (4) (a) and (b)), and then to provide by section 2D a discretionary
power to " disapply " this time limit " if . . . it would be equitable " to do
so. Under section 2D (1) (a) and (b) the court is to have regard to the
degree to which the plaintiff would be prejudiced by the application of the
time limit, and to the degree to which the defendant would be prejudiced
by the court extending the limit. Subsection (3) sets out the main con-
D   siderations to be taken into account by the court in exercising its discretion. This is the technique which has proved successful in the Matrimonial
Causes Act 1973, section 25, which also gives the court very wide discretionary powers. So, under subsection (3) the court is to " have regard
to all the circumstances of the case " and in particular to the six matters
specifically set out in paragraphs (a) to (f) inclusive.

E   The language of the section, in my judgment, is quite clear. Having
laid down the norm, it then gives the court the widest discretion to adapt
this norm to the circumstances of any case in which it would work
inequitably. This is, in fact, a statutory analogy of the old tradition by
which equity was called in to mitigate the rigidity of the common law in
the interests of individual justice.

F   The appellants contend that the section should be construed or applied
not only strictly but, in the interest of public policy, restrictively. So far
as construction is concerned, the words of the section are clear and
unambiguous. It is impossible to construe the word " equitable " narrowly
or liberally. It is either equitable or inequitable to disapply the fixed time
limit in any given set of circumstances, although different people may have
different views of what is equitable in particular cases. The appellants
G   argued that section 2D should be confined to " exceptional cases." That
is precisely what the Act provides, since every case in which the court
decides that the application of the norm would be inequitable is, ex
hypothesi, an exceptional case.

The appellants' main contention was that the section should be read
in the light of the report of the Law Reform Committee in 1974, Twentieth
H   Report. (Interim Report on Limitation of Actions: in Personal Injury
Claims) (Cmnd. 5630). Leaving aside the propriety of looking at such
material when construing a provision in an Act of Parliament, the practical
question is whether it is of any assistance.

In a situation such as this, reference to a report on which legislation
is based involves two further steps, neither of which is easy. First, one
has to construe the report, and, then, if the Act appears to depart from the
recommendations in the report, to decide whether Parliament intended to

18

act on or to depart from the recommendations. In the instant case refer- **A**
ence to the report proved unhelpful from a practical point of view because
the final recommendations in paragraph 69, with which the Act is in line,
are not entirely consistent with certain passages in the body of the report
which seem to suggest that the committee may have had in mind that the
discretionary powers would only be used in "residual" cases. No such
ambiguity appears in the Act itself, which thus provides the answer to the
second stage. **B**

The reasons put forward to support the argument that the court should
apply the section restrictively, in the interests of public policy, were twofold. First, the loss of certainty which would inevitably arise if the discretion were freely used, and, second, the loss of a valuable sanction over
plaintiffs and their solicitors to discourage delay in bringing proceedings,
and, in particular, over solicitors, by allowing them to avoid liability to **C**
their clients for negligence. So far as the first point is concerned Parliament has now decided that uncertain justice is preferable to certain
injustice or, in other words, that certainty can be bought at too high a
price, as these four cases vividly demonstrate. If insurance companies
through their customers choose to take wholly unmeritorious technical
points to avoid liability, they cannot complain if ultimately their ability
to take them is severely restricted. To retain a highly formalistic proce- **D**
dure, the real effect of which is simply to transfer liability from the original
tortfeasor's insurers to the plaintiffs' solicitors' insurers, is not very impressive as a piece of public policy.

In my judgment, therefore, the Act should be applied as it stands,
and we should be careful not to impose judicial fetters on this new and,
to my mind, valuable discretionary power. So applied to the facts of **E**
these appeals (subject in the fourth case to the further point which is
peculiar to that case), the case for disapplying the three-year time limit is
overwhelming. Applying the six considerations set out in subsection (3)
seriatim to the first three cases the position is as follows.

(a) *Delay on the part of the plaintiff;* this was purely formal in each
case, the claims were made in good time, negotiations as to damages were **F**
proceeding, in a desultory manner, there never having been an issue as to
liability; all that happened was that the plaintiffs' solicitors, having issued
their writs within the three-year period, failed to serve them within a year
of issue, and so had to apply to renew them, unfortunately after the expiry
of the limitation period.

(b) *Effect of delay on cogency of the evidence;* it is conceded that the
effect was nil. **G**

(c) and (d) are not applicable.

(e) *Promptitude of plaintiff in taking steps;* there is no criticism under
this head at all.

(f) *Steps taken by plaintiff to obtain advice;* there is no criticism under
this head either.

Upon these facts the court has to decide whether the degree of pre- **H**
judice to the plaintiffs caused by refusing to disapply the normal time limit,
compared to the degree of prejudice to the defendants caused by extending
it, is sufficient to make it equitable to disapply the limit. The answer,
inevitably, is "Yes."

The defendants, however, argued that the plaintiffs will suffer no
prejudice if their actions are statute-barred because in each case they have
an unanswerable claim against their solicitors for damages for negligence.

A The plaintiffs, relying on *Birkett* v. *James* [1978] A.C. 297, contended that this was an irrelevant consideration. I do not think that Lord Diplock's observations in that case, at p. 324, can be applied to cases arising under section 2D, because, under that section, the court is required to have regard to all the circumstances of the case, and this is certainly one of them. I do not think, however, that it carries much weight in these cases. The court is not concerned solely with financial prejudice to the plaintiff. It is prejudicial to be forced to start another set of proceedings and against a party whom one does not particularly wish to sue and to be deprived of a good cause of action against the original tortfeasor. This may not amount to serious prejudice but it has to be balanced against no prejudice to the defendant at all. He, personally, has lost nothing, since no loss falls on him in either event; one or other insurance company will pay the damages and costs and his insurers have lost nothing but a fortuitous bonus arising from a harmless error by the plaintiff's solicitor.

I would therefore dismiss the appeals by the defendants in the first three cases.

In *Down* v. *Harvey and Another*, the plaintiff has a cross-appeal against the refusal of Lawson J. to grant leave to renew the writ under R.S.C., Ord. 6, r. 8. In this and the other two cases the judges in the court below relied on the decision of Megaw J. in *Heaven* v. *Road and Rail Wagons Ltd.* [1965] 2 Q.B. 355, 361, following a line of earlier decisions, that it is contrary to the settled practice of the court to give leave to renew a writ after the expiry of the limitation period. The ratio decidendi of that and the previous cases was that at the expiration of the period of limitation the claim was statute-barred and accordingly that it would be wrong to deprive "the defendant of a defence which he would have had under the relevant statute of limitation" by renewing a time-expired writ. The force of this reasoning was overwhelming as the law then stood, but the change from fixed to flexible time limits effected by the Act of 1975 has largely dissipated it. However, the decision can now be supported on different grounds. The difference to a plaintiff between issuing a new writ and renewing one which has already been issued but not served is very small, whereas the inconvenience of bringing into an application under R.S.C., Ord. 6, r. 8, the serious and possibly complex considerations which arise under section 2D is considerable. From the procedural point of view it seems more satisfactory that cases which involve section 2D should be dealt with as substantive applications under that section and should normally be heard by a judge. I would therefore dismiss the cross-appeal.

The fourth appeal raises rather different considerations but, if section 2D is applicable, it too is an overwhelming case for disapplying the three-year time limit. Again there was nothing but purely formal delay on the part of the plaintiffs and no prejudice to the defendants since they have been involved in the litigation as third parties since 1972. The only delay has been in adding them as defendants which can cause them no difficulty in preparing their defence.

Before leaving this part of the case there are two general points which should be mentioned. First, I agree with Lord Denning M.R. that it is for the parties and the judge to decide how an application for an order under section 2D can most conveniently be made in the circumstances of the individual case. Second, any general observations in this judgment must be read in the light of the facts of these appeals. None of them is

Ormrod L.J.   **Firman v. Ellis (C.A.)**   **[1978]**

what might be called a primary limitation case, that is, a case in which **A**
the plaintiff has made no or no serious attempt to press his claim within
the three-year period. In all these cases the limitation point has arisen
long after the solicitors on both sides have been in contact with each
other, and no difficulty arises about preparing the case for the defendant.
In such circumstances it will usually be difficult for the defendant to show
actual prejudice. In primary cases the position is different. Delay in
putting forward a claim is much more likely to cause real prejudice to **B**
the defendant, with the result that the scales of equity will tend to be
tipped in his favour and great care will be needed before holding that it is
equitable to disapply the three-year limit.

I turn now to Mr. Hutchinson's second submission. He argued that
the respondent plaintiffs in his case were estopped from invoking section 2D
either because it had already been decided by Rees J. in 1974 that their **C**
claim was statute-barred and was, therefore, res judicata, or because they
had " commenced an action " against the appellants in 1974 which had
been disposed of by a " final order " by Rees J. so that the plaintiffs
were precluded by section 3 from inviting the court to exercise the new
discretionary power.

The events of 1974 were very unusual and demonstrate to an extreme **D**
degree the formalistic way in which the Limitation Acts could operate
before the latest reform. In May of that year, just within the three-year
period, the plaintiffs' solicitors issued a summons for leave to amend the
writ to add the appellants, who were already third parties, as defendants.
The appellants' solicitors were served and wrote raising no objection. An
appointment was taken for June 6, 1973, still within the limitation period.
The plaintiffs' solicitor as a result of a slip in his office overlooked that **E**
appointment. A few days later he discovered it and immediately applied
for a new appointment, which was given for July 11, 1973, one day
outside the three-year period. The appellants were not notified of the new
appointment but the registrar made an order giving leave to amend,
recording that he had heard " all parties," though he was in fact acting upon
the appellants' solicitors' letter indicating that they would not oppose the
application. Had the appellants been informed of the later appointment **F**
they would have taken advantage of the statute to oppose it. The writ
was amended and served but was subsequently set aside by another registrar. On appeal to Rees J. he held that the registrar had no power to
make the order of July 11 and dismissed the plaintiffs' appeal. He also
held that in the alternative the registrar was wrong to give leave to amend
after the expiry of the limitation period. **G**

Mr. Hytner, in reply, contended that the judge was right in holding
that the registrar had no power to make the order of July 11, and that
both the order and the writ were void. Consequently, the plaintiffs had
not " commenced an action " within the meaning of section 3, nor could
they be estopped on the res judicata principle. Mr. Hutchinson argued
that the order and the writ were merely voidable for irregularity and that
therefore the plaintiffs had commenced an action which had been disposed **H**
of by a final order under section 3 and also were estopped by res judicata.

In my judgment, the order and the amended writ were void in the
sense that the appellants were entitled ex debito justitiae to have both of
them set aside. Essentially this was a case of non-service: see *Craig* v.
Kanssen [1943] K.B. 256. Alternatively, there was a fundamental
mistake on the part of the court making the order. R.S.C., Ord. 2, r. 1

A does not apply. That is not, however, to say that the order or the amended writ was a nullity. Each was a document emanating from the court and good on its face. Such orders or documents must be acted upon until declared void by the court: see *per* Diplock J. in *O'Connor* v. *Isaacs* [1956] 2 Q.B. 288, 303. Consequently, if the appellants had not challenged the order or the amended writ, the subsequent proceedings would have been validly constituted; but as they did challenge them, the court had no option
B but to declare them void, as Rees J., in effect, did in holding that the registrar had had no power to give leave to amend. Neither was voidable in the sense that the court had a discretion to allow them to stand. (See the judgment of Sir George Baker P. in *Dryden* v. *Dryden* [1973] Fam. 217 and also the judgment of this court in *In re F. (Infants)* [1977] Fam. 165, where the point was fully considered.)
C   In these circumstances the plaintiffs cannot be said to have " commenced an action " because the whole proceedings were void ab initio and there is no res which could found an estoppel.
       Accordingly, Mr. Hutchinson's second submission fails and the fourth appeal too should be dismissed.

D   GEOFFREY LANE L.J. I agree. The issue which is common to all these appeals may be stated thus: do the provisions of the Limitation Act 1975 apply to every type of action involving a claim for damages for personal injury, including a simple claim in negligence, or do they apply only in cases " out of the usual run " or to " difficult cases " (to adopt two of the expressions used by counsel)?
       Those who argue for this latter restricted interpretation point out that
E under the new section 2A (4) a limitation period is provided of three years from the date on which the cause of the action accrued, or from the date (if later) of the plaintiff's knowledge. They suggest that having specified that set term of three years, Parliament would not have taken it upon themselves to emasculate the set term by giving a largely unrestricted discretion to the court to exempt a plaintiff from complying with it. The
F plaintiffs on the other hand say that that is precisely what the Act on its plain wording means.
       The relevant provisions are in the new section 2D to which reference has already been made. The words " If it appears to the court that it would be equitable to allow an action to proceed . . . the court may direct that those provisions [i.e. 2A and 2B] shall not apply to the action " and " the court shall have regard to all the circumstances of the case "
G seem to me to give to the court as wide a discretion as could well be imagined. I find it impossible to understand how any restriction to " difficult " or " unusual " cases can be read into them.
       It is said that if one studies the Report of the Law Reform Committee which was set up to examine the question of Limitation of Actions in Personal Injury Claims (1974 Cmnd. 5630) it is clear that Parliament must
H have meant to give only a restricted discretion to the court to override the three-year limitation period. To that contention there are these answers. First, we are seeking to discover not so much what Parliament meant, but the true meaning of the words which they used. Secondly, where the words of a statutory provision are capable of having only one meaning, as I think is the case here, that is the end of the matter, and no further inquiry from reports of committees is permissible: see *Black-Clawson International Ltd.* v. *Papierwerke Waldhof-Aschaffenburg A.G.* [1975] A.C.

591, 614, *per* Lord Reid. It is true that if one does look at the terms of A
the report, they suggest that the discretion of the court should be restricted,
but that is not carried into effect by the words of the Act. The dictum to
the contrary expressed by Griffiths J. in *Finch* v. *Francis* on July 21, 1977,
namely, that the object of section 2D was " to provide for the occasional
hard case," is not lightly to be dismissed, since he was a member of the
committee which produced the report; but I do not think, with respect, that
it can be supported.   B

Given that the words of section 2D are not to be interpreted in this
restricted sense, there can be no doubt, in each of the cases which are the
subject of appeal, that it is equitable that the plaintiff should be exempted
from compliance with the three-year limitation period, for the reasons
expressed by Lord Denning M.R.

There are a number of subsidiary points which we were asked to clarify C
if possible.

(1) In considering whether or not to relieve the plaintiff under section
2D, is it permissible to have regard to the question whether the plaintiff
has a valid claim against his solicitor in negligence if he is statute-barred
in the original action? The majority of their Lordships in *Birkett* v.
James [1978] A.C. 297 held that in the circumstances of that case,
which was an application to dismiss for want of prosecution not involving D
the Act of 1975, the existence or non-existence of a remedy against the
plaintiff's solicitor was not a material consideration. But section 2D (3)
enjoins the court to have regard to *all* the circumstances of the case, and
I find it impossible to say that the insurance position whether of the plaintiff or of the defendant is not one of those circumstances, when the primary
object of the inquiry is to discover the respective degrees of prejudice. E
What weight should be given to the point is another matter. For example,
if there is any real dispute about the solicitor's liability in negligence, then
the chances of the plaintiff being able to recover against him would no
doubt be largely disregarded. It is plainly undesirable that there should
be any detailed inquiry into the existence of such liability.

(2) What should be the practice in cases such as the first of the present F
appeals, *Firman* v. *Ellis,* where the matter originally comes before the court
on the application of the plaintiff to extend the validity of a writ under
R.S.C., Ord. 6, r. 8? Should the master or registrar consider the application in the light of the new section 2D or should he continue as before to
apply the rule enunciated by Megaw J. in *Heaven* v. *Road and Rail
Wagons Ltd.* [1965] 2 Q.B. 355, dismiss the application, and leave the
plaintiff to issue a fresh writ and make his application under the provisions G
of the Act of 1975? It may at first sight seem cumbersome to take two
steps when one would suffice, and indeed at one stage in the argument I
had formed the view that the whole matter ought properly to be determined
by the master at the hearing of the application to extend. The decision
in *Heaven's* case would no longer constrain him to dismiss the application,
because the basis of that decision, entirely correct when it was made, has H
been undermined and destroyed by the provisions of the Act of 1975. No
longer is it true to say, as Megaw J. said, at p. 358:

     " It follows that, if the validity of the writ were not to be extended,
     and if the plaintiff were left to issue a fresh writ, the defendants would
     have an unanswerable defence by virtue of the three-year period of
     limitation prescribed by the Law Reform (Limitation of Actions, etc.)
     Act 1954."

A   Having heard the arguments of both parties on this aspect of the case, however, it seems to me that the most satisfactory method to adopt is to leave the plaintiff to issue a fresh writ under the 1975 provisions, and for the matter to be considered at a later stage, preferably by a judge. The reason is this. When the matter comes before the master, the information available to him is scanty. There has been no discovery and the parties have scarcely had the opportunity to marshal their evidence.

B   Consequently it would not be practicable for all the circumstances properly to be investigated. Moreover, although there is no reason why the master should not have regard to the provisions of the Limitation Act 1975 in coming to his conclusion, there is no obligation upon him to do so, as there is upon the court deciding whether the plaintiff should be permitted to issue a fresh writ after the expiry of the limitation period.

C   It remains to consider the separate question which arises in the last of the cases before us, namely, *Pheasant & Others* v. *S. T. H. Smith (Tyres) Ltd. and Another.* I have had the opportunity of reading the judgment of Ormrod L.J. on this aspect of the appeal. I respectfully agree with his reasoning and conclusions and it is unnecessary for me to add anything to them.

       I would accordingly dismiss all the appeals.
D

                                   All appeals dismissed with costs in
                                   Court of Appeal.
                                   Cross-appeal dismissed.
                                   Leave to appeal refused.

E   Solicitors: *Badhams; Mayo & Perkins, Eastbourne; Badhams; Thompson & Debenham, Harpenden; Hextall Erskine & Co. for Cartwrights, Bristol; Hextall Erskine & Co. for Toller, Oerton & Balsdon, Barnstaple; Park Nelson, Dennes, Redfern & Co. for Montague Arthur & Skerratt, Barnstaple; Park Nelson, Dennes, Redfern & Co. for Sansbury Hill & Co., Bath; R. E. Warburton & Sons, Liverpool.*

                                                               M. M. H.
F

                          [COURT OF APPEAL]

                   Ex parte ISLAND RECORDS LTD. AND OTHERS
G
                          [1978 I. No. 672]

1978   Feb. 6, 23, 24, 27, 28;   Lord Denning M.R., Shaw and
       March 21   Waller L.JJ.

H   *Practice—Discovery—Motion for—Ex parte application to restrain*
       unauthorised recording of live performances—Statute pre-
       scribing penalties but not for civil remedy—Whether inter-
       ference with property rights sufficient to give court jurisdiction
       to grant order—Dramatic and Musical Performers' Protection
       Act 1958 (6 & 7 Eliz. 2, c. 44), s. 1

       Section 1 of the Dramatic and Musical Performers' Protection Act 1958 provides:
           "... if a person knowingly—(a) makes a record ... of the performance of a dramatic or musical work without

the consent in writing of the performers, or (b) sells or A
lets for hire, or distributes for the purposes of trade . . .
a record made in contravention of this Act . . . he shall
be guilty of an offence under this Act "
and liable to a penalty. The penalties were increased by the
Performers' Protection Act 1972.

Thirty plaintiffs, performers and recording companies with
which the performers had exclusive contracts to record their
performances in the best possible conditions, who complained B
that they were suffering serious damage by reason of the
activities of unauthorised recorders (" bootleggers ") of live
performances and subsequent trading in reproductions of those
recordings, applied ex parte in the Chancery Division for, inter
alia, an injunction to restrain a named defendant from committing any acts in contravention of section 1 of the Act of
1958 or interfering with contractual relations or otherwise
interfering with their business by unlawful means, and an C
order that the defendant deliver up all recordings in his possession. Walton J. held, without looking at the evidence on
affidavit or exhibits thereto, that the court had no jurisdiction
to grant relief to persons who, although they could show damage by the unlawful acts, had no right of property infringed
by those activities.

On appeal ex parte by the plaintiffs on the preliminary
question of jurisdiction: —   D

Held, (1) (per Shaw and Waller L.JJ.) that section 1 of the
Act of 1958 provided only for penalties in criminal proceedings against a person found guilty of the statutory offences
and did not impose any defined duty to any particular class
of persons so that no civil action could be brought for a simple
breach of the statutory provisions.

Per Lord Denning M.R. The determination of the question
whether a criminal statute also created a civil cause of action E
has left the courts with a guess-work puzzle. The dividing
line between the pro-cases and the contra-cases is so blurred
and so ill-defined that you might as well toss a coin to decide
it. The court should seek for other ways to do " therein what
to justice shall appertain " (post, p. 29F, G).

But (2), allowing the appeal (Shaw L.J. dissenting), that
where a private or corporate person could show a private F
right which was being interfered with by a criminal act, thus
causing or threatening to cause him special damage over
and above damage to the public in general, there was
jurisdiction in equity for the court to grant an injunction
ex parte to restrain the defendant from damaging that
private interest; and that where the recording companies and
the performers could show a strong case that the companies
were losing sales of records and the performers were losing G
royalties on those lost sales, that was interference with a
private right which would entitle them to the relief sought.

Anton Piller K.G. v. Manufacturing Processes Ltd. [1976]
Ch. 55, C.A. and dicta in Gouriet v. Union of Post Office
Workers [1977] 3 W.L.R. 300, H.L.(E.) applied.

Institute of Patent Agents v. Lockwood [1894] A.C. 347,
H.L.(Sc.); Musical Performers' Protection Association Ltd. v.
British International Pictures Ltd. (1930) 46 T.L.R. 485 and H
Apple Corps Ltd. v. Lingasong Ltd. (1977) 3 F.S.R. 345 dis-
tinguished.

Per Shaw L.J. Section 1 of the Act of 1958 cannot be
construed as conferring a civil remedy by a penal provision
since it does not define any duty to performers; nor does the
contract between a performer and a recording company impose any obligation on a third party whose only responsibility
is to obey the law and pay the prescribed criminal penalty
if he does not and is found out. It is difficult to see in what

A   way a person committing an offence under section 1 impinges
directly on any definable material right vested by law in the
contracting parties such as to entitle them to legal protection
(post, pp. 33H—34B, 35C–E).
Decision of Walton J. reversed.

The following cases are referred to in the judgments:

B   *Acrow (Automation) Ltd.* v. *Rex Chainbelt Inc.* [1971] 1 W.L.R. 1676;
[1971] 3 All E.R. 1175, C.A.
Anton Piller K.G. v. *Manufacturing Processes Ltd.* [1976] Ch. 55;
[1976] 2 W.L.R. 162; [1976] 1 All E.R. 779, C.A.
Apple Corps Ltd. v. *Lingasong Ltd.* (1977) 3 F.S.R. 345.
Argyll (Duchess) v. *Argyll (Duke)* [1967] Ch. 302; [1965] 2 W.L.R.
790; [1965] 1 All E.R. 611.
Atkinson v. *Newcastle and Gateshead Waterworks Co.* (1877) 2 Ex.
C   D. 441.
Austria (Emperor of) v. *Day and Kossuth* (1861) 6 De G. F. & J. 217.
Benjamin v. *Storr* (1874) L.R. 9 C.P. 400.
Boyce v. *Paddington Borough Council* [1903] 1 Ch. 109.
Chamberlaine v. *Chester and Birkenhead Railway Co. Ltd.* (1848) 1 Exch.
870.
Cutler v. *Wandsworth Stadium Ltd.* [1949] A.C. 398; [1949] 1 All E.R.
D   544, H.L.(E.).
E.M.I. Ltd. v. *Pandit* [1975] 1 W.L.R. 302; [1975] 1 All E.R. 418.
Gouriet v. *Union of Post Office Workers* [1977] Q.B. 729; [1977] 2
W.L.R. 310; [1977] 1 All E.R. 696, C.A.; [1977] 3 W.L.R. 300;
[1977] 3 All E.R. 70, H.L.(E.).
Greig v. *Insole* [1978] 1 W.L.R. 302.
Groves v. *Lord Wimborne* [1898] 2 Q.B. 402, C.A.
E   *Institute of Patent Agents* v. *Lockwood* [1894] A.C. 347, H.L.(Sc.).
Iveson v. *Moore* (1699) 1 L.Raym. 486.
Levy v. *Walker* (1879) 10 Ch.D. 436, C.A.
McCall v. *Abelesz* [1976] Q.B. 585; [1976] 2 W.L.R. 151; [1976] 1 All
E.R. 727, C.A.
Monk v. *Warbey* [1935] 1 K.B. 75, C.A.
Musical Performers' Protection Association Ltd. v. *British International*
F   *Pictures Ltd.* (1930) 46 T.L.R. 485.
National Phonograph Co. Ltd. v. *Edison-Bell Consolidated Phonographic*
Co. Ltd. [1908] 1 Ch. 335, C.A.
Phillips v. *Britannia Hygienic Laundry Co.* [1923] 2 K.B. 832, C.A.
Simmonds v. *Newport Abercarn Black Vein Steam Coal Co. Ltd.* [1921]
1 K.B. 616, C.A.
G   *Solomons* v. *R. Gertzenstein Ltd.* [1954] 2 Q.B. 243; [1954] 3 W.L.R.
317; [1954] 2 All E.R. 625, C.A.
Springhead Spinning Co. Ltd. v. *Riley* (1868) L.R. 6 Eq. 551.
Torquay Hotel Co. Ltd. v. *Cousins* [1969] 2 Ch. 106; [1969] 2 W.L.R.
289; [1969] 1 All E.R. 522, C.A.

The following additional cases were cited in argument:

H   *Anonymous* (1703) 6 Mod.Cas. 27.
Bollinger (J.) v. *Costa Brava Wine Co. Ltd.* [1960] Ch. 262; [1959] 3
W.L.R. 966; [1959] 3 All E.R. 800.
Californian Theatres Pty. Ltd. v. *Hoyts Country Theatres Ltd.* [1959]
N.S.W.R. 188.
Ross v. *Rugge-Price* (1876) 1 Ex.D. 269.
Royal Crown Derby Porcelain Co. Ltd. v. *Russell* [1949] 2 K.B. 417;
[1949] 1 All E.R. 749, C.A.

Ex p. Island Records (C.A.)   [1978]

INTERLOCUTORY APPEAL from Walton J.   A

Thirty plaintiffs, consisting of recording companies, six being incorporated in accordance with the laws of the United States of America, and a number of performers who had exclusive contracts with the companies for making records and tapes of their live performances, issued a writ of summons in the Chancery Division and moved Walton J. ex parte (1) for an injunction against a defendant not named in public to restrain him whether acting by himself his servants or agents or any B of them or otherwise howsoever from doing the following acts: (i) making any record (including gramophone records and tapes) whether directly or indirectly from or by means of the performance by any one or more of the personal plaintiffs of a literary or musical work without the consent in writing of the plaintiff or plaintiffs concerned; (ii) selling, letting for hire, distributing for the purposes of trade or by way of C trade, exposing or offering for sale or using for the purposes of a public performance any such record as is mentioned in sub-paragraph (i) above; (iii) making or possessing any plate or similar contrivance for the purpose of making records as set out in sub-paragraph (i) above or otherwise committing any acts in contravention of the Performers' Protection Acts 1958 to 1972; (iv) interfering with contractual relations between any one or more of the personal plaintiffs and any one or more of the cor- D porate plaintiffs or otherwise interfering with the business of the plaintiffs or one or more of them by unlawful means; (iv) assisting, counselling, procuring, causing, or conspiring with any third party or parties to do any of the aforesaid acts. (2) An order for the delivery up or destruction upon oath of all records (including gramophone records and pre-recorded tapes) and plates and similar contrivances the sale of which or other E dealing in which by the defendant otherwise would be in breach of the aforesaid injunctions or any of them and/or the copying of which by the defendant would constitute a breach of injunction 1 (i) above which were in the possession, power, custody or control of the defendant. (3) An order that the defendant do make and serve on the plaintiffs' solicitors after such delivery up and/or destruction mentioned in paragraph 2 above, an affidavit verifying that the defendant has fully com- F plied with the order in paragraph 2 and no longer has in his possession, power, custody or control any such records, plates, or similar contrivances and further setting forth the names and addresses of all persons, firms, and companies to whom he has supplied and by whom he has been supplied with such records plates and similar contrivances together with the dates and quantities of all such supplies to or by him. (4) An G inquiry as to damages or at the plaintiffs' option an account of profits for unlawful interference with trade and breach of statutory duty together with an order for the payment of all sums found due upon taking such inquiry or account.

On the hearing of the motion the plaintiffs put forward a number of affidavits with exhibits thereto as evidence; but the judge declined H to consider it, since on his view of the authorities he had no jurisdiction to entertain the application for the order sought. He stated that there were serious matters to be argued inter partes and expressed the hope that the matter would be taken to the Court of Appeal to be tested at the earliest possible moment.

The plaintiffs applied ex parte to the Court of Appeal, which ex-

A pressed its wish to have the assistance of an amicus, and to hear the application with his assistance.

Hugh Laddie and *Mark Platts-Mills* for the plaintiffs.
Peter Gibson as amicus curiae.

Cur. adv. vult.

B
March 21. The following judgments were read.

LORD DENNING M.R. If you would like a caption for this case, I can suggest it. It is " Pop Artists want to stop Bootleggers." It needs explanation for the innocents. Take a popular group who play and sing live in a theatre or in a broadcasting studio. They give an exciting per-
C formance. This performance is transmitted on to a tape by a recording company. The company afterwards make records of it and sell them to the public. But there is a person in the audience or beside the wireless set who is listening to the performance. He has in his hand or his pocket one of the latest scientific devices. It is a tiny machine by which he records on tape this exciting performance. It is called a condenser
D microphone. Having recorded it on the one tape, he then uses the tape to make hundreds of copies and sell them in the form of cassettes and cartridges or gramophone records. Sometimes these are poor in quality. Sometimes they are as good as the records made by the recording com-panies themselves. They are sold to the public by small shopkeepers at cut prices and eat into the sales of the recording companies. The per-formers suffer also: because they receive royalties from the recording
E companies according to the number sold.

The performers, however, have no copyright in their performance: nor have the recording companies. No matter how brilliant the per-formance—which no one else could rival—nevertheless it is so intangible, so fleeting, so ethereal, that it is not protected by the law of copyright. The actual musical work which they play or sing may itself be the
F subject of copyright, but the performers have no right in that musical work itself. It may be out of copyright. It may be the work of an old composer who died long ago. Or it may be the copyright of a modern composer or owner, who has already been paid his due. The important thing to notice is that the performers themselves have no copyright.

No matter that the performers have no copyright, nevertheless the making of these secret tapes and records—and the selling of them—is
G quite illegal if it is done without the written consent of the performers. It is a criminal offence, punishable by fine or imprisonment. Those who engage in this trade are called " bootleggers." That is a term which was coined in the United States 100 years ago. Those engaged in illicit trading in liquor used to hide it in the upper part of their tall boots— the leg of the boot.

H We must distinguish these " bootleggers " from the " pirates " in the trade. " Pirates " are different in this way: they do not reproduce live performances. They reproduce existing records. They take the sound records made by the recording companies and reproduce them illicitly on their own tapes and records, and then sell these copies. They can sell them at a very low price, because they have a cheap apparatus for copying, and do not have to maintain studios, or pay artists. They are sold by small shopkeepers in poor surroundings.

These copies are not only illegal. They are infringement of copyright. **A**
They infringe the copyright of the recording companies in their existing
records. These infringers are called "pirates" because "piracy" has
long been used to describe the infringement of copyright, as in the phrase
"literary piracy."

These "pirates" used to do an enormous trade in infringing copies
of recorded music. It was very difficult to catch them. As soon as one
small shopkeeper was sued, he got rid of all infringing material. He **B**
passed his stock to a fellow pirate: and then declared that he never
had any records except the one which the plaintiffs had discovered. This
stratagem was, however, defeated by the enterprise of Mr. Laddie. He
persuaded the judges of the Chancery Division to make an order—ex
parte—on the shopkeeper before the writ is served. This order is
served on him, with the writ, in the presence of a solicitor. It catches **C**
the pirate unawares—before he has had time to destroy or dispose of
his infringing stock or his incriminating papers. It requires him to disclose all relevant material that he has. The order "freezes" the stock
which he has and enables the plaintiff to inspect it. The order contained safeguards to see that no injustice was done. The first reported
case was the order made by Templeman J. in *E.M.I. Ltd.* v. *Pandit*
[1975] 1 W.L.R. 302. The practice was confirmed and consolidated by **D**
the decision of this court in *Anton Piller K.G.* v. *Manufacturing Processes Ltd.* [1976] Ch. 55. The effect of these ex parte orders has been
dramatic. When served with them, the shopkeepers have acknowledged
their wrongdoing and thrown their hand in. So useful are these orders
that they are in daily use—not only in cases of infringement of copyright, but also in passing-off cases, and other cases. They are called **E**
"*Anton Piller*" orders.

Now we have the question whether *Anton Piller* orders can be
made against bootleggers. To a layman there would seem no difference
between pirates and bootleggers. If an *Anton Piller* order can be
made against a pirate, it should be possible, too, against a bootlegger.
But there is a difference in law. A "pirate" is guilty of a civil wrong. **F**
He is infringing the copyright of the recording companies in their tapes
and records. But a "bootlegger" is not guilty of a civil wrong. He is
only guilty of a crime. Many of the judges have ignored this difference.
They have been granted *Anton Piller* orders ex parte against bootleggers.
We are told that Cantley, Plowman, Foster, Whitford, Fox and Slade JJ.
have granted them. None of those cases has been reported. But three
judges have refused them: McCardie J. in *Musical Performers' Pro-* **G**
tection Association Ltd. v. *British International Pictures Ltd.* (1930) 46
T.L.R. 485: Sir Robert Megarry V.-C. in *Apple Corps Ltd.* v. *Lingasong
Ltd.* (1977) 3 F.S.R. 345: and Walton J. in this present case on January 3,
1978. This is an appeal from Walton J.'s decision. It raised a point of
such importance—in which the defendant was not represented—that we
asked the Attorney-General if he would appoint an amicus curiae to help **H**
us. He appointed Mr. Gibson, and his assistance has been invaluable.

The statute

The first point is on the statute. It clearly makes "bootlegging"
a crime. But does it confer a civil cause of action on the performers
and recording companies?

A   There have been two main statutes. The first Dramatic and Musical
Performers' Protection Act in 1925. The second in 1958. There are two
additional statutes increasing penalties. One of 1963. The other is 1972.
I will read only the material parts of section 1 of the present 1958
statute:

B   "... if a person knowingly—(a) makes a record, directly or in-
      directly from or by means of the performance of a dramatic or
      musical work without the consent in writing of the performers, ...
      he shall be guilty of an offence under this Act, and shall be liable"

to a fine of £20 for each record made or punishment of two years or
both.

C *Civil action for damages*

    The courts have discussed on many occasions whether or not the
breach of a statute (which prescribes only criminal penalties) also gives
a civil action for damages. On this point "the only rule" said Lord
Simonds in *Cutler* v. *Wandsworth Stadium Ltd.* [1949] A.C. 398, 407

      "which in all circumstances is valid is that the answer must depend
D   on a consideration of the whole Act and the circumstances, includ-
      ing the pre-existing law, in which it was enacted."

Mr. Laddie submitted that the statutes here were passed for the protection of a particular person or class of persons, namely, the performers. That was seen from the fact that the performers could give or
refuse their written consent. So this case came, he said, within the
E pro-cases, such as *Groves* v. *Lord Wimborne* [1898] 2 Q.B. 402; *Monk*
v. *Warbey* [1935] 1 K.B. 75 and *Solomons* v. *R. Gertzenstein Ltd.* [1954]
2 Q.B. 243. But Mr. Laddie's proposition is not universally true. There
are numerous penal statutes which could be said to be passed for the
protection of a particular class of persons which have been held not to
give rise to a civil action for damages. These are the contra-cases, such
as *Atkinson* v. *Newcastle and Gateshead Waterworks Co.* (1877) 2 Ex.D.
F 441; *Phillips* v. *Britannia Hygienic Laundry Co.* [1923] 2 Q.B. 832 and
Cutler v. *Wandsworth Stadium Ltd.* [1949] A.C. 398.

    The truth is that in many of these statutes the legislature has left the
point open. It has ignored the plea of Lord du Parcq in *Cutler's* case
[1949] A.C. 398, 410. So it has left the courts with a guess-work
puzzle. The dividing line between the pro-cases and the contra-cases
G is so blurred and so ill-defined that you might as well toss a coin to decide
it. I decline to indulge in such a game of chance. To my mind, we
should seek for other ways to do " therein what to justice shall appertain." *

The protection of private rights

    The way was pointed out by Mr. Gibson, who was engaged in the
recent case of *Gouriet* v. *Union of Post Office Workers* [1977] 3 W.L.R.
H 300. He drew attention to the rule of the Court of Equity in these matters. It intervened to protect a private individual in his rights of property,
and in aid of this would grant an injunction to restrain a defendant from
committing an unlawful act, even though it was a crime punishable by the
criminal court: and would supplement its jurisdiction in this regard by its

---

* *Note.* These words are taken from the Commission of Assize which used to
be read on the opening of every Assize.

Lord Denning M.R.　　　　　**Ex p. Island Records (C.A.)**　　　　　**[1978]**

power under Lord Cairns' Act to award damages in lieu of or in addition A to an injunction.

The result of *Gouriet's* case may be summarised thus: when a statute creates a criminal offence—prescribing a penalty for the breach of it but not giving any civil remedy—the general rule is that no private individual can bring an action to enforce the criminal law, either by way of an injunction or by damages. It must be left to the Attorney-General to bring an action, either of his own motion or at the instance B of a member of the public who "relates" the facts to him.

But there is an exception to this rule in any case where the criminal act is not only an offence against the public at large, but also causes or threatens to cause special damage to a private individual. If a private individual can show that he has a private right which is being interfered with by the criminal act—thus causing or threatening to cause him C special damage over and above the generality of the public—then he can come to the court as a private individual and ask that his private right be protected: see *Gouriet's* case [1977] 3 W.L.R. 300, 324F by Viscount Dilhorne, at p. 331B–E by Lord Diplock, at pp. 337D, 343G by Lord Edmund-Davies, and at p. 348D by Lord Fraser of Tullybelton. The court can, in those circumstances, grant an injunction to restrain the offender from continuing or repeating his criminal act. It is no answer D then for the defendant to say: "It is a crime which I am about to commit. If an injunction is granted, I shall be in double jeopardy if I break it—on the one hand for contempt of court in the civil jurisdiction—and on the other hand for a penalty in the criminal jurisdiction." The reply to him is simple: "All the more reason why you should not break the law. You will then be in no jeopardy. If you do E break it, you will not be punished twice over. Whichever court deals with you, it will take into consideration the punishment which has been, or can be, inflicted by the other."

The exception depends, however, on the private individual having a private right which he is entitled to have protected. That was made clear long ago by Holt C.J. in the leading case of *Iveson* v. *Moore* (1699) 1 L. Raym. 486, when he was considering a public nuisance by F stopping up a highway leading to a colliery. It was a criminal act, but it was held that the colliery owner could bring an action against the offender if he could show special damage. Holt C.J. said, at pp. 492–493:

"... actions upon the case for nuisances are founded upon particular rights; but where there is not any particular right, the G plaintiff shall not have an action."

The question, therefore, becomes this: has the plaintiff a particular right which he is entitled to have protected? To this the answer which runs through all the cases is this: A man who is carrying on a lawful trade or calling has a right to be protected from any unlawful interference with it: see *Acrow (Automation) Ltd.* v. *Rex Chainbelt Inc.* H [1971] 1 W.L.R. 1676. It is a right which is in the nature of a right of property. Such as a right to have the access to your premises kept clear without being obstructed by nuisance or smells: see *Benjamin* v. *Storr* (1874) L.R. 9 C.P. 400: or a right to run a ferry for profit across the river Mersey without being injured by rail traffic contrary to the penal statute: see *Chamberlaine* v. *Chester and Birkenhead Railway Co. Ltd.* (1848) 1 Exch. 870, 877, 879: or a right to prevent

3 W.L.R.   **Ex p. Island Records (C.A.)**   **Lord Denning M.R.**

A spurious notes being circulated to the damage of the plaintiff's interests: see *Emperor of Austria* v. *Day and Kossuth* (1861) 6 De G. F. & J. 217, 251–255: or a right to prevent passing-off: see *Levy* v. *Walker* (1879) 10 Ch.D. 436, 448, by James L.J.: or a right to have your servants come unhindered to work, even though it is only made unlawful by a penal statute: see *Springhead Spinning Co. Ltd.* v. *Riley* (1868) L.R. 6 Eq. 551, 561–562: or a right to have your contractual relations maintained

B inviolate without interference by others, unless there is just cause or excuse: see *National Phonograph Co. Ltd.* v. *Edison-Bell Consolidated Phonographic Co. Ltd.* [1908] 1 Ch. 335, 339; *Torquay Hotel Co. Ltd.* v. *Cousins* [1969] 2 Ch. 106, 138 and the recent cricketers' case *Greig* v. *Insole* [1978] 1 W.L.R. 302, 332–338 by Slade J.: or a right in a workman to have his pay slip properly vouched, even though it is only

C made unlawful by a penal statute: see *Simmonds* v. *Newport Abercarn Black Vein Steam Coal Co. Ltd.* [1921] 1 K.B. 616 (where a declaration was granted). In all these cases the unlawful interference may be a tort, such as fraud or passing-off; or it may be a crime, such as a public nuisance; or a breach of a statute which imposes only criminal penalties: but whatever be the nature of the unlawful interference, the party concerned is entitled to come himself to the courts of law and ask to

D be protected from the unlawful interference. It is no answer for the defendant to say: " It is a crime: and so you cannot sue me." It would be a sorry state of the law if a man could excuse himself by such a plea —and thus cause special damage with impunity. For the fact must be faced: the criminal law is a broken reed in some of these cases. At any rate in this particular case. The police have not the men or the means

E to investigate the offence or to track down the offenders or to prosecute them. Nor have they the will. Nor has the Attorney-General. He has, we are told, refused his consent to a relator action—presumably because no public rights are involved. So perforce if the law is to be obeyed— and justice be done—the courts must allow a private individual himself to bring an action against the offender—in those cases where his private rights and interests are specially affected by the breach.

F   This principle is capable of extension so as to apply not only to rights of property or rights in the nature of it, but to other rights or interests, such as the right of a man to his good name and reputation: see *Argyll (Duchess)* v. *Argyll (Duke)* [1967] Ch. 302, 344: and his right to the lawful transmission of his mail: see my illustration in *Gouriet's* case [1977] Q.B. 729, 756–757.

G
The present case

   In the present case both the performers and the recording companies have, to my mind, private rights and interests which they are entitled to have protected from unlawful interference. The recording companies have the right to exploit the records made by them of the performances.

H The performers have the right to the royalty payable to them out of those records. Those rights are buttressed by the contracts between the recording companies and the performers. They are rights in the nature of rights of property. Both the recording companies and the performers suffer severe damage if those rights are unlawfully interfered with. Suppose that the bootlegger in the audience had in his hand or his pocket—instead of a recording device—a distorting device: and by it he could introduce a squeak or a screech into the musical performance:

32

and thus ruin its commercial value. No one could doubt that the **A**
recording company and the performers could bring an action to stop
him and claim damages. That illustration shows that they have a
private right which they are entitled to have protected: and this is so,
no matter whether the interference be by means of a tortious act or
a criminal act. The wrongdoer cannot take advantage of his own crime
so as to damage a private individual with impunity.

All the cases suggested to the contrary can be distinguished. Thus **B**
in *Institute of Patent Agents* v. *Lockwood* [1894] A.C. 347 the plaintiff
had nothing in the nature of a right of property and had suffered no
special damages. In the *Musical Performers'* case before McCardie J.,
46 T.L.R. 485, and the *Apple Corps'* case before Sir Robert Megarry V.-C.,
3 F.S.R. 345, it was thought that the courts can only give relief in the case
of rights of property, strictly so called, whereas the cases I have cited **C**
show that the courts give relief whenever there is unlawful interference
with the plaintiff's trade or calling.

So my conclusion is that the courts have jurisdiction to grant an
Anton Piller order in regard to bootleggers, just as they have regard
to pirates. I am confirmed in this view by the fact that it carries out
to the full the recommendations of the Committee presided over by
Whitford J., 1977 (Cmnd. No. 6732), paragraphs 412 (iii), 414 (iv), **D**
419 (iv). The granting of the " Anton Piller " order is subject to the
safeguards mentioned in the report of that case. I would, therefore,
allow this appeal and remit the case to the judge for him to deal with
bootleggers just as is done in the case of pirates.

SHAW L.J. The world of pop music is in these times richly endowed **E**
and prosperous. It is not therefore surprising that it is much afflicted
by parasites. Pop stars and the recording companies who are their
sponsors and exploiters naturally wish to rid themselves of poachers
who prey upon what they properly regard as their preserve.

The question that arises on this appeal is whether the law has
adequately provided for the protection of that preserve from the activities **F**
of predators who in the pop music scene are described as pirates when
they make and sell copies of discs or tapes in breach of copyright
and as bootleggers when they make an unauthorised direct recording of
a live performance for the purpose of reproducing it for sale to the public.

Whichever of these illicit courses is pursued may, it is asserted,
cause financial detriment to recording companies who contract with pop
musicians for the exclusive right to reproduce their vocal and instru- **G**
mental efforts on discs or tapes for the general delectation of dedicated
votaries of pop music.

There are practical difficulties in the way of the detection and
exposure of these pirates and bootleggers. If any should be suspected
of having in their possession unauthorised discs or tapes, there is no
statutory or other power to grant a search warrant so that their premises **H**
may be entered and their contents scrutinised. Should a writ be
issued in pursuance of some cause of action, the service of the writ
would give advance notice of a prospective order for discovery and the
defendant would have an ample opportunity to dispose of the contraband
in his possession before such an order was made.

It was in the light of these difficulties that following the issue of a writ
on behalf of a number of recording companies and pop musicians against

A   a bootlegger defendant, Mr. Laddie as counsel for the plaintiffs moved ex parte before Walton J. for an *Anton Piller* order in furtherance of the relief claimed in the writ.

The judge declined to make the order sought, holding that the plaintiffs failed to show that they were entitled to any right recognised in law which the order could serve to protect.

B   So far as is material for present purposes the injunction claimed by the writ sought, inter alia, to restrain the defendant by himself his servants or agents from (i) making any record (including gramophone records and tapes) whether directly or indirectly from or by means of the performance by any one or more of the personal plaintiffs of a literary or musical work without the consent in writing of the plaintiff or plaintiffs concerned . . . (iv) interfering with contractual relations

C   between any one or more of the personal plaintiffs and any one or more of the corporate plaintiffs or otherwise interfering with the business of the plaintiffs or one or more of them by unlawful means.

Mr. Laddie founded his case on two alternative propositions. The first was developed from the provisions of the Dramatic and Musical Performers' Protection Act 1958. The contention put forward was that the Act gave rise to a statutory duty to dramatic and musical performers

D   and that the duty was one enforceable by action on the part of those to whom the duty was owed. The Act is expressed to be enacted in order " to consolidate the Dramatic and Musical Performers Protection Act 1925, and the provisions of the Copyright Act 1956 amending it." The inelegant rubric to section 1 is " Penalization of making &c., records without consent of performers." The body of the section reads:

E

> " Subject to the provisions of this Act, if a person knowingly—
> (a) makes a record, directly or indirectly from or by means of the performance of a dramatic or musical work without the consent in writing of the performers, or (b) sells or lets for hire, or distributes for the purposes of trade, or by way of trade exposes or offers for sale or hire, a record made in contravention of this Act, or (c) uses

F

> for the purposes of a public performance a record so made, he shall be guilty of an offence under this Act . . . and shall be liable . . . to a fine. . . ."

Mr. Laddie's submission was that this language on its proper construction had the result of creating a statutory duty to performers which invested them with a cause of action and gave them a right of

G   action for appropriate relief against any person who was in breach of that duty by reason of committing an offence under the section.

The essential issue therefore is whether the terms of the section are to be so construed as to bring contraventions of it within the class of case exemplified by *Groves* v. *Lord Wimborne* [1898] 2 Q.B. 402, or whether they give rise to the interpretation and effect demonstrated by

H   *Cutler* v. *Wandsworth Stadium Ltd.* [1949] A.C. 398. It seems to me to be beyond contention that the section falls within the scope of the later decision. A similar problem fell to be considered in *McCall* v. *Abelesz* [1976] Q.B. 585 in regard to harassment by a landlord in contravention of section 30 of the Rent Act 1965. I ventured there in the course of my judgment (at p. 600), to emphasise that the essential requirement for the conferring of a civil remedy by a penal provision was that the offence created must consist of a failure to perform a defined duty

which the statute imposes on the potential offender for the benefit of a   **A**
particular class of person. In a general sense no doubt every penal
statute imposes a duty owed to the public not to offend against its
provisions. This is very far from a situation in which a duty is defined
for the benefit of a particular class. One looks in vain at section 1 of
the Act of 1958 for any definition in terms of such a duty. It does no
more than provide for the punishment of certain conduct in relation
to dramatic or musical works.   **B**

    To distil from the language of the section a specific duty to per-
formers would involve an illicit process of interpretation. That the
product might be potable cannot justify the method or the result.

    The decision in *Musical Performers' Protection Association Ltd.* v.
British International Pictures Ltd. (1930) 46 T.L.R. 485 was right; and
it was affirmed in *Apple Corps Ltd.* v. *Lingasong Ltd.* (1977) 3 F.S.R. 345.   **C**

    The first proposition advanced on behalf of the appellants is
accordingly, in my view, untenable and should be rejected.

    The second proposition was more widely based. It was submitted that
performers whose performances were " bootlegged," to use the jargon
of the pop world, came within the general rule that

    " a private person is . . . entitled to sue in respect of interference   **D**
    with a public right if either there is also interference with a private
    right of his or the interference with the public right will inflict
    special damage on him. . . ."

per Lord Fraser of Tullybelton in *Gouriet* v. *Union of Post Office
Workers* [1977] 3 W.L.R. 300, 348 citing *Boyce* v. *Paddington Borough
Council* [1903] 1 Ch. 109.   **E**

    Mr. Laddie contended that if on its proper construction section 1 of
the Act was only penal in its character and operation, nonetheless a
contravention of its provisions inflicted special and particular damage
on performers and also on recording companies with whom performers
contracted for the exclusive production and reproduction of their performances. Mr. Gibson, who gave very great assistance to the court   **F**
in the role of amicus, was prepared to concede that having regard to
the contractual rights as between recording companies and their performers there might be said to be vested in those parties a special
interest in the enforcement of the provisions of the section. In regard
to those parties special damage would be suffered by the recording and
reproduction of a performance in contravention of the statute. So the
argument went. Hence, albeit such a contravention was primarily an   **G**
interference with a public right, the recording companies and performers
might have a title to sue. Mr. Laddie cited in support of this *Argyll*
(*Duchess*) v. *Argyll* (*Duke*) [1967] Ch. 302. That decision, however,
was in respect of a special relationship, namely, marriage, and a special
quality or obligation which developed from it, namely, confidentiality.
These are readily identifiable and definable.   **H**

    Another authority on which he sought to rely was *Emperor of
Austria* v. *Day and Kossuth* (1861) 6 De G. F. & J. 217. Lord Campbell
L.C. in his judgment said, at p. 238:

    " Notwithstanding my sincere respect for the authority of that great
    American jurist, Justice Story, I cannot concur with him in his
    recommendation of a mysterious obscurity to be preserved by
    Courts of Equity respecting special injunctions, and the caution

A   which should make them ' decline to lay down any rule which shall
limit their power and discretion as to the particular cases in which
such injunctions should be granted or withheld.' I think that all
branches of the law should, if possible, be made clear and simple,
and should be defined as accurately as possible."

A little later in his judgment, he said, at p. 240:

B   " I consider that this court has jurisdiction by injunction to protect
property from an act threatened, which if completed would give a
right of action. I by no means say that in every such case an
injunction may be demanded as of right, but if the party applying
is free from blame and promptly applies for relief, and shows that
by the threatened wrong his property would be so injured that an
C   action for damages would be no adequate redress, the injunction
will be granted."

As I understand those observations, the interest to be protected must
be of a character which is capable of ready recognition and definition.

The contract between a recording company and a performer imposes
no obligations on third parties save not to procure a breach by one
D   party or the other. It leaves them under no responsibility but the general
one of obeying the law. If they transgress it and are found out they
pay the prescribed penalty. I cannot see in what way they invade or
impinge directly upon any definable material right vested by law in
the contracting parties. Whatever interest there is appears to me too
nebulous and amorphous to carry the aspect of a right susceptible of
legal protection. It may be that this is why the legislature has not
E   attributed a form of quasi-copyright to performances themselves. In my
view the courts cannot make good the hiatus by granting a remedy in
vacuo. It is not unimportant to remember that a search warrant could
not be obtained in a criminal court where a person is suspected of
offences under the section. If the claim for relief put forward is well
founded, the making of an *Anton Piller* order would be at least a
F   possibility. Thus the civil remedy said to arise collaterally from a penal
provision would go beyond what the criminal law permits in the enforcement of that provision. It is not, in my view, a proper function of the
courts indirectly to stiffen the sinews of a criminal statute. I much
regret, therefore, that I come to a different conclusion from that stated
by Lord Denning M.R. in his judgment and from that which I understand will be expressed by Waller L.J. in his judgment. I would dismiss
G   the appeal.

WALLER L.J. This is an appeal from a decision of Walton J. refusing
an *Anton Piller* order in a case arising out of the Dramatic and Musical
Performers' Protection Act 1958. The appeal is upon a preliminary
point because Walton J. held that it was not competent for the plaintiffs
H   to maintain this kind of action against the defendant at all. The court
is not concerned as to whether on the actual facts of the case an *Anton
Piller* order should be made but merely whether, if the facts justified
it, it would be competent to maintain this kind of action.

Section 1 of the Dramatic and Musical Performers' Protection Act
1958 states:

"Subject to the provisions of this Act, if a person knowingly—
(a) makes a record, directly or indirectly from or by means of the

performance of a dramatic or musical work without the consent in A
writing of the performers, or (b) sells or lets for hire, or distributes
for the purposes of trade, or by way of trade exposes or offers for
sale or hire, a record made in contravention of this Act, or (c) uses
for the purposes of a public performance a record so made, he shall
be guilty of an offence under this Act . . . and shall be liable . . .
to a fine. . . ."

B

The factual background to this case is that in the pop music world
star performers make contracts with recording companies for their
exclusive services. The recording company then sells the records and
makes profits from the sales. The performer, on his or her part, obtains
a royalty on each sale. The record company owns the copyright in the
record and if anybody makes a copy of that record there is an infringement of copyright and damages can be claimed. If, on the other hand, C
an unauthorised recording is made at a concert there is no breach of
copyright because there is no copyright in the concert performance.
The remedy lies in the section which I have just quoted. It is submitted
by Mr. Laddie that this statute creates a duty of permission or omission
for the benefit of a particular person or class of persons and that the
language of the section and the surrounding circumstances are such as D
to enable the plaintiffs, who are the record company, to claim damages
for breach of statutory duty. There is an alternative way in which the
case can be put which I will consider hereafter.

Whether or not an individual can bring a common law action in
respect of a breach of duty imposed by a statute depends on whether
the intention of the statute, considered as a whole and in the circumstances in which it was made and to which it relates, was to impose a E
duty which is a public duty only or to impose in addition a duty
enforceable by an aggrieved individual: see *Halsbury's Laws of England,*
3rd ed., vol. 36 (1961), para. 687 and cases there cited. In this case
there are several matters which have to be considered in deciding
whether or not there is a duty, breach of which will give rise to a cause
of action. This Act is an Act to protect performers. The record F
companies are within the scope of the Act and penalties go to the
Crown and not to the performers. It can be said also that there are
no alternative rights. On the other hand, an examination of the section
can be said to show that the only remedy is a criminal remedy and
when one contrasts it with the Copyright Act 1956 there are, in the
Copyright Act, specific remedies in both civil and criminal law which G
are specifically set out. Furthermore it is said that there is no defined
duty under this section.

The words " if a person knowingly . . . makes a record . . . or sells
. . . he shall be guilty of an offence " do not impose a duty. All the
cases in which it has been held that there is a duty imposed which can
be made the subject of a private action are cases where a clear duty
is stated. For example, the "roof and sides of every . . . working place H
shall be made secure": section 49 of the Coal Mines Act 1911.
Dangerous parts of machinery " shall be securely fenced ": see *Groves*
v. *Lord Wimborne* [1898] 2 Q.B. 402: see also *Atkinson* v. *Newcastle
and Gateshead Waterworks Co.* (1877) 2 Ex.D. 441, and *Cutler* v.
Wandsworth Stadium Ltd. [1949] A.C. 398. We were referred to a
number of other cases, but there is no case so far as counsel could
discover where phraseology similar to that in the section we are con-

A sidering has been held to impose a duty on which an action can be
framed. I am satisfied therefore that no action can be brought for a
simple breach of statutory duty under this section.

I next go on to consider the alternative way of putting this case;
one in which the court has had the assistance not only of Mr. Laddie,
on behalf of the plantiffs, but of Mr. Gibson, as amicus curiae. Can
it be said that equity gives a remedy in the circumstances of this case?

B
In *Emperor of Austria* v. *Day and Kossuth*, 6 De G. F. & J. 217, the
court, on appeal from Stuart V.-C., held that the plaintiff was entitled to
the delivery up by the defendants of bank notes printed by the defendants
and of the plate from which they were printed. Turner L.J. said, at
pp. 253–254:

C
"I agree that the jurisdiction of this court in a case of this nature
rests upon injury to property actual or prospective, and that this
court has no jurisdiction to prevent the commission of acts which
are merely criminal or merely illegal, and do not affect any rights
of property, but I think there are here rights of property quite
sufficient to found jurisdiction in this court."

D
Then in *Springhead Spinning Co. Ltd*. v. *Riley* (1868) L.R. 6 Eq. 551, 560,
Malins V.-C. said:

"The truth, I apprehend, is, that the court will interfere to prevent
acts amounting to crime, if they do not stop at crime, but also
go to the destruction or deterioration of the value of property."

The former case involved the printing of unauthorised bank notes, and
E the latter conspiracy to prevent persons working for the plaintiffs.

In *National Phonograph Co. Ltd*. v. *Edison-Bell Consolidated Phonographic Co. Ltd*. [1908] 1 Ch. 335, 361 Buckley L.J. said:

"The act which the defendants did was, I think, a violation of a
legal right of the plaintiffs, because it interfered with the contractual relations subsisting between the plaintiffs and the factors,
F   and there was no sufficient justification for such interference. There
is another ground upon which the same conclusion may be based,
and that is interference with rights of property. The business of
the plaintiff company was property. The sale of phonographic
machines induced the purchase, by the purchasers of such machines,
of accessories to be used with them, the principal subject matter
being records, whose sale produced a profit much larger than that
G   made on the machine itself. The purchase by the defendants of
the 700 or other number of machines which they, in fact, bought
might affect the subsequent sale by the plaintiffs of the records,
and thus affect the plaintiffs' property in their business."

In *Argyll (Duchess)* v. *Argyll (Duke)* [1967] Ch. 302, 244, Ungoed-
H Thomas J. said after quoting *Emperor of Austria* v. *Day and Kossuth*
and *Springhead Spinning Co. Ltd*. v. *Riley*:

"These quotations are hardly reconcilable unless intended as no
more than particular illustrations or applications of the principle
that the old Court of Chancery would not grant an injunction unless
there was a ground which it recognised as giving jurisdiction—
whether the protection of infants, or of property or of civil rights,
which it was bound to protect."

Finally in *Gouriet* v. *Union of Post Office Workers* [1977] 3 W.L.R. A
300, the House of Lords, while denying that the plaintiff could bring
proceedings when he personally had suffered no damage, expressly
reserved the situation where damage was suffered. For example, Lord
Diplock said, at p. 331:

> " For the protection of the private right created by such a statute
> a court of civil jurisdiction has jurisdiction to grant to the person B
> entitled to the private right, *but to none other,* an injunction to
> restrain a certain breach of it by the defendant."

And later:

> " The words italicised "
> " in the last paragraph are important words for they draw
> attention to the fact that the jurisdiction of a civil court to grant C
> remedies in private law is confined to the grant of remedies to
> litigants whose rights in private law have been infringed or are
> threatened with infringement."

In the present case, therefore, assuming that there has been a breach
of section 1 of the Dramatic and Musical Performers' Protection Act
1958, can it be said that there is a right of property which is being D
damaged? The record company has contracted with performers to have
their exclusive services. If therefore somebody makes a record of a
performance by one of the performers to whose services one of the
record companies has the exclusive right, the record company will suffer
an injury to a right of property. That exclusive contractual right would
be interfered with by actions which would be a breach of the law
and would in fact be criminal offences. Similarly the performer who E
is entitled to a royalty for each copy of a recording of his performance
would also suffer injury because a recording of his performance would
be being sold without his drawing the royalty to which he is entitled.

Before coming to a final conclusion there are three other cases to
which I should refer. The first is *Institute of Patent Agents* v. *Lockwood* [1894] A.C. 347, 361, where Lord Herschell L.C. expresses the F
view that where there is a liability to a £20 penalty it would not be right
for the Court of Session to make a declaration that an individual had
been breaking the law when the correct procedure was to go before a
summary court. The second is *Musical Performers' Protection Association Ltd.* v. *British International Pictures Ltd.* (1930) 46 T.L.R. 485
where McCardie J. had to consider a claim under the Dramatic and G
Musical Performers' Protection Act 1925. The judge's decision was
clearly right on the facts because after quoting the passage from Turner
L.J. in the *Emperor of Austria* case he found that on the facts there
was no interference with any right of property. The third case is *Apple
Corps Ltd.* v. *Lingasong Ltd.* (1977) 3 F.S.R. 345, a decision of Sir
Robert Megarry V.-C. on section 1 of the Act of 1958. This also is, if I
may respectfully say so, a decision which was clearly right on the facts H
and arguments put before the court. It was, however, never alleged
before the Vice-Chancellor that this right of property was being infringed
by an unlawful act. It was alleged to be a tort of misappropriation of the
reputations of others, and this the Vice-Chancellor rejected.

Accordingly I am satisfied that in equity there is jurisdiction for a
court to grant an injunction to a person who claims that he suffered
special damage to a property interest of his by a crime and that in the

A circumstances of this case both the record company and the performer
would be entitled to such injunction.
   I should add that in some respects the making of an *Anton Piller*
order resembles the granting of a search warrant. There are however
safeguards in that the consent of the defendant is required before any
search is conducted. Furthermore I entirely agree with the observations
of Ormrod L.J. in *Anton Piller K.G.* v. *Manufacturing Processes Ltd.*
B [1976] Ch. 55, 62 where he laid down the three essential pre-conditions:

> " First, there must be an extremely strong prima facie case.
> Secondly, the damage, potential or actual, must be very serious for
> the applicant. Thirdly, there must be clear evidence that the
> defendants have in their possession incriminating documents or
> things, and that there is a real possibility that they may destroy
C such material before any application inter partes can be made."

Appeal allowed.
No order as to costs.
Case remitted to judge of Chancery
Division for determination as to
D *whether on facts an Anton Piller*
order should be made.

Solicitors: *A. E. Hamlin & Co.; Treasury Solicitor.*

M. M. H.

E ──────────

[COURT OF APPEAL]

JADE INTERNATIONAL STEEL STAHL UND EISEN GmbH &
CO. KG *v.* ROBERT NICHOLAS (STEELS) LTD.
F

1978 Feb. 24   Stephenson, Geoffrey Lane and
                                         Cumming-Bruce L.JJ.

Bill of Exchange—Notice of dishonour—Claim by holder for pay-
ment—Dishonoured bill of exchange returned to drawer by
holder in due course—Drawer applying as holder of bill for
G *summary judgment—Whether his rights to payment those of*
holder in due course—Bills of Exchange Act 1882 (45 & 46
Vict. c. 61), s. 29 (3) [1]

A bill of exchange, payable at 120 days, was drawn by the
plaintiffs on the defendants for DM485,859.50, being the price
of the first of two consignments of steel under a contract dated
January 31, 1977. The bill was discounted by the plaintiffs
H to their bank in Germany, and subsequently transferred
through another bank to the Midland Bank. It was accepted
by the defendants, but dishonoured on presentation for payment because of a dispute about the quality of the steel which
had been supplied and they refused to accept the second

──────────

[Reported by ROBERT WILLIAMS, ESQ., Barrister-at-Law]

[1] Bills of Exchange Act 1882, s. 29: see post, pp. 42G—43A.

Jade International v. Robert Nicholas Ltd. (C.A.)   **[1978]**

A

consignment of steel. The bill was returned after dishonour by the same route to the original discounting bank, who debited the plaintiffs' account with the amount of the bill and handed it back. The plaintiffs sued the defendants for breach of contract in refusing to accept the second consignment of steel and also claimed the amount of the dishonoured bill. On a summons under R.S.C., Ord. 14, Donaldson J. gave judgment for the amount of the bill on the ground that there was no discretion to grant leave to defend, since the plaintiffs derived their title to the bill not as drawers but from the holders in due course and, therefore, they had the right of such holders to immediate payment.

B

On appeal by the defendants: —

Held, dismissing the appeal, that although the plaintiffs were the drawers of the bill, they derived their title from the holders in due course and, by virtue of section 29 (3) of the Bills of Exchange Act 1882, they, as holders of the bill, had all the rights of a holder in due course, and that it was in accordance with that section that their rights were to be determined and not in their capacity as drawers (post, pp. 44F–H, 46B–C, G–H).

C

Decision of Donaldson J. affirmed.

The following case is referred to in the judgments:

Lamont (James) & Co. Ltd. v. *Hyland Ltd.* [1950] 1 K.B. 585; [1950] 1 All E.R. 341, C.A.

D

The following additional case was cited in argument:

Bank of England v. *Vagliano* [1891] A.C. 107, H.L.(E.).

APPEAL from Donaldson J.

E

By a specially indorsed writ dated September 14, 1977, the plaintiffs, Jade International Steel Stahl und Eisen GmbH & Co. KG, claimed DM485,859.50, being the amount of a bill of exchange drawn by them and accepted by the defendants which had been dishonoured on presentation for payment. The bill was the contract price of the first of two consignments of steel under a contract dated January 31, 1977. As a result of a dispute about the quality of the steel the defendants had dishonoured the bill and refused to accept the second of the two consignments. The plaintiffs also claimed damages for breach of contract arising out of that refusal. On a summons under R.S.C., Ord. 14, Donaldson J. gave leave to the defendants to defend the second claim, but gave immediate judgment for the amount of the bill on the ground that there was no discretion to allow leave to defend a claim for a dishonoured bill of exchange where the plaintiffs were not immediate parties to the bill, and that they were not to be treated as immediate parties in the present case because they had discounted the bill to a bank which had returned it to them after dishonour, and they stood in the shoes of the bank, who had the undoubted right to judgment.

F

G

The defendants appealed on the ground that the judge was wrong in holding that the plaintiffs ought to be treated as indorsees of the bill and not as immediate parties, and thus wrong in refusing to exercise his discretion to make an order other than an order for immediate payment of the full amount of the bill.

H

The facts are stated in the judgment of Geoffrey Lane L.J.

Peter Bowsher for the defendants.
Timothy Saloman for the plaintiffs.

A   STEPHENSON L.J.   I will ask Geoffrey Lane L.J. to give the first judgment.

GEOFFREY LANE L.J.   This is an appeal from the order of Donaldson J. which was given on November 22, 1977, by which he gave judgment for the plaintiffs, a West German concern, for some DM485,859.

The facts which lie behind the case can be expressed with comparative B brevity.   The plaintiffs, as their name implies, deal in steel.   Their main place of business is Dusseldorf.   In January 1977 they sold to the defendants, an English limited company, some 2,000 tonnes of steel for delivery in the United Kingdom in two separate lots of 1,000 tonnes each.   A bill of exchange was drawn by the plaintiffs.   The steel in the first consignment in respect of which the bill of exchange had been drawn was C said by the defendants to be sub-standard and not according to the terms of the contract.   They therefore refused to accept the second instalment, and, so far as the first instalment was concerned, when the bill of exchange was presented for payment it was dishonoured.   These proceedings arise out of that dishonour.

The plaintiffs took Order 14 proceedings in respect of both consignments, but only in so far as the bill of exchange was concerned was D there any doubt about leave to defend being given.   As I understand it— I may be wrong, but it is immaterial—there was no dispute so far as the second consignment was concerned that the defendants should have leave to defend; but it was on the bill of exchange that the battle took place before the judge, and it is on the bill of exchange that the battle has taken place before this court too.

E   The defendants before the judge offered to bring the full amount of the bill in to court as a condition of leave to defend, but the judge said that the plaintiffs were entitled to judgment on the bill immediately.

There are, as Mr. Bowsher on behalf of the defendants has rightly said, two points in issue.   The first one is; can it properly be said that there is any discretion in the court to do other than give judgment on the bill of exchange in these circumstances?   And the second point is F this; if there is such a discretion, should it be exercised in favour of the defendants in this case?   At the invitation of counsel what we have done is to consider the first point on its own to begin with, because if that point goes against the defendants it will of course be unnecessary to examine the considerable volume of evidence which would then become relevant on the second point, namely, the question of the exercise of the G discretion.

Mr. Bowsher does not question the general rule, namely, that where money is due under a bill of exchange judgment will be normally given, despite any counterclaim that may be put forward by the defendants. But he prays in aid the exception that gives the court a discretion when the action is between immediate parties to the bill of exchange.   The authority for that proposition, and the case cited in *The Supreme Court* H *Practice* (1976) on that subject, is *James Lamont & Co. Ltd*. v. *Hyland* [1950] 1 K.B. 585.

The main complaint against the judge is this: that he said " although the plaintiffs are the drawers of the bill and although the defendants are acceptors, I will not treat those two parties as being immediate parties to the bill of exchange because the plaintiffs have indorsed the bill of exchange to the bankers and if the bankers had brought their action against the plaintiffs there would have been no defence, and therefore

Geoffrey Lane L.J.   Jade International v. Robert Nicholas Ltd. (C.A.)   [1978]

the plaintiffs, who have got the bill of exchange back from the bankers, A
are entitled to be treated as if they were not immediate parties."

The judgment given by Donaldson J. was very brief and I think it
is right that I should read it.   It is a note taken by counsel who were
present at the time, approved by the judge, although he says he has no
recollection of the case, but he does not doubt that the note is an accurate
one.   It reads:

> " I give judgment for the plaintiffs for the amount of the bill of
> exchange the subject of this action for the following reasons.   The
> bill was for payment in the future, and the plaintiffs indorsed the bill
> to their bankers in order to obtain cash.   The bill was thereafter
> indorsed through German bankers to bankers in England.
>
> " The only reason why the plaintiffs have the bill in their
> possession is because of the activities, lawful or unlawful, of the C
> defendants thereafter in dishonouring the bill.   The bankers have
> taken advantage of their rights of compulsory recovery against the
> plaintiffs to place the bill in the hands of the plaintiffs and debit
> the plaintiffs' account.   The plaintiffs therefore stand in the shoes
> of the banks, each of which have the undoubted right not only to
> judgment but also to immediate payment against the defendants with-
> out the possibility of being met by any set off or counterclaim.   D
>
> " I therefore think it right to treat the plaintiffs as being in the
> same position as the banks would have been had they sued upon
> this bill.   Here the plaintiffs should have ordinary judgment and
> immediate execution.   I will order a stay for seven days."

And he deals with the ancillary matters thereafter.
In his opening address to us Mr. Bowsher treated the matter thus: he   E
posed the question of the capacity in which the plaintiffs were to be
considered in the circumstances of this case.   Are they, he asked
rhetorically, to be treated as drawers or indorsees?   He submitted that
they were to be treated as drawers, and therefore as immediate parties
to the bill, and therefore, on the authorities, as people who should be
given the benefit of the discretion if the circumstances justified the   F
discretion being exercised in their favour.   He drew our attention to
various provisions of the Bills of Exchange Act 1882; section 47 (1), showing the way in which the banks got their money back in due course;
section 29, which he thought might be the section which the judge had
in mind, coupled with *Byles on Bills of Exchange*, 23rd ed. (1972), p. 189
which gives a commentary on that particular section.   He then read to
us section 29 (3), and it is on section 29 (3) that this case may very largely   G
turn.   Let me read the whole of the section to see what it says.

> " (1) A holder in due course is a holder who has taken a bill,
> complete and regular on the face of it, under the following con-
> ditions; namely, (a) that he became the holder of it before it was
> overdue, and without notice that it had previously been dishonoured,
> if such was the fact: (b) that he took the bill in good faith and   H
> for value, and that at the time the bill was negotiated to him he had
> no notice of any defect in the title of the person who negotiated it.
> (2) In particular the title of a person who negotiates a bill is
> defective within the meaning of this Act when he obtained the bill,
> or the acceptance thereof, by fraud, duress, or force and fear, or
> other unlawful means, or for an illegal consideration, or when he
> negotiates it in breach of faith, or under such circumstances as

The Weekly Law Reports, June 23, 1978

43

3 W.L.R.   Jade International v. Robert Nicholas Ltd. (C.A.)   Geoffrey Lane L.J.

A amount to a fraud. (3) A holder (whether for value or not), who derives his title to a bill through a holder in due course, and who is not himself a party to any fraud or illegality affecting it, has all the rights of that holder in due course as regards the acceptor and all parties to the bill prior to that holder."

B Mr. Bowsher submits this. He concedes that at first blush that sub-section (3) would appear to be against him. But what he says is that the drawer cannot deprive himself of his nature as a drawer, whatever may happen thereafter, and accordingly his capacity as drawer ought to be taken into account in any dispute thereafter. And on that basis he submits that the parties never lost their quality as immediate parties to the bill, despite the intervening events which took place between the bill leaving the plaintiffs' hands and eventually coming back into the

C plaintiffs' hands at the end of the story. That was the way he put the matter in his opening address.

But Mr. Saloman in his answer to that put the matter thus. He points out that drawers of a bill simpliciter are in a negative position. They get no title to sue from the mere fact of being drawers, but on dishonour they are exposed to the rights of recourse. Drawers have no

D special rights, he says. But he says in the circumstances of the present case the drawers in the event ceased to be merely drawers and became holders. They became holders because, as one looks at section 2 of the Act, which is the interpretation section, " holder " is expressed to mean " the payee or indorsee of a bill or note who is in possession of it, or the bearer thereof." Section 38 sets out his rights and reads as follows: " The rights and powers of the holder of a bill are as follows: (1) He may

E sue on the bill in his own name: . . ." Carrying on the scheme of the Act one goes to section 55 (1) which reads:

> " The drawer of a bill by drawing it—(a) Engages that on due present-ment it shall be accepted and paid according to its tenor, and that if it be dishonoured he will compensate the holder or any indorser who is compelled to pay it, provided that the requisite proceedings on

F > dishonour be duly taken; . . ."

Then turning back to section 47 (1), that reads:

> " A bill is dishonoured by nonpayment (a) when it is duly presented for payment and payment is refused or cannot be obtained, or (b) when presentment is excused and the bill is overdue and unpaid."

G What happened as a matter of historical sequence in this case was as follows: the drawers, it being a 120 day bill, in the normal way discounted the bill and transferred the title to the Sparkasse, a German bank, and with it went all the rights to sue. One reads section 31 (1) and (4) to see the rights the Sparkasse got in those circumstances. They gave value for the bill and were holders in due course and could accordingly sue on the bill if they wished.

H They in their turn discounted the bill to the Deutsche Bundesbank, and the Deutsche Bundesbank in turn apparently discounted the bill to the Midland Bank. That bank then presented the bill for acceptance. It was duly accepted. It was presented for payment after the 120 days had elapsed and as I have already said it was dishonoured at that stage. The Midland Bank, it having been discounted to them, and assuming it was so discounted as it seems to have been, were holders in due course, and when it arrived to them there was no further transfer. If one looks at

Geoffrey Lane L.J.   Jade International v. Robert Nicholas Ltd. (C.A.)   [1978]

the reverse side of the bill one sees that the Midland Bank simply opened   A
the indorsement; then it was passed back down the line inoculated, so
to speak, with the title of the Midland Bank. The intermediate bankers
had given value for the bill and that made them holders in due course,
which gave them under the sections to which I have already drawn
attention rights against the acceptors. So the bill goes back through the
Deutsche Bundesbank to the Sparkasse; Sparkasse debited the plaintiffs'
current account, and, Mr. Saloman submits, thereby they give value for   B
the bill, although plainly on the terms of section 29 (3), which I have
already read, it does not matter whether they gave value or not, it does
not affect their situation as holders.

Consequently, although they are not holders in due course, because
they have notice of dishonour at that stage, the plaintiffs are holders,
with all the rights of holders; and those rights are expressed to be all   C
the rights of the holder in due course from whom the title has been
derived and all parties to the bill prior to that holder, according to the
terms of section 29 (3).

In his reply to those submissions Mr. Bowsher, if I may say so
respectfully, shifted his ground somewhat, because instead of relying
simply, as he had done in his opening address, upon the position of the
plaintiffs as drawers, he drew attention to the fact, correctly, that not   D
only were the plaintiffs drawers, but they were also payees of the bill;
and as payees they were, under the definition section 2 which I have
already read, holders of the bill. Consequently he suggests that at the
very lowest the plaintiffs were holders in two capacities. First of all
holders as drawers/payees, and secondly holders because they were the
holders from the Sparkasse, who were themselves holders in due course;   E
and he submits that in those circumstances they should certainly be given
the rights which either of those two capacities confers upon them, since,
he says, the capacity of drawer/payee makes them immediate parties to
the bill, and since immediate parties do have a right to have the discretion
situation examined they should be given that right.

I respectfully disagree with that conclusion. It seems to me that once
the drawers/payees (the plaintiffs in this case) have discounted the bill   F
to the Sparkasse (Sparkasse then becoming the holders in due course),
they lose the capacity which they had as immediate parties to the bill
as drawers. Then when in the effluxion of time they once again become
holders of the bill in the way that I have described, it is in that new
fresh capacity of holders via the Sparkasse and the other bank that their
situation must be judged. It is unreal as I see it to regard them as having   G
a dual capacity. Indeed, it is something of a logical difficulty to see
how they could. I repeat, when they discounted the bill they lost the
benefit of their original capacity, and the guise under which they held it
on the second occasion becomes the dominating guise for the purpose of
deciding whether or not the judge was in a position to consider the
question of discretion. Although Donaldson J., a judge of enormous
experience in these matters, did not put the matter quite in that way it   H
seems to me that that was what he in fact meant.

For those reasons, speaking for myself, it seems to me that the judge
was correct in the conclusion to which he came. That being so, if my
brethren are of the same mind, it becomes unnecessary to consider the
further question of whether in any event the judge should have exercised
his discretion in favour of the plaintiffs. On the first ground I would
dismiss this appeal.

A   CUMMING-BRUCE L.J.   Two principles are familiar in relation to the negotiation of bills of exchange and the rights and liabilities that flow therefrom.   One principle is that between the immediate parties contractual rights and liabilities and equities can be raised in any proceedings between them on the bill.   The second principle is that in order to render the bill negotiable those who take the bill for value as holders in due course shall not find themselves subject to any of the contractual
B   rights or liabilities and equities that affect the value of the bill between immediate parties.

This bill was originally drawn, accepted and then held by the plaintiffs as drawers and payees.   Thereafter it was negotiated by them to the Sparkasse Bank, and the indorsements on the back of the bill show its further history of negotiation.   When the Midland Bank were the
C   holders, as holders in due course, the bill was dishonoured.   Then it started its journey backwards, pursuant to section 47 of the Bills of Exchange Act 1882, which provides that on dishonour by non-payment an immediate right of recourse against the drawer and indorser accrues to the holder.   It was pursuant to that right of recourse that when the bill reached Sparkasse Bank for the second time, having a right of recourse against the drawer they debited the drawer's account and there-
D   after delivered the bill to the drawer to take such action as he thought fit.

So the short point which is raised as the first point on this appeal is whether in those circumstances the drawer/payee to whom the bill was delivered pursuant to the Midland Bank or Sparkasse's right of recourse is properly to be regarded as a holder who derives his title to the bill through a holder in due course, within the meaning of section 29 (3) of
E   the Act.

The submission of Mr. Bowsher is that when the plaintiffs recovered the bill pursuant to the Sparkasse Bank's right of recourse they did not thereby derive their title to the bill through the Sparkasse Bank, or through any of the other indorsers, but that it came back to them in their initial capacity as drawer pursuant to their liability as drawer under section 47 (2) of the Act.   Thus, he submits, that whether or not it is right within
F   the meaning of the subsection to regard the plaintiffs at that stage as holders they were not holders who derived their title through a holder in due course.   Initially as drawers they derive title from nobody.   When they negotiated the bill in the first instance they then lost their title.   All that was left was their liability under section 47 (2), the liability to a right of recourse against them in their capacity as drawers.   And so the sub-
G   mission is that the words of section 29 (3) ought to be read strictly so as to limit the meaning of the words " derive title to the bill " to those situations in which the bill is negotiated, what I would call on its way upwards, from the original drawer to indorser and subsequent indorsers.

Some support for that submission is founded on the note which appears in Byles on Bills of Exchange, 23rd ed., p. 189, where the authors write:

H   " When considering a lesser holding than that of a holder in due course and any action which may be brought by such lesser holder, the relationship between him and the defendant must be taken into account.   In this respect parties to a bill may be considered as immediate or remote, the former being parties in direct relation with each other and the latter being those who are not in such relationship."

No authority is cited for such proposition as may be collected from that paragraph.   It is clear that the editors regarded it as limiting the

rights of an immediate party who found themselves as a holder within   A
the meaning of section 29 (3).   But in the absence of any authority the
persuasive value of the note must be limited to its efficacy in the light
of the true construction of the section.

I see the force as a matter of mercantile practice of the submission
of Mr. Bowsher that there is not any good commercial reason to deprive
the defendants of the contractual rights that they initially had before
they discounted the bill merely because in the last stages of the story   B
when the bill was being dishonoured it comes back into the drawer's
hands pursuant to the right of recourse of a party to whom the bill
has been negotiated.   The question which in the absence of authority
I do not find perfectly straightforward is whether it can be right to place
a restricted meaning on the apparently clear words of the subsection so
as to exclude these plaintiffs from a capacity which at first sight they   C
have, namely, a holder deriving title to the bill from a holder in due course;
and faced with the words of the statute I am persuaded that there is not
sufficient reason shown for placing upon those words the restricted meaning for which he contends.

I remain, which may be only a reflection of my inexperience, surprised
that in the year 1977, one hundred years almost since this section was
placed on the Statute Book, that the point does not appear ever to have   D
come up for decision and is without authority.

For the reasons that I have stated on the first point, which is the only
point that has been argued, I would agree that the appeal should be
dismissed.

STEPHENSON L.J.   I also agree.   I also am surprised at the absence of   E
authority; and to some extent I am comforted in finding the point difficult
by the changes which I have observed and to which Geoffrey Lane L.J.
has called attention in the submissions of Mr. Bowsher.   He has obviously
not found it easy to say in what capacity the plaintiffs are bringing this
action on this dishonoured bill of exchange.

He first of all relied on the plaintiffs' rights as drawer of the bill,
something which I think naturally arose from the way in which the   F
statement of claim is pleaded, referring to the bill being drawn by the
plaintiffs, but not referring to them either as holder or as payee.

Then he relied on their rights as payee or drawer/payee.   At one
stage he was prepared to accept that they did in addition or in substitution derive a title from somebody else, but that somebody else, he
said, was the acceptor of the bill, the defendants.   But as I understand   G
his final argument he resiled from that position and was really maintaining that the plaintiffs had no derivative title but an original title from
their original position as holder/payee of the bill.

It seems clear from the note of Donaldson J.'s judgment which
Geoffrey Lane L.J. has read that the judge in his great experience rejected
any argument of that kind and must have held that the plaintiffs' title
to this bill was a derivative title; and I cannot resist the conclusion that   H
whether or not he had reread to himself section 29 (3) he was in fact
applying that subsection and finding that the plaintiffs as a holder of
this bill derived their title to it through the holders in due course, that
is to say one or other of these banks.

For the reasons which Geoffrey Lane and Cumming-Bruce L.JJ. have
given I believe his decision to have been right and I too would dismiss
the appeal on this first point without the necessity of going into the

A   question whether, if the judge had had a discretion to exercise, or had thought he had a discretion to exercise, he would have exercised it for or against the defendants, and whether we should consider further the voluminous fresh matter in deciding which way we ourselves should exercise it.

Appeal dismissed with costs.

B   Solicitors: *Robbins, Olivey & Lake* for *Sampson, Wade & Co.,* *Bradford; Loxley, Sanderson & Morgan.*

[COURT OF APPEAL]

C

CAMDEN LONDON BOROUGH COUNCIL v. HERWALD

1978 Feb. 21, 22, 23;   Megaw, Lawton and Browne L.JJ.
    March 21

D   *Court of Appeal—Jurisdiction—Criminal cause or matter—Dis-*
    tress warrant for non-payment of rates—Justices' refusal to
    issue warrant—Rating Authority's successful appeal to Divi-
    sional Court—Whether appeal to Court of Appeal or House
    of Lords—Supreme Court of Judicature (Consolidation) Act
    1925 (15 & 16 Geo. 5, c. 49), s. 31 (1) (a) (as amended by
    Criminal Appeal Act 1968 (c. 19), s. 52, Sch. 5)[1]*—Administra-*
    tion of Justice Act 1960 (8 & 9 Eliz. 2, c. 65), s. 1 (1) (a)[2]
    Rating—Rateable occupation—Partial occupation—Premises com-
E   *prising two factories and house entered in valuation list as*
    single hereditament—Described as "workshop and store"—
    Ratepayer occupying one factory and room in house as office
    —Whether part occupied within general description of whole
    —Whether ratepayer liable for rates—Test—General Rate Act
    1967 (c. 9), s. 16[3]

F   A group of buildings comprising a three storey house and two small factories were entered in a local valuation list as a single hereditament and described as a "workshop and store." The defendant occupied one of the two factories and a first floor office in the house with the use of a kitchen. The rating authority made demands for rates in respect of the whole hereditament for the period from October 1972 to March 1975 but the defendant refused to pay. On a complaint by the rating authority for a distress warrant for non-payment of
G   rates pursuant to section 97 (1) of the General Rate Act 1967 a magistrates' court held that since the defendant had occupied only parts of the premises he was not liable for rates on the whole and the justices refused to authorise the issue of the warrant. The Divisional Court of the Queen's Bench Division allowed the appeal holding that the parts of the premises which the defendant occupied came within the general

H   [1] Supreme Court of Judicature (Consolidation) Act 1925, s. 31 (1) (as amended): "No appeal shall lie—(a) except as provided by this Act, the Administration of Justice Act 1960 or the Criminal Appeal Act 1968 from any judgment of the High Court in any criminal cause or matter."
    [2] Administration of Justice Act 1960, s. 1 (1): ". . . an appeal shall lie to the House of Lords, . . . (a) from any decision of a Divisional Court of the Queen's Bench Division in a criminal cause or matter; . . ."
    [3] General Rate Act 1967, s. 16: ". . . every occupier of property of any of the following descriptions, namely, (a) lands, (b) houses . . . shall be liable to be assessed to rates in respect of the hereditament or hereditaments comprising that property . . ."

Camden Borough Council v. Herwald (C.A.)   **[1978]**

description "workshop and store" which applied to the pre-   A
mises as a whole and the court remitted the case to the
magistrates' court with a direction to issue the distress warrant.

On appeal by the defendant the Court of Appeal raised the
question whether it had jurisdiction to hear the appeal or
whether it was an appeal in a criminal cause or matter in
respect of which appeal lay to the House of Lords: —

Held, (1) that an application to a magistrates' court for an
order to enforce a general rate under the General Rate Act   B
1967 by the issue of a warrant of distress was not a " criminal
cause or matter " and accordingly an appeal lay to the Court
of Appeal from a decision of the Divisional Court on a case
stated (post, pp. 52B–F, 54G–H).

Southwark and Vauxhall Water Co. v. *Hampton Urban
District Council* [1899] 1 Q.B. 273, C.A. applied.

Seaman v. *Burley* [1896] 2 Q.B. 344, C.A. distinguished.

(2) Allowing the appeal, that the true test was that if the   C
person rated was in occupation of premises which fulfilled
the description in the valuation list that was sufficient for the
issue of a distress warrant; that although the factory which
the defendant occupied could be described as a " workshop,"
and was within the description in the valuation list, on the findings of fact he did not occupy anything which could be
described as a " store ": Moreover, he occupied an office in
the house which was not covered by the description in the   D
valuation list and that in those circumstances the defendant
was not liable for any part of the rates claimed and a distress
warrant could not be issued (post, p. 56D–G).

Overseers of the Poor of Manchester v. *Headlam and
London and North Western Railway Co.* (1888) 21 Q.B.D.
96 applied.

Allchurch v. *Hendon Union Assessment Committee* [1891]
2 Q.B. 436, C.A. considered.   E

Decision of the Divisional Court of the Queen's Bench
Division [1977] 1 W.L.R. 100; [1976] 2 All E.R. 808 reversed.

The following cases are referred to in the judgment:

Allchurch v. *Hendon Union Assessment Committee* [1891] 2 Q.B. 436,
C.A.

Associated Cinema Properties Ltd. v. *Hampstead Borough Council* [1944]   F
K.B. 12; *sub nom. Hampstead Corporation* v. *Associated Cinema
Properties Ltd.* [1944] 1 All E.R. 436, C.A.

Bexley Congregational Church Treasurer v. *Bexley London Borough
Council* [1972] 2 Q.B. 222; [1972] 2 W.L.R. 1161; [1971] 2 All
E.R. 662, C.A.

China v. *Harrow Urban District Council* [1954] 1 Q.B. 178; [1953]
2 All E.R. 1296, D.C.   G

Crease v. *Sawle* (1842) 2 Q.B. 862.

Langford v. *Cole* (1910) 102 L.T. 808, D.C.

McGreavy, In re. Ex parte McGreavy v. *Benfleet Urban District Council*
[1950] Ch. 269; [1950] 1 All E.R. 442, C.A.

Overseers of the Poor of Manchester v. *Headlam and London and North
Western Railway Co.* (1888) 21 Q.B.D. 96.

Seaman v. *Burley* [1896] 2 Q.B. 344, C.A.   H

Southwark and Vauxhall Water Co. v. *Hampton Urban District Council*
[1899] 1 Q.B. 273, C.A.; affirmed *sub nom. Hampton Urban District
Council* v. *Southwark and Vauxhall Water Co.* [1900] A.C. 3,
H.L.(E.).

Vernon v. *Castle* (1922) 127 L.T. 748.

Westminster City Council v. *Southern Railway Co.* [1936] A.C. 511;
[1936] 2 All E.R. 322, H.L.(E.).

A   The following additional cases were cited in argument:

Davis v. *Burrell and Lane* (1851) 10 C.B. 821.

Derby Corporation v. *Derbyshire County Council* [1897] A.C. 550, H.L.(E.).

Edgcombe, In re [1902] 2 K.B. 403, C.A.

London and North Western Railway Co. v. *Buckmaster* (1875) L.R. 10 Q.B. 70; affirmed (1875) L.R. 10 Q.B. 444, C.A.

B   *Reg.* v. *London Justices* [1899] 1 Q.B. 532, D.C.

Spiers and Pond v. *Finsbury Metropolitan Borough Council* (1956) 1 R.R.C. 219.

APPEAL from the Divisional Court of the Queen's Bench Division.

The defendant, Theodore Herwald, appealed with the leave of the
C Court of Appeal from the decision of the Divisional Court (Lord Widgery
C.J., O'Connor and Robert Goff JJ.) [1977] 1 W.L.R. 100 which had
allowed an appeal by the rating authority, Camden London Borough
Council, from a decision of Hampstead Magistrates' Court which, on
May 1, 1977, on a complaint laid by the rating authority under section 97
of the General Rate Act 1967, refused to authorise the issue of a distress warrant for non-payment of general rates in respect of premises
D situate at 63 Loveridge Road, London, N.W.6 of which the ratepayer
occupied part. The Divisional Court, having allowed the appeal, remitted
the case to the magistrates' court with a direction to authorise the issue
of a distress warrant.

The grounds of appeal were (1) that on the facts found by the
magistrates' court the defendant had at all times occupied only certain
E parts of the relevant premises which were described in the local rating
valuation list as a single hereditament, and therefore the magistrates' court
was correct in its opinion that the defendant was not liable to pay rates for
the whole of the premises. The Divisional Court erred in law in holding
that the defendant, on such facts, was liable to pay rates for the whole of
the premises unless and until the description of the premises as a single
F hereditament in the rating valuation list was altered by means of a proposal
under section 69 of the General Rate Act 1967. (2) Further or alternatively, in view of the findings of fact, that the relevant premises appeared
in the local rating valuation list as a " workshop and store " and that in
fact the premises comprised a house, two factories, and two yards, of
which the defendant had occupied only an office on the first floor of the
house with use of the kitchen, and one of the two factories, the Divisional
G Court erred in fact and in law in ruling that the premises occupied by the
defendant fulfilled the description in the valuation list, so as to justify
the issue of a distress warrant. (3) By reason of the matters aforesaid, the
magistrates' court was correct in its decision to refuse to issue a distress
warrant against the defendant and the Divisional Court erred in law in
overruling the decision of the magistrates' court and in directing the
H magistrates' court to issue a distress warrant and the defendant sought an
order that the order of the Divisional Court be set aside.

The facts are sufficiently stated in the judgment of the court.

When the appeal came on for hearing the court raised the question
whether it had jurisdiction to hear the appeal or whether it was an appeal
in a criminal cause or matter in which, by virtue of section 31 (1) (*a*) of
the Supreme Court of Judicature (Consolidation) Act 1925 as amended

by the Criminal Appeal Act 1968, and section 1 (1) (*a*) of the Adminis- A
tration of Justice Act 1960, appeal lay only to the House of Lords.

Sir Peter Rawlinson Q.C. and *Desmond Keane* for the defendant.
Guy Roots for the rating authority.

Cur. adv. vult.

March 21. BROWNE L.J. read the following judgment of the court. B
This is an appeal by Mr. Herwald from a decision of the Divisional Court
of the Queen's Bench Division given [1977] 1 W.L.R. 100 on April 8,
1976. The Divisional Court allowed an appeal by way of case stated
from a decision of the Hampstead Magistrates' Court and refused leave to
appeal, but leave was given by this court on March 28, 1977.

The case relates to distress for rates. On March 13, 1975, the Camden C
London Borough Council laid a complaint in the magistrates' court against
Mr. Herwald for a summons for non-payment of the general rate in respect
of premises at 63 Loveridge Road, London, N.W.6, for the period from
October 1, 1972 to March 31, 1975, amounting to a total of £1,019.80.
On May 1, 1975, the magistrates heard the complaint and refused to
authorise issue of a distress warrant. The Divisional Court, having allowed
the appeal, remitted the case to the justices with a direction to authorise D
the issue of a distress warrant.

When the appeal came on in this court, the court raised the question
whether we had jurisdiction to hear it, in view of the decision of this
court (consisting of Lord Esher M.R., Kay and A. L. Smith L.JJ.) in
Seaman v. *Burley* [1896] 2 Q.B. 344. It was held in that case that there
was no appeal to this court from a decision of a Divisional Court on a E
case stated by justices relating to the grant of a distress warrant to enforce
a poor rate under a local Act, because it was an appeal in a "criminal
cause or matter" within section 47 of the Judicature Act 1873, inasmuch
as the proceedings before the magistrates might end in imprisonment (see
now section 31 (1) (*a*) of the Supreme Court of Judicature (Consolidation)
Act 1925 [as amended by the Criminal Appeal Act 1968, section 52,
Schedule 5] and section 1 (1) (*a*) of the Administration of Justice Act F
1960). Sir Peter Rawlinson, for Mr. Herwald, wished us to deal with the
case; and Mr. Roots for the Camden London Borough Council did not
take any objection to our jurisdiction, and indeed advanced a helpful
argument in support of it.

The statutory provisions as to distress for the general rate are now
contained in Part VI of the General Rate Act 1967, beginning with section G
96 (1).

Section 96 (1) provides:

" . . . if any person fails to pay any sum legally assessed on and due
from him in respect of a rate for seven days after it has been legally
demanded of him, the payment of that sum may, subject to and in
accordance with the provisions of this Part of this Act, be enforced H
by distress and sale of his goods and chattels under warrant issued by
a magistrates' court; and, if there is insufficient distress, he may be
liable to imprisonment under the provisions of this Part of this Act
in that behalf."

Section 97 (1):

" The proceedings for the issue of a warrant of distress under this
Part of this Act may be instituted by making complaint before a

A justice of the peace and applying for a summons requiring the person named in the complaint to appear before a magistrates' court to show why he has not paid the rate specified in the complaint."

Section 98:

"The justices may state a case under the Magistrates' Courts Act 1952 when called upon to issue a warrant of distress under this Part

B of this Act."

Section 99 (1):

"A warrant of distress under this Part of this Act may be directed to the rating authority, to the constables of the police area in which the warrant is issued and to such other persons, if any, as the magistrates' court issuing the warrant may think fit, and the warrant shall

C authorise the persons to whom it is directed to levy the amount which the person against whom the warrant is issued is liable to pay by distress and sale of his goods and chattels."

Section 102 (1):

"If the person charged with the execution of a warrant of distress

D for levying a sum to which some other person has been rated makes a return to the magistrates' court that he could find no goods or chattels (or no sufficient goods or chattels) on which to levy the sums directed to be levied under the warrant on that other person's goods and chattels, a magistrates' court may, if it thinks fit, and subject to the provisions of section 103 of this Act, issue a warrant of commitment against that other person . . . (5) The order in the warrant of

E commitment shall be that the said person be imprisoned for a time therein specified but not exceeding three months, unless the sums mentioned in the warrant shall be sooner paid . . ."

and the subsection goes on to provide for a remission of the term of imprisonment proportionate to the amount of any later payment. Section 103 (1):

F
"Section 102 of this Act shall have effect subject to and in accordance with the following provisions: (a) on the application for the issue of a warrant for the commitment of any person, the magistrates' court shall make inquiry in his presence as to whether his failure to pay the sum to which he was rated and in respect of which the warrant of distress was issued was due either to his wilful refusal or to his culp-

G able neglect; (b) if the magistrates' court is of opinion that the failure of the said person to pay the said sum was not due either to his wilful refusal or to his culpable neglect, it shall not issue the warrant. (2) Where on the application no warrant of commitment is issued, the magistrates' court may remit the payment of any sum to which the application relates, or of any part of that sum."

H   *Seaman* v. *Burley* [1896] 2 Q.B. 344 was decided on the provisions of a local Act relating to the parish of Paddington (5 Geo. IV, c. cxxvi). Section cxx of that Act contained provisions generally corresponding with those of Part VI of the Act of 1967, with one important exception: it contained no provision corresponding to section 103.

In *Ryde on Rating*, 13th ed. (1976), p. 878, the authority of *Seaman* v. *Burley* in the present context is doubted. In two later cases this court has heard and decided appeals from the Divisional Court relating to dis-

tress for rates, though it does not appear that in either of them *Seaman* v. A
Burley was cited or any point taken as to jurisdiction (see *Associated
Cinema Properties Ltd.* v. *Hampstead Borough Council* [1944] K.B. 412
and *Bexley Congregational Church Treasurer* v. *Bexley London Borough
Council* [1972] 2 Q.B. 222). In *In re McGreavy* [1950] Ch. 269 this
court disagreed with what it regarded as an obiter dictum of Lord Esher
M.R. in *Seaman's* case (see pp. 279–280), and in *China* v. *Harrow Urban
District Council* [1954] 1 Q.B. 178 the Divisional Court (we think) B
impliedly distinguished *Seaman*, which was cited in argument. But we do
not think we need refer further to those cases, because two years after
Seaman v. *Burley* was decided it was distinguished by this court on a
ground which in our judgment equally distinguishes it from the present
case. In *Southwark and Vauxhall Water Co.* v. *Hampton Urban District
Council* [1899] 1 Q.B. 273 it was held that an application to a court of C
summary jurisdiction for an order to enforce a general district rate under
the Public Health Act 1875, was not a " criminal cause or matter " and
that an appeal lay to this court from a decision of the Divisional Court
on a case stated. The leading judgment was given by A. L. Smith L.J.,
who had been a party to the decision in *Seaman* v. *Burley,* and Rigby L.J.
and Collins L.J. concurred. The ground on which *Seaman's* case was
distinguished was that in that case the Summary Jurisdiction Act 1879 did D
not apply but in the *Southwark and Vauxhall Water Co.* case it did. The
Act of 1879 contained provisions in section 35 the effect of which was in
our view substantially the same as the effect of the provisions of section
103 (1) of the Act of 1967, and it was held that the proceedings were
therefore not a " criminal cause or matter." The proceedings in the present
case are, therefore, in our view, equally not a " criminal cause or matter." E
This distinction also avoids the startling conclusion that every judgment
summons in a county court under Order 25, rule 33 of the County Court
Rules and section 5 of the Debtors Act 1869 is a " criminal cause or
matter."

In our judgment, this court has jurisdiction to hear this appeal. We
hope that our decision will end the uncertainty referred to in *Ryde.*
We come, therefore, to the substance of the appeal. It is well F
established that an application for a distress warrant to enforce payment
of rates can only be resisted on certain limited grounds. It is also well
established that one of such grounds is that the defendant is not in
occupation of the hereditament in respect of which it is sought to rate
him. The question in this case is whether, and if so in what circumstances,
it is a defence for him to show that he is only in occupation of part of G
that hereditament.

The case stated, having found that the relevant rates were made,
published and demanded, finds the following facts in:

" (ii) That the valuation list shows 63 Loveridge Road as a single
hereditament as a workshop and store. (iii) That Mr. Stephenson,
rates inspector, London Borough of Camden, visited 63 Loveridge H
Road on several occasions the first time being on March 11, 1974.
(iv) That Mr. Herwald had been a subtenant of a Mr. Jellineck from
1960 until six or seven years ago and then of a Miss Marcotics to
whom he had paid a portion of the total rent and rates. (v) That
during Miss Marcotics' lifetime he had occupied certain parts only
of 63 Loveridge Road, namely an office on the first floor of the house,
with use of the kitchen, and area marked ' Factory A ' (see attached

A   rough sketch plan), and that subsequent to her death he continued to
     occupy the same parts of the premises as he had always occupied."

     The sketch plan attached to the case and the legend on it show that
63 Loveridge Road comprises a house of three floors consisting of a shop
and office on the ground floor, four rooms on the first floor (including a
kitchen) and four rooms on the second floor; a one-storey factory (Factory
B   A); a two-storey-factory (Factory B); and two yards separating the
buildings. The case contains no findings about the use made by Mr.
Herwald of the parts which he occupies, nor as to the use or occupation
(if any) of the other parts. Sir Peter Rawlinson emphasised that the effect
of the findings was that during the lifetime of Miss Marcotics Mr. Herwald only paid (to her) the rates in respect of the parts he occupied; that
     after her death he continued to occupy the " same parts of the premises
C   as he had always occupied "; and that he was now being called upon by
the rating authority to pay the rates on the whole.

     The conclusion of the justices and their question to the court were as
follows:

     " We were of opinion that as Mr. Herwald, the [defendant], had at
     all times occupied only certain parts of 63 Loveridge Road, he would
D   not be liable for the rates for the whole premises and accordingly
     refused to authorise issue of a distress warrant.

          " *Question*: The question for the opinion of the High Court is
     whether it is correct that Mr. Herwald is liable only for rates in respect
     of that part of the property in which he has been found to be in sole
     occupation when that part of the property is contained in the valuation
E   list only as part of a single hereditament."

     In view of some criticisms of the Camden London Borough Council
which were made or implied during the argument and of the finding in
paragraph 4 (iii) of the case stated, we think we should emphasise the
division of responsibilities in rating matters which is now embodied in the
General Rate Act 1967. We think this division of responsibilities and
F   procedures is also important in relation to the substance of this case. Mr.
Roots gave us an interesting and helpful summary of the history of the
development of rating procedure from the Poor Relief Act 1601, to the
Lands Tribunal Act 1949. The scheme of the Act of 1967 (re-enacting
earlier legislation) is a division between responsibility for assessment or
valuation and responsibility for collection. Valuation is the responsi-
     bility of valuation officers appointed by the Inland Revenue and collec-
G   tion is the responsibility of the rating authorities. The provisions as to
valuation lists and the duties of valuation officers are contained in Part
V of the Act. It is the duty of valuation officers to prepare a valuation
list for each rating area (section 67 (1)), and to insert in the list the
prescribed particulars " with respect to every hereditament in the rating
area and the value thereof" (section 67 (2)). By section 67 (6) the
H   valuation list is made " conclusive evidence for the purposes of the
levying of [the] rate of the values of the several hereditaments included
in the list." It is not made conclusive evidence of anything else, but it
is obvious that before making a valuation of any hereditament the valuation officer must decide what the hereditament is which he is valuing.
The identification of hereditaments is an essential part of the process of
valuation and so within the province of the valuation officer (see the
definition of " hereditament " in section 115 (1) of the Act). Section 69

Camden Borough Council v. Herwald (C.A.)   **[1978]**

and the following sections contain provisions for the alteration of the **A**
valuation list by means of proposals and for appeals to local valuation
courts and to the Lands Tribunal if there are objections to a proposal.
If the occupier of part of premises included in the list as a single hereditament thinks that his part should be shown as a separate hereditament, he
can and should make a proposal for the alteration of the list under section
69 (1) (*a*) or (*c*) or both. We were told that since the hearing in the
Divisional Court this has been done, and that 63 Loveridge Road is now **B**
shown in the list as two hereditaments. When a proposal takes effect, its
effect relates back to the beginning of the rating period in which it was
made (section 79), but the rates claimed in this case are in respect of
earlier periods. Collection of the rate is the responsibility of the rating
authorities. They have nothing to do with assessment or valuation nor
with the identification or definition of hereditaments. We think that this **C**
is emphasised by their duty under section 85 (1), which is only to give
information to the valuation officer. By section 2, rating authorities are
under a mandatory duty to make and levy the general rate, and by section
2 (4) (*b*) the general rate " shall be made and levied in accordance with
the valuation list in force for the time being. . . ." So long as the entry
in the valuation list remained unaltered, it was therefore the duty of the
Camden London Borough Council to levy the rates in respect of 63 **D**
Loveridge Road in accordance with the list. The rating authority had no
power to split up the hereditament or apportion the rates. We agree with
the Divisional Court that Mr. Herwald's proper remedy was to make a
proposal for the alteration of the list: see [1977] 1 W.L.R. 100, 104B–C.

But this is not the end of the matter. The foundation of Sir Peter
Rawlinson's argument was the incontrovertible proposition that liability to **E**
pay rates depends on the occupation of land (or certain other types of
hereditament); a person is liable to be rated in respect of his occupation
of land. He referred us to section 16 of the Act of 1967, to *Allchurch* v.
Hendon Union Assessment Committee [1891] 2 Q.B. 436, and to *Westminster City Council* v. *Southern Railway Co.* [1936] A.C. 511, especially
Lord Russell of Killowen at p. 529. He submitted that: (a) Mr. Herwald
is not liable to be rated in respect of land of which he is not in occupation; **F**
(b) on the findings of fact he was not in occupation of part of this hereditament; (c) no rate can lawfully be levied in respect of the part of which he
is not in occupation; (d) therefore, no distress warrant can lawfully be
issued for rates which include rates on the part he does not occupy.

As we have said, there is no doubt that on an application for a distress
warrant it is a defence for the defendant to show that he is not in
occupation of the hereditament at all (see, for example, *Associated Cinema* **G**
Properties Ltd. v. *Hampstead Borough Council* [1944] K.B. 412). But
where the defence is that the defendant is only in occupation of part of
the hereditament the position is different. The rating authority relied on
the decision of the Divisional Court in *Overseers of the Poor of Manchester* v. *Headlam and London and North Western Railway Co.* (1888)
21 Q.B.D. 96, and the Divisional Court in the present case accepted their **H**
submission and directed the distress warrant to issue. If we may respectfully say so, we think that the effect of that decision was stated with
complete accuracy in the judgment of Robert Goff J., with which Lord
Widgery C.J. and O'Connor J. agreed. We quote from [1977] 1 W.L.R.
100, beginning at p. 102H:

" It is right that a person is only liable to be rated in respect of
property of which he is the occupier: see section 16 of the General

A   Rate Act 1967. But it does not follow that, merely because he can show that he does not in fact occupy part of premises in respect of which a rate has been made, a distress warrant should not be issued. To resist the issue of a warrant, he must show that the description of the rated property in the valuation list includes on its face property which he does not occupy. The principle was stated by this court in *Overseers of the Poor of Manchester* v. *Headlam and London*
B   *and North Western Railway Co.* (1888) 21 Q.B.D. 96, 98, in a passage which has since been frequently cited and applied: '. . . if one entire assessment be made in terms upon property which he does occupy, and upon other property which he does not occupy, so that upon the true state of facts being ascertained it is impossible to satisfy the description in the rate book without including property which he does
C   not occupy, the rate will be bad and ought not to be enforced.' "

That is the end of the quotation from *Headlam*. Robert Goff J. goes on:

"In that case, property occupied by the railway company had been assessed as ' offices and land with rails,' but in assessing the amount of the rate the overseers had included certain buildings which were not occupied by the company. It was held that, since the property
D   in fact occupied by the company satisfied the description in the rate book, the rate was good on the face of it and a distress warrant must be issued. The proper remedy of the company in such circumstances was to appeal against the assessment; not having appealed, they could not resist the issue of a warrant. By way of contrast, in *Langford* v. *Cole* (1910) 102 L.T. 808, where a single assessment of poor rate was
E   made on property described in the rate book as ' mansion house and grounds' and it was established that the mansion house itself was unoccupied at the date when the rate was made, it was held that the rate made in respect of the whole property could not be enforced and that a distress warrant should not therefore be issued.

"The position is therefore as follows. If the person rated is in occupation of premises which fulfil the description in the valuation
F   list, that is sufficient for the issue of a warrant: but if the description in the valuation list cannot be satisfied without including property which the person rated does not occupy, the rate cannot be enforced against him and a distress warrant should not be issued."

    Applying that test, the Divisional Court held that the part occupied by Mr. Herwald did fulfil the description in the valuation list and that
G   non-occupation of even a substantial part did not prevent him from being liable for the rate in respect of the whole: accordingly, he could not resist the issue of a distress warrant: see p. 104A–C.

    Sir Peter Rawlinson submitted (i) that we should overrule *Headlam* and the later cases which have followed and applied it; (ii) alternatively, that *Headlam* should not be rigidly applied to all cases but only to
H   " trivial matters "; (iii) in the further alternative, that even if the principle of *Headlam* should be applied, the Divisional Court was wrong in holding that the part occupied by Mr. Herwald fulfilled the description in the valuation list.

    As to (i), Sir Peter submitted that the decision in *Headlam* was inconsistent with the fundamental principle that liability to be rated depends on the occupation of land and with the decision of the Court of Appeal three years later in *Allchurch* v. *Hendon Union Assessment Committee* [1891]

2 Q.B. 436. *Headlam* is not binding on us, and Mr. Roots did not feel able A
to submit that the decision of the Exchequer Chamber in *Crease* v. *Sawle*
(1842) 2 Q.B. 862 was binding upon us because of later changes in procedure. But *Headlam* has stood for 90 years, and was followed and
applied in at least the three cases referred to in the judgment of the
Divisional Court, in 1910, 1922 and 1956: we should therefore be very
slow to overrule it. But, in our judgment, it is not inconsistent with the
general principle on which Sir Peter relies. We agree with Mr. Roots that B
the question in this case relates to procedure and jurisdiction rather than
to liability; so it did in *Headlam,* where the proper remedy would have
been to appeal against the rate. *Allchurch* v. *Hendon Assessment Committee* is not, in our view, inconsistent with *Headlam,* because *Allchurch*
related to the assessment process (under the procedure then applicable)
and not to the collection process; it was concerned with the process now C
governed by Part V of the Act of 1967. On an application for a distress
warrant the magistrates have no jurisdiction to alter the valuation list or to
apportion the rates on any such basis. It does not appear to have been
suggested in any of the later cases in which *Headlam* has been applied
that there was anything in *Allchurch* which threw any doubt on it. We
therefore reject Sir Peter's first submission as to *Headlam.* Nor can we
see any reason to limit that decision to "trivial matters." No such D
suggestion seems to have been made in any of the later cases.

But we accept Sir Peter's third submission that, applying the principle
of *Headlam,* these rates cannot be enforced against Mr. Herwald. The
description in the valuation list at the relevant time was " a workshop and
store." "Factory A," which he occupies, can fairly be described as a
"workshop," but on the findings of fact he does not occupy anything E
which can be described as "store." Further, he does occupy the office
in the house, which is not covered by the description in the list. We doubt
whether we are entitled to take into account the later alteration in the list,
but it is interesting to note that we are told that 63 Loveridge Road is
now entered as two hereditaments, the part occupied by Mr. Herwald
described as "Factory and Office" and the rest as "Stores and premises—
void." We do not find any help in the case on which the Divisional F
Court relied—*Vernon* v. *Castle* (1922) 127 L.T. 748; it seems to us that
each case must depend on its own facts and on the construction of the
particular entry in the list.

The appeal will therefore be allowed. The question stated in the
case is not the right question; on our decision, the position is not that
Mr. Herwald is liable only for rates in respect of the part of the property G
which he occupied, but that he is not liable for any part of the rates
claimed. The actual decision of the magistrates in refusing to authorise
issue of a distress warrant was, however, right.

> *Appeal allowed, with costs in Court
> of Appeal and in Divisional Court,
> and of application on March 28,* H
> 1978, *for leave to appeal.*
> *Legal aid taxation of defendant's costs.*

Solicitors: *Walford & Co.; Francis Nickson, Solicitor, Camden London
Borough Council.*

E. M. W.

A

[HOUSE OF LORDS]

DIRECTOR OF PUBLIC PROSECUTIONS . . . RESPONDENT

AND

NOCK AND ANOTHER . . . . APPELLANTS

B

1978 Jan. 12; 31   Lawton L.J., Swanwick and Gibson JJ.

April 5, 6;   Lord Diplock, Lord Edmund-Davies,
May 25   Lord Russell of Killowen, Lord Keith
                    of Kinkel and Lord Scarman

C *Crime — Conspiracy — Agreement to produce cocaine — Method
agreed incapable of producing cocaine—Whether indictable
conspiracy*

The defendants agreed to produce cocaine by separating
it from other substances in a powder which they believed
to be a mixture of cocaine and lignocaine. In fact it was
lignocaine hydro-chloride and contained no cocaine so that
cocaine could not in any circumstances have been produced
D   from it. They were indicted for conspiracy to contravene
section 4 of the Misuse of Drugs Act 1971 in having
" conspired . . . to produce a controlled drug of Class A,
namely cocaine " and were convicted. The Court of Appeal
upheld their conviction.
On appeal: —
Held, that when two or more persons agreed on a course
of conduct with the object of committing a criminal offence
E   but, unknown to them, it was not possible to achieve that
object by that course of conduct, they did not commit the
crime of conspiracy, and accordingly the limited agreement
entered into by the defendants, which could not in any circumstances have involved the commission of the offence created
by the statute, did not amount to the crime of conspiracy
(post, pp. 65D–E, 66C, F, 70F–G).
Reg. v. *Smith (Roger)* [1975] A.C. 476, H.L.(E.) applied.
F   *Reg.* v. *Green (Harry)* [1976] Q.B. 985, C.A. considered.
Haggard v. *Mason* [1976] 1 W.L.R. 187, D.C. distinguished.
Per Lord Diplock. A pickpocket working either with a
confederate or alone would not confine his activities to a
single pocket of a single individual and accordingly, on an
indictment drafted in suitably broad terms, he could be convicted, in the first case, of conspiracy to commit theft or, in
the second, of an attempt to do so, without the prosecution
G   needing to prove that the particular pocket into which he put
his hand in fact contained something which he would have
stolen if he could (post, pp. 64A–C, H—65C).
Decision of the Court of Appeal (Criminal Division), post,
pp. 58H et seq. reversed.

The following cases are referred to in their Lordships' opinions:

H   *Board of Trade* v. *Owen* [1957] A.C. 602; [1957] 2 W.L.R. 351; [1957] 1
All E.R. 411, H.L.(E.).
Haggard v. *Mason* [1976] 1 W.L.R. 187; [1976] 1 All E.R. 337, D.C.
Mulcahy v. *The Queen* (1868) L.R. 3 H.L. 306, H.L.(I.).
Partington v. *Williams* (1975) 62 Cr.App.R. 220, D.C.
Reg. v. *Brown* (1889) 24 Q.B.D. 357.
Reg. v. *Collins* (1864) 9 Cox C.C. 497.
Reg. v. *Easom* [1971] 2 Q.B. 315; [1971] 3 W.L.R. 82; [1971] 2 All E.R.
945, C.A.

D.P.P. v. Nock (C.A.)   **[1978]**

Reg. v. *Green (Harry)* [1976] Q.B. 985; [1976] 2 W.L.R. 57; [1975] **A**
    3 All E.R. 1011, C.A.
Reg. v. *Hussein* (unreported), December 8, 1977, C.A.
Reg. v. *McDonough* (1962) 47 Cr.App.R. 37, C.C.A.
Reg. v. *M'Pherson* (1851) Dears. & B. 197; 7 Cox C.C. 281, C.C.A.
Reg. v. *Ring* (1892) 61 L.J.M.C. 116.
Reg. v. *Smith (Roger)* [1975] A.C. 476; [1974] 2 W.L.R. 1; [1973] 3
    All E.R. 1109, H.L.(E.).   **B**
Rex v. *Percy Dalton (London) Ltd.* (1949) 33 Cr.App.R. 102, C.C.A.

The following additional cases were cited in argument in the House of
    Lords:
Poulterers' Case (1611) 9 Co.Rep. 55b.
Reg. v. *Brown* (1899) 63 J.P. 790.
Reg. v. *Doot* [1973] A.C. 807; [1973] 2 W.L.R. 532; [1973] 1 All E.R. **C**
    940, H.L.(E.).
Reg. v. *Goodchild* (1846) 2 Car. & K. 293.
Reg. v. *Whitchurch* (1890) 24 Q.B.D. 420.

The following cases are referred to in the judgment of the Court of
    Appeal:
Haggard v. *Mason* [1976] 1 W.L.R. 187; [1976] 1 All E.R. 337, D.C.   **D**
Reg. v. *Donnelly* [1970] N.Z.L.R. 980.
Reg. v. *Goodchild* (1846) 2 Car. & K. 293.
Reg. v. *Green (Harry)* [1976] Q.B. 985; [1976] 2 W.L.R. 57; [1975]
    3 All E.R. 1011, C.A.
Reg. v. *Smith (Roger)* [1975] A.C. 476; [1974] 2 W.L.R. 1; [1973] 3
    All E.R. 1109, H.L.(E.).
                                                        E

No additional cases were cited in argument in the Court of Appeal.

APPEAL against conviction.

The appellants, David Michael Nock and Kevin Charles Alsford, were
indicted for conspiracy to contravene section 4 of the Misuse of Drugs
Act 1971. The particulars of offence stated that they " on divers days **F**
before September 23, 1975, conspired . . . to produce a controlled drug
of Class A, namely cocaine." They were tried before Judge Lewisohn
at Snaresbrook Crown Court and on January 26, 1977, they were convicted and sentenced to two years' imprisonment. They appealed to the
Court of Appeal (Criminal Division).

The facts are stated in the judgment of Lawton L.J.
                                                        G

Richard Du Cann Q.C. and *Stephen Batten* for the appellants.
David Tudor Price and *Roy Amlot* for the Crown.

                                                 Cur. adv. vult.

January 31. LAWTON L.J. read the following judgment. On January **H**
26, 1977, in the Snaresbrook Crown Court, after a trial before Judge
Lewisohn, the defendants, David Michael Nock and Kevin Charles
Alsford, were convicted of a number of offences under the Misuse of
Drugs Act 1971, and sentenced to a total of two years' imprisonment.
They appealed on a point of law against their conviction on count 1 of
the indictment. On that count they were each sentenced to 12 months'
imprisonment.

A   After amendment during the trial, that count charged the defendants and others, who were not convicted, with conspiracy to contravene section 4 of the Misuse of Drugs Act 1971. The particulars of offence alleged that they had " conspired together and with other persons unknown to produce a controlled drug of Class A, namely, cocaine."

     On September 22, 1975, the police searched Alsford's home and found a quantity of drugs, some white powder in a number of containers, B and some chemical apparatus. When questioned about a flask of white powder, Alsford said: " Yes, I admit everything: that's cocaine. I've just had it refined." When asked what he meant by " refined," he said: " Well, it wasn't pure, but this is the pure stuff. I've separated it." When asked what he had used to do that, he said: " Chemicals in the bedroom, but people did give us a hand." Later he made a statement in writing C to the effect that he had obtained a sample of powder from a man called Mitchell (who was indicted with Alsford and Nock on count 1 but the jury could not agree about his guilt). Some friends had analysed it and had reported that the powder was a mixture of cocaine and a substance called lignocaine, which is an uncontrolled pharmaceutical product. Encouraged by this report, he and others bought 5 lbs. of the powder and tried to—I use his words—" separate it." At first they were unsuccess- D ful, but in the end they got refined cocaine from the mixture.

     When Nock was interviewed by the police, he admitted that he had been involved with Alsford in the separation of the cocaine from the lignocaine and added: " The process just purified the cocaine and makes it more valuable."

     The process had involved the use of sulphuric acid. When the white E powder was analysed at the Metropolitan Police Forensic Science Labora- tory, it was found to contain no cocaine at all; and cocaine could not have been produced from it.

     The evidence about the chemical composition of the white powder was the foundation of two submissions made by Mr. Du Cann to this court: first, that an agreement to commit an offence which at the date of the agreement could not be committed was not a conspiracy known to the F law; and secondly, that even if such an agreement could be an offence, on the evidence in this case there was no offence, because all they had agreed to do was to separate substances in a mixture, one of which they wrongly believed to be cocaine, and that an agreement to make such a separation could not in law be an agreement to produce a controlled drug.

     The first of these submissions has taken the court into an area of G the law where there is no clear authority, but some speculative writing as to what the law ought to be. For an example, see Glanville Williams, Criminal Law, 2nd ed. (1961), p. 642 et seq. The Law Commission, in its Working Paper No. 50 on Inchoate Offences, tentatively suggested what the law should be: see paragraph 136 (ii) and (iv). There now is some authority touching on this problem. It is partly in the House of Lords decision in Reg. v. Smith (Roger) [1975] A.C. 476, and partly in the H decision of this court in Reg. v. Green (Harry) [1976] Q.B. 985. Reg. v. Smith (Roger), which was concerned with a charge of attempting to handle stolen goods, tends to support the first of the defendants' sub- missions. Reg. v. Green (Harry), which was concerned with an offence of conspiracy to evade the prohibition on the importation of cannabis, gives some support to the prosecution.

     Mr. Du Cann's submission on this issue can, we think, be described as a projection into the law of conspiracy of the reasoning which led the House of Lords to decide that a series of acts done with intent to A commit a specified offence which could not be committed could not be an attempt to commit that offence.

Lord Hailsham of St. Marylebone L.C., in *Reg.* v. *Smith (Roger)* [1975] A.C. 476, 493, critically examined the sixfold classification of attempts to commit a crime, which Turner J. had made in the New Zealand case of *Reg.* v. *Donnelly* [1970] N.Z.L.R. 980. The fifth of these classifications was where someone B

"may find that what he is proposing to do is after all impossible— not because of insufficiency of means, but because it is for some reason physically not possible, whatever means be adopted."

He said, at p. 495E, that this class of "attempt" was not indictable in English law. At p. 498B, Lord Reid examined the proposition which had C been put forward to the effect that

"if the accused does not know the true facts but erroneously believes the facts to be such that his conduct would be an offence if the facts had been as he believes them to be, then he is guilty of an attempt to commit the offence."

He pointed out that in relation to statutory offences (and we are con- D cerned with an alleged conspiracy to commit a statutory offence) that was clearly wrong. The only possible attempt would be to do what Parliament has forbidden, and what the accused in that case had done was to handle goods which had ceased to be stolen goods. Later in his speech Lord Reid commented on the difference between an attempt to commit an offence and the doing of an act with an unlawful intent. In E the latter type of case the offence is committed even though the intent could never have been effected. *Reg.* v. *Goodchild* (1846) 2 Car. & K. 293 was such a case. The offence was to administer a noxious drug with intent to procure a miscarriage. It was no defence that the woman to whom the noxious drug was administered was not with child. But what if the substance was not noxious? Administering an innocuous substance with an unlawful intent was not an act forbidden by law. Men are not F punished because of their wrongful intentions, but for their unlawful acts.

Lord Reid gave some examples of what he considered would be the absurdities arising if intention based upon a mistaken belief as to the facts governed the law relating to attempts. We refer to one. A man lies dead. His enemy comes along and thinks he is asleep, so he stabs the corpse. The theory of intent coupled with belief inevitably requires G the courts to hold that the enemy has attempted to murder the dead man. "The law," said Lord Reid at p. 500, "may sometimes be an ass but it cannot be so asinine at that."

Supported by this line of reasoning, Mr. Du Cann put forward this proposition: if what the parties agreed to do or the specified means they intended to employ to do it did not, either at the moment of agreement H or during the subsistence of the agreement, involve the commission of a criminal offence, then they would not be guilty of the criminal conspiracy. The formulation of this proposition represents an important departure from what Lord Reid was discussing. He discussed intention to do an unlawful act with a mistaken belief as to what the facts were. Mr. Du Cann's proposition involves an agreement to do an unlawful act in the mistaken belief that facts exist which do not. It is the factor of agree-

A   ment which distinguishes attempts to commit crimes from conspiracies to do so.

In *Reg.* v. *Green (Harry)* [1976] Q.B. 985, Ormrod L.J. said, at p. 993, that it was difficult to see how the reasoning in *Reg.* v. *Smith (Roger)* could be applied to conspiracy. We agree. Indeed in *Reg.* v. *Smith (Roger)* [1975] A.C. 476, Lord Hailsham of St. Marylebone L.C. seems to be saying, at p. 497E, that the difficulty arising in that case because of the

B   fact that the goods when handled had ceased to be stolen goods could have been avoided if a conspiracy to handle had been charged.

Mr. Tudor Price, on behalf of the prosecution, put forward a simple proposition. He submitted that as an unlawful conspiracy consists in an agreement between two or more persons to effect a purpose which the law regards as unlawful, all that the prosecution had to prove was

C   the making of such an agreement which the parties to it intended to carry out. In this case, he submitted, there was ample evidence of the making of the agreement and the defendants' subsequent acts showed that they intended to carry it out. The fact that the parties to it could not have carried it out was irrelevant to proof of the offence.

Our first task is to examine carefully what the defendants were proved to have agreed. Counsel on both sides agreed before us that the evidence

D   went to prove that the defendants agreed together to obtain cocaine by separating it from the other substance or substances in the powder which they had obtained from Mitchell, believing that such powder was a mixture of cocaine and lignocaine. Mr. Tudor Price had reservations about the use of the word " separate " in this connection for reasons relating to the issue whether the defendants had agreed to " produce "

E   cocaine. If separating the constituents of a mixture can properly be said to " produce " one of them (which is an issue we will consider later in this judgment), in our judgment the prosecution did prove an agreement to do an act which was forbidden by section 4 of the Misuse of Drugs Act 1971. The fact that the unlawful agreement could not be carried out, in our judgment, is irrelevant, just as in *Reg.* v. *Goodchild,*

F   2 Car. & K. 293 was the fact that the doing of the forbidden act could not have had the effect which was intended. The test is: what is the act forbidden by the law, not what will be the consequences of doing the forbidden act? Thus, in *Haggard* v. *Mason* [1976] 1 W.L.R. 187, the forbidden act was offering to sell lysergide (LSD). This is what the accused did; but what he delivered was not lysergide, although he believed it was. The Divisional Court held that he had been rightly convicted.

G   In our judgment, the first of Mr. Du Cann's submissions must be rejected.

Was the agreement one to produce a controlled drug? Cocaine was a controlled drug. Mr. Du Cann submitted that an agreement to separate a mixture so as to isolate a constituent substance cannot in law be an agreement to produce that substance.

The interpretation section of the Act (section 37 (1)) provides that

H   the word " produce " shall have the meaning assigned to it, namely, " ' produce ', where the reference is to producing a controlled drug, means producing it by manufacture, cultivation or any other method . . ." What the defendants intended to do, and tried to do, was to get cocaine from what they believed to be a mixture of two substances by the use of sulphuric acid. The separation was to be by a chemical process, not a mechanical one. We have no doubt at all that such a method of separation amounted to producing cocaine.

Lawton L.J.   **D.P.P. v. Nock (C.A.)**   [1978]

As a subsidiary point Mr. Du Cann submitted that the judge was   A
wrong in deciding, as he did, to direct the jury as to what the word
" produce " meant. He did so in these terms:

> " If persons agree to subject a powder which contains cocaine to
> elaborate scientific processes with a view to ridding the cocaine of
> the other substance which adulterated it, then what they are doing
> is agreeing to produce cocaine and committing the offence of   B
> conspiracy to produce it."

He should, said Mr. Du Cann, have left the jury to decide whether what
the defendants had agreed to do amounted to producting cocaine. We
do not agree. What the judge was doing was construing a statutory
provision, which is a matter of law for him, not the jury. He may have
gone somewhat beyond the evidence by using the phrase " elaborate   C
scientific processes," but such overstatement as there was did not make
the verdict unsafe or unsatisfactory.

The appeals will be dismissed.

Appeals dismissed.

The court certified, pursuant to section 33 (2) of the Criminal Appeal
Act 1968, that a point of law of general public importance was involved   D
in the decision, namely:

> " Whether an agreement which had as its purpose the production of
> cocaine (being an act forbidden by section 4 of the Misuse of Drugs Act
> 1971) was not an indictable conspiracy because the evidence showed
> that the agreement was to pursue a course of action which could never
> in fact have produced cocaine."   E

Leave to appeal refused.
Bail granted until application to House
of Lords for leave to appeal, and to
continue on application succeeding;
application to be made within 14   F
days, otherwise bail rescinded.
Legal aid for two counsel and solici-
tors for the application, liberty to
apply for further legal aid on
application succeeding.

Solicitors: *Registrar of Criminal Appeals; Director of Public Prosecu-*   G
tions.

[Reported by BERNARD O. AGYEMAN, ESQ., Barrister-at-Law]

APPEAL from the Court of Appeal (Criminal Division).

The defendants appealed to the House of Lords pursuant to leave   H
granted by the Appeal Committee (Lord Diplock, Lord Salmon and Lord
Scarman) on March 9, 1978.

Richard Du Cann Q.C. and *Stephen Batten* for the appellants.
Michael Worsley and *J. G. Boal* for the Crown.

Their Lordships took time for consideration.

A   LORD DIPLOCK. My Lords, I have had the advantage of reading in advance the speech to be delivered by my noble and learned friend, Lord
Scarman, with which I am in full agreement. He draws attention to the
limited terms of the agreement between the conspirators that was proved in
evidence. To use the formulation of this class of conspiracy, now to be
found in section 1 of the Criminal Law Act 1977, the course of conduct to
be pursued was expressed with particularity in the agreement.

B   The classic definition of this class of criminal conspiracy was propounded
by Willes J. in *Mulcahy* v. *The Queen* (1868) L.R. 3 H.L. 306, 317: and
has already been referred to by my noble and learned friend. The full
quotation is worth reciting:

       " A conspiracy consists . . . in the agreement of two or more to do an
       unlawful act, or to do a lawful act by unlawful means. So long as
C   such a design rests in intention only, it is not indictable. When two
       agree to carry it into effect, the very plot is an act in itself, and the
       act of each of the parties, promise against promise, actus contra actum,
       capable of being enforced, if lawful, punishable if for a criminal object
       or for the use of criminal means."

This emphasises the auxiliary nature of the crime and its resemblance to
D that other auxiliary crime " attempt " in which the " proximate act " of
the accused takes the place of the agreement in conspiracy. So to agree
to pursue a course of conduct which, if carried out in accordance with the
intention of those agreeing to it, would not amount to or involve the commission of any offence, would not have amounted to criminal conspiracy at
common law nor does it now constitute an offence of conspiracy under
E section 1 of the Act of 1977.

       Your Lordships' decision to allow this appeal, however, need not cause
the alarm and despondency predicted by those prosecuting authorities who
hoped to find in the law of conspiracy the only available life-buoy in what
appears to be regarded as the shipwreck of *Reg.* v. *Ring* (1892) 61 L.J.M.C.
116 as a result of its collision with the recent decision of this House in *Reg.*
v. *Smith (Roger)* [1975] A.C. 476.

F   *Reg.* v. *Ring* was a typical case of a gang of railway pickpockets. They
were charged with attempting to steal from the person of a person unknown
and with assaulting a person unknown with intent to commit a felony.
They had hustled a woman on the railway platform and had tried to find
the pocket of her clothes, but had not been successful. Their conviction
was upheld by the Court for Crown Cases Reserved. The short judgment
G of the court was delivered by Lord Coleridge C.J. in the course of which
he said that the earlier case of *Reg.* v. *Collins* (1864) 9 Cox C.C. 497 had
been overruled by *Reg.* v. *Brown* (1889) 24 Q.B.D. 357, and was bad law.
It was the purported overruling of *Reg.* v. *Collins* that was repudiated by
this House in *Reg.* v. *Smith.* No member of the Appellate Committee
expressed the view that the actual decision in *Reg.* v. *Ring*, 61 L.J.M.C. 116
was wrong.

H   The facts of the two cases were not dissimilar, but the indictments
were in different terms. In *Reg.* v. *Collins*, 9 Cox C.C. 497, the offence
charged was restricted to an attempt to steal from the person of a woman
unknown property located in the very pocket in which one of the accused had
put his hand, whereas in *Reg.* v. *Ring* the offences charged were an attempt
to steal from the person generally and an assault with intent to commit a
felony. At the time *Reg.* v. *Collins* was decided, in order to support a
charge of stealing property or attempting to steal it, it was necessary to

prove that what was stolen or was the subject of the attempt to steal, **A**
complied strictly with the description of it in the indictment: *Reg.* v.
M'Pherson (1851) Dears. & B. 197.

The modern pickpocket working with a confederate, as is advisable if
success is to be achieved, is hardly likely to have agreed with his confederate
that they will restrict their activities to stealing from a single pocket of a
single individual and desist from all further efforts if that particular pocket
is found to contain nothing. The agreement to be inferred from their **B**
conduct, as no doubt it would have been by the jury in both *Reg.* v.
Collins, 9 Cox C.C. 497 and in *Reg.* v. *Ring,* 61 L.J.M.C. 116, had charges of
conspiracy been brought would not have been so limited. The course of
conduct agreed to be pursued would be to do all that was necessary or
expedient to steal whatever property of value they could find upon whoever was carrying property on their person in an accessible place. **C**

It seems to me, however, that even in relation to the solitary pickpocket
who works alone and is apprehended before he has succeeded in finding
something worth appropriating in any of those pockets or handbags to
which he has been seen to direct his hand, *Reg.* v. *Smith (Roger)* [1975]
A.C. 476 and the earlier case of *Reg.* v. *Easom* [1971] 2 Q.B. 315 have
come to be regarded as authorities for a wider proposition than they or
either of them laid down. **D**

In *Reg.* v. *Easom* the accused had been convicted of stealing a handbag
and its specified contents which were of little value. The accused, in a
darkened cinema, had surreptitiously removed a handbag from where its
owner had placed it by her side. On inspection he had found its contents
not worth stealing and had left it there intact within easy reach of its owner.
He was charged with the complete offence of theft and at his trial the judge **E**
took the view that what had been proved amounted to the full offence or
nothing. He refused to leave to the jury the alternative of attempting to
steal. The appeal was allowed upon the ground of misdirection by the judge
as to the intent of the accused (at the time he took the bag) to deprive the
owner permanently of the property specified in the indictment. In dealing
obiter with the possibility of a conviction for attempted theft the Court of
Appeal said at p. 321: " . . . all, or, at least, much, depends upon the **F**
manner in which the charge is framed." They emphasised that their view
that such a conviction would not lie in *Easom's* case was dependent on
the fact that on that particular indictment the only attempt of which the
accused could have been convicted would have been an attempt to steal
the particular articles specified in the indictment and no others.

Partington v. *Williams* (1976) 62 Cr.App.R. 220 was about a charge **G**
of attempted theft of money from an empty wallet which was not being
carried on the person but was in a drawer. The Court of Appeal there took
the view that this House in *Reg.* v. *Smith* had overruled the actual decision
in *Reg.* v. *Ring,* 61 L.J.M.C. 116 and not merely, as I have suggested, disapproved of the purported overruling of *Reg.* v. *Collins,* 9 Cox C.C. 497
which is to be found in the judgment in *Reg* v. *Ring.* They went on to
suggest that whenever the accused is charged with an attempt to steal **H**
property and the proximate act relied upon as the actus reus (*pace* Lord
Hailsham of St. Marylebone L.C.) is that the accused has inserted his hand
in some place where something worth stealing is likely to be found the onus
lies upon the prosecution to prove that something worth stealing was
actually present in that particular place.

My Lords, this, in relation to pickpockets at least, seems to me to
offend common sense and common justice. The crime which the pick-

A pocket sets out to commit is not confined to stealing from a particular person or a fortiori from a particular pocket in a particular person's clothes or from a particular article carried by a particular person. When he converts intention into attempt by the proximate act of extending his hand to a particular pocket or article, failure at this point to effect his intention of stealing, because where he first puts his hand there is nothing to steal, does not mean that the course of conduct that he intended to

B pursue would have ended with this initial failure and would not have continued until he had found something to steal in some similar place and stolen it. Under an indictment drafted in suitably broad terms I see no reason why even the solitary pickpocket should not be convicted of attempted theft without the prosecution needing to prove that the particular pockets or handbags into which he was seen to put his hand in

C fact contained something which he would have stolen if he could.

LORD EDMUND-DAVIES. My Lords, I have had the advantage of reading in draft the speech prepared by my noble and learned friend, Lord Scarman. I agree with it and with the conclusion that the appeal should be allowed and the conviction of each appellant quashed.

D
LORD RUSSELL OF KILLOWEN. My Lords, I have had the advantage of reading in draft the speech in these consolidated appeals of my noble and learned friend, Lord Scarman. I agree with his conclusion that these appeals should be allowed and with the reasons to which he attributes that conclusion.

The important point to note is that the agreement that is said to have

E been an unlawful conspiracy was not an agreement in general terms to produce cocaine, but an agreement in specific terms to produce cocaine from a particular powder which in fact, however treated, would never yield cocaine. In order to see whether there is a criminal conspiracy it is necessary to consider the whole agreement. The specific limits of the agreement cannot be discarded, leaving a general agreement to produce

F cocaine, for that would be to find an agreement other than that which was made: and that is not a permissible approach to any agreement, conspiracy or other.

It is, I apprehend, clear on authority that neither appellant, discovered in the act of vainly and optimistically applying sulphuric acid (or any other treatment) to this particular powder, would be guilty of an attempt to produce cocaine. It would appear to me strange that the two should be

G guilty of a crime if together they bent over the same test tube, having agreed on the joint vain attempt. These appellants thought that they would succeed in their endeavour. But what if they had doubted success, and their agreement had been to " try it "? That would be an agreement to attempt, and since the attempt would not be unlawful the agreement could not be a criminal conspiracy. But if the conclusion against which these

H appeals are made were correct, it would mean that those erroneously confident of success would be guilty of the crime of conspiracy, but not those who, unconvinced, agreed to try. The gullible would be guilty, the suspicious stainless. That could not be right.

LORD KEITH OF KINKEL. My Lords, I have had the opportunity of reading in draft the speech of my noble and learned friend, Lord Scarman. I agree with it, and for the reasons he gives I would allow the appeal. I

agree also with the supplementary observations of my noble and learned A
friend, Lord Diplock.

LORD SCARMAN.   My Lords, the headnote to the report of *Reg.* v.
Smith (Roger) [1975] A.C. 476 accurately records that the second of the
holdings of your Lordships' House in that case was that steps on the way to
the doing of something, which was thereafter done (or would have been
done, if not interrupted by some supervening event) and which is no crime, B
cannot be regarded as attempts to commit a crime.   In dismissing the two
appeals which are now under consideration by your Lordships, the Court
of Appeal declined to apply this principle to cases of conspiracy, but
certified the point as one of general public importance.   The Court of
Appeal has certified the point in terms specific to the facts of this case.
It is, however, a general question, which, with respect, I think is better C
put as follows: when two or more persons agree upon a course of
conduct with the object of committing a criminal offence, but, unknown
to them, it is not possible to achieve their object by the course of conduct
agreed upon, do they commit the crime of conspiracy?   The question falls
to be considered at common law, the relevant events having occurred
before the coming into force of the Criminal Law Act 1977, section 1 (1)
of which contains a statutory definition of conspiracy superseding the D
common law.   Nevertheless the point is of some importance for the reason
given by the Court of Appeal—that the common law may have to be
investigated for the purpose of construing the section.

The classic description of the crime of conspiracy at common law is
that it consists of an agreement to do an unlawful act or a lawful act by
unlawful means: *Mulcahy* v. *The Queen*, L.R. 3 H.L. 306, 317.   The agree- E
ment itself constitutes the offence.   The mens rea of the offence is the intention to do the unlawful act: the actus reus is the fact of agreement.   The
Court of Appeal—correctly, in my judgment—stressed that it is the factor of
agreement which distinguishes conspiracy from attempt.   But were they
also correct in concluding that because of the factor of agreement the
principle accepted by your Lordships' House in *Reg.* v. *Smith* [1975]
A.C. 476 as applying to attempts is not to be applied to conspiracy.   I have F
reached the conclusion that the Court of Appeal fell into error on this
point, and that *Reg.* v. *Smith* is applicable to cases of conspiracy.

Before giving my reasons for this conclusion it is necessary to determine
the nature and scope of the agreement which in this case is alleged to
constitute the criminal conspiracy.   This calls for a close review of the
facts as found or admitted. G

Five persons, including the two appellants, David Michael Nock and
Kevin Charles Alsford, appeared at the Snaresbrook Crown Court on
January 5, 1977, to answer an indictment charging them with a number
of drug offences.   Nock and Alsford were convicted upon several counts
but your Lordships' House is concerned only with their conviction upon H
the first count in the indictment.   It charged them (and others) with
conspiracy to contravene section 4 of the Misuse of Drugs Act 1971.   The
section provides by subsection (1) that subject to regulations (which are of
no present relevance) it shall not be lawful for a person to produce a
controlled drug and by subsection (2) that it is an offence to produce a
controlled drug in contravention of subsection (1).   The particulars of
offence, after being amended, were as follows:

A   " Kevin Charles Alsford, David Michael Nock [and three other named defendants] on divers days before September 23, 1975, conspired together and with other persons unknown to produce a controlled drug of Class A, namely cocaine."

The indictment makes plain that the Crown is alleging in this case a conspiracy to commit a crime: and no one has suggested that the particulars
B   fail to disclose an offence known to the law.   But the appellants submit, and it is not disputed by the Crown, that the agreement as proved was narrower in scope than the conspiracy charged.   When the case was before the Court of Appeal, counsel on both sides agreed that the evidence went to prove that the appellants agreed together to obtain cocaine by separating it from the other substance or substances contained in a powder which
C   they had obtained from one of their co-defendants, a Mr. Mitchell.   They believed that the powder was a mixture of cocaine and lignocaine, and that they would be able to produce cocaine from it.   In fact the powder was lignocaine hydro-chloride, an anaesthetic used in dentistry, which contains no cocaine at all.   It is impossible to produce, by separation or otherwise, cocaine from lignocaine.   The agreement between the appellants
D   was correctly summarised by the Court of Appeal, when certifying the point of law, as an agreement " to pursue a course of action which could never in fact have produced cocaine."

The appellants made a number of attempts—all of them, of course, unsuccessful—to extract cocaine from their powder.   It was not until after
E   they had been arrested and the powder seized by the police and sent for analysis that they learnt to their surprise that there was no way in which cocaine could be produced from it.

The trial judge in his direction to the jury, and the Court of Appeal in their judgment dismissing the two appeals, treated this impossibility as an irrelevance.   In their view the agreement was what mattered: and there
F   was plain evidence of an agreement to produce cocaine, even though unknown to the two conspirators it could not be done.   Neither the trial judge nor the Court of Appeal thought it necessary to carry their analysis of the agreement further.   The trial judge described it simply as an agreement to produce cocaine.   The Court of Appeal thought it enough that the prosecution had proved " an agreement to do an act which was forbidden
G   by section 4 of the Misuse of Drugs Act 1971."   Both descriptions are accurate, as far as they go.   But neither contains any reference to the limited nature of the agreement proved: it was an agreement upon a specific course of conduct with the object of producing cocaine, and limited to that course of conduct.   Since it could not result in the production of cocaine, the two appellants by pursuing it could not commit the statutory
H   offence of producing a controlled drug.   The appellants, who did get a chemist to take on the impossible job of extracting cocaine from the powder, may perhaps be treated as having completed their agreed course of conduct: if so, they completed it without committing the statutory offence.   Perhaps, however, it would be more accurate to treat them as having desisted before they had completed all that they had agreed to do: but it makes no difference because, had they completed all that they had agreed to do, no cocaine would have been produced.

If, therefore, their agreement, limited as it was to a specific course of   A
conduct which could not result in the commission of the statutory offence,
constituted (as the Court of Appeal held) a criminal conspiracy, the strange
consequence ensues, that by agreeing upon a course of conduct which was
not criminal (or unlawful) the appellants were guilty of conspiring to
commit a crime.

Upon these facts the appellants submit that the evidence reveals no   B
" conspiracy at large," by which they mean an agreement in general terms
to produce cocaine if and when they could find a suitable raw material, but
only the limited agreement, to which I have referred. Counsel for the
appellants concedes that, if two or more persons decide to go into business
as cocaine producers, or, to take another example, as assassins for hire (e.g.
" Murder Incorporated "), the mere fact that in the course of performing   C
their agreement they attempt to produce cocaine from a raw material which
could not possibly yield it or (in the second example), stab a corpse,
believing it to be the body of a living man, would not avail them as a
defence: for the performance of their general agreement would not be
rendered impossible by such transient frustrations. But performance of
the limited agreement proved in this case could not in any circumstances   D
have involved the commission of the offence created by the statute.

The answer sought to be made by the Crown (and accepted by the
Court of Appeal) is that the offence of conspiracy is committed when an
agreement to commit, or to try to commit, a crime is reached, whether or
not anything is, or can be, done to perform it. It is wrong, upon their
view, to treat conspiracy as a " preliminary " or " inchoate " crime: for   E
its criminality depends in no way upon its being a step towards the commission of the substantive offence (or, at common law, the unlawful act).
Upon this view of the law the scope of agreement is irrelevant: all that
is needed to constitute the crime is the intention to commit the substantive
offence and the agreement to try to do so.

If the Court of Appeal is right, *Reg.* v. *Smith* [1975] A.C. 476 can   F
have no application in cases of conspiracy. But neither history nor
principle supports this view of the law. In *Board of Trade* v. *Owen*
[1957] A.C. 602, 623–625 Lord Tucker, quoting with approval some
observations from R. S. Wright J.'s little classic, *The Law of Criminal
Conspiracies and Agreements* (1873) and some passages from Sir William
Holdsworth's (somewhat larger) work, *The History of English Law*,   G
accepted that the historical basis of the crime of conspiring to commit
a crime (the case with which we are now concerned) was that it developed
as an " auxiliary " (R. S. Wright's word) to the law which creates the
crime agreed to be committed. Lord Tucker accepted Holdsworth's
comment (at p. 625) that " It was inevitable therefore, as Stephen has
said, that conspiracy should come to be regarded as a form of attempt   H
to commit a wrong." Lord Tucker concluded his survey with these
words, at p. 626:

> " Accepting the above as the historical basis of the crime of
> conspiracy, it seems to me that the whole object of making such
> agreements punishable is to prevent the commission of the substantive
> offence before it has even reached the stage of an attempt, . . ."

A   Lord Tucker, in whose opinion the other noble and learned Lords sitting with him concurred, by stressing the "auxiliary" nature of the crime of conspiracy and by explaining its justification as being to prevent the commission of substantive offences, has placed the crime firmly in the same class and category as attempts to commit a crime. Both are criminal because they are steps towards the commission of a substantive offence.

B   The distinction between the two is that, whereas a "proximate" act is that which constitutes the crime of attempt, agreement is the necessary ingredient in conspiracy. The importance of the distinction is that agreement may, and usually will, occur well before the first step which can be said to be an attempt. The law of conspiracy thus makes possible an earlier intervention by the law to prevent the commission of the substantive

C   offence. But the distinction has no relevance in determining whether the impossibility of committing the substantive offence should be a defence. Indeed upon the view of the law authoritatively explained and accepted in *Owen's* case [1957] A.C. 602, logic and justice would seem to require that the question as to the effect of the impossibility of the substantive offence should be answered in the same way, whether the crime charged

D   be conspiracy or attempt.

It is necessary, therefore, to analyse the decision in *Reg.* v. *Smith* [1975] A.C. 476 in order to determine whether it can reasonably be applied to cases of conspiracy. The Court of Appeal thought that there were difficulties. But I do not agree.

It was—somewhat half-heartedly—suggested by the Crown that the

E   House might reconsider the decision, which we were told is causing difficulties in some respects. It is, however, a very recent decision; and a unanimous one reached after full argument which brought to the attention of this House the relevant case law and exposed the difficulties. More importantly, the decision is, in my respectful opinion, correct in principle. I would not question the decision, though its proper limits may have to be

F   considered. The House decided the case upon two grounds, either of which would have sufficed, standing alone, to support the decision, but both of which commended themselves to the House. They may be described as the statutory (and narrower) ground and the common law principle.

The statutory ground was provided by sections 22 and 24 (3) of the

G   Theft Act 1968. The offence being considered by the House was one of attempting to handle stolen goods. At the time of the attempted handling, the goods had been (this was conceded) restored to lawful custody. The House ruled that, in the case of a statutory offence:

"The only possible attempt would be to do what Parliament has forbidden. But Parliament has not forbidden that which the accused

H   did, i.e., handling goods which have ceased to be stolen goods. . . . Here the mens rea was proved but there was no actus reus so the case is not within the scope of the section," *per* Lord Reid at p. 498c.

With all respect to the Court of Appeal, there is no difficulty in applying this line of reasoning to a case in which the allegation is not an attempt but a conspiracy to commit a statutory offence. First, there is no logical difficulty in applying a rule that an agreement is a conspiracy to commit

a statutory offence only if it is an agreement to do that which Parliament   A
has forbidden. It is no more than the application of the principle that an
actus reus as well as mens rea must be established. And in the present
case there was no actus reus, because there was no agreement upon a
course of conduct forbidden by the statute. Secondly, the application of
such a rule is consistent with principle. Unless the law requires the actus
reus as well as mens rea to be proved, men, whether they be accused   B
of conspiracy or attempt, will be punished for their guilty intentions alone.
I conclude the consideration of this ground of decision with a further
quotation from Lord Reid's speech, at p. 500: " But such a radical
change in the principles of our law should not be introduced in this way
even if it were desirable."

The second ground of decision—the common law principle—can be   C
summarised in words which commended themselves to all the noble and
learned Lords concerned with the case. In *Rex* v. *Percy Dalton (London)
Ltd.* Birkett J., giving the judgment of the Court of Criminal Appeal
said (1949) 33 Cr.App.R. 102, 110:

> " Steps on the way to the commission of what would be a crime, if
> the acts were completed, may amount to attempts to commit that   D
> crime, to which, unless interrupted, they would have led; but steps on
> the way to the doing of something, which is thereafter done, and which
> is no crime, cannot be regarded as attempts to commit a crime."

In his speech Lord Hailsham of St. Marylebone L.C. added the rider (a
logical one) to the effect " that equally steps on the way to do something   E
which is thereafter *not* completed, but which if done would not constitute
a crime cannot be indicted as attempts to commit that crime," [1975]
A.C. 476, 497c. As in the case of the statutory ground, there is no logical
difficulty in the way of applying this principle to the law relating to
conspiracy provided it is recognised that conspiracy is a " preliminary "
or " auxiliary " crime. And again, as with the statutory ground, common   F
sense and justice combine to require of the law that no man should be
punished criminally for the intention with which he enters an agreement
unless it can also be shown that what he has agreed to do is unlawful.

The Crown's argument, as developed before your Lordships, rests, in
my judgment, upon a misconception of the nature of the agreement proved.
This is a case not of an agreement to commit a crime capable of being   G
committed in the way agreed upon, but frustrated by a supervening event
making its completion impossible, which was the Crown's submission, but
of an agreement upon a course of conduct which could not in any circumstances result in the statutory offence alleged, i.e. the offence of producing
the controlled drug, cocaine.

I conclude therefore that the two parallel lines of reasoning upon which   H
this House decided *Reg.* v. *Smith* [1975] A.C. 476 apply equally to
criminal conspiracy as they do to attempted crime. We were referred to
a recent case in the Court of Appeal, *Reg.* v. *Green (Harry)* [1976] Q.B.
985, in which the contrary view was expressed, but not developed at
any length. The court in that case, as also the Court of Appeal in this
case, attached importance to some observations of Lord Hailsham of St.
Marylebone L.C. in *Reg.* v. *Smith* [1975] A.C. 476, where the indictment

A undoubtedly included, as the second count, a charge of conspiracy with persons unknown to handle stolen goods. The Lord Chancellor (p. 489F) remarked that he was unable to understand why the prosecution did not proceed with this charge. He reverted to the point at p. 497D, and there is an echo of it in Viscount Dilhorne's speech at p. 503E. In *Green's* case [1976] Q.B. 985, 993 Ormrod L.J. treated these remarks as an indication

B that *Reg.* v. *Smith* [1975] A.C. 476 is not applicable in cases of conspiracy. The Court of Appeal in the instant case took the same view. But I do not think that either the Lord Chancellor or Viscount Dilhorne was saying anything of the sort. The conspiracy charged in the second count must have ante-dated the police seizure of the van and the return of the goods to lawful custody. Smith must have agreed to help in the

C disposal of the goods at a time when they were stolen goods and the agreement could be performed. It was an agreement to commit an offence which, but for the police interruption, would have been committed. There is nothing in *Reg.* v. *Smith* which would prevent such an agreement in such circumstances from being treated as a criminal conspiracy.

Our attention was also drawn to two cases, upon which it may be

D helpful to comment very briefly. In *Reg.* v. *McDonough* (1962) 47 Cr.App.R. 37 the Court of Criminal Appeal held that an incitement to receive stolen goods was complete on the making of the incitement even though there were no stolen goods—perhaps even, no goods at all. In *Haggard* v. *Mason* [1976] 1 W.L.R. 187 the Divisional Court held that the offence of offering to supply a controlled drug was committed, even though the drug in fact supplied was not a controlled drug. Neither of

E these cases infringes the principle of *Reg.* v. *Smith*: for in each, as Lord Widgery C.J. pointed out in *Haggard* v. *Mason* (p. 189), the offence was complete. In *McDonough*, 47 Cr.App.R. 37 the actus reus was the making of the incitement and in *Haggard's* case it was the making of the offer.

For these reasons I would allow the appeal. However, counsel for the Crown informed us that *Reg.* v. *Smith* has created difficulties in the

F enforcement of the law. He referred particularly to the pickpocket who finds nothing to steal in the pocket (or wallet) which he picks. In my opinion *Reg.* v. *Smith* provides no escape route for such villains, as Lord Hailsham of St. Marylebone L.C. called them (p. 497D). In *Reg.* v. *Smith* this House reinstated as decisions of authority *Reg.* v. *M'Pherson*, 7 Cox C.C. 281 and *Reg.* v. *Collins*, 9 Cox C.C. 497. In *M'Pherson's*

G case the jury had convicted M'Pherson of an attempt to steal goods other than those mentioned in the indictment. The goods specified in the indictment had been removed before he broke into the house. Quashing his conviction, the Court of Crown Cases Reserved held that " he could not properly be convicted of attempting to commit *the felony charged* " (*per* Cockburn C.J. 7 Cox C.C. 281, 284); my emphasis. This decision

H was followed in *Reg.* v. *Collins*, a pickpocket case. Here also the indictment was limited to an attempt to commit a specific theft, namely to steal the property of the woman in her gown pocket. There was no affirmative proof that there was anything in the pocket. As Bramwell B. commented in *M'Pherson's* case (at p. 285), such cases depend upon the nature of the offence charged; and, I would add, upon the particular facts established or conceded. It is certainly not possible to deduce from

these cases a rule that he who, with intent to steal, picks a pocket but   A
finds nothing to steal must be acquitted of attempted theft: nor do I
think did any of their Lordships in *Reg.* v. *Smith* [1975] A.C. 476 commit
themselves to so sweeping a proposition.

    We were invited by the Crown to express an opinion as to the correct-
ness or otherwise of three decisions of the Court of Appeal, *Reg.* v. *Easom*
[1971] 2 Q.B. 315, *Partington* v. *Williams* (1976) 62 Cr.App.R. 220 and   B
Reg. v. *Hussein* (unreported) December 8, 1977. *Easom* and *Hussein* (to
which I was a party) were, I think, correctly decided: but each, like every
other criminal appeal, turned on its particular facts and on the way in
which the trial judge directed the jury on the law. In *Easom* [1971] 2
Q.B. 315, 319 Edmund Davies L.J. emphasised that in a case of theft the
appropriation must be accompanied by the intention of permanently   C
depriving the owner of his property. This, of course, follows from the
definition of theft in section 1 (1) of the Theft Act 1968. All that *Hussein*
decided was that the same intention must be proved when the charge is
one of attempted theft. Unfortunately in *Hussein* the issue of intention
was summed up in such a way as to suggest that theft, or attempted theft,
could be committed by a person who had not yet formed the intention   D
which the statute defines as a necessary part of the offence. An intention
to steal can exist even though, unknown to the accused, there is nothing
to steal: but, if a man be in two minds as to whether to steal or not,
the intention required by the statute is not proved. In *Partington* v.
Williams, 62 Cr.App.R. 220 the court did, I think, err in its interpretation
of *Reg.* v. *Smith* [1975] A.C. 476: and I respectfully agree with the   E
comments made by my noble and learned friend, Lord Diplock, upon
that case.

Appeal allowed.

    Solicitors: *Clinton Davis & Co.; Offenbach & Co.; Director of Public
Prosecutions.*   F

F. C.

A

[COURT OF APPEAL]

NORWEST HOLST LTD. *v.* SECRETARY OF STATE FOR TRADE
AND OTHERS

B

[1977 N. No. 1112]

1977   July 13, 14, 15, 18, 19, 20, 21; 29   Foster J.

1978   Jan. 30, 31;   Lord Denning M.R., Ormrod and
        Feb. 1   Geoffrey Lane L.JJ.

C
Company—Investigation of affairs—Department of Trade inspectors
—Discretionary power to appoint—Circumstances justifying
use of power—Disclosure of circumstances—Natural justice—
Companies Act 1948 (11 & 12 *Geo.* 6, *c.* 38), *s.* 165 (*b*) (*ii*)—
Companies Act 1967 (*c.* 81), *s.* 109

D
    The plaintiff was a public company with many subsidiaries
and carried on an engineering and construction business in the
United Kingdom and internationally. Its annual report of
September 1976 showed, inter alia, that some 32 per cent. of
its ordinary shares were held by a consortium of which two
of the directors were the principal members, holding over one
million shares each, and that a few months earlier, the City
of London Take-over Panel had not approved a take-over bid
for the company's shares by those two directors, but that the
matter had had "no effect on the conduct of the business."
In November 1976 the Department of Trade, under section 109
E
of the Companies Act 1967,[1] required the company to produce
certain of its books and papers to two appointed officers; and
the company secretary and a director gave such explanations of
the documents as were asked of them. In March 1977 the
department appointed two inspectors to investigate the company's affairs and report to it under section 165 of the Companies Act 1948.[2] The company's board objected, stating that
there appeared no circumstances justifying the appointments,
F
and asked that before any investigation was begun the department should disclose the circumstances and indicate any evidence relied on to justify the appointments. The department
replied that it was neither present practice nor a requirement
under the Act to make such disclosure and stated that the
appointments were made under section 165 (*b*) (ii) of the Act
of 1948. The company protested that that placed a wide category of persons under possible suspicion of having been guilty
G
of serious offences and that the department's failure to disclose
anything seemed hardly just or equitable.
    The company thereupon moved the court for a declaration
that the appointment of the inspectors was unlawful and ultra
vires, and for injunctions restraining the appointed inspectors
from carrying out the investigation. The department in turn
moved to have the company's proceedings struck out under
H
R.S.C., Ord. 18, r. 19, as disclosing no reasonable cause of
action. Their evidence on affidavit stated the nature of the
information in their possession derived from the section 109
inspection and also information from an informant on the
section 109 material and added that disclosure of that information might disclose the informant's identity. Foster J. struck
out the company's action.

[1] Companies Act 1967, s. 109: see post, p. 78D–F.
[2] Companies Act 1948, s. 165: see post, pp. 77G—78A.

Norwest Holst Ltd. v. Dept. of Trade (Ch.D.)   [1978]

On appeal by the company: —   A

Held, dismissing the appeal, (1) that the wide discretion conferred on the department by section 165 (*b*) to appoint inspectors to investigate a company's affairs and report to it was exercised at a preliminary stage for the purposes of good administration, and carried with it no implication that there was any case against the company; accordingly the rules of natural justice were at that stage inapplicable, so that the appointment of inspectors could not be challenged where   B
the Secretary of State had acted in good faith and within the powers conferred by the Acts.

(2) That the court could not and would not review the exercise of that discretion where the company had not discharged the onus on it of showing that there was any lack of good faith on the part of the department.

Per curiam. Limited companies enjoy great advantages under the law; their affairs and management may be in the   C
hands of a few persons who are in reality unaccountable for their activities; it is thus very proper that Parliament has provided power and discretion to investigate the company's affairs and persons concerned in its formation and management so long as the investigation is conducted fairly; and if a well-conducted company should suffer temporary disadvantage by being made the subject of an inquiry it is not unreasonable that it should bear such disadvantage with fortitude (post, pp.   D
88D–E, 90H—91A, 92F–H, 94F–G).

Decision of Foster J., post, p. 76G et seq. affirmed.

The following cases are referred to in the judgments of the Court of Appeal:

Breen v. *Amalgamated Engineering Union* [1971] 2 Q.B. 175; [1971]
      2 W.L.R. 742; [1971] 1 All E.R. 1148, C.A.   E
Cooper v. *Wandsworth Board of Works* (1863) 14 C.B.N.S. 180.
Durayappah v. *Fernando* [1967] 2 A.C. 337; [1967] 3 W.L.R. 289;
      [1967] 2 All E.R. 152, P.C.
Fisher v. *Keane* (1878) 11 Ch.D. 353.
Padfield v. *Minister of Agriculture, Fisheries and Food* [1968] A.C. 997;
      [1968] 2 W.L.R. 924; [1968] 1 All E.R. 694, C.A. and H.L.(E.).
Pergamon Press Ltd., *In re* [1971] Ch. 388; [1970] 3 W.L.R. 792; [1970]   F
      3 All E.R. 535, C.A.
Reg. v. *Barnet and Camden Rent Tribunal, Ex parte Frey Investments
      Ltd.* [1972] 2 Q.B. 342; [1971] 3 W.L.R. 985; [1971] 3 All E.R. 759,
      D.C.
Secretary of State for Education and Science v. *Tameside Metropolitan
      Borough Council* [1977] A.C. 1014; [1976] 3 W.L.R. 641; [1976] 3
      All E.R. 665, C.A. and H.L.(E.).
Secretary of State for Employment v. *ASLEF (No. 2)* [1972] 2 Q.B.   G
      455; [1972] 2 W.L.R. 1370; [1972] 2 All E.R. 949, C.A.
Wallersteiner v. *Moir* [1974] 1 W.L.R. 991; [1974] 3 All E.R. 217, C.A.
Wiseman v. *Borneman* [1971] A.C. 297; [1969] 3 W.L.R. 706; [1969]
      3 All E.R. 275, H.L.(E.).

The following additional cases were cited in argument in the Court of   H
Appeal:

Asher v. *Secretary of State for the Environment* [1974] Ch. 208; [1974]
      2 W.L.R. 466; [1974] 2 All E.R. 156, C.A.
Associated Provincial Picture Houses Ltd. v. *Wednesbury Corporation*
      [1948] 1 K.B. 223; [1947] 2 All E.R. 680, C.A.
Breetveldt v. *Van Zyl* 1972 (1) S.A. 304.
Buckingham v. *Combined Holdings and Industries Ltd.* 1961 (1) S.A.
      326.

A
  D. v. *National Society for the Prevention of Cruelty to Children* [1978]
      A.C. 171; [1977] 2 W.L.R. 201; [1977] 1 All E.R. 589, H.L.(E.).
  Drummond-Jackson v. *British Medical Association* [1970] 1 W.L.R. 688;
      [1970] 1 All E.R. 1094, C.A.
  Irvin & Johnson Ltd. v. *Gelcer & Co. (Pty.)* 1958 (2) S.A. 59.
  NAFTE v. *Allied Minerals Ltd.* 1966 (3) S.A. 94.
  Ridge v. *Baldwin* [1964] A.C. 40; [1963] 2 W.L.R. 935; [1963] 2 All
B   E.R. 66, H.L.(E.).

  The following cases are referred to in the judgment of Foster J.:

  Asher v. *Secretary of State for the Environment* (unreported), Megarry J.,
      December 21, 1973; [1974] Ch. 208; [1974] 2 W.L.R. 466; [1974]
      2 All E.R. 156, C.A.
  Associated Provincial Picture Houses Ltd. v. *Wednesbury Corporation*
C   [1948] 1 K.B. 223; [1947] 2 All E.R. 680, C.A.
  Cannock Chase District Council v. *Kelly* [1978] 1 W.L.R. 1; [1978] 1
      All E.R. 152, C.A.
  D. v. *National Society for the Prevention of Cruelty to Children* [1978]
      A.C. 171; [1977] 2 W.L.R. 201; [1977] 1 All E.R. 589, H.L.(E.).
  Golden Chemical Products Ltd., In re (unreported), December 9, 1976.
  Maxwell v. *Department of Trade and Industry* [1974] Q.B. 523; [1974]
D   2 W.L.R. 338; [1974] 2 All E.R. 122, C.A.
  Padfield v. *Minister of Agriculture, Fisheries and Food* [1968] A.C. 997;
      [1968] 2 W.L.R. 924; [1968] 1 All E.R. 694, C.A. and H.L.(E.).
  Parry-Jones v. *Law Society* [1969] 1 Ch. 1; [1968] 2 W.L.R. 397; [1968]
      1 All E.R. 177, C.A.
  Pergamon Press Ltd., In re [1971] Ch. 388; [1970] 3 W.L.R. 792; [1970]
      3 All E.R. 535, C.A.
E *Reg.* v. *Barnet and Camden Rent Tribunal, Ex parte Frey Investments
      Ltd.* [1972] 2 Q.B. 342; [1971] 3 W.L.R. 985; [1971] 3 All E.R.
      759, D.C.

  The following additional cases were cited in argument before Foster J.:

  Breen v. *Amalgamated Engineering Union* [1971] 2 Q.B. 175; [1971]
      2 W.L.R. 742; [1971] 1 All E.R. 1148, C.A.
F *Bristol District Council* v. *Clark* [1975] 1 W.L.R. 1443; [1975] 3 All E.R.
      976, C.A.
  Drummond-Jackson v. *British Medical Association* [1970] 1 W.L.R. 688;
      [1970] 1 All E.R. 1094, C.A.
  Durayappah v. *Fernando* [1967] 2 A.C. 337; [1967] 3 W.L.R. 289; [1967]
      2 All E.R. 152, P.C.
  Leigh v. *English Property Corporation Ltd.* [1976] 2 Lloyd's Rep. 298,
      C.A.
G *Merricks* v. *Heathcoat-Amory* [1955] Ch. 567; [1955] 3 W.L.R. 56; [1955]
      2 All E.R. 453.
  Pearlberg v. *Varty* [1972] 1 W.L.R. 534; [1972] 2 All E.R. 6, H.L.(E.).
  Pinder v. *Spurr* (unreported), Lawton L.J., sitting as Queen's Bench Judge,
      February 14, 1972.
  Reg. v. *Gaming Board for Great Britain, Ex parte Benaim and Khaida*
H   [1970] 2 Q.B. 417; [1970] 2 W.L.R. 1009; [1970] 2 All E.R. 528, C.A.
  Reg. v. *Lewes Justices, Ex parte Secretary of State for Home Department*
      [1973] A.C. 388; [1972] 3 W.L.R. 279; [1972] 2 All E.R. 1057,
      H.L.(E.).
  Ridge v. *Baldwin* [1964] A.C. 40; [1963] 2 W.L.R. 935; [1963] 2 All
      E.R. 66, H.L.(E.).
  Secretary of State for Education and Science v. *Tameside Metropolitan
      Borough Council* [1977] A.C. 1014; [1976] 3 W.L.R. 641; [1976] 3
      All E.R. 665, C.A. and H.L.(E.).

Norwest Holst Ltd. v. Dept. of Trade (Ch.D.)   **[1978]**

Secretary of State for Employment v. *ASLEF (No. 2)* [1972] 2 Q.B. 455;   **A**
   [1972] 2 W.L.R. 1370; [1972] 2 All E.R. 949, C.A.
Smith v. *Inner London Education Authority, The Times,* July 20, 1977,
   C.A.
Town Investments Ltd. v. *Department of the Environment* [1978] A.C.
   359; [1977] 2 W.L.R. 450; [1977] 1 All E.R. 813, H.L.(E.).
Wilover Nominees Ltd. v. *Inland Revenue Commissioners* [1974] 1 W.L.R.
   1342; [1974] 3 All E.R. 496, C.A.   **B**

MOTIONS

By notice of motion dated May 13, 1977, the plaintiff company,
Norwest Holst Ltd., sought against the first defendant, Secretary of State
for Trade, a declaration that the appointment or purported appointment
of Lewis John Davies Q.C. and Thomas Garrard Harding, a chartered
accountant, the second and third defendants respectively, as inspectors   **C**
under section 165 of the Companies Act 1948 to investigate the company's
affairs and to report thereon was unlawful and ultra vires and, accordingly,
invalid and of no effect. Against the second and third defendants the
company sought an injunction restraining them from exercising or purporting to exercise any of the powers conferred by the Act of 1948 pursuant
to their purported appointment.   **D**

By notice of motion dated May 25, 1977, the first defendant (for the
Department of Trade) and the second and third defendants sought (1) an
order under R.S.C., Ord. 18, r. 19 or the inherent jurisdiction of the
court, striking out the proceedings on the grounds that the company's
writ and statement of claim disclosed no reasonable cause of action or
were frivolous or vexatious or otherwise an abuse of the process of the
court and that the action be dismissed accordingly; (2) if and so far as   **E**
necessary an order under R.S.C., Ord. 3, r. 5 extending the time for
delivery of a defence until after the final determination of the defendants'
application.

The facts are stated in the judgment of Foster J.

Stanley Brodie Q.C., Michael J. Beloff and *E. G. Goldrein* for the   **F**
plaintiff company.
   Peter Gibson for the defendants.

                                        Cur. adv. vult.

July 29. FOSTER J. read the following judgment.

                                                G

The motions

Before me there were originally two motions, one by Norwest Holst Ltd.,
the plaintiff company, for summary judgment under R.S.C., Ord. 14, and
the second by the Department of Trade for an order that the plaintiff's
action should be struck out. The motion by the plaintiff company sought
a declaration against the department that the appointment of the second   **H**
and third defendants as inspectors under section 165 of the Companies
Act 1948 was unlawful, ultra vires and of no effect. Against the second
and third defendants the plaintiff company sought injunctions to restrain
them from carrying out the investigation. Where a final injunction is
sought in the Chancery Division under R.S.C., Ord. 14, the application
should be made by summons before the master: (see Ord. 14, r. 2) and
I allowed the plaintiff to issue a pro forma summons to comply with the

The Weekly Law Reports, June 30, 1978

77

3 W.L.R.   Norwest Holst Ltd. v. Dept. of Trade (Ch.D.)   Foster J.

A   rules.   In the Chancery Division the summons is returnable before the master in the first instance whether or not a final injunction is sought.

The defendants' motion is to strike out the writ and statement of claim, both under R.S.C., Ord. 18, r. 19 and under the inherent jurisdiction of the court.   Ord. 18, r. 19 (1) is in these terms:

B
> " The court may at any stage of the proceedings order to be struck out or amended any pleading or the indorsement of any writ in the action, or anything in any pleading or in the indorsement, on the ground that—(a) it discloses no reasonable cause of action or defence, as the case may be; or (b) it is scandalous, frivolous or vexatious; or (c) it may prejudice, embarrass or delay the fair trial of the action; or (d) it is otherwise an abuse of the process of the court; and may order the action to be stayed or dismissed or
C   judgment to be entered accordingly, as the case may be."

Under the first head, (a), by r. 19 (2) no evidence is admissible.

The statutory provisions

Under the Companies Act 1948 powers were given to the relevant government department (now the Department of Trade), by section 164
D   and the following sections, to appoint persons to investigate the affairs of a company.   This power was always in the original Companies Act and in the Joint Stock Companies Acts before that, though the extent of the power has in each later Act been strengthened.   The present statutory provisions with which I am concerned are section 165 of the Act of 1948 and section 109 of the Act of 1967.   As regards the Act of 1948 I
E   should look also at the surrounding sections.   Section 164 is headed " Inspection " and provides:

> " (1) The Board of Trade may appoint one or more competent inspectors to investigate the affairs of a company and to report thereon in such manner as the board direct—(a) in the case of a company having a share capital, on the application either of not
F   less than 200 members of or members holding not less than one-tenth of the shares issued; (b) in the case of a company not having a share capital, on the application of not less than one-fifth in number of the persons on the company's register of members."

Subsection (2) I need not refer to.   This case primarily deals with section 165, which is in two parts and reads as follows:

G
> " Without prejudice to their powers under the last foregoing section, the Board of Trade—(a) shall appoint one or more competent inspectors to investigate the affairs of a company and to report thereon in such manner as the board direct, if—(i) the company by special resolution; or (ii) the court by order; declares that its affairs ought to be investigated by an inspector appointed by the board; and (b) may do so if it appears to the board that there are
H   circumstances suggesting—(i) that its business is being conducted with intent to defraud its creditors or the creditors of any other person or otherwise for a fraudulent or unlawful purpose or in a manner oppressive of any part of its members or that it was formed for any fraudulent or unlawful purpose; or (ii) that persons concerned with its formation or the management of its affairs have in connection therewith been guilty of fraud, misfeasance or other misconduct towards it or towards its members; or (iii) that its

A members have not been given all the information with respect to its affairs which they might reasonably expect."

Section 166 gives the inspectors powers to investigate the affairs of the related companies, that is to say, subsidiaries and sub-subsidiaries of the company. Section 167 gives the inspectors powers to order the production of documents and evidence on investigation. By subsection (2) an inspector may examine on oath the officers and agents of the company, B or other body corporate in relation to its business and may administer an oath accordingly; and by subsection (4):

"If an inspector thinks it necessary for the purpose of his investigation that a person whom he has no power to examine on oath should be so examined, he may apply to the court and the court may if it sees fit order that person to attend and be examined on C oath before it on any matter relevant to the investigation, . . ."

By section 168 the inspectors have to report to the Board of Trade (now the Department of Trade) and may furnish an interim report ". . . and may also cause the report to be printed and published." Then there are further provisions with which I am not concerned.

Section 109 of the Companies Act 1967 is in these terms: D

"(1) The Board of Trade may at any time, if they think there is good reason so to do, give directions to any such body as follows, namely,—(a) a company formed and registered under the Companies Act 1948; (b) an existing company within the meaning of that Act;" —and then there are a number of other headings—". . . requiring the body, at such time and place as may be specified in the directions, E to produce such books or papers as may be so specified, or may at any time, if they think there is good reason so to do, authorise any officer of theirs, on producing (if required so to do) evidence of his authority, to require any such body as aforesaid to produce to him forthwith any books or papers which the officer may specify."

The facts   F

The plaintiff was incorporated in 1969 as a result of a merger of two companies. It is a public company engaged in construction and engineering, both in England and internationally. Its paid up capital is some £2·2 million and apart from a loss in the year ending March 31, 1975, it has made steady progress and made record profits in the years ending March 31, 1976, of some £2·3 million and March 31, 1977, of some £3·5 G million, both before taxation. There was no evidence to show that the solvency of the company was in question, nor that any shareholder had made a complaint, nor that there had been any adverse comment of the company's affairs in the press, and the certificate of its auditors has never been qualified. Nevertheless, on November 29, 1976, the Secretary of State for the Department of Trade authorised a Mr. Howard and a Mr. Pink of his department (to whom I will refer as the section 109 inspectors) H to look at certain books and papers of the plaintiff company and two subsidiaries under section 109 of the Act of 1967. On March 11, 1977, the Secretary of State appointed the second defendant (a Queen's Counsel) and the third defendant (a chartered accountant) to investigate the affairs of the company under section 165. There then ensued certain correspondence which I will read. The group secretary wrote to the Secretary of State on March 25:

The Weekly Law Reports, June 30, 1978

79

3 W.L.R.   Norwest Holst Ltd. v. Dept. of Trade (Ch.D.)   Foster J.

A   " I have been instructed by the board of directors of the above-
     named company to reply to the letter of March 11 from Mr. H. C.
     Gill, the Inspector of Companies, with which was enclosed a notice of
     your appointment of Mr. Davies and Mr. Harding as inspectors to
     investigate the affairs of a company pursuant to the provisions of
     section 165. I am authorised to say that it does not appear to my
     board that there are any circumstances which would justify the
B   exercise of your discretionary power under the section to appoint
     inspectors. The board have therefor instructed me to request you
     to disclose to it the circumstances, together with an indication of
     the evidence in support thereof, upon which you relied in exer-
     cising or purporting to exercise your discretionary power to appoint
     inspectors. The board consider that this information should be
C   provided to it before any investigation is begun."

The Secretary of State replied to that letter on April 4, 1977, in these
terms—it comes from his private secretary:

     " The Secretary of State has asked me to thank you for your letter
     of March 25 regarding the appointment of inspectors to investigate
     the affairs of your company under the provisions of section 165.
D   There is no requirement laid down in the Act to provide this infor-
     mation, but I can tell you that the appointment has been made under
     the provisions contained in section 165 (b) (ii)."

On April 19 the group secretary replied in these terms:

     " I have been asked by my board of directors to acknowledge receipt
E   of your letter. . . . My board regrets the refusal of the Secretary
     of State to accede to the request contained in the third paragraph of
     my letter of March 25. Disclosure of the circumstances (and an
     indication of the evidence in support thereof) upon which the
     Secretary of State relied in exercising or purporting to exercise his
     discretion to appoint inspectors would enable the company itself to
     take appropriate steps to rectify the supposed matters of complaint
F   of which it is being kept in ignorance. Your reference to the pro-
     visions of section 165 (b) (ii) of the Act places a wide category of
     persons within the company under possible suspicion of having been
     guilty of most serious offences. The board considers that the failure
     of the Secretary of State to give any indication of the nature of the
     alleged offences or of the person or persons allegedly responsible,
G   seems hardly just or equitable. Moreover, the business of the com-
     pany, client relationship and the shareholders' interests have been
     and are being adversely affected until the matter is resolved. The
     board has authorised me to repeat that it does not appear to it that
     there are any circumstances which would justify the exercise of
     the discretionary power to appoint inspectors. As the Secretary of
H   State has declined to disclose the information requested in my letter
     of March 25, it is not accepted that Mr. Davies and Mr. Harding
     have been validly and lawfully appointed as inspectors to investigate
     the affairs of the company. I am further authorised to say that if
     in these circumstances the Secretary of State is intent on the inspec-
     tors carrying out an investigation into the affairs of the company
     then there would appear to be no alternative left to the company but
     to contest the matter by legal proceedings. . . ."

80

That was answered on April 27 by the Secretary of State's private A
secretary:

"I am directed to inform you that, following the recommendations
of the Jenkins Committee on company law it is not the practice of
the department to disclose to the company concerned details of the
information leading to the appointment of inspectors. Further the
department has been advised by counsel that there is no legal obli- B
gation to do so. I regret to observe from your letter that your board
of directors is not prepared to accept Mr. Davies and Mr. Harding
as having been legally appointed by the Secretary of State in this
case. I have to inform you that the Secretary of State has no
intention of withdrawing the appointment, and, in the circumstances,
it is for your board to take such action as it may be advised."

C
The plaintiff company's solicitors replied to that on April 29, 1977, and
the second paragraph reads:

"By a majority decision the board of directors have decided to
challenge the validity of the appointment by the Secretary of State
of Mr. Davies and Mr. Harding to investigate the affairs of the
company and to report thereon. Pursuant to that decision a writ D
has been issued and is being served today on the solicitor for your
department. We enclose a copy for the attention of the Secretary
of State. Counsel has also been instructed to draft a statement of
claim and we anticipate that service of the same will be effected
within the next seven days. We assume that in these circumstances
the Secretary of State will instruct Mr. Davies and Mr. Harding not
to seek to commence the investigation until such time as the matter E
may be resolved by the courts and would be pleased to have your
confirmation to that effect. We should in any event inform you
that until that time neither the board nor any of the officers or
employees of the company intend to co-operate with the inspectors."

On May 18 the solicitor for the Department of Trade replied and said
in the second paragraph: F

"As to your letter of April 29, 1977, the Secretary of State is advised
that the appointment of the inspectors was validly made, and he has
no intention of instructing Mr. Davies and Mr. Harding not to
proceed with the investigation."

The proceedings   G

The writ was issued on April 29, 1977, and on May 13 the motion
for final judgment was brought by the plaintiff under R.S.C., Ord. 14.
It was supported by an affidavit sworn on May 16, by Mr. Bosdet, the
group secretary of the plaintiff company, exhibiting the 1976 annual
report and part of the correspondence. The motion to strike out the
proceedings was served on May 25, 1977, and supported by an affidavit H
of Mr. H. C. Gill, who is the Inspector of Companies in the Department
of Trade. He states in that affidavit:

"8. At the time of the appointment there was available to the Secretary of State the following material (1) copies of books and papers, or
extracts therefrom, of the plaintiff of Norwest Holst Group Administration Ltd. and Rampart Holdings Ltd. and the said explanations
thereof, all obtained under the said section 109 by the section 109

The Weekly Law Reports, June 30, 1978

81

3 W.L.R.   Norwest Holst Ltd. v. Dept. of Trade (Ch.D.)   Foster J.

A   officers. (2) The comments of the section 109 officers on those books, papers and explanations. (3) Other information volunteered by an informant relating to the matters dealt with in the same books, papers and explanations.

"9. From a careful consideration of the said material there appeared to the Secretary of State acting through me circumstances suggesting that the case was one to which the said section 165 (b) (ii) applied.

B   "10. I think that there is a real danger that if the information referred to in paragraph 8 (3) were revealed the identity of the informant might be ascertained therefrom."

Meanwhile, on May 5, 1977, the statement of claim was served. On June 21, 1977, Mr. Bosdet swore a further affidavit, in paragraph 3 of C which he says that at his final meeting with the section 109 inspectors, and I quote: ". . . both officers individually expressed their appreciation of the co-operation and assistance that I had shown." He also put in evidence the injury done to the plaintiff company's business by reason of the appointment of the inspectors. In his affidavit he mentions four persons as interviewed, but Mr. Gill, in a further affidavit sworn on July 13, 1977, says that there was also interviewed Mr. James MacMillan, a former D director of the plaintiff company. It is interesting to note that Mr. Bosdet never says that the answers given ever satisfied the section 109 inspectors.

On July 12, 1977, the amended statement of claim was served and on July 13, 1977, Mr. Bosdet, having presumably seen Mr. Gill's original affidavit, nevertheless on oath says: "I verily believe that none of the defendants to this action have any defence thereto." In view of this, it is E perhaps a good thing that the plaintiff company no longer seeks to obtain summary judgment but admits that the defendants are entitled to have unconditional leave to defend.

The amended statement of claim

The plaintiff company raises two issues. First, that there are no facts F or circumstances known to the company which would justify the exercise by the Secretary of State of the section 165 (b) (ii) power, and that by reason of the failure of the Secretary of State to give reasons, the proper inference to be drawn is that there were no circumstances suggesting matters of complaint and that he misdirected himself or acted unlawfully in appointing inspectors. It was suggested by the plaintiff company that this claim could be amended by confining the facts and circumstances G to the matters set out in paragraph 8 of Mr. Gill's first affidavit, though the company does not know who the informer is or what evidence he gave to the Secretary of State; second, that before appointing inspectors the Secretary of State should act fairly by " stating in outline the nature of the case against [the company] and by giving [the company] an opportunity of answering it," and that as this was not done the Secretary of State was in breach of natural justice. No allegation of bad faith is made H against the Secretary of State.

The first claim

It is idle to say that the plaintiff company knows of nothing which would justify the exercise of the power. I recently had a case where the damage was done in a sub-subsidiary company. It is also idle to say that the section 109 inspectors were satisfied. Mr. Bosdet says no such thing.

It may be that they found exactly what they were looking for.   The inquiry   A
under section 165 (b) (ii) is not against the company but against persons
who may be acting wrongly to the company and is instigated for the
benefit of the company and its shareholders.   Counsel for the plaintiff
admitted that the onus was on the plaintiff to prove that no circumstances
existed.   How such an onus can be discharged I cannot imagine.   The
plaintiff has, if my mathematics are right, some 36 subsidiaries, some
incorporated abroad.   If the Secretary of State fails to give reasons for   B
the appointment, I can find nothing in the provisions of the Acts making
him liable to do so.   Must he do so as a matter of natural justice?

Natural Justice

   In the last 10 years the number of cases in which the actions of
ministers have come in for scrutiny by the court has multiplied to an   C
extraordinary extent.   Mostly this is due to the fact that ministers are
given wider and wider powers which, hopefully Parliament thinks, will
escape the scrutiny of the courts.   In contrast, the courts have taken a far
closer look at the exercise of a minister's power.   I had cited to me some
30 cases, and was told that this was a mere selection, nearly all decided
within the last 10 years.   On the one hand is *Associated Provincial Picture*   D
Houses Ltd. v. *Wednesbury Corporation* [1948] 1 K.B. 223, and which I
will refer to as the *Wednesbury* case.   On the other hand there is *Reg.* v.
Barnet and Camden Rent Tribunal, Ex parte Frey Investments Ltd. [1972]
2 Q.B. 342, to which I will refer as the *Frey* case.   In *Asher* v. *Secretary*
of State for the Environment (unreported) but a transcript of which I had
before me, there is a decision of Megarry J. on December 21, 1973.   He
says: E

   " There was considerable discussion of the standards which have to
   be applied in determining whether an exercise of statutory power is
   ultra vires.   It was common ground that the burden lay on him who
   asserted that an act was ultra vires to establish that this was so: see
   for example the *Wednesbury* case [1948] 1 K.B. 223, 228.   That case
   also establishes the general proposition that in exercising the power   F
   the authority must have regard to all that is relevant, and disregard all
   that is irrelevant, and must not act in bad faith or in a way that no
   reasonable person would have acted.   However, this has to be considered in relation to the power that is being exercised.   In the
   Wednesbury case the decision of the authority was to attach a particular condition to licences for cinematograph performances, so that
   the authority was deciding the whole matter itself and not merely   G
   setting some other body or person in motion.   In the *Frey* case [1972]
   2 Q.B. 342 the decision of the authority was merely to refer certain
   tenancy agreements to a rent tribunal; the substantive decision
   whether or not to reduce the rents would be made by the rent
   tribunal after a hearing of the contentions on either side, and was
   not being made by the local authority.   In the Court of Appeal   H
   Salmon L.J. at p. 358 doubted whether the *Wednesbury* principles
   applied to such cases: a decision on the substantive rights was one
   thing, a mere decision that another body ought to investigate and
   decide on those substantive rights was another.   (I summarise the
   point in my own language.)   The local authority must not exercise
   any power vested in it in bad faith, or frivolously or vexatiously, but
   unless any of this is shown, a case of ultra vires will not be made out.

The Weekly Law Reports, June 30, 1978

83

3 W.L.R.   Norwest Holst Ltd. v. Dept. of Trade (Ch.D.)   Foster J.

A   In such cases, a failure to regard all that is relevant or to disregard
everything that is irrelevant may assist in demonstrating mala fides
or a frivolous or vexatious approach, but it will not per se suffice to
establish ultra vires. I think Edmund Davies L.J. in effect took
the same view, while Stamp L.J. went even further and held that the
court should not even consider whether or not the local authority
had made mistakes in deciding whether to refer the tenancy agree-
B   ments to the rent tribunal. Now in this case the decision of the
Secretary of State is a mere decision to order an extraordinary audit.
Like the local authority in *Frey's* case he has no power to demand
information before deciding whether or not to order the audit.
Like the rent tribunal in *Frey's* case, on the other hand, the district
auditor has wide powers to require information to be provided: see
C   section 225 of the Act of 1933. Both on the authority of *Frey's*
case, and on principle, I would hold that in deciding whether or not
to order an extraordinary audit the Secretary of State is bound not
by the *Wednesbury* standards but by the *Frey* standards."

The plaintiff's counsel mainly relied on *Padfield* v. *Minister of Agriculture, Fisheries and Food* [1968] A.C. 997. In that case the minister
D   had refused to exercise his power to appoint a committee of investigation
under section 19 of the Agricultural Marketing Act 1958. Lord Denning
M.R. in his dissenting judgment in the Court of Appeal, said, at p. 1006:

" It is said that the decision of the minister is administrative and not
judicial. But that does not mean that he can do as he likes, regardless of right or wrong. Nor does it mean that the courts are power-
E   less to correct him. Good administration requires that complaints
should be investigated and that grievances should be remedied.
When Parliament has set up machinery for that very purpose, it is
not for the minister to brush it on one side. He should not refuse
to have a complaint investigated without good reason. But it is said
that the minister is not bound to give any reason at all. And that,
if he gives no reason, his refusal cannot be questioned. So why does
F   it matter if he gives bad reasons? I do not agree. This is the only
remedy available to a person aggrieved."

The judgment of Lord Denning M.R. was upheld in the House of Lords,
and Lord Reid said, at p. 1030:

" It is implicit in the argument for the minister that there are only
G   two possible interpretations of this provision—either he must refer
every complaint or he has an unfettered discretion to refuse to refer
in any case. I do not think that is right. Parliament must have
conferred the discretion with the intention that it should be used to
promote the policy and objects of the Act; the policy and objects
of the Act must be determined by construing the Act as a whole and
construction is always a matter of law for the court. In a matter
H   of this kind it is not possible to draw a hard and fast line, but if
the minister, by reason of his having misconstrued the Act or for
any other reason, so uses his discretion as to thwart or run counter
to the policy and objects of the Act, then our law would be very
defective if persons aggrieved were not entitled to the protection of
the court. So it is necessary first to construe the Act."

And Lord Upjohn said, at p. 1061:

" My Lords, I would only add this: that without throwing any A
doubt upon what are well known as the club expulsion cases, where
the absence of reasons has not proved fatal to the decision of
expulsion by a club committee, a decision of the minister stands
on quite a different basis; he is a public officer charged by Parliament with the discharge of a public discretion affecting Her
Majesty's subjects; if he does not give any reason for his decision it
may be, if circumstances warrant it, that a court may be at liberty to B
come to the conclusion that he had no good reason for reaching that
conclusion and order a prerogative writ to issue accordingly."

But in that case the whole purpose of the section was being frustrated
by the minister. In the present case the Secretary of State is fulfilling
the purpose of the Act by starting an investigation. Once the inspectors C
start their investigation they must conduct it in a fair and proper manner:
see *In re Pergamon Press Ltd.* [1971] Ch. 388 and *Maxwell* v. *Department of Trade and Industry* [1974] Q.B. 523. It is fair to say that there
has been no case where a minister has given no reasons for a decision
and the court has, by inference, concluded that he had no good reason
(a situation envisaged by Lord Upjohn in the *Padfield* case). And so
far as I am aware this is the first occasion since 1948 that the appoint- D
ment of inspectors under section 165 has been challenged in the courts.
    Counsel for the Crown mainly relied on *Parry-Jones* v. *Law Society*
[1969] 1 Ch. 1. Lord Denning M.R. says, at p. 8:

" Then Mr. Parry-Jones raised another point. He said that if the
council act under rule 11 (1) (c) on a written complaint lodged by
a third party, then that complaint should be shown to him, the E
solicitor. He says he is entitled to know who is making the complaint and the nature of it. Such is required, he says, by natural
justice. I would point out that under rule 11 (4) it is provided that,
before instituting an inspection on a written complaint alleged by a
third party, the council shall require prima facie evidence that the
ground of complaint exists. That shows that the council have only
to inquire whether there is prima facie evidence. As we held a few F
days ago in *Wiseman* v. *Borneman* [1968] Ch. 429, a prima facie
case stands on a very different footing from an actual determination.
Where the only inquiry is as to whether there is prima facie
evidence, natural justice does not require that the party should be
given notice of it. Nor do I think the solicitor is entitled to know
whether the council are acting under (a), (b) or (c) of rule 11 (1). G
The rule does not require it. The council are entitled to send their
accountant to make an investigation without disclosing on which
ground they are acting. The solicitor is not entitled to be told the
particulars of the complaint."

    In the present case the words " circumstances suggesting " in section
165 (b) (ii) of the Act do not in my judgment amount to a prima facie H
case but something much less. In *In re Golden Chemical Products Ltd.*
(unreported), the judgment of Mr. Michael Wheeler Q.C., sitting as a
deputy judge of the Chancery Division, being given on December 9, 1976,
the question concerned section 35 of the Companies Act 1967 which
provides that the Secretary of State may bring a petition to wind-up if it
appears to the Secretary of State " it is expedient in the public interest " to
do so. There the company sought to cross-examine the persons appointed

The Weekly Law Reports, June 30, 1978

85

3 W.L.R.   Norwest Holst Ltd. v. Dept. of Trade (Ch.D.)   Foster J.

A   under section 109 to see whether it could base a challenge to the petition on the ground that there was no evidence on which the Secretary of State could reasonably form a view that it was expedient in the public interest that the company should be wound up. The decision was that no such cross-examination could take place, a decision with which I respectfully agree. In *Cannock Chase District Council* v. *Kelly* [1978] 1 W.L.R. 1, the Court of Appeal held that a local authority need not give reasons for serving a notice to quit.

B

Mr. Gill says in his affidavit that there is a real danger, if he divulges the information given to him by the informant, that his identity may be ascertained. The House of Lords recently held in *D.* v. *National Society for the Prevention of Cruelty to Children* [1978] A.C. 171 that the N.S.P.C.C. need not disclose the identity of an informant, even where the information turned out to be wholly wrong.

C

Conclusion

In the absence of any allegation of bad faith, the whole purpose of section 165 and the following sections would be frustrated if this action were to proceed. In my judgment the action falls squarely within the *Frey* case principle and is frivolous and vexatious and an abuse of the process of the court, and I propose to strike it out.

D

Order accordingly.

Solicitors: *Bull & Bull; Treasury Solicitor.*

K. N. B.

E

INTERLOCUTORY APPEAL from Foster J.

The company appealed on the grounds that the judge had erred in law (1) if and in so far as he held that the company's amended writ and/or amended statement of claim was frivolous and/or vexatious and/or an abuse of the process of the court and/or exercised his discretion in ordering that the pleadings be struck out; (2) if and in so far

F   as he failed to hold that there was an obligation on the Secretary of State for Trade (" the minister ") to inform the plaintiffs of the nature of the case against them and to give them an opportunity of answering it before appointing inspectors to investigate their affairs pursuant to the provisions of section 165 of the Companies Act 1948 and/or in holding that the company's contention that there was such an obligation

G   was obviously unsustainable; (3) if and in so far as he held that the company's contention that there was no evidence on which the minister could properly conclude that there were circumstances suggesting the existence of any of the matters of complaint referred to in section 165 (*b*) (ii) of the Act was obviously unsustainable; (4) if and in so far as he held that the company's contention that no reasonable minister could conclude that there were such circumstances as aforesaid on the basis

H   of the material referred to in paragraph 8 of the affidavit of Harold Clifford Gill [the department's Inspector of Companies] sworn herein on May 25, 1977, was obviously unsustainable; (5) if and in so far as he held that the company's contention that in all the material circumstances no reasonable minister could have exercised the discretionary power to appoint inspectors was obviously unsustainable; (6) if and in so far as he held that the company's contention that in all the material circumstances the proper inference to draw from the minister's refusal

to give reasons for the appointment was that he had no proper or unlaw-   A
ful reasons for making the same was obviously unsustainable; (7) if and
in so far as he held that the only basis on which the appointment of
inspectors could be reviewed by the court was if it could be proved
that the minister in making such appointment acted in bad faith; (8) he
misdirected himself if and in so far as he held that in the absence of an
allegation of bad faith the whole purpose of section 165 of the Act and   B
the following sections would be frustrated if the company were allowed
to pursue the action to trial; (9) the judge's finding that Mr. Bosdet
[the company secretary] had not said that the answers given to section
109 inspectors satisfied them was wholly contrary to the evidence before
him; (10) he misdirected himself if and in so far as he held that the
company could not properly discharge the onus of proof of showing that
the minister had wrongfully exercised his discretionary power to appoint   C
inspectors on the ground that the company had 36 subsidiary companies
and that the section 109 inspectors might have found what they were
looking for when on the evidence of Mr. Gill the inspectors confined
themselves to the material referred to in paragraph 8 of his affidavit;
and (11) if and in so far as the judge took into account the objections
made by the defendants with regard to the information provided to them
by the " informer " misdirected himself and erred in law in that such   D
considerations were irrelevant to the issues he had to decide.

The respondents, the Department of Trade and the two appointed
inspectors, filed a respondent's notice of additional grounds on which
they proposed on the hearing of the appeal to contend that the judge's
decision be affirmed; but as counsel for the respondents were not called on
to reply those grounds are irrelevant to the report.   E

Stanley Brodie Q.C. and *Michael Beloff* for the company.
Peter Archer Q.C., S.-J. and *Peter Gibson* for the department and
the appointed inspectors.

LORD DENNING M.R. Ever since 1948 there has been a valuable
provision of the Companies Act by which the Board of Trade can   F
appoint inspectors to investigate the affairs of a company. Many
investigations have been held by inspectors, usually one of Queen's
Counsel, and the other an accountant. In a case we had fairly recently,
In re Pergamon Press Ltd. [1971] Ch. 388, we had to consider the
position of the inspectors under such an inquiry. It was held by this
court that the inspectors were under a duty to act fairly in the conduct   G
of their inquiry.

Now we have to consider a different point. It is said that the
minister himself has done wrong. His conduct is challenged. It is said
that the minister has acted beyond his powers in appointing inspectors.
He ought, it is said, to have warned the company beforehand and given
them a chance of being heard. Furthermore, it is said that the minister
exercised his discretion erroneously. He ought to have had sufficient   H
reasons, and he had none in this case. It is said further that he is
acting on the information of informers, which is inadmissible as being
against the public interest.

On these grounds the company has brought an action to try to
stop the inspectors proceeding with the inquiry. The minister applied
to strike it out. Foster J. struck it out. The company appeal to this
court.

The Weekly Law Reports, June 30, 1978

87

3 W.L.R.   Norwest Holst Ltd. v. Dept. of Trade (C.A.)   Lord Denning M.R.

A   The company is Norwest Holst Ltd. It is a public company. We know nothing about it, except what we find in the annual report for 1976. It has very many subsidiaries. It carries on an engineering and construction business all over the world by itself and its subsidiaries. As at March 1976, 31·89 per cent. of its ordinary shares were held by a consortium, of which two of the directors, Mr. Lilley and Mr. Slater, were the principal members, holding over one million shares each.
B   Those two directors made a take-over bid for the shares of the company. It went before the Takeover Panel of the City of London. The panel did not approve the bid. The annual report said:

"... Following the decision of the Takeover Panel in regard to the proposed bid for the company from two of its directors, Messrs. Slater and Lilley, it might appear that this left a situation which
C   was not helpful to the group, but I must emphasise most strongly that the entire board is unanimous in its support for the Chief Executive and the management, and therefore the matter has no effect on the conduct of the business."

That report was dated September 1976. On November 29, 1976, the Secretary of State appointed two officers of the Department of Trade
D   to look into the company's documents. That was done by virtue of section 109 of the Companies Act 1967. It authorised the officers to require the company to produce any books and papers they wanted and to take copies, and to require explanations.

Those two officers were given the books. They were provided with explanations by Mr. Lilley, the director, and Mr. Bosdet the secretary.
E   We have no information as to what the documents contained or what the explanations were, but we do know that four months later, on March 11, 1977, the Secretary of State ordered the inquiry now in question. He did it under section 165 (*b*) (ii) of the Companies Act 1948. It said:

"Without prejudice to their powers under the last foregoing
F   section "—I will come back to that later—" the Board of Trade— (*a*) shall appoint one or more competent inspectors to investigate the affairs of a company and to report thereon ... (*b*) may do so if it appears to the Board that there are circumstances suggesting ... (ii) that persons concerned with its formation or the management of its affairs have in connection therewith been guilty of
G   fraud, misfeasance or other misconduct towards it or towards its members; ..."

It was under that section that the minister appointed two gentlemen, Mr. Lewis John Davies Q.C. and Mr. Thomas Garrard Harding, a chartered accountant, as inspectors to investigate the affairs of the company.
H   On March 25, 1977, the secretary of the group wrote:

"I am authorised to say that it does not appear to my board that there are any circumstances which would justify the exercise of your discretionary power under the section to appoint inspectors."

He asked: What were the circumstances? Would they be disclosed? The Secretary of State declined to give that information. The company wrote back on April 19, saying:

"Your reference to the provisions of section 165 (b) (ii) of the Act places a wide category of persons within the company under possible suspicion of having been guilty of most serious offences. The board considers that the failure of the Secretary of State to give any indication of the nature of the alleged offences or of the person or persons allegedly responsible seems hardly just or equitable."

As the minister gave no information, the company started this action. They delivered a statement of claim, which they afterwards amended. The burden of the statement of claim is that the company know of no wrongdoing which has been done by them or any of their people; and therefore it was wrong that the minister should appoint inspectors without, as they say, any proper justification. They put it in these words in their final amended pleadings:

". . . It is implicit in the provisions of section 165 (b) (ii) of the said Act that the discretionary power to appoint inspectors is to be exercised fairly and/or in accordance with the principles of natural justice."

They ask for a declaration that the appointment or purported appointment was ultra vires and invalid.

It is important to know the background of the legislation. It sometimes happens that public companies are conducted in a way which is beyond the control of the ordinary shareholders. The majority of the shares are in the hands of two or three individuals. These have control of the company's affairs. The other shareholders know little and are told little. They receive the glossy annual reports. Most of them throw them into the wastepaper basket. There is an annual general meeting but few of the shareholders attend. The whole management and control is in the hands of the directors. They are a self-perpetuating oligarchy: and are virtually unaccountable. Seeing that the directors are the guardians of the company, the question is asked: Quis custodiet ipsos custodes—Who will guard the guards themselves?

In these courts two or three years ago we had a good illustration of the need for some oversight of public companies. In *Wallersteiner* v. *Moir* [1974] 1 W.L.R. 991, 1016–1017 I described what had happened:

"This case discloses grave breaches of company law. Dr. Wallersteiner obtained control of a public company, Hartley Baird Ltd., by means which were quite unlawful. He acquired 80 per cent. of the shares by using its own money. He paid nothing himself. He operated by means of puppet concerns of his own making. Puppet trusts in Liechtenstein. A puppet finance company in the Bahamas. A puppet banking company in the City of London. All these he brought into his service to further his unworthy ends. Much of it took place 14 years ago in 1962. His solicitors refused to act further for him. But still he went on. He has managed to keep it from the light until now. But Nemesis has overtaken him. The Board of Trade has ordered an inquiry under the Companies Act. The liquidator of Camp Bird has brought proceedings against him. In this case the judge has condemned him. I would affirm his condemnation."

It is because companies are beyond the reach of ordinary individuals that this legislation has been passed so as to enable the Department of Trade to appoint inspectors to investigate the affairs of a company.

The Weekly Law Reports, June 30, 1978

89

3 W.L.R.   Norwest Holst Ltd. v. Dept. of Trade (C.A.)   Lord Denning M.R.

A   Mr. Brodie, who appears for Norwest Holst Ltd., drew our attention
to the practice of the Board of Trade from 1948 to 1962. It was given
in evidence to Lord Jenkin's Company Law Committee (1962) (Cmnd.
1749). The Board of Trade said (at p. 79) that it was

> " very necessary to hear both sides before deciding whether or not
> an inspector should be appointed. By so doing it is often possible
B > in cases where no fraud is alleged to bring the parties together or
> for them to reach a mutually satisfactory arrangement so that an
> investigation is not necessary."

That was the practice before 1962. Mr. Brodie submitted that that
practice was required by the common law. He said that the principles of
natural justice are to be applied; and, accordingly, both sides should be
C   heard before an inspector is appointed.
     That may have been the practice of the Board of Trade in those
years: but I do not think that it was required by the common law.
There are many cases where an inquiry is held—not as a judicial or quasi-
judicial inquiry—but simply as a matter of good administration. In
these circumstances there is no need to give preliminary notice of any
D   charge, or anything of that sort. Take the case where a police officer
is suspected of misconduct. The practice is to suspend him pending
inquiries. He is not given notice of any charge at that stage, nor any
opportunity of being heard. The rules of natural justice do not apply
unless and until it is decided to take proceedings. Other instances can
be given in other fields. For instance, the Stock Exchange may suspend
dealings in a company's shares. They go by what they know, without
E   warning the company beforehand.
     Equally, so far as section 109 is concerned, when the officers of the
Department of Trade are appointed to examine the books, there is no
need for the rules of natural justice to be applied. If the company was
forewarned and told that the officers were coming, what is to happen
to the books? In a wicked world, it is not unknown for books or papers
to be destroyed or lost.
F
     So also with the appointment of inspectors, under section 165 (b)
(ii). The inspectors are not to decide rights or wrongs. They are to
investigate and report. This inquiry is a good administrative arrangement for the good conduct of companies and their affairs. It is not a
case to which the rules of natural justice apply. There is no need for
them to be given notice of a charge, or a fair opportunity of meeting it.
G   Mr. Brodie made much of section 164. But that is very different.
It applies only where shareholders themselves want inspectors to be
appointed. Mr. Brodie cited to us four cases from South Africa on a
similar section there. But the statute contained express provisions as
to giving notice, and so forth, before an investigation was held. So
those cases have no application here. In any case section 164 is not in
H   point here. It is little used.
     All we are concerned with is section 165. As to it, I would say
that, so long as the minister acts in good faith, it is not incumbent upon
him to disclose the material he has before him, or the reasons for the
inquiry.
     As it happens we do know something of the material which the depart-
ment had in their possession. They had the report of the officers appointed
under section 109, and the books and papers which were produced to those

officers. They had the comments of the officers on those books and A
papers, and the explanations given to them. They had other "information volunteered" by an informant relating to the matters dealt with
in the same books, papers and explanations. Mr. Brodie commented
on the information which was volunteered. He said that it might be
very prejudicial and it was unfair for the minister to be influenced by it
without the company having an opportunity of dealing with it. The
minister had declined to disclose it on the grounds stated in one of their B
affidavits:

> "The disclosure of information by an informer will often enable
> the identity of the informer to be ascertained therefrom and may
> well have the effect of causing information from such a source to
> cease to be made available in the future."
>   C

So the minister might well claim privilege on the ground that it was
contrary to the public interest to disclose it.

I see no reason why the minister should disclose the information he
has before he makes the order. Nor does it matter whether it would be
privileged or not in litigation. Such questions do not arise at that stage.
It is sufficient that there are "circumstances suggesting . . . misconduct"
within section 165 (*b*) (ii).   D

The only remaining point is that Mr. Brodie asked us to review the
minister's decision itself. He cited such cases as *Padfield* v. *Minister
of Agriculture, Fisheries and Food* [1968] A.C. 997; *Breen* v. *Amalgamated Engineering Union* [1971] 2 Q.B. 175; *Secretary of State for
Employment* v. *ASLEF (No. 2)* [1972] 2 Q.B. 455 and *Secretary of State
for Education and Science* v. *Tameside Metropolitan Borough Council* E
[1977] A.C. 1014. He said that the minister's discretion in many cases
is subject to review by the court. None of us would disagree with that
proposition. Time and time again lately we have reviewed the discretion
of a minister if it has not been properly exercised, or if it has been misused.

But in this case there is no ground whatever for thinking that the
minister's discretion has been in any way improperly used. Mr. Brodie
put it this way. He said: "This is a completely innocent company; F
there is nothing whatever against it at all; and it follows there can have
been no reasonable ground for the minister's decision."

There may be nothing against the company itself, but can the
company speak for all the persons concerned with the management of
its affairs? Clearly not. Section 165 (*b*) (ii) is not concerned only
with the company itself. The company may be the innocent dupe of G
others. The section is concerned with the "persons concerned with its
formation or the management of its affairs." They may have been
guilty of misconduct such as to merit inquiry.

We know that, when these inquiries are held, those persons who are
the subject of them often complain about them. They say that the
machinery operates unfairly against them. Such complaints are usually H
unfounded. They are made so as to delay the inquiry, or to lessen the
effect of the report of the inspectors. But, whether well founded or
unfounded, it is no reason for abandoning this machinery. It is the only
means given to the public by which the conduct of companies can be
investigated. Parliament has clearly enacted that there should be power
—under the control of the Board of Trade, on behalf of the public at
large—for an inquiry to be made into the conduct of the affairs of a

The Weekly Law Reports, June 30, 1978

91

3 W.L.R.   Norwest Holst Ltd. v. Dept. of Trade (C.A.)   Lord Denning M.R.

A   company, if there are circumstances which appear to the minister to suggest " fraud, misfeasance or other misconduct." I do not think we should encourage or support any attempt to delay or hold up the inquiry. To my mind the action is without foundation. The judge was quite right to strike it out. I would dismiss the appeal, accordingly.

B   ORMROD L.J. I agree. In the course of his judgment Foster J. drew attention to the recent proliferation of proceedings of this kind. This is the second case within a week in which this court has had to deal with almost exactly the same point.

The phrase " the requirements of natural justice " seems to be mesmerising people at the moment. This must, I think, be due to the apposition of the words " natural " and " justice." It has been pointed out

C   many times that the word " natural " adds nothing except perhaps a hint of nostalgia for the good old days when nasty things did not happen. If, instead, we omit it and put the question in the form of *Fisher* v. *Keane* (1878) 11 Ch.D. 353: " Have the ordinary principles of justice been complied with?", it at once becomes much more realistic and even mundane. It is just possible that the pleader in the present case might have hesitated a little longer if he had been deprived of the use of that

D   romantic word " natural." Another source of confusion is the automatic identification of the phrase " natural justice " with giving the person concerned an opportunity of stating his side of the story, and so on. In many cases, of course, the two are synonymous but not by any means in all.

There is no doubt, as Lord Denning M.R. has said, that this rule of

E   the common law is a most powerful weapon to prevent injustice, but like all powerful weapons it can cause great damage if it is not used skilfully and properly. As Byles J. said in *Cooper* v. *Wandsworth Board of Works* (1863) 14 C.B.N.S. 180, 194: " . . . the justice of the common law will supply the omission of the legislature "; but it is not to be used to frustrate the intention of the legislature.

F   In the present case we are concerned with the making of a decision by the minister to appoint inspectors under section 165 (*b*) of the Companies Act 1948. The purpose of the appointment is to investigate the company in order to find out what has been going on—in other words, to find the facts. At such an inquiry the company and its officers will be asked to answer the allegations or complaints against them, if there are any, and give any explanation which they wish to give. So in this

G   case what we are concerned with is only the preliminary stage—the decision of the minister to appoint inspectors. It is said that such an appointment is likely to damage the company whose affairs are to be investigated: therefore the minister must act in accordance with the ordinary principles of justice, which means notifying the company of the basis on which the investigation is to proceed and giving it an opportunity, in advance, of

H   being heard.

In my judgment the ordinary principles of justice do not require anything of the kind. At this stage the minister is not required to notify the company or seek its comments before ordering an investigation. It is only necessary to refer very shortly to a passage in Lord Reid's speech in *Wiseman* v. *Borneman* [1971] A.C. 297, 308, which is conveniently cited in Sachs L.J.'s judgment in the *Pergamon Press* case [1971] Ch. 388, 403. The passage reads:

Ormrod L.J.   Norwest Holst Ltd. v. Dept. of Trade (C.A.)   [1978]

A

"Every public officer who has to decide whether to prosecute or raise proceedings ought first to decide whether there is a prima facie case, but no one supposes that justice requires that he should first seek the comments of the accused or the defendant on the material before him. So there is nothing inherently unjust in reaching such a decision in the absence of the other party."

B

To my mind that passage applies precisely to the present case. The only conceivable distinction between the present case and that passage is the use of the words " to prosecute or raise proceedings." Here the raising of proceedings has taken the form of ordering an investigation by the inspectors at which the persons involved will have their opportunity of stating their case. That to my mind is a distinction without a difference.

C

The House of Lords and this court have repeatedly emphasised that the ordinary principles of natural justice must be kept flexible and must be adapted to the circumstances prevailing in any particular case. One of the most important of these circumstances, as has been said throughout the argument, is, of course, the provisions of the statute in question: in this case sections 164 and 165 of the Companies Act 1948. Looking at those sections, the role of the minister can be seen, quite plainly, not always to be the same. Under section 164 he is dealing with a complaint by a group of members against the company. Such a complaint may affect anything properly described as the affairs of the company. Not surprisingly, the minister may require adequate evidence before ordering such an inquiry. In some cases the minister might want to hear the company's comments before reaching his decision: in others he might feel that he could reach a fair decision without calling for such comment.

D

E

Under section 165 (a) the minister has no discretion: in the two events specified there he must appoint inspectors. But under section 165 (b) the minister may do so if it appears to him that there are circumstances suggesting one or other of the various matters set out in paragraphs (i), (ii) and (iii) of that subsection, most of which are fraud, misfeasance, and so on. Clearly in such a case it is the minister who initiates an inquiry; and, in my judgment, all he is required to do at that stage is to act fairly in reaching that decision. But it seems to me it is quite impossible—as Mr. Brodie in argument would require him to do—in reaching that decision, which is simply a decision to cause further inquiries to be made, to hear what the company has to say about it in advance. It is unfortunate if the announcement by the minister that he is appointing inspectors causes damage to the company's trading position or its credit or if it causes great inconvenience or puts the company to expense, but all these are unfortunate side effects of the absolute necessity that someone should exercise some form of supervision over the activities of a limited company. They have great advantages, and it is not altogether unreasonable that they should accept certain corresponding disadvantages.

F

G

H

The argument which Mr. Brodie pressed upon us very hard indeed that damage of that kind to this company was to be equated with the sort of damage to property rights or to reputation which lie at the foundation of most of the cases in which the principles of natural justice have been applied seems to me to be wholly unsound. The two things are entirely different except that they can both be estimated in terms of money.

The Weekly Law Reports, July 7, 1978

93

3 W.L.R.   Norwest Holst Ltd. v. Dept. of Trade (C.A.)   Ormrod L.J.

A   Then Mr. Brodie pressed us very hard with the corresponding legislation in South Africa—the Companies Act of 1952. Speaking for
myself, I did not find that excursus very helpful. The only point to be
made is that in that Act the South African legislature have included an
express provision that the minister should give notice to the company
before ordering such an inquiry unless he is of the opinion that to do so
would defeat the objects of this section. Had there been a similar
B provision in the Companies Act 1948 at the end of section 165, I have
no doubt that the minister's answer would have been just that. So it
does not, in my judgment, carry the argument any further at all. I
therefore come to the same conclusion as Lord Denning M.R. In my view
the minister is under no obligation to inform the company of the basis of
the complaint on which he proposes to act by way of appointing inspectors
C or to ask them to comment upon it. That, therefore, is the end of the
" natural justice " argument.

So far as the appellants' other contention is concerned, that they are
entitled in the circumstances to go on with this action in order to obtain
a judicial review of the exercise of the minister's discretion, I can only
say that that argument seems to me capable of being disposed of in about
two sentences. Once it is held that the minister is not obliged in accord-
D ance with the ordinary principles of justice to disclose the information
upon which he has exercised his discretion, it must follow that the company cannot establish a prima facie case for reviewing the discretion
unless, of course, the minister has already disclosed all the material upon
which he based his decision, which he clearly has not done. In my
judgment, therefore, the action is bound to fail on this second head also.

E   Therefore I entirely agree with the judge that the action should be
struck out for the reasons which he gave.

GEOFFREY LANE L.J. I also agree. First, dealing with the argument
based on what is called " natural justice," it is important to remember
that natural justice and the principle audi alteram partem are not synonymous because there are occasions—and very many occasions—when
F natural justice does not demand that the other side should be heard on
the question.

In every investigation or allegation of fraud or misfeasance there are,
it seems to me, by and large three different phases. First of all, the
administrative phase; next, the judicial phase; and, finally, the executive
phase when the orders of the court or the tribunal are, if necessary,
G executed or promulgated. Quite plainly, fairness to the suspect (if one
may call him that) demands that he should be given a chance of stating
his case before the final period—the execution. That is set out plainly
in Cooper v. Wandsworth Board of Works, 14 C.B.N.S. 180, and also
in Durayappah v. Fernando [1967] 2 A.C. 337. Equally fairness
demands that the suspect shall be given a chance of putting his side of
the case before the judicial inquiry is over. That scarcely needs illustra-
H tion, but if it does it is to be found in the Pergamon case [1971] Ch.
388. But on the other side—and the other side are entitled to fairness
just as the suspect is—fairness to the inquirer demands that during the
administrative period he should be able to investigate without having at
every stage to inquire from the suspect what his side of the matter may
be. Of course it may be difficult to find out the particular point at
which the administrative phase ends and the judicial phase begins. In
other words, when do the judicial proceedings start? Having heard the

argument of Mr. Brodie, put forward so forcibly in this court, it seems   A
to me quite plain, first of all, that the section 109 investigation was still
administrative; and that indeed is not called into question by the appellant
here.   It seems to me equally that the inquiry by the inspectors is a
judicial inquiry, but how can it be argued that anything judicial is
taking place before the inception of that inquiry?   I do not think it can.
It seems to me quite plain that the first moment at which it can be said   B
that natural justice demands that the suspect be given an opportunity to
state his case is at the beginning or during the inquiry by the two inspectors
appointed under section 165 (*b*).

　　Various arguments to the contrary were put forward by Mr. Brodie.
It is said that basic rights are in issue here and therefore audi alteram
partem must apply.   But it seems to me that basic rights are not in
issue here any more than they were in *Reg.* v. *Barnet and Camden Rent*   C
Tribunal, Ex parte Frey Investments Ltd. [1972] 2 Q.B. 342, 361–362,
where Salmon L.J. said:

> " I recognise that when a reference is made by the local authority
> to the tribunal, although it is true that no decision has been taken
> against the landlords which affects their basic rights in the sense that
> I have indicated, it follows that they may be put to expense and incon-   D
> venience.   Nevertheless, in my judgment, the landlords are given
> all the protection which is reasonably necessary, if the Act of 1968
> requires, as in my view it does require, only that the local authority
> shall act bona fide and not make a decision capriciously or vexa-
> tiously.   The assumption must be, until the contrary is proved—
> and the onus of proving the contrary is upon the landlords—that the
> local authority did act properly."   E

　　The second main point made by Mr. Brodie was that the South
African similar Act—that is, Act No. 46 of 1952—contains the express
provision which has been referred to by Ormrod L.J.   For the reasons
which he put forward, I agree that that provision casts no light upon
the duty of the minister under this English Act.   Nor does it seem to me
that it makes any diffence that the tribunal may in the upshot here not   F
come to any adverse conclusion about anyone, nor that their inquiry may
be very far-reaching indeed.   Nor does it make any difference that the
very institution of an inquiry or the appointment of inspectors may or
will have an adverse effect upon the company's affairs and reputation.
As Lord Denning M.R. and Ormrod L.J. have said, companies enjoy
very many advantages, and such disadvantages which may accrue from   G
the appointment of inspectors must be borne by them with fortitude.
The fact that other people may jump to the wrong conclusion when
they hear that inspectors have been appointed and there is going to be
an inquiry should not affect the decision of whether or not a company
should be asked for an explanation of events.

　　In short, the company here is doing this, when one comes to analyse
it: it is asking the court in these proceedings to carry out the very   H
investigation which the tribunal was to have made.   The fact that it
may have been in the past the practice of the ministers to hear the
other side under the provisions of section 164 (2) of the Act of 1948 does
not affect the totally different wording of section 165 (*b*).   That previous
practice does not bind the minister any more than it binds the court.

　　So far as the minister's discretion is concerned, it is quite plain, and
no one will question it for a moment, that any discretion of the minister

The Weekly Law Reports, July 7, 1978

95

3 W.L.R.   Norwest Holst Ltd. v. Dept. of Trade (Ch.D.)   Geoffrey Lane L.J.

A must be exercised bona fide. The court is always entitled—indeed it has the duty—if the minister can be shown to have acted otherwise than bona fide and otherwise than honestly in the exercise of his discretion, to say so and declare that his actions are unlawful. But the wording of this particular section under which he is acting is this:

B " Without prejudice to their powers under the last foregoing section, the Board of Trade—(a) shall appoint . . . (b) may do so if it appears to the Board that there are circumstances suggesting," and so on.

It is difficult to imagine words which would give a wider discretion to the minister than those. Secondly, the burden is firmly and heavily upon the company in question to make out that the minister is not acting
C bona fide in accordance with his powers under that section. There is in fact no evidence in the present case at all, so far as I have been able to discover, that he is acting other than properly in this case.

Mr. Brodie seems to say that the burden has been discharged by showing that the company knows of no basis for the investigation ordered by the minister, no basis for suspicion, and therefore, since there is nothing in the documents to support it, the minister must be acting other than
D bona fide. To that the reply is simple, as Lord Denning M.R. has pointed out, when looking at the passage in Mr. Gill's affidavit dealing with the informant's evidence. " Ah," said Mr. Brodie in reply, " but that is not going to be used in the inquiry by the minister because it is privileged and therefore it cannot be used in order for him to come to a conclusion on section 165 (b)." But that is precisely what it can be used for under
E the wording, " may do so if it appears to the Board that there are circumstances." " Circumstances " is the word used, not " evidence," nor " admissible evidence." It seems to me that that argument founders on that very point. It is indeed the purpose of the inquiry—the investigation which the minister has ordered—to discover whether the view of the minister about those circumstances in the upshot is an accurate one or not.

One further point, and it is this. It seems to me that it would be
F much more unfair to give particulars at this stage than it would be to wait until the inquiry and then to adduce the evidence substantiating or otherwise the suspicions or circumstances which the minister had in mind. If at this stage the minister were to publish the grounds on which the preliminary view had been founded, it might very well be that the company or its officers or other people concerned would have a legitimate
G complaint that this so far incomplete information was being bruited abroad for everyone to hear.

In my judgment, the judge was right in the conclusion which he reached and he was right in the reasons on which he based that conclusion. I too for those reasons and those also expressed by my Lords would dismiss this appeal.

Appeal dismissed with costs.

H
April 27. The appeal committee of the House of Lords (Lord Wilberforce, Lord Salmon and Lord Fraser of Tullybelton) dismissed a petition by the plaintiff company for leave to appeal.

Solicitors: *Bull & Bull; Treasury Solicitor.*

M. M. H.

[1978]

A

[WINCHESTER CONSISTORY COURT]

In re ST. NICHOLAS, BROCKENHURST

1977 Aug. 3   Phillips Ch.

*Ecclesiastical Law—Faculty—Memorial tablet—Mural tablet in B
memory of members of prominent local family — Similar
family tablets erected since early 19th century—No likelihood
of further tablets—Whether faculty to be granted*

The petitioners sought a faculty to authorise the erection of
a memorial tablet in the church commemorating two brothers,
naval officers who, although they had preserved no more than
a tenuous link with the church, were the last relevant male C
members of a prominent local and church family. The church
already contained 12 such family tablets dating from the early
19th century. The petition was unopposed.

On the petition:—

Held, granting a faculty, that, although worthy members
of their family, the brothers had not been so exceptional as
to justify commemoration by a mural tablet in the church;
that membership of a particular family could not be regarded D
as in itself entitling a person to the privilege of a memorial
tablet; but that, as the memorial tablets of the family could
be regarded as an interesting contribution to local history and
there was no possibility of any future application based on
family connection, the erection of a single additional tablet,
which would complete the family record and not noticeably
affect the general appearance of the church, could be E
authorised.

No cases are referred to in the judgment.

PETITION

By petition dated January 19, 1977, the petitioners, Mr. Derek Seaton
and Mrs. Evelyn Seaton, sought a faculty authorising the erection in the F
parish church of St. Nicholas, Brockenhurst, of a mural tablet in memory
of Nigel and John Bowden-Smith, brothers of Mrs. Seaton. The petition
was unopposed.

The facts are stated in the judgment.

P. B. Rustom, solicitor, for the petitioners.

G

PHILLIPS Ch. The petitioners, Mr. and Mrs. Seaton, apply in this case
for a faculty to authorise the erection in the parish church of St. Nicholas,
Brockenhurst, of a mural tablet in memory of Nigel and John Bowden-
Smith, brothers of Mrs. Seaton. The church already contains 12 such
tablets commemorating members of the same family (one of them a
former incumbent of the parish) and covering a period from the early H
part of the 19th century onwards.

As an indication of the law and practice applicable to the placing of
memorial tablets in churches, I quote from an explanatory statement issued
by this court in 1975:

" A faculty is always necessary for this purpose, and according to a
well-established rule, observed by a succession of chancellors in this
diocese and elsewhere, the granting of such a faculty is to be regarded

A   as a special privilege reserved for exceptional cases. Evidence would normally be required that the person to be commemorated had rendered outstanding service to the church and/or the community as a whole—and even then the granting of permission would not follow as a matter of course. Consideration would have to be given to the character of the church, the design of the proposed memorial, the availability of suitable wall-space, etc.; on such matters the chancellor would take particular note of the recommendation of the diocesan advisory committee for the care of churches.

" The strictness with which the court's discretion is exercised may sometimes, on a short-term view, appear excessive; but it is the chancellor's duty to protect the interests of future generations. If faculties were freely granted, albeit in deserving cases, the walls of a church might in the course of years become crowded with tablets to the detriment of the church's appearance.

" It is happily true in many parishes that each generation sees examples of devoted and meritorious service by churchwardens and others which clearly deserves to be kept in remembrance. It is suggested that an acceptable mode of commemoration may often be the provision of some article or feature, suitably inscribed, which can be dedicated as a permanent addition to the contents or perhaps the structure of the church. Examples in this diocese include memorial windows, panelling, pews, candlesticks, communion plate, altar frontals and dorsals, font-covers, lecterns and service books.

" Any person who has a legitimate interest may of course present a petition seeking authorisation for a memorial tablet. But it should be understood that a substantial burden of proof will normally rest on the petitioner and that, even in the absence of formal objection by other parties, a hearing in court may well be required. Intending petitioners would usually be well advised to seek the opinion of the parochial church council and the advice of the diocesan registrar at an early stage, before detailed designs are prepared and submitted to the diocesan advisory committee."

Reference may be made also to *Halsbury's Laws of England* 4th ed., vol. 14 (1975), para. 1316, where a statement on this subject by the late Dr. Wigglesworth is quoted.

In the present case the petition was supported by a resolution of the parochial church council which was, however, not unanimous, the motion being carried by 12 votes to 5, with two members (apparently the church-wardens) abstaining. The petitioners were not successful in obtaining a favourable recommendation from the diocesan advisory committee.

Prima facie, the case did not appear to be one in which the grant of a faculty was manifestly appropriate, and although on citation no appearance was entered in opposition, it was decided that in accordance with accepted practice the petitioners must, if they wished to proceed further, move for a faculty in open court.

The case as presented to the court on behalf of the petitioners is based, first, on the individual merits of the two brothers and, secondly, on their membership of a family which has been prominent in the life of Brockenhurst and its church for a number of generations.

I have no hesitation in accepting what has been said about the careers of Nigel and John Bowden-Smith. Both were naval officers, and it is evident that they worthily upheld their family's fine tradition of service

to the Crown and to the community. Nigel was awarded the Distinguished **A**
Service Cross, and there is evidence in addition that he was an active
and valued member of his local church in another diocese. On the
other hand, neither of the brothers seems to have preserved more than a
tenuous link with the parish church at Brockenhurst, and its churchyard
does not contain their mortal remains. On this aspect of the case my
finding is that while these men had admirable records, deserving of the
B
fullest respect, those records are not in themselves of such an exceptional
character as to justify commemoration by a mural tablet in Brockenhurst
church. Hence if permission is to be granted for such a tablet it can only
be on the ground of membership of the Bowden-Smith family. As was
pointed out by this court in 1974 (when a faculty was granted for the
latest of the Bowden-Smith tablets), membership of a particular family
cannot in these latter days be regarded as ipso facto entitling a person to **C**
the privilege of a memorial tablet in the church, even when such a
privilege has been allowed without question in the past.

It is fair to say, however, that Mr. Rustom has presented the argument
from family connection in a rather more acceptable form. He suggests
that the monumental record of the Bowden-Smiths of Brockenhurst can
be regarded as an interesting contribution to local history, and that it
would be a pity if that record were not completed by the addition of the **D**
names of Nigel and John, who were, I am told, the last male members
of the family to have any personal link with Brockenhurst. I think this
argument, coupled with the assurance that there is no possibility of any
future application based on the family connection, deserves consideration;
it enables me at any rate to treat this as a borderline case, and one in
which there is no risk of setting an undesirable precedent. **E**

I am influenced also by the impression which I received on a recent
inspection of the church. The existing Bowden-Smith memorial tablets
are located, not in the medieval body of the church, but in a corner of
the north aisle, which was built (according to Pevsner and Lloyd) in 1832.
I am satisfied that a single additional mural tablet would not noticeably
affect the general appearance of that part of the church.

As was said by Dr. Wigglesworth (in the statement concerning memorial **F**
tablets that is quoted in *Halsbury*), ". . . a chancellor must exercise a
judicial discretion in every case which comes before him; no hard and
fast rule can therefore be made; each case must be considered on its
merits." In the present case I have come to the conclusion that I am
justified in exercising my discretion in the petitioners' favour.

A faculty will be granted authorising the erection of a mural tablet in **G**
memory of Nigel and John Bowden-Smith, subject to approval by the
court (i) of an amended design which the petitioners have undertaken to
produce and submit for the opinion of the diocesan advisory committee
and (ii) of the position in which the tablet is to be placed on the wall.

Faculty granted.
H

Solicitors: *Heppenstalls, Lymington.*

C. N.

A

[EUROPEAN COURT OF JUSTICE]

REGINA *v.* NATIONAL INSURANCE COMMISSIONER,
Ex parte WARRY

[Case 41/77]

B

1977 Nov. 9   Judge H. Kutscher (President), Judges M. Sørensen and
G. Bosco (President of Chambers), Judges A. M. Donner,
J. Mertens de Wilmars, P. Pescatore, Lord Mackenzie Stuart,
A. O'Keeffe, and A. Touffait
J.-P. Warner (Advocate-General)

C *European Economic Community — Social security — Invalidity
pension — National insurance contributions paid partly in
Britain and partly in Germany—Claimant falling ill in
Germany—Receipt of German sickness benefit—Entitlement to
British invalidity pension—Precondition of receipt of British
sickness benefit not fulfilled—E.E.C. Council Regulation No.
1408/71, art. 45 (1) (as amended)*

D   The claimant, a British national was insured for social
security purposes in Britain from 1933 until 1971, apart from
one period in Germany between 1947 until 1951. In August
1971, he moved to Germany, and was insured under German
legislation from that time until he became ill in June 1973.
He received sickness benefit in Germany from August 1973
until July 1974 when he started to receive disability pension
commensurate with the period he had been insured in that
E country.
     In 1974 the claimant claimed an invalidity pension in
Great Britain, although he had not paid contributions in
Britain during the prescribed period and his claim was out
of time. An insurance officer refused his claim under section
3 of the National Insurance Act 1971 [1] on the ground that
he had not been entitled to sickness benefit for 168 days, a
precondition under national legislation to entitlement to an
F invalidity pension. The claimant's appeal from the insurance
officer's decision to a local tribunal was dismissed. He
further appealed, however, to a National Insurance Commissioner who allowed his appeal. The commissioner ruled
that, although under national law the claimant had not
satisfied the requirements entitling him to an invalidity pension,
by virtue of articles 45 (1) and 46 (2) of Regulation 1408/71
of the Council [2] he was entitled to receive an invalidity pension.
G The insurance officer applied to the Divisional Court for an
order of certiorari to quash the decision of the commissioner.
     On a reference by the Divisional Court to the Court of
Justice of the European Communities to determine the effect
in such cases of Community law on national legislation : —
     Held, (1) that where the relevant legislation, or one of the
relevant codes of legislation, made the entitlement to invalidity
benefit dependent upon a specific period of entitlement to
H sickness benefit, the institution to which a claim for invalidity
benefit was made was required by article 45 (1) of Regulation
1408/71 of the Council to take into account insurance periods

---

[Reported by PETER SURMAN, ESQ., Barrister-at-Law]

[1] National Insurance Act 1971, s. 3 (1): see post, p. 108E–G.
[2] Regulation No. 1408/71, art. 45 (1), as amended: see post, p. 102G–H.
Art. 46 (2), as amended: see post, p. 103C–F.

completed under the legislation of any other member state A
as though they had been completed in accordance with the
national legislation administered by that institution (post,
pp. 115A–B, 116C).

(2) That where a claim had to be made in a prescribed
manner and within a prescribed time, those conditions were
satisfied if such a claim had been duly made in accordance
with the legislation of the claimant's state of residence (post,
pp. 115F–H, 116D).   B

The following cases are referred to in the judgment:

D'Amico v. *Landesversicherungsanstalt Rheinland-Pfalz* (Case 20/75)
[1975] E.C.R. 891.

Golati v. *Landesversicherungsanstalt Schwaken* (Case 33/75) [1975]
E.C.R. 1323.

N. V. Algemene Transport v. *Netherlands Inland Revenue Administration* C
(Case 26/62) [1963] E.C.R. 1.

Reyners v. *Belgian State* (Case 2/74) [1974] E.C.R. 631.

Salgoil v. *Italian Ministry for Foreign Trade* (Case 13/68) [1968] E.C.R.
453.

Salvatore Murru v. *Caisse Régionale d'Assurance Maladie de Paris* (Case
2/72) [1972] E.C.R. 333.

D
The following additional cases were cited in the opinion of Mr. Advocate-
General, J.-P. Warner:

Sotgiu v. *Deutsche Bundespost* (Case 152/73) [1974] E.C.R. 153.

Württembergische Milchverwertung-Südmilch-A.G. v. *Ugliola* (Case 15/69)
[1969] E.C.R. 363.

REFERENCE by Divisional Court of the Queen's Bench Division.   E

On February 15, 1977, the Divisional Court referred to the Court of
Justice of the European Communities certain questions which had arisen
in the course of an application by Christine Margaret Warry, an insurance
officer, to the Divisional Court for an order of certiorari to quash a
decision of a National Insurance Commissioner. The commissioner, on
March 11, 1976, had allowed an appeal by the claimant, John Patrick F
Kelly, from the decision of a local tribunal which had upheld the insurance
officer's decision that the claimant was not entitled to an invalidity pension.

The facts and the questions referred to the court are set out below
in the opinion of Mr. Advocate-General, J.-P. Warner.

October 18. MR. ADVOCATE-GENERAL J.-P. WARNER delivered the
following opinion.   G

Introductory

This case comes before the court by way of a reference for a preliminary ruling by a Divisional Court of the Queen's Bench Division of
the High Court of Justice of England and Wales.

The circumstances in which it does so are these. Mr. John Patrick H
Kelly, who is a British national, now in his sixties, was insured for social
security purposes in the United Kingdom, either as a member of the
forces or as an employed person, from 1933 to 1971, save for a period
from 1947 to 1951 which he spent in Germany. In 1971 he returned
to Germany, where he worked and was insured until June 1973, when he
became sick, it seems permanently. He is still resident in Germany.
He was paid sickness benefit there from August 1973 to July 1974, since

A   when he has received a small German invalidity pension, calculated by reference to the relatively short period for which he was insured in Germany.

In 1974 an application was made on Mr. Kelly's behalf to the Department of Health and Social Security in England for the payment to him of a British invalidity pension. (I say " British " rather than " United Kingdom " because the legislation under which he claimed the pension
B   is applicable only to Great Britain. Northern Ireland has, I understand, its own legislation on social security).

On June 19, 1974, the responsible insurance officer decided that no British invalidity pension was payable to Mr. Kelly, because he had not been in receipt of British sickness benefit. The scheme of the relevant British legislation is, as was explained to us at the hearing, that a person
C   whose employment is interrupted by reason of incapacity for work becomes entitled in the first instance to sickness benefit. If his incapacity continues for more than 168 days, he then becomes entitled to an invalidity pension (which is at a higher rate) instead. The relevant provisions in force at the time when Mr. Kelly made his claim were section 19 of the National Insurance Act 1965 and section 3 of the National Insurance Act 1971. Those provisions are now replaced, without material alteration,
D   by sections 14 and 15 of the Social Security Act 1975, which was a consolidating Act. It is held to be a consequence of the way in which the British legislation is framed that entitlement to sickness benefit for 168 days is a precondition for entitlement to an invalidity pension. Nor is the receipt of German sickness benefit regarded as satisfying that precondition.

E   Against the decision of the insurance officer, Mr. Kelly appealed to the local tribunal at Newcastle-upon-Tyne. On June 3, 1975, that tribunal dismissed his appeal, upholding the insurance officer's reasoning. Thereupon Mr. Kelly further appealed to a National Insurance Commissioner. That appeal was successful. On March 11, 1976, the National Insurance Commissioner delivered a decision reversing that of the local tribunal and holding that Mr. Kelly was entitled to a British invalidity pension
F   by virtue of the provisions of article 46 (2) of Regulation No. 1408/71 of the Council (*Official Journal,* English Special Edition 1971 (II), p. 416).

The National Insurance Commissioner accepted that, under the British legislation taken alone, Mr. Kelly was not entitled to invalidity benefit because he had not been entitled to sickness benefit. The commissioner
G   observed that there were, under that legislation, at least two obstacles to Mr. Kelly obtaining sickness benefit. First, he did not satisfy the relevant contribution conditions, in that he had not paid British national insurance contributions in a period sufficiently proximate to the date when he became sick: see, for the details of those contribution conditions, paragraph 1 of Schedule 2 to the National Insurance Act 1965, now replaced by paragraph 1 of Schedule 3 to the Social Security Act 1975.
H   Secondly, a person could not, under the British legislation, receive benefit whilst absent from Great Britain; see section 49 (1) (*a*) of the National Insurance Act 1965, now replaced by section 82 (5) (*a*) of the Social Security Act 1975; there were exceptions to the latter rule, but none that was applicable in Mr. Kelly's case. It seems that a further point taken on behalf of the insurance officer was that Mr. Kelly was precluded from receiving sickness benefit because he had not made a claim therefor in the prescribed manner and within the prescribed time: see section 48

A

of the National Insurance Act 1965 and the National Insurance (Claims and Payments) Regulations 1971 (S.I. 1971 No. 707), now replaced by section 79 of the Social Security Act 1975 and the Social Security (Claims and Payments) Regulations 1975 (S.I. 1975 No. 560).

In essence the commissioner decided that those difficulties as to the receipt by Mr. Kelly of an invalidity pension were overcome by the provisions of Regulation No. 1408/71.

B

In the course of reaching that decision, the commissioner considered the question whether the precondition to title to British invalidity benefit that there should have been previous entitlement to British sickness benefit was compatible with article 51 of the E.E.C. Treaty or, alternatively, should, by virtue of Community law, be regarded as satisfied in this case by Mr. Kelly's receipt of German sickness benefit. The commissioner referred in that connection to the opinion of Mr. Advocate-General Trabucchi in *D'Amico* v. *Landesversicherungsanstalt Rheinland-Pfalz* (Case 20/75) [1975] E.C.R. 891, 901. In the end, however, the commissioner found it unnecessary to express a concluded opinion on those questions, having regard to the view he had formed on the interpretation of the relevant provisions of Regulation No. 1408/71.

C

Your Lordships are familiar with the fact that Chapter 2 of Title III of that Regulation, which relates to invalidity, has regard to the circumstance that there exist in the member states two different types of legislation as to invalidity benefits: that generally known as "Type A," under which the amount of invalidity benefit is independent of insurance periods; and that generally known as "Type B," under which the amount of such benefit depends on the length of insurance periods. The rights of a worker who has been successively or alternately subject to legislation exclusively of Type A are dealt with by articles 37 to 39, whilst, in the case of a worker who has been successively or alternately subject to legislation of which one at least is of Type B, article 40 prescribes that the provisions of Chapter 3, relating to "Old Age and Death (Pensions)" are to be applied by analogy. So far as the present case is concerned, the relevant British legislation is of Type A, but the relevant German legislation is of Type B, so that article 40 is in point.

D

E

F

Of the provisions of Chapter 3 that are thus rendered relevant, the most important are articles 45 (1) and 46. Both of them have been successively amended by the Act of Accession, (Annex I, point IX (1)) and by Regulation No. 2864/72 of the Council (*Official Journal*, English Special Edition, 1972 (December 31), p. 15). My references to them will be, as were those of the National Insurance Commissioner, to their texts as so amended. Article 45 (1), as so amended, reads:

G

"An institution of a member state whose legislation makes the acquisition, retention or recovery of the rights to benefits conditional upon the completion of insurance periods or periods of residence shall take into account, to the extent necessary, insurance periods or periods of residence completed under the legislation of any member state as though they had been completed under the legislation which it administers."

H

The National Insurance Commissioner took the view, as I understand his reasoning, that, to put it shortly, article 45 (1) overcame two obstacles in the way of Mr. Kelly's entitlement to British invalidity benefit. First, that provision enabled the insurance periods completed by him in Germany to be taken into account as if they had been completed in Great Britain,

A so as to enable him to be deemed to have satisfied the requisite contribution conditions.   Secondly, it enabled his period of residence in
Germany to be treated as if it had been one of residence in Great Britain,
so as to enable his actual absence from Great Britain to be disregarded.
The remaining difficulty that the commissioner felt (and it is, to my mind,
the central difficulty in this case) was that article 45 (1) did not in terms
authorise the further or consequential assumption that Mr. Kelly had been
B entitled to British sickness benefit during the necessary 168 days.

At this point the commissioner's reasoning took a course which, I
confess, I find difficult to follow.   On the footing that article 45 (1) did
not, alone, enable that further assumption to be made, he turned to article
46.   Paragraph 1 of that article prescribes, your Lordships remember,
what benefit is to be awarded to a worker " where the conditions for
C entitlement to benefit have been satisfied without application of the provisions of article 45 being necessary."   That paragraph could not of course
be relevant in such a case as this.   Article 46 (2) provides:

" Where a worker has been subject to the legislation of any member
state and where he does not satisfy the conditions for entitlement
to benefits unless account is taken of the provisions of article 45,
D the responsible institution of that member state shall apply the
following rules: (a) the institution shall calculate the theoretical
amount of benefit that the person concerned could claim if all the
insurance periods or periods of residence completed under the legislation of the member state to which the worker has been subject
had been completed in the state in question and under the legislation administered by it on the date the benefit is awarded.   If,
E under that legislation, the amount of the benefit does not depend
on the length of the periods completed then that amount shall be
taken as the theoretical amount referred to in this sub-paragraph; (b)
the institution shall then establish the actual amount of the benefit
on the basis of the theoretical amount referred to in the preceding
sub-paragraph, pro rata with the length of the periods of insurance or
F residence completed before the occurrence of the event insured against
under the legislation applied by it, as compared with the total length
of the periods of insurance and residence completed under the legislations of all the member states concerned before the occurrence of
that event; . . ."

The commissioner took the view that sub-paragraphs (a) and (b) of
G article 46 (2) were expository of article 45 (1) and that it was impossible
to say whether a person was entitled to anything under article 45 (1)
without making the calculations required by those paragraphs.   On the
assumptions that fell to be made by virtue of article 45 (1), i.e. the
assumptions of continuous insurance and of continuous residence in Great
Britain, Mr. Kelly would, subject to his making the appropriate claim,
have been entitled to sickness benefit for 168 days and thereafter to
H invalidity benefit.   The calculation under article 46 (2) (a) did therefore
yield a " theoretical amount of benefit."   The fact that no actual claim
for sickness benefit had been made by Mr. Kelly could not be material,
since the calculation was of a " theoretical " amount on a hypothetical
basis.   From that theoretical amount the " actual amount " of invalidity
benefit could be established under article 46 (2) (b).

The insurance officer now applies in the Queen's Bench Division for
an order of certiorari quashing the decision of the National Insurance

Reg. v. Nat. Ins., Ex p. Warry (E.C.J.)   [1978]

Commissioner on the ground that it is erroneous in law. By order dated   A
February 15, 1977, the Divisional Court referred to this court, under
article 177 of the Treaty, the following questions:

> " Where the legislation of a member state makes the acquisition of
> a right to invalidity benefit conditional upon the person concerned
> having been entitled to sickness benefit under that legislation for a
> total of 168 days in the immediately preceding period, that condition   B
> being subject to, so far as material, (a) the completion of insurance
> periods (b) the making of a claim therefor in a prescribed manner
> and within a prescribed time—(i) do the provisions of article 51 of
> the Treaty of Rome preclude the application of such a condition to
> a case to which article 40, 45 or 46 of Regulation No. 1408/71
> relates? (ii) do the provisions of (a) article 45 or (b) article 46
> relate to such legislation? (iii) do all or any of the said articles 40,   C
> 45 or 46—(a) enable such a condition to be treated as wholly or
> partly satisfied; or (b) require such a condition to be wholly or partly
> disregarded; and if so to what extent?"

I think it convenient to deal with those questions under two headings:
(1) the interpretation of the Treaty, and in particular article 51; and (2)
the interpretation of Regulation No. 1408/71, and in particular articles   D
45 and 46.

The interpretation of the Treaty, and in particular article 51

It is a feature of this case that Mr. Kelly did not appear and was
not represented before the National Insurance Commissioner, before the
Divisional Court or before this court. As far as this court is concerned,   E
he contented himself with writing to the registrar that there was nothing
constructive which he could " add to the information already given to
the courts and insurance authorities in England." The Divisional Court,
however, had the assistance of an amicus curiae and I imagine, though
we do not of course know, that that court's first question was prompted
by an argument put forward by him, and which may very well itself have
been suggested by the remarks of the National Insurance Commissioner   F
to which I have referred.

At all events the insurance officer and the Commission (on whose
behalf only observations have been submitted to this court) are at one
in saying that article 51 of the Treaty does not preclude the existence in
the legislation of a member state of a provision making it a precondition
to the acquisition of a right to invalidity benefit that the person con-   G
cerned should have been entitled under that legislation to sickness benefit
for a specified number of days in the immediately preceding period.

In support of that proposition they rely to some extent on the decision
of the court in D'Amico's case (Case 20/75) [1975] E.C.R. 891. I do
not, however, for my part think that that decision is in point. It was
there held that no provision of Community lay precluded the existence in
the legislation of a member state of a provision making it a precondition   H
to the acquisition of a right to an early retirement pension that the person
concerned should have been registered as unemployed for a specified
period in that state. But the decision turned on the consideration that the
relevant Community regulations themselves were framed on the footing
that the right to benefit in respect of unemployment in general pre-
supposed that the person concerned was available for employment where
such benefit was claimed. No such consideration is applicable here.

A   Receipt by a person of sickness benefit cannot be regarded as any sort of
quid pro quo for his receipt of invalidity benefit later.

What however is, in my opinion, undoubtedly correct is that, as the
insurance officer and the Commission also both point out, article 51 does
not have direct effect, in the sense of conferring, of itself, on private
persons, rights that they can enforce in the courts of member states.
All that article 51 does, in terms, is to confer on the Council a power,
B   and a duty, to adopt certain measures. Thus, so far as that article is
concerned, only the adoption of such measures by the Council can confer
on a worker a right on which he can rely in a national court.

Nor do I find in the opinion of Mr. Advocate-General Trabucchi in
D'Amico's case (Case 20/75) [1975] E.C.R. 891 anything that casts doubt
on the correctness of that view. As I read that opinion, Mr. Advocate-
C   General Trabucchi deduced from certain earlier decisions of the court the
existence of a general principle that, in certain circumstances, a member
state must, even in the absence of any specific provision to that effect, treat
facts occurring on the territory of another member state as if they had
occurred on its own territory, even though its legislation regards such facts
as relevant only if occurring on its territory. In accordance with such a
principle the United Kingdom might here be required to treat the receipt
D   by Mr. Kelly of German sickness benefit as equivalent to the receipt by
him of British sickness benefit. If such a principle exists, however, it
cannot be derived directly from article 51, nor indeed did Mr. Advocate-
General Trabucchi suggest that it was. Of the decisions to which he
referred, two, namely *Württembergische Milchverwertung-Südmilch A.G.*
v. *Ugliola* (Case 15/69) [1969] E.C.R. 363 and *Sotgiu* v. *Deutsche*
E   *Bundespost* (Case 152/73) [1974] E.C.R. 153, were based on the
principle of non-discrimination enshrined in article 48 of the Treaty and
in certain regulations of the Council not here in point, whilst the third,
Salvatore Murru v. *Caisse Régionale d'Assurance Maladie de Paris* (Case
2/72) [1972] E.C.R. 333, turned on the interpretation of article 1 (*r*)
of Regulation No. 3, which was the predecessor of article 1 (*s*) of Regulation No. 1408/71. Therefore, for the general principle suggested by
F   Mr. Advocate-General Trabucchi to apply it must at least be shown
that, without it, there would be discrimination against a migrant worker
of a kind prohibited by article 48. Since, as your Lordships will see, I
have formed on the interpretation of Regulation No. 1408/71 a view
that accords in its result with the view of the National Insurance Commissioner, and since, moreover, the Divisional Court has not asked any
G   question as to the interpretation of article 48, I need not, I think, pursue
that topic further.

I turn to the questions of interpretation of Regulation No. 1408/71.

*The interpretation of Regulation No. 1408/71, and in particular articles
45 and 46*

It is of course manifest that, if Regulation No. 1408/71 is ineffective
H   to render Mr. Kelly entitled to a British invalidity pension, it has, in
that respect, glaringly failed to achieve its purpose. This is recognised
both by the insurance officer and by the Commission. Both of them
say, however, that the situation results from a lacuna in the regulation
and that that lacuna can only be cured by further legislation. They draw
attention to a proposal for a Council regulation amending Regulations
No. 1408/71 and No. 574/72, which has been drawn up after consultation
with the Administrative Commission on Social Security for Migrant

Workers, and which was submitted by the Commission to the Council on A
June 30, 1977 (OJ No. C 171/2 of 19.7.77).   One effect of that proposed
regulation would be to insert a new paragraph in article 40 of Regulation
No. 1408/71, making it possible in a case like the present for (briefly and
so far as material) sickness benefit received in one member state to be
treated as having been received in the other.   There is provision for that
new paragraph to apply retroactively as from July 1, 1976.   The fact that
new legislation is proposed cannot, however, be a relevant consideration B
for this court in interpreting existing legislation.

　　Your Lordships will have observed that, of the two main obstacles
that the National Insurance Commissioner saw as being in Mr. Kelly's
way to obtaining British sickness benefit, namely (1) the fact that he did
not satisfy the requisite contribution conditions and (2) the fact that he
was at the material time absent from Great Britain, only the first, is C
adverted to by the Divisional Court in its questions to this court.   One
infers that, for some reason into which it is not for this court to inquire,
the Divisional Court did not attach importance to the second.   Nonetheless arguments were developed before this court, both on behalf of the
insurance officer and on behalf of the Commission, designed to show that
the references in article 45 (1) of Regulation No. 1408/71 to " periods
of residence " could not have the effect that the National Insurance Com- D
missioner attributed to them.   Those arguments were based on the fact
that those references were introduced by the Act of Accession, as was the
definition of " periods of residence " in article 1 (s) (a) of the Regulation,
and on the contrast between the wording of those provisions in the Act
of Accession and their wording as substituted by Regulation No. 2864/72.
If I understood the arguments correctly, they logically led to the con- E
conclusion that the commissioner would have been right if Mr. Kelly
had gone to Denmark instead of to Germany, but that, because the
German social security legislation does not define or recognise " periods
of residence," he was wrong.   Why the authors of the legislation should
have intended that a worker's rights in Great Britain should differ according to whether he migrated thence to Denmark or to Germany was not
explained.   Despite the temptation that I feel to deal fully with those F
arguments, I apprehend that it would not be right for me, in the circumstances, to take up your Lordships' time in doing so.

　　So I turn to those of the arguments put forward on behalf of the
insurance officer and of the Commission that bore on the questions
referred to this court by the Divisional Court.   In essence there were
two.   First it was said that the provisions of article 45 (1) requiring an G
institution of a member state, whose legislation made the acquisition
of a right to invalidity benefit conditional upon the completion of insurance
periods, to take into account, to the extent necessary, insurance periods
completed under the legislation of another member state, as though they
had been completed under its own legislation, could not be interpreted
as requiring it to take such periods into account for the purpose of
ascertaining whether a worker would have been entitled to sickness benefit H
where prior entitlement to sickness benefit was a precondition to entitlement to invalidity benefit.   Secondly, it was said that that lacuna in article
45 (1) could not be filled by article 46 (2).

　　I will say at once that, with that second point, I agree; so that, to
that extent, I respectfully dissent from the views expressed by the National
Insurance Commissioner.   The purpose of article 46 (2) is to specify the
consequences of the application of article 45.   There is of course a close

A   nexus between article 45 and article 46 (2), and it is no doubt right to interpret them in the light of each other. But article 46 (2) cannot confer on a worker a right to benefit if his case is such that article 45 does not apply.

So one comes back to the real question in this case, which I described earlier as the central difficulty in it, viz. whether the assumptions that an institution of a member state (in this case the Department of Health and
B   Social Security) is required to make under article 45 (1) are limited in the way contended for by the insurance officer and the Commission, or whether, on the contrary, that institution is required to take into account any relevant consequences flowing from those assumptions.

I have, after some hesitation, come to the conclusion that the latter is the correct answer. To my mind there is in article 45 (1) not so much
C   a lacuna as an ambiguity. How far is an institution of a member state to go in taking into account " insurance periods or periods of residence completed under the legislation of any member state as though they had been completed under the legislation which it administers "? The answer, in so far as it is to be found in the words of article 45 (1) itself, is " to the extent necessary." That being so, it does not seem to me to do violence to the language of article 45 (1) to hold that, where, on those
D   assumptions, a worker would have been entitled, in the member state concerned, first to sickness benefit for a specified period and thereafter to invalidity benefit, the hypothesis enjoined by that provision includes the receipt by him of sickness benefit where that is a precondition to the receipt by him of invalidity benefit. And, if that interpretation, not only does no violence to the language of the provision, but is also (as it
E   manifestly and undisputedly is) the only one consistent with its purpose, it must, so it seems to me, in accordance with the canons of interpretation laid down over and over again by this court, be the correct interpretation.

On that footing, the other difficulty mentioned by the Divisional Court, arising from the requirement in the British legislation that a claim for sickness benefit should be made in a prescribed manner and within a prescribed time, can clearly be disregarded. As to that I agree entirely
F   with the National Insurance Commissioner. When one is in a world of statutory hypotheses as to substantive rights, the absence of fulfilment of the formalities that would be required to secure those rights in the real world cannot be material.

Conclusions

G   In the result I am of the opinion that, in answer to the questions referred by the Divisional Court, your Lordships should rule:

(1) Article 51 of the E.E.C. Treaty does not of itself confer on private persons any rights on which it is open to them to rely in the courts of member states.

(2) Where the legislation of a member state makes the acquisition of a right to invalidity benefit conditional upon the person concerned having
H   been entitled to sicknes benefit under that legislation for a specified number of days in the immediately preceding period, entitlement to such sickness benefit being itself subject to (a) the completion of insurance periods and (b) the making of a claim therefor in a prescribed manner and within a prescribed time, the combined effect of articles 40, 45 and 46 of Regulation No. 1408/71 (in a case where the person concerned has been successively or alternatively subject to the legislation of two or more member states, of which at least one is not of the type referred to in

article 37 of that regulation) is to enable such condition to be treated   A
as satisfied to the extent to which it would have been satisfied if insurance
periods completed by that person under the legislation of any member
state had been completed under the legislation of the first-mentioned
member state and if the appropriate claim for sickness benefit had been
made in the prescribed manner and within the prescribed time.

    Harry Woolf for the insurance officer.   B
    Mr. Allen for the Commission.
    Mr. Kelly was not present and was not represented.

    November 9, 1977.   The following judgment was delivered in open
court in Luxembourg.

FACTS AND ISSUES   C

The facts, the procedure and the written observations submitted under
article 20 of the Protocol on the Statute of the Court of Justice of the
E.E.C. may be summarised as follows:

I. *Facts and procedure*

    John Patrick Kelly, of British nationality, was insured in Great Britain   D
from 1933 until July 1971, apart from a period spent in Germany from
1947 or 1948 until 1951.   He went to Germany in July 1971 where he
worked and was insured under the German insurance legislation from
August 1971 until he became ill in June 1973.   He continued to live in
Germany and received sickness benefit there from August 1973 until
July 1974, since when he has received a limited invalidity pension   E
calculated by reference to his period of insurance in Germany.   He has
now claimed also invalidity pension in Great Britain.
    At the time of his claim the relevant provision of the legislation in the
United Kingdom was section 3 (1) of the National Insurance Act 1971,
which provided:

    " Subject to the following provisions of this section where, in respect   F
    of any period of interruption of employment, a person has been
    entitled to sickness benefit for 168 days, then—(*a*) he shall cease to be
    entitled to that benefit for any subsequent day of incapacity for work
    falling within that period; and (*b*) unless he is over pensionable
    age and has retired from regular employment, he shall be entitled
    to an invalidity pension for any day of incapacity for work in that
    period for which, by virtue of (*a*) above, he is not entitled to sickness   G
    benefit."

This provision has been replaced by a similar provision contained in
section 15 (1) of the Social Security Act 1975.
    Claims for invalidity benefit under the legislation of the United
Kingdom are dealt with by an insurance officer in the first instance.   A
dissatisfied claimant has a right of appeal against a decision of the   H
insurance officer to a local tribunal.   There is a further right of appeal
by the claimant or the insurance officer from the local tribunal to a
National Insurance Commissioner, who is the final appellate tribunal.
    The insurance officer rejected Mr. Kelly's claim on the ground that
he had not been and could not be treated as having been entitled to
sickness benfit for 168 days.   The local tribunal dismissed Mr. Kelly's
appeal to it from the decision of the insurance officer.   The National

A Insurance Commissioner on March 11, 1976, allowed Mr. Kelly's appeal and decided:

"> . . . invalidity benefit is, when not reduced to nothing by the provisions for the elimination of overlapping benefits hereinafter referred to, payable to [Mr. Kelly] in accordance with the provisions of article 46 (2) of Council Regulation No. 1408/71. . . ."

B Although the National Insurance Commissioner is the final authority in the statutory benefit appeals system, the High Court of Justice exercises, in accordance with general rules of English law, a certain supervisory jurisdiction over his decisions and one of the methods of the exercise of that jurisdiction is the order of certiorari, by which the High Court can quash a decision of an inferior tribunal. In the present case the insurance officer applied in the Divisional Court of the Queen's Bench Division of C the High Court for an order of certiorari to quash the decision of the National Insurance Commissioner. The Divisional Court, pursuant to article 177 of the E.E.C. Treaty, referred the following questions to the court for a preliminary ruling:

"Where the legislation of a member state makes the acquisition of a right to invalidity benefit conditional upon the person concerned having been entitled to sickness benefit under that legislation for a D total of 168 days in the immediately preceding period, that condition being subject to so far as material (a) the completion of insurance periods (b) the making of a claim therefor in a prescribed manner and within a prescribed time—(i) Do the provisions of article 51 of the Treaty of Rome preclude the application of such a condition to a E case to which article 40, 45 or 46 of Regulation (EEC) No. 1408/71 relates? (ii) Do the provisions of (a) article 45 or (b) article 46 relate to such legislation? (iii) Do all or any of the said articles 40, 45 or 46 (a) enable such a condition to be treated as wholly or partly satisfied; or (b) require such a condition to be wholly or partly disregarded; and if so to what extent?"

F Pursuant to article 20 of the Protocol on the Statute of the Court the insurance officer and the Commission submitted written observations. Mr. Kelly, who was notified of the proceedings, decided not to submit any observation or to be represented before this court. After hearing the report of the Judge-Rapporteur and the views of the Advocate-General, the court decided to open the oral procedure without a preparatory inquiry.

G II. *Observations submitted under article 20 of the Protocol on the Statute of the Court of Justice of the E.E.C.*

A. Observations of the insurance officer

The insurance officer explains that the conditions for entitlement to invalidity benefit under the United Kingdom legislation are, first, that the person concerned should have been entitled, in the immediately H preceding period, to sickness benefit for 168 days, and, secondly, that he should have paid at any time between his entry into insurance under the Great Britain scheme and the expiry of the said 168 days a specified number of contributions. The reference to a specified number of contributions which must have been paid would fall within the definition of " insurance periods " contained in article 1 (r) of Regulation No. 1408/71. Further, it is a precondition of entitlement to sickness benefit that a claim is made for it in a prescribed manner and within a prescribed time:

section 48 (1) of the National Insurance Act 1965. If a person makes A
a claim for benefit outside the prescribed time limit, it is provided by
section 49 (3) of the same Act that he shall be disqualified for the receipt
of that benefit unless he can show the insurance officer that he has good
cause for the delay. Whether insurance periods have been completed and
whether or not a claim has been made in the prescribed manner are
questions for determination by the Secretary of State and not for
determination by the insurance officer. To acquire a right to invalidity B
benefit a person must, in order to have been entitled to sickness benefit
for 168 days, have completed insurance periods and have made a claim
for such sickness benefit.

As to the first question she submits that article 51 of the Treaty
cannot be held to preclude the application of the legislation of a member
state which makes a period of entitlement to sickness benefit under that C
legislation a precondition for acquiring a right to invalidity benefit.
Article 51 could be held to have such an effect only if construed as
conferring on individuals a right to be exempted from any requirement
of national legislation in the field of social security which can be said to
discourage freedom of movement for workers within the Community. This
would involve a departure from the principles settled by the court in a
number of cases: *N. V. Algemene Transport* v. *Netherlands Inland* D
Revenue Administration (Case 26/62) [1963] E.C.R. 1; *Salgoil* v. *Italian
Ministry for Foreign Trade* (Case 13/68) [1968] E.C.R. 453 and *Reyners*
v. *Belgian State* (Case 2/74) [1974] E.C.R. 631. Article 51 may require
the adoption by the Council of a measure to provide that a period during
which a person has been entitled to sickness benefit in another member
state should be taken into account for the purpose of United Kingdom E
legislation and the insurance officer understands that a proposal for such
an amendment to the relevant regulation has already been submitted by
the Commission to the Council.

In *D'Amico* v. *Landesversicherungsanstalt Rheinland-Pfalz* (Case
20/75) [1975] E.C.R. 891, the court held that Community legislation
did not prohibit a rule of law which required, for the acquisition
of a right to early retirement pension, that the person concerned should F
have been unemployed for a certain time and available to the unemployment bureau of the member state in question. The present case should
be considered by analogy with that case.

As to the second question the insurance officer submits that article 45
of the regulation does not apply. Although " benefits " is defined in
article 1 (*t*) of the regulation as meaning " all benefits," in the context G
of article 45 it must be construed only as referring to benefits to which
Chapter 3 applies, that is to say, invalidity benefits. Chapter 3 and
article 45 do not apply to sickness benefit. Under the legislation of Great
Britain residence is only directly relevant for sickness and invalidity
benefit purposes to avoid disqualification for receipt of benefit by reason
of residence abroad. Article 45 as originally made by the Council referred
only to the completion of insurance periods and a reference to periods of H
residence was inserted when the article was modified by article 1 (13) of
Regulation No. 2864/72 upon the accession of Denmark, whose legislation
makes entitlement to benefit dependent upon periods of residence. Article
45 is concerned with determining acquisition of a right to (or, as the case
may be, the retention or recovery of) benefit by taking periods of insurance
or residence into account so far as is necessary for establishing entitlement to such benefit. Article 46 is directed only towards determining the

A   amount of benefit. Therefore, the provisions of article 46 can only apply after it has first been established that there is entitlement to, in this case, invalidity benefit.

B. Observations of the Commission

The Commission, in its observations, points out that the United Kingdom legislation is of Type A, while that of the Federal Republic of
B   Germany is of Type B. Accordingly article 40 (1) of Regulation No. 1408/71 applies. Chapter 3 of the regulation, which is to be applied by analogy, states that an award in respect of a claim for benefit must be made having regard to all the legislation to which the worker has been subject. Regard needs therefore to be paid to the legislation of both the Federal Republic of Germany and the United Kingdom.
C   Article 45 in its original form referred to " insurance periods." As amended on the accession of the three new member states and by Regulation No. 2864/72 of the Council, it refers also to " periods of residence," which expression, under the provisions of article 1 (s) (a) of Regulation No. 1408/71 means periods of residence as defined or recognised as such by the legislation under which they were completed or deemed to have been completed. These amendments were made to
D   give effect to the Danish social security legislation.

Three cases decided by the court may be of assistance in answering the questions asked. In *Salvatore Murru* v. *Caisse Régionale d'Assurance Maladie de Paris* (Case 2/72) [1972] E.C.R. 33, the court held that in order to determine to what extent a period of unemployment is to be assimilated to a period of employment, regard must be had to the legis-
E   lation under which the period was accomplished. In *Golati* v. *Landesver- sicherungsanstalt Schwaben* (Case 33/75) [1975] E.C.R. 1323, Mr. Advocate-General Reischl expressed the view that the term " insurance periods " is clearly dependent on the legal system under which the periods were completed and the determining factor is whether that legal system recognises them as insurance periods. The third case is *D'Amico* (Case 20/75), referred to by the insurance officer.
F   In the view of the Commission article 51 of the Treaty does not prohibit a rule of national law which requires as a condition of entitle- ment to a social security benefit either formalities as to the manner and time of claiming the benefit or the existence of a factual situation as to previous entitlement to benefit. In *D'Amico's* case (Case 20/75) [1975] E.C.R. 891 the compatibility of a condition that the claimant should have
G   been unemployed in the member state in question was not questioned and its compatibility with Regulation No. 1408/71 was affirmed by the court.

For article 45 of the regulation to relate to legislation containing conditions of the type cited it would be sufficient that the law of the member state concerned recognised that the condition related to an in- surance period or periods of residence for account to be taken of other such periods recognised as such by one or more other member states.
H   For article 46 to apply, however, there must be entitlement to benefit, either without reference to article 45 or by virtue of it.

The Commission proposes that the questions referred by the High Court should be answered as follows.

1. The provisions of article 51 of the E.E.C. Treaty do not preclude the legislation of a member state from making the acquisition of a right to invalidity benefit conditional upon the person concerned having been entitled to sickness benefit under that legislation for a total of

168 days in the immediately preceding period, that condition being subject A
to, so far as material, (a) the completion of insurance periods, (b) the
making of a claim therefor in a prescribed manner and within a prescribed
time.

2. The provisions of articles 45 and 46 of Regulation No. 1408/71
relate to such legislation where the law of that member state recognises
such conditions as making benefit depend upon insurance periods or
periods of residence and there are such periods completed under the legis- B
lation of other member states to be taken into account.

3. Article 45 of Regulation No. 1408/71 enables such a condition to
be treated as satisfied to the extent to which the conditions are treated
as conditions making the benefit depend upon insurance periods or periods
of residence and such periods completed under the legislation of other
member states are taken into account.   C

At the hearing on September 27, 1977, the insurance officer, represented
by Mr. Woolf, and the Commission of the European Communities,
represented by its agent, Mr. Allen, presented oral submissions.

The Advocate-General delivered his opinion at the hearing on October
18, 1977.

DECISION   D

1. By order of February 15, 1977, received at the court registry on
April 12, 1977, the Queen's Bench Divisional Court referred to the
court under article 177 of the E.E.C. Treaty certain questions concerning
the interpretation of article 51 of the Treaty and of articles 40, 45 and 46
of Regulation No. 1408/71 of the Council of June 14, 1971, on the
application of social security schemes to employed persons and their   E
families moving within the Community (*Official Journal*, English Special
Edition 1971 (II), p. 416).

2. Those questions arose within the context of an action concerning the
right to the payment of an invalidity pension under British legislation of
a United Kingdom national, Mr. Kelly, who completed insurance periods
in Great Britain for the greater part of the period from 1933 to July 1971
and in the Federal Republic of Germany from July 1971 to June 1973,   F
when he fell ill.

3. The file shows that he continued to live in the Federal Republic of
Germany and received sickness benefit there from August 1973 to June
1974, since when he has received a limited invalidity pension calculated
by reference to his period of insurance in Germany.

4. Mr. Kelly also applied for an invalidity pension in Great Britain G
but his application was refused by the insurance officer, who is competent
in the first instance, on the ground that he had not been and could not
be treated as having been entitled to sickness benefit for the period of
168 days laid down by British legislation as a precondition for entitlement
to an invalidity pension.

5. The local tribunal dismissed Mr. Kelly's appeal to it from the   H
decision of the insurance officer.

6. However, the National Insurance Commissioner allowed Mr. Kelly's
appeal against the decision of the local tribunal on the ground:

" invalidity benefit is, when not reduced to nothing by the provisions
for the elimination of overlapping benefits hereinafter referred to,
payable to the claimant in accordance with the provisions of article
46 (2) of Council Regulation No. 1408/71."

A   7. However, the insurance officer applied to the Divisional Court of the Queen's Bench Division of the High Court of Justice for an order of certiorari to quash the decision of the National Insurance Commissioner.

8. As it considers that a decision on the following points is necessary in order for it to give judgment, the Divisional Court asks:

B   " Where the legislation of a member state makes the acquisition of a right to invalidity benefit conditional upon the person concerned having been entitled to sickness benefit under that legislation for a total of 168 days in the immediately preceding period that condition being subject to so far as material (a) the completion of insurance periods (b) the making of a claim therefor in a prescribed manner and within a prescribed time—(i) Do the provisions of article 51 of the Treaty of Rome preclude the application of such a condition to

C   a case to which article 40, 45 or 46 of Regulation No. 1408/71 relates? (ii) Do the provisions of (a) article 45 or (b) article 46 relate to such legislation? (iii) Do all or any of the said articles 40, 45 or 46—(a) enable such a condition to be treated as wholly or partly satisfied; or (b) require such a condition to be wholly or partly disregarded; and if so to what extent?

D   9. The questions are raised by the Divisional Court in the context of legislation under which the right to an invalidity pension is dependent upon entitlement to sickness benefit for a period of 168 days.

10. The British legislation in force at the relevant time provided that in order to gain entitlement to sickness benefit a claimant had to have paid contributions over a certain period and to have made a claim for

E   benefit in the prescribed manner and within a certain period following the materialisation of the risk.

11. It is established that Mr. Kelly had not paid contributions in Great Britain during the prescribed period and had not submitted a claim within the period laid down.

12. It appears that, under the provisions of the legislation in question,

F   even if, having paid contributions and submitted a claim, Mr. Kelly was entitled to benefit, payment would be suspended during the whole period during which he was absent from Great Britain.

13. Since the question raised makes no reference to this condition of residence the court may assume that the Divisional Court considers it sufficient for the purposes of the requirements of the British legislation on invalidity pensions that Mr. Kelly be deemed to be entitled to sickness

G   benefit for a period of 168 days, even though payment of that benefit was suspended by virtue of the operation of a residence clause.

14. Article 18 of Regulation No. 1408/71 provides:

" The competent institution of a member state whose legislation [on sickness benefits] makes the acquisition, retention or recovery of the right to benefits conditional upon the completion of insurance periods

H   shall, to the extent necessary, take account of insurance periods . . . completed under the legislation of any other member states as if they were periods completed under the legislation which it administers."

15. Therefore, for the acquisition of the right to sickness benefit under British legislation, insurance periods completed in the Federal Republic of Germany must be taken into account as if they were periods completed under British legislation.

16. However, Mr. Kelly, who at the relevant time resided in the   A
Federal Republic of Germany, was unable to receive payment of the
benefit, since article 10 of Regulation No. 1408/71, which waives residence
clauses, does not refer to sickness benefit.

17. The submission of a claim for invalidity benefit by Mr. Kelly in
the prescribed form and within the period laid down by British legislation would therefore be purposeless.

18. Article 51 of the Treaty requires the Council to adopt such   B
measures as are necessary to provide freedom of movement for workers,
providing for the aggregation, in particular for the purpose of acquiring
and retaining the right to benefit and of calculating the amount of benefit,
of all periods taken into account under the laws of the several countries.

19. According to the fifth and sixth recitals of the preamble to
Regulation No. 1408/71 of the Council: C

"the provisions for co-ordination of national social security legislations fall within the framework of freedom of movement for workers
who are nationals of member states and should, to this end, contribute
towards the improvement of their standard of living and conditions
of employment, by guaranteeing within the Community firstly equality
of treatment for all nationals of member states under the various
national legislations and secondly social security benefits for workers   D
and their dependents regardless of their place of employment or of
residence," those being objectives which "must be attained in particular by aggregation of all the periods taken into account under
the various national legislations for the purpose of acquiring and
retaining the right to benefits and of calculating the amount of
benefits, and by the provision of benefits for the various categories   E
of persons covered by the regulation regardless of their place of
residence within the Community."

20. Under the German legislation on invalidity pensions the amount
of benefit awarded is not independent of the length of the insurance
periods completed, that is, it is legislation of the type known as " Type B."

21. Article 40 of Regulation No. 1408/71 provides that a worker   F
who has been successively or alternately subject to the legislation of
two or more member states, of which at least one is not of the type
referred to in article 37 (1), that is, that known as " Type A," shall receive
invalidity benefits under the provisions of Chapter 3, which apply by
analogy.

22. Therefore, where a worker has been successively subject to the
legislation of two member states, of which at least one is of Type B,   G
the provisions of article 45 of the regulation, which form part of Chapter
3, are applicable by analogy to invalidity benefits.

23. Article 45 (1), as amended by the Act of Accession of the new
member states and by Regulation No. 2864/72 of the Council of December
19, 1972 (Official Journal, English Special Edition 1972 (December 31),
p. 15), is worded: H

"An institution of a member state whose legislation makes the
acquisition, retention or recovery of the rights to benefits conditional
upon the completion of insurance periods or periods of residence
shall take into account, to the extent necessary, insurance periods or
periods of residence completed under the legislation of any member
state as though they had been completed under the legislation which
it administers."

A   24. By virtue of that provision insurance periods completed in the Federal Republic of Germany are taken into account, to the extent necessary, for the acquisition of the right to invalidity benefits, as though they had been completed under British legislation.

25. It follows that, irrespective of the provisions of article 18 of the regulation, those insurance periods must be taken into account for the acquisition of the right to sickness benefit, in so far as the national
B   legislation in question makes the right to invalidity benefits conditional upon entitlement to sickness benefit.

26. Nevertheless, the British institution argued that, not being resident in Great Britain during the period in question, Mr. Kelly had not submitted a claim for sickness benefit in the required manner and within the specified period, which benefit, even if he was entitled to it, could not be paid to
C   him as he was residing outside Great Britain.

27. Article 36 of Regulation No. 574/72 of the Council of March 21, 1972 (*Official Journal*, English Special Edition 1972 (I), p. 159), fixing the procedure for implementing Regulation No. 1408/71 provides that in order to receive benefits under articles 40 to 51 of Regulation No. 1408/71, except in the cases referred to in article 35 of Regulation No. 574/72:

D   " the person concerned shall submit a claim to the institution of the place of residence in accordance with the procedure provided for by the legislation administered by that institution . . . A claim for benefits sent to the institution of one member state shall automatically involve the concurrent award of benefits under the legislation of all the member states in question whose conditions the claimant satisfies . . ."

E   28. That provision was laid down with the aim of simplifying administration in order to exempt migrant workers, who have rights to assert in different member states, from the requirement to lodge with the institutions in each of those states an application for the grant of the benefits which they may claim.

29. Even if it is true that that provision does not apply to sickness
F   benefit, it would be contrary to the aim of article 51 of the Treaty and to the general scheme of Regulation No. 1408/71 that a worker who has submitted a claim for invalidity benefit in accordance with that provision should have his claim refused on the ground that, at an earlier stage, he had not submitted a claim for sickness benefit to the competent institution of another member state.

G   30. Therefore, article 45 of Regulation No. 1408/71 must be understood to mean that where the legislation of a member state makes the acquisition of a right to invalidity benefit conditional upon the person concerned having been entitled to sickness benefit under that legislation for a given period in the immediately preceding period—that condition being subject to, so far as material, (a) the completion of insurance periods
H   (b) the making of a claim therefor in a prescribed manner and within a prescribed time—(i) the competent institution of the said member state shall take into account insurance periods completed under the legislation of any member state as though they had been completed under the legislation which it administers; (ii) the condition that a claim must be made in a prescribed manner and within a prescribed time shall be regarded as satisfied in so far as such a claim has been duly made in accordance with the legislation of the state of residence.

Costs   A

31. The costs incurred by the Commission, which has submitted observations to the court, are not recoverable.

32. As these proceedings are, in so far as the parties to the main action are concerned, in the nature of a step in the action pending before the national court, the decision on costs is a matter for that court.

On those grounds, the court in answer to the question referred to it by the High Court of Justice, Queen's Bench Divisional Court, by order of February 15, 1977, hereby rules: Article 45 of Regulation No. 1408/71 must be understood to mean that where the legislation of a member state makes the acquisition of a right to invalidity benefit conditional upon the person concerned having been entitled to sickness benefit under that legislation for a given period in the immediately preceding period—that condition being subject to, so far as material, (a) the completion of insurance periods (b) the making of a claim therefor in a prescribed manner and within a prescribed time—(i) the competent institution of the said member state shall take into account insurance periods completed under the legislation of any member state as though they had been completed under the legislation which it administers; (ii) the condition that a claim must be made in a prescribed manner and within a prescribed time shall be regarded as satisfied in so far as such a claim has been duly made in accordance with the legislation of the state of residence.

B

C

D

E

[CHANCERY DIVISION]

THOMAS MARSHALL (EXPORTERS) LTD. *v.* GUINLE

[1977 T. No. 2906]

1978   Feb. 13, 14; 21, 22, 23, 24;   Megarry V.-C.   F
          March 10

> *Employment — Contract of service — Repudiation — Managing director carrying on business in competition with employer after purporting to resign—Whether contract automatically determined—Court's power to restrain continuing breach of obligations under contract*
> *Confidential Information—Company director—Disclosure and use of information — Managing director's breach of fidelity and good faith to company—Whether express or implied obligation not to disclose or use information—Test of confidential information*

G

> The defendant was appointed managing director of the plaintiff company for a period of 10 years from September 2, 1972. His service agreement provided that he was not to engage in any other business without the company's consent while he was employed as managing director; that during and after his employment, he was not " to disclose " confidential information in relation to the affairs, customers or trade secrets of the company and its group; and that after

H

[Reported by IAN SLACK, ESQ., Barrister-at-Law]

A   ceasing to be managing director he was neither " to use or disclose " confidential information about the suppliers and customers of the group nor, for a period of five years, employ any person who had worked for the company during the last two years of his appointment. Without the company's knowledge, the defendant began to trade on his own account and on behalf of his two companies in competition with the company and, in doing so, he bought from the company's

B   suppliers and sold to the company's customers. Four of the company's former employees appeared to be either employed by or associated with the defendant or his companies. The defendant purported to resign as managing director on December 5, 1977, at a time when his contract had another $4\frac{1}{2}$ years to run.

    The company brought proceedings against the defendant and his companies and applied for interim injunctions to

C   restrain the defendant from (a) soliciting orders from or otherwise dealing with any customer of the company for goods of the nature sold by the company and from soliciting orders for the supply of goods of such nature from or otherwise dealing with any supplier of such goods to the company and (b) from disclosing or using any confidential information or trade secret of the company during or after his employment as managing director : —

D   *Held*, granting the application, (1) that, although a unilateral repudiation of a contract of employment usually destroyed the essential relationship of confidence and trust between a master and servant, a contract of employment was no exception to the general rule that repudiation did not automatically discharge the contract; that the defendant's repudiation did not release him from his obligations under the contract; and that, although the court was powerless to

E   force the defendant to work in accordance with his contract, the court could restrain him from committing other breaches of his obligations during the period of his contract (post, pp. 125B–E, 127E–F, 130G—131B).

    Lumley v. *Wagner* (1852) 1 De G.M. & G. 604; *William Robinson & Co. Ltd.* v. *Heuer* [1898] 2 Ch. 451, C.A. and *Warner Brothers Pictures Incorporated* v. *Nelson* [1937] 1 K.B. 209 applied.

F   *Vine* v. *National Dock Labour Board* [1956] 1 Q.B. 658, C.A.; *Denmark Productions Ltd.* v. *Boscobel Productions Ltd.* [1969] 1 Q.B. 699, C.A.; *Sanders* v. *Ernest A. Neale Ltd.* [1974] I.C.R. 565, N.I.R.C. and *Hill* v. *C. A. Parsons & Co. Ltd.* [1972] Ch. 305, C.A. considered.

    (2) That the defendant was in breach of an employee's obligation of fidelity and good faith to his employer and

G   in breach of a director's fiduciary duty to the company in dishonestly buying from the company's suppliers and selling to the company's customers on his own behalf; and that, since the company had established the basis for the grant of interlocutory relief, the court would grant an interim injunction restraining the defendant from dealing with the company's customers and suppliers until trial of the action or further order (post, pp. 132D, F—133C, 135A).

H   (3) That, although the defendant's obligation during the period of the contract was limited to a restriction on disclosing confidential information and in the context " disclosing " could not be construed as including " using," the use of the company's confidential information by the defendant for his own purposes was a breach of an employee's duty of fidelity and good faith towards his employer, and the defendant would therefore be restrained from using that information (post, pp. 134F–H, 135B–C).

    Per curiam. Four elements may be discerned which may

be of some assistance in identifying confidential information **A**
or trade secrets which the court will protect. First, the owner
must believe that the release of the information would be
injurious to him or of advantage to his rivals. Second, the
owner must believe that the information is confidential or
secret. Third, his belief under the two previous heads must
be reasonable. Fourth, the information must be judged in the
light of the usage and practices of the particular industry or
trade concerned (post, p. 136A–C).   **B**

The following cases are referred to in the judgment:

American Cyanamid Co. v. *Ethicon Ltd.* [1975] A.C. 396; [1975] 2 W.L.R.
 316; [1975] 1 All E.R. 504, H.L.(E.).
Boston Deep Sea Fishing and Ice Co. v. *Ansell* (1888) 39 Ch.D. 339, C.A.
Cable (Lord), decd., In re [1977] 1 W.L.R. 7; [1976] 3 All E.R. 417.
Chappell v. *Times Newspapers Ltd.* [1975] 1 W.L.R. 482; [1975] I.C.R. **C**
 145; [1975] 2 All E.R. 233, Megarry J. and C.A.
Coco v. *A. N. Clark (Engineers) Ltd.* [1969] R.P.C. 41.
Cook v. *Deeks* [1916] 1 A.C. 554.
Decro-Wall International S.A. v. *Practitioners in Marketing Ltd.* [1971]
 1 W.L.R. 361; [1971] 2 All E.R. 216, C.A.
Denmark Productions Ltd. v. *Boscobel Productions Ltd.* [1969] 1 Q.B.
 699; [1968] 3 W.L.R. 841; [1968] 3 All E.R. 513, C.A.   **D**
Ehrman v. *Bartholomew* [1898] 1 Ch. 671.
Hill v. *C. A. Parsons & Co. Ltd.* [1972] Ch. 305; [1971] 3 W.L.R. 995;
 [1971] 3 All E.R. 1345, C.A.
Hivac Ltd. v. *Park Royal Scientific Instruments Ltd.* [1946] Ch. 169;
 [1946] 1 All E.R. 350, C.A.
Howard v. *Pickford Tool Co. Ltd.* [1951] 1 K.B. 417, C.A.
Lumley v. *Wagner* (1852) 1 De G.M. & G. 604.   **E**
Morris (Herbert) Ltd. v. *Saxelby* [1915] 2 Ch. 57, C.A.; [1916] 1 A.C.
 688, H.L.(E.).
Printers & Finishers Ltd. v. *Holloway* [1965] 1 W.L.R. 1; [1964] 3 All
 E.R. 54; [1964] 3 All E.R. 731.
Robinson (William) & Co. Ltd. v. *Heuer* [1898] 2 Ch. 451, C.A.
Saltman Engineering Co. Ltd. v. *Campbell Engineering Co. Ltd.* (1948)
 65 R.P.C. 203; [1963] 3 All E.R. 413n.   **F**
Sanders v. *Ernest A. Neale Ltd.* [1974] I.C.R. 565; [1974] 3 All E.R. 327,
 N.I.R.C.
Suisse Atlantique Société d'Armement Maritime S.A. v. *N.V. Rotterdamsche
 Kolen Centrale* [1967] 1 A.C. 361; [1966] 2 W.L.R. 944; [1966] 2
 All E.R. 61; [1966] 1 Lloyd's Rep. 529, H.L.(E.).
Vine v. *National Dock Labour Board* [1956] 1 Q.B. 658; [1956] 2
 W.L.R. 311; [1956] 1 All E.R. 1, C.A.; [1957] A.C. 488; [1957] 2
 W.L.R. 106; [1956] 3 All E.R. 939, H.L.(E.).   **G**
Warner Brothers Pictures Incorporated v. *Nelson* [1937] 1 K.B. 209;
 [1936] 3 All E.R. 160.
Wessex Dairies Ltd. v. *Smith* [1935] 2 K.B. 80, C.A.
Whitwood Chemical Co. v. *Hardman* [1891] 2 Ch. 416, C.A.

The following additional cases were cited in argument: **H**

Esso Petroleum Co. Ltd. v. *Harper's Garage (Stourport) Ltd.* [1968] A.C.
 269; [1967] 2 W.L.R. 871; [1967] 1 All E.R. 699, H.L.(E.).
Hounslow London Borough Council v. *Twickenham Garden Developments Ltd.* [1971] Ch. 233; [1970] 3 W.L.R. 538; [1970] 3 All E.R.
 326.
Kores Manufacturing Co. Ltd. v. *Kolok Manufacturing Co. Ltd.* [1957]
 1 W.L.R. 1012; [1957] 3 All E.R. 158; [1959] Ch. 108; [1958] 2
 W.L.R. 858; [1958] 2 All E.R. 65, C.A.

A   *Littlewoods Organisation Ltd.* v. *Harris* [1977] 1 W.L.R. 1472; [1978] 1
          All E.R. 1026, C.A.
       Seager v. *Copydex Ltd.* [1967] 1 W.L.R. 923; [1967] 2 All E.R. 415, C.A.
       White and Carter (Councils) Ltd. v. *McGregor* [1962] A.C. 413; [1962] 2
          W.L.R. 17; [1961] 3 All E.R. 1178, H.L.(Sc.).

       SUMMONS

B   The plaintiff company, Thomas Marshall (Exports) Ltd., who were
       dealers in textiles, were members of the Thomas Marshall Investments
       Group. They employed the defendant, Nigel Edgar Bertrand John Guinle,
       as managing director and joint chairman. The service agreement, dated
       September 29, 1972, contained clauses the purpose of which was to prevent
       disclosure of confidential information obtained by the defendant while he
   C   was in the service of the company relating to the affairs, customers, or
       trade secrets of the group. While managing director, the defendant was
       not to engage, with certain exceptions, in any other business without
       the company's consent. If he ceased to be managing director he was
       to be under no restriction in relation to customers or suppliers to the
       company provided that he did not " use or disclose " any confidential
       information belonging to any of the companies in the group. On
   D   December 5, 1977, the defendant purported to resign. He contended that
       he was entitled to leave at once and to carry on business in competition
       with the company. The company sought an interlocutory order restraining
       the defendant from, inter alia, soliciting orders from or dealing with
       the company's customers or suppliers and restraining him from disclosing
       or using any confidential information or trade secret of the company either
   E   during or after his employment as managing director.

           Andrew Morritt Q.C. and *Charles Aldous* for the plaintiffs.
           Michael Hutchison Q.C., Alexander Irvine and *Anthony Blair* for the
       defendant.
                                                          Cur. adv. vult.

F   MEGARRY V.-C. This is a heavy motion. Over two dozen affidavits
       have been put before me, with exhibits to match, and much law; and it
       took a week to hear. The writ and notice of motion were issued on
       December 14, 1977. The plaintiffs are a company called Thomas Marshall
       (Exports) Ltd.: I shall call it " the company." Prior to two agreements
       made in September 1972, it was a dormant company owned by a holding
   G   company called Thomas Marshall Investments Ltd.: I shall call this
       company " Investments.' The companies in the Investments group deal
       in the import, export, manufacture and marketing of textile products,
       and especially clothing. The defendant, Mr. Nigel Edgar Bertrand John
       Guinle, had been a successful senior executive of another company with
       similar interests, and owned or controlled its whole share capital. He
       had had some five years experience in this type of business. The essence
   H   of the transaction in September 1972 was to bring the company to life
       in order to amalgamate the business of one of Investments' subsidiaries
       with the business of the defendant's company, both companies becoming
       subsidiaries of the company. The company's issued share capital was to
       be increased from £2 to £50,000, with Investments holding three-quarters
       and the defendant one-quarter. Investments (referred to as " T.M.I." in
       the contract) agreed to provide loan finance for the company up to
       £100,000 " and to such sum in excess of £100,000 as T.M.I. may from

time to time in its sole discretion decide," at 2 per cent. over bank base   A
rate. It was agreed that the parties would ensure that the aggregate
borrowing by the company and its subsidiaries from this and any other
source " shall not exceed £100,000 unless otherwise agreed." The agreement which carried out these arrangements was made on September 28,
1972. It contained many detailed provisions, but I do not think that I
need refer to any more.

The next day, September 29, 1972, a service agreement was entered   B
into between the company and the defendant; and this is at the heart of
the case. By this agreement, the defendant was appointed managing
director and joint chairman of the company; and as managing director
he was to have

> " the sole management and control of the day to day running of the
> company's business subject to any directions or directives of the   C
> board of directors of the company on matters of policy for the benefit
> of the company."

The other joint chairman was a Mr. Parr, the chairman of Investments,
and it was he who took the chair at directors' meetings of the company.

The service agreement contained two important provisions relating to
duration and remuneration. First, the defendant's appointment was for   D
10 years from September 2, 1972; and it was further provided in effect
that unless he gave the company notice at least two years before the end
of the 10 years, the appointment would be extended for a second 10
years after the first 10. Second, the defendant's remuneration was not
to be a salary, but was to be a commission of 20 per cent. of the aggregate
net profits of the company and its subsidiaries before tax. The defendant   E
says that he asked for a 10-year contract so as to provide security within
the group, and that he asked to be paid by commission only as he
knew full well that within two years he would be able to build up a
substantial business. The service agreement contained no provision for
varying the terms as to remuneration or for shortening the period of
employment, save that the company reserved the right of summary dismissal for serious breaches of obligation, and so on, and the right to   F
give three months notice of determination for prolonged incapacity. These
and other provisions of the agreement are spelled out in some detail; I
merely give the broad effect.

The service agreement required the defendant to manage and control
the day to day running of the company's business " and for such purposes
to devote the whole of his time and attention to the duties of his office."
It also contains three provisions, most of which I must set out verbatim.   G
The first applies both during the period of his appointment and after its
termination, the second only during the period of his employment, and
the third only when his employment has ceased. The first is clause F.7.:

> " Not at any time during the period of his appointment or after the
> termination thereof to disclose any confidential information relating
> to the affairs customers or trade secrets of the group of which he   H
> shall become possessed whilst in the service of the company under
> this or any other agreement."

The second provision is clause J.1.:

> " During the period of his appointment the managing director shall
> not save with the consent in writing of the company be directly or
> indirectly engaged concerned or interested in any other business save

The Weekly Law Reports, July 7, 1978

121

3 W.L.R.   Thomas Marshall Ltd. v. Guinle (Ch.D.)   Megarry V.-C.

A   that of the company provided that nothing herein contained shall prohibit the managing director from: (a) Retaining his present interests in the business of commodity broking but so that any activities in relation to such business are carried on by the managing director outside normal business hours; (b) Taking a financial interest in any business which does not compete with the company but without devoting any time and attention to any such business;
B   (c) Holding either directly or indirectly through nominees or otherwise investments in any public company."

The third provision is clause J.2.:

"If the managing director shall cease for any reason to be managing director of the company or of any of its subsidiaries he shall be
C   under no restriction in relation to any person firm or company who was or were customers of or suppliers to the company or any of its subsidiaries any rule of law to the contrary notwithstanding provided that he does not use or disclose any confidential information belonging to any companies in the Thomas Marshall Investments Group, nor within five years employ any person employed by the company during the last two years of his appointment."

D
For a while all went well. The defendant's commission for the first six months (to April 1973) was £2,145. For the next four complete years it was a little under £4,500, a little under £6,500, nearly £25,000, and then a little over £21,000. But then there was a transformation: for the year ending next April his commission will probably be little or nothing. Two connected matters appear to have contributed substantially but not
E   exclusively to this change. First, the defendant, as managing director, engaged a Mr. Chalmers in 1975 to develop business in the Far East. Mr. Chalmers had soon overbought speculative stock to a value of some £400,000. After various discussions he was retained (Mr. Parr asserts that until November 1976 the defendant concealed the size of the overbuying from the board); but again he overbought, and in March 1977 he
F   left without warning. Litigation between the company and Mr. Chalmers is pending.

This overbuying caused severe cash problems for the company. After discussions, Investments agreed to make further money available for the company, over and above the agreed £100,000, but only on terms. These terms, as set out in a letter dated April 14, 1975, and agreed at a board meeting on June 4, 1975, were that a further £300,000 should be made
G   available to the company. This was to be done by Investments guaranteeing the company's bank overdraft, at no additional cost to the company for the first £100,000, but at a surcharge payable to Investments of $7\frac{1}{2}$ per cent. on the next £50,000, 10 per cent. on the next £50,000, and $12\frac{1}{2}$ per cent. on the final £50,000. Letters of credit were, however, to be free of any surcharge. The figures are far from clear: I never received
H   an intelligible explanation of the defendant's figures in the second exhibit to his affidavit sworn on January 5, 1978. But there is no doubt about his complaint. It is that it is the surcharge which has prevented him from receiving the commission which he thinks that he ought to receive.

I turn to the company's business. This largely consists of purchasing clothing from manufacturers in Eastern Europe (particularly Romania and Hungary), and latterly in the Far East as well (especially South Korea), and selling that clothing to large concerns in the United Kingdom, especially the British Mail Order Co. and C. & A. Modes. The sales to these two concerns is of the order of over £2 million a year. An important part of the business was conducted by the defendant travelling to these countries, sometimes accompanied and sometimes alone, in order to arrange and monitor orders. Eastern Europe differs from the Far East in that there are state monopolies in the former as contrasted with large numbers of competing concerns in the latter. Timing is also important. The turn of the year is the time for co-ordinating orders from foreign suppliers with orders from customers in the United Kingdom, in time for the mail order catalogues in the following autumn; and much depends upon selling a high proportion of the goods ordered as promptly as possible, so as to minimise cash flow and other problems. There is a further consideration. In Eastern Europe, trade of the nature with which the company is concerned is subject to a quota system, with the foreign government allocating the permitted quota each year as it thinks best. There is an understandable tendency for the company which gets a particular share of the quota one year to get it repeated the next year, and so on.

It is against that background that the events of the second half of 1977 must be seen. At some time in November the company began to hear rumours that the defendant was going to leave the company and start up in competition with the company. On December 5, 1977, Mr. Parr and the defendant met; and the defendant then handed to Mr. Parr a signed letter by which he purported to resign that day as managing director, chairman and director of the company. The defendant contended that he was entitled to leave at once, his service agreement notwithstanding, and that he was entitled to carry on business in competition with the company. There was a board meeting on December 13, at which the defendant was told that if the only reason behind his resignation was the financial difficulties resulting from the fall in his commission, the company would change his basis of remuneration from commission only to a fixed salary plus commission; and the company also offered help if there was any question of repaying borrowed money. In an affidavit sworn three days later (and so two days after the writ was issued) Mr. Parr said that until trial of the action or termination of the service agreement the company would pay the defendant £10,000 a year, to be non-repayable but to be debited against his commission, if he would resume fully his duties and responsibilities to the company. All was to no avail: the defendant was adamant about leaving. The company, on the other hand, has made it plain throughout that the service agreement remains in being despite the defendant's acts; and although the company was willing to consider working towards an orderly termination of the agreement, the defendant would have none of it.

At that time the company knew far less of the defendant's activities than is now known. It has become clear that for many months before December 5, 1977, the defendant, while ostensibly engaged on the business of the company, had been arranging purchases and sales of the type of goods in which the company dealt not on behalf of the company but on behalf of himself and two companies of his. Rindalbourne Ltd. was formed in January 1977; and the defendant says that he acquired control of Lakepoint Tailoring Ltd. in July 1977. He bought goods from the company's suppliers and sold goods to the company's customers: but none of the profits from any of these transactions would go to the company. In addition, four employees of the company have left the

The Weekly Law Reports, July 7, 1978

123

3 W.L.R.   Thomas Marshall Ltd. v. Guinle (Ch.D.)   Megarry V.-C.

A company's employment and appear to be employed by or associated with the defendant or his companies. In those circumstances, the writ, which was originally issued only against the defendant, has been amended so as to add as defendants the two companies and the four former employees of the company that I have mentioned, claiming various forms of injunctions and damages.

B On this motion the only relief claimed by the company is, in its amended form, an interlocutory order restraining the defendant in two respects, namely, from:

"(a) Soliciting orders from or otherwise dealing with any customer of the plaintiffs for any goods of the nature sold by the plaintiffs (including men's suits) and from soliciting orders for the supply of goods of such nature from or otherwise dealing with any supplier of
C such goods to the plaintiffs. (b) Disclosing or using any confidential information or trade secret of the plaintiffs either during or after the termination of his employment as managing director of the plaintiffs under a service agreement made between himself and the plaintiffs dated September 29, 1972."

For brevity, I may call these the "soliciting order" and the "breach of
D confidence order" respectively. In this motion I say what I say solely in relation to the defendant, who is alone the subject of this motion; I make no fiindings against the other six defendants, who are not at present before me.

I do not think I need recount all the interlocutory steps that had been taken before this motion came on for hearing before me. I should,
E however, mention an order made by Whitford J. on January 13, 1978. The order was made on an ex parte application by the company, though only after counsel for all the defendants (except Lakepoint Tailoring Ltd., which had not then been joined) had addressed the court. To put it shortly, the order required the defendant within seven days after the service of the order to disclose to the company full particulars of all negotiations and contracts for the supply or sale of goods during the
F preceding three months with which he had been concerned. It also restrained the defendant, until further order, in much the same terms as the injunctions now sought against him, apart from the reference to men's suits. There were also restraints put on the other defendants that I need not mention. Under the mandatory order the defendant has given various particulars to the company. They reveal substantial transactions
G with suppliers in Romania, Poland and Korea and with customers in the United Kingdom (mainly C. & A.), the orders in each case having been placed at various dates in September 1977 onwards.

For the purposes of this motion, Mr. Hutchison, who has appeared for the defendant, has not sought to deny that the defendant committed breaches of the service contract before December 5, 1977, for which he may be liable in damages. The whole thrust of his contention has
H been that this is not a case in which any injunction should be granted against the defendant. He reaches that conclusion in various ways, but in the forefront there has been his contention that on December 5, 1977, the defendant's service agreement was brought to an end by his unilateral repudiation of it. Thereafter, he said, the defendant was bound by none of its terms save those which were expressed to apply after its termination.

Mr. Hutchison accordingly accepted that clause F.7 of the service agreement, which applied both during the appointment and "after the

termination thereof," required the defendant not "to disclose any con- A
fidential information relating to the affairs customers or trade secrets of
the group " which he acquired while in the company's service. But he said
that this merely related to disclosure and not to use: unlike the words
" use or disclose " in the first proviso to clause J.2, clause F.7 used the
single word " disclose." There was thus nothing in clause F.7 to prevent
the defendant from making any use of confidential information that he
chose, provided that he did not disclose it to any others. Provided that B
he kept the information to himself, he was free to make full use of his
knowledge of the company's suppliers and customers, and the individuals
in them with whom he could best deal, the company's costs, prices, ranges
of goods, current customers' requirements and successful and unsuccessful
purchases, and so on. Furthermore, Mr. Hutchison contended that none
of this or any other information claimed by the company to be con- C
fidential was in fact confidential, though he accepted that for some of
it the point was arguable. Subject only to that, the defendant was free
from any restraint. Clause J.1, which prohibited the defendant from being
concerned in any business except the company's, did not apply, for that
was limited to the period of his employment, and this, he said, terminated
on December 5. Clause J.2, of course, applied after December 5; but
that merely gave the defendant freedom from non-existent restrictions. It D
therefore did not matter whether the provisos were satisfied, thereby making
the main body of the clause operative, although in fact they did so, so
far as they were valid.

Throughout the argument, there was much discussion of the ambit
of injunctions that could be granted to enforce any of the provisions of
a contract of service. Mr. Hutchison contended that there was in this E
case no basis for the grant of any injunction, whereas Mr. Morritt, who
appeared for the company, contended that the case was one which plainly
justified and required the grant of the limited forms of injunction which
he sought. The case is not one, of course, in which the company seeks
to restrain the defendant from engaging in any competing work, but one
in which the company merely seeks restraints in terms of what I have
called the soliciting order and the breach of confidence order. Mr. Morritt F
made it explicit that he did not seek to restrain the defendant from carrying out any contracts that he had made for himself and his companies
before January 13, 1978, when Whitford J. made his order.

Before I turn to consider the rival contentions, I should say that on all
hands it was accepted and asserted that what mattered most to the
parties was the outcome of this motion. This was not a case in which G
either side would be content with some stop-gap order pending the trial
of the action. That trial must of necessity be some way off, and in the
meantime both the company and the defendant were closely and immediately affected by whether or not the injunctions sought by the company
should be granted. The company's business, which has already been
gravely affected by the defendant's acts, will be still further injured if
the injunctions are refused, while the defendant's activities will be greatly H
hampered if the injunctions are granted; and as I have mentioned, this
is an important time of the year for this type of business. Accordingly,
although the decision of the House of Lords in *American Cyanamid Co.*
v. *Ethicon Ltd.* [1975] A.C. 396 had as one of its objects the shortening
of applications for interlocutory injunctions, it seemed to me that this was
a case of a type which justified the full argument that has been put before
me, and so I did not attempt to curtail it. Without departing from either

The Weekly Law Reports, July 7, 1978

125

3 W.L.R.   Thomas Marshall Ltd. v. Guinle (Ch.D.)   Megarry V.-C.

A   the letter or the spirit of the *Cyanamid* case, it seemed to me that there still remain some cases, such as this, in which both justice and the needs of the parties justify the type of interlocutory hearing that was more common before that decision.   At the same time, although both the hearing and what I say in this judgment may be more ample than is strictly necessary under that decision, the actual result must still be governed by the principles which it laid down.

B   I shall take first Mr. Hutchison's submission that the defendant's service agreement was terminated by his unilateral repudiation of it on December 5, 1977, even though the company never accepted it as ending the agreement.   This is a striking contention.   It means that although the defendant and the company contractually bound themselves together for ten years from September 2, 1972, so that the agreement still has over $4\frac{1}{2}$ years to

C   run, the defendant, and also the company, was able at any time, without the consent of the other, to bring the contract to an end simply by saying so; and that is just what the defendant has done.   Mr. Hutchison accepted that the general rule was that a contract was not determined merely by the wrongful repudiation of it by one party, and that it was for the innocent party to decide whether to treat the contract as having determined or as continuing in existence.   That rule, however, did not apply to

D   contracts of employment, for they were subject to a special exception. Under the exception, any contract of employment could at any time be brought to an end by either party repudiating it.   This exception, however, was itself subject to an exception, and that was where despite the repudiation the mutual confidence between the parties remained unimpaired.   In that exceptional case the normal rule for contracts still applied,

E   and the contract remained in being unless the innocent party elected to treat the repudiation as terminating it.

        In support of his proposition, Mr. Hutchison cited a number of authorities.   He accepted that none of them was a decision on a repudiation by a servant: all were cases of repudiation by the employer, as where he had dismissed the servant.   But the same rule, he said, must apply to repudiation by the servant.   I do not propose to go into the

F   cases in any great detail; but I must say something about most of them. The starting point seems to be in the judgment of Jenkins L.J. in *Vine* v. *National Dock Labour Board* [1956] 1 Q.B. 658, 674.   There Jenkins L.J. said:

G   ". . . in the ordinary case of master and servant the repudiation or the wrongful dismissal puts an end to the contract, and the contract having been wrongfully put an end to a claim for damages arises. It is necessarily a claim for damages and nothing more.   The nature of the bargain is such that it can be nothing more."

The case was not one of master and servant, but one of a statutory scheme for dock workers, and the question that was being considered was whether a declaration should be granted.   This was a point on which

H   Jenkins L.J. was dissenting, so that the dictum was plainly not of the ratio.   However, on appeal Viscount Kilmuir L.C. said that in the ordinary master and servant case " if the master wrongfully dismisses the servant, either summarily or by giving insufficient notice, the employment is effectively terminated, albeit in breach of contract ": see *Vine* v. *National Dock Labour Board* [1957] A.C. 488, 500.   That puts it a little differently. In *Denmark Productions Ltd.* v. *Boscobel Productions Ltd.* [1969] 1 Q.B. 699 the plaintiff was a joint manager of a pop group.   Both Salmon

and Harman L.JJ. observed at pp. 726, 737, that if a man employed under **A**
a contract of personal service was dismissed, it was clear that he could
not treat the contract as still subsisting and claim remuneration or an
account of profits under it, but must sue for damages for the wrongful
dismissal which had prevented him from earning under the contract.

I turn to *Hill* v. *C. A. Parsons & Co. Ltd.* [1972] Ch. 305. There,
the employer had reluctantly given the servant notice dismissing him
because he had refused to join a trade union. The notice was shorter **B**
than the contract of service required, and the servant refused to accept
that the contract of employment had terminated; the impending coming
into force of a statute would assist him if his contract was still subsisting.
By a majority, the Court of Appeal held that the contract still subsisted.
Lord Denning M.R. said, at p. 313, that " a notice which is too short
does not terminate a contract of employment," and then went on to say, **C**
at p. 314, that if the master insists on the employment terminating on
the named day, in the ordinary course of things " the relationship of
master and servant thereupon comes to an end: for it is inconsistent
with the confidential nature of the relationship." He then proceeded to
emphasise that this was the rule in the ordinary course of things, though
it was not inflexible; there were exceptions, and the case before him was
one of those exceptions. On this view, the case was an exception to an **D**
exception from the general rule for contracts.

Sachs L.J. put it differently. He rejected the contention that a wrongful
repudiation of a contract of service terminated the contract, irrespective
of whether the innocent party accepted it, and said that he was convinced
that this contention was wrong: pp. 318, 319. On this basis he went on
to agree with Lord Denning M.R. in holding that on the facts of the **E**
case an interlocutory injunction restraining the employer from implementing the notice of dismissal should be granted. That injunction was, of
course, very different from the injunction sought in this case. Stamp L.J.,
who dissented, assumed, without expressing an opinion, that the contract
still subsisted, the servant not having accepted the repudiation. His
dissent was in the main directed to the propriety of granting an injunction
of the width there is in question. **F**

Next, there is *Sanders* v. *Ernest A. Neale Ltd.* [1974] I.C.R. 565, a
decision of the National Industrial Relations Court. There, Sir John
Donaldson P. held that only in very exceptional cases could a wrongful
dismissal leave the contract of employment in existence, as where the
relationship of mutual confidence between the parties remained intact.
He said, at p. 571: **G**

" . . . the repudiation of a contract of employment is an exception to
the general rule. It terminates the contract without the necessity for
acceptance by the injured party."

This, I think, is the high-water-mark of what may be called the doctrine
of automatic determination, making it explicit that the contract is at an
end. Mr. Hutchison also relied on *Chappell* v. *Times Newspapers Ltd.* **H**
[1975] 1 W.L.R. 482. I do not think that he found anything in my
judgment to help him; but he pointed out that on appeal Lord Denning
M.R. referred to *Hill* v. *C. A. Parsons & Co. Ltd.* [1972] Ch. 305 as
an exceptional case in which the parties had complete confidence in each
other. Stephenson L.J. spoke of it in a similar way, and agreed with
Sir John Donaldson's description of it in *Sanders* v. *Ernest A. Neale Ltd.*
[1974] I.C.R. 565, 571, as being " unusual, if not unique."

The Weekly Law Reports, July 7, 1978

127

3 W.L.R.   Thomas Marshall Ltd. v. Guinle (Ch.D.)   Megarry V.-C.

A   Mr. Hutchison also considered *Decro-Wall International S.A.* v. *Practitioners in Marketing Ltd.* [1971] 1 W.L.R. 361, which was against him; and he was concerned to emphasise, as is plainly the fact, that it was not a master and servant case, but a case on commercial dealings between two companies. However, the question arose whether a repudiation of a contract determined it forthwith; and this gave rise to a number of dicta on contracts of service. Salmon L.J. said, at p. 370: " I doubt

B whether, in law, a contract of service can be unilaterally determined by the master's breach " ; but he continued by pointing out that the servant, who would have a claim for damages as his only money remedy, would have to take steps to minimise his loss, and so usually he would be far better off if he treated the contract as being at an end. Sachs L.J. expressed similar views at pp. 375, 376. He favoured the view that

C contracts of personal service were not an exception to the rule that, faced with a repudiation, the innocent party has an election, but that in practice that party was usually obliged to accept the repudiation as terminating the contract, since it was of no benefit to him to keep the contract alive. What was limited in such cases was not the right to elect, but the range of remedies available to the innocent party. Buckley L.J. went little further than saying that " it may be " that contracts of service between

D master and servant " should be " regarded as an exception to the general rule that repudiation does not itself discharge a contract, so that the servant's cause of action arose immediately on the breach: see p. 381. Mr. Hutchison said that it was clear that what Salmon L.J. and Sachs L.J. had said on the point was obiter (as indeed it was) and contrary to authority (which I doubt). The decision was, of course, duly cited in

E *Hill* v. *C. A. Parsons & Co. Ltd.* [1972] Ch. 305, and what Sachs L.J. said there represented a hardening of the tentative views that he had expressed in the earlier case.

At least one thing is plain, and that is that the authorities on the point are in a far from satisfactory state. Let me say at the outset that I have great difficulty in accepting the view that contracts of employment are an exception to the general rule for repudiation, and that they

F are terminated forthwith by the repudiation, whether or not the innocent party elects to accept it as doing this. Indeed, Mr. Hutchison was unable to contend that such a doctrine was right, and in order to make his proposition viable he had to narrow it to a substantial degree. Let me attempt to summarise the matter.

First, there will usually be a wide range of acts and omissions which

G will constitute a repudiation of a contract, whether for service or otherwise. In addition to an outright refusal to perform the contract, there are many other acts and omissions which can amount to a repudiation which will entitle the innocent party to treat the contract as being at an end. Such acts or omissions may consist either of a fundamental breach of the contract or the breach of a fundamental term of it: I adopt the dis-

H tinction made by Lord Upjohn in *Suisse Atlantique Société d'Armement Maritime S.A.* v. *N.V. Rotterdamsche Kolen Centrale* [1967] 1 A.C. 361, 421, 422. If cases of master and servant are an exception from the rule that an unaccepted repudiation works no determination of the contract, and instead are subject to what I have called the doctrine of automatic determination, the result would be that many a contract of employment would be determined forthwith upon the commission of a fundamental breach, or a breach of a fundamental term, even though the commission

128

of this breach was unknown to the innocent party, and even if, had he   **A**
known, he would have elected to keep the contract in being.

That would indeed be a remarkable result. I may take as an example
a case that was not cited during argument, *Boston Deep Sea Fishing and
Ice Co.* v. *Ansell* (1888) 39 Ch.D. 339. That case, like this, concerned
a managing director who was faithless to his company. He took a secret
commission, but before he was discovered the company dismissed him;
and this was before his five years' contract had run very long. It was   **B**
held that when the company discovered his fraudulent conduct the
company could sustain his dismissal on that ground. Bowen L.J. pointed
out, at p. 365, that the determination of the contract by the company
could be looked at in two ways. One way was to regard it as the
exercise by the company of its contractual right to dismiss a servant
guilty of a breach of his implied condition to render faithful service. The   **C**
other way was to treat the act as being a wrongful repudiation of the
contract by the managing director which, being accepted by the company,
determined the contract. This determination, it will be observed, occurs
not on the date when the repudiatory act is done, but " from the time
the party who is sinned against elects to treat the wrongful act of the
other as a breach of the contract." It will be obvious how ill the views
of Bowen L.J. accord with the idea that " the repudiation of a contract of   **D**
employment . . . terminates the contract without the necessity for acceptance by the injured party."

In order to avoid difficulties such as these, Mr. Hutchison reformulated
the doctrine of automatic determination. He said that in master and
servant cases a breach of contract amounting to a repudiation did not
forthwith determine the contract unless the party breaking the contract   **E**
intended to bring the contract to an end. This, of course, is a very
substantial narrowing of the doctrine as stated in the cases. It also
emphasises the shift in intention. Whereas for contracts in general it is
the innocent party who decides whether the contract continues or is at
an end, for master and servant it is the guilty party who has the choice,
or at least the initial choice; for presumably if the wrongdoer sought to
keep the contract alive, the innocent party would then be able to elect   **F**
nevertheless to treat it as having come to an end.

It is plain that some such narrowing and reformulation of the doctrine
is necessary if absurd results are to be avoided. It is also plain that
nothing in the cases which have been put before me point to such a
reformulation. It also produces a result which seems to me to be far
from just. Why should a person who makes a contract of service have   **G**
the right at any moment to put an end to his contractual obligations? No
doubt the court will not decree specific performance of the contract, nor
will it grant an injunction which will have the effect of an order for
specific performance: but why should the limitation of the range of
remedies for the breach invade the substance of the contract? Why
should it deprive the innocent party of any right to elect how to treat
the breach, except, perhaps, in remainder and subject to the wrongdoer's   **H**
prior right of election?

Second, it is difficult, if not impossible, to reconcile the doctrine of
automatic determination with a number of authorities which, for the
most part, do not appear to have been cited in any of the cases that I
have mentioned. I need say no more about the *Boston* case, but I must
refer to some others. Johanna Wagner contracted to sing for a period
for Benjamin Lumley, and not to sing for anyone else. She then agreed

The Weekly Law Reports, July 7, 1978

129

3 W.L.R.   Thomas Marshall Ltd. v. Guinle (Ch.D.)   Megarry V.-C.

A   to sing for someone else for a larger sum, but Lord St. Leonards L.C. granted an injunction to restrain her from doing so: *Lumley* v. *Wagner* (1852) 1 De G.M. & G. 604. A company engaged a confidential clerk named Heuer for five years, the clerk agreeing to devote his whole time to the company's service and not during his engagement to engage as principal or servant in any business relating to goods of any description sold or made by the company. After some three years Heuer left and

B   became employed by other manufacturers in the same line of business as the company. The Court of Appeal held that the company was entitled to an interlocutory injunction restraining Heuer from carrying on or being engaged in a business relating to goods of a description sold or made by the company: *William Robinson & Co. Ltd.* v. *Heuer* [1898] 2 Ch. 451. Bette Davis, the film actress, entered into a contract with a film

C   company for a period, agreeing to render her exclusive services as an actress to that company, and not during that period to render any services for any other stage or motion picture production or business. During the period of the contract the actress refused to be bound by it, and contracted with a third person to appear as a film artist. At the trial of the action Branson J. granted an injunction which restrained the actress from rendering services in any motion picture or stage production

D   for anyone save the film company: *Warner Brothers Pictures Incorporated* v. *Nelson* [1937] 1 K.B. 209. Not surprisingly, Mr. Hutchison was obliged to contend that the last two cases were both wrongly decided; and the same would seem to apply to the first of the three.

    To these three cases I may add one where the injunction was refused: *Ehrman* v. *Bartholomew* [1898] 1 Ch. 671. That was a case of a

E   traveller for a firm of wine merchants who was employed for 10 years under a contract to devote the whole of his time during usual business hours to the business of the firm, and not to employ himself in any other business or transact any business with or for any other person. Within a year the traveller had left the firm and had entered the service of other wine merchants. On motion, Romer J. refused the firm an injunction which would restrain the traveller from engaging or employing

F   himself in any other business. This was on the ground that the restriction was too wide, since it extended to all businesses and not merely to special services as in *Lumley* v. *Wagner*, 1 De G.M. & G. 604.

    Apart from the citation of *Lumley* v. *Wagner* in *Hill* v. *C. A. Parsons & Co. Ltd.* [1972] Ch. 305 (see pp. 315, 322, 324), none of these authorities seem to have been considered in any of the recent cases on

G   automatic determination that I have mentioned. Yet if the doctrine of automatic determination is good law, all that Johanna Wagner, Heuer and Bette Davis had to do was to say that their contracts were at an end, and so they were free from the restrictions that they imposed while their employment continued. The claims to an injunction would thus have failed instead of succeeding. Sir William Jowitt K.C. and Mr. J. D. Cassels K.C., who appeared for Bette Davis, ought to have won instead

H   of losing. Nor need the wine traveller have had to base his contentions on the width of the restrictions. I realise, of course, that in his dissenting judgment in *Hill* v. *C. A. Parsons & Co. Ltd.* at pp. 322, 323, 325, Stamp L.J. referred to *Lumley* v. *Wagner* as being "a much criticised decision," and spoke of the "sure and safe guide" propounded by Lindley L.J. in *Whitwood Chemical Co.* v. *Hardman* [1891] 2 Ch. 416, 426–428. At the same time I have to remember that at p. 427 Lindley L.J. accepted *Lumley* v. *Wagner* as having "more or less definitely" laid down that

where there was an express negative prohibition (which was lacking in   A
the case before him) the court could enforce it by injunction. That, of
course, was exactly what Sir Nathaniel Lindley—by then Master of the
Rolls—did some seven years later in *William Robinson & Co. Ltd.* v.
Heuer [1898] 2 Ch. 451. As I have mentioned, Stamp L.J. was considering a very different type of injunction; to restrain an employer from
acting on a notice dismissing a servant is far removed from restraining
the servant from acting in breach of his obligations to the employer.   B

There is one other case that I should refer to, although it was not
mentioned in argument. That is *Howard* v. *Pickford Tool Co. Ltd.*
[1951] 1 K.B. 417. This was cited in *Hill* v. *C. A. Parsons & Co. Ltd.*
[1972] Ch. 305 (though only in argument), but was not cited in any
of the other automatic determination cases. There, a company contracted to employ the plaintiff as managing director for six years. Within   C
six months the plaintiff, while continuing to act as managing director,
brought proceedings against the company. In these, he claimed that the
conduct of the chairman was such as to show that the company no
longer intended to be bound by the contract; and he sought a declaration
that the company had repudiated the contract, and that it no longer
bound him. On the full doctrine of automatic determination, the
chairman's conduct, if established, determined the contract. On the   D
watered-down version, it determined the contract if the company intended
it to do this. What happened in fact was that the Court of Appeal
struck out the statement of claim. At p. 421 Sir Raymond Evershed
M.R. said that as the plaintiff had not accepted the repudiation but had
gone on performing his part of the contract, " the alleged act of repudiation
is wholly nugatory and ineffective in law." On the same page Asquith   E
L.J. said that " an unaccepted repudiation is a thing writ in water and
of no value to anybody: it confers no legal rights of any sort or kind."
It seems to me to be quite impossible to add the gloss " except in master
and servant cases, where an unaccepted repudiation is etched in granite
and is beautiful to the repudiator "; for the case was itself a master and
servant case. Yet some gloss of this sort seems to be required if any
doctrine of automatic determination is good law.   F

Quite apart from that case, there is the question whether I am required
to treat the *Lumley* v. *Wagner* line of authorities, which include a decision
of the Court of Appeal, as having been overturned sub silentio in the
automatic determination cases. I do not think that I can be. Those cases
speak in a voice which is far from clear; and of the conflicting dicta,
there seems to me to be great force in what was said in the *Decro-Wall*   G
case, and by Sachs L.J. in *Hill* v. *C. A. Parsons & Co. Ltd.* I can see no
ratio decidendi in any of the automatic determination cases which is
necessarily inconsistent with the ratio decidendi in any of the *Lumley* v.
Wagner line of cases. Further, none of the automatic determination cases
have had to deal with the question whether, by unilaterally refusing to
serve, the servant can thereby release himself not merely from any further
obligation to serve but also from any restrictions, whether imposed by his   H
contract or implied by law, which apply only while the contract of service
exists. Furthermore, I think the courts must beware of allowing a
restriction of the range of remedies which it is proper to grant to destroy
or unduly impair the rights of the parties.

Above all, I think the courts must be astute to prevent a wrongdoer
from profiting too greatly from his wrong. If without just cause a servant
who has contracted to serve for a term of years refuses to do so, it is

The Weekly Law Reports, July 7, 1978

131

3 W.L.R.   Thomas Marshall Ltd. v. Guinle (Ch.D.)   Megarry V.-C.

A easy to see that the court is powerless to make him do what he has contracted to do: neither by decreeing specific performance nor by granting an injunction can the court make the servant perform loyally what he is refusing to do, however wrongfully. If such an order were to be made, the ultimate sanction for disobedience is committal to prison; and this, far from forcing the servant to work for his master, would effectively stop him from doing this. But why should the court's inability to make a
B servant work for his employer mean that as soon as the servant refuses to do so the court is forthwith disabled from restraining him from commiting any breach, however flagrant, of his other obligations during the period of his contract? I would wholly reject the doctrine of automatic determination, whether in its wide form or in its narrowed version.

I accept, of course, that there are difficulties in almost any view that
C one takes. To say that a contract of service remains in existence despite the servant's resolute refusal to do any work under it produces odd results. Here, however, I am concerned only with the issue whether the servant's wrongful refusal to serve has set him free of the obligations which bound him while his contract of service continued. Furthermore, since what is before me is a mere motion for an interlocutory injunction, strictly speaking all that I have to do before I turn to consider the
D balance of convenience is to see whether there is a serious question to be tried, and whether the company has any real prospect of succeeding at the trial: see *In re Lord Cable, decd.* [1977] 1 W.L.R. 7, 19. To these questions I would answer with an unhesitating Yes. But, as I have mentioned, the interlocutory stage is so important to both parties that I have examined the authorities in some detail, and I think it right, for
E their assistance, to express my views more fully. I may summarise them as follows. First, in my judgment the service agreement between the parties has not been determined but remains still in force. Second, the defendant is subject to all the obligations that flow from his being bound by the service agreement. Third, as the service agreement is still in force, clause J.2, which provides for the defendant to be free from restrictions when he ceases to be managing director, has not come into operation,
F and that is so whether or not the two provisos are satisfied. Fourth, there is ample jurisdiction in the court to grant an injunction to restrain the defendant from doing acts contrary to his obligations under the service agreement, subject always to the exercise of the court's discretion whether to grant an injunction at all, and, if so, in what width.

The next question is that of the restrictions to which the defendant
G is subject. Mr. Morritt relied upon three heads. First, he relied upon the implied duty of a servant to serve his employer with fidelity and in good faith. The existence of this duty depends upon whether the service agreement is, as I have held, still in being and binding on the defendant. Second, he relied upon the fiduciary duty of a director of a company to apply the company's property for the benefit of the company and not of himself. This, said Mr. Morritt, was not dependent upon the continued
H existence of the service agreement, since a director who breaks his obligations under this head remains accountable until the duty is discharged. Third, Mr. Morritt relied on clause F.7 of the service agreement, requiring the defendant not to disclose confidential information. As in terms this applies both during the period of the defendant's appointment and after its termination, it too does not depend upon the service agreement remaining in force. I will take these heads in turn.

First, then, there is the servant's implied duty of fidelity and good

faith. For this, Mr. Morritt cited two decisions of the Court of Appeal, **A**
Wessex Dairies Ltd. v. *Smith* [1935] 2 K.B. 80 and *Hivac Ltd.* v. *Park
Royal Scientific Instruments Ltd.* [1946] Ch. 169. In the *Wessex* case, a
milk roundsman employed by a company solicited the company's customers
to transfer their custom to him when he ceased to be employed by the
company. The Court of Appeal held that, apart from any express term
of his employment, to do this was a breach of the servant's implied
obligation to serve his master with good faith and fidelity, and to look   **B**
after his master's interests and not his own; and he was held liable in
damages. I need not set out the rather more complex facts of the *Hivac*
case, which related to skilled workers secretly working in their spare time
for a trade rival of their employers. I need only say that in it the
Court of Appeal reaffirmed the servant's implied duty of fidelity, and
applied it to acts done by the servant outside his hours of work for his   **C**
employer, in addition to acts done within those hours. An interlocutory
injunction was granted to restrain the rival firm from employing the
workers in question.

In the case before me acts done by the defendant in the past sound
in damages and in that respect are not before me for decision. What
I say must therefore not be taken as having determined matters for that
purpose. I am concerned only with the question whether or not an inter-   **D**
locutory injunction should now be granted. It is impossible to deny
that the defendant has been guilty of gross and repeated breaches of his
implied obligation to be faithful to the company. While still in office
as managing director of the company he travelled abroad, ostensibly on
the company's business, and without the company's knowledge placed
orders for the benefit of himself and his companies with the company's   **E**
suppliers. He also, while still managing director and without the
company's knowledge, sold goods for the benefit of himself and his
companies to customers of the company. In the *Boston* case, 39 Ch.D.
339, the receipt by the managing director of what may have been a single
secret commission was said in the Court of Appeal to be dishonest and a
fraud. I can apply no milder description to the defendant's prolonged
duplicity. His contention is that he is entitled to go on doing this, and   **F**
that the company is not entitled to any injunction restraining him from
doing it. The injunctions claimed do not seek to restrain him from
carrying on a similar business: all that is claimed is that he should not
solicit orders from the company's customers or suppliers, or otherwise
deal with them, and that he should not disclose or use any confidential
information or trade secrets of the company. Subject to what I shall   **G**
say later, particularly about confidential information, I think it clear that
injunctions to this effect ought to be granted. It was indeed said at one
stage on his behalf that an injunction ought not to be granted because that
would diminish the defendant's ability to pay damages. Such a proposition
would indeed establish a new rogue's charter: the poorer the defendant
and the more his wrongful diversion of the plaintiff's business to himself
is injuring the plaintiff, the smaller would be the prospects of obtaining   **H**
an injunction against him.

I turn to the second main head of Mr. Morritt's contention, based on
the fiduciary duty of a director of a company to apply the company's
property for the benefit of the company and not himself. For this, Mr.
Morritt cited *Cook* v. *Deeks* [1916] 1 A.C. 554. That case established
that it is a breach of duty for a company director to take for himself the
benefit of a contract which he has ostensibly been negotiating on behalf

The Weekly Law Reports, July 7, 1978

133

3 W.L.R.   **Thomas Marshall Ltd. v. Guinle (Ch.D.)**   Megarry V.-C.

A of the company whose interests he should be protecting; and if he does he will hold the benefit of the contract in trust for the company. The way in which Mr. Morritt uses this decision is to say that it was by acting as managing director of the company that the defendant had established his relationship with the suppliers and customers of the company, and that even if he ceased to be managing director of the company or to be subject to the service agreement, he could not claim
B instant freedom to use for himself the relationship which he had established on behalf of the company. Some diversion of the company's business from the company to the defendant and his companies has already occurred: but at least for the immediate future any further diversion should be restrained.

C It seems to me that the company has at least a good arguable case on this point. Applying the *Cyanamid* principles as best I can, I think that the balance of convenience, and not least the status quo existing before the defendant began the conduct of which the company complained so promptly on discovering it, point to granting a suitable injunction to enforce this duty. Certainly if damages have to be paid one way or another, on the evidence as it stands the prospects of the company being able to pay seems to me to outweigh substantially the prospects of the
D defendant being able to pay, especially in view of what has been said on his behalf. Furthermore, I think that the quantum of damages would be much harder to assess for the company than for the defendant. One matter on which Mr. Morritt understandably placed much weight was the threat that the defendant's solicitations of foreign suppliers posed to the shares of the quotas that the company had previously enjoyed. Shares
E of the quota that previously had gone to the company were now going to the defendant and his companies, leaving the company with great problems in seeking to recover for the future what had been diverted from the company.

Third, there is clause F.7 of the service agreement. The obligation of the defendant not to " disclose any confidential information relating to the affairs customers or trade secrets of the group " of which he became
F possessed while in the company's service is clear enough; and it plainly continues after the service agreement terminates. However, Mr. Hutchison contended, as I have mentioned, that this provision did not justify the injunctions claimed. He contended that the only obligation was against disclosure. The contrast in language between the single word " disclose " in this clause, and the phrase " use or disclose " in the first proviso to
G clause J.2, was striking and significant; it showed that the defendant could use the information as he wished, provided that he did not disclose it. In any case, he said, Lord Atkinson's speech in *Herbert Morris Ltd.* v. *Saxelby* [1916] 1 A.C. 688, 698, refers approvingly to words of Joyce J. which point out that an injunction against " using " information ought not to be granted unless there is a covenant not merely against divulging or communicating the information but a covenant against " using " it.
H The reference is, I think, to the judgment of Joyce J. when sitting in the Court of Appeal in the same case: see *Herbert Morris Ltd.* v. *Saxelby* [1915] 2 Ch. 57, 88. There, Joyce J. says that he supposes that an injunction against using information would include making use of it in the defendant's own mind, possibly unconsciously, without disclosing any facts to another person, and that no such injunction should be granted unless there was an express agreement which prohibited using the information.

Mr. Hutchison also relied on *Printers & Finishers Ltd.* v. *Holloway* A
[1965] 1 W.L.R. 1, a case concerning a secret printing process. The
plaintiff company employed a manager and instructed him to preserve
the secrecy of the process, but took no covenant from him to restrict him
from working for competitors when he left them. Cross J. held that in
those circumstances no injunction should be granted to restrain the
manager from using information that he had acquired while working for
the plaintiff company. The basis of this decision was that it would put B
the manager in an impossible position if, after leaving the plaintiff
company and starting to work for a rival concern, he were to be obliged
to refrain from making any use of information or skills that he had
acquired while working for the plaintiff company. This, said Mr.
Hutchison, should be applied in the case before me. If the defendant
was free to work for a rival concern, it was unrealistic to say that he C
must not use his stock of knowledge of methods of work, even if he had
acquired much of it while working for the company.

I can see much force in this. At the same time, I observe that Cross
J., at p. 6, pointed out that to recall information or skills was quite
unlike memorising a formula or a list of customers, or what was said in
confidence at a particular meeting: and he drew a distinction between
such matters on the one hand, and, on the other hand, drawing on a D
fund of knowledge and experience which the employee might well not
realise that it was improper to use. The test that I think he indicated
was whether a man of average intelligence and honesty would think that
there was anything improper in his putting his memory of the matters
in question at the disposal of his new employers. Judged by that standard, I
think it would be remarkable if a man of average intelligence and E
honesty were to think that there was nothing improper in using his
detailed knowledge of his employer's suppliers and customers for the
purpose of dealing with them in place of his employer. I do not think
think that the *Printers* case disposes of the company's claim to an
injunction in the case before me.

I return, then, to Mr. Hutchison's distinction between " disclose " and
" use or disclose." Mr. Morritt contended that the obligation in clause F
F.7 not to "disclose" any confidential information should be read as
including an obligation not to use that information: the words " or use "
ought, he said, to be implied into it. I can see no basis upon which
such an implication could be made, especially in view of the contrast with
the "use or disclose" of the first proviso to clause J.2. I think
"disclose" means what it says, and does not extend to "use." Of G
course, I can conceive of methods of use which would amount to making
a disclosure. If an employee were to use his secret knowledge in such
a way as to make it plain to others what the secret process or information
was, that might well amount to a disclosure. The mode and circumstances of use may be so ostentatious that they plainly constitute a disclosure. But apart from such cases, I do not think that a prohibition
on disclosure prevents use. It therefore seems to me that clause F.7 H
provides no basis for granting an injunction to restrain the defendant
from using confidential information or trade secrets, as distinct from disclosing them.

With that, I turn to the injunctions sought by the company. First,
there is the soliciting order, to restrain the defendant from soliciting orders
from, or otherwise dealing with, any of the company's customers for goods
of the nature of those sold by the company, and from soliciting orders

A for the supply of such goods from, or otherwise dealing with, any of the company's suppliers. From what I have said it can be seen that in my judgment the implied duty of fidelity and good faith plainly warrants the grant of an injunction in such terms. I feel less certain about the claim based on the duty of a director, based on *Cook* v. *Deeks,* but on the whole I think that this too suffices to support the soliciting order. The third head, clause F.7, does not apply to this order. I think that the

B evidence sufficiently supports the insertion of the words " (including men's suits) " after " sold by the plaintiffs."

Second, there is the breach of confidence order. This, in its wide form, restraining the disclosure or use of confidential information or trade secrets, seems to me to be fully supported by the implied duty of fidelity and good faith. On the other hand, I would hesitate to base it on *Cook*

C v. *Deeks,* although it may be that the duty under this head extends not only to taking the benefit of negotiations but also to a misuse of confidences or secrets. That, I think, would have to be examined more fully before I would rest a decision on it. On the other hand, clause F.7 fully supports the breach of confidence order so far as disclosing is concerned, but not as to using.

D I think questions might well arise as to the proper duration of any injunctions in the terms of those sought. However, as this is a motion, and so any injunction will be granted only until trial of the action or further order, any question of duration can be raised on a motion to vary or discharge the order I will therefore not pursue this point now.

There remains the question of the meaning of " confidential information or trade secret." It seems to me to be desirable, if no more, that

E the parties should have a clearer indication of what must not be disclosed or used than is conveyed by the use of these bare terms. The matter was much debated in argument. The defendant was at something of a disadvantage as to evidence because his affidavit on the point was not ready until Mr. Morritt had closed his case, and I refused to admit it at that stage. Indeed, the defendant was at something of a disadvantage generally, because some while after the notice of motion was issued he

F changed his advisers, and then sought, late in the day, to put in issue some matters which previously he had not challenged. However, Mr. Hutchison, duly instructed, no doubt, by the affidavits that he could not use, was able in his address to me to offer informed criticism of the company's claim.

It is far from easy to state in general terms what is confidential infor-

G mation or a trade secret. Certain authorities were cited, but they did not carry matters very far. Plainly " something which is public property and public knowledge " is not confidential: see *Saltman Engineering Co. Ltd.* v. *Campbell Engineering Co. Ltd.* (1948) 65 R.P.C. 203, 215, *per* Lord Greene M.R. On the other hand, " something that has been constructed solely from materials in the public domain may possess the necessary quality of confidentiality: for something new and confidential may have

H been brought into being by the application of the skill and ingenuity of the human brain. Novelty depends on the thing itself, and not upon the quality of its constituent parts ": *Coco* v. *A. N. Clark (Engineers) Ltd.* [1969] R.P.C. 41, 47, a case that was not cited, but in part draws on the *Saltman* case, which was. Costs and prices which are not generally known may well constitute trade secrets or confidential information: see *Herbert Morris Ltd.* v. *Saxelby* [1916] 1 A.C. 688, 705, referring to prices.

If one turns from the authorities and looks at the matter as a question A
of principle, I think (and I say this very tentatively, because the principle
has not been argued out) that four elements may be discerned which may
be of some assistance in identifying confidential information or trade
secrets which the court will protect. I speak of such information or
secrets only in an industrial or trade setting. First, I think that the information must be information the release of which the owner believes would
be injurious to him or of advantage to his rivals or others. Second, I B
think the owner must believe that the information is confidential or
secret, i.e. that it is not already in the public domain. It may be that
some or all of his rivals already have the information: but as long as
the owner believes it to be confidential I think he is entitled to try and
protect it. Third, I think that the owner's belief under the two previous
heads must be reasonable. Fourth, I think that the information must be C
judged in the light of the usage and practices of the particular industry or
trade concerned. It may be that information which does not satisfy
all these requirements may be entitled to protection as confidential information or trade secrets: but I think that any information which does
satisfy them must be of a type which is entitled to protection.

Now the evidence of Mr. Parr states that there are 11 categories of
information which in particular are confidential. They are set out at D
p. 4 of his affidavit sworn on February 21, 1978; I shall merely summarise
the headings. They are the names and telex addresses of the company's
manufacturers and suppliers and their individual contacts; the negotiated
prices paid by the company; the names of some overseas buying agents
through whom the company deals; the company's new ranges, actual or
proposed; information as to the requirements (such as styles) of the E
company's customers; details of the company's current negotiations;
negotiated prices paid by customers to the company; the company's
samples; and the company's current " fast-moving " lines. Despite Mr.
Hutchison's criticisms, I think that all of these forms of information are
at least capable of being confidential; and he very properly conceded
that this must be the case for a number of them. Even in the Eastern
European countries with state monopolies, a knowledge of the particular F
officials with whom business can most satisfactorily be done may be an
important and confidential matter; and in the Far East, with many rival
sources of supply, a detailed knowledge of the cheapest, most reliable and
most efficient sources must be something that a skilled buyer would
firmly keep to himself as a valuable asset. I would regard all the heads
claimed by the company to be confidential as being heads which have G
real prospects of being established at the trial as proper heads of confidential information.

It was, of course, said that if the defendant was restrained from using
confidential information under all these heads, then that would in effect
restrain him from trading in this field altogether, and that this would be
wrong. I do not think it is. This is a case of a defendant who had
contracted to work for the company for 10 years asserting that he should H
not be restrained from using for his own purposes confidential information
that he acquired while in the employment of the company at a time
when there is still some $4\frac{1}{2}$ years of his contract left to run. From first
to last I have been unable to see any merits in his case, or the slightest
justification for the months of deliberate deceit on his part while he was
diverting to himself what he should have been obtaining for the company
of which he was managing director. Mr. Hutchison said that the

The Weekly Law Reports, July 7, 1978

137

3 W.L.R.   Thomas Marshall Ltd. v. Guinle (Ch.D.)   Megarry V.-C.

A imposition of the surcharge was a breach of contract by the company, or at least a breach of understanding. He was unable to make good this assertion, and in any case, though he said that it explained the defendant's conduct, he wisely disclaimed any contention that it excused it. I cannot see any ground on which the defendant should be left free to continue the conduct which has plainly injured the company most materially. If the law is to be held powerless to restrain the defendant from continuing

B to reap the advantages of his wilful breach of contract, that will have to be decided by some other court. In my judgment, the company is entitled to the injunctions claimed, subject to any question that there may be on the wording.

Application for injunctions granted.

C

Solicitors: *Clintons for Kuit, Steinart, Levy & Co., Manchester; Nicholson, Graham & Jones.*

D

[COURT OF APPEAL]

TILLING AND ANOTHER *v.* WHITEMAN

1978 March 8, 9; 22   Stephenson, Shaw and Eveleigh L.JJ.

E *Landlord and Tenant—Rent restriction—Joint owners—Letting by joint owner-occupiers—House required as residence for one owner-occupier—Whether jurisdiction to make order for possession—Rent Act 1968 (c. 23), s. 10 (2), Sch. 3, Pt. II, Case 10* [1]

The joint owner-occupiers of a dwelling house let it furnished in 1975 for a period of two years. The tenancy agreement contained a notice to the tenant that the landlord might recover possession of the premises under Case 10 of Part

F II of Schedule 3 to the Rent Act 1968. The tenant remained in occupation after the expiry of the term and the owners started proceedings for possession in the county court claiming that the dwelling house was formerly occupied by them as their residence and was now required as a residence for one of them (the first plaintiff). On a preliminary issue as to whether one of two joint owners of a dwelling house let on a regulated tenancy who occupied it as his residence was an

G owner-occupier entitled to recover possession of it under Case 10 of Schedule 3 to the Rent Act 1968 if the court was satisfied that the dwelling house was required as a residence for himself, the judge in the county court decided that the owners were not entitled to recover possession because the house was required as a residence for one of them only and he dismissed the claim.

On appeal by the first plaintiff: —

H *Held*, dismissing the appeal (Eveleigh L.J. dissenting), that the " owner-occupier " who qualified under Case 10 was not the first plaintiff alone but the first plaintiff together with the co-owner of the house and therefore an order for possession

---

[Reported by EVERARD CORBALLY ESQ., Barrister-at-Law]

[1] Rent Act 1968, s. 10 (2): see post, p. 140F.
Sch. 3, Pt. II Case 10: see post, p. 140G–H.

under Case 10 could not be made when the house was required   A
as a residence for the first plaintiff alone (post, pp. 145A,
146E–G).

    McIntyre v. *Hardcastle* [1948] 2 K.B. 82, C.A. applied.

    Per Eveleigh L.J. *McIntyre* v. *Hardcastle* was a decision
upon the different wording of Case 8 and does not govern the
interpretation of Case. 10. Upon the wording of Case 10 the
first plaintiff is a person who occupied the dwelling house as
her residence. She is a person who let it on a regulated   B
tenancy. She is therefore an owner-occupier and if the dwelling house is required as a residence for her an order for
possession can be made (post, pp. 146H, 147F, 148H—149A).

The following cases are referred to in the judgments:

Baker v. *Lewis* [1947] K.B. 186; [1946] 2 All E.R. 592, C.A.   C
Howson v. *Buxton* (1928) 97 L.J.K.B. 749.
Lloyd v. *Sadler* [1978] 2 W.L.R. 721, C.A.
McIntyre v. *Hardcastle* [1948] 2 K.B. 82; [1948] 1 All E.R. 696, C.A.
Wetherall & Co. Ltd. v. *Stone* [1950] 2 All E.R. 1209, C.A.

The following additional case was cited in argument:

Leek and Moorlands Building Society v. *Clark* [1952] 2 Q.B. 788; [1952]   D
    2 T.L.R. 401; [1952] 2 All E.R. 492, C.A.

APPEAL from Judge Sumner sitting at Canterbury County Court.

    The first plaintiff, Mrs. Irene Elizabeth Tilling, and the second plain-
tiff, Miss Gertrude Louise May Dossett, joint owners of a dwelling house
in Canterbury, commenced proceedings against Miss Josephine Whiteman,
the tenant of the house, for possession claiming that the house was   E
formely occupied by them as their residence and was now required as a
residence for the first plaintiff. On a preliminary issue as to whether one
of two joint owners of a dwelling house let on a regulated tenancy who
occupied the dwelling house as her residence was an owner-occupier
entitled to recover possession of it under Case 10 of Schedule 3 to the
Rent Act 1968 if the court was satisfied that the dwelling house was   F
required as a residence for herself, Judge Sumner decided that the plaintiffs
were not entitled to recover possession because the house was required
as a residence for one of them only and he dismissed the claim.

    The first plaintiff appealed on the ground that on a proper construction
of Case 10 joint lessors might rely on it if one of them was the owner-
occupier as defined in the case.   G

    The facts are stated in the judgment of Stephenson L.J.

    Christopher Sumner for the first plaintiff.
    Robin Laurie for the tenant.

                                   Cur. adv. vult.

March 22. The following judgments were read.   H

STEPHENSON L.J. This is an appeal from an order of Judge Sumner
made in the Canterbury County Court on May 3, 1977, deciding on a
preliminary point that the plaintiffs have no claim to possession against
the defendant. The preliminary issue and the appeal raise a short point
of construction. What has to be construed is the language of Case 10
in Schedule 3 to the Rent Act 1968, which is first found—with minor

A   differences—in section 14 of the Rent Act 1965, and has since been repeated word for word in Case 11 of Schedule 15 to the Rent Act 1977.

The plaintiffs are two elderly ladies who jointly own a dwelling house known as St. Leonard's, The Street, Staple, Canterbury, Kent. On February 19, 1975, they made an agreement with the defendant, of Keynes College, the University of Kent at Canterbury, in these terms:

B   "Whereby it is agreed as follows: — 1. The landlord lets and the tenant takes all that furnished dwelling house known as St. Leonard's, The Street, Staple, Canterbury, Kent (hereinafter called 'the premises'). 2. There is included in the letting the furniture and effects specified in the schedule annexed hereto. 3. The premises and the furniture and effects shall be held from February 21, 1975, for a period of two years. 4. The tenant shall pay for the premises and the
C   furniture the weekly rent of £12·50 four-weekly in advance the first payment to be made on the signing hereof and thereafter every four weeks."

Then there are the usual covenants, and at the foot of the agreement there is this notice typed on it:

D   "To the tenant the said J. Whiteman. Take notice under the Rent Acts 1968 and 1974 that the landlord may recover possession of the premises under the provisions of Case 10 of Part II of Schedule 3 to the Rent Acts 1968."

Under that comes the sentence: "Dated this 19th day of February 1975", with the signatures of both the landlords, and an acknowledgment: "I acknowledge to have received notice as above", signed by the
E   tenant. (The reference to the Rent Act 1974 has no relevance to this case.)

On the expiry of the term on February 19, 1977, the defendant remained in occupation of the house. On March 4, 1977, the plaintiffs began proceedings for possession in the Canterbury County Court. By their particulars of claim they claimed that they were the freeholders and entitled to possession of the dwelling house known as St. Leonard's;
F   the net annual value was £232; the premises, it was alleged, were let on a regulated tenancy by the plaintiffs to the defendant by the agreement in writing which I have just read; the dwelling house, it is said, was formerly occupied by the plaintiffs as their residence "and is now required as a residence for the first plaintiff." That is paragraph 4 of the particulars of claim. Then they add:

G   "On February 19, 1975, the defendant was given notice in writing that possession might be required under the provisions of Case 10 of Schedule 3 to the Rent Act 1968."

That is paragraph 5; and the plaintiffs claim possession and rent or alternatively mesne profits.

By her defence dated April 21, 1977, the defendant raised three
H   defences, one irrelevant and none touching on the issue decided by the judge. However, it was agreed between the parties that a question, which is nowhere formulated in the pleadings and nowhere expressly stated in the approved note of the judge's oral judgment, should be tried as a preliminary issue on agreed facts. The agreed statement of facts is this:

"1. Jointly owned by Miss Dossett and Mrs. Tilling. 2. The owners are not related. 3. Property was not occupied by one of the owners immediately before it was let. Property had been occupied

by Miss Dossett.   4. Property is only alleged to be required for occu- **A**
pation by Mrs. Tilling, the person who is alleged to have occupied
immediately before letting."

Made consistent and intelligible, this statement means that Miss Dossett
and Mrs. Tilling are joint owners of the house; they are not related; Miss
Dossett had occupied the house but had left it before it was let to Miss
Whiteman; Mrs. Tilling had occupied it and was still occupying it **B**
immediately before it was let to Miss Whiteman.

The issue which should have been agreed, recorded in writing and
submitted to the judge was whether the allegation pleaded in paragraph 4
of the particulars of claim gives the plaintiffs any right to recover possession
of the dwelling house under section 10 (2) of and Case 10 in Schedule 3
to the Rent Act 1968, or whether one of two joint owners of a dwelling **C**
house let on a regulated tenancy who occupied the dwelling house as his
(or her) residence is an owner-occupier entitled to recover possession of
it under Case 10 of Schedule 3 to the Rent Act 1968 if the court is
satisfied that the dwelling house is required as a residence for himself
(or herself).

The judge decided that the plaintiffs were not entitled to recover
possession under those provisions of the Act of 1968 because it was **D**
required as a residence for one of them only.

I think it necessary to read the first three subsections of section 10
before I read Case 10.   Section 10 provides:

"(1) Subject to the following provisions of this Part of this Act, a
court shall not make an order for possession of a dwelling house which
is for the time being let on a protected tenancy or subject to a **E**
statutory tenancy unless the court considers it reasonable to make
such an order and either—(a) the court is satisfied that suitable alternative accommodation is available for the tenant or will be available
for him when the order in question takes effect, or (b) the circumstances are as specified in any of the Cases in Part I of Schedule 3
to this Act.   (2) If, apart from the provisions of subsection (1) above, **F**
the landlord would be entitled to recover possession of a dwelling
house which is for the time being let on or subject to a regulated
tenancy, the court shall make an order for possession if the circumstances of the case are as specified in any of the Cases in Part II
of Schedule 3 to this Act.   (3) The provisions of Part III of Schedule
3 to this Act shall have effect in relation to Case 8 in that Schedule
and for determining the relevant date for the purposes of the Cases in **G**
Part II of that Schedule."

I then turn to Schedule 3 and read Case 10 in Part II, which provides:

"Where a person who occupied the dwelling house as his residence
(in this Case referred to as ' the owner-occupier') let it on a regulated
tenancy and—(a) not later than the relevant date the landlord gave
notice in writing to the tenant that possession might be recovered **H**
under this Case, and (b) the dwelling house has not, since December
8, 1965, been let by the owner-occupier on a protected tenancy with
respect to which the condition mentioned in paragraph (a) above
was not satisfied, and (c) the court is satisfied that the dwelling house
is required as a residence for the owner-occupier or any member
of his family who resided with the owner-occupier when he last
occupied the dwelling house as a residence."

A Part III of Schedule 3 deals (1) with Case 8, which I shall have to read later, and (2) with the relevant date. Paragraph 2 (*b*) of Part III provides: " Any reference in Part II of this Schedule to the relevant date shall be construed as follows: — . . . (*b*) in any other case," than that which is provided by (*a*) which I have not read, ". . . the relevant date means the date of the commencement of the regulated tenancy in question."

B I next read the note of the judgment in full, because it is short and clear and, in my opinion, with all respect to those who are of a different opinion, correct. The judge said:

C " This is a preliminary point. There are no direct authorities. I have been referred to some authority. Two ladies claim possession under Case 10 of Schedule 3 of the Rent Act 1968 as amended, their ground being that basically they propose that one of the ladies, Mrs. Tilling, wishes to occupy." He then sets out the provisions of Case 10 and continues: " The first matter to be considered is: ' Where a person who occupies a dwelling house as his residence let it on a regulated tenancy.' This property was let by two plaintiffs as joint owners. I construe ' person ' as plural under the Interpretation Act. The plaintiffs only come within Case 10 if they

D occupied as their residence. It is an agreed fact that they did, Mrs. Tilling immediately before the tenancy, Miss Dossett some time earlier. So far so good. The plaintiffs then asked me to adopt a different construction. In order to come within the first limb the owner-occupier had to be construed as both ladies. They then have to argue for sub-paragraph (*c*) that as only one wants to occupy, ' owner-occupier ' should be construed as one lady. I do not con-

E sider that they satisfy the proviso of sub-paragraph (*c*). I do not consider that one owner is the owner-occupier as defined. It is inevitably a matter of construction: should one construe strictly or take a wider view? This was not done in *McIntyre* v. *Hardcastle* [1948] 2 K.B. 82 in considering Case 8. Here the reference is to person and owner-occupier rather than landlord. Landlord is referred to in Case 8. However, the principle is the same and the

F overriding consideration is that if one construes person and owner-occupier in the plural to bring the plaintiffs within Case 10 at all, one cannot in the same Case construe owner-occupier in the singular. The construction must be consistent. I find the preliminary issue in favour of the defendant. Claim dismissed. Costs scale 2 taxed or agreed."

G Against that judgment, only Mrs. Tilling, the first plaintiff, appeals. Miss Dossett, the second plaintiff, is living in Oxford and uninterested in any part of these proceedings except their expense. We have in fact granted an application made by Miss Dossett's solicitors for a declaration under R.S.C., Ord. 67, r. 6 that they have ceased to be the solicitors acting for her in this case, and we have also granted an application on

H behalf of Mrs. Tilling for leave to amend her notice of appeal to join Miss Dossett as a respondent.

In *Lloyd* v. *Sadler* [1978] 2 W.L.R. 721, decided in the Court of Appeal on January 19, 1978, Megaw L.J. said, at p. 723:

" This case has brought to light two remarkable facts. First, the Rent Acts through all their long history have never made any relevant express provision relating to joint tenants or joint tenancies, whether protected or statutory. Secondly, and perhaps even more

strangely, there seems to have been no previous case decided by any   A
court, or at least no reported case, in which a question such as falls
to be decided in the present case has been raised for consideration
on section 3 (1) of the Act of 1968 or its predecessors."

It is not so strange that there is no previous reported case in which the
question of joint owner-occupiers seeking possession under Case 10 of
the Act of 1968 has been considered, because its provisions go back only   B
to 1965 and section 14 of the Rent Act of that year. And there are two
reported cases in which this court has considered the question of joint
beneficial owners who are landlords seeking possession under what was
Case 8 in Schedule 3 to the Act of 1968 and is now Case 9 in Schedule
15 to the Act of 1977 but goes back, beyond paragraph (h) of Schedule 1
to the Rent and Mortgage Interest Restrictions (Amendment) Act 1933,
to the year 1920. It is therefore even stranger that Parliament has   C
enacted and re-enacted the provisions in respect of the recovery of
possession of owner-occupied houses with which we are concerned in
this appeal, without making any relevant express provision relating to
joint owners or joint owner-occupiers or joint tenants letting dwelling
houses on a regulated tenancy.

The decision which deals with possession of a dwelling house jointly   D
owned by two landlords is *McIntyre* v. *Hardcastle* [1948] 2 K.B. 82,
where this court adopted a dictum of Asquith L.J. in preference to a
dictum of Somervell L.J. in *Baker* v. *Lewis* [1947] K.B. 186 and
decided that two sisters, who sought possession of a house they owned
jointly under paragraph (h) of Schedule 1 to the Act of 1933 on the
ground that the house was required as a residence for one of them, could
not bring themselves within the paragraph and recover possession.   E
Schedule 1 to the Act of 1933 read as follows:

"A court shall, for the purposes of section 3 of this Act, have
power to make or give an order or judgment for the recovery of
possession of any dwelling house to which the principal Acts apply
or for the ejectment of a tenant therefrom without proof of suitable
alternative accommodation (where the court considers it reasonable   F
so to do) if—. . . (h) the dwelling house is reasonably required by
the landlord (not being a landlord who has become landlord by
purchasing the dwelling house or any interest therein after" [a
certain date] " for occupation as a residence for—(i) himself; or (ii)
any son or daughter of his over 18 years of age; or (iii) his father
or mother: . . ."

G
and then there is a proviso. Case 8 is in very similar terms; Case 8,
that is, in Part I of Schedule 3 to the Act of 1968:

"Where the dwelling house is reasonably required by the landlord
for occupation as a residence for—(a) himself, or (b) any son or
daughter of his over 18 years of age, or (c) his father or mother, or
(d) if the dwelling house is let on or subject to a regulated tenancy,
the father or mother of his wife or husband, and the landlord did   H
not become landlord by purchasing the dwelling house or any interest
therein after March 23, 1965, or, if the dwelling house is let on or
subject to a controlled tenancy, after November 7, 1956."

In the leading judgment, Tucker L.J. said [1948] 2 K.B. 82, 90:

"All kinds of difficulties have been suggested to us as likely to follow
whichever interpretation is accepted by us. I do not think that the

A   legislature really contemplated this situation when this paragraph was
framed.   Therefore, I feel driven to interpret it merely in the light of
the actual language used.   Looking at it in that way, I feel convinced that the interpretation put upon it by Asquith L.J. was
the correct one, and I will not attempt to put into better language
what he so clearly expressed in the passage just quoted."

B   In the passage just quoted, Asquith L.J. had said that " landlord " in
paragraph (h) covered two or more joint beneficial owners and in such
a case the dwelling house must be reasonably required by them for
occupation as a residence for themselves (not " himself "), for any son
or daughter of theirs (not " his "), or for their (not " his ") father or
mother.   That decision has been applied by this court to an application
for a new lease of business premises for occupation by two out of three
C   landlords: Wetherall & Co. Ltd. v. Stone [1950] 2 All E.R. 1209.
Mr. Sumner has submitted that Parliament had regard to that decision and used words in Case 10 which intentionally escape the impact of
that decision and distinguish Case 10 from Case 8.   Alternatively, the
actual language used enables or compels the court to distinguish the two
cases and to hold that one of two (or more) joint beneficial owner-
D   occupiers can come within Case 10 if he (or she) satisfies the court that
the dwelling house is required as a residence for himself (or herself).   He
contends that it is not right to construe " owner-occupier " as referring
to both ladies, as the judge did.
For my part, I cannot infer any intention to distinguish Case 10 from
Case 8 or its judicial interpretation.   I accept that difficulties follow
E   whichever interpretation is accepted and it is the actual language used
which must be interpreted and must give Mr. Sumner success or justify
the judge's adverse decision of the preliminary point.   So is Mrs. Tilling
" a person who " (1) " occupied the dwelling house as [her] residence,"
(2) " let it on a regulated tenancy " and (3) requires it as a residence for
such a person?   If the sentence is divided into these three parts, each of
these questions can be answered affirmatively and Mrs. Tilling can be
F   said to be a person who occupied the dwelling house as her residence,
let it on a regulated tenancy and requires it for occupation as her residence.   She is one of the two persons who occupied it and let it, and
she is the only one of those two who requires it for occupation.   But in
my judgment it is not correct to say that she let it or is a person who let
it within the meaning of those words in their context.   The person who
let it, and who is referred to as " the owner-occupier," was not Mrs.
G   Tilling but herself and her co-owner, Miss Dossett.   It is they two, not
Mrs. Tilling, who occupied the dwelling house and were the owner-
occupier of it, and it is both of them, not Mrs. Tilling alone, who have
to satisfy the court that it is required as a residence for them both.
That is a natural construction of the words used even if it is not
the only natural construction.   It is supported by the difficulty which
H   Mr. Sumner's alternative construction introduces for joint owners who
disagree on who should occupy the dwelling house, the tenant or one of
the owners.   One joint owner can sue for rent or give notice to quit,
but all joint owners must sue for possession, and judgment for possession
cannot be given in favour of one only.   Miss Dossett's indifference
might turn to co-operation or hostility; she might prefer getting rent
from Miss Whiteman to letting Mrs. Tilling replace her.   It is also
supported by the general purpose of the Act to protect the security of

144

tenants from eviction by landlords. It is true that Case 10 opens a A
door to a landlord's exercising his contractual right to possession; but
it is one door in a high wall which strictly protects a tenant and it would
accord better with the object of the Act if it opens a little than if it
opens wide. It was probably both these considerations which led this
court in *McIntyre* v. *Hardcastle* to construe " the landlord " in what was
in Case 8 the Act of 1968 as including the plural and to hold that B
one of two joint owners could not recover possession for herself. It was
the second consideration which led this court in *Lloyd* v. *Sadler* [1978]
2 W.L.R. 721 to refuse to apply *McIntyre* v. *Hardcastle* in reverse so
as to deprive one joint tenant of her statutory tenancy when the other
had abandoned occupation during the contractual joint tenancy. Following the majority decision of this court in *Howson* v. *Buxton* (1928) 97
L.J.K.B. 749, this court held that to apply strictly the doctrine of joint C
tenancy would have led to results which were unreasonable or unlikely
to have been intended by the legislature. But in the instant case the
strict application of the doctrine of joint ownership has the opposite
effect and leads to a result which is not unreasonable and is much more
likely to have been intended by the legislature than an extension of the
right to evict from jointly owned dwelling houses. That case and the
case which it follows seem to me to give no support to Mr. Sumner's D
interpretation. If they help at all, they help the defendant's case.

I get no help also from the minor changes made in the language
of the provision conferring this right to possession in the course of its
transfer from the body of the Act of 1965 to a Schedule to the Act of
1968 (and the Act of 1977). I am satisfied that those changes are due
solely to that transfer. Nor do I get help from the definition of " land- E
lord " in section 113 (1) of the Act of 1968. But I do get help from
section 10 of this Act.

Mr. Sumner relies on the fact that in Case 10 the landlord is referred
to only in (*a*), and it is " a person," not " the landlord," who is referred
to as occupying and letting the dwelling house. But it has to be
remembered that this Rent Act, like all the other Rent Acts, deals primarily
with the landlords and tenants of dwelling houses. In section 10 (1) F
" the landlord " is not mentioned, but in Case 8, which is linked with
the subsection, he is. In section 10 (2) " the landlord " is mentioned,
but in Case 10, which is linked with that subsection, he is not, except
in (*a*). Case 10, no less than Case 8, states conditions in which a landlord can (in Case 8) or must (in Case 10) be entitled to recover possession
from his tenant. Landlords, or owners, of dwelling houses may occupy G
or not occupy the dwelling house; an owner-occupier is a landlord or
owner who is residential, not absentee, at the time when he lets his
dwelling house. If he then occupies, it is strictly correct not to call him
a landlord until he actually lets and to call him a landlord when he has let
and gives notice that he may recover possession under Case 10. In the
instant case these owners gave the notice on the same date and in the same H
document as the agreement creating the tenancy. But even then it was
given at the foot of the agreement and it might in other cases be given on a
later date when the owner who had occupied before he let had indeed
become the landlord by letting. These considerations seem to me to
account for the use of the words " the landlord " in (*a*) of Case 10 and of
the words " a person " (including the indefinite article) in the opening
words of Case 10.

A   I am therefore unable to find any distinction between the language of Case 8 and Case 10 in any respect material to the decision in *McIntyre* v. *Hardcastle* or to infer from the language of Case 10 a right in one of two (or more) owner-occupiers to recover possession of their dwelling house for his or her (or their) own occupation. I am of opinion that the judge's decision to dismiss the plaintiffs' claim was right. I would affirm it and dismiss the appeal.

B

SHAW L.J. The circumstances which give rise to this appeal from the decision of Judge Sumner on a preliminary issue have been recounted in the judgment of Stephenson L.J. and need no further elaboration. The issue was as to jurisdiction to entertain a claim for possession under the provisions of section 10 and Case 10 of Part II of C Schedule 3 to the Rent Act 1968.

The real question was whether the claim as pleaded disclosed a claim within those provisions at all. If it did, the combined effect of section 10 and Part II of Schedule 3 is mandatory and the plaintiffs must succeed in their claim. The objection taken at the trial on behalf of the tenant was founded on what was averred in paragraph 4 of the particulars of claim. It was there pleaded: "The said dwelling house was formerly D occupied by the plaintiffs as their residence and is now required as a residence for the first plaintiff." The last four words give rise to the controversial issue. The defendant contends that they demonstrate that the plaintiffs' claim is not within Case 10. Condition (c) of that Case requires that "the court is satisfied that the dwelling house is required as a residence for the owner-occupier . . ." I have omitted the rest of E paragraph (c), which is irrelevant to the present case. The expression "owner-occupier" is defined, or at any rate described, in the opening words of Case 10, which reads: "Where a person who occupied the dwelling house as his residence (in this Case referred to as 'the owner-occupier') let it on a regulated tenancy." It is apparent that the characteristics which serve to identify an owner-occupier in this context F are (i) that he owned the interest out of which the regulated tenancy was granted, and (ii) that he had occupied the dwelling house as his residence at the time that he let it on a regulated tenancy.

As was the position in the appeal of *Lloyd* v. *Sadler* [1978] 2 W.L.R. 721, it seems clear that the draftsman of the Act of 1968 had not in mind the particular situation of joint tenants in relation to statutory or regulated tenancies. In the present case it was contended on behalf of the G tenant that "owner-occupier" comprised all those who by virtue of a joint interest comprised the "owner," so that it necessarily included all the joint tenants. It would follow that in regard to paragraph (c) it was an essential element of a Case 10 claim that the dwelling house be required as a residence for all the joint owners and not merely for one or some of them. This would accord with the view taken in the Court of H Appeal in *McIntyre* v. *Hardcastle* [1948] 2 K.B. 82, 90 by Tucker L.J., approving and following the judgment of Asquith L.J. in *Baker* v. *Lewis* [1947] K.B. 186.

Like Tucker L.J.—and I quote from his judgment—

"I feel driven to interpret [the statute] in the light of the actual language used. Looking at it in that way, I feel convinced that the interpretation put on it by Asquith L.J. was the correct one."

A

While it is true that those observations were not made in precisely the same statutory context, I cannot see on what principle of construction any material distinction can be drawn between the grounds for that decision and those which obtain in the present appeal. Counsel for the appellant Mrs. Tilling (the sole appellant since Miss Dossett has foresworn her erstwhile role of co-appellant) relies on the judgment of this court in *Lloyd* v. *Sadler*, to which reference has been made already. There it was held that one of two joint tenants under a protected tenancy could, on the expiration of that tenancy, claim to be a statutory tenant notwithstanding that the other joint tenant had gone out of occupation and did not intend to return. If, the argument went, one of two joint tenants could claim to be entitled to statutory protection, why should not one of two joint landlords be similarly entitled to statutory relief? The answer to that contention is that the respective legislative provisions fall to be construed not only " in the light of the language actually used," but in relation to the object and purpose of those provisions.

B

C

The statutory provisions which were the subject of consideration in *Lloyd* v. *Sadler* were designed to give a form of security of tenure to tenants under a protected tenancy. It was a reasonable construction of the relevant provisions that that security of tenure was a personal right of individual tenants notwithstanding that they held under a joint tenancy. Case 10 is to be found as an adjunct of Part II of the Act of 1968 which is headed " Security of Tenure," a phrase which is itself followed by the words " Limitations on recovery of possession of dwelling houses let on protected tenancies or subject to statutory tenancies." Thus the theme is the safeguarding of the tenant's right to continue in possession, a theme communicated to Schedule 3 which begins with the heading " Grounds for possession of dwelling houses let on or subject to protected or statutory tenancies."

D

E

The various Cases set out under Parts I and II respectively of the Schedule constitute derogations from that theme. Thus they run counter to the main burden of Part II of the Act. This, in my opinion, indicates the need for a strict interpretation of the relaxations of the principle that security of tenure is to be maintained. Accordingly, the problem of construction in the present case has to be resolved from a diametrically opposed starting point. In this situation I find no difficulty in arriving at the conclusion that " the owner-occupier " in paragraph (c) of Case 10 necessarily involves everyone who was a joint owner at the time the premises were let on a regulated tenancy.

F

In my view, the judge came to the correct conclusion. I respectfully agree with the judgment of Stephenson L.J., and I would dismiss the appeal.

G

EVELEIGH L.J. In the course of argument great reliance was placed by the respondent upon *McIntyre* v. *Hardcastle* [1948] 2 K.B. 82. That case, however, was concerned with section 3 of the Rent Act 1933 and Schedule 1 to that Act. The words were quite different from those found in Case 10 of the Act of 1968 and contained words which are repeated in Case 8 of the Act of 1968. *McIntyre* v. *Hardcastle*, therefore, is a decision upon completely different wording and upon a very different situation, as the separate Case, Case 8 in the Act of 1968, can be said to emphasise. Furthermore, there is no general principle to be drawn from *McIntyre* v. *Hardcastle* and certainly not one which governs the present case or the interpretation of Case 10. Tucker L.J. said, at p. 90:

H

A   " I do not think that the legislature really contemplated this situation
when this paragraph was framed. Therefore, I feel driven to
interpret it merely in the light of the actual language used."

In the absence of any reasons to the contrary, that, in my judgment, is
the approach which I should adopt to the interpretation of Case 10.

In *McIntyre* v. *Hardcastle* it was necessary, in order for the plaintiff
B to succeed, to substitute the plural for the singular in the words
of the Act. This was of course permissible by virtue of the Interpretation Act. The plaintiff was not allowed to pick and choose where the
substitution should be made but was required to be consistent and
substitute the plural wherever the singular occurred. In the present case
the appellant claims that she is not asking for the alteration of any of the
words of the Act, not even by substituting the plural for the singular. If
C this contention is wrong and it is necessary to substitute, then says the
appellant " I do no more than substitute consistently."

It has been argued that the appellant's claim runs counter to the policy
of the Act. It is said that the intention of the Rent Act is to protect the
tenant. That may well be; but it is equally true that the introduction of
a new ground for possession as that contained in Case 10 was done for
D the benefit of the landlord. Furthermore, it is clear that there was an
overriding intention to encourage persons in occupation of their homes to
be prepared to let them and not refrain for fear of being kept out for
ever. Therefore, if policy considerations are to play a part in the interpretation of the Act in relation to the present claim, it would in my view
favour the appellant.

E   It has also been said that as the Act makes no specific reference to
the position of the joint owner as landlord and as *McIntyre* v. *Hardcastle*
rejected the claim of one of two joint owners, then this court should
proceed upon the basis that the die is still loaded against one of joint
owners. I do not accept this contention. The words of Case 10 are
quite different from those of Case 8; and, while it may be that the legislature did not have joint tenants in mind, I can have no confidence that
F this was so.

I now turn to consider the relevant words of the Act of 1968 actually
found in Case 10. Case 10 begins: Where a person who occupied the
dwelling house as his residence (in this Case referred to as ' the owner-
occupier ') let it on a regulated tenancy. . . ." The appellant did occupy
the dwelling house as her residence. (We are not concerned in this
G present appeal to decide whether the occupation must be immediately
before the letting or whether occupation at any previous time will do.
However, as the past perfect tense is used for both verbs, there is much
to be said for the contention that the occupation has to be the last
occupation of the dwelling house before the letting). Further, in my
opinion the appellant is a person who let on a regulated tenancy.
It is argued that because her joint owner joined in the lease, the
H appellant cannot be heard to say that she let. Counsel for the respondent says that she is forced to say " they let." I do not accept this
argument. Case 10 is concerned to consider the qualifications of a
person. The emphasis is upon occupation. A person in occupation should
not be deterred from making way for a tenant by the thought that
he or she may be kept out of the house permanently. There are two
conditions which have to be fulfilled to allow a person back into occupation. That person must have occupied and that person must have let.

The benefit of Case 10 is given to one who can stand in the way of A
freedom of letting not only by virtue of occupation, but also having the
power to refuse to let. It seems to me to be wholly truthful for the
appellant to say that she let the house on a regulated tenancy. One of
two joint owners can in law deal with the property without the concurrence of the other in so far as the rest of the world is concerned. The
fact that two people do a thing together does not, in my understanding
of the English language, prevent either one claiming that he himself did B
it. The argument to the contrary entails reading into the Act words
something like " on his own." If the appellant had come to an arrangement with the other joint owner that only the appellant's name would
appear in the lease, the tenant would have had no answer to the claim for
possession. Conscious as I am of the technicalities of the Rent Act, I
do not believe that one should encourage a situation where yet another C
technicality arises unless there is a compelling case.

Notice in writing was given to the tenant, but it is argued that the
use of the words " the landlord " is of some significance. It is said that
the appellant is not *the* landlord, but only one of two. Reference is
then made to section 10 (2) of the Act:

> " If, apart from the provisions of subsection (1) above, the landlord D
> would be entitled to recover possession of a dwelling house which is
> for the time being let on or subject to a regulated tenancy, the court
> shall make an order for possession if the circumstances of the case
> are as specified in any of the Cases in Part II of Schedule 3 to this
> Act."

Again it is argued that " the landlord " can only mean all those who are E
the landlords when there are more than one. In my opinion, section 10
(2) is not laying it down as a condition that the plaintiff must be *the*
landlord. It is stating what must be shown before the person claiming
possession shall be given an order, and what has to be shown is that the
case falls within Part II of Schedule 3. It is nowhere stated that the
plaintiff must prove that he is *the* landlord.

However, if this argument is wrong, I see no difficulty in reading F
" landlord " to include the plural. If in section 10 (2) we read " the
landlords," all that consistency requires is that we shall read the plural
also when the word " landlord " appears in Case 10. Section 10 (2)
would then read: " If, apart from the provisions of subsection (1) above,
the landlords would be entitled to recover possession " (in our case they
would) " the court shall make an order for possession if the circumstances G
of the case are as specified in any of the Cases in Part II of Schedule
3 to this Act." Then on the same basis we proceed to inquire whether the
circumstances are as specified. The relevant case is Case 10. Part II of
Schedule 3 is headed: " Cases in which court must order possession where
dwelling house subject to regulated tenancy." As I have said, in my
judgment Mrs. Tilling is a person who occupied the dwelling house and
let it on a regulated tenancy. The first condition, (*a*), if we substitute H
the plural, now reads: " not later than the relevant date the landlords gave
notice in writing to the tenant." The landlords did. It is agreed that the
next provision (*b*), is fulfilled. The final provision, (*c*), reads: " the court is
satisfied that the dwelling house is required as a residence for the owner-
occupier "; in other words, " is required as a residence for the person who
occupied the dwelling house and let it on a regulated tenancy." That
person was and is Mrs. Tilling.

A   In my view therefore, subject to the facts pleaded being established and to any possible argument as to the date when the owner-occupier is required to have been in occupation, the plaintiff's claim succeeds.

Having done this exercise of substituting the plural consistently, I am far from conceding that joint tenants were not in the minds of the legislature. The change in wording from "owner-occupier" to "land-lord" in Case 10 must be deliberate and, in my judgment, achieves
B   the result of giving protection to one of two joint owners. The fact that the expression "joint owners" is not used may well be because there are other forms of shared interests in real property that may also be envisaged and a specific reference to joint owners might be unduly limiting. The Schedule to the Act clearly attempts to deal with situations in a new and simplified manner by setting them out as Cases in what no doubt it was
C   hoped would be treated as straightforward language. That language, in my opinion, covers the present claim.

> *Appeal dismissed with costs, to be paid by legal aid fund unless Law Society gives notice of objection within six weeks.*
> *Leave to appeal.*
D   *Liberty to apply as to terms on which leave granted.*

Solicitors: *Williamson & Barnes, Deal; Furley, Page, Fielding & Pembrook, Canterbury.*

E

[CHANCERY DIVISION]

MIDLAND BANK TRUST CO. LTD. AND ANOTHER
F   *v.* GREEN AND ANOTHER

[1970 G. No. 334]

1977 Oct. 17, 18, 19, 20, 21   Oliver J.

Estoppel—Per rem judicatam—Issue estoppel—Affidavit sworn by father in Beddoes application—Action against father's executors
G   *—Plaintiffs pleading estoppel based on information obtained from father's affidavit—Plea struck out—Subsequent application to introduce affidavit as evidence of facts—Issue estoppel —Whether affidavit admissible*
Vendor and Purchaser—Purchaser for value—Minimal consideration—Grant by father to son of option to purchase farm— Subsequent conveyance of farm by father to wife for £500 —Whether sale and conveyance to wife genuine sale—Whether
H   *wife "purchaser"—Land Charges Act 1925 (15 & 16 Geo. 6 c. 22), ss. 13, 20 (8)*

In 1961, W, in consideration of £1, agreed to grant to his son, G, an option, exercisable over a period of ten years, to purchase at £75 per acre a 300-acre farm, which G was then farming under a lease from his father. The option was not registered under the Land Charges Act 1925. On August 17, 1967, W sold and conveyed the farm to his wife, E, for the sum of £500. On September 5, 1967, another member of the

Midland Bank Trust Co. v. Green (Ch.D.)   **[1978]**

firm of solicitors who had drawn up the option, registered A
the option and on October 6, 1967, G gave formal notice in
purported exercise of the option. Neither W nor E complied
with the notice. On March 28, 1968, E died, and probate of
her will was granted on November 29, 1968, to her executors,
W, G and another son, D. Negotiations for a possible
purchase by G of the farm proved abortive and, on January
27, 1970, G commenced the present proceedings, by issuing
a writ against W and D, as E's executors seeking a declaration B
that the option was binding on E's estate and claiming specific
performance. As later amended, there was also a claim for
damages for conspiracy against E's estate and against W
personally. On February 8, 1972, W died, and thereafter
his personal representative was added as a defendant. The
existing defence was adopted, but on October 7, 1975, the
defence was struck out for failure to comply with an order
for discovery, so that thereafter, as against W's estate, the C
action became undefended. On May 11, 1973, G died, and the
action was continued by his executors as plaintiffs.

After the commencement of the action, an application was
made by the executors of E's estate for the directions of the
court and for that purpose W swore an affidavit, the contents
of which became known to G, despite his exclusion from
part of the hearing. On the information thus received G
sought to raise an estoppel in his reply on the basis of an D
election by W and D to treat the conveyance as a sham or
as being not a bona fide transaction. The relevant paragraph
of the reply was struck out by order of Templeman J., dated
February 19, 1976, on the ground of the confidentiality attaching to the affidavit. The plaintiffs, under the Civil Evidence
Act 1968, sought to introduce the affidavit in evidence and
to rely upon it as evidence of facts supporting the contention
that the sale and conveyance of the farm to E was a sham E
and did not constitute a bona fide sale by a vendor to a
purchaser.

On the hearing of the action and on the question whether
W's affidavit was inadmissible by reason of issue estoppel per
rem judicatam resulting from the order of Templeman J. and
on the basis of the confidential nature of the affidavit: —

Held, (1) that no issue estoppel per rem judicatam arose
which would prevent the plaintiffs from relying on W's affidavit, F
sworn on a *Beddoes* application, as proof of the facts therein
set out; that it was doubtful whether there was any general
principle protecting affidavit evidence of facts, given on a
summons in a *Beddoes* application, from being used or
referred to in any other proceedings than the summons itself
and especially after the deponent's death but, even if there
was such a principle, that confidentiality had been waived by
their publication by W to G, and by their inclusion, without G
claim of privilege, in a list of documents served by D on the
plaintiffs (post, pp. 160c–e, 161c–e, 163c–g).

In re Moritz, decd. [1960] Ch. 251 considered.

(2) That in so far as W's estate was concerned there would
be no answer to the plaintiffs' claim for damages and, accordingly, an inquiry as to such damages would be ordered, but
that the plaintiffs' claim to damages against E's estate must H
fail, since their claim, being a claim in tort, had not been
commenced within six months after the grant of representation
to her estate and, therefore, had already become statute barred
under the Law Reform (Miscellaneous Provisions) Act 1934
(post, p. 164d–f).

(3) That, despite the fact that the transaction contained a
substantial and almost overwhelming element of gift, the
transaction of sale and conveyance of the farm by W to E
was a genuine sale by a vendor to a " purchaser " as defined

A   in section 20 (8) of the Land Charges Act 1925, whereby E acquired the legal estate in the farm for money or money's worth and, accordingly, the plaintiffs' claim to specific performance of the option failed (post, p. 166B–H).

    H. L. Bolton (Engineering) Co. Ltd. v. *T. J. Graham & Sons Ltd.* [1957] 1 Q.B. 159, C.A. considered.

B   The following cases are referred to in the judgment:

Bolton (H. L.) (Engineering) Co. Ltd. v. *T. J. Graham & Sons Ltd.* [1957] 1 Q.B. 159; [1956] 3 W.L.R. 804; [1956] 3 All E.R. 624, C.A.

Carl Zeiss Stiftung v. *Rayner & Keeler (No. 2)* [1967] 1 A.C. 853; [1966] 3 W.L.R. 125; [1966] 2 All E.R. 536, H.L.(E.).

Eton College v. *Minister of Agriculture, Fisheries and Food* [1964] Ch. 274; [1962] 3 W.L.R. 726; [1962] 3 All E.R. 290.

C   *Green* v. *Green* (unreported), February 19, 1976, Templeman J.

Hollington Brothers Ltd. v. *Rhodes (Note)* [1951] 2 All E.R. 578.

Inland Revenue Commissioners v. *Gribble* [1913] 3 K.B. 212, C.A.

Jones v. *Trinder, Capron & Co.* [1918] 2 Ch. 7, C.A.

Monolithic Building Co., In re [1915] 1 Ch. 643, C.A.

Moritz, decd., In re [1960] Ch. 251; [1959] 3 W.L.R. 939; [1959] 3 All E.R. 767.

Vane v. *Vane* (1873) L.R. 8 Ch.App. 383.

D   The following additional cases were cited in argument:

Fidelitas Shipping Co. Ltd. v. *V/O Exportchleb* [1966] 1 Q.B. 630; [1965] 2 W.L.R. 1059; [1965] 2 All E.R. 4, C.A.

Fry v. *Lane* (1888) 40 Ch.D. 312.

Holder v. *Holder* [1968] Ch. 353; [1968] 2 W.L.R. 237; [1968] 1 All E.R. 665, C.A.

E   *Hollingsworth* v. *Lee* [1949] V.L.R. 140.

Lindsay Petroleum Co. v. *Hurd* (1874) L.R. 5 P.C. 221, P.C.

Mountford v. *Scott* [1975] Ch. 258; [1975] 2 W.L.R. 114; [1975] 1 All E.R. 198, C.A.

ACTION

F   By a writ and statement of claim, dated January 27, 1970, as amended the plaintiffs, Midland Bank Trust Co. Ltd. and Margaret Ann Green, as executors of Thomas Geoffrey Green, claimed against the defendants, Beryl Rosalie Kemp, as executrix of Walter Stanley Green, and against Robert Derek Green as the surviving executor of Mrs. Evelyne Green, the following relief, namely, against both defendants (1) a declaration

G   that the option granted on March 24, 1961, by Walter Stanley Green to his son Thomas Geoffrey Green to purchase at a price of £75 per acre a 300-acre farm known as Gravel Hill Farm, Thornton-le-Moor, Lincolnshire was binding on the estate of Evelyne Green, (2) specific performance of the contract arising by reason of the grant of the option and the notice exercising the same dated October 6, 1967, or alternatively by reason of the option and the letter before action, (3) all necessary accounts and

H   inquiries, (4) damages in lieu of or in addition to specific performance, (5) damages for conspiracy, and, (6) as against the estate of Walter Stanley Green damages for conspiracy, further or other relief and costs.

    The facts are stated in the judgment.

    Jeremiah Harman Q.C. and *Jonathan Parker* for the plaintiffs.

    Leonard Hoffmann Q.C., Gavin Lightman and *F. P. Hinks* for the defendants.

Midland Bank Trust Co. v. Green (Ch.D.)   **[1978]**

OLIVER J. This is in many ways a tragic and very unhappy family A
dispute. Walter Stanley Green was a Lincolnshire farmer. He was married and his wife was Evelyne Green. They had two sons, Geoffrey and
Derek, and three daughters. I hope it will not be considered disrespectful
if, for convenience, I refer to all the members of the family by their
Christian names.

Now Walter appears to have been a man of some substance. He was
the freehold owner of more than one farm, and one farm which he owned B
was known as "Thoresway," which was a farm of 600–700 acres and
which appears to have been farmed originally by him and his younger
son, Derek, together, either in partnership or under some other arrangement. Another farm was Gravel Hill Farm at Thornton-le-Moor in
Lincolnshire. That was a smaller farm amounting to some 300 acres, and
it was farmed by Walter's elder son, Geoffrey. Geoffrey had a tenancy C
of the land at £3 an acre, or thereabouts, which was granted to him in
1954.

Walter retired from active farming in 1960, and at that time, or
thereabouts, he sold Thoresway—or his interest in Thoresway—to Derek
at a price of £75 an acre, which was well below the market value at
the time. Geoffrey wanted to buy Gravel Hill Farm at a similar price, but
it seems that Walter had some knowledge, or that he had been advised, D
of the death duty advantages attendant upon the possession of agricultural
property, and he was desirous, at that time at any rate, of retaining
agricultural investment. So he and Geoffrey went to a firm of solicitors in
Brigg, Messrs. Hett, Davy & Stubbs—now Messrs. Hett, Stubbs & Kemp
—and those solicitors drew up, and Walter signed, an option agreement
which was dated March 24, 1961. That agreement was in these terms. E
It was addressed to

> "Thomas Geoffrey Green Gravel Hill Farm Thornton-le-Moor. In
> consideration of the sum of £1 paid by you to me I hereby give you
> the option of purchasing the Gravel Hill Farm now in your occupation
> at the sum of £75 . . . per acre. This option to remain effective for
> ten years. Dated this March 24, 1961."
>   F

It bore a sixpenny stamp and was signed by Walter.

The evidence of Geoffrey's widow—she was not cross-examined on this
and I accept her evidence—is that thereafter the existence of the option
and the possibility of Geoffrey's exercising it were discussed on frequent
occasions between Walter and Geoffrey in the presence of Walter's wife,
Evelyne. It appears that Geoffrey and his wife were in the habit of G
visiting Walter and Evelyne at weekends; and Mrs. Geoffrey Green's
evidence was, and again I accept it, that Evelyne must have known all
about the option, or about its existence at any rate. Whenever it was
discussed, Mrs. Green told me, Walter said that he still wanted to retain
an agricultural investment and, in the result, up to August 1967 the
option had not been exercised. It had not only not been exercised but
it had not been registered under the Land Charges Act 1925; so that H
as a matter of law Walter could still sell the land elsewhere free from
the option although, of course, that would be a clear breach of his contract
with Geoffrey.

On August 14, 1967, a Mr. Harrod, a partner in a well-known firm
of solicitors in Spalding, Messrs. Roythorne, received a telephone call
from Walter's younger son, Derek. It appears that Mr. Harrod had
previously acted for Derek in various matters. He was the litigation

A partner in Roythorne's. Derek asked him to come over to his—that is Derek's—farm and Mr. Harrod did so and he was introduced to Walter, whom, he told me, he had not previously met. Walter then gave Mr. Harrod certain instructions. Now, although these are in fact privileged they were introduced in evidence, and Mr. Hoffman took no objection to Mr. Harrod telling me about them. Walter told Mr. Harrod that he had signed what he " thought " was an option in favour of his son. That,

B on Mrs. Green's evidence, which as I have said I accept, was, I think, somewhat disingenuous because Walter knew perfectly well that he had signed a document which was an option. There is no question of his " thinking " that it was an option; he knew quite well that it was an option. He instructed Mr. Harrod there and then to prepare a conveyance of Gravel Hill Farm in favour of his, Walter's, wife Evelyne, who was

C not present on this occasion and whom Mr. Harrod had not at this stage ever met, for a consideration of £500, and there is no dispute between the parties in this action—and indeed it is a matter of plain common sense—that £500 was a totally inadequate consideration for a farm of 300 acres whether tenanted or not. Walter, at the same time, gave an authority to Mr. Harrod addressed to the National Provincial Bank Ltd. at Brigg, where, apparently, he had his account, to collect the title deeds:

D and he also gave him an authority addressed to Hett, Stubbs & Kemp, who had been, up to that time, his solicitors, to hand over all the documents which they had relating to his affairs. The latter authority certainly, and probably the former, were prepared by Mr. Harrod and signed by Walter. In fact the documents with Hett, Stubbs & Kemp turned out, in the end, to consist of very little. They were, I think,

E Walter's will and the title deeds to his and Evelyne's house, The Old Rectory, Croxby.

On that same evening, Mr. Harrod sent off a search requisition to the land registry with a request to notify the result by telephone. He was notified by telephone, or his firm was notified by telephone, that the search was negative and that was confirmed on August 15. Mr. Harrod told me that he was unable to deal with the matter personally on August

F 16 because he was then involved in some planning inquiry at Brigg, which kept him rather late, but on the morning of August 17 he gave instructions to his conveyancing partner, Mr. Jenkinson, to go to Brigg, to go to the bank, pick up the title deeds, to arrange for the use with a friendly firm of solicitors in Brigg of a secretary and a typewriter and office space and, there and then, to prepare a conveyance for £500 and to take it to a

G nursing home at Cleethorpes for execution by Walter and his wife. Walter had apparently, at that time, been going to Cambridgeshire to stay with a daughter, but Mr. Harrod had learned that Walter had been taken ill and was going to a nursing home in Cleethorpes. Mr. Jenkinson, as one would expect, did as he was instructed. He collected the deeds, he prepared a conveyance, and he took it to Cleethorpes for execution by Walter and his wife. That conveyance is a conveyance in the ordinary

H form of a conveyance on sale. It is made on August 17, expressed to be between Walter Stanley Green who is described as " the vendor " and Evelyne Green his wife, who is described as " the purchaser." It recites Walter's seisin in fee simple and an agreement to sell to the purchaser for a like estate at the price of £500. Then there is the operative part. The document is in some respects curious because Mr. Jenkinson had inserted in it a certificate of value which certified that the transaction was one in respect of which the amount or value, or the aggregate amount or

value, of the consideration did not exceed £5,500. This was palpably
wrong in a conveyance of a valuable estate of this sort at what was,
quite obviously, a grotesque under-value, and I do not think that Mr.
Jenkinson could really have thought about it very seriously. No doubt
he was in a hurry at the time. I think in the witness box he was disposed
to admit himself that if he had been served with a document of this
sort in the course of investigating title he would, on the face of the document, have felt that it was a matter about which he would at least be
justified in raising a requisition. But I accept from him that there was
nothing sinister in this. I think he made an error of judgment.

As I say, he took the conveyance, when prepared, to Cleethorpes. He
told me that he read it and explained it to Walter and his wife and they
executed it and Evelyne gave Mr. Jenkinson a cheque for £500, drawn on
her bank account, and he took it, together with the conveyance and the
title deeds, back to his office. The very next day, August 18, that
cheque was negotiated and paid into Roythorne & Co.'s client account
to the credit entry of " W. S. Green re your affairs " and the conveyance
was dated August 17.

In September 1967, Geoffrey, having made up his mind to exercise
the option, visited his parents and it appears from his widow, Mrs. Green's,
evidence that he learned that the land had been conveyed to his mother
at a sum of £500. Mrs. Green told me that his understanding was that
they were not prepared to discuss with him the exercise of the option and,
indeed, he was very upset and immediately went and took legal and other
advice. No doubt it was as a result of that that on September 5, 1967,
an estate contract was registered, but that was a case of bolting the stable
door after the horse had gone.

On October 6 Geoffrey, through his solicitors, gave a formal notice of
exercise of the option. Nothing turns on that and I do not think that it
is in dispute that, if and so far as the option was still capable of being
exercised, that notice was an effective exercise which brought into being
—subject to one point which has not been very strenuously argued by
Mr. Hoffman—a contract between Walter and Geoffrey for the sale of the
farm—a contract which, of course, Walter at this stage had disabled himself from performing.

There followed correspondence between the respective solicitors in
which Messrs. Roythorne pointed out that the option was, at the material
time—that is the date of the conveyance to Evelyne—unregistered.
Perhaps, not surprisingly, neither Walter nor his wife Evelyne complied
with the option notice and Geoffrey continued as tenant of the farm; the
rent due in March was tendered on a " without prejudice " basis and then
on March 28, 1968, the picture changed suddenly because Evelyne died
quite unexpectedly. By her will, which was dated December 20, 1967, she
had appointed Walter, Geoffrey and Derek to be her executors and she
gave a life interest to her husband Walter and the residue on trust for
sale, and for equal division of the proceeds of sale between her five
children.

After her death, not altogether surprisingly, the Inland Revenue
declined to accept a 10 shilling deed stamp and assessed stamp duty on a
value of £40,000, which was the value which had been agreed between
Roythorne and the district valuer.

Between March and November correspondence between the solicitors
concerning the question of whether Geoffrey would join in proving the
will took place. He ultimately determined to prove and he signed an

A Inland Revenue affidavit on October 14, 1968, which showed the farm as an asset of the estate valued at £40,000 but without any notation of any adverse claim against the estate either by him or anybody else. At the same time, however, Geoffrey's solicitors were threatening proceedings against Walter for damages. On September 30, 1968, Walter executed a deed of gift of his property at Croxby to Derek and his sisters and I have been told, although I do not think there is any specific evidence of B this, that at the same time he gave away substantially the whole of such other property as he had. I do not think that this is in issue and the inference seems to me, so far as it is material in these proceedings, to be irresistible that he was taking steps to put assets out of his control— to put them out of his control and also out of the reach of Geoffrey against whose claim for breach of contract there really could be no C defence. Such proceedings as had been threatened were, in fact, commenced on November 25, 1968, and a statement of claim was endorsed on the writ pleading the grant of the option, its exercise, Walter's failure to comply and that the property was, as indeed is clearly the case, very much more valuable than the price contained in the option; and then there was a claim for damages. That was a claim based entirely, at that stage of course, on breach of contract. These are events which D have assumed some importance in the case because they have been relied on by the defendants as establishing that Geoffrey had elected in some way to affirm the purchase by his mother, and to proceed for damages. It should, however, be mentioned that all this was being done against the background of negotiations which were then in train between Geoffrey, through his solicitors, and the other executors and the family generally, to E try to settle the dispute on the basis of Geoffrey's purchasing the farm. The price proposed was, no doubt, in excess of the option price but nevertheless the basis was that he should become the purchaser of the farm. That applies equally to another act relied on by the defendants, which is the concurrence by Geoffrey, as executor, in paying the stamp duty assessed on the conveyance, an act which he did in response to an express request to the then executors' solicitors, Messrs. Roythorne in March F 1969. On November 29, 1968, probate was granted, and on April 14, 1969, Walter and Derek, on the one hand, as executors of Evelyne, and Geoffrey for himself, agreed a new rent of £2,250 for Gravel Hill Farm with his co-executors. That is yet another act relied on as an election to affirm the transaction with his mother Evelyne.

A defence was served in Geoffrey's action for damages against his G father and a list of documents was served, but otherwise that action seems to have remained more or less inactive for the next nine months and part of the explanation for that may well have been due to the fact that, as appears from the correspondence, Walter, at some stage in 1969, decided to consult some other solicitors, he apparently having—temporarily at any rate—repented of what he had done. Geoffrey also changed his solicitors and on January 27, 1970, he started this action against his father Walter H and Derek, as executors of his mother, seeking a declaration that the option was binding on her estate and specific performance. That was amended in October 1970 to include a claim for damages for conspiracy against her estate and against Walter personally. There was also a claim that the land was held by the estate as trustee for Walter, but that has not, I think, been seriously pursued before me.

On February 8, 1972, Walter died and on January 19, 1973, his sole personal representative, Mrs. Kemp, was added as a defendant. She served

a defence formally adopting the defence already served by the other A
defendants. On October 7, 1975, that defence was struck out for failure
to comply with an order for discovery. So far, therefore, as Walter's
estate is concerned, the action is undefended. On May 11, 1973, Geoffrey,
the plaintiff in the action, died and his will was subsequently proved by
the present plaintiffs, Midland Bank Trustee Co. Ltd. and his widow,
Margaret Ann Green, on October 2, 1973. On November 16, 1973, it
was ordered that the action be carried on by them as plaintiffs. B

So as the matter now comes before the court, it is a claim by Geoffrey's
executors against Derek as the sole surviving personal representative of
Evelyne, for specific performance of the option and for damages for conspiracy, and against Walter's executrix for damages, the latter claim being
undefended.

I have stated facts which are not substantially in dispute. What is C
in issue on the pleadings is the question of whether the conveyance constituted a bona fide sale by a vendor to a purchaser or whether it was, in
truth, a fraudulent and colourable transaction or a sham. There are
certain facts, here, which it has been necessary to investigate and I must,
I think, state my conclusions. In the first place, no evidence has been
adduced to suggest that the conveyance did not do, and was not intended D
to do, what, on the face of it, it did, namely to vest the legal estate in the
land in Evelyne and to vest it in her beneficially. Secondly, there was
nothing illusory, I am quite satisfied, about the £500. It was paid to
Walter and there is no reason to suggest or believe that it was not retained
by him for his own use and benefit. Thirdly, there is no reason to suppose
that it did not genuinely come from Evelyne's own pocket. This is a case
where I am bound to say—and I made some remarks during the course E
of the hearing about it—discovery has left something to be desired. That
may be something of an understatement. But very late in the day there
was produced a copy of Evelyne's bank account which shows that this
sum of £500 was raised on overdraft from the bank on her current account.
Mr. Harrod, the partner in Roythorne who was responsible for the litigation, very frankly admitted before me that the failure to produce this
before was entirely his responsibility and was due to an oversight on his F
part, and I entirely accept that. In the event I do not think that any harm
has been done by the late production.

There remains the question of the state of mind of the parties at the
date of the execution of the conveyance. The instructions given to Mr.
Harrod must, I think, lead to the conclusion that Walter had obtained
from somewhere advice that an option could be defeated by a sale to a G
third party. Mr. Harrod recollects giving no such advice but I find on the
evidence before me that the conclusion is really irresistible that, prior to
the conveyance, Walter and Evelyne thought, and intended, that the effect
of it would be to defeat the option. In support of this I have, first of all,
Mrs. Green's unchallenged evidence that the option and her husband's
desire to exercise it were subjects of discussion in the presence of Walter H
and Evelyne. Secondly, I have the admission which is contained in a
letter written by Mr. Harrod in December 1969. Mr. Harrod thinks he
must have written it with hindsight but even if that is so, he can, I think,
only have got the information in it from Walter who, after all, knew his
own state of mind better than anybody else. I need not read the letter
in full. It was a letter written by Messrs. Roythorne to Walter's then
solicitors. As I have said, he changed solicitors, temporarily at any rate,

The Weekly Law Reports, July 7, 1978

157

3 W.L.R.   **Midland Bank Trust Co. v. Green (Ch.D.)**   Oliver J.

A in 1969 and consulted a firm called Beckett and Co. They communicated with Messrs. Roythorne and Messrs. Roythorne sent a reply on December 15, 1969, in which they said:

"... At the time when we were first consulted by Mr. W. S. Green he was very anxious to find some way of avoiding the option in favour of his son Mr. Geoffrey Green. Whether he should have
B done so or not was a matter upon which we were not asked to advise."

Thirdly, there is the conduct of both Walter and Evelyne after the conveyance, when it would have been so easy to put things right if it had not been intended to defeat Geoffrey's option. Fourthly, there is the almost unseemly haste with which the transaction was effected. And finally, and
C perhaps conclusively, there is an affidavit by Walter himself. This has given rise to a curious and unusual point on which I was required to rule, although it may, perhaps, be said that there were already strong enough circumstances in the undisputed facts in the correspondence to enable the court to draw any necessary inferences. Paragraphs 7 and 9 of the statement of claim contain pleas of conspiracy and that the conveyance was a fraudulent and colourable transaction. Paragraph 7 states:
D
"... if contrary to the plaintiff's contention, the purchase price of £500 " was paid—that was then in issue—"... then (i) the said expressed purchase price ... was a very small fraction of the real value of Gravel Hill Farm at the date of the ... conveyance "—and that, I think, is indubitable—" and (ii) the said conveyance did not constitute a bona fide sale by a vendor to a purchaser but was on the
E contrary a fraudulent or colourable transaction or sham."

And in paragraph 9 it is pleaded alternatively:

"... the conveyance was executed pursuant to an agreement or arrangement made between ..." Walter and Evelyne "... whereby they conspired together to defraud and injure the plaintiff by completing a sale or what purported to be a sale of Gravel Hill Farm
F by ..." Walter to Evelyne "... and to deprive the plaintiff of the benefit of the said option."

I need hardly mention the difficulty of direct proof of allegations of this sort in view of the deaths of Walter, Evelyne and Geoffrey. Apart from Derek, who was not called to give evidence before me, these were the only people who could have had any personal knowledge of the trans-
G action, apart perhaps from Mr. Harrod who, of course, was in a position where any advice that he gave or anything that he was told for the purpose of giving advice, was privileged. This has brought to light the question of evidence upon which I had to rule.

After the commencement of the action, Evelyne's executors made a *Beddoes* application for directions which came before Brightman J. It
H was an application in the usual way by originating summons, and in that application both Walter and Geoffrey swore affidavits. Geoffrey of course, as an executor and also a beneficiary, was a party, and a necessary party, to that application.

Shortly before the trial but in good time—although not the time required by the rules—the plaintiffs' solicitors gave notice under the Civil Evidence Act 1968 to put in those affidavits as evidence of the facts therein stated. That of Walter in particular contains an important admis-

sion. Walter's affidavit had already been relied on, without objection A
being taken, in some particulars which were served in 1971. The introduction of the affidavit as evidence at the trial under the Civil Evidence
Act 1968 was, however, objected to by Mr. Hoffmann on the ground that
the use of the affidavit in evidence at the trial—initially I think he was
prepared to go further and say " or anywhere else " although he subsequently modified that—would be a breach of confidentiality and I have B
been referred to an interlocutory judgment of Templeman J. in this action
on February 19, 1976, which, it is submitted by Mr. Hoffmann, concludes
the matter against the plaintiffs. I have heard a considerable argument
about this and I must therefore state the facts about the application
because although I do not think that in the result the introduction of this
evidence seriously affects the legal result of the case, on the view of the
law which I take, I ought, I apprehend, to make and state my findings of C
fact and findings of law on this, in case the matter goes further or the
question arises again in other proceedings.

On December 18, 1972, the plaintiff delivered a reply which contained
this paragraph:

" Further or alternatively:— in proceedings the short title and
reference to the record whereof are . . ." and there then follows the D
reference to the record of the *Beddoes* application—" the second
defendant "—that is Derek—" (jointly with the above named Walter
Stanley Green) sought for and obtained relief on the basis of an
election to treat the transaction effected by the said conveyance as
a sham, and not or alternatively not a bona fide transaction. Such
election was made by reason of the evidence adduced by the second
defendant and the said Walter Stanley Green in the said proceedings. E
The plaintiff was a party to the said proceedings and appeared
therein, and further was represented and made submissions by counsel in the said proceedings on the footing that the second defendant
and the said Walter Stanley Green accepted that the said transaction
was a sham and not a bona fide transaction. In the premises the
second defendant is now estopped from contending that the said
transaction was a bona fide sale." F

So the plea there was one of estoppel based upon the attitude which had
been taken up by Walter and Derek in the *Beddoes* application.

On November 5, 1975, application was made to strike this out as
scandalous and that came before Templeman J. as a procedure summons.
Before referring to the transcript of his judgment which is before me on G
this matter, I must state some of the background facts. The *Beddoes*
application was made by Walter and Derek, and Geoffrey was made a
party. I have been told by Mr. Harman, on instructions, that the plaintiffs
on the summons, i.e. the defendants in this action, availed themselves of
what they conceived to be the privilege which was conferred on them by
the practice, sanctioned by *In re Moritz, decd.* [1960] Ch. 251, of
withholding the evidence from Geoffrey and excluding Geoffrey and his H
counsel from part of the hearing of the summons. As I shall subsequently
point out, I am not sure that the privilege conferred on them by the
decision in *In re Moritz, decd.* in fact enables them to withhold an
affidavit. However, they did not, apparently, serve the affidavit upon
Geoffrey. It appears from Geoffrey's affidavit that Walter, who, I think it
is obvious from correspondence before me now, was then acutely unhappy about what had happened, had personally shown him the draft of

A the affidavit and he was thus able to comment on it in an affidavit which he filed in those proceedings. On those affidavits and after hearing arguments, Brightman J. gave directions to Walter and Derek, Geoffrey and his counsel being excluded from part of that hearing while the argument was in process. Thereafter, Derek, in his list of documents on behalf of the defendants on the present proceedings, disclosed the *Beddoes* summons and the affidavits in schedule 1, part 1, of the list of documents.

B They claimed no privilege and raised no objection to production. I mention this because on the assumption that that is correct, it seems that Templeman J. may possibly have given his judgment under some mis- apprehension about how Walter's affidavit had in fact come into the hands of Geoffrey and his advisers.

I do not propose to read the whole of the judgment which Templeman J.

C then gave. What he said for material purposes was this. He referred to the *Beddoes* application and the nature of such an application, and he said:

"... of course, it is necessary for defendants to open their hearts to the judge and tell him exactly what the action looks like. The judge is acting in some respects as though he were the adviser and trustee giving guidance. The application is invariably heard in chambers,

D and nothing is published because of the jurisdiction of the judge to look after the estate, and because any information made public would be available to the plaintiff in the action, and might well be prejudicial to the defence and the estate which the judge is there to protect. Over the whole of such an application there is an aura of confidentiality, which is preserved by hearing everything in chambers.

E It so happened that the plaintiff [Geoffrey], apart from being the plaintiff in these proceedings, was the son of the deceased, and inter- ested in her estate, and, therefore, he was interested in the application and therefore, rightly or wrongly, the affidavit evidence sworn in support of that application was served upon him, and he turned up in chambers."

F Then he mentions that Brightman J. gave certain directions and continued:

"The plaintiff, having, as I have said (because he was interested in the estate) received a copy of the affidavit sworn in this highly con- fidential application, thought himself justified in making use of the affidavit for the purposes of this action."

Templeman J. refers to the paragraph in the reply which I have read and

G he says that it was

"... a bold claim that somehow in that application some kind of election was made by the defendants, and that election estops them from putting forward part of the defence they have put forward and wish to persist in. Well, that struck me at first blush as a scandalous assertion in the reply, and if it is scandalous I must strike it out. If

H the plaintiff thinks that the order made in chambers by Brightman J. was wrong, or anything ought to be disclosed, he can always go back to the judge. It is a matter entirely for him. But that does not justify the plaintiff pleading at the moment confidential matters without the slightest attempt to refer back to Brightman J., who decided these confidential matters. It is said: 'Oh, well, we have the affidavit, and the affidavit is not now in chambers, so we can go along and tell everybody about it. We won't tell anyone what was said before the

judge in chambers but we will produce this affidavit.' In my judg- A
ment, the same aura of confidentiality hangs over that affidavit as
hangs over the whole of the proceedings in chambers and I am
surprised that any attempt should be made to exploit it."

It is this last sentence that Mr. Hoffmann relies upon as creating an
estoppel per rem judicatam, but I think it is important to place it in its
proper context. The question before the court on that occasion was B
whether, when a party to a *Beddoes* application has taken up a particular
attitude either through his counsel or in his affidavit, that can be seized
on by the other party in his pleading as the foundation for a plea of
estoppel or election. Templeman J. was clearly of the view that as a
matter of practice and policy, that was wrong because it is important that
parties in a fiduciary position should be able to take the directions of the
court without feeling that they are going thereby to be restricted in some C
way in the prosecution of their case. And, if I may say so with respect,
I would in no way dissent from that. But he was not in any way concerned, nor, so far as I know, was it argued before him at all, with the
very much broader question of whether, when a party has put on affidavit
evidence of facts and that affidavit has been filed by or on behalf of the
party to a *Beddoes* application, after the deponent's death that affidavit D
can be tendered as evidence of the same facts either by or against the
party or his representatives and whether in the same or some other proceedings. That point, which is the point that I am concerned with, was
not so far as I am aware argued before him, and I do not for one moment
think that he intended to decide it or even considered it.

Assuming therefore that the broad statement that "the same aura of E
confidentiality hangs over the affidavit as hangs over the whole of the
proceedings in chambers," were wide enough to cover the point now in
issue—of which, taken in its context, I am by no means convinced—I find
myself unable to accept Mr. Hoffmann's primary submission on this matter
which is that the point is, so far as this trial is concerned, res judicata.
If there is any estoppel per rem judicatam it is what is called an issue
estoppel and without referring in detail to the speeches in the House of F
Lords in *Carl Zeiss Stiftung* v. *Rayner & Keeler Ltd.* (*No. 2*) [1967] 1
A.C. 853, I can, I think, take the principles from *Spencer-Bower and Turner, Res Judicata*, 2nd ed. (1969), p. 18 where he sets out what is involved
in the burden of showing res judicata. He lists there six matters: (i) that
the alleged judicial decision was what in law is deemed such; there is no
doubt about that in this case; (ii) that the particular judicial decision relied
upon was in fact pronounced, as alledged; which of course is the case; G
(iii) that the judicial tribunal pronouncing the decision had competent jurisdiction in that behalf; there is no dispute about that; (iv) that the judicial
decision was final; and in the sense in which that word is used here I
think that this decision was a final decision, though made on an interlocutory application; (v) that the judicial decision was, or involved, a
determination of the same question as that sought to be controverted in H
the litigation in which the estoppel is raised; and (vi) that the parties to
the judicial decision, or their privies, were the same persons as the parties
to the proceedings in which the estoppel is raised, or their privies, or that
the decision was conclusive in rem.

In elaboration of that, at p. 179, he points out that the determination
must be fundamental and not collateral and he states that what one has
to look at is the record—the formal judgment or order. Where an express

A declaration as to any particular question or issue appears on the face of the record of a formal judgment or where from the judgment itself the actual grounds of the decision can be clearly ascertained, there is no necessity for further search. But it is not in general permissible where there is no such express declaration in the formal record to examine what was said by judges in delivering their judgment for the purpose of dis-

B covering what were the real grounds of their decision. He adds that that was considered inconvenient and points out that it is legitimate to look at the report of the judgment as delivered to ascertain, not what the fundamental grounds of the decision actually *were*, but for what they *were not*, for the purpose of negativing any contention that some one particular ground was the only possible and necessary basis of the decision.

The wide statement, on the assumption still that it bears the meaning
C which Mr. Hoffmann seeks to attribute to it, was not one which, in my judgment, *necessarily* arose for decision. The only issue on the procedure summons was whether, where proceedings have taken place in chambers in this way, it can be subsequently relied upon as an estoppel in some way prejudicial to him that a party took up a particular attitude or made a particular submission. It is true, of course, that, in arriving at his conclusion, Templeman J. based himself upon what was said in the
D affidavits; but he was not concerned there at all with the question of whether the affidavit could be used as proof of the facts which were set out in it. That is the only purpose for which the documents are sought to be used on this occasion.

On the point which it falls to me to decide, therefore, I can see no issue estoppel here. Indeed, I think it would be most surprising if there
E were, for the order which was made on the record is one which was made " upon reading the pleadings " which included at that date particulars referring in terms to the facts contained in Walter's affidavit but as facts to be relied on under paragraph 7 of the statement of claim and not in support of some pleaded estoppel or election. Those particulars were not struck out or sought to be struck out.

F Mr. Hoffmann, however, has submitted that even if there is no issue estoppel here, nevertheless there is some general principle that protects evidence of facts given on a *Beddoes* application from being used or referred to. He was, I think, inclined at first to put it as generally as that —that no affidavit filed on a *Beddoes* summons could be used or referred to in any other proceedings than that summons. Such a proposition clearly does not in my judgment bear examination. In the absence of a
G direction by the judge that there should be no publication—and there was no such direction here—the publication of matters in chambers is not per se a contempt of court any longer. The affidavits are filed and formerly could be inspected by anybody on payment of the appropriate fee, which was why, as I understand it, the practice grew up of giving confidential evidence by way of an exhibited statement which was not
H filed. Although the affidavits are not now open to immediate public inspection, they are open to inspection once they get into the Public Records Office. That, no doubt, is a fairly lengthy process, but at the time when the practice in relation to *Beddoes'* applications grew up, they could be inspected by anybody on payment of the appropriate fee and it is difficult to see how any general confidentiality could be claimed for documents which then were—and still are, ultimately—open to public inspection.

162

Quite apart from this, suppose that affidavits are filed containing false A
statements which lead the court to give directions for an action to be
prosecuted or defended by trustees.   Beneficiaries subsequently challenge
the payment by the trustees of the costs of the unsuccessful proceedings
on the ground that the court's directions were procured by fraud.   Is it
to be said that they cannot refer to the affidavits by which the fraud
was perpetrated?   That cannot, in my judgment, be right and I think that
Mr. Hoffmann was disposed to concede it.   B

Mr. Hoffmann confined himself to the much more modest proposition
that an affidavit sworn in a *Beddoes* summons cannot be referred to in
the proceedings which are the subject matter of the summons without
the consent of the party on whose behalf the affidavit was sworn.   I am
bound to say that I know of no authority for such a proposition.   Indeed
it seems to me to contradict what is implicit in *In re Moritz, decd.* C
[1960] Ch. 251 namely that if the exhibits to the affidavit *are* furnished
to or get into the hands of the opposite party to the litigation, they can be
used by him to the detriment of his opponent.   *In re Moritz, decd.*
enshrines the practice of the Chancery Division which entitles an applicant
for directions as to litigation to withhold from the other party the exhibits
to his affidavits and the argument conducted before the judge.   The
reasoning behind that is, of course, that the party would otherwise be D
entitled to use it as a weapon to the prejudice of the applicant.   At the
time of *In re Moritz, decd.* the former R.S.C., Ord. 61, rr. 17 and 18
were in force which enabled inspections to take place of all filed documents
on payment of the prescribed fee and although the right has since been
restricted, that restriction cannot, I think, have altered the basis of the
Chancery practice.   If, as Mr. Hoffmann suggests, there is some general E
principle of confidentiality which protects the use of all material delivered
to anyone in the course of a *Beddoes* application, it would, it seems to
me, be unnecessary to withhold it, at any rate so far as its use in evidence
is concerned, although it might well be, I suppose, that there were other
reasons for withholding exhibited material, such as counsels' opinions.   In
exercising its jurisdiction to give directions, the court, as Wilberforce J.
pointed out in *Eton College* v. *Minister of Agriculture, Fisheries and Food* F
[1964] Ch. 274, is exercising an essentially administrative function, and
will adapt its practice so far as is practicable in order to do justice in
the particular circumstances of the case.

I am bound to say that I know of no general principle which would
prevent any party to the litigation from inspecting and making use of a
filed document.   Indeed, the rules of court make express provision for G
him to be given notice of filing and R.S.C., Ord. 63, r. 4, whilst now
restricting the right of public examination, makes an express exception so
far as the parties are concerned.   Rule 4 (3) provides:

> " Nothing in the foregoing provisions shall be taken as preventing any
> party to a cause or matter searching for, inspecting and taking or
> bespeaking a copy of any affidavit or other document filed in the H
> central office in that cause or matter or filed therein before the com-
> mencement of that cause or matter but made with a view to its
> commencement."

Indeed, it is clear from *Jones* v. *Trinder, Capron & Co.* [1918] 2 Ch. 7
that a filed document may be used even after an order removing it from
the file has been made.

A   That, as it seems to me, is the whole point of the practice generally adopted of dealing with confidential matter by exhibited statements or documents which are not filed. I doubt, in fact, whether the direction given in *In re Moritz, decd.* [1960] Ch. 251 could have been given in the case of the affidavit itself although the point did not arise there because the only question with which the court was concerned was inspection of the exhibits. It seems to me, however, that the Rules of the B   Supreme Court give an express right to a party to see and take copies of filed material.

In any event, I do not think I have to decide any such general question in this case and I must be cautious of expressing wide general propositions which go beyond the immediate case before me. I am concerned with a particular limited question here and on these facts it seems to me that C   even if there was any such confidentiality as to the admissions or statements which are contained in Walter's affidavit as Mr. Hoffmann claims, that was waived by their publication, first by Walter himself to Geoffrey and secondly by their inclusion without any claim of privilege in the list of documents served by Derek.

Mr. Hoffmann argues that such affidavits are akin to "without D   prejudice" correspondence and therefore cannot be used even in cross-examination and even if the deponent is called at the trial and gives evidence which flatly contradicts what he has said in his affidavit. I do not think that this analogy really runs; the privilege conferred by "without prejudice" negotiations is based, as I understand it, upon some express or implied agreement that it should not be referred to in evidence except in the event of a final and concluded agreement of compromise. I can see E   no such implication where a party, who may be under the Chancery practice entitled to withhold any exhibited controversial evidence from his opponent on a *Beddoes* application, deliberately discloses it to him. What Mr. Hoffmann seeks to suggest, in effect, is that the fact that an affidavit is sworn on a *Beddoes* application confers some sort of proprietary interest not, I think, in the deponent but in the party on whose behalf the affidavit F   is sworn. I do not think that there can be any proprietary interest in evidence and it would seem to me lamentable if, when a deponent is dead and his affidavit on a *Beddoes* application prior to the proceedings may be the only available direct evidence of relevant or even critical facts, it cannot be referred to except by permission of one or other party to the litigation who may have a direct interest in suppressing it. If there is any such principle of confidentiality in respect of filed evidence it must, G   I think, be one which it is open to the trial judge to over-ride in an appropriate case. But in any event, as I say, I am clearly of the view that in this case the privilege of confidentiality, if there be such, was waived and I have admitted the affidavits in evidence.

Having said that, they contain, I think, very little that adds to what was already pretty clear from the correspondence and the surrounding H   circumstances. Walter gives some evidence about the value of the farm which he puts at £150 an acre at the time of the grant of the option and about £185 an acre at the time when he swore his affidavit in 1970. The material passage upon which Mr. Harman relies is in paragraph 4. Speaking of the date of the conveyance to Evelyne, Walter said:

"At this date and for a few months prior thereto, there was and had been a serious quarrel between Geoffrey and the testatrix and myself. Neither the option nor any estate contract constituted by the

option and the notice of intention to exercise it had been registered A
at the land charges registry, and the testatrix and I were advised by
our solicitors that in these circumstances if I transferred the farm to
a purchaser, the purchaser would take free of Geoffrey's rights thereunder. Thereupon in order to defeat Geoffrey's option over the farm,
on August 17, 1967, I sold and conveyed the farm (subject to the
tenancy) to the testatrix in consideration of the payment by her to
me of £500."   B

That is, of course, a clear admission of his motives as against Walter
himself and against his estate. The only material passage which I find in
the other affidavit which was filed on behalf of Geoffrey is the statement,
which I see no reason to doubt, that in March 1970 Geoffrey saw his
father Walter who showed him a copy of the draft of his affidavit.
                                                                       C
On that evidence and in the light of the other matters I have referred
to, I am unable to resist the conclusion that both Walter and Evelyne
knew of the option, that they conceived and became parties to the conveyance in the belief that it would frustrate the effective exercise of the
option and that the defeat of the option was their primary purpose and
intent in entering into and completing the transaction. What then are the
consequences? First, there cannot, I think, be any answer so far as D
Walter's estate is concerned to a claim for damages. There will therefore
be judgment against the defendant, Beryl Rosalie Kemp, in her capacity
as executrix of Walter, for an inquiry as to damages, with liberty to apply.
So far as Evelyne's estate is concerned, there is however what appears
to me to be a complete answer to any such claim. The claim, being one
in tort, is one which under the old law would not have survived the death E
of Evelyne; under the Law Reform (Miscellaneous Provisions) Act 1934,
it would have survived but only if the action was commenced within six
months of the grant of representation to her estate, i.e. November 29,
1968. Since this action was not commenced until January 1970, it is, as
I say, clearly out of time. Although the relevant provisions of the Act
of 1934 relating to the time limitation were repealed by the Proceedings
Against Estates Act 1970, section 3 (3) of that Act prevents the revival of F
any cause of action which was already barred, as this one was, when the
Act came into force. Mr. Harman, although not making any concession,
felt unable to argue against those propositions.
The only live question, therefore, so far as Evelyne's estate is concerned, is specific performance and, as one would expect, Mr. Hoffmann
relies upon section 13 of the Land Charges Act 1925, which was the G
relevant legislation in force at the material time. That section provides
in subsection (2) that " A land charge of class B, class C or class D,"—and
of course an option or estate contract is a class C (iv):

> " created or arising after the commencement of this Act, shall (except
> as hereinafter provided) be void as against a purchaser of the land
> charged therewith, or of any interest in such land, unless the land H
> charge is registered in the appropriate register before the completion
> of the purchase: "—and then there is this important proviso—
> " Provided that, as regards a land charge of class D and an estate
> contract created or entered into after the commencement of this Act,
> this subsection only applies in favour of a purchaser of a legal estate
> for money or money's worth."

A   If Evelyne was a purchaser of the legal estate for money or money's worth within that proviso that must be the end of the case. Mr. Harman argues thus. First of all, he says, in the proviso which I have just read, the word " purchaser " is used to refer and to refer only to a person who comes into a matter as a commercial matter—one who acquires the legal estate under a contract of sale. He has referred me to a number of cases, for instance, *Vane* v. *Vane* (1873) L.R. 8 Ch.App. 383; *Inland Revenue Com-*
B   *missioners* v. *Gribble* [1913] 3 K.B. 212 and *H. L. Bolton (Engineering) Co. Ltd.* v. *T. J. Graham & Sons Ltd.* [1957] 1 Q.B. 159 for the various meanings of the term and for the ordinary meaning of the term. The present transaction, he says, bears none of the badges of a purchase. There was no negotiation of the price. There were no normal con-veyancing stages and there was no conceivable commercial purpose in
C   the transaction; it was merely a gift dressed up to look like a sale. The difficulty, I feel, about that submission is that the statute with which I am concerned contains its own artificial definition of a purchaser and the question is not, as it seems to me, whether Evelyne was a purchaser in the ordinary sense of the term as outlined in, for instance, *H. L. Bolton (Engineering) Co. Ltd.* v. *T. J. Graham & Sons Ltd.*, but whether she was a purchaser within the statutory definition which is contained in the Act.
D   That statutory definition is in section 20 (8) which is in these terms:

> " ' Purchaser ' means any person (including a mortgagee or lessee) who, for valuable consideration, takes any interest in land or in a charge of land; and ' purchase ' has a corresponding meaning; . . ."

Mr. Harman seeks to escape from this by pointing out that section 20 expressly provides that the definitions only apply " unless the context
E   otherwise requires." The context does here, he says, " otherwise require " because if you write out the statutory definition in full in the proviso to section 13 (2) in place of the word " purchaser " it makes no sense at all; in fact it makes nonsense and is contradictory. Therefore, he says, " purchaser " in the proviso has some other meaning. The meaning he ascribes to it is the ordinary meaning which in common parlance one
F   would have, i.e. a purchaser under a contract.

I am bound to say, with respect and with regret, that I find that too facile a test. The main subsection applies only to a purchaser as defined. It is then provided that that which, ex hypothesi, applies only to a statutory purchaser shall apply only in particular circumstances, that is to say, in the case of the " purchaser of a legal estate for money or money's worth " in the case of particular land charges. I can see no
G   reason for giving a restricted meaning to the word " purchaser " beyond that which the section requires, the only requirements being, as I see it, the substitution of the legal estate for " any interest in the land " and of " money or money's worth " for " valuable consideration." Mr. Harman also relies on the definition of purchaser which is contained in section 205 (i) (xxi) of the Law of Property Act 1925 which is in these terms:

H   > " ' Purchaser ' means a purchaser in good faith for valuable con-sideration and includes a lessee, mortgagee or other person who for valuable consideration acquires an interest in property . . ."

Then there is an exception for Part I of the Act which I do not think I need trouble with—and it continues:

> " ' purchase ' has a meaning corresponding with that of ' purchaser '; and ' valuable consideration ' includes marriage but does not include a nominal consideration in money; . . ."

He also refers to section 199 of the Act which provides: **A**

" A purchaser shall not be prejudicially affected by notice of—(i) any instrument or matter capable of registration under the provisions of the Land Charges Act 1925, or any enactment which it replaces, which is void or not enforceable as against him under that Act or enactment, by reason of the non-registration thereof; . . ."

He translates section 199 into a positive provision by implication that a **B** purchaser in bad faith *is* affected, using " bad faith " in the sense of a deliberate design to take advantage of the statutory provisions of the Land Charges Act 1925 or of a fraudulent intention. This, he says, was not a real purchase at all; it was a sham; it was a disguised gift with a consideration put in merely to enable the statutory provisions of the Land Charges Act 1925 to be invoked.   **C**

Again, regretfully, I do not feel that I can accept that submission. The transaction was not in my judgment a sham in the accepted sense of the word at all. There was a genuine passing of the legal estate by Walter to his wife without any reservation of any interest to Walter. It was, and was intended to be, a beneficial transfer of the legal estate. There was a genuine payment of the expressed consideration of £500 and there was an acceptance of that payment. That there may have been **D** some ulterior motive for the transaction does not as it seems to me make the transaction other than what it was. Obviously a substantial and indeed an almost overwhelming element of gift existed here but in my judgment that cannot matter.

Mr. Hoffmann argues that really I have only to look at two main questions. I think in fact, in his argument, he sub-divided them into sub-questions but basically they come to this—(1) was Evelyne a **E** purchaser as defined? and (2) was the consideration for the purchase " money or money's worth " and did she acquire a legal estate?

First of all, did she take any interest in the land? She plainly did; the legal estate was conveyed to her. Secondly, did she take it for valuable consideration? The conveyance recites that the money was paid as consideration for the conveyance, the evidence establishes that she **F** did pay the money and one can see no reason why she should have paid that money except for the conveyance of that land to her. I do not think that it can matter what her motive was in entering into this transaction. She was acquiring a legal estate and paying no doubt a wholly inadequate sum for it; but that she was paying money for it seems to me to be beyond doubt. The fact that she knew and indeed intended that the transaction should have a particular effect as regards Geoffrey's **G** option does not seem to me to make her any less a purchaser within the statutory definition or a purchaser for money or money's worth.

Mr. Hoffman has referred me to some well known cases on this branch of the law, *Hollington Brothers Ltd.* v. *Rhodes (Note)* [1951] 2 All E.R. 578 and *In re Monolithic Building Co.* [1915] 1 Ch. 643 which established that actual knowledge in this context is really immaterial. I **H** therefore find myself compelled to accept Mr. Hoffmann's argument and to hold that Evelyne was a purchaser for money or money's worth of the legal estate against whom Geoffrey's option was, under the statutory provisions, void.

I said in the course of the hearing that the merits appeared to me to be all one way. Mr. Hoffmann cautioned me against jumping to any such conclusion without any full knowledge of the family quarrels which

A have gone on or of the circumstances. I accept that and will qualify it to this extent, that, so far as the evidence before me goes, it seems to me that the merits are all one way. The conclusion I have reached therefore is one which I reach with regret, because as it seems to me Geoffrey had a clear legal right which was deliberately frustrated by his parents in breach of the contract created by the option. Nevertheless I cannot, with the best will in the world, allow my subjective moral judgment to

B stand in the way of what I apprehend to be the clear meaning of the statutory provisions. That, therefore, it seems to me, concludes the case. It is unnecessary for me to deal with the other defences which have been raised by the defendants, defences of laches, acquiescence, election and estoppel. I need only say this, that having considered the circumstances I am not satisfied that, if I were in Mr. Harman's favour on the main

C point, any of those defences could avail the defendants. But they do not in the circumstances arise and regretfully I feel therefore that as against the estate of Evelyne, i.e. against the defendant, Derek Green, in his capacity as surviving executor, I must dismiss the claim.

D
> *Judgment against first defendant for damages and costs, up to date that her defence was struck out, together with costs of first two days of the hearing.*
>
> *Claims against remaining defendants dismissed with costs, save that plaintiff have costs of half a day's hearing to be set off against such costs.*

E
Solicitors: *Sidney Torrance & Co. for J. Levi & Co., Leeds; Simmons & Simmons for Roythorne & Co., Spalding.*

T. C. C. B.

F

[CHANCERY DIVISION]

MIDLAND BANK TRUST CO. LTD. AND ANOTHER
v. HETT, STUBBS & KEMP (A FIRM)

G
[1972 G. No. 2267]

1977 Oct. 25, 26, 27;   Oliver J.
      Nov. 1, 2, 3; 21

Solicitor—Negligence—Tort, whether liable in—Option to purchase
H   *farm—Solicitor's omission to register option as land charge—*
     Option defeated by sale of land to third party—Whether right
     of action against solicitors statute-barred—Whether solicitors
     liable both in tort and contract
Limitation of Action—Contract, breach of—Negligence—Solicitor's
     failure to register option to purchase farm — Land sold to
     defeat option—Whether solicitor's duty continuing one—
     Whether action statute-barred

In March 1961, W agreed to grant his son, G, an option to purchase from him a 300-acre farm which at that time

was let to G at a rent of £900 per annum. They went to the A
defendant firm of solicitors, and S, the senior partner, drew
up a document which W signed and which was dated March
24, 1961, whereby in consideration of £1 paid by G, W thereby
granted to G the option of purchasing the farm at £75 per
acre. The option was expressed to remain effective for 10
years. G duly paid the consideration of £1 but, unfortunately,
S omitted to register the option as an estate contract under
the Land Charges Act 1925. On a number of occasions, G B
consulted the defendant firm on the question whether he
should exercise the option. On August 17, 1967, W, with
the object of defeating the option and having discovered,
through consulting with fresh solicitors, that the option had
not been registered, sold and conveyed the farm to his wife
for £500. After the sale K, a partner in the defendant firm,
sought to remedy his firm's omission by registering the option
under the Land Charges Act 1925 and, on October 6, 1967, C
G served formal notice in purported exercise of the option.
Neither W nor his wife complied with the notice. On March
28, 1968, W's wife died. On January 27, 1970, G commenced
proceedings against W and against his wife's executors, of
whom he was himself one, seeking, inter alia, a declaration
that the option was binding on her estate, and claiming
specific performance. On February 8, 1972, W died, and on
May 11, 1973, G also died. The plaintiffs, G's executors, D
continued the action but the action failed save for an award
of damages against W's estate.

On July 21, 1972, G had commenced an action against
the defendant firm of solicitors, claiming damages for negligence or breach of professional duty in neglecting to register
the option, and in failing to advise G as to the necessity of
so doing.

On the question whether the action against the defendant E
firm, which was continued by G's executors, was barred by
the Limitation Act 1939, and had already become barred
before the date of the sale and conveyance of the farm to
W's wife:—

Held, (1) that there was no general or continuing duty
arising out of G's retainer of the defendant firm of solicitors
to consider the enforceability of the option on every occasion
on which they were consulted as to a possible exercise, nor F
to check, on such occasions, whether it had in fact been duly
registered under the Land Charges Act 1925 (post, pp. 180F—
181D).

Duchess of Argyll v. *Beuselinck* [1972] 2 Lloyd's Rep.
172; *Griffiths* v. *Evans* [1953] 1 W.L.R. 1424, C.A.; *Hall* v.
Meyrick [1957] 2 Q.B. 455, C.A. and *Wood* v. *Jones* (1889)
61 L.T. 551 considered.

(2) That a duty of care was imposed upon the defendant G
firm of solicitors by reason of the relationship of solicitor
and client existing between the parties, and that the defendants were therefore liable in tort, independently of any liability
in contract, for their negligence in omitting to register the
option before a third party had acquired an adverse interest
in the farm; and that, since the cause of action in tort did
not arise until the damage occurred on August 17, 1967, a
date within six years before the date of the writ, the plaintiffs' H
cause of action was not statute-barred under the Limitation
Act 1939 (post, pp. 193G—194B, 208G—209B).

Hedley Byrne & Co. Ltd. v. *Heller & Partners Ltd.* [1964]
A.C. 465, H.L.(E.); *Esso Petroleum Co. Ltd.* v. *Mardon* [1976]
Q.B. 801, C.A. and dictum of Lord Salmon in *Arenson* v.
Arenson [1977] A.C. 405, 434, H.L.(E.) applied.

Groom v. *Crocker* [1939] 1 K.B. 194, C.A.; *Clark* v.
Kirby-Smith [1964] Ch. 506; *Bagot* v. *Stevens Scanlan & Co.*

3 W.L.R.   **Midland Bank v. Hett, Stubbs & Kemp (Ch.D.)**

A *Ltd.* [1966] 1 Q.B. 197; *Cook* v. *Swinfen* [1967] 1 W.L.R. 457, C.A. and *Heywood* v. *Wellers* [1976] Q.B. 446, C.A. not followed.

(3) That since the negligence relied upon was not the giving of wrong and negligent advice, in which case the breach of contract would necessarily have arisen at a fixed point of time, but was a simple nonfeasance, the duty of the defendant firm of solicitors to register the option continued

B to bind them until it ceased to be effectively capable of performance on August 17, 1967, and therefore, since the action against the defendants in contract was not statute-barred, they were also liable to the plaintiffs in contract (post, pp. 210D–H, 213E–F, H—214A).

Bean v. *Wade* (1885) 2 T.L.R. 157, C.A. distinguished.

Observations on the principle of stare decisis (post, pp. 182F—183c).

C

The following cases are referred to in the judgment:

Addis v. *Gramophone Co. Ltd.* [1909] A.C. 488, H.L.(E.).

Allen v. *Sir Alfred McAlpine & Sons Ltd.* [1968] 2 Q.B. 229; [1968] 2 W.L.R. 366; [1968] 1 All E.R. 543, C.A.

Anns v. *Merton London Borough Council* [1977] 2 W.L.R. 1024; [1977]

D   2 All E.R. 492, H.L.(E.).

Anon (1372) *Fitzherbert's smith's case* (1534) *Natura Brevium* 94D (Year Book 46 Edw. III Trin. 19).

Arenson v. *Arenson* [1977] A.C. 405; [1975] 3 W.L.R. 815; [1975] 3 All E.R. 901, H.L.(E.).

Argyll (*Duchess*) v. *Beuselinck* [1972] 2 Lloyd's Rep. 172.

Bagot v. *Stevens Scanlan & Co. Ltd.* [1966] 1 Q.B. 197; [1964] 3 W.L.R.

E   1162; [1964] 3 All E.R. 577.

Bailey v. *Bullock* [1950] 2 All E.R. 1167.

Barnett v. *Chelsea and Kensington Hospital Management Committee* [1969] 1 Q.B. 428; [1968] 2 W.L.R. 422; [1968] 1 All E.R. 1068.

Battley v. *Faulkner* (1820) 3 B. & Ald. 288.

Batty v. *Metropolitan Property Realisations Ltd.* [1978] 2 W.L.R. 500, C.A.

F *Bean* v. *Wade* (1885) 1 T.L.R. 404; 1 Cab. & Ell. 519; 2 T.L.R. 157, C.A.

Blyth v. *Fladgate* [1891] 1 Ch. 337.

Boorman v. *Brown* (1842) 3 Q.B. 511; sub nom. *Brown* v. *Boorman* (1844) 11 Cl. & Fin. 1, H.L.(E.).

Bottomley v. *Bannister* [1932] 1 K.B. 458, C.A.

Brown v. *Howard* (1820) 2 Brod. & B. 73.

Candler v. *Crane, Christmas & Co.* [1951] 2 K.B. 164; [1951] 1 All E.R.

G   426, C.A.

Cartledge v. *E. Jopling & Sons Ltd.* [1963] A.C. 758; [1963] 2 W.L.R. 210; [1963] 1 All E.R. 341, H.L.(E.).

Clark v. *Kirby-Smith* [1964] Ch. 506; [1964] 3 W.L.R. 239; [1964] 2 All E.R. 835.

Coats Patons (*Retail*) *Ltd.* v. *Birmingham Corporation* (1971) 69 L.G.R. 356.

H *Consett Industrial and Provident Society Ltd.* v. *Consett Iron Co. Ltd.* [1922] 2 Ch. 135, C.A.

Cook v. *Swinfen* [1967] 1 W.L.R. 457; [1967] 1 All E.R. 299, C.A.

Davies v. *Hood* (1903) 88 L.T. 19.

Davies v. *Lock* (1844) 3 L.T. O.S. 125.

Dearle v. *Hall* (1828) 3 Russ. 1.

Dutton v. *Bognor Regis Urban District Council* [1972] 1 Q.B. 373; [1972] 2 W.L.R. 299; [1972] 1 All E.R. 462, C.A.

Midland Bank v. Hett, Stubbs & Kemp (Ch.D.) [1978]

East Suffolk Rivers Catchment Board v. *Kent* [1941] A.C. 74; [1940] 4 **A**
All E.R. 527, H.L.(E.).
Edwards v. *Mallan* [1908] 1 K.B. 1002, C.A.
Esso Petroleum Co. Ltd. v. *Mardon* [1976] Q.B. 801; [1976] 2 W.L.R.
583; [1976] 2 All E.R. 5, C.A.
Everett v. *Griffiths* [1920] 3 K.B. 163, C.A.
Fish v. *Kapur* [1948] 2 All E.R. 176.
Great Western Railway Co. v. *Owners of S.S. Mostyn* [1928] A.C. 57, **B**
H.L.(E.).
Griffiths v. *Evans* [1953] 1 W.L.R. 1424; [1953] 2 All E.R. 1364, C.A.
Groom v. *Crocker* [1939] 1 K.B. 194; [1938] 2 All E.R. 394, C.A.
Hall v. *Meyrick* [1957] 2 Q.B. 455; [1957] 3 W.L.R. 273; [1957] 2 All
E.R. 722, C.A.
Hedley Byrne & Co. Ltd. v. *Heller & Partners Ltd.* [1964] A.C. 465;
[1963] 3 W.L.R. 101; [1963] 2 All E.R. 575, H.L.(E.).
Heywood v. *Wellers* [1976] Q.B. 446; [1976] 2 W.L.R. 101; [1976] 1 **C**
All E.R. 300, C.A.
Howell v. *Young* (1826) 5 B. & C. 259.
Hughes v. *Twisden* (1886) 55 L.J.Ch. 481.
Jackson v. *Mayfair Window Cleaning Co. Ltd.* [1952] 1 All E.R. 215.
Jarvis v. *Moy, Davies, Smith, Vandervell & Co.* [1936] 1 K.B. 399, C.A.
Kelly v. *Metropolitan Railway Co.* [1895] 1 Q.B. 944, C.A.
Lake v. *Bushby* [1949] 2 All E.R. 964. **D**
Manby, In re (1856) 26 L.J.Ch. 313.
Miliangos v. *George Frank (Textiles) Ltd.* [1976] A.C. 443; [1975] 3
W.L.R. 758; [1975] 3 All E.R. 801, H.L.(E.).
Ministry of Housing and Local Government v. *Sharp* [1970] 2 Q.B. 223;
[1970] 2 W.L.R. 802; [1970] 1 All E.R. 1009, C.A.
Mutual Life and Citizens' Assurance Co. Ltd. v. *Evatt* [1971] A.C. 793;
[1971] 2 W.L.R. 23; [1971] 1 All E.R. 150, P.C. **E**
Newsholme Brothers v. *Road Transport and General Insurance Co. Ltd.*
[1929] 2 K.B. 356, C.A.
Nocton v. *Lord Ashburton* [1914] A.C. 932, H.L.(E.).
Otto v. *Bolton and Norris* [1936] 2 K.B. 46; [1936] 1 All E.R. 960.
Quinn v. *Leathem* [1901] A.C. 495, H.L.(I.).
Robertson v. *Bannigan,* S.L.T. 318.
Sachs v. *Henderson* [1902] 1 K.B. 612, C.A. **F**
Sawyer v. *Goodwin* (1867) 36 L.J.Ch. 578.
Short v. *M'Carthy* (1820) 3 B. & Ald. 626.
Simmons v. *Pennington & Son* [1955] 1 W.L.R. 183; [1955] 1 All E.R.
240, C.A.
Smith v. *Fox* (1848) 6 Hare 386.
Turner v. *Stallibrass* [1898] 1 Q.B. 56, C.A.
Wilkinson v. *Sibley* [1932] 1 K.B. 194, C.A. **G**
Williams v. *Glasbrook Brothers Ltd.* [1947] 2 All E.R. 884, C.A.
Wood v. *Jones* (1889) 61 L.T. 551.
Young v. *Bristol Aeroplane Co. Ltd.* [1946] A.C. 163; [1946] 1 All E.R.
98, H.L.(E.).

The following additional cases were cited in argument:

Sparham-Souter v. *Town and Country Developments (Essex) Ltd.* [1976] **H**
1 Q.B. 858; [1976] 2 W.L.R. 493; [1976] 2 All E.R. 65, C.A.
Steljes v. *Ingram* (1903) 19 T.L.R. 534.

ACTION

By a writ dated July 21, 1972, issued by Thomas Geoffrey Green, and
a statement of claim dated April 11, 1974, the plaintiffs, Midland Bank
Trust Co. Ltd. and Mrs. Margaret Ann Green, as executors of Thomas

A   Geoffrey Green who had died on May 11, 1973, claimed damages against the defendants, Hett, Stubbs & Kemp, damages for negligence or breach of duty in that they, acting as solicitors for Thomas Geoffrey Green "neglected (at the date of grant of the option and at all material times thereafter) to register and failed (at the said date or at any time thereafter) to advise the plaintiff [Thomas Geoffrey Green] as to the necessity of register-ing an estate contract in respect of an option dated March 24, 1961, granted

B   to him by Walter Stanley Green [his father] to purchase Gravel Hill Farm, Thornton-le-Moor, Lincolnshire, against the estate owner Walter Stanley Green." In the statement of claim there were also claims to further or other relief, all necessary accounts and inquiries, and costs. The defendants contended that if, which was denied, Thomas Geoffrey Green had any cause of action arising during his lifetime, the same was barred under and

C   by virtue of the Limitation Act 1939.

The facts are stated in the judgment.

Jeremiah Harman Q.C. and *Jonathan Parker* for the plaintiffs.
R. A. Gatehouse Q.C. and *Ian McCulloch* for the defendants.

D   *Cur. adv. vult.*

OLIVER J.   The late Mr. Walter Green owned a 300 acre farm known as Gravel Hill Farm, Thornton-le-Moor, in Lincolnshire. His elder son, Geoffrey, had a tenancy of the farm from his father at a rent of £900 per annum. It will be convenient to refer to them by their Christian names. In March 1961 they came to an arrangement under which Geoffrey was

E   to be entitled to an option to purchase the freehold reversion at a price of £75 per acre exercisable at any time during the next 10 years. In order to put this into a regular and enforceable form they together visited a firm of solicitors in Brigg, Messrs. Hett, Davy & Stubbs (now Hett, Stubbs & Kemp), which had previously acted for each of them individually. There they saw the senior partner, Mr. Aymere Albert Fletcher Stubbs, a solicitor

F   of great experience in conveyancing matters and, according to the evidence of his son, a meticulous lawyer. Mr. Stubbs drew up a formal option agreement in his own handwriting and Walter signed it. It was in these terms:

"To: Thomas Geoffrey Green, Gravel Hill Farm, Thornton-le-Moor.
In consideration of the sum of one pound paid by you to me I hereby
G   give you the option of purchasing the Gravel Hill Farm now in your occupation at the sum of £75 (seventy five pounds) per acre. This option to remain effective for ten years. Dated this 24th March 1961."

That was signed over a sixpenny stamp.

An issue has been raised in this action as to whether the £1 was ever
H   paid. Both Walter and Geoffrey have died since this action was com-menced, as has Mr. Stubbs senior, so that the payment is not easily suscep-tible of proof. I have admitted, under the Civil Evidence Act 1968, evidence in the form of affidavits of Walter and Geoffrey and hearsay statements of Geoffrey, and there is a conflict between the testimony of the two persons primarily concerned. Geoffrey has sworn that he did pay it, and with the option being drawn up in the presence of the meticulous Mr. Stubbs, I think that the overwhelming likelihood is that it was paid.

For what it is worth—and I am far from convinced that it makes any A
difference in the result—I so find as a fact.

There can be no shadow of doubt that it was the firm's duty, acting
as it was for both parties to the transaction, to complete the matter by
taking the necessary steps to see that Geoffrey's interest was fully protected
by registering the option as an estate contract under the provisions of the
Land Charges Act 1925. For some reason Mr. Stubbs, meticulous conveyancer though he was, did not do this. Whether he intended to do it B
and put it on one side and then forgot; whether he thought that in a family
transaction of this sort it was practically unnecessary; or whether, for some
reason, it simply slipped his mind, remains a mystery. For whatever
reason, he omitted to do it immediately after the grant of the option, and
that omission remained unremedied until September 1967 when the option
was registered by another member of the firm, his son, Mr. Kenneth Stubbs. C

Unfortunately, when Mr. Kenneth Stubbs finally put in train the steps
which his father had so strangely omitted to take it was already too late.
Walter, having, for some reason, repented of the grant of the option and
having, through some other solicitors whom he consulted, discovered that
it had not yet been registered against him by his former solicitors, had
determined to defeat it by conveying the farm to his wife, Geoffrey's
mother, for a small, but not entirely nominal, consideration of £500. That D
transaction was—unknown to Geoffrey and to Messrs. Hett, Davy & Stubbs
—completed on August 17, 1967, some 6½ years after the grant of the
option. In proceedings by Geoffrey's executors against his father's and
his mother's executors which recently came before me I found myself compelled to hold that the option had been defeated except to the extent, for
what it is worth, of grounding a claim for damages against Walter's estate. E

On July 21, 1972, family negotiations for the settlement of the dispute
having failed to produce any result, Geoffrey commenced this action
against his former solicitors for damages for breach of their professional
duty.

The damage sustained by Geoffrey and his family as a direct result of
the failure of Messrs. Hett, Davy & Stubbs to do, before Augst 17, 1967,
what it was their plain duty to do has been very great. The estimate of his F
accountants in June 1967 was that the exercise of the option, followed
by a sale and lease back of the farm—which was what he then intended
—would have brought him a profit of £37,750. But of course, it does not
end there, because the effect of his inability to acquire the freehold meant
that he stayed on under his existing tenancy, the rent under which was
promptly increased, and that, on his subsequent death, his widow and G
family, as the law then stood, had no security of tenure.

There was no possible way in which, during the 6½ years which
elapsed between the grant of the option and its frustration on August
17, 1967, Geoffrey could have discovered that registration had not been
effected, unless Messrs. Hett, Davy & Stubbs, who continued to act as
his solicitors throughout, had told him; no way in which he could have
complained of or rectified their omission, of which, it must be inferred, H
he remained in total ignorance until he was told about it by Messrs. Hett,
Davy & Stubbs in late 1967. I do not for one moment suppose that, until
then, he had any idea of the purpose of or necessity for registration. He
was a farmer, not a lawyer; and the earliest moment at which he could
possibly have mounted any claim against the defendants was after a
conference with counsel in late 1967, up to which time it seems that
Mr. Stubbs, who had continued to advise him, was still hopeful that there

The Weekly Law Reports, July 7, 1978

173

3 W.L.R.   Midland Bank v. Hett, Stubbs & Kemp (Ch.D.)   Oliver J.

A might be a chance of enforcing the option against the land in the hands of Mrs. Green senior.

To the claim now made the solicitors plead that any action is barred by the Limitation Act 1939—indeed not only is barred now but was barred by about the end of March 1967, which is the expiration of the period of six years from the date upon which *they* say that they ought to have done what they did not do. The plea of limitation is an unattractive

B plea at the best of times. It is doubly unattractive—even when presented by an advocate as skilled as Mr. Gatehouse—when the circumstances are, as it is claimed here that they are, that the claim became barred not only before any damage at all occurred but even before the unfortunate victim of the wrong could, by any conceivable stretch of imagination, have discovered that any damage might occur or could have taken any practical

C steps to prevent it or seek any redress. I say this in no spirit of criticism of Mr. Kenneth Stubbs and his partners, for it is the familiar experience in cases such as this that solicitor defendants are not, practically, entirely free agents in the matter of the defences which may be raised on their behalf. But the fact remains that it is an unattractive plea. Nevertheless, if it is good in law, the defendants are entitled to succeed and the action must be dismissed.

D Before turning to the questions of law raised by this case, I must first expand a little on the history of the matter and state my findings on certain factual issues which are in dispute. One of the issues on the pleadings is raised by the non-admission that the defendants, who are sued as a firm, are the same firm as Hett, Davy & Stubbs in which, at the material time, Mr. Aymere Stubbs was a partner. Mr. Kenneth

E Stubbs however, in his evidence, admits to a partnership between himself and his father at the material time and states that his father was then, and that he himself is now, the senior partner of the firm. And Mr. Gatehouse has not taken any point as to misjoinder of parties although I did, at an early stage, raise a query as to whether any such point arose. The more critical issue is raised by the non-admission of any retainer. The case was opened on the basis that there was a retainer by Geoffrey.

F Throughout, this has not been disputed by Mr. Gatehouse. And it was not until his reply that Mr. Harman took the point that he himself had failed to prove any retainer and that any liability which the defendants might have was, therefore, non-contractual. I am bound to say that when the case has been presented and fought throughout on a particular basis, the adoption of a wholly different approach in reply, even if technically open on the pleadings, strikes me as a little less than satisfactory.

G But since the point has been raised I must state my conclusions.

So far as the documents show, the first approach in the matter seems to have come from Walter, because Mr. Aymere Stubbs' diary entry for March 23, 1961, shows that Mr. Green senior telephoned him in the afternoon re " sale to Derek Green "—that was his younger son—and " option. Geoff." Geoffrey, at a conference with counsel in 1970—a note

H of which was taken by Miss Bush, a legal executive of the plaintiffs' present solicitors—told counsel that he and his father went to Mr. Stubbs' office when the option was drawn up in Mr. Stubbs' handwriting, that he paid the £1 consideration to his father there and then, and that the option was deposited with the solicitors.

Mr. Kenneth Stubbs' evidence—and it is supported by the documents —was that the firm had acted as solicitors for the Green family—an expression which he later identified as meaning Walter and Geoffrey—

since 1939, but there is no trace of any bill for this particular work being   A
rendered to Geoffrey. Geoffrey, at the conference with counsel which I
have mentioned, surmised that it might have been paid by his father.
That is quite possible, if indeed a separate bill was rendered at all. The
probability is that it was absorbed in the general costs attributable to the
sale to Derek Green which was proceeding at the same time.

Who actually paid the bill, however, does not, I think, matter. Hett,
Davy & Stubbs had acted from time to time for each of the parties   B
individually and together—there is a bill rendered to Geoffrey in 1959 for
the preparation of a deed of gift from Walter to Geoffrey—and this was
quite clearly work on which the firm was being instructed by both and
for which they were entitled to charge, whatever arrangements might
have been made between Walter and Geoffrey as to who was to bear the
charge. When the option was signed it was left with Mr. Stubbs and   C
placed in the strong room and was retained by him in safe custody for
Geoffrey. And subsequently Mr. Stubbs opened a file relating to Geoffrey
and the option. I see nothing to suggest that this was being undertaken
merely as a friendly service to Geoffrey and I am not, in any event,
convinced that, on the view that I take of the law, it would make any
difference to the result if it were. But in fact I find the inference irresistible   D
that there was on March 24, 1961, a retainer from Geoffrey under which
Mr. Stubbs was acting and under which he bound himself to act as a
matter of contract.

Aside from all this I bear in mind the observations of Scott L.J. in
Groom v. Crocker [1939] 1 K.B. 194, 222 that a retainer will be presumed
if the conduct of the parties shows that the relationship of solicitor and
client has in fact been established between them.   E

Mr. Aymere Stubbs appears next to have been consulted by Geoffrey
about the option on January 3, 1964—apparently Geoffrey was then
thinking of going into partnership with somebody and was contemplating
exercising the option. Mr. Stubbs made a note of this which was put on
the file and apparently he took the opportunity of looking up the option
and made a note of the strong room reference number. The firm—again   F
I think by Mr. Aymere Stubbs—also acted for Geoffrey during that year
in the purchase of a farm at Linwood, but the option does not seem to
have been mentioned again until February 22, 1965. This time it was
Mr. Kenneth Stubbs who saw the client. He made a note, which was
also put on the file, that Geoffrey had said that he wanted to exercise the
option, and Mr. Stubbs then gave him some advice on the effect that
this might have when his father died, having regard to the loss of agri-   G
cultural relief which would ensue if, for the farm, there were substituted
in the estate a sum of cash.

Mr. Stubbs told me that this was his first contact with the matter,
although he knew about the existence of the option from his father, who
had mentioned it to him at the time when it was granted. Mr. Stubbs told
me that his normal practice, when an application for registration of a land   H
charge was made, was to have a carbon made of the typed insertions on
the application form, which would then be kept in the client's file; and
for the acknowledgment from the registry—which then took the form of
a buff card—to be attached, when received, to the actual document, assuming that that remained in his firm's possession. He told me, too, that he
would expect his father to have followed the same practice. Naturally
no such documents were present, and it was put to him that he ought to

The Weekly Law Reports, July 7, 1978

175

3 W.L.R.   Midland Bank v. Hett, Stubbs & Kemp (Ch.D.)   Oliver J.

A have noticed this. He certainly inspected the option itself because he made a summary of its terms on his father's note of the interview that he had had with Geoffrey on January 3, 1964. He said in evidence that his mind never adverted to the question of registration. He knew his father as a careful conveyancer and he either did assume or would, if he had thought about it, have assumed that his father had taken this obvious and elementary step.

B
The question of the exercise of the option does not seem to have been further pursued at that stage, and Mr. Stubbs had no particular recollection of seeing Geoffrey again during 1965. In 1966, however, the firm did a good deal of work for him. During that year he made arrangements for the sale of Walk Farm, which he had bought in 1964, and Poplar Farm, which belonged to his father, to the Central Board of Finance for the

C Church of England, and for the lease back to him of those farms by the purchaser. It seems that Walter wanted to distribute the proceeds of Poplar Farm to his sons and daughters but arrangements were made for Geoffrey to borrow his sisters' shares and to use them for the purchase of yet another farm, Manor Farm, which was purchased at about the same time, subject to the tenancy of a Mr. Ranby. The sales of Poplar Farm and Walk Farm and the purchase of Manor Farm were completed in

D June 1966. There followed negotiations with Mr. Ranby about rent and dilapidations and, in about October 1966, Messrs. Hett, Davy & Stubbs acted for Geoffrey on the sale of a small piece of land owned by Geoffrey at South Kelsey. The only significance of this to the present dispute is, first, in relation to evidence given by Mrs. Green, Miss Bush, and Mr. Michael Lawrence of the plaintiffs' solicitors, in respect of which notice

E was given—rather late in the day—under the Civil Evidence Act 1968 and, secondly, in relation to submissions which Mr. Harman made as to the defendants' duty at a later stage when they were consulted in the following year.

The notice, to which I need not refer in detail, indicated that it was proposed to give evidence of statements made by Geoffrey (a) to his wife in October, November or December 1966 that he had consulted Mr.

F Kenneth Stubbs concerning the exercise of the option following the sale and lease back of Manor Farm and had been assured that it was valid; (b) to Mr. Lawrence that in June 1967 he had received a similar assurance; and (c) to counsel that at least once a year from 1961 to 1967 Mr. Kenneth Stubbs had assured him that the option was valid.

Mrs. Green, in her evidence, said that they frequently discussed the

G option and that her husband had inquired about it and been assured that it was all right. She was, however, very vague about dates although she said that the correspondence about the land at South Kelsey had reminded her that there had been such a conversation at about that time; that is, in October 1966. In cross-examination she reiterated more firmly that she knew that she had asked him about the option in October 1966 and he had said he had been assured that it was all right.

H
Now Mrs. Green was, I am sure, a perfectly honest witness, but her recollection is obviously at fault in a number of respects. For instance, she could not have discussed the matter with her husband in October 1966 " following the sale and lease back of Manor Farm," as the notice states, because we know from the documents that that sale and lease back did not take place until 1968. Nor, even accepting Mrs. Green's evidence at its face value, is there any indication of what period her husband was referring

to when he said that he had received the assurance that the option was **A** valid. He could have been referring for instance to his meeting with Mr. Aymere Stubbs in 1964.

The date is critical, because it is upon the basis of this testimony that the plaintiffs seek to say that a fresh duty arose in Mr. Kenneth Stubbs to make a search and register the option, and, in order to be of any service to them, the consultation and advice has to fall within a bracket from July 21, 1966 (six years before the writ) to August 17, 1967 (the date of **B** Walter's conveyance to his wife). Mr. Kenneth Stubbs denies that he was ever consulted prior to September 1967 with regard to the enforceability, as opposed to the exercise, of the option, or that he was ever asked for or gave any such assurance. Mr. Harman asks me to reject that testimony because, as he points out, Mr. Stubbs remembers very little beyond what is recorded in the documents. I am, however, bound to say that it seems to **C** me almost overwhelmingly unlikely that he would have omitted to search if his attention had been directed to the question of enforceability, having regard to what in fact happened in September 1967 when he undoubtedly *was* consulted about it. His immediate reaction then was to make a search.

Miss Bush's evidence carries the matter no further because all that Geoffrey said in *her* presence was that he had received an assurance once a year from 1961 to 1967, without putting any date upon it. Mr. Lawrence **D** had little more to add: Geoffrey told him, he said, that "he had been to see Mr. Stubbs and had been assured that the option was valid." This statement, he says, he related to June 1967, but Mr. Kenneth Stubbs' telephone diary entries indicate that Geoffrey was on holiday between June 1 and June 19 and although he had a short telephone conversation with Mr. Stubbs on June 19—in which, I think, he must have mentioned his **E** desire to exercise the option—there is no indication that he went to see Mr. Stubbs during this month.

I have to bear in mind too that the statements made in the presence of Miss Bush and Mr. Lawrence were made some 2½ years after the trouble had arisen and at a time when an action against the defendants was in contemplation, an action in which it must have been obvious that a **F** limitation point was likely to be taken. Miss Bush took a full note of the conference with counsel and it is evident from that that Geoffrey's recollection was at fault in at least two material respects, because he said first, that after the initial grant of the option the only partner whom he consulted was Mr. Kenneth Stubbs, which is clearly wrong, and secondly, that he never discussed the question of registration with his solicitors, whereas he had attended a conference with counsel and it is obvious from counsel's **G** subsequent opinions, which I think Geoffrey must have seen, that the matter was fully discussed.

I do not, in the result, think that I can treat any of this testimony as reliably establishing that there was during the relevant period any consultation with or assurance by Mr. Kenneth Stubbs as regards the enforceability of the option, and I must accept his evidence upon this point. **H**

What there undoubtedly was—and this is common ground—was a considerable consultation about its *exercise*—its desirability and consequences from the point of view of death duties. As I have already mentioned, Geoffrey telephoned Mr. Stubbs on June 19, 1967. It appears to have been a short conversation early in the morning and the subject matter is described as "Ranby rent," but I think that the question of the effect of the exercise of the option must have been mentioned then, and indeed

The Weekly Law Reports, July 7, 1978

177

3 W.L.R.   Midland Bank v. Hett, Stubbs & Kemp (Ch.D.)   Oliver J.

A Mr. Stubbs so recollects, for that afternoon Mr. Stubbs made a fairly long telephone call to Geoffrey's accountant, Mr. Kewley of Messrs. R. N. Storr & Co. I surmise that the subject matter must have been the tax and duty position if the option were exercised. Mr. Kewley had a meeting with Geoffrey that day and took down details of what was the acquisition of the freehold of Gravel Farm and also of an adjoining farm known as Shifty Nooking. He formed the view that counsel's opinion should be

B taken and appears to have telephoned to Mr. Stubbs to express that view. On the following day he wrote this letter to Mr. Stubbs:

"With reference to our telephone conversation yesterday, our client considers, and we agree, that this is a matter on which counsel's opinion should be taken. We trust you concur.

"The salient points are as follows: 1. Gravel Hill Farm, Thornton-

C le-Moor, comprises 300 acres and has for some years been tenanted by our client at an annual rental of £900, the tenant bearing all out-goings doing all repairs and maintenance. 2. As you are aware, our client has an option to purchase. 3. If the option is exercised a private investor will buy Gravel Hill Farm together with an adjoining farm of 235 acres at £200 per acre, and rent back to our client at £9 per acre

D (i.e. $4\frac{1}{2}$ per cent. of £107,000). The lease would be for an indefinite number of years. The adjoining farm is not in our client's ownership or possession at the moment. 4. If this option is exercised there will be an immediate cash profit of £125 per acre on 300 acres, namely £37,500. 5. The position concerning death duties in relation to our client's father is one in which you are no doubt involved. It is desired to know when to exercise the option, and what the position

E would be regarding the incidence of capital gains tax and death duties.

"We shall be pleased to give you any further information you may require."

Following that Mr. Stubbs got out the option and drew some instruc-tions to counsel which started "Instructing solicitors are concerned on behalf of Mr. Walter Stanley Green . . . and his son Mr. Thomas Geoffrey

F Green." They had, in fact, no instructions from Walter, but I suppose that Mr. Stubbs must have assumed that the project was being planned by Geoffrey in consultation with his father. The instructions set out the option verbatim and explained the operations proposed, which consisted of exercising the option and subselling to an investor who would purchase the adjoining farm and let the whole back to Geoffrey at £9 per acre.

G The instructions concluded:

"Mr. T. G. Green is desirous of considering at what stage it would be best for him to exercise the option, whether to do so now or await developments and, if anything unfortunate should happen to Mr. W. S. Green before March 24, 1971, when the option expires, whether to exercise the option at that stage. Counsel is requested to advise:

H 1. As to when he considers it best for Mr. T. G. Green to exercise the option. 2. As to the incidence of capital gains tax and death duties. 3. Generally in the matter."

I have set this out in some detail because it forms the foundation for a submission to which I will return in a moment. But just to complete the history, before counsel's opinion was received, Mr. Stubbs, on August 25, 1967, received a letter from Messrs. Roythorne informing him that Walter had consulted them and asking for his documents. Now it might have

been thought that this would have alerted Mr. Stubbs to the possibility of **A**
disharmony in the family and caused him to consider for a moment, in
the light of the scheme upon which he was taking counsel's advice, whether
the option was properly protected. But even if this is right, it would
have done no good in fact, because the conveyance of the farm had already
taken place.

Mr. Stubbs did not, in fact, become alert to the danger until Septem- **B**
ber 4, when his client telephoned him and voiced a suspicion that something
was going on between his father and his mother. At that stage, without
telling his client, Mr. Stubbs made a search—even then, I note, asking
only for a postal and not a telephonic reply—and upon receiving the
result, which showed no subsisting entries, he effected a registration, again
without consulting Geoffrey. It was, of course, too late and when, a
month later, Geoffrey, on Mr. Stubb's advice, sought formally to exercise **C**
the option, he was met with the response that it had not been registered
and that the land had been sold.

The case raises some important points of principle which have been
extensively canvassed in argument, including questions, which I have not
found at all easy, as to the application of the doctrine of stare decisis.
In deference to the very full argument of counsel, I think that I must **D**
state fully the reasoning by which I have been led to my conclusions even
at risk of overburdening an already lengthy judgment. The argument has
thrown up three principal questions of law, or of mixed law and fact.

First, assuming that an action based on the original failure to register
is statute barred, did anything occur subsequently to impose upon the
defendants a fresh duty, the neglect of which can be made the subject
matter of complaint? Secondly, did the defendants, quite apart from any **E**
contractual obligations which they assumed, owe a general duty to the
plaintiffs' testator, the breach of which would give rise to an action in
tort, when, but only when, damage was occasioned? Concealed in this is a
further question as to the duty of a judge of first instance when confronted
by conflicting or apparently conflicting authorities. Finally, on the footing
of a solely contractual liability, is an action for damages barred by the **F**
Limitation Act 1939?

It will, I think, be convenient if I deal with these matters in order and
under their separate headings even though this may necessitate referring
to the same authority more than once in different contexts.

1. *Did a fresh duty arise after July 21, 1966?*
G
In case this case goes further I must, in any event, state my findings
on certain evidence adduced in support of this submission, but I deal with
it first also because, if it is well founded, it concludes the case in the
plaintiffs' favour and I need not go on to consider the further questions of
law which otherwise arise.

It arises out of an amendment to the pleadings which Mr. Harman
sought leave to make and which I granted, against Mr. Gatehouse's **H**
opposition. As originally pleaded, the case being made—in so far as it
did not rest simply upon a failure to register after March 1961—was that
the defendants acted as Geoffrey's solicitors; that he sought their advice
from time to time as to whether the option was valid and subsisting; and
that they failed to advise him of the need for registration and indeed
wrongly advised him that the option was binding upon the land. That
was denied in the defence although it was admitted that the defendants

The Weekly Law Reports, July 7, 1978

179

3 W.L.R.   Midland Bank v. Hett, Stubbs & Kemp (Ch.D.)   Oliver J.

A were consulted about the matters raised in Mr. Kewley's letter. Particulars were then sought of the occasions upon which it was alleged that the defendants had been consulted as to the validity of the option and a number of occasions were specified. None of those now has any relevance, because they were either before July 21, 1966, or after August 17, 1967.

B In the reply, however, the plaintiffs pleaded:

"3. In so far as the defendants acted in breach of duty as alleged in the said paragraphs, such duty was a continuing duty and the same was subsisting and the defendants were in breach thereof immediately prior to the execution of the conveyance hereinbefore referred to."

The amendment sought by Mr. Harman was in these terms:

C "After paragraph 3, add a new paragraph, as follows: ' 3A. Further or alternatively, it was the duty of the defendants, on each and every occasion when the said Thomas Geoffrey Green sought their advice in relation to the said option, to satisfy themselves that the said option had been registered as an estate contract and—the said option not having been so registered—to advise him that the said option would, unless so registered, be void against a purchaser of a legal D estate in Gravel Hill Farm for money or money's worth.' "

He also sought leave to add some further particulars to the particulars of paragraph 5 of the statement of claim already delivered. The only one I need refer to is this: "(v) That the said Thomas Geoffrey Green sought advice from the defendants in June 1967 concerning the exercise of the said option."

E Mr. Gatehouse resisted this on the ground that it was a new case, but Mr. Harman relied on the reply, interpreting the words "continuing duty" as meaning "duty arising from time to time whenever any advice was sought in relation to the option." At that stage he expressly disclaimed any contention that there was a continuing duty in the sense of one which continued from day to day from March 1961 onwards. That is something F to which I shall have to return later.

I allowed the amendment because it seemed to me that it involved no new cause of action beyond that embraced in the original writ—which specified a neglect to register "at the date of the grant and at all material times thereafter "—nor did it involve evidence of any new facts which had not already been pleaded, but merely a deduction of law from facts already appearing on the face of the pleadings.

G This new plea does however raise an issue of law not apparent upon the original pleadings, namely, what is the scope of a solicitor's duty when he is consulted about a particular aspect of a problem—is he entitled to confine himself to the particular matters for which he is retained to advise or must he consider all the circumstances affecting the underlying data including hypothetical circumstances or risks to which his attention is not H directed and upon which his advice is not specifically sought?

As to this, I have heard the evidence of a number of practising solicitors. Mr. Harman modestly contented himself with calling one; but Mr. Gatehouse—mindful, no doubt, of what is said to be the divine preference for big battalions—called no less than three. I must say that I doubt the value, or even the admissibility, of this sort of evidence, which seems to be becoming customary in cases of this type. The extent of the legal duty in any given situation must, I think, be a question of law for the court.

Clearly, if there is some practice in a particular profession, some accepted A
standard of conduct which is laid down by a professional institute or sanctioned by common usage, evidence of that can and ought to be received.
But evidence which really amounts to no more than an expression of
opinion by a particular practitioner of what he thinks that he would have
done had he been placed, hypothetically and without the benefit of hindsight, in the position of the defendants, is of little assistance to the court;
whilst evidence of the witnesses' view of what, as a matter of law, the B
solicitor's duty was in the particular circumstances of the case is, I should
have thought, inadmissible, for that is the very question which it is the
court's function to decide.

Predictably, the witnesses differed. Mr. Gibbon, an experienced conveyancing solicitor from Grimsby, told me that if he were consulted about
any aspect of an option, he would make a search to see if it had been C
registered—assuming, of course that there was no documentary evidence
of registration already on the file. Mr. Gatehouse's witnesses, on the other
hand, concurred in saying that if they were consulted in the terms of Mr.
Kewley's letter of June 20, 1967, it would not occur to them to query
whether the option was registered or not. It would depend, as Mr.
Stebbings put it, upon whether there was anything in the circumstances or
the instructions to direct the solicitor's mind in that direction. D

This seems to me, if I may say so, to be obvious common sense and I
find nothing in the evidence of these gentlemen, helpful as they all tried to
be, establishing a practice or general standard which assists me in this case.
Mr. Harman sought to rely upon the fact that Mr. Stubbs was Geoffrey's
solicitor under some sort of general retainer imposing a duty to consider all
aspects of his interest generally whenever he was consulted, but that cannot E
be. There is no such thing as a general retainer in that sense. The expression " my solicitor " is as meaningless as the expression " my tailor " or
" my bookmaker " in establishing any general duty apart from that arising
out of a particular matter in which his services are retained. The extent
of his duties depends upon the terms and limits of that retainer and any
duty of care to be implied must be related to what he is instructed to do. F

Now no doubt the duties owed by a solicitor to his client are high, in
the sense that he holds himself out as practising a highly skilled and exacting profession, but I think that the court must beware of imposing upon
solicitors—or upon professional men in other spheres—duties which go
beyond the scope of what they are requested and undertake to do. It may
be that a particularly meticulous and conscientious practitioner would, in
his client's general interests, take it upon himself to pursue a line of inquiry G
beyond the strict limits comprehended by his instructions. But that is not
the test. The test is what the reasonably competent practitioner would do
having regard to the standards normally adopted in his profession, and
cases such as *Duchess of Argyll* v. *Beuselinck* [1972] 2 Lloyd's Rep. 172;
Griffiths v. *Evans* [1953] 1 W.L.R. 1424 and *Hall* v. *Meyrick* [1957] 2
Q.B. 455 demonstrate that the duty is directly related to the confines of H
the retainer. It is not seriously arguable that a solicitor who or whose
firm has acted negligently comes under a continuing duty to take care to
remind himself of the negligence of which, ex hypothesi, he is unaware:
see, e.g., Kekewich J. in *Wood* v. *Jones* (1889) 61 L.T. 551, 552; but Mr.
Harman suggests that in this case, because the exercise of the option was
crucial to the scheme which Geoffrey was proposing in June 1967, it then
became Mr. Kenneth Stubbs' duty to consider and check upon the registra-

The Weekly Law Reports, July 7, 1978

181

3 W.L.R.   Midland Bank v. Hett, Stubbs & Kemp (Ch.D.)   Oliver J.

A tion of the option. But that was not what he was asked to do. The
instructions were given in the context of an agreement between father and
son who were on friendly terms and against the background that Mr.
Stubbs' firm had, for years, acted as solicitors for both parties and would
expect to know if Walter was contemplating any sale of his property.
Mr. Stubbs told me—and I accept—that he had heard of no family discord
and Geoffrey's own evidence, in the affidavit to which I have made previ-
B ous reference, was that he had not quarrelled with his father. Furthermore,
only in the previous year, Walter had, to Mr. Stubbs' knowledge, concurred
with Geoffrey in the arrangements over Poplar and Walk Farms, all of
which pointed to the existence of harmonious family relationships.

The state of Mr. Stubbs' knowledge of the family affairs is illustrated
by the fact that he assumed, when giving instructions to tax counsel, that
C he was acting for both parties. I can, in these circumstances, see no reason
why the possibility of Walter's disposing of the land in defiance of the
option should then have been present to his mind nor why the instructions
to advise as to the tax and death duty consequences should have suggested
to him that he ought to check whether the option had been registered.

If there was no continuing duty to register up to this point, therefore
—and that is the supposition upon which this submission is based—I can
D see nothing in the instructions given in June 1967 which would have
revived it or created some fresh duty in Mr. Stubbs to consider whether
or not the option had been registered.

I cannot, therefore, accept Mr. Harman's submissions upon this part
of the case.

E 2. *Are the defendants liable to the plaintiffs in tort?*

I turn, then, to what is, on one view of the matter, the critical question
in the case. That is, whether the plaintiff's claim was barred by effluxion
of time at or before the date when Walter disposed of the land. I put it
in this form because although the writ was issued five years later, the
logical consequence of the defendants' submissions is that the limitation
F period would have run even if a writ had been issued at that date.

Mr. Gatehouse's case is a very simple one. It rests on three propositions. (1) A solicitor's duty to his client under his retainer is a duty which
arises from the contract, and from the contract alone, and there is no
general duty to exercise care and skill such as would found an action in
tort if damage results from want of care and skill. (2) It is accepted that,
here, there was a breach of contract, but it is well established that in cases
G of breach of contract time under the Limitation Act 1939 runs from the
date of the breach, which is when the complete cause of action accrues,
even if the damages which could be awarded at that date would be nominal
only. (3) The breach of contract, and the only breach of contract, which
could support an action is breach of a contract—whether it be expressed
as a contract to exercise care and skill or as a contract containing a specific
H term is immaterial—to effect registration within a reasonable time. Although
it may be difficult to state with precision the specific date of breach, it
certainly occurred before August 17, 1961, by which date a reasonable
time for registration of the option had expired.

Mr. Harman makes a direct frontal assault on Mr. Gatehouse's first
proposition. There is, he says, an alternative cause of action in tort which
was not complete until the damage was sustained in August 1967, well
within the period of six years before the issue of the writ in this action.

He based this, first, on the proposition that there was no retainer—or, to A
put it more accurately, that, whatever the pleadings say, he has not proved
a retainer. I must, he suggests, therefore approach the case on the footing
that Mr. Aymere Stubbs gratuitously assumed to act for Geoffrey in a
matter in which professional care and skill were required and that, accordingly, he became liable in tort for damage occasioned by his want of care
and skill. Imperitia culpae adnumeratur. I have already said that, in my
judgment, the evidence in this case does establish a retainer, but it seems B
to me that there may, in any event, be another answer to this contention.
I am far from convinced that the giving by a solicitor of gratuitous advice
to a friend could necessarily be said to be something done in the ordinary
course of a partnership business. If Mr. Harman's contention were correct
then it may be that the defendants should be, not the firm of Hett, Stubbs
& Kemp, but Mr. Aymere Stubbs' personal representatives.   C

   The second basis for Mr. Harman's attack is a more general one, and
it is that the result of a recent authority in the Court of Appeal has been
to destroy the validity of the view heretofore generally accepted that the
solicitor's liability is contractual only. Mr. Harman's submission is, in
essence, that since the recent decision of the Court of Appeal in *Esso
Petroleum Co. Ltd.* v. *Mardon* [1976] Q.B. 801, there are two conflicting D
lines of authority of co-ordinate courts and that a judge of first instance
is therefore given a choice which to follow and should follow that which
appears to accord most with authority and common sense. But I think
that ultimately it went further than that and amounted, if not in terms,
at least in substance, to a submission that the effect of the House of Lords
decision in *Hedley Byrne & Co. Ltd.* v. *Heller & Partners Ltd.* [1964]
A.C. 465, taken in conjunction with other cases—and, in particular, the E
case just mentioned—has been, by necessary implication, to overrule the
Court of Appeal's decision in *Groom* v. *Crocker* [1939] 1 K.B. 194 and
the cases which followed it. The *Esso* case and the *Hedley Byrne* case
formed the bedrock of Mr. Harman's submission.

(a) *The doctrine of stare decisis*

   I have been led by counsel through a bewildering complex of authori- F
ties many of which are not easy to reconcile with the principles established
in subsequent cases in superior courts or, in some cases, with one another.
The task of a judge of first instance faced with this situation is not an easy
one. Our system of courts is hierarchical and he must on the one hand
follow and apply those principles of law which have been clearly laid down
by higher authority whilst, at the same time, avoiding the risk of arrogat- G
ing to himself a function which properly belongs only to a higher tribunal
and which he has no power to exercise even where reason might tempt
him to do so. Even the principles which he should follow when confronted by apparently conflicting decisions of superior courts are not
always clear and, where they are clear, they are not always easy to apply,
for their application may itself depend upon a disputable interpretation
of a decision of a superior court. The principles so far as relevant to the H
present case appear to me to be these and I adopt them in my approach
to Mr. Harman's submissions.

   (1) A decision of the House of Lords resting upon or establishing a
general doctrine binds all inferior courts and represents the law of the
land until it is altered by legislation or, nowadays, departed from by the
House itself: see *Great Western Railway Co.* v. *Owners of S.S. Mostyn*
[1928] A.C. 57, 82 and *Wilkinson* v. *Sibley* [1932] 1 K.B. 194, 200.

The Weekly Law Reports, July 7, 1978

183

3 W.L.R.   Midland Bank v. Hett, Stubbs & Kemp (Ch.D.)   Oliver J.

A   (2) A decision of an inferior court may be treated as having been over-ruled by a decision of a superior court with which it is shown to be inconsistent, although it has not been expressly so stated by those who concur in such a decision: *Consett Industrial and Provident Society Ltd.* v. *Consett Iron Co. Ltd.* [1922] 2 Ch. 135, 173, 174.

B   (3) An interpretation of a statute or of a decision of the House of Lords by the Court of Appeal is binding upon that court even if it subsequently regards the interpretation as erroneous: see *Williams* v. *Glasbrook Brothers Ltd.* [1947] 2 All E.R. 884 and *Miliangos* v. *George Frank (Textiles) Ltd.* [1976] A.C. 443, 479. A fortiori such interpretation binds an inferior court.

    (4) Where there are conflicting decisions of the Court of Appeal, that court is free to choose which it will follow: *Young* v. *Bristol Aeroplane*
C *Co. Ltd.* [1946] A.C. 163. The position of a judge at first instance when faced with such a conflict is not clear. He must, I think, be equally free to choose unless it is to be suggested that he must follow that decision which is latest in point of time.

(b) *Authorities leading up to* Groom v. Crocker

D   Mr. Harman's submission seems, at first sight, a bold one, for there is a formidable and continuous line of cases, some of them decided since the *Hedley Byrne* case [1964] A.C. 465, which assert that a solicitor's relationship with his client is a contractual one only and gives rise to no liability in tort. But boldness and wrongness are not synonyms and although justice is said to be blind, the doctrine of precedent does not prescribe that the court must blindly follow previous decisions without considering their
E rationale and the impact upon them of subsequent authority. In order to test Mr. Harman's submissions I must, I think, first seek to trace and analyse the genesis of the rule which found its expression in *Groom* v. *Crocker* [1939] 1 K.B. 194 and the cases which followed; then consider how, if at all, it was affected by what appeared, at the time, to be the revolutionary decision of the House of Lords in the *Hedley Byrne* case
F and finally I must look at the cases on solicitors' liability decided since the *Hedley Byrne* case and assess the effect upon them of *Esso Petroleum Co. Ltd.* v. *Mardon* [1976] Q.B. 801 upon which Mr. Harman relies. In *Clark* v. *Kirby-Smith* [1964] Ch. 506 Plowman J. said that a line of cases going back for nearly 150 years showed that the client's action against his solicitor was in contract and not in tort, and he cited *Howell* v. *Young* (1826) 5 B. & C. 259.

G   Mr. Gatehouse has referred me to that case and a perusal of it raises, in my mind at least, a serious doubt whether it did in fact decide that a solicitor's sole liability was in contract. It has to be remembered that it was decided at a time when English law was still bedevilled by the technicalities of the forms of action and when the general concept of negligence as a separate tort was still developing. Lack of care and skill in the per-
H formance of their duties by those professing certain callings or offices had, since mediaeval times, been regarded by the law as wrongful and the duty to display ordinary care and skill had attached beyond the sphere of the so-called common callings to professions such as those of the apothecary, the surgeon and the attorney: see Winfield, *Select Legal Essays* (1952), pp. 74–77.

    It was clearly established, however, that if a plaintiff sued in assumpsit, he was bound by that pleading to a reliance upon the contract which he

alleged and time under the Statute of Limitation 1623 was treated, as one A
would expect, as running from the date of the breach alleged. In *Battley*
v. *Faulkner* (1820) 3 B. & Ald. 288, for instance, Holroyd J. pointed out
at p. 294 that subsequently sustained damage could not be considered as
a substantive ground of action " in this form of action." *Short* v. *M'Carthy*
(1820) 3 B. & Ald. 626 and *Brown* v. *Howard* (1820) 2 Brod. & B. 73
were both cases of actions against solicitors pleaded in assumpsit where
the same consequence followed. *Howell* v. *Young*, 5 B. & C. 259, how- B
ever, was an action on the case, but it was a case where the damage—the
acceptance of a bad title to a mortgage security—had accrued at the same
time as the negligent act which constituted the breach of duty although it
did not then become apparent. The breach and the immediately consequent damage, therefore, had occurred simultaneously, as indeed they had
in *Short* v. *M'Carthy*, 3 B. & Ald. 626 (as Bayley J. pointed out in that C
case) and the only question was whether the consequential special damage
pleaded gave rise to a further and different cause of action.

   Howell v. *Young*, 5 B. & C. 259, was a case which raised directly the
question of when the cause of action accrued, the particular misconduct
alleged being the defendant's negligent assurance as to the title to certain
properties upon the security of which the plaintiff had lent money, all of
which had occurred over six years before the commencement of the pro- D
ceedings, although it was not until later that default was made in payment
of the interest and the lack of title came to light. It was held that the
plaintiff's action was barred and that the special damage claimed—the loss
of interest—did not give rise to a fresh cause of action. It is, however,
far from clear that the court regarded the defendant's liability as an
exclusively contractual one and that was certainly not decided in terms. E
Although it is true that, at p. 265, Bayley J. thought that the case was
analogous to the earlier case of *Short* v. *M'Carthy*, 3 B. & Ald. 626, he
seems to have differentiated between a cause of action founded upon a
promise and one founded upon what he called " breach of duty " although
he held that the result was the same because "the breach of duty is
substantially the cause of action " : see p. 266. He does, it is fair to say,
at one point say that an award of nominal damages could have been made F
if the action had been commenced in time, which might suggest that he
regarded the action as a purely contractual one; but in another part of his
judgment, at p. 264, he refers to the special damage pleaded as " part
only " of the damage suffered.

   Holroyd J. was even more equivocal. He too, at p. 266, employed the
dichotomy of " breach of promise " and " breach of duty," and held that G
it made no difference which way the plaintiff elected to put his case,
because, on the facts, in either event the cause of action accrued at the
same moment. He does not, however, suggest that there was only one
cause of action arising by virtue of a breach of contract. Indeed, he said
expressly that the plaintiff could sue in either assumpsit or case and the
final passage in his judgment suggests that an action in tort was equally H
appropriate for, having pointed out that if the plaintiff had sued immediately
the security was given the jury would have been bound to award damages
for the probable loss, he went on to say, at p. 268, that " therefore " the
subsequent special damage pleaded did not constitute a fresh cause of
action. Nor does the exclusively contractual nature of the solicitor's
liability emerge from the subsequent case of *Smith* v. *Fox* (1848) 6 Hare
386, another negligence action where the plaintiff sued in case rather than

The Weekly Law Reports, July 7, 1978

185

3 W.L.R.   Midland Bank v. Hett, Stubbs & Kemp (Ch.D.)   Oliver J.

A assumpsit. This merely followed *Howell* v. *Young*, 5 B. & C. 259 without any discussion as to the basis of the cause of action.

It seems to me, therefore, to be open to doubt whether these early decisions really establish the proposition for which they were subsequently cited as authority. It does not appear to have been the view at least of Stuart V.-C. that they had this effect, for he is recorded as saying, in a

B case where a solicitor had wrongly conducted litigation in the name of a person from whom he had no instructions, that " the law of tort, as applied in cases of *Howell* v. *Young*, 5 B. & C. 259 and *Smith* v. *Fox*, 6 Hare 386 was inapplicable to a case of this kind ": *In re Manby* (1856) 26 L.J. Ch. 313, 317, and see also *Sawyer* v. *Goodwin* (1867) 36 L.J.Ch. 578, 582, where he clearly contemplated tort and contract as alternative causes of action.

C But so far as the court of first instance was concerned the question became an academic one in 1885, for whether they did or did not have the effect referred to, they were accepted by the Court of Appeal as so doing and the proposition was clearly established as a matter of direct decision in *Bean* v. *Wade* (1885) 2 T.L.R. 157. I have ventured to look at the underlying basis for that decision only because of Mr. Harman's

D submission that I am now faced with conflicting authorities of the Court of Appeal and am entitled to choose which I shall follow. The report of *Bean* v. *Wade* is not a particularly satisfactory one, it being, as was the custom with the Times Law Reports at the time, in oratio obliqua. On this point, however, it seems entirely unequivocal. Lindley L.J., who was sitting with Lord Esher M.R. and Cotton L.J., is recorded, in delivering the judgment of the court, as saying, at pp 158–159, that:

E " . . . according to *Howell* v. *Young*, 5 B. & C. 259, *Smith* v. *Fox*, 6 Hare 386 and *In re Hindmarsh* (1860) 1 Drew. & Sm. 129 . . ."— a case concerned with the different point of a solicitor's fiduciary liability—" . . . the right of action in cases of this kind was treated as arising from a breach of contract, and not from negligence apart from contract or from any breach of trust. Therefore, the statute

F began to run in favour of Mr. G. Wade from the date of his breach of his duty to his clients. . . ."

The decision does not seem to have achieved a great notoriety, possibly because it never got into the official Law Reports. A similar question arose in the following year in *Hughes* v. *Twisden* (1886) 55 L.J.Ch. 481, and it was not cited, the court merely contenting itself with saying

G that the facts came to the same as in *Howell* v. *Young*, 5 B. & C. 259. And in 1890 in *Blyth* v. *Fladgate* [1891] 1 Ch. 337, 366, Stirling J. was still evidently of the view that there were alternative liabilities which could be asserted either in tort or in contract. Again in *Davies* v. *Hood* (1903) 88 L.T. 19 Ridley J. considered that the action might be either in contract or in tort.

H Perhaps even more significantly we find no less an authority than Viscount Haldane L.C. saying in *Nocton* v. *Lord Ashburton* [1914] A.C. 932, 956:

" My Lords, the solicitor contracts with his client to be skilful and careful. For failure to perform his obligation he may be made liable at law in contract or even in tort, for negligence in breach of a duty imposed on him. In the early history of the action of assumpsit this liability was indeed treated as one for tort."

It should be added, perhaps, that Lord Dunedin, at p. 964 of the same case, **A**
put the liability in contract.

Even if, however, the point remained open at all after *Bean* v. *Wade*,
2 T.L.R. 157, in any court below the House of Lords, it was conclusively
determined again by a unanimous Court of Appeal over 50 years later in
Groom v. *Crocker* [1939] 1 K.B. 194. The question at issue was whether
damages for injured feelings and reputation—which clearly could not then
be claimed in contract as a result of the House of Lords' decision in *Addis* **B**
v. *Gramophone Co. Ltd.* [1909] A.C. 488—were nevertheless claimable
in tort.

Sir Wilfrid Greene M.R. in *Groom* v. *Crocker* [1939] 1 K.B. 194,
205 said:

> "In my opinion, the cause of action is in contract and not in tort. **C**
> The duty of the appellants was to conduct the case properly on behalf
> of the respondent as their client, subject to any proper exercise by
> the insurers of the right of control conferred upon them by the policy.
> The relationship of solicitor and client is a contractual one: *Davies* v.
> *Lock* (1844) 3 L.T.(O.S.) 125; *Bean* v. *Wade*, 2 T.L.R. 157. It was
> by virtue of that relationship that the duty arose, and it had no
> existence apart from that relationship." **D**

Scott L.J. concurred. He said, at p. 222:

> "Mr. Pritt argued for the respondent that he had a cause of action in
> tort for breach of duty. I do not think so. A solicitor, as a pro-
> fessional man, is employed by a client just as much as a doctor, an
> architect, or a stockbroker, and the mutual rights and duties of the **E**
> two are regulated entirely by the contract of employment. The cases
> of *Bean* v. *Wade*, 2 T.L.R. 157 and *Jarvis* v. *Moy, Davies, Smith,
> Vandervell & Co.* [1936] 1 K.B. 399 cited to us, both recognise this
> basic principle. . . . The retainer when given puts into operation the
> normal terms of the contractual relationship, including in particular
> the duty of the solicitor to protect the client's interest and carry out
> his instructions in the matters in which the retainer relates, by all **F**
> proper means. It is an incident of that duty that the solicitor should
> consult with his client on all questions of doubt which do not fall
> within the express or implied discretion left him, and should keep
> the client informed to such an extent as may be reasonably necessary
> according to the same criteria. But in all these aspects the tie between
> the two is contractual. There is today no common law duty similar
> to that which survives in the case of a bailee or carrier, and no action **G**
> lies in tort for the breach of the above duties, unless, of course,
> particular circumstances disclose such a case—fraud, for instance."

MacKinnon L.J.'s view was expressed much more shortly, at p. 229:

> "Next as to the £1,000 damages for breach of duty. I am clear that
> this is a claim for damages for breach of contract, and that the plaintiff **H**
> can only recover the pecuniary loss that he can show he has suffered."
> suffered."

Apart from *Bean* v. *Wade*, 2 T.L.R. 157 the only other authority
referred to by Sir Wilfrid Greene M.R. was an elderly case of *Davies* v.
Lock which was partially heard before the Court of Queen's Bench in
May 1844. It is reported in 3 L.T.O.S., on its first hearing, at p. 100,

The Weekly Law Reports, July 7, 1978

187

3 W.L.R.   Midland Bank v. Hett, Stubbs & Kemp (Ch.D.)   Oliver J.

A   when the court suggested to counsel that they should dispose of the matter
by entering a non-suit by consent, and again at p. 125 where there is a
report of an adjourned hearing. But the case can hardly be called an
authority, and such guidance as it gives is provided not by the court but
by the reporter who expressed the view in the headnote that the liability
of a solicitor is a contractual one and preceded his view with the word
" semble."

B
    It was an action for negligence against partners in which the jury had
found a verdict against one defendant and not against others and the
submission being made was that, inasmuch as partners are jointly liable
on the firm's contractual obligations, the verdict should have been against
all or against none. There appears to have been no argument on the point
and certainly no decision. Counsel for the plaintiff conceded that the
C   liability was ex contractu, and the court simply suspended the argument
to enable counsel to make an application to the trial judge to amend the
verdict.

    The only other authority relied upon was that referred to in the
judgment of Scott L.J., namely *Jarvis* v. *Moy, Davies, Smith, Vandervell
& Co.* [1936] 1 K.B. 399 in which Greer L.J. said, at p. 405 :

D   " The distinction in the modern view, for this purpose, between con-
        tract and tort may be put thus: where the breach of duty alleged
        arises out of a liability independently of the personal obligation
        undertaken by contract, it is tort, and it may be tort even though there
        may happen to be a contract between the parties, if the duty in fact
        arises independently of that contract. Breach of contract occurs where
        that which is complained of is a breach of duty arising out of the
E   obligations undertaken by the contract."

    But that was a case which was concerned with the question of whether
an action was one " founded on a contract " or " founded on a tort " for
the purposes of section 11 of the County Courts Act 1919—a question in
regard to which it was well established that what had to be regarded was
the substance of the matter even though there might be alternative
F   liabilities (see, for instance, *Sachs* v. *Henderson* [1902] 1 K.B. 612 and
Edwards v. *Mallan* [1908] 1 K.B. 1002) and in saying what he did
Greer L.J. was merely applying the principle which had been expressed by
A. L. Smith L.J. in *Turner* v. *Stallibrass* [1898] 1 Q.B. 56, 58, as
follows:

        " The rule of law on the subject, as I understand it, is that, if in order
G   to make out a cause of action it is not necessary for the plaintiff to
        rely on a contract, the action is one founded on tort; but, on the other
        hand, if, in order successfully to maintain his action, it is necessary
        for him to rely upon and prove a contract, the action is one founded
        upon contract."

    That, of course, is quite different from saying that there cannot be
H   overlapping liabilities both in contract and tort. Indeed, it appears to me
to be saying the opposite. It is true that in *Jarvis* v. *Moy, Davies, Smith,
Vandervell & Co.* [1936] 1 K.B. 399 the Court of Appeal held that it was
necessary, in order to found the cause of action there, to rely on the contract, but that is scarcely surprising on the facts of the case, for it had not
been pleaded as a claim in negligence resting upon any breach of a general
duty, but upon a disregard of the plaintiff's specific instructions: see, for
instance, the judgment of Slesser L.J. at p. 406.

Now it is fair to say that the duties alleged in the statement of claim **A**
in *Groom* v. *Crocker* [1939] 1 K.B. 194 and set out in the judgment of
Scott L.J., went rather beyond any implied general duty to exercise reasonable care and skill.   Nevertheless there can be no doubt that the decision
proceeded on the basis that there was no liability beyond and apart from
liability for duties imposed by the contract.   And that, subject to Mr.
Harman's contention as to the effect of *Esso Petroleum Co. Ltd* v. *Mardon*
[1976] Q.B. 801, has been treated as the law ever since.   *Groom* v. **B**
Crocker [1939] 1 K.B. 194 has consistently been followed and applied.
In *Lake* v. *Bushby* [1949] 2 All E.R. 964, 968 Pritchard J. said that the
authorities showed " beyond doubt that the duty which a solicitor owes to
his client arises ex contractu," and that " apart from the contract between
him and his client the duty does not exist at all."   In *Bailey* v. *Bullock*
[1950] 2 All E.R. 1167, 1169 Barry J. likewise described the proposition **C**
as " beyond doubt."   It was applied too by Hodson L.J. in *Hall* v.
Meyrick [1957] 2 Q.B. 455, 478.

(c) *The decision in Hedley Byrne*

Now if there was, in the House of Lords' decision in *Hedley Byrne* [1964]
A.C. 465, anything that was inconsistent with and destroyed the reasoning **D**
upon which *Groom* v. *Crocker* [1939] 1 K.B. 194 was based, I should
not, I apprehend, be any longer bound by it nor bound to follow those
subsequent cases at first instance which nevertheless applied it—and that
would include even a case carrying the high authority of Diplock L.J.,
who, in *Bagot* v. *Stevens Scanlan & Co. Ltd.* [1966] 1 Q.B. 197, was
sitting as an additional judge of the Queen's Bench Division.   I have
to confess that, unassisted by prior authority, I think that I should have **E**
felt myself compelled to the conclusion that the ratio of *Groom* v. *Crocker*
[1939] 1 K.B. 94—which, of course, was decided before the doctrine of
tortious negligence arising from special relationships enunciated in the
Hedley Byrne case had been fully developed—could not stand alongside
that overriding decision of the House of Lords.

The principle was stated by Lord Morris of Borth-y-Gest as a perfectly **F**
general one and it is difficult to see why it should be excluded by the
fact that the relationship of dependence and reliance between the parties
is a contractual one rather than one gratuitously assumed, in the absence,
of course, of contractual terms excluding or restricting the general duties
which the law implies.   Logically, as it seems to me, this could be so only
if there is read into every contract not only an implied term to employ
reasonable care and skill in the performance of the contract, but a further **G**
term to the effect that the contract shall be the conclusive and exclusive
source of all duties owed by one party to the other to the exclusion of
any further or more extensive duties which the general law would otherwise impose.   Lord Morris of Borth-y-Gest expressed the principle when
he said, at pp. 502–503 :

"   My Lords, I consider that it follows and that it should now be **H**
regarded as settled that if someone possessed of a special skill undertakes, quite irrespective of contract, to apply that skill for the assistance of another person who relies upon such skill, a duty of care
will arise.   The fact that the service is to be given by means of or
by the instrumentality of words can make no difference.   Furthermore, if in a sphere in which a person is so placed that others could
reasonably rely upon his judgment or his skill or upon his ability to

The Weekly Law Reports, July 7, 1978

189

3 W.L.R.   Midland Bank v. Hett, Stubbs & Kemp (Ch.D.)   Oliver J.

A make careful inquiry, a person takes it upon himself to give information or advice to, or allows his information or advice to be passed on to, another person who, as he knows or should know, will place reliance upon it, then a duty of care will arise."

Now this was a perfectly general statement of principle and even if it be treated as qualified to the extent indicated in the majority view of B the Board in *Mutual Life & Citizens' Assurance Co. Ltd.* v. *Evatt* [1971] A.C. 793 there seems to me to be no ground for confining its operation to non-contractual relationships. Indeed, the exposition of the principle in the majority judgment of Lord Diplock in that case at pp. 801–803, suggests just the contrary, for Lord Diplock there ascribes the origin of the principle to the duty imposed by the law by reason merely of the carrying on of particular professions or trades and summarised in the C maxim " spondet peritiam artis et imperitia culpae adnumeratur."

That there is no such restriction is, I think, clear not only from the speech of Lord Morris of Borth-y-Gest but from other speeches as well. Lord Pearce in *Hedley Byrne* [1964] A.C. 465, 538 for instance, adopted and approved the dissenting judgment of Denning L.J. in *Candler* v. *Crane, Christmas & Co.* [1951] 2 K.B. 164, 179–180. Denning L.J. said:

D " Let me now be constructive and suggest the circumstances in which I say that a duty to use care in statement does exist apart from a contract in that behalf. First, what persons are under such duty? My answer is those persons such as accountants, surveyors, valuers and analysts, whose profession and occupation it is to examine books, accounts, and other things, and to make reports on which other E people—other than their clients—rely in the ordinary course of business. Their duty is not merely a duty to use care in their reports. They have also a duty to use care in their work which results in their reports. Herein lies the difference between these professional men and other persons who have been held to be under no duty to use care in their statements, such as promoters who issue a prospectus: *Derry* v. *Peek* (1889) 14 App.Cas. 337 (now altered by statute), and F trustees who answer inquiries about the trust funds: *Low* v. *Bouverie* [1891] 3 Ch. 82. Those persons do not bring, and are not expected to bring, any professional knowledge or skill into the preparation of their statements: they can only be made responsible by the law affecting persons generally, such as contract, estoppel, innocent misrepresentation or fraud. But it is very different with persons who engage in a calling which requires special knowledge and skill. From G very early times it has been held that they owe a duty of care to those who are closely and directly affected by their work, apart altogether from any contract or undertaking in that behalf. Thus Fitzherbert, in his new *Natura Brevium* (1534) 94D, says that: ' if a smith prick my horse with a nail . . . , I shall have my action upon the case against him, without any warranty by the smith to do it well '; and he supports H it with an excellent reason: ' for it is the duty of every artificer to exercise his art rightly and truly as he ought.' This reasoning has been treated as applicable not only to shoeing smiths, surgeons and barbers, who work with hammers, knives and scissors, but also to shipbrokers and clerks in the custom house who work with figures and make entries in books, ' because their situation and employment necessarily imply a competent degree of knowledge in making such entries ': see *Shiels* v. *Blackburne* (1789) 1 H.Bl. 158, 162, *per* Lord

Loughborough, which was not referred to by Devlin J., in *Heskell* v. **A** *Continental Express Ltd.* [1950] 1 All E.R. 1033, 1042, The same reasoning has been applied to medical men who make reports on the sanity of others: see *Everett* v. *Griffiths* [1920] 3 K.B. 163, 182, 217. It is, I think, also applicable to professional accountants."

Now, in that passage, I think that it is abundantly clear that Denning L.J. was seeking to enunciate a general principle of liability arising from the **B** relationship created by the assumption of a particular work or responsibility, quite regardless of how the relationship arose. In the case of *Fitzherbert's Smith*, Anon. Year Book 46 Edw. III Trin. 19, the relationship was contractual. In *Everett* v. *Griffiths* [1920] 3 K.B. 163 it arose out of the performance of a statutory function.

The inquiry upon which the court is to embark is " what is the relationship between plaintiff and defendant? " not " how did the relationship, if **C** any, arise? " That this is so appears, I think, with complete clarity from subsequent cases.

Ministry of Housing and Local Government v. *Sharp* [1970] 2 Q.B. 223 was concerned with the negligent performance of the statutory duty of a local authority to answer inquiries about charges in the local land charges register. Undoubtedly, in addition to any statutory duty, there **D** must, I think, have been a contractual duty to the inquirer who paid the fee for the service. The actual question at issue was as to liability to a third party injured by a negligent answer. The Court of Appeal found such liability but it is interesting to note that they assumed that exactly the same duty was owed to the inquirer. And the case is a clear authority that the principle in the *Hedley Byrne* case [1964] A.C. 465 is one which **E** in no way depends upon the voluntary assumption of the relationship which gives rise to the duty.

Fisher J. in *Ministry of Housing and Local Government* v. *Sharp* said, at p. 243:

"Legal responsibility . . . can arise either from the voluntary making of a particular statement, or the voluntary entry into a continuing relationship which involves the making of such statements, or the **F** voluntary assumption of an office or appointment which involves the making of such statements."

There he was quoting from the submission which counsel had made to him. He rejected that in these terms on the same page:

"As I see it, the emphasis on the voluntary nature of the representa- **G** tion in *Hedley Byrne* [1964] A.C. 465, was dictated by the facts of that case, and the limitations in the statements of principle were not intended to be universally applicable. . . ."

On the following page Fisher J. quoted from the speech of Lord Pearce saying:

"Another principle is to be discerned in the speeches, and in cases **H** cited with approval therein, namely, that ' persons who hold themselves out as possessing a special skill are under a duty to exercise it with reasonable care ': see, for instance, Lord Hodson, at p. 505, and Lord Pearce, at p. 538. Lord Pearce said: ' In those cases there was no dichotomy between negligence in act and in word, nor between physical and economic loss. The basis underlying them is that if persons holding themselves out in a calling or situation or profession

A   take on a task within that calling or situation or profession, they have a duty of skill and care. In terms of proximity one might say that they are in particularly close proximity to those who, as they know, are relying on their skill and care although the proximity is not contractual.' "

Although Fisher J.'s decision was reversed in the Court of Appeal,
B his expression of opinion about the ambit of the *Hedley Byrne* principle was affirmed by all three members of the court. Lord Denning M.R. said, at p. 268:

"I have no doubt that the clerk is liable. He was under a duty at common law to use due care. That was a duty which he owed to any person—incumbrancer or purchaser—whom he knew, or ought
C   to have known, might be injured if he made a mistake."

A little further on, Lord Denning M.R. continued:

"Mr. Hunter submitted to us, however, that the correct principle did not go to that length. He said that a duty to use due care (where there was no contract) only arose when there was a voluntary assumption of responsibility. I do not agree. He relied particularly
D   on the words of Lord Reid in *Hedley Byrne's* case [1964] A.C. 465, 487, and of Lord Devlin at p. 529. I think they used those words because of the special circumstances of that case (where the bank disclaimed responsibility). But they did not in any way mean to limit the general principle. In my opinion the duty to use due care in a statement arises, not from any voluntary assumption of responsi-
E   bility, but from the fact that the person making it knows, or ought to know, that others, being his neighbours in this regard, would act on the faith of the statement being accurate. That is enough to bring the duty into being. It is owed, of course, to the person to whom the certificate is issued and whom he knows is going to act on it."

F Salmon L.J. said, at p. 279:

"It has been argued, in the present case, that since the council did not voluntarily make the search or prepare the certificate for their clerk's signature they did not voluntarily assume responsibility for the accuracy of the certificate and accordingly owed no duty of care to the Minister. I do not accept that, in all cases, the obligation
G   to take reasonable care necessarily depends upon a voluntary assumption of responsibility."

Finally, Cross L.J. said, at p. 291:

"Again I do not think that the fact that the searcher did not undertake the function of making the statement in question 'voluntarily' —except in the sense that he could have refused to accept employ-
H   ment in so potentially hazardous an occupation—is relevant to the problem in hand. It is true that the phrase 'voluntary assumption of risk' occurs frequently in the speeches in the *Hedley Byrne* case [1964] A.C. 465, but I agree with the judge that that case did not purport to lay down any metes and bounds within which legal liability in tort for false statements, on which the parties to whom they are made rely, has to be confined: see in particular *per* Lord Devlin, at pp. 530–531. I see no sufficient reason why in an appro-

priate case the liability should not extend to cases in which the　A
defendant is obliged to make the statement which proves to be false."

Lord Denning M.R. spoke to the same effect in *Dutton* v. *Bognor Regis
Urban District Council* [1972] 1 Q.B. 373, 394–395, where he said:

"Nowadays since *Hedley Byrne & Co. Ltd.* v. *Heller & Partners
Ltd.* [1964] A.C. 465 it is clear that a professional man who gives
guidance to others owes a duty of care, not only to the client who　B
employs him, but also to another who he knows is relying on his
skill to save him from harm. It is certain that a banker or accountant
is under such a duty. And I see no reason why a solicitor is not
likewise. The essence of this proposition, however, is the *reliance.*
In *Hedley Byrne* v. *Heller* it was stressed by Lord Reid at p. 486,
by Lord Morris of Borth-y-Gest at pp. 502–503, and by Lord Hodson　C
at p. 514. The professional man must know that the other is *relying*
on his skill and the other must in fact rely on it."

This seems to me to be quite inconsistent with the restrictive view of
a solicitor's liability enunciated in *Groom* v. *Crocker* [1939] 1 K.B. 194
and to be expounding a basis of liability which was not contemplated in
that case either in the argument or the judgments. I do not think that　D
in the speech of Lord Morris of Borth-y-Gest in the *Hedley Byrne* case
the words, at p. 502, " quite irrespective of contract " can legitimately be
read as " only where there is no contract." That seems to me to be
putting a wholly unwarranted gloss on the decision and to be out of line
with the subsequent authorities in which the doctrine has been expounded and, to some extent, expanded. The matter becomes, in my
judgment, even clearer when one looks at the speech of Lord Devlin in　E
the *Hedley Byrne* case [1964] A.C. 465, for he treats the existence of a
contractual relationship as very good evidence of the general tortious duty
which he is there discussing. He said, at pp. 528–529:

"I think, therefore, that there is ample authority to justify your
Lordships in saying now that the categories of special relationships
which may give rise to a duty to take care in word as well as in　F
deed are not limited to contractual relationships or to relationships of
fiduciary duty, but include also relationships which in the words of
Lord Shaw in *Nocton* v. *Lord Ashburton* [1914] A.C. 932, 972
are ' equivalent to contract,' that is, where there is an assumption of
responsibility in circumstances in which, but for the absence of
consideration, there would be a contract. Where there is an express　G
undertaking, an express warranty as distinct from mere representation, there can be little difficulty. The difficulty arises in discerning
those cases in which the undertaking is to be implied. In this respect
the absence of consideration is not irrelevant. Payment for information or advice is very good evidence that it is being relied upon and
that the informer or adviser knows that it is. Where there is no　H
consideration, it will be necessary to exercise greater care in distinguishing between social and professional relationships and between
those which are of a contractual character and those which are not."

A little further down he seems to have had in mind the very case of a
solicitor as a typical example of the type of situation in which the duty
arises. Lord Devlin said, at p. 259:

The Weekly Law Reports, July 7, 1978

193

3 W.L.R.   Midland Bank v. Hett, Stubbs & Kemp (Ch.D.)   Oliver J.

A   " I do not understand any of your Lordships to hold that it is a responsibility imposed by law upon certain types of persons or in certain sorts of situations. It is a responsibility that is voluntarily accepted or undertaken, either generally where a general relationship, such as that of a solicitor and client or banker and customer, is created, or specifically in relation to a particular transaction."

B   Again, Lord Devlin said, at p. 530:

" I shall therefore content myself with the proposition that wherever there is a relationship equivalent to contract, there is a duty of care. Such a relationship may be either general or particular. Examples of a general relationship are those of solicitor and client and of banker and customer. For the former *Nocton* v. *Lord Ashburton*
C   [1914] A.C. 932 has long stood as the authority and for the latter there is the decision of Salmon J. in *Woods* v. *Martins Bank Ltd.* [1959] 1 Q.B. 55 which I respectfully approve. There may well be others yet to be established. Where there is a general relationship of this sort, it is unnecessary to do more than prove its existence and the duty follows."

D   Nor, as I read the decision, can its operation be confined to cases where the service undertaken takes the form of a representation or of a statement of fact, opinion, or advice. It must logically, I think, apply where the service involves some other positive action such as the giving of a notice as in *Bean* v. *Wade,* 2 T.L.R. 157. Once the duty is established it cannot, in my judgment, matter whether the breach takes the form of malfeasance or nonfeasance: see, for instance, *Barnett* v. *Chelsea*
E   *and Kensington Hospital Management Committee* [1969] 1 Q.B. 428.
Nor, if I may respectfully say so, do I follow the argument advanced by counsel in *Bagot* v. *Stevens Scanlan & Co. Ltd.* [1966] 1 Q.B. 197, 200, that the cause of action there was necessarily in contract alone because the architects in that case had " failed to do the very thing which they contracted to do." Well, so they had, but the form of the
F   breach cannot affect the nature of the duty, nor does an obligation imposed by law become an obligation different in quality simply because the obligee agrees to accept money for its performance.
If an accountant gratuitously undertakes to render a careful and accurate report on a company's affairs to one who, as he knows, is relying and will act upon it, and he renders a careless and inaccurate report, he has failed to do the very thing that he undertook to do. But that is
G   merely a description of his failure, not an analysis of his duty.
The case of a layman consulting a solicitor for advice seems to me to be as typical a case as one could find of the sort of relationship in which the duty of care described in the *Hedley Byrne* case [1964] A.C. 465 exists; and if I am free to do so in the instant case, I would, therefore, hold that the relationship of solicitor and client gave rise to a
H   duty in the defendants under the general law to exercise that care and skill upon which they must have known perfectly well that their client relied. To put it another way, their common law duty was not to injure their client by failing to do that which they had undertaken to do and which, at their invitation, he relied upon them to do. That duty was broken, but no cause of action in tort arose until the damage occurred; and none did occur until August 17, 1967. I would regard it as wholly immaterial that their duty arose because they accepted a retainer which

entitled them, if they chose to do so, to send a bill to their client. And, if I felt free so to hold, it would encourage me to find that my decision was in line with the law which has been applied in another part of the United Kingdom. A similar point to that which arises in the instant case fell for decision in Scotland after the decision of the House of Lords in the *Hedley Byrne* case [1964] A.C. 465. In *Robertson* v. *Bannigan,* S.L.T. 318 it was held that time under the Limitation Act 1939 ran from the accrual of the damage and not from the date of the breach of the contractual duty imposed by the retainer. Lord Hunter observed, at p. 319:

> " But, in any event, I am unable to accept the proposition that a client does not have a remedy in delict against a negligent solicitor in addition to such remedy as may be available to him in contract."

I would respectfully arrive at the same conclusion in this case.

It is—as has been said recently—certainly no part of the function of a puisne judge to criticise decisions of higher courts and I do not venture to do so. He does, however, have to analyse their effect and the effect upon them of general doctrines subsequently established by yet higher courts. The question which I am called upon to answer is whether the principle in the *Hedley Byrne* case [1964] A.C. 465, as it has since been interpreted and applied, not only in the Court of Appeal but in the House of Lords itself, so destroys the only reasoning upon which *Groom* v. *Crocker* [1939] 1 K.B. 194 rested and has since stood that I can no longer be bound, or indeed entitled, to follow it but must apply what I conceive to be the overriding principle.

The effect of the authorities, if Mr. Gatehouse is correct in saying that the law is still represented by *Groom* v. *Crocker* in a case where a retainer exists, is a curious one. The solicitor who gratuitously assumes to advise a relative and does it negligently remains liable to suit at any time within six years of damage occurring. The solicitor who charges a substantial fee to a client who retains his services in the normal way escapes any liability at all if the damage does not occur or is not discovered until six years has elapsed from the date on which the negligent advice is given.

As Lord Devlin has said [1964] A.C. 465, 516: " The common law is tolerant of much illogicality, especially on the surface; but no system of law can be workable if it has not got logic at the root of it." On the other hand, Lord Reid remarked that " the life blood of the law is not logic but common sense." Both the logic and the common sense of this position may be apparent to lawyers, but I doubt whether they would be readily discernible by the man on the Clapham omnibus or even, I venture to think, by the man in the company car.

(d) *Decisions since Hedley Byrne*

It is, however, Mr. Gatehouse's submission that even if, which I think he would contest, the reasoning which has led me to the conclusion which I have expressed above is sound, that conclusion is not open to me because of the current of authority since. The impact of the *Hedley Byrne* principle upon a solicitor and client relationship came directly in question very shortly after the decision of the House of Lords in the *Hedley Byrne* case. In *Clark* v. *Kirby-Smith* [1964] Ch. 506, a solicitor whose express instructions were to give a notice under the Landlord and

The Weekly Law Reports, July 7, 1978

195

3 W.L.R.   Midland Bank v. Hett, Stubbs & Kemp (Ch.D.)   Oliver J.

A Tenant Act 1954 failed to do so, so that his client lost his right of renewal. The basis of the solicitor's liability arose in connection with the measure of damages. Plowman J. followed *Groom* v. *Crocker* [1939] 1 K.B. 194 and rejected the argument that the effect of the *Hedley Byrne* case [1964] A.C. 465 was to create, in the case of a solicitor and his client, any liability for the tort of negligence.

B Plowman J. pointed out that *Howell* v. *Young,* 5 B. & C. 259 had, only in the previous year, been recognised and applied by the House of Lords in *Cartledge* v. *E. Jopling & Sons Ltd.* [1963] A.C. 758. That was so, but the approval was not on the point for which he was citing it as authority, but on the point that, where damage is suffered as a result of negligence but remains undetected, the occurrence of subsequently emerging damage does not ground a fresh cause of action so as to give rise to
C a further period of limitation. That proposition itself has been recently reconsidered in *Anns* v. *Merton London Borough Council* [1977] 2 W.L.R. 1024. Furthermore, it looks very much, from the context, as if Lord Pearce, who delivered the leading speech in *Cartledge* v. *E. Jopling & Sons Ltd.* [1963] A.C. 758, was treating the case as one of tortious negligence, for he said, at p. 782–783:

D   " It was held that his cause of action accrued at the time when the solicitor was negligent (*and the plaintiff was damaged by receiving inadequate security*) although the plaintiff was then unaware of any negligence *or damage.*" (The emphasis is mine.)

Now in the light of the very specific references in the speech of Lord Devlin in the *Hedley Byrne* case [1964] A.C. 465 to the very relationship
E of solicitor and client, the question arises how *Clark* v. *Kirby-Smith* [1964] Ch. 506 can be justified. What was there, apart from the bare fact of the decision in *Groom* v. *Crocker* [1939] 1 K.B. 194—a case decided at a time when it was conceived that there was no liability for negligent misstatement apart from contract—to dictate that the general *Hedley Byrne* duty did not apply where the services of a solicitor were
F retained by a client? Plainly Plowman J. considered that there *was* nothing in *Groom* v. *Crocker* [1939] 1 K.B. 194 which was inconsistent with the *Hedley Byrne* case [1964] A.C. 465 or he would not and could not have followed it. But if there was no inconsistency, that can—so far as I can see—have been for only one or more of four possible reasons. First, it might be because *Groom* v. *Crocker* [1939] 1 K.B. 194 established some doctrine peculiar either (i) to the profession of solicitors or
G (ii) to professional men generally which absolved them from a duty affecting every other relationship of the type described in the *Hedley Byrne* case [1964] A.C. 465 as giving rise to a duty of care. Secondly, it might be because there falls to be implied in the retainer of every solicitor some term to the effect that any duty which would otherwise arise under the general law is excluded. Thirdly, it might be because
H of some general principle of law that a plaintiff who has rights against a defendant both in contract and in tort is bound to rely upon his contractual rights alone. And, fourthly, it might be because the doctrine of the *Hedley Byrne* case applies *only,* and the duty arising under that doctrine *attaches* only, to relationships gratuitously—or at least non-contractually—assumed and does not and cannot apply where the relationship between the parties out of which the duty is alleged to arise is a contractual relationship. Standing *Groom* v. *Crocker* [1939] 1 K.B.

194 and the *Hedley Byrne* case [1964] A.C. 465 side by side, I can   A
see no other way beyond one or more of these four in which they can
be reconciled.

The first ground cannot, in my judgment, be seriously arguable. In
the first place, apart from the fact that it would be wholly irrational, it is
noticeable that, in *Groom* v. *Crocker* [1939] 1 K.B. 194, both Sir Wilfrid
Greene M.R. and Scott L.J. treat the solicitor as being in the same position as a doctor. Scott L.J. relied upon *Jarvis* v. *Moy, Davies, Smith,*   B
Vandervell & Co. [1936] 1 K.B. 399 as establishing the basic principle
for his decision, and that was a case of a stockbroker. And in *Bagot* v.
Stevens Scanlan & Co. Ltd. [1966] 1 Q.B. 197, Diplock L.J. followed
Clark v. *Kirby-Smith* [1964] Ch. 506 and applied the same principle
to an architect. As Harman J. put it in *Simmons* v. *Pennington & Son*:
" I do not think I need deal at any great length with the question of a   C
solicitor's liability for negligence. It is the same as anybody else's
liability . . . "; and that was approved and adopted by Hodson L.J. in
the Court of Appeal [1955] 1 W.L.R. 183, 188–189. Nor is it a
tenable proposition that there is something about what may be termed
loosely " professional activity " generally which excludes the general duty
of care in tort. Cases of tortious liability in the professions of medicine,   D
dentistry, surgery and accountancy are legion.

The second ground to which I have referred seems to me equally
unsustainable. Contractual relationships are a matter of agreement in
individual cases and, apart from statute, I know of no authority for
importing into contracts some universal term which applies whether the
parties could be contemplated as intending it or not.

Nor does the third ground bear examination. There is not and never   E
has been any rule of law that a person having alternative claims must
frame his action in one or the other. If I have a contract with my dentist
to extract a tooth, I am not thereby precluded from suing him in tort
if he negligently shatters my jaw: *Edwards* v. *Mallan* [1908] 1 K.B.
1002; nor does the contractual duty assumed by a local authority to
answer inquiries prevent its being sued both in tort and in contract if it   F
does so carelessly: *Coats Paton (Retail) Ltd.* v. *Birmingham Corporation*
(1971) 69 L.G.R. 356. I am left, therefore, with the fourth ground,
namely, that the *Hedley Byrne* duty either never arises at all where the
relationship existing between the parties, although otherwise such as
would give rise to it, is a relationship created by a contract between them
or alternatively, that if such a relationship did exist before or independently of a contract being made, it is totally excluded by or merges in   G
the contractual relationship assumed.

This seems in fact to be the reasoning behind *Groom* v. *Crocker*
[1939] 1 K.B. 194. That most clearly emerges from the judgment of
Scott L.J. when he said, at p. 222, " the mutual rights and duties of the
two are regulated entirely by the contract of employment." I confess
that I find this difficult to understand in the context. Scott L.J. was   H
referring here not only to solicitors but to doctors, architects, stock-
brokers and others in a like situation. But there has never, so far as
I know, been any doubt of the tortious liability of a medical man even
though he may be in a contractual relationship with his patient; see
Edwards v. *Mallan* [1908] 1 K.B. 1002; and the distinction between the
case of a medical man and some other profession cannot, I think, lie
simply in the type of damage which arises—which, in the case of the

The Weekly Law Reports, July 7, 1978

197

3 W.L.R.   Midland Bank v. Hett, Stubbs & Kemp (Ch.D.)   Oliver J.

A   medical man, normally takes the form of direct physical injury. Any
distinction based on that ground was firmly rejected in *Ministry of
Housing and Local Government* v. *Sharp* [1970] 2 Q.B. 223: see, for
example, Salmon L.J. at p. 278.

That the mere fact that the relationship is contractual is the ground
for excluding the case of, inter alios, the solicitor from the ambit of the
Hedley Byrne principle appears, I think, clearly from the judgment of
B   Diplock L.J. in *Bagot* v. *Stevens Scanlan & Co. Ltd.* [1966] 1 Q.B.
197. That was a case in which the plaintiff sued for damage arising from
the alleged neglect of his architects to supervise properly the laying of
drains to his property. The architects' retainer had expired more than
six years before the damage became apparent. Diplock L.J. held that
the action was barred by the Limitation Act 1939, and in doing so
C   followed *Clark* v. *Kirby-Smith* [1964] Ch. 506. He said, at p. 204:

> " It seems to me that, in this case, the relationship which created the
> duty of exercising reasonable skill and care by the architects to their
> clients arose out of the contract and not otherwise. The complaint
> that is made against them is of a failure to do the very thing which
> they contracted to do. That was the relationship which gave rise
D   > to the duty which was broken. It was a contractual relationship, a
> contractual duty, and any action brought for failure to comply with
> that duty is, in my view, an action founded on contract. It is also,
> in my view, an action founded upon contract alone."

He expressed the view that the only relationships where a contractual
duty to take care continued to subsist alongside a common law duty
E   were those cases where the law, in the old days, recognised something in
the nature of a public calling—such as the common carrier, or an inn-
keeper—or cases of master and servant. As to the argument that there
subsisted a liability on the principle of the *Hedley Byrne* case [1964]
A.C. 465, he dismissed this by simply quoting from and adopting the
judgment of Plowman J. in *Clark* v. *Kirby-Smith* [1964] Ch. 506. The
F   same principle, he said, applied not only to solicitors but to other professional relationships such as the one in the case before him where someone
undertakes to exercise by contract his professional skill in relation to the
matter.

The relevant principle of law was, he held, that expressed by Greer
L.J. in *Jarvis* v. *Moy, Davies, Smith, Vandervell & Co.* [1936] 1 K.B.
399. But as I have mentioned, that case must, in my judgment, be looked
G   at in the context of the question which there fell for decision, namely,
that of the costs recoverable under the County Courts Act 1919. I have
already referred to *Turner* v. *Stallibrass* [1898] 1 Q.B. 56 but the same
distinction occurs again in *Kelly* v. *Metropolitan Railway Co.* [1895] 1
Q.B. 944, another case in the Court of Appeal. A. L. Smith L.J. said,
at p. 947:

H   > " The distinction is this—if the cause of complaint be for an act of
> omission or nonfeasance which without proof of a contract to
> do what has been left undone would not give rise to any cause of
> action (because no duty apart from contract to do what is complained
> of exists), then the action is founded upon contract and not upon
> tort. If, on the other hand, the relation of the plaintiff and the
> defendants be such that a duty arises from that relationship, irres-
> pective of contract, to take due care, and the defendants are negligent,

then the action is one of tort, and as regards the County Court Acts   A
and costs this is what was laid down in the above-mentioned case."

This appears to me to be a clear recognition that the mere existence
of a contractual duty of care does not exclude a similar independent
duty which arises from the relationship of proximity between the parties.
Nevertheless the effect of *Bagot* v. *Stevens Scanlan & Co. Ltd.* [1966]
1 Q.B. 197 is that any duty in tort is excluded in the case of any pro-   B
fessional relationship involving the exercise of care and skill which is
undertaken as a result of a contract between the parties. But I ask
again: what about the dentist?   No one has suggested that his is a
common calling.   But the Court of Appeal had held quite unequivocally
that he could be sued in tort for breach of the duty to take care.   I quote
from the judgment of Vaughan Williams L.J. in *Edwards* v. *Mallan*   C
[1908] 1 K.B. 1002, 1005:

" As I understand the law, if there is either a special contract or an
implied contract arising from the relation of dentist and patient, and
an action is brought upon the contract for a breach of the duty
arising out of that relation, then, in *either* case, if the plaintiff
substantially does not rely upon any *special* term in the special
contract, and only relies (so far as the implied contract is concerned)   D
upon a contract the implication of which depends solely upon the
relation of dentist and patient, in neither case would it be right
that the action should necessarily be treated as one of contract."
(the emphasis is mine).

That case was followed by Lynskey J. in *Fish* v. *Kapur* [1948] 2
All E.R. 176.   He held in terms that the action was an action in tort.   E
So I find myself faced with what appear to me to be conflicting lines
of authority—one which would exclude all contractual professional
relationships from the ambit of the *Hedley Byrne* principle and another
which would, if followed logically, bring them in.

Nor can the restrictive view of the *Hedley Byrne* duty be logically
confined to the exclusion simply of contractual *professional* relationships,
if that adjective is used to differentiate those relationships from relation-   F
ships entered into in the course of carrying on a trade or business.
There is nothing magical which distinguishes a " professional " contract
in that sense from any other commercial contract.   So that the underlying
basis of *Clark* v. *Kirby-Smith* [1964] Ch. 506 and *Bagot* v. *Stevens
Scanlan & Co. Ltd.* [1966] 1 Q.B. 197 must, I think, be that the duty
of care which would otherwise arise from a relationship of the sort   G
described in the *Hedley Byrne* case [1964] A.C. 465 has no existence
where that relationship is a contractual one.

And here again, the authorities are not easy to reconcile. The contractual obligations of a window-cleaner include an obligation to exercise
reasonable care in carrying out his work.   But if he is engaged to clean
my chandelier and, in doing so, he negligently shatters it, it is clear that,
whilst no doubt he can be sued in contract, there is an independent   H
and co-existing liability in tort.   That was what happened in *Jackson* v.
Mayfair Window Cleaning Co. Ltd. [1952] 1 All E.R. 215.   That is an
instructive case, both because of Barry J.'s approach to the question and
also for the interpretation which he placed on *Jarvis* v. *Moy, Davies,
Smith, Vandervell & Co.* [1936] 1 K.B. 399, one of the cases relied
on by Mr. Gatehouse and forming part of the foundation of the reasoning
in *Bagot* v. *Stevens Scanlan & Co. Ltd.* [1966] 1 Q.B. 197.   It is quite

The Weekly Law Reports, July 7, 1978

199

3 W.L.R.   Midland Bank v. Hett, Stubbs & Kemp (Ch.D.)   Oliver J.

A clear that Barry J. did not regard *Jarvis* v. *Moy, Davies, Smith, Vandervell & Co.* [1936] 1 K.B. 399 as establishing that the only duty lay in contract, but merely as an application of the test established in *Turner* v. *Stallibrass* [1898] 1 Q.B. 56 for whether an action is to be treated as substantially in tort or substantially in contract for the purposes of the County Courts Act 1919. Having referred to the judgment of Greer L.J. in *Jarvis* v. *Moy, Davies, Smith, Vandervell & Co.* [1936] 1 K.B. 399,

B Barry J. said [1952] 1 All E.R. 215, 217–218:

> " That there was a contract between the plaintiff and the first defendants is, of course, not in dispute. Moreover, the acts complained of might well have been pleaded as a breach of that contract. What I have to ask myself, however, is whether, in essence, the plaintiff must rely on that contract in order to establish her claim or whether
>
> C she can properly treat the contract as a mere matter of history, explaining the presence of the defendants' workman in her flat, and establish a breach of duty independent of any obligations undertaken by the defendants to her under that contract. In my judgment, the present claim falls within the latter category. The plaintiff does not complain of mere nonfeasance, nor does she say that the defendants failed to clean her chandelier at the time or in the manner stipulated
>
> D by their contract. Her case is based on a broader duty, independent of any contractual obligation undertaken by the defendants. She says that if the defendants, through their workmen, interfere with her property—whether with or without her permission and whether in pursuance of a contract or otherwise—they are under an obligation not to damage that property as a result of their negligence, or, in
>
> E other words, they are bound to take reasonable care to keep it safe. This is, I think, the true foundation of the plaintiff's claim.
>
> " I reach that conclusion largely because I am satisfied that, on the evidence in this case, the plaintiff would have been equally entitled to recover damages had the defendants carried out this work gratuitously or had the contract for cleaning been made by some third
>
> F party, not her agent, on which contract she could found no right of action. In either of those hypothetical cases the defendants would, I think, owe a duty to the plaintiff—independently of contract—to take due care not to damage her property. Any breach of this duty would render them liable to an action for negligence."

G Another case of liability under a duty of care both in contract and in tort, where the same question arose as to the substance of the action for the purposes of the County Courts Act 1919, is *Sachs* v. *Henderson* [1902] 1 K.B. 612, another decision of the Court of Appeal. Collins M.R., referring to *Turner* v. *Stallibrass* [1898] 1 Q.B. 56, said, at p. 616:

> " I agree that the distinction between tort and contract is not a
> H logical one, and that it is sometimes difficult to say whether a particular thing is a wrong or a breach of contract. If the claim of the plaintiff had been set out at large pointing to some particular stipulation in the contract, which stipulation had been broken, the action would be founded on contract; but where it is only necessary to refer to the contract to establish a relationship between the parties, and the claim goes on to aver a breach of duty arising out of that relationship, the action is one of tort."

But wherever logic may lead me—or wherever I think that it may lead A me—it is suggested that I am bound to follow *Clark* v. *Kirby-Smith* [1964] Ch. 506 and *Bagot* v. *Stevens Scanlan & Co. Ltd.* [1966] 1 Q.B. 197 by the decision of the Court of Appeal in *Cook* v. *Swinfen* [1967] 1 W.L.R. 457. I say " it is suggested " but, in fact, the reference to the case was passed to me by Mr. Gatehouse, with Mr. Harman's permission, after the conclusion of the argument—neither side desiring the case to be restored for further argument—and, in so saying, I am merely voicing B what I think would have been Mr. Gatehouse's submission if the case had been available in court during the argument.

The case was one which raised, as did *Groom* v. *Crocker* [1939] 1 K.B. 194, a question of the correct measure of damages in an action against a solicitor for negligence in conducting the client's affairs. The defendant had badly misadvised the plaintiff in relation to divorce pro- C ceedings so that a decree was granted to her husband on his undefended petition whereas she could have cross-petitioned on the ground of his adultery. The defendant had also failed to make an application for maintenance of the child of the marriage. The plaintiff claimed, inter alia, damages for loss of earnings attributable to a breakdown in health as a result of the mishandled proceedings and the question arose whether this was a recoverable head of damage. Lawton J. held that the damages D claimed were too remote because the claim was one in contract. In so holding he merely followed and applied *Groom* v. *Crocker* [1939] 1 K.B. 194.

The plaintiff appealed to the Court of Appeal and the only judgment is that of Lord Denning M.R. The court upheld the result at which Lawton J. had arrived because on the facts they did not regard the E damage claimed as a foreseeable consequence of the negligence. It was therefore too remote but not for the reason that Lawton J. had given. He had arrived at that result *because* the action was one in contract. The Court of Appeal considered the damage too remote however the claim was put, because the measure in both tort and contract was the same and depended simply on foreseeability. The significance of the case, F however, is that Lord Denning M.R. dealt with the claim as if it were a solely contractual claim. He said, at p. 461 :

"The cause of action, it must be remembered, is one for breach of contract. An action against a solicitor is always one for breach of contract, as was held in *Groom* v. *Crocker* [1939] 1 K.B. 194 "; and after discussing the test of foreseeability he continued " In these circumstances I think that, just as in the law of tort, so also in the G law of contract, damages can be recovered for nervous shock or anxiety state if it is a reasonably foreseeable consequence."

So here, Mr. Gatehouse would say, is a decision of a unanimous Court of Appeal after the *Hedley Byrne* case [1964] A.C. 465, affirming yet again the exclusively contractual nature of the solicitor's liability. But was it dictum or decision? I do not find this an easy question to answer. H

Contractual liability certainly formed the underlying assumption upon which the decision at first instance was based and this was equally assumed in the Court of Appeal. It was not, however, so far as I can see, argued in either court that the liability was a tortious liability and the question was how far the underlying assumption limited the damages recoverable. The decision was that the claim was too remote, but the ratio in the Court of Appeal was that that result ensued, not because the claim was a

The Weekly Law Reports, July 7, 1978

201

3 W.L.R.   Midland Bank v. Hett, Stubbs & Kemp (Ch.D.)   Oliver J.

A   contractual claim—although they averred that it was—but because it failed to satisfy a universal test of foreseeability. In my view the observations of Lord Denning M.R. on the exclusively contractual nature of the claim were obiter and formed no essential part of the decision, for which they were strictly unnecessary.

The line of authority directly concerned with solicitor's liability does not, however, end there. In November 1975, very shortly before *Esso*
B   *Petroleum Co. Ltd.* v. *Mardon* [1976] Q.B. 801, the question of remoteness of damage again came before the Court of Appeal in *Heywood* v. *Wellers* [1976] Q.B. 446. Here the plaintiff claimed damages for an anxiety state arising from molestation by a man to whom she had lent money, and the basis of her claim was that the defendants, her solicitors, had negligently failed to advise her to take steps to enforce an injunction
C   which she had obtained. Counsel for the defendants relied upon *Groom* v. *Crocker* [1939] 1 K.B. 194 and *Cook* v. *Swinfen* [1967] 1 W.L.R. 457. His contention was rejected, and Lord Denning M.R. remarked, at p. 459, that those cases might have to be reconsidered.

James L.J., at p. 461, approached the case on the assumption that the action was indeed one in contract only, which he described as " well known and settled law." Bridge L.J. expressed no view on this point. The court
D   was unanimous in holding that damages were recoverable under the head claimed, on the ground that, as Bridge L.J. put it, they were not merely an incidental consequence of the solicitor's mishandling of litigation but the direct and inevitable consequence of his negligent failure to secure the relief which was the whole purpose of the litigation. As a matter of decision, therefore, this case carries the matter no further. The plaintiff
E   was in person and the argument was, therefore, necessarily of a rather limited order. The case does, however, contain a dictum of James L.J. in favour of Mr. Gatehouse's proposition and a, perhaps rather tentative, hint of doubt on the part of Lord Denning M.R.—a doubt which was to find much more forceful expression in *Esso Petroleum Co. Ltd.* v. *Mardon* [1976] Q.B. 801 where the underlying proposition upon which *Groom* v. *Crocker* [1939] 1 K.B. 194 was based formed part of the plain-
F   tiff's argument. Before I come to *Esso Petroleum Co. Ltd.* v. *Mardon* [1976] Q.B. 801, however, it is worth noting, in passing, that at the end of 1975—in fact only two days before the decision in *Heywood* v. *Wellers* [1976] Q.B. 446—the House of Lords had delivered judgment in *Arenson* v. *Arenson* [1977] A.C. 405, which concerned the liability of a firm of accountants. The case is not directly in point here because the point
G   which the House was called upon to decide was whether a third party brought in to value property and valuing it negligently, could claim immunity from suit on the ground that he was exercising a judicial or quasi-judicial function. But what clearly emerges from the speeches of all their Lordships—apart from that of Lord Fraser of Tullybelton who does not deal with the point—is that the doctrine of the *Hedley Byrne* case applies *wherever* the necessary relationship of confidence and reliance
H   exists. It depends upon the relationship not upon how the relationship has been brought into being. Lord Simon of Glaisdale said, at p. 419:

" There is a primary and anterior consideration of public policy, which should be the starting point. This is that, where there is a duty to act with care with regard to another person and there is a breach of such duty causing damage to the other person, public policy in general demands that such damage should be made good to the party to whom

the duty is owed by the person owing the duty. There may be a A
supervening and secondary public policy which demands, nevertheless,
immunity from suit in the particular circumstances. . . . But that
the former public policy is primary can be seen from the jealousy
with which the law allows any derogation from it."

Lord Wheatley said, at p. 426:

" Since *Hedley Byrne* . . . it is clear, if it ever was in doubt, that all B
persons who express an opinion which is negligent are liable for that
negligence to persons who are within a relationship which is recognised
by the law and who have suffered as a result thereof."

Lord Kilbrandon said, at pp. 429–430:

" My Lords, I entirely agree that it would be absurd if the situation C
were that, where an expert is asked by one customer to value a picture,
he is liable in damages if he is shown to have done so negligently, but
that if two customers had jointly asked him to value the same picture
he would have been immune from suit. The latter is precisely the
situation displayed here, leaving out what I think is not relevant at
this stage, that the formal request was made by a third party (the
company) on behalf of the customers. Two people wanted to know, D
for reasons which are immaterial, the value of a parcel of shares.
They had contracted with one another that in such a situation a particular expert should be asked to give his opinion, which opinion they
were bound to accept as final in accordance with their contract. This
is just the same as two customers employing a valuer. It does not
matter whether there has arisen between the customers and the valuer E
a relation of ' neighbourhood ' which fixes on the latter an obligation
to act with reasonable care, or whether—and more rationally as I
would have thought—one holds that the contract between them and
the valuer includes an implied term that he will exercise proper skill
and care. The formality that the secretary of the company made the
contract on behalf of the ' customers ' (shareholders) is of no significance. He made it for the shareholders, not for the company. It is F
not a case of looking for a cause of action in the shareholders on a
contract between the valuer and a third party. The result, whether
in tort or contract, is the same—a liability in damages arising out of
negligence—and conceptual subtleties, however edifying, are not helpful.
I do not think there can be much doubt as to the nature of the
relationship from which such liability, at least in a case like the G
present, must be held to arise. It is seen in a wider range of activities,
and can by no means be confined today to the relation between a
professional man and his client. If I engage a man to exercise his
expertise on my behalf, and it matters not whether he is to prepare a
conveyance of land or to drive a straight furrow across it, then spondet
peritiam artis, et imperitia culpae adnumeratur."

  H

Finally Lord Salmon was quite unequivocal about this. He said, at p. 434:

" We do not know whether the respondents were asked to make the
valuation on behalf of the company (which presumably was interested
in the value of its own shares) or on behalf of Mr. Archy Arenson and
the appellant, nor do we know whether the respondents charged any
fee for this valuation and, if so, to whom, or whether they made their
valuation as part of their ordinary duties as the company's auditors.

A   Nor do I think that this matters because since the decision of this House in *Hedley Byrne* . . . it is clear that quite apart from any contractual obligation, the respondents must have owed a duty both to Mr. Archy Arenson and to the appellant to use reasonable care and skill in making their valuation."

Beyond this, there is an implicit rejection of the notion that the duties
B   created by contractual relationships exclude the general duty in tort in the judgments both of Lord Denning M.R. and Sachs L.J. in *Dutton* v. *Bognor Regis Urban District Council* [1972] 1 Q.B. 373. There, at p. 393, Lord Denning M.R. expressly disapproved the rule laid down in *Bottomley* v. *Bannister* [1932] 1 K.B. 458 and applied in *Otto* v. *Bolton and Norris* [1936] 2 K.B. 46 that there was no liability, apart from con-
C   tract, for the letting or selling of a defective house, even though the defects were the result of negligent construction by the defendant himself. This was, perhaps, only indirectly in issue because the claim against the builder in that case had been compromised Nevertheless, Lord Denning M.R. [1972] 1 Q.B. 373, 394, said in the clearest terms that the liability of a man who builds on his own land, whether to his purchaser or to a third party, is exactly the same as the liability of a contractor who builds on
D   someone else's land. The fact that the defendant is the vendor, so that the relationship between him and the purchaser is a contractual one, clearly does not here exclude a parallel liability in tort.

Lord Denning M.R.'s view has since been expressly approved by the House of Lords in *Anns* v. *Merton London Borough Council* [1977] 2 W.L.R. 1024. That again was not a case concerned directly with a con-
E   tractual liability but it is worth noting the very general terms in which, again, the duty of care was expressed by Lord Wilberforce. He said, at p. 1032:

"Through the trilogy of cases in this House—*Donoghue* v. *Stevenson* [1932] A.C. 562, *Hedley Byrne & Co. Ltd.* v. *Heller & Partners Ltd.* [1964] A.C. 465 and *Dorset Yacht Co. Ltd.* v. *Home Office*
F   [1970] A.C. 1004, the position has now been reached that in order to establish that a duty of care arises in a particular situation, it is not necessary to bring the facts of that situation within those of previous situations in which a duty of care has been held to exist. Rather the question has to be approached in two stages. First one has to ask whether, as between the alleged wrongdoer and the person who has suffered damage there is a sufficient relationship of proximity or
G   neighbourhood such that, in the reasonable contemplation of the former, carelessness on his part may be likely to cause damage to the latter—in which case a prima facie duty of care arises."

Subsequently, in referring to *East Suffolk Rivers Catchment Board* v. *Kent* [1941] A.C. 74, he said, at p. 1037:

H   " My Lords, I believe that the conception of a general duty of care, not limited to particular accepted situations, but extending generally over all relations of sufficient proximity, and even pervading the sphere of statutory functions of public bodies, had not at that time become fully recognised."

It remains true, however, that although, as it seems to me, this is really implicit in the *Hedley Byrne* case itself [1964] A.C. 465 and in the other cases in which the principle has been applied and expounded since,

there was no case prior to *Esso Petroleum Co. Ltd.* v. *Mardon* [1976]   A
Q.B. 801—at any rate at the level of the Court of Appeal and above
—which *expressly* decided that the *Hedley Byrne* duty and a co-extensive
contractual duty were *not* mutually exclusive and none in which anything
but the most tentative doubt had been expressed with regard to the basis
or the continuing validity of the Court of Appeal's decision in *Groom* v.
Crocker [1939] 1 K.B. 194.

B

(e) *Esso Petroleum Co. Ltd.* v. *Mardon*

I turn therefore to the *Esso* case [1976] Q.B. 801. This was a case,
it will be remembered, where the plaintiffs had treated with the defendant
with a view to his taking from them a tenancy of a garage. In the
course of the negotiations they had provided him with certain estimates
of annual throughput which it was found as a fact were prepared   C
negligently. In reliance on those estimates he entered into the contract
with them and suffered very severe loss, for which, when sued by the
plaintiffs for the price of petrol supplied, he counterclaimed.

The claim was put both in tort, on the basis of the *Hedley Byrne*
case [1964] A.C. 465, and in contract, on the footing that there was a
warranty that the estimates were correct. At first instance, Lawson J.   D
found that the negotiations had created a special relationship of the type
envisaged in the *Hedley Byrne* case and that the plaintiffs were, therefore,
liable in tort. He rejected the claim based on contract. The defendant
appealed and the Court of Appeal unanimously held that the facts did
give rise to a contractual liability. There was, they held, a warranty, not
that the estimates were correct, but that they were made with reasonable
care and skill. That had been broken and therefore the defendant was   E
entitled to recover damages for the breach of that contract.

The noticeable feature of this, in the present context, is that the
contractual duty found by the Court of Appeal not only covered the same
ground as, but was, in practical terms, identical and co-terminous with,
the duty arising from a special relationship of the *Hedley Byrne* type.

The Court of Appeal went on to find that, in addition to and quite   F
apart from the contractual liability referred to above, the plaintiffs were
liable to the defendant in tort under the *Hedley Byrne* doctrine. Now
this was no unconsidered view. It had been specifically argued on behalf
of the plaintiffs that the two duties, contractual and tortious, could not
subsist together and that *Groom* v. *Crocker* [1939] 1 K.B. 194 and the
cases which followed it were authority for the proposition that any duty
in tort which might otherwise exist was merged and extinguished in the   G
contract between the parties which must then be considered as the conclusive and exclusive source of the rights between them. That argument
was rejected, and rejected unanimously; and Lord Denning M.R., in a
passage at p. 819 which I will read in a moment and upon which Mr.
Harman heavily relies, explicitly disapproved and declined to follow the
Groom v. *Crocker* line of cases which he said were wrong and contrary   H
to previous authority. The other members of the court did not expressly
mention those cases, but it is suggested that the conclusion is inescapable
that the unanimous decision cannot stand with them, for it amounts to a
clear rejection by a court of co-ordinate jurisdiction of the fundamental
reasoning upon which—so far as I can see at any rate—*Groom* v. *Crocker*
[1939] 1 K.B. 194 and its successors are based.

Ormrod L.J. said, [1976] Q.B. 801, 827–828:

The Weekly Law Reports, July 7, 1978

205

3 W.L.R.   Midland Bank v. Hett, Stubbs & Kemp (Ch.D.)   Oliver J.

A   " Had I taken the same view as Lawson J. on the warranty point I would certainly have held, with him, that Mr. Mardon had proved his case in negligence. The parties were in the kind of relationship which is sufficient to give rise to a duty on the part of the plaintiffs. There is no magic in the phrase ' special relationship '; it means no more than a relationship the nature of which is such that one party, for a variety of possible reasons, will be regarded by the law as under a duty of care to the other."

B

Shaw L.J. was, perhaps, less explicit, because he dealt with the case on the footing of alternative liabilities. But there is nothing in his judgment to suggest that he regarded the remedies in contract and in tort as mutually exclusive, except where this was expressly or by necessary implication a term of the contract, and, as I read his judgment, its effect

C is that he upheld the trial judge's decision on the *Hedley Byrne* liability quite regardless of any contractual liability. Shaw L.J. said, at pp. 832–833 :

    " In this regard I would differ from the finding of the judge below in holding as he did that no warranty was given by Esso. Lawson J. did, however, decide that Esso owed Mr. Mardon a duty to take care in relation to the statement made to him as to the potential

D of the filling station and that they were in breach of that duty. I agree entirely with the reasons and conclusions of the judge on this part of the case. Thus, even if it were right that Esso did not give a warranty to Mr. Mardon, they would be liable to him in negligence, following the principle enunciated in *Hedley Byrne & Co. Ltd.* v. *Heller & Partners Ltd.* [1964] A.C. 465, unless a

E further argument advanced by Mr. Ross-Munro stood in the way.

    " He contended that where the negotiations between the parties concerned actually culminate in a contract between them they cannot look outside that contract in the assertion of any claim by one against the other which is founded on the subject matter of the negotiations and of the contract. To such a situation, Mr. Ross-Munro submitted, the *Hedley Byrne* principle had no application.

F It would follow that, notwithstanding the fact that one party to the negotiations induced the other by a negligent misrepresentation to enter into the contract, the other would have no remedy unless one were available under the Misrepresentation Act 1967. As the matters of which Mr. Mardon complained occurred in 1963, his only available means of redress would be such as his contract with Esso afforded: so

G that if there were no warranty he would have no remedy at all.

    " It is difficult to see why, in principle, a right to claim damages for negligent misrepresentation which has arisen in favour of a party to a negotiation should not survive the event of the making of a contract as the outcome of that negotiation. It may, of course, be that the contract ultimately made shows either expressly or by

H implication that, once it has been entered into, the rights and liabilities of the parties are to be those and only those which have their origin in the contract itself.

    " In any other case there is no valid argument, apart from legal technicality, for the proposition that a subsequent contract vitiates a cause of action in negligence which had previously arisen in the course of negotiation."

This, as it seems to me, necessarily implies a rejection of the argument   **A**
which had been founded by counsel on *Groom* v. *Crocker* [1939] 1 K.B.
194. Lord Denning M.R., in rejecting that argument, expressly disapproved *Groom* v. *Crocker* and the cases which followed it. I had
better read the whole passage from his judgment because Mr. Harman
strongly relies on it. Lord Denning M.R. said, at p. 819:

> " In arguing this point, Mr. Ross-Munro took his stand in this way.   **B**
> He submitted that when the negotiations between two parties resulted
> in a contract between them, their rights and duties were governed by
> the law of contract and not by the law of tort. There was, therefore,
> no place in their relationship for *Hedley Byrne* [1964] A.C. 465,
> which was solely on liability in tort. He relied particularly on *Clark*
> v. *Kirby-Smith* [1964] Ch. 506 where Plowman J. held that the
> liability of a solicitor for negligence was liability in contract and not   **C**
> in tort, following the observations of Sir Wilfrid Greene M.R. in
> *Groom* v. *Crocker* [1939] 1 K.B. 194, 206. Mr. Ross-Munro might
> also have cited *Bagot* v. *Stevens Scanlan & Co. Ltd.* [1966] 1
> Q.B. 197, about an architect; and other cases too. But I venture to
> suggest that those cases are in conflict with other decisions of high
> authority which were not cited in them. These decisions show that,   **D**
> in the case of a professional man, the duty to use reasonable care
> arises not only in contract, but is also imposed by the law apart
> from contract, and is therefore actionable in tort. It is comparable
> to the duty of reasonable care which is owed by a master to his
> servant, or vice versa. It can be put either in contract or in tort: see
> *Lister* v. *Romford Ice and Cold Storage Co. Ltd.* [1957] A.C. 555,
> 587 by Lord Radcliffe and *Matthews* v. *Kuwait Bechtel Corporation*   **E**
> [1959] 2 Q.B. 57. The position was stated by Tindal C.J., delivering
> the judgment of the Court of Exchequer Chamber in *Boorman* v.
> *Brown* (1842) 3 Q.B. 511, 525–526: ' That there is a large class of
> cases in which the foundation of the action springs out of privity of
> contract between the parties, but in which, nevertheless, the remedy
> for the breach, or non-performance, is indifferently either assumpsit   **F**
> or case upon tort, is not disputed. Such are actions against attorneys,
> surgeons, and other professional men, for want of competent skill or
> proper care in the service they undertake to render: . . . The principle
> in all these cases would seem to be that the contract creates a duty,
> and the neglect to perform that duty, or the nonfeasance, is a ground
> of action upon a tort.' That decision was affirmed in the House of
> Lords in (1844) 11 Cl. & Fin. 1, when Lord Campbell, giving the   **G**
> one speech, said, at p. 44: ' . . . wherever there is a contract, and some-
> thing to be done in the course of the employment which is the
> subject of that contract, if there is a breach of duty in the course
> of that employment, the plaintiff may either recover in tort or in
> contract.' To this there is to be added the high authority of Viscount
> Haldane L.C., in *Noeton* v. *Lord Ashburton* [1914] A.C. 932, 956 "
>   **H**

—and then there is quoted the passage to which I have already made
reference. Lord Denning M.R. continued, at p. 820:

> " That seems to me right. A professional man may give advice under
> a contract for reward; or without a contract, in pursuance of a
> voluntary assumption of responsibility, gratuitously without reward.
> In either case he is under one and the same duty to use reasonable
> care: . . . In the one case it is by reason of a term implied by law.

The Weekly Law Reports, July 7, 1978

207

3 W.L.R.   Midland Bank v. Hett, Stubbs & Kemp (Ch.D.)   Oliver J.

A   In the other, it is by reason of a duty imposed by law. For a breach of that duty he is liable in damages. . . ."

There seem to be three possible approaches to the case as an authority. The first is that it is authority only for the proposition that there was, on the facts, a liability for breach of warranty and that everything else is dictum. That I do not think is tenable. The court was unanimous

B   in upholding the trial judge's decision on the *Hedley Byrne* liability and clearly put that forward as an alternative ground of decision. And where a superior court gives two reasons for its decision I am, I apprehend, bound by both of them. Secondly, it may be said that the Court of Appeal was advancing two alternative, but mutually exclusive, heads of liability and that a decision that the plaintiffs were liable under one

C   or the other head is not irreconcilable with those cases which decide that a contractual and a tortious liability cannot co-exist. On this view, the case is authority only for the proposition that a supervening contract does not, in the absence of express or implied term, supersede or extinguish a duty which has already arisen from a relationship formed prior to contract. It does not, so the argument would run, touch the case where the duty did not pre-exist but arose from the contract itself. The third

D   view is that the case demonstrates that there are co-existing duties in both contract and tort.

The second view might seem superficially to derive some support from the introductory words of Lord Denning M.R. at p. 818: "Assuming there was no warranty, the question arises . . ."; from Ormrod L.J.'s statement at p. 827: "Had I taken the same view as Lawson J. on the warranty point . . ."; and from Shaw L.J.'s words at p. 832: ". . . even

E   if it were right that Esso did not give a warranty. . . ." I do not, however, think that this really bears examination. Despite the opening words referred to above, Lord Denning M.R. made it perfectly clear, as his references to *Boorman* v. *Brown*, 3 Q.B. 511 show, that he regarded the duties in contract and tort as interchangeable and co-existing. It is clear, I think, also that Ormrod L.J. and Shaw L.J. were of the same

F   view, for they both emphasised that the critical factor was the nature of the relationship not the manner of its origin.

The judgments are really only explicable on the footing that the Court of Appeal regarded the duties as cumulative and that they did not regard the contractual right arising from the warranties which they found as the sole and exclusive source of his claim, for on no other footing would it have been necessary even to consider the question of *Hedley Byrne*

G   liability. It would have been concluded once and for all by the finding of the warranty. Not only is there not a hint of this in any of the judgments, but they lead in fact to a contrary conclusion.

As I read the case it is authority for the proposition that the existence of a contractual duty of care—in that case created by the warranty which the court found—does not preclude a parallel claim in tort under the

H   *Hedley Byrne* principle. It seems to me that it is an authoritative interpretation of the *Hedley Byrne* decision in a way which is in line with what was said by their Lordships in *Arenson* v. *Arenson* [1977] A.C. 405 and which is, on analysis, irreconcilable with *Groom* v. *Crocker* [1939] 1 K.B. 194 and *Clark* v. *Kirby-Smith* [1964] Ch. 506.

To summarise:

(1) In my judgment the *Hedley Byrne* case [1964] A.C. 465 establishes a general duty arising by law from a relationship of the type therein

described however that relationship is created. It is therefore in my   A
view inconsistent with the underlying reasoning of *Groom* v. *Crocker*
[1939] 1 K.B. 194 and the cases which followed.

(2) On the view I take and in the light of the opinions expressed
in *Arenson* v. *Arenson* [1977] A.C. 405, and particularly that of Lord
Salmon, I would, with the greatest deference, not follow *Clark* v. *Kirby-
Smith* [1964] Ch. 506 and *Bagot* v. *Stevens Scanlan & Co. Ltd.* [1966]
1 Q.B. 197.   B

(3) I do not think that *Cook* v. *Swinfen* [1967] 1 W.L.R. 457 and
Heywood v. *Wellers* [1976] Q.B. 446 so compel me, because the references there to the contractual nature of the liability formed no necessary
part of the rationes decidendi.

(4) Even if I am wrong about that, those cases are, so far as they
pass on that point, in my judgment in conflict with the Court of Appeal's   C
interpretation in *Esso Petroleum Co. Ltd.* v. *Mardon* [1976] Q.B. 801
by which I am bound.

(5) If I am not so bound, there is at least a conflict between decisions
of the Court of Appeal and I must, I conceive, elect which to follow
or, if I am not free to elect, I must follow the later decision.

I would respectfully follow what was said by Lord Denning M.R. in
Esso Petroleum Co. Ltd. v. *Mardon* [1976] Q.B. 801, save that, again   D
respectfully, I would have some reservations about the very wide statement of Lord Campbell in *Boorman* v. *Brown*, 3 Q.B. 511. As Mr.
Gatehouse has pointed out, the actual decision in that case was on
the very narrow point of whether, *after verdict*, a judgment could be
arrested on the ground that the cause of action had been wrongly stated
in the declaration. I think, incidentally, that Lord Denning M.R. must   E
have been misreported in his reference to Lord Campbell in *Brown*
v. *Boorman*, 11 Cl. & Fin. 1 giving " *the* one speech." In fact there
were speeches also from Lord Brougham and Lord Cottenham. Mr.
Gatehouse, in the course of his argument, described the passage which I
have quoted from the judgment of Lord Denning M.R. as " heretical."
For my part I think that, if there was heresy at all, it lay in the extraction
from the earlier authorities, in *Bean* v. *Wade*, 2 T.L.R. 157, of a rule   F
of law that they did not really support, a rule which has been productive of anomaly if not of injustice and which subsequent authority
has shown cannot be supported. But if I am wrong, I have at least the
consolation of knowing that I shall have distinguished company at the
stake.

In my judgment, the instant case is one in which there was clearly   G
between the defendant firm and Geoffrey a relationship of the sort which
gave rise to a duty of care under the *Hedley Byrne* principle. And, in
my judgment, the interpretation of that principle by the Court of Appeal
in *Esso Petroleum Co. Ltd.* v. *Mardon* [1976] Q.B. 801 leads to the
conclusion that there was here a liability in tort which arose when the
damage occurred on August 17, 1967. Accordingly, the claim in my
view is not barred by the Limitation Act 1939. I am, of course, conscious   H
that, in reaching the conclusion to which I have felt compelled, I am
departing from what has long been considered a firm and settled rule
of law. It is for that reason and because the point is obviously one of
considerable importance both to clients and solicitors and to their insurers,
that I have felt it right to set out my reasoning in extenso. I ought,
perhaps, to add that since writing this judgment my attention has been
drawn by counsel to a very recent decision of the Court of Appeal

The Weekly Law Reports, July 7, 1978

209

3 W.L.R.   Midland Bank v. Hett, Stubbs & Kemp (Ch.D.)   Oliver J.

A in *Batty* v. *Metropolitan Property Realisations Ltd.* [1978] 2 W.L.R. 500 (in which judgment was given on November 8, 1977. No report of that decision is yet available. I have been able to obtain a transcript of the judgment but since it has not yet been corrected and approved I ought not, I think, to refer to it, beyond saying that I can find nothing in it which would cause me to revise or alter the conclusion at which I have arrived.

B   I turn to the final point which arises.

3. *Are the defendants liable in contract?*

    Let me, however, assume that I am wrong in the conclusion at which I have arrived on Mr. Harman's first submission, and that the obligation owed by the defendant firm to Geoffrey was a contractual one only. I

C must then consider Mr. Gatehouse's third proposition. What was the contractual duty which was broken and when was it broken? An action is barred by the Limitation Act 1939 after the expiration of the appropriate period from the accrual of the cause of action, that is to say from the occurrence of every fact which it would be necessary to prove, if traversed, in order to support his right to the judgment of the court.

D   It is perhaps a truism to say that what those facts are can be ascertained only by reference to the right asserted, or, to put it another way, in the case of an action for breach of contract, by reference to the particular contractual duty the breach of which is asserted as the ground for the claim. Mr. Gatehouse says that there was only one duty in this case, namely, a duty to register the option within a reasonable time and that was broken once and for all when a reasonable time had elapsed. It

E was, therefore, then that the cause of action accrued. If that is right, it must conclude any claim in contract. Mr. Harman, however, says that that simply is not the failure of which he complains and upon which the action is based. The breach of contract which gave rise to the action was the non-performance of the defendants' obligation to register before a third party acquired an interest. That was the obligation which the

F defendants assumed, and it was an obligation which continued to bind them until August 17, 1967. This submission was advanced at a very late stage in the case and it involved a withdrawal of Mr. Harman's disclaimer of a reliance upon a continuing duty. I took the view, however, that it would not be right to shut out the submission so long as Mr. Gatehouse was afforded an opportunity to answer it.

    Unassisted by authority, I would again favour Mr. Harman's sub-

G mission. The reality is that the plaintiffs' complaint is not that the option was not registered within a reasonable time—which caused no conceivable loss to anyone—but that it was not registered at all. The defendants simply did not perform their contract and if their continued failure constituted a repudiation it was not one which was known to Geoffrey and, not being accepted, gave rise to no cause of action until

H events put it out of their power any longer to perform. Indeed, I asked Mr. Kenneth Stubbs whether, when he registered the option in September 1967 without informing his client or seeking his instructions, he conceived that he was doing anything more than seeking to fulfil, rather belatedly, the contractual obligation which his firm has assumed to Geoffrey. His answer was a quite unequivocal negative. The classical formulation of the claim in this sort of case as " damages for negligence and breach of professional duty " tends to be a mesmeric phrase. It concentrates

attention on the implied obligation to devote to the client's business that   A
reasonable care and skill to be expected from a normally competent and
careful practitioner as if that obligation were not only a compendious,
but also an exhaustive, definition of all the duties assumed under the
contract created by the retainer and its acceptance. But, of course, it
is not. A contract gives rise to a complex of rights and duties of which
the duty to exercise reasonable care and skill is but one.

If I employ a carpenter to supply and put up a good quality oak   B
shelf for me, the acceptance by him of that employment involves the
assumption of a number of contractual duties. He must supply wood of
an adequate quality and it must be oak. He must fix the shelf. And he
must carry out the fashioning and fixing with the reasonable care and
skill which I am entitled to expect of a skilled craftsman. If he fixes
the brackets but fails to supply the shelf or if he supplies and fixes a   C
shelf of unseasoned pine, my complaint against him is not that he has
failed to exercise reasonable care and skill in carrying out the work but
that he has failed to supply what was contracted for. He may fix the
brackets and then go away for six months, but unless and until I accept
that conduct as a repudiation, his obligation to complete the work remains.

It is, I think, important in the instant case to note that it is not a
case of the giving of wrong and negligent advice—where the breach of   D
contract necessarily occurs at a fixed point of time—but of simple nonfeasance. If one were to seek to write out in longhand the obligations
which Mr. Stubbs senior assumed when he engaged to act in the matter
of the grant of the option, they were (1) to draw and have completed
a proper and enforceable option agreement which would bind the parties;
(2) to take such steps as were necessary and practicable to ensure that   E
it was binding on the land into whosesoever hands it might come before
any third party acquired a legal estate; and (3) to carry out his work with
the care and skill which a normally competent practitioner would bring
to it.

So far as the client is concerned, it is a matter of total indifference
to him at what date the solicitor chooses to fulfil his contractual obligation
under (2) above so long as it is effectively fulfilled. No doubt a normally   F
careful practitioner would fulfil that obligation as soon as is reasonably
practicable. In an appropriate case he might give a priority notice. But
if he fails to do so and an effective registration can still be and is effected,
his client can have no complaint except the purely technical one that he
has been a bit careless and might have done it sooner. He has, no
doubt, exhibited a failure to show the normal competence and care for   G
his client's affairs by carelessly allowing a period to elapse during which
a third party might have, but has not in fact, acquired an interest. But
such a failure cannot, I should have thought, affect, much less discharge,
the primary obligation to effect registration timeously, which continues
until it is performed or becomes impossible of performance or until the
client elects to treat the continued non-performance as a repudiation of
the contract.   H

Suppose that Mr. Stubbs had woken up to the fact that he had failed
to register the option in, say, May 1961 and had then registered it. And
suppose that, four years later, Geoffrey had caused a search to be made
and had discovered that the charge had not been registered until two
months after the date of the option? Could Geoffrey have successfully
sued the firm for breach of contract on alleging those facts? Mr.
Gatehouse says yes. There would he says have been a technical cause

The Weekly Law Reports, July 7, 1978

211

3 W.L.R.   Midland Bank v. Hett, Stubbs & Kemp (Ch.D.)   Oliver J.

A of action for breach of the duty to exercise reasonable care and skill which would have entitled Geoffrey to nominal damages. I think that the action would have been struck out as an abuse of the process of the court.

I find Mr. Gatehouse's argument from authority, however, more convincing. The point is, he submits, concluded against Mr. Harman's submissions by *Bean* v. *Wade*, 2 T.L.R. 157, to which reference has already

B been made. In order to appreciate this argument it is necessary to state the facts of that case, at least in outline. A husband, having an interest in certain trust funds, had assigned his interest to the trustee of his marriage settlement. No notice was given to the trustees of the fund of this assignment. Proceedings were started by the wife for the removal of the trustee of the marriage settlement and the appointment of the

C plaintiffs in their place, and the defendants acted as her solicitors in those proceedings. An order was obtained for the appointment of the plaintiffs and directions were given for the preparation and execution of a deed of assignment from the former trustee to them and for the payment by the plaintiffs of the defendants' fees out of the fund. That was effected and the matter concluded in 1875, but the defendants, apparently assuming that notice of the marriage settlement had already been given to the trustees

D of the head settlement, omitted to give any notice to them of the assignment to the plaintiffs so as to preserve their priority under the rule in *Dearle* v. *Hall* (1828) 3 Russ. 1.

In February 1879 the husband executed a mortgage of his interest under the head settlement in favour of a mortgagee who took without notice of the prior assignment to the plaintiffs. On April 9, 1879, notice

E of the mortgagee's interest was given to the trustees of the head settlement and, in the result, he gained priority and there was a loss of interest and a deficiency in capital which the plaintiffs had to make good to the widow. They sued the defendants, but as regards one of the partners, Mr. G. Wade, he did not become a party to the action until 1883. He pleaded the Statute of Limitation 1623.

Cave J. (1885) 1 T.L.R. 404, 405 at first instance said that he

F found the cases unhelpful because in all of them there had been a definite time at which the act out of which the damage had arisen had been done. He held the defendants, including Mr. G. Wade, liable on the ground, so far as that defendant was concerned, that the " act "— which I think must have meant the omission to act—had been done on April 8, 1879, and that time, therefore, started to run only from that

G date. It is evident, therefore, that he considered the defendants as having a duty to give notice which continued up to the date upon which it could no longer be effective to preserve priority.

The Court of Appeal reversed this on the ground that more than seven years had elapsed between the date of the assignment to the plaintiffs and the commencement of the action against Mr. G. Wade, and therefore more than six years had elapsed between the time when

H notice should have been given and the commencement of the action. The instant case, Mr. Gatehouse submits, is substantially indistinguishable. The terms of a retainer are, of course, a question of fact and no decision on fact is binding, but the decision of the court involved, on substantially indistinguishable facts, a conclusion of law, namely, that the solicitors' retainer involved an obligation to give notice within a reasonable time, and there was no separate or co-existing continuing duty upon which the action could be founded. That conclusion of law formed the ground for

the court's reversal of the decision below and is, Mr. Gatehouse submits,   **A**
binding upon me. If the facts of *Bean* v. *Wade*, 2 T.L.R. 157 and
the claim made in that case are in substance indistinguishable from the
instant case, then I think that must be right.

As Scrutton L.J. said in *Newsholme Brothers* v. *Road Transport and
General Insurance Co. Ltd.* [1929] 2 K.B. 356, 375:

> " The decision of the Court of Appeal on fact is not binding on   **B**
> any other court, except as between the same parties. When the
> decision is that from certain facts legal consequences follow, the
> decision is, I think, binding on the Court of Appeal in any case
> raising substantially similar facts."

At the same time, one must be careful of deducing wide general
propositions from expressions of opinion on particular circumstances and   **C**
that must, I think, particularly be the case where the particular facts
supporting the expression are not fully or satisfactorily set out in the
report. A fortiori is this the case where the report does not set out the
ipsissima verba of the court or give any clue as to the arguments put
before it. I approach the problem, therefore, having in mind the caution
uttered by the Earl of Halsbury L.C. in *Quinn* v. *Leathem* [1901] A.C.
495, 506:   **D**

> ". . . there are two observations of a general character which I
> wish to make, and one is to repeat what I have very often said
> before, that every judgment must be read as applicable to the par-
> ticular facts proved, or assumed to be proved, since the generality of
> the expressions which may be found there are not intended to be
> expositions of the whole law, but governed and qualified by the   **E**
> particular facts of the case in which such expressions are to be
> found. The other is that a case is only an authority for what it
> actually decides. I entirely deny that it can be quoted for a pro-
> position that may seem to follow logically from it. Such a mode of
> reasoning assumes that the law is necessarily a logical code, whereas
> every lawyer must acknowledge that the law is not always logical at   **F**
> all."

The duties of a solicitor depend upon the particular retainer and upon
the particular circumstances of each individual case. In *Bean* v. *Wade*,
2 T.L.R. 157 the retainer was not in fact from the plaintiffs in the
first instance but from a proposed incumbrancer of the husband's interest
and the next friend of the beneficiary widow. The reported judgment of   **G**
Cave J., 1 T.L.R. 404, 405, states:

> " It was shown by the result rather than by any express instructions
> that the defendants had been employed to file a bill in Chancery
> against Mr. Cooper and to see that the trust property was duly
> conveyed to the plaintiffs."

For that, they were paid out of the trust funds, but there is no indication   **H**
in the report whether or not they continued to act thereafter. It looks
as if they were treated as functi officio once the assignment to the plaintiffs
was concluded, for the judgment continues at p. 405: "In a letter
by one of the defendants to one of the plaintiffs asking him to execute
the conveyance, it was distinctly said that that would complete the matter."
How far these matters were considered as significant by the court it is
not easy to see from the report, but obviously the case bears a very

The Weekly Law Reports, July 14, 1978

213

3 W.L.R.   Midland Bank v. Hett, Stubbs & Kemp (Ch.D.)   Oliver J.

A   striking resemblance to the instant case. There, as here, there was brought into being a document which was perfectly valid and effective inter partes but which required a further step to be taken in order to protect it against claims by third parties. There, as here, the requirement was a perfectly well known one. There, as here, the solicitor failed to take the necessary step. Nevertheless, the decision in one case on one set of facts cannot necessarily be treated as a decision on similar,
B though not identical facts, in another case, because the matter may very well depend, not simply on the facts, but upon what is alleged and pleaded.

  It is, I think, important to note what the question was that was being raised for decision in *Bean* v. *Wade*, 2 T.L.R. 157—at any rate so far as it can be gleaned from the report. The note of the facts states that the plaintiff trustees had paid interest on the sum lost to the widow
C and claimed to recover this and the principal lost by the first charge (see 1 T.L.R. 405) ". . . on the ground that its loss had been due to their negligence in having failed to *have given notice within a reasonable time of their* (the plaintiffs') appointment as trustees." It appears, therefore, that the only breach of duty being alleged by the plaintiffs was the failure to give notice " within a reasonable time " and the court, having decided that the only claim lay in contract, was concerned solely with
D the question of when that breach occurred, or, in other words, at what point a reasonable time could be said to have expired. In my judgment *Bean* v. *Wade*, 2 T.L.R. 157 is not conclusive of the question in the instant case.

  It is perhaps worth noting that in *Bagot* v. *Stevens Scanlan & Co. Ltd.* [1966] 1 Q.B. 197 the time was treated as running not from the
E date of the failure, which, presumably, was when the drains to the property were laid and covered in, but from the date when the architects had completed, whether adequately or not, their work under the retainer.

  The defendants here never treated themselves as functi officio in relation to the option. They kept the document on Geoffrey's behalf in their strongroom. They opened a file relating to the matter. They were consulted about it at intervals over the next $6\frac{1}{2}$ years. In my judgment
F the obligation to register which they assumed when they were first consulted continued to bind them. It was an obligation to protect the interest from third parties by registration and without their client's knowledge they failed to perform it until it ceased to be effectively capable of performance on August 17, 1967. It seems to me that it was then that the contract was broken once and for all.

G   Take, for instance, the analogous case of a solicitor engaged in litigation. Suppose that he is so dilatory in taking out a summons for directions that the action goes to sleep for six years and is then struck out for want of prosecution. Is it then to be said that the client's action against him for negligence is barred because he ought to have taken out a summons " within a reasonable time " of the close of pleadings, so that the longer his default the better off he is? If that were right then
H the client in *Allen* v. *Sir Alfred McAlpine & Sons Ltd.* [1968] 2 Q.B. 229, where the defence was delivered in January 1961 and the action was struck out in May 1967, would have had no remedy. Yet both Diplock L.J. and Salmon L.J. considered that she clearly would have (see pp. 256, 262, 272) and that could only be on the basis of a continuing duty.

  In my judgment the breach of contract on which this action is based occurred on August 17, 1967, and the defence of limitation fails under

Oliver J.　　　　Midland Bank v. Hett, Stubbs & Kemp (Ch.D.)　　　　[1978]

this head also. In the circumstances, the plaintiffs' claim succeeds and I
must give judgment for an inquiry as to the damages and I will discuss
with counsel the form of that order. Before parting with the case, I
ought to say how indebted I am to counsel for the lengthy submissions
which they put before me.

> *Judgment for plaintiffs.*
> *Consideration of terms of order*
> *adjourned.*

Solicitors: *Sidney Torrance & Co., for J. Levi & Co., Leeds; Park
Nelson, Dennes, Redfern & Co.*

T. C. C. B.

[COURT OF APPEAL]

NATIONAL VULCAN ENGINEERING INSURANCE GROUP LTD. *v.* WADE

1978　Jan. 26, 27　　　　　　　　　Lord Denning M.R., Ormrod
　　　　　　　　　　　　　　　　　　and Geoffrey Lane L.JJ.

*Discrimination—Sex—Equal pay—Variation due to material dif-
ference—Woman clerk paid less than male clerk doing " like
work "—Wages fixed according to employers' grading scheme
based on ability and performance—Whether variation in pay
due to material difference other than sex—Burden of proof—
Equal Pay Act 1970 (c. 41), s. 1 (3) (as amended by Sex Discrimination Act 1975 (c. 65), s. 8 (1))*

An insurance company graded its clerks in accordance
with their experience, capacity, skill and application. All the
clerks, male and female, in the company's policy department
were employed in "like work," but were paid according to
their grade. A woman clerk applied to the industrial
tribunal for equality of pay on the ground that she was doing
the same work as male clerks who, being in higher grades,
were paid more than she was. The industrial tribunal, awarding the applicant equality of pay, held that the company had
failed to establish that the variation between the applicant's
contract and that of a higher-graded male clerk was genuinely
due to a material difference in their cases pursuant to section
1 (3) of the Equal Pay Act 1970.[1] The tribunal's decision was
upheld by the Employment Appeal Tribunal.

On appeal by the company: —

Held, allowing the appeal, that a grading scheme such as
that operated by the company was not contrary to the Equal
Pay Act 1970 so long as it was genuinely applied irrespective
of sex (post, pp. 220B, C, H, 223C); that the burden of proof
required of an employer by section 1 (3) of the Act was no
higher than the civil standard of proof on the balance of
probabilities (post, pp. 219G, 220G, 222A); and that on the
evidence the company had plainly discharged that burden

---

[1] Equal Pay Act 1970, s. 1 (3), as amended: see post, p. 218F.

A   and established that the variation between the applicant's
contract and that of her male colleague was genuinely due
to a material difference in their skill and capacity (post, pp.
219H, 221E, 222G).

  Decision of the Employment Appeal Tribunal [1977] I.C.R.
455; [1977] 3 All E.R. 634 reversed.

  The following cases are referred to in the judgments:

B   *Clay Cross (Quarry Services) Ltd.* v. *Fletcher* [1977] I.C.R. 868, E.A.T.
  Electrolux Ltd. v. *Hutchinson* [1977] I.C.R. 252, E.A.T.
  Hornal v. *Neuberger Products Ltd.* [1957] 1 Q.B. 247; [1956] 3 W.L.R.
    1034; [1956] 3 All E.R. 970, C.A.
  Navy, Army and Air Force Institutes v. *Varley* [1977] 1 W.L.R. 149;
    [1977] I.C.R. 11; [1977] 1 All E.R. 840, E.A.T.
C   *Snoxell* v. *Vauxhall Motors Ltd.* [1978] Q.B. 11; [1977] 3 W.L.R. 189;
    [1977] I.C.R. 700; [1977] 3 All E.R. 770, E.A.T.

  The following additional cases were cited in argument:

  Capper Pass Ltd. v. *Lawton* [1977] Q.B. 852; [1977] 2 W.L.R. 26;
    [1977] I.C.R. 83; [1977] 2 All E.R. 11, E.A.T.
  Greene v. *Broxtowe District Council* [1977] I.C.R. 241; [1977] 1 All E.R.
D   694, E.A.T.
  Waddington v. *Leicester Council for Voluntary Service* [1977] 1 W.L.R.
    544; [1977] I.C.R. 266; [1977] 2 All E.R. 633, E.A.T.

  APPEAL from Employment Appeal Tribunal.
  On March 10, 1976, Mrs. Edna Wade, a clerk employed by National ·
Vulcan Engineering Insurance Group Ltd., made an application to the
E   industrial tribunal, claiming equal pay with male colleagues who were
graded higher and paid more. The industrial tribunal sitting at Manchester on June 3, 1976, held that the employers were in contravention
of an equality clause in the applicant's contract of employment and
made an award accordingly. The Employment Appeal Tribunal dismissed an appeal by the employers on February 17, 1977.

F   The employers appealed by notice dated March 9, 1977, on the
grounds, inter alia, that (1) the Employment Appeal Tribunal erred in
law in holding that an employer who placed an employee in a grade
on his assessment of her skill by reason of which grading her pay was
determined had failed to show a material difference under section 1 (3)
of the Equal Pay Act 1970; (2) the Employment Appeal Tribunal erred
in law or misdirected itself in holding that, a grading scheme, which
G   assessed the personal skill of employees, was less satisfactory and less
able to demonstrate a material difference under section 1 (3) if (a) it was
not jointly negotiated, (b) it left the final decision to management, and
(c) although it was demonstrated to be unisex, it had succeeded a discriminatory scheme; and (3) the Employment Appeal Tribunal erred in
law in holding that it was not incumbent on an industrial tribunal to
H   come to a conclusion as to (a) whether there had or had not been
sexual discrimination in relation to the employee and (b), where there
was a scheme of general application, whether or not the scheme was in
general operated in a discriminatory manner.
  The facts are stated in the judgment of Lord Denning M.R.

  Martin Collins Q.C. and *Giles Wingate-Saul* for the company.
  Christopher Rose Q.C. and *John Hand* for the appellant.

LORD DENNING M.R. This case concerns a grading system which   A
operates in many government departments and business houses. Each
man or woman is paid a salary in accordance with the grade in which he
is placed. The higher his grade, the higher his salary. Within one
grade there may be six "performance ratings." A man or a woman
of experience and skill may be allotted a higher percentage rating than
a newcomer who is yet to learn his business. He may be in the same
grade, but he receives a higher salary because of his higher percentage   B
rating.

The employers are the National Vulcan Engineering Insurance Group
Ltd., which is a big insurance company dealing with the insurance of
engineering equipment and engineering works. It employs very many
clerks. It divides them into grades, starting with grade 1 and going up to
grade 8. Grade 1 is the lowest grade in which the newcomers are placed.   C
They start as very junior clerks. They gradually progress up through
the various grades. The very best may reach grade 8 and become a
supervisor in charge of many.

Within each of those grades the clerks differ very much according to
their ability and capacity. So the company allocates them performance
ratings. In each grade the lowest rating is " F," which is given to the   D
very poor performer. Then comes " E," which is given to a better
performer. " C " is given to the good average performer. " B " is
higher. " A " is first class. So, there are six performance ratings
within each grade: and, of course, the higher the performance rating
the higher the salary.

The performance ratings overlap the gradings. A person with a good
performance rating in a lower grade, such as grade 6B, may do better   E
than a person with a low performance rating in a higher grade such as
grade 7E. To give an example, a person in grade 6B will receive a salary
of £2,301 whereas a person in grade 7E will only get £2,223.

That is the background in which we have to apply the Equal Pay
Act 1970. The object of the Act is that there should be equal pay for
men and women doing like work. But that Act did not come into   F
operation in 1970. It was amended and brought up to date by the
Sex Discrimination Act 1975, and only came into force on December 29,
1975. In passing that statute the legislature of the United Kingdom
was carrying out its duty under the E.E.C. Treaty, article 119 of which
says:

> "Each member state shall during the first stage ensure and sub-   G
> sequently maintain the application of the principle that men and
> women should receive equal pay for equal work."

Although the statute only came into force at the end of 1975, nevertheless,
business and commerce had previously been given warning of its coming
into operation so as to be able to make the necessary arrangements.

The Vulcan Insurance company had a grading system starting from   H
grade 1 and going up to grade 8. In all the lower grades up to grade 5
the company had for many years paid men and women equally for
equal work. But in grades 6 and 7 up to early 1975, the company had
made a difference in that women were paid only 85 per cent. of what
the men received for equal work. But at the beginning of 1975 the
company felt it necessary to prepare for the new Act. Accordingly, by
October 1, 1975, they had altered their system so as to provide equal

The Weekly Law Reports, July 14, 1978

217

3 W.L.R.   National Vulcan Insurance v. Wade (C.A.)   Lord Denning M.R.

A   pay for men and women doing equal work. In particular in grades 6 and 7 (where there had previously been a difference) they eliminated the difference between men and women altogether. They issued a table showing the new payments for grade 6 and grade 7. It showed that men and women in those grades would receive equal pay for equal work: but according to their performance ratings.

B   Now I come to the claim of Mrs. Wade. She is aged 50. She was employed as a policy clerk with the company. She had to prepare new policies of insurance, amend existing ones, calculate charges and rebates and so forth. She was assessed by the management early in January 1975 as category 6D. Her assessment was as follows: " Mrs. E. M. Wade (grade 6D: no change). Mrs. Wade has a fair knowledge of the procedures and works quite well when concentrating, but unfortunately
C   is easily distracted."

There was a man also in the same grade as Mrs. Wade, that is 6D. He was Mr. I. He was getting the same salary. The assessment said of him: " Has a fair knowledge of the procedures, is willing and can be a good worker when he concentrates on the job. However, he is easily distracted which results in careless mistakes." So there it was. Mrs.
D   Wade and Mr. I were placed on an equal footing. Both were easily distracted: both were put in the same grade and received the same salary of £2,028.

Mrs. Wade was working in a department where there were 18 policy clerks all told, all doing the same work, 14 men and 4 women. The work of all 18 was the same. Each of them was handed a bundle of papers estimated to take two hours to process, and they were expected
E   to process them in that time. But the quality and accuracy of the work done by those 18 varied according to each individual. Some needed more supervision than others. The management made a difference in grading and rating according to the quality of each individual's performance.

We have a table of the grading of each of those 18. I am afraid that Mrs. Wade and Mr. I were the lowest graded of all. One man was
F   graded above them at 6C: he received £2,202. One man was graded at 6B, and he received £2,301. There was one man at 7E who received £2,223. I will speak of him later: he is a Mr. McCann. Then in grade 7D there were five men and one woman all getting the same, £2,334. In grade 7C there were five men and two women, all getting £2,535.

That is the table which was put before the court by the employers, showing how their grading scheme operates. It applies equally, as far
G   as can be observed, for men and women. Indeed they put two cases before the tribunal of a man, Mr. F, and a woman Mrs. L, who were both in grade 7C. The assessment of Mr. F was " has a good overall knowledge of the procedures gained through his experience, but he tends to lack confidence in his own abilities," and that Mrs. L

H   " is one of the more experienced members of the S.A.L. section who has been useful this year in teaching other members of the staff the finer points of the various periodics done on the section."

So there it is. According to that evidence before the tribunal (which I am afraid they did not analyse as we have had it analysed before us) the employers were operating their scheme fairly and evenly according to the skills and experience of the individuals and not according to their sex.

I now come back to the Equal Pay Act 1970. It came into operation A
on December 29, 1975. I need not read all the clauses, but an equality
clause is written into contracts by that Act. Section 1 (2) (a) of the
Act, as amended by section 8 of the Sex Discrimination Act 1975, reads:

" . . . (a) where the woman is employed on like work with a man
in the same employment—(i) if (apart from the equality clause) any
term of the woman's contract is or becomes less favourable to the B
woman than a term of a similar kind in the contract under which
that man is employed, that term of the woman's contract shall be
treated as so modified as not to be less favourable . . ."

That is when it is like work.

Mrs. Wade claims that she was employed on like work with a man
because all 18 employees were doing the same work. On March 10, C
1976, she applied to the industrial tribunal and made this claim in her
own handwriting:

" I claim that the work I am doing is the same as that being done
by my male colleagues who are graded higher and paid more than
myself. I therefore claim equal pay for equal work."

At the hearing before the tribunal on June 3, 1976, on behalf of D
Mrs. Wade there was called a young man, Mr. McCann, who was graded
higher than her and was doing like work. He was graded 7E, because
he had been assessed by the management " as a young man going places."
He had not been employed by them as long as Mrs. Wade, but they
evidently rated his skill and ability as more than hers. Mrs. Wade called
that young man as a witness and said that she ought to be graded as E
high as he was and that she ought to be receiving the same pay.

If one stopped at section 1 (2) one might think Mrs. Wade had a
case, but the employers rely on an exception to that clause, in section
1 (3), which says:

" An equality clause shall not operate in relation to a variation
between the woman's contract and the man's contract if the
employer proves that the variation is genuinely due to a material F
difference (other than the difference of sex) between her case and
his."

That is what the employers are saying here. They say that this
variation is genuinely due to the difference in the skill, capacity and
experience of the individual. It has nothing to do with the sex. A better
person, whether he be man or woman, is given a higher grading and more G
pay than a worse man or a worse woman. They say that the difference
is due to the employees' skill, capacity and experience and is not due to
their sex at all.

I will read what the manager of the policy department said in
evidence:

" If two-hour bundles are given to a 7C clerk I would expect them H
to be done better than if they were done by a 6D clerk and a 6D
clerk's work would be positively checked by the supervisor. I look
for quality and accuracy, quantity is not the prime consideration.
We try to reflect these matters in the grading a person received.
. . . Nothing in the assessments contains a built in bias against
the female sex, the applicant's assessment of 6D in April 1975 was
a genuine judgment by me as to her value."

The Weekly Law Reports, July 14, 1978

219

3 W.L.R.   National Vulcan Insurance v. Wade (C.A.)   Lord Denning M.R.

A   The Employment Appeal Tribunal seem to have accepted that view. This is what they said, [1977] I.C.R. 455, 460:

" . . . the assignment of a particular individual, and therefore his remuneration, depended upon the personal assessment of the individual, which was of necessity a subjective judgment."

Later in their judgment they said, at p. 461:

B   " A scheme for grading of jobs and personal assessment to which a great deal of time and thought has been given, but one which can be shown in action to be obscure in certain respects, and in the end to rest for its operation in particular cases upon the personal assessment of the qualities of an individual, determined by the management."

C   In those very findings the Employment Appeal Tribunal seems to have accepted that the grading was a personal assessment dependent upon the qualities of the individual: but they took it as a point against the employers. I must say that I can see nothing against the employers' case on that. There was ample evidence that the grading had nothing to do with the sex of the individual. That is borne out by the evidence
D   I have read out about the 18 persons in the department. All of them were doing like work. Some were better workers than others, and therefore were given a better grading and a bigger salary. No distinction was drawn between the men and the women: all in the same grade were paid the same salary.

There is one intervening point which I must mention. During the course of the hearing it was disclosed that a few weeks before the hearing
E   there had been a re-grading assessment. Mrs. Wade had improved. She had been up-graded from 6D to 7E. That was in some way taken against the employers by the tribunal: but for myself I cannot see any reason whatever why that should be taken against them.

All this makes me wonder why, on those facts, the industrial tribunal and the Employment Appeal Tribunal found against the employers.
F   I am afraid that it must rest on a misconception as to the burden of proof on the employers. We have been shown a series of judgments of the Employment Appeal Tribunal where many phrases have been used which come very near to the burden of proof required to prove a serious crime: "It must be clear and convincing," "not fanciful," and such like. As we said long ago in *Hornal* v. *Neuberger Products Ltd.* [1957]
G   1 Q.B. 247 the burden of proof required depends upon the nature and gravity of the subject matter. It depends on whether it is a grave offence or a minor one. In a civil case the burden is usually on the balance of probabilities. In these cases, under section 1 (3), it seems to me that this court must say that the burden of proof upon the employer is not a very heavy burden of proof. It is the ordinary burden of proof in a civil case. It is on the balance of probabilities. If that test is
H   applied in this case, it seems to me that there can be no doubt on the evidence whatsoever that the employers discharged the burden upon them. They proved that the difference between Mrs. Wade and Mr. McCann was due to a material difference in their skill and capacity and was not due to any difference in sex at all.

I must say that the consequences of any other decision would be most serious for any business. It would mean that in a department where all were doing like work, any low-paid woman amongst, say,

18 people could put in a claim and say that she ought to be paid the   A
same amount as the highest paid man, or vice versa. In other words,
everyone in the department, men and women, where both are employed,
would have to be raised up to the highest wage paid to anyone in the
department.   Alternatively, it might operate very badly for the employees
eventually, because they all might be paid at the lowest rate so that
none could claim higher than the other.

If it were to go forth that these grading systems are inoperative and   B
operate against the Equal Pay Act 1970, it would, I think, be disastrous
for the ordinary running of efficient business. It seems to me that a
grading system according to ability, skill and experience is an integral
part of good business management: and, as long as it is fairly and
genuinely applied irrespective of sex, there is nothing wrong with it at
all.   It ought not to be challenged and made inoperative by reason of the   C
Equal Pay Act 1970.   The contrary view would leave grading systems
open to challenge.

I am afraid I think that both the tribunals below were wrong and I
would reverse the decision and give judgment for the employers.

ORMROD L.J. I agree. This is the first case to come before this   D
court under section 1 of the Equal Pay Act 1970, as amended, and it
seems to me highly desirable that the object of this legislation should
not be lost sight of. It was in simple terms to bring into force what
was loosely described as the policy of equal pay for equal work. It is
an Act which has to be applied by hundreds and thousands of ordinary
people who are not lawyers, and it should therefore be kept as simple
and as free from legalistic complications as is possible.   E

For that reason Parliament placed the decision as to whether or not
the Act was contravened in the hands of the industrial tribunal.   People
on the spot were made judges of fact.   In my judgment, the crucial thing
is to keep the issue which the tribunal has to decide, as a matter of
fact, to as simple a matter of fact as it can be and not to complicate their
task by an ever-increasing number of technical legal decisions which must   F
be completely bewildering to those who have to administer this sort of
legislation on the ground.

I entirely agree with all that Lord Denning M.R. has said. It seems
to me that the way in which this Act has been set up is quite simple.
It starts with a presumption in favour of a woman who is doing like
work with a man, and of a man who is doing like work with a woman,
and then provides the employers in section 1 (3) with an opportunity   G
of showing on balance of probabilities that the difference in pay for
like work is due to some other material difference between the individuals
of opposite sex, and that, it seems to me, should be quite a simple
question of fact.

Here the employers said that they were operating a differential scheme
based on performance or personal assessment. That in itself, I would have   H
thought, was enough, provided only that they can show that they were
genuinely operating the scheme. It could be, of course, that an employer
had so set up a scheme to conceal an underlying sex discrimination in
rates of pay. If so, he fails under section 1 (3).

But, with respect to the Employment Appeal Tribunal, the complexity
which they appear to have found in this case astonishes me. I cannot
think that many of the considerations mentioned by the judge below

The Weekly Law Reports, July 14, 1978

221

3 W.L.R.   National Vulcan Insurance v. Wade (C.A.)   Ormrod L.J.

A in the course of his judgment are anything but entirely neutral when it comes to the question of deciding whether or not the employers have been genuinely operating a grading scheme. The fact that they formerly operated a discriminatory scheme before they changed their policy must be wholly neutral. The fact that they, like very many other employers, paid women a lower rate than men for comparable work in the past adds absolutely nothing to the question as to whether this is a genuine

B scheme. Although I do not wish to go through them in detail, the same comment would apply to the criticisms of the fact that this was a subjective scheme which had not been negotiated.

The only question is, was it genuinely operated? To answer that question, we turn to the schedule showing the gradings of the 18 people employed in this department, and that document (unless I am quite

C misled) seems to me to establish positively that there is no sexual discrimination in this case. To put it in a single sentence, analysing that schedule, it shows that 75 per cent. of the women and 80 per cent. of the men are in the same grade (grade 7) and 25 per cent. of the women and 20 per cent. of the men are in the lower grade 6. One can refine that analysis a little further, but it is not worth taking up time in doing

D so. It is perfectly obvious that the distribution of the 18 people in that department over the scale cannot be due to a sexual difference, and I am surprised that neither the industrial tribunal nor the Employment Appeal Tribunal really paid any attention to it.

Mr. Rose submitted that the employers had not established that each of these gradings was a genuine one not coloured by the sex of the person concerned. I would only say this: look at the schedule and it

E stands out a mile that that argument simply will not run.

For those reasons I, too, agree that this appeal must be allowed. In my judgment, the employers have plainly discharged the burden of proof which was upon them under section 1 (3).

GEOFFREY LANE L.J. I agree. This case demonstrates how easily the simple can become complex and the short long. There was no

F dispute that Mrs. Wade was being paid less by her employers than others in her section, the majority of whom were men, and in particular less than Mr. McCann, who was selected by her as the point of comparison. There was no dispute that the work which she was doing was broadly the same or similar to the work done by her colleagues in that section.

By section 1 (1) of the Equal Pay Act 1970 as amended by the Act

G of 1975, those facts caused to be implied into her contract of employment what is called "an equality clause." So far there is no difficulty. The employers then in their turn, as they are entitled to, relied on section 1 (3) of the Act, which reads as follows:

"An equality clause shall not operate in relation to a variation between the woman's contract and the man's contract if the

H employer proves that the variation is genuinely due to a material difference (other than the difference of sex) between her case and his."

Note the wording. The word used is "case." It is not "contract," it is not "skill," it is not "employment," it is "case."

I am prepared to assume that there was the necessary variation between the two contracts—that is, the contract of Mrs. Wade and that of Mr. McCann—and on that assumption two matters then fell to be

Geoffrey Lane L.J.   National Vulcan Insurance v. Wade (C.A.)   [1978]

decided. First of all, what was the standard of proof which the   A
employer had to achieve in order to discharge the burden imposed upon
him by section 1 (3) and, secondly, what does he have to prove?
Even if this were a criminal charge against the employer, the burden of
proof being on him, he would only have to discharge it on the balance
of probabilities. This is not a criminal charge, and the burden of proof
is a civil burden. Accordingly, it is quite plain that the Employment
Appeal Tribunal were wrong in imposing, as they seem to have imposed,   B
the obligation on the employer to prove the matter beyond reasonable
doubt.

We have been referred to other cases in which expressions were used
(most of them, be it said, obiter) indicating that something more than
the civil standard of proof is required. Those cases were *Snoxell* v.
Vauxhall Motors Ltd. [1978] Q.B. 11; *Electrolux Ltd.* v. *Hutchinson*   C
[1977] I.C.R. 252; *Navy, Army and Air Force Institutes* v. *Varley* [1977]
1 W.L.R. 149; and *Clay Cross (Quarry Services) Ltd.* v. *Fletcher* [1977]
I.C.R. 868. In so far as those cases appear to require the criminal
standard of proof they were wrongly decided.

The industrial tribunal did not fall into that error, probably because
none of those cases had been decided (certainly not reported) before they
came to consider this matter.   D

The employer then has to show that it is more probable than not that
the variation was due to a material difference, and a genuine material
difference, not based on sex. In other words, that the difference between
Mrs. Wade's salary and that of her male colleagues was bona fide due
to some difference other than the difference of sex.

What did the employer prove here? He proved that he had had for   E
years a system in operation which graded each employee in the section
according to capacity, skill and application. Up to the date of the Act
there was a rider super-added to that system which kept the women's
pay at only 85 per cent. of that paid to the men, but that was eliminated
before the Act came into force, very properly. There was before the
industrial tribunal and before the appeal tribunal the list containing   F
the names of 18 members of the section with their grading and salary,
and that was proved. Some were men and some were women. There
was also strong oral evidence given before the tribunal to the effect that
the difference in sex had nothing to do with the disparity in pay. That
indeed was obvious from the list. The employers further produced two
sets of assessments of various employees which equally made it clear
that any differentiation was not due to differences of sex.   G

Those pieces of evidence were not even challenged in cross-
examination. Consequently, it seems to me perfectly plain that there
was overwhelming evidence adduced by the employers to establish their
case under section 1 (3).

Mr. Rose on behalf of the employee suggests that there were two
matters which could be placed in the other side of the balance on behalf   H
of Mrs. Wade: (1) that the employers had before the Act paid to the
women only 85 per cent. of the men's wage; and (2) that Mrs. Wade
had been told when she had complained about her grading at 6D that
she ought to ascend to a grading of 6C before she could be considered
for a promotion to grade 7. That is simply telling her, " Do better and
you may be promoted." The complaint is that Mr. McCann was promoted to grade 7 without any such rider having been imposed on him.

The Weekly Law Reports, July 14, 1978

223

3 W.L.R.   National Vulcan Insurance v. Wade (C.A.)   Geoffrey Lane L.J.

A   I confess that I cannot understand how either of those two matters make any impact on the case at all. They seem to me to be neutral at the best and irrelevant at the worst.

The only question which remains then is whether the grading system was genuine or was merely a colourable attempt, if you like, to conceal a policy of discrimination being operated secretly by the employers—discrimination, that is, on the ground of sex. That proposition only

B   has to be stated to demonstrate its fatuity. There was no proper evidence at all to contradict the employers' assertion that they had differentiated solely on the basis of competence. The system was obviously a genuine and true one. One only has to look, as I say, at the list of employees in the section, of which there were 18, and couple that with the oral evidence which was given to make that point abundantly

C   clear.

I should add this. It is not for the tribunal to examine the employers' system with the object of seeing whether it is operating efficiently or even fairly. The only inquiry is whether it is genuine—that is to say, designed to differentiate between employees on some basis other than the basis of sex.

For those reasons I too would allow this appeal.

D

Appeal allowed.
No order as to costs.

Solicitors: *Gregory, Rowcliffe & Co.* for *Addleshaw, Sons & Latham,* Manchester; *Brian Thompson, Esq., Manchester.*

E   C. N.

——————

[CHANCERY DIVISION]

F   *In re* EARL OF STRAFFORD, DECD.

ROYAL BANK OF SCOTLAND LTD. *v.* BYNG AND OTHERS

[1976 S. No. 2325]

1978   May 2, 3, 4, 5, 8, 10   Megarry V.-C.

G

Trusts—Trustee—Compromise of litigation—Testator settling his chattels on successive life interests—Testatrix bequeathing her chattels to beneficiaries—Allegation that chattels given to beneficiaries were property of testator—Summons for directions —Court's direction that executors take proceedings to recover chattels—Beneficiaries offering compromise—Whether trustees empowered to accept compromise—Trustee Act 1925 (15 & 16

H   *Geo. 5, c. 19), s. 15*

Certain valuable chattels, the property of the testator, were settled by his will on a long succession of life interests. Other similar chattels, the property of his wife, the testatrix, were bequeathed by her absolutely to the third and fourth defendants. The testator and testatrix died in 1951. The first defendant, the son of the third defendant and the nephew of the fourth, now contended that some of the chattels given to the third and fourth defendants were the property not of

the testatrix but of the testator, and that they should be held A
on the trusts of the settlement under the testator's will. The
testator's executors issued a summons for directions whether
they should take proceedings against the third and fourth
defendants for the recovery of the disputed chattels. Megarry
V.-C. heard the summons in chambers and held that they
should issue proceedings. Thereupon the third and fourth
defendants offered to compromise on terms, inter alia, that
the executors should abandon the claim as to those chattels B
which the defendants had either sold or given away and that,
subject to the third defendant retaining her life interest in
certain items, the remaining chattels should be divided as to
one-fifth to the third and fourth defendants absolutely and as
to the remaining four-fifths to the executors to hold on the
trusts of the testator's will, with the qualification that neither
the third nor fourth defendant, nor the latter's sons, should C
claim any interest under those trusts, thus surrendering their
life interests in the four-fifths and accelerating the first
defendant's life interest from third to first place.

On a preliminary point taken by the first defendant, that
under section 15 of the Trustee Act 1925 [1] the trustees were
not empowered to accept the compromise: —

Held, that, on the true construction of section 15 of the
Trustee Act 1925, the trustees (and where they surrendered
their discretion, the court) had power to accept a compromise D
if they thought it to be desirable and fair to all the beneficiaries; that the section did not, expressly or impliedly, make
it necessary for all the beneficiaries to consent before the
trustees accepted the compromise; and that accordingly the
trustees, and so the court, had power under the section to
accept such a compromise (post, p. 229c–g).

In re Ezekiel's Settlement Trusts [1942] Ch. 230, C.A.
applied. E

The following cases are referred to in the judgment:

Chapman v. *Chapman* [1954] A.C. 429; [1954] 2 W.L.R. 723; [1954]
1 All E.R. 798, H.L.(E.).
Chesterfield's (Earl of) Trusts, In re (1883) 24 Ch.D. 643.
Ezekiel's Settlement Trusts, In re [1942] Ch. 230; *sub nom. National*
Provincial Bank Ltd. v. *Hyam* [1942] 2 All E.R. 224, C.A. F
Howe v. *Earl of Dartmouth* (1802) 7 Ves. 137.

PRELIMINARY POINT
The facts are stated in the judgment. The case was heard in chambers
and judgment was given in open court.

G

P. M. F. Horsfield Q.C. for the plaintiff executors.
E. G. Nugee Q.C. and *David Lowe* for the first and second defendants.
Robert Walker for the third to sixth defendants.
Grant Crawford for the seventh to ninth defendants.

MEGARRY V.-C. This judgment is an outcropping of strongly contested proceedings in chambers which lasted some five days. At the end H
of those proceedings I ruled that certain proposed terms of compromise
were of a nature which fell within the powers of the trustees of a
settlement to accept by virtue of the Trustee Act 1925, section 15.
Mr. Nugee, who appears on behalf of one of the beneficiaries under
the settlement, has contended that there was no power to compromise

[1] Trustee Act 1925, s. 15: see post, p. 226d–f.

A the dispute on terms such as those put forward, and he now wishes to have a reasoned judgment on the point to consider before deciding whether to appeal against my rejection of his contentions. I have therefore adjourned the proceedings into court for judgment on this one matter.

B Let me say at the outset that I do not propose to say more about this unhappy family dispute than is necessary to resolve the one point in issue. The dispute arises over chattels which consist mainly of pictures and furniture of considerable value. Some were owned by the testator and some by his wife, the testatrix. The testator's were settled by his will on a long succession of life interests, whereas those owned by the testatrix were given outright to the third and fourth defendants. The testator and testatrix both died in 1951. The essence of the dispute
C is that it is now contended by the first defendant, who is the son of the third defendant and nephew of the fourth defendant, that many of the chattels which previously were believed to have belonged to the testatrix in fact belonged to the testator, so that they should be held on the trusts of the settlement created by his will, and not be treated as the sole property of the third and fourth defendants and those who
D claim title through them. Under the trusts of the settlement the first life interest is in the third defendant, the next life interest in the fourth defendant, and the third in the first defendant, followed by other life interests and ultimately entails and other remainders. On any footing the third and fourth defendants are thus entitled to enjoy the chattels during their respective lives: it is after their deaths that the resolution of the dispute will determine whether the first defendant is entitled to
E enjoy them, or whether they are free from the settlement, and can remain with the third and fourth defendants or those who claim under them.

In those circumstnces the plaintiffs, a bank, which is the sole executor of the testator's estate, took out an originating summons under R.S.C., Ord. 85, for directions whether the bank should take proceedings against
F the third and fourth defendants for the recovery of the disputed chattels; and I held that it should. The third and fourth defendants then put forward certain proposed terms of compromise, whereupon the bank sought the directions of the court whether the proposed compromise should be accepted; and for this purpose the bank surrendered its discretion to the court. I do not propose to set out the proposed terms in detail, and I shall omit a number of matters which do not bear upon
G the point of jurisdiction. Broadly, the terms are, first, that the bank should abandon the claim as regards those chattels which the third and fourth defendants have either sold or given away. Second, that subject to the third defendant retaining her life interest in certain items, and subject to enough of the other chattels being sold to pay the costs of these proceedings, the remaining chattels should be divided as to one-
H fifth to the third and fourth defendants absolutely, and as to the remaining four-fifths to the bank to hold on the trusts of the testator's will, with the important qualification that neither the third nor fourth defendants (nor the fourth defendant's sons) would claim any interest under those trusts. There would thus in effect be a surrender by the third and fourth defendants of their respective life interests in the remaining four-fifths, with the consequent acceleration of the first defendant's life interest in them from third place to first.

It is this surrender of life interests that is at the centre of Mr. A
Nugee's contention, on behalf of the first defendant, that the proposed
compromise is outside the powers of section 15. So far as the first
defendant is concerned, the compromise would benefit him as to the
four-fifths, since his life interest would be accelerated; but he would lose
all prospects of enjoying the one-fifth, and I think that this is a major
factor in his objection, quite apart from his contention that although
he will benefit, the ultimate remaindermen will suffer. Technically, B
however, the objection is that the surrender would amount to a variation
of the beneficial interests under the trusts, and this, said Mr. Nugee,
was not authorised by section 15. The trustees cannot, he said, under
the guise of compromising a dispute, bring about a variation of the
trusts affecting the property that they hold; and this applies also to the
court when the trustees have surrendered their discretion to the court. C
Statute apart, the court has no power to sanction the variation of trusts
save in the very limited circumstances recognised by *Chapman* v.
Chapman [1954] A.C. 429.

I turn to the Trustee Act 1925, section 15. I think that I had better
set it out in full:

> " A personal representative, or two or more trustees acting together, D
> or, subject to the restrictions imposed in regard to receipts by a sole
> trustee not being a trust corporation, a sole acting trustee where by
> the instrument, if any, creating the trust, or by statute, a sole
> trustee is authorised to execute the trusts and powers reposed in
> him, may, if and as he or they think fit—(*a*) accept any property,
> real or personal, before the time at which it is made transferable or
> payable; or (*b*) sever and apportion any blended trust funds or E
> property; or (*c*) pay or allow any debt or claim on any evidence that
> he or they think sufficient; or (*d*) accept any composition or any
> security, real or personal, for any debt or for any property, real
> or personal, claimed; or (*e*) allow any time of payment of any debt;
> or (*f*) compromise, compound, abandon, submit to arbitration, or
> otherwise settle any debt, account, claim, or thing whatever relating F
> to the testator's or intestate's estate or to the trust; and for any of
> those purposes may enter into, give, execute, and do such agree-
> ments, instruments of composition or arrangement, releases, and
> other things as to him or them seem expedient, without being
> responsible for any loss occasioned by any act or thing so done by
> him or them in good faith."
                                                                          G
The section replaces the Trustee Act 1893, section 21, with some
expansion of the powers conferred. It will be seen that the section is
very wide in its terms, particularly as regards the wording of paragraph
(*f*). Furthermore, it refrains from making any stipulation about the
consideration that the trustees may accept in return for compromising
compounding, abandoning or otherwise settling any debt, account, claim
or thing whatever relating to the trust. That is left at large. Moreover, H
the section was treated by the Court of Appeal in *In re Ezekiel's Settlement Trusts* [1942] Ch. 230 as having a wide operation. The trustees
must listen to the beneficiaries and pay attention to their wishes, but
even if all of them oppose the proposed compromise, the trustees have
power under section 15 to agree a proposed compromise; and if the
matter is put before the court, the court must, as Lord Greene M.R. said,

A   at p. 234, decide "what the trustees ought to do having regard to the interests of everybody concerned."

    I think that it has to be borne in mind that section 15 is concerned with what may be called external disputes, or cases in which there is some issue between the trustees on behalf of the trust as a whole and the outside world. It is not concerned with internal disputes, where one beneficiary under the trusts is at issue with another beneficiary under the trusts. It is in this latter territory that the learning associated with *Chapman* v. *Chapman* [1954] A.C. 429 is particularly concerned. Where there is an external dispute, prima facie that learning plays no part. The question is whether the trustees are properly exercising the powers which section 15 confers upon them. I need hardly say that there is here no suggestion that section 15 is being used as a device to

C   effect the variation of beneficial interests. Obviously in exercising these powers, like other powers, the trustees must act in good faith in the interests of all concerned, without preferring one beneficiary to another. Given that, what limitation is there upon their powers? If in order to induce a compromise two of the beneficiaries agree to surrender their life interests, thus accelerating the interest of the beneficiary with the next life interest under the settlement, and also the interests of all

D   subsequent beneficiaries, I do not see why this per se should take the case out of section 15. Of course, the normal form of compromise may well involve the extraneous party in transferring some property to the trustees to hold on the trusts of the settlement, in return for the trustees relinquishing some claim of theirs; and that property, being added to the trust assets, will augment the interests of all the beneficiaries under the

E   settlement. But if in addition the extraneous party, owning some beneficial interest under the settlement, augments the interests of all the other beneficiaries under the settlement by relinquishing his beneficial interest to them, I do not see why that should be incapable of forming part of a perfectly proper consideration for the compromise if the trustees consider it to be in the interests of the beneficiaries as a whole.

F   Of course it may be said that the release of a life interest under the settlement is liable to operate unequally, in that it confers an obvious and immediate benefit upon the next life tenant by putting him in possession instead of keeping him in remainder, whereas it may confer little or no benefit upon the remoter remaindermen, as where the life tenant who is put into possession in fact outlives the life tenant who surrenders his interest. That, of course, is so. But life is so uncertain that even an

G   apparently remote remainderman may benefit from the surrender by reason of the unexpected deaths of intervening beneficiaries. Nor is a strict mathematical and actuarial calculation of benefits the only criterion: a compromise which, on the best estimate available, confers unequal financial benefits may nevertheless be a good compromise which ought to be accepted if it is likely to resolve long-standing family disputes and promote family peace. A beneficiary who benefits least

H   in money may benefit most in the value that he or she places on peace of mind. It will be remembered that in the Variation of Trusts Act 1958 the word "benefit" has been construed as not being confined to financial benefit.

    There is a further consideration. Let me suppose a settlement which in terms excludes the rule in *Howe* v. *Earl of Dartmouth* (1802) 7 Ves. 137, the rule in *In re Earl of Chesterfield's Trusts* (1883) 24

Ch.D. 643, and all other equitable rules for apportionment, and has a   A
very wide investment clause. Suppose also that in a dispute with a
stranger to the trust an offer is made to compromise the dispute by
transferring to the trustees, in satisfaction of their claim, a leasehold
interest or other wasting asset, or a reversionary interest. Of course
the trustees will be able to sell the asset when they have acquired it: but
can it be said that they have no power to settle the dispute under section
15 because what they are obtaining is an asset which will not be of   B
equal benefit to all the beneficiaries? Alternatively, could it be said
that although the transaction can be brought within section 15, this is
conditional upon the immediate sale of the asset in question?

    Without in terms answering these questions, let me consider another
aspect of the matter. Suppose the offer made by the stranger to compromise the dispute is one which the trustees consider to be fair, but   C
one of the beneficiaries strongly objects to it because, for instance, it
involves surrendering to the stranger some chattels which, for the
beneficiary, have a pretium affectionis. If to overcome this objection
the stranger improves his offer so as to include some additional element
which will be of greater advantage to the objecting beneficiary than the
other beneficiaries, will that improvement in the offer drive the proposed   D
compromise outside the bounds of section 15?

    Now in answering these questions I think it is important to draw a
firm line between what trustees have power to do under section 15, and
whether a particular exercise of that power is proper. Mr. Nugee's
fundamental objection is under the first head: he contends that there is
no jurisdiction to approve a compromise on the lines put forward. If
there is jurisdiction, then he takes the further objection that the proposed   E
compromise is not a proper one. This latter point is one which does
not arise for decision at this stage, since it is agreed on all hands that
there should be an up-to-date valuation of the chattels in question, and
that after this has been made the precise details of the offer should then
be reconsidered and, if thought desirable, revised terms put forward.
I have said that some compromise along the general lines put forward   F
seems to me to be the one which could be approved, but of course I
have not yet in fact approved anything. The one question before me
for decision is that of the jurisdiction under section 15.

    Ultimately the question of jurisdiction comes back to the terms of
section 15. Mr. Nugee contended that it was a purely administrative
provision, and that it could not be read as permitting the alteration of
beneficial interests under the trust. Plainly it must authorise the   G
alteration of beneficial interests in one sense. If trustees compromise a
dispute by giving up their claim to property A in return for the waiver
of all adverse claims to property B, the compromise has altered the
interests of the beneficiaries in property A by destroying all the beneficial
interests that they claim to have in it. Furthermore, if the beneficiaries
interested in property A differ from those interested in property B, the   H
compromise will alter the balance of their beneficial interests; and
although this would be a matter of serious concern in deciding whether
the compromise is fair in the interests of all the beneficiaries, I do not
think that such a compromise would be outside the powers of section 15.
However, such compromises would not alter the beneficial interests in
the trust property as a whole, and I think it was in that sense that Mr.
Nugee was speaking.

A   In the end, I think that Mr. Nugee's contentions (or at least one aspect of them) came down to saying that unless all the beneficiaries consent, any consideration for a compromise under section 15 must consist entirely of assets to be held by the trustees upon the existing trusts of the settlement, and must not include any surrender of any beneficial interests under the trusts; for that would alter the beneficial interests under those trusts, and the trustees cannot, under the purely
B   administrative provisions of section 15, effect any compromise which would bring about any such alteration. He accepted, of course, that there was nothing to prevent the life tenants from voluntarily surrendering their life interests: but if they sought to do this as part of the terms of compromise, that drove the compromise outside the bounds of the powers conferred by section 15.

C   A number of authorities were cited, but they had little real bearing on the point before me. As I have said, the question of jurisdiction comes back to the terms of section 15. I can see in it no limitations or restrictions of the kind that Mr. Nugee suggests, whether express or implied. There is not a word in it to restrict or define what it is that is to constitute the consideration for any compromise; and I should be
D   very slow to imply or read into a section couched in such wide and general terms any restrictions of the nature for which Mr. Nugee contends. It is in the mode of exercising the powers, and not in the existence of the powers themselves, that any restrictions are to be found; and this suffices to prevent any misuse of the section. I think that Mr. Horsfield, who appeared for the bank, and Mr. Walker, who appeared for the third and fourth defendants, were right in the essentials of their
E   contentions. These were, first, that the powers conferred by section 15 are not limited or restricted in any way by reference to the consideration to be given as part of the compromise. The only question on jurisdiction is whether what is done falls fairly within the words of the section, such as the term " compromise . . . any . . . claim." Second, in exercising the power, the only criterion is whether the compromise is desirable and fair as regards all the beneficiaries. It is in the exercise
F   of the power, and not in its existence, that any disparity of benefit between the beneficiaries must be considered. The greater the disparity, the less likely it is that the compromise will be regarded as being fair in the interests of all the beneficiaries, and so the less likely it is that the making of the compromise will be a proper exercise of the power. Nevertheless, as I have already indicated, financial parity is not all.

G   In the result, therefore, I hold that a compromise on the lines put forward by the third and fourth defendants and the bank is one that lies within the powers of the trustees, and so of the court where (as here) the trustees have surrendered their discretion to the court. Whether the particular compromise should in fact be approved remains to be determined when the terms of the proposed compromise are in their
H   final state after the valuations of the disputed chattels have been made and considered by all concerned.

Ruling accordingly.
Leave to appeal.

Solicitors: *Farrer & Co.; Boodle, Hatfield & Co.; Charles Russell & Co.; Frere Cholmeley & Co.; Gamlens.*

A. R.

[1978]

A

[COURT OF APPEAL]

M.E.P.C. LTD. *v.* CHRISTIAN-EDWARDS AND OTHERS

1978 May 4, 5, 8, 9   Stephenson, Orr and Goff L.JJ.

B

*Vendor and Purchaser—Contract—Requisition on title—Evidence
of contract 60 years earlier for sale of property—No evidence
that earlier contract ever completed—Whether specific performance to be granted—Whether good title shown by vendors in
accordance with contract—Land Registration Act 1925 (15 &
16 Geo. 5, c. 21), s. 13 (c)* [1]

In 1973 freehold premises were sold at auction to a property   C
company for £710,000. The vendors sold as trustees for sale
under the will of M, who had died in 1911. On examination
of the title it came to light that in about 1912 the then trustees
had entered into a contract with M's son, P, to sell him the
property for £23,750, subject to and with the benefit of a 21-year
lease granted by the trustees to P on December 14, 1911. No
copy or note of the contract had survived, but it was referred
to in two deeds of 1912 and 1930 respectively, the latter of   D
which also recited that it had been suspended, without, however, setting out the terms of the suspension. In January 1933
P had taken a second lease for 21 years from December 25,
1932. P died in 1942 without ever having been in possession
or occupation of the premises as purchaser and no one had
taken out representation to his estate or sought to enforce the
contract. Neither the second lease nor an appointment of
new trustees in 1936 contained any reference to the contract of   E
1912, although the latter recited that P's option to purchase
had never been exercised. On a vendor and purchaser summons, Goulding J. held that since the trustees were unable
to show the terms on which the completion of the contract
of 1912 was suspended they had failed to provide a good
title in accordance with the contract of sale of 1973.
On appeal by the trustees : —

Held, allowing the appeal, (1) that the court would presume   F
facts on which the title to land depended in circumstances
where, if the question had been referred to a jury, the judge
would have directed the jury to make the presumption rather
than have allowed them to decide the question themselves
and that although there were no longer juries in vendor and
purchaser summonses, the test remained the same; and that
in the circumstances there was overwhelming evidence to   G
support the presumption that performance of the contract of
1912 had been abandoned (post, pp. 234F, G, 238D).

Hillary v. *Waller* (1806) 12 Ves.Jun. 239; *Emery* v.
Grocock (1821) 6 Madd. 54 and *Games* v. *Bonnor* (1884)
54 L.J.Ch. 517 applied.

In re Atkinson and Horsell's Contract [1912] 2 Ch. 1
C.A. and *In re Spollon and Long's Contract* [1936] Ch. 713
considered.   H

(2) That since the court had no original jurisdiction over
registration under section 13 of the Land Registration Act

[Reported by ROBERT WILLIAMS ESQ., Barrister-at-Law]

⸳ Land Registration Act 1925, s. 13 (c): see post, p. 240B.

A   1925 and there were no objectors before it the trustees were
not entitled to a declaration, which was unnecessary in the
circumstances, that the property was fit to be registered with
title absolute (post, p. 239G).
        Per curiam. Even if, contrary to the court's view, the
contract of 1912 was still subsisting, specific performance
could not possibly be obtained 35 years after P's death since
P's personal representatives, if and when constituted, could
B   only stand in P's shoes and could not escape laches by
pleading want of knowledge (post, pp. 238E, F, 239A–C).
        Nwakobi v. *Nzekwu* [1964] 1 W.L.R. 1019, P.C.
distinguished.
        Decision of Golding J. [1977] 1 W.L.R. 1328; [1978] 1
All E.R. 295 reversed.

C   The following cases are referred to in the judgment:

Atkinson and Horsell's Contract, In re [1912] 2 Ch. 1, C.A.
Emery v. *Grocock* (1821) 6 Madd. 54.
Games v. *Bonnor* (1884) 54 L.J.Ch. 517.
Hepworth v. *Pickles* [1900] 1 Ch. 108.
Hillary v. *Waller* (1806) 12 Ves.Jun. 239.
D   *Nwakobi* v. *Nzekwu* [1964] 1 W.L.R. 1019, P.C.
Spollon and Long's Contract, In re [1936] Ch. 713.
Stone and Saville's Contract, In re [1962] 1 W.L.R. 460; [1962] 2 All
        E.R. 114.

The following additional cases were cited in argument:

Alley v. *Deschamps* (1806) 13 Ves.Jun. 225.
E   *Barnwell* v. *Harris* (1809) 1 Taunt. 430.
Cooke v. *Dawson* (1861) 3 De G.F. & J. 127.
Cooke v. *Soltau* (1824) 2 Sim. & St. 154.
Hopkinson v. *Chamberlain* [1908] 1 Ch. 853.
Johnson v. *Clarke* [1928] Ch. 847.
Levy v. *Stogdon* [1899] 1 Ch. 5, C.A.
F   *Mills* v. *Haywood* (1877) 6 Ch.D. 196, C.A.
South Eastern Railway Co. v. *Knott* (1852) 10 Hare 122.

APPEAL from Goulding J.
        M.E.P.C. Ltd. were purchasers at auction of a freehold property
known as 8, Storey's Gate, Westminster. By a summons dated August
5, 1975, they sought to determine whether the vendors of the property,
G   Thomas Guy Christian-Edwards, Jessie Marie Wyles and Margaret
Hornby, the trustees for sale under the will of William Paul Metchim,
had shown a good title to the property in accordance with the contract.
Goulding J. held that they had not, since the trustees had, in about 1912,
entered into a contract with a son of the testator for him to purchase
the property, and although the facts showed that the performance of
H   the contract, no copy of which had survived, had been suspended, the
terms of the suspension were no longer ascertainable.
        The trustees appealed on the grounds, inter alia, (1) that the contract
of 1912 was incapable of being an incumbrance on the title; (2) that the
contract was unenforceable by reason of lapse of time; (3) that from
1933 onwards, when the trustees had granted the son a lease of the
property for 21 years, the contract was treated as no longer subsisting,

and the son had died in 1942.   The trustees also asked for a declaration   A
that the property was fit to be registered with title absolute.

The facts are stated in the judgment of the court.

G. B. H. Dillon Q.C. and *E. W. H. Christie* for the trustees.
Richard Scott Q.C. and *J. F. Parker* for the purchasers.

STEPHENSON L.J.   The judgment of the court will be delivered by   B
Goff L.J.

GOFF L.J.   This is an appeal from a judgment of Goulding J. given
on May 17, 1977, on a vendor and purchaser summons.   The appellants were the vendors and were defendants to the summons.   The
property was some business premises know as 8, Storey's Gate, Westminster, formerly Abbey Buildings, 8, Princes Street.   It was sold by   C
auction on April 10, 1973, at the price of £710,000 to the purchasers,
who are a property company.   The vendors sold as trustees for sale
under the will of William Paul Metchim, who died on December 14,
1911, probate being dated February 2, 1912.

Apart from one difficulty which gives rise to this case the title is a
straightforward one, consisting really simply of the probate, an appoint-   D
ment of new trustees and some leases.   The trouble is that it came to
light on examination of title that the then trustees had at some time
between the death of the testator on December 14, 1911, and July 1,
1912, entered into a contract to sell the property to a son of the
testator, one Percy Bridgman Metchim, since deceased, at the price of
£23,750.   Many of the trust papers were lost by enemy action during   E
the war, when the offices of the solicitors and of the managing agents
for the trustees suffered war damage, and neither that contract (which
we will call the contract of 1912), nor any copy or note of it is known
to survive.   But the fact that it was made appears from recitals in a
deed of family arrangement dated July 1, 1912, and a deed of covenant
dated February 11, 1930.

By the will the son Percy was given an option to purchase, which he   F
did not exercise, and in that event the will directed that he should be
granted a lease, which was done.   That lease, of which also no copy
survives, though that is not, we think, of much significance, was for a
term of 21 years and 11 days from December 14, 1911.

Then in 1912 there was the deed of family arrangement which we
have mentioned, which was made for the purpose of dealing with a
number of matters which had arisen in the administration of the estate.   G
That has no direct bearing on the question at issue, but it contains these
important recitals:

"And whereas the said Percy Bridgman Metchim has not exercised
the option to purchase Abbey Buildings given to him by the said
will AND whereas the trustees of the said will have granted a
lease for a term of twenty-one years at the yearly rental fixed by   H
a properly qualified valuer of £950 of the business premises known
as Abbey Buildings aforesaid to the said Percy Bridgman Metchim ...

"AND whereas the trustees of the said will have agreed with the
said Percy Bridgman Metchim for the sale to him at the sum of
£23,750 of the said Abbey Buildings for all the interest therein of
the said testator and subject to and with the benefit of the said
lease."

A   Under the will three of the testator's daughters were entitled to a one-quarter share of income of the residuary estate with limitations over in favour of the survivors, the whole capital finally going to the ultimate survivor.   One of the three having died, the other two wished to make some provision for their niece, the daughter of the deceased sister, and so they entered into a deed of covenant dated February 11,
B   1930, to provide her with a share of the income of the property pending sale and thereafter an annuity.   Again the terms of that deed are not in themselves material, but it contains the following recital:

"AND whereas the said Percy Bridgman Metchim did not exercise the option to purchase the said premises Abbey Buildings given him by the said will but the trustees of the said will granted to the said Percy Bridgman Metchim a lease of the said premises for a term
C   of 21 years and 11 days from the said December 14, 1911, at the yearly rental fixed by a properly qualified valuer of £950 AND whereas since the grant of such lease the trustees agreed with the said Percy Bridgman Metchim for the sale to him of the said premises at the price of £23,750 subject to the said lease but such purchase has not yet been completed and by consent of all parties
D   interested the performance thereof has been suspended."

In the operative part of the deed:

"The donors do hereby covenant that the donee shall as from August 23, 1929, be entitled so long as she is living and the sale of the said premises shall be incomplete to receive and be paid out of the share of the rents of Abbey Buildings to which they became
E   absolutely entitled on the death of the said Beatrice Louise Metchim the yearly sum of £80 to commence as from August 23 last and be paid to her by quarterly payments.   And further that if and whenever during the lifetime of the donee the sale of the said premises shall be duly completed an annuity of the same amount of £80 for the life of the donee shall be purchased for and in the name of the
F   donee out of the proceeds of sale."

The only parties to that deed were the two surviving daughters and the niece.

It will be seen that the recital is somewhat bald in that it does not state at what date performance of the contract was suspended and whether it was indefinitely or on some and if so what conditions.
G   The lease to Percy having expired at December 25, 1932, the trustees granted and Percy accepted a new lease dated January 19, 1933, for a further 21 years from December 25, 1932.

Down to the end of 1933 Percy and his brother Ralph were in occupation of the premises and carrying on business there in partnership as printers and stationers, but, of course, under the two successive leases, Percy was never in possession or occupation as purchaser under the 1912
H   contract.   In December 1933 a company was formed to take over the business, which it did.   Percy and Ralph were the subscribers to the memorandum and articles of association and were named by the articles as the first directors.   Percy died on November 6, 1942, and Ralph on December 26, 1947.

The second lease having expired on December 25, 1954, the trustees granted to the company and the company accepted a new lease dated March 25, 1954, for 21 years from December 25, 1953, at a rental of

£3,000 per annum. That lease is still subsisting and the present sale was   A
expressly made subject thereto. It is also very important to mention
that there was an appointment of new trustees dated March 18, 1936,
to which we must later more specifically refer.

The judge held that the title could not be forced upon the purchasers
and declared that a good title had not been shown. He dismissed a
counterclaim by the trustees, but that necessarily followed as it merely
set up the converse of the purchasers' case by saying that a good title   B
had been shown.

The trustees appeal to this court.

As appears from the counterclaim the trustees present their case in
two alternative ways. First, they ask for "a declaration that the defendants have shown a good title to the above-mentioned property in
accordance with the above-mentioned contract of sale," and secondly,   C
for "a declaration that the property held in accordance with the said
title is fit to be registered with title absolute and unconditionally."

Before analysing the evidence and what conclusions should be drawn
from it we think it important to consider by what principles we should
be guided. First, whilst it is clear that a vendor may be able to force
a purchaser to accept a title different from that which he contracted to   D
give (see *In re Atkinson and Horsell's Contract* [1912] 2 Ch. 1), yet
apart from any case in which the conditions of the contract may otherwise require, and the present is not such a case, the purchaser is entitled
to require not merely a good holding title but a good marketable one.
As Luxmoore J. said in *In re Spollon and Long's Contract* [1936] Ch.
713, 718:
                                                                           E
> "The purchaser having bought on an open contract, was entitled
> to have a good marketable title, which, as I understand it, is a title
> which will enable him to sell the property without the necessity of
> making special conditions of sale restrictive of the purchaser's
> rights."

This, however, does not mean that the court will not in a proper case   F
presume the facts on which the title depends, and, of course, the first
submission for the trustees is that we should presume that the contract
of 1912 was abandoned. It is established by ancient authority that such
a course should be taken only where the position is such that under the
position which obtained in the days of the old Court of Chancery if the
question were referred to a common law court the judge would direct
the jury to make the presumption and not merely leave it to them to   G
decide as they might think fit. This, in our judgment, is correctly stated
in *Fry on Specific Performance,* 6th ed. (1921), p. 417, para. 890 (v),
which reads:

> "Where the title rests on a presumption of fact of such a kind
> that if the question of fact were before a jury, it would be the
> duty of the judge not to give a clear direction in favour of the fact,   H
> but to leave the jury to draw their own conclusion from the
> evidence."

That sub-paragraph is given as an example of a case in which a
court would consider the title doubtful. Then, at pp. 420–421, para.
891 (v), which is dealing with cases where the title would not be considered doubtful, the converse is given:

A   " Where the title depends on a presumption, provided it be such,
that if the question were before a jury, it would be the duty of the
judge to give a clear direction in favour of the fact, and not to
leave the evidence generally to the consideration of the jury."

These passages are, in our judgment, established by *Emery* v. *Grocock*
(1821) 6 Madd. 54; *Hillary* v. *Waller* (1806) 12 Ves.Jun. 239, and *Games*
B v. *Bonnor* (1884) 54 L.J.Ch. 517.

The first of those cases concerned a portions term. There was no
evidence that the portions had been satisfied, but the portioners had all
attained 21 at least 60 years previously, and all were dead. The court
presumed a surrender of the portions term, and Sir John Leach said,
at 6 Madd. 54, 57: " A court of equity will not compel the acceptance
C of a title where there is reasonable doubt in law or in fact." In view
of later cases that proposition so far as law is concerned has to be
taken with some reservation, but that does not affect the position before
us. Later he went on to say, at p. 57:

" . . . and the only rule that they can adopt in cases of presumption
like the present seems to be, that if the case be such, that sitting
before a jury, it would be the duty of a judge to give a clear
D   direction in favour of the fact; then it is to be considered as without
reasonable doubt; but if it would be the duty of a judge to leave
it to the jury to pronounce upon the effect of the evidence, then
it is to be considered as too doubtful to conclude a purchaser."

In the second there was a conveyance to raise charges. The vendor
E and his predecessors in title had been in possession for 140 years, but
the purchaser objected that there was an outstanding legal estate. Sir
William Grant M.R. presumed the legal estate had been got in (see
12 Ves.Jun. 239, 254) and on appeal Lord Erskine L.C. affirmed this,
saying, at pp. 269–270:

" There is a defect and omission in the deed; not providing, that,
when the annuities are satisfied, there shall be a conveyance of the
F   other moiety. My judgment is, that at this distance of time I ought
to presume, that this re-conveyance has been made. I agree, I
must make that presumption. My judgment is founded upon this;
and I make the presumption without sending it to law; being confident, a judge must tell a jury, they ought to presume, and they
would presume, that this re-conveyance had been made."

G
Games v. *Bonner*, 54 L.J.Ch. 517 is not quite so strong, because in
that case there was evidence which, if accepted, proved the title, though
it was not strict proof. In the Court of Appeal the problem was set at
rest, because the purchaser, having been offered an inquiry, refused it,
and it was held therefore that he could not object to the evidence. But
in the court below Pearson J. relied upon *Emery* v. *Grocock*, 6 Madd
H 54, and said, at p. 519:

" The facts here are these: Lewis died in 1835. If he left a son,
he must have been more than 21 in 1869, when Mrs. Williams died.
I am asked to conjecture that he had a descendant under disability.
Before a jury I should say they had no right to assume such a
conjecture. I conclude, therefore, that a title is clearly shown, so
far as regards possession, and any possibility of a claim through
Lewis against the mortgagee in possession."

One further reference to *Fry*, 6th ed., is apposite at this juncture; A
where the author was giving examples of cases where it is conceived
that the court would consider the title not to be doubtful, and said, at
pp. 419–420:

> " And in cases where the circumstances led to a presumption that
> a restrictive covenant affecting the user of the property sold had
> been released or waived, the title has been forced on the purchaser," B

citing the well known case *Hepworth* v. *Pickles* [1900] 1 Ch. 108.

Today, of course, law and equity are decided together and there is
no jury in a specific performance action or a vendor and purchaser
summons, but the test is, we think, still in effect the same.

This test can only apply to the question of abandonment, because
the question whether the 1912 contract, if still subsisting, could or C
would be ordered to be specifically performed could never have been
a jury question; nor is there anything to presume. The problem is how
the court would exercise its discretion if an action for specific performance were brought.

By analogy, however, we think the court ought to hold the title
good if on the facts before him the judge can see plainly that specific D
performance would not be granted in any reasonably conceivable circumstances. Germane to this is the well established maxim that a
purchaser will not be required to buy a law suit, but that means no more
than that the title will not be forced upon him if there is a realistic
prospect of litigation. This position is summarised in *Fry*, 6th ed.,
p. 416, para. 890 (i): E

> " Where the probability of litigation ensuing against the purchaser
> in respect of the matter in doubt is considerable, or, as it was put
> by Alderson B., where there is a ' reasonable decent probability of
> litigation.' The court, to use a favourite expression, will not compel
> the purchaser to buy a lawsuit."

Whatever else may be true in this case we do not see any such F
prospect. Mr. Scott sought to overcome this difficulty by saying that
the vendor and purchaser summons is itself such litigation. In our
judgment, however, that cannot possibly be right. It would stultify the
whole purpose of the Vendor and Purchaser Act 1874. The purchaser
must make up his own mind whether he is satisfied with the title, and G
if not he can either rescind at his peril or get the point which worries
him summarily determined upon a summons under the Act; but if then
the court should hold the title good and such as he ought to have
accepted he cannot turn round and say " Ah no, because although I
was wrong and the title was good I had to come to court for a ruling."
We are not, of course, considering any question of the costs of the H
summons, but whether a title otherwise good cannot be forced upon a
purchaser because the purchaser will not accept it until the court has
ruled upon it.

With these principles in mind we turn to the first question: whether
we ought to presume that the contract of 1912, which in 1930 was
clearly alive but under suspension, whatever that may mean, was subsequently abandoned. We do not attach much, if any, significance to

A the first lease of 1911 or 1912, because the contract of 1912 was made subsequently thereto, and was subject to and with the benefit thereof, and because the deed of covenant shows that some members of the family at all events regarded the contract of 1912 as still subsisting in 1930, since we agree with the judge that it is impossible to read the words " But such purchase has not yet been completed," and the words " If and whenever during the lifetime of the donee the sale of the said
B premises shall be duly completed," as referring to anything other than completion of that particular contract.

Some question may arise as to the effect of the deed upon the beneficial interests in the event of a sale otherwise than under the contract of 1912, although that will probably be overcome by implication. However, that does not concern us for present purposes.

C The lease of January 19, 1933, is, however, much more significant, since it was nearly three years after the deed of covenant.

It was made in consideration of Percy doing certain repairs or making improvements, and Mr. Dillon relied strongly upon that, but we do not think that that factor really tells us very much. Even if the contract were still subsisting but not likely to be speedily performed the trustees
D might well require Percy to put the premises in better shape, and, of course, as tenant, he would enjoy the benefit of these works, and should he complete the purchase he would have improved his own property. What is telling, however, in our view is that there was a preliminary agreement for the lease which contains no reference to the contract of 1912, nor does the lease itself. Taking a lease for 21 years was, prima
E facie, inconsistent with the contract of 1912, and we would have expected some saving clause to have appeared at least in the preliminary agreement.

The matter does not rest there, however, because we come to the appointment of new trustees in 1936, which contained meticulous recitals as to what had so far happened in the administration, and
F specified the property remaining subject to the trusts which included the freehold of the property, and was said to be subject to the lease of January 19, 1933; but there is no mention at all of the contract of 1912. It recited, however, that Percy had not exercised his option to purchase and contains the following further recitals:

"(O) The present trustees with the consent of the said Henrietta
G Lilian Blackwood Maud Bridgman Whitley Wilson and Violet Gladys Bridgman Wyles on January 19, 1933, granted to the said Percy Bridgman Metchim the lease of the said Abbey Buildings particulars of which appear in Part II of Schedule 2 hereto.

"(P) The property now held by the present trustees on the trusts of the will consists of . . . the freehold property known as Abbey
H Buildings more particularly described in Part I of Schedule 2 hereto subject to and with the benefit of the lease in Part II of such Schedule mentioned which said freehold property is held on the trusts declared concerning the same by the said will."

Moreover, the son Ralph was a party to that deed as a present or continuing trustee.

Then the company took yet another lease on March 25, 1954. It is

true we do not know whether the company had the benefit of the contract A
of 1912, if it still existed, and Percy was by then deceased and had been
for some 12 years, but we cannot altogether discount this further act of
ownership by the trustees.

Moreover, there is a further very important feature in that, as we
have said, neither the contract itself nor any copy of it, nor the suspension agreement, appear to have survived. It is true that when the
offices of the trust solicitors and of their estate agents suffered war B
damage, many records were destroyed, but the formal deeds were not
lost, and it is difficult to see, therefore, why the contract of 1912, if
still subsisting in 1939, even if suspended in some way, was not to be
found with them, to say nothing of any record of the suspension itself.
Further, there was a probate valuation on October 13, 1937, which
refers to the second lease, but not the contract of 1912, although this C
would have been highly relevant to the valuation. Moreover, this shows
that Percy's firm were having difficulty in paying the rent, let alone
completing the contract of 1912.

Finally Percy died at the age of 65 on November 6, 1942. No one
troubled to take out representation to his estate, and over 35 years have
elapsed since them.
                                                                         D
Weighing all these factors, and particularly the appointment in 1936
of new trustees, there is ample, and indeed overwhelming, evidence to
support the presumption of abandonment and nothing to the contrary,
apart from the deed of 1930, which is ancient history. We have no
doubt but that we ought to presume abandonment, and subject to the
impact of section 13 of the Land Registration Act 1925, which we will
presently consider, we ought to allow this appeal.   E

In the circumstances it is not strictly necessary to consider the
alternative question whether even if the contract of 1912 be still subsisting specific performance of it could possibly now be obtained, but
we do so, because we think this second line of argument greatly fortifies
the trustees' case. Even if, which we do not believe, the contract of
1912 is still subsisting, and even if somebody sought to set it up, which F
we cannot imagine will ever happen, we cannot see how specific performance could be a possible remedy. The judge found it so only by
what he himself admitted was mere speculation, and, with the greatest
possible respect, in our judgment he founded it upon a postulate which
is really inconceivable.

It being a family matter we can conceive that the brothers and G
sisters might say: " We know you are are not doing very well and we
will not press you, but, of course, if and when it is necessary to sell,
then you must either perform your contract or give it up." But surely
the parties would never have agreed, or even thought of the idea, that
Percy should not in the meantime be entitled to enforce it, however
well his business prospered; that he must go on paying rent as tenant, H
and indeed if the lease expired before a sale became necessary then he
could not complete his ex hypothesi still subsisting contract but must
seek to negotiate terms for a new lease. We, therefore, reject this
supposition. But that is not conclusive so far as Percy's lifetime is
concerned, though it goes a long way. Possibly he would not have
been unable to get specific performance during the 14 years that he
survived 1930, but even so over 35 years have elapsed since his death.

A   That long further time and the rise in value of the property must in any event, we think, present formidable difficulties in the way of a claim to specific performance by his personal representatives if and when constituted, even if they and their beneficiaries had none of them any knowledge or means of knowledge of the contract of 1912. But it seems to us that Mr. Dillon's answer is complete, that they could only stand in Percy's shoes and could not escape laches by pleading want of
B   knowledge. *Nwakobi* v. *Nzekwu* [1964] 1 W.L.R. 1019 in the Privy Council is distinguishable, since there the Onitshas were not claiming through the Crown but setting up an independent right.

Mr. Scott argues that this court could not or should not hold that the case is free from doubt seeing that the judge below had doubts. We cannot accept that. Although both points were argued before him it is
C   clear that the judge was directing his mind more to the question of specific performance than abandonment, but the two do not depend on entirely the same considerations. In any case, however, his doubt was largely, if not exclusively, based upon his postulated example which we cannot share with him. In our judgment we are free to hold, and with respect do hold, that the matter is free from doubt, despite the judge's doubts, and we would refer in this connection once again to *Fry*, 6th
D   ed., p. 415, para. 887, which reads:

"Again, as regards the decision of an inferior court; —the judges of the Court of Appeal have held that they are in no wise bound by such decisions, and that where they consider that there is no reasonable doubt, the adverse decision of the inferior court will not be a sufficient reason to refuse the plaintiff relief. 'With respect to the
E   common cases of doubtful title,' said Lord St. Leonards [in *Sheppard* v. *Doolan* (1842) 3 Dr. & War. 1, 8], 'I cannot agree with the proposition, that an unfavourable decision in the court of inferior jurisdiction renders the title doubtful. The judge of the superior court would still be bound to exercise his own discretion and decide according to his own judgment.' This language has been cited with
F   approval by the Court of Appeal in Chancery in England."

We turn then to the one point we reserved earlier in this judgment, namely the effect of section 13 of the Land Registration Act 1925. I read again the trustees' alternative claim:

"A declaration that the property held in accordance with the said
G   title is fit to be registered with title absolute and unconditionally."

Mr. Dillon submitted that we could and should make this declaration, but we do not think it would be right to do so, because we have no original jurisdiction over registration, and in any event have no objectors before us. The point is not directly relevant because taking the view that we do, that the title is good, the trustees do not have to rely on
H   their alternative argument. We have, however, been concerned whether it might be argued that the title cannot or should not be forced on the purchaser because the registrar might, nevertheless, enter the contract of 1912 as an encumbrance, and reliance was placed by analogy on *In re Stone and Saville's Contract* [1962] 1 W.L.R. 460. That, of course, was a different case, because there was an actual entry; and even then the judge did not express a concluded opinion, and nor do we, upon that

state of affairs.   It seems to us, however, that there is nothing in this   A
point so far as this case is concerned.   The object of section 13 was to
give the registrar a wider power than the court has on a vendor and
purchaser summons or in a specific performance action.   He can accept
a mere holding title.   Sub-paragraph (c) of that section reads:

> " If the registrar, upon the examination of any title, is of opinion
> that the title is open to objection, but is nevertheless a title the   B
> holding under which will not be disturbed, he may approve of such
> title, or may require the applicant to apply to the court, upon a
> statement signed by the registrar, for its sanction to the registration."

Surely if we decide, as we do, that there is a good marketable title
the registrar would never turn the section round and make it more
restrictive by qualifying the title.   Secondly, however, even if that were   C
to happen, and we cannot believe it would, surely the purchasers would
be in no difficulty after our decision in satisfying a prospective mortgagee or purchaser.   In any case, however, it cannot, we think, be
right that the question should be decided one way if the property be
not in a compulsory registration area, and another if it be, or that, on
the ground that before the conveyance passes off the title, the area may
become a compulsory one, we should be deterred from what we think   D
ought to be decided.   In taking this view of the effect our decision
should have in its impact upon section 13 we do not feel that we are in
any way listening to a siren song.

For these reasons we allow the appeal, and on the counterclaim we
declare that a good title has been shown according to the contract.

It only remains to say that this case was exceptionally well argued on   E
both sides and we are grateful to counsel for their assistance.

> *Appeal allowed.   Declaration that
> good title shown according to con-
> tract as from October 16, 1976.
> Trustees to pay costs to that date,
> purchasers thereafter.*   F
> *Leave to appeal.*

Solicitors: *Monro, Pennefather & Co.; Simmons & Simmons.*

G

H

A

[HOUSE OF LORDS]

PONSFORD AND OTHERS . . . . . RESPONDENTS

AND

H.M.S. AEROSOLS LTD. . . . . . . APPELLANTS

B

1978 May 3, 4;   Lord Wilberforce, Viscount
       June 29   Dilhorne, Lord Salmon, Lord Fraser
                           of Tullybelton and Lord Keith of Kinkel

Landlord and Tenant—Rent—" Reasonable rent "—Rent review
clause providing for assessment of " reasonable rent for the
C   *demised premises "—Premises burning down and being rebuilt*
—Improvements at tenant's own expense—Whether assessment
of " reasonable rent " to include improvements

The plaintiffs' predecessors in title granted the defendants
a lease of factory premises for 21 years from June 1968 at a
yearly rent of £9,000 for the first seven years. The rent review
clause provided that for the second and third period of seven
D   years the rent should be £9,000 or such a sum, whichever would
be the higher, as would be assessed as "a reasonable rent
for the demised premises." It further provided that the assessment should be made by agreement of the parties or, in
default of agreement, by an independent surveyor. In 1969
the premises were burnt down and rebuilt out of the insurance
proceeds. At the same time, the defendants, at their own
expense and after obtaining the plaintiffs' licence to carry out
E   the work, made extensive improvements and alterations to the
factory premises at a cost of nearly £32,000. It was common
ground that the improvements, once made, became part of the
demised premises. Further, by a term of the licence all the
conditions of the lease were to apply to the premises " when
and as altered and shall extend to all additions." When the
rent for the second seven-year period fell to be assessed, the
parties disagreed as to the amount of a reasonable rent and a
F   surveyor was appointed. The plaintiffs then issued a summons
to determine whether the proper basis for assessing a reasonable
rent under the rent review clause should have regard to the
premises in their existing state or whether the works of
improvement made at the defendants' expense should not be
taken into account. The judge held that a reasonable rent
should be assessed without having regard to the improvements
made by the defendants on the basis, inter alia, that it would
G   be unreasonable for the plaintiffs to have both the benefit of
the improvements to the property and an increased rental.
The Court of Appeal reversed his decision.
On appeal: —
Held, dismissing the appeal (Lord Wilberforce and Lord
Salmon dissenting), that on the true construction of the rent
review clause " a reasonable rent for the demised premises "
was that which was reasonable for the premises and not what
H   would be reasonable for the tenant to pay; that the improvements became part of the demised premises to which the
conditions of the lease applied and that, accordingly, a reasonable rent was to be assessed by having regard to their improved
condition, without considering who had paid for the improvements (post, pp. 246G–H, 247C–E, 252G–253A, 255G–H).
Cuff v. *J. & F. Stone Property Co. Ltd.* (*Note*) [1978] 3
W.L.R. 256 approved.
Decision of the Court of Appeal [1977] 1 W.L.R. 1029;
[1977] 3 All E.R. 651 affirmed.

242

Ponsford v. H.M.S. Aerosols Ltd. H.L.(E.) [1978]

The following cases are referred to in their Lordships' opinions: A

Cuff v. *J. & F. Stone Property Co. Ltd.* (*Note*) [1978] 3 W.L.R. 256.
Kay (John) Ltd. v. *Kay* [1952] 2 Q.B. 258; [1952] 1 All E.R. 813, C.A.
United Scientific Holdings Ltd. v. *Burnley Borough Council* [1977] 2
　W.L.R. 806; [1977] 2 All E.R. 62, H.L.(E.).

The following additional cases were cited in argument:

Smith v. *Lucas* (1881) 18 Ch.D. 531. B
White & Co. Ltd. v. *Toronto City* [1955] O.R. 320.

APPEAL from the Court of Appeal.

The respondents to this appeal were Ian Reginald Ponsford, Peter
Philip Rough and Edward John Posey (suing as trustees of the G. M.
Posey Voluntary Settlement). The appellants, H.M.S. Aerosols Ltd.,
were appealing by leave of the Court of Appeal (Cairns and Roskill L.JJ. C
and Sir Gordon Willmer) from the judgment of that court dated February
8, 1977.

The issue in the case was whether the words "reasonable rent"
in a rent review clause in a lease meant simply a rent which was reasonable for the demised premises, having regard only to those premises and
to no other consideration, or whether they meant a rent which it was D
reasonable for the lessors to exact and the lessees to pay, having regard
to all the circumstances of the case and in particular to the fact that the
demised premises in respect of which the reasonable rent was to be
assessed had been improved at the lessees' expense during the term of the
lease.

The facts are stated in the opinions of Lord Wilberforce and Viscount
Dilhorne. E

Peter Millett Q.C. and *Michael Rich* for the appellant company.
Leolin Price Q.C. and *Bruce Coles* for the respondents.

Their Lordships took time for consideration.

June 29. LORD WILBERFORCE. My Lords, this case concerns the F
interpretation of a rent review clause, and is one of impression. Of the
four judges who have considered it, two favour one interpretation, two
another. Your Lordships are, unfortunately, also divided in view.

The clause is contained in a lease of industrial premises for 21 years
from June 24, 1968, at an initial rent for the first seven years of £9,000 per
annum. For the second and third seven years of the term it is to be G
£9,000 " or such sum whichever be the higher as shall be assessed as a
reasonable rent for the demised premises for the appropriate period."
There follow provisions for fixing this reasonable rent by an independent
surveyor.

Soon after the granting of the lease the buildings were burnt down.
The lessors, having received insurance money, undertook to reconstruct
them, but at the same time the lessee desired to make some improvements. H
It applied to the lessors for a licence, and on November 14, 1969, this
was granted by a formal document under seal. It contained this clause:

　" 3. It is hereby agreed and declared that all the lessees' convenants
　and conditions contained in the lease which are now applicable to
　the premises demised thereby shall continue to be applicable to the
　same when and as altered and shall extend to all additions which
　may be made thereto in the course of such alterations."

A   The improvements, including I understand the construction of a new bay, and the installation of sprinkler equipment and a central heating system, were carried out at a cost of about £32,000, which sum was paid by the lessee.

Now, at the end of the first seven years, the question which arises is this: on what basis is the independent surveyor to fix the reasonable rent? It is not disputed that he must fix that rent for the premises as improved

B   —they are now " the demised premises." But can he take into account the fact that the improvements have been paid for by the lessee? The answer depends solely on the construction of the words " a reasonable rent for the demised premises."

Many arguments great and small have been used by either side. I start by discarding some which, for my part, I find inconclusive or

C   unhelpful.

1. The lessors, and the majority judges in the Court of Appeal, place great reliance on the words " for the demised premises." They show, it is said, that the surveyor only has to look at the premises and value them as they are: he cannot consider anything else. For my part I find these words neither conclusive, nor even indicative. They state the obvious. What else could the rent be for? The question is not what the rent is

D   payable for but on what basis the surveyor is to fix it—on the market value, the rack-rent value or, whatever this means, on the basis of what is reasonable.

2. The clause, it is said, prescribes merely " a reasonable rent." If the surveyor were to consider other matters than the visible character of the premises it would say " reasonable in all the circumstances." A distinc-

E   tion is thus made between this clause and the statutory provision considered by the Court of Appeal in *John Kay Ltd.* v. *Kay* [1952] 2 K.B. 258 in which it was held that the words " such rent . . . as the court in all the circumstances thinks reasonable " gave to the court a wide discretion. I cannot find the least substance in this argument. The word reasonable has no abstract or absolute meaning: it only has significance when related to a set of facts. What is reasonable in some circumstances may be

F   unreasonable in others. I find no difference between the two expressions.

3. It is said that if the lessee had wished to protect himself against paying rent based on the improvements, it could, and should, have done so when the licence was granted. I do not agree. If the review clause has the meaning for which it contends there was no need for it to do so. If it bears the opposite meaning, it loses its case. The question which is

G   right remains to be decided.

4. It is said that the lessee's argument involves reading the clause as if it said " a reasonable rent for the tenant to pay " and that there is no justification for reading in the latter words.

I do not follow this argument. There is no need, on the lessee's argument, to read in any words. The rent which has to be fixed is a rent

H   payable by this tenant under this lease which has 14 years to run and which may be renewed thereafter. It is not a rent, to follow the words of section 34 of the Landlord and Tenant Act 1954, at which the holding might reasonably be expected to be let in the open market by a willing lessor. The contrast in language is plain: the lessor's contention, indeed, is that the words mean just that which, in my opinion, they cannot do.

I turn to arguments of substance. The clause exists and must be interpreted in the context of this lease and of what the parties must have

been aware of at the time they agreed to it.   They must have known the   A
following:

1. That a lessee has the right to make improvements subject to the
lessors' approval which cannot be unreasonably withheld.   The lessors
cannot as a condition of granting approval demand an increased rent.
They did not of course do so in 1969.

2. If, when the lease expires, the lessee is in a position to call for a
new lease, the rent then payable must be fixed without regard to the   B
improvements: see the Landlord and Tenants Acts 1954–1969.

3. If, when the lease expires, the lessee goes out, he may be entitled
to compensation in respect of the improvements to the extent to which
they add to the letting value.

These facts would be known to any surveyor called on to fix a
reasonable rent.   C

In the light of this one has to ask: would a rent, taking into account
the physical existence of the improvements and nothing more, be a
reasonable rent?   The answer to this is surely negative.   It is not reasonable: (a) For a lessee who has spent £32,000, at an interest cost maybe of
£3,200 per annum, to pay rent on the product of this expenditure for the
rest of the term—even if it gets some compensation at the end of the
lease.   (b) For a lessee, who on a renewed lease would pay rent on a   D
basis which disregarded the improvements, to pay rent during the current
lease on a basis which did not disregard them.   (c) For a lessor, who
could not exact an increased rent on licensing the improvements, to obtain
one at a later date by use of the rent review clause, the purpose of such a
clause being to adjust the rent for inflation and market changes.

If, at the present time, the lessors were to say to the lessee " we are   E
asking you to pay an increased rent which, of course, takes account of the
improvements you have made to my premises " the lessee would surely
say " That is most unreasonable."   And conversely, if the lessee were to
say " I offer to pay you an increased rent taking into account inflation
since 1968, the rise/fall in market demand and the fact that I paid
for the improvements made in 1969 " the lessors would surely say " Fair
enough."   F

If the meaning of " reasonable " is not such as to admit the considerations to which I have referred, I must ask what is its meaning or what is
the " reasonable rent " referred to in the clause.   The answer given to
this is that the rent is the market rent.   Then, when the question is asked
why, if this is so, the clause does not so state, the answer given is that the
word reasonable is put in so as to exclude a freak rent which some extra-   G
ordinary lessee might offer.   I must say that I find this a very lame
argument.   A market rent, or a rack rent, is one thing: a reasonable rent
is another.   A reasonable market rent is a hybrid which I cannot understand, and the clause, understandably, does not use these words.

In support of their argument, the respondents and the majority in
the Court of Appeal appeal to a judgment of Megarry J. in a case: *Cuff*
v. *J. & F. Stone Property Co. Ltd. (Note)* [1978] 3 W.L.R. 256.   The   H
actual decision in that case could not be supported except upon the
basis of a concession made by counsel in the case which was plainly
wrong.   But reliance was, naturally, having regard to its source, placed
upon the reasoning of the judge.   I hope I do justice to it by summarising it in this way: to allow the surveyor to explore questions who
paid for the improvements would be to embark upon an uncharted
sea of what might be moral and ethical considerations—such as might

A interest a philosopher or a theologian, but could not be part of a valuation process. And the lessee's contention involves other difficulties: what would happen if the improvements were paid for not by the lessee but by a subsidiary or related company? I am not impressed by these latter difficulties: if such payments were made they must surely be on account of or on behalf of the lessee and taken into account as such. And that to take them into account is a normal process of valuation is surely shown
B by the terms of section 34 of the Landlord and Tenant Act 1954 which requires a market rent to be fixed, there being disregarded any effect on rent of any improvement carried out by the tenant. "Disregards" of this kind are part of the daily work of surveyors, which they can and do carry out without assuming the mantle of other callings.

My Lords, clear words may sometimes force the courts into solutions
C which are unjust and in such cases the court cannot rewrite the contract. This is not such a case: in my opinion logic and justice point in the same, not opposite, directions. I cannot attribute any other meaning to "reasonable rent" in this context than one which takes into account (or disregards) what any lessor, any lessee, or any surveyor would consider it reasonable to take into account (or disregard). In this case the surveyor should disregard any effect on rent of improvements carried out (viz.
D paid for) by the lessee.

I agree with the judgment of Roskill L.J. and would allow the appeal.

VISCOUNT DILHORNE. My Lords, by a lease dated August 19, 1968, the respondents' predecessors in title leased to the appellants a factory at Barking for a term of 21 years from June 24, 1968, at a yearly rent of
E £9,000 during the first seven years of the term and during the second and third seven years of the term at a rent of £9,000 " or such sum whichever be the higher as shall be assessed as a reasonable rent for the demised premises for the appropriate period."

The lease made provision for the reasonable rent for the demised premises for those periods to be agreed between the parties, and if they failed to agree, for it to be assessed by an independent surveyor appointed
F by them. If they failed to agree on a surveyor, it provided for his appointment by the President of the Royal Institute of Chartered Surveyors.

The factory buildings were destroyed by fire. They were rebuilt with the use of the insurance moneys with improvements wanted and paid for by the lessees who obtained a licence dated November 14, 1969, from
G the lessors to make them. These improvements included the addition of a bay to the factory and the installation of central heating. They cost £31,780.

It is common ground that the improvements made by the lessees formed part of the demised premises and the question on which there has been and is much division of judicial opinion is whether, when assessing a reasonable rent for the demised premises, regard should be had to the
H fact that the improvements were paid for by the lessees. If in consequence of them, the rent was assessed at a higher figure than it would otherwise have been, the lessees say that is not fair. They should not, they say, be required to pay rent on account of expenditure they have made on their landlord's property. They point out that if the lease had been for only seven years and they had been granted a new tenancy by order of the court under Part II of the Landlord and Tenant Act 1954 as amended by the Law of Property Act 1969 and the rent for that tenancy

fell to be determined by the court, the effect of the improvements on the   A
rent for which the holding might reasonably be expected to be let in the
open market by a willing lessor would have had to be disregarded by
section 34.   It would be highly anomalous that they should have to pay a
higher rent on a review under the lease they had for the second and, it
may be, for the third periods of seven years than that which they would
have had to pay on the grant of a new lease under the Act.   What, they
say, has to be determined on a review of the rent is what is a reasonable   B
rent for them to pay for the demised premises and they contend that it
would not be reasonable to require them to pay anything on account of
the improvements they had made.

Our task can indeed be simply stated.   It is just to decide the meaning
of the words " assessed as a reasonable rent for the demised premises."
Their meaning is not altered or affected by the fact that in 1954 Parlia-   C
ment decided that in assessing the rent of a new tenancy granted under
the Landlord and Tenant Act, the effect of improvements such as those
made in this case was to be disregarded.   Lessors and lessees are usually
advised by lawyers on the terms of leases.   If the parties to this lease had
agreed that the effect of improvements was to be disregarded in assessing
the rent, that could easily have been stated and if that had been agreed,
I expect it would have been.   A precedent which could be adapted is in   D
section 34 of the Landlord and Tenant Act.   In the absence of any such
express provision as Parliament thought it necessary to include in section
34, I do not think that one is entitled to conclude that by the use of the
words " assessed as a reasonable rent for the demised premises " the
parties were seeking to express their agreement that in assessing the rent,
the effect of improvements made by the lessees was to be disregarded.   E

If it be thought to be unfair, as Parliament clearly thought it unfair,
that a tenant should pay a rent which reflected the value of the improvements made by him, that is no ground for interpreting the words in
question as the appellants contend.   It is not for us to re-write the lease.
It may be that the parties in 1968 did not consider what was to be the
effect on the assessment of the rent if the lessees made improvements.
One does not know, but just as I see no grounds for supposing that they   F
did consider it, I see no ground for concluding, if they did consider it,
that the landlords agreed that the effect of improvements should be
excluded.

Rent review provisions are now commonly included in leases at the
instance of lessors to give them some protection against inflation.   If
they were not included, landlords might only be disposed to let for a   G
shorter term.   Their object is to secure that in real terms the rent payable
does not fall below that initially agreed on.   It was not disputed in this
case that that is their main object.   In the present case and in many
others provision is made for the assessment to be made by an independent
surveyor.   What has he to do?   Surely it is to assess what rent the
demised premises would command if let on the terms of the lease and
for the period the assessed rent is to cover at the time the assessment falls   H
to be made.   That rent may depend to some extent on local factors such
as deterioration of the neighbourhood.   In assessing it, the surveyor will
be assessing the reasonable rent that others, not just the sitting tenant,
would be prepared to pay for the use and occupation of the premises.   He
will not consider the tenant's position separately.

It may be said that this is treating a reasonable rent for the demised
premises as the rent obtainable on the open market and that the decision

A   in *John Kay Ltd.* v. *Kay* [1952] 2 Q.B. 258 shows this to be wrong.   That
was a decision on section 12 of the Leasehold Property (Temporary
Provisions) Act 1951 which gave the court power to grant a tenancy " at
such rent and on such terms and conditions as the court in all the circumstances thinks reasonable," and it was held that that did not mean the
rent which the property would fetch if offered in the open market as
property to let.   If the wording of this lease had been similar to that,
B   the surveyor would in my opinion have been entitled, indeed would have
been bound, to have regard to the particular circumstances of the tenant.
I do not think that the decision in that case affords any support for the
view that the task of the surveyor under the lease was not to assess what
would be paid in rent for the use and occupation of the demised premises
if offered to let on the open market.   What significance then is to be
C   attached to the word " reasonable "?   I think that it was included to give
the surveyor some latitude.   He might know that if the premises were to
let, there was someone who would be prepared to offer an exceptionally
high rent for their use.   The use of the word " reasonable " would enable
him to disregard that.

   The rent payable by the lessees will of course be rent for the demised
premises but as I see it, the task of the surveyor is not to assess what
D   would be a reasonable rent for the lessees to pay but what is a reasonable
rent for the premises.   That, when assessed, is payable by the lessees.   If
the effect of the improvements on the rent payable is to be disregarded,
then the lessees will not be paying a reasonable rent for the demised
premises but a reasonable rent for the demised premises less the improvements; but it is recognised that the improvements are part of the demised
E   premises.   If the effect on the rent of the improvements is to be disregarded then in my opinion an express provision is required to effect that
as was necessary in the Landlord and Tenant Act.

   In *Cuff* v. *J. & F. Stone Property Co. Ltd. (Note)* [1978] 3 W.L.R.
256, Megarry J. also had to consider a provision for the review of rent
in a lease in all material respects similar to that under consideration in
F   this case.   He too had to consider the meaning of the words " assessed as
a reasonable rent for the demised premises."   In the course of his judgment which I found illuminating and with which I respectfully entirely
agree he said, at p. 259c:

   " There is nothing save the expression ' reasonable rent ' to give
   colour to the view that anything save pure matters of valuation are
   to be considered . . . it seems to me to put an impossibly heavy burden
G   on the word ' reasonable ' in this lease to say that it allows and
   requires the surveyor to explore questions of who paid for the improvements, and in appropriate cases to allow some discount for this,
   calculated on an unspecified basis."

He held, at p. 259H that " the surveyor must take the premises as he finds
them, and then determine what he considers to be a reasonable rent for
H   those premises, regardless of who provided them or paid for them."

   Roskill L.J. in his dissenting judgment in the present case attached
great importance to the different factual background in that case.   There
the improvements had been made some 12 years before and so the
phrase " the demised premises " clearly included the improvements when
the lease was executed.   In the present case it is not disputed that
" demised premises " included the improvements made after the lease was
executed and this being so, I do not myself see that the fact that in *Cuff*

v. *J. & F. Stone Property Co. Ltd. (Note)* [1978] 3 W.L.R. 256 the   A
improvements were made before the lease was entered into affords any
ground for distinguishing that case from this. In that case there had
been a lease to J. & F. Stone Lighting and Radio Ltd. and on March 3,
1966, when the lease was expiring, the court made an order for the grant
of a new lease. No doubt the rent fixed by the court disregarded the
effect of the improvements but the defendants in the action tried by
Megarry J. were not the lessees in whose favour the court had made the   B
order. It appears from Megarry J.'s judgment that the form of the lease
they entered into was agreed between them and their landlords. Whether
the rent review provision he had to consider was a term of the tenancy
which the court ordered to be granted, the judgment does not reveal, but
it would not affect the meaning of the provision in my opinion if it was.

Roskill L.J. also wondered whether Megarry J. would have reached   C
the same conclusion if it had not been conceded for the lessees that the
improvements were not simply to be disregarded but I do not see any
reason to suppose that Megarry J. would have come to a different conclusion if that concession had not been made.

Megarry J. had to decide the meaning of the words used in the lease,
as we have to do, and I do not see how the factual background or the
concession to which I have referred can properly be considered as aids to   D
the determination of the meaning of ordinary English words.

In my opinion Cairns L.J. and Sir Gordon Willmer came to the right
conclusion in this case, and were it not for the division of opinion in this
House, I would have been content simply to say that I agreed with them
and Megarry J. and with their reasoning.

In my opinion this appeal should be dismissed.   E

LORD SALMON. My Lords, the relevant facts and the terms of the
lease have been fully set out in the speech of my noble and learned
friend, Lord Wilberforce, and I shall not repeat them in any detail. I
would however emphasise that the lease was for a period of 21 years and
provided for a rent of £9,000 a year reviewable in the seventh and
fourteenth year of the term so that in the second and third seven year   F
periods, the rent should be £9,000 a year " or such sum whichever be the
higher as shall be assessed as a reasonable rent for the demised premises."

This appeal turns solely upon the true meaning of the words " a
reasonable rent." Considerable stress was laid by Mr. Price and the
majority of the Court of Appeal on the words " for the demised premises."
I am afraid that I do not understand how those words can afford any real   G
help in construing the words " a reasonable rent " as used in the lease.
After all, the rent fixed by the lease could hardly be a rent for anything
other than the demised premises. Moreover, it is plain, as the landlords
have always conceded, that when the demised premises were rebuilt,
extended and improved after the fire which took place in the first year of
the 21-year term, the cost of the extension and improvements, amounting
to £31,780, was voluntarily paid by the tenants. By a well established   H
legal principle the extension and improvements became part of the
demised premises, but this does not mean that in assessing a reasonable
rent for the tenant to pay, it would be possible to increase the rent because
of the additions and improvements to the landlords' premises which the
tenant had made at his own expense.

The case for the landlords really turns on the argument, with which I
disagree, that " a reasonable rent " for the demised premises must mean

A the open market rent for the demised premises. If the parties had meant the open market rent, they would, no doubt, have said so, as they usually do.

Two appeals were recently heard together in your Lordships' House namely *United Scientific Holdings Ltd.* v. *Burnley Borough Council* [1977] 2 W.L.R. 806 and *Cheapside Land Development Co. Ltd.* v. *Messels Service Co.* [1977] 2 W.L.R. 806. As appears from your Lordships' speeches,

B virtually every reported case relating to rent revision clauses was drawn to your Lordships' attention upon the hearing of those appeals. I have again looked at these cases, and in each of them the rent revision clause clearly provides that the tenant shall pay the open market rent at the time of review or the original rent whichever should be the higher. If the provision in the present lease for revising the rent had been couched in

C similar terms, I would agree with the majory of the Court of Appeal. Had the parties agreed that the rent should be revised on the basis of open market value, the lessees would be bound by their agreement to accept a revision on that basis however unfair and unreasonable the result might turn out to be in the special circumstances of the case.

In the present case, however, the rent revision provision calls for the rent to be revised on the basis of " a reasonable rent," which, for reasons

D I shall presently attempt to explain, can, and in this case does, mean something quite different from an open market rent. Although there may be cases in which a rent review clause has provided for review on the basis of a reasonable rent, I have been unable to discover any such case which has come before the courts other than the present case and the unreported case of *Cuff* v. *J. & F. Stone Property Co. Ltd.* (*Note*) [1978]

E 3 W.L.R. 256 to which I shall later return. One, if only one, of the reasons why that case was apparently thought not to be worth reporting may have been that its rent revision clause may have seemed to be sui generis.

A lease constitutes a contract between a landlord and a tenant, binding them, their successors and assigns, under which it is agreed that the landlord shall let and the tenant shall rent premises on the terms set out

F in the lease. If the lease provides for a rent review in the same terms as the lease under consideration, I am convinced that the surveyor who, in default of agreement between the parties, assesses the reasonable rent cannot do so in blinkers or in a vacuum. He necessarily must have regard to the relevant circumstances of the case. I know of no other method of deciding what " reasonable " means in a contract, whether it

G be " reasonable time," " reasonable price " or " reasonable rent."

No doubt, in many cases, the reasonable rent will turn out to be the open market rent of the demised premises—but not always; certainly not, in my view, if the demised premises, as in the present case, have been extended and improved by the tenant at his own expense. It is well settled law that the extension and improvements enure for the benefit of

H the landlord—but not twice over, unless this has been expressly agreed by the tenant, as, for example, when the rent review clause provides that the rent shall be reviewed to coincide with the open market rent at the date of the review. I imagine, however, that even in such a case, a tenant who proposed spending a substantial sum of money in making additions and improvements to the demised premises would, before carrying them out, if properly advised by his solicitors, normally insist upon the landlords entering into an agreement that any increase in the open market rental of the premises caused by these additions and improvements should be A disregarded in future rent reviews.

There is, however, no need to enter into a new agreement, if, as in the present case, the lease calls for " a reasonable rent " to be assessed upon the rent review—and means what, in my view, it says, not by implication, but expressly and plainly. Whether or not either party to the lease foresaw, at the time it was executed, all the relevant facts which existed at the date of the rent review, is, to my mind, irrelevant. I agree entirely with B Roskill L.J. that the reviewed rent must be reasonable as between the parties to the lease—a reasonable rent for the lessors to accept and for the lessees to pay, having regard to all the relevant circumstances of the case existing at the date of the rent review.

I do not consider that the ordinary surveyor would have the slightest difficulty in assessing a reasonable rent on the basis I have indicated: C indeed I think he would be astonished to be asked to assess it on any other basis. He would have been called in only because the landlord and the tenant were unable to agree between themselves what would be a reasonable rent for the tenant to pay during the next seven years. I do not know of any legal principle or sound authority which requires the surveyor, in assessing the reasonable rent, to shut his eys to what any surveyor would regard as a vitally relevant factor, namely that the exten- D sions and improvements to the demised premises had been paid for by the tenant out of his own pocket. He would recognise that the additions and improvements to the premises would, in all probability, enure to the benefit of the lessor when he recovers possession of the premises and that, quite apart from a possible double benefit for the lessor, it would be most unreasonable for him to recover a higher rent from the tenant on account E of additions and improvements which the tenant had made to the premises entirely at his own expense and with the landlords' consent.

I think that any competent and experienced surveyor would estimate the open market rent of the whole of the demised premises at the date of the review and, in fixing the reasonable rent, would discount from the open market rent that part of it attributable solely to the additions and improvements which had been made at the tenant's expense. This F appears to me to accord with common sense and justice.

Nor am I discouraged in this view by the fact that section 34 of the Landlord and Tenant Act 1954, as amended by section 1 (1) of the Law of Property Act 1969, provides:

" The rent payable under a tenancy granted by order of the court under this Part of this Act . . . may be determined by the court to G be that at which, having regard to the terms of the tenancy (other than those relating to rent), the holding might reasonably be expected to be let in the open market by a willing lessor, there being disregarded—. . . (c) any effect on rent of an improvement to which this paragraph applies."

I refer to this section solely because the reason why Parliament made H this provision is obviously because Parliament realised that it would be unreasonable for a tenant who, at his own expense, had made improvements to the demised premises to have his rent increased as a result of those improvements; and that it would be none the less unreasonable because the tenant might, at some future date, obtain some compensation for those improvements from the landlord under sections 1 and 2 of the Landlord and Tenant Act 1927.

A   I do not understand how in assessing a " reasonable rent," a surveyor
can be required to take an element into account which would make the
rent unreasonable. Nor do I understand how the majority of the Court
of Appeal who recognised that the decision at which they arrived with
reluctance was unfair could have regarded the rent which that decision
produced as reasonable. This seems to me to be a contradiction in terms.
As appears from their judgment they were however very much influenced
B by *Cuff* v. *J. & F. Stone Property Co. Ltd.* *(Note)* [1978] 3 W.L.R. 256,
Before dealing with that authority, I must refer to one of the arguments
on behalf of the landlords in support of their proposition that " a reasonable rent " should be construed as necessarily having the same meaning
as the open market rent. The argument was that the word " reasonable "
was introduced into the lease before the word " rent " to give the surveyor
C some latitude, which he has in any event. It would enable the surveyor,
so the argument ran, to disregard a freak rent which he knew that someone might be prepared to offer for the demised premises. This, in my
respectful view, is a wholly untenable argument. No self-respecting
surveyor would take into account a fantastically high or fantastically
low rent in assessing an open market rent any more than he would do so
in assessing a reasonable rent.

D   I will now deal shortly with *Cuff* v. *J. & F. Stone Property Co. Ltd.*
which raised exactly the same question for consideration as the instant
case. In my opinion, the decision in *Cuff's* case was wrong and the
grounds on which it was based are unsound for the reasons I have already
indicated, and which are as applicable to that case as they are to the
present case. It is fair to say that in *Cuff's* case, counsel for the tenant
E conceded that the improvements made at the tenant's expense could not
be wholly disregarded by the surveyor in assessing " a reasonable rent for
the demised premises " under the rent revision clause. It may be that but
for that unfortunate concession the learned judge might have come to a
different conclusion. The learned judge said, at pp. *(Note)* [1978] 3
W.L.R. 259D–F, in a passage quoted with approval by Cairns L.J. [1977]
1 W.L.R. 1029, 1034–5:

F   " . . . it seems to me to put an impossibly heavy burden on the word
          ' reasonable ' . . . to say that it . . . requires the surveyor to explore
          questions of who [had] paid for the improvements, and . . . to allow
          some discount for this, calculated on an unspecified basis. . . . If one
          accepts to the full that ' reasonable ' means ' right and fair,' one
          may still say that it means ' right and fair ' in a valuation sense,
G   without extending it to the whole range of moral and ethical con-
          siderations. I say nothing of the improbable case of a reasonable
          rent which is to be assessed not by a surveyor but by a philosopher
          or theologian; but I do say that . . . a provision for a reasonable rent
          to be assessed by a surveyor . . . will not cast the survey loose upon
          uncharted and perhaps unchartable ethical seas such as these."

H   To assess " a reasonable rent " does not call for the surveyor to
embark upon charted or unchartable moral or ethical seas. All he has to
take into consideration are the relevant business factors applying to the
case. I cannot see that it would cast any burden on the surveyor to find
out as easily as the judge did what additions and improvements the tenant
had made to the demised premises at his own expense, and then to assess a
reasonable rent on the basis I explained earlier in this speech.
          The following passage in the judgment in *Cuff's* case, at post, 259H,

A

was also quoted with approval by Cairns L.J.: " The question is not that of the rent ' which it would be reasonable for the tenant to pay,' but that of a ' reasonable rent for the demised premises. . . .' " I can see no difference between these two formulations. In my opinion, they both mean a rent which, in all the relevant circumstances, it would be reasonable for the tenant to pay and for the landlord to accept. It cannot, in my opinion, be reasonable to increase the rent to be paid by the tenant because of the additions and improvements the tenant has made to the demised premises at his own expense. Any rent increased because of such additions and improvements could not, in my opinion, sensibly be regarded as a " reasonable rent " within the ordinary and natural meaning of those words.

B

My Lords, for the reasons I have indicated I would allow the appeal.

C

LORD FRASER OF TULLYBELTON. My Lords, I need not repeat the facts of this case, as they have already been fully set out in the speech of my noble and learned friend, Viscount Dilhorne, with whose reasoning and conclusions I entirely agree.

The only question for decision in the appeal relates to the proper construction of a few words in the lease. The words occur in clause 1 which provides that, during the second and third seven-year periods of the lease, the yearly rent shall be £9,000 " or such sum whichever shall be the higher as shall be assessed as a reasonable rent for the demised premises for the appropriate period . . ." There is no dispute that " the demised premises," which originally meant the factory described in clause 1 of the lease, now means the factory as rebuilt after the fire, including the improvements made at the expense of the tenants, with the approval of the landlord given in a licence dated November 14, 1969. The premises would have included the improvements without express provision to that effect, on the principle that anything made part of the premises by the tenants enures to the landlord, but provision to that effect was in fact made in clause 3 of the licence, which is in the following terms:

D

E

F

" It is hereby agreed and declared that all the lessees' covenants and conditions contained in the lease which are now applicable to the premises demised thereby shall continue to be applicable to the same when and as altered and shall extend to all additions which may be made thereto in the course of such alterations."

G

The question therefore becomes what is meant by " a reasonable rent " in the context, and the reference to the demised premises is relevant only as part of the context. In my opinion the words point unambiguously to the result contended for by the landlords (the respondents), and they mean the reasonable rent assessed on an objective basis, without reference to the particular landlord or the particular tenant or to the history of how the premises came to be built or paid for. Regard must, of course, be had to the terms of the lease, because its provisions with regard to duration, responsibility for repairs and other matters may affect the rent, but their effect would be the same whoever the landlord or the tenant might be. It is true that the words " for the demised premises " do not add anything new, because there is no doubt about the identity of the premises for which the rent is payable, but in my opinion the words are of importance because they emphasise that the assessment is to be made by reference to the premises and not by reference to wider considerations or to what would

H

A be reasonable between this particular landlord and tenant. I respectfully agree with Sir Gordon Willmer in the Court of Appeal, and with
Megarry J. in his opinion in the *Cuff* v. *J. & F. Stone Property Co. Ltd.*
(Note) [1978] 3 W.L.R. 256, that the position might have been different if
the lease had provided for the rent fixed on a review to be that " which it
would be reasonable for the tenants to pay." The emphasis would then
have been shifted to the circumstances affecting the particular tenant as in
B *John Kay Ltd.* v. *Kay* [1952] 2 Q.B. 258. But those are not the words
we have to construe.

The whole weight of the tenants' case rests on the word " reasonable." It is said that if the rent were to be increased because of the
improvements for which the tenants themselves have paid, that would be
unfair and the rent would therefore not be reasonable. With all respect
C to those who think otherwise, that argument seems to me to be unsound
for several reasons. In the first place the description of the rent as
" reasonable " is quite insufficient to displace the objective standard which
in my opinion is indicated by the clause as a whole. I think that the effect
of the word " reasonable " is to exclude any exceptional or freak rent that
might have had to be taken into account if the clause had referred to the
open market rent. In the second place, having regard to the provisions
D contained in sections 1 and 2 of the Landlord and Tenant Act 1927 for
compensation to tenants in certain circumstances for improvements made
by them, I am not satisfied that the result of the landlords' construction
of the clause is so unfair as has been suggested. Those sections are not
referred to in the opinions of any of the learned judges in the Court of
Appeal and they may not have been present to the minds of Cairns L.J.
E and Sir Gordon Willmer when they said that they reached their decision
with regret. The possibility of compensation at the end of the lease may
not be so satisfactory to the tenants as a lower rent during the remainder
of the lease after the first review date, but it goes some way to meet their
complaint. Thirdly, whether I am right or wrong in regarding the
possibility of compensation under the Act of 1927 as relevant, and even
if the result may seem harsh or unfair from the tenants' point of view,
F I would not regard that as sufficient reason for departing from what seems
to me to be the proper construction of the words used. The lease is an
elaborate document and the tenants presumably took legal advice before
entering into it. They are a business concern, able to look after their
own interest, and there is nothing to suggest that they were misled or
taken advantage of in any way. It is most unlikely that either party had
this problem in mind when the terms of the lease were agreed. If the
G parties intended that the general law was to be varied by special provisions
in favour of the tenants, the time to make such provisions would have
been when the licence for improvements was granted by the landlords, but
that was not done. The problem has therefore to be solved by reference
to the lease alone: it contains no express provisions in favour of the
tenants on this matter and in my opinion it cannot, without distortion, be
H construed as making such provisions by implication.

The meaning of the clause appears to me to be free from ambiguity,
and I do not consider that your Lordships would be justified in giving it an
artificial construction because of any apparent anomaly that may exist
between it and section 34 of the Landlord and Tenant Act 1954. The
effect of that section is that, when a new lease is granted under Part II
of the Act of 1954, the rent is not liable to be increased because of
improvements carried out by the tenant or his predecessors in title, but

circumstances in which section 34 applies are not those in which the   A
question arises here.   It is not material for the present purpose.

I would dismiss the appeal.

LORD KEITH OF KINKEL.   My Lords, this appeal raises a short but
very difficult question as to the proper construction of a rent review
clause in a lease.

The lease is one on industrial premises for a term of 21 years from   B
June 26, 1968.   It provided for a yearly rent of £9,000 during the first
seven years of the term and during the second and third seven years the
sum of £9,000 " or such sum whichever be the higher as shall be assessed
as a reasonable rent for the demised premises."   That assessment was to
be made, failing agreement between the parties, by an independent
surveyor.   C

The particular problem to be resolved arises in this way.   At an early
stage in the life of the lease the tenants desired that, in the course of the
reconstruction of the premises following a fire, certain improvements
should be incorporated at their expense.   The landlords granted a formal
licence for these improvements dated November 16, 1969, which provided
inter alia,

> " all the lessees' covenants and conditions contained in the lease   D
> which are now applicable to the premises demised thereby shall
> continue to be applicable to the same when and as altered and shall
> extend to all additions which may be made thereto in the course of
> such alterations."

The improvements were duly carried out at a cost to the tenants of some
£32,000.   The question to be determined is whether, upon a proper con-   E
struction of the words I have quoted above, account is to be taken in
assessing a reasonable rent for the demised premises for the second period
of seven years of the circumstance that the improvements in question
were paid for by the tenants.

At first impression the words " reasonable rent for the demised premises " suggest that what has to be ascertained is simply the rent that is   F
reasonable for the premises as such in their actual state, the situation
being viewed entirely objectively. " The demised premises " must mean
the demised premises as improved, by virtue both of the ordinary law
and of the passage I have quoted from the licence agreement.   So upon
this view any contribution the improvements might have made to rental
value would have to enter into the assessment.   G

It was however argued for the tenants that to proceed in that way
would involve assessment of the rent on the basis of market value,
whereas the lease provided for a different basis, namely that of a " reasonable " rent.   It was not maintained that the assessment should be made
upon the assumption that the improvements did not exist, but it was said
that any assessment of a " reasonable " rent could not ignore that the
improvements had been paid for by the tenants.   Otherwise an unreason-   H
able result would be reached and one which was unfair to the tenants,
considering that the landlords had not contributed to any increase of
rental value resulting from the improvements and that their capital value
would enure to the landlords' benefit at the expiry of the lease.

It must be recognised, in my view, that, if the approach is to be a
purely objective one, it is difficult to perceive any difference in meaning
between " a reasonable rent " and " the market rent," and so there is

A force in the argument that if the parties had intended a purely objective
assessment they would have used the latter expression, which is in
common use in contexts such as this one. I am not impressed by the
suggestion that the expression " a reasonable rent " might have been used
merely in order to exclude any freak or special rent that a prospective
tenant might be prepared to pay, because I think that in estimating the
market rent a valuer would proceed on the general level of rents for
B comparable premises without reference to any such freak or special rent.
I regard it as a proper inference that when agreeing on the terms of the
rent review clause the parties did not have present to their minds the
situation which might arise by reason of the execution by the tenants of
improvements, because I consider that if they had they would have made
specific provision about the application of the clause to that situation.
C But whether or not that is correct the clause must have been envisaged
as capable of operating in respect of the original unimproved premises.
Would the surveyor then have reached any different result than if he had
simply been instructed to ascertain the market rent? I would think not,
because I am not able to envisage any circumstances which he would take
into or leave out of account in one case but not in the other. It may be,
of course, that in the surveying profession " a reasonable rent " is well
D known to bear a particular meaning distinct from that of " the market
rent," but there is no available material to indicate whether or not that is
so. As it is, I consider that in either case the surveyor would have regard
to the condition of the premises, the terms and provisions of the lease, and
the general level of rent for comparable premises in the same locality or
in similar localities, and I would not expect any difference in the resulting
E assessment. Even if the difference of wording were intended to lead to
a different approach to the rent review, it is to be expected that the
different approach would be capable of application where there had been
no improvements.
   That being so in the normal case, does the difference of wording lead
to a different result when the tenant has carried out improvements at his
own expense? I think it could do so only if there were ground for
F inferring that the particular wording used here was used in contemplation
of that particular situation, and, as I have already said, I do not consider
that such grounds exist. Further, I cannot think that parties can have
had in view the additional factor that any licence agreement for improvements would fail to make provision for the manner in which the improvements were to be dealt with on a rent review.
G   In my opinion the words " a reasonable rent for the demised premises "
simply mean " the rent at which the demised premises might reasonably
be expected to let." Considering that the demised premises necessarily
include the improvements, to arrive at a lower rent by reason that the
tenants paid for the latter would in substance mean that a rent for part
only of the demised premises was being assessed. The fact that the
assessed rent leads to an unreasonable result as between the particular
H tenant and the particular landlord does not mean that it is not a reasonable rent for the premises. The unreasonable result is due to circumstances which were not in contemplation when the terms of the rent
review clause were agreed, and which were therefore not expressly provided for. They might have been expressly provided for at the stage
when the licence for the improvements came to be granted, but they
were not. I consider that the construction which the tenants would place
upon the review clause involves a severe straining of the language used

and is not the correct one. I therefore reach the conclusion that the A
decision of the majority of the Court of Appeal was right.

Reference was made in the course of the argument to a number of
statutory provisions regulating, in certain circumstances, the relationship
of landlord and tenant of business premises, in particular section 34 of
the Landlord and Tenant Act 1954. Section 34 is of some significance, in
my view, as indicating the need, when it is desired that certain matters
including improvements carried out by a tenant, should be disregarded in B
the assessment of a rent, to provide expressly for this. But apart from
that I do not consider that any of the provisions referred to are of
assistance in resolving the present problem of construction.

Reference was also made to the decision of Megarry J. in *Cuff* v. *J. &
F. Stone Property Ltd. (Note)* [1978] 3 W.L.R. 256, finding in favour
of the landlords in circumstances closely akin to those of the instant case. C
While I should not be disposed to adopt the whole of the reasoning
of the judge in that case, I agree with him at pp. 259E–F, H, that the
expression " reasonable rent " is to be read in a valuation sense, and that
" the surveyor must take the premises as he finds them, and then determine what he considers to be a reasonable rent for those premises,
regardless of who provided them or paid for them."

My Lords, for these reasons I would dismiss the appeal. D

Appeal dismissed.

Solicitors: *Tarlo, Lyons & Aukin; Gamlens.*

F. C.

E

NOTE

[CHANCERY DIVISION]

CUFF *v.* J. & F. STONE PROPERTY CO. LTD. F

1973   Dec. 13   Megarry J.

*Landlord and Tenant — Rent — " Reasonable rent " — Rent review
clause providing for " such sum as shall be assessed as a
reasonable rent for the demised premises "—Improvements by
previous tenants—Whether assessment to have regard to who G
made improvements*

ORIGINATING SUMMONS

On November 21, 1966, Hugh Jerome Cuff (" the landlord ")
granted to J. & F. Stone Property Co. Ltd. (" the tenants ") a lease
for 14 years of No. 80 High Street North in the London Borough
of Newham. The clause material herein was as follows:

" . . . the yearly rent payable by the lessee during the last H
seven years of the term hereby granted shall be the sum of
£2,400 . . . or such sum as shall be assessed as a reasonable
rent for the demised premises for the said period "

When the review clause fell to be operated differences arose as
to whether or not certain improvements made to the premises were
to be disregarded in the assessment. An originating summons
was issued on behalf of the landlord to determine this question,
the tenants being defendants.

The facts are set out in the judgment of Megarry J.

A   The following cases are referred to in the judgment:

English Exporters (London) Ltd. v. *Eldonwall Ltd.* [1973] Ch. 415;
　　[1973] 2 W.L.R. 435; [1973] 1 All E.R. 726.
Kay (John) Ltd. v. *Kay* [1952] 2 Q.B. 258; [1952] 1 All E.R. 813, C.A.
"Wonderland," Cleethorpes, In re [1965] A.C. 58; [1963] 2 W.L.R. 1426;
　　[1963] 2 All E.R. 775, H.L.(E.).

B   E. J. *Prince* for the plaintiff.
C. B. *Priday* for the defendant company.

MEGARRY J. I have before me an originating summons seeking a declaration. The facts which give rise to the summons may be shortly stated. In
1945 the plaintiff, to whom I shall refer as " the landlord," granted a 21-year
lease of business premises to a company called J. & F. Stone Lighting &
C   Radio Ltd., which I shall call the " lighting company." The lease was at the
modest rent of £275 a year, rising by stages to £325. In 1954 the lighting
company sought and obtained the landlord's permission to make certain
substantial alterations to the premises; and in due course the work was done.
These were building alterations which materially increased the area of the
buildings.

In 1966, when the lease was running to its end, there were proceedings in
D   the Bow County Court in which the lighting company sought a new tenancy
under the Landlord and Tenant Act 1954. On March 3, 1966, the court made
an order for the grant of a new tenancy at a rent of

" £2,400 per annum with rent review at the end of seventh year. New
tenancy for 14 years to commence at termination of current tenancy.
(Under section 64 of the Landlord and Tenant Act)."

E   The rent fixed by the court no doubt gave effect to section 34 of the Landlord
and Tenant Act 1954, which included a provision for the disregarding of

" (c) any effect on rent of any improvement carried out by the tenant or a
predecessor in title of his otherwise than in pursuance of an obligation to
his immediate landlord."

Having obtained that order for a new tenancy, the lighting company requested
F   the landlord to grant the lease not to it, but to another company named
J. & F. Stone Property Co. Ltd., which I shall call the " property company."
That company is the defendant to this summons. There is no evidence before
me as to the relationship between these two companies, though one would
infer from their names and the events that there is some connection.

A form of lease was duly agreed between the landlord and the property
company, and a lease for 14 years was granted, bearing date November 21,
G   1966. This was a demise of

" All that messuage or dwelling house shop and premises known as
Number 80 High Street North in the London Borough of Newham
together with the yard or garden thereto."

In accordance with the order of the county court, provision was made for rent
review. The clause in question reads as follows:

H   " Provided also and it is hereby declared that the yearly rent payable by
the lessee during the last seven years of the term hereby granted shall be
the sum of £2,400 aforesaid or such sum as shall be assessed as a reasonable rent for the demised premises for the said period such assessment
to be made in the following manner that is to say:— either (a) such
assessment as shall be agreed between the parties hereto in writing before
December 25, 1972, (b) in the event of the parties hereto failing to reach
such agreement as aforesaid on or before the date appointed (in respect
of which time is to be deemed to be of the essence of the contract) then

A

the reasonable rent for the last seven years of the term hereby granted shall be fixed or assessed by an independent surveyor appointed for that purpose by the parties hereto or failing agreement as to such appointment by March 25, 1973, (time in this respect to be deemed to be the essence of the contract) then by an independent surveyor appointed for that purpose by the President for the time being of the Royal Institute of Chartered Surveyors. The assessment fixed by the independent surveyor shall be communicated to the parties hereto in writing and immediately upon such communication the rent so assessed as a reasonable rent for the last seven years of the term hereto granted shall be the rent payable for that period under the terms hereof."

B

When the rent review clause fell to be operated, there were at first negotiations between the parties, but in the end a surveyor was appointed. The valuers of each party nevertheless continued their negotiations, and there is some evidence before me to the effect that if the improvements are to be disregarded, the rent will be something of the order of £3,500, whereas if the improvements are to be taken into account, the rent will be of the order of £4,600. A consequence of this difference was that the originating summons was issued; and before me Mr. Prince has appeared for the landlord and Mr. Priday for the property company.

C

What from the summons and the evidence initially appeared to be the question for decision was whether or not the surveyor was to have regard to the improvements. The summons sought a declaration that the rent was to be assessed " without disregarding any improvements " to the demised premises effected by the property company or the lighting company. However, as the argument proceeded it became apparent that this was not the real question between the parties, for Mr. Priday advanced no contention, whether based on section 34 or otherwise, that the improvements should be wholly disregarded. His case was that while he accepted that the improvements should not be wholly disregarded, he asserted that, to put it shortly, the surveyor should temper the effect to be given to the improvements by what he considered to be reasonable. This assertion Mr. Prince rejected. Accordingly, if I were simply to answer the question asked by the summons in its original form, resolving the real issue merely by what I said in my judgment, it seemed to me that there might be difficulties if the unsuccessful party wished to appeal from my order; for an appeal lies against the order rather than the judge's reasons for the order, and an appeal against an order which, in effect, was supported by both parties would present obvious difficulties. The parties therefore agreed an amendment to the summons, so that the plaintiff is now seeking a declaration that the rent is to be assessed without any regard to the fact that the improvements to the premises have been effected by the property company or the lighting company.

D

E

F

Mr. Prince's case was of elemental simplicity. When the lease was granted in 1966 the improvements admittedly formed part of the demised premises. What is to be assessed is " a reasonable rent for the demised premises." In default of agreement, that assessment is to be made by an independent surveyor. Therefore the question is a pure matter of valuing the demised premises in their actual physical condition, disregarding the provenance of the improvements. The valuation is to be on the basis of what rent is reasonable for those premises. Mr. Priday, on the other hand, stressed the distinction between the " market rent " and a " reasonable rent," and pointed to *John Kay Ltd.* v. *Kay* [1952] 2 Q.B. 258, 267. There, Evershed M.R. said:

G

H

" The reasonable rent is arrived at by applying the subjective test of what the judge thinks is right and fair, as distinct, for example, from the objective test of what the evidence shows is the market value."

The surveyor must therefore, said Mr. Priday, say what was the right and fair rent for the premises as they stood; but in doing that he must consider

The Weekly Law Reports, July 21, 1978

259

3 W.L.R.   Cuff v. J. & F. Stone Property Co. (Ch.D.)   Megarry J.

A   not only what was physically there, but also all matters put before him by the parties, including the circumstances in which the improvements were made. He must then duly reflect those circumstances in saying what was a right and fair rent. To the objection that it might be very difficult to say how much of a discount should be allowed for the fact that an improvement had been provided by the tenant or someone associated with him, Mr. Priday answered that just as the question of the rent "which it would be reasonable for the tenant to pay" as an interim rent under the Landlord and Tenant Act 1954,

B   section 24A, might depend on the length of the judge's foot (see *English Exporters (London) Ltd.* v. *Eldonwall Ltd.* [1973] Ch. 415, 433), so in this case the length of the surveyor's foot might be decisive.

I go back to the lease. When it was executed, the improvements had already been made some 12 years earlier. The demise plainly included the improvements as being part of the premises. Not a word is said in the

C   lease about the improvements. The provision for assessing the rent is expressed solely in valuation terms. There is nothing save the expression "reasonable rent" to give colour to the view that anything save pure matters of valuation are to be considered. The ancient principle is that what the tenant makes part of the demised premises enures for the landlord's benefit, subject to rules such as those relating to tenant's fixtures and to any statutory qualifications of the principle. The limited qualification made by section 34 (*c*)

D   of the Landlord and Tenant Act 1954 (on which see *In re "Wonderland," Cleethorpes* [1965] A.C. 58) admittedly contributes nothing to the determination of this case. Though this qualification was relevant when the Bow County Court was determining the initial rent, the rent for the second seven years is purely a creature of the lease. In those circumstances, it seems to me to put an impossibly heavy burden on the word "reasonable" in this lease to say that it allows and requires the surveyor to explore questions of who paid for the improvements, and in appropriate cases to allow some discount

E   for this, calculated on an unspecified basis. What sort of deduction should be allowed if the improvements were paid for by the tenant itself, or partly by the tenant and partly by a subsidiary company, an associated company, or a related company, or wholly by such a company? If one accepts to the full that "reasonable" means "right and fair," one may still say that it means "right and fair" in a valuation sense, without extending it to the whole range of moral and ethical considerations. I say nothing of the improbable case of

F   a reasonable rent which is to be assessed not by a surveyor but by a philosopher or theologian; but I do say that in the absence of provisions sufficiently indicating the contrary, a provision for a reasonable rent to be assessed by a surveyor to be appointed, in default of agreement, by the President of the Royal Institution of Chartered Surveyors will not cast the surveyor loose upon uncharted and perhaps unchartable ethical seas such as these. The word "reasonable" no doubt requires the surveyor to reject a rent which, though

G   obtainable in the open market by reason of special circumstances, appears to him to exceed the rent for the premises which is right and fair; but I do not think that it does more than that.

If the formula used in the lease had been the formula relating to interim rent that fell to be considered in the *Eldonwall* case [1973] Ch. 415, namely, the "rent which it would be reasonable for the tenant to pay," Mr. Priday's hand might perhaps have been strengthened; for such language more readily

H   admits of a construction which allows regard to be paid to the individual circumstances of the particular tenant. But here there is the bare phrase "reasonable rent," used in relation to the demised premises: the question is not that of the rent "which it would be reasonable for the tenant to pay," but that of "a reasonable rent for the demised premises," and that, as it seems to me, is a matter not affected by who paid for the premises or any part of them. In my view the surveyor must take the premises as he finds them, and then determine what he considers to be a reasonable rent for those premises, regardless of who provided them or paid for them. The point is not

capable of any great elaboration, but it seems to me that the landlord's conten-   A
tions are right, despite Mr. Priday's gallant endeavours to establish the contrary, and that subject to any question that there may be on the precise form
of wording, I should make a declaration as prayed in the amended summons.

Declaration accordingly.

Solicitors: *Moon, Beever & Hewlett; Paisner & Co.*   B

F. C.

[COURT OF APPEAL]

C

HILLBANK PROPERTIES LTD. *v.*
HACKNEY LONDON BOROUGH COUNCIL

TALISMAN PROPERTIES LTD. *v.* SAME

1978   May 10, 11, 12; 26   Lord Denning M.R., Geoffrey Lane   D
and Eveleigh L.JJ.

*Housing—Repairs—Local authority notice—Works required to
bring property to reasonable standard—Cost of required works
exceeding value of house with sitting tenant after repair—
Value of house—Appeal against notices—Discretion of judge
—Financial implications for owners—Relevance—Housing Act
1957 (5 & 6 Eliz. 2, c. 56), ss. 9 (1A) (inserted by Housing Act   E
1969 (c. 33), s. 72), 11 (1) (3), 39 (1)*

Two property companies each owned a terraced house
in Hackney built nearly 100 years ago. Each house had a
sitting tenant and both houses were managed by the same
property managers. The surveyors to the local authority
inspected the houses and notices were served on the owners
under section 9 (1A) of the Housing Act 1957[1] stating that   F
although the houses were not unfit for human habitation
substantial repairs were needed to bring them up to a reasonable standard having regard to their age, character and locality.
Each company was required to execute the works specified in
the notice served on it. The cost of the repairs of each
house was greater than the value of the property with a sitting
tenant both before and after repair but less than the value of
the property with vacant possession after repair. The owners   G
appealed to the county court under section 11 (1) of the Act
of 1957. The judge held that in each case the cost of the
works required to be executed would exceed the value of the
house after repair and that the notices would cause considerable financial loss to the owners; and he quashed the notices.
On appeals by the local authority: —
Held, allowing the appeals, that the local authority had
properly had regard to the matters stated in section 9 (1A)   H
of the Act of 1957 and the notices had been properly served
under that section (post, pp. 264G–H, 270H—271B, 273H); that the
judge had erred in the exercise of his discretion under section
11 (3) of the Act in failing to consider that the owners

[1] Housing Act 1957, s. 9 (1A): see post, p. 266G–H.
S. 11 (1) (3): see post, p. 269A–B.
S. 16 (5): see post, p. 269H.
S. 39 (1): see post, p. 271G.

3 W.L.R.   **Hillbank Properties v. Hackney Council (C.A.)**

A
might have made a substantial profit by getting vacant possession of the houses, by giving undue weight to the
owners' alleged impecuniosity without any conclusive evidence
as to their financial position and by holding that an improvement grant was necessary before notice could be given under
section 9 (1A) of the Act (post, pp. 267c–D, H, 268c, 273A, c, G,
274A); and that accordingly the notices should be restored.

B
    Victoria Square Property Co. Ltd. v. *Southwark London
Borough Council* [1978] 1 W.L.R. 463, C.A. considered.

The following cases are referred to in the judgments:

Bacon v. *Grimsby Corporation* [1950] 1 K.B. 272; [1949] 2 All E.R. 875,
    C.A.
National Coal Board v. *Thorne* [1976] 1 W.L.R. 543; [1976] 2 All E.R.
    478, D.C.

C
Salford City Council v. *McNally* [1976] A.C. 379; [1975] 3 W.L.R. 87;
    [1975] 2 All E.R. 860, H.L.(E.).
Stepney Borough Council v. *Joffe* [1949] 1 K.B. 599; [1949] 1 All E.R.
    256, D.C.
Victoria Square Property Co. Ltd. v. *Southwark London Borough Council*
    [1978] 1 W.L.R. 463; [1978] 2 All E.R. 281, C.A.

D
The following additional case was cited in argument:

Betts v. *Penge Urban District Council* [1942] 2 K.B. 154; [1942] 2 All E.R.
    61, D.C.

APPEALS from Judge Willis sitting at Shoreditch County Court.
    On March 30, 1977, the appellant local authority, the Hackney London
E
Borough Council, served notices under section 9 (1A) of the Housing Act
1957 on Hillbank Properties Ltd. and Talisman Properties Ltd., the
owners of 65, Glyn Road, London, E.5 and 48, Coopersale Road, London,
E.9 respectively, requiring the execution of works of repair. 68, Glyn
Road was occupied by a tenant who sublet half, both tenant and sub-
tenant being protected under the Rent Act 1977. 48, Coopersale Road
had one protected tenant. The owners appealed against the notices.

F
    On December 16, 1977, at the Shoreditch County Court, Judge Willis
held, inter alia, that since the local authority had "never exercised any
discretion at all" he was entitled to substitute his discretion for theirs
under section 9 (1A) that "in the case of each house a capital sum
greatly in excess of the value of the property will . . . have to be spent
and still the value of the house after repairs will be less than the capital
G
sum spent on the repairs," that "the notices will cause considerable
financial loss to the appellants," that "money must be borrowed to carry
out the work," that "it is not reasonable to require the spending of
all this money, when no public funds have been spent on the house"
and he quashed the notices.
    The local authority appealed on the grounds that the judge mis-
directed himself (1) in holding that the authority was only entitled to
H
serve a notice under the section in relation to a property where public
funds had been spent or were available to be spent on it, (2) in taking
into account possible financial detriment to the owners; alternatively, if
possible financial detriment to the owners was a relevant consideration
then the judge failed to take into account all matters relevant to the issue
and in particular whether the house was owner/occupied; what sum has
been paid for the house by the owners and when the same had been
purchased; and what sums, if any, the owners had expended upon the

262

A
house since purchase; (3) in holding that the local authority had not
exercised their discretion under section 9 (1A) of the Act of 1957 and
further that because of this or in any event when considering the matter
himself he should give no weight at all to the decision of the local
authority to serve the notice under the section.

The facts are stated in the judgments of Lord Denning M.R. and
Geoffrey Lane L.J.

B

Anthony Scrivener Q.C. and *William Birtles* for the local authority.
John Colyer Q.C and *Richard Fawls* for the owners.

Cur. adv. vult.

C
May 26. The following judgments were read.

Lord Denning M.R. In Hackney there are two roads of terraced
houses. They were built nearly 100 years ago. The houses have two floors
and are occupied by tenants. They have been inspected by the surveyor
to the local council. He found that they were fit for human habitation,
but that they were in need of repair. He reported it to the local council:
and they served notices on the owners, requiring them to do the repairs
D
necessary to bring them up to a reasonable standard. But the owners
objected. They said that the repairs would cost much more than the
houses are worth. In the face of this objection the circuit judge has set
aside the notices. The local council appeal to this court.

The cases are in the nature of test cases and for this reason: if the
owners do not do the repairs, the houses will in due course become so
E
dilapidated that they will be unfit for human habitation. Once they are
unfit the owners will be in a position to evict the tenants by this means:
they will give an undertaking to the local council that the houses will not
be used for human habitation. On the owners giving such an undertaking, the tenants will no longer be protected by the Rent Acts: see
section 16 (5) of the Housing Act 1957. The owners will then get orders
for possession of the houses. The local council will have to rehouse the
F
tenants. The owners will get vacant possession: and then deal with the
houses to their great advantage. They will do them up and sell them
with vacant possession.

I should have thought that socially this was most undesirable. It
means that the owners are at liberty to let houses get in a state of
gross disrepair: and use it as a means of depriving tenants of their homes.
G
One other thing must be remarked. It is the emergence of the " one
house " company. This is a new phenomenon in the housing world. It
is comparable to the " one ship " company in the shipping world. It can
be used with great advantage by people who form private companies,
sometimes Irish companies or other overseas companies. Such a company
buys one house on mortgage, and then—if liabilities accrue to outside
creditors—the company can be wound up. The mortgagees can sweep up
H
the only asset and the other creditors will go away empty-handed. Often
enough, the promoters will themselves be the mortgagees: and will then
operate so as to take all possible benefit to themselves and inflict all
possible losses on others.

With this introduction, I turn to the two houses in this case. One
is 68, Glyn Road, E.5. It is owned by a company called Hillbank
Properties Ltd. The other is 48, Coopersale Road, E.9. It is owned by

The Weekly Law Reports, July 21, 1978

263

3 W.L.R.   Hillbank Properties v. Hackney Council (C.A.)   Lord Denning M.R.

A a company called Talisman Properties Ltd. Both companies have their address at 27, Victoria Square, London, S.W.1. We know nothing about these two companies. No information was given to the court below about them. All we do know is that both houses are managed by the same property managers. These managers gave evidence that neither company has any money with which to pay for any repairs. Any work on the houses will have to be financed by a loan at normal interest rates
B of 14 per cent. Both houses are occupied, in whole or in part, by sitting tenants.

In 1976 the surveyors to the council inspected the houses and made a detailed list of work required to put them into a reasonable standard of repair, having regard to their age, character and location. The surveyors submitted their reports to the appropriate committee of the council. In
C consequence the council on March 30, 1977, served notice on the owners' agents requiring them to do the works of repair set out in the schedule. The cost of the works was in each case more than the house was worth— if a sitting tenant was there who was protected by the Rent Acts—but the cost was well worth while if the house was vacant. These are the figures:

D
    68, Glyn Road

Value of house in its unrepaired state with sitting tenant therein	£1,700
Cost of repairs	£2,750
	£4,450

E
Value of house after repairs carried out with sitting tenant therein	£2,300
Value of house with vacant possession after works carried out	£7,500

The result is that, with a sitting tenant, the repairs done result in a loss of £2,150: but if, with vacant possession, they result in a profit of £3,050.

F
    48, Coopersale Road

Value of house in its unrepaired state with sitting tenant therein	£1,700
Cost of repairs	£2,900
	£4,600

G
Value of house repaired but with sitting tenant therein	£2,500
Value of house repaired but with vacant possession	£7,500

The result is that, with a sitting tenant, the repairs result in a loss of £2,100: but with vacant possession they result in a profit of £2,900.

I must observe, however, that we do not know the price for which these companies bought the houses. If they bought them at a very low
H price because of the sitting tenants, their profit with vacant possession would be greatly increased.

It is obviously, therefore, of no financial advantage to the owners to repair the houses with a sitting tenant there; because that would involve them in a loss. It is far more to their advantage to allow the houses to go unrepaired and become unfit for human habitation: because in these circumstances they may be able to get the tenant evicted, obtain vacant possession and make a large profit. At any rate, they do not

Lord Denning M.R. Hillbank Properties v. Hackney Council (C.A.) **[1978]**

want to do any repairs. They object very strongly to the notices of repair A
which have been served on them. The judge has quashed the notices.
Was he right?

The law

In considering the problem, it is necessary to bear in mind throughout that these houses were *fit* for human habitation. They were, no B
doubt, in need of repair, but they were *fit* in this sense: that they were
worth repairing. If they had been *unfit*—because the cost of repairs was
more than the houses were worth—the local authority would have had
to condemn them and serve a notice preliminary to a demolition order
under the procedures contained in sections 9 to 39 of the Housing Act
1957 as explained in *Bacon* v. *Grimsby Corporation* [1950] 1 K.B. 272.

The Act of 1957 did not, however, contain any provision for houses C
which were fit for human habitation: that needed repairs to keep them
up to a reasonable standard. This was first provided for in 1969 by
section 72 of the Housing Act 1969. Parliament introduced a new section
into the Housing Act 1957. It is section 9 (1A). It says that the local
authority may serve a notice requiring the owner to do repairs when
they are needed so as to bring a house up to a reasonable standard D
" having regard to its age, character and locality."

The discretion of the local authority

In applying that section the judge said:

" In order to exercise a discretion properly, it is my opinion that the
local authority must put themselves in possession of all the relevant E
facts. They will, of course, pay attention to any official representation or a report from any of their officers or other information
in their possession, but they must also find out about the owner of
the property, the cost of the works, and the value of the property.
These are examples and I do not pretend they are exhaustive."

If the statute had afforded no appeal—or no means of challenging or F
questioning this notice—I would have agreed wholeheartedly with the
judge. I go further. If fairness had demanded that the owner should be
given a hearing before the notice was served, I would agree also. But I
regard this notice as a preliminary step—a preliminary notification—
made by an administrative authority. It is designed to ensure that the
stock of houses is kept in good repair and not allowed to fall into decay. G
So long as the local authority have regard to the matters stated in section
9 (1A) they are not bound to look further. They need not give any prior
warning to the owner. They need not hear him. They need not make
any inquiries of him. They need not inquire into the cost of the works
or the value of the property. So long as they are satisfied that substantial
repairs are required to bring the house up to a reasonable standard,
having regard to its age, character, and locality, that is sufficient to justify H
them in serving the notice: and they can properly be so satisfied by
receiving a report from their officers who have examined the house and
set down its condition and the repairs that are required.

The protection afforded to the owner is his right of appeal to the
county court. If any owner is aggrieved by the notice, he can appeal to
the county court: and on such appeal the judge will hear any objections
that the owner may wish to make against the notice: and may quash

The Weekly Law Reports, July 21, 1978

265

3 W.L.R.   Hillbank Properties v. Hackney Council (C.A.)   Lord Denning M.R.

A it or vary it as he thinks fit: see section 11 (1) (a) and (3) of the Act of 1957, and *Victoria Square Property Co. Ltd.* v. *Southwark London Borough Council* [1978] 1 W.L.R. 463, 473. But here is the point: to what matters is the judge to have regard?

The discretion of the judge

B   The judge held that he was entitled to take into account the individual facts, including " the value of the property, the capital cost of the works and the financial position" of the owners. Applying that principle, he said:

"I have no doubt that the house is not unfit for human habitation and that substantial repairs are required to bring it up to a reasonable standard, but it cannot be right in my view that an individual
C   owner can be required, upon the say-so of [the council], to spend thousands of pounds when at no time were the individual facts considered. In the case of each house, a capital sum in excess of the value of the property will, if the [council] are right, have to be spent and still the value of the house after repairs will be less than the capital sum spent on the repairs. The notices will cause considerable
D   financial loss to the [owners]. Money must be borrowed to carry out the work and still not be recovered by any increase of rent."

       The question is whether the judge directed himself aright in that passage. Each side before us—no doubt for its own purposes—said that the judge was not entitled to take into account the financial position of the owner or his means. But there was a difference as to whether the
E judge was entitled to take into account the fact that the cost of the works exceeded the value of the house.
       In order to determine this question, I propose to consider the meaning of the word " value " in section 39 of the Housing Act 1957.

" The value " in section 39

F   These are the crucial words in section 39. We all know that the value of a house depends greatly on whether it is sold with vacant possession or not. If the purchaser can get vacant possession, he will pay far more than if the house is occupied by a tenant who is protected under the Rent Acts. These two houses are excellent examples. Take no. 68, Glyn Road. It would cost £2,750 to put it into proper repair. If it was put into proper repair and sold with vacant possession, it would
G fetch £7,500. If sold with a protected sitting tenant, it would fetch only £2,300. Similarly with no. 48, Coopersale Road.
       What is the " value " that is spoken of in section 39? Is it the value with vacant possession? Or the value with a sitting protected tenant? Or something in between?
       There is a sentence in *Bacon* v. *Grimsby Corporation* [1950] 1 K.B.
H 272, 283, which looked as if it might be the value with a sitting tenant, but the matter was not discussed in that case, and I do not think it should be regarded in any way as binding. To my mind the value is primarily the value with vacant possession. It must be remembered that, when the Housing Act 1957 was passed, most of the houses in the country had been decontrolled by the Rent Act 1957, so that the owners could obtain vacant possession by giving notice to quit to the tenants. Many of the remaining houses were let furnished and were equally not

protected by the Rent Acts. There were some houses of low rateable **A**
value in which the tenant was still protected if he had been living there
for many years: but these were so few as not to affect the principle.
Parliament can never have intended that the question—Should the house
be condemned or not?—should depend on whether the tenant was protected by the Rent Acts or not. It should depend on whether the house
was so dilapidated that it was not worth the cost of repairing it, irrespective
of the quality of the tenancy.   **B**

This view is confirmed by the fact that, if the house was so dilapidated
as to be condemned, the tenant was no longer protected by the Rent Acts.
The owner could evict him by giving an undertaking to the local authority
under section 16 (4) of the Act of 1957. So he could get vacant possession. This shows that the value of the house (which Parliament had
in mind) was primarily its value with vacant possession.   **C**

In my opinion, therefore, in applying section 39, the " value " of the
house is primarily the value it will have if sold with vacant possession
when the works are completed.

In 1965, control was brought back again. Many tenants became
protected tenants under the Rent Acts. But that does not alter the
meaning of the word in the Act of 1957.   **D**

Applying " value " to these two houses

In the case of these two houses, the value of each of them, when
repaired, with vacant possession was so great that the local authority could
not possibly have condemned them under sections 16 to 18. If the
local authority had considered them *unfit* for human habitation, their
duty would have been to compel the owner to do the repairs by serving **E**
a notice under section 9 (1) and enforcing it by the measures stated in
section 10.

But the local authority did not consider them *unfit* for human habitation. They considered them to be fit. They could not, therefore,
condemn them under sections 16 to 18: nor could they require the owners
to do the repairs under section 9 (1): nor could they invoke the provisions **F**
of the Public Health Act 1936 to secure the doing of the repairs: see
Salford City Council v. *McNally* [1976] A.C. 379, 389, *per* Lord
Wilberforce and *National Coal Board* v. *Thorne* [1976] 1 W.L.R. 543.
Their only recourse therefore—to secure the execution of the repairs—
was section 9 (1A) which was introduced in 1969 by section 72 of the
Housing Act 1969. It reads:

> " (1A) Where a local authority, upon consideration of an official **G**
> representation, or a report from any of their officers, or other infor-
> mation in their possession, are satisfied that a house is in such state
> of disrepair that, although it is not unfit for human habitation,
> substantial repairs are required to bring it up to a reasonable standard,
> having regard to its age, character and locality, they may serve upon
> the person having control of the house a notice requiring him, within **H**
> such reasonable time, not being less than 21 days, as may be specified
> in the notice, to execute the works specified in the notice, not being
> works of internal decorative repair."

The matters to be considered by the judge under section 9 (1A)

There was much discussion before us as to the matters to which the
judge should have regard. I would not myself limit his inquiry by any

The Weekly Law Reports, July 21, 1978

267

3 W.L.R.   Hillbank Properties v. Hackney Council (C.A.)   Lord Denning M.R.

A set limits. So long as the matters are relevant to the issue, he should consider them. Let me take a few instances:

(i) We are told that the local authority never serves notices under section 9 (1A) on any owner-occupiers. This is no doubt a wise policy: but it should not be regarded as inflexible. They assume, no doubt, that every owner-occupier will do his best to keep his house in good repair—to the extent of his resources. So in many cases it would be unduly

B harsh to press him with a notice to do more. If, by some oversight or misunderstanding, a local authority did serve an owner-occupier with a section 9 (1A) notice, the judge would be entitled to set it aside on appeal, if he thought it right to do so.

(ii) There was a question raised as to whether the judge could consider the means or financial position of the owner. Both sides seemed to think

C that he could not do so. But I would not limit the judge in this respect. I can envisage a poor widow who has only one house which she lets out to bring in some rent. If she could not afford to do the repairs, I think the judge could quash the notice or reduce the requirements so as to bring the cost within her means. So in this case, I think the judge could consider the financial position of these two companies. But I think he had too little evidence to form an opinion about them or their

D means. He should have torn aside the corporate veil and have seen the strength of the resources at their command. I should expect to find a strong property-owning company at the back of them.

(iii) Next, I think that the judge could consider the cost of the works as compared with the "value" of the house. But in this respect I am inclined to think that the "value" could in many cases be taken as the

E value with vacant possession (as in section 39): and not the "value" with a sitting protected tenant. And on this reckoning of value, each house was well worth the cost of the works. The cost of the works to 68, Glyn Road was £2,750: and, when the work was done, the house would be worth, with vacant possession, £7,500. And very probably the company may have bought it at a very low figure.

It would, I think, be very mischievous to take the "value" of the

F house with a sitting protected tenant. If that were taken, the owner could get the notice quashed—and then by good strategy deprive the tenant of the protection of the Rent Acts—and sell with vacant possession. So its real value to him may be its value with vacant possession.

At any rate, the judge should not take—as the sole measure of value—the "value" as the value with a sitting protected tenant in the house.

G For that is not its real value to the owner of the property. The sitting tenant may be old and soon die: or he may move elsewhere to live: and thus lose any protection. In one way or another the owner may soon get vacant possession: especially if he uses the device of letting the house get so bad that it is unfit for human habitation. So it may be very proper for the judge to consider the value as the value with vacant possession—or at any rate a value approaching it. Even if he took a

H midway value in this case, the house was of sufficient value to justify the cost of the repairs.

(iv) One final point: the judge said that, if public money had been expended on the property by way of improvement grants, it would be proper for the local authority to serve a notice under section 9 (1A): but that, if no grant had been spent on it, the local authority should not put the owner to the expense of repairs. I do not think that an owner (who had received no grant) should be exempt from a notice under 9 (1A).

Lord Denning M.R. Hillbank Properties v. Hackney Council (C.A.) [1978]

Conclusion A

This case throws up a problem of great social importance. It seems to me that the policy of Parliament was to make the owners of houses keep them in proper repair. Not only so as to keep up the stock of houses, but also to see that protected tenants should be able to have their houses properly kept up. It would be deplorable if there were no means of compelling owners of old houses keeping them in proper repair: or if the owners could let them fall into disrepair—as a means of evicting the tenants. Of course if the state of a house is so bad that it should be condemned—whoever was occupying it—then let it be demolished or closed or purchased. But if it is worth repairing, then it should be repaired, no matter whether it is occupied by a protected tenant or an unprotected tenant. The owners of these houses should not be allowed to evade their responsibilities under the cloak of the company law system. C I think that the judge misdirected himself in taking the " value " as it is: and when he said that the " notice will cause considerable financial loss to the owners." There was no evidence to warrant any such inference before him. If he had directed himself properly, on the evidence before him, it seems to me that there could only have been one answer. He should have upheld the notices. I would therefore allow the appeal and uphold these notices and not quash them. D

B

GEOFFREY LANE L.J. These appeals concern two Victorian terraced dwelling houses in Hackney. One is at 68, Glyn Road, and the other at 48, Coopersale Road. Each is occupied by tenants. Each is owned by a different property company though the companies are apparently connected. There are a few insignificant differences of fact between the E two appeals, but they raise the same problems. The circuit judge heard them together as a matter of convenience, and so do we.

In 1976 the tenants complained to the local authority that the houses required repair. An environmental health officer inspected the houses and came to the conclusion that neither of them was unfit for human habitation, but that each suffered from a number of defects which required remedying if they were to be brought up to local standards for such F dwellings. He accordingly recommended that the local authority should serve notices under section 9 (1A) of the Housing Act 1957, which runs as follows:

> "Where a local authority, upon consideration of an official representation, or a report from any of their officers, or other information in their possession, are satisfied that a house is in such state of G disrepair that, although it is not unfit for human habitation, substantial repairs are required to bring it up to a reasonable standard, having regard to its age, character and locality, they may serve upon the person having control of the house a notice requiring him, within such reasonable time, not being less than 21 days, as may be specified in the notice, to execute the works specified in the notice, not being H works of internal decorative repair."

The officer in question before reaching a decision in the matter had considered and taken into account, as the judge found, the age, character and locality of the houses, the landlords' interests and the cost of the work. In due course these recommendations were put before the relevant council committee by the chief environmental officer, Mr. White. The practice of the committee, followed on this occasion, was to accept

The Weekly Law Reports, July 21, 1978

269

3 W.L.R.   Hillbank Properties v. Hackney Council (C.A.)   Geoffrey Lane L.J.

A recommendations made under section 9 (1A) without further inquiry and with little if any discussion. Notices were served on the landlords accordingly.

By section 11 of the Act:

" (1) Any person aggrieved by—(a) a notice under the foregoing provisions . . . requiring the execution of works . . . may . . . appeal to
B the county court . . . (3) On an appeal to the county court under this section the judge may make such order either confirming or quashing or varying the notice, demand or order as he thinks fit . . ."

The landlords exercised their right of appeal under this section. In their original notice of appeal to the county court they set out the following grounds:

C " (1) The house is unfit for human habitation. (2) Alternatively . . . (a) Execution of the works specified in the notice will not bring the house up to a reasonable standard . . . (b) In the alternative to (a), the works specified in the notice are excessive to those required to bring the house up to a reasonable standard . . . (c) In any event, it is unreasonable to demand of the [landlords] the execution to the
D house of the works specified in the notice."

In the upshot all these grounds of appeal save the last were abandoned before the hearing, and the judge was left with the task of deciding simply whether the requirement to repair was reasonable. Particulars had been requested of the remaining ground but they were not forthcoming.

Section 9 (1A) was added to the Act of 1957 by section 72 of the
E Housing Act 1969. Section 9 (1) of the Act of 1957 deals with houses which are unfit for human habitation. It runs as follows:

" Where a local authority, upon consideration of an official representation, or a report from any of their officers, or other information in their possession, are satisfied that any house is unfit for human habitation, they shall, unless they are satisfied that it is not capable
F at a reasonable expense of being rendered so fit, serve upon the person having control of the house, a notice—(a) requiring him, within such a reasonable time, not being less than 21 days, as may be specified in the notice, to execute the works specified in the notice, and (b) stating that, in the opinion of the authority, those works will render the house fit for human habitation."

G Paradoxically though it may be, we are told that there may be great advantages to a landlord in having his house declared unfit for human habitation. One of the reasons is that under section 16 of the Act the landlord can give an undertaking that the house shall not be used for human habitation until the authority, on being satisfied that it has been rendered fit for such purpose, cancel the undertaking. By section 16 (5):

H " Nothing in the Rent Acts shall prevent possession being obtained of any premises by any owner thereof in a case where an undertaking has been given under this section that those premises shall not be used for human habitation."

Thus when the house has reached such a state of dilapidation that it is no longer fit to be occupied, the landlord can, if the authority serve a section 16 notice, obtain possession of the house (thus vastly increasing its value), repair it and sell it at a great profit to himself. Meanwhile

Geoffrey Lane L.J.   **Hillbank Properties v. Hackney Council (C.A.)**   **[1978]**

the local authority will be under an obligation to house the dispossessed   A
tenant. It follows that there may be a temptation for landlords to let
their houses reach a state of unfitness of such a degree that they are not
capable at a reasonable expense of being rendered fit for human habitation, thus producing the opposite result to that plainly intended by the
Act.

In the present case the local authority considered that the houses
were fit for human habitation. Consequently they fell to be dealt with   B
under section 9 (1A) and not under section 9 (1) (unfit and capable of
being repaired economically) or under section 16 (unfit and not capable of
being repaired economically).

Before the judge the landlords called two witnesses. The first was a
Mr. Toms, property manager employed by a firm of estate agents who
managed the houses for the two landlord companies. He gave evidence-   C
in-chief that Talisman Properties Ltd. had a substantial overdraft and
Hillbank Properties Ltd. had a small credit balance.

The landlords' second witness was Mr. Eburn, the environmental
officer who had made the original inspection of the two houses. In his
view there was no method available for putting these houses in order
other than a section 9 (1A) notice. The judge's findings as to the value
of the two houses and the cost of carrying out the required repairs were   D
as follows:

68, Glyn Road

The cost of carrying out the works was approximately £2,750. The
value of the house unrepaired with a sitting tenant was £1,700. Repaired
and with a sitting tenant it was £2,300. The registered rent was £5 per   E
week. The work would have to be financed by means of a loan at about
14 per cent. interest. Repaired and with vacant possession it would be
worth £7,500 to £8,000.

48, Coopersale Road

Estimated cost of the works was £2,900. The value of the house   F
unrepaired with a sitting tenant was £1,700. Repaired and with a sitting
tenant it was £2,500. The work would have to be financed in the same
way as no. 68, Glyn Road. The rent and value with vacant possession
were the same as the other house.

In coming to the conclusion on value the judge rejected the evidence
of the local authority's valuer and accepted that of the landlords' estate   G
agent.

The first matter for consideration is the extent of the inquiries which
the local authority ought to make before serving a notice under section
9 (1A). The judge rightly drew attention to the distinction between the
mandatory terms of section 9 (1) (" shall . . . serve . . . a notice ") and
the permissive words of section 9 (1A) (" may serve . . . a notice ")
and pointed out that the latter words give a discretion to the local   H
authority whether to serve a notice or not. However, he went on to hold
that it was incumbent upon them to find out at least about the owner of
the house, the cost of the works and the value of the property. Since
they had not done so they had failed to exercise any discretion at all.
The local authority are understandably concerned to know whether it is
incumbent upon them to make all these inquiries before serving a notice.
I do not think it is. The use of the word " may " means no more in

The Weekly Law Reports, July 21, 1978

271

3 W.L.R.   Hillbank Properties v. Hackney Council (C.A.)   Geoffrey Lane L.J.

A this context than that they are not bound to serve a notice even though they are satisfied that the house is in the requisite state of disrepair, and that substantial repairs are required to bring it up to the reasonable standard. It may be they will have had representations from the owner; it may be that other information about the circumstances is available to them which makes it appear that the service of a notice would be inexpedient or unjust. In that case no notice need be served. All that the B local authority are required to do before serving the notice is to satisfy themselves in accordance with the terms of section 9 (1A). There is no obligation on them to go further.

That error on the part of the judge does not necessarily affect the outcome of the appeal, because, as he rightly went on to point out, the fact that he had heard evidence from both sides (which the local authority C had not) meant that any discretion which had to be exercised in the matter could be exercised by him. The fact that the local authority had not made inquiries merely made their conclusions less weighty: see *per* Lord Goddard C.J. in *Stepney Borough Council* v. *Joffe* [1949] 1 K.B. 599, 602.

The next question before us was whether the judge in considering the appeal from the local authority was entitled to have regard to matters D not mentioned in section 9 (1A) and if so how far his inquiries should properly range. What the judge in fact did was to point to the cost of the required repairs and to draw attention to the fact that they exceeded the value of the respective houses with sitting tenants even after repair. He said: " I am entitled to take into account the value of the property, the capital cost of the works and the financial position of " E the landlords. The landlords in support of the judge's approach contend that the words of section 11 (3) are very wide (" such order . . . as he thinks fit ") and that they necessarily imply a power to take into consideration all the surrounding circumstances. The local authority agree that the *powers* given to the judge are wide but argue that that is not to say that the proper ambit of his *inquiries* can be wide. In particular they point to the following matters. The words in section 9 (1), ". . . they shall, F unless they are satisfied that it is not capable at a reasonable expense of being rendered so fit, serve . . . a notice," have no counterpart in section 9 (1A). The irresistible inference from that, it is said, is that any such provision was intended to be excluded from section 9 (1A). Secondly, section 39 (1) reads:

G " In determining for the purposes of this Part of this Act whether a house can be rendered fit for human habitation at a reasonable expense, regard shall be had to the estimated cost of the works necessary to render it so fit and the value which it is estimated that the house will have when the works are completed."

This is referable to section 9 (1). Again there is no corresponding provision relating to section 9 (1A), and a similar inference, it is suggested, H should be drawn.

Finally on this aspect of the appeal, under section 10 provision is made for various methods of enforcement. The local authority can execute the works themselves and recover the cost from the owner. They can declare the expenses to be payable by instalments over as long as 30 years with interest. They can leave the expenses as a charge on the premises—which we are told is often done. All these methods are subject to review by the judge under section 11. It is at that stage of the pro-

Geoffrey Lane L.J.   Hillbank Properties v. Hackney Council (C.A.)   [1978]

ceedings and not before, it is argued, that any hardship or lack of funds   A
or unreasonable expense should be considered.

It may be that by a strict application of the canons of construction
this result can be reached. But it seems to me that injustice may very
well result from such a conclusion. We were told that this particular
local authority would never serve a section 9 (1A) notice on an owner-
occupier. There is however nothing in the Act to prohibit that being
done. Assume that a notice was served on an elderly and impecunious   B
owner-occupier who was quite content to go on living in a sub-standard
house and had no money with which to carry out repairs. Would the
judge in such circumstances be powerless to quash that notice? Put in
another way, are the local authority not permitted to take such matters
into account if they know about them? Because if they can take them
into account, so can the judge.   C

Again, are the local authority not permitted to take into account
when deciding whether or not to serve the notice the fact that the cost
of repairs far exceeds the value of the house? Mr. White, the chief
environmental health officer, said this in evidence:

> " If my office reported that cost of works was out of all proportion
> to benefit to the tenant from the work and because of the age of   D
> the property, I should not recommend this matter to the committee."

So he is saying that he would at least take cost compared with benefit to
the tenant into consideration at that stage. I agree with him on this
point. The absence from section 9 (1A) of the conditional sentence found
in section 9 (1) and the fact that there is no section applicable to section
9 (1A) which corresponds with section 39 is not to my mind an oblique   E
method of restricting the discretion of the local authority or of the judge.
It is due to the fact that section 9 (1A) was an afterthought. Had it been
part of the original Act of 1957 the inference might well have been
different.

Accordingly there is no fetter (apart from admissibility and relevance)
upon those matters which the local authority or the judge can take into
account. The estimated cost of the required repairs compared with the   F
value of the premises is obviously an important consideration: see
Victoria Square Property Co. Ltd. v. *Southwark London Borough Council*
[1978] 1 W.L.R. 463, 474H, *per* Bridge L.J. But it is at this point that one
runs into difficulties. There are in the present cases, as there usually will
be, two different house values for comparison. The " sitting tenant "
value, which is less than the cost of the repairs, and the " vacant pos-   G
session " value, which is a great deal more. The reasonableness or otherwise of the local authority's notice to repair may largely depend upon
which of those two values one selects for purposes of comparison. It
may be that evidence is available to show that the tenancy is unlikely
to come to an end in the foreseeable future, in which case the landlords
should adduce it; it may be that there is evidence to the contrary, in
which case the local authority should do the same. If there is no   H
evidence one way or the other, as was the case here, what is the judge
to do? It seems to me that in such a case it is wrong to take either the
tenanted value or the vacant possession value without qualification as
the standard of comparison. In those circumstances any disparity between
the cost of repairs and the value of the property will have much less
weight, because one of the figures is necessarily imponderable. It may
be that the judge will come to the conclusion that the true value of the

The Weekly Law Reports, July 28, 1978

273

3 W.L.R.   **Hillbank Properties v. Hackney Council (C.A.)**   Geoffrey Lane L.J.

A house is too uncertain to enable him to base any conclusion upon it at all
It may be that he will take the mean figure between the two extremes,
which in this case would have been about £5,750. I feel the judge here
was in error. Although he did properly set out the various values which
had been ascribed to the houses he does not seem to have considered the
possibility that the landlords might in the near future make a handsome
B profit by getting vacant possession. He seems to have assumed, without
any evidential basis, that the tenants were there to stay.

It may be helpful to mention one or two other matters which may be
taken into consideration by the judge in considering appeals under this
section. Owner-occupation would be in most cases a powerful argument
against allowing a notice to repair. The financial means of the landlord where the premises are tenanted is of marginal significance, if any.
C In the present case such evidence of the landlords' means as there was,
was given, not by an officer of the property companies themselves but by
Mr. Toms, the employee of the landlords' estate agents. That was
probably hearsay and certainly valueless. If a landlord in these circumstances is not prepared to adduce proper evidence as to means through
a witness who is in a position to meet questions asked in cross-examination
D then the wealth or indigence of the landlord should be disregarded.

The final point argued by the local authority arises from what was
almost a postscript to the judgment. The judge said:

"It seems to me . . . that what the legislature intended was to enable
a local authority to serve a notice requiring the execution of works,
where public money by way of improvement grants has been spent
E on property. . . . Taking this view it provides another matter which
should have been taken into account by the [local authority] when
purporting to exercise discretion, and so I do. It is not reasonable
to require the spending of all this money when no public funds
have been spent on the house. . . ."

There is nothing in the Act of 1957 or that of 1969 which in any way
F expresses or impliedly makes improvement grants relevant to section
9 (1A). The fact that no improvement grant has been made in respect
of the premises is certainly not something which the local authority or
judge has to take into account. On the other hand, the fact that there
has been such a grant may well be material.

The judge, therefore, in exercising the discretion which is given to
G him by the Act, fell into understandable error in the respects I have
indicated. One is loth to interfere with the exercise of this type of
discretion, but it seems to me that the judge's conclusions were in the
circumstances wrong. If he had applied the correct criteria he would
have come to the opposite conclusion. I would allow the appeal and
restore the notices issued by the local authority.

H
EVELEIGH L.J. I do not think that the local authority are bound
to consider all the matters which are relevant to the decision of the
judge. He, however, should consider all the matters which are relevant
and given in evidence and then, in my view, he should give them such
weight as he thinks fit in all the circumstances. However, in these
present cases he took the view, wrongly in my opinion, that there must
be an improvement grant before notice can be given under section 9 (1A).

Eveleigh L.J.   Hillbank Properties v. Hackney Council (C.A.)   [1978]

He also gave considerable weight to the alleged impecuniosity of the   A
landlord when there was no proper evidence of this. In these and in the
other respects referred to in the judgments just delivered he erred.

I agree that these appeals should be allowed and the notices restored.

> *Appeal allowed with costs in Court*
> *of Appeal and below. Notices*
> *restored.*   B
> *Leave to appeal refused.*

Solicitors: *R. A. Benge; Stafford, Clark & Co.*

A. H. B.
                                                                                  C

_____

[HOUSE OF LORDS]

C. CZARNIKOW LTD. . . . . APPELLANTS

AND   D

CENTRALA HANDLU ZAGRANICZNEGO
ROLIMPEX . . . . RESPONDENTS

1978 May 18, 22, 23;   Lord Wilberforce, Viscount Dilhorne, Lord
      July 6   Salmon, Lord Fraser of Tullybelton and
                               Lord Keith of Kinkel
                                                                                  E

Contract—Frustration—Force majeure clause—Polish state organi-
sation contracting to sell sugar on terms of Refined Sugar
Association — Force majeure and licence clauses — Sellers
obtaining necessary export licences—Governmental decree ban-
ning export of sugar—Whether sellers part of government—
Whether entitled to rely on act of own government to escape
liability—Licence clause excluding reliance on force majeure
—Whether sellers excused from liability for breach of contract   F

   Under the Polish national economic plan the greater part
of home-produced beet sugar was allocated to the domestic
market and a proportion was sold on world markets through
a Polish state enterprise, Rolimpex, which was a separate
legal entity in Polish law. It claimed no sovereign immunity,
and, although subject to ministerial directions, had considerable freedom of decision and action.   In May and July   G
1974 Rolimpex contracted with an English company to
sell them 200,000 metric tons of sugar, part of the export
quota.   The contract terms incorporated the Rules of the
Refined Sugar Association, rule 18 (a) of which—the force
majeure clause—provided that if delivery was prevented,
inter alia, by " government intervention . . . beyond the seller's
control " the contract would be void without penalty.   Rule
21 made the seller " responsible for obtaining any necessary   H
export licence " and added that " the failure to obtain such
licences shall not be sufficient grounds for a claim of force
majeure if the regulations in force . . . when the contract was
made, called for such licences to be obtained."

   Owing to floods and heavy rain the 1974 sugar beet
crop was so poor that the whole of it was required for home
needs, and on November 5, 1974, the Council of Ministers
resolved on an immediate ban on the export of all sugar and
a formal decree was issued on the same date giving legal

A   effect to the ban, though it did not in terms revoke the export licences already obtained timeously by Rolimpex in compliance with rule 21.

Rolimpex thereupon in reliance on the force majeure clause informed the buyers that the contracts could not be fulfilled by reason of " government intervention beyond their control "; and they carried out all consequential steps required by the contracts.

B   On a reference of the dispute to a panel of the Refined Sugar Association in London, the arbitrators unanimously found in favour of Rolimpex that it was a legal entity separate from the Polish government and could rely on the force majeure rule 18 (a). Kerr J. on an award stated by the arbitrators dismissed the buyers' appeal. The Court of Appeal affirmed his decision.

On appeal by the buyers: —

C   Held, dismissing the appeal, (1) that on the findings of the arbitrators the sellers had established that they were not an organ or a department of the Polish government but an independent state enterprise, and accordingly their contracts with the buyers were frustrated by " government intervention . . . beyond the seller's control " within rule 18 (a) so as to release them from liability under the contracts (post, pp. 279D–F, 282B–D, 284D–E, 287C).

D   Commissioners of Crown Lands v. Page [1960] 2 Q.B. 274, C.A. considered.

(2) (Lord Salmon dissenting) that the sellers were not precluded from relying on rule 18 (a), since the obligation under rule 21 to " obtain " any necessary export licence, which they had done, imported no obligation or warranty to maintain it in force (post, pp. 279F–G, 283A–C, 287E–F).

Decision of the Court of Appeal [1978] Q.B. 176; [1977] 3 W.L.R. 677; [1978] 1 All E.R. 81 affirmed.

E

The following cases are referred to in their Lordships' opinions:

Board of Trade v. Temperley Steam Shipping Co. Ltd. (1926) 26 Ll.L.Rep. 76.

Commissioners of Crown Lands v. Page [1960] 2 Q.B. 274; [1960] 3 W.L.R. 446; [1960] 2 All E.R. 726, C.A.

F   Société d'Avances Commerciales (London) Ltd. v. A. Besse & Co. (London) Ltd. [1952] 1 Lloyd's Rep. 242; [1952] 1 T.L.R. 664.

The following additional cases were cited in argument:

British Broadcasting Corporation v. Johns [1965] Ch. 32; [1964] 2 W.L.R. 1071; [1964] 1 All E.R. 923, C.A.

Cassidy (Peter) Seed Co. Ltd. v. Osuustukkukauppa I. L. [1957] 1 W.L.R.
G   273; [1957] 1 All E.R. 484.

Partabmull Rameshwar v. K. C. Sethia (1944) Ltd. [1951] 2 All E.R. 352n; [1951] 2 Lloyd's Rep. 89, H.L.(E.).

Pfizer Corporation v. Ministry of Health [1965] A.C. 512; [1965] 2 W.L.R. 385; [1965] 1 All E.R. 450, H.L.(E.).

Société Co-operative Suisse des Céréales et Matières Fourragères v. La Plata Cereal Co. S.A. (1947) 80 Ll.L.Rep. 530.

H   Tamlin v. Hannaford [1950] 1 K.B. 18; [1949] 2 All E.R. 327, C.A.

Trendtex Trading Corporation v. Central Bank of Nigeria [1977] Q.B. 529; [1977] 2 W.L.R. 356; [1977] 1 All E.R. 881, C.A.

Walton (Grain & Shipping) Ltd. v. British Italian Trading Co. Ltd. [1959]1 Lloyd's Rep. 233.

APPEAL from the Court of Appeal.

The appellants C. Czarnikow Ltd. appealed from a judgment of the Court of Appeal (Lord Denning M.R. and Cumming-Bruce L.J., Geoffrey

Lane L.J. dissenting) dated May 26, 1977, affirming the judgment of A
Kerr J. dated December 13, 1976, which upheld an award in the form of
a special case by a panel of arbitrators of the Council of the Refined
Sugar Association. The arbitrators dismissed the appellants' claims for
damages for non-delivery of about 14,300 tonnes of Polish white sugar
f.o.b. Polish ports in November/December 1974. The broad issue raised
by the appeal was whether a state trading organisation could rely on the
act of its own government as a defence to claims for non-performance of B
commercial contracts. The particular issue was whether the respondents,
Centrala Handlu Zagranicznego, Rolimpex, who were established by the
Minister of Foreign Trade in Poland for the purpose of exercising the
state monopoly in (inter alia) the export and import of sugar, could
rely on a decree published by the minister as a case of force majeure
under rules 18 and 21 of the Refined Sugar Association.   C

The facts are stated in their Lordships' opinions.

Anthony Evans Q.C. and *David Johnson* for the appellants.
Michael Mustill Q.C., Andrew Longmore and *Timothy Salomon* for
the respondents.

Their Lordships took time for consideration.   D

LORD WILBERFORCE. My Lords, this appeal arises out of two contracts
for the purchase of sugar by the appellant from the respondent. Each
contract was made subject to the rules of the Refined Sugar Association
and expressly provided that the performance of the contract was subject
to force majeure as defined in the association's rules. There are two E
relevant rules. Rule 18 (a) applies if the delivery in whole or in part
within the delivery time should be prevented or delayed directly or
indirectly by (inter alia) government intervention and provides, as is
usual, for an extension and ultimately for cancellation of the contract.
Rule 21 deals with licences and is in the following terms:

> "The buyer shall be responsible for obtaining any necessary import F
> licence and the seller shall be responsible for obtaining any necessary
> export licence. The failure to obtain such licence/s shall not be
> sufficient grounds for a claim of force majeure if the regulations in
> force at the time when the contract was made, called for such licence/s
> to be obtained."

The contracts were made in May and July 1974 (subject to addenda of
later dates) and were forward sales for delivery in November/December G
1974. The seller thus assumed the risk of a rise in the price of sugar
between the contract date and the date of delivery.

Since the seller failed to deliver any of the 11,000 m.t. provided for by
the first contract and part of the tonnage provided for by the second
contract, it would be liable to the buyer for substantial damages unless
it could rely on force majeure.   H

The respondent (seller) Rolimpex is a state trading organisation of
the Polish state: it obtains sugar required for export from the Sugar
Industry Enterprises represented by the Union of Sugar Industries in
Poland. The relation between the latter body and Rolimpex is that
Rolimpex sells as "commission merchant," i.e., it sells in its own name
but only for a commission and on account of the Sugar Industry Enterprises
concerned. The contracts now in question were no doubt intended to

A be satisfied from the 1974 sugar crop in Poland. It is found that the Polish National Economic Plan required a total sugar production of 1,835,000 m.t. for the season 1974/75. Of this, 1.500,000 m.t. was required for the domestic market and the balance was authorised for export. In May 1974 Rolimpex was authorised to contract for the export of 200,000 m.t.

B In August 1974 there was heavy rain and flooding in the sugar beet producing areas: the result was that only 1,432,000 m.t. were produced— a shortfall even on the amount required for domestic consumption. On November 5, 1974, a resolution of the Council of Ministers was passed banning the export of sugar with effect from November 5, 1974, and cancelling export licences. This resolution was found not to have the force of law. However, later on November 5, 1974, the Minister of

C Foreign Trade and Shipping signed a decree providing:

"1. From November 5, 1974, it is prohibited to release export deliveries of sugar specified by present contracts. 2. Customs authorities shall immediately stop the deliveries of sugar prepared for export and notify disposers about the prohibition of sugar export. 3. The rule is in force from the date of its signature."

D This made the export of sugar illegal by Polish law.

It was found by the arbitrators that on November 5, 1974, there was a considerable quantity of sugar at the port of Gdynia and a further quantity on the way to Gdynia by rail. But for the ban, sugar would have been available for the performance by Rolimpex of both contracts. It was also found that both before and after November 15, 1974 (the date when the buyer was able to ship) there was Polish sugar of the contract quality

E available on the market. If there were insufficient quantities available, there was a market for the purchase and sale of other sugar of equivalent quality. In the condition of the market any purchaser would have accepted any sugar of equivalent quality in substitution for Polish sugar. The market value of the relevant quality of sugar on November 15 was however FF. 7,500 per m.t. as compared with FF. 3,064, the price fixed

F for one contract and about FF. 4,000 for the other.

The export ban remained in operation until July 1, 1975. Rolimpex declared force majeure on November 6, 1974, and, if it was entitled to do so, both contracts became void.

The seller referred the matter to the council of the Refined Sugar Association in accordance with the association's rules. The council appointed a panel of six arbitrators in respect of the dispute. They heard

G evidence over a hearing of 10 days. In their award the arbitrators found (inter alia) that sugar was available on the world market to meet the shortage in the Polish market but the Council of Ministers resolved not to purchase sugar on the world market because of the high price and the loss of foreign exchange that such a purchase would have entailed; that the ban was imposed to relieve the anticipated shortage in the

H domestic market; that its effect was to throw the losses caused by the partial failure of the Polish sugar crop on overseas traders and consumers, thus saving the Polish state having to bear any financial loss in replacing the sugar sold well in advance of the 1974/75 campaign. They added this unusual observation:

"(a) (v) We very much regret that the Council of Ministers authorised the ban rather than permitting the purchase of sugar on the world market, so enabling Rolimpex to honour its contractual obligations."

Lord Wilberforce   **Czarnikow Ltd. v. Rolimpex (H.L.(E.))**   **[1978]**

A further group of findings contained the following: A

"(b) The persons employed in Rolimpex did not induce the Council
of Ministers to authorise the ban and did not influence its continuance
or effect. (c) Rolimpex is an organisation of the Polish state. (d)
Rolimpex is not so closely connected with the Government of Poland
that it is precluded from relying on this ban (imposed for the reasons
set out above) as 'government intervention' within rule 18 (A) of   B
the rules of the Refined Sugar Association. (e) Rolimpex is accordingly entitled to rely on rule 18 (A) as a defence to Czarnikow's
claims."

The award having been stated in the form of a special case, the matter
came before the court with two main questions for decision. 1. Was
this a case of government intervention within rule 18 (a)? 2. Was the   C
case taken out of rule 18 (a) by the provisions of rule 21? There was
also a question (of very considerable difficulty) as to the measure of
damages.

Questions 1 and 2 were answered by Kerr J. in favour of the seller,
i.e., Yes and No respectively. The Court of Appeal (Lord Denning M.R.
and Cumming-Bruce L.J.) affirmed this decision. Geoffrey Lane L.J.
dissented holding that Question 2 should be answered in the affirmative.   D

Consideration of Question 1 can conveniently start from the arbitrators'
finding (b) above. It was the case of the buyer before the arbitrators
that there was some kind of collusion or conspiracy between Rolimpex
and the government of Poland by which the government was persuaded,
in the interest of Rolimpex, to impose the ban. In order to deal with
this, Rolimpex produced a quantity of evidence to show that there was   E
no such collusion or conspiracy; on the contrary, when the possibility of
a ban on exports was mentioned to the director and general manager
of Rolimpex before November 6, 1974, he protested about it and the
persons employed in Rolimpex were not consulted about the imposition
of the ban and were not informed of the ban until after its imposition.
The arbitrators found that Czarnikow had failed to prove its allegation
that the ban was imposed after consultation between the persons employed   F
in Rolimpex and the Ministry of Foreign Trade and Shipping. The
ban was in fact requested by the Minister of Food and Agricultural
Industries on the grounds that it was unacceptable to put the people of
Poland on short rations and other alternatives were unacceptable. There
being disagreement among the ministers (including the Minister for
Foreign Trade and Shipping who supervises Rolimpex) the matter was   G
referred to the Council of Ministers which passed the resolution of
November 5, 1974 (see above). There was thus ample evidence to support
the arbitrators' finding against collusion or conspiracy.

Before the courts and this House the buyer took a different line. It
appealed to a group of English cases dealing with actions taken by or
on behalf of the Crown in which a distinction has been made, broadly,
between the acts which are performed by a government for the public   H
good or for a general executive purpose and acts which a government does
so as to avoid liability under a contract or contracts (see *Board of
Trade* v. *Temperley Steam Shipping Co. Ltd.* (1926) 26 Ll.L.Rep. 76,
and *Commissioners of Crown Lands* v. *Page* [1960] 2 Q.B. 274 *per*
Devlin J.). Lord Denning M.R. was disposed to hold that this distinction
might be applied to the present case if, but only if Rolimpex was to be
regarded as a department of government: he then proceeded to hold

A that it was not. I have very great doubt whether the doctrine developed by these cases, which is very much one of English constitutional law, can viably be transplanted into the constitutional climate of foreign States—particularly such states as Poland which we are entitled to know have an entirely different constitutional structure from ours. Such a transplantation, if possible at all, would involve English courts in difficult and delicate questions as to the motivation of a foreign State, and as to
B the concept of public good, which would be unlikely to correspond with ours. I am not saying that there may not be cases when it is so clear that a foreign government is taking action purely in order to extricate a state enterprise from contractual liability, that it may be possible to deny to such action the character of government intervention, within the meaning of a particular contract, but that result cannot, in my opinion, be
C achieved by means of the doctrine mentioned above: it would require clear evidence and definite findings. It is certain that no such evidence or findings exist in the present case. On the contrary, the evidence is that the action was taken to avoid serious domestic, social and political effects and to avoid loss of foreign exchange if high price sugar were to be brought on the world market. The arbitrators indeed so found.

I agree, however, wholly with Lord Denning M.R. that Rolimpex
D cannot on the evidence be regarded as an organ of the Polish state. The award does indeed use the words " an organisation of the Polish state " but read with the evidence this can mean no more than that it was set up by the Polish state and controlled by the Polish state: in their next finding quoted above, the arbitrators find that Rolimpex is not so closely connected with the government of Poland that it is
E precluded from relying on the ban as government intervention—a finding not as clear as it might be but, in the light of the evidence, meaning necessarily that Rolimpex is not an organ or department of the state. The independence of Rolimpex from the government is in my opinion amply demonstrated by the facts set out at length in the award. Together with all four learned judges who have considered this point, I find the conclusion clear, and I therefore hold that the seller makes good the
F contention that there was government intervention within rule 18.

The second question is whether rule 21 operates as a saving clause which, in the circumstances, takes the case out of rule 18. I am afraid that I can find no substance in this argument. Rule 21 appears in a section of the rules headed " Licences." In my opinion it does no more than to place on the seller the obligation to obtain an export licence
G (and on the buyer to obtain an import licence) and to state that failure to fulfil this obligation shall not be a sufficient ground for a claim of force majeure. The word " obtain " in this context means " obtain " or " get " and I cannot read in to it any obligation or warranty to maintain it in force. The seller complied with this obligation and the clause is satisfied. I agree entirely with the disposition of this point by Kerr J.

I would dismiss the appeal.
H

VISCOUNT DILHORNE. My Lords, under two contracts made in 1974 the appellants agreed to buy from the respondents quantities of sugar f.o.b. Each contract incorporated the rules of the Refined Sugar Association and this appeal is as to the meaning and effect of rules 18 (a) and 21 of those rules.

Under the Polish Economic Plan 1,835,000 metric tons of sugar were to be produced in the 1974/75 season. It was estimated that 1,500,000

tons would be required for domestic consumption and 335,000 tons were
allocated for export. In May 1974 the respondents were authorised to
contract for the export of 200,000 tons thereof and the contracts made
with the appellants were pursuant to that authority.

In that season due to bad weather only 1,432,000 tons were produced,
and in October 1974 the Minister of Food and Agricultural Industries
told the Prime Minister of Poland that the sugar produced would not
cover domestic needs, and that the respondents were insisting nevertheless
on the export of 200,000 tons for which they had concluded contracts.
He suggested that there should be an immediate ban on the export of
sugar " as it was socially and politically unacceptable to put the people
of Poland on short rations and other alternatives were also unacceptable."

On November 5, 1974, this was considered at a meeting of the Council
of Ministers. It was decided that an immediate ban on the export of
sugar should be imposed and it was resolved:

" 1. Sugar export is banned commencing November 5, 1974. 2. Export
licences granted hitherto are cancelled. 3. Minister of Foreign Trade
and Shipping shall issue without delay respective decrees in order to
strictly execute this provision. 4. The resolution is carried into effect
on the passing date."

That afternoon a decree, which had force of law in Poland, was
signed by the Minister of Foreign Trade and Shipping. It read as
follows:

" On the basis of paragraph 3 of the resolution of the Council of
Ministers on November 5, 1974, related to a prohibition to export
sugar, the following is made to apply: 1. From November 5, 1974, it
is prohibited to release export deliveries of sugar specified by present
contracts. 2. Customs authorities shall immediately stop the deliveries
of sugar prepared for export and notify disposers about the prohibition
of sugar export. 3. The rule is in force from the date of its signature."

This ban remained in force until July 1, 1975, so from November 5,
1974, till then the export of sugar from Poland was illegal. Sugar which
the respondents had contracted to deliver to the appellants f.o.b. could
not consequently be delivered. By telex on November 5 the respondents
told the appellants of the ban and the appellants replied saying that
they did not accept that delivery of sugar already contracted for could
be stopped in that manner. The next day the respondents told the
appellants that it was a case of force majeure.

The rules of the Refined Sugar Association contain a chapter headed
" Force Majeure." The chapter contains rules 17–20. Rule 18 (a) is
relevant to this case and so far as material reads as follows:

" Should the delivery in whole or in part within the delivery time
specified be prevented or delayed directly or indirectly by government
intervention . . . beyond the seller's control, the seller shall immediately advise the buyer . . . of such fact and of the quantity so affected,
and the period of delivery shall be extended by 30 days for such
quantity. . . . If delivery is still prevented by the end of the extended
period, the buyer shall have the option of cancelling the contract for
the affected quantity or of taking delivery at the contract price without claiming damages as soon as the sugar can be delivered. . . .
Should the buyer elect not to cancel the contract but delivery of
the sugar in whole or in part still remains impossible 60 days after

A   the last delivery date provided for by the contract, the contract shall be void for such quantity without penalty payable or receivable."

It is in my opinion clear beyond all doubt that delivery of the sugar in pursuance of the contracts within the delivery time was prevented by the intervention of the government of Poland. It is, I think, equally clear that the action taken by the government was beyond the respondents'
B control. The facts found by the arbitrators show, as I have said, that the respondents had insisted on the export of the 200,000 tons they had contracted to sell, and also that on November 5 when informed of the possibility of the ban, the respondents' director and general manager had protested. Nevertheless the ban was imposed.

The appellants contended that "government intervention" in rule
C 18 (a) should be interpreted to mean only intervention for what was called a general executive purpose; that the decree was imposed to achieve a particular result in relation to the contracts for the export of sugar, and that intervention for such a purpose was not to be regarded as government intervention within the meaning to be given to those words in rule 18 (a).

The particular result which it was the respondents' purpose to achieve
D was, it was alleged, to throw the losses caused by the failure of the sugar crop on to overseas traders and consumers and to avoid it being borne by the Polish state.

Rule 18 (a) clearly requires it to be established if the force majeure relied on is government intervention, that the cause of the delivery being prevented or delayed was government intervention. It does not stipulate
E that, if there is such intervention, one has to go on to consider for what purpose the intervention was made. I do not find it necessary in this case to consider whether a government intervention which in fact occurred, can be treated as not having occurred if it be established that it was to secure a particular result such as that alleged by the appellants, for the facts found by the arbitrators in their award, in my view clearly negative the contention that it was for that particular purpose. They found that
F Poland was faced with a shortage of sugar if all contracts for the export of sugar were performed, that the Council of Ministers feared that the shortage of sugar in the home market would have serious domestic social and political effects, that sugar was available on the world market to meet the shortage but that the Council of Ministers resolved not to purchase on the world market because of the high price of sugar and the
G loss of foreign exchange that such a purchase would have entailed and that the ban " was accordingly imposed to relieve the anticipated shortage in the domestic market." Presumably this purpose was achieved. The arbitrators say that the effect of the ban was

> " to throw the losses caused by the partial failure of the Polish sugar crop on overseas traders and consumers thus saving the Polish state having to bear any financial loss in replacing the sugar sold well in
H advance of the 1974/75 campaign."

While this was a consequence of the ban, its purpose as stated by the arbitrators was not that but to relieve the anticipated shortage on the home market.

The foundation for this contention by the appellants is not there and so it is unnecessary to consider what effect, if any, it would have had it been.

The appellants do not say that the respondents are to be identified   A
with the Polish government. The respondents are an organisation of the
state. Under Polish law they have a legal personality. Though subject
to directions by the appropriate minister who can tell them " what to do
and how to do it," as a state enterprise they make their own decisions
about their commercial activities. They decide with whom they will do
business and on what terms and they have considerable freedom in their
day to day activities. They are managed on the basis of economic   B
accountability and are expected to make a profit. The arbitrators in
my opinion rightly found as a fact that the respondents were not so
closely connected with the government of Poland as to be precluded from
relying on the ban imposed by the decree as government intervention.

The appellants also asserted that the respondents bought and sold for
the state. This while no doubt true, does not in my view help the   C
appellants. The facts found by the arbitrators stated above show that
they were not a department of the government but have a separate
identity. They were, it was found as a fact, employed as " a commission
merchant " to sell sugar intended for export on behalf of Sugar Industry
Enterprises which were also state enterprises.

The fact that they did so cannot in my opinion invalidate the decree
made on November 5.   D

So if rule 18 (a) stood alone, the respondents are in my opinion
entitled to rely on it as excusing them from liability for non-delivery
of the sugar within the period stipulated in the contract.

The appellants, however, say that they are prevented from doing so
by rule 21. That rule is headed by the word " Licences," and is clearly
designed to deal with the situation where at the time when a contract   E
is made a licence is required for export or for import. It reads as follows:

" The buyer shall be responsible for obtaining any necessary import
licence and the seller shall be responsible for obtaining any necessary
export licence. The failure to obtain such licence/s shall not be
sufficient grounds for a claim of force majeure if the regulations
in force at the time when the contract was made called for such
licence/s to be obtained."   F

Export licences for sugar were required when the contracts were made
between the appellants and the respondents. The first sentence of this
rule imposes a collateral obligation on the buyer to obtain any necessary
import licence and on the seller to obtain any necessary export licence.
But what is the extent of this obligation? The appellants contend that the
respondents undertook by undertaking to obtain any necessary export   G
licence, not only to get but also to have at the time that delivery was
required to be made, a valid licence under which the delivery could be
made, and that the licences they had having been cancelled by the decree,
they were in breach of this obligation. In those circumstances, they say,
the second sentence of the rule prevents the respondents from relying on
force majeure.   H

If this is the right construction of the rule, it would mean that where
a licensing system was in force at the time of the contract, the words
" government intervention " in rule 18 (a) would have little, if any, significance. Never could the seller in any country rely on that rule if the
government of that country placed an embargo on export and a licence
for export was required both at the time of the contract and at the time
for delivery.

A   I do not think that this is the right construction to be placed on the rule. I do not think that it was ever intended to have such a far-reaching effect. I see no reason for giving the word " obtaining " which appears twice in the rule and " obtained " any other than their natural meaning which in my view is " getting " and " got," and I agree with my noble and learned friend, Lord Fraser of Tullybelton, whose speech in draft I have now had the advantage of reading, that for the reasons he gives, the word

B   " necessary " in rule 21 gives no assistance to the appellants.

If it was the intention of the parties that in addition to the getting of any necessary licence, the buyer in the case of an import licence and the seller in the case of an export licence undertook to have and warranted that he would have a valid import or export licence when the time came for importation or for delivery, I would have expected express provision

C   to have been made for that as it was in a clause in the c.i.f. contract under consideration in *Société d'Advances Commerciales (London) Ltd. v. A. Besse & Co. (London) Ltd.* [1952] 1 Lloyd's Rep. 242. The word " obtaining " is in my view too slender a peg to sustain the weight of such a far-reaching obligation.

The second sentence of the rule is in my opinion of limited effect. It merely provides that failure to get a necessary licence shall not of

D   itself suffice to justify a claim of force majeure.

In this case the cause of the non-delivery was government intervention not failure to obtain an export licence.

For these reasons in my opinion this appeal fails and should be dismissed. It is not necessary to consider to what damages the appellants would have been entitled had their appeal succeeded.

E
LORD SALMON. My Lords, I need not recite the two contracts entered into between the sellers and the buyers in May and July 1974, nor rule 18 (a) of the Refined Sugar Association's rules incorporated in these contracts, nor the export ban imposed by the Polish government on November 5, 1974, nor the basic facts concerning the dispute between the parties to this appeal, for these are all fully and lucidly set out in the speeches

F   of my noble and learned friends, Lord Wilberforce and Viscount Dilhorne.

One of the allegations which had been unsuccessfully made in the arbitration by the buyers was that the ban which I have mentioned had been planned or plotted between the sellers and the Polish government in order to force a substantial increase in the price of the sugar sold under the contracts to which I have referred. The arbitrators held that

G   this allegation had no foundation in fact (see paragraph 19 of the award). Mr. Evans, quite rightly, never challenged this finding; the evidence referred to in the award clearly established that the sellers had no knowledge of the ban until after it was made and that the Minister of Foreign Trade and Shipping, who supervised the sellers' business, had strongly opposed the imposition of the ban.

Mr. Evans did, however, argue that the sellers were, in fact, part of

H   the Polish government and that therefore the ban caused by the intervention of that government could not be recognised as being " beyond the control of the sellers " within the meaning of those words in rule 18 (a); and that accordingly it followed that the sellers could not be excused on the ground of " force majeure " from fulfilling their obligations under the contracts of sale. This argument was most skilfully developed but it faced the insuperable difficulty that it was contrary to the arbitrators' findings of fact.

Lord Salmon   Czarnikow Ltd. v. Rolimpex (H.L.(E.))   [1978]

The arbitrators' found in paragraph 50 (d) of the award that the   A
sellers were not so closely connected with the Polish government that they
were precluded from relying on the ban. I do not overlook the finding
in paragraph 50 (c) of the award that the sellers were " an organisation
of the Polish state." These words, are, however, very loose and imprecise
and must be read in the light of the findings of fact in paragraphs
21–29 of the award. It is clear from these findings that the sellers were   B
set up by the state as a separate entity. They were known as a state
enterprise and registered as such. This gave them in Polish law a
" legal personality." Some of the consequences of the sellers' legal
personality and economic accountability are that the State Treasury is not
responsible for their obligations and they are not responsible for the
obligations of the State Treasury; nor are they entitled, under Polish
law, to claim sovereign immunity. Although the sellers are under the   C
general supervision of the Minister for Foreign Trade and he has the
power to tell them " what to do and how to do it," the sellers generally
make their own decisions about their own business and have substantial
freedom in their day-to-day activities. The sellers carry on business as
commission merchants on a very large scale. They have a virtual
monopoly of selling, on commission, in their own name, all the sugar
intended for export and produced by the various state enterprises. They   D
also sell on commission many other commodities intended for export and
produced by other state enterprises. In my view, the arbitrators were
justified in refusing to hold that the sellers were an organ or a department of the government or the state. Accordingly, I agree that but for
rule 21 (which I shall presently consider) the sellers would have a complete
defence under rule 18 (a) to the claim brought against them by the buyers   E
for failure to perform their obligations under the contract.

I do not express any concluded opinion as to what the position might
have been, in law, had the facts as found by the arbitrators established
that the sellers were an organ or department of the government or of the
state. I am inclined to the view that, in such circumstances, the facts
as found in paragraph 50 (a) of the award may nevertheless have been
expressed without sufficient clarity to establish with the necessary certainty   F
that the ban was not imposed " for the public good " or for " a general
executive purpose " but only for the purpose of extricating the government from its obligation under the contracts of sale. If the findings had
been so expressed, I would agree with Lord Denning M.R. that the
sellers, in the circumstances postulated, would have been precluded from
relying on rule 18 (a)—see *Commissioners of Crown Lands* v. *Page* [1960]   G
2 Q.B. 274, 293–294 *per* Devlin J.; *Board of Trade* v. *Temperley Steam
Shipping Co. Ltd.* (1926) 26 Ll.L.Rep. 76 *per* Roche J.

In my view paragraph 50 (a) of the award is somewhat ambiguous.
Naturally the Council of Ministers feared that a shortage of sugar in the
home market would have serious domestic, social and political effects.
But there was no risk of such a shortage because the council had one
of two alternative means of preventing it. A. There was plenty of sugar   H
available for sale on the world market to avoid the shortage which would
otherwise have occurred on the home market if the sellers had honoured
their obligations under their contracts with the appellant and other buyers
for exporting 200,000 tonnes of sugar; or, B. The contracts for exporting
200,000 tonnes of sugar could all have been torn up and a total ban on
exports imposed; then the home produced sugar, freed from export,
would have supplied virtually all the sugar required on the home market.

A   If the latter course were followed, it could have been accompanied by paying reasonable compensation to all the foreign buyers. The sellers did adopt the latter course but did not pay any compensation.

According to the findings in paragraph 50 (a) (iii) of the award, "the Council of Ministers resolved not to purchase sugar on the world market because of the high price and the loss of foreign exchange that such a purchase would have entailed." There is no finding as to whether this
B loss of foreign exchange would or would not have seriously affected Polish currency. If it would have done so, then the ministers' decision to do as they did could have been justified on the ground that they were acting for the public good and for a general executive purpose.

If, on the other hand, the currency would not have been affected and the sellers had been part of the government or the state, they would only
C have been evading a financial loss on the forward contracts into which they had entered and could not, in my view, have sheltered behind rule 18 (a).

Paragraph 50 (a) (iv) of the award makes it plain that the ban had been imposed to relieve the anticipated shortage in the domestic market: but this step was taken only because it had been decided not to buy the
D sugar which was readily available on the world market and would equally have relieved any home shortage. For my part I am not at all surprised by the comment in paragraph 50 (a) (v) of the award: "We very much regret that the Council of Ministers authorised the ban rather than permitting the purchase of sugar on the world market, so enabling [the sellers] to honour [their] contractual obligations."

Since, however, the sellers were not found to be an organ or depart-
E ment of the government or the state, it is unnecessary to express any concluded view on what should have been the result had such a finding been made.

I now turn to consider the effect of rule 21 of the Refined Sugar Association's rules which was also incorporated in the contracts of sale. It reads as follows:

F   "The buyer shall be responsible for obtaining any necessary import licence and the seller shall be responsible for obtaining any necessary export licence. The failure to obtain such licence/s shall not be sufficient grounds for a claim of force majeure if the regulations in force at the time when the contract was made called for such licence/s to be obtained."

G   The regulations in force in Poland at the time the contracts were made called for such licences to be obtained.

Someone had to take the risk that the necessary export licences might become unobtainable or be cancelled. In my opinion, it was the sellers who accepted the responsibility for obtaining such licences and the risk that they might fail to do so. If they failed from any cause, obviously,
H they could not deliver the sugar they had sold: but they would then be liable to compensate the buyers for any damage the buyers had suffered as a result of the non-delivery.

I do not think that there is any difficulty about the meaning of the word "obtain" in rule 21. It means simply to "get." The obligation is merely to get "any necessary export licence." This prompts the question "necessary for what?" In my opinion, in order to make any commercial sense out of the rule, it can only be referring to a licence necessary to

enable the sugar sold to be cleared through customs and loaded on   A
board ship.

If the sellers obtain a document purporting to be an export licence,
but before the shipment is due, the document is cancelled, or for any
other cause does not enable the sugar to be cleared through customs and
loaded on board then, in my view, the sellers have failed to obtain or
get a " *necessary* " export " licence "; and they are precluded from relying
on force majeure to escape from their liability to pay compensation to   B
the buyers for their failure to deliver under the contracts. I would add
that it is, in my view, impossible for a seller to know for certain whether
he has obtained a necessary export licence until he presents it to the
customs authorities and they clear the goods on the strength of it.

It was argued on behalf of the sellers that the rules of the game were
changed when the ban on exports came into force on November 5, 1974,   C
because the whole licensing system was temporarily put out of action by
government intervention and rule 21 no longer had any application. I
am afraid that I cannot accept that argument. I entirely agree with the
judgment of Geoffrey Lane L.J. and gratefully adopt the following passage
in his judgment [1978] Q.B. 176, 201:

> " To say that that which caused the failure to deliver was the ban   D
> on exports rather than the absence of a valid licence, . . . is to draw
> a distinction without a difference. A ban on exports means a refusal
> to permit exports. A licence to export is a permit to export. There-
> fore the ban is no more and no less than a withdrawal of any existing
> licences and a refusal to grant any further licence for the time being."

It seems to me that one of the most obvious risks which rule 21   E
envisaged and the sellers accepted was that the necessary export licences
might be unobtainable by reason of government intervention whether in
the form of a ban on the export of sugar or in any other form. Once
the sellers contracted to shoulder the risk of failing to obtain the necessary export licences, the reasons why they failed to do so became irrelevant.
In my opinion, an export licence is, in reality, no more and no less than
government permission to export.   F

Export licences are wholly unlike dog licences or television licences
which are issued automatically upon the payment of a fee and the completion of a form. It is incredible that there should be government intervention of any kind in respect of such licences. Not so in respect of
export licences. These are normally issued by a department of government and depend upon government policy—which alters from time to
time. The department concerned may, on behalf of the government,   G
decide not to issue a licence or to cancel an issued licence, in its own
discretion, or as a result of a decree or direction emanating from the
government itself.

At the time when these forward contracts were entered into, it must
have been foreseen that before the stipulated delivery date, the Polish
government might well intervene by preventing export licences from   H
being issued and cancelling any such licences as had been issued. This,
in my opinion, was a risk which fell upon the sellers under rule 21. To
construe this rule otherwise emasculates it and deprives the buyers of
the protection which it purports to afford them.

Rule 18 (a) cites, first, government intervention and then ten other
specific examples of force majeure. Any of these, unless excluded by
some provision in the contract, would afford a valid defence to the sellers

A if it prevented or delayed delivery under the contract. So far as the sellers' contractual obligations are concerned, rule 21 preserves only their obligation to obtain the necessary export licences: otherwise, the sellers' escape routes under rule 18 (a) for failure to deliver, or a delay in delivery, are left intact. I consider, however, that rule 21 makes it plain that the sellers cannot escape from their failure to obtain the necessary export licence on the ground of government intervention or any other ground of force majeure; certainly not without implying or writing into rule 21 after the words "force majeure," the words "unless caused by government intervention." I cannot find any justification for doing so. Far from it being necessary to emasculate rule 21 in order to give business efficacy to the contract, I consider that it makes far better commercial sense as it stands.

C   I would accordingly allow the appeal.

LORD FRASER OF TULLYBELTON. My Lords, I have had the advantage of reading in draft the speech of my noble and learned friend, Lord Wilberforce, and I agree with it.

On the arbitrators' findings in this case there is no doubt that there was government intervention in the sense of rule 18. At one time I was inclined to attribute more importance than some of your Lordships do to rule 21, and to think that it was intended to place on the seller an obligation to obtain an export licence which would be effective at the time of exporting. But further reflection has satisfied me that for the reasons stated by my noble and learned friend, Viscount Dilhorne, to construe rule 21 in that way would involve reading into the word "obtain" more than it can fairly bear. Nor does it seem to me that the word "necessary" helps the appellants. In the context of rule 21, the word must imply that there is in force a licensing system of such a character that, if the necessary licence is obtained, it would be effective to allow the seller to export the goods which he had contracted to sell. But if the licensing system is abolished or (as in the present case) superseded, with the result that no licence can be effective during the period of suspension, rule 21 does not have the effect of imposing on the seller an absolute obligation to obtain government permission to export the goods; if it did, it would remove almost the whole of the protection against government intervention given to him by rule 18. I agree with Cumming-Bruce L.J. in the Court of Appeal [1978] Q.B. 176, 204 that:

"His [the seller's] obligation though absolute is more restricted, and is only to obtain from the licensing department or authority evidence of such permission to export as is within the ordinary scope of the licensing system that that department is concerned with."

I would dismiss the appeal.

LORD KEITH OF KINKEL. My Lords, I have had the opportunity of reading in draft the speech of my noble and learned friend, Lord Wilberforce. I agree with it, and for the reasons he gives I too would dismiss the appeal.

Appeal dismissed.

Solicitors: *William A. Crump & Son; Norton, Rose, Botterell & Roche.*

F. C.

[1978]

A

[FAMILY DIVISION]

DEAN v. DEAN

1978 Feb. 22, 23, 24;　　　　　　　　　　　　　　　　　　　Bush J.
March 20, 21

B

Husband and Wife—Financial provision—Agreement—Order of Court—Undefended suit—Certificate of approval granted by registrar—Wife seeking to resile from agreement before hearing—Jurisdiction to review agreement—Matrimonial Causes Act 1973 (c. 18), s. 25

The parties married in 1965 and had two children, a girl born in 1965 and a boy born in 1968. The husband was a wealthy business man with homes in Spain and France. The wife who had an adulterous relationship with a Spanish national was anxious for divorce. Following negotiations between the respective solicitors, agreement was reached on the wife's financial provision. Each party signed a copy of the draft minutes of the agreement. The agreement was headed: " Draft minutes of order to be submitted for approval by registrar with a view to incorporation in the order made on decree nisi." The husband filed a petition for dissolution of the marriage under section 1 (2) (*a*) of the Matrimonial Causes Act 1973.

C

D

Shortly after signing the agreement the wife changed her mind and sought to resile from the agreement. Judge Figgis ordered that the suit be transferred to a judge of the Family Division and that the wife show cause why the minutes of agreement should not be made an order of the court: —

E

Held, (1) that so far as financial arrangements were concerned, the court had a discretion whether an order was made under section 23 or under section 24 of the Matrimonial Causes Act 1973; that discretion was to be exercised at the time of granting the decree or later and, in exercising it, the court had a duty under section 25 to consider whether the arrangements agreed by the parties were reasonable (post, p. 292C–D, F–H).

F

(2) That although, under the special procedure, a registrar might certify that the petitioner was entitled to an order in agreed terms and the judge might be satisfied by such, he was not thereby relieved of his primary duty under section 25 although his consideration of the conduct of the parties would include the fact and nature of the agreement voluntarily arrived at between the parties (post, p. 294D–E, G).

G

(3) That although collusion was no longer a bar to divorce, it was still a matter of public policy that the court should retain its jurisdiction over matters of maintenance (post, p. 293G–H).

Bennett v. *Bennett* [1952] 1 K.B. 249, C.A. applied.

(4) That the court in performing its duty under section 25 where there was an agreement between the parties should adopt the broad rather than the particular approach; whilst it had a duty under section 25 it also owed a duty to uphold agreements especially where made between parties at arm's length negotiated by legal advisers, where there had been no change of circumstances, and which were not against public policy; accordingly, in all the circumstances, the court would approve the agreement (post, pp. 297B, 298F–G, 299A–B).

H

The following cases are referred to in the judgment:

Bennett v. *Bennett* [1952] 1 K.B. 249; [1952] 1 All E.R. 413, C.A.

A   *Brockwell* v. *Brockwell*, November 5, 1975, Court of Appeal (Civil
        Division) Transcript No. 468 of 1975, C.A.
    M. v. *M.* [1967] P. 313; [1967] 2 W.L.R. 1333; [1967] 1 All E.R. 870.
    Smallman v. *Smallman* [1972] Fam. 25; [1971] 3 W.L.R. 588; [1971] 3
        All E.R. 717, C.A.

    The following additional cases, supplied by the courtesy of counsel, were
B   cited in argument:

    Backhouse v. *Backhouse* [1978] 1 W.L.R. 243; [1978] 1 All E.R. 1158.
    Barnard v. *Barnard* (1961) 105 S.J. 441, C.A.
    Carpenter v. *Carpenter* (1976) 6 Family Law 110.
    Dennett v. *Dennett*, The Times, March 24, 1977, C.A.
    Harte v. *Harte*, The Times, December 3, 1976, C.A.
    L. v. *L.* [1962] P. 101; [1961] 3 W.L.R. 1182; [1961] 3 All E.R. 834,
C   C.A.
    Ladbrook v. *Ladbrook* (1977) 121 S.J. 710.
    Minton v. *Minton* (1978) 122 S.J. 31, C.A.
    Practice Direction (Decrees and Orders: Agreed Terms) [1972] 1 W.L.R.
        1313; [1972] 3 All E.R. 704.
    Practice Direction (Matrimonial Causes: Special Procedure) (No. 2) [1977]
        1 W.L.R. 320; [1977] 1 All E.R. 844.
D   *Wales* v. *Wadham* [1977] 1 W.L.R. 199; [1977] 2 All E.R. 125.
    Wright v. *Wright* [1970] 1 W.L.R. 1219; [1970] 3 All E.R. 209, C.A.

    PETITION

    The parties were married on January 1, 1965. On July 14, 1977, the
husband presented a petition for dissolution of the marriage. The cause
was entered in the county court special procedure list. It came before
E Judge Figgis on October 17, 1977, who transferred the issue to a judge
of the Family Division.

    After a hearing in chambers, Bush J. gave judgment in open court
on February 24, 1978 on the point of law. The substantive issue was
adjourned until March 20, 1978.

    The facts are stated in the judgment.

F
    John Peppitt Q.C. and *John Jarvis* for the wife.
    Joseph Jackson Q.C. and *Robert Johnson* for the husband.

    BUSH J. This is an application by a respondent wife to show cause
why the minutes of an agreement arrived at between herself and her
husband should not be made an order of the court.
G   The issue is the extent to which a court is bound by an agreement made
by the parties, the effect of which is to compromise a wife's claim for
financial provision under section 23 or 24 of the Matrimonial Causes Act
1973, which requires for its implementation an order of the court.

    The husband says that there is no power to review the agreement. The
wife says that the court has a duty to review.

H   The parties were married on January 1, 1965. There are two
children: a girl, aged 12 years 9 months, and a boy, aged 9 years 5
months. The husband was an extremely successful business man. The
last matrimonial home was in Spain. The marriage finally broke up
towards the end of 1975. The wife lives in Spain at the former matrimonial home and the husband lives in France. The wife was anxious
for a divorce; the husband was not really concerned about divorce.

    Negotiations took place as to custody and financial provision between solicitors and eventually minutes of agreement were arrived at. One A copy was signed by the wife on September 12, 1977, and the other by the husband, on September 21, 1977. The draft minutes so signed were headed: "Draft minutes of order to be submitted for approval by a registrar with a view to incorporation in the order made on decree nisi." It is accepted by both sides that this agreement, negotiations in respect of which began in 1976, was arrived at at arm's length, with both parties represented by solicitors and without improper pressure either way. In B arriving at that agreement, the solicitors were content to proceed on the basis that the husband was a very, very rich man, but there was no discovery of documents as such, or, as I understand it, any specific details of capital, income and liabilities supplied or seriously required.

On July 14, 1977, the husband filed his petition alleging adultery by the wife. The matter proceeded undefended in the special procedure C list under rule 48 of the Matrimonial Causes Rules 1977. The husband's solicitors had conduct of the proceedings.

On September 12, 1977, the registrar granted his certificate. On September 29, 1977, Mr. Registrar Artro-Morris, having had presented to him the draft minutes, wrote a note:

> "I am prepared to amend the registrar's certificate . . . but first D the [wife] must lodge a written undertaking to return the [boy] to the jurisdiction if called upon to do so. Second—who is to have care and control of the [girl]—if the [husband], will [she] live in France? If so, undertaking from the [husband] is required."

On September 30, 1977, the note read, in red, "I have amended the registrar's certificate accordingly." As amended, the registrar's E certificate read:

> "I am satisfied that the requirements of rule 33 (1) of the Matrimonial Causes Rules 1977 have been complied with, and I direct that this cause be entered in the County Court Special Procedure List."

That was dated August 31, 1977. The registrar's certificate:

F
> "I certify that the [husband] has sufficiently proved the contents of the petition herein and is entitled to a decree of divorce/judicial separation on the ground of the [wife's] adultery with a man against whom the charge has not been proved."

Then the amendment, in red:

> "And to an order in the terms of the draft minutes of order signed G by the [wife] on September 12, 1977, and signed by the [husband] on September 21, 1977, both as amended by me on September 30, 1977."

By September 27, 1977, it was clear that the wife was resiling from the agreement. Indeed, on September 24, 1977, she had sent a telegram to her solicitors, which read: "Stop all court proceedings. Having second H thoughts." It is clear from the notes of attendance by the husband's solicitors that the wife was in effect saying that she was not going to move out of the former matrimonial home in accordance with the agreement, and was denying that she had signed any agreement. On October 5, 1977, the registrar was told that the ex-wife had changed her mind and on that date he re-amended the certificate by deleting the amendment of September 30, 1977.

A   The suit came before Judge Figgis on October 17, 1977, under the special procedure, and he stood the suit over for 14 days, directing the wife to file an affidavit to show cause why the minutes of agreement should not be made an order of the court and he transferred the issue to a judge of the Family Division. To complete the history, on December 2, 1977, a decree nisi was pronounced by Judge Everett, clearly without prejudice to the present inquiry.

B   The first point taken by the wife is that the registrar, by his amendment of the minutes on September 30, 1977, when he inserted above the arrangements for the custody of the children and after the words " By consent," the words: " Subject to the appropriate undertakings being lodged by the parties and subject to the approval of the judge," was thereby making a new agreement for the parties and therefore the wife

C   is discharged from the original agreement. I reject this argument since the amendment by the registrar was merely to put into the document what would have been common form of any order made by the court relating to the children and the parties must be taken to know that such undertakings would be required of them, it being the court's duty and prerogative to require such undertakings.

D   By virtue of the agreement, the wife receives a capital lump sum payment of £30,000 and a two-bedroom flat at Altea, bringing in £47 or so a month, with a capital value of approximately £15,000. On her evidence this was purchased for her in discharge of a loan for the purchase of the matrimonial home. She believed that it was in her name in any event, but be that as it may. In addition, she has most of the contents of the matrimonial home and gives up everything else. The wording is:

E   "The [wife] by agreement accepts the said sum in full and final satisfaction of all her claims of any kind for financial provision, orders and property adjustment orders, and then save as aforesaid, upon decree absolute, the [wife's] said claims do stand dismissed."

        The husband, on the other hand, gets a four-bedroomed Sierra Nevada flat, valued at about £33,000, which had originally been bought

F   in joint names; the matrimonial home, which was in joint names until November 1974, with a capital value of something like £60,000; and he also gets the family's share, which is a half share, in a motel at Alicante, though at one time the wife had had 48 per cent. of that half, as opposed to her husband's 52 per cent., and though the husband says—and it does not seem for the present at any rate to be seriously contested—that that

G   is not really an asset but a liability. The husband gets everything else, including a valuable business, which he values at £111,000 to £141,000.

        On the authority of Smallman v. Smallman [1972] Fam. 25 the agreement is binding on the parties unless and until it is not approved by the court. Lord Denning M.R. said, at p. 31:

        " It is very common for agreements to be made in divorce proceedings
H   ' subject to the approval of the court.' This has been so ever since the enactment of the Matrimonial Causes Act 1963 (now section 5 of the Matrimonial Causes Act 1965) which validates a bargain which represents an honest negotiation between the parties provided it is disclosed to the court. In Nash v. Nash [1965] P. 266, 277, Scarman J. said that it was in these days quite proper to come to an agreement which is intended to make reasonable provision for the parties: . . ."

Lord Denning M.R. quoted Scarman J. in *Nash* v. *Nash* and went on: A

"Since the Divorce Reform Act 1969 also it is common for agreements to be made 'subject to the approval of the court' and to seek the opinion of the court under section 7 as to the reasonableness of them. In my opinion, if the parties have reached an agreement on all essential matters, then the clause 'subject to the approval of the court' does not mean there is no agreement at all. There is   B
an agreement, but the operation of it is suspended until the court approves it. It is the duty of one party or the other to bring the agreement before the court for approval. If the court approves it, it is binding on the parties. If the court does not approve, it is not binding."

Although the agreement in this case refers to the registrar's approval,   C
whose is the ultimate responsibility? It seems clear from *M.* v. *M.* [1967] P. 313 and *Brockwell* v. *Brockwell*, November 5, 1975, Court of Appeal (Civil Division) Transcript No. 468 of 1975 that the court has ultimate discretion so far as financial arrangements are concerned and that discretion applies whether the orders are to be made under section 23 or section 24 of the Matrimonial Causes Act 1973. In exercising that discretion, the court must have regard to the principles laid down in section   D
25, which provides:

"(1) It shall be the duty of the court in deciding whether to exercise its powers under section 23 (1) (*a*), (*b*) or (*c*) or 24 above in relation to a party to the marriage and, if so, in what manner, to have regard to all the circumstances of the case including the following matters . . ."   E

and then it goes on to set out the matters.

The discretion by virtue of sections 23 and 24 of the Act of 1973 becomes exercisable on the granting of a decree or at any time thereafter, since that is the language used at the commencement of each of those sections:

"On granting a decree of divorce, a decree of nullity of marriage   F
or a decree of judicial separation or at any time thereafter . . . the court may make any one or more of the following orders . . .".

Section 25 is mandatory and is the modern authority for the retention by the court of its powers over agreements by the parties.

What the parties here are asking the court to do in part is to exercise its powers of making a lump sum payment order under section 23 of the   G
Matrimonial Causes Act 1973. Therefore the court must have regard to the provisions of section 25 of the Act of 1973 and the time when it must have such regard is on granting a decree of divorce, a decree of nullity of marriage or a decree of judicial separation or at any time thereafter. Under section 7 of the Matrimonial Causes Act 1973 the court may express an opinion before or after the presentation of a petition of   H
an agreement or arrangement, but if a court does express an opinion, that does not relieve it of its duty to re-consider the matter under section 25 at the appropriate time.

In *Brockwell* v. *Brockwell*, November 5, 1975, Court of Appeal (Civil Division), Transcript No. 468 of 1975 Stamp L.J. said:

"There is nothing in the Matrimonial Causes Act 1973 enabling parties to contract out of the provisions of section 23 or 24 of that

A   Act which provides under section 23 for periodical payments or lump
     sum payments, and under section 24 for property adjustment orders
     in connection with divorce proceedings, or to preclude the court
     from performing the duties imposed upon it under section 25 (1). . . .
     Sir Gordon Willmer in *Wright* v. *Wright* [1970] 1 W.L.R. 1219, 1223
     said ' There is no doubt that no agreement made inter partes can ever
     deprive the court of its right to review the question of maintenance
B   for a wife, as was decided by the House of Lords in *Hyman* v. *Hyman*
     [1929] A.C. 601. I do not think that anything contained in the new
     provisions of the Act of 1965, giving the court the power to approve
     reasonable arrangements between the parties, is such as to cast any
     doubt at all upon the continuance in force of the doctrine enunciated
     by the House of Lords in *Hyman* v. *Hyman* [1929] A.C. 601. There
C   is, therefore, scope for two diametrically opposite views. On the
     one hand, it may be said that the court has an absolute right to go
     behind any agreement between the parties so far as the question of
     maintenance for a wife is concerned. On the other hand, there is
     the judge's approach to the problem, that is, that where there is an
     agreement between the parties approved by the court, effect must
     be given to it. Under the one view, the right to award maintenance
D   would be completely uninhibited, whereas under the other it would
     be strictly curtailed by the arrangement made between the parties and
     approved by the court at the time of the trial.' So in my judgment
     here no agreement between the parties could deprive the court of its
     powers and duties under sections 23, 24 and 25 of the Matrimonial
     Causes Act 1973. In *Wright* v. *Wright* [1970] 1 W.L.R. 1219 the
E   court concluded that the proper order was that the agreement there
     in question entered into with full knowledge of all the circumstances
     and on the advice of both parties' legal advisers was something to
     which considerable attention must be paid. Sir Gordon Willmer
     accepted the view, at p. 1224, ' that it would not be right to say that
     it has to be construed like a statute, or that it absolutely forbids any
F   possible award of maintenance, except upon the strictest proof of
     the existence of the circumstances mentioned.'—the circumstances
     mentioned being a change of circumstances—' If and in so far as
     the judge so decided, I would not agree wholly with his conclusion.
     But I do not think that he went so far as that.' "

     There is also a public policy reason why the court should retain
G   control over orders which it makes, and that was adumbrated as early
     as 1952, in *Bennett* v. *Bennett* [1952] 1 K.B. 249, 262, where Denning
     L.J. said:

        " *Agreements for permanent maintenance on a divorce.* An award
     of permanent maintenance on a divorce is peculiarly a matter for the
     Divorce Court, and the jurisdiction of that court in regard to it
H   cannot be ousted by the private agreement of the parties. The
     reason lies in public policy. First, it is in the public interest that
     the wife and children of a divorced husband should not be left
     dependent on public assistance, or on charity, when he has the
     means to support them. They should therefore be able to come
     to the Divorce Court for maintenance, notwithstanding any agree-
     ment to the contrary: *Hyman* v. *Hyman* [1929] A.C. 601."

Bush J.   **Dean v. Dean (Fam.D.)**   **[1978]**

Public policy has, in my view, survived the disappearance of collusion,   A
first as an absolute and then as a discretionary bar to divorce.

Mr. Jackson, on behalf of the husband, has urged that the court is
bound by the agreement and that the approval of the court is limited to
the judge or registrar satisfying himself that the orders sought are
within the jurisdiction of the court or are not against public policy. He
grasps the nettle and says, by way of argument, that he fundamentally
disputes the proposition that it is the duty of the court in consent matters   B
to satisfy itself as to the reasonableness of the provisions. The answer
to that is that if the court is to be asked to make an order under section
23 or section 24 of the Act of 1973 then the mandatory effect of section
25 operates.

Mr. Jackson further raises the fear that the courts would have an
impossible task, particularly under the special procedure, if they had   C
minutely to examine every proposed financial consent order. In the
general run of cases, all that would be needed is that the solicitors for
the parties or party are present at the appropriate stage ready to answer
any relevant questions. The agreement itself will provide prima facie
evidence of the reasonableness of the provisions. Probably formal discovery of documents would be unnecessary, for the court would no doubt
give great weight to an agreement arrived at by the parties who are   D
both legally represented and who have conducted their negotiations at
arm's length. It may, under the special procedure, be convenient for
the registrar to certify that the petitioner is entitled to an order in agreed
terms and it may be that this will be sufficient to satisfy the judge, who
under the special procedure pronounces the decree and other orders in
open court, and does so without any of the parties being in attendance.   E
But it does not relieve the judge from making an order by virtue of
section 23 or section 24 of his primary duty under section 25 of the
Matrimonial Causes Act 1973.

It is clear from the wording of the registrar's certificate in this case
that at the stage of granting the certificate the registrar is only saying,
and can only say, that in his view the husband is entitled to the order in
due course. He does not make the order, and there is no jurisdiction to   F
make the order until on or at any time after decree nisi. Clearly, not
only has the court jurisdiction; it must assume it.

Judge Figgis very properly directed the wife to show cause why the
concluded agreement of the parties should not be made an order of the
court. For the purpose of the exercise, I, at this stage, am the judge
who has to perform that duty. In exercising that duty, I would of
course have regard to the provisions of section 25 of the Act of 1973,   G
but also the conduct of the parties in all the circumstances. The conduct of the parties in this context must include the fact of and the nature
of an agreement voluntarily arrived at between the parties.

In *Brockwell* v. *Brockwell,* Court of Appeal (Civil Division) Transcript
No. 468 of 1975 Ormrod L.J. dealt with the matter in this way. It was
a case where he said in relation to a lump sum application, where there   H
had been an apparent agreement between the parties:

"But it must be a matter entirely for the judge to look at all the
facts and the financial situation of each party and taking into account
the fact that they made this agreement which to my mind is a very
important piece of conduct under section 25 of the Matrimonial
Causes Act 1973 because what the court is required to arrive at
eventually is such an order as will be just and practicable having

A   regard, among other things, to the conduct of the parties, and clearly
when people make an agreement like this it is a very important factor
in considering what is the just outcome of the proceedings. It may
or may not represent what they themselves felt to be fair at the
time when they made the agreement, and that is as good a guide to
justice perhaps as anything."

B   In the instant case it has not been said that there has been any change
of circumstances since the agreement was arrived at. What is said is
that the wife really has not got a very good bargain and has changed her
mind. To this end she has filed an affidavit, sworn on October 28, 1977.
In that affidavit she sets out in great detail what she alleges is her husband's financial position and sets out also her claims to shares, now or
at one time, in various family assets. The husband, without prejudice,
C has filed an affidavit of means, which shows substantial assets, though
not as substantial as suggested by the wife. Nevertheless this is not one
of those cases where the wife is in ignorance of the true financial status of
the husband.

    Mr. Peppitt has asked for an adjournment so that there can be full
discovery of documents and detailed investigation of the husband's
D financial affairs and he wishes to argue the question of whether the provision of maintenance or the agreement made reasonable provision for
the wife. For my part, as at present, I do not feel that I ought to accede
to such a request for an adjournment, but I will of course hear further
argument on it and further argument on the question of whether there
has been proper provision.

Adjournment granted.
E
Order for discovery refused.

    The following judgment was delivered in chambers on March 21, 1978,
and is reported by permission of the judge.

    BUSH J. This judgment is supplemental to the judgment I gave on
F the preliminary issue on February 24, 1978. Having said it was the duty
of the court before making an order under section 23 or section 24 of
the Matrimonial Causes Act 1973 to have regard to section 25 of the
same Act, I now go on to consider whether the wife has shown cause
why the minutes of agreement should not be made a rule of court.

    After further argument I granted Mr. Peppitt his application for an
adjournment, but refused his application for discovery of documents.
G For the purposes of a consideration of this aspect, I did not regard it as
right that the parties should be put to yet further delay and expense.
I have been content to assume that the husband is a very rich man indeed.
The wife says he is a millionaire and the negotiations for the agreement
proceeded on the basis that he was worth at least £500,000. A good deal
of his wealth, however, must be tied up in his business.

H   The basis of the negotiations was set out in the affidavit of the husband's solicitor, Mr. Sylvester, where he said that the third issue was
the husband's worth, both in net terms and in terms of what could be
regarded as reasonably realisable assets:

        " Mr. Wood [the wife's solicitor]—and I both accepted that what-
      ever the gross value of his assets we were negotiating for this purpose
      on the basis that the figure might certainly be in excess of half a
      million pound sterling. His net worth would be less than the

gross. Moreover, there was the familiar problem of achieving an A
arrangement that was practicable having regard to the nature of
the assets."

He went on to say that Mr. Wood strenuously asserted on behalf of the
wife that the husband was a man of very considerable wealth, and set
out some of the properties that it is alleged he had.

[His Lordship described the terms of the agreement between the B
parties and continued:] Upon implementation of the agreement the
wife's income would comprise £53 per month, subject to tax, which
would be her income from her occupation as a physiotherapist in Spain
(it would arrive in her hands in pesetas); and an estimated £47 per month
in respect of the rent from the flat. The wife is a state registered nurse
and has no wish to return to England where her qualification would be of
financial value.   C

Further additional facts which it is important to bear in mind are,
(a) she is 37 and the husband is 50 years of age; (b) the wife's adultery
commenced in 1972, the marriage having been in 1965, and continued
thereafter; (c) the wife was anxious to obtain a divorce and anxious to
stay in Spain with the other man; (d) the husband, at the beginning at
any rate, was not anxious for a divorce and initially was seeking a recon- D
ciliation; (e) the wife was anxious about the position in Spanish law of
her lover, who was and is a married man. It is common ground that
as the law then was in Spain that concern, which was that the lover
might in certain circumstances be imprisoned, was not without foundation.
Let me emphasise that at no time did the husband or his legal advisers use
the possible Spanish legal position as a weapon or as a threat. (f) The
husband was and is resident in France, which in itself produced a com- E
plication. The wife's legal adviser wrote to her about that on March 2,
1977, when he said:

"Further, with regard to any divorce proceedings, I presume that
these would be brought by your husband in this country, in which
event I could act and he would be required to disclose the whole
of his property in the United Kingdom. However, I understand F
that he lives most of his time in France and if he should wish to
bring proceedings under French law you would need the advice of
a lawyer in France. If this happens I could let you have the name
of a reputable firm of solicitors who could act for you."

In fact the wife never took the advice of a French lawyer. It is now
said by the wife's advisers that there would have been no jurisdiction in G
France for the husband to bring proceedings, though he had received,
apparently, advice to the contrary effect. It is not necessary for me to
decide that issue. Indeed, the fact that there was a problem of jurisdiction was a fact that of course the parties would have had in mind
throughout the negotiations. (g) As part of the agreement the husband
brought his petition in England. It is said that as the petition was
dated July 14, 1977, and the minutes of agreement were only signed by H
the wife on September 12, 1977, this cannot have been in pursuance
of the agreement. One has only to look at the correspondence to see
the falsity of this argument. In fact, the substance of the terms was
agreed on July 13, 1977, and the petition was filed the next day. Further,
as part of the agreement the husband sought no finding or relief against
the second respondent. I doubt if the husband, had he so wished,
would have found any difficulty in obtaining evidence against the second

A respondent, though the enforcement of an order for costs would of course have been another matter. In the event, there was a finding of adultery by the wife with a man against whom the charge has not been proved. It is true that the divorce was pronounced after the wife had sought to resile from her agreement, but the husband was entitled to seek to hold her to that agreement.

B In the present case the wife had legal advice throughout. She knew all the relevant facts so far as her husband's financial position was concerned. The negotiations were conducted at arm's length. Since the agreement there has been no change of circumstances, unforeseen or otherwise. Duress, mistake, undue influence are not alleged. The wife is not left destitute.

The wife says in her affidavit of March 17, 1978:

C   " I changed my mind about the agreement when I was being asked to leave the matrimonial home within three months. I realised that I would not have adequate money to purchase a new house. In the meantime I was to be housed in a temporary small flat where there would be no separate bedroom for [the girl]."

The girl is at boarding school in England but spends holidays, or part D of them, with her mother.

"I realised that I would get no support in Spain, that my physiotherapy business was not prospering, and the fear of being abroad with no means of supporting myself either in England or Spain frightened me. I have never had to maintain myself. I strongly felt that the agreement was not in accordance with the [husband's] agreement E   with me that I would not have to worry about money again. I realised that I needed income as well as capital."

The wife says in amplification of that through her counsel that the bargain is not as good a bargain as the bargain that she would have got if she had either stood out for more or had left the court to decide. I can only stigmatise that argument as, in the circumstances, unmeritorius, F however rich the husband.

Secondly, the wife says that on the evidence she made the agreement on manifestly bad advice. Whether this would represent a valid objection to the agreement it is not necessary for me to decide, because I cannot accept that the advice she received was bad, manifestly or otherwise. One has only to look at the correspondence between the wife and her G solicitors as a whole to see the care with which her case was handled. There had been quite prolonged negotiations where an offer by the husband had been submitted to the wife and rejected by her, and then eventually about June 14, 1977, a telex message was sent by the husband's solicitor to her solicitor—this was after the wife and the husband had met in Spain—and it said:

H   " I have been given to understand that our respective clients have met and as a result I am to put the following offer which I understand will be acceptable to [the wife],"

and then they set out the terms of the agreement. Then on July 5, 1977, the wife wrote to her solicitor:

"Dear Mr. Wood, I have today received a copy of the settlement paper. I am rather surprised that I have not had anything more from you, particularly after my telephone conversation one week

ago. I am not squabbling about the money settlement but I cannot
sign this paper until I have other things settled that are worrying
me. One, I want a written promise that my son will not be taken
from me, certainly not before the age of 11 when I am prepared to
let him go to boarding school. Two, as mother I feel a right to be
part of the choosing of a suitable boarding school with the agreement
of my husband and myself. Three, the agreement that the two
children will be coming to spend a large part of their holidays with
me whether I remain in Spain or not. That my husband is prepared to pay the fares to and from school to wherever I may be
living. A definite quotation of a certain sum for the children's
maintenance while they are staying with me. That the capital sum
settlement be paid to me in English currency. I know these may
only be details, but as they are very important to me I will not
sign anything until this is added to the final papers for signing. I
hope you can let me have the final settlement with these particulars
included."

Then her solicitor wrote to her:

" I refer to our recent various telephone conversations, particularly
that of today when you instructed me that you were now prepared
to agree the terms which I have now been able to negotiate with
your husband's solicitor, Mr. Sylvester."

In fact, all the terms that she was insisting on in the previous letter had
been conceded and the letter goes on to set them out. Indeed, it goes
into some detail at a later stage about the furniture and property.

It may be that on one view of the matter the wife got less than she
might otherwise have done. However, what is or is not a good bargain
does not depend entirely on the financial aspect: other considerations
may apply. For example, though it is not so in this case, a wife's
intention may be to remarry: this would make her want a lump sum
and she would be prepared to appear to bargain away her right to
periodical payments in order to get it, knowing full well that when
she did remarry her periodical payments would cease. It would be
undesirable under such circumstances that a court exercising its power
under section 25 of the Act of 1973 should have to cross-examine the
wife as to her intentions. The court must, in performing its duty under
section 25 in circumstances where there is an agreement between the
parties, adopt the broad rather than the particular approach. On the one
hand, the court has a duty under section 25, but at the same time the
court owes a duty to uphold agreements validly arrived at and which are
not on the face of them, or in fact, against public policy. In general
terms also, it is wrong for the court to stir up problems with parties who
have come to an agreement.

In so far as the wife complains about the arrangements for the
children, which she does in her affidavit of October 28, 1977, questions
of maintenance and provision for the children are always open, and if
she wishes to air her complaints in this respect and seek a different
order then it is open to her to do so.

In one respect the minutes are in error. They do not correctly set
out what was in fact agreed between the parties, namely that the wife
should have the care and control of both children. In those circumstances
the minutes will accordingly be amended to represent the true agreement
of the parties.

A   Finally, I take into account all the provisions of section 25 of the
Act of 1973, which includes the agreement of parties, and all the circumstances which includes a close study of the correspondence between
the solicitors, and in particular the wife's correspondence with her own
solicitors and her own solicitors' correspondence with her.

       I find that in all the circumstances reasonable provision has been
made for the wife and she should be held to her bargain. Indeed, it
B   would be unconscionable in my view not to hold her to her agreement.
Consequently, I order that the draft minutes be incorporated as an
order of the court.

                              Order accordingly.
                              Wife to pay half of husband's costs.

C   Solicitors: *Howlett & Clarke, Cree & Co.; Clintons.*

                                                              M. B. D.

                              _____

D   [PRIVY COUNCIL]

BRISBANE CITY COUNCIL AND MYER SHOPPING
       CENTRES PTY. LTD. . . . . APPELLANTS

                              AND

ATTORNEY-GENERAL FOR QUEENSLAND
E   (AT THE RELATION OF ARTHUR THOMAS SCURR AND
    WILLIAM PERCIVAL BOON) . . . . RESPONDENT

       [ON APPEAL FROM THE FULL COURT OF THE SUPREME COURT OF
                              QUEENSLAND]

F   1978 March 14, 15, 16 20;   Lord Wilberforce, Lord Hailsham of
         May 23   St. Marylebone, Lord Russell
                                      of Killowen, Lord Keith of Kinkel and
                                                  Sir John Pennycuick

*Australia—Queensland—Charity—Charitable purposes—Conveyance
    to council on conditions—Area to be set aside for "show-
    ground, park and recreational purposes"—Whether intention
G   to create trust—Whether exclusively charitable—Earlier plan-
    ning consent appeals—Whether question of trust res judicata*

       In 1938 the trustees of a society whose main function was
    to organise a district annual show conveyed about 20 acres of
    land to Brisbane City Council in consideration of the council's
    discharging a debt of £450 owed by the society and on the
    following conditions (recorded in the minutes of the council
H   and in a letter of October 25, 1937, from the council to the
    trustees):
          " (a) the area to be set apart permanently for showground,
       park and recreation purposes; (b) the show ring to be
       levelled off; (c) the show society to be granted the exclu-
       sive use of the ground without charge for a period of two
       weeks in each and every year, for the purposes of and
       in connection with the district annual show."
    In 1970 developers applied under the City of Brisbane Town
    Planning Act 1964 for consent to use the land as a shopping

centre and the council contracted to sell the land to them. A
The relator S. gave notice of objection to the granting of
planning consent: his appeal to the Local Government Court
eventually reached the High Court of Australia.   Another
appeal against the granting of planning consent by the relator
to the Local Government Court was dismissed in December
1975. In March 1971, during the pendency of the planning
appeals, the Attorney-General at the relation of S. brought an
action against the council and the developers for a declaration B
that the purported sale to the developers was ultra vires and
void.   That action was dismissed. In the present proceedings,
the Attorney-General on the relation of S. and B. sought, as
against the council and the developers, a declaration that the
land was subject to a valid and enforceable charitable trust.
The trial judge found as a fact that a " show " in Queensland
operated to encourage agriculture and horticulture and made C
an order granting the declaration. The council and the
developers appealed on the grounds that the council did not
hold the land as trustee; that there was no valid and enforceable public charitable trust and that even if there were the
Attorney-General was debarred from asserting it in that, inter
alia, the existence of the trust could and should have been
asserted in the previous litigation against the council.   The
Full Court of the Supreme Court dismissed the appeal. D

On appeal by the council and the developers to the Judicial
Committee: —

Held, dismissing the appeal, (1) that the terms of paragraph
(*a*) of the conditions that the land was to be set apart permanently for specified purposes showed unequivocally an
intention to create a trust for the purposes specified binding on
the land in the council's hands and, there being nothing in
paragraphs (*b*) and (*c*) inconsistent with that intention, the E
council had acquired the land as trustee (post, p. 304E–F).

(2) That, since on the trial judge's findings a " show "
operated in Queensland to encourage agriculture, a trust for
" showground purposes " could properly be construed as a
trust for the promotion of agriculture and as such was a charitable activity beneficial to the community within the fourth head
of *Pemsel's* case and, therefore, since on authority " park and
recreational purposes " were also charitable objects, the pur- F
poses specified in paragraph (*a*) of the conditions were
exclusively charitable and the land was subject to a valid and
enforceable public charitable trust and that that validity was
not impaired by the terms of paragraph (*c*) which permitted
the trusts to be implemented in part by the land's being placed
at the disposition of private individuals (post, pp. 306B–F, 307B).

Income Tax Special Purposes Commissioners v. *Pemsel* G
[1891] A.C. 531, H.L.(E.) and *Inland Revenue Commissioners*
v. *Yorkshire Agricultural Society* [1928] 1 K.B. 611, C.A.
applied.

(3) That the basis of the defence of res judicata in its
wider sense, by which a party was precluded from raising an
issue which he could and should have raised in earlier proceedings, was that to raise such an issue was an abuse of
process and that (even assuming that in the present case the H
existence of the trust was known at the time of the earlier
proceedings and that there was the necessary identity of
parties), since it would have been inappropriate to assert the
existence of the trust either in the planning consent appeals or
in the 1971 action against the council, the bringing of the
present action was not an abuse of process and the defence
failed (post, pp. 307H—308A, D–F).

Judgment of the Full Court of the Supreme Court of
Queensland affirmed.

301

A   The following cases are referred to in the judgment of their Lordships:

Dunne v. *Byrne* [1912] A.C. 407, P.C.
Greenhalgh v. *Mallard* [1947] 2 All E.R. 255, C.A.
Hadden, In re [1932] 1 Ch. 133.
Henderson v. *Henderson* (1843) 3 Hare 100.
Hoystead v. *Commissioner of Taxation* [1926] A.C. 155, P.C.
Income Tax Special Purposes Commissioners v. *Pemsel* [1891] A.C. 531,
B   H.L.(E.).
Incorporated Council of Law Reporting for England and Wales v.
        Attorney-General [1972] Ch. 73; [1971] 3 W.L.R. 853; [1971] 3 All
        E.R. 1029, C.A.
Incorporated Council of Law Reporting (Q.) v. *Federal Commissioner of
        Taxation* (1971) 125 C.L.R. 659.
Inland Revenue Commissioners v. *Baddeley* [1955] A.C. 572; [1955]
C   2 W.L.R. 552; [1955] 1 All E.R. 525, H.L.(E.).
Inland Revenue Commissioners v. *Yorkshire Agricultural Society* [1928]
        1 K.B. 611, C.A.
Monds v. *Stackhouse* (1948) 77 C.L.R. 232.
Spence, In re [1938] Ch. 96.
Yat Tung Investment Co. Ltd. v. *Dao Heng Bank Ltd.* [1975] A.C. 581;
        [1975] 2 W.L.R. 690, P.C.

D
    The following additional cases were cited in argument:

Ashton's Estate, In re [1938] Ch. 482; [1938] 1 All E.R. 707, C.A.;
        sub nom. *Farley* v. *Westminster Bank Ltd.* [1939] A.C. 430; [1939]
        3 All E.R. 491, H.L.(E.).
Attorney-General v. *Proprietors of Bradford Canal* (1866) L.R. 2 Eq. 71.
Attorney-General v. *Southampton Corporation* (1858) 1 Giff. 363.
E   *Associated Minerals Consolidated Ltd.* v. *Wyong Shire Council* [1975]
        A.C. 538; [1975] 2 W.L.R. 81, P.C.
Alexandra Park Trustees v. *Haringey London Borough* (1967) 66 L.G.R.
        306.
Barby v. *Perpetual Trustee Co. Ltd.* (1937) 58 C.L.R. 316.
Bones, In re [1930] V.L.R. 346.
Brunsden v. *Humphrey* (1884) 14 Q.B.D. 141, C.A.
F   *Crystal Palace Trustees* v. *Minister of Town and Country Planning. In
        re Town and Country Planning Act* 1947 [1951] Ch. 132.
Congregational Union of New South Wales v. *Thistlethwayte* (1952) 87
        C.L.R. 375.
D'Aguiar v. *Inland Revenue Commissioner* (unreported), January 19,
        1970, P.C.
Dingle v. *Turner* [1972] A.C. 601; [1972] 2 W.L.R. 523; [1972] 1 All
        E.R. 878, H.L.(E.).
G   *Erlanger* v. *New Sombero Phosphate Co.* (1878) 3 App.Cas. 1218, H.L.(E.).
Hadaway v. *Hadaway* [1955] 1 W.L.R. 16, P.C.
Harpur's Will Trusts, In re [1961] Ch. 38; [1960] 3 W.L.R. 607; [1960] 3
        All E.R. 237.
Hood, In re [1931] 1 Ch. 240, C.A.
Inland Revenue Commissioners v. *City of Glasgow Police Athletic
        Association* [1953] A.C. 380; [1953] 2 W.L.R. 625; [1953] 1 All E.R.
H   747, H.L.(Sc.).
Kok Hoong v. *Leong Cheong Kweng Mines Ltd.* [1964] A.C. 993; [1964]
        2 W.L.R. 150; [1964] 1 All E.R. 300, P.C.
Leahy v. *Attorney-General (N.S.W.)* [1959] A.C. 457; [1969] 2 W.L.R.
        722; [1959] 2 All E.R. 300, P.C.
Lindsay Petroleum Co. v. *Hurd* (1874) L.R. 5 P.C. 221.
Lysons v. *Commissioner of Stamp Duties* [1945] N.Z.L.R. 738.
Mitford v. *Reynolds* (1842) 1 Ph. 185.

Brisbane City Council v. Attorney-General (P.C.)   [1978]

Morgan v. *Wellington City Corporation* [1975] N.Z.L.R. 416.   A

Murray v. *Thomas* [1937] 4 All E.R. 545.

New Brunswick Rail Co. v. *British and French Trust Corporation Ltd.*
    [1939] A.C. 1; [1938] 4 All E.R. 747, H.L.(E.).

Nightingale v. *Goulbourne* (1848) 2 Ph. 594.

Oxford Group v. *Inland Revenue Commissioners* [1949] 2 All E.R. 537.

Royal National Agricultural and Industrial Association v. *Chester* (1974)
    48 A.L.J.R. 304.   B

St. Mary Magdalen, Oxford v. *Attorney-General* (1857) 6 H.L.Cas. 189,
    H.L.(E.).

Schebsman, In re [1944] Ch. 83, C.A.

Schellenberger v. *Trustees Executors and Agency Co. Ltd.* (1952) 86
    C.L.R. 454.

Smith, In re [1967] V.R. 341.

Smith v. *Kerr* [1902] 1 Ch. 774.   C

Stratton v. *Simpson* (1970) 125 C.L.R. 138.

Trades House of Glasgow v. *Inland Revenue*, 1970 S.L.T. 294.

Tribune Press, Lahore (Trustees) v. *Income Tax Commissioners, Punjab,
    Lahore* [1939] 3 All E.R. 469.

Wanganui Borough v. *Wanganui Fire Board* [1919] N.Z.L.R. 767.

Williams' Trustees v. *Inland Revenue Commissioners* [1947] A.C. 447;
    [1947] 1 All E.R. 513, H.L.(E.).   D

Wrexham, Corporation of v. *Tamplin* (1873) 28 L.T. 761.

APPEAL (No. 18 of 1977) by Brisbane City Council and Myer Shopping
Centres Pty. Ltd., the developers, from a judgment (March 18, 1977) of
the Full Court of the Supreme Court of Queensland (Hanger C.J., Stable
and D. M. Campbell JJ.) dismissing by a majority (Stable J. dissenting) E
an appeal from a judgment (December 7, 1976) of Hoare J. in the Supreme
Court. On a claim by the Attorney-General for Queensland at the
relation of Arthur Thomas Scurr and William Percival Boon, Hoare J.
declared that land at Mount Gravatt, Brisbane, described as subdivisions
2 and 3 of portions 332 and 333 in the county of Stanley, parish of Bulimba,
was presently held by the council on trust for showground, park and
recreation purposes and that the council was bound by the terms of its F
resolution of October 19, 1937, which set out the conditions on which
the trustees of the Mount Gravatt Agricultural, Horticultural and
Industrial Association, the show society, conveyed the land to the council
on September 15, 1938.

The facts are stated in the judgment of their Lordships.

G. E. Fitzgerald Q.C. and *John Gallagher* (both of the Queensland G
Bar) for the council and the developers.

C. W. Pincus Q.C. (of the Queensland Bar) and *John G. C. Phillips*
for the Attorney-General.

                                                    Cur. adv. vult.

May 23. The judgment of their Lordships was delivered by Lord H
Wilberforce.

These consolidated appeals are from the Full Court of the Supreme
Court of Queensland, which by a majority affirmed a judgment of
Hoare J. in the Supreme Court. A declaration was made by the judge
that certain land at Logan Road, Mount Gravatt, Brisbane, owned by the
Brisbane City Council, and which the council had contracted to sell to
the developers, Myer Shopping Centres Pty. Ltd., was subject to a valid

A and enforceable charitable trust, so that the council was not free to sell it. The issues raised are: 1. whether the council holds the land on a charitable trust; 2. whether the respondent is precluded by laches from asserting that the land is so held; 3. whether the issue whether the land is so held is " res judicata " (using this expression in an extended sense) as between the parties to this present litigation.

B The land in question is about 20 acres in extent: the council is the registered proprietor for an estate in fee simple.   Before the land was acquired by the council, in 1938, the registered proprietors were two persons as trustees for the members of the Mount Gravvat Agricultural, Horticultural and Industrial Association.   This unincorporated body has at various times also been known as the Mount Gravatt Agricultural Horticultural and Industrial Society, the Mount Gravatt A.H. & I. Society and the Mount Gravatt Show Society: their Lordships will refer to it as " the show society," or " the society."   It appears to have no defined objects or constitution: its main function however was to operate a showground on the land and to conduct a district show there each year.   In 1938 the land was subject to a mortgage in favour of the Bank of New South Wales securing a debt of £450 with interest.   It was clear at that time that the show society was in financial difficulties such as would prevent it from continuing to use the land as a showground.   It therefore entered into negotiations with a view to persuading the council to take it over.   There was a deputation to the Lord Mayor in September 1937 and this was followed by a number of communications and resolutions passed by the council and the society.   The first discussions, recorded in a memorandum from the office of the Lord Mayor, focused on the advantages to the city and to the society which would follow from transfer of the land to the city.   The society on its side desired that the bank mortgage should be discharged, that the city should undertake to level and improve the show ring, and that the show society should be granted the free use of the showground for two weeks in each year, when it should be used entirely for the purpose of holding the district annual show.   The city for its part would gain a park area in a district where none then existed, and would hold the ground " in perpetuity " as a recreation reserve and showground.   Proposals on these lines were referred to the finance committee of the council which reported in favour of their adoption, and a resolution of the council recorded in a minute dated October 19, 1937, accepted the committee's report.   This was followed by a letter from the town clerk to Mr. W. H. Clarke, one of the trustees for the society, dated October 25, 1937, the relevant part of which is as follows:

> " In reply I have to inform you that provision is to be made in the estimates for the next financial year for a sum, not exceeding £450, for the liquidation of the overdraft on the property, the council then to take over the fee simple of the land under the following conditions:
> " (a) The area to be set apart permanently for showground, park and recreation purposes;
> " (b) The show ring to be levelled off;
> " (c) The show society to be granted the exclusive use of the ground without charge for a period of two weeks in each and every year, for the purposes of and in connection with the district annual show."

At the annual general meeting of the society held on December 15, 1937, **A** the council's proposals were approved, and on September 20, 1938, the land was transferred to the council and the mortgage paid off.

It is necessary to refer to four other matters in connection with the transfer. First, in the correspondence which followed the letter of October 25, 1937, there were proposals to vary the terms in certain details, including the period for which the show society should have exclusive use of the showground, but these were inconclusive, and, in their **B** Lordships' opinion, nothing occurred which amounted to an effective variation of the terms set out in the letter. Second, although a draft was prepared of a formal agreement between the council and the society, this was not proceeded with. Third, although a suggestion was made for an express definition of trusts upon which the council should hold the land, this too was not proceeded with. Fourth, in a letter from the **C** town clerk of August 24, 1938, which preceded the transfer of the land to the council, it was stated that the council undertook to hold the land for the purposes of a public park, recreation reserve, or show ground, " or other purposes not inconsistent therewith ". This letter did not however purport to make or record any fresh proposals beyond those already agreed, and their Lordships do not regard it as varying or extending the terms on which the council was to acquire and hold the land: indeed **D** it could not do so in the absence of formal action by the council. The words " other purposes not inconsistent therewith ", if not mere verbiage, can only refer to purposes purely ancillary to those already stated in the letter of October 25, 1937. It is these terms which their Lordships now proceed to consider.

The first question is whether the council acquired the land as trustees **E** upon any trust. To create a trust no formal words are required once the intention is clear. The relevant intention, if a trust is to be held to be created, must be that the council's legal ownership of the land is to be held beneficially, in the case of a private trust, for ascertained persons, or in the case of a permanent public trust, for charitable purposes. Their Lordships are clearly of opinion that paragraph (a) of the letter of October 25, 1937, stating that the area is: (i) " to be set apart "; (ii) " per- **F** manently "; (iii) " for [specified] purposes ", are words entirely appropriate for, and only consistent with, an intention to create a trust binding the land in the council's ownership. There is nothing in paragraphs (b) and (c) inconsistent with the existence of a trust. Paragraph (b) simply creates a contractual obligation on the part of the trustee, as one of the terms, i.e. part of the consideration upon which it acquired the **G** land; it has the same status as the agreement to liquidate the overdraft of £450, an amount which was clearly inferior to the value of the land. Paragraph (c) defines one of the methods by which the use of the area for showground purposes is to be carried out. Their Lordships agree with the majority of the Full Court in considering that this paragraph is incidental to paragraph (a); it amounts, in effect, to a partial definition of the purposes referred to in paragraph (a) by means of an obligation to **H** allow the society to use the land for the purposes of the district annual show. It becomes, in the end, necessary to consider whether the trust declared in paragraph (a), one of the means of implementing which is spelt out in paragraph (c), is valid or invalid. This is the central issue in the present case.

It is common ground that the trust is only a valid charitable trust if it falls within the fourth class of charitable purposes defined in *Income*

A *Tax Special Purposes Commissioners* v. *Pemsel* [1891] A.C. 531 as a trust beneficial to the community within the spirit and intendment of the preamble to 43 Eliz. 1, c. 4. The lack of precision of the latter's words has to be made good by reference to decided authorities which, as has been said, are legion and not easy to reconcile (*Williams' Trustees* v. *Inland Revenue Commissioners* [1947] A.C. 447, 455). It has been said in the Court of Appeal in England (*Incorporated Council of Law Reporting for*

B *England and Wales* v. *Attorney-General* [1972] Ch. 73, 88 per Russell L.J. and endorsed by the other members of the court) that, if a purpose is shown to be beneficial to the community or of general public utility, it is prima facie charitable, an approach which might help to simplify the law, but this doctrine, even assuming it to be established in the law of England, does not yet seem to have been received in Australia: see *Incorporated Council of*

C *Law Reporting (Q)* v. *Federal Commissioner of Taxation* (1971) 125 C.L.R. 659, 666–7, per Barwick C.J. Their Lordships will therefore follow the route of precedent and analogy in the present appeal.

The task of the court is made no easier by the lack of precise evidence as to the normal activities which should be understood as associated with showgrounds in Queensland. Even as regards the use made of the Mount Gravatt ground by the show society, before transfer to the council,

D which might have been expected to throw some light upon the purposes to which the council was to put the land, the evidence, such as it is, is meagre and not easy to interpret.

Of the purposes associated in paragraph (*a*) of the letter of October 25, 1937 with those of a showground, park or recreation purposes may be accepted as charitable purposes. " Recreation " was held to be a charit-

E able purpose in *In re Hadden* [1932] 1 Ch. 133, a decision approved by members of the House of Lords at least as regards recreation in a park or garden in *Inland Revenue Commissioners* v. *Baddeley* [1955] A.C. 572, 589, 594–6, 615. However the ground on which such purposes as " park and recreation " purposes have been accepted as charitable, namely as conducing towards the health and wellbeing of the public, is not one which can easily be extended so as to cover " showground " purposes. If an

F element of public benefit is to be found in the latter, it must be sought in another direction. A closer analogy can be found in trusts for the promotion of agriculture. In England, a society formed with the object of holding an annual meeting for the exhibition of farming stock, implements, etc. for the general promotion of agriculture was held to be established for a charitable purpose. Atkin L.J. said that a bequest for

G the general improvement of agriculture, " including, if you please, specific mention of the encouragement or holding of an agricultural show " would be a charitable bequest: *Inland Revenue Commissioners* v. *Yorkshire Agricultural Society* [1928] 1 K.B. 611, 630. This was accepted as correct by Barwick C.J. in *Incorporated Council of Law Reporting (Q)* v. *Federal Commissioner of Taxation*, 125 C.L.R. 659, 669:

H   " Agriculture ", he said, " partakes of that fundamental social quality which can give a charitable nature to a trust or purpose relating thereto which is beneficial to the community. So it would seem does horticulture."

—words which are flexible if slightly tentative. Is it, then, legitimate to extrapolate from such trusts as these to a trust for showground purposes? Or, reversing this question, is it possible to extract from the trusts stated in the present case a trust for the promotion of agriculture—including

one for the holding of agricultural shows?   The point of departure for   A
this lies in the words " for ... showground purposes ".

" Showground " is a word of normal parlance; not a term of art
requiring interpretation with expert assistance.   It is a word to be interpreted by the judge, using his knowledge of the language, and his
acquaintance with accepted applications of the word to situations arising
in the normal life of the community in which he lives.   Judicial knowledge
is the knowledge of the ordinary wide-awake man, used by one who is   B
trained to express it in terms of precision.   The judges in the courts
below seem to have had no doubt as to the kind of purposes which would
be accepted as included in " showground purposes " :

> " It is ... common knowledge that voluntary associations exist in
> scores of towns and districts of Queensland for the purpose of holding
> an annual ' show ' or exhibition.   The ' showground ' is the area   C
> where that show or exhibition is held. . . . The activities of the
> ' shows ' according to the evidence in this case are broadly similar.
> To the extent that there is an exhibition of agricultural and horti-
> cultural produce it would scarcely be disputed that this activity would
> probably operate to encourage agriculture and horticulture in the
> region and thus would be a charitable purpose " (per Hoare J.).   D

Their Lordships note the cautious and qualified language used but nevertheless this is a positive finding as to the normal show of which, as Hoare
J. proceeds to find, the Mount Gravatt could be regarded as typical.   In
his view (and their Lordships agree) the evidence showed that the show
society conducted an annual show at Mount Gravatt for many years,
similar in type to the various agricultural shows held throughout the   E
state.   Such shows, as was that promoted at Mount Gravatt, were
managed by voluntary associations; a circumstance which would both
explain the lack of definite and clear-cut evidence as to the objects of
the shows and also serve to indicate that they did not have a directly
commercial purpose.   All such shows, as the judge accepted, would
include a number of miscellaneous activities, from the provision of food
and drink to entertainments and " side shows " of various kinds and no   F
doubt sale of agricultural products: but he was prepared to regard these
as ancillary to the main purpose—" intended to assist in ensuring a
successful show ".

In the Full Court, Campbell J. reached the same conclusion.   Endors-
ing the opinion of Hoare J. as to the meaning of " showground " in
Queensland, he said that the word was used in connection with land   G
occupied by show societies throughout the state.

> " It would not have occurred to me to doubt that a gift of land to a
> city, town or shire for ' showground, park and recreational purposes '
> was a charitable gift."

In so far as Campbell J. is, in this passage relying upon the public
character of the trustee to establish the charitable character of a   H
stated purpose, their Lordships would not, with respect, follow him: where
the purposes of the trust are expressed in plain language, the nature of the
trustee cannot be appealed to in order to impart a charitable character:
Dunne v. Byrne [1912] A.C. 407, 410.   The character of the expressed
purposes must be decided on their own merits.   The observations of
Luxmoore J. in In re Spence [1938] 1 Ch. 96, 102, to which the judge
appeals, in their Lordships' opinion are out of line with other cases and

A   are not authoritative. But the judge proceeds unequivocally to hold that
the purposes expressed in the whole phrase " park, recreation or showground purposes " are beneficial to the community within the fourth
category of charitable purposes—without specific reliance upon the
promotion of agriculture. Their Lordships while not dissenting from this
approach are of opinion that, in so far as the judgment of Hoare J. does
place such reliance, it is on firmer ground.

B   Their Lordships are therefore, on the whole, in agreement with the
majority of the Full Court in holding that a valid charitable trust was
created as regards the land in 1937. If this is so, i.e. if the trusts declared
in paragraph (a) of the letter of October 25, 1937, are valid as charitable
trusts, their validity is not impaired by a provision which permits these
trusts to be implemented, in part, by being placed at the disposition of
C   private individuals: see Monds v. Stackhouse (1948) 77 C.L.R. 232.

Their Lordships now consider the two particular defences put forward
in the present case. The first is that of laches. There have been a number of proceedings relating to the land over a period of about six years.
In 1970 application was made under the City of Brisbane Town Planning
Act 1964 by the developers for consent to the use of the land for a shopping centre, and notice of objection was given by the relator Scurr.
D   There was an appeal to the Local Government Court by the relator
Scurr and others which was carried to the Full Court and eventually to
the High Court of Australia. Later, there was a further appeal by the
relator and others to the Local Government Court in which judgment
was delivered in December 1975. In addition to these appeals there was
an action brought in 1971 by the Attorney-General on the relation of
E   Scurr against the Brisbane City Council, in which the developers were
joined as defendants: the issue was whether the council had acted ultra
vires in accepting the developers' tender and whether it had acted in bad
faith.

In none of these proceedings was the question raised of a charitable or
other trust binding the council. The reason for this was that until shortly
before he brought the present action, the relator Scurr did not know of
F   the council minutes which recorded the transaction with the society in
1937–38. He seems to have had some suspicion of the existence of a trust,
and there was an application for discovery in the Local Government Court
proceedings which the council successfully resisted. It is true that he was
entitled by law to inspect the council's minutes, but failure to go through
the records of 1937–38 can hardly be held against him. It is true also
G   that being a member and in 1955 on the committee of the show society—
and later a vice-president of it—he might have been able to inspect the
latter's records, but he did not do so. In the course of his evidence at
the trial no questions were put to him as to his knowledge or means of
knowledge of the trust or why he did not take earlier action to ascertain
whether it existed. The courts below held that, on these facts, no case
of laches was made out. Their Lordships agree and would only add that
H   in addition to the factual weakness of the appellants' case they see serious
legal difficulties in the way of asserting a defence of laches in proceedings
against an express trustee who is still the legal owner of the trust property,
and who holds the land on a trust for the benefit of the public. They
consider it unnecessary however to enter upon these in this case.

The second defence is one of " res judicata ". There has, of course,
been no actual decision in litigation between these parties as to the
issue involved in the present case, but the appellants invoke this defence

Brisbane City Council v. Attorney-General (P.C.)   **[1978]**

in its wider sense, according to which a party may be shut out from A
raising in a subsequent action an issue which he could, and should, have
raised in earlier proceedings. The classic statement of this doctrine is
contained in the judgment of Wigram V.-C. in *Henderson* v. *Henderson*
(1843) 3 Hare 100 and its existence has been reaffirmed by this Board in
Hoystead v. *Commissioner of Taxation* [1926] A.C. 155. A recent
application of it is to be found in the decision of the Board in *Yat Tung*
Investment Co. Ltd. v. *Dao Heng Bank Ltd.* [1975] A.C. 581. It was, in B
the judgment of the Board, there described in these words:

> " . . . . there is a wider sense in which the doctrine may be appealed
> to, so that it becomes an abuse of process to raise in subsequent
> proceedings matters which could and therefore should have been
> litigated in earlier proceedings." (p. 590)
C
This reference to " abuse of process " had previously been made in
Greenhalgh v. *Mallard* [1947] 2 All E.R. 255 *per* Somervell L.J. and
their Lordships endorse it. This is the true basis of the doctrine and it
ought only to be applied when the facts are such as to amount to an abuse:
otherwise there is a danger of a party being shut out from bringing
forward a genuine subject of litigation.

In their Lordships' opinion there is no room for application of this D
doctrine here. To assert the existence of a trust (even assuming that it
was known to exist) in the Local Government Court proceedings would
have been entirely out of place. And the same is true of the earlier action
in the Supreme Court. This, though a relator action, like the present,
was in effect a ratepayers' action brought against the authority to restrain
an alleged excess of power. The present is an action instigated by two E
members of the public asserting a right belonging to the public at large.
It must be doubtful whether in these circumstances the necessary identity
of parties between the two proceedings exists, but in any event it cannot be
claimed that to bring the second after the first has failed involves any
abuse of process. Furthermore, the fact that the relator who was
ignorant of the trust would have had to search the records of the council
in order to discover its existence, and that he was to some extent obstructed F
by the council in his attempt to obtain the relevant documents, makes
this a totally unsuitable case for the introduction or admission of this
defence. Their Lordships agree with the judgment of Lucas J. dated
August 9, 1976, at an interlocutory stage of the present action.

For these reasons their Lordships will humbly advise Her Majesty that
the appeal be dismissed. The appellants must pay the costs of the appeal. G

Solicitors: *Coward Chance; Maxwell Batley & Co.*

T. J. M.

H

The Weekly Law Reports, August 4, 1978

309

3 W.L.R.   Federal Commerce Ltd. v. Molena Alpha Inc. (Q.B.D.)

A

[COURT OF APPEAL]

FEDERAL COMMERCE & NAVIGATION CO. LTD. *v.*
MOLENA ALPHA INC.

B

SAME *v.* MOLENA BETA INC.

SAME *v.* MOLENA GAMMA INC.

1978   Jan. 30, 31;
       Feb. 1, 2, 3; 23   Kerr J.

       April 4, 5, 6, 7, 10, 11,   Lord Denning M.R.,
C   12, 13; 18   Goff and Cumming-Bruce L.JJ.

*Shipping—Charterparty—Time charter—Hire—Right to make valid
   claim to deductions by equitable set off—Owners' insistence on
   hire payments without disputed deductions—Instructions on
   legal advice to masters to withdraw charterers' authority to
   sign bills of lading—Whether repudiatory breach of contract—
   Whether law as to freight applies to hire*

D
Ships' Names—Lorfri—Nanfri—Benfri

By time charters of November 1974 the owners let three
ships to the charterers for periods of about six years to carry
grain from the Great Lakes to Europe and, on the return
voyage, steel. Most of the cargoes were carried on c.i.f.
terms, the shippers paying the freight in advance and receiving
" freight pre-paid " bills of lading. Clause 6 of the charters
E   provided for the payment of hire twice monthly in advance; in
default of payment the owners to have the right of withdrawing
the vessel, but before invoking any right or remedy the owners
had to notify the charterers of the non-receipt of the hire
payment when due. Clauses 11 and 14 of the charters provided
for permissible deductions from hire. By clause 9 the masters
were to be under the orders of the charterers as regards
employment, agency or other arrangements; and accordingly
F   the bills of lading were issued and signed by the charterers on
behalf of the master and freight was paid to the charterers or
their agents. Clause 18 gave the owners a lien on all cargoes,
sub-freights belonging to the time charterers and any bill of
lading freight.

The charterers made deductions from hire under clauses 11
and 14, sometimes without the owners' prior agreement. On
G   September 6, 1977, the owners asserted that the charterers
were not entitled to make deductions from hire in respect of
any disputed item. The charterers did not agree to proposed
limitations on their right to make deductions from hire, but
offered to place the amount of any disputed item in escrow.
On September 19, 1977, the charterers gave notice that they
intended to deduct $47,122 from the hire payable on October
1 under the *Nanfri* charter in respect of alleged loss of speed
H   of that vessel during a voyage in 1975, a claim first made in
November 1975. The owners demanded the full hire instalment due, and on September 21 gave notice requiring an
arbitration to decide whether the charterers had correctly
calculated the items deducted on September 1 and whether
they were " entitled unilaterally to deduct disputed items from
charter hire." The charterers deducted the $47,122 from the
hire due on October 1.

Acting on legal advice the owners by telex on October 4,
1977, informed the charterers that the masters of all three ships

Federal Commerce Ltd. v. Molena Alpha Inc. (Q.B.D.)   **[1978]**

were being instructed "to withdraw all direct or implied   A
authority to charterer or its agents to sign bills of lading"; and
that the masters would not sign any bill of lading endorsed
"freight pre-paid" or not bearing an indorsement incorporating the lien under clause 18 on bill of lading freight. Instructions in those terms were given by the owners to the masters.

On October 5, 1977, a series of telex exchanges took place.
The charterers maintained that they had been put in "an
impossible position commercially" and demanded a withdrawal   B
of the owners' instructions to the masters. The owners
insisted that the instructions to the masters would stand.
Finally the charterers accepted the totality of the owners'
conduct as a repudiation of the charters which was accepted.

The question whether the charters had been determined
by repudiation and acceptance was referred to arbitration. In
the interim, by a "without prejudice" agreement, the ships
remained in service as before October 1977 and the charterers   C
paid disputed deductions and agreed to make no more deductions without the owners' approval.

The two arbitrators disagreed. The umpire held in favour
of the charterers that the owners' conduct amounted to a
repudiation of the charterparties and that the charterers had
validly terminated them on October 5, 1977. A special case
in respect of each ship was stated under section 21 (1) (b) of
the Arbitration Act 1950, the questions for the court (to which   D
the umpire gave the answers "yes") being: (1) whether on the
true construction of the charterparty the charterers were
entitled to deduct from hire without the consent of the owners
valid claims which (a) arose under clause 11 of the charterparty or (b) constituted an equitable set off; (2) whether the
charterers validly terminated the charterparty on October 5,
1977. Kerr J. held that the answer to question (2) was "No"
and the answers to question 1 (a) and (b) "Yes."   E

On appeal by the charterers and cross-appeal by the
owners: —

Held, allowing the appeal and dismissing the cross-appeal,
(1) that the charterers were entitled to deduct from hire
valid claims, i.e., sums quantified by reasonable assessment
made in good faith, which (a) arose under clause 11 of the
charterparty or (b) (Cumming-Bruce L.J. dissenting)
constituted an equitable set off (post, pp. 340F, H, 343B, E, H,   F
350D, 355F, G).

Mondel v. *Steel* (1841) 8 M. & W. 858, 871 and *Sea and
Land Securities Ltd.* v. *William Dickinson & Co. Ltd.* [1942]
2 K.B. 65; 72 Ll.L.Rep. 159, C.A.

Henriksens Rederi A/S v. *T.H.Z. Rolimpex (The Brede)*
[1974] Q.B. 233, C.A. and *Aries Tanker Corporation* v. *Total
Transport Ltd. (The Aries)* [1977] 1 W.L.R. 185, H.L.(E.)   G
distinguished.

Compania Sud Americana de Vapores v. *Shipmair B.V.
(The Teno)* [1977] 2 Lloyd's Rep. 289 approved.

Seven Seas Transportation Ltd. v. *Atlantic Shipping Co.
Ltd.* [1975] 2 Lloyd's Rep. 188 disapproved.

Per Cumming-Bruce L.J. The exception of "freight" in
Mondel v. *Steel* (1841) 8 M. & W. 858, 871, applies to a
contract incorporated in a time charter (post, p. 359C, D).   H

Per Lord Denning M.R. and Goff L.J. The law as to
"freight" applicable to a voyage charter does not apply indiscriminately to "hire" in a time charter (post, pp. 337B,
345B–E, 350D).

Per Lord Denning M.R. When a shipowner is guilty of
a breach of contract which deprives the time charterer of part
of the consideration for which the hire has been paid in
advance, the charterer can deduct an equivalent amount out
of the hire falling due for the next month (post. p. 340B).

3 W.L.R. **Federal Commerce Ltd. v. Molena Alpha Inc. (Q.B.D.)**

A (2) That the owners' telex of October 4, 1977, was a breach of clause 9 of the charters, under which the masters were to be under the orders of the charterers as regards employment and agency; that the owners knew that the implementation of the instructions set out in that telex would have had disastrous commercial consequences for the charterers; and that, since the owners, notwithstanding that they had acted on legal advice, had evinced an intention not to be bound by their contractual

B obligations, they had committed an anticipatory breach of the charters which was repudiatory, and the charterers had accepted that repudiation as they were entitled to do (post, pp. 341H—342B, F, G, H, 353E, 355F, G).

Dicta of Lord Blackburn in *Mersey Steel and Iron Co. Ltd.* v. *Naylor Benzon & Co.* (1884) 9 App.Cas. 434, 442–444, H.L.(E.) applied.

James Shaffer Ltd. v. *Finlay Durham & Brodie* [1953] 1

C W.L.R. 106, C.A. and *Sweet & Maxwell Ltd.* v. *Universal News Services Ltd.* [1964] 2 Q.B. 699, C.A. distinguished.

Per Lord Denning M.R. A party who breaks a contract cannot excuse himself by saying that he did it on legal advice, or under an honest misapprehension (post, p. 342E–F).

Decision of Kerr J., post, p. 314C et seq., varied.

D The following cases are referred to in the judgments in the Court of Appeal:

Aries Tanker Corporation v. *Total Transport Ltd.* (*The Aries*) [1977] 1 W.L.R. 185; [1977] 1 All E.R. 398, H.L.(E.).

Associated Bulk Carriers Ltd. v. *Koch Shipping Inc.*, The Times, August 10, 1977, C.A.

Compania Sud Americana de Vapores v. *Shipmair B.V.* (*The Teno*) [1977]

E 2 Lloyd's Rep. 289.

Dawnays Ltd. v. *F. G. Minter Ltd. and Trollope and Colls Ltd.* [1971] 1 W.L.R. 1205; [1971] 2 All E.R. 1389, C.A.

Ellis Mechanical v. *Wates* (1976) 2 B.L.R. 57.

French Marine v. *Compagnie Napolitaine d'Eclairage et de Chauffage par le Gaz* [1921] 2 A.C. 494, H.L.(E.).

Halcyon Steamship Co. Ltd. v. *Continental Grain Co.* (1943) 75 Ll.L.Rep. 57; [1943] K.B. 355; [1943] 1 All E.R. 558; 75 Ll.L.Rep. 80, C.A.

F *Hanak* v. *Green* [1958] 2 Q.B. 9; [1958] 2 W.L.R. 755; [1958] 2 All E.R. 141, C.A.

Havelock v. *Geddes* (1809) 10 East 555.

Henriksens Rederi A/S v. *T.H.Z. Rolimpex* (*The Brede*) [1974] Q.B. 233; [1973] 3 W.L.R. 556; [1973] 3 All E.R. 589, C.A.

Mardorf Peach & Co. Ltd. v. *Attica Sea Carriers Corporation of Liberia* [1976] Q.B. 835; [1976] 2 W.L.R. 668; [1976] 2 All E.R. 249, C.A.

G *Mersey Steel and Iron Co. Ltd.* v. *Naylor, Benzon & Co.* (1884) 9 App. Cas. 434, H.L.(E.).

Modern Engineering (Bristol) Ltd. v. *Gilbert-Ash (Northern) Ltd.* [1974] A.C. 689; [1973] 3 W.L.R. 421; [1973] 3 All E.R. 195, H.L.(E.).

Mondel v. *Steel* (1841) 8 M. & W. 858.

Morgan & Son Ltd. v. *Martin Johnson & Co. Ltd.* [1949] 1 K.B. 107; [1948] 2 All E.R. 196, C.A.

H *Mottram Consultants Ltd.* v. *Bernard Sunley & Sons Ltd.* [1975] 2 Lloyd's Rep. 197, H.L.(E.).

Naxos Shipping Corporation v. *Thegra Shipping Co. S.A.* (*The Corfu Island*) (unreported), April 10, 1974, Ackner J.

Nippon Yusen Kaisha v. *Acme Shipping Corporation* (*The Charalambos N. Pateras*) [1971] 2 Lloyd's Rep. 42.

Nova (Jersey) Knit Ltd. v. *Kammgarn Spinnerei G.m.b.H.* [1977] 1 W.L.R. 713; [1977] 2 All E.R. 463, H.L.(E.).

Rawson v. *Samuel* (1841) Cr. & Ph. 161.

Federal Commerce Ltd. v. Molena Alpha Inc. (Q.B.D.)   **[1978]**

Russell v. *Pellegrini* (1856) 6 E. & B. 1020.

Sea and Land Securities Ltd. v. *William Dickinson and Co. Ltd.* [1942] 1 K.B. 286; [1942] 1 All E.R. 88; [1942] 2 K.B. 65; [1942] 1 All E.R. 503; 72 Ll.L.R. 159, C.A.

Seven Seas Transportation Ltd. v. *Atlantic Shipping Co. Ltd.* [1975] 2 Lloyd's Rep. 188.

Shaffer (James) Ltd. v. *Findlay Durham & Brodie* [1953] 1 W.L.R. 106, C.A.

Smyth (Ross T.) & Co. Ltd. v. *T. D. Bailey, Son & Co.* [1940] 3 All E.R. 60; 56 T.L.R. 825, H.L.(E.).

Steelwood Carriers Inc. of Monrovia, Liberia v. *Evimeria Compania Naviera S.A. of Panama (The Agios Giorgis)* [1976] 2 Lloyd's Rep. 192.

Sweet & Maxwell Ltd. v. *Universal News Services Ltd.* [1964] 2 Q.B. 699; [1964] 3 W.L.R. 356; [1964] 3 All E.R. 30, C.A.

Tagart, Beaton & Co. v. *James Fisher & Sons* [1903] 1 K.B. 391, C.A.

Tankexpress (A/S) v. *Compagnie Financière Belge des Petroles S/A* (1946) 79 Ll.L.Rep. 451. (1947) 80 Ll.L.Rep. 365, C.A.; [1949] A.C. 76; [1948] 2 All E.R. 939, H.L.(E.).

United Scientific Holdings Ltd. v. *Burnley Borough Council* [1977] 2 W.L.R. 806; [1977] 2 All E.R. 62, H.L.(E.).

The following additional cases were cited in argument in the Court of Appeal:

Admiral Shipping Co. Ltd. v. *Weidner, Hopkins & Co.* [1916] 1 K.B. 429; [1917] 1 K.B. 222, C.A.

Aegnoussiotis Shipping Corporation of Monrovia v. *A/S Kristian Jebsens Rederi of Bergen* [1977] 1 Lloyd's Rep. 268.

Attica Sea Carriers Corporation v. *Ferrostaal Poseidon Bulk Reederei G.m.b.H. (The Puerto Buitrago)* [1976] 1 Lloyd's Rep. 250, C.A.

Brankelow Steamship Co. Ltd. v. *Canton Insurance Office Ltd.* [1899] 2 Q.B. 178, C.A.; [1901] A.C. 462, H.L.(E.).

Dakin v. *Oxley* (1864) 15 C.B.N.S. 646.

Decro-Wall International S.A. v. *Practitioners in Marketing Ltd.* [1971] 1 W.L.R. 361; [1971] 2 All E.R. 216, C.A.

Forslind v. *Bechely-Crundall*, 1922, S.C.(H.L.) 173, H.L.(Sc.).

Freeth v. *Burr* (1874) L.R. 9 C.P. 208.

Heyman v. *Darwins Ltd.* [1942] A.C. 356; [1942] 1 All E.R. 337, H.L.(E.).

Hongkong Fir Shipping Co. Ltd. v. *Kawasaki Kisen Kaisha Ltd.* [1962] 2 Q.B. 26; [1962] 2 W.L.R. 474; [1962] 1 All E.R. 474, C.A.

Inman Steamship Co. Ltd. v. *Bischoff* (1881) 6 Q.B. 648; (1882) 7 App.Cas. 670, H.L.(E.).

Merchant Shipping Co. Ltd. v. *Armitage* (1873) L.R. 9 Q.B. 99.

Mihalis Angelos, The [1971] 1 Q.B. 164; [1970] 2 W.L.R. 907; [1970] 1 All E.R. 673; [1971] 1 Q.B. 164; [1970] 3 W.L.R. 601; [1970] 3 All E.R. 125, C.A.

Molthes Rederi Aktieselskabet v. *Ellerman's Wilson Line Ltd.* [1927] 1 K.B. 710.

Sheels v. *Davies* (1814) 4 Camp. 119.

Shillito, The (1897) 3 Com.Cas. 44.

Stimson v. *Hall* (1857) 1 H. & N. 831.

Sunbeam Shipping Co. Ltd. v. *President of India* [1973] 1 Lloyd's Rep. 482.

Turner v. *Haji Goolam Mahomed Azam* [1904] A.C. 826, P.C.

Wehner v. *Dene Steam Shipping Co.* [1905] 2 K.B. 92.

The following cases are referred to in the judgment of Kerr J.

Aries Tanker Corporation v. *Total Transport Ltd. (The Aries)* [1977] 1 W.L.R. 185; [1977] 1 All E.R. 398, H.L.(E.).

3 W.L.R.   Federal Commerce Ltd. v. Molena Alpha Inc. (Q.B.D.)

A   *Aktieselskabet Pitwood* v. *J. W. Baird & Co. Ltd.* (1926) 24 Ll.L.Rep. 282, C.A.

Brankelow Steamship Co. Ltd. v. *Canton Insurance Office Ltd.* [1899] 2 Q.B. 178, C.A.; [1901] A.C. 462, H.L.(E.).

Clausen v. *Canada Timber & Lands Ltd.* [1923] 4 D.L.R. 751.

Compania Sud Americana de Vapores v. *Shipmair B.V.* (*The Teno*) [1977] 2 Lloyd's Rep. 289.

B   *Decro-Wall International S.A.* v. *Practitioners in Marketing Ltd.* [1971] 1 W.L.R. 361; [1971] 2 All E.R. 216, C.A.

Freeth v. *Burr* (1874) L.R. 9 C.P. 208.

Hansen v. *Harrold Brothers* [1894] 1 Q.B. 612, C.A.

Hongkong Fir Shipping Co. Ltd. v. *Kawasaki Kisen Kaisha Ltd.* [1962] 2 Q.B. 26; [1962] 2 W.L.R. 474; [1962] 1 All E.R. 474, C.A.

Manuel De Fribis Arrospe v. *Thomas Barr* (1881) 8 R. 602.

C   *Mersey Steel & Iron Co. Ltd.* v. *Naylor, Benzon & Co.* (1884) 9 App. Cas. 434, H.L.(E.).

Modern Engineering (Bristol) Ltd. v. *Gilbert-Ash (Northern) Ltd.* [1974] A.C. 689; [1973] 3 W.L.R. 421; [1973] 3 All E.R. 195, H.L.(E.).

Sea and Land Securities Ltd. v. *William Dickinson and Co. Ltd.* [1942] 2 K.B. 65; [1942] 1 All E.R. 503; 72 Ll.L.Rep. 159, C.A.

D   *Shaffer (James) Ltd.* v. *Findlay Durham & Brodie* [1953] 1 W.L.R. 106, C.A.

Shillito, The (1897) 3 Com.Cas. 44.

Smyth (Ross T.) & Co. Ltd. v. *T. D. Bailey, Son & Co.* [1940] 3 All E.R. 60, H.L.(E.).

Sweet & Maxwell Ltd. v. *Universal News Services Ltd.* [1964] 2 Q.B. 699; [1964] 3 W.L.R. 356; [1964] 3 All E.R. 30, C.A.

E   The following additional cases were cited in argument before Kerr J.

Aegnoussiotis Shipping Corporation of Monrovia v. *A/S Kristian Jebsens Rederi of Bergen* [1977] 1 Lloyd's Rep. 268.

Canada, The (1897) 13 T.L.R. 238.

Mardorf Peach & Co. Ltd. v. *Attica Sea Carriers Corporation of Liberia* (*The Laconia*) [1977] A.C. 850; [1977] 2 W.L.R. 286; [1977] 1 All E.R. 545, H.L.(E.).

F   *Peek* v. *Larsen* (1871) L.R. 12 Eq. 378; 25 L.T. 580.

Seven Seas Transportation Ltd. v. *Atlantic Shipping Co. S.A.* [1975] 2 Lloyd's Rep. 188.

Steelwood Carriers Inc. of Monrovia, Liberia v. *Evimeria Compania Naviera S.A. of Panama* [1976] 2 Lloyd's Rep. 192.

Universal Cargo Carriers Corporation v. *Citati* [1957] 2 Q.B. 401; [1957] 2 W.L.R. 713; [1957] 2 All E.R. 70.

G

SPECIAL CASES stated by umpire.

By three charter parties on Baltime 1939 forms dated New York, November 1, 1974, the claimant charterers, Federal Commerce and Navigation Ltd., of Montreal, Quebec, Canada, hired three motor vessels, the *Nanfri, Benfri* and *Lorfri* from the Molena Trust Inc., as bareboat
H   chartered owners, for periods of time. Subsequently the Molena Alpha Inc., owners of the *Nanfri*, the Molena Beta Inc., owners of the *Benfri*, and the Molena Gamma Inc., owners of the *Lorfri*, were substituted for the Molena Trust Inc. as parties to the charterparties. The charter-parties provided for disputes to be referred to arbitration in London. Disputes arose between the parties. The charterers determined each of the charterparties on or about October 5, 1977, and sought a declaration that their determination was justified. The arbitrators were unable to

agree and the umpire, Clifford Albert Lawrence Clark, made three A awards each in the form of a special case.

The umpire stated questions for the court, namely, (1) whether on the true construction of the charterparty (in each case) the charterers were entitled to deduct from hire without the consent of the owners valid claims which (a) arose under clause 11 of the charterparty or (b) constituted an equitable set off; and (2) whether the charterers validly terminated the charterparty on October 5, 1977. Subject to the opinion B of the court the umpire answered " yes " to each question.

The facts are stated in the judgments of Kerr J. and Lord Denning M.R.

Michael Mustill Q.C., *A. G. S. Pollock* and *P. Gross* for the charterers.
Anthony Evans Q.C. and *Nicholas Phillips* for the owners.

Cur. adv. vult.

February 23. KERR J. read the following judgment. These are three special cases. Like so many nowadays, they arise out of disputes between shipowners and time charterers in connection with the charterers' obligation to pay the hire. The due performance of this obligation is usually D safeguarded by the owners' express right to withdraw the vessel in the event of default, and in recent years many cases have come to the courts on the question whether or not the right to withdraw had arisen and had been properly exercised. The background to those cases was always that the market rate was substantially above the charter rate, with the result that the owners wished to free themselves from the charter if they E could in order to employ the vessel more profitably elsewhere. But then the freight market collapsed and has remained very low for some years. Arbitrators and the courts are therefore nowadays constantly faced with long-term charters fixed at times when the market was still high. It is now the charterers who would like to rid themselves of the charters, since the hire often greatly exceeds the amounts which they can recoup by employing the vessel on the market. Conversely, the owners' right to F withdraw the ship in the event of a non-payment or short payment of hire is no longer economically realistic; they wish to retain the charters and not to be left with having to employ their vessels in the present depressed conditions. The upper hand has therefore passed to the charterers, and this often gives rise to what have come to be called " reverse withdrawal " situations. A frequent instance is that charterers G make deductions from instalments of hire on the basis of disputed claims, in particular for loss of time due to alleged under-performance of the vessel. Their right to do so by way of equitable set off in the absence of any express provision in the charter is a moot point on which there are four evenly divided decisions of this court. But so long as the charter rate exceeds the market rate the charterers run substantially no risks. In this way the payment of every monthly instalment of hire can H become the subject of dispute, with threats and counter-threats and tactical moves as in a game of chess. If it is then alleged that one side has over-stepped the line between threat or breach and repudiation, the episode usually ends with a " without prejudice " agreement under which the ship remains in the charterers' service and the question whether she continues at the charter rate or the market rate, according to who was right, is referred to arbitration, which usually leads to a special case.

The Weekly Law Reports, August 4, 1978

315

3 W.L.R.   Federal Commerce Ltd. v. Molena Alpha Inc. (Q.B.D.)   Kerr J.

A   This is also the background to the present dispute. The issue is whether or not the owners have wrongfully repudiated three valuable time charters for about six years by their reaction to the charterers' deduction of a claim from an instalment of hire. I have been told that the amount involved lies within a bracket of U.S. $6,000,000 to $15,000,000.

The claimants in each of the three cases is the Canadian parent company of a subsidiary which was the actual charterer, but nothing turns
B   on the distinction and I will simply refer to the claimants as the charterers. The owners in each case were one-ship companies in the Molena Group, but again nothing turns on the distinction and I will simply refer to them as the owners. Their managers were Seven Seas Ship Management Ltd. to whom I will refer as the managers. The three ships, the *Benfri*, *Lorfri* and *Nanfri* were operated as units of a single
C   fleet on both sides, and it was common ground that for present purposes all three charters stand or fall together. They were in virtually identical terms. All were concluded on November 1, 1974, for a period of 72 to 75 months, i.e., about six years, in continuation of previous charters. The trading limits were world-wide within institute warranty limits subject to certain exclusions, but the vessels were designed and built for Great Lakes trading and were used by the charterers throughout for trading to
D   and from the Great Lakes during the Great Lakes seasons. The great majority of this trade follows the pattern that grain cargoes are carried from the Great Lakes to Europe and steel or steel products from Europe to the Great Lakes, most of such cargoes being sold on c.i.f. or c & f terms. The charters were in the Baltime form and I must set out certain of their provisions. [His Lordship read clauses 6, 9, 11 (A) and (C) and
E   18 of the charterparties, post, pp. 330E, F, G, H, 333B, E and continued:] Clause 23 provides for arbitration in London by two arbitrators, one to be nominated by each party, and an umpire to be appointed by them in the event of disagreement. Clause 43:

F   " Owner and charterer agree that the vessel hereby chartered is of special interest to the charterer because of her particulars and the trade in which she is to be employed and that so long as charterer is not in default in the payment of hire or in breach of any of its fundamental obligations under the charter, charterer shall have the right . . . to compel specific performance of this charter," subject to certain other provisions which are not relevant.

Then clause 12 of an addendum no. 2:

G   " In the event that any payment of hire is not paid to owners' account when due under clause 6, owners, before invoking any right or remedy which they may have as a result of such non-payment, must notify charterers in writing by telex or personal delivery that the hire payment was not received when due."

I must now set out or summarise a number of findings from the special
H   case:

" 10. From the beginning of the charterparties the pattern of deductions from hire—whether for owners' disbursements, off-hire or cross-claims—was as follows: (i) Sometimes the charterers and Seven Seas would discuss and agree in advance that deductions were to be made from hire. (ii) Sometimes the charterers would simply deduct from hire the sums to which they thought they were entitled without prior discussion or agreement; in so far as the owners or

their agents wished to challenge any deduction, whether in whole or   A
in part, correspondence and/or meetings would take place; in the
usual course of matters any disputes would be resolved in the course
of such correspondence or meetings. (iii) On at least one occasion
the charterers made deductions from hire in respect of items which,
prior thereto, had been indicated as disputed by Seven Seas.
" 11. In early June 1977 a meeting took place between the charterers
and Seven Seas at which all outstanding disputed deductions from hire   B
were settled."

I have set out these findings by way of background, but I do not think
that anything turns on them. Neither party relied on any previous
course of dealing for the purposes of the disputes which thereafter arose.

In July and September 1977 the charterers made a number of deductions from hire. It is not clear whether hire was in fact paid twice-   C
monthly as provided in clause 6, but the argument proceeded on the basis
that the relevant payments of hire and the deductions were made on the
1st of the month. Some of these deductions were subsequently disputed
by the owners. The total deductions for all three ships in July amounted
to about $182,000, of which less than $10,000 was disputed by the owners.
The September deductions involved more dispute; they totalled about   D
$109,000 of which $38,000 was disputed. A few items were resolved at
a meeting on September 13, but about $46,000 still remained in dispute.
These evidently related to all three ships to some extent, but there is no
finding as to the nature of the charterers' claims on which they were
based, and in particular whether or not they fell within clause 11 (A) or
(C). The special case finds that the owners believed these deductions to
have been invalid.   E

From September 1, 1977, onwards the parties were in open dispute,
and I must summarise the subsequent events. On September 2 the
owners gave a telex notice under clause 12 of addendum no. 2 with
regard to the deductions made on September 1. The charterers replied
on the same day, giving a breakdown of the deductions and referred to
detailed justifications for deductions previously sent to the owners. On   F
September 6 the owners telexed to the charterers, asserting that they were
not entitled to make any deductions from hire unless (a) the deduction
was supported by vouchers signed by the master (see clause 14), or (b)
the deduction was accepted by the owners, or (c) any dispute about the
deduction had been resolved by a proper tribunal in the charterers'
favour. This remained the owners' contention throughout and was at
all times challenged by the charterers.   G

In legal terms the issues between the parties at this stage can be stated
as follows. First, in so far as the charter does not give any express
right to make any deduction from hire, or to make a deduction by
reference to a particular head of claim, may such deduction nevertheless
be made under the equitable right of set off? Secondly, even if there is
a right to deduct, what is the position about disputed claims? Can the   H
charterers deduct any amount claimed by them even if it ultimately turns
out that the claim was unwarranted in whole or in part? This would
leave the owners at the mercy of the charterers and in fact frequently
appears to happen nowadays. Or must the charterers obtain the owners'
agreement, or establish any disputed claim by arbitration, before they can
make any deduction? This would preclude them from deducting anything meanwhile, although their claims to do so may well be justified, at

The Weekly Law Reports, August 4, 1978

317

3 W.L.R.   Federal Commerce Ltd. v. Molena Alpha Inc. (Q.B.D.)   Kerr J.

A least in part. Or does the solution lie in a half-way position whereby—
assuming that the right to deduct exists—the charterers can deduct any
sum which they claim bona fide and assess on a reasonable basis? All
these are moot points on which both sides have an arguable case. As
already mentioned, the issues whether a right to deduct by way of equitable set off exists at all has been the subject of four evenly divided judgments of this court. The issue when and what deductions are
B permissible, if the right exists, has not, I think, ever been decided
specifically, though the last of these judgments, that of Parker J. in *Compania Sud Americana de Vapores* v. *Shipmais B.V.* (*The Teno*) [1977]
2 Lloyd's Rep. 289, contains obiter dicta which support the half-way
position. I will hereafter refer to all these issues compendiously as " the
deduction issues."

C   I return to the history of the dispute. On September 19 the charterers
wrote to the managers to give notice that they intended to deduct
$47,122.43 from the hire payable on October 1 under the *Nanfri* charter
in respect of an alleged loss of speed during a voyage from Antwerp to
Durban in the latter part of 1975, nearly two years earlier. The umpire
was not asked to reach any final determination of the validity of this
claim, but he made certain provisional findings which can be summarised
D as follows. The vessel had suffered a main engine breakdown which had
necessitated deviations to ports of refuge on two occasions. The off-hire
amounts for the delays in port during the repairs had been settled. After
these breakdowns the vessel's speed and engine revolutions appeared
from the log abstracts supplied to the charterers to be below normal,
and the charterers reasonably inferred that these were consequences of
E defects in, or partial breakdowns of, the vessel's engines. The charterers
reasonably concluded that they had a claim under clause 11 (C) of the
Nanfri charter which at least raised a case for the owners to answer. The
sum of $47,122.43 was based on the difference between the time actually
taken for the voyage and the time which the vessel would have taken at
an average speed of 15 knots, which was her optimum speed in good
weather and smooth water. On this basis the umpire concluded pro-
F visionally, without prejudice to any future arbitration, that in his opinion
a deduction in respect of slow steaming was justified but in an amount
less than that claimed. The charterers had first put this claim forward
at the end of November 1975. It was rejected on behalf of the owners
on February 26, 1976. There was then a telephone conversation on
March 2, 1976, in which the managers again rejected the claim and
G suggested that if the charterers wished to persist in it they should resort to
arbitration. Nothing further was then heard about the claim for about
18 months until the receipt on September 20, 1977, of the charterers'
letter announcing their intention to deduct this sum from the *Nanfri* hire
due on October 1, although the parties had meanwhile met on a number
of occasions to settle outstanding claims, including other slow steaming
claims of more recent origin.

H   The managers immediately telexed on September 20 protesting against
the proposed deduction and demanded that the hire be paid in full. On
September 21 the owners gave notice of arbitration to the charterers
with regard to (a) the disputed deductions of about $46,000 already made
which the owners believed to be invalid, and (b) the principle of what I
have compendiously called the deduction issues. Notwithstanding this,
however, the charterers in fact made the deduction of $47,122.43 from
the *Nanfri* hire paid on October 1.

The owners were clearly incensed. They took legal advice in New   A
York and London, and it was agreed before me that they were advised
that they were entitled to take the action to which I come in a moment.
It was therefore common ground that the owners were acting bona fide
in what they did. This was the following. First, on October 4 they
instructed the masters of all three vessels (i) to withdraw all authority to
issue or sign bills of lading on their behalf, (ii) to refuse to sign bills of
lading marked " freight pre-paid," and (iii) to insist that all bills of lading   B
should bear an endorsement reading:

> " All terms, conditions and exceptions of the time charter dated
> November 1, 1974, as amended, including the lien under clause 18
> on bill of lading freight as well as sub-freight belonging to the time
> charterers are herein incorporated."

On the same day the managers sent the following telex to the charterers: C

> " The masters of the *Benfri, Nanfri* and *Lorfri* are being instructed
> to withdraw all direct or implied authority to charterers or its agents
> to sign bills of lading. Please present all bills of lading to the master
> for signature. Note that the masters will not sign any bill of lading
> (1) endorsed ' freight pre-paid ' or (2) which does not bear an
> endorsement reading . . ."   D

and there then followed the endorsement which I have already read.

The charterers appear to have received this on the following day,
October 5. On that day the position of the vessels was as follows. Each
had been sub-chartered by the charterers to an important shipper, Continental Grain, on the terms of a voyage charter which required the issue
of freight pre-paid bills of lading. The *Nanfri* completed loading a cargo   E
of soya beans during the afternoon of October 5. The *Benfri* was on
passage to Chicago to discharge the balance of her cargo and was then to
load a cargo of grain in Duluth from Continental Grain. The *Lorfri* was
loading a cargo of grain at Chicago for Continental Grain. She had
loaded a parcel on October 3 for which a separate bill of lading was to be
issued, and she was then due to load the balance of her cargo from   F
Continental Grain at other Great Lakes ports.

The special case finds that the consequences for the charterers of the
orders issued by the owners were extremely serious, in that:

> " (i) Unless the charterers could ensure the issue of freight prepaid
> bills of lading which were not claused with any reference to a time
> charterparty the vessels were largely debarred from use by the   G
> charterers in the grain and steel trades, since nearly all of the
> shippers of grain and steel would not agree to accept bills of lading
> if they were either non-freight pre-paid or claused with a reference
> to a time charter. (ii) The charterers would be unable to comply
> with their existing obligations to sub-charterers. (iii) The charterers
> were likely to be blacklisted as grain carriers by Continental Grain,
> which is one of the world's largest shippers of grain. In consequence   H
> the charterers' reputation would be very seriously damaged and they
> would probably have been unable to obtain business for the vessels
> from other major shippers of grain. (iv) The charterers were likely
> to incur very substantial liabilities to Continental Grain if the
> cargoes which were being loaded or which were about to be loaded
> on October 5 were not completed and if freight pre-paid unclaused
> bills of lading were not issued promptly."

The Weekly Law Reports, August 4, 1978

319

3 W.L.R.   Federal Commerce Ltd. v. Molena Alpha Inc. (Q.B.D.)   Kerr J.

A   There was some discussion before me about the degree of urgency
implied in the word " promptly " in relation to the issue of freight pre-
paid bills of lading. It is used twice in the special case, but understandably not defined. It was submitted on behalf of the charterers that
it involved a matter of hours. But it was not contested that masters are
always entitled to a reasonable time to consider their position concerning
the signature of bills of lading, and in my view the charterers' submission
B goes too far. The bill of lading for the parcel loaded on the *Lorfri* on
October 3 was still outstanding, apparently without complaint. I think
that a day or two would be more reasonable, as the owners submitted,
but they also rightly accepted that the position had to be resolved as a
matter of urgency.

There then followed an exchange of telex messages, all on October
C 5. The deduction of about $47,000 on October 1 had only related to the
Nanfri, but in the telex exchanges no clear distinction was drawn by
either side between this vessel and the others. Most of the telexes
expressly referred to all three ships, and I was told that no distinction
between them had been drawn in the arbitration. [His Lordship set out
the telex messages of October 5, post, pp. 334G—335A, C–F, and continued:]
The telex of the charterers, post, p. 335E, F, was only headed *Nanfri* whereas
D most of the earlier ones had been sent in relation to all three vessels.
However, no point was taken on behalf of the owners to the effect that
the alleged repudiation had only been accepted in relation to this vessel.
As in the arbitration, the argument before me proceeded on the basis
that all three charterers must stand or fall together in the result.

The special case contains a number of findings about the parties'
E states of mind at this time. I must return to these findings in a moment,
but it is convenient first to set out the subsequent course of events. The
ships remained in service throughout without interruption. As frequently
happens in these situations, a " without prejudice " agreement was concluded. When this happened is not found, but since no bills of lading
were ever presented or refused despite their urgency, it presumably
happened on the following day. Under this agreement the three vessels
F remained in the charterers' service. The charterers paid all disputed
deductions and agreed to make no more without the owners' approval.
Freight pre-paid bills of lading were issued without any endorsement
referring to the charters. Both sides then co-operated in a speedy
arbitration. It did not prove possible to hold it in October, as the
owners wished, but the hearing took place on Saturday and
Sunday, November 12 and 13 before two arbitrators and the umpire
G in case the arbitrators should disagree. As already mentioned, the
owners had previously given notice of arbitration on September 19 to
resolve the disputes concerning the July and September deductions and
the charterers' right to make disputed deductions in principle. However,
after October 5 the main issue had become the question whether or not
the owners would have been entitled to act in relation to the issue of bills
H of lading as they threatened to do and, if not, whether their conduct
constituted a wrongful repudiation of all three charters. The arbitrators
disagreed. The umpire thereupon entered upon the reference, and on
January 12, 1978, he made his award in the form of the special case
before me in favour of the charterers. On Friday, January 27 the judge
in charge of the Commercial List, Donaldson J., was asked to fix a date
for the hearing of the special case and he fixed it to be heard by me as a
matter of urgency on Monday, January 30, during the adjournment of

another hearing. These facts speak for themselves for the speed with   A
which urgent commercial disputes can often be resolved by arbitration
and before this court. It is a pity that this could not have been done on
or about October 5, but there are of course limits to what is possible.

I now return to a number of findings made in the special case about
the parties' states of mind on October 5. As already mentioned, the
owners took legal advice in New York and London and it was agreed
before me that what they did, or rather threatened to do, was in accord-   B
ance with the advice received, and that they acted bona fide. There are
then the following further findings in relation to the owners:

> " 26. At the time of the aforesaid telex correspondence the following
> was the state of knowledge of the owners (including Seven Seas): (i)
> they knew, as at all material times they had known, that in the
> ordinary course of events the charterers would wish to use the vessels   C
> for Great Lakes trade during the Great Lakes season—namely grain
> out and steel in; (ii) they knew that both steel shipments into the
> Great Lakes and grain shipments out from the Great Lakes were
> usually carried on c.i.f. terms; (iii) they knew that where carriage
> was effected on c.i.f. terms, it would be usual for freight pre-paid
> bills of lading to be issued, clean of any reference to a time charter;   D
> and that such requirement as regards freight pre-paid bills of lading
> was likely to be the subject of an express contractual obligation on
> the charterers; (iv) they knew that the refusal to issue freight pre-paid
> bills was likely to cause the charterers severe commercial embarrass-
> ment and the possibility of substantial liability to third parties for
> breach of contract; (v) that the charterers were likely to suffer
> consequences . . . unless they could ensure the prompt issue of   E
> freight pre-paid bills of lading clean of any incorporation of time
> charter terms; (vi) they were aware of the identity of the shippers
> of cargo in at least one of the three vessels; (vii) they were aware of
> the general nature of the contracts pursuant to which cargo was to
> be carried in the three vessels; (viii) as experienced operators in the
> Great Lakes trade, they knew the types of bills of lading generally
> used in the Great Lakes trading; . . .   F
>
> " 27. The owners intended that the effect of the aforesaid telex
> correspondence would be that the charterers would pay the disputed
> deductions under protest and that all issues between the parties
> would shortly be resolved by arbitration. The issuing of the order
> of October 4, 1977, was not to secure their claim for disputed deduc-
> tions (the offer for an escrow deposit having been rejected by owners   G
> as ' meritless ') but rather to compel the charterers to pay over all
> sums deducted from hire by the charterers which the owners dis-
> puted, irrespective of whether such deductions should ultimately be
> determined to be valid or invalid, in whole or in part, and to ensure
> that in the future the charterers made no deductions whatsoever
> from hire unless they had previously been expressly approved by
> the owners or they were supported by vouchers signed by the master   H
> or a proper tribunal had pronounced on their validity. At the same
> time, the owners knew that part of the amounts, payment of which
> they were demanding as a condition of the withdrawal of their
> orders, were due to the charterers."

On the material before me the last sentence can only relate to the
claim of about $47,000 in respect of the slow steaming of the *Nanfri* in

The Weekly Law Reports, August 4, 1978

321

3 W.L.R.   Federal Commerce Ltd. v. Molena Alpha Inc. (Q.B.D.)   Kerr J.

A 1975, since it is also found that in relation to the disputed balance of about $46,000 deducted in July and September the owners believed the charterers' deductions to have been invalid. It therefore appears that in this finding the umpire concluded, no doubt entirely reasonably, that his preliminary view that the charterers had a good claim under this head, but for a lesser amount than claimed, was shared by the owners. However, since the claim was based on a comparison with the vessel's

B maximum performance under optimum conditions it would no doubt also have been apparent to the charterers that they would be unlikely to succeed in full and that to this extent, even assuming that a right to deduct existed, the deduction was to some extent excessive.

Turning then to the findings about the charterers' state of mind, these are as follows:

C   " 29. The charterers regarded the orders issued by the owners on October 4, 1977, as a deliberate and fundamental breach of the latters' obligations under the charterparties. They further believed, correctly, that the owners fully realised the severe commercial difficulties which would be caused to them by such orders. The charterers further believed, reasonably in view of the conduct and communications of the owners, that the owners would issue such

D   orders again in the future whenever they, the owners, wished to force the charterers to comply with the owners' demands in similar circumstances."

It was not disputed before me on behalf of the charterers that the latter finding must be read subject to two qualifications. First, the words

E " in similar circumstances " were intended to refer to future instances, if they should arise, of unilaterial deductions by the charterers of disputed claims. In other words, the charterers reasonably believed that if they were again to make such deductions, then the owners would again react in the same way. However, it was also common ground that the charterers had no knowledge that the owners had taken legal advice, and it is clear from the finding in the first sentence of this paragraph that

F they did not believe that the owners were acting bona fide, though it is now accepted that they did. The second qualification is that the owners at all times intended that the deduction issues should be resolved by arbitration as soon as reasonably possible and that they would not maintain their standpoint thereafter if the result went against them.

Finally, it is found that at the time of the telex communications on

G October 5 " the charterers knew that, if they paid the disputed deductions, the instructions to the master would be withdrawn."

Paragraph 31 of the special case is in the following terms:

    " In so far as they are questions of fact I find, and in so far as they are question of law I hold that: a. The conduct of the owners constituted breaches of contract going to the root of the charter-

H   parties. b. The conduct of the owners did not constitute an absolute refusal to perform the charterparties, but did constitute an intention to perform the charterparties in a fundamentally different manner."

It was common ground that these were not findings of fact but conclusions of law which are not binding on the court, though the court would of course give weight to them in forming its own conclusion on the relevant question of law. This is in each of the cases " whether the charterers validly terminated the charterparty on October 5, 1977." It **A** was accepted in the argument before me that the answer must be the same in each case.

I therefore turn to the legal issues involved in this question. The first, before one gets to the question of repudiation, is logically whether or not the owners' actions and threatened actions constituted breaches of the charters. I think that most people familiar with shipping cases would instinctively feel that the answer must be in the affirmative. **B** Neither counsel nor I had ever come across a case in which a shipowner had claimed against a time charterer that he was entitled to refuse to issue freight pre-paid bills of lading and to clause them so as to incorporate all the terms of the time charter, including in particular the lien for unpaid hire. This was also clearly the impression of Barnes J. in *The Shillito* (1897) 3 Com.Cas. 44, the only reported case cited to me **C** which raised a somewhat similar issue, in which he summarily dismissed a claim by an owner against his master for negligence because he had failed to take some similar action. However, the point is undoubtedly arguable the other way, as Mr. Evans demonstrated, and in relation to voyage charters there is strong authority to support the argument.

One starts with the fact, which Mr. Evans rightly accepted against himself, that the second sentence of clause 9 of the charters, which is **D** often referred to as the employment and indemnity provision, ordinarily implies that the master is bound to sign bills of lading as presented and at any rate of freight. In practice the charterers' agents would nowadays sign and issue the bills of lading on his and the owners' behalf, but this does not affect the position. However, though the authorities are not very clear, they lend support to the view, at any rate in relation to voyage **E** charters, that the owners may object to bills of lading which would put them in a worse position than the terms of the charter, in particular to the extent to which the charter expressly provides for a lien. In this connection it was submitted by Mr. Evans that the express incorporation in the charter of rights of lien must have been designed to confer on the owners greater rights by way of security than the indemnity to compensate them for any greater liabilities which might be imposed on them **F** under the bills of lading than under the charter. The security of these rights will however be lost unless the bills of lading are endorsed accordingly, so that if " freight pre-paid " bills of lading are demanded and issued, then any right of lien will to that extent have gone.

This is a plausible argument which has strong support from the authorities on voyage charters, though it is not easy to see how far they **G** go: see *Manuel de Fribis Arrospe* v. *Thomas Barr* (1881) 8 R. 602; *Hansen* v. *Harrold Brothers* [1894] 1 Q.B. 612 and *Brankelow Steamship Co. Ltd.* v. *Canton Insurance Office Ltd.* [1899] 2 Q.B. 178; [1901] A.C. 462. Their discussion in the textbooks leaves the position inconclusive, and the relevant passages in the judgments should perhaps best be regarded as directed to the particular facts and the wording of the **H** charters in question: see *Scrutton on Charterparties*, 18th ed. (1974), art. 39, and *Carver, Carriage by Sea*, 12th ed. (1971), *British Shipping Laws*, vol. 2, art. 429. However, it seems to me that time charters are in any event in a different position. They are not contracts for the voyage or voyages to which the bills of lading relate, and the shipowners' remuneration is not freight but periodic hire. In dealing with the incorporation of the terms of a charterparty into a bill of lading, the

The Weekly Law Reports, August 4, 1978

323

3 W.L.R.   Federal Commerce Ltd. v. Molena Alpha Inc. (Q.B.D.)   Kerr J.

A   editors of *Scrutton on Charterparties* are in my view right in doubting
whether a time charter would ever be treated as intended to be incorporated, and when they state that " The court might well hesitate to hold
the consignee liable for, say, unpaid time charter hire ": see art. 34, note
46.   There is also another consideration.   The lien clause must be construed in the context of the time charter as a whole.   The shipowners'
primary remedy for a default in the payment of hire is the express right
B   to withdraw the ship from the service of the charterers.   It is true that
the lien clause purports to give them additional remedies, but I think
that these must be limited by reference to normal shipping practice.   The
normal way of exercising the lien is to try to intercept sub-freights or bills
of lading freights before they reach the charterers by giving the appropriate notices: see *Scrutton on Charterparties*, 18th ed., art. 188, note 47,
C   or perhaps by claiming that even thereafter the effect of the notices is
that the moneys are held in trust by the charterers for the owners.
Effect can also be given to the reference to bill of lading freights in the
lien clause by confining it to freight payable after shipment and
excluding advance freight.   In my judgment it would be wrong, in the
face of all these considerations, to elevate the lien clause in a time
charter to a level where it entitles the owners to refuse to issue freight
D   pre-paid bills lading, at any rate when the ship is being employed in a
trade in which the issue of such bills of lading is customary and of
paramount importance, as here.   I think that in the face of all these considerations the lien clause must give way and be construed restrictively.
To do so does not by any means deprive it of all efficacy.   As between
the owners and charterers it still operates as something in the nature of
E   an equitable assignment which can be perfected by giving the proper
notices if and when the charterers are in default in the payment of some
sum due to the owners.   But it would be unnecessary, and on the findings
before me contrary to business efficacy, to construe it so as to entitle
the owners to paralyse the charterers' use of the ship by acting in the way
in which the owners did in this case.   Furthermore, even if this be
wrong, the owners clearly went further than they were entitled.   Their
F   threatened action related to all three ships, but the October deduction
only related to the *Nanfri* and the earlier deductions had already been
referred to arbitration.   Secondly, there was on any view no acceptable
basis for threatening to incorporate " all the terms, conditions and exceptions " of the time charter, even if the threatened incorporation of the
lien clause could be justified.   On the facts found in the special case this
G   phraseology was bound to make the bills of lading virtually unacceptable,
and on any view it went further than was necessary to protect the owners'
interests concerning any unpaid hire.

I therefore hold that the managers' telex of October 4, setting out the
instructions to the masters was a threat to commit a breach of each of
the charters, in the sense that the owners would have been in breach if
H   freight pre-paid bills of lading had been presented for signature and any
of the masters had then acted in accordance with these instructions.   The
crucial question is then whether this telex, coupled with the instructions
to this effect which had in fact been given (though in my view they do
not add anything, since they did not cross the line between the parties),
constituted an anticipatory breach which amounted to a repudiation of
the three charters.

Mr. Mustill submitted on behalf of the charterers that it did.   He

relied on the consequences to the charterers, which I have already set out   A
from the special case.   Mr. Evans on behalf of the owners submitted that
it did not, even assuming against him that the owners were threatening
to commit breaches of each of the charters, as I have already held.

Both sides relied on numerous authorities, and it is convenient to deal
first with those cited on behalf of the owners.   Mr. Evans referred to
the classic authorities on repudiation such as *Freeth* v. *Burr* (1874) L.R.
9 C.P. 208 and *Mersey Steel & Iron Co. Ltd.* v. *Naylor, Benzon & Co.*   B
(1884) 9 App.Cas. 434.   The leading authorities on either side of the line are
well summarised in *Chitty on Contracts*, 24th ed. (1977), vol. 1, arts.
1479, 1480, under the heading of " Renunciation."   Mr. Evans referred
to some of the classic expressions which have been used to describe the
test whether a breach or anticipatory breach has this character, such as
" whether the acts or conduct of the one do or do not amount to an intima-   C
tion of an intention to abandon and altogether to refuse performance of the
contract," or whether they " evince an intention no longer to be bound
by the contract ": see Lord Coleridge C.J. in *Freeth* v. *Burr* at p. 213.
Another classic phrase to which he referred was " an absolute refusal to
perform the contract, such as would amount to a rescission if he "—the
guilty party—" had the power to rescind ": *per* Earl of Selborne L.C.,
in the *Mersey Steel* case at p. 439.   Mr. Evans submitted that this was   D
clearly not the attitude of the owners here, since they obviously wished
to retain the charters in the present market conditions, and he pointed
out that similar considerations had been taken into account in both
these cases.   However, none of these matters are in any way conclusive.
An anticipatory breach which the innocent party may treat as a repudiation can occur if the guilty party evinces an intention only to perform   E
the contract in a manner substantially inconsistent with that which the
contract requires.   If authority is required for this it is to be found in
the speech of Lord Wright in *Ross T. Smyth & Co. Ltd.* v. *T. D. Bailey,
Son & Co.* [1940] 3 All E.R. 60, 72 :

> " I do not say that it is necessary to show that the party alleged to
> have repudiated should have an actual intention not to fulfil the   F
> contract.   He may intend in fact to fulfil it, but may be determined
> to do so only in a manner substantially inconsistent with his obliga-
> tions, and not in any other way.   However, a mere honest mis-
> apprehension, especially if open to correction, will not justify a
> charge of repudiation."

I think that the words " especially if open to correction " were intended   G
to refer to the possibility of the situation being remedied before it had
gone too far, rather than to the possibility of persuading the party in
question that he was in fact under a misapprehension about his
obligations.   I must return to this point later.

Mr. Evans' second and main argument was based on two well-known
more recent authorities in this field, *James Shaffer Ltd.* v. *Findlay*   H
Durham & Brodie [1953] 1 W.L.R. 106 and *Sweet & Maxwell Ltd.* v.
Universal News Services Ltd. [1964] 2 Q.B. 699.   In both these cases
one party to the contract put forward to the other an erroneous construction of its contractual obligations, in the sense of maintaining that
his contractual obligation was X and no more, and firmly intimating that
this was how he proposed to perform the contract.   In both cases X was
a wrong interpretation of a term of substantial importance, but the party

The Weekly Law Reports, August 4, 1978

325

3 W.L.R.   Federal Commerce Ltd. v. Molena Alpha Inc. (Q.B.D.)   Kerr J.

A in question had a bona fide belief in the correctness of his view, and his interpretation, although incorrect, was not unreasonable. In both cases the Court of Appeal reviewed the leading authorities and concluded that there had been no repudiation. Mr. Evans submitted that the same position applied here, if, contrary to his submissions and as I have already decided, the owners would have been in breach if bills of lading had been presented and the masters had carried out the instructions set out in

B the telex of October 4. In this connection I should point out that neither side suggested, in my view rightly, that in deciding whether or not there had been a repudiation any distinction was to be drawn—at any rate for present purposes—between an anticipatory breach by giving notice that a certain action will be taken and an actual breach by taking the action in question. Mr. Evans pointed out that the owners were

C acting bona fide and indeed on legal advice, that their belief that they were entitled to deal with the bills of lading in this manner was not unreasonable, and that they at all times intended that all disputes between them and the charterers should be decided by arbitration as soon as reasonably possible. He stressed the fact that the owners were not insisting on taking this action whether they were entitled to or not, but only pending a decision by arbitration.

D   Mr. Mustill submitted that the *actual* intention and bona fides of the guilty party is irrelevant; what matters is his outward conduct. If he is in breach or intimates that he will not perform the contract according to its terms, then his subjective state of mind will not help him. With this I agree, but the character and consequences of the actual or threatened breach must still be assessed against the background of all the circum-

E stances before one can decide whether or not it goes far enough to be repudiatory. For instance, if damages would provide adequate compensation, or if the gravity or duration of the breach, whether actual or threatened, does not go to the roots of the contract when it is measured against the contractual transaction as a whole, then it seems to me on the modern authorities that it is not to be treated as a repudiation. Parties must not snatch at breaches in order to seek to free themselves

F from their contracts, and repudiation is not to be inferred lightly. The decision of the Court of Appeal in *Decro-Wall International S.A.* v. *Practitioners in Marketing Ltd.* [1971] 1 W.L.R. 361 is a recent example of the application of the modern doctrine. But Mr. Mustill disputed the correctness of this approach and relied on two older decisions, one of the Privy Council and one of the Court of Appeal, which appear to

G conflict with this view, at any rate where one party makes a statement concerning the interpretation of the contract which on its true construction is erroneous. These are *Clausen* v. *Canada Timber & Lands Ltd.* [1923] 4 D.L.R. 751, in the judgment of Lord Sumner, and *Aktieselskabet Pitwood* v. *J. W. Baird & Co. Ltd.* (1926) 24 Ll.L.Rep. 282, in the judgments of Bankes, Warrington and Atkin L.JJ. Neither of these appears ever to have been judicially considered, nor are they

H referred to in any of the standard textbooks. There was no time for lengthy argument on these cases before me, but I think that their approach is difficult, if not impossible, to reconcile with the approach in the *Ross T. Smyth, James Shaffer, Sweet & Maxwell* and *Decro-Wall* cases. In particular the *Pitwood* case, suggests that an intimation by one party to commit what Atkin L.J. refers to as " only a little breach " is nevertheless by itself sufficient to constitute a repudiation. I do not think that this accords with the modern view as illustrated in the cases to which

I have referred; nor perhaps with the emergence of " innominate terms," A
which are neither necessarily " conditions " nor " warranties " but whose
character and effect depend on their gravity and consequences in all the
circumstances: see *Hongkong Fir Shipping Co. Ltd.* v. *Kawasaki Kisen
Kaisha Ltd.* [1962] 2 Q.B. 26. Nor do I think that this approach can be
reconciled with the statement of Lord Wright in the *Ross T. Smyth* case
[1940] 3 All E.R. 60 which I have already cited, where he refers to an
honest misapprehension which is open to correction. The approach of B
the Court of Appeal in the *Pitwood* case, 24 Ll.L.Rep. 282, would
also appear to lead to the conclusion that an intimation that a party
proposes to do something which on the true construction of the contract
amounts to a " little breach " can be treated as a repudiation, whereas
the actual breach would not. I think that I should follow the modern
authorities. If a party can be seen to have the intention of performing C
the contract, but misconstrues it in a way which is not unreasonable, and
in a respect which does not go to the roots of the contract but can be
compensated by damages, then I do not think that he should be held to
have repudiated the whole contract more or less accidentally. As submitted by Mr. Evans, the correct test, in my view, is nowadays that, in
determining whether or not a breach, anticipatory or actual, has the
character of a repudiation, the court must ask itself whether it goes to D
the roots of the contract, so that, when set against the terms of the contract and all the circumstances, its effect would be analogous to a frustration. In the *Decro-Wall* case [1971] 1 W.L.R. 361, 379–380 Buckley
L.J. summed up the position as follows in a passage which clearly
represented the views of Salmon L.J. and Sachs L.J. as well:

> " Each party to an agreement is entitled to performance of the con- E
> tract according to its terms in every particular, and any breach,
> however slight, which causes damage to the other party will afford
> a cause of action for damages; but not every breach, even if its
> continuance is threatened throughout the contract or the remainder
> of its subsistence, will amount to a repudiation. To constitute
> repudiation, the threatened breach must be such as to deprive the F
> injured party of a substantial part of the benefit to which he is
> entitled under the contract. The measure of the necessary degree
> of substantiality has been expressed in a variety of ways in the cases.
> It has been said that the breach must be of an essential term, or of
> a fundamental term of the contract, or that it must go to the root of
> the contract. Various tests have been suggested: . . ."

G
and then he referred to authorities to which I have already referred. Then
he went on:

> " I venture to put the test in my own words as follows: Will the
> consequences of the breach be such that it would be unfair to the
> injured party to hold him to the contract and leave him to his remedy
> in damages as and when a breach or breaches may occur? If this
> would be so, then a repudiation has taken place." H

When the special cases before me are considered on these lines I feel
no doubt that the owners did not repudiate the charters merely by giving
these instructions to the masters and sending the telex of October 4.
Their actions were consistent with a belief—which it is now conceded
they had, supported by legal advice—that they were entitled to react in
this way by way of riposte to the charterers' repeated deductions from

The Weekly Law Reports, August 4, 1978

327

3 W.L.R.   Federal Commerce Ltd. v. Molena Alpha Inc. (Q.B.D.)   Kerr J.

A hire. They were not so much acting as re-acting, and they were doing so in the context of a deduction of a stale claim, after the points of principle involved in the deduction issues had already been referred to arbitration. I was reminded during the argument of the old French saying " Cet animal est tres méchant, quand on l'attaque il se défend." In comparison with the commercial adventure as a whole which these charters represented, the owners' threatened action should not in my
B view be regarded as a repudiation. The charters had three more years to run, and the owners were only creating a temporary impasse. The practicalities were speedily resolved, as was to be expected. The charterers always knew that the impasse could be resolved by their paying the disputed deduction of about $47,000, or at most also the earlier disputed sum of about $46,000, making about $93,000 in total. As
C against the monthly hires of about three times $180,000 this was not a very large sum. There is no suggestion that the owners would not have been good for the money if they were liable to repay it, and if the charterers' right to make the deductions were upheld in the pending arbitration, then they always had the security of future payments of hire from which these could be held back. If they succeed on the deduction issues they can be compensated by an appropriate award of interest. If
D the owners had simply refused to issue or to authorise the issue of bills of lading on one or more particular cargoes pending the full payment of the hire, the impasse would equally have been resolved, but I do not think that anyone would have regarded the owners as having thereby repudiated the charters altogether. What the owners did was to intimate what (in my judgment) was a breach of the charters, but only temporarily,
E pending the resolution by arbitration of a bona fide dispute. They were in effect compelling the charterers to preserve the status quo until then, without being able to make any disputed deductions, but they were really doing no more. If it had come to an actual breach, the charterers could have been compensated in damages. To use the words of Lord Wright, I think that the owners were under an honest misapprehension which
F was open to correction in the context of the charters as a whole. What the charterers did, however, was to snatch at this intimation as a means of getting rid of the charters. In the present state of the market they ran no risks other than having to pay costs. In my judgment they were not entitled to do so, and, to use the words of Buckley L.J., it would not be unfair to them to hold them to the charters. On the contrary, in all the circumstances I think that this would be unfair to the owners,
G although they overstepped the line.

In each of the three special cases the question of law is: " Whether the charterers validly terminated the charterparty on October 5, 1977." In my view the answer is " No." I accordingly do not uphold the umpire's award but remit the special cases to him as he requests.

Each of the special cases also contains a further question of law as
H follows:

> " Whether on the true construction of the charterparty the charterers were entitled to deduct from hire without the consent of owners valid claims which (a) arose under clause 11 of the charterparty, or (b) constituted an equitable set off."

This raises all the points to which I have referred compendiously as the deduction issues, and one can see at once the difficulty of determining

the meaning of " valid claims " in this context. Due to the limited A
time available I did not hear full argument on these issues, which might
in any event turn out to be hypothetical as between these parties in the
future. It was at first agreed that the argument and determination of
these issues should be adjourned. However, it was also pointed out that
this would prevent the determination of these issues in the present cases
in the Court of Appeal and possibly higher if they should go there, though
the time is clearly ripe for their determination. I then intimated that B
rather than add a further swing to the judicial pendulum I would in
any event probably decide to follow the most recent authority, the judgment of Parker J. in *The Teno* [1977] 2 Lloyd's Rep. 289 and to leave
the determination of these important issues to a higher level. It was
then agreed that I should take this course, and I therefore formally
answer both (a) and (b) affirmatively, as did the arbitrator. In doing so I C
interpret " valid claims " to mean " bona fide claims assessed on a
reasonable basis," which represents the half-way position to which I have
already referred. Whether or not the disputed deductions satisfy this
test will no doubt ultimately be resolved by agreement or decided in these
arbitrations if necessary.

There are passages in the judgment in *The Teno* which might be taken
to suggest that the conclusion reached by Parker J. was in accordance D
with what had generally been thought to be the legal position before this
series of cases reached the Commercial Court. I do not think that a
careful reading of the judgment really supports this interpretation; I think
that the judge was merely expressing his view of the cases to which he
referred. I heard no argument on behalf of the charterers on this or
any other point concerning the deduction issues. However, since I have E
a clear impression of what was thought to be the legal position and was
asked to state it by Mr. Evans with Mr. Mustill's consent, I will mention
it for what it may be worth. Speaking for myself, I have no doubt that
the belief generally held among commercial practitioners was as follows.
It was generally thought that there was no right to set off any cross-
claim against a claim for freight, as was confirmed by the House of Lords F
in *Aries Tanker Corporation* v. *Total Transport Ltd.* (*The Aries*) [1977]
1 W.L.R. 185. It was also thought that if this was the position concerning freight, then the position concerning time charter hire would be the
same. The brief passages from the judgments cited by Parker J. were not
regarded as authorities the other way; the most frequently cited passage
was from the judgment of MacKinnon L.J. in *Sea and Land Securities
Ltd.* v. *William Dickinson and Co. Ltd.* (1942) 72 Ll.L.Rep. 159, 163, G
where he referred to the " continuous and unbroken liability " of the
charterers to pay the hire. Time charterparties of course commonly
provide expressly, as in the present cases, for permitted deductions from
hire. The general view, in my experience, was that the permitted deductions were exhaustive. If a claim or cross-claim did not fall within them,
then the general view was that hire was payable continuously and in full; H
it could only be raised by way of a separate cross-claim in debt or damages
The continuity and security of payments of hire, subject to the expressly
permitted deductions, were considered the essential safeguards of the
owners under time charters, in the same way as in relation to freight under
voyage charters. However, while I feel confident that this was the generally
held view, I am in no way impugning the conclusion reached in *The Teno*
[1977] 2 Lloyd's Rep. 289, particularly since the decision of the House of

The Weekly Law Reports, August 4, 1978

329

3 W.L.R.   Federal Commerce Ltd. v. Molena Alpha Inc. (Q.B.D.)   Kerr J.

A Lords in *Modern Engineering (Bristol) Ltd.* v. *Gilbert-Ash (Northern) Ltd.*
[1974] A.C. 689.

> *Award remitted to umpire with direction
> to answer question* (1) (a) *and* (b) *in
> affirmative and* (2) *in negative.*

B Solicitors: *Ince & Co.; Richards, Butler & Co.*

[Reported by RACHAEL DAVIS, Barrister-at-Law]

APPEALS from Kerr J.

C The charterers appealed on the grounds that the judge was wrong in law and/or in fact in holding that the charterers had not validly terminated the charterparties on October 5, 1977, and in holding that the owners had not committed a breach and/or repudiation of the charterparties which justified them in determining them.

The owners gave notices of cross-appeals on the grounds that the judge was wrong in law and/or in fact in holding that the charterers D were entitled to deduct amounts from time charter hire without the consent of the owners in respect of valid claims which (a) arose under clause 11 of the charterparties or (b) constituted an equitable set off; and that the owners' managers' telex on October 4, 1977, did not contain a threat to commit a breach of the charters.

E *A. G. S. Pollock* and *Peter Gross* for the charterers.
Anthony Evans Q.C., Nicholas Phillips Q.C. and *A. M. Ginsberg* for the owners.

Cur. adv. vult.

April 18. The following judgments were read.

F LORD DENNING M.R. Time charters have become the sport of the shipping markets. There is always a provision by which the hire is to be paid punctually in advance. There is also a withdrawal clause which enables the shipowner to withdraw the vessel if the charterer makes default in payment. In the days when vessels were fully employed—and the freight market was rising—shipowners used to watch for a chance to determine the charter and withdraw the ship—long before the expiry G date. If the charterer made the slightest slip, the shipowner used to pounce and give notice of withdrawal: and thus force the charterer to pay the high current rate. You will find the story in *Mardorf Peach & Co. Ltd.* v. *Attica Sea Carriers Corporation of Liberia (The Laconia)* [1976] Q.B. 835, 848–849. Since those cases, some shipping people have made alterations in the terms of the charterparties. They have inserted a H provision by which the owners are not allowed to invoke their right of withdrawal unless they give 24 hours' notice in banking hours. This gives the charterers an opportunity to remedy their slip and avoid the withdrawal.

The market has now gone into reverse. There has been a disastrous slump in shipping. Shipowners are seeking employment for their vessels and the freight market has dropped dramatically. When ships are on long time charters, it is now the charterers who wish to bring them to an

end—if a chance arises—and it is the shipowners who wish to keep them   A
in force.   The shipowners want to receive their full hire.   The charterers
want to get out of paying it.   Sometimes they adopt unusual tactics for
the purpose.   A familiar device is to manufacture counterclaims as a
pretext for getting out of the hire.   You will find it described in a recent
case *Associated Bulk Carriers Ltd.* v. *Koch Shipping Inc.*, The Times,
August 10, 1977.   No unusual tactics however by the charterers in this case.
They are of first-class standing: and are and always have been ready and   B
willing to pay the full hire if properly due from them.

The time charters

There are three vessels—the *Nafri, Benfri* and *Lorfri.*   They fly the
Liberian flag.   They were built for Great Lakes trading.   They carry
grain cargoes from the Great Lakes to Europe, and on return carry   C
steel cargoes from Europe to the Great Lakes.   Most of such cargoes are
carried on c.i.f. terms: so that the shippers pay the freight for the
carriage in advance and receive bills of lading marked " Freight
pre-paid."

All three vessels are operated as part of a single fleet.   Each is owned
by a one-ship company and is mortgaged up to the full amount of the   D
present value.   They are operated from New York.   Each was let on
time charter in 1974 to first-class charterers, Federal Commerce Co.
Ltd., of Canada.   They operate from Montreal.   The charters were for
six years.   They were on the Baltime 1939 form, and contained several
variations and addenda.   I will take the *Lorfri* as typical.

The provision for payment of hire   E

The vessel carried about 35,700 tons deadweight.   The charterers
were to pay as hire U.S. $5 per ton deadweight per calendar month.
That is, $178,500 a month.   Clause 6 of the charter reads:

> " Payment of hire to be made in cash, in Montreal, on the 1st and
> 16th day of each month, without discount, in advance, to owner's
> account . . . In default of payment, the owners to have the right of   F
> withdrawing the vessel. . . ."

Clause 12 of addendum no. 2 reads:

> " In the event that any payment of hire is not paid . . . owners,
> before invoking any right or remedy . . . must notify charterers in
> writing . . . that the hire payment was not received when due. . . ."   G

The permissible deductions

Clause 11 reads:

> " (A) In the event of . . . breakdown of machinery . . . no hire to
> be paid in respect of any time lost thereby during the period in
> which the vessel is unable to perform the services immediately
> required.   Any hire paid in advance to be adjusted accordingly. . . .   H
> (C) If upon the voyage the speed be reduced by defect in or break-
> down of any part of her hull, machinery or equipment, the time so
> lost and the cost of any extra fuel consumed in consequence thereof
> and extra expenses to be deducted from hire."

Clause 14 reads:

> " The charterers or their agents to advance to the master, if required,

A   necessary funds for ordinary disbursement for the vessel's account
. . . and such advances to be deducted from hire, when supported
by vouchers signed by the master."

During the first 2½ years of the charter, the charterers made deduction from hire in respect of those clauses, sometimes by agreement
beforehand, and sometimes by deductions first and agreement afterwards.
B On at least one occasion the charterers deducted an item which the
owners had indicated was disputed.   But in June 1977 a meeting took
place at which all outstanding disputed deductions from hire were settled.

The events leading up to the crisis

July 1977.   In July 1977 the charterers deducted $65,274.22 from the
C hire due for the *Lorfri.*   The whole of this deduction was afterwards
agreed, save for a small item of $1,608.63 which was disputed.   In the
same month, the charterers also deducted $17,866.53 due for the *Benfri,*
all of which was afterwards agreed.   The charterers also deducted
$98,565.45 for the *Nanfri,* all of which was afterwards agreed, save for a
small item of $6,809.26.

August 1977.   The charterers appear to have made no deductions.
D
September 1977.   On September 1, 1977, the charterers made several
deductions, and gave detailed justifications for them. $67,775.39 for the
Nanfri of which the larger part was afterwards agreed, but $23,184.78
was disputed. $35,379.38 for the *Benfri* of which $14,823.95 was subsequently disputed. $6,531.69 for the *Lorfri,* all of which was afterwards
agreed.

E

The opening round

The owners took exception to those deductions being made by the
charterers.   They now for the first time asserted that the charterers were
not entitled to make any deductions which they (the owners) disputed.
In order to enforce this assertion, the owners on September 2, 1977,
F fired their opening shot.   They telexed the charterers giving them notice
under clause 12 of addendum no. 2 that the hire payment had not been
received when due.   They thus opened the way for themselves to exercise
" any right or remedy " available to them in respect of the non-payment.
The charterers replied immediately, giving a breakdown of the deductions, and referring to the detailed justifications previously sent to the
owners.
G
By a telex of September 6 the owners firmly asserted that the
charterers were not entitled to make deductions in respect of any disputed
item.

At all times from September 6, 1977, onwards the owners have contended that the charterers were not entitled to make any deduction from
hire by way of off-hire or set off (even if the sum deducted was in fact
H due to the charterers) unless prior to such deduction (a) the owners had
accepted the validity of the deduction; or (b) it was supported by vouchers
issued by the master; or (c) a proper tribunal had pronounced on its
validity.

In answer the charterers did not agree to those limitations on their
right to deduct from hire, but offered to place the amount of any disputed item in escrow: and this they have always remained ready and
willing to do.

332

The first reference to arbitration   A

On September 21, 1977, the owners gave notice to the charterers requiring an arbitration to decide whether the charterers had correctly calculated the items deducted on September 1, 1977: and also on the question of principle whether or not the charterers were in any event " entitled unilaterally to deduct disputed items from charter hire."

It is to be noticed that at that time there was no question of the   B
owners withdrawing the vessel from charter. After all, the owners wanted the hire at the high rate: so they did not want to determine the charter. There was only a difference about the deduction of disputed items. This was referred to arbitration.

The deduction by the charterers for the slow steaming in 1975
       C
It was at this juncture that the charterers brought up an outstanding claim. As long ago as 1975 the *Nanfri* had suffered engine breakdown whilst she was on a voyage from Antwerp to Durban. She had put into a port of refuge for repairs on two occasions. She was off-hire for the period of those repairs. Deductions had been made on that account and agreed. But the log abstract showed that, after the breakdown, the vessel's speed was reduced below normal. The charterers attributed this   D
slow steaming to the engine breakdown. So they claimed to deduct $47,122.43 on account of it. They calculated the sum in this way: they took the vessel's optimum speed in good weather and smooth water. This was 15 knots. They assumed that she could have done that speed for every day on that voyage if she had not suffered the engine breakdown. This was probably too favourable to themselves, because she may have encountered bad weather. Undoubtedly the charterers were   E
entitled to make some deduction, but not as much as the sum claimed of $47,122.43.

The charterers had made this claim in November 1975, but in February 1976 the owners had rejected it—at any rate in the full amount claimed —saying that it could only be considered for any day of actual reduced speed. On March 2, 1976, the owners told the charterers by telephone   F
that if they wished to pursue this claim, they should resort to arbitration.

The charterers for some time did nothing about this claim. They did not make any deductions from hire on account of it. They did not refer it to arbitration. It lay fallow from March 1976 until the opening shot had been fired in the beginning of September 1977, which I have described. The charterers then seem to have looked up their papers and   G
found this outstanding claim. On September 19, 1977, they wrote to the owners claiming the sum of $47,122.43 for the slow steaming.

The reaction by the owners

The owners reacted sharply. The managers telexed on September 20, 1977, rejecting the reduction. I will set out the telex:
       H
> ". . . we, on owner's behalf, under no condition shall authorise this deduction. We therefore demand a full hire instalment be made on September 30, 1977."

The charterers nevertheless insisted on making the deduction. They deducted $47,122.43 from the hire due on October 1, 1977. It was the only deduction that they made on any of the three vessels from that month's hire. It was the casus belli. The owners took legal advice and

The Weekly Law Reports, August 4, 1973

333

3 W.L.R.   Federal Commerce Ltd. v. Molena Alpha Inc. (C.A.)   Lord Denning M.R.

A took counteraction based on various clauses in the charterparty to which
I now turn.

The employment and indemnity clause

In the ordinary course of these time charters, the master did not
sign the bills of lading himself. They were signed by the charterers'
B agents on behalf of the owners. The freight was always pre-paid. This
was necessary so as to implement the contracts of sale of the cargo on
board which was always c.i.f. The charterers were entitled to insist on
this by reason of clause 9 of the charterparty, which said:

> " . . . The master to be under the orders of the charterers as regards
> employment, agency or other arrangements. The charterers to
> indemnify the owners against all consequences or liabilities arising
C > from the master, officer or agent signing bills of lading or other
> documents or otherwise complying with such orders. . . ."

In right of that clause, the bills of lading were issued and signed by the
charterers on behalf of the master and the freight was paid to the
charterers or their agent. So the owners never had any control over
D it—unless they got it by way of the lien clause to which I now turn.

The lien clause

The charterparty contained this clause in favour of the owners. It is
clause 18:

> " The owners to have a lien upon all cargoes and sub-freights belong-
E > ing to the time-charterers and any bill of lading freight for all claims
> under this charter, and the charterers to have a lien on the vessel
> for all moneys paid in advance and not earned."

The owners placed much reliance on that lien clause. It gave them a
lien on any sub-freights and any bill of lading freights. It is obvious
that, if such freights were pre-paid, there would be nothing on which the
F lien could operate. So in this trade (where freight was always pre-paid)
the clause was not much use to the owners. The only way in which they
could take advantage of the lien was like this: if hire was unpaid, the
owners had to intervene before the freight was paid to the charterers:
see *Tagart, Beaton & Co.* v. *James Fisher & Sons* [1903] 1 K.B. 391.
They could give notice to the sub-charterer or the shipper, telling them
of the lien clause, and requiring the freight to be paid to them, the owners
G (up to the amount of the unpaid hire): but the sub-charterer or shipper
would not pay on that notice except with the agreement of the charterers.
If the charterers did not agree, the sub-charterer or shipper would interplead: and place the freight in escrow. So the lien clause itself was of no
use to the shipowners. It did not enable them to get hire paid clear of
any deductions.

H
The coup de main—the shattering blow

In this situation the owners turned to their lawyers in London and
New York. They asked them whether there were any means by which
they could get the hire paid in full every month without any deductions.
They were advised that there was a way of doing it. They could take
away all authority from the charterers to sign bills of lading, and vest the
sole authority in the master on their own behalf: and he could require

Lord Denning M.R.   Federal Commerce Ltd. v. Molena Alpha Inc. (C.A.)   [1978]

the bills of lading to be in a form which incorporated the terms of the   A
charterparty, thus giving the owners a lien on the freight for the hire.
The master could then receive the freight and pay the owners out of it
the hire without any deductions.

Acting an their lawyers' advice, the owners on October 4, 1977, sent
this telex to the charterers:

> " The masters of the *Benfri, Nanfri* and *Lorfri* are being instructed   B
> to withdraw all direct or implied authority to charterer or its agents
> to sign bills of lading.   Please present all bills of lading to the master
> for signature.   Note that the masters will not sign any bill of lading
> (1) endorsed ' freight pre-paid ' or (2) which does not bear an
> endorsement reading: ' All terms, conditions and exceptions of the
> time charter dated November 1, 1974, as amended, including the lien
> under clause 18 on bill of lading freight as well as sub-freight   C
> belonging to the time charter, are herein incorporated.' "

At the same time, the owners actually gave instructions to the masters
of the three vessels in those very terms.

The effect on the charterers
                                                                            D
That stroke by the owners was a pistol at the head of the charterers.
If the owners carried out their threat—for that is what it was—it would
mean disaster for the charterers.   Each of the three vessels had been
sub-chartered to big suppliers of grain called Continental Grain who were
themselves the shippers.   The *Nanfri* was just on the point of completing
the loading of a cargo of soya beans at Toledo on Lake Erie.   The
Lorfri was in the course of loading a cargo of grain at Chicago for   E
Rotterdam.   The *Benfri* was on passage to Chicago to discharge a cargo
of grain and from there to Duluth on Lake Superior to load a cargo for
Rotterdam.   It was vital to the charterers that these shipments should be
concluded and the bills of lading should be issued " freight pre-paid "—
because otherwise there would be a default under all the contracts of sale
to Northern Europe, which were all on c.i.f. terms.
                                                                            F
The owners fully realised the difficulties in which they put the
charterers: and their very object was to bring irresistible pressure on the
charterers to pay the hire without any deduction of disputed items.   They
were issuing a threat equivalent to " Your money or your life "—that
is to say " Pay up the hire in full without deductions or else we will play
havoc with your trade."
                                                                            G
The telex interchanges

The charterers' reply to the threat was contained in a telex of October
5, 1977, which set out their case very well, and I will read it:

> " We are most distressed by your action which has placed us in an
> impossible position commercially.   It is both customary and
> necessary for us to issue freight pre-paid bills of lading in order to   H
> meet the requirements of letters of credit and other commercial
> agreements.   For the same reason the clausing of bills of lading
> as instructed by you is non-workable.   We cannot understand why
> you are taking this position particularly since we have previously
> offered to put all disputed deductions from hire in escrow pending
> arbitration and we are still prepared to do so.   It is our belief that
> the charterparty requires the master to sign bills of lading as pre-

The Weekly Law Reports, August 4, 1978

335

3 W.L.R.   Federal Commerce Ltd. v. Molena Alpha Inc. (C.A.)   Lord Denning M.R.

A   sented and therefore your instructions to the contrary indicate an unwillingness on your part to comply with the charter agreement. In view of the immediate problems created by your message we must insist that by not later than 4 p.m. today you confirm to us that you have withdrawn unequivocally these instructions to the master and have told the master that he is to sign bills of lading freight pre-paid or otherwise as ordered in the same way as has been customary since
B   the beginning of our relationship."

This plea did not move the owners. They at once replied describing the proposal of an escrow as " meritless " and insisting on payment of hire in full without " unilateral deductions " by 3 p.m. If they did not pay in full the instructions to the captains of the vessels would stand. The charterers replied saying:
C
"clause 11 of the charter quite clearly gives us a right to make deductions from hire in specified circumstances and we have exercised that right from time to time and intend to continue doing so."

The owners were still unmoved. They replied:

D   " . . . the instructions to the masters concerning bills of lading will stand unless full payments for unauthorised and unilateral deductions are paid."

The coup de grace—the knock-out blow

The charterers then administered the coup de grace—the knock-out
E   blow—if they were right. Their final telex was:

" . . . Owners, by their conduct, have clearly evinced an intention not to be bound by the terms of the charter (notwithstanding your protestations to the contrary) and we accept the totality of their conduct as a repudiation of the charter and we accept such repudiation without prejudice to any rights that we may have, including our claim for damages. Accordingly we consider the charter
F   terminated effective immediately and we demand that owners remit payment of all hire paid in advance and not earned, together with the value of the bunkers now on board the vessel."

If that telex was justifiable, the legal effect was tremendous. It meant that the time charters had come to an end after only three years. For
G   the remaining three years of the charters, the vessels reverted to the shipowners for them to use as best they could. They would only get the very low market rate in 1977 as compared with the high market rate in the charter of 1974. Instead of getting over $500,000 a month coming in on the three vessels, they would get a minimal amount. We are told that $15,000,000 are at stake in the case: as well as important questions of law.

H
The " without prejudice " agreement

In point of fact the parties avoided any disaster at that stage. They made a " without prejudice " agreement of which we know nothing except that the three vessels have remained in service, the charterers have paid all disputed deductions and agreed to make no more deductions without the owners' approval; and freight pre-paid bills of lading have been issued without any endorsement referring to the charterparties. Meanwhile

A

the contest—whether or not the charter has been determined by repudiation and acceptance—was referred to arbitration.

So pending the decision of the arbitration—and of the case stated—everything has gone on in the same way as if the time charterparties had never been determined. The charterers have suffered no extra loss except that they have paid about $93,000 to the owners direct instead of in escrow. The owners have gained no extra benefit except that they have had $93,000 in hand in lieu of in escrow. This minimal effect is the strongest card in the shipowners' hands: and they have played it well. It led Kerr J. to decide in their favour.

B

The arbitration

The two arbitrators disagreed. The umpire (Mr. Clifford Clark) held that the conduct of the owners amounted to a repudiation of the charterparties and that the charterers validly terminated them on October 5, 1977.

C

Kerr J. reversed the umpire. He held that the conduct of the owners created only a temporary impasse which was speedily resolved. It was not a repudiation and the charterparty continued at the full rate of hire.

D

The legal position

To my mind the best way to tackle this case is to take each difference between the parties in chronological order and decide which of them was in the right about it.

Difference No. 1: The deductions from the hire payments due on September 1, 1977

E

On September 1, 1977, the monthly hire due on all three vessels together was $530,000. The charterers deducted $109,000 for various reasons of which they gave detailed justifications. On September 13, 1977, the owners agreed that these deductions were justified save for $38,000. So all was paid except $38,000—that is about 7 per cent.

The owners contested these deductions. They did so on the ground:

F

"the charterers were not entitled to make any deduction from hire by way of off-hire or set off (even if the same was in fact due to the charterers) unless prior to such deduction either the owners had accepted the validity thereof or it was supported by vouchers signed by the master or a proper tribunal had pronounced on its validity."

G

This contention was founded on the proposition that hire payable under a time charterparty is in the same position as freight payable under a voyage charterparty: and that under a settled rule of law freight is payable in full without deduction. Even if cargo is short-delivered, or delivered damaged, there can be no deduction on that account. Any cross-claim must be left to be decided later by the courts or by arbitration. That is well-established now for " freight " in such cases as H *Henriksens Rederi A/S* v. *T.H.Z. Rolimpex (The Brede)* [1974] Q.B. 233 and *Aries Tanker Corporation* v. *Total Transport Ltd. (The Aries)* [1977] 1 W.L.R. 185.

At one time it was common to describe the sums payable under a time charterparty as " freight." Such description is to be found used by judges and textbook writers of great distinction. But in modern times a change has come about. The payments due under a time charter are

3 W.L.R.   Federal Commerce Ltd. v. Molena Alpha Inc. (C.A.)   Lord Denning M.R.

A usually now described as " hire " and those under a voyage charter as
" freight." This change of language corresponds, I believe, to a recognition that the two things are different. "Freight" is payable for carrying a quantity of cargo from one place to another. "Hire" is payable
for the right to use a vessel for a specified period of time, irrespective of
whether the charterer chooses to use it for carrying cargo or lays it up,
out of use. Every time charter contains clauses which are quite inappro-
B priate to a voyage charter, such as the off-hire clause and the withdrawal
clause. So different are the two concepts that I do not think the law as
to " freight " can be applied indiscriminately to " hire." In particular the
special rule of English law whereby " freight " must be paid in full (without deductions for short delivery or cargo damage) cannot be applied
automatically to time charter " hire." Nor is there any authority which
C says that it must. It would be a mistake to suppose that the House of
Lords had time charter hire and so forth in mind when they decided *The
Aries* [1977] 1 W.L.R. 185 or the *Nova (Jersey) Knit Ltd.* v. *Kammgarn
Spinnerei G.m.b.H.* [1977] 1 W.L.R. 713, or that anything said in those
cases can bind this court. Many of us, I know, in the past have assumed
that the rule as to " freight " does apply: and some judges have said so.
But now, after full argument, I am satisfied that the " freight " rule does
D not apply automatically to " time charter " hire: and we have to consider
the position on principle.

Equitable set off in general

It is often necessary to distinguish between a set off or defence properly so called; and a counterclaim or cross-action. For instance in the
E case of a statute of limitation or a time bar under the Hague Rules, a
set off or defence properly so called is never defeated by the lapse of time:
but a counterclaim or cross-action is liable to be defeated: see *The Brede*
[1974] Q.B. 233, 245–249 and *The Aries* [1977] 1 W.L.R. 185. Again
in the case of a submission to arbitration when a " dispute " is to be
referred, then if there is a sum payable under the contract to the creditor,
but the debtor has a cross-claim seeking to reduce it, then the question
F whether the whole has to be referred—or only the cross-claim—may
depend on whether the cross-claim is a set off or a defence properly
so called (thus reducing the claim) or is a counterclaim: see *Russell* v.
Pellegrini (1856) 6 E. & B. 1020, as explained by Lord Russell of Killowen
in *Nova (Jersey) Knit Ltd.* v. *Kammgarn Spinnerei* [1977] 1 W.L.R.
713, 739; *Naxos Shipping Corporation* v. *Thegra Shipping Co. S.A.* (*The
G Corfu Island*) (unreported) April 10, 1974, Ackner J. and *Ellis Mechanical*
v. *Wates* (1976) 2 B.L.R. 57.

Again take the case where the contract gives a creditor a right to
take the law into his own hands—to take a particular course of action if
a sum is not paid—such as to forfeit a lease for non-payment of rent,
or to withdraw a vessel for non-payment of hire. There the distinction
between set off and cross-claim is crucial. When the debtor has a true
H set off it goes in reduction of the sums owing to the creditor. If the
creditor does not allow it to be deducted, he is in peril. He will be liable
in damages if he exercises his contractual right of withdrawal wrongly.
But when the debtor has no set off or defence properly so called, but only
a counterclaim or cross-action, then the creditor need not allow any
deduction to be made. He can exercise his contractual right without
fear; and leave the debtor to bring an action for damages on his counterclaim.

Lord Denning M.R.   Federal Commerce Ltd. v. Molena Alpha Inc. (C.A.)   [1978]

In making the distinction between set off and cross-claim, the courts   A
of common law had their own special rules.   For instance in a series of
cases they formulated rules saying when there could be an abatement of
rent or an abatement of the sums due for work and labour done, or an
abatement of the price of goods sold and delivered.   So that the defendant
could make deductions accordingly.   But the courts of equity, as was
their wont, came in to mitigate the technicalities of the common law.
They allowed deductions—by way of equitable set off—whenever there   B
were good equitable grounds for directly impeaching the demand which
the creditor was seeking to enforce: see *Rawson* v. *Samuel* (1841) Cr. &
Ph. 161, 178–179, *per* Lord Cotterham L.C.   These grounds were never
precisely formulated before the Judicature Act 1873.   It is now far too
late to search through the old books and dig them out.   Over 100 years
have passed since the Judicature Act 1873.   During that time the streams   C
of common law and equity have flown together and combined so as to
be indistinguishable the one from the other.   We have no longer to ask
ourselves: what would the courts of common law or the courts of equity
have done before the Judicature Act?   We have to ask ourselves: what
should we do now so as to ensure fair dealing between the parties?   See
United Scientific Holdings Ltd. v. *Burnley Borough Council* [1977] 2
W.L.R. 806, 812, *per* Lord Diplock.   This question must be asked in each   D
case as it arises for decision: and then, from case to case, we shall build
up a series of precedents to guide those who come after us.   But one
thing is quite clear: it is not every cross-claim which can be deducted.
It is only cross-claims that arise out of the same transaction or are closely
connected with it.   And it is only cross-claims which go directly to
impeach the plaintiff's demands, that is, so closely connected with his   E
demands that it would be manifestly unjust to allow him to enforce
payment without taking into account the cross-claim.   Such was the case
with the lost vehicle in *Morgan & Son Ltd.* v. *Martin Johnson & Co. Ltd.*
[1949] 1 K.B. 107 and the widow's misconduct in *Hanak* v. *Green*
[1958] 2 Q.B. 9.

Equitable set off in this case   F

So I turn to the problem here.   A shipowner has contracted to
give a charterer the right to use the vessel for a period of time—
six years in fact.   In return the charterer has agreed to pay a stated
sum of hire monthly in advance.   Then let us suppose that, after the
charterer has paid his month's hire in advance, the shipowner wrongly
declines to allow the charterer to have the use of the vessel for   G
some days during the ensuing month.   He may put the vessel
perhaps to some more profitable use.   He, by his conduct, deprives the
charterer of part of the consideration for which the hire was paid.   I
should have thought it plain that the charterer should in fairness be able
to recoup himself by making a deduction from the next month's hire—
so as to compensate him for the loss of use for those days—equivalent to
the hire of those lost days.   Likewise if the shipowner has been guilty of   H
some other wrongful conduct which has deprived the charterer of the
use of the ship during some days—or prejudiced the charterer in the use
of the ship—then the charterer should in fairness be able to recoup himself by making a deduction from the next month's hire.   If the charterer
quantifies his loss by a reasonable assessment made in good faith—and
deducts the sum quantified—then he is not in default.   The shipowner
cannot withdraw his vessel on account of non-payment of hire nor hold

The Weekly Law Reports, August 4, 1978

339

3 W.L.R.   Federal Commerce Ltd. v. Molena Alpha Inc. (C.A.)   Lord Denning M.R.

A him guilty at that point of any breach of contract.   If it subsequently turns out that he has deducted too much, the shipowner can of course recover the balance.   But that is all.   This point of view is supported by a score of judges versed in commercial matters over the last 30 to 40 years.   As the matter is so important, I will summarise those cases, particularly emphasising the facts, as the facts do influence decisions.

    The first case is where a shipowner withdrew a ship from the use of B the time charterer for one day and 13 hours so as to fit de-gaussing apparatus.   If the withdrawal had been a breach of contract—not assented to by the charterer—then it was clearly stated by Atkinson J. and by MacKinnon L.J. that the charterers could recoup themselves by deducting the equivalent amount from the next month's hire.   The material passage in MacKinnon L.J.'s judgment is not to be found in the law C report of *Sea and Land Securities Ltd.* v. *William Dickinson and Co. Ltd.* [1942] 2 K.B. 65, 71, but it is in 72 Ll.L.Rep. 159, 165.

    In the next year 1943 that view was accepted as correct by both Mr. Devlin and me as counsel—we were both young and very often appearing in cases of this kind about charterparties—and by the Court of Appeal. This was in *Halcyon Steamship Co. Ltd.* v. *Continental Grain Co.* (1943) 75 Ll.L.Rep. 57, 80.   The master of a ship under a time charter refused to D sign bills of lading for goods already on board: and thereupon the charterers stopped loading for a certain time until the bills of lading were signed.   The charterers were not justified in stopping loading and so full hire was payable: but, if the charterers had been justified, they would have been entitled to deduct the time lost from the hire.   That is what I understood—and I believe the others in the *Halcyon* case understood—where E MacKinnon L.J., at p. 84, repeated what he had said in the *Sea and Land* case.

    The same opinion was expressed by a good judge in Admiralty, who was also well-versed in commercial matters, Bucknill L.J. in *Tankexpress (A/S)* v. *Compagnie Financière Belge des Petroles S/A* (1947) 80 Ll.L.Rep. 365, 380, a year or two later.   It was suggested there that the shipowners could wrongfully withdraw the vessel from the use of the F charterers—and nevertheless cancel the charter for non-payment of hire. Bucknill L.J., said at p. 380: "This result appears to me to be so very inequitable that I cannot think it to be the law." (When the case reached the House of Lords, Lord Porter preferred not to express any opinion on the point: see [1949] A.C. 76, 91.)

    In 1971 there was *Nippon Yusen Kaisha* v. *Acme Shipping Corporation* G *(The Charalambos N. Pateras)* [1971] 2 Lloyd's Rep. 42 where a master wrongfully refused to enter a port ordered by the charterers and thus deprived the charterers of the use of the vessel for some days.   Mocatta J. said that they would have been entitled to deduct a sum for the loss of use except for an exceptions clause.

    Then in 1974 there was *The Corfu Island* (unreported).   The vessel had been in breach of the warranty as to speed; and by reason of it the H time charterers had lost the use of the vessel for part of the time to which they were entitled—in return for the hire.   Ackner J. held that, if the breach of warranty was proved, it would be a ground of deduction from hire.   There was therefore a " dispute " as to the amount of hire due and it should be referred to arbitration.

    Lastly there is *Compania Sud Americana de Vapores* v. *Shipmair B.V.* *(The Teno)* [1977] 2 Lloyd's Rep. 289.   There the master sailed away from the loading port, short of 769 tonnes of soya beans, in breach

of the contract. He did so because, if he had loaded those additional   A
tonnes, the vessel would have been too deep in the water and he would
have had to wait four days longer: during which time she would have
been off-hire under the clause. The charterers claimed damages in
respect of cargo shut out. Parker J. held that this claim could be
deducted from the owners' claim for hire.

This line of cases is so convincing that I would hold that, when the
shipowner is guilty of a breach of contract which deprives the time   B
charterer of part of the consideration for which the hire has been paid
in advance, the charterer can deduct an equivalent amount out of the
hire falling due for the next month.

I would as at present advised limit the right to deduct to cases when
the shipowner has wrongly deprived the charterer of the use of the vessel
or has prejudiced him in the use of it. I would not extend it to other   C
breaches or default of the shipowner, such as damage to cargo arising
from the negligence of the crew. This was the view of Parker J. in *The
Teno*. A parallel situation may be seen in the case about building contracts *Mottram Consultants Ltd.* v. *Bernard Sunley & Sons Ltd.* [1975]
2 Lloyd's Rep. 197 where the majority of the House of Lords did not
allow a deduction to be made for damage done for want of care in
preparing imprest accounts.   D

It follows that I find myself differing from the the view of Donaldson
J. in *Seven Seas Transportation Ltd.* v. *Atlantic Shipping Co. Ltd.* [1975]
2 Lloyd's Rep. 188 and Mocatta J. in *Steelwood Carriers Inc. of Monrovia,
Liberia* v. *Evimeria Compania Naviera S.A. of Panama* (*The Agios
Giorgis*) [1976] 2 Lloyd's Rep. 192, 201 and the views expressed in
Carver, Carriage by Sea, 12th ed. (1971), vol. I, para. 402 and *Scrutton*   E
on Charterparties, 18th ed. (1974), p. 358.

I do not think the cases on building contracts help much. *Modern
Engineering (Bristol) Ltd.* v. *Gilbert-Ash (Northern) Ltd.* [1974] A.C. 689
and *Mottram Consultants Ltd.* v. *Bernard Sunley & Sons Ltd.* [1975] 2
Lloyd's Rep. 197 turn on the construction of the conditions in a particular building contract. There was no particular discussion as to the
scope of equitable set off. In my opinion therefore in a time charter,   F
if the shipowner wrongly and in breach of contract deprives the
charterer for a time of the use of the vessel, the charterer can deduct a
sum equivalent to the hire for the time so lost.

The special clauses

Thus far I have considered only cases where the shipowner has him-   G
self been guilty of a breach of contract in depriving the charterer of the
use of the vessel. Now I come to cases where the shipowner has not been
guilty of any breach of contract, or is protected by exceptions clauses. In
such cases the charterer is often given a right of deduction by express
clauses such as the off-hire clause or a clause allowing deductions for
disbursements. There is no doubt that the charterer can make the
deduction, but the question is when? Have they to be agreed or esta-   H
blished before he can make the deduction? There is no authority that
I know of to that effect. It seems to me that he is entitled to quantify
his loss by a reasonable assessment made in good faith—and deduct the
sum so quantified from the hire. Then the actual figures can be ascertained later: either by agreement between the parties: or, failing agreement, by arbitration. That was what the parties did in the present case
for the first three years of the charters. The right to deduct would be

The Weekly Law Reports, August 4, 1978

341

3 W.L.R.   Federal Commerce Ltd. v. Molena Alpha Inc. (C.A.)   Lord Denning M.R.

A useless to the charterer if he had to wait until a figure was agreed or established—for then it might be postponed indefinitely. This seems to have been the view of Kerr J. in the present case. It is the " half-way position " to which he refers.

This is borne out by the interpretation placed by the House of Lords on the clause in *Modern Engineering (Bristol) Ltd.* v. *Gilbert-Ash (Northern) Ltd.* [1974] A.C. 689 where the contractor was given the right

B to deduct the amount of any " bona fide contra account and/or other claim." Lord Morris of Borth-y-Gest said, at p. 704:

> " To have a process of deduction from such a sum there must clearly be some other stated sum . . . There could not be a deduction of something that lacked any kind of specification. But need the sum to be deducted be a liquidated sum or an ascertained sum in the
C sense of an agreed sum or of a sum assessed by a court? The wording of the provision does not so indicate."

Nor does it in these clauses in this charter.

Conclusion on difference No. 1

D This brings me to a conclusion on the first question. In my opinion the charterers were entitled to make the deductions which they did from the hire due on September 1, 1977. The deductions were calculated on a reasonable basis in good faith with detailed justifications. The greater portions were accepted as correct: and the actual figures were agreed on September 13, 1977. I see no justification whatever for the owners'
E contention that they were entitled to insist on full payment of hire without deduction of any items except those which they agreed.

Difference No. 2. The deductions made from the hire payment on October 1, 1977

On October 1, 1977, the charterers paid the full hire on all three vessels save that they deducted the one payment of $47,122.33 for the hire
F due on the *Nanfri*. This deduction was made for slow steaming: and was claimed by virtue of clause 11 (C). It was calculated in good faith on a reasonable basis—indeed on the only basis on which the charterers had any information. The owners were better placed than the charterers. They would have the relevant information as to the number of revolutions of the engine and so on: and could easily check the validity of the deduction. So it seems to me that the charterers were entitled to make
G that deduction. Instead of allowing them to make that deduction, the shipowners insisted that the charterers were not entitled to make any unilateral deductions from the hire at all. This was, I think, a mistake on their part. They knew that the charterers were entitled to some deduction for slow steaming: and they were not entitled to refuse any deduction at all. The owners were no doubt upset at having this claim of slow-steaming revived after it had lain fallow. But that did not justify
H them in reacting as they did.

Difference No. 3. The telex of October 4, 1977

To my mind the conduct of the owners on October 4, 1977, was a clear breach of the charterparty. They had expressly agreed in clause 9 that the master was to be under the orders of the charterers as regards employment, agency or other arrangements. Yet here they were them-

Lord Denning M.R.   **Federal Commerce Ltd. v. Molena Alpha Inc. (C.A.)**   **[1978]**

selves giving orders to the masters of the three vessels which were in   A
flat contradiction of the charterers' arrangements. If these orders to the
masters had been implemented, it would have had disastrous consequences
to the charterers. It was a plain threat: "Pay up the hire in full or we
will play havoc with your trade." The owners seek to excuse their breach
by saying: "We knew that you would pay up in full and would not suffer
any disturbance in your trade." That plea was accepted by the judge.
He spoke of the threat as creating only a "temporary impasse" which   B
was speedily resolved by the "without prejudice" agreement. I am
afraid that I cannot so view it. It was to my mind a completely unjustifi-
able threat—to do an unlawful act—so as to gain their own ends. The
threat was not confined to these particular deductions. It would be
repeated month after month, if need be, so as to compel the charterers
to pay the hire in full without any deductions.   C

The owners sought to justify their threat by reference to the lien clause
18 in the charterparty: as if that excused it. But it did nothing of the
sort. In order to exercise a lien on sub-charter freight, they would have
had to give notice to the sub-charterers—with the likely consequence
that the sub-charterers would place the amount of freight in joint hands
pending a decision as to whether the shipowners were entitled to it. A
lien does not give a party a right to the money. It is only a security for   D
sums properly due. So the shipowners would be no better off than they
would have been if they had accepted the charterers' counter-offer—to
place the amount of the disputed deduction in escrow.

The owners further sought to justify their threat on the ground that
they had taken the advice of their lawyers in New York and London and
were advised that they could properly give the instructions to the masters   E
as set out in the telex; and they relied upon *James Shaffer Ltd.* v. *Findlay
Durham & Brodie* [1953] 1 W.L.R. 106 and *Sweet & Maxwell Ltd.* v.
Universal News Services Ltd. [1964] 2 Q.B. 699; and also they said that
they were under an honest misapprehension as to their rights which was
open to correction, relying on the words of Lord Wright in *Ross T.
Smyth & Co. Ltd.* v. *T. D. Bailey, Son & Co.* (1940) 56 T.L.R. 825, 830.
I have yet to learn that a party who breaks a contract can excuse himself   F
by saying that he did it on the advice of his lawyers: or that he was
under an honest misapprehension. Nor can he excuse himself on those
grounds from the consequences of a repudiation. In those three cases the
conduct of the party concerned was entirely innocent. It did not evince
any intention to break his contractual obligations. I would go by the
principle as I have always understood it that if the party's contract—   G
objectively considered in its impact on the other party—is such as to evince
an intention no longer to be bound by his contractual obligations, then it
is open to the other party to accept his repudiation and treat the contract
as discharged from that time onwards. A most important point here is
that the conduct of the owner was such as to lead the charterers reasonably to believe that the owners would issue such orders again in the future
whenever they, the owners, wished to force the charterers to comply   H
with the owners' demands in similar circumstances. In short, the owners
were determined to give orders to the masters—in flat contradiction of
the charterparty—time and time again so long as the contract continued so
as to enforce their demand that hire should be paid in full without any
deductions unless the owners agreed. To my mind such conduct
amounted to a repudiation of the contract within the principles laid down
by Lord Blackburn in *Mersey Steel and Iron Co. Ltd.* v. *Naylor Benzon &*

The Weekly Law Reports, August 4, 1978

343

3 W.L.R.   Federal Commerce Ltd. v. Molena Alpha Inc. (C.A.)   Lord Denning M.R.

A *Co.* (1884) 9 App.Cas. 434, 442–444 and followed ever since. It was open to the charterers to accept the repudiation, as they did, and to treat themselves as discharged from any further performance. It was then at an end for the future. It cannot be revived by any subsequent " without prejudice " agreement.

B So at long last I turn to the question asked by the umpire. I regard the words " valid claims " as denoting claims which are made to deduct sums quantified by a reasonable assessment made in good faith. To the questions so interpreted I come to the same conclusion on each of these as the umpire, Mr. Clifford Clark. I would hold that the charterers were entitled to deduct from hire without the consent of the owners valid claims which arose under clause 11 of the charterparty or valid claims which constituted an equitable set off. I would hold that the charterers C validly determined the charterparty on October 5, 1977. So I would answer with the umpire " Yes, yes, yes."

I differ from the judge only on the point of repudiation. It seems to me that the shipowners, by making the threats, launched a petard with which to destroy the charterers. It has blown up in their faces. They are hoist with their own petard. They must nurse their wounds as best they can.

D I would allow the appeal accordingly.

GOFF L.J. I will not recapitulate the facts which, if I may say so with respect, have been stated by Lord Denning M.R. with his usual clarity of thought. The first question which arises on this special case has two limbs and is as follows. (1) Whether on the true construction of the E charterparty the charterers were entitled to deduct from hire without the consent of the owners valid claims which (a) arose under clause 11 of the charterparty or (b) constituted an equitable set off. The first limb (a) raises pure questions of construction and is itself divided into two, since the language of clause 11 (A) of the charterparty is different from clause 11 (C). In paragraph (C) deduction is expressly provided for, so that the only problem is whether it may be made before the amount F cross-claimed has been agreed or awarded. Paragraph (A), however, raises a preliminary point whether it authorises deduction at all but, in my judgment, it does. The words are:

" In the event "—and then a number of events are specified—" no hire to be paid in respect of any time lost thereby during the period in which the vessel is unable to perform the service immediately G required. Any hire paid in advance to be adjusted accordingly."

It is said on behalf of the owners that this means the charterers are to go on paying hire which has ceased and then later recover it back. To my mind, however, the natural meaning of a provision that hire shall cease, and if it has already been paid in advance it shall be adjusted, is that the hire which should not have been paid because it ceased before the end H of the period covered by the payment in advance should be recouped by extinguishment or reduction of the next payment. In my judgment, therefore, although the language of the two paragraphs is different, the result is the same and each authorises deduction.

Then can those deductions be made before the amount has been agreed or awarded? I agree with the umpire and the judge that the answer must be in the affirmative. The line of reasoning which has led me to construe paragraph (A) as authorising deduction tends towards that

answer, and it seems to me that the express power to deduct in para- A
graph (C) must prima facie operate that way also, because the natural or
more ordinary meaning of the words is that there should be a deduction
from the next payment, and not at some future uncertain time.

Before reaching a final conclusion, however, it seems to me that we
have to balance two conflicting considerations. One which tells against
the prima facie view is that it weakens the effect of the power given to the
owners by clause 6 to determine the charter in the event of the hire being B
in arrears. If deductions may be made before ascertaining the right to
make them, then, if the owners dispute the deduction, they can only
exercise that power at their peril and, if it should turn out that the
deduction is wholly justified, then their purported determination will
be a repudiatory breach. The other which tells in the opposite direction
is that unless the power to deduct can be exercised when the charterers C
claim they have a right to exercise it without waiting for their claim to
be agreed or established, then they may have to pay money which they
are not liable to pay and be kept waiting for months, and it may be even
years, pending arbitration before they can recoup themselves. That is
stressed by the fact that in the present case even the owners admit that
something is due to the charterers under clause 11 (C) in respect of " slow
steaming." Moreover, should the ship be lost or should the charterparty D
be of short duration or nearing its end, the charterers may in practice
be wholly deprived of any effective right of deduction.

In my judgment, the latter considerations overbear the former, particularly as the charterers will themselves be acting at their peril which
on one state of the market at least may serve to inhibit any overclaims.
In my judgment, therefore, the prima facie view is confirmed, and I agree E
that on this first question, paragraph 32 (1) (a) of the award, the judge
was right and the cross-appeal fails.

I next turn to the second limb of the question posed by sub-paragraph
(1) (b). It must first be observed that equitable set off, which is really a
defence, does not arise in every case where there are cross-claims or even
always where the cross-claims arise out of the same contract. The
circumstances must be such as to make it unfair for the creditor to be F
paid his claim without allowing that of the debtor if and so far as well-
founded and thus to raise an equity against the creditor or, as it has
been expressed, impeach his title to be paid.

Secondly, if it be possible in the case of a time charterparty such as
we have before us that such an equity may arise on the facts, then we must
assume such a case, for the question of law submitted to us is whether G
valid claims may be deducted.

Thirdly, in my judgment, it is obvious that such a case can arise where
the owner through his neglect or default deprives the charterer of the use
of the vessel or hinders or prejudices his use thereof, though I would agree
with Lord Denning M.R. not where the cross-claim arises merely from
damage to cargo. In any given case the arbitrator or trial judge will
have to decide for himself whether the facts establish an equitable set H
off, assuming of course that the defence of equitable set off against hire
is in any case allowable in the case of a time charterparty and is not
excluded by the terms of the particular contract.

Fourthly, in my judgment, this defence by its nature is such that it
must be open to the charterer to set it up before ascertainment, not
merely as a means of preventing the owner obtaining judgment or, at any
rate, execution, but also as an immediate answer to his liability to pay

The Weekly Law Reports, August 4, 1978

345

3 W.L.R.   Federal Commerce Ltd. v. Molena Alpha Inc. (C.A.)   Goff L.J.

A hire otherwise due. Of course he acts at his peril and, if he is wrong, he will enable the owner to determine the charterparty if he is willing for his part to act at his peril the other way. It cannot be right, in my judgment, that this defence is not operative until the claim has been agreed or awarded or, in other words, that the hire must be deemed due upon the due date for payment notwithstanding the subsistence of a potentially valid equitable set off.

B   In my judgment, therefore, the answer given by the umpire and the judge to the second limb of the question must also be correct unless (1) the defence of equitable set off is excluded in the case of hire under a time charterparty by the ancient rule now finally established beyond doubt by the Court of Appeal in *The Brede* [1974] Q.B. 233 that the legal defence of abatement (*Mondel* v. *Steel* (1841) 8 M. & W. 858) and

C also that of equitable set off cannot be set up against freight properly so called—or perhaps I should say in its narrow meaning—that is to say, bill of lading freight or voyage charter freight or, in other words, if that rule also applies to hire. (2) If not so excluded, nevertheless it is excluded as a matter of construction by the terms of this particular charterparty which with a few modifications is of course in a very well-known form.

D   I turn now to consider the major question whether the old rule which I have mentioned does apply to hire and, unless I am bound so to hold, I would not think it right to do so, for in the type of case I have envisaged equity in a sense of common fairness which, after all, is the basis of the equitable doctrine clearly calls for its application; and I agree with Donaldson J. in the *Seven Seas* case [1975] 2 Lloyd's Rep. 188 in saying that this old rule should not be extended, although I part company with

E him in the end because he felt that to apply it to hire would not be an extension whereas I have come to the contrary conclusion. Counsel on both sides have taken us most carefully and thoroughly through the history of the old rule and of freight and charterparties and, for my part, I am most grateful to them for the help they have given me.

      I start with the premise that *The Aries* [1977] 1 W.L.R. 185 decided

F that there is a strict rule of common law that the defence of abatement (*Mondel* v. *Steel*, 8 M. & W. 858) does not apply to contracts of any kind of carriage. Lord Wilberforce said [1977] 1 W.L.R. 185, 190:

      " In this House, that the rule of deduction, or abatement, is one confined to contracts for the sale of goods or for work and labour and does not extend to contracts generally, was recognised in *Modern Engineering (Bristol) Ltd.* v. *Gilbert-Ash (Northern) Ltd.*

G   [1974] A.C. 689, 717, *per* Lord Diplock. There is no case of its having been extended to contracts of any kind of carriage. The rule against deduction in cases of carriage by sea is, in fact, as well settled as any common law rule can be."

      It was also decided that equity has never attacked that rule and cannot

H now do so. This I cite also from Lord Wilberforce in *The Aries*, where he said, at p. 191:

      " But in this case counsel could not suggest, and I cannot detect, any such equity sufficient to operate the mechanism, so as, in effect, to over-ride a clear rule of the common law on the basis of which the parties contracted. It is significant that in no case since the Judicature Act 1873 or at a time before that Act when equitable jurisdiction was available to a court dealing with the claim, was any such equit-

able set off or equitable defence upheld or, until *The Brede* [1974]   A
Q.B. 233, suggested."

The question is, however, whether that means freight in the narrow
sense I have mentioned, of bill of lading or voyage charterparty freight,
or extends to freight or hire under a time charterparty and, of course,
time charterparties and voyage charterparties are in many respects
different; and Lord Denning M.R. has mentioned some of the clauses   B
which one finds in the one but not in the other.

Secondly, the old rule may well have owed its origin to the fact that
the master would require to be paid the freight in full at the end of the
voyage to pay off his crew and to re-fit and victual his ship. He could
not wait a long time for funds to be remitted to him in the days when communications were slow. The time charter, however, which began life as
an actual demise, is of much more modern origin and does not really   C
appear in its modern form until 1940 or thereabouts, and the cash flow
principle no longer holds as a basis of itself for excluding equitable set
off since the decision of the House of Lords in the *Gilbert-Ash* case [1974]
A.C. 689.

There are, of course, very strong dicta in *The Aries* [1977] 1 W.L.R.
185 and also in the *Nova (Jersey) Knit* case [1977] 1 W.L.R. 713 that the   D
rule of equitable set off does not apply to freight. But the House was not
considering the problem that we have before us of the possible distinction
between the narrow meaning of " freight " and " freight " in the sense of
hire payable under a charterparty. Indeed, as I have already mentioned,
Lord Wilberforce in *The Aries* [1977] 1 W.L.R. 185, 191, said that the
equitable set off or equitable defence had not been upheld or even
suggested prior to *The Brede* [1974] Q.B. 233. That is, of course, if   E
I may say so with respect, perfectly correct so far as the limited meaning
of " freight " is concerned, but not as to hire since the defence was
adumbrated in 1941 and at first instance upheld. It was not found bad
in the Court of Appeal, although there the point was held not to arise
because the Court of Appeal came to the conclusion that the owners
were not at fault.   F

The strongest approach that I can find to the assimilation of the two
cases is to be found in *Sea and Land Securities Ltd. v. William Dickinson
and Co. Ltd.* [1942] 2 K.B. 65, 69, where MacKinnon L.J. said:

> " A time charterparty is, in fact, a misleading document, because
> the real nature of what is undertaken by the shipowner is disguised
> by the use of language dating from a century or more ago, which   G
> was appropriate to a contract of a different character then in use.
> At that time a time charterparty (now known as a demise charter-
> party) was an agreement under which possession of the ship was
> handed by the shipowner to the charterer for the latter to put his
> servants and crew in her and sail her for his own benefit. A demise
> charterparty has long been obsolete. The modern form of time
> charterparty is, in essence, one by which the shipowner agrees with   H
> the time charterer that during a certain named period he will render
> services by his servants and crew to carry the goods which are put
> on board his ship by the time charterer. But certain phrases which
> survive in the printed form now used are only pertinent to the older
> form of demise charterparty. Such phrases, in the charterparty now
> before the court, are: ' the owners agree to let,' and ' the charterers
> agree to hire ' the steamer."

The Weekly Law Reports, August 4, 1978

347

3 W.L.R.   Federal Commerce Ltd. v. Molena Alpha Inc. (C.A.)   Goff L.J.

A   Even so, it seems to me both from what MacKinnon L.J. went on to say later in that case and from the authorities since 1941 generally that the question is open in this court, and I therefore proceed to review the authorities.

The cases which bear on the problem of equitable set off in the case of time charters begin with *Sea and Land Securities Ltd.* v. *William Dickinson and Co. Ltd.* at first instance [1942] 1 K.B. 286, but there is

B   nothing which amounts to a decision until we come down to two or three years ago. In that case at first instance Atkinson J. held that as there was a total withdrawal, albeit for a limited period, hire ceased; and he added by way of obiter only that if the claim had to be in damages it could be set off. He said, at p. 298:

C   " I hold that the view taken by the umpire was right. In my opinion, under this charterparty the freight was not payable during the period occupied by degaussing the ship, inasmuch as the charterers had no use of her during that time, and the withdrawal of the ship from their use was due to the voluntary act of the owners for their own purposes. If I am wrong, if the only remedy open to the charterers is a claim for damages, such damages could, of course, be

D   set off against the freight."

The matter came before Atkinson J. in *Halcyon Steamship Co. Ltd.* v. *Continental Grain Co.* (1943) 75 Ll.L.Rep. 57, where he said, at p. 63:

        " In view of what the Court of Appeal said lately in regard to that matter, it would seem that in any event hire would continue, and that the charterers' remedy would be damages."

E   He seems perhaps there to have resiled from his former view that there could be a set off unless possibly where there was total deprivation, albeit for a limited time.

The question propounded by the special case in the *Halcyon* case was whether the steamer was off-hire under the charterparty while lying idle under the discontinuance of loading, and all that was decided was

F   that it was not because the case did not fall within the off-hire clause, but in the Court of Appeal, 75 Ll.L.Rep. 80, 84–85 MacKinnon L.J. said:

        " In truth, question (d) seems only to be asked as concerning a matter which may be relevant in the consideration of the remaining questions, (e) and (f). Those are directed to the question whether the charterers can claim to be relieved from payment of hire during

G   the period while the master was refusing to sign bills of lading and the charterers stopped the loading. It was pointed out in a recent case in this court "—which is *Sea and Land Securities* v. *William Dickinson and Co. Ltd.* [1942] 2 K.B. 65—" that under such a time charter the charterers can only be relieved from the continuous payment of the agreed hire in two events: firstly, if the cesser of hire clause applies to the facts "—and this is the significant part—" and,

H   secondly, if they can set off or counterclaim hire for a certain time as the whole or part of their claim for damages caused to them by a breach on the part of the shipowner of his duties under the charterparty."

So he clearly envisaged that equitable set off could in some circumstances at all events apply.

The matter came before Atkinson J. again for a third time in *A/S*

Goff L.J.   Federal Commerce Ltd. v. Molena Alpha Inc. (C.A.)   **[1978]**

Tankexpress v. *Compagnie Financière Belge des Petroles S/A* (1946) A
79 Ll.L.Rep. 451.   Here he held there was a right of set off, but I think
again only if one has total deprivation for a limited period.   In that
case Atkinson J. said, at pp. 456–457:

> " Swinfen Eady L.J. has pointed out that an owner does not agree
> to give the use of the ship absolutely and unconditionally, but only
> if not prevented by some cause mentioned in the exceptions clause. B
> But apart from anything in any exceptions clause, or any other
> clause limiting their obligations, prima facie the owner is agreeing
> ' that the ship shall be at your service, and the captain and crew shall
> be at your service and shall obey your orders.' "

That is the end of the quotation from Swinfen Eady L.J.   Then Atkinson
J. continued: C

> " If the shipowner during any particular period of time fails to render
> the services which he has agreed to render, for some reason outside
> the exceptions clause, as, for example, if the ship is withdrawn without
> justification, the charterers, if they paid in advance, can recover
> the hire paid as for a consideration which has failed, or as damages
> for breach, either by deducting the appropriate sum from the next
> payment, or, if the final payment has been made, then by action. D
> If hire is not payable in advance the charterers are not bound to pay
> for the period of failure to render services.   The hire, in my judg-
> ment, is not due; but at any rate, let there be no question about this,
> a claim for hire can be defeated by setting off damages or by
> application of the principle stated by Lord Dunedin in *French Marine*
> v. *Compagnie Napolitaine d'Eclairage et de Chauffage par le Gaz* E
> [1921] 2 A.C. 494, 511."

In that case in the Court of Appeal, 80 Ll.L.Rep. 365, one of the lords
justices unfortunately became ill, and a decision was given by the other
two who disagreed, one accepting Atkinson J.'s view and the other
rejecting it; and the whole matter went off in the House of Lords [1949]
A.C. 76, where it was found that having regard to the course of dealing F
between the parties there was no hire in arrear in any case.
    Donaldson J., in certain unreported cases, held that there was no set
off because of the cash flow doctrine advanced by the Court of Appeal in
Dawnays Ltd. v. *F. G. Minter Ltd. and Trollope and Colls Ltd.* [1971]
1 W.L.R. 1205, which was later rejected by the House of Lords in the
Gilbert-Ash case [1974] A.C. 689.   Then came *The Corfu Island* G
(unreported), of which we have a transcript, in which Ackner J. considered that the decision must now go the other way because of the
decision of the House of Lords in the *Gilbert-Ash* case.
    So I come to the two latest express decisions, one of Donaldson J.
and the other of Parker J., which are in direct conflict.   In the former,
Seven Seas Transportation Ltd. v. *Atlantic Shipping Co. Ltd.* [1975]
2 Lloyd's Rep. 188, Donaldson J. held that set off was not open because H
hire and freight are really the same thing; and, secondly, because it would
be incorrect to allow it since it would cause great confusion in the operation of the power to determine the charterparty.   The second reason is
not, in my judgment, a sound one because that confusion is already
inherent in the express power to make deductions.
    Then I turn to the decision of Parker J. which went the other way in
The Teno [1977] 2 Lloyd's Rep. 289.   He declined to follow Donaldson

The Weekly Law Reports, August 4, 1978

349

3 W.L.R.   Federal Commerce Ltd. v. Molena Alpha Inc. (C.A.)   Goff L.J.

A   J., and I think it necessary to cite extensively from his analytical and carefully reasoned judgment on the subject. He posed the question in this way, at p. 293:

"In *The Aries* [1977] 1 Lloyd's Rep. 334; [1977] 1 W.L.R. 185 it was finally settled by the House of Lords that a claim in respect of cargo could not be asserted by way of deduction from freight or used
B   by way of equitable set off against a claim for freight. Although only finally settled in that case the rule has been in existence for a very long time. The question which now arises is whether or not the same rule applies to claims for time charter hire. If it does, then the charterer's claim in respect of cargo shut out will not avail them as a defence or create a dispute as to any part of the claim for hire."
C

Then he began to review the cases and, when he came to *Sea and Land Securities Ltd.* v. *William Dickinson and Co. Ltd.* [1942] 2 K.B. 65, he said, at p. 295:

"It is to be noted that no criticism whatever was made of the passage which I have quoted from Atkinson J.'s judgment and that of
D   MacKinnon L.J. treats the charterparty as being ' like any other contract.' He does, it is true, use words which are referable to total loss of use but I do not consider that this was due to anything more than that the facts of the case before him were of such a nature. Having referred to a failure for any particular period of time he then said quite generally ' that is to say if they committed a breach of contract.' "
E

Then he referred to the passage in the judgment of MacKinnon L.J. in the *Halcyon* case, 75 Ll.L.Rep. 80, where he referred to the only two cases in which the charterer could be relieved from hire, namely the off-hire clause, and if he could set off his claim for damages. Parker J. says of that, at p. 296:

F   "The foregoing cases show a continuous recognition since 1941 of a right to set off against a claim for time charter hire damages for breach of contract where, at any rate, the breach consists in wrongful withdrawal of the vessel for a certain time. None of them were cited to the House of Lords in *The Aries* or to the Court of Appeal in *The Brede*, a somewhat curious circumstance, if it is well recognised
G   that time charter hire and freight are indistinguishable for set off purposes."

Then I would quote from the judgment of Parker J., at p. 297:

"Be that as it may, the cases in my judgment establish that equitable set off is, in principle, available against a claim for hire and that the existence of such a defence has been recognised since at the latest
H   1941. It would be as wrong to change it now as the House of Lords in *The Aries* held it would have been wrong to change the recognised rule with regard to freight . . . The next question is whether the equitable set off is limited to cases where there is a total withdrawal for a specified time. I can see no reason in principle why it should be so limited. If the defence lies in equity it may be that in some particular cases it will be denied but that is a wholly different matter. If the defence is available at all there is no reason why it should be

A

any the less applicable to a case where the master wrongfully refuses to load any save one of four holds than to a case where he refuses to load any holds at all.   In the latter case the charterer is not getting any use and in the former only 25 per cent. of the use . . . The whole matter of the development of the equitable right of set off was exhaustively dealt with by Morris L.J. in *Hanak* v. *Green* [1958] 2 Q.B. 9 in a judgment described by Lord Diplock in his speech in *Modern Engineering (Bristol) Ltd.* v. *Gilbert-Ash (Northern) Ltd.* [1974] A.C. 689, 717 as giving ' a masterly account ' of the subject. From that judgment I conclude that where the cross-claim not only arises out of the same contract as the claim but is so directly connected with it that it would be manifestly unjust to allow the claimant to recover without taking into account the cross-claim there is a right of set off in equity of an unliquidated claim. These conditions are clearly satisfied where an owner claims hire in respect of a period in which he has not provided his ship at all.   They are in my judgment equally satisfied when, as here, he claims hire in respect of a period when, in breach of contract, he has provided less than the full use of the vessel."

B

C

That reasoning to my mind, with respect, is impeccable, and I would follow that case in preference to the decision of Donaldson J.   Following and applying it to this case, I agree that the answer to question 1 (b) of the case is in the affirmative.

D

It will be apparent from what I have said that I have not overlooked the important dicta in *The Aries* [1977] 1 W.L.R. 185 and in the *Nova (Jersey) Knit* case [1977] 1 W.L.R. 713.   I trust that I do no disrespect to their Lordships and am fully conscious of my duty to accept, and that I am bound by, what is decided in their Lordships' House; but, in my judgment, those cases are distinguishable as the question before the House was different, and the question we have to decide was not argued.

E

Having reached the conclusion that equitable set off is not excluded as a matter of law, I then have to determine whether it is excluded in this particular case by the terms of the charterparty as a matter of construction.   First, it may be said that this charterparty contains express provisions in clauses 11 and 14 allowing deductions and therefore on the principle expressio unius est exclusio alterius they should not be allowed in any other cases.   In my judgment, however, that is not sufficient because equitable set off is part of the general law and can only be excluded by clear provisions to that effect, and such an inference as I am now considering is not sufficient.

F

G

In support of that, I make a brief reference again to the *Gilbert-Ash* case [1974] A.C. 689, 707, where Viscount Dilhorne, after referring to the express deduction provisions in that case, said:

" The existence of these provisions in the contract lends no support to the contention that the amount certified is of a special sacrosanct character which must be paid without deduction.   If these deductions can be made, as they clearly can, from the amount certified, the amount which clause 30 (1) says the contractor is entitled to be paid, why should it be inferred that the contract impliedly, for there is nothing express, excludes reliance by the employer on his common law and equitable rights to counterclaim and set off if sued for the amount certified.   I see no ground for any such inference."

H

The Weekly Law Reports, August 4, 1978

351

3 W.L.R.   Federal Commerce Ltd. v. Molena Alpha Inc. (C.A.)   Goff L.J.

A Then from the speech of Lord Diplock, at p. 717:

"It is, of course, open to parties to a contract for sale of goods or
for work and labour or for both to exclude by express agreement a
remedy for its breach which would otherwise arise by operation of
law or such remedy may be excluded by usage binding upon the parties
(cf. Sale of Goods Act 1893, section 55). But in construing such a
B contract one starts with the presumption that neither party intends
to abandon any remedies for its breach arising by operation of law,
and clear express words must be used in order to rebut this presumption."

Moreover, it is to be observed that the express deduction provisions,
at all events so far as clause 11 is concerned, are no fault provisions and
C were required in any case not merely to give a right to make a deduction
but to give any right at all.

The only other relevant consideration is that which I have already
dealt with in considering the effect of clause 11, namely the impact of the
power of determination in clause 6, and for the reasons I there gave in
my judgment this cannot be sufficient to exclude equitable set off, particularly since on the construction which I have given to clause 11 that
D clause itself already imports the practical difficulty in giving full effect
to that power. In my judgment, therefore, the umpire and the judge
were right and the cross-appeal fails on this point also.

I now turn to the last, and at any rate as between the parties the most
important question, namely, did the owners commit an anticipatory
breach of the charterparty which was repudiatory, and which, if it were,
E was accepted by the charterers? Here the umpire and the judge disagreed
and, with the utmost respect to the latter, I prefer the former. I have the
greatest respect for the skill and knowledge of Kerr J. particularly in the
Commercial Court, but on this occasion I fear he was led to a line of
thought not consistent with the findings of fact by which he was of course
bound and to drawing inferences which were certainly not inevitable and,
therefore, not open to him.

F In particular, with all respect, on the findings of the umpire I do not
agree that the charterers could be accused of snatching at an opportunity
of escaping from the charterparty which in the state of the market may
have been onerous, or that their position could be likened to that of
charterers who put forward ill-founded or exaggerated claims for that
purpose, since the umpire found that they were first-class charterers.
G Secondly, in my judgment, it was wrong to absolve the owners as having
reacted rather than acted, that is to say, treating them as aggrieved persons
driven to desperation. Rather, as it seems to me, the inevitable inference
from the findings is the other way round. The cause of the trouble was
the high-handed and unwarranted conduct of the owners. Thirdly, in
my judgment, it is not right to say that all the dispute really involved was
the disputed total of some $93,000 and not the disastrous consequences
H found by the umpire, or to place any reliance against the charterers on
the without prejudice agreement.

Subject to giving due notice under clause 12 of the addendum, the
owners could, but at their peril, have said: "We do not recognise these
deductions. Therefore, hire is in arrear and so we determine the charterparty under clause 6." Having regard to the state of the market, however,
they did not wish to do this. So they went off and gave instructions to
the masters as follows:

" (i) Withdraw all authority to issue or sign bills of lading on their   A
behalf; (ii) Refuse to sign bills of lading marked ' freight pre-paid ';
(iii) Insist that all bills of lading should bear an endorsement reading:
' All terms, conditions and exceptions of the time charter dated
November 1, 1974, as amended, including the lien under clause 18
on bill of lading freight as well as sub-freight belonging to the time
charter ' "—that must mean " time charterer "—" ' are herein
incorporated.' "   B

They also notified the charterers that they had done this.

The charterers having given the owners a few hours to withdraw and
warned them that if they did not they the charterers would treat this as a
repudiation, and the owners not having withdrawn, the charterers did
accept the owners' conduct as a repudiation.

Now the owners say this could not be a repudiation because they were   C
neither committing nor threatening to commit any breach of their
obligations since they were entitled to do what they did or threatened to
do by virtue of the lien on bills of lading freight or perhaps cargo freight
under clause 18 of the charterparty.

In my judgment this defence fails for at least two reasons. First, they
failed to give notice under clause 12 of addendum no. 2, which notice is   D
required not only before exercising the right under clause 6 to terminate
the charter but " any right." Even, therefore, if the owners were otherwise right they put themselves out of court. Mr. Evans submitted that
this was only a technical breach and could not be repudiatory. That
however, with all respect to his argument, is not the point. Clause 12
created a condition precedent which was not performed and therefore
the owners were not entitled to exercise any right under clause 18.   E

Secondly, they were not exercising or threatening to exercise any lien.
That they could do only if there were freight payable which they could
intercept, which there was not, and then only by notice given to the party
liable to pay that freight, which was not given or at that stage threatened
to be given. All that the owners can urge—and they did present this
argument very forcibly—is that they were entitled to give, and if necessary   F
act upon, the instructions they did in fact give to the masters in order to
secure that any freight becoming payable would be amenable to their
lien. That, however, could only be so, if at all, if they were entitled
nothwithstanding clause 9 of the charterparty to refuse to issue freight
paid and unclaused bills of lading, which is what they assert. They would
read this clause as without prejudice to the charterparty and therefore as
entitling them to direct the master not to sign bills of lading which might   G
be in terms different from those of the charterparty. But, in my judgment, that is not the true construction of the clause. Under clause 9 the
master was bound to sign bills of lading laid before him in any proper form,
and the trading for which this vessel was intended clearly required freight
paid bills of lading and unclaused bills of lading to be issued by the owners.

In my judgment, therefore, the owners were plainly not entitled to act
upon the instructions they were giving and if freight paid and unclaused   H
bills of lading had been presented and rejected I have no doubt that the
owners would have committed an actual breach of their obligations under
the charterparty. Moreover—and I did not understand this to be disputed—such a breach would clearly have been repudiatory having regard
to the requirements of the trade for which the vessel was chartered and
the findings in the case as to the disastrous consequences which would
ensue.

The Weekly Law Reports, August 4, 1978

353

3 W.L.R.   Federal Commerce Ltd. v. Molena Alpha Inc. (C.A.)   Goff L.J.

A   It is important to observe that the case found that bills of lading were
required to be issued forthwith or certainly very speedily, because one
vessel had just finished loading, one vessel had loaded part of her cargo and
was proceeding to the next port to load the rest.

        Then the owners contend that as the breach never became actual but
remained anticipatory that makes all the difference, and they make the
following submissions.   They say (1) that they are entitled to rely upon
B   the fact that subjectively it never was their intention to determine the
charterparty; (2) that having regard to the state of the market, no
right-minded charterer would think that it was; (3) that in any case this
was simply a situation in which they and the charterers were putting
forward their respective and differing views of their rights and duties under
the charterparty; that their view was tenable and not stupid; and that
C   advancing such a view on construction is not repudiatory.   They rely on
Sweet & Maxwell Ltd. v. *Universal News Services Ltd.* [1964] 2 Q.B. 699
and *James Shaffer Ltd.* v. *Findlay Durham & Brodie* [1953] 1 W.L.R.
106; (4) that in any case the consequences found by the umpire neither
did nor would ensue because it was inevitable that there would be some
such agreement as the without prejudice agreement which was in fact
made; (5) that it was the duty of the charterers to minimise the con-
D   sequences of the owners' conduct by entering into such an agreement and
by paying the whole of the disputed $93,000.   Lastly (6), that they had
already given notice requiring arbitration not only as to these particular
disputed amounts but also on the point of principle set out in paragraph
16 of the award:

            "The owners also claimed a decision on the question of principle
E   of whether or not the charterers were in any event entitled
            unilaterally to deduct disputed items from the charter hire."

        In my judgment the first of these answers cannot be right.   The
question is not what the owners wanted or wished in the recesses of their
minds, but did they by their conduct evince an intention no longer to
be bound by the contract or to perform it only in a way inconsistent with
F   their obligations under the charter?

        The second answer is similarly ineffective.   By the same test, what did
their conduct evince?   Surely as the umpire concluded:

            "The conduct of the owners did not constitute an absolute refusal
            to perform the charterparties, but did constitute an intention to
            perform the charterparties in a fundamentally different manner."

G
        The third point fails on the findings and the cases relied upon are
clearly distinguishable on the facts.   The finding in the second part of
paragraph 27 is entirely destructive of the owners' case:

            "The issuing of the order of October 4, 1977, was not to secure
            their claim for disputed deductions (the offer for an escrow deposit
            having been rejected by owners as ' meritless ') but rather to compel
H   the charterers to pay over all sums deducted from hire by the
            charterers which the owners disputed, irrespective of whether such
            deductions should ultimately be determined to be valid or invalid,
            in whole or in part, and to ensure that in the future the charterers
            made no deductions whatever from hire unless they had previously
            been expressly approved by the owners or they were supported by
            vouchers signed by the master or a proper tribunal had pronounced
            on their validity.   At the same time, the owners knew that part of

the amounts, payment of which they were demanding as a condition   A
of the withdrawal of their orders, were due to the charterers."

The two cases relied upon are in my judgment clearly distinguishable
on the facts. In the *James Shaffer* case [1953] 1 W.L.R. 106 in my
judgment no question of repudiation ever arose. It is true that the
defendants said, "We are not bound to provide the specified number
of orders," but that was only a defence to a claim for damages. They   B
made it perfectly clear that they wanted to get those orders and perform
the contract in that way if they could. In *Sweet & Maxwell Ltd.* v.
Universal News Services Ltd. [1964] 2 Q.B. 699 there was already an
effective lease in equity because the agreement was capable of specific
performance; but, quite apart from this, in my view the position was
quite different from anything we have in this case. There a negotiation
was in progress between the solicitors as to the proper way of giving   C
effect to the agreement. What Harman L.J. said, at p. 730, was:

"That again is the test, and judged by that test I do not think the
defendants in this case made it plain that they did not intend to
perform the contract. It was attractively suggested that what they
did was to say 'we will only perform the contract upon our terms
and not on yours,' and that the contract they offered was a different   D
contract from that which they were bound to perform and that,
therefore, they repudiated. But I do not think that a person who
maintains his view of the construction of what is, after all, a not
very perspicuous document is repudiating because he says 'my view
of it is this, and this I will do' and the other man says 'well, my
view is different.' Let them go to the court and have the matter   E
determined as they can. But to seize upon an attitude of that sort
and call it repudiation in order to serve an object which was then
of course dear to the hearts of the plaintiffs, who wanted to get rid
of this deed, is not in my opinion justified, and I would therefore
differ from the judge's view on that."

In the present case it seems to me that the irresistible inference is   F
that they were saying, "We will only perform the contract upon our
terms and not on yours" and, as Lord Denning M.R. has said, they
were holding a pistol to the heads of the charterers and we have the
finding as to their true purpose which I have read from the award.

I cannot accept the defence (4). It cannot be right that a party can
say, "I will break my contract with you in a fundamental way which
will cause you tremendous loss unless you accept my terms and accept   G
my view of your rights under the contract." (5) falls by the same test.
The judge's view really turns the without prejudice agreement into a
prejudicial one. Moreover, it was not only that the $93,000 had to be
paid but also the charterers had to agree not without the consent of the
owners to make any future deductions however unassailable until adjudicated by arbitration. (6) is the only point which causes me any difficulty.   H
Mr. Pollock says that the proposed arbitration would not have settled
the dispute between the parties, and that may be so because we do not
know what caused the rift which obviously occurred in September.
On the face of it, however, it would seem that a decision on the question
stated in paragraph 16 of the case would have set the deduction issue
at rest. Either it would be held that the charterers could not deduct
claims not agreed or awarded or that they could; and in the latter case

The Weekly Law Reports, August 4, 1978

355

3 W.L.R.   Federal Commerce Ltd. v. Molena Alpha Inc. (C.A.)   Goff L.J.

A it seems hardly likely that the owners would oppose subsequent deductions by the same or similar threats. The deduction issue as actually brought on for arbitration made it less likely to be conclusive because it seems only to determine the bare legal question whether the charterers could deduct valid claims and not to cover the question whether they could do so before the validity was established by agreement or award.

B There is, however, the finding in paragraph 29 of the case that the charterers:

"further believed, reasonably in view of the conduct and communication of the owners, that the owners would issue such orders again in the future whenever they, the owners, wished to force the charterers to comply with the owners' demands in similar circumstances."

C In any case, arbitration was not likely to be speedy. Mr. Evans was instructed that it was fixed for a date in October, but the correspondence shows that there was some misapprehension. The case was expedited because of the urgency which the repudiation issue imported into it, but apart from that it would not have been heard for some months, and the owners' solicitors were themselves saying that a date in January they D thought would be too soon.

Therefore, as it seems to me, it cannot be said that the position was simply that the charterers were being asked to pay the $93,000 pending a speedy arbitration, and I cannot see that this argument saves the owners any more than the others I have considered.

E Moreover it must not be forgotten that the owners threatened this drastic action at a time when bills of lading were immediately required.

There is, I think, one further point to be weighed against the owners. there were three companies each owning one ship, and there were outstanding moneys due to each from September, though very little in one case. The October deduction which brought the matter to a head concerned the *Nanfri* only. Yet each company demanded payment not of what was due to it but of the whole $93,000.

F In my judgment, therefore, there can be no doubt that the owners were threatening without justification to commit a fundamental breach of their obligations, and actually taking steps to implement this by the instructions which they gave to the masters at a crucial moment. As I see it, this was a clear anticipatory breach which the charterers were entitled to and did accept. I would, therefore, allow the appeal on this G point and restore the award of the umpire.

CUMMING-BRUCE L.J. For the reasons stated by Lord Denning M.R. and Goff L.J. I agree with the order proposed by them on the questions in the case numbered 1 (a) and 2.

As to the question in the case whether on the true construction of the charterparty the charterers were entitled to deduct from hire without H the consent of the owners valid claims which constituted an equitable set off I find difficulty, with regret, in accepting the analysis propounded by Lord Denning M.R. and Goff L.J. The solution of the question brings into play consideration of the principles of equity as applied to this particular branch of shipping law. I am conscious that in respect of shipping law the experience and erudition of Lord Denning M.R. is incomparably greater than any experience or knowledge that I have, and that in relation to the application of the principles of equity the experi-

ence and erudition of Goff L.J. is incomparably greater than the   A
experience and knowledge which I have in the field of equity. Nonetheless, with natural diffidence and great regret, I cannot accept their
conclusions.

As my reasoning will not affect the result, I propose to give my
reasons as briefly as possible. As a matter of the general law of contract
there is now no doubt that the defence of equitable set off, if that is the
right terminology, would apply to this contract and would avail the   B
charterers unless there is some exception firmly established in our law
that excludes that defence. The starting point must inevitably be the
judgment in *Mondel* v. *Steel*, 8 M. & W. 858, 871, where Parke B. stated
as settled law that an abatement of consideration could not be raised as
a defence in an action for freight.

So the matter on which a difference of judicial opinion in recent years   C
has emerged at first instance is whether the exception in relation to an
action for freight has any application to a claim for hire in a time
charter. That difference of opinion has been illustrated in the judgments
of Ackner J. and Parker J. who have decided that hire in a time charter
is distinguishable from freight and of Donaldson J. who has taken the
view that there is no relevant distinction.
                                                                          D
In *The Aries* [1977] 1 W.L.R. 185 their Lordships expressed strong
views to the effect that in relation to a time charter being a contract of
carriage by sea the *Mondel* v. *Steel* exception did apply; but, as has been
pointed out by Mr. Pollock and has been clearly elaborated in the
judgment of Parker J. in *The Teno* [1977] 2 Lloyd's Rep. 289, the question
was not in issue and there is an inaccuracy or at least an ellipsis in the
speech of Lord Simon of Glaisdale [1977] 1 W.L.R. 185, 193, when he   E
said there is no record of equity having in fact intervened and that an
equitable defence would be available had never been suggested.

The history of the authorities can be summarised in this way. There
is no case on the subject between Lord Ellenborough in *Havelock* v.
Geddes (1809) 10 East 555 and *Mondel* v. *Steel*, 8 M. & W. 858, which
asserts the principle that in a time charter the charterers had a defence   F
by way of abatement to a claim for hire. But there is the trilogy of
cases to which Lord Denning M.R. and Goff L.J. have referred and to
which Goff L.J. has adverted in some detail wherein Atkinson J. and
MacKinnon L.J. clearly expressed the view that in a time charter a
cross-claim on the part of the charterers could be relied upon by way of
set off as a defence to the claim of the owners for hire. The three cases
are *Sea and Land Securities Ltd.* v. *William Dickinson and Co. Ltd.* [1942]   G
2 K.B. 65, the *Halcyon* case, 75 Ll.L.Rep. 57, 80, and the *Tankexpress* case,
79 Ll.L.Rep. 451. I am conscious of the experience of Atkinson J.
in this field and of the very great authority which MacKinnon L.J.'s
views have always been held to have; but I have observed that in those
cases there does not appear to have been any explicit analysis of the
problem whether the *Mondel* v. *Steel*, 8 M. & W. 858, exception did   H
apply, and it appears to me that Atkinson J.—who in the second case
may be observed to have recanted somewhat—and MacKinnon L.J. were
approaching the question as a matter of the general law of contract and
were not thinking about the question whether the exception in *Mondel*
v. *Steel* did apply in a claim for hire under a time charter.

The term " freight " as compared to the term " hire " is a term which
as far as my researches go was used throughout the 19th century and

The Weekly Law Reports, August 4, 1978

357

3 W.L.R.   Federal Commerce Ltd. v. Molena Alpha Inc. (C.A.)   Cumming-Bruce L.J.

A   indeed into the 20th century both in a wide sense and in a narrow sense.
As Mr. Phillips submitted, freight may be simply a consideration paid by
charterers of a vessel to carry goods by sea or may have a more narrow
meaning, being the consideration to be paid for carrying goods to their
destination. The problem that arises in this case is whether the law
as stated in *Mondel* v. *Steel,* where the freight exception received
acknowledgment, stated an exception that related to freight in its wider
B   meaning or only in its narrow meaning.

When one examines the chapters in the textbooks—in particular I think
Scrutton on Charterparties and *Carver, Carriage by Sea*—one sees the
earlier editions regarding freight and hire as frequently synonymous. It
is only in the most recent editions that one finds the classification and
analysis of the problem presented in such a way that hire in a time
C   charter is treated as something separate from freight in a voyage charter—
including time freight in a voyage charter—and distinguished therefrom.
From my attempt to observe how the word "freight" has been used
throughout the 19th century I have come to the conclusion that at the
date of *Mondel* v. *Steel* the overwhelming probability is that Parke B.
was using the word "freight" in its wide sense and not restricted to its
D   narrow meaning. I also take the view that in the observations of
Atkinson J. (in one case perhaps it can fairly be called a decision
although it was not necessary for the Court of Appeal to pronounce on
it) and in the observations of MacKinnon L.J. (which were not I think
necessary for decision in the two cases to which I have referred) there is
no sign that those judges were addressing their minds to the question
whether Parke B.'s exception was inconsistent with the view that they
E   in those cases were expressing.

I accept Parker J.'s observation [1977] 2 Lloyd's Rep. 289, 296, that in
The Aries [1977] 1 W.L.R. 185 their Lordships' House did not appear
to have been reminded of the trilogy of cases to which I have referred
and that therefore the observations in the speeches may pro tanto apply
less widely at first sight. But as those three cases themselves were cases
F   in which the *Mondel* v. *Steel* rule was not critically examined, I do not
myself think that the authority with which Lord Wilberforce spoke in
The Aries [1977] 1 W.L.R. 185, 189–191, in the speech with which
Viscount Dilhorne at p. 191 agreed and the authority with which Lord
Simon of Glaisdale spoke at pp. 191–194 in the same case is materially
weakened by the fact that their Lordships did not consider *Sea and Land
Securities* [1942] 2 K.B. 65 or the *Halcyon,* 75 Ll.L.Rep. 57, 80, or the
G   *Tankexpress,* 80 Ll.L.Rep. 365, cases.

In relation to the *Tankexpress,* 80 Ll.L.Rep. 365, in the Court of
Appeal I would add this, that the two Lords Justices who considered the
case on appeal disagreed. Bucknill L.J. accepted the view propounded by
Atkinson J. but Tucker L.J. did not. It was not necessary for their Lordships when the case reached their Lordships' House to consider the
H   question, but it certainly looked to me, on reading the speech of Lord
du Parcq [1949] A.C. 76, 106–107, that Lord du Parcq regarded with
great doubt the proposition put forward by Bucknill L.J.

Therefore I have formed the view that if it is right (Lord Denning
M.R. and Goff L.J. have held that it is not right) to regard a contract of
hire charter as being for relevant purposes significantly like a voyage
charter, the observations of the House in *The Aries* [1977] 1 W.L.R.
185 give strong support to the view that a defence of equitable set off is

not available to overcome any difficulty in the charterers' way arising   A
from the exception in *Mondel* v. *Steel*, 8 M. & W. 858.

In relation to a voyage charter, the matter of course is put beyond
doubt by the decision of this court in *The Brede* [1974] Q.B. 233, which
has been expressly affirmed by their Lordships in *The Aries* [1977] 1
W.L.R. 185, a decision anyway which would be binding on this court.

So one returns to the basic problem: is there any relevant distinction
for the purposes of the proposition formulated by Parke B. in *Mondel* v.   B
Steel, 8 M. & W. 858, 871, between remuneration payable under a voyage
charter and remuneration payable under the name of hire in a time
charter? There I am fortified—it may seem improbably—by the observations of MacKinnon L.J. in *Sea and Land Securities Ltd.* [1942] 2 K.B.
65, 69, because there MacKinnon L.J. dwells upon the fact that a time
charterparty is a misleading term: C

"because the real nature of what is undertaken by the shipowner
is disguised by the use of language dating from a century or more
ago, which was appropriate to a contract of a different character
then in use," namely, "a demise charterparty."

The term "hire," as MacKinnon L.J. observed, is really wholly
inappropriate as a description of the consideration payable by the   D
charterer for the use of a vessel, its master and crew, put at the charterer's
disposal for the purposes of the use of the vessel for the carriage of goods
by sea on bills of lading signed by the master on behalf of the owners,
although under most time charterparties the master acts on the direction
of the charterer. If you look at the mutual obligations of owner and
charterer at the time of the charterparty there is no express provision for   E
the carriage of cargo, yet the whole object of the adventure comprised in
the charterparty is an adventure for carriage of goods by sea and the
provisions of the charterparty expressly make that perfectly plain. When
one looks at the history of the word "freight" as used to describe the
consideration in shipping contracts paid by the charterer, as a matter of
common sense "freight" is a more apt description of the consideration
payable by the charterer on a hire charter than the term "hire." This   F
explains the fact, which I regard as emerging clearly from an examination
of the authorities, that that was the way in which the consideration in a
hire charter was described throughout the 19th century and the early years
of the 20th century. "Freight" and "hire" seem frequently to have
been used indistinguishably in innumerable judgments.

For those reasons I am not satisfied that there is any solid and relevant   G
distinction between a time charter and a voyage charter for the purposes
of the application of what is described as the exception in the rule of
Mondel v. *Steel*, 8 M. & W. 858, 871.

As what is under consideration is whether at the time of the dispute
the law enabled the charterer, quite apart from the express terms of the
charter, to rely upon an equitable defence of set off, the fact that it is only
in the observations in the trilogy of cases which I have described that   H
there is any indication of such a doctrine seems to me of great weight. I
accept the inference drawn by Lord Simon of Glaisdale in *The Aries*
[1971] 1 W.L.R. 185, 193, from the fact that equity did not bark at all
in a claim for freight during the century-long night from 1873 until 1977.
I am aware that the problem of trying to discern how equity approached a
question of remuneration in a hire charter is greatly complicated by the
fact that equitable relief was not available after the Common Law Pro-

The Weekly Law Reports, August 4, 1978

359

3 W.L.R.   Federal Commerce Ltd. v. Molena Alpha Inc. (C.A.)   Cumming-Bruce L.J.

A cedure Act 1852 save where a perpetual injunction should be claimed.
Also it is probably true to say that it was only Morris L.J.'s judgment in
Hanak v. *Green* [1958] 2 Q.B. 9 that brought clearly to the attention
of the legal profession and the commercial world the possibilities of
equitable set off as a defence.   But, in the light of what I have said,
I find myself in this difficulty.   As I understand the judgments of Lord
Denning M.R. and Goff L.J., they agree that a cross-claim for cargo
B damage could not be relied upon as an equitable defence because there
would not be a sufficient equity.   Therefore the only cross-claim that
Lord Denning M.R. and Goff L.J. envisage as being available as an
equitable defence is one that operates by way of abatement, facts which
have the effect of impeaching the title to the claim or part of the claim.
But that is exactly the ground covered by the defence of abatement in
C *Mondel* v. *Steel*, 8 M. & W. 858.   It is clear from *The Brede* [1974] Q.B.
233 and *The Aries* [1977] 1 W.L.R. 185 that in relation to a voyage
charter equity cannot be invoked to avoid the rigours of the rule in
Mondel v. *Steel*, 8 M. & W. 858, at law.   Therefore, if I am right in
taking the view that the exception in *Mondel* v. *Steel* does apply to a
contract incorporated in a time charter, it would not be right to invoke
a rule of equity to avail the charterer when faced with the fact that at
D law no defence is available.   In this situation I would think that equity
must follow the law.

For those reasons I regret that I am unable to agree with the answer
given by Lord Denning M.R. and Goff L.J. to the question put in the
case as question 1 (b), and to that question I would answer No.

E   *Appeal allowed and cross-appeal dis-*
                                     missed with costs in Court of Appeal
                                     and below.
                                     Leave to appeal with conditions.

Solicitors: *Ince & Co.; Richards, Butler & Co.*

F   A. H. B.

[1978]

A

[COURT OF APPEAL]

FLOOR v. DAVIS (INSPECTOR OF TAXES)

1977 Nov. 15, 16, 17;   Buckley and Eveleigh L.JJ. and
1978 March 17   Sir John Pennycuick

B

*Revenue—Capital gains tax—Disposal of assets—Scheme to avoid
tax on sale of shares—Company incorporated to transfer shares
to ultimate purchaser and to pass purchase price to overseas
company—Taxpayer acquiring shares in new company in
exchange for his shareholding—Whether taxpayer disposing
of shares direct to ultimate purchaser—Whether deemed disposal of shares—Finance Act 1965 (c. 25), Sch. 7, paras. 4 (2),
6 (1)* [1]

C

*Revenue—Capital gains tax—Control of company—Resolution to
wind up company and thereby cause value to pass out of its
shares to overseas company—Whether " person having control "
includes plural—Whether winding up resulting from taxpayer
" exercising control "—Finance Act 1965, Sch. 7, para. 15 (2)*

In 1969 the taxpayer and his two sons-in-law held the
majority of the share capital of IDM. In common with the   D
remaining shareholders they wished to sell all IDM's shares
to an American company, KDI, for £833,333. Before that
sale was agreed the taxpayer caused a scheme to be put into
effect for the purpose of avoiding or reducing the liability
to capital gains tax that would arise on the sale. The scheme
involved the incorporation of FNW, a company that had its
share capital divided into ordinary and preferred shares. Under
its articles of association the ordinary shares carried rights to   E
six-sevenths of its surplus assets on a winding-up. In February
1969 the taxpayer and his family's IDM shares were transferred
to FNW in exchange for 100,000 of FNW's preferred shares
of 1s. each. The taxpayer received 43,954 of those shares.
FNW then sold the shares it had acquired in IDM to KDI for
£560,889. The next step in the scheme involved an application
in March 1969 by D Ltd., a company registered in the Cayman
Islands, to purchase 100 preferred shares in FNW for £500.   F
At a board meeting of FNW it was agreed to accept that application and to offer to all preferred shareholders a rights issue
of the ordinary shares in the company. The only shareholder
to accept the offer of the rights issue was D Ltd. who, in April
1969, was issued with 50 ordinary shares. Shortly thereafter
FNW was voluntarily wound up and as a result six-sevenths of
its surplus assets passed to D Ltd., being the only holder of its
ordinary shares.   G
In respect of those transactions the taxpayer was assessed
to capital gains tax of £235,000. On appeal against the assessment, the special commissioners reduced the amount to
£104,655 but dismissed the appeal in principle. Goulding J.
allowed an appeal by the taxpayer holding (1) that there was no
disposal of the shares by the taxpayer direct to KDI and as, in
consequence of the taxpayer's share exchange, control of IDM
was acquired by FNW, the exemption from the tax that was   H
contained in paragraphs 4 and 6 of Schedule 7 applied to the

[Reported by MRS. HARRIET DUTTON, Barrister-at-Law]

[1] Finance Act 1965, Sch. 7, para. 4 (2): see post, p. 369A.
Para. 6: see post, p. 368B.
Para. 15 (2): see post, p. 369D.

A   taxpayer on that exchange, and (2) that paragraph 15 (2) of
that Schedule did not extend to a situation where a group of
people had the control of a company and that in any event
there was no " exercise of control " by the taxpayer on the
winding up of FNW and thus no deemed disposal to bring the
taxpayer within the charge to the tax.

On appeal by the Crown: —

Held, (1) (Eveleigh L.J. dissenting), that as the clear legal
B   effect of the 1969 agreement and of the share transactions was
to transfer the taxpayer's shareholding in IDM to FNW without
creating any contractual obligation on FNW to sell on those
shares to KDI, the taxpayer could not be held to have disposed
of those shares direct to KDI; that in consequence of that share
exchange FNW acquired control of IDM and thus the exemption from tax contained in paragraphs 4 and 6 of Schedule 7
to the Act applied to the transactions (post, pp. 371A–D, 372F–H,
C   377H—378B).

Inland Revenue Commissioners v. *Duke of Westminster*
[1936] A.C. 1, H.L.(E.) applied.

(2) Allowing the appeal, that section 45 (1) and paragraph
3 (1) of Schedule 18 to the Act gave an extended definition of
" control " requiring paragraph 15 (2) of Schedule 7 to extend
to cover a situation where two or more persons had control
of a company; that the series of operations represented a
D   scheme planned in advance by the taxpayer and his sons-in-law
that included the resolution to wind up FNW and as such
should be regarded as an exercise of control by those individuals
that caused value to pass out of FNW's shares and into the
shares of the Cayman Island company; and that accordingly,
by virtue of paragraph 15 (2) of Schedule 7, the taxpayer
must be deemed to have disposed of his shares in FNW and thus
to come within the charge to capital gains tax (post, pp.
E   373B–E, 374H—375B, 378B).

Decision of Goulding J. [1976] 1 W.L.R. 1167; [1976] 3
All E.R. 314 reversed.

The following cases are referred to in the judgments:

Campbell v. *Inland Revenue Commissioners* [1970] A.C. 77; [1968] 3
W.L.R. 1025; [1968] 3 All E.R. 588; 45 T.C. 427, H.L.(E.).
F   *Dawes* v. *Tredwell* (1881) 18 Ch.D. 354, C.A.
Inland Revenue Commissioner v. *Europa Oil (N.Z.) Ltd.* [1971] A.C.
760; [1971] 2 W.L.R. 55, P.C.
Inland Revenue Commissioners v. *Duke of Westminster* [1936] A.C. 1;
19 T.C. 490, H.L.(E.).
MacKenzie v. *Childers* (1889) 43 Ch.D. 265.
Ransom v. *Higgs* [1974] 1 W.L.R. 1594; [1974] 3 All E.R. 949; 50 T.C.
G   1, H.L.(E.).

The following additional cases were cited in argument:

Bailey, Hay & Co. Ltd., In re [1971] 1 W.L.R. 1357; [1971] 3 All E.R.
693.
Cleveleys Investment Trust Co. v. *Inland Revenue Commissioners* (1971)
47 T.C. 300.
H   *Feversham's (Earl of) Contract, In re* [1942] Ch. 33; [1941] 3 All E.R.
100.
Inland Revenue Commissioners v. *Park Investments Ltd.* [1966] Ch. 701;
[1966] 3 W.L.R. 65; [1966] 2 All E.R. 785; 43 T.C. 200, C.A.
Nichols, decd., In re [1975] 1 W.L.R. 534; [1975] 2 All E.R. 120, C.A.
Quistclose Investments Ltd. v. *Rolls Razor Ltd. (In Liquidation)* [1970]
A.C. 567; [1968] 3 W.L.R. 1097; [1968] 3 All E.R. 651, H.L.(E.).
Sturge (John & E.) Ltd. v. *Hessel* (1975) T.C. Leaflet No. 2571, C.A.

APPEAL from Goulding J.   A

The taxpayer, Major Ides Maria Floor, held a large part of the share capital in IDM Electronics Ltd. Together with all the other shareholders, he wished to sell the IDM shares to KDI International Corporation for £833,333. As a result of a scheme devised to avoid or reduce the amount of capital gains tax payable on that sale, a large proportion of the proceeds from the sale of the shares passed to Donmarco Ltd., a company registered in the Cayman Islands. In respect of those trans- B actions, the taxpayer was assessed to capital gains tax for the year 1968–69 in the sum of £235,000.

The taxpayer appealed against the assessment to the Commissioners for the Special Purposes of the Income Tax Acts. The relevant part of the case stated read as follows:

4. The following facts were admitted between the parties: C

(1) The taxpayer was the father-in-law of Mr. Wellesley-Wesley and Mr. Naylor-Leyland (' the vendors ').

(2) On February 27, 1969, the vendors between them held the majority of the share capital in IDM, although none of the three of them was by himself able to control IDM. By that date it had been agreed, subject to contract, by all the shareholders in IDM to sell the shares in IDM to D KDI, an American corporation, for a cash consideration of £833,333, of which £560,889 would be payable to the vendors.

(3) Had that transaction gone ahead in a straightforward way, a very considerable capital gains tax liability would have arisen to the shareholders in IDM. For the purpose of avoiding such a liability the vendors decided to put into effect the following series of transactions whereby the value of their original IDM shareholdings would eventually enure to the E benefit of themselves and their families: (i) On February 27, 1969, an agreement was made between the vendors and FNW. FNW, which had been incorporated for the purpose of those transactions three days earlier on February 24, had its authorised share capital divided into two classes of shares, ordinary shares and preferred shares of 1s. each. Under article 4 of its articles the ordinary shares when issued and paid up were to F carry rights to one-seventh of total declared dividends and six-sevenths of surplus assets on a winding up; the preferred shares when issued and paid up were to carry the rights to six-sevenths of all declared dividends and one-seventh of all surplus assets on a winding up. All issued shares were to have equal voting rights. Under the agreement made on February 27 the vendors were to transfer their majority shareholding in IDM in G consideration for the issue by FNW of 100,000 preferred shares of 1s. each in FNW. The taxpayer received 43,954 preferred shares in FNW for the transfer of 38,075 ordinary shares in IDM and 38,075 " A " ordinary shares in IDM. The agreement recited that negotiations had been concluded subject to contract for the purchase by KDI of all the issued share capital in IDM, and the vendors undertook with FNW to use their best endeavours to procure IDM and all other necessary parties to co-operate H to enable a formal agreement for the sale of all the issued share capital of IDM to KDI to be entered into as soon as possible. The proposal by FNW to purchase their IDM shares from the vendors had been approved by the board of FNW at a meeting on February 27. The only other shares in FNW in issue at the relevant date were the two subscribers' preferred shares which were transferred to the taxpayer and Mr. Naylor-Leyland. (ii) On February 28 FNW agreed (with the other shareholders

A in IDM) to sell its IDM shares to KDI for a cash consideration of
£560,889. (iii) On March 27 Donmarco, a company registered in the
Cayman Islands, applied to the board of FNW for 100 preferred shares
of 1s. each, offering a price of £5 per share and enclosing a cheque of
£500. FNW was requested, in the event of the application for subscription being accepted, to issue its shares to a nominee, Roycan Nominees
Ltd., being a nominee company run by the Royal Bank of Canada. (iv)
B On March 27 a board meeting of FNW was held at which it was agreed
to accept the subscription requests from Donmarco. It was also resolved
that a rights issue of ordinary shares of 1s. each in the capital of FNW
should be offered to the preferred shareholders in FNW on the basis of
one ordinary share of 1s. payable in cash at par in respect of each two
preferred shares of 1s. each already in issue. Letters offering the rights
C issue were despatched on March 27 to each of the vendors and Roycan
Nominees Ltd. (v) The time for acceptance of the rights issue expired
on April 3. By that date Donmarco was the only shareholder to accept
the rights issue. On April 3 another board meeting of FNW was held
at which it was resolved to issue the 50 ordinary shares offered by way
of rights issue to Donmarco. It was also resolved to convene an extraordinary general meeting of the members in FNW to be held at short
D notice on April 5 to consider a resolution for the voluntary winding up
of FNW. (vi) The extraordinary general meeting of the members of
FNW was held on April 5 attended by a Mr. Surman, accountant, as
proxy for Mr. Wellesley-Wesley and a Mr. Blackburn, solicitor, as proxy
for Roycan Nominees Ltd. At this meeting a special resolution for the
voluntary winding up of FNW was duly passed. By virtue of article 4
E of the FNW articles the effect of the winding up was to pass six-sevenths
of the surplus assets of FNW to Donmarco (through Roycan Nominees
Ltd. as nominee) being the only ordinary shareholder, the remaining one-
seventh going to the vendors and Donmarco (through its nominee) being
the only preferred shareholders. (vii) On February 27 the taxpayer's
shareholding in IDM was 38,075 ordinary shares and 37,075 " A " ordinary
F shares out of a total issued share capital of 128,702 ordinary shares and
128,702 " A " ordinary shares. At all material times the taxpayer's shareholding in FNW consisted of 43,954 preferred shares (plus one subscriber's
preferred share) out of a total issued share capital of 100,102 preferred
shares and 50 ordinary shares. None of the other shareholders in either
IDM or FNW was an " associate " of the taxpayer within the meaning of
section 303(3) of the Income and Corporation Taxes Act 1970.

G   5. It was contended on behalf of the appellant (1) that in paragraph
15 (2) of Schedule 7 to the Finance Act 1965 the reference to a " person "
should not be read as a reference to " persons " since a contrary intention
appeared from the following, among other, circumstances (i) because the
concept of control being exercised by more than one person would be
incapable of any coherent application in the context of paragraph 15 (2);
H (ii) because, as paragraph 16 of Schedule 7 indicated, a clear distinction
was made in the schedule between references to a person and references
to persons; (iii) because, as paragraph 21 (5) (b) and (7) of Schedule 7
indicated, in relation to the exercise of control a specific distinction was
made in Schedule 7 between control exercised by a single person and by
two or more or by a group of persons; and (iv) because where reference
was intended to be made to the exercise of control by two or more
persons such reference was identified in terms as in paragraph 3 (1) of

Schedule 18; (2) that support of the resolution to wind up FNW by Mr. A
Wellesley-Wesley's proxy did not amount to an exercise of control by
Mr. Wellesley-Wesley; (3) that in consequence of the vendors' exchange
of their IDM shares for FNW shares FNW had control of IDM, and
that, therefore, paragraph 4 of Schedule 7 to the Act of 1965 applied
and there was no disposal by the taxpayer of his IDM shares when he
exchanged them for FNW shares; (4) that the transactions which resulted
in value passing out of the shares in FNW owned by the taxpayer and B
into the shares owned by Donmarco involved no exercise of control by
the vendors but were the consequence of their refraining from any exercise
of control; (5) that if, contrary to the foregoing contention, the relevant
transaction or transactions involved any exercise of control, such exercise
was not by the taxpayer himself but by the taxpayer and either Mr.
Wellesley-Wesley or Mr. Naylor-Leyland, or both of them; and (6) that C
paragraph 15 (2) of Schedule 7 to the Act of 1965 had no application
to an exercise of control by more than one person.

　　6. It was contended on behalf of the Crown (1) that paragraph 6 of
Schedule 7 did not apply to the vendors' exchange of their IDM shares
for shares in FNW because FNW's control of IDM was in the circumstances no more than " paper " or artificial control and not real control D
so that the requirement mentioned in paragraph 6 (2) was not satisfied,
and on that basis the taxpayer must be taken to have disposed of his
IDM shares at that stage; alternatively, if paragraph 6 applied; (2) that
nothing in the context of paragraph 15 (2) of Schedule 15 to the Act of
1965 overrode the presumption that the use of the singular ' person ' in
that paragraph included the plural; (3) that the terms of paragraph 15 (2)
were satisfied since the vendors as a controlling group so exercised their E
control that value passed out of their FNW shares into the shares in
FNW held for Donmarco; and (4) that, in the alternative, such value
passed in consequence of the exercise by Mr. Wellesley-Wesley, through
his proxy, of control at the meeting which approved the resolution to
wind up FNW. . . .

　　8. The commissioners who heard the appeal took time to consider F
their decision and gave it in writing on March 5, 1974, as follows:

　　" In accordance with a scheme, as carefully executed as it was in-
　　geniously devised, the [taxpayer], Major Floor, and his two sons-
　　in-law, being ' connected persons ' but not ' associates,' transferred
　　their majority interest in IDM to FNW in exchange for preferred
　　shares in FNW. The sole reason for FNW's existence was to pro-
　　vide a vehicle for the transfer of the shares in IDM to KDI, the G
　　ultimate American purchaser, and for the siphoning off of six-sevenths
　　of the purchase consideration to Donmarco, the non-resident holder
　　of ordinary shares in FNW. No question of the [taxpayer's] liability
　　for tax in respect of any gain which accrued to Donmarco on the
　　winding up of FNW is before us. The sole issue for us, as it was
　　put on behalf of the [taxpayer], is whether or not the trick works: H
　　whether or not paragraphs 4 and 6 of Schedule 7 of the Finance Act
　　1965 require the consideration shares in FNW to be identified with
　　the IDM shares acquired in exchange, and whether or not paragraph
　　15 (2) of Schedule 7 requires the [taxpayer] to be treated as having
　　made a part disposal of his shares.

　　　" It is argued on behalf of the revenue that the crucial condition
　　for the application of paragraph 6 Schedule 7 is not satisfied because

A   FNW did not have control of IDM: see paragraph 6 (2) of Schedule
7. It is not disputed that FNW had control as a matter of form
within the definition in paragraph 3 of Schedule 13 to the Finance
Act 1965. But this, it is argued, was mere ' paper' control to be
distinguished from ' real ' control. Two general propositions were
advanced in support of the argument that paragraph 6, and there-
B   fore paragraph 4, did not apply. First, it was said that in appropriate
circumstances the veil of incorporation must be pierced and the
transactions of companies looked through to see what really
happened. *Littlewoods Mail Order Stores Ltd.* v. *McGregor* [1969]
1 W.L.R. 1241 was relied on as an example of the application of this
principle. Secondly, it was said that just as in the dividend stripping
cases, such as *Lupton* v. *F.A. & A.B. Ltd.* [1969] 1 W.L.R. 1627 the
C   existence of a tax avoidance motive could result in an apparent trading
transaction not being accepted as such, so a tax avoidance scheme
devised to give the appearance of control could be defeated on the
ground that the control was artificial and not real.

" We derive no great assistance from figures of speech which
identify the circumstance of incorporation with a veil which cloaks a
D   company's transactions. Once it is accepted that the company existed
and carried out certain transactions by resolutions being passed and
agreements being executed, it seems to us that there is no choice but
to observe whether the wide description in paragraph 3 of Schedule
18 of what constitutes ' control ' was satisfied. The only relevant
' control ' is ' control ' within the meaning of that paragraph. It
was no part of the argument before us, and seemingly there was no
E   evidence available to support such an argument, that FNW's acquisition of the IDM shares was subject to a binding condition that the
shares would be sold on, or subject to a contract to sell already made
with KDI, so that FNW never acquired a beneficial title to the shares.
Clearly on that basis the position might have been different.

" *Littlewoods Mail Order Stores Ltd.* v. *McGregor* [1969] 1
F   W.L.R. 1241 and *Lupton* v. *F.A. & A.B. Ltd.* [1969] 1 W.L.R. 1627
we take to illustrate a principle which is not directly in point in
the present case, namely that when it appears in the light of all the
relevant evidence that a payment purporting to have been made for
one purpose, (e.g. as rent or as the price of trading stock), was made
in whole or in part for some other purpose, (i.e., as the price of a
capital asset acquired by a wholly-owned subsidiary or merely as a
G   payment in a dividend stripping operation), the tax consequences
should be adjusted accordingly.

" We find that FNW had control of IDM and we hold that paragraphs 4 and 6 of Schedule 7 accordingly applied with the result that
there was, at that stage of the scheme, no disposal by the [taxpayer]
of the IDM shares which he exchanged for shares in FNW. Para-
H   graph 15 (2) of Schedule 7 in conjunction with paragraph 15 (1)
requires a gratuitous transfer of value derived from shares to be
treated as a part disposal of the shares if a person having control of
a company exercises his control so that value passes out of shares
in the company owned by him and passes into other shares. These
words seem to us to be an apt description of what happened when
Donmarco subscribed for ordinary shares and a resolution was subsequently passed for the winding up of FNW so that value passed

out of the preferred shares into the ordinary shares. Throughout its A
existence the [taxpayer] and his two sons-in-law had control of FNW.
Whatever the company did, it did in consequence of their exercise
of control. The creation of the preferred and ordinary shares with
particular rights, the issue of a small number of preferred shares to
Donmarco, the acquisition of ordinary shares by Donmarco in consequence of the rights issue, and the ultimate liquidation of FNW,
all occurred in consequence of the three original shareholders' exercise B
of control. As a result value passed, as it was intended to pass, from
the [taxpayer's] shares into Donmarco's.

"The critical question is whether 'a person' in paragraph 15 (2)
includes the plural. By virtue of section 1 of the Interpretation Act
1889 'unless the contrary intention appears' we ought to read 'a
person' in paragraph 15 (2) as including 'persons.' We were C
referred on behalf of the [Crown] to In re Earl of Feversham's Contract [1942] Ch. 33 as illustrating how positive an intention to the
contrary needs to be if it is to displace the ordinary presumption
that the singular includes the plural. On the [taxpayer's] behalf we
were referred to paragraph 16 of Schedule 7 and to paragraph 21 (5)
as showing that the author of the Schedule habitually uses the D
singular without impliedly including the plural since, whenever a
significant reference to the plural is intended, it is set out in full to
avoid any possible confusion. It would have been possible in paragraph 16 to refer to several gifts acquired from a person and in
paragraph 21 (5) to the same person having control of two companies
implying in each case that the singular included the plural; but the
spelling out of references to one or more persons or two or more E
persons shows that the draftsman used the singular to indicate one
person and, in terms, referred to more than one person when such
a reference was intended.

"We consider that paragraph 16 is explained by the need to deal
with a succession of gifts from a succession of connected persons,
and paragraph 21 (5) by the need to cover the possible permutations F
where one group is identifiable with another consisting of persons
included in the first group or connected with one or more persons
so included. In neither case would a reference to a person, including
by implication a reference to persons, have conveyed precisely the
same meaning as is conveyed by the words and expressions in fact
used. But even if we accept that there are many other examples,
(and our attention was specially drawn to paragraph 3 of Schedule G
18), of express references to one or more, or two or more, persons,
we find it difficult to infer that the reference in paragraph 15 (2) to
a person was not intended to include persons. Where no particular
difficulty was likely to arise, the draftsman seems to have left a
reference to the plural to be inferred: where an implied reference
would not have been sufficiently precise, the draftsman in several H
instances made the position clear by spelling out express references
to situations involving more than one person or more than one
combination of persons.

"It was argued that paragraph 15 (2) was a case in which difficulties of construction and application would indeed arise if the
reference to a person was taken to include persons. A single con-
troller could always readily be identified; but in view of the com-

A   plexities of paragraph 3 of Schedule 18, it would frequently be difficult, if not impossible, to say whether the members of a controlling group were exercising control in a particular situation. We are not, however, persuaded by this argument that a person in paragraph 15 (2) should not be taken to include persons. There might be more to the argument if the question who controls a company fell to be answered in a void. But the question under paragraph 15 (2) in any particular case is whether a group of persons having control of a company have acted in such a way in relation to the affairs of the company that value has passed from their shares into other shares. At least it is clear in the present case who controlled the company, who manipulated the share rights and what was the consequence of the scheme.

C   "We take paragraph 15 (2) to be covered by the normal presumption, we find no contrary intention, and our conclusion is that the [taxpayer] must be taken to have made a part disposal of his shares. When the figures have been considered, no doubt the parties can agree what gain was realised and we shall be in a position finally to determine the appeal.

D   "An alternative submission was made on behalf of the [Crown] to the effect that one of the [taxpayer's] sons-in-law, who at the date when the meeting was held at which the resolution to wind up FNW was passed held a power of attorney given to him by the [taxpayer], had control of the company and exercised that control at the meeting mentioned. But we do not consider that the agreed facts support the inference that Mr. Wellesley-Wesley, whose proxy was in the chair at the meeting at which it was resolved to liquidate FNW, can be said, by proxy, then to have exercised his control of the company. To attend and vote by proxy at a meeting at which two proxies attend is not, we think, such an exercise of control as is referred to in paragraph 15 (2)."

The special commissioners ordered that the assessment be reduced to an agreed amount of £104,655.

Goulding J. allowed an appeal by the taxpayer on the grounds that the exemption from the tax contained in Schedule 7, paragraphs 4 to 6 applied on the share exchange and that paragraph 15 (2) of that Schedule did not apply to bring the taxpayer within the charge to tax.

The Crown appealed on the grounds that (1) the judge was wrong in law in holding that section 1 (1) (b) of the Interpretation Act 1889 did not apply to paragraph 15 (2) of Schedule 7 to the Finance Act 1965 on the ground that a contrary intention was expressed in that sub-paragraph; (2) the judge was wrong in law in holding that that sub-paragraph did not apply to the taxpayer on the ground that he had neither alone nor in conjunction with his sons-in-law control of FNW; (3) the judge was wrong in law in holding that within the meaning of that sub-paragraph the taxpayer did not exercise either alone or in conjunction with his sons-in-law control of FNW in the material respects; (4) the judge was wrong in law in not holding that the taxpayer disposed of his shares in IDM to KDI; (5) the judge was wrong in law in holding that within the meaning of paragraph 6 (2) of Schedule 7 FNW ever had control of IDM; and (6) the judge was wrong in law in holding that on the facts found paragraph 6 could apply.

The taxpayer, Major Floor, died on July 28, 1976, and under R.S.C.,

Ord. 15, r. 15, his widow Marguerite Marie Mathilde Janssen Floor, was   A
appointed to represent the taxpayer's estate for the purposes of the
appeal.

The facts are set out in the judgment of Goulding J. [1976] 1 W.L.R.
1167, 1169–1172.

Peter Millett Q.C. and *Brian Davenport* for the Crown.   B
C. N. Beattie Q.C. and *G. R. Aaronson* for the taxpayer.

Cur. adv. vult.

March 17. The following judgments were read.

C
BUCKLEY L.J. I have asked Sir John Pennycuick to read the first
judgment.

SIR JOHN PENNYCUICK. This is an appeal from an order dated July 7,
1976, of Goulding J. whereby he reversed a decision in favour of the
Crown by the special commissioners. The appeal is concerned with a
series of transactions effected in February and March 1969 by one Ides   D
Maria Floor, the taxpayer, and his two sons-in-law whereby they sought
to carry through a sale of their respective shares in a company known as
IDM Electronics Ltd. (" IDM ") to an American company known as
KDI International Corporation (" KDI ") in such a way as to minimise
the liability to capital gains tax upon the profit resulting from the sale.

In the barest outline the series of transactions may be summarised   E
thus. *Stage 1*: The taxpayer and the two sons-in-law held respectively
38,075, 29,525 and 19,025 ordinary shares and each held a like number
of " A " ordinary shares out of 257,404 issued shares in IDM. By
an agreement dated February 27, 1969, they agreed to sell their
respective shares to a newly incorporated company known as FNW
Electronic Holdings Ltd. (" FNW ") in consideration of the issue to
them rateably of preferred shares in FNW, in which company they   F
thereby came to own the whole of the issued capital. Next day,
February 28, 1969, FNW sold the shares in IDM so acquired by it to
KDI in consideration of the sum of £560,889. *Stage 2*: between March
27 and April 5, 1967, FNW went through a series of operations whereby,
making use of certain special provisions in its articles, it went into liquidation and distributed six-sevenths of this sum of £560,889 to a foreign   G
company which, through the instrumentality of a rights issue, had
acquired ordinary shares in FNW. The Crown claims that the taxpayer
is chargeable with capital gains tax by reference to a proportion of the
sum paid by KDI to FNW which corresponds to the shares in IDM sold
by him to FNW.

It will be convenient now to refer to the provisions of Part III of
the Finance Act 1965 which are directly relevant to the present appeal.   H
Section 19 and the succeeding sections impose a charge of tax in respect
of capital gains accruing to persons on the disposal of assets. I need not
read those sections. The Act contains no definition of " disposal."
Section 22 (9) introduces the provisions contained in Schedule 7. That
Schedule, which is headed " Capital Gains: Miscellaneous Rules,"
contains the following provisions:

Paragraph 4 (2):

A   "Subject to the following sub-paragraphs, a reorganisation or reduction of a company's share capital shall not be treated as involving any disposal of the original shares or any acquisition of the new holding or any part of it, but the original shares (taken as a single asset) and the new holding (taken as a single asset) shall be treated as the same asset acquired as the original shares were acquired."

B

Paragraph 6:

"(1) Subject to the following sub-paragraphs, where a company issues shares or debentures to a person in exchange for shares in or debentures of another company, paragraph 4 above shall apply with any necessary adaptations as if the two companies were the same company and the exchange were a reorganisation of its share capital.

C   (2) This paragraph shall apply only where the company issuing the shares or debentures has or in consequence of the exchange will have control of the other company . . ."

(These sub-paragraphs are relevant on stage 1 of the series of transactions.)

D   Paragraph 15 (2):

"If a person having control of a company exercises his control so that value passes out of shares in the company owned by him or a person with whom he is connected, or out of rights over the company exercisable by him or by a person with whom he is connected, and passes into other shares in or rights over the com-

E   pany, that shall be a disposal of the shares or rights out of which the value passes by the person by whom they were owned or exercisable."

(This sub-paragraph is relevant upon stage 2 of the series of transactions.)

Finally, paragraph 3 (1) of Schedule 18 contains an extended definition of "control" under which a person shall be taken to have control

F   of a company, inter alia (a) "if he possesses, or is entitled to acquire, the greater part of the share capital or voting power in the company," and concludes:

"Where two or more persons together satisfy any of the conditions in paragraphs (a) to (c) above they shall be deemed to have control of the company."

G   Section 45 (1) of the Act provides:

"In this Part of this Act" (i.e. Part III which includes Schedule 7 as well as Schedule 18) "unless the context otherwise requires . . . control shall be construed in accordance with paragraph 3 of Schedule 18 to this Act."

H   Before the special commissioners the Crown based its case exclusively upon the provisions contained in Schedule 7, i.e. paragraphs 4 (2) and 6 (1) in relation to stage 1 of the series of transactions and paragraph 15 (2) in relation to stage 2. The special commissioners in paragraph 2 of the case stated set out the questions for decision by them in the following terms:

"(i) whether when FNW Electronic Holdings Ltd. ('FNW') issued shares to the [taxpayer] in exchange for his shares in IDM Electronics

Ltd. (' IDM ') FNW had or in consequence of the exchange acquired A
control of IDM within the meaning of paragraph 6 (2) of Schedule
7 to the Finance Act 1965; (ii) whether the reference in paragraph
15 (2) of that Schedule to a person exercising control of a company
is to be read as if it referred to persons exercising such control and
(iii) whether the transactions relating to FNW constituted the
' exercise of control ' of the company within the meaning of paragraph
  B
15 (2) of Schedule 7 to the Finance Act 1965."
In paragraph 4 they set out in detail the facts, none of which was in
dispute. In paragraph 5 they set out the contentions on behalf of the
taxpayer. In paragraph 6 they set out the contentions on behalf of the
Crown. In paragraph 8 they give a full and careful decision, accepting
the contentions on behalf of the taxpayer in relation to stage 1 but
  C
accepting the contentions of the Crown in relation to stage 2. They
accordingly dismissed the taxpayer's appeal. I will treat paragraphs
4, 5, 6 and 8 of the case stated as read into this judgment: see ante,
pp. 362c et seq.

The taxpayer appealed to the High Court and his appeal was heard
by Goulding J. Upon this appeal the Crown raised a new contention,
namely, that for the purpose of capital gains tax there was a disposal D
by the taxpayer of his shares in IDM direct to KDI. This new contention
the judge rightly dealt with first. He rejected the new contention and,
like the special commissioners, he rejected the Crown's contentions in
relation to stage 1. But, unlike the special commissioners, he also
rejected the Crown's contentions in relation to stage 2. He accordingly
allowed the taxpayers' appeal. The appeal before us is brought by the
Crown against that decision. The taxpayer died before the hearing of E
the appeal and his personal representative has been joined as a party in
his place.

The appeal, as it has now developed, raises four distinct issues, namely,
(1) did the taxpayer make a disposal of his shares in IDM direct to KDI?
(2) Did FNW obtain control of IDM within the meaning of paragraphs 4
(2) and 6 (1) of Schedule 7? (3) Did the taxpayer and his two sons-in- F
law together have control of FNW within the meaning of paragraph
15 (2) of Schedule 7? (4) If so, did they exercise that control within the
meaning of paragraph 15 (2) when the resolution for the winding up
of FNW was passed? There is of course no doubt that that resolution
caused value to pass out of the shares in FNW held by them respectively.
I will endeavour to deal with these four issues in the same order.
  G
(1) The critical transactions upon this issue are (a) the agreement
dated February 27, 1969, whereby the taxpayer and the sons-in-law entered
into a binding contract with FNW for the sale to FNW of their
respective shares in IDM in consideration of the issue to them respectively
of shares in FNW and (b) the sale on February 28, 1969, by FNW of the
shares in IDM to KDI for cash. It was not in dispute on the one hand
that these transactions, together with all the other relevant transactions, H
were effected pursuant to a pre-arranged scheme; and on the other hand
that all the transactions were genuine, in contradistinction to colourable,
transactions.

It was contended by Mr. Millett on behalf of the Crown that, even
apart from any contractual or equitable obligation on the part of FNW
to pass on the shares in IDM to KDI, transactions (a) and (b) looked at
together, as they must be, should be regarded as simply a disposal

A   by the taxpayer and the sons-in-law of their shares in IDM to KDI. It was pointed out that the Finance Act 1965 contains no definition of disposal and it was stressed that the combined effect, or end result, of the two transactions was indeed to pass the shares in IDM from the taxpayer and his sons-in-law to KDI, FNW being no more than a conduit pipe through which this passage was achieved. It seems to me that this contention disergards the legal effect of what were admittedly

B   genuine transactions and really seeks to resurrect the conception of substance which was buried by the House of Lords in *Inland Revenue Commissioners* v. *Duke of Westminster* [1936] A.C. 1: see for a recent affirmation of the principle laid down in the *Duke of Westminster's* case the statement by Lord Wilberforce in *Inland Revenue Commissioner* v. *Europa Oil (N.Z.) Ltd.* [1971] A.C. 760, 771. In my

C   judgment it is impossible, upon the plain legal effect of transactions (a) and (b), to maintain that the taxpayer and the sons-in-law sold their shares in IDM to anyone other than FNW or that KDI purchased those shares from anyone other than FNW. That is not a disposal by the taxpayer and the sons-in-law to KDI. This contention of the Crown does not appear to me to derive any support from two decisions relied upon, namely *Europa Oil* and *Ransom* v. *Higgs* [1974] 1 W.L.R. 1594. In the

D   former case it was held that two contemporaneous and closely related contracts must be looked at together in order to determine whether certain expenditure was incurred exclusively for the purchase of trading stock. In the latter case a succession of transactions was examined in order to determine whether a trade was carried on. Each of these questions turned upon considerations fundamentally different from that

E   now under discussion in the present case.

    An alternative contention was founded on preamble (d) of the agreement dated February 27, 1965. I will read that preamble again:

> "The vendors have agreed to sell and the purchaser has agreed to purchase the shares from all liens, charges and encumbrances upon the terms and conditions hereinafter appearing and with a view to
F   the purchaser re-selling the shares to the said KDI International Corporation as hereinbefore recited."

    It was argued that the recital imports a contractual obligation upon FNW to sell the shares in IDM to KDI and accordingly that FNW, having acquired the shares subject to that obligation, was never the unfettered owner of the shares but in law as well as in substance merely

G   a piece of machinery through which the taxpayer and the sons-in-law disposed of the shares directly to KDI. If the premise was well-founded, I should see much force in this contention. But I am unable to accept the premise. Certainly in an appropriate case an instrument may require to be so construed that a binding obligation is to be implied from the recitals. A good instance is afforded by *Mackenzie* v. *Childers* (1889)

H   43 Ch.D. 265 where it was really clear from the recitals in a deed of mutual covenants constituting a building scheme that the vendor as well as the purchasers was to be bound. But I find nothing in the circumstances or apparent intention of the agreement dated February 27 which requires such an implication. The three individuals would be expected to rely on their 100 per cent. control of FNW to ensure that it carried out their plan and would not find it necessary to impose a contractual obligation upon their creature. We were referred in this

connection to *Dawes* v. *Tredwell* (1881) 18 Ch.D. 354 where Sir George   A
Jessel M.R. said, at p. 358:

> " Now the rule is, that a recital does not control the operative part
> of a deed where the operative part is clear.   The recital here, as is
> usually the case, is in general terms; the operative part is in definite
> terms.   There is another rule that the recital of an agreement does
> not create a covenant where there is an express covenant to be   B
> found in the witnessing part relating to the same subject-matter.   If,
> therefore, the covenant is clear, it cannot be controlled or affected
> by the recital."

For a full discussion of this subject, see *Halsbury's Laws of England*,
4th ed., vol. 12 (1973), p. 638.   The former of the rules laid down by
Sir George Jessel M.R. applies here.   That is to say, the operative part   C
of the agreement is perfectly clear.   It was suggested that clause 4 of
the agreement brought the latter rule into play also.   That, I think, is
not so.   Clause 4 is an undertaking by the vendors and would not
exclude the implication of an obligation on the part of the purchaser.

It was contended on behalf of the Crown that one should infer some
collateral contract between the taxpayer and the sons-in-law and FNW.
The existence of such a contract would be a question of fact and there   D
is no finding by the special commissioners of such a contract.   Nor, I
think, had they any material before them which would have supported
such a finding.   It was further contended on behalf of the Crown that
FNW was under some equitable obligation to sell the shares to KDI.
I see no ground for importing such an equitable obligation.   The relation
of the taxpayer and the sons-in-law and FNW was that of vendors and   E
purchaser under a contract of sale for full consideration and FNW's conscience could not be affected by any relevant obligation to the vendors
outside the terms of the contract.   Contrast the case of a voluntary
disposition, e.g. a gift, made with a view to the application by the recipient
of the subject matter to some particular purpose.   There the conscience
of the recipient is indeed affected and he cannot accept the subject
matter without carrying out the purpose.   For a recent instance, see   F
Campbell v. *Inland Revenue Commissioners* [1970] A.C. 77 where a
deed of covenant was made upon the understanding that the covenantee
would apply the sums paid under it to a given purpose.   That is a wholly
different position from that in the present case.

(2) In order to take advantage of the provisions in paragraphs 4
(2) and 6 (2) of Schedule 7 the taxpayer must show that upon a share   G
exchange the company issuing the shares has, or in consequence of the
exchange will have, control of the other company.   That requirement is
manifestly satisfied here.   That is to say, FNW, the company issuing
the shares, in consequence of the exchange, acquired the greater part of
the share capital of IDM and with it the control of IDM.   Once issue
(1) has ben resolved in favour of the taxpayer then issue (2) does not   H
admit of argument.   Perhaps one should mention, in order to avoid
possible misunderstanding, that where paragraphs 4 (2) and 6 (2) provide
that the share transaction is not to be treated as involving a disposal,
that expression clearly denotes a disposal giving rise to a charge of tax.
It is not suggested that the transaction is to be disregarded in the sense
that the acquiring company is to be treated as a mere emanation of the
other company.   Before leaving issues (1) and (2) I would express my

A concurrence with the admirable judgment of Goulding J. upon these issues.

(3) By virtue of the extended definition of " control " in section 45 (1) and paragraph 3 (1) of Schedule 18, unless the context otherwise requires, where two or more persons possess the greater part of the share capital or voting power in a company, then they shall be taken to have control of the company. The context of paragraph 15 (2) of Schedule 7
B emphatically does not otherwise require. There is nothing in the context which renders the provision of that sub-paragraph inappropriate to operations carried out in concert by two or more persons. Extended so as to include the plural, the sub-paragraph would read: " If a person or persons having control of a company exercises or exercise his or their control so that value passes out of shares in the company owned by him
C or them or a person or persons with whom he is or they are connected . . . that shall be a disposal of the shares . . . out of which the value passes by the person or persons by whom they were owned. . . ." So extended, and with no other addition to, or alteration of, its language, the sub-paragraph plainly admits of, and requires, a distributive construction. That is to say, in the case where two or more persons have control, it would read: " If persons having control of a company exercise
D their control so that value passes out of shares in the company owned by them respectively or persons with whom they are respectively connected . . . that shall be a disposal of the shares . . . out of which the value passes by the persons by whom they were respectively owned. . . ." That is a perfectly clear and sensible provision. To take a simple example, suppose that X Ltd. has 100 issued shares, A owns
E 30 shares, Mrs. A 10 shares, B 30 shares, Mrs. B 10 shares, C (a stranger) 10 shares, and D (a stranger) 10 shares; and that A and B exercise their control by passing a resolution such that value passes out of the shares held by A, Mrs. A, B, Mrs. B and C into the shares held by D. Then there is a disposal by A, Mrs. A, B and Mrs. B of the shares owned by them respectively, but no disposal by C.

F Mr. Millett, for the Crown, found great obscurity in the sub-paragraph and in particular in the words " a person with whom he is connected." At one stage in his argument he was disposed to say that these words could have no application at all where more than one person has control. In the end he settled for a contention that the words would apply to a person with whom all the persons having control were connected, an improbable and rather ridiculous provision. Mr. Beattie, for the tax-
G payer, stressed the difficulties of construction which arise on any but a distributive basis. Faced with this consensus of obscurity, Goulding J. made an elaborate analysis of the sub-paragraph and found it equally obscure. Neither counsel nor the judge seemed to have addressed their minds to a distributive construction. The special commissioners had been content to construe the provision in relation to the facts of the
H present case. I have felt some diffidence in applying a construction which does not seem to have occurred to the very experienced counsel or to Goulding J., but for myself I believe this construction to be plainly correct, and so construed the sub-paragraph is free from obscurity.

I have dealt with this question by reference to the definition of " control " in the Act itself. The argument below, and most of the argument before us, was conducted by reference to section 1 of the Interpretation Act 1889. The result is the same. It seems to me more

appropriate to apply the definition in the Act. On this issue, then, I   A
differ from the judge.

(4) It remains to consider whether the taxpayer and the sons-in-law
should be regarded as having exercised their control of FNW when that
company passed its winding up resolution on April 5, 1969. The meeting
at which the resolution was passed was attended by a proxy for Mr.
Wellesley-Wesley, one of the sons-in-law, and a proxy for Roycan
Nominees Ltd., which had now come to hold 50 ordinary shares in the   B
company. Under the articles of FNW the ordinary shares and the
preferred shares rank pari passu as regards voting. Neither the taxpayer
himself nor Mr. Naylor-Leyland, the other son-in-law, was present, nor
was a vote cast on behalf of either of them. The special commissioners
appear to have taken it for granted that the taxpayer and his sons-in-law
must together be treated as having exercised their control when the   C
special resolution was passed. The judge, however, took a different
view. I will quote from the passage in his judgment in which he deals
with this point [1976] 1 W.L.R. 1167, 1177:

> " This is a question of difficulty and of some breadth. Mr. Millett
> submitted quite generally that to refrain from stopping action by a
> company which one has power to prevent and with knowledge of   D
> the consequences, may in suitable circumstances be an exercise of
> control of the company. Of course, one does not need to have
> control of a company in any sense to be able in some circumstances
> to allow a result to happen by abstention. One can think at once
> of the 30 per cent. holder of voting shares who refrains from blocking
> a special resolution although he could do so. He certainly exercises
> no control of the company although his abstention has a certain   E
> result. Of course, Mr. Millett intended his formulation to apply
> only to cases where the person who refrains from acting is one who
> has control in the statutory sense.
>
> " I am unable to accept either Mr. Millett's general submission
> or the assertion of the special commissioners, on the basis of the
> primary agreed facts, that whatever FNW did throughout its exist-   F
> ence it did in consequence of its shareholders' exercise of control.
> In my judgment, to satisfy the words ' exercises . . . control ' in
> paragraph 15 (2) of Schedule 7 some positive act that is capable of
> specific identification as an exercise of control is required. It is not
> everyone who has control who exercises it even though the company
> controlled may in fact do things that he would like it to do. Accord-
> ingly, on this point also I respectfully differ from the special   G
> commissioners."

I do not doubt that in the ordinary case of control by the holding of a
majority of shares the expression " exercise control " indicates the casting
of the votes attached to those shares upon the relevant resolutions, and
that a shareholder could not be treated as exercising control when he is
absent or inactive when the resolution is proposed. But the expression   H
" exercise control " is not a term of art denoting by its own force the
casting of votes and nothing else, and there may be circumstances, in
the case of control by more than one person, where those persons should
indeed be treated as collectively exercising control without all of them
actually casting their votes. It seems to me that the circumstances here
are of that character. The taxpayer and the sons-in-law acquired voting
control of FNW as the first step in a series of operations designed to

A eventuate in the proceeds of their shares in IDM passing to a foreign company. This series of operations represented a scheme planned in advance by the three individuals acting in concert. The passing of the winding up resolution by FNW was an integral and essential operation in this scheme and was indisputably carried out in furtherance of a common and continuing intention on the part of the three individuals. Upon these facts it seems to me that the resolution should be regarded
B as an exercise by all three individuals of their collective control. It is, I think, immaterial that two of the individuals did not actually cast their votes in favour of the resolution. So on this issue too I differ from the judge.

I conclude that, although the taxpayer succeeds on the first two issues, he fails on the third and fourth issues. That conclusion is
C sufficient to decide the appeal in favour of the Crown and I would allow the appeal accordingly.

EVELEIGH L.J. I take the view that the shares with which we are concerned were disposed of by the taxpayer to KDI. On all other points I agree with the judgment just delivered.

It is clear that right from the beginning KDI indicated that it would
D purchase the shares. The only reason for avoiding a direct sale to them was the prospect of capital gains tax. In an attempt to avoid paying this, as is frankly accepted, the initial transfer to FNW took place. There was however no real possibility at any time that the shares would not reach KDI. By virtue of their control of FNW the shareholders guaranteed from the moment they parted with the legal ownership that the
E shares would become the property of KDI. No one could prevent this against their wishes. By virtue of the arrangement initially made between them each was under an obligation to the other to do nothing to stop the shares arriving in the hands of KDI. They controlled the destiny of the shares from beginning to end in pursuance of a continuing intention on their part that the shares should be transferred to KDI.

This court is concerned to decide whether any capital gains accruing
F as a result of the transaction can be said to be gains accruing to a person on the disposal of assets within the meaning of section 19 (1) of the Finance Act 1965. There is no legal definition of the word " disposal " and I can see no reason to define it as " the first legal transfer in the ownership of property." Indeed I do not understand counsel for the taxpayer to contend that the meaning should be so limited. Property could
G be disposed of to C by transferring it to B in trust for C. If in the present case FNW had contracted to transfer the shares to KDI and had acquired them on those terms it seemed to me, as this case was argued before the court, that it would have been very difficult for counsel to contend that there was not a disposal by the taxpayer to KDI. However, what he said was that there was no such contract and consequently the only transaction by the respondent was a transfer (or disposal) of the
H shares to FNW. Thereafter he said the transfer to KDI was entirely separate. Emphasis was placed upon the fact that it was conceded that the transfer to FNW was a genuine one. I understand " genuine " in this context to mean that it was what it purported to be, namely, the transfer of the ownership to FNW. The court often meets the contention that a transaction is specious in the sense that it is not the legal transaction it appears to be. Hire purchase agreements masquerading as bills of sale, and so-called furnished tenancies under the Rent Acts, are

examples of this. Without the concession I would have treated the transfer to FNW as genuine, but it was only part of a larger transaction. The question that the court has to determine is whether that transaction was a disposal to KDI. If a man wished to sell his house to his mistress at an artificially low price and conceal it from his wife, he might with the cooperation of a friend who held a controlling interest in a company sell the house to the company at that low price in the knowledge that his friend would ensure that the house was sold to the mistress. There would be no legal obligation on the company to do this. None the less in my opinion the original owner would have disposed of his house to his mistress. Qui facit per alium facit per se is a maxim which does not depend on contractual relationship of principal and agent. A man may act through the hand of another whose conduct he manages to manipulate in some way, and whether or not he has so acted is often a question of fact to be considered by looking at all that is done.

I see this case as one in which the court is not required to consider each step taken in isolation. It is a question of whether or not the shares were disposed of to KDI by the taxpayer. I believe that they were. Furthermore, they were in reality at the disposal of the original shareholders until the moment they reached the hand of KDI, although the legal ownership was in FNW. I do not think that this conclusion is any way vitiated by *Inland Revenue Commissioners* v. *Duke of Westminster* [1936] A.C. 1. In that case it was sought to say that the payments under covenant were not such but were payments of wages. I do not seek to say that the transfer to FNW was not a transfer. The important feature of the present case is that the destiny of the shares was at all times under the control of the taxpayer who was arranging for them to be transferred to KDI. The transfer to FNW was but a step in that process. In the *Westminster* case the legal position was that there existed a covenant imposing upon the Duke a liability to make payments thereunder. The Crown was not permitted to say that those payments were anything else. Effect had to be given to the legal position. Lord Russell of Killowen said, at p. 24:

"I confess that I view with disfavour the doctrine that in taxation cases a subject is to be taxed if in accordance with a court's view of what it considers the substance of the transaction, the court thinks that the case falls within the contemplation or spirit of the statute. The subject is not taxable by inference or by analogy but only by the plain words of a statute applicable to the facts and circumstances of his case."

In deciding that there was a disposal within the plain words of the statute to KDI, I in no way deny the legal effect of the transfer to FNW. Referring to the alleged doctrine that the subject is to be taxed according to the court's view of the substance of the transaction, Lord Russell of Killowen said, at p. 25:

"If all that is meant by the doctrine is that having once ascertained the legal rights of the parties you may disregard mere nomenclature and decide the question of taxability or non-taxability in accordance with the legal rights, well and good. . . . If on the other hand the doctrine means that you may brush aside deeds, disregard the legal rights and liabilities arising under a contract between parties, and decide the question of taxability or non-taxability upon the footing

A　　of the rights and liabilities of the parties being different from what in law they are, then I entirely dissent from such a doctrine."

I hope that in reaching the conclusion I have, I am paying full attention to the words of Lord Russell of Killowen and to the principle established in the *Westminster* case. I am not called upon to decide whether or not the transfer to FNW was a disposal. Paragraphs 6 (1) and 4 (2) of

B　Schedule 7 to the Finance Act 1965 require such a transfer to be treated as a reorganisation of share capital and not as involving any disposal of the shares. Whatever the nature of that transaction, and in ordinary language it could be called a disposal or dealing with the shares, I take the view that the taxpayer was dealing with the shares right up to the time that they reached KDI and that the transfer to FNW was conveyancing

C　machinery. I therefore would allow this appeal on this ground also.

BUCKLEY L.J. I agree with the judgment delivered by Sir John Pennycuick. In my judgment, the transactions which together make up Stage 1 of the series cannot for the present purpose properly be regarded as a disposal by the taxpayer and his sons-in-law of their shares in IDM to KDI. It was conceded that there was a genuine sale of those

D　shares by the three shareholders to FNW. Had that transaction stood alone, it seems to me that the questions whether the shareholders had disposed of their shares, and, if so, to whom, could only be answered in one way: " Yes, to FNW." The fact that the shareholders became in consequence the only shareholders of FNW and controlled that company would not, I think, affect this answer. Paragraphs 4 (2) and 6 (1) of

E　Schedule 7 to the Finance Act 1965 cannot, in my opinion, have that effect. Those paragraphs, as I read them, provide that a disposal of assets to which they apply shall not for the purposes of the charge to tax be treated as a disposal. This does not mean that such a disposal is not a disposal within the meaning of that term in the Act, but that, notwithstanding that it is a disposal, it shall not be taxed as such.

F　If one considers what rights and obligations arose in consequence of the sale and transfer of the shares to FNW it cannot, I think, be disputed that FNW became the legal and beneficial owner of the shares. No trust, whether express or constructive, arose. No obligation in favour of KDI was created. In the improbable event of the taxpayer and his sons-in-law changing their minds and abandoning their pre-existing intention that FNW should sell the shares on to KDI, KDI could have had no ground

G　for complaint. Nor could the taxpayer and his sons-in-law have complained if KDI had decided not to proceed with its purchase of the shares from FNW. Using the word " disposal " in its primary and natural sense, the three shareholders did, in my opinion, dispose of their shares to FNW.

In these circumstances, can the fact that they mutually intended to procure the sale of the shares by FNW to KDI deprive the sale to FNW

H　of its character as a disposal and reduce it to the status of a merely mechanical step in a disposal of the shares by the three shareholders to KDI? It is again conceded that the sale by FNW to KDI was a genuine sale. The contract for this sale was made on February 28, 1969, the day following the transfer of the IDM shares to FNW. It was a distinct transaction from the sale to FNW. Again using the word " disposal " in its primary and natural sense, it is, in my opinion, clear that by that contract FNW disposed of the shares to KDI. To treat both these

Buckley L.J.   **Floor v. Davis (C.A.)**   **[1978]**

transactions together as effecting a single disposal by the three shareholders   A
to KDI by reason of their pre-existing intention that the shares should
ultimately reach KDI and of their control of the proceedings, seems to me
to involve ignoring the principle enunciated in *Inland Revenue Commissioners* v. *Duke of Westminster* [1936] A.C. 1 that to ascertain the
" substance " of a transaction one must determine the rights and obligations of the parties from a consideration of the whole transaction, having
regard to the legal effect of what the parties have done, ascertained upon   B
ordinary legal principles: see *per* Lord Tomlin at p. 20.   So regarding
the present case, I do not think it justifiable to tax the taxpayer upon
the basis that there was only one disposal where in law there were two.
Nevertheless, for the reasons indicated by Sir John Pennycuick I think
that this appeal succeeds upon the third and fourth issues discussed by
Sir John Pennycuick in his judgment.   C

> *Appeal allowed with costs.*
> *Order of commissioners restored.*
> *Leave to appeal.*

Solicitors: *Solicitor of Inland Revenue; Courts & Co.*
                                                                                D

[HOUSE OF LORDS]

HESPERIDES HOTELS LTD. AND ANOTHER . . . APPELLANTS

AND   E

MUFTIZADE . . . . RESPONDENT

[On appeal from HESPERIDES HOTELS LTD. *v.* AEGEAN TURKISH HOLIDAYS
LTD.]

1978 May 8, 9, 10, 11,   Lord Wilberforce, Viscount Dilhorne, Lord   F
        15, 16, 17;   Salmon, Lord Fraser of Tullybelton
   July 6   and Lord Keith of Kinkel

> *Conflict of Laws—Jurisdiction—Tort—Action for conspiracy in
> England to procure trespass to land and chattels situate out-
> side jurisdiction—Greek Cypriot hotels under Turkish Cypriot
> control—Prayer for interim injunction—Whether jurisdiction
> to entertain action in English court*   G
> *Judicial Precedent—House of Lords decision—How far binding—
> No jurisdiction to adjudicate on trespass to land abroad —
> Acceptance in other common law jurisdictions—Possibility of
> modification conflicting with foreign jurisdictions—No suffi-
> cient change of circumstances to justify modification*

Two companies registered under the law of the Republic of
Cyprus owned Greek Cypriot hotels in Kyrenia when it was   H
occupied by troops from Turkey invading the north of the island
in 1974.   They issued a writ in 1977 against an English travel
company and an individual purporting to represent in London
the " Turkish Federated State of Cyprus," claiming damages
and an injunction to restrain the defendants from conspiring to
procure, encourage, or assist trespass to the hotels by circulating
brochures and inviting tourists to book holidays in the hotels.
They also moved the judge in chambers for an interim injunction
in terms of the writ.   May J., after applying for and receiving a

A   Foreign Office certificate which stated that Her Majesty's
Government did not recognise the administration established
under the name " Turkish Federated State of Cyprus " de facto
or de jure, granted an interim injunction in the terms asked for
and refused an application by the individual defendant to set
aside the writ for want of jurisdiction.

The individual defendant appealed. During the appeal the
plaintiff companies amended their writ to claim in addition the
B   same relief in respect of conspiracy to trespass in respect of
the contents of their hotels. The Court of Appeal struck out
the amended statement of claim.

On appeal by the plaintiff companies: —

Held, allowing the appeal in part, (1) that the rule in the
Moçambique case that the Supreme Court of Judicature had
no jurisdiction to entertain an action to recover damages
for trespass to land situate abroad precluded the action for
C   damages for trespass to the hotels in Cyprus even though no
question of title arose; and that the claim for conspiracy was
equally precluded since the unlawfulness on which the con-
᠍spiracy was based depended on proving the intention to effect
a trespass on foreign land on which point the court would
not adjudicate (post, pp. 383D, 384A–C, 385A–C, 389G—390A,
391G—392A, 393F–H).

British South Africa Co. v. *Compania de Moçambique*
D   [1892] A.C. 602, H.L.(E.) followed.

The Tolten [1946] P. 135, C.A. approved.

(2) That, having regard to the fact that the rule was
accepted in other common law jurisdictions; that by its nature
it involved possible conflict with foreign jurisdictions; that its
revision might involve consequential changes in the law and
that, since it was formulated, there had been no such change
in circumstances as to justify the House of Lords in changing
E   it, the House should not modify the rule.

Practice Statement (*Judicial Precedent*) [1966] 1 W.L.R.
1234 considered (post, pp. 385E–F, 386A, E–G, 390B–C, 392H—
393B).

(3) That the rule did not apply to the chattel contents of
the hotels and, since no local laws were relied on as justifying
interference with them, the action could continue in respect of
them (post, pp. 386H—387B, 390E–F, 394H).

F   Decision of the Court of Appeal [1978] Q.B. 205; [1977]
3 W.L.R. 656; [1978] 1 All E.R. 277 reversed in part.

The following cases are referred to in their Lordships' opinions:

Albert v. *Fraser Companies Ltd.* [1937] 1 D.L.R. 39.
Atlantic Star, The [1974] A.C. 436; [1973] 2 W.L.R. 795; [1973] 2 All
E.R. 175, H.L.(E.).
G   *Brisbane* v. *Pennsylvania Railway Co.* (1912) 205 N.Y. 431; 98 N.E. 752.
Companhia de Moçambique v. *British South Africa Co.* [1892] 2 Q.B.
358, D.C. and C.A.; sub nom. *British South Africa Co.* v. *Companhia
de Moçambique* [1893] A.C. 602, H.L.(E.).
Doulson v. *Matthews* (1792) 4 Term Rep. 503.
Gray v. *Manitoba & N.W. Railway Co.* (1896) 11 Man.Rep. 42.
Inglis v. *Commonwealth Trading Bank of Australia* (1972) 20 F.L.R. 30.
H   *Jacobus* v. *Colgate* (1916) 217 N.Y. 235.
Livingston v. *Jefferson* (1811) 15 Fed.Cas. 660; 1 Brock. 203.
London (City) Corporation v. *Cox* (1867) L.R. 2 H.L. 239, H.L.(E.).
MacShannon v. *Rockware Glass Ltd.* [1978] 2 W.L.R. 362; [1978] 1 All
E.R. 625, H.L.(E.).
Miliangos v. *George Frank (Textiles) Ltd.* [1976] A.C. 443; [1975] 3
W.L.R. 758; [1975] 3 All E.R. 801, H.L.(E.).
Mostyn v. *Fabrigas* (1774) 1 Cowp. 161.
Penn v. *Lord Baltimore* (1750) 1 Ves.Sen. 444.

Phillips v. *Eyre* (1870) L.R. 6 Q.B. 1.   A

Potter v. *Broken Hill Pty. Co. Ltd.* (1906) 3 C.L.R. 479.

Practice Statement (Judicial Precedent) [1966] 1 W.L.R. 1234; [1966] 3 All E.R. 77, H.L.(E.).

Ruthven v. *Ruthven* (1905) 13 S.L.T. 409.

Skinner v. *East India Co.* (1666) 6 St.Tr. 710.

Tolten, The [1946] P. 135; [1946] 2 All E.R. 372, C.A.

B

The following additional cases were cited in argument:

Aksionairnoye Obschestvo A. M. Luther v. *James Sagor and Co.* [1921] 1 K.B. 456; [1921] 3 K.B. 532, C.A.

Al-Fin Corporation's Patent, In re [1970] Ch. 160; [1969] 2 W.L.R. 1405; [1969] 3 All E.R. 396.

Arantzazu Mendi, The [1939] A.C. 256; [1939] 1 All E.R. 709, H.L.(E.).

Board v. *Board* [1919] A.C. 956, P.C.   C

Boys v. *Chaplin* [1971] A.C. 356; [1969] 3 W.L.R. 322; [1969] 2 All E.R. 1085, H.L.(E.).

Brereton v. *Canadian Pacific Railway* (1899) 29 O.R. 57.

Broaddus v. *Vanadium Corporation of America* (1963) 244 N.Y.S. 2d 336.

Broome v. *Cassell & Co. Ltd. (No. 2)* [1972] A.C. 1027; [1972] 2 W.L.R. 645; [1972] 1 All E.R. 801, H.L.(E.).   D

Carl Zeiss Stifftung v. *Rayner & Keeler Ltd. (No. 2)* [1965] Ch. 596; [1965] 2 W.L.R. 277; [1965] 1 All E.R. 300, C.A.; [1967] 1 A.C. 853; [1966] 3 W.L.R. 125; [1966] 2 All E.R. 536, H.L.(E.).

Deschamps v. *Miller* [1908] 1 Ch. 856.

Duck v. *Mayeu* [1892] 2 Q.B. 511, C.A.

Ellenwood v. *Marietta Chair Co.* (1895) 158 U.S. 105.

Ellerman Lines Ltd. v. *Read* [1928] 2 K.B. 144, C.A.   E

Exchange Telegraph Co. Ltd. v. *Gregory & Co.* [1896] 1 Q.B. 147, C.A.

Holmes v. *Barclay* (1849) 36 La. 63.

Ingram v. *Great Lakes Pipe Line Co.* (1941) 153 S.W. 2d 547.

Inman v. *Harris* (1951) 52 So. 2d 247.

Johnson v. *Diprose* [1893] 1 Q.B. 512, C.A.

Little v. *Chicago, St. Paul, Minneapolis & Omaha Railway Co.* (1896) 65 Minn. 48.   F

Luigi Monta of Genoa v. *Cechofracht Co. Ltd.* [1956] 2 Q.B. 522; [1956] 3 W.L.R. 450; [1956] 3 All E.R. 769.

Malo and Berthrand v. *Clement* [1943] 4 D.L.R. 773.

Maret, The (1944) 145 F. 2d 431.

Montesano Lumber Co. v. *Portland Iron Works* (1915) 152 Pac. 244.

Oakley v. *Lyster* [1931] 1 K.B. 148, C.A.

Reasor-Hill Corporation v. *Harrison* (1952) 249 S.W. 2d 994.

Reg. v. *National Insurance Commissioner, Ex parte Hudson* [1972] A.C. G
944; [1972] 2 W.L.R. 210; [1972] 1 All E.R. 145, H.L.(E.).

St. Pierre v. *South American Stores (Gath and Choues) Ltd.* [1936] 1 K.B. 382, C.A.

Salimoff & Co. v. *Standard Oil Co. of New York* (1933) 186 N.E. 679.

Sokoloff v. *National City Bank of New York* (1924) 145 N.E. 917.

Stark v. *Howe Sound Co. Inc.* (1933) 269 N.Y.S. 368.

H

Texas v. *White* (1868) 7 Wall. 700.

Upright v. *Mercury Business Machines Co. Inc.* (1961) 213 N.Y.S. 2d 417.

Vandervell's Trusts (No. 2), In re [1974] Ch. 269; [1974] 3 W.L.R. 256; [1974] 3 All E.R. 205, C.A.

Ward v. *Lewis* [1955] 1 W.L.R. 9; [1955] 1 All E.R. 55, C.A.

Werenjchik v. *Ulen Contracting Corporation* (1930) 240 N.Y.S. 619.

Whitwham v. *Westminster Brymbo Coal and Coke Co.* [1896] 2 Ch. 538, C.A.

A   APPEAL from the Court of Appeal.

This was an appeal from the judgment of the Court of Appeal (Lord Denning M.R., Roskill and Scarman L.JJ.) dated May 23, 1977, whereby the order of May J. sitting in chambers in the Queen's Bench Division, made on April 6, 1977, granting the appellants, Hesperides Hotels Ltd. and Catsellis Hotels Ltd., the plaintiffs, an interlocutory injunction against the respondent, Omer Faik Muftizade, the second defendant, was set aside

B   and the appellant's amended statement of claim was struck out with costs. The first defendants were Aegean Turkish Hotels Ltd.

The facts are set out in the opinions of Lord Wilberforce and Viscount Dilhorne.

David Kemp and *George Newman* for the appellant companies.

C   *F. P. Neill Q.C., Gerald Davies* and *Nicholas Padfield* for the respondent.

Their Lordships took time for consideration.

July 6, 1978. LORD WILBERFORCE. My Lords, this appeal is from an order of the Court of Appeal setting aside the appellants' writ against the

D   respondent Mr. Omer Faik Muftizade for want of jurisdiction.

The appellants are two companies registered under the laws of the Republic of Cyprus: they are family concerns owned and controlled by Greek Cypriots. Before 1974, in which year Turkish forces took possession of areas in the north of Cyprus, these companies were owners of two hotels in Kyrenia, on the north coast. Hesperides Hotels Ltd. owned

E   and operated one called the Hesperides; Catsellis Hotels Ltd. one called the Dome. After the Turkish invasion those who controlled the appellants left Kyrenia and went to Limassol, which is on the southern coast and is in the Greek Cypriot area. In 1976 it came to their knowledge that efforts were being made in London to organise holiday tours to the hotels. There was a body calling itself the Turkish Federated State of Cyprus which issued brochures; there was a travel agency called Aegean Turkish

F   Holidays Ltd. which handled these brochures, and, it is said, accepted bookings for the hotels from intending holiday-makers in England. The Turkish Federated State of Cyprus has as its representative in London, Mr. O. F. Muftizade, respondent to this appeal.

On February 16, 1977, the appellants issued a writ with statement of claim endorsed against Aegean Turkish Holidays Ltd. and Mr.

G   Muftizade claiming damages, in effect for conspiracy, an account of profits and an injunction restraining the defendants from conspiring to procure acts of trespass to the appellants' hotels. They also issued, on March 4, 1977, a summons claiming an interim injunction in the same terms. The respondent, Mr. Muftizade, entered a conditional appearance and himself issued a summons for an order setting aside the writ. These summons came for hearing before May J. on April 1, 1977.

H   The respondent's contentions, at this stage, were twofold. First he claimed immunity from suit on the basis that the Turkish Federated State of Cyprus was a foreign sovereign state and that he was its representative. Secondly he contended that the court had no jurisdiction to entertain the action upon the principle established by this House in *British South Africa Co.* v. *Companhia de Moçambique* [1893] A.C. 602 (the " *Moçambique* case "). To enable himself to deal with the first point May J. addressed an inquiry to the Secretary of State, Foreign and Common-

wealth Office, asking whether Her Majesty's Government recognised, de   A
jure or de facto, the Turkish Federated State of Cyprus and whether Her
Majesty's Government accords any diplomatic privilege to the respondent.
On April 6, 1977, the Secretary of State replied giving a negative answer
to each of these questions. These replies disposed of the respondent's
first contention; on the second point the learned judge decided that the
court had jurisdiction to try a claim based upon a conspiracy to procure
trespass to foreign land when the conspiracy took place in this country   B
and there were overt acts in this country. He granted an interim injunction
in the terms claimed and dismissed the respondent's summons.

     On May 13, 1977, a consent order was made against the Aegean
Turkish Holidays Ltd. under which they submitted to a perpetual injunction
restraining them from conspiring or acting in any way to procure trespass
to the hotels and to an order for payment to each appellant of £10 by   C
way of damages for conspiracy to trespass. It is asserted in the respondent's case (their Lordships accept in good faith), in support of his
contention that there had been an accord and satisfaction, that this sum
has been paid, but it was conceded, on the hearing of the appeal, that
this fact could not be established.

     The respondent appealed against the order of May J. to the Court of
Appeal and added, by leave, an additional ground, that the statement of   D
claim disclosed no reasonable cause of action and/or should be struck
out as an abuse of the process of the court. At the hearing of the appeal
the respondent adduced voluminous additional evidence directed to showing the development since 1974 of affairs in Cyprus and to proving the
actual situation prevailing in the island. This was to be the foundation
of an argument in the Court of Appeal and in this House that, in spite   E
of the certificate of the Secretary of State, there was an autonomous
administration in each part of Cyprus of which and of whose " legislation "
the court can take note. The appellants objected to this evidence on
the ground that it contradicted the certificate of the Secretary of State,
that it was contentious, and that they had no opportunity to answer it.
The Court of Appeal however admitted it.

     Further, in the course of the hearing before the Court of Appeal,   F
the appellants amended their statement of claim alleging a conspiracy to
procure trespasses to the contents of the hotels, no doubt with the
expectation of thereby escaping from the consequences of the rule in the
Moçambique case [1893] A.C. 602.

     The Court of Appeal unanimously allowed the respondent's appeal but
differed in the reasons they gave for doing so.   G

     Roskill L.J. and Scarman L.J. held that the action was precluded by
the rule in the Moçambique case, none the less though it was presented
in the form, or guise, of a conspiracy. They also held that the action was
not maintainable as regards the chattels (contents of the hotels) since it
was based upon trespass (not conversion) and since the appellants were
admittedly out of possession.   H

     Lord Denning M.R. held that the Moçambique rule should be confined
to cases where there is a dispute as to title and that the court should have
jurisdiction to try a claim based on a conspiracy in England. He held
however that the action, being an action in tort, was not maintainable
because the acts complained of were not unlawful under the lex loci actus:
notice could be taken of the " laws " of the Turkish Federated State of
Cyprus which authorised the acts. Moreover public policy rendered the

A dispute not justiciable in England there being two conflicting adminis-
trations in Cyprus.

I shall consider first the question whether the present action is precluded
by the rule in the *Moçambique* case [1893] A.C. 602. The appellants'
arguments are threefold:

First they contend that the rule established by that case has no
application where there is no dispute as to the title to foreign land and
B (I use their words) " no real dispute over the right to possession of the
foreign land." This result, they say, can be reached by a process of
interpretation of the decision of this House without departing from it.

Secondly they invite your Lordships to overrule, or depart from, the
decision in the *Moçambique* case, at least to the extent necessary to allow
the present action to be brought.

C   Thirdly they argue that the rule has no application to an action
based on a conspiracy entered into in England even if the conspiracy
is to effect or procure trespass to foreign land.

The rule in the *Moçambique* case can be conveniently stated in the
form in which it is generally accepted, viz., in *Dicey & Morris, The
Conflict of Laws*, rule 79. I quote from the 9th ed. (1973), but it
appears as rule 53 in the same form (except for one letter) in the 3rd
D ed. (1922) edited by Professor Dicey himself and Dr. Berriedale Keith.

> " Subject to the exceptions hereinafter mentioned, the court has no
> jurisdiction to entertain an action for (1) the determination of the
> title to, or the right to the possession of, any immovable situate out
> of England (foreign land); or (2) the recovery of damages for trespass
> to such immovable."

E   The exceptions later mentioned relate to actions in equity (*Penn* v. *Lord
Baltimore* (1750) 1 Ves.Sen. 444) and other special cases on which reliance
cannot be placed in this appeal.

It will be seen that the rule is in two parts—if either applies, the court
has no jurisdiction. The second part refers to the recovery of damages
for trespass and if correctly stated must (subject only to the conspiracy
F point) preclude the action. So the questions are (1) whether this part of
the rule is correct in law, (2) whether it should be read subject to an exception for actions where no question as to title arises. My Lords, the answer
to the first of these questions cannot, in my opinion, admit of doubt. The
history of the rule, which is a long one, was examined in depth in the
Moçambique case, both in this House [1893] A.C. 602, and in the Court of
Appeal [1892] 2 Q.B. 358. Two of the Lords Justices in the Court of
G Appeal were prepared to hold that an action in trespass, being in their view
an action in personam, could lie against a defendant found in England:
Lord Esher M.R. thought otherwise and his opinion prevailed in this House.
In his speech (which I shall not attempt to summarise) Lord Herschell L.C.
traced the development of the rule from *Skinner* v. *East India Co.* (1666) 6
St.Tr. 710 to 1893; it was Lord Mansfield who attempted, in two cases
H decided by himself and referred to in *Mostyn* v. *Fabrigas* (1774) 1 Cowp.
161, to support the doctrine that actions for trespass against a defendant in
England could lie. But this doctrine was decisively rejected *per* Buller J.
in *Doulson* v. *Matthews* (1792) 4 Term Rep. 503, 504:

> " It is now too late for us to inquire whether it were wise or politic to
> make a distinction between transitory and local actions: it is sufficient
> for the courts that the law has settled the distinction, and that an action
> quare clausum fregit is local. We may try actions here which are in their

nature transitory, though arising out of a transaction abroad, but not A
such as are in their nature local."

It has not been revived since in any English reported case.

There is no more doubt, in my opinion, as to the second question. It
is certainly true that in the *Moçambique* case itself the plaintiff's title was
disputed, but the House considered the legitimacy of actions in trespass
in the broadest and most general terms. Lord Herschell L.C. opened his B
speech in these words at p. 617:

"the principal question raised by this appeal is whether the Supreme
Court of Judicature has jurisdiction to try an action to recover damages
for a trespass to lands situate in a foreign country"

and the whole of the discussion is in terms as general as this. The rejection
of Lord Mansfield's doctrine is inconsistent with any supposed limitation of C
the rule to a case where title is disputed, for in neither of the cases decided
by him was there a dispute as to title. But Lord Herschell (as Buller J.
before him), recognising this fact (see p. 624), rejecting the admissibility of
actions in trespass. There are passages no doubt in the speech which are
directed towards the actual facts of the case which the House was considering, in which not only was there a dispute as to title, but the action D
was brought in order that the title should be determined. In these passages
Lord Herschell L.C. draws attention to the particular, and additional,
difficulties which would be involved if the English court were to adjudicate
upon title. But in my understanding these are treated as a fortiori cases,
and there is nothing in the examination of them which supports a proposition that the rule is limited to them.

The speech of Lord Halsbury follows the same course. He states the E
question for decision in the same general way as it had been stated by
Lord Herschell, at p. 630, and he deals with it similarly without a single
reference, even as regards the case under discussion, to support an argument
that the rule applies only when title is disputed.

My Lords, this is not the first time that this supposed limitation of
the rule has been contended for. It was raised in *The Tolten* [1946] P. 135 F
and firmly rejected by Somervell L.J. at p. 163, and by Cohen L.J. at p.
169. It is suggested that Scott L.J. took a different view, but all he said
at pp. 141–142, was this:

"I recognise that in a case where the action is brought by a party in
possession of land and structures, suing merely for damages for negligence, or even, it may be, for trespass quare clausum fregit, and the
plaintiff relies solely on his possession as the foundation for his action, G
the House of Lords might hereafter distinguish the *Moçambique* case.
I do not think, however, that it would be right for this court to attempt
that distinction, as I am satisfied that, in regard to common law actions,
no such distinction was then in the mind of the House . . ."

But, whether or not this House possesses greater powers of distinguishing
earlier decisions than does the Court of Appeal—a question which may H
raise some interesting jurisprudential questions—I hardly find in this
passage any encouragement to exercise such powers as we have.

I therefore regard the formulation in *Dicey*, rule 79 (2) as correctly
stating the law.

Before considering whether we should overrule or depart from the
Moçambique rule in any respect I must deal with the argument that we
have here the distinguishable claim of a conspiracy formed in England.

A   The majority in the Court of Appeal gave short shrift to this argument
and I think they were right.   In my opinion the answer to this argument
is to be found in a passage in the judgment of Scarman L.J. [1978] Q.B.
205, 231:

"But, more significant, the reliance upon the alleged conspiracy as
distinct from the alleged trespass which it is intended to effect is wrong
B   in principle.   The combination or agreement, which is said to constitute
(with overt acts and ensuing damage) the tort of conspiracy, is unlawful
only if there be the intention to effect a trespass upon foreign land.
Unless that be shown, there is nothing unlawful.   And that can be
established only if the court is prepared to adjudicate upon the right
to possession of the foreign land—which is exactly what the House of
Lords said the English courts may not do: see Lord Herschell L.C.
C   in the passage already cited."

I gratefully adopt this passage on which I am unable to improve.
The rule being then as I have stated it, should your Lordships accede
to the appellants' invitation to restate it, in different terms? There is no
doubt that the rule can be criticised.   Although Professor Dicey seems to
have approved it (3rd ed., pp. 223–224) the diligence of the appellants'
D   counsel has assembled a massive volume of academic hostility to the rule
as illogical and productive of injustice: see inter alia *Dicey & Morris*, 9th
ed., pp. 516–518, 525; *Cheshire's Private International Law*, 3rd ed. (1947),
p. 719, 8th ed. (1970), p. 481, 9th ed. (1974), p. 495; *American Law Institute,
Restatement of the Law, Second, Conflict of Laws* (1957), ss. 10, 87; *Beale,
The Conflict of Laws* (1935), s. 614.1; *Goodrich, Conflict of Laws*, 4th ed.
E   (1964), s. 96 and *Ehrenzweig, Conflict of Laws*, (1962), s. 39.
Although these writers are concerned with the conflict of laws, as to
which academic authority is of particular value, rather than with the
English law as to jurisdiction which is what now concerns us, the concensus
as to where considerations of logic and justice might lead if this matter
were tabula rasa is impressive.   But there are other factors to be weighed
when revision of an old established rule, sanctioned by this House is
F   suggested.
First: the rule is accepted with differing degrees of force and emphasis
in other jurisdictions of the common law.   Their Lordships were referred
to cases decided in Australia and Canada which accept the rule and to none
which reject it: see *Potter* v. *Broken Hill Pty. Co. Ltd.* (1906) 3 C.L.R.
479; *Inglis* v. *Commonwealth Trading Bank of Australia* (1972) 20 F.L.R.
G   30 and *Gray* v. *Manitoba and N.W. Railway Co.* (1896) 11 Man.Rep. 42.
In *Albert* v. *Fraser Companies Ltd.* [1937] 1 D.L.R. 39 the Supreme Court
of New Brunswick specifically discussed the question whether the *Moçambique* decision [1893] A.C. 602, can be limited to a case where title is
in dispute, and held that it could not: see also *Sykes, Australian Conflict
of Laws* (1972), p. 202.   In the United States of America the rule appears
to be accepted in the great majority of jurisdictions, Arkansas, Minnesota
H   and Missouri being the only states in which it has been judicially departed
from.   In general the courts have followed the judgment of Marshall,
Circuit Justice (subsequently Chief Justice) in *Livingston* v. *Jefferson*
(1811) 15 Fed.Cas. 660 in which the learned judge seeing no good reason
for the rule, upheld it for the sake of consistency and continuity.   In New
York and Virginia it has been altered by statute (see further below).
In Scotland a similar rule appears to prevail without certainty of definition: see *Anton, Private International Law* (1967), p. 125.

Second: the nature of the rule itself, involving, as it clearly must, A
possible conflict with foreign jurisdictions, and the possible entry into and
involvement with political questions of some delicacy, does not favour
revision (assuming such to be logically desirable) by judicial decision,
but rather by legislation. I am impressed in this context by the judgment
of Cullen Ch.J. in the Court of Appeals of New York in *Brisbane* v.
Pennsylvania Railway Co. (1912) 205 N.Y. 431, 434, which contains this
passage: B

"The authorities in the highest courts of this state are uniform to
the effect that our courts have no jurisdiction of an action for damages
for injuries to real estate lying without the state, and the latest
decisions are quite recent. . . . It was so held by Chief Justice
Marshall in *Livingston* v. *Jefferson*, 15 Fed.Cas. 660; 1 Brock 203,
where he decided that an action could not be maintained in Virginia C
for trespass upon lands in Louisiana. Such, also, is the rule in the
great majority of the states . . . though there are some where the
contrary rule prevails . . . and the old law was changed in Virginia
by statute. Were the question an open one, I would favour the
doctrine that our courts have jurisdiction of actions to recover damages
for injuries to foreign real estate. Chief Justice Marshall in D
Livingston v. *Jefferson*, expressed his personal disapproval of the rule
which he felt bound to give effect under the authorities. In the
century which has elapsed since Chief Justice Marshall's decision,
all the decisions in this state which I have cited have been rendered.
At this late day I think we would not be justified in overruling these
cases, but should leave it to the legislature to change the rule by
statute." E

Thirdly: Revision of the rule may necessitate consequential changes
in the law. In order to prevent "forum shopping" and overlapping, one
such change would have to relate to "forum non conveniens" a principle
not yet fully developed in England (see *The Atlantic Star* [1974] A.C.
436 and *MacShannon* v. *Rockware Glass Ltd.* [1978] 2 W.L.R. 362) and,
if English courts were to be given an extended jurisdiction, requiring F
legislative definition.

Fourthly: It cannot be said thaat since 1893 there has been such a
change of circumstances as to justify this House in changing the rule:
see *Miliangos* v. *George Frank (Textiles) Ltd.* [1976] A.C. 443.

On these considerations I have reached the conclusion that the
necessary conditions to bring into operation the Practice Direction of 1966 G
[*Practice Statement (Judicial Precedent)* [1966] 1 W.L.R. 1234] do not
exist and that the rule should be maintained in this House. The consequence is that the appellants' action, as regards the hotels themselves,
being land situate abroad, cannot be maintained. In view of this conclusion it is not necessary to enter upon the questions raised by the
respondent's counsel as to the degree of notice (if any) which the courts
should take of the situation in Cyprus and of "laws" passed by the H
non-recognised Turkish Federated State of Cyprus. These gave rise to
an interesting and learned argument for which the House is indebted but
having regard to the nature of the issues raised I think that the present is
not the occasion to pass upon them.

There remains the appellants' claim as regards the chattel contents
of the hotels. To this the *Moçambique* rule has no application. Moreover the alleged "laws" passed in the Turkish Federated State of

A Cyprus do not extend to the chattels. The Court of Appeal, however, struck out this part of the appellants' claim on the ground that for such a claim to be admissible the plaintiffs must be in possession of the chattels in questions. But a claim could validly be laid in conversion: the plaintiffs allege sufficient facts to support such a claim and it is not necessary in modern pleadings to attach a specific label to it if the factual basis is there, so the claim can be asserted without amendment.

B The case of *Albert* v. *Fraser Companies Ltd.* [1937] 1 D.L.R. 39 on which the respondent relied does not assist him, for in that case there was no direct allegation in the plaintiff's statement of claim of any trespass to his personal property: see *per* Baxter C.J., at p. 46. In the present case interference with the appellants' chattels is distinctly alleged and, moreover, no local law is relied upon as jusifying the interference.

C I would allow the appellants' appeal so far as to permit the action to continue as regards the chattels but I would uphold the order striking out the writ and substantive claim so far as they relate to land or immovable property in Cyprus.

VISCOUNT DILHORNE. My Lords, on May 23, 1977, the Court of Appeal (Lord Denning M.R., Roskill and Scarman L.JJ.) ordered that

D the writ in these proceedings should be set aside. By that writ endorsed with a statement of claim, the appellants, the owners of two hotels in Kyrenia in northern Cyprus, the first appellant being the owner of the Hesperides Hotel now called the Kyrenia Rocks, and the second appellant being the owner of the hotel called the Dome Hotel, claimed damages from and an injunction against two defendants, the first a travel agency called Aegean Turkish Holidays and the second the respondent to this

E appeal. They alleged that the travel agency and the respondent had " conspired together and with others unknown to effect trespasses to the said hotels and/or have conspired together to obtain advantage for themselves by " the unauthorised use " of the appellants' property.

The alternative conspiracy alleged appears to be in substance also an allegation in different language of a conspiracy to effect trespasses to the

F hotels, and it was not contended on behalf of the appellants that if the court had no jurisdiction to hear the claim in respect of the conspiracy to effect trespasses, it nevertheless had jurisdiction to entertain the claim under the alternative head.

Of these allegations of conspiracy the statement of claim purported to give particulars. They alleged that the travel agency had held itself out

G as willing to book, and had booked, accommodation for holidays at the appellants' hotels, and that the respondent had counselled and procured divers persons to commit trespass to the hotels. The only link between the travel agency and the respondent disclosed by these particulars was the alleged possession by the travel agency of a brochure issued by the Turkish Federated State of Cyprus headed " Hotels 1976," which advertised hotels in the area of Cyprus occupied by Turkish troops including

H the Kyrenia Rocks, and the alleged distribution of the brochure by the respondent.

The statement of claim alleges that in August 1974 the appellants, limited companies, were with their servants or agents forced to flee from their hotels in consequence of the Turkish invasion, and were deprived of all access to them and have consequently lost control and possession of the hotels.

On March 4, 1977, the appellants took out a summons seeking an

interim injunction restraining the travel agency and the respondent from A
conspiring or acting in any way to procure a trespass to the hotels, and
on March 31, 1977, the respondent took out a summons asking that the
writ should be set aside.

Both summonses were heard by May J. on April 6. He granted an
interim injunction against the respondent and dismissed his application
that the writ against him should be set aside.

On May 10 the respondent gave notice of appeal which was amended B
pursuant to leave granted by the Court of Appeal on May 19, and on
May 13 Peter Pain J. by consent granted an injunction against the travel
agency which submitted to judgment for £20 by way of damages for
conspiracy to trespass.

In the course of the hearing before the Court of Appeal the appellants
amended the statement of claim to include an allegation that the travel C
agency and the respondent had conspired together and with others to
effect trespasses to the contents of the hotels. The respondent in his
case presented to this House alleged that each of the appellants had been
paid £10 pursuant to the consent order made by Peter Pain J. and contended that the respondent was thereby released from the appellants'
claim. It subsequently emerged during the course of the argument in
this House that the money had not been paid. As the consent order D
was made before the statement of claim was amended it could not
operate as a bar to the appellants' claim so far as it relates to the
contents of the hotels.

In *British South Africa Co.* v. *Companhia de Moçambique* [1893]
A.C. 602 the headnote states that it was held that the Supreme Court
of Judicature has no jurisdiction to entertain an action to recover damages E
for trespass to land situate abroad. The respondent relies strongly on this
decision. The appellants however contend that the case only decided
that there was no jurisdiction to entertain such a claim when the title to
land abroad was involved. Further, they say that the House should,
in the exercise of its power to depart from a previous decision, review
it and if the headnote correctly states the decision of the House, at least
limit its application to cases where the title to foreign lands is involved. F
They also contend that the decision does not and should not be interpreted
as applying to a claim based on a conspiracy entered into in this country
to procure the commission of a trespass abroad for damages made against
defendants within the jurisdiction. Finally, they say, that this decision
does not operate as a bar to their claim for damages and an injunction
in so far as it relates to the contents of the hotels.   G

A number of interesting questions were fully argued; in particular
whether the courts of this country should and can have regard to legislation of the Turkish Federated State of Cyprus when the Foreign Office
in response to an inquiry by May J. has certified that Her Majesty's
Government do not recognise the administration established under that
name and do not recognise that administration as being the government
of an independent de facto sovereign state. But it is not necessary to H
reach a conclusion on them, and on whether the consent order of Peter
Pain J. releases the respondent from liability in respect of conspiracy to
effect trespasses to the hotels if the decision in the *Moçambique* case
[1893] A.C. 602 is an effective bar to that claim and is adhered to.

In that case the *Moçambique* company sought a declaration of title
to lands in South Africa, damages for trespass and an injunction. The
Divisional Court [1892] 2 Q.B. 358 held that the court would not enter-

A tain the action in so far as it claimed a declaration of title and Wright J. delivering the judgment of the court, said, at p. 368, that, assuming that there was jurisdiction in this country to try an action for damages for trespass to foreign lands where no question of title was raised

> " it would seem that, when an issue of title is directly raised . . . the court must be as incompetent to try that issue as it is to try an action directly brought for the recovery of the land. . .''

B

In the Court of Appeal there was a division of opinion, Lord Esher M.R. at p. 393 observed that the claim for a declaration of title had been persisted in (though the report of the case at p. 385 states that it was abandoned in the course of the argument) and that Sir Henry James Q.C. for the appellant had put forward an alternative argument that, as the claim was for damages only in respect of an intrusion on the plaintiff's possessory title, the action was only in personam and transitory, as on that view of the case it did not raise any question of title to land. He held, at p. 398 that an action for trespass to land abroad could not be entertained in an English court. Fry and Lopes L.JJ. were of the contrary opinion. In this House Sir Henry James sought to establish three propositions. (1) The Queen's courts have jurisdiction over all D persons within the realm; (2) those courts are open to all suitors who can enforce the jurisdiction against all subjects against whom personally effectual relief can be given; and (3) all personal actions can be maintained if the defendants are within the jurisdiction—and that an action for trespass is a personal action.

Lord Herschell L.C. referred to Lord Mansfield's observations in *Mostyn* v. *Fabrigas*, 1 Cowp. 161 in which he said that he had awarded damages for trespass abroad. Lord Herschell pointed out that in *Doulson* v. *Matthews*, 4 Term Rep. 503, an action for trespass to land in Canada, these decisions of Lord Mansfield were not followed, Buller J. delivering the judgment of the court saying, at p. 504:

> " It is now too late for us to inquire whether it were wise or politic to make a distinction between transitory and local actions: it is F sufficient for the courts that the law has settled the distinction, and that an action quare clausum fregit is local. We may try actions here which are in their nature transitory, though arising out of a transaction abroad, but not such as are in their nature local."

Lord Herschell also referred to the judgment of Willes J. in *City of London Corporation* v. *Cox* (1867) L.R. 2 H.L. 239, 261, and in *Phillips* G v. *Eyre* (1870) L.R. 6 Q.B. 1 when Willes J. said that there was no jurisdiction here to try actions for trespass to land abroad and held that such an action was not maintainable. In his view, at p. 629, " the grounds upon which the courts have hitherto refused to exercise jurisdiction in actions of trespass to lands situate abroad were substantial. . ."

I can find nothing in his speech to support the conclusion that he held that the action in the *Moçambique* case [1893] A.C. 602 was not H maintainable because title was involved. The division of opinion in the Court of Appeal was on whether or not an action for trespass to foreign lands was justiciable in the courts of this country, and that was the question this House had to decide. As I read Lord Herschell's speech it was clearly his view that the courts of this country have not and never had exercised jurisdiction in relation to such claims.

In Lord Halsbury's opinion the judgment of Lord Esher M.R. in the Court of Appeal was correct; Lord Macnaghten agreed with what had been said and Lord Morris agreed with the observations of Lord Herschell A L.C.

I see no ground for concluding that the headnote of the case in this House did not correctly state the decision, and if the decision stands, actions for trespass to foreign lands are not justiciable in the English courts whether or not any question of title is involved.

The rule in this case, as stated in the headnote and in *Dicey & Morris, The Conflict of Laws* has been subjected to much criticism by dis- B tinguished persons. Our attention was drawn to the criticisms and we were pressed to revise the rule. In my opinion it would not be right for us to exercise our power to do so. Buller J. said in 1792 it was then too late to inquire whether it was wise or politic to distinguish between transitory and local actions. It is now in my opinion far too late for us to seek to do so. Questions of comity of nations may well be involved C and if any change in the law is to be made it should only be made after detailed and full investigation of all the possible implications which we sitting judicially cannot make. In my view it must be left to Parliament to change the law if after full consideration that is thought to be desirable.

In my view the rule cannot be evaded by alleging conspiracy. To obtain damages the appellants must show that they have suffered loss as the result of it. They must show that a tresspass to the hotels has D been procured. Proof of their claim involves a proof of trespass to the land abroad and in my opinion this the courts of this country cannot try. As in my opinion the rule in the *Moçambique* case is correctly stated in the headnote to the report and in *Dicey*, it follows that that decision is a complete bar to the appellants' claim in relation to trespass to the hotels. In my view that decision should not be altered now by this E House and it follows that those parts of the statement of claim which relate to the allegation of the conspiracy to effect trespasses into the hotels and the alternative claim relating to the hotels should be struck out on the ground that the court has no jurisdiction to hear them.

The rule in the *Moçambique* case however is no bar to the appellants' claim in relation to the contents of the hotels and that part of the statement of claim should stand. F

LORD SALMON. My Lords, I have had the advantage of reading in draft the speech prepared by my noble and learned friend, Lord Wilberforce. I agree with it and would allow the appeal to the extent to which he proposes. I also agree with his proposed order as to costs.

G

LORD FRASER OF TULLYBELTON. My Lords, this appeal raises the important general question of whether the English courts have jurisdiction to entertain an action for damages for trespass to foreign land, in a a case where no question of title to the land or of right to possess it is raised. The answer involves considering the decision of this House in *British South Africa Co.* v. *Companhia de Moçambique* [1893] A.C. 602 ("the *Moçambique* case"), to ascertain whether it covered that H question. If, as I think, for reasons to be explained in a moment, it did, then it is necessary to consider whether we ought now to depart from that decision, relying on the Practice Statement of 1966 ([1966] 1 W.L.R. 1234).

The generally received understanding of what was decided in the *Moçambique* case is summarised in *Dicey & Morris, The Conflict of Laws,* 9th ed. in branch (2) of rule 79. Rule 79 is as follows:

A
" Subject to the exceptions hereinafter mentioned, the court has
no jurisdiction to entertain an action for (1) the determination of the
title to, or the right to the possession of, any immovable situate out
of England (foreign land); or (2) the recovery of damages for trespass
to such immovable."

It was stated in almost exactly the same words as rule 53 in the 3rd
B ed., the last edition for which Professor Dicey himself was responsible.
None of the exceptions apply to the facts of this case. The rule virtually
repeats the headnote of the report in [1893] A.C. 602. But Mr. Kemp
for the appellants pressed us with the submission that the rule is stated
too widely and that the decision in the *Moçambique* case was limited to
cases in which the title to the foreign land was in issue, or at least where
there was an issue as to the right of immediate possession of the land.
C In the *Moçambique* case itself the title to the land was in dispute, and
when the action began the plaintiffs were claiming a declaration of title,
although that claim was abandoned in the Court of Appeal (see [1892]
2 Q.B. 358, 420) and it was not a live issue when the appeal reached
the House of Lords.
The leading speech in the House of Lords was made by Lord
D Herschell L.C. It contains passages which leave room for some doubts
as to whether he was treating the dispute on title as part of the ground
of decision—see p. 624 where the Lord Chancellor referred to two
decisions by Lord Mansfield relating to trespass to foreign land and
commented that in those cases " no question of title to real property was
in issue," and see also pp. 625 to 626. But a reading of the speech as
a whole shows, in my opinion, that it was not intended to be limited to
E cases where there was a dispute as to title. In the first paragraph of
the speech Lord Herschell L.C. said, at p. 617:

". . . the principal question raised by this appeal is whether the
Supreme Court of Judicature has jurisdiction to try an action to
recover damages for a trespass to lands situate in a foreign country."

F He made no mention of disputed title. Among the authorities upon
which he relied was *Doulson* v. *Matthews*, 4 Term Rep. 503 where the
Court of Queen's Bench did not follow Lord Mansfield's decisions on
this point, and where Buller J. said, at p. 504:

" It is now too late for us to inquire whether it were wise or politic
to make a distinction between transitory and local actions: it is
G sufficient for the courts that the law has settled the distinction, and
that an action quare clausum fregit is local. We may try actions
here which are in their nature transitory, though arising out of a
transaction abroad, but not such as are in their nature local."

Finally at p. 629 he stated his conclusion in general terms which exactly
match the question stated at the beginning of his speech. Lord Halsbury
H at p. 630 also stated what he described as " the only real question which
is in debate " in general terms not limited to cases where title was disputed. Similarly Lord Esher M.R., who dissented in the Court of Appeal
and whose view was upheld in the House of Lords, also stated the
question for decision in the widest terms, see [1892] 2 Q.B. 358, 394.
In *The Tolten* [1946] P. 135 the basis of the *Moçambique* case was
considered and all three members of the Court of Appeal took the view
that it was not limited to cases where title was disputed: see especially

Cohen L.J. at pp. 167 to 169. I am of opinion that it is not possible   A
now to distinguish the decision in the *Moçambique* case on the ground
that it was so limited.

That decision, as interpreted in branch (2) of rule 79 in *Dicey* has
been the subject of criticism from many sources. Mr. Kemp submitted
that the criticisms were well founded and that, if the decision could not
be distinguished in the instant appeal, it should be departed from. The
decision was based, as the speech of Lord Herschell L.C. clearly shows,   B
on a historical distinction drawn in English law between local and
transitory actions. Lord Herschell held that actions for trespass to
land were local and that for that reason the English courts had no
jurisdiction to try them if the land was outside England. No criticism
was made in the argument before us of that historical explanation. The
decision was criticised on the ground that, however historically correct it   C
might be, it was illogical and was liable to produce injustice in practice.
I recognise that there is force in these criticisms, and particularly in the
criticism that it may lead to a plaintiff being left without a remedy.
Indeed the instant appeal is one where the plaintiffs, if they have no
remedy in the English courts, will probably be left with no remedy at all.

Those who seek to justify the rule on its merits, apart from its   D
historical origin, have done so mainly on two grounds. The first is that
it is " a legitimate application or extension of the principle of effectiveness "—*Dicey*, 3rd ed., p. 224—that is the principle that a court has
jurisdiction only over matters in which it can give an effective judgment.
The second is that it is in accord with the comity of nations. Neither of
these justifications seems to me wholly convincing. As regards effectiveness, a judgment awarding damages against a defendant is generally   E
regarded as effective if the defendant is subject to the court's jurisdiction,
because it can normally be enforced against him by order of the court.
The effectiveness of the award has nothing to do with the ground on
which it was made; an award of damages for trespass to foreign land
is no less effective than an award for damages for any other wrong. Moreover the courts both in England and in Scotland have asserted jurisdiction   F
in actions to enforce contracts relating to foreign land although enforcement can only be by indirect means: see *Penn* v. *Lord Baltimore*, 1
Ves.Sen. 444 and *Ruthven* v. *Ruthven* (1905) 13 S.L.T. 409. Actions of
that sort seem to affect the foreign land itself hardly less than actions for
damages for trespass to the land. So far as comity of nations is concerned, this may afford some support for the rule although I doubt
whether rule 79 (2) represents one which is generally recognised by the   G
international community. For example the comments on the French
Civil Code that were brought to our attention were far from satisfying
me that rule 79 (2) was in accordance with the law of France.

For these reasons I have serious doubt whether the law as laid down
in the *Moçambique* case [1893] A.C. 602 is either logical or satisfactory in
its result. If the matter were free from authority, there would be much   H
to be said for what Mr. Kemp suggested was the true rule to be extracted
from the *Moçambique* case, videlicet that the English court has jurisdiction to entertain an action for damages for trespass to foreign land
against a person within the jurisdiction in a case where title is not in
dispute and where there is no real dispute as to the plaintiff's right to
possession of the land. But the matter is not free from authority and,
in my opinion, this is not one on which it would be right for the House to

A   depart from its earlier decisions. The main reason is that I do not think
that the House in its judicial capacity has enough information to enable
it to see the possible repercussions of making the suggested change in
the law. One probable repercussion would be that, if the English
courts were to have the wider jurisdiction of the suggested "true rule,"
they might at the same time have to limit their new jurisdiction by
applying to it a rule of forum non conveniens. Since *The Atlantic Star*
B   [1974] A.C. 436 and *MacShannon* v. *Rockware Glass Ltd.* [1978] 2
W.L.R. 362, this might not be a revolutionary step, but it would nevertheless represent a consequential change in the law of some significance.
There may well be other and more important repercussions. I would
apply to this question the words of my noble and learned friend, Lord
Simon of Glaisdale, in *Miliangos* v. *George Frank (Textiles) Ltd.* [1976]
C   A.C. 443, 480:

> " I do not think that this is a ' law reform ' which should or can
> properly be imposed by judges; it is, on the contrary, essentially a
> decision which demands a far wider range of review than is available
> to courts following our traditional and valuable adversary system—
> the sort of review compassed by an interdepartmental committee."

D
There are also other reasons. The law as stated in the *Moçambique*
case was not new. It goes back at least as far as 1792 when *Doulson*
v. *Matthews*, 4 Term Rep. 503 was decided and it has been generally,
though reluctantly, followed in the United States of America, Canada
and Australia—see particularly the decision of Chief Justice Marshall
in *Livingston* v. *Jefferson*, 15 Fed.Cas. 660. In a few American states
E   the courts have declined to follow the *Moçambique* decision, but
such cases seem to have been rare. Secondly, departure from the
Moçambique rule would mean that the House of Lords in its judicial
capacity would be assuming a new jurisdiction for the English courts:
see *Albert* v. *Fraser Companies Ltd.* [1937] 1 D.L.R. 39 (New Brunswick) and *Jacobus* v. *Colgate* (1916) 217 N.Y. 235 (New York). That is
not a step that I think we would be justified in taking, at least in this
F   case where Parliament could have made an opportunity for altering or
modifying the law when dealing with jurisdiction in the Supreme Court
of Judicature (Consolidation) Act 1925. Thirdly, we were told that a
new European convention dealing with jurisdiction of national courts was
in preparation so that legislation is likely to be required before long.
The result is that if this had been an action for damages for, or for
G   an injunction against, trespass to immovable property in Cyprus, it would
in my opinion have failed. It is therefore unnecessary to consider the
interesting questions raised as to the legal status of the Turkish Federated
State of Cyprus.
In my opinion it makes no difference that the action is based on
allegations not of actual trespass in Cyprus but of a conspiracy in England
H   to effect such trespass.
The statement of claim at paragraph 6 is as follows:

> " Since at least June 1976 (if not earlier) to the date hereof the first
> defendants and the second defendant have conspired together, and
> with others unknown, to effect trespasses to the said hotels [and
> contents], and or have conspired together as aforesaid to obtain
> advantage for themselves by the unauthorised use of the plaintiffs'
> said property."

The words in square brackets do not appear in the statement of claim as A
reproduced, but counsel for the appellants explained that they had been
omitted per incuriam and no objection was raised by counsel for the
respondents to the words being read in.

The first thing that strikes one about that paragraph is that it is concerned only with past events—"Since at least June 1976 . . . to the date
hereof." It contains no averment of a continuing wrong or of a wrong
that is threatened in the future. Unless therefore, it is to be read in a B
sense wider than the words themselves bear, the averments would not
justify an injunction. Further, the effect of the paragraph seems to be
to aver two conspiracies, one between the first and second defendants
and "others unknown" to effect trespasses, and the second between the
defendants to obtain advantage for themselves by unauthorised use of
the plaintiff's property. But the particulars that follow do not fit well C
into that framework. They consist of allegations in paragraphs (i) and
(ii) that the first defendants have had dealings with certain named
persons (but with no mention of the second defendant) and in paragraphs
(iii), (iv) and (v) that the second defendant has counselled and procured
other persons to trespass on the plaintiff's property as well as doing
other, and apparently inoffensive acts (but with no mention of the first
defendants). Finally paragraph 7 of the statement of claim contains a D
bald averment that "By reason of the aforesaid the plaintiffs have and
will suffer damage." But there is nothing to show how such damage
could have been caused or could in future be caused to the plaintiffs in
England apart from actual trespass in Cyprus. In my opinion there is
no proper averment of a conspiracy between the defendants even in the
past, still less in the future, nor (assuming that there is such a conspiracy) E
of how damage has been caused or will be caused by it in England. The
case of conspiracy is simply an attempt to dress up the substantive claim,
which is for trespass, in a different guise and in my opinion the attempt
fails.

Finally there is the claim based on trespass to chattels. The
respondents' original answer to this claim was that it could not succeed F
because the appellants were not in actual possession of the chattels. But
Mr. Neill in his reply conceded that there was some authority that a
right to immediate possession was enough to found a claim for trespass
to chattels and that he therefore could not maintain that the claim
should be struck out now. The same result follows from the appellants'
argument to the effect that they have alleged facts which amount to
conversion of the movables and that they are entitled to maintain a G
claim for conversion although they have not stated the legal inference
from the facts alleged. This argument depends on English rules of
pleading and with regard to it I gratefully adopt the reasoning of my
noble and learned friend, Lord Wilberforce, who is so much more familiar
with these rules than I am. The *Moçambique* decision [1893] A.C. 602
has no application to chattels. Moreover there is direct authority for H
distinguishing within a single action between a claim in respect of trespass
to movables situated abroad (where the jurisdiction of the English courts
depends on ordinary principles) and a claim in respect of trespass to
foreign land (where the English courts have no jurisdiction)—see *Skinner*
v. *East India Co.*, 6 St.Tr. 710, 719 where the judges reported to the
House of Lords as follows:

A   " That the matters touching the taking away of the petitioner's ship
and goods, and assaulting of his person, notwithstanding the same
were done beyond the seas, might be determined upon His Majesty's
ordinary courts at Westminster; and as to the dispossessing him of
his house and island, that he was not relievable in any ordinary court
of law."

B   The decision of the Supreme Court of New Brunswick in *Albert* v. *Fraser
Companies Ltd.* [1937] 1 D.L.R. 39 that they had no jurisdiction in a
claim for damages either to real or *personal* property in another province
was made on special facts in respect that the two branches of the claim
were very closely connected to one another.
      I agree that the appeal should be allowed to the extent proposed by
my noble and learned friend, Lord Wilberforce.
C

      LORD KEITH OF KINKEL. My Lords, I have had the advantage of
reading in draft the speech of my noble and learned friend, Lord
Wilberforce. I agree with it and with the order which he proposes.

Appeal allowed in part.
D

      Solicitors: *Lovell, White & King; Theodore Goddard & Co.*

F. C.

E

[QUEEN'S BENCH DIVISION]

ATTORNEY-GENERAL *v.*

F   LEVELLER MAGAZINE LTD. AND OTHERS

1978 May 2, 3, 4, 5; 19   Lord Widgery C.J., Croom-Johnson and
Stocker JJ.

*Contempt of Court—Proceedings completed—Court's ruling—
Witness's name not to be disclosed during committal proceedings—National security—Validity of ruling—Publication
G   of name after proceedings completed—Whether contempt of
court—Official Secrets Act 1920 (10 & 11 Geo. 5, c. 75), s. 8 (4)*

      During committal proceedings before the justices of
defendants charged with offences under the Official Secrets
Acts, the prosecution sought to call a witness but to suppress his
identity by referring to him as Colonel A on the ground that
if his identity was revealed, it would be injurious to national
H   safety and to Colonel A's personal safety. The justices ruled
that he need not disclose his name to the public, but must
write it down and disclose it to them and to defence counsel.
The prosecution were unwilling that that should be done
and instead of calling Colonel A they called Colonel B, whose
personal safety was not at risk. They asserted, however, that
were his identity revealed the national safety might be at risk,

[Reported by MRS. RACHEL DAVIES, Barrister-at-Law]

and the justices permitted him to write his name down and
show it only to defence counsel and to the court, after which
he gave his evidence.

After the committal proceedings had been completed,
Colonel B's name was deliberately published in a periodical
belonging to one of the respondent publishers. The other
two respondent publishers then also published articles in their
periodicals which revealed his identity.

On an application by the Attorney-General for orders com- **B**
mitting the three publishers and their editors for contempt: —

Held, (1) that the court had power to control its own
proceedings and that power included the known practice to
rule that a witness need not disclose his name in evidence but
might merely write it down and hand the paper to the court;
that the justices having ruled that they would permit Colonel
A's name to be written down and the paper shown to the
Bench and defence counsel and, thereafter, having permitted **C**
Colonel B to write his name down in accordance with the
previous direction, had ruled that Colonel B's name was not
to be disclosed during the committal proceedings (post, p.
401A, F–H).

(2) That the ruling that the witness's name was not be to
disclosed could be made without formal evidence that disclosure would be prejudicial to the national safety and, therefore, the ruling was valid and any disclosure of the witness's **D**
name in court in contravention of that ruling was a contempt
of court; that, although the ruling had no direct effect outside
the court, publication of the name outside the court with
the deliberate intention of frustrating the arrangements made
by the court to preserve the witness's anonymity was a flouting
of the court's authority and in itself a contempt and, accordingly, the respondents had been guilty of contempt of court
(post, p. 402A–E, G). **E**

Attorney-General v. *Butterworth* [1963] 1 Q.B. 696, C.A.
applied.

Held further, that the power to exclude the public on the
ground of national safety " during any part of the hearing "
under section 8 (4) of the Official Secrets Act 1920 meant
exclusion from the court and did not include exclusion of the
public from hearing part of the evidence while present in
court; that, although the justices could have excluded the public **F**
from the court room while the witness stated his name, the
justices had properly not invoked that subsection for the
purposes of preserving the witness's anonymity (post, p. 401C–E).

The following cases are referred to in the judgment of the court:

Attorney-General v. *Butterworth* [1963] 1 Q.B. 696; L.R. 3 R.P. 327;
  [1962] 3 W.L.R. 819; [1962] 3 All E.R. 326, C.A.   **G**

Reg. v. *Lewes Justices, Ex parte Secretary of State for Home Department*
  [1973] A.C. 388; [1972] 3 W.L.R. 279; [1972] 2 All E.R. 1057,
  H.L.(E.).

Reg. v. *Socialist Worker Printers and Publishers Ltd., Ex parte Attorney-
  General* [1975] Q.B. 637; [1974] 3 W.L.R. 801; [1975] 1 All E.R.
  142, D.C.

Rex v. *Governor of Lewes Prison, Ex parte Doyle* [1917] 2 K.B. 254.   **H**

Scott v. *Scott* [1913] A.C. 417, H.L.(E.).

The following additional cases were cited in argument:

Attorney-General v. *Times Newspapers Ltd.* [1974] A.C. 273; [1973]
  3 W.L.R. 298; [1973] 3 All E.R. 54, H.L.(E.).

Chandler v. *Director of Public Prosecutions* [1964] A.C. 763; [1962] 3
  W.L.R. 694; [1962] 3 All E.R. 142, H.L.(E.).

A   *Kores Manufacturing Co. Ltd.'s Application, In re* [1958] R.P.C. 448.
     Morris v. *Crown Office* [1970] 2 Q.B. 114; [1970] 2 W.L.R. 792; [1970]
       1 All E.R. 1079, C.A.
     Reg. v. *Bhagwan* [1970] 2 W.L.R. 837; [1970] 1 All E.R. 1129, C.A.;
       [1972] A.C. 60; [1970] 3 W.L.R. 501; [1970] 3 All E.R. 97, H.L.(E.).
     Reg. v. *Border Television Ltd., Ex parte Attorney-General*, The Times,
       January 18, 1978, D.C.
B   *Reg.* v. *Knuller (Publishing, Printing and Promotions) Ltd.* [1973] A.C.
       435; [1972] 3 W.L.R. 143; [1972] 2 All E.R. 898, H.L.(E.).
     Reg. v. *Waterfield* [1975] 1 W.L.R. 711; [1975] 2 All E.R. 40, C.A.

APPLICATION

The Attorney-General applied under R.S.C., Ord. 52 for an order to
C commit for contempt Leveller Magazine Ltd., publishers of the
periodical " The Leveller," Peace News Ltd., publishers of the periodical
" Peace News," and the National Union of Journalists, publishers of the
periodical the " Journalist "; and against David Anthony Clark, Russell
David Southwood, David Nigel Mitchell Thomas, Philip John Kelly,
and Timothy Reginald Gopsill, editors of " The Leveller," and Alison de
Reybekill, Helen Linton, Christopher Jones, Michael Holderness and
D Albert Beale, editors of " Peace News," on the ground that they com-
mitted a contempt of court in publishing the name of a witness to whom
permission to conceal his identity was given by Tottenham Magistrates'
Court in committal proceedings before them under the Official Secrets
Acts in November 1977.

The facts are stated in the judgment.

E

Harry Woolf and *Rodger Bell* for the Attorney-General.
Stephen Sedley for Leveller Magazine Ltd.
Nicholas Blake for Peace News Ltd.
Lord Gifford for Alison de Reybekill, Helen Linton and Christopher
Jones.
John Melville Williams Q.C. and *John Hendy* for the National Union
F of Journalists.

The respondents, David Anthony Clark, Russell David Southwood,
David Nigel Mitchell Thomas, Philip John Kelly, Timothy Reginald
Gopsill, Michael Holderness and Albert Beale, in person.

Cur. adv. vult.

G

May 19. LORD WIDGERY C.J. The judgment which I am about to
read is the judgment of the court in which each member has had a hand.

This matter comes before the court in the form of an application
by Her Majesty's Attorney-General under Order 52 of the Rules of the
Supreme Court to commit for contempt two limited companies, who
are the publishers respectively of the " Peace News " and " The Leveller."
H Similar application is made against the National Union of Journalists, as
publishers of a periodical known as the " Journalist," and against a
number of individuals associated with these three publications.

The case presented on behalf of the Attorney-General is as follows.
Three young men called respectively Aubrey, Berry and Campbell were
committed for trial at the Central Criminal Court for alleged offences
under the Official Secrets Acts. The committal proceedings took place
at Tottenham Magistrates' Court in November 1977. It is important

that we should reconstruct certain aspects of these proceedings as best A
we can on the material available.

Counsel prosecuting for the Director of Public Prosecutions before
the justices opened the case. The first material evidence which he sought
to put before the court was a tape recording of a conversation between the
three accused. He applied for the play-back of this recording to be in
camera, relying on section 8 (4) of the Official Secrets Act 1920, which
provides: B

" In addition and without prejudice to any powers which a court may
possess to order the exclusion of the public from any proceedings
if, in the course of proceedings before a court against any person
for an offence under the principal Act or this Act or the proceedings
on appeal, or in the course of the trial of a person for felony or
misdemeanour under the principal Act or this Act, application is   C
made by the prosecution, on the ground that the publication of any
evidence to be given or of any statement to be made in the course
of the proceedings would be prejudicial to the national safety, that
all or any portion of the public shall be excluded during any part of
the hearing, the court may make an order to that effect, but the
passing of sentence shall in any case take place in public."   D

In support of his application that the tapes should be heard in camera,
counsel made reference to a transcript of the tapes to illustrate the nature
of the material which they contained. The application was opposed, but
was granted by the Bench and the tapes were heard in camera. We
know nothing about the contents of the tapes, save that one witness said
that the playing of them had taken " several hours," so, if that is right, E
they must have been substantial.

After the playing of the tapes, the Crown sought to call an expert
witness to comment upon the tapes and to explain their relevance from
the standpoint of security. No direct application seems to have been
made to hear the evidence of the witness in camera, but the Crown made
it clear that, if the evidence was to be given in open court, the identity of
the witness should be suppressed and that he should be referred to simply F
as " Colonel A." The justices were advised that the identity of Colonel
A must be disclosed to the court and defence counsel, though his name
might be written down. The justices announced this ruling. The
prosecution were unwilling that this should be done, as they regarded a
possible disclosure of Colonel A's identity as injurious to national safety
and dangerous to Colonel A in person. At the next hearing a Colonel B G
was called instead of Colonel A. Colonel B's position is said to differ
from that of Colonel A, in that his personal security does not seem to
have been at risk. Colonel B simply wrote his name on a piece of paper,
which was shown to counsel and to the court, and then gave his evidence
without more ado.

Most of the reconstruction of the proceedings at Tottenham comes
from the evidence of Miss Anne Butler and Mr. Albert Harold Beale, the H
essential parts of which were as follows: first of all Miss Butler said in her
affidavit:

" 1. I am a senior legal assistant in the office of the Director of Public
Prosecutions and on his behalf I was present at the committal proceedings of John Berry, Crispin Aubrey and Duncan Campbell at
Tottenham Magistrates' Court in respect of the charges set out on
the schedule annexed hereto marked ' A.B. 1.' . . .

A   " 3. On November 10, 1977, Mr. Michael Coombe, counsel for the
Crown, made an application to the magistrates that the next witness
should be referred to as ' Colonel A ' and that his name should not
be disclosed for his security and for the reason of national safety.
       " 4. Each of the counsel appearing for the defendants objected
to this course and counsel for Mr. Campbell said that if the justices
were minded to allow the Crown's application he would ask for
B   Colonel A's name to be written down and shown to defence counsel
and the court and the defendants.
       " 5. The justices retired to consider the application.   On their
return the chairman announced the ruling of the justices which was
that Colonel A's name would have to be written down and shown
to the court, the defence counsel and the defendants.   The chairman
C   said that he would have preferred the name not to be made available
to the defendants but he was advised that this was not a practicable
proposition.
       " 6. The Crown did not call ' Colonel A ' and the hearing was
adjourned.
       " 7. On November 14, 1977, in accordance with the ruling which
D   they had given, the justices allowed the Crown to call ' Colonel B '
and for ' Colonel B's ' name to be written on a piece of paper and
shown to the court, the defence counsel and the defendants.   The
reason for the court allowing Colonel B not to disclose his identity
was that the Crown contended that this would not be in the interests
of national security."

E   Paragraphs 5, 6 and 7 that I have read are accepted as correct by Mr.
Pratt, clerk to the justices, in his affidavit.   Turning to Mr. Beale's
affidavit, he says:

       " 3. On the first day, counsel for the prosecution applied for a part
of the proceedings, namely the hearing of the tape recording, to be
in camera.   After objections by counsel for the defence, the court
made an order for the public to be excluded.   I am informed and
F   verily believe that the court resumed the public hearings on the
second day after several hours of in camera hearings.
       " 4. On November 10, 1977, before any witness was called counsel
for Crispin Aubrey stated that he understood that the Crown wished
the identity of the next witness (described as Lieutenant-Colonel A)
to remain wholly secret and not to be disclosed even to the court and
G   the defence.   Mr. Coombe, counsel for the prosecution, confirmed
that he would be so applying.   Defence counsel then made various
objections as to the lawfulness of such a procedure.
       " 5. The ruling of the court was that the name of the witness
would have to be written down and shown to the court and to the
defence.   The chairman added that the court would have preferred
H   the name not to have been disclosed to the defendants but was advised
that this was not a practicable proposition.
       " 6. On November 14, 1977, Colonel B entered the witness box.
He said that he wished to be known for the purposes of this case as
Colonel B.   He was asked by Mr. Coombe to write his name on a
piece of paper and did so.   The paper was passed to the court and the
defence lawyers.   No objection was raised by the defence counsel.
No ruling was made by the court.   Colonel B proceeded to give his

A.-G. v. Leveller Magazine Ltd. (D.C.)   [1978]

evidence, which was in the nature of expert evidence on the alleged   A
damage to national security of certain disclosures made privately
by John Berry."

The committal proceedings finished on or about November 18.   On
December 15, 1977, " The Leveller " published an article which disclosed
the identity of Colonel B.   It is said that the discovery of Colonel B's
identity was achieved by a study of his evidence and other material   B
available to the public.   Be that as it may, the article in " The Leveller "
was the first of a number of publications which Mr. Woolf described as a
campaign to disclose the colonel's identity in the widest possible basis and
to do so as a protest against the Official Secrets Acts 1911–1939, the
particular proceedings against Aubrey, Berry and Campbell, or public
secrecy generally.   It is important to realise that these publications were
a protest (even if somewhat ill-defined) against public secrecy.   All the   C
respondents knew that the writing down of Colonel B's name was intended
to preserve his anonymity.   The respondents formed their own judgment
as to the alleged risk to public security and decided that the grounds for
Colonel B's anonymity were spurious.   They then quite deliberately set
out to frustrate the efforts which had been made at Tottenham to preserve
that anonymity.   Was this, as the Attorney-General contends, a con-   D
tempt of court?

Contempt of court can take many different forms and one is a
deliberate flouting of the court's authority: see *Attorney-General* v.
Butterworth [1963] 1 Q.B. 696.   The history of the matter (that is this
matter), as recited so far, undoubtedly raises a prima facie contempt.
The court had taken steps to preserve the anonymity of the witness and
the respondents quite deliberately set out to frustrate that intention.   E
This, however, is not an end of the matter, because it is open to the
respondents to defeat the prima facie case if they can.   The number of
respondents makes it difficult to consider in this judgment all their contentions in detail, but we will endeavour to deal with the main lines of
argument.

Central to all the respondents' arguments was the contention that this   F
type of contempt requires a direction or mandatory order of a court
and breach of that order, whereas here it is said that there was no order
against disclosure, but merely a request.

This contention seems to have been founded on the fact that in *Reg.* v.
Socialist Worker Printers and Publishers Ltd., *Ex parte Attorney-General*
[1975] Q.B. 637 the trial judge did in fact purport to give a direction
that the names of the witnesses should not be given but that   G
they should be referred to in court by letters.   Consequently,
when that case came before this court, the facts were discussed
on the basis that there might be on the one hand a direction by the court
concealing the identity of the witness and on the other a mere request
that a name actually used in court should not be published outside it.

In the present case there has been a dispute about one matter of   H
fact.   Miss Butler said in her affidavit that at the conclusion of the proceedings on November 14, 1977, the chairman of the justices reminded
the court of his earlier ruling and stressed that no attempt should be made
to disclose the identity of Colonel B.   Mr. Pratt, who was the clerk to
the justices, in his affidavit contradicted that particular paragraph of
Miss Butler's affidavit.   In view of that conflict of evidence, counsel for
the Attorney-General has not sought to rely on any disregard of such a

A statement, but relies on the earlier ruling in conformity with which it is said Colonel B gave his evidence. Indeed, if the chairman of the justices did say what Miss Butler says he said, its direct authority would only have gone to those within the court. The relevant ruling for present purposes was when the court gave permission for Colonel B to write down his name, in accordance with the same decision it had made for Colonel A. It is the authority of that ruling which is for consideration. If it was an B effective ruling, a later so-called " direction " would have added nothing to it, and consequently can be ignored.

The grounds filed on behalf of the Attorney-General, though regrettably leaving much to be desired, are sufficient to found the complaint which he makes. At one stage, counsel appearing for him applied for leave to amend his grounds of application, but leave was refused.

C It is within the knowledge of all of us that the device of allowing a witness to write his name down is widely used. Counsel for the Attorney-General suggested that in the present case this would be making use of section 8 (4) of the Official Secrets Act 1920 which I have already read. His argument was that the words in that subsection " all or any portion of the public shall be excluded during any part of the hearing " covered the situation where the public is " excluded " from hearing a part of the D evidence. He described it as an exclusion pro tanto. We do not think the section is apt to describe that situation. The public is indeed " prevented " from hearing a part of the evidence. But " excluded " means excluded from the court.

On the other hand, if the evidence, in whole or in part, of the witness in question could properly be heard in camera, we see no difficulty in E allowing him to write down his name. This is far less restrictive of the public's rights than a hearing in camera would be. The justices could have sat in camera to hear Colonel B identified, or to hear the whole of his evidence. They could have done that either by virtue of section 8 (4) of the Act of 1920 or the very wide terms of section 6 of the Criminal Justice Act 1967, or, indeed, at common law: see *Rex* v. *Governor of Lewes Prison, Ex parte Doyle* [1917] 2 K.B. 254, which must surely have F provided thus for disclosure likely to be against the national safety. In those circumstances, the suppression of Colonel B's identity would not offend the principle of *Scott* v. *Scott* [1913] A.C. 417. The device of writing down a witness's name is a convenient way of achieving a result which otherwise would only be achieved by the court going into camera.

What is the power to do this? This question has been much debated. G Every court has the power to control its own proceedings, subject to the rules of evidence and general practice. An instance is the power to order witnesses out of court. Disobedience of rulings of that nature may or may not be contempt: it is at any rate capable of being contempt. They are matters on which the court gives a ruling or a decision. The court may add something which can be called a formal direction, but no such formality is required. All such rulings are given, and only purported H to be given, to those in court and not outside it.

A flouting in court of the court's ruling will be a contempt. Equally, a flouting or deliberate disregard outside the court will be a contempt if it frustrates the court's ruling. On this aspect of the case, however, there remain the following questions. (a) Did the justices make a mandatory order or was this a mere request to the press not to publish? Much confusion arose in argument on this question. The question was whether the justices' ruling was intended to be mandatory within the court or

not. We think it clear, beyond argument, that the deliberate disclosure **A**
of Colonel B's identity in court would have been an actionable breach
of the justices' instruction. If a request not to publish had been intended,
the Colonel's identity would have been disclosed, since, in the absence
of disclosure, there would have been no basis for a request not to publish.
The fact that the justices' ruling had no direct effect outside the court
does not prevent the publications here in question from being a contempt
if they were made with the deliberate intention of frustrating the arrange-   **B**
ment which the court had made to preserve Colonel B's anonymity. It
is this element of flouting the court which is the real basis of the contempt
here alleged. It can be sustained without proof that something like a
direction or a specific order of the court has been breached. (*b*) To
what extent does a decision to hear a matter in camera depend upon
evidence?—a matter pursued in detail by Mr. Sedley. It is contended   **C**
that, no matter on what ground the suppression of the Colonel's identity is
justified, there will be a condition of fact which must be satisfied by
evidence before a departure from the rule in *Scott* v. *Scott* [1913] A.C.
417 can be justified. Thus, it is argued that if reliance is placed on
section 8 (4) of the Official Secrets Act 1920, the Crown must provide
sworn evidence that disclosure would "be prejudicial to the national
safety." We cannot accept this. Courts should of course always be alert   **D**
to the importance of keeping proceedings before the public and should
examine with care the argument in favour of secrecy, but it will often
happen that something less than formal proof is all that is available. For
example, it is now established that the court may suppress the identity of
blackmail victims (see the *Socialist Worker* case [1975] Q.B. 637) but
no evidence is appropriate to support such an application. In this type of   **E**
situation, where the public interest is involved, the magistrate must do his
best with what he has and there is authority in the House of Lords to
support this: see *Reg.* v. *Lewes Justices, Ex parte Secretary of State for
Home Department* [1973] A.C. 388, 404–407.

Equally, where a court gives a ruling of a different kind, such as ordering witnesses out of court, it would not be possible to hear evidence on
the likelihood that one of them might trim his evidence if he remained.   **F**

When the time came for Colonel B to give his evidence, the justices
must have had an extensive knowledge of the case and did not require
further formal evidence.

Reference should be made to a further argument, supported primarily
by Mr. Melville Williams, to the effect that the respondents could not
be guilty of contempt, unless it could be shown that the disclosure of   **G**
Colonel B's identity in some way interfered with the course of justice. We
do not find it possible to accept that argument. The contempt here relied
upon is the deliberate flouting of the court's intention. The public has
an interest in having the courts protected from such treatment and that
is the public interest on which the Attorney-General relies.

It should be said that this court seeks to follow the authority of its   **H**
own decision in the *Socialist Worker* case [1975] Q.B. 637. In the course
of argument, grave warnings were given by counsel as to the consequences
of a further extension of the principles adopted in that case. We do not
think that that case, or the present, has done more than provide a ruling
in certain aspects of the law which were previously unexplored.

Whatever the motives of the respondents have been, they appear to
have lost sight of the fact that in pursuing their course of action they

A were flouting a decision of the court—not simply disagreeing with a decision of the Security Service, or campaigning for a reform of the Official Secrets Acts 1911–1939. It is simply for the first of those matters that they are now before this court, and for the reasons given we find that the contempt has been established.

B Counsel addressed the court on penalty.

LORD WIDGERY C.J.   There are a lot of points which touch the question of penalty in this case, but we cannot hope to deal precisely with what is in any event a rather vague field.

We are not going to make any orders against individual respondents for reasons which were disclosed sufficiently in argument this morning.   In
C particular, in the case of " The Leveller," the selection of the individual respondents is a purely random selection, and we see no justice in making a financial penalty on that basis.

Furthermore, we do not propose to make any award of costs against any of the respondents.   I expect they realise therein lies a fairly substantial financial concession.   If we had thought it right to make an order for costs, it would have increased the overall sum to be found to a
D substantial degree.

We must also bear in mind the fact that, whereas the National Union of Journalists have expressed an apology and indicated that they would not be likely to do this again, the other respondents have not, for reasons which I have heard, reached the view that an apology should be given, and have not in any way disabused us of the idea that they might do
E exactly the same all over again.

Bearing those matters in mind, and doing the best we can, we shall impose on the National Union of Journalists the smaller amount for reasons I have already given of £200 by way of fine.   In regard to the other two publications—" The Leveller " and " Peace News "—each will be subjected to £500 by way of fine.

F   *Order accordingly.*

Solicitors: *Director of Public Prosecutions; Seifert, Sedley & Co.; Fisher Meredith; Vizards.*

G July 6, 1978.   The Appeal Committee of the House of Lords (Lord Diplock, Lord Salmon and Lord Russell of Killowen) granted a petition by the respondents for leave to appeal.

H

[1978]

A

[COURT OF APPEAL]

REGINA v. LEMON

REGINA v. GAY NEWS LTD.

1978 Feb. 13, 14, 16;   Roskill and Eveleigh L.JJ. and   B
March 17   Stocker J.

*Crime—Blasphemous libel—Mens rea—Publication of homosexual
poem concerning body of Christ after crucifixion—Subjective
intent to attack Christianity—Whether essential element of
offence*

The defendants, who as the editor and publishers of a news-   C
paper for homosexuals published, with an illustration, a poem
describing acts of fellatio and sodomy committed on Christ's
body immediately after his death, were charged with publishing a blasphemous libel. The trial judge directed the jury that
in order to establish blasphemous libel it was unnecessary for
the prosecution to prove an intent to attack the Christian
religion. The defendants were convicted.

On appeal by both defendants against conviction:—   D

Held, dismissing the appeals, (1) that blasphemous libel was
the publication of any matter that insulted, offended or vilified
the Deity or Christ or the Christian religion; that it was the
publication of an offensive nature, or in offensive terms, to the
Christian religion that constituted the offence and, therefore, it
followed that a moderate and reasoned reference, even though
critical, to the Christian religion was not such an offence (post,
pp. 413c–e, 416h—417a, b–f).   E

Reg. v. *Ramsay and Foote* (1883) 15 Cox C.C. 231 and *Bowman* v. *Secular Society Ltd.* [1917] A.C. 406, H.L.(E.) applied.

(2) That provided there was an intention to publish the
material the absence of an intention to be blasphemous was
irrelevant; that it was for the jury to decide whether the
article offended the contemporary opinion of society in its
reference to Christianity and, accordingly, the judge had
properly directed the jury on the nature of the offence (post,   F
pp. 410b–c, 420a–e).

Dictum of Lord Denman C.J. in *Reg.* v. *Hetherington*
(1841) 4 St.Tr.N.S. 563, 593, applied.

The following cases are referred to in the judgment of the court:

Bowman, In re [1915] 2 Ch. 447, C.A.
Bowman v. *Secular Society Ltd.* [1917] A.C. 406, H.L.(E.).   G
Reg. v. *Anderson* [1972] 1 Q.B. 304; [1971] 3 W.L.R. 939; [1971] 3 All
E.R. 1152, C.A.
Reg. v. *Bradlaugh* (1883) 15 Cox C.C. 217.
Reg. v. *Hetherington* (1841) 4 St.Tr.N.S. 563.
Reg. v. *Holbrook* (1878) 4 Q.B.D. 42.
Reg. v. *Knuller (Publishing, Printing and Promotions) Ltd.* [1973] A.C.
435; [1972] 3 W.L.R. 143; [1972] 2 All E.R. 898, H.L.(E.).
Reg. v. *Morgan* [1976] A.C. 182; [1975] 2 W.L.R. 913; [1975] 2 All   H
E.R. 347, H.L.(E.).
Reg. v. *Moxon* (1841) 4 St.Tr.N.S. 693.
Reg. v. *Ramsay and Foote* (1883) 15 Cox C.C. 231.
Rex v. *Boulter* (1908) 72 J.P. 188.
Rex v. *Carlile (Mary)* (1821) 1 St.Tr.N.S. 1033.

[Reported by MRS. RACHEL DAVIES, Barrister-at-Law]

A   *Rex* v. *Carlile (Richard)* (1819) 1 St.Tr.N.S. 1387.
     Rex v. *Gott* (1922) 16 Cr.App.R. 87, C.C.A.
     Rex v. *Morris* [1951] 1 K.B. 394; [1950] 2 All E.R. 965, C.C.A.
     Rex v. *Taylor* (1676) 1 Vent. 293.
     Rex v. *Williams* (1797) 26 St.Tr. 653.
     Shaw v. *Director of Public Prosecutions* [1962] A.C. 220; [1961] 2
          W.L.R. 897; [1961] 2 All E.R. 446, H.L.(E.).
B   *Shore* v. *Wilson* (1842) 4 St.Tr.N.S.App. 1370, H.L.(E.).
     Sweet v. *Parsley* [1970] A.C. 132; [1969] 2 W.L.R. 470; [1969] 1 All
          E.R. 347, H.L.(E.).

     The following additional cases were cited in argument:

     North Cheshire and Manchester Brewery Co. Ltd. v. *Manchester Brewery
          Co. Ltd.* [1899] A.C. 83, H.L.(E.).
C   *Reg.* v. *Burns* (1886) 16 Cox C.C. 355.
     Reg. v. *Rowell* [1978] 1 W.L.R. 132; [1978] 1 All E.R. 665, C.A.
     Rex v. *Waddington* (1822) 1 St.Tr.N.S. 1339.
     Rex v. *Wicks* (1936) 25 Cr.App.R. 168; [1936] 1 All E.R. 384, C.C.A.

     APPEALS against conviction.
     A private prosecution was instituted by Mrs. Mary Whitehouse against
D   the defendants, Denis Lemon, editor of " Gay News," and Gay News
     Ltd., its publishers, for a blasphemous libel in issue no. 96 of that news-
     paper. The particulars of the offence alleged that they " unlawfully and
     wickedly published or caused to be published . . . a blasphemous libel
     concerning the Christian religion, namely, an obscene poem and illus-
     tration vilifying Christ in his life and in his crucifixion." The defendants
     were convicted of the offence on July 11, 1977, at the Central Criminal
E   Court before Judge Alan King-Hamilton and a jury. The editor was
     sentenced to nine months' imprisonment suspended for 18 months and
     fined £500. The publishers were fined £1,000.
     The defendants appealed against conviction on the grounds, inter alia,
     that the trial judge was wrong in law in directing the jury that an intent
     to blaspheme was not a necessary element in the offence of blasphemous
F   libel; and that an attack on Christ or the Christian religion was not a
     necessary element in the offence of blasphemy.
     The facts are stated in the judgment.

     John Mortimer Q.C. and *Geoffrey Robertson* for the editor.
     Geoffrey Robertson for the publishers.
G   *John Smyth* and *Jeremy Maurice* for the Crown.

                                        Cur. adv. vult.

     March 17. ROSKILL L.J. read the following judgment of the court.
     The defendants, Gay News Ltd., are the publishers of a newspaper for
     homosexuals entitled " Gay News." The defendant Mr. Denis Lemon
     is editor of that paper. The defendants were respectively publishers and
H   editor of that paper when issue no. 96 was published early in June 1976.
     Page 26 of that issue contained a poem by Professor James Kirkup en-
     titled " The Love that Dares to Speak its Name." Printed alongside that
     poem and parallel with the entirety of its text was a drawing. We do not
     propose in this judgment either to read the poem or to describe the draw-
     ing beyond saying that the poem purports to describe in explicit detail acts
     of sodomy and fellatio with the body of Christ immediately after the
     moment of his death.

As a result of that publication criminal proceedings were sought to   A
be begun against the defendants for blasphemous libel. By virtue of
section 8 of the Law of Libel Amendment Act 1888, the leave of a judge
of the High Court to prefer a voluntary bill of indictment was required
for such a prosecution. Such leave was sought and obtained from Bristow J. As a result the defendants were duly indicted for the offence of
blasphemous libel. It is of some importance to note that there was no
second count in the indictment charging an offence against the Obscene   B
Publications Act 1959. The particulars of the offence charged in the
indictment which that judge gave leave to prefer alleged that the defendants
". . . unlawfully and wickedly published or caused to be published in a
newspaper called ' Gay News ' No. 96 a blasphemous libel concerning
the Christian religion, namely an obscene poem and illustration vilifying
Christ in his life and in his crucifixion." We draw attention at this junc-   C
ture to the successive references to " the Christian religion," " an obscene
poem and illustration " and " vilifying Christ in his life and in his crucifixion," and to the absence in the indictment of any reference to intent
on the part of either of the defendants.

After a trial at the Central Criminal Court before Judge King-Hamilton
and a jury, which began on July 4, 1977, and ended on July 12, 1977,
the jury on July 11, 1977, convicted the defendants of blasphemous libel   D
by a majority verdict of ten to two. On July 12, 1977, the judge imposed
on the defendant editor Mr. Lemon a sentence of nine months' imprisonment suspended for 18 months, a fine of £500 and an order to pay one-
fifth of the prosecution's taxed costs, and either his own legal aid costs
or £434, whichever was the less, and on the publishers a fine of £1,000
and an order to pay four-fifths of the prosecution's costs.   E

The defendants appeal against their respective convictions. They are
entitled to do so as of right since these appeals raise questions of law.
They also seek leave to appeal against the sentence imposed by the judge.
At the conclusion of the argument of the appeals against conviction Mr.
Mortimer, who appeared for Mr. Lemon in this court as he had at the
trial, asked this court to hear the applications for leave to appeal against
sentence there and then and irrespective of the result of the appeals   F
against conviction. But after discussion with his client he withdrew this
request. If, therefore, these appeals fail, those applications remain to be
heard.

Save in one respect the arguments for the defendants are identical. In
the court below Mr. Geoffrey Robertson appeared for the publishers. In
this court he appeared with Mr. Mortimer for Mr. Lemon but alone for   G
the publishers. In that capacity he adopted but also added to Mr.
Mortimer's submissions on behalf of Mr. Lemon. Save, therefore, in
that one respect which raises a separate question under section 7 of the
Libel Act 1843 (Lord Campbell's Act), and which, if the argument be
well founded, would afford Mr. Lemon an extra defence not open to the
publishers, it is not necessary for us to consider the cases of the defendants   H
separately.

Mr. Lemon originally advanced a large number of grounds of appeal
and the publishers adopted those grounds in their notice of appeal. In
opening the appeal on behalf of Mr. Lemon, Mr. Mortimer reduced those
grounds to nine. Ultimately, however, without resiling from the last six
of those grounds he very properly accepted that in reality the result of
the appeals turned upon the view which this court took of the first three

A of the grounds and more especially of the first two, the third being perhaps little more than a gloss upon those two.

Before the judge it was strenuously argued that blasphemy or blasphemous libel no longer existed as a common law offence. The judge rejected that submission. This contention was not further pursued in this court, though it was (logically enough) the first of the original grounds advanced. Since it was accepted before us that this common law offence

B still existed, it is unnecessary to mention this point further beyond observing that the relevant provisions of the Criminal Law Act 1967 obviously made this submission difficult for the defendants to sustain.

The original grounds of appeal also complained of the judge's refusal to allow either the prosecution or the defence to call expert theological evidence. Before us no complaint was made of this ruling and we say

C no more about it.

Before we turn to the critical questions which we have to determine on this appeal, there are a number of matters which require mention. First, it would be idle to affect ignorance that this court is aware that this prosecution and these convictions have, to borrow the words used by Lord Widgery C.J. in giving the judgment of this court in *Reg.* v. *Anderson* [1972] 1 Q.B. 304, 309, commonly called " the ' Oz ' case," ". . .

D aroused enormous interest among the public and no doubt the decision of the court today will also excite a certain amount of interest and comment." Later on the same page Lord Widgery C.J. used words which, mutatis mutandis, are of direct application to the present appeal. We quote his words with the necessary adaptation:

" The function of this court is also worth explaining. It is not here

E to consider whether the jury was right or wrong, nor to consider whether the publication was [a blasphemous libel] or not [a blasphemous libel]—that is a decision for the jury and the jury only. The function of this court is to review the proceedings below with the assistance of counsel to see if the proceedings were properly conducted and, if not, to see whether any irregularities which arose in the course of the proceedings were sufficient to render the finding

F of the jury unsafe or unsatisfactory. I stress that because it is important for people to realise that we in this court are not here to clear [Mr. Lemon and ' Gay News '] or to condemn [Mr. Lemon and ' Gay News ']. Our own opinion in regard to the character of the subject matter is totally unimportant. We are here simply to review what happened below and see whether there were such irregularities

G as to justify the convictions being quashed. If we come to the conclusion that there were such irregularities, then we quash the convictions and since there is no machinery in English law for re-trial in such circumstances, the matter rests in that somewhat inconclusive state."

Of course, if there were no such irregularities, the appeals must fail.

H Secondly, we draw attention to the fact that the jury received a full, clear and correct direction from the judge as to the relevant meanings of " obscene " and " vilify." It has not been suggested in argument before us that those directions were in any way open to criticism. The relevant criticisms were against other parts of the summing up. We shall return to those passages and others and the criticisms made of them in more detail hereafter.

The point that we are presently concerned to emphasise is that by

their verdicts under the direction which the judge gave to the jury, the A
jury must be taken to have found that this poem accompanied by this
drawing was " obscene " in the ordinary meaning of that word and
" vilified Christ in his life and crucifixion." If the jury had not reached
that conclusion they could not under the judge's direction as to the ingredients of the offence of blasphemous libel have convicted the defendants
of that offence. If the judge were correct in his direction as to that
meaning, the convictions must of course stand. But if he were wrong, B
then any resulting quashing of the convictions can only be on the basis
that more than proof of " obscenity " and more than proof of " vilification
of Christ in his life and crucifixion " is required to be proved by the
prosecution in this case before a conviction for blasphemous libel can
be obtained. Such quashing would not in any way involve overturning
the conclusions implicit in the jury's verdict of guilty that the allegedly C
offending poem and drawing was obscene in the ordinary meaning of
that word, or that it " vilified Christ in his life and crucifixion " in the
ordinary meaning of that phrase.

Thirdly, we have already mentioned that there was in the indictment
no second count alleging an offence against the Obscene Publications Act
1959. Mr. Mortimer frankly admitted before us that had there been such
a count, the defendants might, subject of course to any defence under D
that statute, have been convicted of an offence against that Act, an admission perhaps easier to make in this court than at the trial. Indeed Mr.
Mortimer went further and strenuously argued that since the prosecution
had included the word " obscene " in the particulars of the offence charged,
a charge under that statute and not under the common law of blasphemy
or blasphemous libel was the proper course to be followed by those seek- E
ing to secure criminal convictions arising from the publication of issue no.
96 of " Gay News."

We asked Mr. Smyth for the Crown why no such second count had
been added, especially in the light of the addition of the word " obscene "
in the particulars, since obscenity, it was common ground, is not an essential ingredient in the common law offence of blasphemy or of blasphemous
libel. Mr. Smyth replied, with commendable frankness, that he regretted F
that that word had been included in the particulars. He sought to justify
the omission of a second count on the ground that the essence of the
publication complained of was blasphemous libel and not obscenity. But
that answer, of course, simply raises in another form what has to be
proved before a conviction for blasphemy or blasphemous libel can be
secured. G

Fourthly, as was logical in the light of his abandonment of the contention that there was no longer any extant offence of blasphemy or of
blasphemous libel at common law, Mr. Mortimer conceded that had the
defendants been convicted of publishing a blasphemous libel after what
he contended would have been a proper direction to the jury, they could
not have complained in this court of their convictions. H

We have thought it right to emphasise these matters for two reasons.
First, this court is in no way concerned with whether there should in
1978 be an offence of blasphemy or of blasphemous libel. Our attention
was drawn by Mr. Mortimer to an opinion of Sir John Simon, when
Attorney-General, written for the Home Office in 1914. This opinion is
reproduced by Mr. Blom-Cooper in his recent book on Law and Morality,
at page 252. The then Attorney-General made certain suggestions for

A   amending the law of blasphemy but no successful legislative action was taken then or has been taken since in that regard. We must, therefore, accept that there is such an offence and it is our duty to apply the law accordingly as we conceive it to be. Secondly, if these convictions were quashed, it could only be because we had been persuaded by Mr. Mortimer and Mr. Robertson that the judge had misdirected the jury. That would not be in any way a matter for criticism but for sympathy, for he was

B   faced under the pressure of an emotive trial with the need for giving a series of immediate or almost immediate rulings on difficult matters of law not previously raised in criminal proceedings for half a century and not fully debated for some 60 years or more, and then only in a very different context in the House of Lords. He did not have, as we have had, the opportunity of hearing four days of sustained and learned argu-

C   ment and of considering those arguments for some considerable while thereafter. Nor did he have, as we have had, the advantage of a full report of the proceedings in *Rex* v. *Gott* (1922) 16 Cr.App.Rep. 87, either at the trial before Avory J. and a jury at the Central Criminal Court in December 1921, or on the hearing of the appeal before the Court of Criminal Appeal in January 1922. We take this opportunity of expressing our gratitude to Mr. Walter of the Rationalist Press Association, who

D   produced those reports from the contemporary files of " The Freethinker." This has enabled us to see, as the judge did not and could not see, the full terms of the direction given by Avory J. to the jury in that case and of the judgment given by Lord Trevethin C.J. in the Court of Criminal Appeal.

    In his opening submissions to us Mr. Mortimer summarised his two

E   principal arguments thus. First, the judge had ruled and then directed the jury that for the defendants to be guilty of publishing a blasphemous libel it was not necessary for the Crown to prove an intent on their part to attack the Christian religion. Mr. Mortimer submitted that proof was required of such a subjective intention on their part. The relevant issue is—as Eveleigh L.J. put it during the argument—must the defendants have had an intention to offend in the manner complained of, or is it enough

F   that he or they intended to publish that which offends? Mr. Mortimer in reply put the same point neatly when he said " When the various cases speak of intent are they speaking of an intent to offend or of an intent to do that which in the eyes of the jury is offensive?"

    Secondly, he complained that the judge had ruled and then directed the jury that the allegedly offending publication could be a blasphemous

G   libel even though it did not attack the Christian religion. Mr. Mortimer complained that the judge had wrongly directed the jury in terms which meant that any writing which spoke ill of Christianity in a manner which offended or caused resentment to ordinary Christians could be blasphemous. He further contended that while accepting that the jury must be taken to have found that this publication vilified Christ in his life and

H   in his crucifixion, that was not enough unless the publication were also an attack upon the Christian religion.

    These submissions were in the first instance advanced as separate arguments. But the more the arguments for the defendants and the Crown proceeded and the more the relevant authorities were cited to us, the more it appeared to us that the two submissions to a considerable extent elided and we did not understand Mr. Mortimer ultimately to disagree with that view. Certainly many of the authorities are relevant

410

to both issues and to a considerable extent can be considered together,   A
and we propose to do so, so far as possible.

As already stated, the judge accepted the relevant submissions for the
prosecution and rejected those advanced for the defence. His directions
to the jury naturally followed his earlier rulings and were very clearly
given on pp. 3, 7, 8, 9, 11A and 16 of volume 5 of the transcript.

Of course one result of the judge's ruling on the first point was, as
he himself very fairly recognised in the summing up, that no evidence   B
from Mr. Lemon or from Professor Kirkup as to their respective intentions in publishing the poem and the drawing, or in writing the poem—
there was no evidence that Professor Kirkup was himself responsible for
the drawing—would have been relevant and therefore admissible. The
relevant question on that issue was in the judge's view not what either
intended, but what was the objective opinion of the jury derived from   C
looking at the matter complained of in the light of the arguments placed
before them by counsel and of the judge's direction to them on the law
as he held it to be.

There was a further point which may conveniently be mentioned here
and which was argued more fully below than in this court; indeed it was
barely argued in this court. The point was that it was an essential ingredient of the crime of blasphemy or of blasphemous libel that there should   D
have been a subjective intention on the part of the accused persons to
provoke a breach of the peace. This submission was rejected by the
judge—in our view quite rightly—for the reasons which he gave on pp. 2
and 3 of vol. 4. His resulting direction to the jury on this point seems
to us quite faultless. This submission on behalf of the defendants is
contrary to all authority and, as already stated, was not seriously pressed   E
in this court.

We now turn to consider whether the judge's two relevant rulings were
right or wrong in law. The determination of these questions unfortunately
involves close consideration of the history of blasphemy and of blasphemous libel in our law and also consideration of some of the relevant
authorities, especially those few during the last 100 years or so at least
to the extent that these questions have there arisen for consideration.   F
There is no doubt that both are common law offences of great antiquity,
though Lord Goddard C.J. in a passage in his judgment in *Rex* v. *Morris*
[1951] 1 K.B. 394, 397 (a decision on a wholly different subject) to
which the court drew counsel's attention, referred to the " somewhat
obsolete offence of blasphemy." The obscurity of the relevant law at
the present time seems due to two matters. First, a determined attempt   G
was made in the 1880s to mitigate the earlier rigours of the law of blasphemy and of blasphemous libel. This no doubt was, as all counsel
accepted in argument before us, the result of the intellectual revolution
—it was no less—in the middle of the last century, of which Charles
Darwin and Thomas Huxley were among the leaders. Had those rigours
not been so mitigated, those great men and others might have been in   H
peril of prosecution for blasphemy or blasphemous libel. This course
might possibly have been acceptable to some contemporary opinion but
without doubt, as history shows, it would have been repugnant to other
and perhaps more enlightened minds: see in this connection the judgment of Lord Cozens-Hardy M.R. in *In re Bowman* [1915] 2 Ch. 447,
462, and his comments upon the views of Lord Coleridge C.J., as shown
by his direction to the jury in *Reg.* v. *Ramsay and Foote* (1883) 15 Cox

A   C.C. 231, a case which we shall have to examine in much more detail
hereafter.

Secondly, of the four cases in the last 100 years, *Reg.* v. *Ramsay and
Foote; Rex* v. *Boulter* (1908) 72 J.P. 188; *Bowman* v. *Secular Society
Ltd.* [1917] A.C. 406; *Rex* v. *Gott*, 16 Cr.App.R. 87 and "The Freethinker" for January 8, 1922, at p. 28 and January 29, 1922, at pp. 75,
91 and 108, in three the relevant law is to be found only in the directions
B   of the trial judges respectively concerned to the juries—in *Rex* v. *Gott*
there was no review of the law in the Court of Criminal Appeal—while
in *Bowman* v. *Secular Society Ltd.* [1917] A.C. 406, the only modern
case where the law of blasphemy has received the consideration of the
House of Lords, their Lordships, who reviewed the law exhaustively,
were not concerned with a criminal prosecution, but with the legality or
C   otherwise of the objects of the Secular Society, the intention of which
was self-evident to any reader of that society's memorandum and articles
of association. Hence, not surprisingly, there is no reference in any of
the speeches in their Lordships' House to any question of intent, subjective or otherwise. That was not an issue in that case. Further, in
Rex v. *Boulter*, 72 J.P. 188 and in *Rex* v. *Gott*, 16 Cr.App.R. 87 the
judges respectively concerned, Phillimore J. and Avory J., in their direc-
D   tions to the jury appear to have borrowed almost verbatim Lord Coleridge
C.J.'s earlier directions to the juries in *Reg.* v. *Bradlaugh* (1883) 15
Cox C.C. 217 and *Reg.* v. *Ramsay and Foote* (1883) 15 Cox C.C. 231
without elaborating upon them.

One consequence of this fact was a tendency in argument before us
to submit those several directions to juries to microscopic textual examina-
E   tion perhaps more suitable to consideration of the language of an Act of
Parliament, rather than seeking to ascertain from their general content
what it was that each trial judge concerned had intended that the jury
listening to his direction should gather from his guidance on the law
which they had to apply.

It is clear that in *Bowman* v. *Secular Society Ltd.* [1917] A.C. 406
the House of Lords accepted as correct what Lord Coleridge C.J. had
F   said in the second of those two cases, and rejected an argument by Mr.
G. J. Talbot K.C., that the law should be declared to be that expressed by
Fitzjames Stephen J. more or less contemporaneously with Lord Coleridge
C.J.'s directions in those two cases. As Lord Sumner tersely said in
Bowman v. *Secular Society Ltd.* [1917] A.C. 406, 465, Lord Coleridge C.J.
was "faithfully dealt with soon afterwards by Stephen J., one of his own
G   puisnes." But nonetheless their Lordships said that Lord Coleridge C.J.
had been right. The problem is how far that approval assists the defend-
ants in the present case.

The history of the offence is discussed in the speeches in the House
of Lords in *Bowman* with such authority that repetition of what is there
stated in superfluous. An even fuller history is set out in G. D. Nokes's
History of the Crime of Blasphemy (1928), a little known work of which
H   few copies seem to have survived. The work is of importance since it
was written after *Bowman's* case and after *Rex* v. *Gott*, 16 Cr.App.R. 87
and after, it would seem from the preface, abortive attempts had been
made to abolish the laws of blasphemy in 1923 and 1925, but before the
also unsuccessful attempt that was made in 1930. The author treats the
crime historically. So does Professor Kenny in an article in (1922) 1
Cambridge Law Journal 127, which contains an interesting account of
the story of and the events following the Bradlaugh prosecutions in 1883.

It is clear that the offence was originally in Christian times ecclesias- A
tical. Fortunately it is not necessary to refer to the offence of blasphemy
in pre-Christian times. The state only became interested in the offence
if the actions of the alleged offender affected the safety of the state. An
attack upon Christianity in general or a total denial of the Deity was
punished by the state upon the assumption that the foundation of the
state and of the society upon which the state was founded was thereby
endangered. Indeed, at one time in our history a person who had received B
religious education, but in spite of it was convicted of blasphemy or of
blasphemous libel, was made liable by statute to a greater penalty than
someone less fortunately placed—no doubt upon the footing that Parliament thought that he should have known better.

In the disturbed history of this country during and following the
Napoleonic Wars there were many prosecutions for blasphemy or for C
blasphemous libel, not perhaps so much for the purpose of vindicating
Christian truths as for fear that their denial in such works as Paine's *Age
of Reason* or some of Shelley's poems might tend to a breach of the
peace, by which in those days was meant serious civil disturbance rather
than violence between individuals at street corners. There is an interesting note in Appendix C, preceding the report of the summing up at the
trial of Richard Carlile in 1819, 1 St.Tr.N.S. 1387, that between January D
1821 and April 1834 (just over 13 years) there had been no less than 73
convictions for blasphemy.

As one reads the mid-19th century cases before coming to *Reg.* v.
Ramsay and Foote, 15 Cox C.C. 231, it becomes clear that, notwithstanding the number of prosecutions that there had been during the troubled
years of the first half of that century, not only for the publication of E
Paine's *Age of Reason,* but even as late as 1841, the case of *Reg.* v.
Moxon (1841) 4 St.Tr.N.S. 693, for publishing Shelley's " Queen Mab "
many years after it had been written, the view gradually if hesitatingly
begins to emerge that the truth of hitherto accepted religious beliefs and
indeed the historical and doctrinal foundation of Christianity itself might
be challenged, and indeed attacked as wrong, provided that the challenge F
or attack was carried out with proper respect and moderation so that
there would be no consequent threat of a breach of the peace. One
finds a reflection of this approach in the summing up of Lord Denman
C.J. to the jury in *Reg.* v. *Hetherington* (1841) 4 St.Tr.N.S. 563, 590–591.
We quote the passage in full :

  " Now, gentlemen, upon the question whether it is blasphemous or G
  not I have this general observation to make, which I have often heard
  from Lord Tenterden in cases of this description, namely, that the
  question is not altogether a matter of opinion, but that it must be,
  in a great degree, a question as to the tone, and style, and spirit,
  in which such inquiries are conducted. Because, a difference of
  opinion may subsist, not only as between different sects of Christians, H
  but also with regard to the great doctrines of Christianity itself; and
  I have heard that great judge declare, that even discussions upon
  that subject may be by no means a matter of criminal prosecution,
  but, if they be carried on in a sober and temperate and decent style,
  even those discussions may be tolerated, and may take place without
  criminality attaching to them; but that, if the tone and spirit is that
  of offence, and insult, and ridicule, which leaves the judgment really

A   not free to act, and, therefore, cannot be truly called an appeal to
the judgment, but an appeal to the wild and improper feelings of
the human mind, more particularly in the younger part of the community, in that case the jury will hardly feel it possible to say that
such opinions, so expressed, do not deserve the character which is
affixed to them in this indictment. With that general observation,
I leave the question of libel to you. Is it, or is it not, a blasphemous
B   libel which the defendant appears to have published in his shop? "

We shall have to return to *Reg.* v. *Hetherington,* 4 St.Tr.N.S. 563 later
in this judgment. The gradual move to what we have called the mitigation
of the earlier rigours of the law was firmly established by Lord Coleridge
C.J., in *Reg.* v. *Ramsay and Foote,* 15 Cox C.C. 231. We shall shortly
have to consider Lord Coleridge C.J.'s direction to the jury in detail. But
C   it is worth at this juncture quoting the headnote to the report at p. 232,
for in our view it accurately summarises the effect of the direction given
by Lord Coleridge C.J. to the jury in that case:

    " The mere denial of the truth of the Christian religion, or of the
Scriptures, is not enough, per se, to constitute a writing a blasphemous
libel, so as to render the writer or publisher indictable. But indecent
D   and offensive attacks on Christianity or the Scriptures, or sacred
persons or objects, calculated to outrage the feelings of the general
body of the community, do constitute the offence of blasphemy, and
render writers or publishers liable at common law to criminal
prosecution."

E   We quote this headnote at this point to emphasise that Lord Coleridge
C.J. in directing the jury in that case was concerned with attacks upon
the truth of Christianity and the mitigation of the old law that any attack
upon the Christian faith or upon Christian doctrine was without more
blasphemy or blasphemous libel. He said this in terms, at p. 235: " Therefore, to asperse the truth of Christianity cannot per se be sufficient to
sustain a criminal prosecution for blasphemy." It was that less strict view
F   of the law which was unsuccessfully attacked by the appellants in the
House of Lords in *Bowman* v. *Secular Society Ltd.* [1917] A.C. 406.
Their Lordships finally and authoritatively disapproved of the view which
had been expressed by Lord Hale C.J. who said, in *Rex* v. *Taylor* (1676)
1 Vent. 293, " Christianity is parcel of the laws of England," and that
therefore to reproach the Christian religion was to speak in subversion of
G   the law: see in particular the speech of Lord Sumner in *Bowman* v.
Secular Society Ltd. [1917] A.C. 406, 454–458, 464. But it must be
observed that this disapproval was not thought by their Lordships to
destroy or indeed in any way to affect in any other respect the authority
of Lord Hale's decision: see, for example, what Lord Sumner said at
pp. 457–458 and Lord Buckmaster at pp. 470 and 472.

H   We therefore turn to consider what it was that Lord Coleridge C.J.
had said in *Reg.* v. *Ramsay and Foote,* 15 Cox C.C. 231, which the House
approved so emphatically in *Bowman* v. *Secular Society Ltd.* [1917] A.C.
406. We begin with the speech of Lord Finlay L.C. at pp. 422 and 423 of
the report. On p. 422 he referred to five cases now well known to those
involved in the present appeal. Those five cases include *Rex* v. *Taylor,*
1 Vent. 293, and *Reg.* v. *Hetherington,* 4 St.Tr.N.S. 563. Lord Finlay
L.C. said, at p. 423:

"The true view of the law of blasphemy appears to me to be that A expressed by Lord Denman in *Reg.* v. *Hetherington,* which is substantially in accordance with that taken by Lord Coleridge in *Reg.* v. *Ramsay and Foote,* and followed by Phillimore J. in *Rex* v. *Boulter,* 72 J.P. 188 . . . The consequences of the view put forward on behalf of the appellants would be somewhat startling, and in the absence of any actual decision to the contrary I think we must hold that the law of England on this point is the same as that of Scotland, B and that the crime of blasphemy is not constituted by a temperate attack on religion in which the decencies of controversy are maintained."

Thus the Lord Chancellor expressly approves Lord Denman C.J.'s direction to the jury in *Reg.* v. *Hetherington.* Lord Dunedin at p. 433 expressed his entire agreement with Lord Finlay L.C. on this matter, adding a C reference to the dictum of Erskine J. as one of the judges advising the House of Lords in *Shore* v. *Wilson* (1842) 4 St.Tr.N.S.App. 1370. Lord Parker of Waddington said, at pp. 445–446:

"My Lords, on the subject of blasphemy I have had the advantage of reading, and I entirely agree with, the conclusions arrived at by my noble and learned friends the Lord Chancellor and Lord Buckmaster. D In my opinion to constitute blasphemy at common law there must be such an element of vilification, ridicule, or irreverence as would be likely to exasperate the feelings of others and so lead to a breach of the peace."

Thus he also expressly agreed with what the Lord Chancellor had said. Lord Sumner reviewed all the authorities in even more detail, and reached E the same conclusion which he expressed in characteristically trenchant language at pp. 466–467. The relevant passage in the speech of Lord Buckmaster is at p. 470.

By those statements of the law in the House of Lords we are, of course, bound. We therefore turn back to Lord Coleridge C.J.'s direction to the jury in *Reg.* v. *Ramsay and Foote,* 15 Cox C.C. 231 to see F what he had said which was the subject of such unanimous and authoritative approval. We must quote the passage on p. 236 in full, for it was much relied upon on behalf of the defendants, especially in connection with the argument as to the requirement of subjective intent. We must also mention that Lord Coleridge C.J., with the qualification to which we have already referred, like the House of Lords subsequently in *Bowman* G v. *Secular Society Ltd.* [1917] A.C. 406, approved what Lord Hale had said in *Rex* v. *Taylor,* 1 Vent. 293. Lord Coleridge C.J. said, at p. 236:

"I have no doubt, therefore, that the mere denial of the truth of Christianity is not enough to constitute the offence of blasphemy. It is my duty to lay down the law on the subject as I find it laid down in the best books of authority, and in *Starkie's Slander and Libel,* H 4th ed. (1876), p. 599, it is there laid down as, I believe, correctly: 'There are no questions of more intense and awful interest than those which concern the relations between the Creator and the beings of his creation; and though, as a matter of discretion and prudence, it might be better to leave the discussion of such matters to those who, from their education and habits, are most likely to form correct conclusions; yet it cannot be doubted that any man has a right, not

A   merely to judge for himself on such subjects, but also, legally speaking, to publish his opinion for the benefit of others. When learned and
acute men enter upon those discussions with such laudable motives,
their very controversies, even where one of the antagonists must
necessarily be mistaken, so far from producing mischief, must in general
tend to the advancement of truth, and the establishment of religion
on the firmest and most stable foundations. The very absurdity and
B   folly of an ignorant man, who professes to teach and enlighten the
rest of mankind, are usually so gross as to render his errors harmless;
but, be this as it may, the law interferes not with his blunders, so
long as they are honest ones, justly considering that society is more
than compensated for the partial and limited mischief which may
arise from the mistaken endeavours of honest ignorance, by the
splendid advantages which result to religion and truth from the exer-
C   tions of free and unfettered minds. It is the mischievous abuse of
this state of intellectual liberty which calls for penal censure. The
law visits not the honest errors, but the malice of mankind. A wilful
intention to pervert, insult, and mislead others, by means of licentious
and contumelious abuse applied to sacred subjects, or by wilful misrepresentations or wilful sophistry, calculated to mislead the ignorant
D   and the unwary, is the criterion and test of guilt. A malicious and
mischievous intention, or what is equivalent to such an intention, in
law, as well as morals—a state of apathy and indifference to the
interests of society—is the broad boundary between right and wrong.'
Now that I believe to be a correct statement of the law."

E   We would add to that quotation from the 4th edition of *Starkie* a reference to the opening passage of Chapter 33 in the 3rd edition (1869) of
that work, of which a copy was made available to us, so as to put the
passage which Lord Coleridge C.J. cited into proper context. Indeed,
the whole of the opening of the chapter repays reading and study. The
opening words are, at p. 583 :

F   " The first grand offence of speech and writing is, speaking blas-
phemously against God, or reproachfully concerning religion, with
an intent to subvert man's faith in God, or to impair his reverence of
him."

On the next page the author said:

G   " Offences of this nature are punishable in the temporal courts with
fine and imprisonment, because they tend to subvert all religion and
morality, which are the foundation of government."

Those passages will be found on pp. 583 and 584 of the 3rd edition.
We think reading that summing up as a whole Lord Coleridge C.J.
was quite plainly telling the jury that, it being admitted that the publications complained of were intended to be an attack upon Christianity
H   and upon the Old Testament, they had to determine in accordance with
his direction and his approval of the passage which he had quoted to
them from *Starkie*, whether the publications there in question had crossed
the line between decent and restrained controversy into the field of what
Starkie had described as " licentious and contumelious abuse applied to
sacred subjects."

But it was said on behalf of the defendants that the direction to the
jury in *Reg.* v. *Ramsay and Foote*, 15 Cox C.C. 231 is authority for the

proposition that a publication cannot be a blasphemous libel unless it is A published with the subjective intent to attack Christianity and the foundations of Christian belief, even though, as in the present case, the jury has found as a fact that the publication amounted to vilification of Christ in his life and crucifixion.

It is at this point that we think it becomes necessary to look at some of the earlier cases, many of which, as already stated, touch upon both the points which we have under consideration. To save undue repetition, B we shall consider these cases as far as possible chronologically. The earliest is *Rex* v. *Taylor*, 1 Vent. 293. The report in Ventris is brief. The reasoning is clear. The words complained of appear in the report. The defendant apparently attempted to say that he meant those words in some different sense from that which they bore in their ordinary and natural meaning. Lord Hale would have none of that submission. He C said:

". . . such kind of wicked blasphemous words were not only an offence to God and religion, but a crime against the laws, state and government, and therefore punishable in this court."

We pause in the 18th century only to mention *Rex* v. *Williams* (1797) 26 St.Tr. 653, 705, where Lord Kenyon C.J. spoke of "the most malignant D purposes" of the publication of Paine's *Age of Reason*. In *Rex* v. *Carlisle (Richard)* (1819) 1 St.Tr.N.S. 1387, Abbott C.J. spoke of "intention" or "endeavour" to bring the Christian religion into disrepute. At another point he said "to endeavour by publication to bring the Christian religion and the Holy Scriptures into disbelief and contempt is an offence." In *Rex* v. *Carlile (Mary)* (1821) 1 St.Tr.N.S. 1033, 1045, E Best J. spoke of "a tendency to vilify the Christian religion" and asked, at p. 1047: "Is this a temperate discussion, or the writing of a person who attempts not to argue, but to vilify and degrade, to excite prejudices in our mind and not to convince our judgment?"

Most important, we think, is what Lord Denman C.J. said in his charge to the jury in *Reg.* v. *Hetherington*, 4 St.Tr.N.S. 563, since it was this statement of the law which received the express approval of the House F of Lords in *Bowman* v. *Secular Society Ltd.* [1917] A.C. 406. The alleged blasphemous libel was directed to certain parts of the Old Testament. Lord Denman C.J. at p. 589, asked the jury to consider whether the passages complained of treated the Old Testament with "contempt and disgrace." He said, at p. 593:

"The question before you, and the only question for you to decide, G is a matter of fact and of opinion. Aye or no, is this in your opinion a blasphemous publication, and has the defendant in point of fact issued it knowingly and wilfully? If these questions are answered in the affirmative, it is the duty of the jury to pronounce a verdict accordingly."

Now as we have already pointed out, in a number of these cases, as H indeed in the directions to the jury by Phillimore J. in *Rex* v. *Boulter*, 72 J.P. 188 and by Avory J. in *Rex* v. *Gott*, 16 Cr.App.R. 87, references will be found to the word "attack" in connection with attacks upon Christianity, Christian doctrines and beliefs and the like. But if those cases are studied with care, it will be found that in each the real question before the jury was whether the dividing line so clearly laid down in *Reg.* v. *Ramsay and Foote*, 15 Cox C.C. 231 and approved by the House of

A   Lords in *Bowman* v. *Secular Society Ltd.* [1917] A.C. 406 and already adumbrated in some of the earlier cases before *Reg.* v. *Ramsay and Foote*, between moderate and reasoned criticism on the one hand and immoderate or offensive treatment of Christianity or sacred subjects on the other, had been crossed. And that was the issue which in each of these cases the jury was directed by the judge concerned to decide.

B   We do not find it surprising that in such contexts the word " attack " has been frequently used. It was treated, we think, by the judges concerned as synonymous with that lack of due moderation and restraint which each jury concerned, as typifying the contemporary opinion of society, might think was appropriate having regard to the subject matter under discussion. The defendants' counsel in argument before us sought almost to elevate these various references to the word " attack " in these several contexts to the status of, as it were, a condition precedent to liability for a conviction for blasphemy or blasphemous libel so that, however much the allegedly offending publication might insult, offend or vilify, to use but some of the words used in the cases we have quoted, the Deity or Christ or the Christian religion or some part of its doctrines, it must amount to an attack upon the whole edifice of Christianity and its foundations.

D   With all respects to the persuasive way in which that argument was presented, we do not think that the authorities viewed as a whole over the centuries will bear that interpretation. Indeed, so to hold would in our view be contrary to the emphasis repeatedly laid in the speeches in the House of Lords in *Bowman* v. *Secular Society Ltd.* [1917] A.C. 406 upon such words as " indecent," " offensive," " insulting," " ridicule," " vilification," " irreverence." The word " attack " in this context is not a word of art. It is a compendious word which embraces many meanings in the relevant respect. A treatise attacking Christian doctrine in one form or another or denying the truth of miracles recorded in the New Testament may well, as a matter of ordinary language, be described as an attack upon Christianity. Yet such publications have long been within the law because they neither insult nor offend nor vilify. But if the " attack " upon the Deity or upon Christ takes another form and, for example, is " insulting " or " vilifying " and a jury is prepared so to hold, then the law still says today, as it always has, that the publisher of such an attack, if vilifying or insulting, is guilty of blasphemous libel.

The judge at p. 16 of the transcript of his summing up said:

G   " The Crown does not have to prove that the poem is an attack. For blasphemy it has got to be about Christianity or Christ or some aspect of the religion, not necessarily an attack at all. It has got to be about it, but about it in such terms as are likely to arouse resentment and so on."

The judge in the passage from which we have quoted was dealing with a statement in the speech of Mr. Robertson in which counsel had argued

H   that it was necessary for the Crown to prove " an outrageous attack on Christianity." The judge was correcting what counsel had stated as being the law. For the reasons we have given, we think that this part of the judge's direction to the jury was correct.

We turn now to give separate consideration, although we have already touched upon the point, to the argument about subjective intent. We have in our approach to this question had three matters very much in mind. First, before 1898 no prisoner could give evidence in his own

defence and therefore it would not have been permissible for a person **A**
accused of blasphemy or blasphemous libel to have given evidence on
oath to assert what his own subjective intention had been in relation to
the words spoken or written and published. Secondly, in many of the
cases, though not, it would seem, in *Rex* v. *Taylor*, 1 Vent. 293, the
accused's own intention clearly accorded with the plain meaning of
the words he or she had published by word of mouth or in writing. The
weight attaching to the first of these two points is perhaps somewhat **B**
lessened by the fact that in some cases the defendants (see, for example,
Rex v. *Carlile* (*Mary*) (1821) 1 St.Tr.N.S. 1033, to which we have already
referred), whether or not at the time such defendants might have been
defended by counsel, managed by their own addresses to the jury or
by their own statements from the dock to convey their own subjective
intentions to the jury without the possible disadvantage of being cross- **C**
examined upon those statements Thirdly, throughout this period and
indeed until comparatively recently, the view that an accused person was
presumed to intend the natural consequences of his acts continued to
prevail.

Much reliance was placed in argument before us upon the latter part
of the quotation from *Starkie*, 4th ed. (1876) which Lord Coleridge C.J.
read to the jury in the passage we have quoted in full, as well as *Starkie's* **D**
reference in the 3rd edition of his work (1869) of which we had a copy,
and to *Holt's Law of Libel*, 2nd ed. (1816), of which we also had the
benefit of a copy. The defendants also relied upon *Odgers, Libel and
Slander*, 1st ed. (1881) (thus before Lord Coleridge C.J.'s direction to the
jury in *Reg.* v. *Ramsay and Foote*, 15 Cox C.C. 231) where the law was
stated, at p. 394:   **E**

> " It is a misdemeanour, punishable by indictment and by criminal
> information, to speak, or write and publish, any profane words vilify-
> ing or ridiculing God, Jesus Christ, the Holy Ghost, the Old or New
> Testament, or Christianity in general, with intent to corrupt the public
> morals, to shock and insult believers, or to bring the established
> religion into hatred and contempt."   **F**

The author wrote, at p. 395:

> " The intent to corrupt the public morals, to shock and insult believers,
> or to bring the established religion into hatred and contempt, is an
> essential element in the crime. Actus non facit reum, nisi mens sit
> rea. The existence of such an intent is a question of fact for the
> jury, and the onus of proving it lies on the prosecution. The best **G**
> evidence of such an intention is usually to be found in the work
> itself."

We will not quote the next two or three pages, though they repay study.
In the 6th edition (1929), the latter passage is repeated verbatim, though
the former has been slightly altered and a reference to *Bowman* v. *Secular* **H**
Society Ltd. [1917] A.C. 406 added. By the time of the 6th edition,
of course, and for some 30 years before, accused persons could give
evidence in their own defence so that it no longer necessarily followed
that the best evidence of their intention was to be found in the work itself.

On the other hand the Crown relied upon successive editions of *Halsbury's Laws of England*. The 1st ed., vol. 9 (1909), pp. 530–531, makes
no reference to any question of intent. In the 2nd ed., vol. 9 (1933), the

A same passage appears unaltered. The same observation applies to the
3rd ed., vol. 10 (1955), p. 661. In the current 4th ed., vol. 11 (1976),
para. 1009, which has the authority of Shaw L.J., the previous passage
has been rewritten but again there is no reference to intent.

   Archbold, 39th ed. (1976), paras. 3405 and 3406 does not mention
any question of intent being required. *Russell on Crime*, 12th ed. (1964),
vol. 2, p. 1519, does not directly discuss the question of means rea. On
B the other hand this question is touched upon in *Smith and Hogan*,
Criminal Law, 3rd ed. (1973), pp. 567, 568. The authors, after discussing
the nature of the actus reus required to be proved, turned to consider the
question of mens rea with the following observations, at p. 577:

> " There seems to be no clear modern authority on the nature of the
>   mens rea required, but it ought to follow in principle from the nature
C >   of the actus reus that there must be proved at least an intention so
>   to ridicule the Christian religion, etc., as to tend to provoke ordinary
>   Christians (or, possibly, those actually addressed) to violence."

   Much time was quite properly spent in argument before us in analysing the earlier cases, such as those of *Rex* v. *Carlile (Richard)*, 1 St.Tr.
N.S. 1387 and *Rex* v. *Carlile (Mary)*, 1 St.Tr.N.S. 1033, to see what, if
D any, help could be garnered from the language of the indictments preferred by the Crown in those cases, or of the various judgments to which
we have already referred. So far as the language of the indictments is
concerned, there is no doubt that, unlike the indictment in the present
case, the word " intent " is referred to. See also the indictment in *Reg.*
v. *Hetherington*, 4 St.Tr.N.S. 563. But contemporary ignorance of the
E rules of criminal pleading 150 years ago make such documents at best
a very uncertain guide to the solution of the present problem. We need
not quote again from the passages in the summing up of Abbott C.J.
in *Rex* v. *Carlile (Richard)*, 1 St.Tr.N.S. 1387, or of Best J. in *Rex* v.
Carlile (Mary), 1 St.Tr.N.S. 1033, where such words as " intention,"
" tendency," " attempts " are used. There is no doubt what Lord Hale's
view was on this issue. The ordinary meaning of the words used was
F enough. In each of the *Carlile* cases, the judges were inviting the jury
to assess not the defendants' own intention, but the quality or tone of
the words used. Were they words of moderate discussion or of violent
abuse? Most relevant of the earlier 19th century cases is, once again,
Reg. v. *Hetherington*, 4 St.Tr.N.S. 563. It seems to us that Lord Denman
C.J. could not have used the language at p. 593 which he did—we have
G already quoted the language, but we do so again for ease of reference—
if he had thought that it was relevant to consider what the defendant's
subjective intention was. He said:

> " The question before you, and the only question for you to decide, is
>   a matter of fact and of opinion. Aye or no, is this in your opinion
>   a blasphemous publication, and has the defendant in point of fact
H >   issued it knowingly and wilfully? If these questions are answered
>   in the affirmative, it is the duty of the jury to pronounce a verdict
>   accordingly."

   Intent in the sense for which the defendants have contended was not a
live issue in *Reg.* v. *Ramsay and Foote*, 15 Cox C.C. 231, for Foote, as
already stated, had admitted his intention. It is, we think, a legitimate
comment that since this was the position in that case, the passages in
Starkie, 4th ed. (1876), p. 599 approved by Lord Coleridge C.J. cannot have

been thought by Lord Coleridge C.J. to have borne the meaning contended A
for by the defendants. The cases before *Reg.* v. *Ramsay and Foote*
seem to us clearly to show that if an accused person deliberately published
that which crossed the line which divided the blasphemous from the
non-blasphemous, he could not be heard to say that he did not know or
realise or intend that that which he had deliberately put into circulation
possessed those characteristics which rendered him liable to conviction
for blasphemy or blasphemous libel, according to whether the words in B
question were spoken or written.

That is, of course, the position in the case of the ordinary civil law
of defamation. If the editor or printer or publisher of a newspaper pub-
lishes or prints or puts into circulation that which defames it is no answer
to a claim for damages for libel that he did not know, realise or intend
that that should be so. We have not, of course, in reaching this con- C
clusion lost sight of the fact that the question of intention was not discussed in *Bowman* v. *Secular Society Ltd.* [1917] A.C. 406. But we
cannot treat that fact as of assistance to the defendants when the earlier
cases, which seem to us so strongly to militate against their contentions,
were expressly approved.

Certainly it is a striking fact that neither in *Reg.* v. *Ramsay and
Foote,* 15 Cox C.C. 231 nor in *Rex* v. *Boulter,* 72 J.P. 188 nor in *Rex* v. D
Gott, 16 Cr.App.R. 87, does one find any clear direction to the jury that
they must not convict unless the Crown had made them sure that the
accused was possessed of that requisite subjective intention without which
on the defendants' case they could not have been properly convicted.
The more we have reflected upon this branch of the defendants' argument,
the less surprising we have found this fact. If subjective intention were E
a necessary ingredient in this offence, whose intention has to be proved?
Is it the intention of anyone concerned in the publication, or only the
intention of the accused? If it is only his, could it be a defence that his
only intention when putting the offending matter into circulation was to
make money, or to inform the world of the writings of another? If it
be the intention of the author that matters, then the fate of the publisher
might depend, at least in the case of a dead writer, upon an intention F
difficult to ascertain save from the language of that which was known
to have been written or spoken in the past.

For the reasons we have given, in our view the further submission on
behalf of the defendants fails.

The defendants relied upon section 8 of the Criminal Justice Act
1967, and what had been said in the House of Lords in *Sweet* v. *Parsley* G
[1970] A.C. 132, a case upon statutory construction, and again in *Reg.*
v. *Morgan* [1976] A.C. 182, 210, by Lord Hailsham of St. Marylebone.
But if the common law never required proof of a subjective intent in
cases of blasphemy or blasphemous libel, the enactment of section 8
cannot help the defendants, while if their main submission be right (contrary to our view) they do not need this additional argument. H

Mr. Smyth for the Crown argued in the alternative that if we were
to come to the conclusion that the law was in doubt and that there was
what he called a " grey area," we should not hesitate to declare the law
to be such, and we quote his words, " as would protect the interests of
sympathisers with Christian ideals about things which they regard as most
sacred." He relied upon the well known passage in the speech of Viscount
Simonds in *Shaw* v. *Director of Public Prosecutions* [1962] A.C. 220,

A 267, 268, as justifying the submission. But in *Reg.* v. *Knuller* (*Publishing, Printing and Promotions*) *Ltd.* [1973] A.C. 435, Lord Reid who had dissented from the views of the majority in *Shaw's* case uttered a formidable warning against legislation by judicial decision. So did Lord Diplock, at pp. 474, 475, in a dissenting speech in the latter case. On the view we take of this appeal we find it unnecessary to consider this submission further. We only mention it for the sake of completeness.

B   It remains to mention Mr. Mortimer's other submissions. We take first the point raised on behalf of Mr. Lemon under section 7 of the Libel Act 1843. It was sufficiently proved in evidence and in any event it was finally admitted that Mr. Lemon was the editor of " Gay News." But there was no direct evidence that he was personally associated with the publication of the libels and it was argued that the fact that he was editor
C was insufficient to prove the necessary connection between him as editor and the publication of the blasphemous libels. Reliance was placed upon what Lord Coleridge C.J. had said in *Reg.* v. *Bradlaugh*, 15 Cox C.C. 217, 228–229, which had resulted, it was said, in Bradlaugh's acquittal because of section 7. But Bradlaugh was not the editor of the paper in question. He asserted that he knew nothing of the contents of the paper or of the allegedly offending material. Section 7 reads:
D

    " . . . whensoever, upon the trial of any indictment or information
    for the publication of a libel, under the plea of not guilty, evidence
    shall have been given which shall establish a presumptive case of
    publication against the defendant by the act of any other person by
    his authority, it shall be competent to such defendant to prove that
    such publication was made without his authority, consent, or know-
E   ledge, and that the said publication did not arise from want of due
    care or caution on his part."

Clearly here there was, by proof or admission, evidence of Mr. Lemon being the editor. There was thus a presumptive case of publication of the alleged blasphemous libel against him.

F   This section was considered in *Reg.* v. *Holbrook* (1878) 4 Q.B.D. 42, a decision to which Lord Coleridge C.J. referred. There the prosecution was of newspaper proprietors and not of an editor. The relevant passage is in the judgment of Lush J., with whom Cockburn C.J. agreed, at p. 50:

    " The effect of it [section 7] read by the light of previous decisions,
    and read so as to make it remedial, must be that an authority from
    the proprietor of a newspaper to the editor to publish what is libellous
G   is no longer to be, as it formerly was, a presumption of law, but a
    question of fact. Before the Act the only question of fact was
    whether the defendant authorised the publication of the paper; now,
    it is whether he authorised the publication of the libel. It is true
    that the publication of the paper which contains the libel, coupled
    with proof that the defendant is the proprietor, is prima facie evidence
H   that he caused the publication of the libel, and the onus is on him
    to prove the negative. But when he has proved that the literary
    department was intrusted entirely to an editor, the question what
    was the extent of the authority which that employment involved is
    to be tried upon the principle which is applicable to all other ques-
    tions of authority."

Clearly here there was sufficient presumptive evidence adduced by the

prosecution or admitted on behalf of the defence. Mr. Lemon could A
have gone into the witness box to say he knew nothing of the matters
complained of and that the publication of the alleged blasphemous libel
was something which arose from functions which he had wholly entrusted
to someone else. He did not do so. He was fully entitled not to do so.
But the decision having been taken that he should not go into the witness
box, there was in our view nothing to displace the inference arising from
his admitted editorship. What Lord Coleridge C.J. said in the context B
of different facts, which related, as we have already pointed out, to proprietors of newspapers and not to an editor, may have been correct in
that particular context. But applying section 7 of the Libel Act 1843 to
the facts of the present case, we can see nothing wrong in the ruling
which the judge gave on this issue.

We can deal briefly with the remainder of the submissions made on C
behalf of the defendants. Complaint was made of the judge's comments
on p. 20 of the summing up. But we think that this complaint adds little
to the main criticisms of the summing up with which we have already
dealt at length. If the judge's direction was right, these comments were
legitimate.

Then it was said, not very forcibly, as we have already pointed out, D
that the prosecution had to prove an intention on the part of the defendants to cause a breach of the peace. We have dealt with this already.
We need say no more. The judge's direction on this was entirely right.

Mr. Mortimer next complained that the judge invited the jury to
consider the matter by reference to their first reaction on reading the
allegedly offending matter. But we think that this part of the summing E
up must be read with the rest and this passage is not really open to
criticism when put into context.

Mr. Mortimer also argued that since the essence of the complaint was
obscenity, a prosecution for blasphemous libel was excluded by section 2
(4) of the Obscene Publications Act 1959. He contended that the judge
was wrong in ruling otherwise. With respect, the short answer to this
contention is that when one looks at the indictment the essence of the F
offence charged was blasphemous libel and not an obscene publication.

Finally, complaint was made of the judge asking the jury whether
they could think of anything more profane. Our comment on this criticism
is the same as we have made in relation to complaints about what the
judge said on p. 20 of the transcript.

In the result, therefore, none of the further points avails the defendants G
and since the arguments on the main issues have failed, it follows that
the appeals against conviction must be dismissed. We cannot part from
this case without thanking all counsel involved for their well researched,
cogent and learned arguments. We would add our thanks to Miss Toohey
of the Registrar's staff whose collection of a massive number of authorities and legal literature not easily obtainable greatly assisted the court's H
preparatory work before the hearing of the appeal began as well as facili-
tated its speedier disposal than would otherwise have been the case.

Counsel addressed the court on sentence.

ROSKILL L.J. We grant leave to appeal to Mr. Lemon. We do not
consider this an appropriate case for a prison sentence. We therefore

A   quash the sentence of nine months' imprisonment suspended for 18 months. The fines will stand.

> *Appeals against conviction dismissed.*
> *Appeal of editor against sentence allowed.*
> *Prosecution costs out of central funds.*

B   April 19. The court certified that a point of law of general public importance is involved in the decision to dismiss the appeals, namely, the question: " Was the learned trial judge correct (as the Court of Appeal held) first in ruling and then in directing the jury that in order to secure the conviction of the appellants for publishing a blasphemous libel: (1) it was sufficient if the jury took the view that the publication C complained of vilified Christ in his life and crucifixion; and (2) it was not necessary for the Crown to establish any further intention on the part of the appellants beyond an intention to publish that which in the jury's view was a blasphemous libel? "

> *Leave to appeal refused.*
> *Legal aid (solicitors and two counsel)*
D   *granted for purpose of proceedings*
> *in House of Lords.*

Solicitors: *Offenbach & Co.; Robbins, Olivey & Lake.*

E   May 17. The Appeal Committee of the House of Lords (Lord Wilberforce, Viscount Dilhorne and Lord Salmon) allowed a petition by Denis Lemon and Gay News Ltd. for leave to appeal.

F
[HOUSE OF LORDS]

COMMISSIONER OF POLICE OF THE METROPOLIS   RESPONDENT

AND

HILLS   .   .   .   .   APPELLANT
G
[On appeal from REGINA *v.* HILLS]

1978   July 4, 5; 27   Lord Diplock, Viscount Dilhorne, Lord Salmon,
                              Lord Russell of Killowen and Lord Keith of Kinkel

Crime—Evidence—Character—Co-accused—Causing death by
H   *dangerous driving—Different counts in same indictment*
charging each co-accused in respect of same death—Whether
" same offence "—Criminal Evidence Act 1898 (61 & 62 Vict.
c. 36), *s.* 1 (*f*) (iii) [1]

The appellant and L were tried together on an indictment which contained two counts. The first count charged L and the second count charged the appellant with having caused

[1] Criminal Evidence Act 1898, s. 1, see post, pp. 426H—427A.

Reg. v. Hills (H.L.(E.))   **[1978]**

the death of K by dangerous driving. The particulars of the   A
offence in each case were the same. The charges arose out of
a collision between vehicles driven by the appellant and L as
a result of which a pedestrian was killed. The appellant gave
evidence against L and the trial judge acceded to an application
on behalf of L for the appellant to be cross-examined as to his
character ruling that for the purposes of section 1 (*f*) (iii) of
the Criminal Evidence Act 1898, both defendants were charged
with " the same offence." Subsequently L was acquitted and   B
the appellant convicted of the charge and he was sentenced to
a term of imprisonment consecutive to one that he was serving
at the time of the trial. The appellant appealed on the ground
that the judge's ruling was wrong in law. The Court of Appeal
dismissed the appeal.

On appeal: —

Held, allowing the appeal, (1) that for the offences charged
to be regarded as the same for the purposes of section 1 (*f*) (iii)   C
of the Criminal Evidence Act 1898, they must be the same
in all material respects including the time at which the offence
was alleged to have been committed, and a distinct and separate
offence similar in all respects to an offence committed later,
no matter how short the interval between the two, could not
properly be regarded as " the same offence " (post, p. 428G).

(2) That where persons were jointly charged with one   D
offence and the charge was not bad for duplicity, they were
charged with the same offence within the meaning of the Act;
that if charged separately with offences, a test of whether
the defendants were charged with the same offence was
whether they could have been charged jointly, and that in the
present case in the light of the case for the prosecution against
each, the defendants could not properly have been charged with
having jointly caused the death of K by dangerous driving; and   E
that, accordingly, the appellant's conviction must be quashed
on the ground that there was a material irregularity in the
course of the trial in allowing cross-examination of the
appellant as to his character (post, pp. 428H—429A, F).

Reg. v. *Russell (George)* [1971] 1 Q.B. 151, C.A. overruled.

Per Lord Diplock, Viscount Dilhorne and Lord Keith of
Kinkel. It does not seem to accord with justice that when one   F
of two accused gives evidence against the other, the right of
the accused against whom evidence is given should depend on
what charges the prosecution has thought it right to bring. It
is hoped that section 1 (*f*) (iii) of the Act of 1898 will be
referred to the Criminal Law Revision Committee for consideration (post, pp. 426A, 429E, 430E–F).

Decision of the Court of Appeal (Criminal Division)
[1978] R.T.R. 320, C.A. reversed.   G

The following cases are referred to in their Lordships' opinions:

Murdoch v. *Taylor* [1965] A.C. 574; [1965] 2 W.L.R. 425; [1965] 1 All
E.R. 406, H.L.(E.).

Reg. v. *Assim* [1966] 2 Q.B. 249; [1966] 3 W.L.R. 55; [1966] 2 All E.R.
881, C.C.A.

Reg. v. *Lauchlan* (unreported), June 15, 1976, C.A.; but see (Note) [1978]   H
R.T.R. 326.

Reg. v. *Lovett* [1973] 1 W.L.R. 241; [1973] 1 All E.R. 744, C.A.

Reg. v. *Rockman* (unreported), November 22, 1977, C.A.

Reg. v. *Russell (George)* [1971] 1 Q.B. 151; [1970] 3 W.L.R. 977; [1970]
3 All E.R. 924, C.A.

Rex v. *Hadwen* [1902] 1 K.B. 882.

Rex v. *Roberts* [1936] 1 All E.R. 23; 25 Cr.App.R. 158, C.C.A.

A   The following additional cases were cited in argument:

Attorney-General for the Colony of Hong Kong v. *Kwok-A-Sing* (1873) L.R. 5 P.C. 179, P.C.

Attorney-General (Ryan) v. *Egan* [1948] I.R. 433.

Reg. v. *Caspar* (1839) 9 C. & P. 289.

Reg. v. *Gosney* [1971] 2 Q.B. 674; [1971] 3 W.L.R. 343; [1971] 3 All E.R. 220, C.A.

B   *Reg.* v. *Hussain* [1969] 2 Q.B. 567; [1969] 3 W.L.R. 134; [1969] 2 All E.R. 1117, C.A.

Reg. v. *Merriman* [1973] A.C. 584; [1972] 3 W.L.R. 545; [1972] 3 All E.R. 42, H.L.(E.).

Reg. v. *Pulham* (1840) 9 C. & P. 280.

C   APPEAL from the Court of Appeal (Criminal Division).

This was an appeal by the appellant, John David Hills, by leave of the House of Lords, from the decision of the Court of Appeal (Orr L.J., Thompson and Milmo J.) dated February 20, 1978, dismissing an appeal by the appellant against his conviction at Knightsbridge Crown Court (Judge Alastair Morton) on April 1, 1977, on count 2 of an indictment which count charged the appellant with causing death by dangerous driving

D   contrary to section 1 (1) of the Road Traffic Act 1972, in that he on September 9, 1975, caused the death of Nora Keane by driving a motor vehicle on a road, namely, Western Avenue, Acton, London, W.3, in a manner which was dangerous to the public. Count 1 charged Gordon Peter Ledwith in respect of the death of Nora Keane in identical terms. On April 1, 1977, Ledwith was acquitted and the appellant convicted and

E   sentenced to a term of nine months' imprisonment consecutive to a term of imprisonment he was then serving.

The Court of Appeal refused leave to appeal but certified that the following point of law of general public importance was involved in their decision namely:

F   " Whether two persons charged in the same indictment, but in separate counts, each with causing the death of the same person by driving in a manner dangerous to the public the acts of dangerous driving alleged being different, are ' charged with the same offence ' for the purpose of section 1 (*f*) (iii) of the Criminal Evidence Act 1898."

The facts are set out in the opinion of Viscount Dilhorne.

G   *Richard Hayden* and *Michael Joyce* for the appellant.
Donald Farquharson Q.C. and *N. H. Freeman* for the respondent.

At the conclusion of the argument their Lordships conferred.

LORD DIPLOCK stated that their Lordships would allow the appeal for reasons to be given later.

H
July 27. LORD DIPLOCK. My Lords, I have read in advance the speech of my noble and learned friend Viscount Dilhorne. I agree with it and for the reasons that he gives I too would allow this appeal; but not without regret for, as it seems to me, the justice of the case required that the jury should be aware of the appellant's history of previous convictions for motoring offences when they came to consider the weight to be attached to the charges of dangerous driving that he had made in the witness-box

against his fellow accused. The words of the statute which prohibit this, A however, are too plain and unequivocal; they leave no discretion to the trial judge. So I share the hope expressed by Viscount Dilhorne that this provision of a statute, which was passed 80 years ago, should be referred to the Criminal Law Revision Committee for their consideration.

VISCOUNT DILHORNE. My Lords, the appellant and Mr. Ledwith were tried together in the Crown Court at Knightsbridge on an indictment which B contained two counts. The first charged Mr. Ledwith with having caused the death of Mrs. Keane by dangerous driving. The second charged the appellant with having done so. The particulars of offence in each count were the same. Each alleged that the accused had on September 3, 1975, caused the death of Nora Keane by driving a motor vehicle on a road, to wit, Western Avenue, Acton, W.3, in a manner which was dangerous to C the public.

Mr. Ledwith, it appears, was driving a van in the eastbound carriageway of Western Avenue and had stopped at an intersection in the central reservation as it was his intention to cross into the westbound carriageway and to enter the entrance to the Unigate factory which was on the near side of the westbound carriageway. As he drove into the outside lane of that D carriageway, he saw a Triumph motor car coming towards him 100 to 150 yards away. He accelerated to get out of its way and then stopped. The Triumph hit his wing, bounced off it on to the near-side kerb and hit and killed Mrs. Keane who was standing in the Unigate factory entrance.

The appellant, the driver of the Triumph, said in evidence that he had been about 150 yards from the intersection when the van turned right out of it in front of him and that there was no room for him to get round it. E

Counsel for Mr. Ledwith sought to cross-examine the appellant as to his character, to establish that he was an unqualified driver without " L " plates and without a qualified driver with him, that he had been convicted of dangerous driving and of driving uninsured in 1973 and that in 1974 and 1975 he had sought to obtain driving licences by falsely stating that he had passed a driving test. That the appellant had given evidence against F Mr. Ledwith was conceded. Mr. Chedlow for Mr. Ledwith contended that though not charged jointly in a count in the indictment, Mr. Ledwith and the appellant were charged with the same offence and that he was consequently by virtue of the Criminal Evidence Act 1898 entitled so to cross-examine. Judge Morton held that each of the accused was charged with the same offence and allowed the cross-examination.

Mr. Ledwith was acquitted. The appellant was convicted, sentenced to G nine months' imprisonment and disqualified from holding or obtaining a driving licence for three years. He appealed to the Court of Appeal (Criminal Division). That court dismissed his appeal but certified that a point of law of general public importance was involved, namely, whether two persons charged in the same indictment but in separate counts, each with causing the death of the same person by driving in a manner dangerous to H the public, the acts of dangerous driving alleged being different, are " charged with the same offence " for the purpose of section 1 (f) (iii) of the Criminal Evidence Act 1898.

The material parts of that section are as follows:

"Every person charged with an offence . . . shall be a competent witness for the defence at every stage of the proceedings, whether the person so charged is charged solely or jointly with any other person.

A   Provided as follows: — . . . (*f*) A person charged and called as a witness in pursuance of this Act shall not be asked, and if asked shall not be required to answer, any question tending to show that he has committed or been convicted of or been charged with any offence other than that wherewith he is then charged, or is of bad character, unless— . . . (iii) he has given evidence against any other person charged with the same offence."

B

Our task in this appeal is to construe the words " the same offence." It is clear that an accused is not liable to be cross-examined as to character merely because he has given evidence against a co-accused. Such cross-examination is only permissible when the accused against whom he has given evidence is charged with the same offence. A number of persons may be indicted in one indictment even though none of them are accused of committing an offence jointly if :

C

"... the matters which constitute the individual offences of the several offenders are upon the available evidence so related, whether in time or by other factors, that the interests of justice are best served by their being tried together," see *Reg.* v. *Assim* [1966] 2 Q.B. 249, 261.

D   It may be that persons are now more frequently joined in one indictment when charged only with separate offences than was the case in 1898, but the review made by Sachs J. in *Reg.* v. *Assim* suggests that in those days no valid objection could have been taken to an indictment against a number of persons none of whom was jointly charged in a count, if the matters on which the counts were based were so related that the interests of justice were best served by their being tried together.

E   If two or more persons are jointly charged in a count, that count will be bad for duplicity if it charges more than one offence. When it is not bad for duplicity, each accused is charged with the same offence and if one accused has given evidence against another accused in that count, it cannot be doubted that proviso (iii) to section 1 (*f*) applies.

F   Where it is alleged by the prosecution that two or more persons have committed the same offence, it would indeed be unusual to find them indicted together but only charged in separate counts. If, though indicted together, they are charged only in separate counts, that may be taken as an indication that the prosecution at least did not regard them as charged with the same offence.

G   Counts in an indictment are not nowadays so detailed as in days gone by. To decide whether two persons are charged in separate counts with the same offence, one must, of course, look at the counts, but one is in my opinion entitled to have regard also to what further particulars of the offence charged would have been given if applied for. When considering the propriety of the joinder of accused in one indictment one is entitled to look at the substance of the case as disclosed in the depositions (*Reg.* v.

H   *Assim* [1966] 2 Q.B. 249) and in my opinion for the purpose of determining whether separate counts charge the same offence one can look at the depositions to judge what further particulars of a count would have been given if applied for.

In this case it is clear that if further particulars of the dangerous driving alleged in each count had been given, they would have alleged that Mr. Ledwith had driven dangerously in turning into the path of an oncoming

vehicle when it was not safe to do so and that the appellant had driven   A
dangerously in driving too fast and not keeping a proper look-out. If
particulars of this kind had been contained in the indictment or given it
could not in my opinion be said that Mr. Ledwith and the appellant were
charged with the same offence within the meaning of the statute.

Since 1898 there have been very few occasions on which the meaning of
the words " the same offence " in this Act have been the subject of judicial
consideration. In *Rex* v. *Hadwen* [1902] 1 K.B. 882, Lord Alverstone C.J.   B
said that the most ordinary case where persons were charged with the same
offence, would be when there were two or more prisoners jointly indicted,
though he agreed that the words would apply where the same offence had
been the subject of other proceedings. In *Rex* v. *Roberts* [1936] 1 All
E.R. 23 two persons were jointly indicted and tried together; one was
charged with fraudulent conversion and the other with false pretences. One   C
accused who gave evidence against the other was cross-examined as to
character. His conviction was quashed. Talbot J., delivering the judgment
of the Court of Criminal Appeal, said that proviso (iii) must be strictly
construed. He recognised that there were arguments for making the
provision more extensive. He said it was impossible to say that the accused
were charged with the same offence. In *Reg.* v. *Russell (George)* [1971]
1 Q.B. 151 Russell and Hurst were charged in separate counts with being in   D
possession of the same forged £5 notes. Hurst gave evidence against Russell
whose counsel was not allowed at the trial to cross-examine Hurst as to
character. Widgery L.J., delivering the judgment of the Court of Appeal,
observed that the offences charged against Russell and Hurst were similar
in really every respect but that it was argued that they were not charged
with the same offence because the possessions alleged against them were   E
not " coincident or concurrent but consecutive." He thought that Lord
Donovan in *Murdoch* v. *Taylor* [1965] A.C. 574 had taken the view that
there should be a wide interpretation of the words " the same offence."
With respect I do not myself see anything in his speech which leads to that
conclusion.

There is no doubt that if Russell and Hurst had been jointly charged
with possession, cross-examination as to Hurst's character would have been   F
permissible. No doubt if the evidence warranted the preferment of a joint
charge that would have been done and the fact that such cross-examination
would have been permissible if it had been, does not lead to the conclusion
that successive possessions constitute the same offence. If a house is burgled
by a burglar and an hour later it is burgled by another burglar, it would be
wrong in my opinion to hold that each burglar was charged with the same   G
offence. In my view for the offences charged to be regarded as the same
for the purposes of the proviso, they must be the same in all material
respects including the time at which the offence is alleged to have been
committed, and a distinct and separate offence similar in all material respects
to an offence committed later, no matter how short the interval between
the two, cannot properly be regarded as " the same offence."   H

For these reasons the decision in this case was in my opinion wrong
and it should be overruled. It was followed by the Court of Appeal in the
present case. As I have said where persons are jointly charged with one
offence and the charge is not bad for duplicity, they are charged with the
same offence within the meaning of the Act. If charged separately with
offences, a test of whether they are charged with the same offence is whether

A they could have been charged jointly. In the present case in the light of the case for the prosecution against each, they could not properly have been charged with having jointly caused the death of Mrs. Keane by dangerous driving.

Our attention was drawn to two unreported cases, *Reg.* v. *Lauchlan,* June 15, 1976, and *Reg.* v. *Rockman,* November 22, 1977. In *Reg.* v. *Lauchlan* two men were indicted together each charged with assaulting the other. It was held rightly that they were not charged with the same offence, Shaw L.J. pointing out that to justify their convictions different facts would have to be proved. In *Reg.* v. *Rockman* two men were indicted together, one charged with assaulting the other and the other charged with wounding the man accused of assault. It was held, in my opinion again rightly, that the proviso did not apply.

C At the end of his judgment in *Reg.* v. *Russell (George)* [1971] 1 Q.B. 151, Widgery L.J. said that it would be a very unsatisfactory result if Russell had been denied the right to cross-examine his co-accused. I agree that the result of so deciding is unsatisfactory but that does not entitle one to amend the statute or to give its language a meaning which it does not in my opinion have. In *Reg.* v. *Lovett* [1973] 1 W.L.R. 241, 243 Edmund Davies L.J. said:

"It has been suggested (and not without good reason) that the law on this matter is unsatisfactory, and that the mischief aimed at in proviso (iii) would be more satisfactorily dealt with if it applied whenever two accused are jointly tried, even though they are not charged with the same offence: ...."

E I agree. It does not seem to me to accord with justice that when one of two accused gives evidence against the other, the right of the accused against whom the evidence is given should depend on what charges the prosecution has thought it right to bring. I hope that the Secretary of State for Home Affairs will invite the Criminal Law Revision Committee to give attention to this without delay.

F In my opinion "same offence" in the proviso means an offence which is the same in all respects. The counts in this indictment did not charge offences the same in all respects and for the reasons I have given I would allow the appeal and quash the appellant's conviction on the ground that there was a material irregularity in the course of the trial in allowing the cross-examination of the appellant as to his character.

G LORD SALMON. My Lords, I agree that this appeal should be allowed.

LORD RUSSELL OF KILLOWEN. My Lords, in one sense the two counts in the indictment charged Ledwith and the appellant Hills respectively with the same offence, viz.: driving a motor vehicle on Western Avenue on September 9, 1975, in a manner dangerous to the public thereby causing the relevant death. But on analysis I do not consider that to be the relevant sense for present purposes. In 1898 when the relevant statute was enacted, the indictment would have been drawn with far greater particularity, and today further particulars could have been required on behalf of the accused. That greater particularity would have revealed that the dangerous driving of which the appellant was accused consisted in driving a motor car too fast westwards in the outer lane of Western Avenue without regard to the

possibility of the emergence through the intersection of Ledwith's van A
across his bows. It would also have revealed that the dangerous driving
of which Ledwith was accused was turning his van from the eastbound
carriageway across part of the westbound carriageway across the bows of
the appellant without regard to the possibility that he could not get across
in time for the appellant to avoid colliding with the van.

Suppose there had been no question of death resulting from the collision,
and each had been charged in the same indictment with the relevant B
dangerous driving. I do not consider that they could have been charged
together in one count: the offence of dangerous driving alleged against one
was factually quite different from the offence of dangerous driving alleged
against the other: they were not " the same offence " in that they were not
identical. The fact that in the instant case a death resulted, and that
causing it is included in the charges, cannot alter that; because the first C
essential step is for the prosecution to prove the dangerous driving, and
only when those dangerous drivings were proved to show that death was
thereby caused.

As was said in the case of *Reg.* v. *Lauchlan* (unreported), June 15, 1976,
in which as a consequence of a fight between A and B each was charged
with assault causing actual bodily harm to the other in separate counts,
" To procure a conviction of [A], or on the other hand to justify a D
conviction of [B], required proof of differing facts."

Whether it is desirable that the ability for an accused to question the
other on the relevant matters should remain thus narrowly confined by the
statute, I do not debate. My impression is that the Court of Appeal in
Reg. v. *Russell (George)* [1971] 1 Q.B. 151 were anxious to escape from
too strait a jacket, and I agree that that led to an erroneous decision. E

I would therefore answer the question posed in the point of law in the
negative and allow the appeal.

LORD KEITH OF KINKEL. My Lords, I have had the benefit of reading
in advance the speech of my noble and learned friend Viscount Dilhorne.
I agree with it and cannot usefully add anything. I, too, would allow the
appeal. F

Appeal allowed.

Solicitors: *Nicholls, Christie & Crocker; Solicitor, Metropolitan Police.*

J. A. G.

G

H

A

[QUEEN'S BENCH DIVISION]

THE RENA K

1977   Dec. 12, 13, 14;   Brandon J.
1978   Jan. 12;
B   Feb. 17

Admiralty—Arrest of ship—Stay of judicial proceedings—Arbitra-
tion clause—Stay of action in rem—Shipowners' lack of
financial resources—Whether stay final—Whether action in
rem merging in arbitral award—Whether shipowners entitled
to unconditional order for release—Arbitration Act 1975 (c. 3),
C   *s. 1 (1) [1]—R.S.C., Ord. 75, r. 13 (4) [2]*
Arbitration—Stay of judicial proceedings—Arbitration agreement
—Cargo owners' claim against shipowners—If successful,
possibility of shipowners being unable to satisfy award—
Whether arbitration agreement " incapable of being per-
formed"—Arbitration Act 1975, s. 1 (1)
Shipping—Charterparty—Arbitration clause—Bills of lading—
Incorporation of terms expressly including arbitration clause in
D   *charterparty—Construction—Intention of parties*
Ships' Names—Rena K

A vessel belonging to the shipowners, a Panamanian company, was chartered for the shipment of sugar from Mauritius
to Liverpool. The charterparty contained a clause which
provided that any dispute arising under the charter should be
settled by arbitration in London. There were two bills of
E   lading relating to the shipment of sugar both of which contained clauses incorporating all the terms, clauses, conditions
and exceptions of the charterparty, including by express
description the arbitration clause. During the voyage, seawater
entered one of the holds so that 2,440 metric tons of sugar
was ruined and had to be jettisoned. Before the vessel reached
Liverpool, the cargo owners commenced an action in rem
against the ship and in personam against the shipowners claim-
F   ing damages for £549,000. The ship arrived at Liverpool
and began to discharge her cargo. On July 27, 1977, she was
arrested. The next day, the shipowners applied for a stay
of all proceedings in the action under section 1 of the
Arbitration Act 1975, on the ground that the matter was a
dispute which the parties had agreed to refer to arbitration
and that consequently the ship should be released from arrest.
The parties agreed to adjourn the hearing of the motion on
G   the terms that the insurers (the club) would put up security on
behalf of the shipowners in the form of a letter of undertaking
for £390,000 (the estimated value of the ship); that the letter
of undertaking would be cancelled and returned by the cargo
owners if the court should subsequently decide that on July 28,
1977, the shipowners were entitled to a stay of the action

H   [1] Arbitration Act 1975, s. 1: " (1) If any party to an arbitration agreement . . .
or any person claiming through or under him, commences any legal proceedings
in any court against any other party to the agreement, . . . in respect of any matter
agreed to be referred, any party to the proceedings may at any time after appearance, and before delivering any pleadings or taking any other steps in the
proceedings, apply to the court to stay the proceedings; and the court, unless
satisfied that the arbitration agreement is null and void, inoperative or incapable
of being performed or that there is not in fact any dispute between the parties with
regard to the matter agreed to be referred, shall make an order staying the
proceedings."

[2] R.S.C., Ord. 75, r. 13: " (4) A release may be issued at the instance of a party
interested in the property under arrest if the court so orders, . . ."

under the Act of 1975 and so were further entitled to the
unconditional release of the ship from arrest, and that the
cargo owners were not entitled, by way of alternative security
for their claim, to a *Mareva* injunction restraining the shipowners from removing the ship from the jurisdiction; and that
the ship should meanwhile be released from arrest. The ship
was released, and proceeded to Greece where she was laid up in
circumstances which suggested, as she was the shipowners' only
asset other than the charterparty, freight and any sum due
under the charter for demurrage, that the shipowners would be
incapable of paying out of their own resources the full amount
of the cargo owners' claim.

On the questions whether the action should have been
stayed as being referable to arbitration and, if it should,
whether as at July 28 the ship should have been released
unconditionally consequent on such stay: —

Held, (1) that by using the express words " including the
arbitration clause " in the general words of incorporation
in the bills of lading the parties had shown an intention to
provide for arbitration in disputes arising under the bills of
lading so that the arbitration clause in the charterparty applied
to such disputes despite the need to adapt part of the wording and therefore the dispute which concerned damage to
cargo was one which the parties had agreed should be referred
to arbitration (post, pp. 439H—440B).

The Annefield [1971] P. 168, C.A. distinguished.

(2) That the words " incapable of being performed " in
section 1 (1) of the Arbitration Act 1975 referred only to the
question whether an arbitration agreement was capable of
being performed up to the stage when it resulted in an award
and should not be construed as extending to the question
whether, once an award had been made, the party against
whom it was made had the financial resources to satisfy that
award; and, accordingly, the shipowners were entitled under
the Act of 1975 to a stay of the cargo owners' action (post,
p. 442C–D).

(3) That the distinction between the choice of forum and
the right to security should be recognised and given effect to
in arbitration cases, and that where the stay of the proceedings
might not be final the discretion given to the court by R.S.C.,
Ord. 75, r. 13 (4), should be exercised either by refusing to
release the security at all or only releasing it subject to a term
that alternate security should be provided for the payment of
any award in the arbitration; that since a cause of action in rem
did not become merged in an arbitral award, the stay in the
present case might well not be final; and, in the exercise of the
court's discretion, the shipowners were not entitled to the
unconditional release of the ship (post, pp. 452C–D, E–F, H,
454D–F).

The Golden Trader [1975] Q.B. 348 distinguished.

Per curiam. The rights given to the plaintiffs by the Supreme
Court of Judicature (Consolidation) Act 1925 and the Administration of Justice Act 1956 are cumulative not alternative.
That being so, the circumstance that the cargo owners cannot
(if it be the case) maintain security for their claim by having
the ship kept under arrest by the court in the exercise of its
jurisdiction in rem should not be a reason why they should not
be entitled to obtain alternative security for their claim by
means of a *Mareva* injunction relating to the ship granted by
the court in the exercise of its jurisdiction in personam. On
the contrary, the fact that they are unable, in their efforts to
ensure security for their claim to use one of the two methods
potentially available for the purpose seems to afford a very
good reason why they should be permitted to use the other
(post, p. 457C–E).

3 W.L.R.   **The Rena K (Q.B.D.)**

A

The following cases are referred to in the judgment:

Annefield, The [1971] P. 168; [1971] 2 W.L.R. 320; [1971] 1 All E.R. 394, C.A.

Athenee, The (1922) 11 Ll.L.Rep. 6, C.A.

Atlantic Star, The [1974] A.C. 436; [1973] 2 W.L.R. 795; [1973] 2 All E.R. 175, H.L.(E.).

Bengal, The (1859) Swab. 468.

B

Bremer Oeltransport G.m.b.H. v. *Drewry* [1933] 1 K.B. 753, C.A.

Cap Bon, The [1967] 1 Lloyd's Rep. 543.

Cella, The (1888) 13 P.D. 82, C.A.

Eleftheria, The [1970] P. 94; [1969] 2 W.L.R. 1073; [1969] 2 All E.R. 641.

Fehmarn, The [1957] 1 W.L.R. 815; [1957] 2 All E.R. 707; [1958] 1 W.L.R. 159; [1958] 1 All E.R. 333, C.A.

Foresta Romana S.A. v. *Georges Mabro (Owners)* (1940) 66 Ll.L.Rep. 139.

C

Gascoyne v. *Edwards* (1826) 1 Y. & J. 19.

Golden Trader, The [1975] Q.B. 348; [1974] 3 W.L.R. 16; [1974] 2 All E.R. 686.

Hamilton & Co. v. *Mackie & Sons* (1889) 5 T.L.R. 677, C.A.

John and Mary, The (1859) Swab. 471.

Makefjell, The [1975] 1 Lloyd's Rep. 528; [1976] 2 Lloyd's Rep. 29, C.A.

Merak, The [1965] P. 223; [1965] 2 W.L.R. 250; [1965] 1 All E.R. 230, C.A.

D

Njegos, The [1936] P. 90.

Phonizien, The [1966] 1 Lloyd's Rep. 150.

Rasu Maritima S.A. v. *Perusahaan Pertambangan Minyakdangas Bumi Negara (Government of the Republic of Indonesia intervening)* [1977] 3 W.L.R. 518; [1977] 3 All E.R. 324, C.A.

Siskina (Owners of cargo lately laden on board) v. *Distos Compania Naviera S.A.* [1977] 3 W.L.R. 818; [1973] 3 All E.R. 803, H.L.(E.).

E

Sylph, The (1867) L.R. 2 A. & E. 24; 17 L.T. 519.

Thomas (T. W.) & Co. Ltd. v. *Portsea S.S. Co. Ltd.* [1912] A.C. 1, H.L.(E.).

Yeo v. *Tatem (The Orient)* (1871) L.R. 3 P.C. 696, P.C.

The following additional cases were cited in argument.

F

Carl Zeiss Stiftung v. *Rayner & Keeler Ltd. (No. 2)* [1967] 1 A.C. 853; [1966] 3 W.L.R. 125; [1966] 2 All E.R. 536, H.L.(E.).

King v. *Hoare* (1844) 13 M. & W. 494.

Macabe v. *Joynt* [1901] 2 Ir.R. 113, D.C.

Nelson v. *Couch* (1863) 15 C.B.N.S. 99.

Purser and Co. (Hillingdon) Ltd. v. *Jackson* [1977] Q.B. 166; [1976] 3 W.L.R. 700; [1976] 3 All E.R. 641.

Speak v. *Taylor* (1894) 10 T.L.R. 224, D.C.

G

MOTION

By a voyage charterparty dated April 13, 1977, the first plaintiffs, the Mauritius Sugar Syndicate, chartered the motor vessed *Rena K* from the second defendants, the Black Lion Shipping Co. S.A., a Panamanian company managed and controlled from Greece by the

H first defendants, the owners of the *Rena K* for the carriage of 11,150 metric tons of sugar from Port Louis, Mauritius, to Liverpool. By a writ dated June 24, 1977, the first plaintiffs, together with the second plaintiffs, Tate & Lyle Refineries Ltd. (the cargo owners), the third plaintiffs, Emcar Ltd. (agents of the first plaintiffs) and the fourth plaintiffs Adam & Co. Ltd. (also agents of the first plaintiffs) began an action in rem against the vessel the *Rena K* and in personam against the Black Lion Shipping Co. S.A. for damages for loss of and/or damage

to cargo during the voyage from Port Louis to the United Kingdom in A
or about the months of May/June/July 1977 sustained by reason of
the defendants' breach of contract and/or duty and/or negligence and/or
conversion of their cargo and the carriage thereof on board the *Rena K.*
The plaintiffs also invited the court to grant an injunction restraining the
second defendants by themselves, their servants or their agents from
removing the vessel *Rena K* from or taking or disposing of any assets
out of the jurisdiction pending determination of the plaintiffs' claim by B
the court. On July 27, 1977, the writ in rem was served on the *Rena K*
and she was arrested. By a notice of motion dated July 28, 1977, the
defendants sought an order for a stay of the proceedings in the action
under section 1 of the Arbitration Act 1975 and an order setting aside
the warrant of arrest.

It was agreed between the parties (a) that the London Steamship C
Owners' Mutual Insurance Association Ltd. (the P. & I. Club) should
put up security for the claim on behalf of the defendants in the form of
a letter of undertaking in the sum of £390,000; (b) that the letter of
undertaking would be cancelled and returned by the plaintiffs to the
P. & I. Club if the court subsequently decided that as at July 28, 1977,
(1) the defendants were entitled to a stay of the action on the ground D
that there was an agreement to refer the dispute to arbitration, (2) as
a consequence, that the defendants were entitled to the unconditional
release from arrest of the *Rena K,* and (3) that the plaintiffs were not
entitled, by way of alternative security for their claim, to a *Mareva*
injunction restraining the defendants from removing the *Rena K* from
the jurisdiction; and (c) that the *Rena K* should meanwhile be released
from arrest. In accordance with the agreement, the *Rena K* was E
released from arrest and the hearing of the defendants' motion was
adjourned.

On December 8, 1977, the defendants, the Black Lion Shipping Co.
S.A. and the P. & I. Club, by originating summons (which named the
plaintiffs in the proceedings commenced on June 24, 1977 as defendants)
asked the court whether the P. & I. Club was in effect entitled to the F
cancellation and delivery up of its letter of undertaking. By agreement,
the originating summons was heard at the same time as the adjourned
motion.

The facts are stated in the judgment.

M. N. Howard for the shipowners.
David Grace for the cargo owners.   G

Cur. adv. vult.

February 17, 1977. BRANDON J. read the following judgment.
These proceedings arise out of the carriage of a cargo of about 11,150
metric tons of sugar from Port Louis, Mauritius, to Liverpool in the
Greek ship *Rena K* during May, June and July, 1977.   H

The sugar concerned was sold by the Mauritius Sugar Syndicate to
Tate & Lyle Refineries Ltd. on c.i.f. terms. The *Rena K* was chartered
for the carriage by the Mauritius Sugar Syndicate from her owners,
Black Lion Shipping Co. S.A., under a voyage charterparty dated London
April 13, 1977. The latter is a Panamanian company managed and
controlled from Greece.

The cargo was shipped for the Mauritius Sugar Syndicate by two

A   agents of theirs, Emcar Ltd. and Adam & Co. Ltd., and two bills of
lading were issued in respect of such shipment.   One bill of lading was
on Emcar Ltd.'s form and the other on Adam & Co. Ltd.'s form.   In
either case the agent was named as shipper in the bill of lading although
acting as agent only.

The *Rena K* left St. Louis on May 17, 1977.   On May 20, 1977, there
was an entry of sea water into her no. 4 hold.   As a result of this a
quantity of about 2,440 metric tons of sugar in that space was ruined.
Later, after the *Rena K* had proceeded to Durban for examination and
temporary repairs, the whole of the ruined sugar was jettisoned.

On June 24, 1977, while the voyage was still in progress, the Mauritius
Sugar Syndicate, Tate & Lyle Refineries Ltd., Emcar Ltd., and Adam
& Co. Ltd., began an action in this court both in rem against the *Rena K*
C   and in personam against Black Lion Shipping Co. S.A.   The claim
endorsed on the writ was for damages for breach of contract and duty
in and about the carriage of the cargo.   The amount claimed is said by
the plaintiffs to be £549,000 with interest and costs, that figure being
calculated on the basis of a total loss of 2,440 metric tons of sugar with
a sound arrived value of £225 per metric ton.

D   On July 11, 1977, the *Rena K* arrived at Liverpool, and on July 24
or 25 discharge of the rest of her cargo began.   On July 25, 1977, the
plaintiffs applied ex parte for a *Mareva* injunction restraining the
defendants from dealing with moneys payable to their bankers in
London in respect of freight due under the charterparty.   An interim
injunction effective for 28 days or until further order was granted, with
liberty to the defendants to apply on short notice to vary or discharge
E   the order.

On July 27, 1977, the writ, in so far as it was in rem, was served on
the *Rena K* and she was arrested in the action.   At the same time
solicitors acting for the defendants accepted service of the writ in so
far as it was in personam.   On July 28, 1977, the defendants entered an
appearance in the action, and on the same day they issued a notice of
F   motion asking, first, for a stay of the action on the ground that the
dispute to which it related was one which the parties had agreed to refer
to arbitration, and, secondly, along with and consequent on such stay,
for the release of the *Rena K* from arrest.

It was then the last day but one of the Trinity sittings, and there was
insufficient time for the questions raised by the notice of motion to be
adequately argued and decided.   In these circumstances an agreement
G   was reached between the plaintiffs on the one hand and the defendants
and their P. & I. Club (the London Steamship Owners' Mutual Insurance
Association Ltd.) on the other hand, which would allow the *Rena K* to
be released while preserving for the plaintiffs all such rights as they
might at that stage have had to retain security for their claim by keeping
the *Rena K* under arrest, or, if such arrest was not maintainable, by
H   obtaining comparable security in the form of a *Mareva* injunction
relating to the ship which they would in that event have applied for in
the alternative.

The principal terms of the agreement to which I have referred are
contained in a telex from Messrs. Ince & Co., the solicitors for the
plaintiffs, to Messrs. Hill Dickinson & Co., the solicitors for the
defendants, dated July 27, 1977, and can be summarised as follows.
(a) That the P. & I. Club should put up security for the claim on behalf

of the defendants in the form of a letter of undertaking in the sum of $\quad$ A
£390,000. (b) That this letter of undertaking should be cancelled and
returned by the plaintiffs to the P. & I. Club if the court should subsequently decide that as at July 28, 1977: (1) the defendants were entitled
to a stay of the action on the ground that there was an agreement to
refer the dispute to which it related to arbitration; (2) as a consequence
of such stay the defendants were further entitled to the unconditional $\quad$ B
release of the *Rena K* from arrest; and (3) the plaintiffs were not
entitled, by way of alternative security for their claim, to a *Mareva*
injunction restraining the defendants from removing the *Rena K* from
the jurisdiction. (c) That the *Rena K* should meanwhile be released
from arrest.

The sum of £390,000 referred to in term (a) above was based on
the estimated value of the *Rena K* in the condition in which she was at $\quad$ C
that time.

In accordance with that agreement, the P. & I. Club put up security
in the form of a letter of undertaking in the sum of £390,000 and the
Rena K was released from arrest. A consent order was further made
adjourning the hearing of the defendants' application for a stay to
December 12, 1977. $\quad$ D

On December 8, 1977, a further proceeding was begun by originating
summons in which Black Lion Shipping Co. S.A. and the London
Steamship Owners' Mutual Insurance Association Ltd. were named as
plaintiffs and the Mauritius Sugar Syndicate, Tate & Lyle Refineries Ltd.,
Emcar Ltd. and Adam & Co. Ltd. as defendants. In that originating
summons, as subsequently amended, the plaintiffs ask the court to
determine in effect whether, by virtue of the agreement summarised $\quad$ E
above, the P. & I. Club is entitled to the cancellation and return to it
of the letter of undertaking in the sum of £390,000 given by it pursuant
to the agreement.

On December 9, 1977, the four defendants to the originating summons
entered an appearance to it, and it was agreed by all the parties concerned that the originating summons should be heard at the same time $\quad$ F
as the adjourned application for a stay in the original action.

As I have indicated above, four persons, the Mauritius Sugar Syndicate, Tate & Lyle Refineries Ltd., Emcar Ltd. and Adam & Co. Ltd.,
were named as plaintiffs in the original action and again as defendants
in the further proceedings begun by originating summons. It is, however, common ground that the title to sue for substantial damages in $\quad$ G
respect of the cargo which was lost is vested in Tate & Lyle Refineries
Ltd., and in them alone, as endorsees of the two bills of lading to which
I referred earlier, and that the existence of the other three plaintiffs
can, therefore, for all practical purposes be disregarded. It is further
common ground that, in these circumstances, the relevant terms of
carriage for the purposes of the claim are those contained in those bills $\quad$ H
of lading.

In the rest of this judgment I shall refer to the effective plaintiffs,
Tate & Lyle Refineries Ltd., as the cargo owners, to Black Lion Shipping
Co. S.A. as the shipowners, to London Steamship Owners' Mutual
Insurance Association Ltd. as the club, and to the *Rena K* as the ship.
Before I state and examine the various questions which arise in this
matter, I think it is right to say something about the nature and strength

A of the prima facie case which the cargo owners have shown in respect of their claim.

There was put in evidence a report of T. R. Little & Co. dated June 13, 1977, of a survey made by them of the ship at Durban on June 1, 1977, and following days. According to that report the ingress of sea water into no. 4 hold resulted from defects in the hull of the ship of such a character that they must have been in existence at the commencement

B of the voyage and have made her unseaworthy at that time. Since the carriage of the cargo was on Hague Rules terms, it would be for the shipowners, in order to resist the cargo owners' claim successfully, to show that, although the ship was unseaworthy, they had exercised due diligence to make her seaworthy. While the possibility of the ship-owners' discharging the burden of proof which would be on them in this

C respect cannot be excluded, the inference which I draw from the survey report is, to put the matter no higher, that they would be likely to have considerable difficulty in doing so.

In these circumstances I am of opinion that the cargo owners have shown a very strong prima facie case on the merits in support of their claim.

D Four main questions were argued before me as follows: (1) Is the dispute to which the cargo owners' action relates one which the parties have agreed should be referred to arbitration? (2) If so, were the ship-owners entitled, as at July 28, 1977, to a stay of the action? (3) If so, were the shipowners also entitled, as at July 28, 1977, along with and consequent on such stay, to the unconditional release of the ship from

E arrest? (4) If so, were the cargo owners entitled, as at July 28, 1977, by way of alternative security for their claim, to a *Mareva* injunction in respect of the ship? I shall examine each of these four questions in turn.

(1) *Is the dispute to which the cargo owners' action relates one which the parties have agreed should be referred to arbitration?*

F The charterparty between the Mauritius Sugar Syndicate and the shipowners dated April 13, 1977, contains the following provision:

" Arbitration: Any dispute which may arise under this charter to be settled by arbitration in London, each party appointing an arbitrator, and should they be unable to agree, the decision of an umpire selected by them to be final. The arbitrators and umpire all to be commercial men. This submission may be made a rule of

G the High Court of Justice in England by either party."

The bill of lading on Emcar Ltd.'s form, which has terms printed or typed on both its face and its reverse side, contains several references to the charterparty. On the main part of the face of the bill of lading there are words acknowledging the shipment of the goods at the port of loading and providing for their delivery at the port of discharge to order.

H Then there follow, mainly in print but partly in type, these two sentences:

" Freight for the said goods to be paid as laid down in the charter-party. All conditions of the charterparty dated April 13, 1977, including exception clause, incorporated in the bill of lading."

On the left hand side of the face of the bill of lading these words appear again in type: " Freight payable as laid down in charterparty." On the reverse side of the bill of lading there are a number of standard

printed clauses, some of which, as appear from their terms, are designed A
for inclusion in a charterparty rather than in a bill of lading. Right at
the end, following this series of standard clauses, comes the following
further printed clause:

> " All other terms, conditions, clauses and exceptions including the
> arbitration clause as well as the negligence clause and cesser clause
> as per charterparty. In case of conflict between the terms of the
> charterparty and those of the bill of lading, the former shall B
> prevail."

The bill of lading on Adam & Co. Ltd.'s form, which has terms printed
or typed on its face only, also contains several similar references to the
charterparty.

There are two references, one in the main part of the bill of lading C
about a third of the way down, and the other on the left hand side about
half way down, to freight being paid or payable " as laid down in
charterparty dated London April 13, 1977." In addition there is a
clause on the left hand side of the bill of lading towards the top which
reads:

> " All terms, clauses, conditions and exceptions including the arbi-
> tration clause, the negligence clause and the cesser clause of the D
> charterparty dated London April 13, 1977, are hereby incorporated."

This clause is all in print except for the date of the charterparty which is
typed.

Those being the relevant terms of the charterparty and the two bills
of lading, the problem of construction which arises is this. Both bills of
lading contain clauses incorporating all the terms, clauses, conditions E
and exceptions of the charterparty, including, by express description,
the arbitration clause contained in the latter contract. That clause itself
however, by its own terms relates only to disputes arising under the
charterparty. What then is the effect, if any, of its incorporation?

For the cargo owners it was contended that the incorporation had no
effect at all because, when the arbitration clause was read into the bills F
of lading, it did not by its terms apply to disputes arising under them,
but only to disputes arising under the charterparty. Nor, it was further
argued, was there any justification for manipulating or adapting the
wording of the clause, when read into the bills of lading, so as to make
it apply to disputes arising under the bills of lading instead of disputes
arising under the charterparty.

For the shipowners, on the other hand, it was contended that the G
fact that the arbitration clause was expressly incorporated by description
showed clearly that the parties to the bills of lading intended the provisions of that clause to apply in principle to disputes arising under the
bills of lading. It followed, so the argument went on, that some
manipulation or adaptation of the wording of the clause, when read into
the bills of lading, was justified in order to give effect to that clearly H
shown intention.

A long series of authorities has established that, where a charterparty
contains an arbitration clause providing for arbitration of disputes
arising under it, general words in a bill of lading incorporating into it
all the terms and conditions, or all the terms, conditions and clauses,
of such charterparty, are not sufficient to bring such arbitration clause
into the bill of lading so as to make its provisions applicable to disputes

A   arising under that document: *Hamilton & Co.* v. *Mackie & Sons* (1889) 5 T.L.R. 677; *Thomas (T. W.) & Co. Ltd.* v. *Portsea S.S. Co. Ltd.* [1912] A.C. 1; *The Njegos* [1936] P. 90; *The Phonizien* [1966] 1 Lloyd's Rep. 150 and *The Annefield* [1971] P. 168.

By contrast it has been held that, where an arbitration clause in a charterparty provides for arbitration of disputes arising not only under the charterparty itself, but also under any bill of lading issued pursuant
B   to it, general words of incorporation in such a bill of lading of the kind referred to above, are sufficient to bring in the arbitration clause so as to make it applicable to disputes arising under that bill of lading: *The Merak* [1965] P. 223.

In the authorities mentioned above a distinction has been drawn between clauses in the relevant charterparty which are directly germane
C   to the shipment, carriage and delivery of the goods covered by the bill of lading and other clauses which are not directly germane to such matters.

Referring to this distinction Lord Denning M.R. said in *The Annefield* [1971] P. 168, 184:

D   "I would say that a clause which is directly germane to the subject matter of the bill of lading (that is, to the shipment, carriage and delivery of goods) can and should be incorporated into the bill of lading contract, even though it may involve a degree of manipulation of the words in order to fit exactly the bill of lading. But if the clause is one which is not thus directly germane, it should not be incorporated into the bill of lading contract unless it is done explicitly in clear words either in the bill of lading or in the charter-
E   party."

Mr. Grace for the cargo owners argued, on the basis of these authorities, that an arbitration clause in a charterparty, being a clause which was not directly germane to the shipment, carriage and delivery of the goods, could never be brought into a bill of lading and made
F   applicable to disputes arising under that document, if it was necessary to manipulate the wording of the clause in order to achieve that end. He contended that it made no difference, for this purpose, whether the words of incorporation contained in the bill of lading were general words without any specific reference to the arbitration clauses in the charterparty, as in all the authorities relied on, or general words to which a specific reference to such clause was added, as in the present case.

G   I cannot accept this last contention. It was an essential element in the facts of the cases referred to that the words of incorporation in the bill of lading were general words without specific reference to the arbitration clause in the charterparty; the conclusions reached on the questions of construction involved depended entirely on that circumstance; and the judgments of the judges who decided the cases must be
H   read and understood in the light of it.

The present case is, in my view, clearly distinguishable, in that there are added to the usual general words of incorporation in the two bills of lading the further specific words " including the arbitration clause." The addition of these words must, as it seems to me, mean that the parties to the bills of lading intended the provisions of the arbitration clause in the charterparty to apply in principle to disputes arising under the bills of lading; and, if it is necessary, as it obviously is, to manipulate

or adapt part of the wording of that clause in order to give effect to that   A
intention, then I am clearly of opinion that this should be done.

For the reasons which I have given I prefer the argument for the
shipowners to that for the cargo owners on this part of the case. I hold
that, on the true construction of the bills of lading, the provisions for
arbitration contained in the arbitration clause of the charterparty were
brought into the bills of lading and made applicable to disputes arising
under them.   B

The cargo owners' claim in the action is brought under the bills of
lading, so that the dispute to which the action relates is a dispute arising
under those documents.   It follows, on the view which I have expressed
above, that the dispute is one which the parties have by the terms of the
bills of lading, agreed to refer to arbitration.

                                                                               C
(2) *If the dispute to which the action relates is one which the parties*
have agreed to refer to arbitration, were the shipowners entitled, as at
July 28, 1977, to a stay of the action?

Section 1 of the Arbitration Act 1975, which came into operation on
December 23, 1975, provides so far as material:

> " (1) If any party to an arbitration agreement to which this section   D
> applies . . . commences any legal proceedings in any court against
> any other party to the agreement . . . in respect of any matter
> agreed to be referred, any party to the proceedings may at any
> time after appearance, and before delivering any pleadings or taking
> any other steps in the proceedings, apply to the court to stay the
> proceedings; and the court, unless satisfied that the arbitration   E
> agreement is null and void, inoperative or incapable of being
> performed or that there is not in fact any dispute between the
> parties with regard to the matter agreed to be referred, shall make
> an order staying the proceedings.   (2) This section applies to any
> arbitration agreement which is not a domestic arbitration agreement;
> and neither section 4 (1) of the Arbitration Act 1950 nor section 4
> of the Arbitration Act (Northern Ireland) 1937 shall apply to an   F
> arbitration agreement to which this section applies. . . . (4) In
> this section ' domestic arbitration agreement ' means an arbitration
> agreement which does not provide, expressly or by implication, for
> arbitration in a state other than the United Kingdom and to which
> neither—(a) an individual who is a national of, or habitually
> resident in, any state other than the United Kingdom; nor (b) a   G
> body corporate which is incorporated in, or whose central manage-
> ment and control is exercised in, any state other than the United
> Kingdom; is a party at the time the proceedings are commenced."

On the basis of the court's answer to question (1), it was conceded
for the cargo owners that, since the shipowners were a body corporate
incorporated in Panama, and since also their central management and   H
control were exercised in Greece, the arbitration agreement concerned
was not a domestic arbitration agreement within section 1 (4) above,
and that section 1 (1) was accordingly applicable to the case.

At the commencement of the hearing before me it was further
conceded for the cargo owners that, since section 1 (1) of the Act of 1975
applied to the case, the court was bound to make an order staying
their action. Subsequently, however, this further concession was, with

A   the leave of the court, withdrawn, and it was contended instead for the cargo owners that an order staying the action should be refused on the ground that the shipowners did not have the financial resources with which to satisfy an award against them if made, and that the arbitration agreement was therefore "incapable of being performed" within the meaning of that expression as used in section 1 (1) of the Arbitration
B   Act 1975. This contention was, not surprisingly, strongly disputed on behalf of the shipowners.

    This contention for the cargo owners raises two questions. The first question is one of law. It is whether an arbitration agreement is "incapable of being performed" within the meaning of section 1 (1) of the Arbitration Act 1975 if the financial position of one of the parties to it is such that, in the event of an award being made against him in
C   an arbitration held pursuant to the agreement, he would not be able to pay the amount of the award. The second question is one of fact. It is whether the financial position of the shipowners in this case is such that, if the cargo owners were to succeed in an arbitration against them and obtain an award in respect of their claim, the shipowners would be unable to satisfy such an award.

D   So far as the first question, that of law, is concerned the argument for the cargo owners was as follows. Any person who enters into an arbitration agreement impliedly undertakes that he will pay any award made against him in an arbitration held pursuant to such agreement: *Bremer Oeltransport G.m.b.H.* v. *Drewry* [1933] 1 K.B. 753. Performance of an arbitration agreement involves, therefore, not only the appointment of an arbitral tribunal in accordance with such agreement;
E   the conduct before that tribunal of such proceedings as may be appropriate; and, following such proceedings, an adjudication by the tribunal on the matters referred to it and the issue of an award. Performance of an arbitration agreement involves also, as an essential element in the whole process, the payment of the amount of the award by the party against whom it is made.

F   That being so, where a claim by "A" against "B" is the subject matter of an arbitration agreement, and it is shown that, in the event of "A" suceeding in an arbitration held pursuant to such agreement and obtaining an award in respect of his claim against "B," "B" will not be able, by reason of his impecuniosity, to pay the amount of the award, then the arbitration agreement concerned is, in that essential respect, incapable of being performed, and should be so treated for the purposes
G   of section 1 (1) of the Arbitration Act 1975.

    In considering whether this argument is sound or not it is necessary to have regard to the background and purpose of the Act of 1975. The Act was passed to give effect to the New York Convention on the Recognition and Enforcement of Foreign Arbitral Awards 1958. It is an essential preliminary to the recognition and enforcement of arbitral
H   awards that the arbitration agreements capable of resulting in such awards being made <u>should</u> themselves first be recognised and enforced. Section 1 of the Arbitration Act 1975, giving effect to paragraph 3 of article II of the convention, compels the recognition and enforcement of convention (i.e. non-domestic) arbitration agreements by requiring a court, except in certain specified cases, to stay any legal proceedings brought in respect of a matter referred to arbitration under such agreement. Sections 2, 3 and 4 of the Arbitration Act 1975, giving effect to

articles III, IV and V of the Convention, go on to deal with the A
recognition and enforcement of the awards themselves after they have
been made.

   The exceptional cases in which the court is not bound to recognise and
enforce a convention arbitration agreement by granting a stay of legal
proceedings are defined in section 1 (1) of the Arbitration Act 1975 as
those in which the court is satisfied that the arbitration agreement B
concerned is " null and void, inoperative or incapable of being performed," or that " there is not in fact any dispute between the parties
with regard to the matter agreed to be referred." The whole of the
expression " null and void, inoperative or incapable of being performed,"
as so used, is taken directly from paragraph 3 of article II of the
convention.

   It follows from what is said above that the context in which the C
words " incapable of being performed " are used is the context of the
recognition and enforcement or arbitration agreements which, if valid
and effective, will result in awards being made; and not the context of
the recognition and enforcement of such awards themselves after they
have been made. Having regard to that context it appears to me that
the words " incapable of being performed " should be construed as D
referring only to the question whether an arbitration agreement is
capable of being performed up to the stage when it results in an award;
and should not be construed as extending to the question whether, once
an award has been made, the party against whom it is made will be
capable of satisfying it.

   There is the further point that, even if the words " incapable of E
being performed " were given the extended meaning discussed above,
the fact that, if an award were made against one party, he would be
incapable of satisfying it, would not necessarily mean that the arbitration
agreement was incapable of being performed. This is because the
arbitration might also result in the award being made against the other
party, in which case the incapacity concerned would be irrelevant.

   For the reasons which I have given I decide this first point of law F
against the cargo owners. I hold that the fact that one of the parties
to an arbitration agreement would be incapable of satisfying an award
if it should be made against him does not make such agreement
" incapable of being performed " within the meaning of section 1 (1)
of the Arbitration Act 1975.

   Since I may be wrong on the point of construction, however, I shall G
go on to consider whether it is in this case shown that, if an award were
to be made against the shipowners, they would be incapable of satisfying
it. This involves consideration of the financial position of the shipowners, including their rights as members of the club, a subject which
will in any case be highly material in relation to questions (3) and (4)
later.   H

   I shall consider first the financial position of the shipowners apart
from such rights as they may have as members of the club. They are, as
I indicated earlier, a company incorporated in Panama whose central
management and control are exercised in Greece. Their only asset,
apart from the charterparty freight in respect of which a *Mareva*
injunction was granted earlier, and possibly also some further moneys
payable to them by way of demurrage under the same charterparty, is

A the ship herself. That, at any rate, is the inference which I feel bound
to draw in the absence of any evidence from the shipowners themselves
to the contrary.

    I understand that separate security representing the freight, and
possibly also the demurrage, has been provided unconditionally by the
club, and that the amount of such security is about £75,000. There was,
B however, no clear evidence about these matters before me, and the
actual figure may be a little different.

    The ship, according to affidavit evidence from the managers of the
club, A. Bilbrough & Co. Ltd., is at present laid up in Greece. There
is no evidence about her present value, but, since she has been laid up
for a considerable period of time without permanent repairs being done
to her, I infer that it is substantially less than the £390,000 at which she
C was valued in July 1977.

    If the cargo owners were to succeed fully in an arbitration in respect
of their claim, the amount of the award, including interest and costs,
would be likely to be about £700,000. It is clear that, even after allowing
for part of such award being met out of the separate security representing
the freight and possibly also the demurrage, realisation by the ship-
D owners of their only other asset in the form of the ship would provide
a fund quite insufficient to satisfy the balance of the award.

    The conclusion to which I feel bound to come, therefore, is that, if
the cargo owners were to succeed in an arbitration and obtain an award
in respect of the full amount of their claim, the shipowners would be
incapable, out of their own resources alone, of satisfying more than a
E part, probably less than half, of the amount of the award. This proportion would, moreover, be much decreased if the shipowners, between
now and the time when the award becomes payable, sold the ship and
disposed of the proceeds in one way or other.

    The question then arises whether the award would be satisfied by the
club on the shipowners' behalf. The ship was entered in the club at
the material time and the shipowners' calls have been paid up to date.
F They were therefore entitled, subject to the relevant rules of the club,
to be indemnified by the club in respect of liability for loss of or damage
to cargo carried in the ship.

    The relevant rules, however, which come under the heading " Class
5. The Protection and Indemnity Rules," include rules 6 and 8 (k).
Rule 6 provides that, unless the committee otherwise decides, the club
G is not obliged to indemnify a member in respect of a liability unless and
until the member has himself first discharged the liability out of moneys
belonging to him absolutely and not by way of loan or otherwise.
Rule 8 (k) provides that the club may, whenever it thinks fit, reduce the
amount of a member's claim on the ground that he has not taken such
steps to protect his interests as he would have done if the ship had not
H been entered for protection and indemnity.

    The affidavit from the club's managers, A. Bilbrough & Co. Ltd.,
to which I referred earlier, contained evidence also about the way in
which rules 6 and 8 (k) mentioned above are applied in practice. As
regards rule 6 the evidence amounts to this: that, in the case of large
claims like that involved in the present case, the committee often agree
to a member's request that the club should pay the claimant direct
without insisting on the member discharging the claim out of his own

resources first. No indication is, however, given by the deponent as to A
the criteria by which the committee makes its decisions on these matters.

As regards rule 8 (*k*), the evidence is that the committee very
seldom exercises its powers under this rule, even though there may be
circumstances which would justify it in doing so.

The result of the above is that the question whether, if the shipowners
could not pay the award or a large part of it themselves from their own B
resources, the club would pay it directly on their behalf, is left entirely
open. The shipowners have no legal right to insist on the club doing so,
and the club has an unfettered discretion, exercised on no principles
revealed in evidence, to decline to do so. On the other hand, the club
often agrees to make such payments, and it is at least possible that it
would do so in this case.

The burden of proof on the question whether, if the cargo owners C
were to succeed in an arbitration and obtain an award in respect of the
whole of their claim, the shipowners would be incapable of satisfying the
award, lies, in my view, on the cargo owners. So far as satisfaction of
the award, except in part, out of the shipowners' own resources is
concerned, I consider that the cargo owners have discharged that burden
of proof. So far as satisfaction of the award in full by the club on D
the shipowners' behalf is concerned, however, I consider that the cargo
owners have not discharged the burden, because the evidence shows a
clear possibility that the club would satisfy the award direct on their
member's behalf and the cargo owners are unable to eliminate that
possibility.

The result of the conclusions to which I have come on the matters
discussed above is that the contention for the cargo owners, that the E
court should in this case refuse a stay under section 1 (1) of the
Arbitration Act 1975 on the ground that the arbitration agreement is
incapable of being performed, fails both on the law and the facts.

It follows that I answer question (2) by holding that the shipowners
were, as at July 28, 1977, entitled under that subsection to a stay of the
cargo owners' action   F

(3) *If the shipowners were, as at July 28, 1977, entitled to a stay of the
cargo owners' action, were they also entitled, along with and consequent
on such stay, to the unconditional release of the ship from arrest?*

It was contended for the shipowners that, whenever an action in rem
in which a ship is under arrest is stayed under section 1 (1) of the G
Arbitration Act 1975, an order for the unconditional release of the ship
from arrest must also be made, and that the court has no discretion,
whatever the circumstances of any particular case, to refuse such order.

In support of this contention counsel for the shipowners relied on
two comparatively recent cases decided by me in this court which he
said were together conclusive of the matter. These were *The Cap Bon* H
[1967] 1 Lloyd's Rep. 543 and *The Golden Trader* [1975] Q.B. 348.

In *The Cap Bon* there was a claim by charterers against shipowners
for damage to cargo carried under a charterparty containing a London
arbitration clause. The charterers began two proceedings against the
shipowners in respect of the claim: first, an action in rem in the
Liverpool District Registry, in which they arrested the ship concerned,
and in which the shipowners, having appeared, gave bail in order to

A obtain her release; and, secondly, arbitration proceedings under the arbitration clause in the charterparty. The charterers did not proceed with the action but were ready and willing to proceed with the arbitration, their plan being that, if and when they obtained an award in their favour in the arbitration, they would be able to enforce it against the bail in the action. The shipowners applied by summons to the district registrar B for an order that the action either be proceeded with by the charterers or else be dismissed and the bail given in it released. The district registrar refused the order sought, but on appeal I took a different view and made an order that, unless the charterers proceeded with the action by serving a statement of claim within 21 days, the action should stand dismissed and the bail bond should be cancelled.

My decision was based on two propositions of law, one positive and C one negative, which I considered flowed from the nature and form of the provisions in the Administration of Justice Act 1956, by which jurisdiction in rem is conferred on the Admiralty Court. The first and positive proposition is that the purpose of arresting a ship in an action in rem is to provide the plaintiff with security for the payment of any judgment which he may obtain in such action, or of any sum which may D become payable to him under a settlement of such action. The second and negative proposition is that it is not the purpose of arresting a ship in an action in rem to provide the plaintiff with security for payment of an award which he may obtain in an arbitration of the same claim as that raised in the action, and the court therefore has no jurisdiction to arrest a ship, or keep her under arrest, for such other purpose.

On the basis of these propositions I held that the charterers' plan was E misconceived, in that they could never enforce any award which they might obtain in the arbitration against the bail given in the action. That being so, I thought that the charterers should be compelled to choose between the two courses available to them: either pursuing their claim in the action with the advantage of the security obtained by them in it; or pursuing their claim in the arbitration without that advantage.

F It is to be observed that this was not a case where a defendant to an action was seeking to have it stayed, either because he preferred to arbitrate or because he wished to have the security which he had been compelled to give released. It was rather a case in which one party, who was asserting a claim against another party, had set on foot at the same time two separate proceedings in respect of such claim, one an action in rem and the other an arbitration. He wished, however, to have G the claim decided in the arbitration, and was only using the action as a means of obtaining security for the award which he hoped to obtain in the former proceeding. The other party contended that he was not entitled as as matter of law, to do that, and I upheld that contention.

In *The Golden Trader* [1975] Q.B. 348 the facts were in many respects similar to those in the present case. A ship had been chartered H by Dutch charterers from shipowners residing and carrying on business in Eire. The charterers had a claim against the shipowners for alleged breaches of the charterparty. The charterers began an action in rem against the ship in this court in respect of their claim and arrested her in that action. The shipowners then applied, first, for a stay of the action on the ground that the dispute to which it related was covered by the arbitration clause in the charterparty, and secondly, along with and consequent on such stay, for the release of the ship from arrest.

The Arbitration Act 1975 had not been passed at that time, and the A
application for a stay had to be decided under section 4 of the Arbitration
Act 1950, which dealt separately in two subsections with non-protocol
cases on the one hand and protocol cases on the other. So far as non-
protocol cases are concerned, section 4 (1) gave the court, subject to
certain specified conditions, a discretionary power to stay an action
relating to a matter agreed to be referred to arbitration. So far as
protocol cases are concerned, section 4 (2) imposed on the court, again B
subject to certain specified conditions, a mandatory duty to stay an
action relating to a matter agreed to be so referred.

Section 28 of the Arbitration Act 1950 further drew a distinction,
so far as attaching terms to orders for a stay is concerned, between
discretionary orders in non-protocol cases made under section 4 (1), and
mandatory orders in protocol cases made under section 4 (2). The C
effect of the distinction was that the court had power to attach terms
as to costs or other matters to orders made under section 4 (1), but had
no power to do so in the case of orders made under section 4 (2).

I pointed out in my judgment in *The Golden Trader* [1975] Q.B. 348
that, although the question for decision in that case arose on a stay granted
under section 4 (2) of the Arbitration Act 1950, it was part of a larger D
problem which arose whenever an action in rem, in which the property
proceeded against had been arrested, or bail or other security had been
given to prevent or obtain release from arrest, was subsequently stayed on
the ground that the dispute ought properly to be decided by another
tribunal. The same problem arose in three other kinds of case, which
I described shortly for convenience as " non-protocol arbitration cases,"
" foreign jurisdiction clause cases " and " vexation cases " respectively: E
it was what to do with the security when the action was stayed.

I went on to say that there were, in principle, three ways in which this
problem, which arose in these three other kinds of case also, could be
dealt with. The first method was for the court to retain the security to
satisfy any judgment or award of the other tribunal. I called this
" the retention method," and pointed out that it was the method con- F
templated by the International Convention for the Arrest of Seagoing
Ships 1952 (" the Brussels Arrest Convention "), to which the United
Kingdom was a party: see article 7, paragraphs 1 to 4. The second
method was for the court to release the security, but only subject to a term
that the defendants provided other equivalent security outside the court
to satisfy the judgment or award of the other tribunal. I called this
" the alternative security method," and gave examples of its use in G
foreign judgment clause cases: *The Eleftheria* [1970] P. 94 and in
vexation cases: *The Atlantic Star* [1974] A.C. 436. It appeared to me
then that the alternative security method could also be used in non-
protocol arbitration cases (i.e. cases under section 4 (1) of the Arbitration
Act 1950), where the grant of a stay, as in foreign jurisdiction clause
cases and vexation cases, was discretionary and not mandatory. I still H
think that to be so, although the cases concerned should now, as a result
of the Arbitration Act 1975, be re-named " domestic arbitration cases."

It was common ground in *The Golden Trader* [1975] Q.B. 348 that
the case was a protocol case to which section 4 (2) rather than section
4 (1) of the Arbitration Act 1950 applied. If the decision in *The Cap
Bon* [1967] 1 Lloyd's Rep. 543 was correct, the court had no jurisdiction
to use the retention method of dealing with the security; and, since it

A　was a protocol case under section 4 (2), section 28 meant that the alternative security method, in the form of attaching a term to the order for a stay, was not available either.

　　In this situation it would have been open to counsel for the charterers to invite me to treat my earlier decision in *The Cap Bon,* that the court had no jurisdiction to use the retention method, as wrong and to depart from it.　He did not, however, do this, but accepted that *The Cap Bon*
B　[1967] 1 Lloyd's Rep. 543 had been correctly decided and sought to resist the shipowners' application for the release of the ship on other grounds.

　　His contention was that, although the court was bound to make an unconditional order for a stay, it was not also bound to make at the same time an order for the release of the ship.　His main ground for
C　this contention was that the stay was not final, and that the security therefore could and should be retained by the court to cater for the possibility of the stay later being removed and the action then pro-
ceeding to judgment.　This argument did not conflict with the decision in *The Cap Bon* [1967] 1 Lloyd's Rep. 543 for what was being suggested was not retention of the security for the inadmissible purpose of
D　satisfying an award in the arbitration, but retention of the security for the proper purpose of satisfying a judgment in the action which might still, in certain hypothetical events, be obtained by the charterers.

　　Counsel for the charterers relied on a second and alternative ground for the court not releasing the ship.　This was that, once the charterers had begun an arbitration, they would be entitled to apply to the court under section 12 (6) (*f*) of the Arbitration Act 1950 for an order
E　securing the amount in dispute, and the court would have power, on such application, to order the arrest of the ship in order to provide such security.　In these circumstances the existing arrest should be maintained at least until the charterers had had an opportunity of making such application and the court had adjudicated one way or the other upon it.

　　A further possibility was canvassed in argument, at my suggestion
F　if I remember correctly.　This was that, if the court would be justified, on the first ground relied on by counsel for the charterers, in refusing an order for the release of the ship, it might also be justified in making such an order for release but attaching to it a term with regard to the provision of alternative security.　That would involve using, in effect, the alternaive security method of dealing with the problem, but employing slightly different procedural means, which did not conflict
G　with section 28 of the Arbitration Act 1950, for the purpose.

　　The conclusions with regard to these matters which I reached were as follows:

　　(1) That the court had no jurisdiction to keep the ship under arrest in order to provide the charterers with security for an award in the arbitration.　It only had jurisdiction to keep her under arrest in order
H　to provide security for a judgment or settlement in the action.　This conclusion accorded with my earlier decision in *The Cap Bon* [1967] 1 Lloyd's Rep 543, which was not, as I have said, challenged by counsel for the charterers, and which appeared to me in any event to derive support from the approach adopted in three earlier cases which I examined: *The Athenee* (1922) 11 Ll.L.R. 6; *Foresta Romana S.A.* v. *Georges Mabro (Owners)* (1940) 66 Ll.L.R. 139 and *The Fehmarn* [1957] 1 W.L.R. 815; [1958] 1 W.L.R. 159.　(2) That a stay of the action,

not being final, could later be removed for good cause, in which case the A
action could still proceed to judgment or settlement.   (3) That good
cause for removal of the stay might arise if the arbitration subsequently
(in the words of section 4 (2) of the Arbitration Act 1950) became
inoperative or could not proceed.   There was, however, no evidence of
there being more than a remote possibility of events of that kind supervening in that case.   The court would not, therefore, be justified in B
keeping the ship under arrest in order to cater for the possibility of the
stay being removed and the action proceeding by reason of such supervening events.   (4) That failure by the shipowners to satisfy any award
which the charterers might later obtain in the arbitration would not
necessarily be good cause for the removal of the stay.   In the event of
such failure the charterers would be entitled either to enforce the award
as a judgment under section 26 of the Arbitration Act 1950, or to sue C
for breach of the arbitration agreement (see *Bremer Oeltransport
G.m.b.H.* v. *Drewry* [1933] 1 K.B. 753 to which I referred earlier).
There was no evidence before the court to suggest that the shipowners, if
an award were to be made against them, would not pay under it.   The
court would not, therefore, be justified in keeping the ship under
arrest in order to cater for the possibility of the stay being removed and D
the action proceeding by reason of the shipowners not paying under an
award.   (5) That section 12 (6) (*f*) of the Arbitration Act 1950 did not
give the court power to arrest a ship, or to keep her under arrest, in
order to provide security for the claim of a claimant in an arbitration.
The argument for the charterers based on that provision accordingly
failed.   (6) That since, in all probability at least, the stay would be final
and there would be no judgment or settlement in the action to be E
satisfied, the court should make an unconditional order for the release
of the ship, and should not qualify such order by attaching to it a term
with regard to the provision of alternative security.

In *The Golden Trader* [1975] Q.B. 348 the question of stay was, as
I explained, governed by section 4 (2) of the Arbitration Act 1950.
That subsection was repealed by the Arbitration Act 1975 and replaced F
by the provisions of section 1 of the latter Act which I set out earlier.
The Arbitration Act 1975 further repealed the proviso to section 28 of the
Arbitration Act 1950, which had prohibited the attachment of any terms
as to costs or other matters to orders made under section 4 (2).

It might perhaps have been contended in the present case that, since
the Arbitration Act 1975 contained no express prohibition against G
attaching terms as to costs or other matters to orders for a stay under
section 1 (1) of that Act, the court had a discretion to do so.   Mr. Grace
for the cargo owners, however, did not argue that this was so, but
accepted that orders for a stay made under section 1 (1) of the Arbitration Act 1975, like orders for a stay made under section 4 (2) of the
Arbitration Act 1950, had to be unconditional, that is to say without any H
terms of any kind attached to them.

I think that this concession was rightly made for, where a statute
requires the court, in a specified situation, to make an order of a
particular kind, the court can, in general, only attach terms to such
order if the statute gives it express power to do so.   The situation under
the Arbitration Act 1950 was that section 28 expressly gave the court
power to attach terms to various kinds of orders, including orders made

A   under section 4 (1), while providing that the court should not have the same power in relation to orders made under section 4 (2). The situation under the Arbitration Act 1975 is that no power to attach terms to orders for a stay is expressly given, and I do not think that any such power can be implied.

B   Mr. Howard for the shipowners contended, as I indicated earlier, that the question whether, upon a stay being granted, the ship should be unconditionally released, was concluded in the shipowners' favour by the previous decisions of this court in *The Cap Bon* [1967] 1 Lloyd's Rep. 543 and *The Golden Trader* [1975] Q.B. 348. Mr. Grace for the cargo owners did not accept that this was so, because the present case was, he said, distinguishable from *The Golden Trader* [1975] Q.B. 348. If he was wrong about that, however, he fell back on the submission that

C   the two cases were wrongly decided and ought not to be followed.

In considering these matters it is, I think, necessary to distinguish between two aspects of the problem. The first aspect is whether the view which I expressed in *The Cap Bon* [1967] 1 Lloyd's Rep. 543 and followed in *The Golden Trader* [1975] Q.B. 348, that the court has no jurisdiction to arrest a ship, or keep her under arrest, in order to provide

D   a plaintiff with security for payment of an arbitration award, as distinct from payment of a judgment or settlement in the action in rem concerned, is correct or not. The second aspect is whether, assuming that view to be correct, the court nevertheless has a discretion, when it grants a mandatory stay under the Arbitration Act 1975 of an action in rem in which a ship has been arrested, to refuse to release the ship from arrest unless alternative security for payment of an award in the arbi-

E   tration is provided; or, to put the same thing in a different way, to attach to any order made for the release of the ship, as distinct from the order for the stay of the action, a term relating to the provision of such alternative security.

I shall refer to these two aspects of the problem as the jurisdiction point and the discretion point respectively.

F

The jurisdiction point

The conclusion on the jurisdiction point which I reached in *The Cap Bon* [1967] 1 Lloyd's Rep. 543 and followed in *The Golden Trader* [1975] Q.B. 348 was, from the point of view of what I believe that the law on the matter ought to be, as distinct from what I felt obliged to

G   hold that it was, an unsatisfactory conclusion.

I say this for two reasons. The first reason is that I think that, quite apart from any international convention relating to the matter to which the United Kingdom is a party, the court should have power, when it grants a stay, on the ground that the dispute should be decided by another tribunal, of an action in rem in which security has been obtained, to

H   retain such security to satisfy any judgment or award of the other tribunal. When the grant of a stay is discretionary, as in domestic arbitration cases, foreign jurisdiction clause cases, and vexation cases, the court can get round the lack of such power, and has in practice got round it, by using the alternative security method. It would, however, be more satisfactory, in my view, even in those cases, to use the retention method, which is both more simple and direct, and which is, I believe, commonly used in other jurisdictions.

The second reason is that article 7 of the International Convention for A the Arrest of Seagoing Ships 1952 to which the United Kingdom is a party, contemplates that a court, which stays an action on the ground that the dispute should be decided by another tribunal, will have power to retain any security obtained in the action for the purposes mentioned above. I drew attention to this fact, as I said earlier, in the course of my judgment in *The Golden Trader* [1975] Q.B. 348. I further thought B it right to point out at the end of my judgment in that case that, if the view on the jurisdiction point which I have formed was correct, this court did not have the power which the International Convention for the Arrest of Seagoing Ships 1952 contemplated that it would have, and this was a situation which could not be regarded as satisfactory and which it would be desirable for Parliament to remedy.

I have said that Mr Grace for the cargo owners submitted, by way C of alternative argument in support of his case, that the opinion on the jurisdiction point which I formed in *The Cap Bon* [1967] 1 Lloyd's Rep. 453 and followed in *The Golden Trader* [1975] Q.B. 348 was wrong. In view of that submission I have reconsidered carefully the reasons which led me to form that opinion, and it will be apparent, from the observations which I have made above, that I should be in no way D reluctant to change it if I were persuaded that it would be right to do so. Having re-examined the whole question, however, I remain of the same opinion that, without some statutory authority which does not unfortunately at present exist (although it could, of course, easily be given), the court has no jurisdiction to use the retention method, that is to say to retain security not for the purpose of satisfying a judgment or settlement in the action in which the security has been given, but to E satisfy the judgment or award of another tribunal.

The discretion point

There was controversy before me as to what *The Golden Trader* [1975] Q.B. 348 actually decided. For the shipowners it was said that it decided that, in every case where the court grants a mandatory stay F of action in rem in which the ship proceded against has been arrested, it is bound to make an unconditional order for the release of the ship. If the case decided that, and decided it correctly, then it follows that the shipowners in this case were entitled, as at July 28, 1977, along with a stay of the cargo owners' action, to an unconditional order for the release of the ship.   G

For the cargo owners it was said that the decision in *The Golden Trader* [1975] Q.B. 348, that the shipowners were entitled to an unconditional order for the release of the ship, was related to the finding made by the court in that case, that in all probability the stay would be final and that there would therefore be no judgment in the action to be satisfied. In these circumstances, the decision left open the question H whether, in other cases where it was shown that the stay might well not be final and there might well therefore still be a judgment in the action to be satisfied, the court might not be justified in keeping the ship under arrest or only releasing her subject to a term for the provision of alternative security. Alternatively, if the case laid down the general rule which the shipowners said it did, it was to this extent at least wrong.

A   The relevant passage in my judgment in *The Golden Trader* [1975] Q.B. 348, 359–360, reads:

"In theory I do not see why, if it is appropriate to use the alternative security method in non-protocol arbitration cases, foreign jurisdiction clause cases and vexation cases, where the grant of a stay is discretionary, it should not also be appropriate to use

B   it in protocol arbitration cases, where the grant of a stay is mandatory, even if the procedure employed for the purpose has to be slightly different. On further examination of the point, however, I think that protocol arbitration cases must, in this respect, be treated differently. Counsel for the defendants argued that to attach a term for the provision of alternative security to the order for release, while not offending against the letter of section 28 of

C   the Act of 1950, would offend against its spirit. While this may be the right way to put the matter, I should prefer to put it differently as follows. The starting point, if *The Cap Bon* [1967] 1 Lloyd's Rep. 543 is right, is that the court can only retain the security to satisfy a judgment or compromise in the action itself. It follows that, if the court stays the action, *so that there will, in all probability

D   at least, be no judgment or compromise in the action to be satisfied,* it must then release the security. Putting it shortly, if there is a stay, there must, as a necessary consequence, be a release. In cases where the grant of a stay is discretionary, the court can refuse a stay unless alternative security is provided. The defendant then has to choose between having a stay subject to a term for the provision of such security and not having a stay at all. If he

E   chooses the former, then, subject to his complying with the term, he gets both stay and release; if he chooses the latter, he gets neither. By contrast, in protocol arbitration cases, where the grant of a stay is mandatory, the court cannot refuse a stay unless alternative security is provided. It is bound to grant a stay in any event, and, since release is a necessary consequence of a stay, it

F   is bound also to grant a release."

The emphasis on the words "so that there will, in all probability at least, be no judgment or compromise to be satisfied" is mine.

I can well understand this passage being read as meaning that, in all cases where the stay of an action in rem is mandatory, the security obtained in it must be unconditionally released. It was, however, not

G   necessary for me to go so far as that in order to decide the case before me, and the words emphasised in italics show that my views were being expressed in relation to a case in which in all probability the stay of the action would be final and there would therefore be no judgment in the action to be satisfied. In these circumstances I think that counsel for the cargo owners was right in saying either that the case left open the

H   question as to what order should be made in other cases in which it was shown that the stay might well not be final and that there might well therefore still be a judgment in the action to be satisfied; or alternatively that, if the case did not leave that question open, it ought to have done so and was to that extent wrong.

On the footing that the question is an open one, it was suggested for the shipowners that a party to an arbitration agreement should be treated as having, by entering into such an agreement, abandoned the

452

rights which he would otherwise have had to security for any claim   A
covered by the agreement.

I do not accept this proposition at all. The choice of forum for the
determination of the merits of a dispute is one thing. The right to
security in respect of maritime claims under the Admiralty law of this
country is another. This distinction has been recognised and given
effect to by the way in which the court has exercised its discretion in
foreign jurisdiction clauses and vexation cases, in which it has either   B
treated the plaintiff's right to security as a material factor in refusing
a stay (*The Athenee* (1922) 11 Ll.L.Rep. 6 and *The Fehmarn* [1957]
1 W.L.R. 815), or else has only granted a stay subject to a term for
the provision of alternative security: *The Eleftheria* [1970] P. 94 and
The Atlantic Star [1974] A.C. 436, and more recently *The Makefjell*
[1975] 1 Lloyd's Rep. 528; [1976] 2 Lloyd's Rep. 29.   C

If this distinction between choice of forum on the one hand and right
to security on the other is recognised and given effect to in foreign
jurisdiction clause cases and vexation cases, I cannot see any good reason
why it should not equally be recognised and given effect to in arbitration
cases, whether the grant of a stay is discretionary under section 4 (1) of
the Arbitration Act 1950, or, as in the present case, mandatory under   D
section 1 (1) of the Arbitration Act 1975.

I would like to stress again in this connection also that the distinction
in question is clearly recognised and given effect to by the International
Convention for the Arrest of Seagoing Ships 1952.

The process by which property, which has been lawfully arrested in
an action in rem, can be released at the instance of the party interested
in it, is the making by the court of an order for the issue of a release   E
under R.S.C., Ord. 75, r. 13 (4). That rule provides, so far as material:
" A release may be issued at the instance of a party interested in the
property under arrest if the court so orders, . . ." That rule, as I understand it, gives the court a discretion, when an application for an order
for the issue of a release is made, whether to make such order or not.
The discretion so given is, so far as the terms of the rule go unfettered,   F
but it must, like any other discretion, be exercised judicially.

There is nothing in section 1 (1) of the Arbitration Act 1975 which
obliges the court, whenever it grants a stay of an action in rem in which
security has been obtained, to make an order for the unconditional
release of such security. Nor did section 4 (2) of the Arbitration Act
1950, now repealed, impose any such obligation. That being so, I
think that it is a matter for the discretion of the court, acting under the   G
rule referred to above, what order it should make with regard to such
security, and that the way in which it exercises that discretion must
depend on the circumstances of each particular case.

If, on the one hand, the case is one where in all probability the stay
will be final and there will therefore never be any judgment in the action
to be satisfied, the court should exercise its discretion by releasing the   H
security unconditionally, as was done in *The Golden Trader* [1975]
Q.B. 348. If, on the other hand, the case is one where the stay may well
not be final and there may well therefore still be a judgment in the
action to be satisfied, the court should exercise its discretion either by
refusing to release the security at all, or by only releasing it subject to
a term that the defendants shall provide alternative security for payment
of any award in the arbitration.

A   On this view of the law it is necessary to consider, in relation to the facts of this particular case, whether in all probability the stay will be final and there will therefore never be any judgment in the action to be satisfied, or whether the stay may well not be final and there may well therefore still be a judgment in the action to be satisfied.

It is in this respect that Mr. Grace contended that the present case was clearly distinguishable from *The Golden Trader* [1975] Q.B. 348.
B   There was, he said, ample evidence to show that, if the cargo owners obtained an award in respect of the full amount of their claim, the shipowners might well be unable to satisfy it, even if all available steps to enforce the award were taken. In that event the cargo owners would be entitled to have the stay of action removed and to obtain a judgment in rem against the shipowners in it. That judgment would, however, be
C   worthless unless there were security still available against which it could be satisfied. Justice to the cargo owners therefore demanded that the court should either, as at July 28, 1977, have kept the ship under arrest to serve as such security, or alternatively should only have released her subject to a term that the shipowners provided alternative security to satisfy an award in the arbitration.

D   Mr. Howard for the shipowners contended that it was wrong to suggest that, if an award should be made against the shipowners and they should be unable to satisfy it, the cargo owners' would then be in a position to have the stay of the action removed and to obtain a judgment in rem in it. It was wrong, he said, because, once an award was made, the cargo owners' cause of action would become merged in the award and would therefore no longer be available to them for pro-
E   secution in the action. In these circumstances the whole argument for the cargo owners broke down, and the whole basis for keeping the ship under arrest, or only releasing her subject to a term for the provision of alternative security, disappeared.

This contention involves a consideration of the law of merger in relation, firstly, to arbitral awards, and, secondly, to causes of action in
F   rem. I am prepared to assume, without finally deciding, that, just as a cause of action in personam which is adjudicated upon by an English court merges in the judgment of that court, so also a similar cause of action which is adjudicated upon by an English arbitral tribunal merges in the award of that tribunal. That is the view which is expressed in *Spencer Bower and Turner, Res Judicata*, 2nd ed. (1969), p. 362, and
G   it appears to be supported at least by *Gascoyne* v. *Edwards* (1826) 1 Y. & J. 19, and possibly also by certain other cases to which I was referred.

It has, however, been held that a cause of action in rem, being of a different character from a cause of action in personam, does not merge in a judgment in personam, but remains available to the person who has it so long as, and to the extent that, such judgment remains unsatis-
H   fied: *The Bengal* (1859) Swab. 468; *The John and Mary* (1859) Swab. 471; *The Cella* (1888) 13 P.D. 82; see also *The Sylph* (1867) L.R. 2 A. & E. 24 (although this may have turned partly on an express reservation made in the submission to arbitration concerned) and *Yeo* v. *Tatem (The Orient)* (1871) L.R. 3 P.C. 696. The situation must, in my view, be the same in the case of an arbitral award, which is likewise based on a cause of action in personam.

It was argued for the shipowners that this exception to the general

rule of merger applied only when the cause of action in rem was A
founded on a maritime lien, which the cargo owners' claim in the present
case is not. The first two cases referred to above, *The Bengal*,
Swab. 468 and *The John and Mary*, Swab. 471, were certainly maritime lien cases, the claim in the former being for wages and in the
latter for damages by collision. But the observations of Sir James
Hannan P. in the third case, *The Cella*, 13 P.D. 82, 85 related to a
claim for repairs and necessaries made under section 4 of the Admiralty B
Court Act 1861, in respect of which the plaintiff had no maritime lien,
but only, like the cargo owners in the present case, a statutory right of
action in rem. I cannot see any good reason in principle for distinguishing in this respect between a cause of action founded on a maritime
lien and one founded on a statutory right in rem. It appears to me,
therefore, both on principle and authority, that the distinction suggested C
is not a valid one.

The result is that I accept the argument of counsel for the cargo
owners that, if an award should be made against the shipowners and
they should be unable to satisfy it, the cargo owners would be entitled
to have the stay of the action removed and to proceed to a judgment
in rem in it. D

I examined earlier, in relation to question (2), the financial situation
of the shipowners and the position of the club in the matter. As a
result of that examination I have no hesitation in concluding that this
is a case in which, if the cargo owners should obtain an award in respect
of the full amount of their claim, the shipowners might well be unable
to satisfy it, either themselves or through the medium of the club. It
follows, on my view that a cause of action in rem does not, as a matter E
of law, become merged in an arbitral award, that this is a case where
the stay might well not be final and there might well therefore still be a
judgment in the action to be satisfied.

In these circumstances, applying the principles for the exercise of
the court's discretion which I concluded earlier were the right principles
to apply, I consider that the court ought in this case to have exercised F
its discretion, as at July 28, 1977, by either keeping the ship under
arrest or by only releasing her subject to a term for the provision of
alternative security.

It follows that I answer question (3) by saying that the shipowners
were not entitled, as at July 28, 1977, along with and consequent on the
stay of the action, to the unconditional release of the ship from arrest. G

(4) *If, as at July 28, 1977, the shipowners were entitled to the unconditional release of the ship from arrest, were the cargo owners then
entitled, by way of alternative security for their claim, to a Mareva
injunction in respect of the ship?*

This further question only arises if I am wrong on question (3). H

The power of the High Court to grant *Mareva* injunctions under
section 45 of the Supreme Court of Judicature (Consolidation) Act 1925
has been established by a series of recent decisions of the Court of Appeal
culminating in *Rasu Maritima S.A.* v. *Perusahaan Pertambangan Minyakdangas Bumi Negara (Government of the Republic of Indonesia intervening)* [1977] 3 W.L.R. 518. Further the House of Lords, while
reserving the question of the correctness of those decisions, was prepared

A   to assume the existence of the power, in principle, for the purpose of its decision in *Siskina (Owners of cargo lately laden on board)* v. *Distos Compania Naviera S.A.* [1977] 3 W.L.R. 818.

A *Mareva* injunction is granted in a case where a plaintiff has brought an action here against a foreign defendant, and the latter has moneys or chattels within the jurisdiction which, if he were not prevented from doing so, he would be free to remove out of the jurisdiction
B   before the plaintiff could bring the action to trial, and, if successful, obtain and enforce a judgment against him.

The injunction takes the form of an order restraining the defendant, by himself, his servants or agents, from selling, disposing of or otherwise dealing with such moneys or chattels or from removing them out of the jurisdiction, usually until further order. Its purpose is to ensure
C   that, if the plaintiff succeeds in the action, there will be property of the defendant available here out of which the judgment which the plaintiff obtains in it can be satisfied.

On the footing that the procedure is available to provide a plaintiff, in a case where no question of arbitration arises, with security for any judgment which he may obtain in an action, I see no good reason in principle why it should not also be available to provide a plaintiff,
D   whose action is being stayed on the application of a defendant in order that the claim may be decided by arbitration in accordance with an arbitration agreement between them, with security for the payment of any award which the plaintiff may obtain in the arbitration. I have further been informed by counsel that the Commercial Court has granted injunctions on this extended basis in a number of unreported
E   cases.

I doubt whether specific statutory authority, beyond the general authority conferred on the court by section 45 of the Supreme Court of Judicature (Consolidation) Act 1925, is required to justify this extension of the *Mareva* injunction procedure. If such specific authority is required, however, I think that it is to be found in section 12 (6)
F   of the Arbitration Act 1950, which provides so far as material:

"The High Court shall have, for the purpose of and in relation to a reference, the same powers of making orders in respect of— . . . (f) securing the amount in dispute in the reference; . . . (h) interim injunctions; . . . as it has for the purpose of and in relation to an action . . ."

G   As I mentioned earlier, it was argued for the charterers in *The Golden Trader* [1975] Q.B. 348 that section 12 (6) (f) above gave the court power to arrest a ship in order to secure the amount in dispute in an arbitration once such arbitration had been commenced. Counsel for the cargo owners in the present case went a stage further and argued that the provision gave the court power to do this not only once the
H   arbitration concerned had been commenced, but also in anticipation of its commencement.

I was unable to accept the basic argument with regard to section 12 (6) (f) put forward for the charterers in *The Golden Trader* [1975] Q.B. 348, because it appeared to me that, on the true construction of that provision, it did not cover the arresting of a ship, or the keeping of a ship under arrest, in the exercise of the court's jurisdiction in rem at all. The provision refers to the power of "making orders in respect of securing the amount in dispute." This did not seem to me to be **A** appropriate language to describe the process of arrest in an action in rem, because such arrest does not result from the making of any order by the court, but from the party concerned himself causing a warrant of arrest to be issued under R.S.C., Ord. 75, r. 5, subject to the requirements of that rule. The matters to which I thought the provision related were the court's powers of securing amounts in dispute in various other ways, for instance by making orders under R.S.C., Ord. 29, rr. 2 **B** (3) and 6.

I still think that section 12 (6) (*f*) of the Arbitration Act 1950 does not cover the arresting of a ship, or the keeping of a ship under arrest, in the exercise of the court's jurisdiction in rem. It follows that I am equally unable to accept the extended argument as to the effect of that provision put forward for the cargo owners in the present case. The **C** point involved in the extension itself, however, is a separate one, and I shall return to it shortly.

Although I cannot, for the reasons which I have given, accept that section 12 (6) (*f*) of the Arbitration Act 1950 covers the arresting of a ship, or the keeping of a ship under arrest, it appears to me that both section 12 (6) (*f*) and (*h*) cover the granting of a *Mareva* injunction, and **D** so give the court the same power to grant such an injunction for the purpose of and in relation to an arbitration as it has for the purpose of and in relation to an action or matter in the court.

As to the question whether the court can exercise such power not only once the arbitration concerned has been commenced but also in anticipation of its commencement, it is to be observed that R.S.C., Ord. 29, r. 1 (3), gives the court power to grant interim injunctions, for **E** the purpose of and in relation to an action or matter in the court, before the writ or originating summons by which the cause or matter is to be begun has been issued, and, in such cases, to impose terms providing for the issue of the writ or originating summons, together with such other terms as it thinks fit.

It follows, in my view, that the court has power under section 12 **F** (6) (*f*) and (*h*) to grant a *Mareva* injunction for the purpose of and in relation to an arbitration which has not yet been commenced, and to do so subject to a term providing for the arbitration to be commenced within a specified time, together with such other terms, if any, as it thinks fit.

Various arguments were advanced for the shipowners against the **G** application of the procedure of *Mareva* injunctions to ships. First, it was said that, because the Administration of Justice Act 1956 provided for the arrest of ships in Admiralty actions in rem, it impliedly excluded ships from the categories of chattels in respect of which a *Mareva* injunction could be granted under section 45 of the Supreme Court of Judicature (Consolidation) Act 1925. If that were not so, it was said, a plaintiff with a maritime claim might obtain a *Mareva* injunction in **H** respect of two or more ships, or proceed in rem against one ship and obtain a *Mareva* injunction in respect of one or more other ships, and by these means obtain security for a larger amount than he could by proceeding in rem against a single ship (which was all he was allowed to do) under the Administration of Justice Act 1956.

Secondly, it was said that, if a plaintiff was in the difficulty that he was not entitled, in a case like the present one, to ensure security for

A his claim by having a ship kept under arrest in the exercise of the
court's jurisdiction in rem, he should not be allowed to get round that
difficulty and achieve substantially the same result by obtaining a
Mareva injunction relating to the same ship.

Thirdly, it was said that the grant of a *Mareva* injunction in respect
of a ship gave rise, or might well give rise, to a number of incon-
veniences. The ship would not be in the custody of the Admiralty
B marshal, so that the control and effective enforcement of her detention
provided by such custody would not be available. The detention of the
ship might further create an obstruction in a port or elsewhere to the
prejudice of a port authority or other third parties.

I do not find these arguments at all convincing. As regards the first
and second arguments, it is to be observed that the shipowners entered
C an unconditional appearance to the cargo owners' action, so that it is
not only an action in rem against the ship but also an action in personam
against them. The rights given to the plaintiffs by the Supreme Court
of Judicature (Consolidation) Act 1925 and the Administration of Justice
Act 1956 are cumulative, not alternative: see particulary section 43 of
the Act of 1925. That being so, I cannot see why the circumstance
that the cargo owners cannot (if it be the case) maintain security for
D their claim by having the ship kept under arrest by the court in the
exercise of its jurisdiction in rem should be a reason why they should
not be entitled to obtain alternative security for their claim by means
of a *Mareva* injunction relating to the ship granted by the court in the
exercise of its jurisdiction in personam. On the contrary, the fact that
they are unable in their efforts to ensure security for their claim to use
E one of the two methods potentially available for the purpose, seems to
me to afford a very good reason why they should be permitted to use
the other.

The questions of a plaintiff obtaining a *Mareva* injunction in respect
of several ships, or of combining an arrest of one ship in proceedings
in rem with the obtaining of a *Mareva* injunction in respect of one or
F more other ships in proceedings in personam, do not arise for consideration in this case. I would, however, just say that the prospect of
a plaintiff being able to obtain several kinds of security cumulatively in
respect of the same claim, if the size of such claim justifies it, is not
one which fills me with any consternation or dismay.

As regards the third argument, I do not think that the fact that the
ship will not be in the custody of the Admiralty marshal is of any
G particular significance. The court grants injunctions in the expectation
that they will be obeyed, not disobeyed, and a *Mareva* injunction relating
to a ship does not differ in principle, so far as enforcement is concerned,
from a similar injunction in respect of any other moveable chattel. As
to third parties, if they should be adversely affected by the injunction,
I think that they would be entitled to intervene in the proceedings in
H order to protect their interests.

The result is that I approach this matter on the basis that the court
had power, as at July 28, 1977, to grant a *Mareva* injunction in this case,
and that the only question is whether, in the words of section 45 of the
Supreme Court of Judicature (Consolidation) Act 1925, it would have
appeared to the court just and convenient to do so. That would have
been a matter for the discretion of the court, having regard to the
particular circumstances of the case.

Considering the matter as at July 28, 1977, there were two strong A
points in favour of granting a *Mareva* injunction. The first point was
that the cargo owners had a very strong prima facie case in support of
their claim. The second point was that, if an injunction were not
granted, the cargo owners, assuming that they obtained an award,
might well be unable to recover more than a comparatively small part
of it. I have explained earlier why each of these matters should be so,
and do not need to do so again here.   B

There was one apparently strong point against granting an injunction.
It was that the ship was a trading asset, and that, if the shipowners were
compelled by an injunction to keep her here, they would lose the benefit
of trading her. The strength of the point is, however, apparent only,
for we now know that, since the ship was released, the shipowners have
not used her for trading but have laid her up in Greece without carrying C
out permanent repairs to her. It may be said that this circumstance
could not have been known in advance as at July 28, 1977. The intentions of the shipowners at that time would, however, have had to be
investigated, and it would have been for them to prove that they intended
to continue trading the ship. They adduced no evidence to show that,
whatever it is now known in fact happened, it was then their intention
to do so.   D

In any case there is a certain artificiality about the concept that, if
a *Mareva* injunction had been granted, the ship would have remained
here, for it is obvious from what in fact happened that the club would
have given a letter of undertaking rather than have allowed their
member's ship to be detained here indefinitely.

Having considered all the relevant circumstances of the case, includ- E
ing particularly the main points discussed above, I should on July 28,
1977, if it had been necessary for me to decide whether to grant a
Mareva injunction or not, have exercised my discretion by granting
such injunction, subject, I think, to a term providing for the arbitration
to be commenced within a specified time. It follows that I answer
question (4) in the affirmative.   F

I have now examined and answered each of the four main questions
which were argued before me. The result of my answers to questions
(1) and (2) is that, on the shipowners' adjourned application in the cargo
owners' action, there must be an order for a stay of the action. The
result of my answer to question (3), or, if that is wrong, of my answer
to question (4), is that, on the originating summons issued by the shipowners and the club, there must be a declaration that the club is not G
entitled to the return and cancellation of its letter of undertaking.

Declaration accordingly.
Shipowners to pay 15 *per cent. of*
cargo owners' costs.
Leave to appeal. H

Solicitors: *Hill, Dickinson & Co.; Ince & Co.*

M. B. D.

A

[COURT OF APPEAL]

INLAND REVENUE COMMISSIONERS *v.* PLUMMER

1978 April 4, 5, 6;   Buckley and Bridge L.JJ and
B   May 5   Foster J.

*Revenue—Tax avoidance—Sale of annuity to charity—Surtax
payer selling five-year annuity to registered charity—Yearly
sum equalling £500 after deduction of income tax paid by
taxpayer in consideration for receiving £2,480 from charity—
Whether payment of " any annuity or other annual payment "
—Whether yearly payments made for " valuable and sufficient
consideration "—Whether scheme expressly designed to avoid*
C   *tax falling within statutory definition of " settlement "—
Whether yearly payments deductible from total income for
tax purposes—Income and Corporation Taxes Act* 1970 (c. 10),
ss. 52 (1), 434, 454 (3), 457

      The taxpayer, a taxation manager, supervised and par-
ticipated in a taxation saving scheme aimed at surtax payers.
The scheme provided for a registered charity to purchase
D   annuities from those wishing to participate in the scheme.
The charity was thought to be able to recover the tax deducted
when the surtax payers paid the annuity to it and the surtax
payers would be able to deduct the amount of the annuity from
their income for tax purposes.   In 1971 the taxpayer personally
took advantage of the scheme; he agreed that in consideration
of payment to him of £2,480 by the charity he would make to
the charity five yearly payments of a sum which after deduction
E   of standard rate tax would each equal £500.   To provide the
charity with sufficient funds to make the capital payments to
the taxpayer and to give it security against possible failure by
the taxpayer to pay a due instalment, financing arrangements
were made which complicated an otherwise simple scheme.
Additionally, the charity took out a life insurance to protect it
against the possibility of the taxpayer's death before all five
F   payments had been made.   The taxpayer appealed against
three assessments to surtax for the years from 1970 to 1973
on the ground that no deductions had been made under the
provisions of section 52 (1) of the Income and Corporation
Taxes Act 1970 [1] from his total income in respect of the

[Reported by MRS. HARRIET DUTTON, Barrister-at-Law]

G

[1] Income and Corporation Taxes Act 1970, s. 52 (1): " (1) Where any annuity
or other annual payment charged with tax under Case III of Schedule D, not being
interest, is payable wholly out of profits or gains brought into charge to income tax—
(*a*) no assessment to income tax (other than surtax) shall be made on the person
entitled to the annuity or other annual payment, and (*b*) the whole of the profits
or gains shall be assessed and charged with income tax on the person liable to the
annuity or other annual payment, without distinguishing the annuity or other annual
payment, and (*c*) the person liable to make the payment, whether out of the profits or
H   gains charged with income tax or out of any annual payment liable to deduction, or
from which a deduction has been made, shall be entitled on making the payment to
deduct and retain out of it a sum representing the amount of income tax thereon at
the standard rate for the year in which the amount payable becomes due, and (*d*) the
person to whom the payment is made shall allow the deduction on receipt of the
residue of the payment, and the person making the deduction shall be acquitted and
discharged of so much money as is represented by the deduction, as if that sum had
been actually paid."
      S. 434: " (1) Any income which, by virtue or in consequence of any disposition
made, directly or indirectly, by any person (other than a disposition made for
valuable and sufficient consideration), is payable to or applicable for the benefit of

annuity payments made to the charity. The special com- A
missioners, allowing the appeal, held that the payments were
payments of " any annuity or other annual payment " within
section 52 (1) and were deductible.

Walton J., dismissing an appeal by the Crown, upheld the
commissioners' decision that the payments fell within section
52 (1), and were not disallowed as deductions under the
provision either of section 434 or of section 457.

On appeal by the Crown: —   B

Held, dismissing the appeal, (1) that in order to ascertain
whether the payments made by the taxpayer were " payments
of any annuity " it was necessary to look at the whole transaction to determine their true character; that the Crown's
contention that the payments were repayments of a loan and
thus of a capital nature was not supported by the facts with
the result that the character of " annuity payments " had to be
attributed to them and that as under the scheme the payments C
were to be treated as paid out of the taxpayer's taxed income,
section 52 (1) of the Act did operate to allow deduction of
income tax from those payments (post, pp. 467G, H, 468B,
469A–C, 474C, D).

Sothern-Smith v. *Clancy* [1941] 1 K.B. 276, C.A.; *Inland
Revenue Commissioners* v. *Frere* [1965] A.C. 402, H.L.(E.)
and *Chancery Lane Safe Deposit and Offices Co. Ltd.* v.
Inland Revenue Commissioners [1966] A.C. 85, H.L.(E.) D
applied.

(2) That as the transaction between the parties was a bona
fide commercial transaction devoid of any element of bounty,
notwithstanding that its sole object was to avoid payment of
tax, the only possible conclusion that could be reached was
that the price paid for the annuity, albeit viewed as an amount
paid net of tax, was " valuable and sufficient consideration "
and that accordingly section 434 of the Act could not operate E
to disallow the deductions (post, pp. 471H—472D, 473H—
474C, D).

(3) That as the transaction was effected for full consideration it could not come within the definition of a " settlement " and that accordingly section 457 of the Act could not
be applied to disallow the deduction and thus the annual payments were deductible in computing the taxpayer's income
for surtax purposes (post, pp. 470C, D, G, H, 474C, D).   F

Bulmer v. *Inland Revenue Commissioners* [1967] Ch. 145
and *Inland Revenue Commissioners* v. *Leiner* (1964) 41 T.C.
589 applied.

Per Buckley L.J.   (i) Fiscal consequences are nowadays
incidents of many business transactions and as such affect the
amount of consideration given or accepted by any party and
they must therefore be elements to be taken into account in
determining whether the consideration given by either party G
to a transaction is sufficient (post, p. 471F, G).

(ii) *Bulmer* v. *Inland Revenue Commissioners* [1967] Ch.
145 has no bearing on section 434 of the Income and
Corporation Taxes Act 1970 (post, p. 472G).

Decision of Walton J. [1977] 1 W.L.R. 1227; [1977] 3 All
E.R. 1009 affirmed.

any other person for a period which cannot exceed six years shall be deemed for all H
the purposes of the Income Tax Acts to be the income of the person, if living, by
whom the disposition was made, and not to be the income of any other person. (2)
In this chapter, unless the context otherwise requires, ' disposition ' includes any
trust, covenant, agreement or arrangement."

S. 454 (3): see post, p. 470A, B.

S. 457: " (1) Where, during the life of the settlor, income arising under a settlement made on or after April 7, 1965, is, under the settlement and in the events that
occur, payable to or applicable for the benefit of any person other than the settlor,
then, . . . the income shall be treated for the purposes of surtax as the income of
the settlor and not as the income of any other person."

A

The following cases are referred to in the judgments:

Ball v. *National and Grindlays Bank Ltd.* [1973] Ch. 127; [1972] 3
 W.L.R. 17; [1971] 3 All E.R. 485; 47 T.C. 287, C.A.
Bulmer v. *Inland Revenue Commissioners* [1967] Ch. 145; [1966] 3
 W.L.R. 672; [1966] 3 All E.R. 801; 44 T.C. 1.
Campbell v. *Inland Revenue Commissioners* [1970] A.C. 77; [1968]
 3 W.L.R. 1025; [1968] 3 All E.R. 588; 45 T.C. 427, H.L.(E.).

B

Copeman v. *Coleman* [1939] 2 K.B. 484; [1939] 3 All E.R. 224; 22 T.C.
 594.
Chancery Lane Safe Deposit and Offices Co. Ltd. v. *Inland Revenue Commissioners* [1966] A.C. 85; [1966] 2 W.L.R. 251; [1966] 1 All E.R.
 1; 43 T.C. 83, H.L.(E.).
Foley v. *Fletcher* (1858) 3 H. & N. 769.
Inland Revenue Commissioners v. *Church Commissioners for England*

C

 [1977] A.C. 329; [1976] 3 W.L.R. 214; [1976] 2 All E.R. 1037,
 H.L.(E.).
Inland Revenue Commissioners v. *Frere* [1965] A.C. 402; [1964] 3 W.L.R.
 1193; [1964] 3 All E.R. 796; 42 T.C. 125, H.L.(E.).
Inland Revenue Commissioners v. *Leiner* (1964) 41 T.C. 589.
Inland Revenue Commissioners v. *Wesleyan & General Assurance Society*
 [1948] 1 All E.R. 555; 30 T.C. 11, H.L.(E.).

D

Perrin v. *Dickson* [1930] 1 K.B. 107; 14 T.C. 617, C.A.
Ransom v. *Higgs* [1974] 1 W.L.R. 1594; [1974] 3 All E.R. 949; 50 T.C.
 1, H.L.(E.).
Secretary of State for India v. *Scoble* [1903] A.C. 299; 4 T.C. 618, H.L.(E.).
Sothern-Smith v. *Clancy* [1941] 1 K.B. 276; 24 T.C. 1, C.A.

The following additional cases were cited in argument:

E

Black Nominees Ltd. v. *Nicol* (1975) 50 T.C. 229.
Inland Revenue Commissioners v. *Goodwin* [1976] 1 W.L.R. 191; [1976]
 1 All E.R. 481; T.C. Leaflet No. 2589, H.L.(E.).
Inland Revenue Commissioners v. *Joiner* [1975] 1 W.L.R. 1701; [1975]
 3 All E.R. 1050, H.L.(E.).

APPEAL from Walton J.

F

The taxpayer, Ronald Anthony Plummer, was taxation manager of
Slater Walker Ltd. He supervised and participated in a tax saving scheme
whereby he agreed to sell to a registered charity, Home and Overseas
Voluntary Aid Services Ltd., a five-year annuity which after tax was
deducted was equal to a yearly sum of £500 in consideration of payment to
him of £2,480. He was assessed to surtax for 1970–71 in the sum of
£3,485; for 1971–72 of £3,476 and for 1972–73 of £4,165. The special

G

commissioners allowed his appeal against the assessments on the ground
that the yearly payments made by him to H.O.V.A.S. were payments of
" any annuity or other annual payments " and thus fell within the relieving
provisions of section 52 (1) of the Income and Corporation Taxes Act
1970. They discharged the assessments for 1970–71 and for 1971–72 and
reduced the assessment for 1972–73 to £3,349.

H

Walton J., dismissing an appeal by the Crown, upheld the commissioners' decision in relation to section 52 (1) of the Act. Additionally,
he held that neither section 434 nor section 457 of the Act operated to
disallow deduction of the payments from the taxpayer's income for
surtax purposes.

The Crown appealed on the grounds that (1) the payments made by
the taxpayer to H.O.V.A.S. in pursuance of the agreement of March 15,
1971, were capital payments and not income payments and, therefore,

were not deductible in the computation of the taxpayer's total income   A
from all sources for the purposes of surtax; (2) alternatively, if, contrary
to the Crown's contention in ground (1), the said payments were income
payments, (a) the payments were not payments made out of profits or
gains brought into charge to tax within the meaning of section 52 of the
Act, and therefore the taxpayer was not entitled to deduct the sums in
computing his total income from all sources for the purposes of surtax;
(b) the payments were payments of income which by virtue of a disposition   B
made by the taxpayer, namely the agreement of March 15, 1971, were
payable to another person, namely H.O.V.A.S., for a period which could
not exceed six years. As the disposition was not made for valuable and
sufficient consideration within the meaning of section 434 of the Act, the
payments were to be deemed, by virtue of that section, to be the income
of the taxpayer for all the purposes of the Income Tax Acts. Therefore   C
the taxpayer was not entitled to deduct the sums in computing his total
income from all sources for the purposes of surtax; (c) the payments were
(within the meaning of section 457 of the Act) payments of income arising
under a settlement of which the taxpayer was the settlor and were,
under the settlement, payable to H.O.V.A.S. and were therefore, by
virtue of the provisions of that section, to be treated as the income of the
taxpayer for the purposes of surtax—the payments not falling within the   D
provisions of any of the exceptions set out in that section; (3) the judge
was wrong in law in holding that the agreement of March 15, 1971, was a
disposition made by the taxpayer for valuable and sufficient consideration
within the meaning of section 434 of the Act; (4) the judge was wrong in
law in holding that the ratio decidendi of *Bulmer* v. *Inland Revenue Commissioners* [1967] Ch. 145 was applicable to the present case because, (a)   E
the principle enunciated in *Bulmer* was not applicable to cases falling with
the provisions of section 434 of the Act, which itself expressly limited the
class of dispositions to which the section applied by the words in
brackets, and (b) on a proper construction of the relevant legislation the
principle enunciated in *Bulmer* did not apply to a " disposition " or " settlement " the whole raison d'être of which was tax avoidance; and (5)
alternatively, if, contrary to the Crown's contentions in ground (4), the   F
principle enunciated in *Bulmer* was applicable to cases falling within
section 434 or to cases where the whole raison d'être of the " disposition "
or " settlement " was tax avoidance, the Crown would contend that *Bulmer*
was wrongly decided.

The facts are set out in the judgment of Buckley L.J.

  G

Patrick Medd Q.C., *Peter Gibson* and *Brian Davenport* for the Crown.
Michael Nolan Q.C. and *David Milne* for the taxpayer.

Cur. adv. vult.

May 5. The following judgments were read.

BUCKLEY L.J. This is an appeal from Walton J. who on July 1,   H
1977, dismissed an appeal by the Crown from a decision of the special
commissioners for the income tax, who had allowed appeals by the taxpayer, Mr. Plummer, against three assessments to tax in respect of the
years 1970–71, 1971–72 and 1972–3. The case involves considering the
effect of an ingenious tax avoidance scheme devised by Slater Walker Ltd.
(" Slater Walker "), the objects of which were: (1) to reduce the surtax
liability of any surtax payer who availed himself of the scheme; and (2) to

A enable a charitable body to build up a fund applicable for its charitable purposes by means of tax reclaimed from the revenue in respect of five-year annuities sold by the surtax payers to the charity and paid subject to deduction of tax, without in effect either the surtax payer or the charitable body having to find any cash from their own resources. The facts are set out in the case stated. It will be sufficient if I explain how the scheme worked in respect of the taxpayer.

B At the relevant time the taxpayer was employed as taxation manager by Slater Walker and acted in that capacity for the whole of the Slater Walker group of companies. It was part of his duties to ensure that the scheme to which I have referred worked efficiently. The Slater Walker group included a company called Baldrene Ltd. (" Baldrene ") of which the taxpayer was a director, and also a company called Old Change Court

C (Investments) Ltd. (" O.C.C."). On December 30, 1970, Home and Overseas Voluntary Aid Services Ltd. (" H.O.V.A.S.") was incorporated ad hoc for the purposes of the scheme. Its authorised and issued share capital was £10 divided into ten shares of £1 each. It was formed for charitable purposes and registered under the Charities Act 1960. It had a close business association with Slater Walker, but was not, as I understand it, one of the companies in the Slater Walker group. It has not

D been suggested that the personal relationship of the taxpayer to Slater Walker or Baldrene has any bearing on this case.

H.O.V.A.S., with the aid of moneys borrowed from Baldrene, held itself out as prepared to purchase annuities on terms attractive to persons who paid a high rate of surtax. Insurance and investment brokers named S. Cardale & Co. Ltd. (" Cardale ") sought to interest clients in

E the scheme. The taxpayer decided to take advantage of the scheme himself and approached Cardale accordingly. By March 11, 1971, negotiations were concluded under which the taxpayer was to promise to pay to H.O.V.A.S. for a period of five years or during the remainder of his life, if shorter, a yearly sum which would after deduction of income tax at the standard rate for the time being in force be equal to £500 in consideration of a price of £2,480 to be paid by H.O.V.A.S. to him.

F On the same day H.O.V.A.S. wrote to the taxpayer confirming that H.O.V.A.S. would accept as security for the yearly sum payable by the taxpayer promissory notes to the value of £2,500 issued by O.C.C. and a cheque for £300 to be invested in the taxpayer's name in bank stock which he proposed to lodge with H.O.V.A.S. as part of the security. On March 12, 1971, the taxpayer opened a banking account with Slater

G Walker, remitting £40 as an opening credit. He informed Slater Walker that they would be receiving £2,480 from H.O.V.A.S. on March 15, 1971, to be credited to his account, following which Slater Walker should make the following payments out of the account, viz., £15 to Cardale (a fee for negotiating the agreement with H.O.V.A.S.) and £2,500 to O.C.C. in return for which O.C.C. would issue ten promissory notes payable to bearer. The taxpayer asked Slater Walker to accept the promissory notes

H and lodge them on his behalf with H.O.V.A.S. as security for the due performance of his obligations under his agreement with H.O.V.A.S. He explained that, as his obligations were fulfilled, a proportion of the security given by him would be released, and he requested and authorised Slater Walker to accept each release on his behalf. In the event of his account being overdrawn at the time of a release Slater Walker were to present an appropriate number of the notes to O.C.C. for payment and to credit his account with the sums paid. The taxpayer gave Slater Walker a stand-

ing order for payment out of the account of the five yearly sums of £500, A
the first to be paid on March 29, 1971.

On March 15, 1971, at a meeting referred to as the completion meeting, at which all parties concerned were present or represented, the
taxpayer entered into a written agreement with H.O.V.A.S. and a
memorandum of agreement to deposit with H.O.V.A.S. securities having
a value equivalent to twice the aggregate amount of the net yearly sums
due under the agreement or such other security as H.O.V.A.S. should B
from time to time be prepared to accept to secure the due payment of
the annual sums payable under the agreement. At the completion
meeting H.O.V.A.S. paid £2,480 to Slater Walker, which was credited
to the taxpayer's account with them. Slater Walker paid £15 to Cardale
and £2,500 to O.C.C. O.C.C. issued ten promissory notes to bearer
payable on demand for an aggregate amount of £2,500. O.C.C. entered C
into a written agreement with the taxpayer to pay him interest on the
amounts of the said notes at the rate of $6\frac{1}{2}$ per cent. per annum less income
tax at the standard rate until demand for payment. Slater Walker
lodged the notes with H.O.V.A.S. H.O.V.A.S. in turn lodged the notes
with Baldrene as part of the security for Baldrene's loan to H.O.V.A.S.
The taxpayer gave H.O.V.A.S. a cheque for £300 and by way of further
security assigned to H.O.V.A.S. his right to interest under his agreement D
with O.C.C. The £300 was invested by H.O.V.A.S. in the taxpayer's
name and the investment was retained by them as security as arranged.
The taxpayer signed five certificates of deduction of income tax pursuant
to section 55 of the Income and Corporation Taxes Act 1970 and
handed these to Slater Walker with instructions to complete them on his
behalf for use by H.O.V.A.S. when claiming repayments of tax as and E
when each of the yearly sums was paid. All the documentation of these
transactions was in standard pre-prepared forms.

H.O.V.A.S. for a small premium effected a life assurance policy covering the risk of the taxpayer's death before April 16, 1975, in annually
reducing amounts. The taxpayer was 34 years of age at the time and
in good health. In the agreement, which I shall call " the annuity F
agreement," the taxpayer is described as " the annuity payer " and
H.O.V.A.S. is described as " the annuitant." Clause 1 of the agreement
is in these terms:

" In consideration of the sum of £2,480 (hereinafter called ' the
purchase price ') now paid by the annuitant to the annuity payer
(the receipt whereof the annuity payer hereby acknowledges) (a) the
annuity payer hereby agrees to pay to the annuitant for the period G
of five years from the date hereof or during the remainder of the
annuity payer's lifetime (whichever period shall be the shorter) an
annuity (hereinafter called ' the annuity ') at such rate as shall after
deduction of income tax at the standard rate for the time being in
force be equal to £500 per annum which annuity shall be payable in
accordance with the provisions of clause 2 hereof."   H

Paragraphs (b) and (c) of that clause relate to a warranty by the annuity
payer concerning his age and medical history. Clause 2 reads:

" The first payment hereunder shall be made 14 days from the date
hereof and subsequent payments hereunder shall be made on the
anniversary of the first payment in each year during the continuance
of this agreement each payment (if not paid on the due date) to carry

A   interest at the rate of 18 per cent. per annum from the due date until payment."

Clause 3 reads:

" Notwithstanding anything in the Apportionment Act 1870 the annuity payments hereunder shall only become payable on the due dates and shall not be deemed to accrue from day to day."

B

The memorandum of agreement to deposit was satisfied by the deposit with H.O.V.A.S. of the promissory notes and the £300. The first payment under the annuity agreement was made on March 29, 1971, when Slater Walker debited the taxpayer's account and credited the account of H.O.V.A.S. with the sum of £500. The taxpayer's account with Slater Walker thus went into overdraft. Promissory notes amount-
C ing to £500 in value were released by H.O.V.A.S. on March 31, 1971, to Slater Walker and on the same date O.C.C. at Slater Walker's request paid £500 into the taxpayer's account with Slater Walker. The two days' delay between March 29 and March 31, 1971, was caused by the fact that the promissory notes lodged with H.O.V.A.S. by the taxpayer had been lodged by H.O.V.A.S. with Baldrene as security for the moneys lent by
D Baldrene to H.O.V.A.S. for the purchase of the taxpayer's promise to make the yearly payments. Baldrene would not release any of its security until satisfied that its account had been effectively credited with an appropriate repayment. A precisely similar procedure was adopted on and after March 29 in each of the succeeding years under the annuity agreement.

E   It will be appreciated that the purchase price paid by H.O.V.A.S. for the five annual payments was borrowed from Baldrene, paid by H.O.V.A.S. to Slater Walker for the account of the taxpayer, and applied by Slater Walker at the direction of the taxpayer in purchase of the promissory notes, which provided the security for the payment of the five annual sums and also for the loan by Baldrene to H.O.V.A.S. Apart from the small sum of £20, being the difference between £2,480 and
F £2,500, no cash had to be found by anyone other than Baldrene. It will also be appreciated that as each of the five annual payments was made, the taxpayer paid £500 to H.O.V.A.S., H.O.V.A.S. paid £500 to Baldrene, Baldrene released promissory notes to the value of £500 to H.O.V.A.S., H.O.V.A.S. released the same notes to Slater Walker for the account of the taxpayer, and those notes were encashed, thus restoring the tax-
G payer's account with Slater Walker to the state in which it was before he made the payment. The gross amount, equivalent to £500 net of income tax at the standard rate then in force, was £851·06. As each yearly payment was made, H.O.V.A.S. was provided with a certificate of deduction of tax, and in due course claimed repayment of tax under section 360 of the Income and Corporation Taxes Act 1970. The Inland Revenue Commissioners, however, refused to admit such claims.
H H.O.V.A.S. appealed against such refusal to the special commissioners, who dismissed the appeal. Although H.O.V.A.S. required a case to be stated under section 56 of the Taxes Management Act 1970 for the opinion of the High Court, the appeal from that decision of the special commissioners has not been pursued.

The taxpayer was assessed to surtax in the three years of assessment under appeal upon the footing that the annual payments which he made in those years under the annuity agreement were not deductible from his

income for surtax purposes.   He appealed against such assessments to the   A
special commissioners contending: (a) that the sum of £500 paid in each
of the years under appeal was paid as an " annuity or other annual payment " and therefore fell to be deducted in computing his total income
for surtax purposes; (b) that he was not under any legal obligation before
March 15, 1971, to take or procure the taking of any of the steps taken
at the completion meeting of that date; (c) that the said sums were paid
for valuable and sufficient consideration and accordingly were not under   B
section 434 of the Income and Corporation Taxes Act 1970 to be
deemed to be his income; and (d) that, even if the said sums were
not paid for valuable and sufficient consideration, the annuity agreement
was a commercial transaction without any element of bounty and accordingly neither section 434 nor section 457 of the Income and Corporation
Taxes Act 1970 applied so as to cause such sums to be deemed to be his   C
income.

The Crown's contentions, stated shortly, were to the following effect:
(a) that the proper conclusion on the facts was that the taxpayer and
H.O.V.A.S. entered into a binding agreement at some time before March
15, 1971, to take all the steps eventually taken by each of them, and
that upon analysis the effect of such agreement was that the annual payments made by the taxpayer were repayments of moneys lent to him by   D
H.O.V.A.S. and were therefore not payments of an income nature which
would qualify for deduction in computing the taxpayer's total income for
tax purposes; (b) that, if contrary to (a) the annual payments had the
quality of income, they were not made for valuable and sufficient consideration within the meaning of section 434 (1) of the Income and
Corporation Taxes Act 1970 and so were to be deemed to be the income   E
of the taxpayer under that section; and that in considering whether the
payments were or were not made for valuable and sufficient consideration
for the purposes of section 434, fiscal advantages were not to be taken
into account, not being consideration moving from the promisee; (c) that
bona fide commercial transactions without any element of bounty were
not by implication excepted from section 434, and that in any event a
transaction designed solely and primarily to obtain tax advantages was   F
not a bona fide commercial transaction; and (d) that, if section 434 did
not apply, the payments were to be treated as the taxpayer's income under
section 457 of the same Act.

The commissioners held that no contractual obligation to implement
the scheme arose before March 15, 1971.   They rejected the Crown's
contention that the payment by H.O.V.A.S. to the taxpayer of £2,480   G
had the quality of a loan, and held that that payment was an outright
payment to the taxpayer in return for his promises under the annuity
agreement and was not returnable to H.O.V.A.S. either in whole or in
part at any time.   They treated the case as covered by Sothern-Smith v.
Clancy [1941] 1 K.B. 276 and accordingly held that the sums paid by the
taxpayer under the annuity agreement were payments of an annuity or
other annual payments and not repayments of a capital sum lent to him.   H

The commissioners were not satisfied that the consideration moving
from H.O.V.A.S. under the annuity agreement was sufficient for the purposes of section 434.   They felt constrained by Bulmer v. Inland Revenue
Commissioners [1967] Ch. 145 to proceed on the basis that neither section
434 nor section 457 applies to a bona fide commercial transaction without
any element of bounty, and they held that this transaction was a bona fide
commercial transaction without any element of bounty.   The com-

A missioners consequently allowed the appeal and discharged the first two assessments under appeal and reduced the third assessment to £3,349. The Crown asked for a case to be stated and this in due course came before Walton J. The arguments before the judge were similar to those before the commissioners. Walton J. rejected the Crown's contention that the real nature of the taxpayer's payments under the annuity agree-
B ment was that they were all capital payments, either as repayments of a loan or on some other basis. He also rejected a contention that the pay-ments were not made out of profits or gains brought into charge to tax within section 52 of the Income and Corporation Taxes Act 1970. He held that under the annuity agreement the taxpayer had obtained a fair equivalent, that is to say, a sufficient consideration, for his obligations. Finally, he held that *Bulmer* v. *Inland Revenue Commissioners* [1967]
C Ch. 145 applies to both section 434 and section 457. Before Walton J. the question whether *Bulmer* v. *Inland Revenue Commissioners* was rightly decided was kept open for possible argument in this court, but Mr. Medd has not suggested before us that that case was wrongly decided.

Where any annuity or other annual payment charged with tax under Case III of Schedule D, not being interest, is payable wholly out of profits or gains brought into charge to income tax, the payer bears tax at the
D standard rate on the amount of the annual payment but is not liable for any surtax in respect of it: see sections 52 (1) and 3 (2) of the Income and Corporation Taxes Act 1970. He may, however, deduct tax at the standard rate from the amount paid to the recipient of the annual pay-ment. It was under these provisions that the scheme was designed to benefit surtax payers who sold " annuities " to H.O.V.A.S. So the first
E question for consideration is whether the payments made by the taxpayer under the annuity agreement were payments of an annuity or other annual payments within the meaning of those sections. Under Case III of Schedule D, which is to be found in section 109 of the Act, tax is charged in respect of any annuity or other annual payment payable as a personal debt or obligation by virtue of any contract. The five annual payments to be made by the taxpayer under the annuity agreement were clearly
F annual payments payable under a personal debt or obligation of the taxpayer by virtue of a contract, viz., the annuity agreement. Never-theless they do not fall within the charge to tax if on the true view they are payments of capital: see *Secretary of State for India* v. *Scoble* [1903] A.C. 299; *Foley* v. *Fletcher* (1858) 3 H. & N. 769 and *Perrin* v. *Dickson* [1930] 1 K.B. 107. If upon the true view of the facts the annual payments
G have the character of payments of capital, section 52 (1) does not apply, even if they are made wholly out of profits or gains brought into charge to income tax.

The fact that the payments are described in the annuity agreement as an " annuity " and that the parties are described as " the annuity payer " and " the annuitant " is not conclusive of the true character of the pay-ments. The term " annuity " is not a term of art in our law. One has
H to look at the whole transaction to ascertain the true character of the payments: see *Secretary of State for India* v. *Scoble* [1903] A.C. 299; *Inland Revenue Commissioners* v. *Wesleyan & General Assurance Society* [1948] 1 All E.R. 555 and *Inland Revenue Commissioners* v. *Church Commissioners for England* [1977] A.C. 329. In so doing one must pay due regard to the terms and legal effect of any formal legal documents employed. One may also have regard to extrinsic evidence, not to contradict the terms and effect of those formal legal documents,

but to supplement them in throwing light on the true nature of the whole
transaction: see *Perrin* v. *Dickson* [1930] 1 K.B. 107 and *Inland Revenue
Commissioners* v. *Church Commissioners for England* [1977] A.C. 329.
If the transaction involves a series of preconceived steps, the performance
of each of which is dependent on the others being carried out in accordance
with a common intention of the parties, the nature and effect of the whole
scheme may have to be taken into consideration in determining the
nature of the annual payments: see *Ransom* v. *Higgs* [1974] 1 W.L.R.
1594, *per* Lord Wilberforce at p. 1612. If the true nature of the annual
payments, so ascertained, is that they constitute repayment of an existing
debt by annual instalments, or payment of the purchase price of property
by annual instalments, they will not, so far as the instalments constitute
payment of principal, be chargeable with income tax, although to such
extent, if any, as an instalment comprises an element of interest on
principal, the instalment will be taxable: see *Secretary of State for India*
v. *Scoble* [1903] A.C. 299 and *Sothern-Smith* v. *Clancy* [1941] 1 K.B.
276, 281, *per* Sir Wilfred Greene M.R. If the recipient is bound contractually or otherwise to apply the annual payments for capital purposes,
the effect of the transaction may, and in my opinion almost certainly must,
be such that the payments will not constitute income in the hands of the
recipient and so will not be payable subject to deduction of tax by the
payer: see *Campbell* v. *Inland Revenue Commissioners* [1970] A.C. 77. I
may say that I am not at all sure that the author of the headnote to
that report in 45 T.C. 427 has correctly analysed the rationes decidendi of
the Lords who decided that case.

Mr. Medd said that in consequence of that fact that the only purpose
of the scheme was to secure tax advantages it is particularly incumbent
on the court in this case to look behind the way in which the transaction
is dressed up to see what its true nature is. It is to be distinguished, he
said, from a case in which the parties have some legitimate object which
they wish to attain other than a mere fiscal advantage, for which purpose
they have devised machinery which will incidentally also produce the
most satisfactory fiscal consequences. He has pointed out certain
features which would be unusual in any ordinary case of a sale of an
annuity such as: (1) that the payer of the annuity was required by the
scheme to secure due payment of it and to employ the whole purchase
price in providing such security; (2) that the period of the annuity was
not made dependent on the life of the purchaser or anyone whom he
wished to benefit but on the life of the annuity payer; and (3) that the
purchaser insured the life of the annuity payer. I may say in passing that
this last feature is obviously a consequence of or connected with the second
feature. It was not stipulated in the annuity agreement nor, so far as
I can see, was it in any other way a contractual feature of the scheme.
The insurance was effected at the cost of H.O.V.A.S. and was, it seems to
me, a unilateral act on their part.

In support of his primary submission that the annual payments in this
case were in truth payments of capital, Mr. Medd emphasised the circular
nature of the financial operations which, he said, were designed to ensure
that H.O.V.A.S. should get back by yearly instalments the whole of the
sum paid by H.O.V.A.S. to the taxpayer. There seem to me to be two
formidable objections to this view. First, the taxpayer's primary obligation under the annuity agreement was to pay in each year the gross
amount of £851, amounting over the five years to much more than the
£2,480 paid by H.O.V.A.S. to the taxpayer. The excess might perhaps be

A explicable as consideration for the loan and the arrangement for repayment over five years, but it is only if the taxpayer was entitled to make the yearly payments subject to deduction of tax, which he could only do if the payments were not of a capital nature, that one achieves any coincidence between the £2,480 and the aggregate amount of the five yearly payments, that is, £2,500. More significant, in my opinion, is the consideration that, if the taxpayer had

B died after March 15, 1971, but before March 29, 1971, neither he nor his estate would have been liable to make any payment to H.O.V.A.S. This seems to me to be irreconcilable with the view that the £2,480 was paid to the taxpayer by way of loan. If the yearly payments were not repayments of a loan, I can see no other character that can be attributed to them except that of a fixed term annuity determinable on the death of

C the taxpayer within five years. If that is what they are, as I think is the case, we are in my opinion bound by the decision in *Sothern-Smith* v. *Clancy* [1941] 1 K.B. 276 to hold that they are income payments: and see *Inland Revenue Commissioners* v. *Church Commissioners for England* [1977] A.C. 329, 340, *per* Lord Wilberforce.

D Mr. Medd rightly, in my opinion, did not contend that in the present case H.O.V.A.S. was bound to apply the yearly payments for capital purposes. Although it may be inferred from the case stated that H.O.V.A.S. used each payment as it was received in making a payment of that amount to Baldrene in order to secure the release of £500 worth of promissory notes, there was no contractual obligation upon H.O.V.A.S. to do so. They could have used any other available money for this

E purpose and were no doubt in receipt of other like annual sums from annuity payers under the scheme which could have been so applied. So I am in agreement with Walton J. in rejecting Mr. Medd's primary submission that on a true view of the transaction the yearly payments were, or were analogous to, repayments of a loan.

The next question is whether they were payable wholly out of profits or gains brought into charge to income tax. It was conceded that, where

F a taxpayer has taxable income of a larger amount than the gross amount of any annuity or annual payments which he is obliged to make, he is entitled to be treated as having made such payments out of that income: see *Inland Revenue Commissioners* v. *Frere* [1965] A.C. 402, 419, *per* Viscount Radcliffe, unless the taxpayer has treated the payment as made out of capital in circumstances having practical results which are inconsistent with an attribution of the payments to his fund of taxed income:

G see *Chancery Lane Safe Deposit and Offices Co. Ltd.* v. *Inland Revenue Commissioners* [1966] A.C. 85, particularly *per* Lord Morris of Borth-y-Gest at p. 115 and *per* Lord Wilberforce at p. 136. Mr. Medd submitted that the taxpayer's account with Slater Walker was an account of capital moneys, being concerned only with capital receipts and payments. He said that the operations in that account were carefully segregated from

H all dealings with his taxed income. Walton J. rejected this submission and in this respect also I agree with him. The taxpayer was not bound to make the payments out of his account with Slater Walker nor was there any reason why he should not have fed that account from his fund of taxed income. It was clearly part of the scheme that the payments should be attributed to his taxed income and treated as paid thereout. In my judgment, the taxpayer did nothing which made it inappropriate for him to claim to have the payments treated in this way.

The next question for consideration is the application to this case of A
sections 434 and 457 of the Income and Corporation Taxes Act 1970.
Both these sections are contained in Part 16 of the Act which is headed
" Settlements." Section 434 is in Chapter 1 of that Part of the Act,
which is headed " Dispositions for short periods," and section 457 is in
chapter 4, which is headed " Surtax liability of settlors in certain cases."
By virtue of section 459 and of section 454 (3) " settlement " in chapter
4 " includes any disposition, trust, covenant, agreement or arrangement." B
By virtue of section 434 (2) " disposition " in chapter 1 includes any
trust, covenant, agreement or arrangement. From the language of these
sections it appears that the term " settlement " may be capable of a wider
interpretation than the term " disposition." Section 434 expressly
excludes from its operation any disposition made for valuable and sufficient
consideration. Section 457 on the other hand contains no comparable C
exclusion. In *Bulmer* v. *Inland Revenue Commissioners* [1967] Ch. 145,
however, Pennycuick J., applying earlier decisions of Lawrence J. in
Copeman v. *Coleman* [1939] 2 K.B. 484 and Plowman J. in *Inland
Revenue Commissioners* v. *Leiner* (1964) 41 T.C. 589 held that a commercial transaction without any element of bounty could not constitute a
" settlement " for the purposes of section 415 (1) of the Income Tax Act
1952, which was the predecessor of section 457 (1) of the 1970 Act. D
Pennycuick J. said, at p. 165:

> " In the case of this definition, i.e., the definition of settlement, it
> must, I think, be at any rate legitimate to hold that a sufficient
> context exists for a restriction in the scope of the definition. Indeed,
> unless one implies some restriction, the definition, standing where it
> does in this Part of the Act, represents as odd a provision as one E
> would anywhere find in a taxing statute."

It has not been suggested to us that that decision was wrong and for the
purposes of the present appeal I assume it to have been right. Mr. Medd
submitted that in using the word " commercial," Pennycuick J. intended
to indicate that the transaction referred to must be one effected in the
course of commerce or trading, which I take to mean one effected in F
the course of carrying on a business. I feel unable to accept this view,
for it seems to me that the judge was not using the word " commercial "
in so restricted a sense. In my judgment, the sale by a private individual,
not in the course of his business, of his house to another individual who
buys it for his private occupation is a commercial transaction in the
proper sense of that term, although it is not carried out in the course of G
carrying on any business or trade. In my opinion it is clear from the
judgments of Pennycuick J. in *Bulmer* v. *Inland Revenue Commissioners*
[1967] Ch. 145 and of Plowman J. in *Inland Revenue Commissioners* v.
Leiner (1964) 41 T.C. 589 that those judges were there using the term
" commercial transaction " to indicate any transaction in which there was
no element of bounty. It follows that a transaction effected for full consideration in money or money's worth is not a " settlement " for the H
purposes of section 457.

The express exception contained in section 434 of " a disposition
made for valuable and sufficient consideration " appears to me to have a
similar effect. In *Ball* v. *National and Grindlays Bank Ltd.* [1973] Ch.
127, Ungoed-Thomas J., construing the words " valuable and sufficient
consideration " in section 52 (4) (*b*) of the Finance Act 1965, said, at p.
136:

A   " So in our case it seems to me that ' valuable and sufficient ' must be given a meaning in this tax statute independent of any common law reluctance to consider adequacy in consideration. It was submitted —rightly, in my view—that ' valuable ' consideration is, as it so familiarly is in a legal context, in contrast with ' good ' consideration, even though ' good ' consideration might hardly relate to a corporation; and ' sufficient ' goes to quantum in the sense of ' adequate,' or, B   what doubtless comes to the same thing, ' fair equivalent.' "

In the Court of Appeal Russell L.J. said, at p. 139: " Now there is no problem as to the meaning of the word ' sufficient '; it connotes adequacy, an adequate quid pro the quo of the liability incurred . . ." So, in my judgment, it is also true to say that a transaction effected for full con- C sideration in money or money's worth is not a " disposition " for the purposes of section 434.

      The transaction with which we are concerned was the sale of an annuity by the taxpayer to H.O.V.A.S. for a price in money. Was it, on the facts of the case, a transaction which was devoid of any element of bounty? Should the price paid be regarded as full consideration? In sub-paragraph 3 (b) of their decision the commissioners stated that they D were not satisfied on the evidence before them that the consideration moving from H.O.V.A.S.—that is to say, the purchase price—was sufficient consideration. They went on to explain their reason for this by a calculation of the interest which H.O.V.A.S. would receive on its outlay. They made no positive finding in this respect, but in the next sub-paragraph of the decision they found that it had been common ground E between the parties that the transaction was carried out at arm's length. In the same paragraph they found that the taxpayer knew of no other organisation which would have been prepared to purchase an annuity from him, and that from his point of view, if the expected tax advantages materialised, he would have laid out his money to excellent advantage. They said:

F   " We regard it as a fair description of the transaction to say that it was a bona fide commercial transaction without any element of bounty notwithstanding that the benefits from it were largely to be derived from the tax advantages which the parties expected would accrue to them."

      Mr. Medd contended that a transaction, the sole object of which is tax G avoidance, cannot be a bona fide commercial transaction. Nowadays, fiscal consequences are incidents of a very large number and variety of business transactions. These must inevitably affect the willingness of the parties to any transaction to enter into it. They must also necessarily affect the amount or value of the consideration which any party is willing to give or to accept in order to close a bargain. They must consequently be elements to be taken into account in determining whether the con- H sideration given by either party is sufficient. In the present case both parties entered into the transaction in the anticipation that the taxpayer would be able to deduct the annuity payments from his total income for surtax purposes and to pay the annuity subject to deduction of tax at the standard rate, and that H.O.V.A.S. would be able to recover the tax so deducted. These were expected incidents of the transaction, and I can see no reason why the parties should have excluded them from considera-tion in negotiating the price which H.O.V.A.S. was prepared to pay, and the taxpayer was prepared to accept, for the annuity. It may be true that £2,480 would in other circumstances be a low price for the right to receive over five years gross sums amounting to £4,255, but H.O.V.A.S. knew that the taxpayer expected to be able to deduct tax at the standard rate and expected the transaction to afford him substantial surtax relief, so that, considering the sale of the annuity in isolation from the rest of the scheme, it would cost the taxpayer much less on balance than £4,255 to provide the annuity. In the face of the finding that the negotiation was at arm's length it seems to me impossible to reach any other conclusion than that the price of £2,480 was full, and so sufficient, consideration for the purchase of the annuity, taking all the expected consequences into account. Indeed this seems to have been the commissioners' own ultimate view having regard to their final conclusion that the transaction was a bona fide commercial transaction without any element of bounty. This is a finding of fact which could only be disturbed if it could be shown that it is insupportable on some ground of law. It appears to me that it was a finding which the commissioners were fully entitled to make upon the basis that the transaction was negotiated at arm's length. The price of £2,480 was consequently presumably the lowest which H.O.V.A.S. considered that they could reasonably hope to induce the taxpayer to accept and the highest which the taxpayer considered that he could reasonably expect to induce H.O.V.A.S. to give. The fact that each party would have been influenced by fiscal considerations in reaching this decision does not in any way detract from the interest of each party to negotiate a price as advantageous as possible to that party. It is, in my opinion, quite fallacious to regard the fiscal advantages as constituting any part of the consideration for the bargain as Mr. Medd was inclined to do. They were incidents of the bargain and no more. The consideration was the purchase price on the one hand and the grant of the annuity on the other. In these circumstances it would, I think, be wrong to read sub-paragraph 3 (b) of the commissioners' decision as containing an inferential finding of fact that the consideration moving from H.O.V.A.S. was insufficient consideration for the purposes of section 434. Had they made such a finding, I should regard it as a finding which could not be supported upon the commissioners' own findings of primary fact.

For these reasons I agree with the conclusion of Walton J. that section 434 does not apply to the present case. For these reasons also I agree with his further conclusion that section 457 also does not apply to the present case.

In the concluding passage of his judgment, Walton J. said that he could see no escape from the conclusion that the *Bulmer* principle applied to section 434 as well as to section 457, notwithstanding that this might involve an element of tautology in section 434 in expressly excepting any disposition made for valuable and sufficient consideration. In my judgment the decision in *Bulmer* has no bearing upon section 434. The presence in section 434 (1) of the exception of any disposition made for valuable and sufficient consideration, in my opinion, makes it unnecessary to imply in section 434 any such limitation on the meaning of " disposition " as was implied in *Bulmer* in respect of the meaning of " settlement " in section 457.

For these reasons I would dismiss this appeal.

BRIDGE L.J. I agree, and wish to add some words of my own only with reference to the application of section 434 of the Income and Cor-

A poration Taxes Act 1970. The effect of this section is that the annual payments by the taxpayer to H.O.V.A.S. under the annuity agreement are deemed to be the income of the taxpayer and not of H.O.V.A.S. unless the consideration moving from H.O.V.A.S. was " sufficient." The relevant passage from the decision of the special commissioners reads:

B "As to the question whether the consideration moving from H.O.V.A.S. was sufficient consideration for the purpose of the words in parenthesis in section 434 (1) we were not satisfied on the evidence before us that it was. [The taxpayer] was aged 34 in March 1971 and was to receive £2,480 in return for gross payments, before deduction of tax, of some £4,255 over five years. As in the H.O.V.A.S. appeal it was not suggested to us that the possible depreciation of money over the five years was a factor to be taken into account and C we therefore ignore it. On this footing, assuming, as was the probability, that [the taxpayer] survived the period, H.O.V.A.S. would receive the equivalent of compound interest at the rate of some 36 per cent. on its outlay assuming no undue delay in repayment of tax or 27 per cent. assuming a delay of one year, both yields being well in excess of yields of 6½ to 9 per cent. available in the market at the time."
D

Walton J., having set out this passage, commented [1977] 1 W.L.R. 1227, 1238:

"I am afraid that, in this finding, the special commissioners have fallen into manifold errors. In the first place, they have asked themselves the wrong question. The question is not whether E H.OV.A.S. made a bargain (if they did, which I shall examine later) but whether or not the taxpayer received the market price for that which he had to sell. As to that, I think one has only to look at the matter from a purely commercial point of view—an immediate payment of £2,480 in return for five payments of £500 spread over five years—to appreciate at once that the discount for immediate payment F is so slight (£20) as to constitute an extremely good bargain so far as the [taxpayer] was concerned. In my view, there can be no question but that he received ' sufficient ' consideration; it was obviously more than he could have hoped to obtain elsewhere."

These two passages reveal a fundamental difference of approach, in that the special commissioners ask whether the consideration was G sufficient for the gross amount to be paid by the taxpayer whereas Walton J. takes the net amount after deduction of tax. The first approach shows the taxpayer paying interest to H.O.V.A.S. at an exorbitant rate, for which is could well be said that the consideration given by H.O.V.A.S. was not sufficient. The second approach shows the taxpayer paying over five years an aggregate sum to H.O.V.A.S. which is only marginally in excess of the capital sum he receives at the outset; on this basis the consideration given by H.O.V.A.S. is clearly ample. It seems to me, therefore, that H we must decide which of these two approaches is correct. I was at first much impressed by the argument of Mr. Medd that one cannot, in deciding the sufficiency of consideration for the purposes of section 434, look at anything but the gross figures. He submitted that to take the net figures after deduction of tax for this purpose is to assume the answer to the very question which falls to be decided, viz., whether the section applies and whether the gross payments will be eligible for deduction of

tax. But Mr. Nolan has satisfied me that the effective counter to this A
argument is found in section 435. The effect of this section is that when
section 434 applies to a disposition so that the income paid under it is
deemed to be that of the payer he becomes entitled as against the payee
to deduct from the payments the amount of the income tax chargeable
on and paid by him in respect of the deemed income. It must follow from
this that when a person is contemplating making a disposition to which
section 434 may or may not apply according to whether or not the con- B
sideration he receives is sufficient, he will know that in any event his
liability will be limited to making the payment net of income tax at the
basic rate. Accordingly, this represents the commercial reality of the
transaction and it must, in my judgment, be by reference to this commercial reality that the sufficiency of the consideration should be judged.
I conclude that in the two passages quoted the approach of Walton J. C
was correct and that of the special commissioners mistaken. For this
reason in addition to the reasons given by Buckley L.J. I agree with the
judge's rejection of the Crown's argument that section 434 applied to the
disposition in question. On all the other points canvassed I am in full
agreement with the reasons given by Buckley L.J. for concluding that
the appeal should be dismissed.

D

FOSTER J. I agree with the judgment of Buckley L.J. and with the
reasons which he gave.

> *Appeal dismissed with costs.*
> *Leave to appeal on condition that*
> *no application be made by the*
> *Crown for costs in Court of Appeal*   E
> *or in House of Lords.*

Solicitors: *Solicitor of Inland Revenue; Roney, Vincent & Co.*

F

[CHANCERY DIVISION]

In re TILTWOOD, SUSSEX
BARRETT *v.* BOND AND OTHERS

G

[1976 S. No. 10105]

1978   Feb. 1, 2; 14   Foster J.

Restrictive Covenant—Enforceability—Purchase from common
vendor—Owner of benefited land purchasing burdened land—
Sale of burdened land—Whether restrictive covenants extin-
guished

H

> In June 1951, L, the purchaser of the agricultural land
> forming part of an estate surrounding a mansion house and
> grounds, covenanted with the vendor to use the four parcels
> thereof for agricultural purposes only and not permit the erec-
> tion of any building thereon. The vendor took the covenant to
> protect the view to the south of the mansion house. In February
> 1952 the vendor conveyed to S the mansion house and grounds
> with the benefit of the covenants as to the four parcels which
> were contained in the 1951 conveyance. The vendor also

A   conveyed to S a strip of land to the south of the parcels, with
      the grant of a right of way to the strip from the mansion
      house. In August 1952, S purchased from L three of his
      four parcels (in area about half the burdened land). Having
      sold off the western part of the mansion house and some ground
      without any express assignment of the benefit of the covenant,
      S divided up the rest of the benefited and burdened land into
      six lots. The first four lots, each with an express assignment
B   of the benefit of the covenants, were sold to the defendants
      (part of lot 3 going to the plaintiff). The remaining two lots,
      each consisting of burdened land, were sold to the plaintiff.
           On the plaintiff's summons for a declaration that the two
      lots of burdened land were no longer subject to the covenants
      in the 1951 conveyance on the ground that the purchase by
      S of part of the burdened land had created unity of seisin of
      the benefited and burdened land: —
C   *Held*, that where the fee simple of land benefited and
      land burdened by restrictive covenants became vested in the
      same person, the restrictive covenants were extinguished unless
      the common owner recreated them; that, accordingly, since S, the
      common owner, had not re-imposed the covenants when
      dividing up and selling the land, the plaintiff, as purchaser
      of the burdened land, was entitled to a declaration that she
      was no longer bound by the covenants which were extinguished
D   (post, pp. 482H—483A).
           Dictum of Lord Cross of Chelsea in *Texaco Antilles Ltd.* v.
      Kernochan [1973] A.C. 609, 626, P.C. applied.

      The following cases are referred to in the judgment:
      Brunner v. *Greenslade* [1971] Ch. 993; [1970] 3 W.L.R. 891; [1970] 3
           All E.R. 833.
E   *Miles* v. *Etteridge* (1692) 1 Show. 349.
      Sunnyfield, In re [1932] 1 Ch. 79.
      Texaco Antilles Ltd. v. *Kernochan* [1973] A.C. 609; [1973] 2 W.L.R. 381;
           [1973] 2 All E.R. 118, P.C.

      The following additional cases were cited in argument:
      Bolton v. *Bolton* (1879) 11 Ch.D. 968.
F   *Holmes* v. *Goring* (1824) 2 Bing. 76.
      London and South Western Railway Co. v. *Gomm* (1881) 20 Ch.D. 562,
           C.A.
      Simper v. *Foley* (1862) 2 Johns. & Hem. 555.
      Union of London and Smith's Bank Ltd.'s Conveyance, In re [1933] Ch.
           611, C.A.
G   *Wheeldon* v. *Burrows* (1879) 12 Ch.D. 31, C.A.

      SUMMONS
           By summons dated December 8, 1976 (as amended and reissued on
      February 15, 1977), the plaintiff, Florence Lilian Barrett, applied for a
      declaration under section 84 (2) of the Law of Property Act 1925 that
      parcels of land at Tiltwood, Sussex, designated O.S. nos. 267B, 267C
H   and 267D in a conveyance dated June 18, 1951, were no longer subject
      to any of the restrictive covenants contained in that conveyance. Out
      of eleven defendants to the application, five defendants, Shaun Walter
      Duggan, Lavinia D. H. Duggan, Sheila Margaret Parker, Andrew A. H.
      Graham and Donald Driver, appeared by counsel claiming to be entitled
      to the benefit of and to enforce the covenants in the conveyance in
      relation to the entirety of the land expressed to be bound thereby.
           The facts are stated in the judgment

In re Tiltwood, Sussex (Ch.D.) [1978]

George Newsom Q.C. and *J. M. Henty* for the plaintiff. A
Nathaniel Micklem for the five defendants.
The remaining six defendants did not appear and were not represented.

Cur. adv. vult.

February 14. FOSTER J. read the following judgment. In this case B
the plaintiff, Mrs. Barrett, seeks a declaration that the land which she
owns is not bound by a restrictive covenant. The claim is made under
section 84 of the Law of Property Act 1925, subsection (2) and (5) of which
read:

> " (2) The court shall have power on the application of any person
> interested—(*a*) To declare whether or not in any particular case any
> freehold land is affected by a restriction imposed by any instrument; C
> . . . (5) Any order made under this section shall be binding on all
> persons, whether ascertained or of full age or capacity or not, then
> entitled or thereafter capable of becoming entitled to the benefit of
> any restriction, which is thereby discharged, modified, or dealt with,
> and whether such persons are parties to the proceedings or have
> been served with notice or not. . . ." D

There are five defendants who appear before me by counsel to oppose
the declaration but I must first be satisfied that all other possible
defendants have been given an adequate chance of appearing before me.
In *In re Sunnyfield* [1932] 1 Ch. 79, 83, Maugham J., in an unopposed
case, said:

> " When such an order as this is asked for, the court ought to make E
> every effort to see that all persons who may wish to oppose the
> making of the order have the opportunity of being heard, stating
> their objections in argument before the court, and inviting the court
> to refuse to exercise its powers. In the present case, it seems that
> every effort has been made to give notice to all persons having a
> probable interest in the property, and accordingly I ought not to F
> refuse to proceed to the hearing of the matter."

Mr. Newsom for the plaintiff submitted that sufficient notice had
been given. Mr. Micklem for the opposing defendants was in no way
concerned with this aspect of the case. However I asked him if he
would act as amicus curiae on the matter and I am indeed grateful to
him for doing so. He assured me that sufficient notice had been given G
to those who might be concerned. On his and Mr. Newsom's submissions I am satisfied that all those who might wish to oppose and who
do not appear before me have had sufficient notice, and particularly as
the five defendants who appear by Mr. Micklem oppose strongly the
application. I can therefore proceed to consider the application as an
opposed and strongly opposed case on its merits. H

Conveyancing history prior to June 1951
By conveyances dated respectively March 25, 1911, and November
20, 1928, the Tiltwood Estate at Crawley Down, consisting of some 500
acres, a mansion house and a farm, Hophurst Farm, became vested for
an estate in fee simple in Mr. A. G. Scaramanga. He made his will
dated May 2, 1944, and died on November 4, 1946. Probate of his will

A and a codicil dated October 28, 1946, was granted to his executors on
March 20, 1947. By his testamentary dispositions he gave a life interest
in the mansion house and immediate gardens together with a field both
to the east and west to his widow, and he gave the remainder of the
estate and the reversionary interest expectant on the widow's death in
the mansion house and other grounds to his son, Mr. G. A. Scaramanga.
By an assent dated April 27, 1948, the testator's executors assented to
B the vesting in the son of all the portions of the estate other than those
in which the widow had a life interest. The son decided to sell the
agricultural portions of the estate, i.e., those lands in which the widow
had no life interest, and it was put up for auction in June 1951. Lot 1,
which comprised the land around the mansion house and grounds, was
by a conveyance dated June 18, 1951, conveyed by Mr. G. A. Scaramanga
C to Mr. H. J. Longinotto. By clause 3 of that conveyance:

"The purchaser hereby covenants with the vendor (but not so that
he the purchaser shall be liable for any breach thereof after he
shall have parted with the property or any part thereof in respect
of which a breach of this covenant shall hereafter occur) that he
the purchaser and his successors in title will use the enclosures
D numbered 267 267B 267C and 267D more particularly referred to
in the schedule hereto for agricultural purposes only and that no
building or other structure or erection whatsoever whether permanent or temporary shall at any time hereafter be built erected or
placed or suffered to be upon any part of the aforesaid enclosures."

It is with these covenants that I am concerned. The mansion house
E had a fine view to the south over the ordnance survey numbers 267 and
267B, C, and D, and it was to protect this that the covenant was taken.

Conveyance of February 11, 1952

The widow, Mrs. Nina Scaramanga, died on August 21, 1951, and
as there had been no assent in her favour as life tenant, the executors
F of the testator's will assented to the vesting in the son, Mr. G. A.
Scaramanga, of the freehold in the mansion house and its grounds and
fields on November 29, 1951. By a conveyance dated February 11, 1952,
Mr. Scaramanga conveyed the mansion house and grounds to Mrs. Netta
Mountford Spence, with the benefit of the restrictive covenants contained
in the 1951 conveyance by Mr. Longinotto in respect of the parcels 267,
and 267B, C, and D. To the south of those parcels there was a strip of
G land consisting of woods and some ponds which was also conveyed to
Mrs. Spence and she was granted a right of way from the mansion house
to this piece of land. The right of way divided ordnance survey no. 267
on the east from ordnance survey no. 267B, C, and D on the west.
Thus I find that Mrs. Spence has become the owner of the mansion
house and other lands (the benefited lands) and Mr. Longinotto is the
H owner of the parcels 267, 267B, C, and D, which I will call "the
burdened land," by the restrictive covenant in the 1951 conveyance.

Events prior to the 1952 auction

It is clear that Mrs. Spence had no intention of retaining the mansion
house and land as a unity and immediately started to break up the
mansion house into various lots to be put up for auction, which was
to have taken place on October 30, 1952. Before I consider what took

place just before this auction, there are two conveyances which are of   A
some significance in this case. (i) On July 15, 1952, Mrs. Spence conveyed to Colonel Clark the western part of the mansion house and
some ground. In this conveyance there was no express assignment of
the benefit of the restrictive covenant in respect of the land to the south.
(ii) On August 28, 1952, Mrs. Spence purchased the land, being ordnance
survey numbers 267B, C, and D, but not 267, back from Mr. Longinotto.   B
The evidence showed that the reason for this was that in exercising her
right of way to visit her land to the south she had been attacked by a
bull and wished to have her own land over which she could visit the
southern part. This land 267B, C, and D is of course part and in area
about half of the burdened land, and she owned the benefited land,
other than that part of the mansion house and land sold to Colonel
Clark, though with no express assignment of the benefit. I must notice   C
the conveyance of August 28, 1952, in greater detail. The relevant
words in paragraph 1 are:

> " Excepting and reserving unto George Ambrose Scaramanga and
> his successors in title being the owner or owners occupier or
> occupiers for the time being of the adjoining land known as Tilt-
> wood a right of way at all times and for all purposes over the way   D
> not exceeding 12 feet in width as indicated on the said plan by the
> letters A B and C and also excepting and reserving unto the vendor
> all timber or timberlike and other trees on any part of the land
> hereby conveyed with the right for the vendor and all other persons
> authorised by him to enter upon the said land hereby conveyed or
> any part thereof from time to time as he shall think fit to remove
> such timber or timberlike and other trees or any part of them. To   E
> hold (except and reserved as aforesaid) unto the purchaser in fee
> simple subject to the rights and covenants contained in a conveyance
> dated June 18, 1951, and made between the said George Ambrose
> Scaramanga of the one part and the vendor of the other part so far
> as the same relate to the property hereby conveyed and are sub-
> sisting and capable of being enforced."   F

And in paragraph 2:

> " With the object of affording to the vendor a full and sufficient
> indemnity but not further or otherwise the purchaser hereby coven-
> ants with the vendor that she will perform and observe the covenants
> contained in the beforementioned conveyance dated June 18, 1951,
> so far as the same relate to the property hereby conveyed and are   G
> still subsisting and capable of being enforced and will keep the
> vendor and his estate and effects effectually indemnified from and
> against all actions claims and demands in any wise relating thereto."

As Mrs. Spence owned the benefited land and was purchasing part
of the burdened land, the exception of a right of way over the land
she was purchasing was wholly unnecessary and there was no necessity   H
to convey it subject to the covenants in the conveyance of June 18, 1951.
Further, paragraph 2 of that conveyance was wholly otiose.

The 1952 auction

This was scheduled to take place on October 30, 1952, and particulars
of the sale were prepared. Colonel Clark had already acquired Tiltwood

A West. The remainder of the mansion and its grounds was divided into six lots. The centre of the mansion house was the subject of lot 1 and called Tiltwood South though it is now known as Tiltwood House. Lot 2 was the eastern portion of the mansion house known as Tiltwood East and there were four other lots. It is common ground that all the lots were sold prior to the auction but that the contracts were all made in accordance with the auction particulars and the conditions of sale.

B Condition 10 of the conditions of sale is in these terms:

"In his conveyance the purchaser of each lot shall enter into a covenant for himself and his successors in title with intent so as to bind so far as practicable the property agreed to be sold into who-soever's hands the same may go and to benefit and protect the remainder of the Tiltwood Estate: — (a) not at any time to use any

C building for any other purpose whatsoever than as a private dwelling house or residence or for agricultural or horticultural purposes and that nothing shall be done or suffered to be done upon any lot or any part thereof which may be or become a nuisance annoyance or injury or which may tend to depreciate the value of any other lot or any part of the Tiltwood Estate."

D Sub-paragraph (b) is not I think relevant. There is no mention in the auction particulars or the conditions of sale of the restrictive coven-ants affecting the southern aspect, i.e. ordnance nos. 267 or 267B, C, and D. The fact that in certain conveyances there was an express assignment of the restrictive covenant occurred because of certain requisitions on title.

E

The defendants' properties

There are four properties owned by the five defendants. 1. Tiltwood West is now owned by the defendant Mr. Driver. This consists of part of the mansion house and grounds conveyed to Colonel Clark on July 15, 1952, with no express assignment, but further land was later bought

F which had an express assignment of the benefit of the restrictive coven-ants. 2. Tiltwood House, which consisted of the centre part of the mansion house, is now owned by the defendants Mr. and Mrs. Duggan, who have also an express assignment. 3. Tiltwood East is owned by the defendant Dr. Graham, also with an express assignment of the covenant. 4. The defendant Dr. Parker owns a property to the south west of the mansion house on which she has built a house called Pasture Wood.

G That property too has been conveyed with an express assignment of the covenants.

It is therefore common ground that all the defendants have express assignments of parts of the land benefited by the restrictive covenants, and on their behalf it is submitted that those covenants remain valid and enforceable.

H

The plaintiff's land

The plaintiff also bought just before the 1952 auction part of lot 3 and lots 5 and 6. Lot 5 consisted of the west part of the burdened land purchased by Mrs. Spence on August 28, 1952, from Mr. Longinotto. Lot 6 is the remainder of the burdened land, namely ordnance survey no. 267. It is admitted by the plaintiff that so far as ordnance survey no. 267 is concerned, the restrictive covenant is unaffected.

Conveyance to the plaintiff dated December 30, 1952   A

I will read the main provisions.   It reads:

" 1. . . . To hold the same unto the purchaser in fee simple subject
to but with the benefit of the exceptions and reservations stipulations
and covenants contained or referred to in a conveyance of the
neighbouring property now known as Tiltwood West dated July 15,
1952, and made between the vendor of the one part and Harold   B
Ernest Clark of the other part so far as the same relate to or affect
the property hereby conveyed and are still subsisting and capable of
taking effect and subject to a covenant contained in a conveyance
dated June 18, 1951, and made between George Ambrose Scaramanga of the one part and Henry John Longinotto of the other
part that the said Henry John Longinotto and his successors in   C
title would use the enclosures 267, 267B 267C and 267D (being
part of the land hereby conveyed) for agricultural purposes only
and that no building or other structure or erection whatsoever
whether permanent or temporary should at any time thereafter be
built erected or placed or suffered to be upon any part of the
aforesaid enclosures.   2.   The purchaser hereby covenants with the
vendor with intent so as to bind as far as practicable the property   D
hereby conveyed unto whosoever hands the same may go and to
benefit and protect the remainder of the property known as the
Tiltwood Estate that she the purchaser and her successors in title:
(a) will not at any time use any building upon the property hereby
conveyed for any other purpose whatsoever than as a private dwelling
house or residence or for agricultural or horticultural purposes and   E
will not do or suffer to be done upon the property hereby conveyed
or any part thereof anything which may be or become a nuisance
annoyance or injury or which may tend to depreciate the value of
any other part of the property known as the Tiltwood Estate. . . ."

Whoever drafted and approved that conveyance knows little of conveyancing.   How could the plaintiff be bound to use the land for agri-   F
cultural purposes only and at the same time for a private house only?
In fact the plaintiff has received planning permission to develop the
burdened land at a density of 8 houses to the acre.   She admits that she
is bound by the express covenants in her conveyance to build only
houses for domestic purposes but submits that she is not bound by the
1951 restrictive covenants because when Mrs. Spence bought the   G
enclosures in question the restrictive covenants were extinguished because
part of the burdened land came into the common ownership of the
benefited land.

Submissions

It is clear that by the conveyance of August 28, 1952, Mrs. Spence   H
who was then the owner in fee simple of the benefited land (except
the part conveyed to Colonel Clark) purchased the fee simple in some
half part of the burdened land.   The question of law is whether in those
circumstances the restrictive covenants on that part of the burdened land
are for ever extinguished unless a fresh express covenant is taken from the
purchaser of the part of the burdened land, or whether the restrictive
covenants are thereby suspended and are revived when part of the

A benefited land is sold with an express assignment of the covenant. It is
curious that this question has never before been decided by the courts.

Counsel for the defendants made three submissions: (i) That the
answer depended on the intention of the seller of the benefited land.
I do not think that the question of intention arises as in a question of
merger. But even if it did arise it is I think clear that the only
covenants which the seller intended to impose were those set out in
B the conditions of sale. (ii) That it would be inequitable for the plaintiff
to succeed. Even if equity does affect the question, which I do not
think it does, I do not think that the plaintiff's claim is inequitable.
Again the restrictions were to be the same for all purchasers under the
1952 auction particulars and conditions of sale. (iii) That the plaintiff
only purchased part of the burdened land. But this is a difficult sub-
C mission as the defendants only own part of the benefited land and the
part sold to Colonel Clark which had no express assignment cannot in
any event claim the benefit of the covenants.

The law

For the plaintiff it was submitted that the covenants are extinguished
when there is unity of seisin. The question is: does unity of seisin
D extinguish restrictive covenants or merely suspend them, and they
revive on an express assignment of the benefit? The legal pronounce-
ments on the subject are indeed jejune. In *Jolly on Restrictive Covenants Affecting Land,* 2nd ed. (1931), p. 52 I find this under the heading
" Merger: " " Upon the analogy of an easement it is conceived that the
benefit of a restrictive covenant would be merged and extinguished by
E unity of title and possession, if the dominant and servient tenements
pass into the same hands." In that sentence the benefited land is called
" the dominant tenement " and the burdened land " the servient tenement." In *Preston & Newsom on Restrictive Covenants Affecting Freehold Land,* 1st ed. (1939), I was informed by Mr. Newsom that Chapter 3
on the burden of covenants was entirely written by Mr. Preston who
unfortunately never returned from Dunkirk. That chapter reads, at
F p. 42:

"Similarly, it is submitted that restrictive covenants are destroyed
when the fee simple in the benefited and in the burdened land
become vested in the same person. Then there ceases to be land to
be protected; and as in the case of an easement, the fact the
owner exercises certain forbearances on part of his land is merely
G the particular user which as owner he chooses to have. Upon the
subsequent partition of the land, however, the covenant can scarely
be said to revive: it cannot be ' of necessity ' like a way nor
' continuous and apparent.' It is accordingly submitted, though
there is no authority on the point, that such unity of seisin destroys
the covenant, and does not merely suspend it."

H It is my duty to provide that authority.

This case is not part of a building scheme where different considerations apply and the plaintiff admits that the covenant was taken
in respect of ascertainable land. Both the text books to which I have
referred apply the law in regard to easements. It is well settled in the
law of easements that unity of seisin of the dominant and servient tenements
destroys all existing easements but that upon severance those quasi-ease-
ments which have been enjoyed by the owner and as are continuous or

apparent or arise from necessity are created as implied easements by the fact of severance: see *Gale on Easements,* 14th ed. (1972), pp. 309–311. In respect of profits à prendre I find in Hall on *Profits à prendre and Rights of Common* (1871), p. 335 this passage:

> "It follows from the doctrine above stated that, where the whole of the dominant tenement and the whole of the servient tenement are vested in the same person, a profit à prendre is either suspended or extinguished: if there be only unity of possession, they are suspended; if there be unity of seisin in fee simple, they are extinguished."

And it has long ago been decided that a release of part of a right of common extinguishes the rights over the whole common: *Miles* v. *Etteridge* (1692) 1 Show. 349.

I turn to the modern dicta. In *Brunner* v. *Greenslade* [1971] Ch. 993 Megarry J. was dealing with a scheme of development of land in several lots and he said, at p. 1005:

> "The major theoretical difficulties based on the law of covenant seem to me to disappear where instead there is an equity created by circumstances which is independent of contractual obligation. Further, whatever arguments there may be about unity of seisin destroying a covenant, by analogy to easements, I do not think that it precludes the application of a scheme of development as between purchasers of lots merely because they were initially in one hand."

In *Texaco Antilles Ltd.* v. *Kernochan* [1973] A.C. 609, a Privy Council case in which there was a building scheme, Lord Cross of Chelsea said, at p. 626:

> "It is no doubt true that if the restrictions in question exist simply for the mutual benfit of two adjoining properties and both those properties are bought by one man the restrictions will automatically come to an end and will not revive on a subsequent severance unless the common owner then recreates them. But their Lordships cannot see that it follows from this that if a number of people agree that the area covered by all their properties shall be subject to a ' local law ' the provisions of which shall be enforceable by any owner for the time being of any part against any other owner and the whole area has never at any time come into common ownership an action by one owner of a part against another owner of a part must fail if it can be shown that both parts were either at the inception of the scheme or at any time subsequently in common ownership. The view which their Lordships favour is supported by dicta of Sir H. H. Cozens-Hardy M.R. in *Elliston* v. *Reacher* [1908] 2 Ch. 665, 673 and of Simonds J. in *Lawrence* v. *South County Freeholds Ltd.* [1939] Ch. 656, 677–683, but at the time when this case was heard by the Court of Appeal there was no decision on the point. Subsequently, however, in *Brunner* v. *Greenslade* [1971] Ch. 993 which raised the point, Megarry J. followed those dicta. The appellants submitted that his decision was wrong but in their Lordships' view it was right."

Although the dictum in regard to restrictive covenants which exist simply for the benefit of two adjoining properties is strictly obiter, it carries great weight coming as it does from Lord Cross.

A *Conclusion*

I propose to follow that dictum and the text books to which I have referred and hold that where the fee simple of the benefited and the burdened land is vested in one person, the restrictive covenants are extinguished unless the common owner recreates them. In this case the common owner did not recreate them and they are therefore extinguished.

B It follows that the plaintiff is entitled to the declaration which she seeks.

> *Declaration accordingly.*
> *Plaintiff to pay defendants' costs.*

Solicitors: *Lewis, Lewis & Co.; Thomson, Snell & Passmore, Tunbridge Wells.*

C
K. N. B.

June 13, 1978. The defendants' appeal to the Court of Appeal (Buckley, Roskill and Goff L.JJ) was dismissed by agreement between the parties on terms endorsed on counsels' briefs.

D

_____

E
[CHANCERY DIVISION]

In re SPENCE, DECD.

OGDEN *v.* SHACKLETON AND OTHERS

[1976 S. No. 5850]

F 1978 April 6; 13
Megarry V.-C.

Charity—Cy-près doctrine—Misdescription—Residuary bequest for
benefit of patients of blind home—Home specified by name and
address—Association for blind carrying on two homes at
different places—Whether gift to association's endowments or
to specified home
Charity—Cy-près doctrine—Gift to discontinued charity—Gift for
G *benefit of patients of " Old Folks Home at Hillworth Lodge "*
—Home in existence at date of will—Home no longer in
existence at date of death—Whether gift capable of accomplish-
ment—Whether general charitable intention

The testatrix, by her will dated December 4, 1968, after appointing executors and trustees and giving a number of pecuniary legacies, bequeathed her residuary estate on trust
H " to pay and divide . . . equally between The Blind Home Scott Street Keighley and the Old Folks Home at Hillworth Lodge Keighley for the benefit of the patients," and declared that " the receipt of the treasurer for the time being of each of the above-mentioned institutions " should be a sufficient discharge to her trustees. She died on May 30, 1972. No institution by the name of " The Blind Home " existed at Keighley but a charity known as " The Keighley and District Association for the Blind " had been in existence since 1907. The association had changed its name thrice and had been

484

In re Spence (Ch.D.)   [1978]

running a blind home at Scott Street for over 25 years. There   A
had been no other premises or association connected with the
blind in Keighley, but the premises of the association were
quite often called the " Blind Home." The association also
carried on a home for the blind at Bingley.

Hillworth Lodge was built as a workhouse in 1858 and
was closed in 1939. In 1948, before the testatrix made her
will, it became an aged persons' home under the National
Assistance Act 1948, but was closed down as such in 1971,   B
before the testatrix's death. Since then the building had been
used as government offices. Over the years the aged of the
area were accommodated in purpose-designed old people's
homes.

On a summons by one of the trustees to determine whether
the gifts of residue were valid charitable gifts: —

Held, (1) that the testatrix made the gift for the benefit
of the patients for the time being at the home usually known   C
as The Blind Home in Scott Street, Keighley, so that it could
be used exclusively for the benefit of those patients and not
for general purposes of the association which ran the home;
and that the testatrix's purpose could be achieved by giving the
money to the association but confining its use to the patients for
the time being at the Scott Street home (post, p. 489B, C).

In re Lucas [1948] Ch. 424, C.A. distinguished.

(2) That where a testatrix took pains to identify a particular   D
charitable purpose which at the date of the will was capable
of being carried out but which at the date of the death was
not, then, as with gifts to institutions rather than purposes, the
court would be slow to find a general charitable intention;
that although a general charitable intention might be inferred
when the gift appeared in association with a number of other
gifts to undoubted charities with kindred objects, in the present
case neither the single associated charitable gift nor any other   E
circumstances showed any general charitable intention; and
that the gift for the benefit of the patients of the Old Folks
Home accordingly could not be applied cy-près, so that it
failed and the moiety of residue passed as on intestacy (post,
pp. 491A–D, 493F, G, 494B–D).

In re Harwood [1936] Ch. 285 applied.

In re Knox [1937] Ch. 109 distinguished.

F

The following cases are referred to in the judgment:

Biscoe v. *Jackson* (1887) 35 Ch.D. 460, C.A.

Davis, In re [1902] 1 Ch. 876.

Finger's Will Trusts, In re [1972] Ch. 286; [1971] 3 W.L.R. 775; [1971]
3 All E.R. 1050.

Hartley, decd., In re (unreported), March 15, 1978.

Harwood, In re [1936] Ch. 285.   G

Knox, In re [1937] Ch. 109; [1936] 3 All E.R. 623.

Lucas, In re [1948] Ch. 175; [1947] 2 All E.R. 773; [1948] Ch. 424;
[1948] 2 All E.R. 22, C.A.

Satterthwaite's Will Trusts, In re [1966] 1 W.L.R. 277; [1966] 1 All
E.R. 919, C.A.

Stemson's Will Trusts, In re [1970] Ch. 16; [1969] 3 W.L.R. 21; [1969]
2 All E.R. 517.   H

Wilson, In re [1913] 1 Ch. 314.

The following additional cases were cited in argument:

Rymer, In re [1895] 1 Ch. 19, C.A.

Slatter's Will Trusts, In re [1964] Ch. 512; [1964] 3 W.L.R. 18; [1964]
2 All E.R. 469.

White's Trusts, In re (1886) 33 Ch.D. 449.

A   ORIGINATING SUMMONS

On July 20, 1976, Agnew George Ogden, one of the executors of the will of Beatrice Spence deceased, issued an originating summons seeking to determine whether, on the true construction of the will dated December 4, 1968, the gift of a moiety of the residuary estate to The Blind Home, Scott Street, Keighley, was a valid charitable gift and whether in the absence of any institution called The Blind Home, Scott Street, Keighley,
B   the executors, the plaintiff and the second defendant, John Driver, ought to transfer the moiety to the Keighley and District Association for the Blind, whose chairman, Frank Shackleton, was the first defendant in the present proceedings. Further, it was sought to determine whether the gift of the other moiety of the residuary estate to the Old Folks Home at Hillworth Lodge, Keighley, for the benefit of the patients was a valid
C   charitable gift or, as the home no longer existed, the gift failed and the fund was undisposed of.

The facts are stated in the judgment.

D. Gidley Scott for the plaintiff.
J. B. W. McDonnell for the first defendant, the chairman of the Keighley and District Association for the Blind.
D   *J. F. Mummery* for the seventh defendant, the Attorney-General.

The second to sixth defendants, the next-of-kin, took no part in the proceedings.

Cur. adv. vult.

April 13. MEGARRY V.-C. read the following judgment. The facts of
E   this case lie in a narrow compass. But for the authorities, my judgment would have been correspondingly short. However, this is a case about charities; and those words almost of necessity expel brevity. The testatrix, Mrs. Spence, was a childless widow who lived at Keighley in Yorkshire. She made her will on December 4, 1968, and died on May 30, 1972. After appointing executors and trustees, her will gave 17 pecuniary legacies to relations and friends. She then gave her residuary estate to her
F   trustees on trust to sell it and to pay her funeral and testamentary expenses and debts, and then

"to pay and divide the residue thereof equally between The Blind Home Scott Street Keighley and the Old Folks Home at Hillworth Lodge Keighley for the benefit of the patients."

G   The will next provided that the receipt of the treasurer for the time being of "each of the above mentioned institutions" should be a sufficient discharge to her trustees. There was then a professional charging clause, and that was all. Subject to the expenses of administration and to the costs of these proceedings, the net residue is now worth some £17,000.

The question before me is the effect of this residuary gift. The plaintiff in the originating summons is one of the executors and trustees
H   under the will; and Mr. Gidley Scott appeared for him. Those believed to be the next-of-kin have been joined as defendants, and all of them (save one, who is in default of appearance) have entered appearances but have not been represented and have taken no part in the proceedings. At my request, Mr. Gidley Scott has assisted the court by arguing the claims of those entitled on intestacy. The first defendant is the chairman of the Keighley and District Association for the Blind, which is a registered but unincorporated charity; and Mr. McDonnell appeared for

him. Finally, Mr. Mummery appeared for the seventh defendant, the ⒜ Attorney-General.

I shall first consider the gift to " The Blind Home Scott Street Keighley . . . for the benefit of the patients." I think it is clear that these last six words apply to the gift to the Blind Home as they apply to the gift to the Old Folks Home; and nobody contended to the contrary. The question is whether this gift carries a moiety of residue to the Keighley and District Association for the Blind and, if so, on what terms. That ⒝ charity was founded in 1907 and, over the years, it has changed its name thrice. It has borne its present name for nearly 20 years, and is at present governed by a trust deed dated October 25, 1963. For over 25 years it has been running a blind home at 31 Scott Street, Keighley, which provides permanent accommodation for the blind in Keighley and district. Since 1907 there have been no other premises or associations connected with ⒞ the blind in Keighley. The premises in Scott Street are often called " The Blind Home "; and a memorandum of the appointment of new trustees made on June 9, 1970, refers to the meeting for that purpose held at " The Blind Home Scott Street Keighley." Other names are used. A board on the building calls it " The Keighley and District Home for the Blind," and a brochure in evidence calls it " Keighley Home for the Blind." It seems clear beyond a peradventure that the language of the will fits the ⒟ home run by the charity at these premises.

In those circumstances, Mr. Gidley Scott felt unable to advance any argument that the gift of this moiety failed and passed as on intestacy; and in this I think he was right. That, however, does not dispose of the matter, since the charity also carries on a home for the blind at Bingley, and may of course expend some or all of its funds on this or other ⒠ purposes within its objects. There is therefore the question whether the moiety should go to the charity as an accretion to its endowment, and so be capable of being employed on any of its activities, or whether it is to be confined to the particular part of the charity's activities that are carried on at The Blind Home in Scott Street, Keighley. I confess that but for the decision of the Court of Appeal in In re Lucas [1948] Ch. 424, I should have had little hesitation in resolving this question in the latter ⒡ and narrower sense, confining the moiety to the particular Blind Home in Scott Street, Keighley.

In In re Lucas the testatrix made her will on October 12, 1942, and died on December 18, 1943. The will made gifts to " the Crippled Children's Home, Lindley Moor, Huddersfield "; and it provided that the receipt of the treasurer or other officer for the time being should be ⒢ a sufficient discharge. From 1916 there had been an establishment called " The Huddersfield Home for Crippled Children " at Lindley Moor, governed by the charitable trusts established by a deed dated March 29, 1915; but according to the statement of facts in the report, at p. 425, " On October 17, 1941, this home was closed and a scheme for the future administration of its assets was made by the charity commissioners." Under that scheme the charity thereby created was to be known as " The ⒣ Huddersfield Charity for Crippled Children," and the income was to be applied in sending poor crippled children to holiday or convalescent homes.

During the argument before me the question arose (for reasons that will appear) whether the words " On October 17, 1941," which plainly applied to the closing of the home, also applied (as appeared to be the case) to the making of the scheme and the consequent change of the name of the charity. To this no definite answer could be given, for the report

A at first instance (*In re Lucas* [1948] Ch. 175, 176) stated the facts in the same way. However, the matter is resolved by the reports of *In re Lucas* in the All England Reports which I examined after reserving judgment: [1947] 2 All E.R. 773, 774; [1948] 2 All E.R. 22, 24. There, passages in the judgments which are omitted from the Law Reports explicitly state that the scheme of the charity commissioners was sealed on October 17, 1941. They also show that the home had been closed not on that day

B but some two and a half years before, on April 6, 1939, when the lease had run out. The statement of facts in the Law Reports is thus wrong in this respect. When the testatrix came to make her will on October 12, 1942, the home had been closed for some three and a half years, and the charity had for almost a year had a name which, in accord with its new objects, had had the word " Home " in it replaced by " Charity."

C The All England Reports also show that the original name, " The Huddersfield Home for Crippled Children," had been given to the charity by the trust deed. The question for resolution in *In re Lucas* was thus whether the gifts to " the Crippled Children's Home Lindley Moor Huddersfield " took effect as gifts to " The Huddersfield Charity for Crippled Children," or whether they were gifts for the upkeep of a particular home for crippled children which had ceased to exist before the

D will had been made, so that they failed.

At first instance, Roxburgh J. held that the latter was the correct view: *In re Lucas* [1948] Ch. 175; [1947] 2 All E.R. 773. On appeal, Lord Greene M.R. delivered the reserved judgment of himself, Somervell L.J. and Jenkins J. This reversed the decision below, and held that the gifts were gifts which contributed to the endowment of the charity, and so did

E not fail. I have found the judgment puzzling in places. Lord Greene M.R. discussed the misdescription in the will [1948] Ch. 424, 428: " As to the misdescription (i.e. ' The Crippled Children's Home ' for ' the Huddersfield Home for Crippled Children ') the description given by the testatrix was no more an accurate description of the particular home than it was of the charity." Later on the same page the judgment considers the position if the testatrix " did know the correct name of the charity

F (i.e. ' the Huddersfield Home for Crippled Children ') . . ."

I find this puzzling. I say that with much hesitation, not least because the judgment is a reserved judgment of a Court of Appeal of such eminence. It would be wrong, however, for me to pass over in silence what I do not understand. My difficulty is this. Nearly a year before the will was made, the correct name of the charity had ceased to be

G what the judgment says it was. The " description given by the testatrix " was " The Crippled Children's Home, Lindley Moor, Huddersfield." This, said the judgment, was " no more an accurate description of the particular home " (that is, the Huddersfield Home for Crippled Children which was at Lindley Moor) " than it was of the charity." Yet when the will was made the name of the charity had for nearly a year been: " The Huddersfield Charity for Crippled Children," a name which did

H not include the word " Home." I find it difficult to see why a gift to a " Home " does not fit an entity with " Home " in its title better than it fits an entity without the word " Home " in its title, but the word " Charity " instead. If in referring to the " correct name " of the charity the judgment intends to refer to what had once been the correct name of the charity, I cannot see what it was that made the court reject the state of affairs when the will was made in favour of the past, particularly when there appears to have been no evidence about what the testatrix knew about the charity. I say what I say with all due humility, **A** and a ready recognition that the fault may be an inability on my part to see what is plain to others; but, though humble, I remain puzzled.

During the argument, counsel referred me to difficulties of this sort not on p. 428 but on p. 429. On that page there are three references to "The Huddersfield Home for Crippled Children" as being the name of the charity. There is also a sentence which refers to the use of the word "Home" in the inaccurate description used by the testatrix, **B** and states that the "correct description itself contains similar references." This, I think, may readily be explained. The explanation (or an explanation) is provided by the first sentence on the page. This shows that what is being considered is what the position would have been if the home at Lindley Moor had remained subject to the original trust deed, and in use in accordance with its provisions until after the **C** testatrix had died. Though the judgment does not in terms say so, I think it is reasonably plain that the hypothetical state of affairs being assumed necessarily implies that it is also to be assumed that the scheme had not been made and so the charity had not changed its name. On that footing, of course, the use of the word "Home" in the title of the charity is entirely accurate, and the difficulty disappears. Unfortu- **D** nately this provides no help in understanding the difficulties in the judgment on the previous page, p. 428, which I encountered only when I came to consider my judgment.

The main factors in the decision of the Court of Appeal seem to have been that the words used in the will fitted the home that had been closed down no better than the charity which continued in existence, and that the will had omitted to make any specific reference to the **E** upkeep or maintenance of the home which would indicate that the gifts were to be confined to the upkeep of the home. The gifts were accordingly gifts to the charity, and so did not fail. The question for me is whether on the case before me there ought to be a similar result, so that the moiety of residue would go to the Keighley and District Institution for the Blind as an addition to its endowment generally, and **F** would not be confined to the Blind Home in Scott Street, Keighley, carried on by the institution.

Mr. McDonnell submitted that there were two substantial points of distinction between the present case and *In re Lucas.* First, the words of the will fitted the Blind Home far better than they fitted the institution. Indeed, although the Blind Home was from time to time described by different names, all the names used included both "Blind" and **G** "Home": and, as I have mentioned, the appointment of new trustees in June 1970 uses the name "The Blind Home Scott Street Keighley," which is the precise expression used in the will. The title of the charity, "The Keighley and District Association for the Blind," is very different. True, it has the word "Blind" in common with the title used in the will. There is also the word "Keighley," though this is used adjectively **H** and not as part of the address. But otherwise there is nothing in common. In particular, there is not the use of the word "Home" in both titles which the Court of Appeal in *In re Lucas* said was present in that case; and I think the words "Home" and "Association" are different in a real and significant sense.

Second, in the case before me, there are the words "for the benefit of the patients" which follow and govern the expression "The Blind

A Home Scott Street Keighley." In *In re Lucas* there was no counterpart to this. Indeed, the absence of any reference to the upkeep or maintenance of the home in that case was, as I have indicated, one of the grounds on which the decision was based. Here, there is no reference to upkeep or maintenance as such: but I think " patients " must mean " patients of the Blind Home," and the upkeep and maintenance of the home is an obvious means of providing a benefit for the patients in it.

B In my judgment both these distinctions are valid and substantial. It therefore seems to me that the case before me is distinguishable from *In re Lucas,* so far as I have correctly understood that case. The testatrix was making provision for the benefit of the patients for the time being at a particular home, namely, the home usually known as The Blind Home at Scott Street, Keighley. She was giving the money not to

C augment generally the endowment of the charity which runs that home, with the consequence that the money might be used for purposes other than the benefit of the patients at that home, but was giving the money so that it would be used exclusively for the benefit of those patients. The only way in which this can conveniently be done is to give the money to the charity but to confine its use to use for the benefit of the patients for the time being at the home. That, I think, requires a

D scheme; but I see no need to direct that a scheme should be settled in chambers. Instead, I think that I can follow the convenient course taken by Goff J. in *In re Finger's Will Trusts* [1972] Ch. 286, 300. I shall therefore order by way of scheme (the Attorney-General not objecting) that the moiety be paid to the proper officer of the charity to be held on trust to apply it for the benefit of the patients for the time

E being of the home known as The Blind Home, Scott Street, Keighley.

I now turn to the other moiety of residue, given by the will to " the Old Folks Home at Hillworth Lodge Keighley for the benefit of the patients." Hillworth Lodge was built as a workhouse in 1858. Shortly before the outbreak of war in 1939 the West Riding County Council, in whom it had become vested, closed it down: but during the war it was

F used to house what were generally but inelegantly called " evacuees." In 1948 it became an aged persons' home under the National Assistance Act 1948, and it continued as such until on January 28, 1971, it was finally closed down. There had been between 120 and 140 residents in it as late as 1969, but the numbers were then progressively run down, until in January 1971, just before it closed, only 10 residents were left; and these were transferred to another establishment in Pudsey. The

G aged of the area had over the years been increasingly accommodated in purpose-designed old people's homes which provided better accommodation for the aged than could the old workhouse, despite many improvements to it. Since the building ceased to house old people it has been used as divisional social services offices.

When the testatrix made her will in 1968 the building was accordingly

H still in use as an old people's home run by the local authority in accordance with their duty under the National Assistance Act 1948. As an old people's home it had no assets of its own, and residents contributed towards their maintenance in accordance with the Ministry of Social Security Act 1966, Part III. When the testatrix died on May 30, 1972, the building was no longer used as an old people's home, and was being used, or was soon to be used, as offices. The home had been run neither as nor by a charity. It formerly provided homes for those

living in a large area of the West Riding, and not merely Keighley; and   A
it has not been replaced by any one home. Instead, there are many old
people's homes serving the area.

    Now without looking at the authorities, I would have said that this
was a fairly plain case of a will which made a gift for a particular
purpose in fairly specific terms. The gift was for the benefit of the
patients at a particular home, namely, the Old Folks Home at Hillworth
Lodge, Keighley. At the date of the will there were patients at that   B
home. When the testatrix died, there was no longer any home there,
but offices instead; and so there were no longer any patients there, or
any possibility of them. The gift was a gift for a charitable purpose
which at the date of the will was capable of accomplishment and at the
date of death was not. Prima facie, therefore, the gift fails unless a
general charitable intention has been manifested so that the property   C
can be applied cy-près. Buttressed by authority, Mr. Gidley Scott contended that the court would be slow to find a general charitable intention
where the object of the gift is defined with some particularity, as it was
here.

    Against that, Mr. Mummery, on behalf of the Attorney-General,
advanced two main contentions. First, he said that as a matter of   D
construction it was wrong to construe the gift as being merely for the
benefit of patients who were actually at the Old Folks Home at Hillworth Lodge; admittedly, of course, there are none of these. Instead,
those who were intended to benefit included all those who would have
been sent to that home if it had still existed, irrespective of the type of
home in which in fact they are being or will be accommodated. He
emphasised that the gift was essentially a gift for old people in Keighley,   E
and the home was merely a means of providing a benefit for them.

    I do not think that this argument can be right. When the testatrix
made her will there were patients at the Old Folks Home at Hillworth
Lodge. The gift to that Home "for the benefit of patients" is, on this
construction, to be treated as being a gift for the benefit not only of the
patients who successively were for the time being at the Home, but of   F
others who never go near the Home but who might or would have
been sent to it in certain circumstances. The words of the will were
perfectly capable of being satisfied by confining their meaning to their
natural sense, namely, as relating to those who are or will in the future
be patients at the Home. Why is there to be forced on to those words
a notional extension of uncertain effect? If at the time they were
being written those words could not have their natural effect, one   G
might indeed look round for a secondary meaning; but that is not the
case.

    There are further difficulties. If the notional extension is made, who
are within it? As I have said, the defunct Home provided for a large
area of the West Riding, and not merely Keighley. How is it to be
determined who can hope to benefit under the gift? Which of the   H
occupants of the other old people's homes in such an area (the extent
of which is undefined) can claim to be objects of the testatrix's bounty?
Who is to decide whether any particular individual could (or would) have
been sent to the defunct Home had it still existed, and so would fall
within the scope of the gift? I do not see how such an extension of
meaning can fairly be placed on the words of the will. No doubt a
scheme could cure much, but my difficulty is in seeing what, on this

A footing, was the intention of the testatrix. For the reasons that I have given, I reject this contention.

Mr. Mummery's other contention was that the will displayed a sufficient general charitable intention for the moiety to be applied cy-près. In doing this he had to contend with *In re Harwood* [1936] Ch. 285. This, and cases which apply it, such as *In re Stemson's Will Trusts* [1970] Ch. 16, establish that it is very difficult to find a general charitable B intention where the testator has selected a particular charity, taking some care to identify it, and the charity then ceases to exist before the testator's death. This contrasts with cases where the charity described in the will has never existed, when it is much easier to find a general charitable intention.

These cases have been concerned with gifts to institutions, rather than C gifts for purposes. The case before me, on the other hand, is a gift for a purpose, namely, the benefit of the patients at a particular Old Folks Home. It therefore seems to me that I ought to consider the question, of which little or nothing was said in argument, whether the principle *In re Harwood*, or a parallel principle, has any application to such case. In other words, is a similar distinction to be made between, on the one D hand, a case in which the testator has selected a particular charitable purpose, taking some care to identify it, and before the testator dies that purpose has become impracticable or impossible of accomplishment, and on the other hand a case where the charitable purpose has never been possible or practicable?

As at present advised I would answer Yes to that question. I do not think that the reasoning of the *In re Harwood* line of cases is directed E to any feature of institutions as distinct from purposes. Instead, I think the essence of the distinction is in the difference between particularity and generality. If a particular institution or purpose is specified, then it is that institution or purpose, and no other, that is to be the object of the benefaction. It is difficult to envisage a testator as being suffused with a general glow of broad charity when he is labouring, and labouring F successfully, to identify some particular specified institution or purpose as the object of his bounty. The specific displaces the general. It is otherwise where the testator has been unable to specify any particular charitable institution or practicable purpose, and so, although his intention of charity can be seen, he has failed to provide any way of giving effect to it. There, the absence of the specific leaves the general undisturbed. It follows that in my view in the case before me, where G the testatrix has clearly specified a particular charitable purpose which before her death became impossible to carry out, Mr. Mummery has to face that level of great difficulty in demonstrating the existence of a general charitable intention which was indicated by *In re Harwood*.

One way in which Mr. Mummery sought to meet that difficulty was by citing *In re Finger's Will Trusts* [1972] Ch. 286. There, Goff J. H distinguished *In re Harwood* and held that the will before him displayed a general charitable intention. He did this on the footing that the circumstances of the case were "very special." The gift that failed was a gift to an incorporated charity which had ceased to exist before the testatrix died. The "very special" circumstances were, first, that apart from a life interest and two small legacies, the whole estate was devoted to charity, and that this was emphasised by the direction to hold the residue in trust for division "between the following charitable institutions

and funds." Second, the charitable donee that had ceased to exist was **A**
mainly, if not exclusively, a co-ordinating body, and the judge could
not believe that the testatrix meant to benefit that body alone. Third,
there was evidence that the testatrix regarded herself as having no
relatives.

In the case before me neither of these last two circumstances applies,
nor have any substitute special circumstances been suggested. As for
the first, the will before me gives 17 pecuniary legacies to relations and **B**
friends, amounting in all to well over one third of the net estate.
Further, in *In re Rymer* [1895] 1 Ch. 19, which does not appear to
have been cited, the will had prefaced the disputed gift by the words
" I give the following charitable legacies to the following institutions
and persons respectively." These words correspond to the direction
which in *In re Finger's Will Trusts* was regarded as providing emphasis, **C**
and yet they did not suffice to avoid the conclusion of Chitty J. and
the Court of Appeal that a gift to an institution which had ceased to
exist before the testator's death lapsed and could not be applied cy-près.
I am not sure that I have been able to appreciate to the full the cogency
of the special circumstances that appealed to Goff J.; but however that
may be, I can see neither those nor any other special circumstances
in the present case which would suffice to distinguish *In re Harwood* **D**
[1936] Ch. 285.

The other way in which Mr. Mummery sought to meet his difficulty
was by relying on *In re Satterthwaite's Will Trusts* [1966] 1 W.L.R.
277 (which he said was his best case), and on *In re Knox* [1937] Ch. 109,
which I think may possibly be better. The doctrine may for brevity
be described as charity by association. If the will gives the residue **E**
among a number of charities with kindred objects, but one of the
apparent charities does not in fact exist, the court will be ready to find
a general charitable intention and so apply the share of the non-existent
charity cy-près. I have not been referred to any explicit statement of
the underlying principle, but it seems to me that in such cases the court
treats the testator as having shown the general intention of giving his **F**
residue to promote charities with that type of kindred objects, and then,
when he comes to dividing the residue, as casting around for particular
charities with that type of objects to name as donees. If one of more of
these are non-existent, then the general intention will suffice for a cy-près
application. It will be observed that, as stated, the doctrine depends,
at least to some extent, upon the detection of "kindred objects" (a
phrase which comes from the judgment of Luxmoore J. in *In re Knox* **G**
[1937] Ch. 109, 113, in the charities to which the shares of residue are
given; in this respect the charities must in some degree be ejusdem
generis.

In *In re Satterthwaite's Will Trusts* [1966] 1 W.L.R. 277 the residuary
gift was to nine charitable bodies which were all concerned with kindness
to animals; but the gifts to two of them failed as no bodies could be found **H**
which sufficiently answered the descriptions in the will. Harman L.J.
said that he " felt the gravest doubts " (p. 284) whether a general
charitable intent had been shown. However, at first instance the judge
had held that in respect of one of the bodies a sufficient general charitable
intention had been displayed, and as there had been no appeal as to that
share, he (Harman L.J.) would reach the same conclusion in respect
of the other share, which was the subject of the appeal. On the other

A hand, Russell L.J. had no doubt that a general charitable intention had been shown: p. 287. Diplock L.J. delivered a single-sentence judgment agreeing with both the other judgments. The support which this case provides for Mr. Mummery accordingly seems to me to be a trifle muted.

In *In re Knox* [1937] Ch. 109 Luxmoore J. distilled a general charitable intention out of a residuary gift in quarters to two named
B infirmaries, a named nursing home and Dr. Barnado's Homes. No institution existed which correctly answered the description of the nursing home, and it was held the the quarter share that had been given to it should be applied cy-près. I am not entirely sure what genus the judge had in mind as embracing the infirmaries and Dr. Barnado's Homes when, at p. 113, he said that " the object of each of the other charities is
C a kindred object to that which might be inferred from the name " of the nursing home: perhaps it was the provision of residential accommodation for those in need. Perhaps I should also mention *In re Hartley, decd.* (unreported), a decision of mine on March 15, 1978, in a case in which the Attorney-General was one of the parties. In that case, *In re Knox* [1937] Ch. 109 was applied to a will when the residue was given in
D quarters between service charities of a benevolent nature. It was held that a general charitable intention had been shown which sufficed for the cy-près application of the share given to a body of that nature which did not exist at the date of the will. A body which might have answered the description in the will had existed some years earlier.

It will be observed that these are all cases of gifts to bodies which did not exist. In such cases, the court is ready to find a general
E charitable intention: see *In re Davis* [1902] 1 Ch. 876, especially at p. 884. The court is far less ready to find such an intention where the gift is to a body which existed at the date of the will but ceased to exist before the testator died, or, as I have already held, where the gift is for a purpose which, though possible and practicable at the date of the will, has ceased to be so before the testator's death. The case before me is,
F of course, a case in this latter category, so that Mr. Mummery has to overcome this greater difficulty in finding a general charitable intention.

Not only does Mr. Mummery have this greater difficulty: he also has, I think, less material with which to meet it. He has to extract the general charitable intention for the gift which fails from only one other gift: the residue, of course, was simply divided into two. In *In re Knox* and *In re Hartley* the gifts which failed were each among three other
G gifts, and in *In re Satterthwaite's Will Trusts* [1966] 1 W.L.R. 277 there were seven or eight other gifts. I do not say that a general charitable intention or a genus cannot be extracted from a gift of residue equally between two: but I do say that larger numbers are likely to assist in conveying to the court a sufficient conviction both of the genus and of the generality of the charitable intention.

H A further point occurred to me which I think that I should mention. There are, of course, cases where there is merely a single gift, but the court is nevertheless able to see a clear general charitable intention underlying the particular mode of carrying it out that the testator has laid down. Thus in the well known case of *Biscoe* v. *Jackson* (1887) 35 Ch. D. 460, which I read in the light of *In re Wilson* [1913] 1 Ch. 314, the gift was to provide a soup kitchen and cottage hospital " for the parish of Shoreditch." Despite a considerable degree of particularity about the soup kitchen and the cottage hospital that were to be provided, the court A found a general charitable intention to provide a benefit for the sick and poor of the parish. In that case, of course, there would have been no real difficulty in ascertaining those who were intended to benefit. Whatever the practical difficulties, at least the concept of those who were to be included is clear enough. The only real difficulty or impossibility lay in the particular method of carrying out that intention which the testator had specified. In the present case, on the other hand, the B difficulty lies not only in the particular method but also in the very nature of the general charitable intention that is said to underlie that method. For the reasons that I have already given, I find it far from clear which "patients" are intended to benefit once the touch-stone of the Old People's Home at Hillworth Lodge is removed. There is no geographical or other limitation to provide a guide. Where the difficulty C or impossibility not only afflicts the method but also invades the concept of the alleged general charitable intention, then I think that the difficulty of establishing that the will displays any general charitable intention becomes almost insuperable.

From what I have said it follows that I have been quite unable to extract from the will, construed in its context, any expression of a D general charitable intention which would suffice for the moiety to be applied cy-près. Instead, in my judgment, the moiety was given for a specific charitable purpose which, though possible when the will was made, became impossible before the testatrix died. The gift of the moiety accordingly fails, and it passes as on intestacy.

Declaration accordingly.   E

Solicitors: *Roche Son & Neale for Wright, Atkinson & Pearson, Keighley; Hatchett, Jones & Kidgell; Treasury Solicitor.*

A. R.

F

[CHANCERY DIVISION]

GRAVESHAM BOROUGH COUNCIL AND ANOTHER
v. BRITISH RAILWAYS BOARD

G

PORT OF LONDON AUTHORITY *v.* SAME

[1977 G. No. 541]

[1977 P. No. 782]

1977 May 9, 10, 11, 12, 13, 16, 17;   H
June 24   Slade J.

Ferry—Ancient franchise—Curtailment of services—Ferries vested in railways board—Proposal to curtail services—Ferries operating at loss—Services not much used—Actions by local authorities in interests of inhabitants—Action by port authority as suffering particular damage—Locus standi—Duty of ferry owner

A   Two ancient common law ferries across the river Thames between Gravesend and Tilbury became vested in the defendants, British Railways Board, one under a conveyance in fee simple of 1880, and the other under a lease dated December 31, 1951, for a term of years expiring on September 29, 1980. By letters dated February 11, 1977, the defendants informed the borough councils of Gravesham and Thurrock and the Port of London Authority, which operated Tilbury docks, of their

B   intention to reduce both the hours of operation and the frequency of services of each of the ferries. In particular, the defendants intended to discontinue the first early morning service and the last five night services in each direction. Since 1964, British Rail had run the ferries at a substantial annual loss, the most recent loss for 1976 being some £55,000. By the proposed reduction of services they could dispense with the services of a fourth crew and a ticket collector, and save

C   fuel, the total saving being estimated at £20,500. By writs dated February 17, 1977, the two borough councils and the P.L.A. in separate actions sought identical relief, namely, a mandatory injunction ordering the defendants to " maintain the period and frequency of operation as at the date of issue hereof." Subsequently, the plaintiffs sought injunctions merely requiring maintenance of the early morning and late night services until the date of termination of the lease of the

D   southbound ferry, i.e. September 29, 1980. The average number of inhabitants of the areas of the two plaintiff councils using the late night sailings for social purposes was assessed at about 21 per day. The number of those using the early and late ferries for going to and from work was estimated at 34 per day. In running the Tilbury docks the P.L.A. operated a three-shift system, and some of its employees living south of the river were accustomed in travelling to

E   and from work to rely on the ferry services proposed to be discontinued. The number of P.L.A. employees who would be affected by the curtailment of the late night services was assessed at 50, 1 per cent. of its entire work force and less than 10 per cent. of those employed on the three-shift system. And of those only 25 were actual dock workers who might have to be replaced by men requiring a special training which would cost some £14,000.

F   At trial of the action the P.L.A. claimed the right to bring proceedings by reason of the obstruction likely to be caused to its employees through the discontinuance of such services and the disruption which would be caused to its business: —

     Held, (1) that the duty of a ferry owner under the common law was to be ready to carry passengers, not at any time of day or night but at all reasonable hours, and that the test

G   of what was reasonable in that context had to be assessed according to all the circumstances, it being necessary to strike a balance between, on the one hand, the extent of the demand for the ferry service at particular hours and the inconvenience and hardship, if any, which would be caused to the public if such services were not provided, and, on the other hand, the burden that would fall on the ferry owner in providing such services; and that the onus of proving that the proposed

H   new time-table was unreasonable was on the plaintiffs (post, pp. 507F–H, 515H—516A).

     Hammerton v. *Earl of Dysart* [1916] 1 A.C. 57, H.L.(E.) and dictum of Stirling L.J. in *Attorney-General* v. *Simpson* [1901] 2 Ch. 671, 717, C.A. applied.

     Letton v. *Goodden* (1866) L.R. 2 Eq. 123; *Dibden* v. *Skirrow* [1907] 1 Ch. 437 and *Attorney-General* v. *Colchester Corporation* [1955] 2 Q.B. 207 considered.

     (2) That the P.L.A. had a locus standi to bring proceedings

Gravesham B.C. v. British Rail (Ch.D.)   **[1978]**

to restrain the introduction of the proposed new time table   A
as being an alleged threatened breach by the defendants of
their duty as a ferry owner, because interference with the
P.L.A.'s business and expense caused by its servants being
prevented from using the ferry were capable of being regarded
as particular damage, giving it a locus standi to sue for
public nuisance and because the potential injury and loss,
which the authority would be likely to suffer in replacing
those employees who would be forced to change their jobs,   B
constituted injury and loss beyond the general hardship likely
to be suffered by members of the public (post, pp. 511H—
512B, H—513C, 517B–C).

   Blundy Clark & Co. Ltd. v. *London & North Eastern
Railway Co.* [1931] 2 K.B. 334, C.A. applied.

   (3) That in the circumstances and on the evidence the
plaintiffs had failed to discharge their onus of showing that
the proposed new timetable was unreasonable so as to con-   C
stitute a breach by the defendants of their common law duty
as a ferry owner, and accordingly the plaintiffs' actions must
be dismissed with costs (post, p. 517B–C).

   Per curiam. It cannot be regarded as an absolute and
inflexible rule that the court will never grant an injunction
requiring a person to do a series of acts requiring the continuous employment of people over a number of years.
Nevertheless the paucity of authority illustrating the grant of   D
injunctions of this nature indicates that the jurisdiction is one
that will be exercised only in exceptional circumstances (post,
pp. 518H—519A).

The following cases are referred to in the judgment:

Attorney-General v. *Colchester Corporation* [1955] 2 Q.B. 207; [1955] 2
   W.L.R. 913; [1955] 2 All E.R. 303.   E
Attorney-General v. *Simpson* [1901] 2 Ch. 671, C.A.; *sub nom. Simpson*
   v. *Attorney-General* [1904] A.C. 476, H.L.(E.).
Benjamin v. *Storr* (1874) L.R. 9 C.P. 400.
Blundy Clark & Co. Ltd. v. *London & North Eastern Railway Co.* [1931]
   2 K.B. 334, C.A.
Dibden v. *Skirrow* [1907] 1 Ch. 437.
Fortescue v. *Lostwithiel and Fowey Railway Co.* [1894] 3 Ch. 621.   F
Giles (C.H.) & Co. Ltd. v. *Morris* [1972] 1 W.L.R. 307; [1972] 1 All
   E.R. 960.
Greene v. *West Cheshire Railway Co.* (1871) L.R. 13 Eq. 44.
Hammerton v. *Earl of Dysart* [1916] 1 A.C. 57, H.L.(E.).
Harper v. *Haden & Sons Ltd.* [1933] Ch. 298, C.A.
Iveson v. *Moore* (1699) 1 Ld.Raym. 486.   G
Letton v. *Goodden* (1866) L.R. 2 Eq. 123.
Lumley v. *Wagner* (1852) 1 De G.M. & G. 604.
North & South Shields Ferry Co. v. *Barker* (1848) 2 Exch. 136.
Paine v. *Partrich* (1691) Carth. 191.
Ricket v. *Metropolitan Railway Co.* (1867) L.R. 2 H.L. 175, H.L.(E.).
Shiloh Spinners Ltd. v. *Harding* [1973] A.C. 691; [1973] 2 W.L.R. 28;
   [1973] 1 All E.R. 90, H.L.(E.).   H
Tito v. *Waddell (No. 2)* [1977] Ch. 106; [1977] 3 W.L.R. 972; [1977]
   3 All E.R. 129.
Wilkes v. *Hungerford Market Co.* (1835) 2 Bing N.C. 281.

The following additional cases were cited in argument:

Bidwell v. *Holden* (1890) 63 L.T. 104.
Kennard v. *Cory Brothers and Co. Ltd.* [1922] 1 Ch. 265.

3 W.L.R.   Gravesham B.C. v. British Rail (Ch.D.)

A   *Overseas Tankship (U.K.) Ltd.* v. *Miller Steamship Co. Pty.* [1967] 1
A.C. 617; [1966] 3 W.L.R. 498; [1966] 2 All E.R. 709, P.C.
Turner v. *Bladin* (1951) 82 C.L.R. 463.

ACTIONS

On February 17, 1977, two separate actions were commenced by writ
against British Railways Board, one jointly brought by Gravesham
B   Borough Council and Thurrock Borough Council, and the other by the
Port of London Authority, in each case claiming the same relief, namely,
a mandatory injunction that the defendants should " maintain the period
and frequency of operation as at the date hereof " of two ancient common
law ferries which were vested in British Railways Board across the river
Thames, linking Gravesend in Kent with Tilbury in Essex, and vice
C   versa. The injunction sought was not a perpetual one, but merely until
September 29, 1980, the date on which the British Railways Board's
lease in respect of the south-bound ferry from Tilbury to Gravesend was
due to expire.

The facts are stated in the judgment.

Nicholas J. C. Stewart for the plaintiffs.
D   *David Gidley Scott* for the defendants.

Cur. adv. vult.

June 24. SLADE J. read the following judgment. These are two
actions concerning the same subject matter, to each of which British
Railways Board is sole defendant. In one action, Port of London
E   Authority is sole plaintiff. In the other action there are two plaintiffs,
namely Gravesham Borough Council and Thurrock Borough Council.

The actions concern two ancient common law franchise ferries across
the river Thames. One of them runs northwards from Gravesend in the
county of Kent to Tilbury in the county of Essex. The other runs south-
wards from Tilbury to Gravesend. Both these public ferries are now
vested in and operated by British Railways Board. The Port of London
F   Authority, which I will henceforth call " the P.L.A.," is concerned with
the ferries because it runs the Tilbury docks complex on the north side
of the river Thames. The two plaintiff councils are suing in exercise of the
powers conferred on them by section 222 (1) (*a*) of the Local Government
Act 1972, which empowers a local authority to institute civil proceedings
in its own name where it considers it expedient for the protection of the
interests of the inhabitants of its area. The borough of Gravesend on
G   the south side of the river has a population of about 97,700 persons. The
borough of Thurrock on the north side, which includes Tilbury, has a
population of about 127,600.

A ferry service between Gravesend and Tilbury has existed for centuries and is still a most important link between the north and south
banks of the river Thames in that area. The nearest alternative pedes-
H   trian crossing of the river is at Woolwich, some 15 miles up-stream,
where there is a free ferry and pedestrian tunnel. The Dartford tunnel,
which was opened in 1963, is about eight miles up-stream from the
Tilbury-Gravesend ferry. It caters for vehicular but not for pedestrian
traffic, and a toll is payable for the journey through this tunnel. Because
it becomes congested at peak hours and holiday times, a second tunnel
is being constructed alongside the existing one, and is expected to open
in the summer of 1978.

The writs in both actions were issued on February 17, 1977, and the   A
relief sought in both is precisely the same, namely an order that the
defendants, which I will henceforth call "British Rail," do "maintain
the period and frequency of operation as at the date of issue hereof" of
the Gravesend-Tilbury and Tilbury-Gravesend ferries. The relief sought
is thus relief by way of mandatory injunction.

Following the issue of the two writs, the respective plaintiffs sought
interlocutory relief designed to preserve the existing timetable of the ferries   B
until the hearing of the action. Their motions were heard by Brightman J.
effectively on February 24, 1977, when they were resolved by means of
undertakings given on behalf of British Rail until after judgment or
further order in the meantime, to maintain, unless prevented by circumstances beyond its control, the period and frequency of operation of the
two ferries as at the date of issue of the writs. At the same time, various   C
directions were given, including directions for a speedy trial, an order
that the affidavits sworn on the motions should stand as pleadings in the
action and an order for exchange of proofs.

The time tables currently operated by British Rail in relation to the
ferries provide the following services for pedestrians, motor cyclists and
pedal cyclists. [His Lordship then summarised the effect of such time-
tables, which provided (inter alia) for a first sailing from Gravesend at   D
5.15 a.m. on Mondays to Saturdays, a first sailing from Tilbury at 5.25
a.m. on Mondays to Saturdays, a last sailing from Gravesend at 11.40
p.m. on Mondays to Saturdays and a last sailing from Tilbury at 11.50 p.m.
on Mondays to Fridays and at 11.59 p.m. on Saturdays, and continued:]
The present proceedings have arisen as a result of a recent decision
of British Rail, made in the interests of economy, to reduce both the   E
hours of operation and the basic frequency of the ferry service. The
intention of British Rail to implement a decision of this nature was announced in letters written to the respective plaintiffs in the two actions
on February 11, 1977. The effects of the proposed new timetable can be
summarised as follows: (i) the first sailing either way on Monday to
Friday would be one at 5.45 a.m. from Gravesend, a half an hour later
than at present; (ii) the last sailing either way on every day of the week   F
would be one at 10.20 p.m. from Tilbury, compared with 11.50 p.m. or
11.59 p.m. on Saturday; (iii) the basic service, broadly between 9 a.m.
and 5 p.m. and from 8 p.m. onwards, would be every 30 minutes, compared with every 20 minutes at present; (iv) the peak service, operating,
broadly, on Monday to Friday between 6.15 a.m. and 9 a.m. and then
between 5 p.m. and 8 p.m., would be every 20 minutes, instead of every   G
15 minutes.

Though the writs in the two actions seek relief, inter alia, designed to
maintain the frequency of operation of the two ferries, Mr. Stewart, in
opening the case on behalf of the plaintiffs in the two actions, indicated
that on further consideration, his clients were content at present not to
press their claim in relation to *frequency of operation*, it being their   H
understanding that there was no intention on the part of British Rail
to reduce frequency of sailings within the hours of operation to intervals
greater than 30 minutes; this is the longest interval that would be provided
for under the proposed new timetable. Nevertheless, Mr. Stewart indicated that the respective plaintiffs did intend to press strongly their
claims in relation to the proposed reduction of *periods of operation* of the
ferries.

A   The plaintiffs in the two actions, however, are no longer seeking
perpetual injunctions even in relation to the maintenance of the period
of operation. They are now seeking injunctions requiring British Rail
to maintain the existing period of operation merely until September 29,
1980. The reason for this is that the southbound ferry is vested in British
Rail for a term of years expiring on September 29, 1980, under a lease
dated December 31, 1951, made between (1) His late Majesty King
B   George VI, (2) the Commissioners of Crown Lands and (3) the British
Transport Commission, and by virtue of the Transport Act 1962. I think
that nothing turns on the provisions of this lease, which is referred to in
Part II of Schedule 7 to the British Transport Commission Act 1960,
except for the date of its determination. In the light of this date, Mr.
Stewart for the plaintiffs, without invitation, accepted that it would not
C   be appropriate for them to seek relief in the present proceedings extend-
ing beyond September 29, 1980.

      The northbound Gravesend-Tilbury ferry is vested in British Rail in
fee simple by virtue of a conveyance dated May 19, 1880, to the London,
Tilbury and Southend Railway Co. and various enactments which are
specified in Part I of Schedule 7 to the British Transport Commission Act
1960 and also by virtue of the Transport Act 1962.
D
      Before further considering the position of the plaintiffs and those
whom they represent, and before examining the legal issues that arise
in this case, it will be convenient to summarise the practical considerations
which have led British Rail, according to its evidence, to the decision that
the hours of operation of the two ferries should be curtailed.

      Since November 18, 1964, and as a result of section 58 of the British
E   Transport Commission Act 1960, the duties and obligations of British
Rail in relation to the two ferries have been restricted to the carrying
of passengers and their hand luggage and such motor bicycles (equipped
with pedals with which they are capable of being propelled) motor
scooters, bicycles, invalid carriages and perambulators as can safely and
conveniently be embarked and accommodated on board the ferry vessels.
F   The ferries ceased to carry motor vehicles in 1964. Since then, they have
operated at first with three and subsequently with two vessels each carrying up to 475 passengers; only one vessel is required to maintain this
service, the second being held in reserve and used in the event of breakdown or of the other being out of service for repair, overhaul or annual
survey.

      Until 1963, when the Dartford tunnel was opened, the ferries operated
G   at a substantial profit. Mr. D. J. Ainsworth, who is the deputy traffic
manager (Irish and Estuarial) of the Shipping and International Services
Division of British Rail, has given figures in an affidavit showing that
for each of the years 1961, 1962 and 1963 over three million passengers
were carried and an annual profit ranging between £83,000 and £95,000
was made. In his oral evidence, though speaking from memory, he said
H   that he thought the profits for the previous years 1958, 1959 and 1960
had been in the region of £5,000, £35,000 and £60,000. Since the opening
of the Dartford tunnel, however, there has been a drastic and continuing
reduction in the numbers of passengers carried and in every year since
1963 the ferries have made a substantial loss. The number of passengers
carried in 1964 dropped immediately to about 2,100,000; since then this
number has dropped each successive year, with one single exception,
until in 1976 it fell to about 700,000. Correspondingly, since 1964 there

has been a continuing pattern of severe loss in respect of the operation **A** of the ferries. The loss in 1974 would have been as high as £72,000 but for grants received by British Rail from the Kent and Essex county councils in respect of the ferries. The loss for 1975 would have been £98,000, and for 1976 £105,000, but for such grants. These grants only eliminated a modest proportion of the losses and have now, for the time being, ceased altogether.

In these circumstances, according to Mr. Ainsworth's evidence, from **B** 1975 onwards strenuous efforts have been made on behalf of British Rail to effect economies in the running of the ferries and also with a view to trying to persuade the county councils to continue their grants. The latter attempts were unsuccessful. The grants from the two county councils were discontinued as from April 1, 1976, on economic grounds and Mr. Ainsworth has been informed that there is no prospect whatever of the **C** grants being reinstated before April 1, 1978. He further states that he is satisfied that it is unlikely that any county council grants will be reinstated in the foreseeable future.

In 1976, after consultation between management and staff and between management and trade unions earlier in the year, a joint working party consisting of five management representatives and six staff representatives of British Rail spent a working week considering the background **D** and observing the operation of the ferries. The working party in due course reported, in October 1976, its principal joint recommendations being as follows: (i) a reduction in the hours of the service, broadly corresponding with that now proposed; (ii) a reduction in the frequency of the sailings, broadly corresponding with that now proposed; and (iii) a reduction in staffing levels. **E**

Mr. Ainsworth's evidence is that both management and staff of British Rail regard the first two of these three recommendations as important, because they would reduce the overall hours worked to $16\frac{3}{4}$ and thus enable British Rail to operate the ferries with three complete crews, instead of four crews as at present. The four crews working at present are three crews on shifts and the fourth crew as a relief crew. The proposed reductions would enable the ferries to be worked on two shifts **F** instead of three, so that there would be two shift crews and one relief crew. This reduction from four crews to three could not be achieved without a curtailment in the hours of operation of the service as proposed.

Two new and much smaller vessels were acquired by British Rail in January 1977. Each of these will carry 150 passengers, as compared with the capacity of the vessels at present in use, which is 475. This will be **G** adequate for current requirements since the greatest number of passengers carried on any one sailing at the present time is usually about 120. These new vessels require some modifications and overhaul, but it is hoped that they will be ready for service in July or August 1977, when the present vessels will be disposed of. Mr. Ainsworth told me that British Rail would intend to bring these new vessels into service whatever my decision **H** in the present actions. Since the new boats are much smaller than those at present being operated, he indicated that British Rail hoped agreement would be reached with the unions concerned for a reduction in the manning of them to a crew of three, compared with four on the present boats, and possibly to a reduction to a crew of two. My impression of his evidence was that while he was reasonably confident that the smaller reduction in manning might be agreed, he was less confident of achieving

A   the greater reduction. A further reduction in the potential loss from running the ferries should be achieved as the result of a recent application to the Price Commission. During the course of the trial, the news came through that the commission had approved British Rail's proposal for an increase in the ordinary single fare from 25p to 30p and of the children's fare from 13p to 15p with pro rata increases for season tickets and the conveyance of articles. I understand that this increase will come into effect

B   in about July 1977. Mr. Ainsworth expects that, after allowance for reduction in the number of passengers carried, it should achieve an increase of revenue of about £26,000 for a full year.

On the assumption, which seems the most reasonable assumption, that agreement will be reached for a reduction in the manning of the new boats to a crew of three, Mr. Ainsworth's evidence is that the savings

C   which would be effected by introducing the new boats, but retaining the service provided for by the present timetable, coupled with the consequent inevitable retention of four complete crews, would be in the region of £55,000 a year. However, even when this saving is added to the increased revenue of £26,000, which should come in from the increase in fares, a substantial deficit in respect of running the ferries appears

D   inevitable. Mr. Ainsworth's unchallenged estimate of the budgeted loss for 1977 before allowing for these two sums is £136,000, which, even after allowing for them, leaves a loss of some £55,000.

Under section 3 (1) of the Transport Act 1962 British Rail are under a statutory duty in providing their ferry services " to have due regard . . . to efficiency, economy and safety of operation." Under section 41 (2) of the Transport Act 1968 they are further under a duty so to operate their

E   undertakings including their subsidiaries that the combined revenues of them and their subsidiaries taken together are not less than sufficient to meet their combined charges properly chargeable to revenue account taking one year with another. British Rail's evidence is that the overall deficit of itself and its subsidiaries on revenue account for 1976 was £350,000,000 which was recovered from the Government under revenue

F   support arrangements and that a deficit of the same order is expected in 1977. It appears that while section 3 of the Railways Act 1974 contains provisions enabling British Rail to obtain subsidies from central public funds for uneconomic railway services, these operate by reference to Council Regulation (EEC) No. 1191/69 * and neither the statutory provision nor the Regulation applies to the ferry services.

Mr. Scott, who has appeared on behalf of British Rail, has not sought

G   to submit, and I do not think it could be submitted, that section 3 (1) of the Transport Act 1962 and section 41 (2) of the Transport Act 1968 can operate actually to relieve British Rail of its common law duties as ferry owner or indeed even to vary those duties. He has, however, submitted in effect that, in so far as it may do so consistently with its duties at common law as a ferry owner, it is right that British Rail should use

H   its best endeavours to effect all reasonable economies in the operation of the ferry service. So long as the point is put no higher than this, I accept this submission. Broadly it would seem to me right that British Rail should seek to achieve the maximum economies in the running of the ferry service, provided at least that these do not conflict with the discharge of its common law duties and do not cause unreasonable hardship to the

* See *Halsbury's Statutes of England*, 3rd ed., vol. 42A (1975), p. 174 et seq.

public. The primary question in the present case is, of course, what are   A
the nature and extent of its duties at common law as a ferry owner?

Substantially the present dispute arises because British Rail, in an
effort to reduce the estimated annual deficit of £55,000 still further,
wishes to operate the ferries with three crews instead of four as at present, and on the evidence, as has not been disputed by any of the plaintiffs,
such reduction cannot be achieved without the curtailment of the service
now proposed.   [His Lordship, after reviewing the evidence, concluded   B
that it was a fair assumption that the further annual saving which would
be achieved at 1977 levels by the proposed restriction in the hours of
operation as opposed to reduction of frequency of service would be between
£15,500 and £17,500 per annum.]

I now turn to consider the practical consequences of curtailing the
hours of the ferry services, still for the time being regarding the matter   C
from the point of view of British Rail. If the proposed timetable were
to be introduced, 12 early morning or late evening sailings would in all
be eliminated as follows:

Sailings from Gravesend
    5.15 a.m., 10.20 p.m., 10.40 p.m., 11.00 p.m., 11.20 p.m., 11.40 p.m.   D

Sailings from Tilbury
    5.25 a.m., 10.30 p.m., 10.50 p.m., 11.10 p.m., 11.30 p.m., 11.50 p.m.
(11.59 p.m. Saturdays).

In these circumstances, in March of this year, 1977, British Rail
arranged for the taking of a census of passengers using the ferries, limited
to the 12 early morning and late evening sailings in both directions to   E
which I have referred. The persons taking the census were also instructed
to ascertain from the passengers, so far as possible, if their journey was
a social one or in connection with work. The census began on Thursday,
March 31, and continued until the late evening of Sunday, April 24. On
such an operation there was clearly room for minor errors, particularly
in the drawing of the distinction between the passengers travelling on
social journeys and those going to and from work. The census however   F
appears to have been professionally and carefully conducted; and very
sensibly, if I may say so, Mr. Stewart, on behalf of the plaintiffs, has
accepted the figures contained in the census as being sufficiently accurate
to be relied on for the purposes of the present proceedings. This concession has clearly saved a lot of time in avoiding the need to call a
number of further witnesses. It also provides the court with some firm   G
statistics, indeed the only firm statistics, in this regard. For, though a
census of sorts has also been taken by the P.L.A., as will appear, it could
not be contended that this afforded anything approaching firm statistical
evidence.

The results of British Rail's census have been conveniently extracted
and summarised in an agreed document, which has become exhibit " D.5 "
in the proceedings. This analysis shows, inter alia, the following statistics   H
relating to the 5.15 a.m. sailing from Gravesend and the 5.25 a.m. sailing
from Tilbury:

Average number of passengers on any one 5.15 a.m.
    sailing from Gravesend 5.89
Average number of passengers on any one 5.25 a.m.
    sailing from Tilbury 3.45

A It is common ground that all passengers travelling on these early sailings would be travelling to or from work.

In regard to the five late evening sailings from Tilbury to Gravesend, exhibit D.5 reveals, inter alia, the following statistics for the period of 25 days covered by the census:

B
Average total number of passengers on all five late evening sailings on any one day	19.16
Average number of passengers on any one such sailing .	3.83
Average total number of passengers travelling to and from work on such five sailings on any one day . . .	13.33
Average number of passengers travelling to and from work on any one such sailing	2.67

C In regard to the five late evening sailings from Gravesend to Tilbury, exhibit D.5 reveals, inter alia, the following statistics for the period of 25 days covered by the census:

Average total number of passengers on all five late evening sailings on any one day	26.84
Average number of passengers on any one such sailing .	5.37
Average total number of passengers travelling to and from work on such five sailings on any one day . . .	11.04
Average number of passengers travelling to and from work on any one such sailing	2.21

D

A few more statistics are worth mentioning when considering the relative strength of the demand for the sailings in question. On an average throughout 1976, British Rail carried approximately 1,900 passengers per E day on the ferries, of whom an average total number of about 55 passengers travelled on all the 12 early morning and late evening Tilbury-Gravesend-Tilbury sailings now in question.

On the basis of these various statistics, among others, British Rail submits that there appears to be very little demand for sailings before 5.45 a.m. and after 10.15 p.m., and that a curtailment of the ferry F services, so as to eliminate these uneconomic sailings and thereby to save the cost of employing one entire crew of four men, would not result in its becoming in breach of its common law duties as owner of the ferries. This necessitates consideration of the nature and extent of such duties.

The nature and extent of the duties of British Rail as ferry owner

G   By way of introduction to the general law relating to ferries, I was referred to *Halsbury's Laws of England*, 3rd ed., vol. 17 (1956), paras. 391–402. Certain points appearing from the paragraphs are, I think, common ground. A public ferry is a public highway of a special description, whose termini must be in places where the public have rights. It exists in connection with the use of a right of way. The right is wholly unconnected with the ownership or occupation of land. The ferry owner H merely has a right to make a special use of the highway over the river; the right to charge tolls is usually incident to the ferry and a right of ferry is primarily a toll franchise, which may be created or acquired by Royal grant or Act of Parliament or by prescription at common law. Neglect of a ferry owner's duties does not ipso facto destroy his franchise. One consequence of such neglect, however, may be that the Crown may by proceedings in the nature of scire facias annul the grant of the ferry and, if necessary, vest it in some other person. Another consequence of

neglect is that the ferry owner is liable to be indicted and fined if he does
not keep his ferry in readiness and in good repair. He is also liable to
an action at the suit of a person who has suffered special damage by his
neglect.

The editor of *Halsbury's Laws*, para. 401, goes on to say:

" . . . but the court will not make a declaration that the owner of
the ferry is bound to operate the ferry or grant a mandatory
injunction to compel him to do so."

This statement of the law is based on the decision in *Attorney-General* v.
Colchester Corporation [1955] 2 Q.B. 207. In that case a municipal
corporation, which owned the franchise of a public ferry crossing the
river Colne, discontinued the operation of the ferry. The ferry had not
been extensively used and the receipts from the tolls charged were insufficient to pay the wages of the ferryman. The Attorney-General
brought a relator action for a declaration that the corporation was obliged
to maintain and operate the ferry at all reasonable times and carry foot
passengers willing to pay the toll and for a mandatory injunction ordering
them to do so. The corporation admitted its obligation to operate the
ferry, but contended that it had become so burdensome that no mandatory
injunction ought to be granted. Lord Goddard C.J. held that although
a ferry owner who failed to perform his obligations to the public could
be indicted for breach of a public duty and might also be the subject of
a scire facias at the suit of the Crown to repeal the franchise, an injunction should not be granted to compel the owner to continue to run a
ferry which was so little used that it could only be run at a loss, since
it would be inequitable to do so; and as in that case a bare declaration
would be of no assistance to the relator or the residents of the parish
concerned, no declaration should be made.

This decision if correct, would seem to be fatal to the respective
plaintiffs' claims in both the present actions, since it would seem to
indicate that the desired relief by way of injunction should not be granted
to them, even if they could establish a threatened breach of the defendants' duty as ferry owners. Mr. Stewart, however, on the plaintiff's
behalf has submitted so far as necessary that, in relation to the question
of remedy, the case was not rightly decided. I shall revert to this question
hereafter.

Mr. Stewart furthermore relied on a passage from the judgment of
Lord Goddard C.J., in which he described the common law obligation
of the owner of an ancient ferry at p. 213:

" His duty, as I understand it, would be to have the ferry in operation
at all hours, and to convey foot passengers across the river at any
time that they required the facility."

Lord Goddard C.J., in describing the duty of a ferry owner as being to
have the ferry in operation " *at all hours,*" went beyond the terms of the
declaration claimed by the plaintiffs in that action, being a declaration
that the duty was one to operate the ferry " *at all reasonable times.*" This
illustrates a point which does not seem to have been much canvassed in
the *Attorney-General* v. *Colchester Corporation* case, but has been fully
argued before me. Is the duty of a ferry owner a duty to have the ferry
in operation at all hours of the day or night whatsoever, as the plaintiffs
assert? Or is it, as British Rail asserts, merely a duty to have it in
operation at all reasonable times?

A   There have been cited to me a number of authorities which contain apparently conflicting judicial dicta on this point. In *Letton* v. *Goodden* (1866) L.R. 2 Eq. 123, Sir Richard Kindersley V.-C. said, at pp. 130–131:

" A ferry has been said to be the continuation of a public highway across a river or other water for the purpose of public traffic from the termination of the highway on the one side to its recommence-
B   ment on the other side; and as such the existence of a ferry is obviously for the benefit of the public. The advantage to the public is so great that the Crown has from time to time granted rights of ferry, and all common ferries have their origin in Royal grant, or in prescription, which presumes such grant. Such a right of ferry is an exclusive right or monopoly, and, as such, it is in itself an evil, being in derogation of common right, for by common right any
C   person may carry passengers across a river. But as a compensation for that derogation of common right, there is this great advantage to the public, that they have at all times at hand, by reason of the ferry, the means of travelling on the King's highway, of which the ferry forms a part; for the owner of the ferry is under the obligation of always providing proper boats, with competent boatmen, and all
D   other things necessary for the maintenance of the ferry in an efficient state and condition for the use of the public, and this he is bound to do under pain of indictment; and if he be found in default, he would, as it is expressed, be liable to be grievously amerced."

Accordingly, though on the particular facts of that case it was not relevant to inquire whether the duty of a ferry owner was to provide a
E   boat on the one hand at all times or on the other hand at all reasonable times, the language used by Sir Richard Kindersley V.-C. suggests that he took the former view.

Mr. Stewart, on behalf of the plaintiffs, laid emphasis on the point made in that case, and indeed in other decisions such as *North and South Shields Ferry Co.* v. *Barker* (1848) 2 Exch. 136, 149, *per* Parke B.
F   that a ferry forms part of the means of travelling on the Queen's highway. As such, he submitted, it should be kept permanently open at all hours like any other part of the Queen's highway.

This at first sight is a logically attractive proposition. Closer examination, however, reveals difficulties attached to its acceptance. In many cases, no doubt, ancient common law ferries would have been granted to one man only. A ferryman like anyone else would need occasional rest
G   and sleep, which would have been denied him if he had been expected to be on duty for 24 hours a day at all times and in all circumstances. Furthermore if the ferry owner found himself obliged to employ one or more persons to assist him in the performance of his duties, circumstances might have arisen in which it became impossible for him to find persons to work for him or alternatively to pay such persons.

H   Since neglect of a ferry owner's duties involves a criminal offence, it is not surprising to find that Sir Matthew Hale, in a passage at the beginning of Chap. II of his treatise *De Jure Maris* (see *Hargrave's Collection of Law Tracts* (1787)), expresses an important limitation in regard to such duties:

" The King by an ancient right of prerogative hath had a certain interest in many fresh rivers, even where the sea doth not flow or reflow, as well as in salt or armes of the sea; and those are these

which follow: First, a right of franchise or privilege, that no man   A
may set up a common ferry for all passengers, without a prescription
time out of mind, or a charter from the King. He may make a
ferry for his own use or the use of his family, but not for the
common use of all the King's subjects passing that way; because it
doth in consequence tend to a common charge, and is become a thing
of public interest and use, and every man for his passage pays a toll,
which is a common charge, and every ferry ought to be under a   B
public regulation; viz. that it give attendance at due times, keep a
boat in due order, and take but reasonable toll; for if he fail in
these, he is fineable."

This passage which was quoted with approval by Stirling L.J. in
Attorney-General v. *Simpson* [1901] 2 Ch. 671, 717, thus expresses the
duty as being one to give attendance " at due times," a very different   C
matter from " at all times." I read the phrase " at all due times " as
bearing substantially the same meaning as " at all reasonable times."

When the latter case went to the House of Lords as *Simpson* v.
Attorney-General [1904] A.C. 476, Lord Macnaghten, in the course of
his speech said, at p. 490:

"Within the limits of an ancient ferry no one is permitted to convey   D
passengers across but the owner of the ferry. No one may disturb
the ferry. The ferry carries with it an exclusive right or monopoly.
In consideration of that monopoly the owner of the ferry is bound
to have his ferry always ready."

In *Dibden* v. *Skirrow* [1907] 1 Ch. 437, Neville J. said, at p. 443:

"I think that what is pointed out in the passage in Sir Matthew   E
Hale's treatise *De Jure Maris*, cited in *Attorney-General* v. *Simpson*,
assists one to that conclusion, because it is there laid down that the
granting of a franchise to a ferry owner which involves a monopoly
is not granted for the benefit of the ferry owner, but is granted for
the benefit of the public, as a means whereby the public may be
certain of finding means of transit across the river. The monopoly   F
is given in return for an obligation on the ferryman's part to maintain boats and means so that the public may be transferred across
and may go from one side to the other at any time."

The wording of this passage from Neville J.'s judgment would suggest
that he regarded the duty as being one to carry passengers " at any time."
Since, however, his observations were based on the passage from Sir   G
Matthew Hale's treatise cited in *Attorney-General* v. *Simpson* [1901] 2
Ch. 671, 717, and since Neville J. apparently did not advert to the point
that that treatise had described the duty as being one to convey " at due
times," I think that the dicta in *Dibden* v. *Skirrow* [1907] 1 Ch. 437,
443 carry little weight for present purposes.

In *Hammerton* v. *Earl of Dysart* [1916] 1 A.C. 57, Lord Summer
said, at p. 103:   H

"At all reasonable times the ferryman must be prepared to ferry
those who wish to be ferried. He must be provided with a reasonable
and sufficient number of men and craft. He must charge only
reasonable and uniform tolls. He must carry all peaceable wayfarers
who are ready and willing to pay his toll."

This is an interesting passage, because later in his speech, at p. 103,

A   Lord Sumner referred to the reason why the law has treated the grantee of a ferry as being " so to speak, chained to his oar " as being ". . . in order that the public may have assured to it the perpetual convenience of the ferry. . . ." Nevertheless, he clearly did not regard the public interest as requiring that the ferry owner should be chained to his oar at every hour of every day or night, reasonable or unreasonable.

B   Apart from the judgment of Lord Goddard C.J. in *Attorney-General* v. *Colchester Corporation* [1955] 2 Q.B. 207, this passage from Lord Sumner's speech is, I think, the most recent judgment cited to me dealing with the nature and extent of the obligations of a ferry owner. With so many conflicting judicial dicta, the law on this point as to times of operation is not entirely clear. Perhaps the reason for this uncertainty stems from the fact that in contrast to the present case, in none of the C cases cited to me were the precise times of operation of a particular ferry in issue. The courts did not therefore have specifically to consider the issue of law which I now have to decide.

In my judgment the statement of the law by Lord Sumner in *Hammerton* v. *Earl of Dysart* [1916] 1 A.C. 57 backed as it is by the passage from Sir Matthew Hale's treatise, and Stirling L.J.'s judgment in *Attorney-General* v. *Simpson* [1901] 2 Ch. 671 should be regarded as representing a D correct statement of the law. It is in my judgment highly material first that the breach of a ferry owner's obligation at common law to operate his ferry has at all times been regarded as a criminal offence, and, secondly, that he has not been entitled of his own volition to disclaim his ferry. I cannot believe that, even in the harsher conditions of two or three centuries ago, the courts would have regarded it as a criminal offence E for a ferryman to refuse to carry a passenger seeking carriage at a time of day or night which in all the circumstances was an unreasonable time to expect to be carried. Rather similarly, Mr. Stewart on behalf of the plaintiffs in the present case, tempering the strict logic of his argument with regard to practical realities, more or less conceded that no court would in practice grant an injunction compelling a ferry owner such as F British Rail to operate its ferries at all hours of the day and night, though he made no such concession in regard to the definition of the strict duties of a ferry owner.

In my judgment, the obligation of British Rail under the common law, as owner of the two ancient common law ferries in the present case, is an obligation to carry passengers across the river Thames at all reasonable hours. Reasonableness in this context must be assessed according to all G the circumstances of the case. For this purpose it is necessary to strike a balance between (a) the extent of the demand for the ferry service at particular hours and the inconvenience and hardship, if any, to the public which would be caused if such service were not provided and (b) the extent of the burden in terms of money and otherwise that would fall on the ferry owner in providing such service at the hours in question. How-H ever, the onus must in my judgment fall on the plaintiffs to show that the time-table which British Rail now intends to introduce is *unreasonable*.

I appreciate that this attempted statement of the law, if correct, may in some instances leave a difficult area of uncertainty both for ferry-owners and for those seeking to enforce the duties of ferry-owners. In my judgment, however, the introduction of the concept of reasonable times leads to fewer anomalies than would an obligation unrestricted in regard to hours of operation.

508

Finally in this context I should mention that Mr. Scott, on behalf of A
British Rail, produced some interesting historical facts as to the mode of
operation of the ferries in question in past centuries. It was not, however,
suggested on either side that the actual mode of operation over past years
either limited or extended the present obligations of British Rail as the
owners of two ancient common law ferries. Over the year, circumstances
may change and reasonable hours of operation may correspondingly alter
from time to time. Reasonableness in this context must in my judgment B
be determined on an ad hoc basis. This point would have some further
relevance, if liability were to be established and questions of form of
relief were to arise.

The effect of the proposed new timetable on the Port of London Authority

I now turn to consider the position of the P.L.A. If it has a cause of C
action at all in the present case—a question to which I will revert—this
can in my judgment only arise from potential injury or loss which may
be caused to the P.L.A. itself by the proposed curtailment of the ferry
service. Accordingly, though it has filed evidence suggesting that the
curtailment will cause loss and hardship to individual persons or bodies
in addition to itself, I do not propose to consider such evidence in the D
context of the P.L.A.'s case, except in so far as the P.L.A. can itself be
said to be affected by such loss and hardship.

The P.L.A. employs a total number of 4,757 persons at Tilbury docks
of whom 1,757 are registered dock workers and 3,000 are in other
categories such as clerical, executive, management, marine services or
police. About 30 other companies including, among others, shipping companies and stevedoring contractors have employees working at the docks. E
Many of those working at Tilbury docks live on the south side of the
river and it is usual for them to travel to and from work by the ferry.
Of the persons employed by the P.L.A. at the docks, some work on a
two-shift system and others on a three-shift system. The three-shift
system, which is particularly significant for present purposes, operates at
berths 39, 40, 41, 43 and 45. Berth 39 is occupied by Overseas Containers F
Ltd. as tenants of the P.L.A. Berths 40, 41, 43 and 45 are occupied and
operated by the P.L.A. for the use of ships and cargo of any owners and
are therefore called " multi-user berths." The three-shift system at these
berths involves shifts from 7 a.m. to 3 p.m., from 3 p.m. to 11 p.m. and
from 11 p.m. to 7 a.m., operating seven days a week. Employees
normally work four or five shifts a week. The total number employed
by the P.L.A. at the multi-user berths and working on the three-shift G
system (including dock workers, engineers and other staff) is about 560.
The registered dock workers and staff are divided into eight shift groups
each consisting of 37 registered dock workers, 25 clerical staff and eight
engineers. The night staff from 11 p.m. to 7 a.m. consists of one shift
group. The 7 a.m. to 3 p.m. and 3 p.m. to 11 p.m. shifts each consist of
two shift groups, comprising 74 registered dockworkers and 50 clerical H
staff and 16 engineers. The number of consecutive days worked by a
shift group varies depending on the period of the shift. A morning shift
group for example works seven days, whereas an afternoon shift group
may work two, four, five days or even six if the period includes a Sunday.
[His Lordship then referred to a survey recently conducted by the P.L.A.
from the office of its docks manager, Mr. R. F. White, amongst personnel
employed at Tilbury Docks as to their use of the ferry in travelling to

A and from work and concluded that the detailed statistics embodied in this survey could not be regarded as reliable. His Lordship continued:] The P.L.A.'s survey has, however, served at least two useful purposes. First, Mr. White's original view was that the loss of the 5.15 a.m. ferry from Gravesend to Tilbury would create problems for those employees working at No. 39 berth, where the morning shift begins at 6.00 a.m.
B This view, however, has not been borne out by the survey, which showed that during the period of the survey only one P.L.A. employee and two other workers used the 5.15 a.m. ferry. The P.L.A. itself, though not the two councils, has therefore abandoned before me any claim arising out of the proposed discontinuance of the early ferries. Nor has it pursued any claim arising out of the proposed discontinuance of the late Gravesend-Tilbury ferries.

C Secondly, Mr. White was able to give in evidence a figure derived from the forms relating to the late Tilbury-Gravesend ferries which it has been common ground can be regarded as reasonably accurate. About 50 P.L.A. employees use the last five ferries, i.e. at 10.30 p.m., 10.50 p.m., 11.10 p.m., 11.30 p.m. and 11.50 p.m., for the purpose of making the crossing from Tilbury to Gravesend not, of course, all on the same night,
D but whenever they are for the time being working on the 3 p.m. to 11 p.m. shift.

It is the proposal for the discontinuance of these last five sailings from Tilbury which causes the P.L.A. the most concern, because if the new time-table is introduced, the last ferry will leave Tilbury for Gravesend 40 minutes before the end of the shift finishing at 11 p.m. If the last ferry were to leave Tilbury for Gravesend at 10.20 p.m., those
E 50 or so employees, who work on the shift finishing at 11 p.m. and have to get back to the other side of the river, would have to make alternative arrangements for this purpose. Since they would not be able to get home by public transport and since the P.L.A. itself has no alternative form of transport to offer, the only way for them to get back would be by leaving work at least 45 minutes before the end of their shift and catching the
F 10.20 p.m. ferry, unless they possessed and were prepared to use their own private motor vehicle or obtained a lift from one of their workmates.

In the circumstances, the P.L.A. would find itself confronted with a dilemma, after introduction of the new time-table. It attaches importance to its employees working until the end of the time of their shift, except on those particular occasions when there is no work left for a man to do and he is allowed to leave early. According to Mr. White's evidence, it
G already has severe time-keeping problems in respect of the shift ending at 11 p.m. Nor for practical purposes could it alter the times of that shift, since the times of the three shifts were introduced about seven years ago after delicate and difficult industrial negotiations and any attempt to amend them now would affect the whole port and be liable to cause dangerous dislocation throughout the port. The P.L.A. could
H not therefore agree to persons working on the 3 p.m. to 11 p.m. shift leaving about 45 minutes early in order to catch the last ferry. It would have to attempt to discipline persons who did so leave, just as it attempts to discipline early leavers at present. However, in Mr. White's view, attempts to discipline men who were leaving early, simply in order to catch a curtailed ferry service, would not be likely to be very successful for practical purposes, particularly in view of probable opposition from the unions involved. It would therefore probably be difficult in practice

to stop those persons working on the 3 p.m. to 11 p.m. shift and living   A
on the south bank of the Thames from leaving work about 45 minutes
early in order to catch the last ferry. If employees working on this shift
left work early in this manner and for this reason, this would encourage
other persons similarly to drift away early, with the consequence that
work would be left undone, which in turn would lead to complaints by
those using the P.L.A.'s docks and services. This is a prospect which it
views with concern, especially since today there is fierce competition   B
between ports both to win new trade and retain their present trade,
particularly in the field of container handling.

    According to Mr. White's evidence which I see no reason to doubt in
this context, the proposed curtailment of the ferry service would cause
others of the 50 employees of the P.L.A. who live on the south bank of
the Thames and work on the three-shift system, instead of merely   C
anticipating the proper hour of their departure from work, either to
leave the employment of the P.L.A. altogether or to apply to join the
two-shift system. Employees working at the multi-user berths are all
volunteers, in the case of registered dockworkers. Though they are paid
increased wages, the increase averaging about £15 per week, for working
on the three-shift rather than the two-shift system, Mr. White envisaged
a number of employees leaving the former for the latter system with its   D
more attractive hours (7 a.m.–2 p.m. and 2 p.m.–9 p.m. alternately each
week) if the new time-table were introduced. [His Lordship, after
analysing the relevant evidence, concluded that it was a reasonable
estimate that, if the proposed curtailment of the ferry service were
implemented, of the 50 P.L.A. employees who had previously been using
the last five ferries departing from Tilbury, 25 would go on to the two-   E
shift system of working, 10 would leave the P.L.A.'s employment altogether
and 15 would somehow or other continue on the three-shift system. His
Lordship also considered it a reasonable assumption that about half of
those 50 employees would be registered dockworkers, with the result that
the introduction of the new time-table would require the replacement of
some 18 registered dockworkers at present working on the three-shift
system by other workers who would cost the P.L.A. about £14,000 to   F
train. He referred to the evidence of Mr. White on behalf of the P.L.A.
to the effect that, even after a four-week course, it would take another
eight months before such other workers became fully efficient and to the
evidence of Mr. R. A. Firth, a plant engineer employed by British Rail,
to the effect that persons could be trained within four to five weeks to
operate straddle-carriers fully effectively. His Lordship continued:]   G
I suspect that Mr. Firth's evidence in this context was a little on the
optimistic side. Likewise, however, I suspect that Mr. White's evidence
on this matter and indeed on other aspects in relation to all the consequences of the proposed curtailment of the ferry service, may tend
towards the pessimistic. The matter must be brought into proper
perspective. Though the potential consequences to the P.L.A. resulting   H
from the proposed curtailment of the ferry service at first sight sound
serious, the following points must be borne in mind: (1) The P.L.A. will
not be substantially affected by the curtailment of the early morning
sailings or of the late night sailings from Gravesend to Tilbury. It will
only be affected by the curtailment of the late night sailings from Tilbury
to Gravesend. (2) It will be affected in this manner solely because of
the effect that such curtailment will have on some 50 of its employees

A　who live south of the Thames, representing about 1 per cent. of its entire
work force and less than 10 per cent. of its total work force employed
on the three-shift system. (3) Of these 50 employees, it is fair to assume
that about 25 are engineers and members of the clerical staff. There is
no evidence that any persons in these categories who left the P.L.A.'s
employment or changed to the two-shift system as a result of the curtail-
B　ment of the ferry service could not be satisfactorily replaced by persons
living on the north bank of the Thames, without appreciable loss or
inconvenience to the P.L.A. (4) It appears that those of the 25 dockworkers comprised in these 50 persons who left the P.L.A.'s employment
or changed to the two-shift system could likewise be fairly readily
replaced in due course. The only disadvantage in this case would be that
the replacement would involve training, which in turn would involve the
C　P.L.A. in some expense (not exceeding about £14,000) and some disruption during the weeks before the men concerned had become fully
competent—such disruption consisting of less than complete efficiency on
their own part coupled with a degree of possible restiveness among their
fellow workers. (5) While the potential disruption referred to should not
be regarded as negligible, it does not appear to me potentially very grave.
D　For on the figures postulated it appears unlikely that (a) the 37 registered
dockworkers comprising a one-shift group would on any one occasion
have to include more than about four newly trained replacements, or
(b) the 74 registered dockworkers comprising two-shift groups would on
any one occasion have to include more than about eight newly trained
replacements.

In short, in all the circumstances, I envisage that the proposed
E　curtailment of the ferry service would involve the P.L.A. in some expense
(though minimal in relation to its weekly wage bill) and a limited degree
of disruption and inconvenience extending over a period of a few months.

Has the P.L.A. a locus standi to sue?

There has been no dispute that the two plaintiff councils have a right
F　to bring their action in exercise of the powers conferred on them by the
Local Government Act 1972. It has, however, been submitted on behalf
of British Rail that the P.L.A. itself has in any event no locus standi to
bring its action. This will be a convenient moment to deal with this point.

Since a public ferry is a public highway, albeit of a special description,
it is a public nuisance to obstruct or hinder the free passage of the public
G　along such highway. It has also been common ground that it would
similarly constitute a public nuisance for a ferry owner to withdraw the
ferry service in breach of his duties as a ferry owner. The debate on the
law has centred on the questions (a) whether a breach is in fact contemplated in the present case (b) whether the P.L.A. has a locus standi
to sue in respect of it and (c) if a breach is contemplated, whether or not
H　relief should be granted by way of mandatory injunction as prayed.

A private individual or a corporation such as the P.L.A. has a right
of action in respect of a public nuisance if, but only if, he or it can prove
that he or it has sustained particular damage other than and beyond the
general inconvenience and injury suffered by the public, and that the
particular damage which he has sustained is direct and substantial (see
for example *Benjamin* v. *Storr* (1874) L.R. 9 C.P. 400). Mr. Scott on
behalf of British Rail, if I understood him correctly, raised two principal

points in support of his contention that the P.L.A. has no right of action   A
in the present case.

First, no reported case was cited on behalf of the P.L.A. in which a
plaintiff has succeeded in an action for public nuisance on the basis of
damage suffered of a nature precisely analogous to that which would be
suffered by the P.L.A. in the present case, namely disruption of its
business and expense caused by its servants being prevented from using   B
a highway or ferry. The most relevant authorities cited have related to
the question whether a plaintiff has a right of action in respect of an
obstruction to a highway as a result of which prospective customers are
diverted from his place of business, causing him loss of business. And
even on the latter point there has been a conflict of judicial opinion. In
Wilkes v. *Hungerford Market Co.* (1835) 2 Bing. N.C. 281, it was held
that an action of this nature was sustainable. The earlier decision in   C
Iveson v. *Moore* (1699) 1 Ld.Raym. 486 was one to the same effect.
In *Ricket* v. *Metropolitan Railway Co.* (1867) L.R. 2 H.L. 175, however,
Lord Cranworth, at p. 199, said he had great difficulty in agreeing with
the *Wilkes* decision, 2 Bing. N.C. 281, adding that the relief to which
the plaintiff was there held to be entitled was not founded on any suggestion of injury to the land or to the house, but on an injury to the
occupier, which he said " the court must have held, in the language of   D
Tindal, C.J. to have been the direct, necessary, natural and immediate
consequence of the obstruction." In that same case Lord Chelmsford L.C.
at p. 188, also expressed doubt as to the correctness of the decision. However, in *Blundy Clark & Co. Ltd.* v. *London & North Eastern Railway Co.*
[1931] 2 K.B. 334, Greer L.J., at p. 362, expressed the view that the
Wilkes case had not been overruled by *Ricket's* case. Scrutton L.J. ex-   E
pressed the same view by inference, since he made it clear in his judgment,
at pp. 353, 354, that he regarded *Ricket's* case as a decision based on
the special provisions of the Lands Clauses Consolidation Act 1845. The
like opinion that the *Wilkes* case was still good law was expressed by
Lord Hanworth M.R. in *Harper* v. *Haden & Sons Ltd.* [1933] Ch. 298,
306.

In all the circumstances there is, in my judgment, sufficient authority   F
for the statement of the law by Greer L.J. in the *Blundy Clark* case
[1931] 2 K.B. 334, where he said at p. 365:

" In my judgment it is the law that where a plaintiff has property
near a highway which he uses for the purpose of his business, and
the highway, whether a canal or a roadway, is unlawfully obstructed,
and he is thereby put to greater expense in the conduct of his   G
business, or suffers loss by the diminution of his business, he is
entitled to recover damages as a person who has suffered special or
peculiar damage beyond that which has been suffered by other
members of the public wanting to use the highway or waterway."

Earlier in his judgment Greer L.J. said, at pp. 362–363 :
                                                                          H
" If the diminution in value of business premises due to an unauthorised obstruction gives the owner a good cause of action, it seems
to me that the interference with his business which gave rise to the
loss of business earnings ought a fortiori to be regarded as particular
damage giving him a cause of action."

I respectfully agree with both the statements of law and the reasoning
of Greer L.J. in that case. Accordingly I reject Mr. Scott's first sub-

A mission in this context, which was, in effect, that an interference with the P.L.A.'s business of the nature alleged by it was not capable of being regarded as particular damage giving it a cause of action. I can see no difference in principle between the case where the relevant interference with a business consists of the obstruction of its customers and the case where it consists of obstruction of its employees.

B   The second submission made on behalf of British Rail in this context was that the relevant damage likely to be suffered by P.L.A. is in any event not sufficiently direct and substantial to give it a locus standi to sue. Quite apart from the degree of general disruption of its business which the curtailment of the ferry time-table is likely to cause it, the P.L.A. has shown that it will probably suffer a specific item of financial loss amounting to about £14,000 in the training of new employees on

C the three-shift system. This, though a small item in relation to the P.L.A.'s total wage bill, in my judgment constitutes genuine and particular damage other than and beyond the general inconvenience and injury likely to be suffered by the public.

    For these reasons I conclude that the P.L.A. has a locus standi to bring its proceedings.

D

The effect of the proposed new time table on other users of the ferry

    Mr. Stewart made it plain that unlike the P.L.A. in its action, the two plaintiff councils in their action, in their concern to protect the interests of the inhabitants of their areas, wished to complain of the intended curtailment of the two earliest Gravesend-Tilbury-Gravesend sailings and also of the five latest Gravesend-Tilbury sailings, as well as

E the proposed curtailment of the five latest Tilbury-Gravesend sailings.

    In so far as the claim of the plaintiff councils relates to the five latest Tilbury-Gravesend sailings, they rely, as they are entitled to do, inter alia, both on the effect which their curtailment would have on the P.L.A. itself, as an important rate-payer to the Thurrock Borough Council, and also on the position of individual employees of the P.L.A., who will be

F affected in the manner which I have described. Mr. Rousell is a typical example of such employees. As I have indicated, however, there is no evidence that the curtailment of the early morning service or of the five latest Gravesend-Tilbury sailings will cause any real hardship to the P.L.A. or its employees. Other evidence therefore has to be relied on by the plaintiff councils in this context.

G   Mr. T. C. Oliver, a senior administrative assistant with Thurrock Borough Council has given evidence on behalf of the two councils in relation to the effect which the proposed curtailment of the ferry service will have on other persons living in the area. He says that many people living in Gravesend, Northfleet and Tilbury and neighbouring areas use the ferry to travel to and from work and that frequent journeys are made on the ferry for commercial shopping and recreational purposes. The

H plaintiff councils, he says, consider it important that for economic and social reasons the existing ferry services should not be reduced. He points out that the shortest distance by road between the two ferry terminals through the Dartford tunnel is some 14 miles compared with the river crossing of five minutes, over less than half a mile. He gives an estimate that a non-stop bus service between these points would take about 40-50 minutes in good traffic conditions, but says that there is no such service at present. He observes that even if at certain times in the evening the passengers are all or nearly all travelling for social purposes, the plaintiff A councils consider it to be in the interests of their inhabitants that this important link between the two sides of the river should nevertheless be maintained throughout the current operating hours.

This is a readily intelligible point of view but does not, of course, greatly assist in providing an answer to the question whether British Rail would be in breach of its duty if it were to curtail the present services. In regard to the probable effects of such curtailment on the persons or B bodies living or operating in the area other than the P.L.A. I am bound to say that there is a conspicuous lack of hard facts in the evidence adduced on behalf of the plaintiff councils.

Mr. Oliver says that the flow of work is predominantly from the south to the north of the river, because passengers are either going on from Tilbury Riverside Station to London Fenchurch Street or because more C varied job opportunities are available on the northside. In the latter context he mentions Tilbury docks, West Thurrock industrial area, Corringham oil refinery, Tilbury power station and the Bata shoe factory at East Tilbury, all of which are within the Thurrock Borough Council area. He mentions also that construction workers from Essex travel to work at the Littlebrook and Isle of Grain power stations in Kent.

In this present case, however, I am concerned not so much with what D persons use the ferry service generally as with what persons use the early morning and late night services. In this context, I think it is fair to say that apart from a hearsay statement by Mr. Oliver that two or three people who work at the Bata shoe factory would be affected by the curtailment, the only specific evidence adduced on behalf of the plaintiff councils relates to the Central Electricity Generating Board ("the E C.E.G.B."). And since no representative of the C.E.G.B. was called even this evidence was based on hearsay, though it was admitted without objection from Mr. Scott, British Rail's counsel, for what it was worth. [His Lordship, after summarising the evidence relating to the C.E.G.B., concluded that the percentage of its employees who would be affected by the proposed curtailment was even smaller than the percentage of the F P.L.A.'s employees who would be so affected and further that, in relation to the C.E.G.B., there was no evidence comparable with that of the P.L.A. as to potential disruption or financial loss. His Lordship continued:] The two councils in their evidence laid stress on the fact that in their annual bill promoted in Parliament during the 1975-76 session which ultimately became the British Railways Act 1976, British Rail included, as clause 19, a provision designed to extinguish the common law rights and G duties of British Rail in relation to each of the two ferries and to substitute a statutory obligation. The plaintiff councils together with two other councils presented a petition against the clause. An amendment to clause 19 was devised in an attempt to meet the objections raised in the petition. The effect of clause 19 as amended, if it had become law would, briefly, have been that (a) British Rail would have been relieved of any H obligations to maintain work or use the northbound ferry and all its rights therein would have been extinguished; (b) the lease of the southbound ferry would have been extinguished; (c) notwithstanding (a) and (b), an obligation would have been placed on British Rail to continue to provide a ferry service between Tilbury and Gravesend, until such time as the Secretary of State should have given his consent to its discontinuance, certain specified restrictions being placed on the circumstances in

A which such consent might be given. On May 12, 1976, after evidence on the bill had been taken, a select committee of the House of Commons decided to omit clause 19 from the bill altogether. It therefore did not appear in any form in the British Railways Act 1976. The plaintiff councils have put in evidence copies of extracts from the transcript of the hearing before the select committee which contains the opening and closing of the case for British Rail by its counsel and the closing of the

B case for the petitioners by their counsel.

The plaintiff councils in the present action by them have sought to rely on certain extracts from such speeches of counsel, as well as on the fact that the select committee, after full consideration, rejected the proposed clause 19 and thereby left British Rail's obligations as ferry-owner unaffected. In my judgment, however, these matters have only marginal

C relevance for present purposes. They cannot operate to enlarge or extend the duties of British Rail as owner of the two ancient common law ferries. At most they might be among the factors which I would be entitled to take into account if it had been otherwise established that British Rail were in breach of its duties and questions were to arise as to the form of relief which should be granted.

D Apart from the evidence to which I have referred, there is, I think no hard evidence before me that the inhabitants of the areas of the two plaintiff councils will suffer any substantial loss, inconvenience or hardship if the proposed curtailment of the ferry service takes effect. On any one day, according to the agreed statistics, an average total of some 55 persons will travel on the 12 sailings in question. But the inference cannot possibly be drawn from this that by any means all such persons would suffer any serious inconvenience through the introduction of the new time-table. The

E agreed statistics indicate that, of the persons who travel on one or other of the five late evening sailings from Tilbury to Gravesend, one-third—say a total of about six persons a day—are travelling for social reasons and that of the persons who travel on one or other of the five late evening sailings from Gravesend to Tilbury about three-fifths—say a total of about

F 15 persons a day—are travelling for such reasons. Mr. Ainsworth gave evidence that a number of these passengers are persons returning from public houses on the other side of the river. Others, doubtless, include persons returning from visiting friends or relatives. There is, however, no more detailed evidence than this. Furthermore there is no evidence before me of any outcry or protest by members of the public, who say they would suffer social hardship if the proposed curtailment took effect.

G No member of the public, as such, has given evidence before me, and, for all I know, many or most of the persons who use the late evening sailings for social purposes may be spasmodic or casual users, who would in fact mind little if the sailings were cancelled in the future.

Conclusions

H As I have already indicated, in my judgment the onus falling on the plaintiffs in the present actions is to show that, in introducing its new time-table, British Rail would be failing in its obligation to carry passengers across the river Thames at all reasonable hours. As has already been stated, reasonableness for this purpose must in my judgment be assessed according to all the circumstances, in particular by striking a balance between, on the one hand, the extent of the demand for the 12 sailings in question and the inconvenience and hardship, if any, to the

public which would be caused if they were cancelled and, on the other A
hand, the extent of the burden in terms of money and otherwise that
would fall on British Rail providing these sailings.

On the evidence before me—and the matter can only be dealt with on
such evidence—I find it impossible to conclude that, in introducing the
new time-table, British Rail would be causing substantial inconvenience
or hardship to the small numbers of persons who might wish to travel
on the 10 late night sailings for *social* purposes. B

The position of the persons who use the two early morning sailings or
the 10 late night sailings for the purpose of going to or from their work
gives rise to rather different considerations. Many of them (unlike persons
using the ferries for social purposes) will have little choice in the matter,
so long as they retain their present employments, on the present terms
of such employments. If the ferry service is curtailed, the workers C
affected who live on the north or south side of the Thames, whether they
be employees of the P.L.A. or of any other employers in the neighbourhood, will be obliged either to make new arrangements with their employers in regard to the hours over which they work, which may be
difficult, or to arrange alternative means of transport by motor vehicle,
which may be difficult or expensive, or to leave their present employment D
and seek new employment on the opposite side of the Thames. Mr.
Rousell is a typical example of such persons.

I do not underestimate the potential hardship which the proposed
alteration in the time-table may involve for the workers to whom I have
just referred. I have no doubt that in a few individual cases it may be
real and substantial. Nevertheless the number of individuals involved is
relatively very small. The statistics already quoted for example indicate E
that an average of some six persons per day use the early Gravesend-
Tilbury sailing for the purpose of travelling to and from work and that an
average of three to four persons per day use the early Tilbury-Gravesend
sailings for the like purpose. They also indicate that an average of 13 to
14 persons per day in all use one or other of the five late Tilbury-Gravesend sailings for the like purpose and that an average of 11 persons per F
day in all use one or other of the five late Gravesend-Tilbury ferries
for the like purpose. In short the six Tilbury-Gravesend ferries in issue
in the present action accommodate in all an average of a total of only
about 17 persons going to or from work a day and the six Gravesend-
Tilbury ferries in issue accommodate in all about the same numbers.

Against the real inconvenience and hardship which these persons may
suffer if the 12 relevant sailings are cancelled has to be set the cost and G
hardship to British Rail in continuing to provide them. Their continuation
would mean that it had to maintain 12 sailings for the benefit of, on
average, never more than about five passengers, each time a substantial
proportion of whom were using them for purely social purposes. It would
further mean that British Rail had to employ four complete crews,
instead of the three crews which would otherwise suffice under the pro- H
posed new time-table, and that it had to incur effectively increased expenses of between £15,500 and £17,500 per annum.

The mere desire of British Rail to effect economies would, of course,
provide no defence whatever if it were to cease to provide a ferry service
at all reasonable times. Nevertheless the extent of the additional cost
and loss that would be incurred by British Rail in providing the 12 sailings
in question is in my judgment some measure of the lack of substantial

A   public demand for them. Evidence has been given as to the times of
certain of the last buses and trains leaving from Tilbury and Gravesend.
These times range over a period extending from 9.56 p.m. until 11.49 p.m.
A fairly typical time for last buses, however, seems to be about 10.30 p.m.
so that I do not think that potential users of the ferry service could
justifiably claim that the proposed new time-table was wholly out of line
with the times of other local public transport.

B
   The curtailment of any public transport service must cause hardship
to some persons and I have sympathy for the persons who will be affected
in the present case. In the end, however, balancing all the relevant factors
against each other as best I can, I have not been convinced on the
evidence before me that the introduction of the new time-table will
involve British Rail in any breach of its common law duties to provide
C   a ferry service at all reasonable times.

   This of course, means that the two actions must each fail. I should,
however, add some further observations in regard to a further important
question of principle, which has been fully argued. The primary relief
sought in each action has been relief by way of mandatory injunction.
Lord Goddard C.J. in *Attorney-General* v. *Colchester Corporation* [1955]
D   2 Q.B. 207, having found that the ferry owner was in breach of its common
law duty, continued as follows, at p. 215:

   " So I have now to consider whether the court can, in accordance
   with established principles, grant a mandatory injunction to compel
   the corporation to work the ferry. There is no case to be found
   in the books of such an injunction ever having been granted, nor
E   any hint or suggestion of there being such a remedy."

A little later in his judgment, at p. 216, Lord Goddard C.J. pointed out
that it had been said more than once that it is not easy to be precise as
to when Equity will or will not grant a mandatory injunction. He referred
there to the judgment of Lord St. Leonards in *Lumley* v. *Wagner* (1852)
1 De G.M. & G. 604 as authority for the proposition that the court will
F   not grant injunctions requiring a person to perform personal services. He
referred to the decision in *Powell Duffryn Steam Coal Co.* v. *Taff Vale
Railway Co.* (1874) L.R. 9 Ch.App. 331 as authority for the proposition
that an injunction will not be granted compelling a company or an individual to do a continuous act which requires the continuous employment
of people. He asked how the court could compel a person to maintain
and work a ferry which would require him either to do the work himself
G   or maintain and pay ferrymen as his servants. Finally in this context
he said, at p. 217:

   " No authority has been quoted to show that an injunction will be
   granted enjoining a person to carry on business, nor can I think that
   one ever would be, certainly not where the business is a losing
   concern. The franchise of a ferry is granted for the public benefit,
H   and the public, by using it and paying the toll, enable the owner
   to maintain and work it and probably obtain a profit for his trouble.
   If it is so little used that it can only be maintained at a loss, it would
   seem to be inequitable to order the owner to continue working it, on
   pain of imprisonment if he is an individual, or sequestration if a
   corporate body, for the continued working of the ferry might force
   an individual into bankruptcy. It seems reasonable to assume in this
   case that if the franchise were forfeited no other person would be

found willing to accept such a damnosa hereditas. I therefore refuse A
to grant an injunction."

In the *Powell Duffryn* case (1874) L.R. 9 Ch.App. 331, James L.J.
with whose judgment Mellish L.J. agreed, said, at p. 335:

" . . . it is not the practice of this court to compel by injunction
either a company or an individual to do a continuous act which
requires the continuous employment of people."   B

This decision and that in the *Colchester Corporation* case [1955] 2 Q.B.
207 would by themselves have presented formidable obstacles to the
plaintiffs in their plea for relief by way of mandatory injunction to compel
continuance of the present time-table, even if they had succeeded in
satisfying me that the introduction of the new time-table would involve
a breach of duty on the part of British Rail. It is, I think, still true to C
say that there is no case to be found in the books of such an injunction
having been granted, nor any hint or suggestion of there being such a
remedy.

Mr. Stewart, however, in the course of his strenuous and able argument submitted that even if it has ever been the practice of the court
not to compel by injunction the performance of a continuous act which D
requires the continuous employment of people, this was never more than
rule of practice which could be departed from in an appropriate case. He
pointed out that it used to be thought that covenants to do work to
property would not be specifically enforceable, on the grounds that there
would be difficulty in the court supervising its execution, but that this
particular objection to the making of an order for specific performance E
has been disposed of since *Shiloh Spinners Ltd.* v. *Harding* [1973] A.C.
691, 724 *per* Lord Wilberforce, and *Tito* v. *Waddell* (*No. 2*) [1977]
Ch. 106, 322 *per* Megarry V.-C. He referred me also to the decision
of Megarry V.-C. in *C. H. Giles & Co. Ltd.* v. *Morris* [1972] 1 W.L.R.
307. He submitted that cases such as these show that the courts nowadays are more willing than hitherto to grant specific performance of F
agreements to do a positive act or acts; by the like token, he submitted,
they should and would be more willing to grant mandatory injunctions in
an appropriate case, even though the relevant act would require the
continuous employment of persons.

Nevertheless Mr. Stewart for all his industry was not, I think, able
to point to any decided case whether the court has actually granted an G
injunction requiring a person to do a series of acts requiring the continuous employment of people. Perhaps the nearest he came to this was
to refer to the decision of Bacon V.-C. in *Greene* v. *West Cheshire Railway Co.* (1871) L.R. 13 Eq. 44 and *Fortescue* v. *Lostwithiel and Fowey
Railway Co.* [1894] 3 Ch. 621 in which judgments were given against
railway companies for specific performance of agreements, where the H
carrying out of such agreements would have involved a measure of continuous employment of persons to do the acts in question.

In the light of these and the more recent authorities to which I have
referred, I would accept that it cannot be regarded as an absolute and
inflexible rule that the court will never grant an injunction requiring a
person to do a series of acts requiring the continuous employment of
people over a number of years. Nevertheless the paucity of authority

A illustrating the grant of injunctions of this nature in my judgment indicates that the jurisdiction is one that will be exercised only in exceptional circumstances.

Even if, contrary to my conclusion, the proposed time-table would by a narrow margin (and I do not think it would be more) involve a breach of British Rail's duties, I still would not think that in all the circumstances this would be an appropriate case for the court to intervene by way of

B mandatory injunction. A number of considerations lead me to this conclusion: First, if contrary to my view, British Rail were to fail to perform its obligations to the public, it would be liable to indictment; in this sense therefore, all the interested parties have an alternative remedy available. Secondly, in this contingency, in respect of the special damage suffered by it, for example in regard to the cost of training new employees, the

C P.L.A. in my judgment would have a remedy in damages against British Rail: see *Paine* v. *Partrich* (1691) Carth. 191. The like remedy would be available to any member of the public who had suffered special damage through the neglect of its duties. This remedy, it is true, would not adequately compensate the P.L.A. for any additional loss caused to the disruption of its business which could not be reflected in terms of money. Nor would it compensate those comparatively few members of the public

D who would suffer inconvenience but no special damage beyond other members of the public. On the evidence before me, however—and this is the third point—I have formed the view that the hardship caused to the P.L.A. by such additional loss and to a few members of the public by such inconvenience would be outweighed by the hardship that would be caused to British Rail by compelling it to maintain the sailings in

E question at a heavy additional loss for the benefit of a relatively very small number of passengers. In this context, while it is not relevant that British Rail happens to represent a nationalised industry, it is in my judgment relevant that, like any other owners of a common law ferry, it is not entitled to disclaim its obligations. Fourthly, I would foresee the risk of potential practical difficulties in regard to enforcement arising from the grant of an injunction compelling British Rail to operate its ferry service

F to a particular time-table, even if the limits of the relevant times were fairly broadly defined and even if the period of the injunction were, as suggested, no more than about three and a quarter years.

These are some of the reasons why in the present case I would have been minded to follow the decision of Lord Goddard C.J. in the *Colchester Corporation* case [1955] 2 Q.B. 207 in refusing relief by way of mandatory

G injunction, even if I had concluded that the proposed new time-table would involve a breach of British Rail's duties.

As things are, however, the question of relief does not arise and I must dismiss both actions.

Actions dismissed with costs.

Solicitors: *Solicitor, Gravesham Borough Council; Solicitor, Thurrock*
H *Borough Council; Solicitor, Port of London Authority; Solicitor, British Railways Board.*

T. C. C. B.

[1978]

A

[PRIVY COUNCIL]

MELWOOD UNITS PTY. LTD. . . . . . APPELLANT

AND

COMMISSIONER OF MAIN ROADS . . . . RESPONDENT

B

[ON APPEAL FROM THE FULL COURT OF THE SUPREME COURT OF QUEENSLAND]

1978 March 7, 8, 9, 13; Lord Wilberforce, Lord Hailsham
     May 23 of St. Marylebone, Lord Simon of Glaisdale,
          Lord Russell of Killowen and Lord Keith of Kinkel

C

*Compulsory Purchase—Compensation—Assessment —Australia—
Resumption (compulsory acquisition) of land in Queensland for
expressway severing holding—Planning permission for shopping
centre on larger part of severed land—Sale of larger part after
resumption—Whether all of land to be treated as having
potential as part of shopping centre—Principles of assessment
—Relevance of sale price and knowledge of resumption—Main
Roads Acts 1920 to 1952, s. 26A (5)*
*Australia—Queensland—Land—Compulsory resumption — Assess-
ment—Main Roads Acts 1920 to 1952, s. 26A (5)*

D

In December 1964 a developer acquired 37 acres of land
in Brisbane from five separate vendors. The land was then
subject to an expressway proposal entailing the resumption
(compulsory acquisition) by the Commissioner of Main Roads
of a strip which when resumed would sever the land into two
parts, " the north land " and " the south land." In April 1965   E
the local planning authority gave outline planning permission
for the north land to be developed as a drive-in shopping centre,
on September 11 the commissioner resumed the strip and in
December the planning authority approved a layout plan for
the north land submitted in accordance with the permission
granted in April. In June 1966 the developer sold the north
land at $40,000 an acre and then filed a claim in the Land Court   F
for compensation for the value of the strip and for the diminution in value due to severance of the south land. The
court made an award and the developer appealed to the Land
Appeal Court, which assessed compensation on the basis that
the strip and the south land had never had any potential as
part of a 37 acre shopping centre and disregarded as irrelevant
to valuation the 1966 sale of the north land on the grounds
that the local planning authority's approval of the layout plan   G
had been given after the date of resumption and that on the
facts the sale was not relevant where the test for valuation
was what would a buyer desiring to buy the land have to pay
to a vendor willing but not desirous to sell. The developer
appealed by case stated to the Full Court of the Supreme
Court, which declined to answer the questions posed by the
case stated on the ground that an error in arriving at a
valuation could not involve a question of law.   H
On appeal by the developer to the Judicial Committee: —
Held, allowing the appeal, (1) that compensation for
resumption was to be assessed without reference to any
diminution in value of the land caused by the scheme of which
the resumption formed an integral part and that was so notwithstanding a proprietor's knowledge of the scheme at the
time he acquired the land; that that principle was part of the
common law and that in Queensland the absence of any
expression of it in section 26A (5) of the Main Roads Act

A   1920 to 1952 did not impliedly alter the law; and that,
accordingly (accepting that, but for the expressway proposal,
planning permission would have been granted to develop the
whole of the 37 acres as a drive-in shopping centre and that
there would have been a purchaser for it), the Land Appeal
Court should have left out of account the diminution in value of
the south land due to severance and assessed compensation by
reference to the value of the strip and the south land both
B   used as part of the 37 acres and as if the planning permission
had been granted for the entire holding (post, pp. 525D–H,
526D–F, 529F—530A).
     Pointe Gourde Quarrying and Transport Co. Ltd. v. *Sub-*
Intendent of Crown Lands [1947] A.C. 565, P.C. applied.
     (2) That a tribunal assessing compensation was not required
to disregard transactions made after the date of resumption;
and that, since on the facts the approval of the layout plan
C   had had no effect on the value of the north land, the price paid
on the 1966 sale of the north land was relevant when considering what a desirous purchaser would have had to pay to
a not unwilling vendor for the strip and the south land in
September 1965 and the court should have considered it
(post, pp. 525A–B, 527E–F, 529F—530A).
     (3) That any disregard by a tribunal of a principle of
assessment of compensation or of a transaction affording
D   evidence of the value of resumed land was an error of law
and that, therefore, the Full Court of the Supreme Court
ought to have remitted the case to the Land Appeal Court for
reconsideration according to the principles stated in their
Lordships' opinion (post, p. 523F–H).
     Order of the Full Court of the Supreme Court of
Queensland reversed.

E   The following cases are referred to in the judgment of their Lordships:

Pointe Gourde Quarrying and Transport Co. Ltd. v. *Sub-Intendent of*
     Crown Lands [1947] A.C. 565, P.C.
Spencer v. *Commonwealth of Australia* (1907) 5 C.L.R. 418.
Woollams v. *The Minister* (1957) 2 L.G.R.A. 338.

F   The following additional cases were cited in argument:

Castle Hill Brick, Tile & Pottery Works Pty. Ltd. v. *Baulkham Hills Shire*
     Council (1961) 7 L.G.R.A. 139.
Cedars Rapids Manufacturing and Power Co. v. *Lacoste* [1914] A.C.
     569, P.C.
Chapman v. *The Minister* (1966) 13 L.G.R.A. 1.
Commonwealth of Australia v. *Arklay* (1952) 87 C.L.R. 159.
G   *Corrie* v. *MacDermott* [1914] A.C. 1056, P.C.
Forssberg, Ex parte; In re Warringah Shire Council (1927) 27 S.R.(N.S.W.)
     200.
Fraser v. *City of Fraserville* [1917] A.C. 187, P.C.
Googong Pty. Ltd. v. *Commonwealth of Australia* (1977) 13 A.L.R. 449.
Ismail v. *Polish Ocean Lines* [1976] Q.B. 893; [1976] 2 W.L.R. 477;
     [1976] 1 All E.R. 902, C.A.
H   *Little* v. *Fairfield Municipal Council* (1962) 8 L.G.R.A. 64.
Lloyd v. *Robinson* (1962) 107 C.L.R. 142.
Minister, The v. *Stocks & Parkes Investments Pty. Ltd.* (1973) 129 C.L.R.
     385.
Nelungaloo Pty. Ltd. v. *The Commonwealth* (1948) 75 C.L.R. 495.
Royal Sydney Golf Club v. *Federal Commissioner of Taxation* (1957) 97
     C.L.R. 379.
Rugby Joint Water Board v. *Shaw-Fox* [1973] A.C. 202; [1972] 2 W.L.R.
     757; [1972] 1 All E.R. 1057, H.L.(E.).

Melwood Units Ltd. v. Main Roads Comr. (P.C.)   **[1978]**

San Sebastian Pty. v. *Housing Commission of New South Wales* **A**
(unreported), October 14, 1977: Court of Appeal of the Supreme Court
of New South Wales.
Vyricherla Narayana Gajapatiraju (Raja) v. *Vizagapatam Revenue
Divisional Officer* [1939] A.C. 302, P.C.
Wright, Ex parte; In re Concord Municipal Council (1925) 7 L.G.R.
(N.S.W.) 79.
Wunderlich Ltd. v. *Valuer-General* (1959) 5 L.G.R.A. 50.   **B**

APPEAL (No. 26 of 1976) by Melwood Units Pty. Ltd. (the developer)
with leave granted on July 30, 1976, by the Full Court of the Supreme
Court of Queensland against a judgment (June 23, 1976) and order of
the Full Court (Wanstall S.P.J., Matthews and Dunn JJ.) on an appeal
by case stated from a decision (December 4, 1972) of the Land Appeal
Court (Stable J., P. F. Wright and S. Dodds) in favour of the respondent, **C**
Commissioner of Main Roads, on an appeal by the developer from an
assessment (September 11, 1970) of compensation for resumption by
the commissioner of four acres, two roods and 15 perches of land in the
county of Stanley, parish of Yeerongpilly, Queensland. The majority of
the Full Court (Matthews and Dunn JJ.) declined to answer questions in
the case stated by the Land Appeal Court (set out in the order of the Full **D**
Court granting leave to appeal to the Queen in Council: see post, p. 529A–E)
on the ground that it did not contain or give rise to any questions of law
which an answer to those questions would involve or determine.
   The facts are stated in the judgment of their Lordships.

   Kenneth Gifford Q.C. (of the Bars of Victoria, Queensland and **E**
Tasmania) and *Nicholas Phillips* for the developer.
   J. M. Macrossan Q.C., W. C. Lee Q.C. (both of the Queensland Bar)
and *John G. C. Phillips* for the commissioner.

                                              Cur. adv. vult.

   May 23. The judgment of their Lordships was delivered by LORD **F**
RUSSELL OF KILLOWEN.
   This appeal from the Full Court of the Supreme Court of Queensland
arises in connection with a claim for compensation by the appellant
developer for the compulsory resumption by the Commissioner of Main
Roads on September 11, 1965, of an irregular central strip of the
developer's property in Brisbane, and for severance and injurious
affection of other property of the developer adjoining that strip to the **G**
south. The strip was to be the site of part of an expressway project
from Brisbane to Combabah. The project for the expressway had
reached a stage of detailed planning by the end of 1962, so that it was
then a reasonable assumption that the central strip of the developer's
land would in due course form part of the site of the expressway and
be resumed for that purpose.   **H**
   In December 1964 the developer exercised a series of earlier options
and thus obtained a contractual right to acquire from five separate
owners a total area of some 37 acres, at an average price of some
$7,700 an acre. This area was bounded on the north by Logan Road
and Kessels Road, on the west by Wadley Street and other land, on
the south by Doone Street and on the east by other land. The area
was irregular in shape and is shown in a plan at p. 27 of the record.

3 W.L.R.   Melwood Units Ltd. v. Main Roads Comr. (P.C.)

A   The projected expressway site which was subsequently resumed in September 1965 embraced two areas of the developer's land, one triangular and one a parallelogram, totalling slightly over four acres. An effect of the resumption was to sever from the northern part of the developer's land (some 25 acres) that part of that land lying to the south of the parallelogram (backing on Doone Street)—some seven acres. The total area of the land acquired by the developer is con-
B   veniently referred to as the 37 acres. That part lying to the north of the resumed land is referred to as the 25 acres and as the north land, and that part lying to the south of the resumed land as the south land.

The developer, having in June 1966 sold the north land, filed in October 1966 in the Land Court a claim for compensation totalling some $280,000 for the value of the resumed land and loss due to
C   severance of the south land. Being dissatisfied with the conclusion of the Land Court the developer appealed to the Land Appeal Court, which appeal involves a rehearing. The Land Appeal Court delivered a judgment on December 4, 1972, arriving at a figure of compensation of $83,000-odd made up as to $42,000-odd from the value of the resumed land and $40,000-odd as loss to the south land due to severance.
D   Neither side was satisfied with this outcome. Appeal from the Land Appeal Court to the Supreme Court is by way of case stated. The Land Appeal Court was asked to state a case, and did so after the lapse of some considerable time. The case stated appended as part of it the judgment which the Land Appeal Court had delivered so that there is considerable overlap between the former and the latter. The case stated concluded with a series of questions, some expressed to be
E   posed at the request of the developer and some at the request of the commissioner. As to two questions the Full Court answered that the Land Appeal Court, in connection with its inspection of the land on its own, had infringed the principles of natural justice and on that ground set aside the determination of compensation and remitted the matter for determination of the developer's claim according to law.
F   Their Lordships are not concerned with that, nor with any questions other than questions (a), (b) and (c) in the order of the Supreme Court giving leave to appeal to Her Majesty in Council. The details of those questions are best understood after a fuller statement of the facts of this case. Suffice it for the present to say that the Full Court declined to answer them on the ground, to state it shortly, that an error in arriving at a valuation could only be a question of fact and could not
G   involve a question of law. Neither the developer nor the commissioner supported that proposition and in their Lordships' opinion it is erroneous. If it should appear that the Land Appeal Court ignored a principle of assessment of compensation for compulsory acquisition (resumption), such as for example that commonly known as the *Point Gourde* principle, that in their Lordships' opinion would be an error in law. So
H   also if the Land Appeal Court rejected as wholly irrelevant to assessment of compensation a transaction which prima facie afforded some evidence of value and rejected it for reasons which were not rational, that in their Lordships' opinion would be an error in law. And as will be seen, it is on those lines that the developer contends that the Land Appeal Court erred in this case.

To return to the narrative. The 37 acres, at the time when by contract in December 1964 the developer acquired them, could not be

524

used under the relevant planning law otherwise than for residential A
purposes unless a permit was obtained under that law for another use.
The developer sought planning permission in January 1965 for development of the area as a drive-in shopping centre with ancillary parking
space, the latter an obvious essential to such a project. The application was in terms applicable to the whole 37 acres but having regard
to the impact of the expressway project, the course of which was indeed
shown on the plans accompanying the application, it is now accepted B
that the application was rightly treated as an application for the 25
acres north land and any consequential permit was also so limited.

On February 23, 1965, the developer was informed by letter from
Brisbane City Council that the Greater Brisbane town planning committee had decided to recommend the drive-in shopping centre in
principle to the registration board. That board was the decision-making C
body on applications for planning permissions such as this. On April
15, 1965, by letter the developer was informed by Brisbane City Council
that its registration board:

> " has granted the necessary permission, in principle, to use land
> [describing it in detail] and to erect buildings on such land for the
> purpose of a drive-in shopping centre." D

The letter concluded by pointing out that the approval gave permission
to use and erect buildings on " only that part of the land north of the
proposed arterial road, as determined by the main roads department."
The permission was expressed to be subject to a long list of conditions,
of the kind which might be expected in a permission in principle or
outline permission. The first condition was that a plan of the proposed E
layout satisfactory to the board be submitted showing inter alia
facilities within the site for loading and unloading and for parking of
not less than 2,500 vehicles. Their Lordships can have no doubt that
from the viewpoint of value of the 25 acres of the north land this
permission in principle was the vital event, and that when, as happened
in December 1965, the registration board reiterated its approval on the F
basis of a layout plan submitted in accordance with the first condition
of the April permission this would not have significantly added to the
value of those 25 acres of north land in the hands of the developer.
On this occasion their Lordships observe that substantially the same
long list of conditions was attached as was attached to the April 1965
permission.

The Land Appeal Court referred to certain evidence set out in the G
case as " uncontradicted and unchallenged." Their Lordships add to
the many occasions on which appellate courts have deplored the practice
in stated cases of rehearsing evidence rather than directly finding facts.
But in the relevant respects their Lordships conclude that the rehearsal
of the uncontradicted and unchallenged evidence, as such, is tantamount
to a finding of fact of the contents of that evidence. The following are H
what their Lordships, on that basis, accept as findings of fact. First:
that but for the expressway project and its impact on the 37 acres an
application to develop the whole area for a drive-in shopping centre
with ancillary parking area would have been granted by the registration
board, including the resumed land and south land. Second: that had
that been done there would have been a market available to the developer
for the whole 37 acres for that purpose. Moreover, it is clear that

The Weekly Law Reports, October 6, 1978

525

3 W.L.R.   Melwood Units Ltd. v. Main Roads Comr. (P.C.)

A   David Jones Ltd. would have been one of the, perhaps limited, number
of hypothetical purchasers in the market at resumption date for the 37
acre area for that purpose.   David Jones Ltd. in June 1966 bought the
25 acres of north land for an average price of approximately $40,000
an acre.   This purchase appears to their Lordships to be a highly
relevant piece of evidence for the evaluation of compensation in this
case when it is considered in the context of the assumed findings of
B   fact already mentioned.   Their Lordships by no means say that it
follows that David Jones Ltd. as a notional purchaser, willing to buy
the whole 37 acres, as shopping centre plus ancillary parking, would
have paid for the extra 12 acres (resumed land and south land) at the
same rate per acre: the extra 12 acres would have been parking area
more remote from the assumed actual buying area, though avoiding
C   in part a need for nearer expensive vertical car park building.
       Their Lordships consider now various aspects of the Land Appeal
Court decision in order to see whether they show error in law.   The
Land Appeal Court purport to premise their assessment on the fact that
the developer when it bought was aware that because of the commissioner's road project there was no prospect of a drive-in shopping
centre other than for the north land 25 acres.   In so far as this indi-
D   cates a view that, as a consequence, the value of the resumed land
and the loss by severance of the south land is to be based on the
hypothesis that they never had a potential as part of a 37 acre drive-in
shopping centre, it discloses in their Lordships' opinion an error in law.
Under the principle in *Point Gourde Quarrying and Transport Co.
Ltd.* v. *Sub-Intendent of Crown Lands* [1947] A.C. 565 the landowner
E   cannot claim compensation to the extent to which the value of his land
is enhanced by the very scheme of which the resumption forms an
integral part: that principle in their Lordships' opinion operates also in
reverse.   A resuming authority cannot by its project of resumption
destroy the potential of the whole 37 acres for development as a drive-in
shopping centre, and then resume and sever on the basis that that
F   destroyed potential had never existed.   Moreover, in their Lordships'
opinion the principle remains applicable in a case such as the present,
notwithstanding that planning permission had not been given for the
whole 37 acres and would not have been given, when the lack of such
permission was manifestly due to the expressway project, and it is
established that, without the expressway project, such planning permission would have been given for the whole 37 acres.   To hold other-
G   wise in this case would enable the acquiring authority to inflict by its
project the same injustice at one remove.   Further, as to the premise
of the Land Appeal Court abovementioned, if it is meant thereby that
because the developer bought the land with knowledge he should not,
on some principle, be allowed compensation except on the basis of
what he knew, this would be doubly wrong: a person buying land buys
H   with it the right to compensation for resumption and severance.   In
their Lordships' opinion the only light cast upon the matter by the developer's knowledge of the expressway project is that he considered that the
north land alone could be a viable area for a drive-in shopping centre:
and this in itself might be a factor in determining the value per acre of
the resumed land and south land for that purpose in comparison with
the value per acre of the north land.
       Although there are strong indications of departure from principle

The Weekly Law Reports, October 6, 1978

526

Melwood Units Ltd. v. Main Roads Comr. (P.C.)   [1978]

on the above lines by the Land Appeal Court, when they come to the   A
estimate of value of the resumed land and loss by severance of the
south land it may be arguable that ultimately, and in apparent contradiction of their " premise," they adjusted to the principles stated above.
Their approach to valuation (which was for a different reason, later
stated, in their Lordships' view erroneous in principle and therefore in
law) was to take the whole 37 acres at the price of $7,700 per acre
payable by the appellant in December 1964 as residential area value,   B
add something for an assumed inflationary increase in value as such at
10 per cent. per annum for nine months to resumption date, and then
add a further sum of about $1,000 per acre for the market potential
generated by the April 1965 permit—a total of $9,250 per acre. This
figure was applied to the resumed area and as the basis for assessment
of loss due to severance, and did not distinguish (apparently) between   C
the potential of the three different zones of the 37 acres. If this were
so, and the passage is in some respects obscure, it would mean that the
Land Appeal Court were not discounting as a result of the expressway
project the value as part of a drive-in shopping centre of the resumed
and south land, and were not infringing the reverse *Point Gourde*
principle. On the other hand, the Land Appeal Court in discussing   D
Woollams v. *The Minister* (1957) 2 L.G.R.A. 338 pointed out that that
decision was based upon a section of the relevant New South Wales
statute which, so to speak, embraced both the *Point Gourde* principle
and its reverse operation, and distinguished the relevant operative section
[section 26A (5)] of the Main Roads Acts 1920 to 1952 as only forbidding consideration of *increase* in value attributable to the relevant
project. This suggests that the Land Appeal Court thought that effect   E
could be given to a decrease in value so attributable, which as their
Lordships have indicated would be wrong in principle and in law. In
their Lordships' opinion it is a part of the common law deriving as a
matter of principle from the nature of compensation for resumption or
compulsory acquisition, that neither relevantly attributable appreciation
nor depreciation in value is to be regarded in the assessment of land   F
compensation. The relevant New South Wales section merely reflects
the law, as it did in England section 9 of the Land Compensation Act
1961, and the absence of the reverse of the medal in the relevant section
of the Queensland Main Roads Acts is not to be taken as altering the
law. Immediately after that passage in the judgment of the Land
Appeal Court, they say:
                                                                      G
   " Apart from that, however, there is no evidence before us that,
   prior to the resumption, foreknowledge of the proposed expressway
   had a depressing effect upon land values in their neighbourhood of
   the resumed land."

Their Lordships venture to think that this overlooks the true question,
which is whether such foreknowledge had a depressing effect upon the   H
development potential of the resumed and south land.
   Having been left in some uncertainty on the question of departure
in principle on the lines above mentioned, their Lordships turn to the
second alleged error in principle and law. It has already been noted
that the Land Appeal Court worked forward to a figure of $9,250 per
acre as a value basis at resumption date of September 1965. But David
Jones Ltd. in June 1966 bought the 25 acres of north land for the

The Weekly Law Reports, October 6, 1978

527

3 W.L.R.   Melwood Units Ltd. v. Main Roads Comr. (P.C.)

A purpose of a drive-in shopping centre at a price of about $40,000 per acre. While it may well be that this average price should not be attributed without qualification to every part of the 25 acres, however important the more southerly part as a parking facility (which facility David Jones Ltd. later found desirable to increase), this was the only tangible evidence of the value of land in this area for that purpose, and in respect of which there would have been availability of planning permission and demand from David Jones Ltd. for the whole 37 acres.

B This was wholly rejected by the Land Appeal Court as irrelevant to the assessment of value to the developer of the resumed land and the assessment of loss due to severance of the south land. What was the reason for this rejection, which led to an alternative build up which attributed no more than about $1,000 per acre to the commercial

C potential, a figure in support of which no evidence is referred to by the Land Appeal Court? The Land Appeal Court considered that by September 1965 (the date of resumption) the fact that in April 1965 there had been permission in principle to the relevant use would have become fairly widely known by September 1965. Their Lordships fail to see the relevance of this: the only relevant knowledge would be that

D of a narrow market of potential purchasers for the given purpose, who would be assumed to know of the April permission. Having attributed to this general knowledge some particular rise in the value of " the land " beyond the December 1964 values the Land Appeal Court thought the price paid in June 1966 by David Jones Ltd.—which as their Lordships have remarked was not less than an average $40,000 per acre for the north land 25 acres—not to be a reliable guide to the value

E of the resumed land at the date of resumption in September 1965. Now it is plain that in assessing values for the purpose of compensation for resumption on compulsory acquisition a tribunal is not required to close its mind to transactions subsequent to the date of resumption: they may well be relevant or of assistance to a greater or lesser degree, and in the instant case the figure paid by David Jones Ltd. was the

F only figure available at the date of assessment of the value of adjacent land to a person wishing to develop the land for its " highest and best use." Why then did the Land Appeal Court reject any consideration of this transaction in their evaluation? The reasons were stated by the court. The first was that at the date of resumption planning permission had only been granted (in April) in principle, and then subject to a long list of conditions. But the December 1965 permission was subject to

G substantially the same conditions, and David Jones Ltd. agreed to buy at an average price of $40,000 per acre nevertheless: and the Land Appeal Court considered that after the April permission in principle re-zoning was virtually ensured. Moreover, the Land Appeal Court did not seek to attribute to the December 1965 planning permission the startling increase to an average price of $40,000 per acre.

H   The other reason for rejection of the David Jones figure as not relevant was that the witness for the developer had advanced a figure based not only on the David Jones purchase price from the developer but also on the price per acre of adjacent land, which David Jones Ltd. paid in 1969 and 1970 as a desirable adjunct to its expected expansion of the drive-in shopping centre, which opened in 1970. The Land Appeal Court referred to the " circumstances surrounding " all three purchases by David Jones Ltd. in 1966, 1969 and 1970 as preventing them com-

The Weekly Law Reports, October 6, 1978

528

Melwood Units Ltd. v. Main Roads Comr. (P.C.)   [1978]

plying, for relevance to valuation, with the requirements of *Spencer* v. A
Commonwealth of Australia (1907) 5 C.L.R. 418. Counsel for the commissioner suggested that in relation to the 1969 and 1970 purchases the
"circumstances surrounding" were the pressure to buy exerted by the fact
of being committed to the major 1966 purchase. That may be so, and
the price per acre paid in 1969 and 1970 may not consequently be a
reliable guideline in this case: though the acquisition may in part
incidentally stress the value to such a project of parking space. But B
no suggestion was advanced to suggest that the 1966 average price per
acre was not some guideline except that David Jones Ltd. had been
for some time in negotiation in relation to the 25 acre site. If this, as
their Lordships must suppose in default of any other suggestion, was
the reason for total rejection from consideration of the average price
for the relevant purpose of some $40,000 an acre (quite apart from C
additional benefits on the sale to associated companies of the developer)
it was a rejection of evidence, and indeed the only relevant evidence, of
value which no properly instructed valuation tribunal should have made,
and was therefore an error in principle and of law. Their Lordships
do not of course say that the average price paid in June 1966 per acre
for the 25 acres is necessarily to be applied for compensation purposes D
to the rest of the 37 acres. Maybe some value is to be attributed to
the more definitive planning permit of December 1965. Maybe the
south land, or the more southerly parts of it, as being more remote as a
parking area from the actual shopping centre in the north land, would
have been of less value per acre to a hypothetical purchaser such as
David Jones Ltd., although no doubt the alternative cost of building
vertical car parks (mentioned by the Land Appeal Court) would have E
been a material consideration. But taking for example the resumed
land there does not seem any justification for ignoring a value of the
immediately adjacent north land at an arms length sale in June 1966
of well over $31,000 per acre above inflated residential use value and
deciding upon a comparable figure only nine months earlier of about
$1,000 per acre. The slight extra distance from the actual proposed F
shopping buildings coupled with the December permit can scarely be
justification for a difference of $30,000 per acre. In marking these
value contrasts their Lordships are not to be thought to overlook the
fact that $40,000 is an average figure and that it may be that the value
per acre of the land for the stated purpose diminishes with its increasing
remoteness in a southerly direction from the proposed site of the shop- G
ping area in the northern part of the north land.

Their Lordships have indicated the respects in which in their opinion
the Land Appeal Court erred in principle and therefore in law: and it
might well be that this opinion would suffice as a direction to the Land
Appeal Court when they come to reconsider the quesion of value to
the developer of the resumed land and loss to the developer as a con- H
sequence of severance of the south land, on the remission ordered by
the Full Court of the Supreme Court of Queensland. And any answers
given by their Lordships to the questions posed will be interpreted in
the light of the opinions here expressed. Nevertheless it is as well to
set out the questions referred to in the order giving leave to appeal,
being some of those extracted from the case stated. These were as
follows:

The Weekly Law Reports, October 6, 1978

529

3 W.L.R.   Melwood Units Ltd. v. Main Roads Comr. (P.C.)

A   " (a) Was the Land Appeal Court in error or mistaken in law in the method which it adopted for assessing the value of the resumed land?

" (b) Was the Land Appeal Court in error or mistaken in law in assessing the value of the resumed land and the effect of severance: (i) by reference to the facts that (A) at the time when the contracts for the purchase of [the developer's] land were signed
B   in December 1964 [the developer knew about the proposed location of the expressway proposal? (B) at all relevant times from 1962 at the latest [the developer] was aware that the only land available to it for the drive-in regional shopping centre was the northern land and that at no time did [the developer] have any reasonable expectation of receiving a permit to use the southern area for
C   purposes of a drive-in regional shopping centre? (C) the centre line of the expressway proposal through the resumed land and in its vicinity was finally fixed in 1962? . . . (ii) by reference to the market value of the [developer's] land unaffected by proposals for its use as a drive-in regional shopping centre? (iii) by excluding from consideration the sale of the northern land by [the developer]
D   to David Jones Ltd. and the payments by David Jones Ltd. to other companies within the . . . group of companies of which [the developer] was a member?

" (c) Having regard to the evidence set out in . . . the case stated should the Land Appeal Court have assessed compensation on the basis that but for the resumption (i) a town planning consent would or would probably have been granted by Brisbane City Council by
E   its registration board for the whole of the [developer's] land to be developed as a drive-in regional shopping centre? (ii) the resumed land and the severance area would have been used for the purpose of a drive-in regional shopping centre? "

Taken by themselves the answers to these questions, on the basis of their Lordships' opinion, would be:
F
        (a) Yes, to some extent. (b) (i) (A) Yes, if it did. (B) Yes, if it did. (C) Yes, if it did. (ii) Yes, if it did. (iii) Yes, as to the direct payment at the average rate of about $40,000 per acre. (c) (i) Yes. (ii) Yes. These answers by themselves may not serve any very useful purpose. The developer at the hearing of this appeal reformulated the proper answers to the questions as follows: (a) (i) Yes. (ii) In assessing
G   the value of the developer's land (including the resumed land and the south land) the Land Appeal Court should: (A) Leave out of account any diminution in value attributable to the proposal for the expressway. (B) Ascertain the highest and best use of the land on the basis that, there being for this purpose no expressway proposal, planning permission would have been obtainable for the use of the resumed land and of the
H   south land as part of the drive-in regional shopping centre. (iii) Neither the reasons given nor the material contained in the Land Appeal Court's reasons for judgment and in the case stated precludes the purchase by David Jones Ltd. in 1966 from complying with the test in *Spencer* v. *The Commonwealth* (1907) 5 C.L.R. 418. (iv) In assessing compensation for severance and injurious affection the Land Appeal Court should have regard to the existence of the expressway. (b) and (c) need not be answered having regard to the answer to (a). Their Lordships do not

regard these answers, when read in the light of their opinions, as really   A
being different save by way of formulation, and are prepared to adopt
them.

Their Lordships are of opinion that the Full Court of the Supreme
Court, in declining to answer certain of the questions posed, were for
the reasons already stated in this opinion in error, and should in their
order have remitted the case to the Land Appeal Court not only on the   B
matters referred to in their order but also upon the matters referred to
in, and upon the basis of, this opinion. The order of the Full Court of
the Supreme Court must be varied accordingly and the appeal allowed,
so that the Land Appeal Court shall on the reconsideration of the
question of compensation have regard both to the order of the Full Court
and to this opinion. In all the circumstances their Lordships are not
minded to interfere with the order for costs in the Full Court but are of   C
opinion that the Commissioner should pay to the developer its costs of
this appeal.   Their Lordships will humbly advise Her Majesty accordingly.

Solicitors: *Maxwell Batley & Co.; Freshfields.*

T. J. M.

D

[PRIVY COUNCIL]

PORT SWETTENHAM AUTHORITY   .   .   .   .   APPELLANT   E

AND

T. W. WU AND CO. (M) SDN. BHD.   .   .   .   .   RESPONDENT

[ON APPEAL FROM THE FEDERAL COURT OF MALAYSIA]

1978 April 4, 5, 6, 10;   Lord Wilberforce, Viscount Dilhorne,
      June 19   Lord Salmon, Lord Fraser of Tullybelton   F
                                    and Sir Garfield Barwick

Bailment—Burden of proof—Loss of goods—Goods in custody of
port authority—No evidence of how loss occurred—Liability
—Contracts (Malay States) Ordinance (No. 14 of 1950), ss. 104,
105, 114
Malaysia—Bailment—Loss of goods—Port authority's liability for
loss—By-law limiting authority's liability—Whether by-law   G
ultra vires—Port Swettenham Authority By-Laws 1965, by-law
91 (1)—Port Authorities Act 1963 (No. 21 of 1963), s. 29 (1) (g)

A consignment of 93 cases of pharmaceutical goods was
shipped from Hong Kong to Port Swettenham under bills of
lading nominating the plaintiffs as consignees. The consignment passed into the custody of the defendants (the port
authority) and the port charges were paid. While the consign-   H
ment was in the defendants' custody 64 of the cases disappeared. The plaintiffs brought an action against the defendants alleging that the loss had been due to the defendants'
negligence and claiming damages. At the trial the defendants
adduced evidence as to their system of taking care of goods
entrusted to them but adduced no specific evidence as to their
care of the 64 lost cases. The judge held that the burden was
on the defendants to show that the loss had not been caused
by their negligence and found that they had failed to discharge

A   that burden. He gave judgment for the plaintiffs. The Federal Court, on appeal, upheld that decision.

On appeal by the defendants to the Judicial Committee on the grounds, inter alia, that sections 104 and 105 of the Contracts (Malay States) Ordinance 1950 [1] did not put the burden of proving that he had not been negligent on the bailee and alternatively that by-law 91 of the Port Swettenham Authority By-Laws 1965 [2] (made under powers conferred by

B   section 29 of the Port Authorities Act 1963) limited the defendants' liability to loss caused "solely" by their misconduct or negligence which it was for the plaintiffs to prove: —

Held, dismissing the appeal, (1) that under sections 104 and 105 of the Contracts Ordinance and at common law where bailed goods were lost from the custody of the bailee (whether he was a gratuitous bailee or bailee for reward) the onus was

C   on him to prove that the loss was not due to his failure to exercise the care required by law and that, therefore, since under section 104 of the Contracts Ordinance the defendants were under a duty to take as much care of the goods as a reasonable port authority would take of its own similar goods and they had lost them and had shown neither how the loss had occurred nor that they had not been negligent, they were liable to the plaintiffs for the loss (post, pp. 534A–B, G–H;

D   536D–E).

Giblin v. *McMullen* (1868) L.R. 2 P.C. 317 and *Cheshire* v. *Bailey* [1905] 1 K.B. 237, C.A. and dictum of Sir Walter Phillimore in *Dwarka Nath* v. *Rivers Steam Navigation Co. Ltd.*, A.I.R. (1917) P.C. 173, 175, P.C. disapproved.

Morris v. *C. W. Martin & Sons Ltd.* [1966] 1 Q.B. 716, C.A. approved.

(2) That the defendants had no power under section 29

E   (1) (*g*) of the Port Authorities Act to make a by-law limiting their liability for loss due to their actual fault or privity and that, accordingly, in purporting to exclude liability for loss except that caused "solely" by the negligence or misconduct of the defendants or their officers or servants, by-law 91 (1) was ultra vires section 29 (1) (*g*) and invalid and its defects could not be cured by striking out any part of it and that therefore the defendants' liability was not limited by the by-

F   law and they were liable for any loss caused by their negligence (post, pp. 537G–H—538A).

Decision of the Federal Court of Malaysia affirmed.

The following cases are referred to in the judgment:

Asiatic Petroleum Co. Ltd. v. *Lennard's Carrying Co. Ltd.* [1914] 1 K.B. 419, C.A.; sub nom. *Lennard's Carrying Co. Ltd.* v. *Asiatic Petroleum*

G   *Co. Ltd.* [1915] A.C. 705, H.L.(E.).

Cheshire v. *Bailey* [1905] 1 K.B. 237, C.A.

Dwarka Nath v. *Rivers Steam Navigation Co. Ltd.*, A.I.R. (1917) P.C. 173.

Giblin v. *McMullen* (1868) L.R. 2 P.C. 317, P.C.

Hunt & Winterbotham (West of England) Ltd. v. *B.R.S. (Parcels) Ltd.* [1962] 1 Q.B. 617; [1962] 2 W.L.R. 172; [1962] 1 All E.R. 111, C.A.

Kush Kanta Barkakati v. *Chandra Kanta Kakati* (1923) 28 C.W.N. 1041; 83 I.C. 151.

H   *Lloyd* v. *Grace, Smith & Co.* [1912] A.C. 716, H.L.(E.).

Morris v. *C. W. Martin & Sons Ltd.* [1966] 1 Q.B. 716; [1965] 3 W.L.R. 276; [1965] 2 All E.R. 725, C.A.

Sharikat Lee Heng Sdn.Bhd. v. *Port Swettenham Authority* [1971] 2 M.L.J. 27.

---

[1] Contracts (Malay States) Ordinance 1950, s. 104: see post, p. 533G–H. S. 105: see post, p. 533H.

[2] Port Swettenham Authority By-Laws 1965, by-law 91 (1): see post, p. 537F.

The following additional cases were cited in argument: A

Abdul Rhaman v. *Arriffin* (1956) 22 M.L.J. 89.
British Traders & Shippers Ltd. v. *Ubique Transport & Motor Engineering
   Co. (London) Ltd.* [1952] 2 Lloyd's Rep. 236.
Bullen v. *Swan Electric Engraving Co.* (1907) 23 T.L.R. 258, C.A.
Calcutta Credit Corporation Ltd. v. *Prince Peter of Greece,* A.I.R. (51)
   1964 Calcutta 374.
Copland v. *Brogan* 1916 S.C. 277.   B
Gee Hup & Co. v. *Yeo Swee Hern trading as Chop Yong Bee Huat* (1935)
   4 M.L.J. 66.
Houghland v. *R. R. Low (Luxury Coaches) Ltd.* [1962] 1 Q.B. 694; [1962]
   2 W.L.R. 1015; [1962] 2 All E.R. 159, C.A.
Karuppan Bhoomidas v. *Port of Singapore Authority* [1978] 1 W.L.R. 189;
   [1978] 1 All E.R. 956, P.C.
Kruse v. *Johnson* [1898] 2 Q.B. 91, D.C.   C
Leesh River Tea Co. Ltd. v. *British India S.N. Co. Ltd.* [1967] 2 Q.B.
   250; [1966] 3 W.L.R. 642; [1966] 3 All E.R. 593, C.A.
Malayan Thread Co. Sdn. Bhd. v. *Oyama Shipping Line Ltd.* [1973] 1
   M.L.J. 121.
Norman, The [1960] 1 Lloyd's Rep. 1, H.L.(E.).
Rustenberg Platinum Mines Ltd. v. *South Africa Airways* [1977] 1 Lloyd's
   Rep. 564.   D
Samuel v. *Westminster Wine Co. Ltd.,* The Times, May 16, 1959.
Secretary of State v. *Ramdhan Das Dwarka Das Firm* (1934) A.I.R.
   Calcutta 151.
Smith (H.C.) Ltd. v. *Great Western Railway Co.* [1922] 1 A.C. 178,
   H.L.(E.).
Trustees of the Harbour, Madras v. *Best & Co.* (1899) 22 I.L.R. (Madras)
   524.   E
Wiehe v. *Dennis Brothers* (1913) 29 T.L.R. 250.

APPEAL (No. 6 of 1976) by the Port Swettenham Authority (the
defendants) with leave of the Federal Court of Malaysia from its judgment
of March 8, 1975 (Suffian L.P., Lee Hun Hoe C.J. (Borneo) and Ali F.J.),
dismissing the defendants' appeal from an order (June 27, 1974) of Abdul
Hamid J. in the High Court of Malaysia at Kuala Lumpur ordering the   F
defendants to pay $21,236.84 damages to the plaintiffs, T. W. Wu and Co.
(M) Sdn. Bhd. (the respondents) in respect of the loss of 64 cases of
pharmaceutical goods, the property of the plaintiffs, from the custody of
the defendants.
   The facts are stated in the judgment of their Lordships.

John Vinelott Q.C. and *Mark Potter* for the defendants.   G
   J. S. Hobhouse Q.C., Mark Havelock-Allan and *Cecil W. M. Abraham*
(of the Bar of West Malaysia) for the plaintiffs.

                                          Cur. adv. vult.

June 19. The judgment of their Lordships was delivered by LORD
SALMON.   H
   A consignment of 93 cases of pharmaceutical goods was shipped,
under two bills of lading dated March 28, 1970, on board the vessel *Sansei
Maru* for carriage from Hong Kong to Port Kelang (Port Swettenham) in
Malaysia. The bills of lading nominated the plaintiffs (respondents in this
appeal) as consignees. The *Sansei Maru* arrived at Port Swettenham on
April 5, 1970. The trial judge found as a fact (1) that on that day, all the
93 cases were unloaded on to the wharf and passed into the custody of the

A port authority (the defendants) who transferred them into shed no. 8; and
(2) that on April 8, the chief forwarding clerk of the plaintiffs' forwarding
agents and a customs' officer inspected and counted all of the 93 cases in
shed no. 8, and (3) that the inward cargo charges and customs duty were
paid in respect of each of the 93 cases on the following day. By April 15,
1970, only 29 of the 93 cases could be found. The balance of 64 cases
weighing about 5·65 tons had disappeared. The defendants at first
B contended that the 64 cases had been short-landed and therefore had never
been in their custody. Their counsel, however, abandoned this contention
at the trial after having heard the evidence adduced on behalf of the
plaintiffs.

No. 8 shed was about 400 feet long and 100 feet wide. It had eight
doors in front and eight doors behind. It was in the charge of a chief clerk
C who had a number of other clerks to assist him in looking after the contents
of the shed. They worked in three shifts around the clock. None of them
was called as a witness at the trial. The doors in front of the shed faced
the ship, and cargo was taken by the defendants' servants from the ship's
side and transported by forklift and pallets to the shed: a distance of
about 40 feet. It was admitted on behalf of the defendants that they had
no system for counting any of the cases brought into the shed. At no time
D did the defendants have any idea of how many cases the shed should have
contained. Cargo was usually kept in the shed for up to three days and
then if not delivered to the consignee within that period transferred into
the warehouse. Whilst the goods were kept in the shed, no extra fees were
charged for this was all part of the service offered by the defendants and
covered by the inward cargo charges. If and when the cargo was transferred
E to the warehouse, then extra dues were charged as long as the cargo
remained there. It is obvious that the missing 64 cases, weighing over five
tons, could not have been taken out of the defendants' custody save by
loading them on to a vehicle. Some of the contents of the cases were later
found in a local chemists's shop. It is obvious that goods of this bulk and
weight could not have been spirited out of the defendants' custody if due
care for their safety had been taken by the servants into whose care the
F goods had been entrusted by the defendants for safe keeping.

The trial judge found that the onus lay upon the defendants to prove
that the goods had not been lost because of their negligence or misconduct
or that of their servants: and that they had failed to discharge that onus.
Accordingly he gave judgment for the plaintiffs for $21,236·84 being the
undisputed value of the missing 64 cases. The defendants' appeal from that
G judgment to the Federal Court of Malaysia was dismissed, and they now
appeal to this Board from the decision of the Federal Court.

The law in relation to bailment is set out in sections 104 and 105 of the
Contracts (Malay States) Ordinance of 1950 which read as follows:

" 104. In all cases of bailment the bailee is bound to take as much
care of the goods bailed to him as a man of ordinary prudence would,
under similar circumstances, take of his own goods of the same bulk,
H quality, and value as the goods bailed.
" 105. The bailee, in the absence of any special contract, is not
responsible for the loss, destruction, or deterioration of the thing bailed,
if he has taken the amount of care of it described in section 104 of this
Ordinance."

It will be observed that these sections apply to all bailments and make no
distinction between bailments for reward and gratuitous bailments.

Port Swettenham Authority v. T. W. Wu & Co. (P.C.) [1978]

Their Lordships consider that the onus is upon the defendants under A sections 104 and 105 to prove that they had taken as much care of the plaintiffs' goods as a port authority of ordinary prudence would, under similar circumstances, have taken of its own goods of the same bulk, quality and value as the 64 lost cases. See *Sharikat Lee Heng Sdn. Bhd.* v. *Port Swettenham Authority* [1971] 2 M.L.J. 27, 29 and *Indian Contract and Specific Relief Acts* by Pollock and Mulla, 6th ed. (1931), in which the authors, who are generally regarded as authorities of great weight, state, B at p. 521:

> " In cases governed by the provisions of sections 151 and 152, [which correspond exactly with sections 104 and 105] the loss or damage of goods entrusted to a bailee is prima facie evidence of negligence, and the burden of proof, therefore, to disprove negligence lies on the bailee." C

Their Lordships respectfully agree with this statement of the legal position. It has, however, been argued on behalf of the defendants that neither sections 104, 105 nor 114 spell out that the onus lies upon them to prove that they took the degree of care specified in section 104 in respect of the 64 missing cases. Section 114, for example, reads: D

> " If, *by the fault of the bailee*, the goods are not returned, delivered, or tendered at the proper time, he is responsible to the bailor for any loss . . . of the goods from that time." (My italics)

If there is nothing in the sections to establish with certainty whether the onus is upon the bailor to prove the default, or upon the bailee to disprove it, these sections must be interpreted in the light of the common law. E Pollock and Mulla, however, comment upon section 161 of the Indian Contract Act (which is in exactly the same terms as section 114) at p. 531, as follows: " Unexplained failure to return the thing bailed is presumed to be by the bailee's default." For this proposition they cite an Indian authority, *Kush Kanta Barkakati* v. *Chandra Kanta Kakati* (1923) 28 C.W.N. 1041; 83 I.C. 151, where, as they rightly say: " the English auth- orities on which this section is founded are cited at some length." The F Civil Law Act 1956 provides:

> " 3 (1) Save so far as other provision has been made or may hereafter be made by any written law in force in Malaysia, the court shall (*a*) in West Malaysia or any part thereof, apply the common law of England and the rules of equity as administered in England on April 7, 1956." G

It is true that Malaysian law sets a single standard of care for all bailees— whether they are bailees for reward or gratuitous bailees—and it corre- sponds to the standard required of a gratuitous bailee at common law. This standard, although high, may be a less exacting standard than that which the common law requires of a bailee for reward. But the line between the two standards is a very fine line, difficult to discern and impossible to H define. After all, a man of ordinary prudence would presumably take reasonable care of his own goods. However this may be, there is no doubt that under Malaysian law interpreted in the light of the common law, as it always has been by the Malaysian courts and by this Board, the onus is on the bailee to show that he has taken the care required by the law, of the goods entrusted to him.

Their Lordships recognise that, under the common law, there is some

A authority for holding that, in the case of a gratuitous bailment, the onus of proving that the loss of goods bailed was caused by the negligence or misconduct of the bailee rests upon the bailor; see *Giblin* v. *McMullen* (who represented the Union Bank of Australia) (1868) L.R. 2 P.C. 317 upon which the defendants relied. Their Lordships however gravely doubt whether that case was correctly decided. There is no compelling authority that a gratuitous bailee who fails to return the goods left in his custody

B is not obliged to explain why he is not able to return them and to show that their loss is not due to his failure to have taken as much care of the goods as a man of ordinary prudence would have taken of his own goods in similar circumstances. In any event, a bank, which offers its customers, in the ordinary course of business, the service of looking after goods deposited with it, can hardly be described as a gratuitous bailee. The bank

C must realise that were it to refuse a customer such a service it would probably lose the customer who would have no difficulty in finding another bank which would be happy to render the service which is normally offered by banks to their customers. Moreover, in *Giblin* v. *McMullen* the plaintiff had deposited a box containing valuable securities with the defendant bank for safe custody and one of the bank's cashiers (who was employed to look after boxes deposited with the defendant bank) had stolen certain

D debentures from the box. That case was decided long before *Lloyd* v. *Grace, Smith & Co.* [1912] A.C. 716 in days when it was still thought to be the law that a master could not be liable to his customer for a theft by his own servant in any circumstances except when the master benefited from or connived at the theft.

   The undisputed facts of the present case already recited in this judgment

E establish that the defendants were clearly bailees for reward. However this may be, in their Lordships' view the onus is always upon the bailee, whether he be a bailee for reward or a gratuitous bailee, to prove that the loss of any goods bailed to him was not caused by any fault of his or of any of his servants or agents to whom he entrusted the goods for safe keeping. Accordingly the onus of proving that the loss of the goods deposited with the defendants for safe custody was not caused by the

F negligence or misconduct of their servants in the course of their employment, without any doubt, lies on the defendants: see *Hunt & Winterbotham (West of England) Ltd.* v. *B.R.S. (Parcels) Ltd.* [1962] 1 Q.B. 617:

   " If an owner of goods leaves them with another person who undertakes to mind them for reward, and then fails to produce them when they are wanted, it is a reasonable inference, in the absence of any

G explanation, that he cannot have looked after them properly: in other words, that he has at least been negligent. Accordingly, it is right to say in such a case . . . that it is for the depositee to show that he has not been negligent . . ." *per* Donovan L.J. at p. 635.

   Great reliance was placed by the defendants upon a passage in a judgment of this Board given by Sir Walter Phillimore in *Dwarka Nath* v. *Rivers*

H *Steam Navigation Co. Ltd.* A.I.R. (1917) P.C. 173. In that case a vessel belonging to the defendants, laden with a cargo of jute belonging to the plaintiff, was moored to two buoys in a river. Another vessel was moored alongside and fastened to the same two buoys. This latter vessel caught fire which spread to the defendants' vessel, and although this vessel ultimately got clear and was towed down the river, the greater part of the cargo of jute was destroyed. The plaintiff sued the defendants as bailees for not taking proper care of the cargo by getting away from the fire more

quickly than they did. The case was decided in favour of the defendants A
on the ground that they were faced with a sudden emergency of extreme
peril and difficulty, and the fact that in the agony of the moment, they
took a course which turned out not to be the best which they could have
taken did not amount to negligence. The passage in Sir Walter Phillimore's
judgment, on which the defendants rely, reads as follows, at p. 175:

> " It is true that under the Evidence Act of 1872, section 106, [which B
> corresponds with section 106 of the Malaysian Evidence Act 1950 as
> revised in 1971] ' when any fact is especially within the knowledge of
> any person, the burden of proving the fact is on him; ' and it was
> therefore right that the defendant company should call the material
> witnesses who were on the spot . . . But this provision of the law of
> evidence does not discharge the plaintiffs from proving the want of due
> diligence, or . . . the negligence, of the servants of the defendant C
> company. It may be for the company to lay the materials before
> the court; but it remains for the plaintiffs to satisfy the court that
> the true inference from these materials is that the servants of the
> defendant company have not shown due care, skill and nerve."

Their Lordships with great respect are unable to accept that passage (which
having regard to the decision was entirely obiter) as correctly stating the D
law in relation to the onus of proof which lies upon a bailee.

In their Lordships' view the defendants have conspicuously failed to
discharge the onus which lay upon them. They called only two witnesses,
and those witnesses knew nothing at all about the lost goods. They spoke
of nothing except the nature of the system and security measures which
the defendants adopted for taking care of the goods committed to their E
custody. Both the trial judge and the Federal Court took the view that
the system of control and the security measures left much to be desired and
should have been tightened up. Their Lordships consider that there was
every justification for that view. In particular, it seems most unfortunate
that no record was kept of the goods which were stored in shed no. 8 for
safe custody; and this, of course, must have been known to the defendants'
servants whose role it was to look after these goods whilst in the shed. F
Even if the system and security precautions had been perfect, the best of
systems sometimes breaks down through the human factor, viz. through
negligence or misconduct on the part of those who are employed to work it.
The defendants elected not to call as witnesses any of the men working
in the shed whose duty it was to safeguard the goods—not even the man in
charge of the shed. There was accordingly no evidence that these men had G
taken due care of the goods or that the 64 cases had not been lost as a
result of their negligence or misconduct. For the reasons already stated, it
seems virtually certain that the cases were stolen and could not have been
stolen without the negligence or misconduct of the defendants' servants
who were employed to keep them in safe custody. When a bailee puts
goods which have been bailed to him in the care of his servants for safe H
custody, there can be no doubt that the bailee is responsible if the goods
are lost through any failure of those servants to take proper care of the
goods. The heresy that any dishonest act on the part of a servant employed
to take care of the goods is necessarily outside the scope of his employment,
and that the master cannot be liable for the dishonest act unless done for
his benefit or with his privity, was exorcised by *Lloyd* v. *Grace, Smith &
Co.* [1912] A.C. 716. It was on the basis of this heresy that *Cheshire* v.

A *Bailey* [1905] 1 K.B. 237 laid down the startling proposition of law that a master who was under a duty to guard another's goods was liable if the servant he sent to perform the duty for him performed it so negligently as to enable thieves to steal the goods, but was not liable if that servant joined with the thieves in the very theft. This proposition is clearly contrary to principle and common sense, and to the law: *Morris* v. *C. W. Martin and Sons Ltd.* [1966] 1 Q.B. 716, 740. Their Lordships agree with the decision

B in *Morris* v. *C. W. Martin and Sons Ltd.* and consider that *Cheshire* v. *Bailey* mis-stated the common law.

It is now necessary to turn to by-law 91 (1) of the Port Swettenham Authority By-Laws 1965, made by the Port Swettenham Authority with the approval of the Minister and in exercise of the powers conferred by section 29 of the Port Authorities Act 1963. The defendants relied strongly

C upon this by-law which, so far as material, reads as follows:

> " The authority shall not be liable for any loss . . . of goods . . . from any . . . cause, unless such loss, . . . has been caused solely by the misconduct or negligence of the authority or its officers or servants."

It was at one time suggested on behalf of the defendants that this by-law altered the onus of proof and put the onus upon the plaintiffs to prove

D that the loss of the missing 64 cases had been caused solely by the misconduct or negligence of the defendants or their officers or servants. It is unnecessary to make any comment about this submission save that it was attractively presented but is without substance. Even if the submission were right it would only afford an added reason for finding the by-law invalid in that it purported to alter the general law. The defendants, how-

E ever, relied on the by-law mainly for the proposition that if the goods were stolen as the result of misconduct or negligence of the defendants, their officers or servants, it could not be said that their loss was caused solely by that misconduct or negligence since it was also caused by the criminal conduct of the thieves who stole them. In their Lordships' view, the by-law is ultra vires section 29 (1) (*g*) of the Port Authorities Act 1963. That section, so far as relevant, reads as follows:

F
> (1) The authority may with the approval of the Minister make by-laws for—(*g*) limiting the liability of the authority in respect of any loss . . . occurring without the actual fault or privity of the authority . . ."

Clearly, any by-law which purports to limit the authority's liability in

G respect of a loss occurring with the actual fault or privity of the authority would be ultra vires; and that is precisely what by-law 91 (1) does. It distinguishes between the misconduct or negligence of the authority itself and that of its servants for which it is also responsible. If anyone who could properly be described as the alter ego of the defendants, for example, their managing director, had been privy to the theft of the 64 missing cases, this would constitute a loss occurring with the actual fault or privity of

H the defendants (see *Lennard's Carrying Co. Ltd.* v. *Asiatic Petroleum Co. Ltd.* [1915] A.C. 705, 715), yet the defendants would be exempt from liability because the loss would have been caused partly by the actual thieves and therefore not solely by the fault of the defendants. There is, however, no power under section 29 to make a by-law which limits the liability of the authority in respect of any loss occurring with its actual fault or privity. The by-law, in their Lordships' view, would also be ultra vires because it does not only limit, it wholly excludes, the defendants'

Port Swettenham Authority v. T. W. Wu & Co. (P.C.)   **[1978]**

liability for the loss of any goods caused by their own misconduct or   A
negligence: and section 29 (1) (*g*) of the Act of 1963 confers no power to
exclude but only to limit liability. Further, in their Lordships' opinion,
the defects in the by-law cannot be cured by striking out any part of it.

For these reasons, their Lordships will advise His Majesty the Yang
di-Pertuan Agong that the appeal should be dismissed with costs.

Solicitors: *Stephenson, Harwood; Waltons & Morse.*   B

T. J. M.

[HOUSE OF LORDS]   C

JOHNSON AND ANOTHER   .   .   .   .   .   APPELLANTS

AND

MORETON   .   .   .   .   RESPONDENT

1978 June 19, 20, 21, 22;   Lord Salmon, Lord Hailsham of   D
      July 27   St. Marylebone, Lord Simon of Glaisdale,
                               Lord Edmund-Davies and Lord Russell
                                                     of Killowen.

*Agricultural Holding—Notice to quit—Counter-notice—Tenant
covenanting in lease not to serve counter-notice—Whether
covenant enforceable—Agricultural Holdings Act 1948 (11 &*   E
*12 Geo. 6, c. 63), s. 24 (1) (2) (e) (as amended by Agriculture
Act 1958 (6 & 7 Eliz. 2, c. 71) s. 3).*

Landlords granted to a tenant a lease of an agricultural
holding for 10 years from January 1, 1967. Clause 27 of the
lease provided:

"The tenant agrees to give possession of the whole of the
farm to the landlords immediately upon the determination
of the term hereby granted and not in any event to serve   F
a counter-notice under section 24 (1) of the Agricultural
Holdings Act 1948 or to take any steps to claim the
benefit of any statutory provision granting security of
tenure which may be in force at the time of the determination thereof."

On November 27, 1975, the landlords served on the tenant
a notice to quit the holding on December 31, 1976. On
December 16, 1975, the tenant served a counter-notice on the   G
landlords requiring that section 24 (1) of the Agricultural
Holdings Act 1948 [1] should apply to the notice to quit. On
December 22, 1975, the landlords served a second notice to

---

[1] Agricultural Holdings Act 1948 (as amended), s. 24: "(1) Where notice to
quit an agricultural holding or part of an agricultural holding is given to the tenant
thereof, and not later than one month from the giving of the notice to quit the
tenant serves on the landlord a counter-notice in writing requiring that this   H
subsection shall apply to the notice to quit, then, subject to the provisions of
the next following subsection, the notice to quit shall not have effect unless the
Agricultural Land Tribunal consents to the operation thereof. (2) The foregoing
subsection shall not apply where— . . . (e) at the date of the giving of the notice
to quit the interest of the landlord in the agricultural holding to which the notice
relates had been materially prejudiced by the commission by the tenant of a
breach, which was not capable of being remedied, of any term or condition
of the tenancy that was not inconsistent with the fulfilment by the tenant of his
responsibilities to farm in accordance with the rules of good husbandry, and it is
stated in the notice that it is given by reason of the matter aforesaid; . . ."

A   quit on the tenant under section 24 (2) (e) of the Act giving
      as reasons that the tenant's service of the counter-notice was
      a breach of clause 27 of the lease not capable of being
      remedied and that the landlord's interest had thereby been
      materially prejudiced. The tenant contested those reasons
      and the matter was referred to an arbitrator under the
      Agricultural Holdings Act 1948.
           The arbitrator stated a special case to the county court as
B   to whether the reasons given in the second notice to quit were
      good. The judge held that the Agricultural Holdings Act
      1948 did not preclude the parties to a lease from agreeing to
      exclude the operation of section 24 (1); that, therefore, clause
      27 was enforceable, the service of the counter-notice was a
      breach of the clause falling within section 24 (2) (e) of the
      Act and that, accordingly, the second notice to quit was a
      valid notice terminating the tenancy on December 31, 1976.
C   The Court of Appeal allowed the tenant's appeal.
           On the landlords' appeal: —
           Held, dismissing the appeal, that section 24 (1) of the
      Agricultural Holdings Act 1948 gave the tenant of an agri-
      cultural holding an option to serve a counter-notice in
      response to a notice to quit served on him by his landlord
      and that both the words of the subsection and the policy of
      the Act made it clear that the tenant could not by agreement
D   deprive himself of that option in advance; and that, accord-
      ingly, the agreement in clause 27 not to serve a counter-notice
      was unenforceable and, since the rest of the clause was also
      unenforceable, the tenant was entitled to serve the counter-
      notice and thereby render the notice to quit subject to the
      consent of the Agricultural Land Tribunal (post, pp. 542F, G,
      543H—544G, 554C–G, 559G, 561F, H—562A, 563G—564A, G—
      565B).
E   Decision of the Court of Appeal affirmed.

      The following cases are referred to in their Lordships' opinions:
      Admiralty Commissioners v. Valverda (Owners) [1938] A.C. 173, H.L.(E.).
      Artizans, Labourers & General Dwellings Co. v. Whitaker [1919] 2
           K.B. 301.
      Attorney-General v. Prince Ernest Augustus of Hanover [1957] A.C.
F   436; [1957] 2 W.L.R. 1; [1957] 1 All E.R. 49, H.L.(E.).
      Barrow v. Isaacs & Son [1891] 1 Q.B. 417, C.A.
      Barton v. Fincham [1921] 2 K.B. 291, C.A.
      Bowmaker Ltd. v. Tabor [1941] 2 K.B. 1, C.A.
      Brandling v. Barrington (1827) 6 B. & C. 467.
      Brisbane City Council v. Attorney-General for Queensland [1978] 3
           W.L.R. 299, P.C.
G   Farrell v. Alexander [1976] Q.B. 345; [1975] 3 W.L.R. 642; [1976]
           1 All E.R. 129, C.A.; [1977] A.C. 59; [1976] 3 W.L.R. 145; [1976]
           2 All E.R. 721, H.L.(E.).
      Gladstone v. Bower [1960] 2 Q.B. 384; [1960] 3 W.L.R. 575; [1960]
           3 All E.R. 353, C.A.
      Graham v. Ingleby (1848) 1 Ex. 651.
      Griffiths v. Earl of Dudley (1882) 9 Q.B.D. 357, D.C.
H   Hill v. Barclay (1811) 18 Ves. 56.
      Hunt v. Hunt (1862) 4 De G. F. & J. 221.
      Hyman v. Hyman [1929] A.C. 601, H.L.(E.).
      Incorporated Council of Law Reporting (Q.) v. Federal Commissioner
           of Taxation (1971) 125 C.L.R. 659.
      Inland Revenue Commissioners v. Yorkshire Agricultural Society [1928]
           1 K.B. 611, C.A.
      Kennedy v. Johnstone, 1956 S.C. 39.
      Mears v. Callender [1901] 2 Ch. 388.

National Westminster Bank Ltd. v. *Halesowen Presswork & Assemblies* A
    Ltd. [1972] A.C. 785; [1972] 2 W.L.R. 455; [1972] 1 All E.R.
    641, H.L.(E.).
Premier Dairies v. *Garlick* [1920] 2 Ch. 17.
Printing and Numerical Registering Co. v. *Sampson* (1875) L.R. 19 Eq.
    462.
Rajenback v. *Mamon* [1955] 1 Q.B. 283; [1955] 2 W.L.R. 21; [1955]
    1 All E.R. 12.
River Wear Commissioners v. *Adamson* (1877) 2 App.Cas. 743, H.L.(E.).   B
Salford Guardians v. *Dewhurst* [1926] A.C. 619, H.L.(E.).
Sanders v. *Pope* (1806) 12 Ves.Jr. 282.
Soho Square Syndicate Ltd. v. *E. Pollard & Co.* [1940] Ch. 638.
Stock v. *Frank Jones (Tipton) Ltd.* [1978] 1 W.L.R. 231; [1978] 1 All
    E.R. 948, H.L.(E.).
Vacher & Sons Ltd. v. *London Society of Compositors* [1913] A.C. 107,
    H.L.(E.).   C

The following additional cases were cited in argument:
Coates v. *Diment* [1951] 1 All E.R. 890.
Fender v. *St. John-Mildmay* [1938] A.C. 1; sub nom. *Fender* v. *Mildmay*
    [1937] 3 All E.R. 402, H.L.(E.).
Land Settlement Association Ltd. v. *Carr* [1944] K.B. 657, C.A.
Scala House & District Property Co. Ltd. v. *Forbes* [1974] Q.B. 575;   D
    [1973] 3 W.L.R. 14; [1973] 3 All E.R. 308, C.A.

APPEAL from the Court of Appeal.

This was an appeal by the landlords, Henry Leslie Johnson and
Caroline Johnson, from the judgment of the Court of Appeal (Megaw,
Lawton and Geoffrey Lane L.JJ.) dated February 15, 1977, allowing   E
the appeal of the tenant, Samuel Moreton, from an order of Judge
Harrison-Hall sitting at Warwick County Court made on October 13, 1976,
on a special case stated by Mr. E. G. Righton M.C., F.R.I.C.S., an
arbitrator appointed under the Agricultural Holdings Act 1948.

The facts are stated in their Lordships' opinions.

F

Leolin Price Q.C. and *Peter Langdon-Davies* for the landlords.
G. B. H. Dillon Q.C. and *Derek Wood Q.C.* for the tenant.

Their Lordships took time for consideration.

July 27. LORD SALMON. My Lords, this appeal raises an important
point of law relating to the degree of security of tenure which the   G
Agricultural Holdings Act 1948, as amended by the Agriculture Act
1958, affords a tenant farmer.

By a lease dated August 11, 1967, the present landlords' (the
appellants) predecessors in title granted to the tenant (the respondent)
a lease of Village Farm, Offchurch, Warwickshire (a farm of some 236
acres) for a term of 10 years from January 1, 1967. The rent was   H
£1,888 for the first three years of the term and £2,360 for the remainder
of the term subject to a rent review in respect of the last three years
of the term. Clause 27 of the lease reads as follows:

    " The tenant agrees to give possession of the whole of the farm to
    the landlords immediately upon the determination of the term
    hereby granted and not in any event to serve a counter-notice under
    section 24 (1) of the Agricultural Holdings Act 1948 or to take any

A   steps to claim the benefit of any statutory provision granting
     security of tenure which may be in force at the time of the
     determination thereof."

The clear intention of this clause was to deprive the tenant of the
security of tenure afforded him by the Act of 1948 or any other Act
which might be passed by Parliament for the protection of tenant
B   farmers.

     I must now set out the relevant parts of sections 3, 23 and 24 of
the Act. The result of this appeal depends entirely upon the true
construction of section 24 (1). Section 3:

     "(1) A tenancy of an agricultural holding for a term of two years
     or upwards shall, instead of terminating on the expiration of the
     term for which it was granted, continue (as from the expiration of
C   that term) as a tenancy from year to year, but otherwise on the
     terms of the original tenancy so far as applicable, unless, not less
     than one year nor more than two years before the date fixed for
     the expiration of the term, a written notice has been given by either
     party to the other of his intention to terminate the tenancy. (2)
     A notice given under the foregoing subsection shall be deemed,
D   for the purposes of this Act, to be a notice to quit. . . . (4) This
     section shall have effect notwithstanding any agreement to the
     contrary."

Section 23 (1):

     "A notice to quit an agricultural holding or part of an agricultural
     holding shall (notwithstanding any provision to the contrary in the
E   contract of tenancy of the holding) be invalid if it purports to
     terminate the tenancy before the expiration of 12 months from
     the end of the then current year of tenancy: . . ."

Section 24:

     "(1) Where notice to quit an agricultural holding or part of an
     agricultural holding is given to the tenant thereof, and not later
F   than one month from the giving of the notice to quit the tenant
     serves on the landlord a counter-notice in writing requiring that
     this subsection shall apply to the notice to quit, then, subject to the
     provisions of the next following subsection, the notice to quit shall
     not have effect unless the Agricultural Land Tribunal consents to
     the operation thereof. (2) The foregoing subsection shall not apply
     where— . . . (e) at the date of the giving of the notice to quit the
G   interest of the landlord in the agricultural holding to which the
     notice relates had been materially prejudiced by the commission
     by the tenant of a breach, which was not capable of being remedied,
     of any term or condition of the tenancy that was not inconsistent
     with the fulfilment by the tenant of his responsibilities to farm in
     accordance with the rules of good husbandry, and it is stated in the
H   notice that it is given by reason of the matter aforesaid; . . ."

     On November 27, 1975, the landlords served the tenant with a notice
under section 3 (1) of their intention to terminate his tenancy on
December 31, 1976. I will call this the first notice to quit. On
December 16, 1975, the tenant served the landlords with a counter-
notice under section 24 (1) requiring that that subsection should apply
to the first notice to quit so that that notice to quit should have no effect
unless the Agricultural Land Tribunal consented to its operation. On

Lord Salmon   **Johnson v. Moreton (H.L.(E.))**   **[1978]**

December 22, 1975, the landlords served the tenant with a second notice   A
to quit in precisely the same terms as the first notice save that it added:

> " And further take notice that this notice is given under section
> 24 (2) (*e*) [of the Act of 1948] for the following reasons:—that at
> the date of the giving of this notice the interest of the landlord . . .
> has been materially prejudiced by the commission by you, of a
> breach, which is not capable of being remedied, of a term or   B
> condition of the . . . lease . . . namely serving a counter-notice
> contrary to clause 27 of your . . . lease."

On December 23, 1975, the tenant served a notice on the landlords that
he wished to contest the reasons stated in their second notice to quit
and that he required that issue to be determined by arbitration under
the Act.

    An arbitrator was accordingly appointed; and the parties agreed   C
that he should state a special case for the opinion of the court.   The
question of law propounded in the special case was whether the reasons
stated in the landlords' notice of December 22, 1975, were good or not.
The special case was argued before Judge Harrison-Hall who in a full
and careful judgment held that the Act did not preclude the parties from
agreeing to exclude the operation of section 24 (1); and that accordingly   D
the tenant's counter-notice of December 16, 1975, which was in breach of
clause 27 of the lease, fell within section 24 (2) (*e*) and therefore the second
notice to quit was a valid notice which terminated the lease on December
31, 1976.   The tenant's appeal to the Court of Appeal was allowed and
the landlords now appeal from that decision to your Lordships' House.

    The case for the landlords and for the tenant has been argued with   E
outstanding ability by both leading and junior counsel.   The first, and
by far the most important question which arises is whether that part of
clause 27 of the lease which purports to exclude the tenant's right to
serve a counter-notice under section 24 (1) is enforceable.   The second
question, which arises only if the answer to the first question is in the
affirmative, is (a) whether the landlord has been materially prejudiced
by the service of the counter-notice and (b) whether the tenant's breach   F
of clause 27 of the lease by serving the counter-notice is capable of
being remedied.

    As to the first question, it has been rightly conceded on behalf of
the landlords that the first part of clause 27 of the lease which provides
that the tenant shall give the landlords possession of the whole farm on
December 31, 1977, and the third part of clause 27 which provides that   G
the tenant shall take no steps to secure the benefit of any future
statutory provision granting him security of tenure are each unenforceable.   The first part because it offends against section 3 of the Act and
the third part because it is contrary to public policy.   It has however
been strongly argued that the second part of clause 27 of the lease
which prohibits the service of a counter-notice is enforceable.   It, of
course, does not always necessarily follow that, because one can see   H
that most of an apple is rotten, there is no part of it which may be sound
and severable from the rest.

    The first point taken on behalf of the landlords is that what I have
called the second part of clause 27 is sound because there is nothing in
the Act of 1948 which expressly prohibits an agreement between a
landlord and tenant that the tenant shall not serve a counter-notice
under section 24 (1).   It has been pointed out that sections 3, 11, 15,

A 23, 65 and 77 of the Act have expressly excluded contracting out by some such words as " this section shall have effect notwithstanding any agreement to the contrary." The argument is that if that had been the intention of the legislature in relation to section 24 (1), why had similar words been omitted from that section? Sections 12 and 30 (2), however, expressly permit contracting out; and it might be argued why, if the legislature intended to permit contracting out in relation to section

B 24 (1) did it not expressly say so? In my opinion, neither of these arguments carries much weight: indeed, they cancel each other out. For the reasons I will presently explain, I think the answer to the argument formulated on behalf of the landlords is that the language of section 24 (1) as it stands, coupled with the policy of the Act, makes it crystal clear that prohibitory words, such as are incorporated in the

C six sections upon which the landlords rely, would be entirely otiose if included in section 24 (1).

The second point taken on behalf of the landlords relates to the sanctity of the freedom to contract and the sanctity of a contract once it has been made. I certainly do not wish to cast any doubt upon this sanctity. It does not, however, derogate from the power of Parliament to make certain contracts unenforceable; and there are many well

D known examples (which I need not recite) of statutes which have done so. The question here is—does section 24 (1) do so? We have been helpfully referred to all the authorities which could throw any light on this question. I doubt whether any of them except those which state or restate the familiar principles to be applied in construing statutes will further the argument very much one way or the other, for none of

E them concerns section 24 (1) nor any similar statutory provision.

The relevant principles of construction for construing section 24 (1) are:

1. "If the language of a statute be plain, admitting of only one meaning, the legislature must be taken to have meant and intended what it has plainly expressed, and whatever it has in clear terms enacted must be enforced though it should lead to absurd or mischievous result." *Vacher*

F *& Sons Ltd.* v. *London Society of Compositors* [1913] A.C. 107, *per* Lord Atkinson at p. 121.

2. The courts have no power to fill in a gap in a statute, even if satisfied that it had been overlooked by the legislature and that if the legislature had been aware of the gap, the legislature would have filled it in: *Gladstone* v. *Bower* [1960] 2 Q.B. 384; *Brandling* v. *Barrington* (1827)

G 6 B. & C. 467, *per* Lord Tenterden C.J. at p. 475. 3. If the words of a statute are capable, without being distorted, of more than one meaning, the courts should prefer the meaning which leads to a sensible and just result complying with the statutory objective and reject the meaning which leads to absurdity or injustice and is repugnant to the statutory objective: *River Wear Commissioners* v. *Adamson* (1877) 2 App.Cas. 743 *per* Lord Blackburn at p. 763; *Attorney-General* v. *Prince Ernest Augustus of*

H *Hanover* [1957] A.C. 436 *per* Viscount Simonds at p. 462; *Stock* v. *Frank Jones (Tipton) Ltd.* [1978] 1 W.L.R. 231 *per* Lord Simon of Glaisdale at p. 236.

I reject the argument that there is any gap in section 24 (1) notwithstanding that there are no words in the subsection expressly forbidding or permitting the parties to enter into an agreement which provides that no counter-notice shall be served by the tenant. In my opinion, the language of this subsection is capable of only one meaning—the

Lord Salmon   Johnson v. Moreton (H.L.(E.))   **[1978]**

meaning for which the tenant contends; and that meaning does not lead A
to any absurd or mischievous result but to a sensible and just result
which is consonant with the clear objective of the Act. If you carve
out of section 24 (1) the words:

> ". . . and not later than one month from the giving of the notice
> to quit the tenant serves on the landlord a counter-notice in writing
> requiring that this subsection shall apply to the notice to quit, . . ." B

you are left with the words:

> "Where notice to quit an agricultural holding or part of an
> agricultural holding is given to the tenant thereof, . . . then,
> subject to the provisions of the next following subsection, the notice
> to quit shall not have effect unless the Agricultural Land Tribunal
> consents to the operation thereof." C

In my opinion, these words are clearly mandatory and would make any
agreement to the contrary unenforceable. I cannot believe that the
words relating to the counter-notice were inserted into the subsection
with the intention or effect of stripping it of its mandatory character.
They were, in my opinion, inserted, as Mr. Wood so ably argued, in
order to save the time and money which would otherwise be wasted if D
every notice to quit an agricultural holding had to be submitted to the
Agricultural Land Tribunal for consent to its operation. It was
obviously foreseen that there might well be, as no doubt there are, a
substantial number of cases in which a tenant served with a notice to
quit is willing to go. If, however, he is unwilling to go, as I suspect he
is in the large majority of cases, he has only to serve a counter-notice E
within a month of the notice to quit; and then he cannot be ejected
without the consent of the Agricultural Land Tribunal. The Act gives
him a statutory option to decide at the time when he receives the notice
to quit whether or not he wants to leave the land. By that time he will
probably have had considerable experience of working the land and so
will be able to judge how best to make up his mind.

I do not consider that any question of implication arises in relation F
to section 24 (1). Its meaning is plain and unambiguous. It gives the
tenant a statutory option to be exercised within one month of receiving
a notice to quit. The option is to go voluntarily or to serve a counter-
notice and remain in possession unless the Agricultural Land Tribunal
exercises its very restricted powers of allowing the notice to quit to
become effective. The option cannot be exercised any sooner or any G
later than the subsection prescribes. Nor can it, in my view, be
renounced by the tenant in advance. The language of the section
makes this plain. Moreover the statutory option was conferred on
tenant farmers, not for their personal protection alone, but for the
public good.

I now pass to the policy or objective of the Act of 1948. Sections
3 and 23 of that Act (which I have recited earlier in this speech) intro- H
duced nothing new. They reproduced, in substance, sections 23 and 25 of
the Agricultural Holdings Act of 1923 (which was also a consolidation Act).
The protection afforded to tenants by these sections was no doubt quite
useful; but it was of no real significance when compared with the
immense protection conferred on tenant farmers by section 31 of that
Act, which in reality gave all tenant farmers who farmed their land
efficiently, complete security of tenure save in most exceptional circum-

A stances. That section was, in substance, reproduced by sections 24, 25 and the procedural section 26 of the Act of 1948.

Section 25 (as amended) enacted that the Agricultural Land Tribunal should consent to the operation of any notice to quit any agricultural holding only if the tribunal was satisfied that to consent would be in the interests of efficient farming, sound estate management, agricultural research, education and the like, or, in certain other circumstances,
B that greater hardship would be caused by the tribunal withholding than by granting its consent. The proviso to section 25, however, laid down that even if the tribunal was satisfied of the existence of any of the foregoing reasons for consenting to the operation of a notice to quit, it should nevertheless withhold its consent if, in all the circumstances, it appeared to the tribunal that a fair and reasonable landlord would not
C insist upon possession.

I have not thought it necessary to set out section 25 in detail. It is, however, I think quite plain from a summary of the section that, as a rule, a landlord would be faced with a most daunting task were he to attempt to obtain the tribunal's consent to the operation of a notice to quit.

During the last war, the submarine menace was such that it would
D have been virtually impossible to import into this country any more goods vital for our survival than we, in fact, did. Accordingly, it is extremely doubtful whether we could have survived had it not been for the food produced by our own farms. Even in 1947 when the Agriculture Act of that year was passed, food rationing was still in existence. It must have been clear to all that it was then and always
E would be of vital importance, both to the national economy and security, that the level of production and the efficiency of our farms should be maintained and improved. This could be achieved only by the skill and hard work of our farmers and the amount of their earnings which they were prepared to plough back into the land from which those earnings had been derived. A very large proportion of those farmers were tenant farmers. They were tenants because they did not have the
F necessary capital to buy land or they could not find any land which they wanted that was for sale—or for sale at a price which they could afford. In spite of section 23 and 25 of the Act of 1923 which had put them in a somewhat better position than did the common law, the sword of Damocles was always hanging over their heads. If they were tenants for a term of years, they might receive an effective notice to quit on the
G date when the term expired—and this term was rarely for more and usually for less than 10 years. If they were tenants from year to year, and very many of them were, they might in any year receive an effective notice to quit at the end of the next ensuing year. Accordingly there was no great inducement for these farmers to work as hard as they could, still less to plough money back into land which they knew they might well lose sooner or later.

H The security of tenure which tenant farmers were accorded by the Act of 1947 was not only for their own protection as an important section of the public, nor only for the protection of the weak against the strong; it was for the protection of the nation itself. This is why section 31 (1) of the Act of 1947, reproduced by section 24 (1) of the Act of 1948, gave tenant farmers the option to which I have referred and made any agreement to the contrary void. If any clause such as clause 27 was valid landlords might well insist upon a similar clause being

introduced into every lease; and prospective tenants, having no money   A
with which to buy the land they wanted to farm, would, in reality, have
had little choice but to agree. Accordingly if clause 27 is enforceable
the security of tenure which Parliament clearly intended to confer, and
did confer upon tenant farmers for the public good would have become
a dead letter.

There are two other factors which support the proposition that the
second part of clause 27 is clearly as unenforceable as the rest of that   B
clause. First, the Act of 1947 covered all leases whether made before
or after the passing of that Act. Those made before that date could not
have contained any clause similar to clause 27, unless landlords had the
gift of prophecy, because no such thing as a counter-notice to a notice
to quit then existed. To my mind, it is not feasible that Parliament
intended to give any less security of tenure to tenants who entered into   C
a lease after the date upon which the Act of 1947 came into operation
than it gave to tenants who had entered into a lease before that date.
Moreover section 8 of the Act of 1948, as amended by the Act of 1958,
amongst other things, gave the landlords the protection of having a rent
review by arbitration should there be a rise in the open market rent of
the land during the continuance of the tenancy. Secondly, it has been
acknowledged and indeed argued on behalf of the landlords that the   D
counter-notice served by the tenant on December 16, 1975, was an
effective counter-notice under section 24 (1), notwithstanding clause 27
of the lease; and this was the cornerstone of their case. It would be
strange indeed if a tenant by availing himself of a statutory provision
obviously designed to give him security of tenure, should be taking a
step which gave his landlord the right to eject him.   E

Having come to the conclusion that clause 27 of the lease was wholly
unenforceable, for the reasons I have stated, it is unnecessary for me to
express any opinion about the arguments addressed to this House concerning the true meaning of section 24 (2) (e) of the Act of 1948; and
I shall refrain from doing so. My Lords, I would dismiss the appeal
with costs.
                                                                          F

LORD HAILSHAM OF ST. MARYLEBONE. My Lords, approximately
nine out of ten appeals which come before your Lordships' House are
concerned with disputes about the correct construction of Acts of
Parliament. This appeal is concerned with the correct construction of
section 24 of the Agricultural Holdings Act 1948 as amended. In
particular it is concerned with the question whether, to what extent,   G
and in what sense it is permissible for the parties to an agricultural
tenancy to contract out of the provisions of section 24 (1) of that Act
in such a way as to prevent the tenant from serving under that section a
counter-notice making a notice to quit ineffective unless consented to
by the Agricultural Land Tribunal on one of the grounds sanctioned
under section 25 of the Act. Since the proceedings have taken a
somewhat tortuous course before reaching your Lordships' House it   H
will be convenient if I set out the facts and statutory provisions
applicable before dealing with the arguments.

By a lease dated August 11, 1967, the predecessors in title of the
appellants let to the respondent an agricultural holding in the county
of Warwick known as Village Farm. The lease was for 10 years
reckoned from January 1, 1967, so that, apart from any statutory provision to the contrary, the contractual tenancy would have ended on

A December 31, 1976. Clause 27 of the lease, with which alone we are concerned, was in somewhat unusual terms. It provided as follows:

> " The tenant agrees to give possession of the whole of the farm to the landlords immediately upon the determination of the term hereby granted and not in any event to serve a counter-notice under section 24 (1) of the Agricultural Holdings Act 1948 or to take any
B > steps to claim the benefit of any statutory provision granting security of tenure which may be in force at the time of the determination thereof."

On the face of it this clause which, as will be seen, consists of three possibly severable parts, was an open, not to say brazen, attempt to get round the provisions of the agricultural holdings legislation both as it
C had existed up to that point and as Parliament might enact it in the future at least so far as it provided security of tenure to the tenant.

The first part, which consisted of a covenant to give up possession on December 31, 1976, whilst not in itself illegal, is clearly displaced by section 3 of the Agricultural Holdings Act 1948. This section provides that notwithstanding any such clause instead of terminating on the expiration of the term, a tenancy of this length must operate as a
D tenancy from year to year unless terminated by a notice under section 3 (1) which, for the purposes of the Act, is deemed to be a notice to quit. In this case there is no difficulty or dispute about this since, in the events which happened, the appellants exercised their rights under section 3 (1) to regain possession of the holding on December 31, 1976, by notices dated November 27, 1975. These notices duly complied
E with the requirements of section 3 of the Act of 1948. The last limb of clause 27 purports to forbid the tenant to:

> ". . . claim the benefit of any statutory provision granting security of tenure which may be in force at the time of the determination of the tenancy."

This likewise gives no rise to difficulty or dispute. The appellants did
F not rely upon it and made no serious effort to defend it. It would appear to be an attempt on the part of the landlords to deprive the tenant of the benefit of any future Act of Parliament conferring security of tenure upon him. I would have thought that this part of the clause was clearly contrary to public policy and I confess to some surprise at seeing it embodied in a professionally drawn lease. For the purposes
G of this opinion I assume in the appellants' favour, without necessarily deciding, that this part of the clause is severable from the rest.

The controversy in the appeal revolves round the intermediate limb of clause 27, which, it will be remembered, enjoins the tenant " not in any event to serve a counter-notice under section 24 (1) of the Agricultural Holdings Act 1948. . . ." The controversy arises since this is precisely what the respondent did upon receipt of the appellants' notices
H of November 27, 1975, which purported to determine the tenancy on the original contractual date. On December 16, 1975, and despite clause 27, he served a counter-notice, which, apart from clause 27, complied exactly with the requirements of section 24 (1) of the Act. At this stage the appellants took what might at first sight seem an ingenious but surprising step. Despite clause 27 of the lease they did not challenge, and have never challenged, the validity of the respondent's counter-notice. Perhaps they were deterred by the express and seem-

ingly mandatory language of section 24 (1) itself, which it will be A
remembered as amended expressly provides:

> "Where notice to quit an agricultural holding or part of an
> agricultural holding is given to the tenant thereof, and not later
> than one month from the giving of the notice to quit the tenant
> serves on the landlord a counter-notice in writing requiring that this
> subsection shall apply to the notice to quit, then, subject to the
> provisions of the next following subsection, the notice to quit
> shall not have effect unless the Agricultural Land Tribunal consents
> to the operation thereof."

B

Instead of claiming that the respondent's counter-notice was invalid as
contrary to his obligations under clause 27 of the lease, the appellants
themselves made use of the machinery of section 24 (2) of the Act to C
which, as will be observed, section 24 (1) is expressly made subject.
On December 22, 1975, the appellants served fresh notices to quit on
the same date as that prescribed by the original notices. These fresh
notices were based on the assertion, that by serving his counter-notice
under section 24 (1), the respondent had broken a term or condition of
the tenancy which was not capable of being remedied and which
had materially affected the appellants' interest in the holding. In D
other words they claimed that, in spite of the fact that the counter-notice
was effective to achieve the purposes of section 24 (1), the respondent
had deprived himself of the right to the security conferred upon him by
that section by the very act of claiming it, since this act on his part was
itself a breach of clause 27 of the lease. In order to achieve this object
it was necessary for the appellants to invoke the aid of section 24 (2) (e)
of the Act of 1948. This subsection provides:

E

> " (2) The foregoing subsection " (viz section 24 (1)) " shall not apply
> where— . . . (e) at the date of the giving of the notice to quit the interest
> of the landlord in the agricultural holding to which the notice relates
> had been materially prejudiced by the commission by the tenant of
> a breach, which was not capable of being remedied, of any term or
> condition of the tenancy that was not inconsistent with the fulfilment F
> by the tenant of his responsibilities to farm in accordance with the
> rules of good husbandry, and it is stated in the notice that it is given
> by reason of the matter aforesaid; . . ."

The appellants' new notices of December 22, 1975, so far as form goes
complied with the requirements of section 24 (2) (a) and were in the
following terms:

G

> " . . . We hereby give you notice that the said Caroline Anne John-
> son and Henry Leslie Johnson intend to terminate the tenancy of
> the holding known as Village Farm, Offchurch, which you hold of
> them under a lease dated August 11, 1967, and made between
> Graham Stanley Pearson and John Davenport Siddeley Ainscow as
> landlords and yourself as tenant on December 31, 1976, being the H
> date fixed by the said lease for the expiration of the term thereby
> granted. And further take notice that this notice is given under
> section 24 (2) (e) of the Agricultural Holdings Act 1948 for the
> following reasons: —that at the date of the giving of this notice the
> interest of the landlords in the above mentioned holding has been
> materially prejudiced by the commission by you of a breach, which
> is not capable of being remedied, of a term or condition of the said

A   lease being a term or condition which is not inconsistent with the
fulfilment of your responsibilities to farm in accordance with the
rules of good husbandry, namely serving a counter-notice contrary to
clause 27 of your said lease
" Dated this 22nd day of December 1975."

The appellants therefore claim that by their second notice they had
B   successfully by-passed the security of tenure conferred by section 24 (1),
since they had successfully invoked section 24 (2) which over-rides
section 24 (1).   On receipt of this second series of notices the respondent
then invoked the arbitration machinery provided under the Act by the
Agriculture (Notices to Remedy and Notices to Quit) Order 1964 (S.I.
1964 No. 706) stating that he wished to contest the reasons in the
appellants' second series of notices and required the question to be
C   determined by arbitration under the Act.   This he did by a series of
notices dated December 23, 1975.   At this point the stately minuet
of notices and counter-notices comes to an end and the question of the
validity of the appellants' second series of notices was duly referred
under the Act and Order to the arbitration of Mr. E. G. Righton, M.C.,
F.R.I.C.S.   Since the question is purely one of law the arbitrator duly
D   stated a question for the opinion of the court in the form of a special
case.   The sole question he stated for the opinion of the court was
" whether, on the agreed facts of this case the said reason (viz. that
stated in the appellants' notices of December 22, 1975) is good or not."
This is the only question to be determined by your Lordships.

Thus the matter came before the courts.   On October 13, 1976,
E   Judge Harrison-Hall, sitting in the Warwick County Court, decided the
question in favour of the appellants.   After a hearing lasting three days,
the Court of Appeal (Megaw, Lawton and Geoffrey Lane L.JJ.) reversed
the decision of the county court judge and gave a unanimous judgment
in favour of the respondent. By leave of your Lordships' House the appellants now appear before the House of Lords asking your Lordships to
restore the order of the county court judge.

F   In my opinion, although I would prefer to formulate my reasons in
my own terms rather than in those of the judgment of the Court of
Appeal, the appeal fails and should be dismissed.   In doing so I rely
solely on the construction of the Agricultural Holdings Act 1948 viewed
as a whole, and in particular on the wording of section 24 (1) of the
Act.   This Act is a consolidating Act to which the observations of a
G   majority of your Lordships in Farrell v. Alexander [1977] A.C. 59,
72 (Lord Wilberforce), 82 (Lord Simon of Glaisdale) and 97 (Lord
Edmund-Davies) clearly apply.   Even if I were not bound by these
observations I would respectfully agree with them.   In my view the
whole purpose of consolidation would be defeated if they were not
observed and rigidly adhered to or if endeavours were made to split the
various components of the consolidation Act apart and construe them
H   by reference to their individual histories.   If, in the course of these
remarks, I refer to the history of the legislation before and after 1948
it is not in order to construe the words of the Act, which, as will be seen,
are in my view unambiguous as they stand, but simply to place them in
their proper historical and social context as at 1948.   In doing so I am
only observing the wise counsel of Viscount Simonds in Attorney-
General v. Prince Ernest Augustus of Hanover [1957] A.C. 436, 461,
when he said:

"... words, and particularly general words, cannot be read in   A
isolation: their colour and content are derived from their context.
So it is that I conceive it to be my right and duty to examine
every word of a statute in its context, and I use 'context' in its
widest sense, which I have already indicated as including not only
other enacting provisions of the same statute, but its preamble,
the existing state of the law, other statutes in pari materia, and
the mischief which I can, by those and other legitimate means,   B
discern the statute was intended to remedy."

This is also entirely in conformity with the observations of Lord Simon
of Glaisdale in *Farrell* v. *Alexander* [1977] A.C. 59, 84.

Appellants' counsel founded their well reasoned, lucid and persuasive
arguments on three propositions, each unassailable, and for each of   C
which they found no difficulty in discovering authority. The first is the
undoubted silence of section 24 (1) on the question of contracting out.
In itself this silence is neutral, but, as they pointed out, there are sections
of the Act of 1948 which expressly prohibit, exclude or displace, contrary agreement. Such sections include sections 3, 11, 15, 23, 65 and
77 and appellants' counsel invited the inference that had the prohibition
of contracting out in any form been contemplated a similar clause   D
would have been inserted in section 24. The argument would be even
more persuasive were there not other sections, for instance, sections 2,
8, 13, 17 which are silent on the question of contracting out, one at least
of which, namely section 2, must be prohibitory, and others which are
expressly permissive of contracting out, e.g. section 12, section 30 (2).
This must indicate that mere silence is not necessarily conclusive.

  E

The second proposition is that it is the policy and presumption of
English and other systems of law that there should be freedom of contract and that contracts freely entered into should be enforceable. The
appellants found no difficulty in adducing authority for this proposition,
embellished, and perhaps even reinforced, but hardly improved, by trans-
lating it into Latin and saying: "pacta sunt servanda." See for
instance *Griffiths* v. *Earl of Dudley* (1882) 9 Q.B.D. 357; *Hunt* v. *Hunt*   F
(1862) 4 De G. F. & J. 221; *Hyman* v. *Hyman* [1929] A.C. 601 and
Kennedy v. *Johnstone* 1956 S.C. 39, especially *per* Lord Sorn. I myself
share the doubts of Lord Wright in *Admiralty Commissioners* v. *Valverda*
(Owners) [1938] A.C. 173, 185 as to whether the first of these cases was
correctly decided; the point is now academic and cannot be tested since
the Employers Liability Act 1880 is now past history. But of the   G
general principle there can hardly be controversy.

The third proposition is that a person may renounce a right which
exists solely for his own use or benefit. This again is not improved by
legal Latin cant and saying "cuilibet licet" (or "quilibet potest")
"renuntiare" (or "renunciare") "juri" (or "jure") "pro se introducto" as have numerous authorities, including the county court judge
in the present issue, or the transcriber of his judgment, with varying   H
degrees of deviation from correct Latin grammar and orthography. But
it is undoubtedly good law where, as Lord Westbury said in *Hunt* v.
Hunt, 4 De G. F. & J. 221, the right in question is "nothing ... more than
a private remedy and a private right." See also *Mears* v. *Callender*
[1901] 2 Ch. 388, as to which, however, I have some doubt, under the
then agricultural holdings legislation, and *Premier Dairies* v. *Garlick*
[1920] 2 Ch. 17, when, as counsel for the respondent pointed out, the

The Weekly Law Reports, October 13, 1978

551

3 W.L.R.   Johnson v. Moreton (H.L.(E.))   Lord Hailsham of
                       St. Marylebone

A statutory scheme was different in some important respects. The key however to the interpretation of the maxim lies, as Lord Simon of Glaisdale pointed out in *National Westminster Bank Ltd.* v. *Halesowen Presswork & Assemblies Ltd.* [1972] A.C. 785, 808 in discovering whether the particular liberty or right conferred by the statute or rule of law is entirely for the benefit of the person purporting to renounce it. If there is a public as well as a private interest a contrary Latin
B maxim applies.

In the course of their arguments, counsel for the appellants candidly accepted that there must be certain exceptions to these general principles. The main example of these was when the terms of the enactment under consideration was sufficiently explicit and unqualified to render an agreement contracting out of the statute impossible, inappropriate or
C inconsistent with the policy of the Act. I shall come to the policy of the Act in a moment, but in the meantime there is a clear argument on the phraseology of section 24 (1) of the Act of 1948 which would seem at first sight to bring the terms of the section within the exception. The subsection says that IF a proper counter-notice is given by the tenant the notice to quit SHALL NOT have effect, unless the consent pro-cedure is complied with. Nothing could be more explicit or mandatory
D than the words SHALL NOT in the above section, and it sounded somewhat strange on the lips of appellants' counsel to reply to this criticism that these words followed only on the " if " clause which it was argued left the service of the counter-notice solely within the discre-tion of the tenant. The argument a silentio, if it applies at all, should cut both ways. The section appears to say explicitly that if certain
E events happen certain legal consequences must follow.

It seems to me that the whole validity of the appellants' argument depends upon their being able to establish, to borrow the words of Lord Westbury in *Hunt* v. *Hunt,* 4 De G. F. & J. 221 that the remedy and right conferred on the tenant by section 24 (1) of the Act of 1948 is " *nothing . . . more* than a private remedy and a private right," (my italics),
F or, to use the phrase of Lord Simon of Glaisdale quoted above that the pro-cedure prescribed by section 24 (1) is one *entirely* in the favour of a particular tenant, without any element of public policy. (The emphasis in each case is mine.) I myself am satisfied that this is not so on at least two separate but closely connected heads. The first is the nature of farming itself. At least since the 1880's successive Parliaments have considered the fertility of the land and soil of England and the proper
G farming of it as something more than a private interest. Fertility is not something built up as the result of a mere six months' activity on the part of a cultivator, which was all the period of notice given by the common law to the individual farming tenant, by whom in the main the land of England was cultivated then, as now, mainly under a yearly tenancy. It takes years (sometimes generations) of patient and self-
H abnegating toil and investment to put heart into soil, to develop and gain the advantage of suitable rotations of crops, and to provide proper drains, hedges and ditches. Even to build up a herd of dairy cattle, between whose conception and first lactation at least three years must elapse, takes time and planning, whilst to disperse the work of a lifetime of careful breeding is but the task of an afternoon by a qualified auctioneer. Even within the space of a single year the interval between seed time and harvest, between expenditure and return with all the divers

dangers and chances of weather, pest or benignity of climate is sufficient   A
to put an impecunious but honest cultivator at risk without adding to his
problems any uncertainty as to his next year's tenure. At first Parliament was concerned simply with compensation for cultivation, manuring
and improvement. But it never regarded these as matters simply for
private contract, or something wholly unconnected with any public
interest. From the first, Parliament was concerned with the management of the soil, the land of England which had grown gradually into   B
its present fertility by the toil of centuries of husbandmen and estate
owners. By the 1920's Parliament similarly concerned itself with the
length of notice to which the yearly tenant was entitled. Such provisions are now to be found in sections 3 and 23 of the Act of 1948.
But they date from this time. In 1947 a new and momentous step
was taken. The landlord's notice to quit, save in certain specified   C
instances, was at the option of the tenant to be subject to consent, at
first of the Minister, but latterly of a quasi-judicial tribunal, the Agricultural Land Tribunal, whose jurisdiction clause 27 of this lease seeks
by its express terms to eliminate and oust. Even the consent of the
Agricultural Land Tribunal is carefully regulated by section 25 of
the Act of 1948 (consolidating and amending the 1947 provisions). The
circumstances in which its consent may be accorded are thus defined   D
and limited by objective and justiciable criteria. These are not simply
matters of private contracts from which the landlord can stipulate that
the tenant can deprive himself as if it were a " jus pro se introductum."
It is a public interest introduced for the sake of the soil and husbandry
of England of which both landlord and tenant are in a moral, though
not of course a legal, sense the trustees for posterity. Silence is not an   E
argument, particularly when the words are prima facie mandatory, for
excusing a term in a contract introduced for the purpose of annulling
the protection given to the tenant by section 24.

But there is another ground, closely related to the first, for disagreeing with the appellants' contention. It is not only the tenants of
agricultural holdings that Parliament has increasingly sought to protect
by statute from an improvident use of their contractual powers. The   F
policy of the law has been repeatedly used to protect the weaker of two
parties who do not contract from bargaining positions of equal strength.
The protection given to minors by the courts is, of course, immemorial
but has been reinforced by statute. The exigencies of war have provided
a whole bundle of interferences with contractual obligations, and these
have often developed into permanent features of peacetime legislation.   G
The rent restrictions Act are an example. We were referred to the
momentous decision of Astbury J., under the Act of 1915, in *Artizans,
Labourers & General Dwellings Co.* v. *Whitaker* [1919] 2 K.B. 301,
304, subsequently embodied by Parliament in the Act of 1920. The
reasoning of Astbury J.'s judgment was accepted as valid generally in
the rather different case of *Bowmaker Ltd.* v. *Tabor* [1941] 2 K.B. 1,
7, 20, to which I will shortly make reference.   H

There was also the line of cases beginning with *Salford Guardians* v.
Dewhurst [1926] A.C. 619, especially *per* Lord Cave at pp. 624 and 625
(based on a statutory pensions scheme) which fortified the robust treatment by Farwell J. of the war time emergency legislation of 1939 in
Soho Square Syndicate Ltd. v. *E. Pollard & Co.* [1940] Ch. 638,
644, 645. Farwell J.'s reasoning was subsequently endorsed by the
Court of Appeal in *Bowmaker Ltd.* v. *Tabor* [1941] 2 K.B. 1. These

A last two decisions were all the more striking in view of what had been
the contrary attitude of the courts during the currency of comparable
provisions of the 1914–18 emergency legislation. Farwell J. made short
work of the earlier decisions in the light of subsequent economic and
social developments between the wars and in so doing he was supported
by an experienced Court of Appeal. The truth is that it can no longer
be treated as axiomatic that, in the absence of explicit language, the
B courts will permit contracting out of the provisions of an Act of
Parliament where that Act, though silent as to the possibility of contracting out, nevertheless is manifestly passed for the protection of a
class of persons who do not negotiate from a position of equal strength,
but in whose well being there is a public as well as a private interest.
Such acts are not necessarily to be treated as simply " jus pro se intro-
C ductum," a " private remedy and a private right " which an individual
member of the class may simply bargain away by reason of his freedom
of contract. It is precisely his weakness as a negotiating party from
which Parliament wishes to protect him. See also per Lord Simon of
Glaisdale in National Westminster Bank Ltd. v. Halesowen Presswork &
Assemblies Ltd. [1972] A.C. 785, 808 in his treatment of the Latin maxim
as cited in Broom, Legal Maxims, to which I have already referred. I
D would not have it supposed that the examples I have given of the policy of
recent Parliaments to limit freedom of contract in the interest of the
weaker party to contracts of a particular class are limited to the
examples I have given. Almost every session of Parliament provides
fresh examples in the field, for instance, of consumer protection, or
employer and employee. I have limited myself, however, to classes of
E legislation, examples of which were cited in argument in the instant
case. It is not for the courts to decide whether the policy underlying
these statutes is always wise or productive of the results intended. The
point is that, once the court has identified the point of such legislation,
it should be cautious about permitting " contracting out."

I have however a certain reluctance in this case to use the phrase
" contracting out " without some further qualification. This is because
F there is clear authority that, whilst a purely executory contract to contract out of statutory provisions may be unenforceable for the reasons
stated above, an executed agreement for good consideration which has
been executed by the weaker party may none the less be enforceable
against the stronger. See for instance the distinction drawn between
Barton v. Fincham [1921] 2 K.B. 291, especially at p. 297: and Rajen-
G back v. Mamon [1955] 1 Q.B. 283. I see no reason why this reasoning should not apply to contracts under section 24 of the Agricultural
Holdings Act 1948 and there may be many other cases where the same
distinction applies.

At the end of the day I feel convinced that to allow this appeal
would be, adopting the phrase used in some of the authorities, to permit
section 24 of the Act of 1948, which was designed in the public interest
H to give the agricultural tenant security of tenure, and for a generation
has been thought appropriate to do so, to become a dead letter. If
the appellants are right there is no reason why a clause 27 should not
be written into every agricultural lease. Admittedly if this were a
genuine casus omissus by Parliament as in Gladstone v. Bower [1960]
2 Q.B. 384, we should have no alternative but to say so. In that event
we should have to adopt the carefree attitude of the Mikado in the
Gilbert and Sullivan opera:

Johnson v. Moreton (H.L.(E.))   [1978]

"That's the slovenly way in which these Acts are always drawn. A
However, cheer up, it'll be all right. I'll have it altered next
session. Now, let's see about your execution—will after luncheon
suit you? Can you wait till then?"

But despite the argument delivered in reply by appellants' counsel I do
not regard the salutary observations of Lord Simon of Glaisdale or
Lord Scarman in *Stock* v. *Frank Jones (Tipton) Ltd.* [1978] 1 W.L.R. B
231 as an invitation to take such a course. Before the courts adopt the
somewhat cavalier attitude of Gilbert's Mikado, they would be well
advised to consider whether Parliament, or its experienced drafting
counsel, have been quite so slovenly as the draftsman in the opera. In
my opinion in this case at least they have not. It may well be that
the historical origins of the different sections of the consolidating Act
have something to do with the draftsman's silence, but I am inclined to C
think that the true explanation is that he regarded section 24 as
something outside the terms of any agreement altogether, but as a
necessary part of a procedure designed to initiate the consent jurisdiction, at first of the Minister and latterly of the Agricultural Land
Tribunal, who are bound by the terms embodied in section 25 of the Act
in order to guarantee the tenant security of tenure. In any event my D
opinion is that the terms of section 24 are sufficiently unqualified as to
render nugatory any clause in the lease which runs counter to them.
The silence in section 24 as to the possibility of contracting out is thus
explained by the simple fact that the section is plainly mandatory in its
effect and an express prohibition unnecessary. If a counter-notice is
given, certain consequences are prescribed by law to follow and one of
them is that the matter has to be decided by the Agricultural Land E
Tribunal in accordance with the objective criteria contained in section
25 of the Act. The service of the counter-notice is not a part of the
tenancy agreement on whose terms the parties are free to contract but
a means by which the tenant may invoke a quasi-judicial proceeding
before a tribunal on a matter in which it is thought by Parliament to
be in the interest of the public and not merely of the individual to F
enforce his security of tenure and limit the landlord's right of possession.
It follows that an agreement to oust the jurisdiction of the tribunal by
prohibiting the tenant from initiating the proceeding before it is contrary
to public policy, like any other agreement the purpose of which is to
oust the jurisdiction of a court. To use the words of the authorities
relevant to this case, to argue otherwise would be to make the Act a
dead letter. Since it follows from what I have said that the appeal G
should be dismissed with costs, it is not necessary to consider the other
ingenious, logical and particular arguments by which the parties sought
to illustrate or enforce their conclusions. I would not, however, think
that these are necessarily without weight, and what weight they have
lies in the same scale as my main conclusion. If the tenant can contract
out of exercising his right of counter-notice under section 24 (1), can H
the landlord equally contract out of exercising his rights or any of them
under section 24 (2)? If he is so entitled and breaks such a contract,
what remedy has the tenant? Is there a logical contradiction in the
argument of the landlord that the tenant can lose his right under section
24 (1) by the very act of asserting it? If I had come to a different conclusion on the main issue, I believe that the least I could have done
would have been to face some of the above difficulties. As I have not

A come to a different conclusion they are not difficulties, for such questions
   do not arise. Thus, in the result, the appeal should be dismissed with
   costs because clause 27 of the lease between the parties is as unenforceable in its intermediate limb as in the other two.

       LORD SIMON OF GLAISDALE. My Lords, this appeal raises an
   important point relating to such security of tenure as was accorded to
B agricultural tenants by the Agricultural Holdings Act 1948—in effect,
   whether such security may be excluded by the terms of the lease. In
   order to understand the facts which raise the issues in this appeal, it is
   convenient first to set out or refer to certain relevant statutory provisions.
   The 1948 statute was a consolidation Act. Any provision in it must
   therefore be construed in the context of the whole of the statute in which
C it now stands (Farrell v. Alexander [1977] A.C. 59); though it is
   legitimate (indeed, incumbent) to investigate the statutory history in so
   far as that throws light on the objective of a particular provision (at p.
   84); the ascertainment of the parliamentary objective is an important—
   generally, an essential—part of the process of statutory interpretation. I
   cite the Act of 1948 as it now stands, having been subsequently amended.
D Section 1 defines " agricultural holding." Section 2 places restrictions
   on letting agricultural land for less than from year to year. It re-enacts
   a provision originally introduced into the code in order to prevent
   obviation (by the device of a tenancy for 364 days) of provisions (now
   sections 3 and 23 of the Act of 1948) enacted for the protection and
   benefit of tenants of agricultural holdings. His Lordship read sections
   3 (1) (2) (4), 23 (1), 24 (1) (2) (e) (see ante, pp. 541B–H) and section 25 (1),
E which provided:

       " 25 (1) The Agricultural Land Tribunal shall consent under
       the last foregoing section to the operation of a notice to quit an
       agricultural holding or part of an agricultural holding if, but only
       if, they are satisfied as to one or more of the following matters,
       being a matter or matters specified by the landlord in his application
F   for their consent, that is to say—(a) that the carrying out of the
       purpose for which the landlord proposes to terminate the tenancy
       is desirable in the interests of good husbandry as respects the land
       to which the notice relates, treated as a separate unit; or . . ."

   His Lordship continued: Section 27 provides for applications for certificates of bad husbandry for purposes of notices to quit. Subsequent sections
G provide elaborately for compensation, notably on the termination of the
   tenancy in the interest of the tenant for improvements effected by him,
   though also in the interest of the landlord for deterioration of the holding.
       Section 3 of the Act of 1948 corresponds to section 23 of the
   Agricultural Holdings Act 1923, itself a consolidation Act. Section 23
   of the Act of 1948 corresponds to section 25 of the Act of 1923. Sections
H 24 and 25 of the Act of 1948 are provisions taken from the Agricultural
   Holdings Act 1947, which, in section 11 (still unrepealed), describes what
   is meant by good husbandry. Sections 3 and 23 of the Act of 1948,
   deriving from the Act of 1923, make some modification of contractual
   terms in agricultural tenancies. But it was in 1947 that the profound
   revolution was carried out (by what is now sections 24 and 25 of the
   Act of 1948) which conferred security of tenure on agricultural tenants.
   This was done by meshing the machinery of sections 24 and 25 into that

of sections 3 and 23. Whatever the contractual terms of the tenancy, **A** the landlord had to serve a 12 months' notice to quit. The tenant could then serve a counter-notice; and, on his doing so, he could only be dispossessed after the matter was considered by (now) an Agricultural Land Tribunal; and the tribunal could only give effect to the notice to quit on certain specified and narrow grounds, of which the most material for instant purposes relates to good husbandry.

The material facts giving rise to the present appeal are as follows. **B** An agricultural holding was let by the predecessors in title of the appellants to the respondent by a lease dated August 11, 1967, for a term of 10 years from January 1, 1967. By clause 27 of the lease the respondent covenanted:

> ". . . to give possession of the whole of the farm to the landlords immediately upon the determination of the term hereby granted / and **C** not in any event to serve a counter-notice under section 24 (1) of the Agricultural Holdings Act 1948 / or to take any steps to claim the benefit of any statutory provision granting security of tenure which may be in force at the time of the determination thereof."

(I have divided the clause into its three limbs by inserting oblique strokes.) **D** On November 27, 1975, the appellants gave the respondent a notice (" the first notice ") to terminate the tenancy on December 31, 1976, " being the date fixed by the said lease for the expiration of the term thereby granted," pursuant to the provisions of section 3 of the Act of 1948. On December 16, 1975, the respondent served counter-notices on the appellants requiring section 24 (1) of the Act to apply to the first notice. Since the first notice could not thereafter take effect unless an Agri- **E** cultural Land Tribunal consented thereto, the appellants served on December 22, 1975, a fresh notice to quit on December 31, 1976 (" the second notice "). The second notice was stated to be served for the reasons specified in section 24 (2) (*e*) of the Act of 1948. The breach relied on in the second notice was the service of the counter-notices in response to the first notice, being an alleged breach of clause 27 of the **F** lease. (It will be noted that the first notice was served in time to allow service of a second 12-month notice to quit on December 31, 1976.) On December 23, 1975, the respondent notified the appellants that he required the validity of the second notice to be referred to arbitration in accordance with the provisions of the Act. The facts being agreed and the arbitrator being faced with a pure question of law, he stated a special case for the opinion of the court. On October 13, 1976, **G** Judge Harrison-Hall delivered a reserved judgment. He had to answer two questions. The first was whether the provisions of clause 27 of the lease were void and/or illegal on the ground that they were contrary to public policy and/or the provisions of the Agricultural Holdings Act 1948 and therefore unenforceable against the tenant. The second was whether, assuming the provisions of clause 27 were valid, **H** the service of the counter-notices was such as to be a breach within the meaning of section 24 (1) (*e*) of the Act. The judge answered both questions in favour of the instant appellants. The Court of Appeal reversed him on both issues. The appellants now appeal to your Lordships. In order to succeed the appellants must make good their contention on both issues: the second does not arise if the appellants fail on the first. I therefore turn to consider the first issue.

A   The first limb of clause 27 is admittedly invalid by reason of section 3 of the Act of 1948. The last limb is also invalid; since it would preclude the tenant from claiming the benefit of any statutory provision granting security of tenure, even though the statute might say that no such claim could be excluded by contract. The issue in this appeal is whether the middle limb was a term which could be validly made and enforced. The case has throughout been argued on the assumption
B   that the middle limb is severable.

The appellants rely on the principle of law expressed in the maxim Quilibet potest renunciare juri pro se introducto (" Anyone may, at his pleasure, renounce the benefit of a stipulation or other right introduced entirely in his own favour "): see *Broom's Legal Maxims,* 10th ed. (1939), p. 477. The right to serve a counter-notice was, the appellants argue, a
C   statutory provision entirely in favour of the agricultural tenant—it is completely up to him whether or not he serves a counter-notice—and he can therefore contract not to do so. (In argument this has been referred to as " contracting out of the statute." But this may be a little misleading; since if *Barton* v. *Fincham* [1921] 2 K.B. 291 was correctly decided—as to which I feel some reservation—it suggests that even though
D   a covenant not to take advantage of a statutory provision for security of tenure cannot be enforced as an executory contract, if it is executed and specific consideration has been given for the covenant—in that case a sum of money paid to the tenant specifically for the obligation not to claim security of tenure by virtue of the statute in question there—a court would give effect to the covenant. But the phrase " contracting out " is convenient; and, having noted this possible qualification, I shall
E   myself continue to use it hereafter.)

The appellants claim that the applicability of the maxim Quilibet, etc., is reinforced by the fact that other provisions than section 24 (1) of the Act specifically exclude contracting out: see, for example, sections 3 (4), 11 (1), 23 (1), 65 (1). If Parliament had intended to exclude contracting out of section 24 (1) also, it would equally have so provided
F   specifically, it was argued. I turn to this argument before dealing with the general applicability of the maxim. It is, in my view, cancelled out by two considerations. First, in certain other sections of the Act there is express provision that there may be contracting out of the statutory provision—see, e.g., sections 12 (1) and 16 (3). It can therefore be argued with matching cogency that, if Parliament had intended to permit contracting out of section 24 (1) also, it would equally have so
G   provided specifically. Secondly, section 2, an anti-evasion provision which I have already summarised, is undoubtedly unsusceptible of contracting out, though it has no express provision to that effect. I return therefore to consider the applicability of the maxim Quilibet, etc., in a context which provides neither reinforcement nor contra-indication.

The maxim exemplifies Maine's famous observation (*Ancient Law*
H   (1861), 1st ed. (Chapter 5) that the movement of progressive societies had thitherto been a movement from status to contract—that is, from on the one hand societies where legal relationships between persons arise from their membership of classes to which the law ascribes peculiar rights and obligations, capacities and incapacities, to on the other hand societies where those relationships arise from private agreements between the parties which will be enforced by the law. It was natural for Maine, writing in the middle of the 19th century, to discern such a movement.

The laisser-faire laisser-aller ideology was dominant. Human felicity, A
it was argued, was best promoted by leaving to every person to seek
his own maximum advantage in competition with his fellows. A free
market—including a free labour market—would ensure that the individual's effort was directed to anticipating and satisfying with maximum efficiency the wants of his fellows. The most powerful motive
force in the universe—man's pursuit of his own interest—would thus be
harnessed to drive a whole society forward. " Man's selfishness is God's B
providence," they said.

     The development of the law, as so often, reflected the dominant
ideology. Freedom and sanctity of contract tended to be considered as
pre-eminent legal values. It is unnecessary to expatiate after Dicey's
classic study: it is sufficient to note, for example, Equity's increasing
reluctance to relieve against contractual forfeitures (cf. *Sanders* v. *Pope* C
(1806) 12 Ves.Jr. 282 with *Hill* v. *Barclay* (1811) 18 Ves.Jr. 56 and the
latter's evolution to produce *Barrow* v. *Isaacs & Son* [1891] 1 Q.B.
417), and Sir George Jessel M.R.'s representative pronouncement in
Printing and Numerical Registering Co. v. *Sampson* (1875) L.R. 19 Eq.
462, 465:

     " . . . if there is one thing which more than another public policy D
     requires it is that men of full age and competent understanding
     shall have the utmost liberty of contracting, and that their contracts
     when entered into freely and voluntarily shall be held sacred and
     shall be enforced by courts of justice."

But well within the lifetimes of Maine and Jessel the ideology which lay
behind their juristic views was questioned. By some it was directly E
attacked: society's objective should be not wealth but welfare (with the
implication that the pursuit and achievement of wealth were destructive
of welfare), which was best promoted by the direct intervention of the
organs of the state and could not be left to the bargain of the
marketplace. " Competition " came to have the cliché " cut-throat "
attached to it. Others, more subtly, argued that, for the laisser-faire F
system to work felicitously as claimed, there must be a genuinely free,
open and abundant market in which there is equality of bargaining
power—equality of knowledge of the market and of staying-power in
holding out for a bargain: this called for at least a limited intervention
by the state to prevent or counteract rigging of the market by monopolies
or oligopolies and to redress inequalities of bargaining power. And
consonantly, even in the 19th century, the law began to back-pedal. G
The maxim Quilibet, etc., was held to be inapplicable to a matter in
which the public had an interest (*Graham* v. *Ingleby* (1848) 1 Exch. 651,
per Pollock C.B. at p. 655, per Parke B. at pp. 656–657, per Alderson B.
at p. 657 " . . . an individual cannot waive a matter in which the public
have an interest," Platt B. concurring: and see also *National Westminster
Bank Ltd.* v. *Halesowen Presswork & Assemblies Ltd.* [1972] A.C. 785, H
808): it was apparently no longer accepted by the law that freedom and
sanctity of contract were conclusive of the public interest.

     There was one economic and social relationship where it was claimed
that there were palpably lacking the prerequisites for the beneficent
operation of laisser-faire—that of landlord and tenant. The market
was limited and sluggish: the supply of land could not expand immediately and flexibly in response to demand, and even humble dwellings

A took more time to erect than those in want of them could spare. Generally, a man became a tenant rather than an owner-occupier because his circumstances compelled him to live hand-to-mouth; the landlord's purse was generally longer and his command of knowledge and counsel far greater than the tenant's. In short, it was held, the constriction of the market and the inequality of bargaining power enabled the landlord to dictate contractual terms which did not necess-
B arily operate to the general benefit of society. It was to counteract this descried constriction of the market and to redress this descried inequality of bargaining power that the law—specifically, in the shape of legislation—came to intervene repeatedly to modify freedom of contract between landlord and tenant. Since Maine the movement of many " progressive " societies has been reversed. The holding of a
C statutory or a protected tenancy is rather a status than a pure creature of contract. The Agricultural Holdings Act 1948 exemplifies such legis-lative activity specifically where the tenancy is of agricultural land.

The movement from status to contract was largely a creature of the common law. The reverse movement has been largely a creature of legislation. As a result lawyers sometimes tend to regard freedom and
D sanctity of contract as still of special and supervening juristic value. But freedom of contract and its consequences are quite likely to be " mischiefs " as that word is used in statutory construction. Courts of law do not nowadays hold themselves out to judge public policy in the light of ideologies. But since statutory construction almost always calls for consideration of the statutory objective, it is incumbent to hold in mind the palpable objective of section 24 (1)—namely, to vouchsafe
E to the good tenant-husbandman a security of tenure which went beyond the lease he had bargained for. Can he nevertheless bargain by the lease that he shall not lose that security? The Court of Appeal noted the paradox of answering Yes. They said:

"... is the Act to be read as permitting its general purpose of overriding a contractual provision for a fixed term itself to be
F overridden by another contractual provision?"

But the fixed term is not statutorily overridden if a notice to quit is served: section 3. In the instant case a notice to quit *was* served. That notice to quit would be effective in the absence of a counter-notice. Had the respondent validly bound himself not to serve a counter-notice?
G There are two main reasons why, in my view, the principle of law expressed in the maxim Quilibet, etc., is inapplicable to section 24 (1). The first is the inherent limitation, manifested by what was said in *Graham* v. *Ingleby*, 1 Exch. 651 and *National Westminster Bank Ltd.* v. *Halesowen Presswork & Assemblies Ltd.* [1972] A.C. 785, that the rule expressed in the maxim has no applicability where the matter
H of alleged private waiver is one in which the public has an interest. To establish a public interest in the instant case the respondent has to make good two propositions: first, that the public has an interest in good husbandry (or that Parliament thought so); and, secondly, that security of tenure is (or was regarded by Parliament as) conducive to good husbandry.

As for the public interest in good husbandry, contemporanea expositio makes it legitimate to recall that the Acts of 1947 and 1948 were passed

on the morrow of the second occasion within a half-century when this A
country faced mortal peril through its dependence on imports of food
in consequence of the long agricultural decline when an unprotected
farming interest had to face the competition of cheap food from abroad.
We relearnt that one must dig to survive. Society came once again to
treasure the productivity of its agricultural land, and the heart follows the
treasure. The law, indeed, in its continuity—its conservatism, if you will—
never lost this insight: a bequest for the general improvement of agriculture B
was charitable because that was beneficial to the general community: Atkin
L.J. in *Inland Revenue Commissioners* v. *Yorkshire Agricultural Society*
[1928] 1 K.B. 611, 630; see also Barwick C.J. in *Incorporated Council of
Law Reporting (Q)* v. *Federal Commissioner of Taxation* (1971) 125 C.L.R.
659, 669; *Brisbane City Council* v. *Attorney-General for Queensland*
[1978] 3 W.L.R. 299. What is more—and crucial—the public interest C
in good husbandry appears clearly from the statute itself. The terms
" good husbandry " themselves imply value. The provisions for compensation for improvements and deterioration of the holding are a further
indication. Most significant of all, the very security of tenure has to
yield in the face of bad husbandry: see sections 25 (1) (*a*) and 27. As
for the connection between good husbandry and security of tenure, I
have had the advantage of reading in draft the speech just delivered by D
my noble and learned friend, Lord Hailsham of St. Marylebone. As I
could not hope to emulate what he says on this issue, I content myself
with gratefully adopting it.

I am therefore of opinion that there is sufficient public interest in
security of tenure, as conducive to good husbandry, to make inapplicable
the principle of law expressed in the maxim on which the appellants E
rely; and that this public interest is manifested in the statute itself. But
there is another, more fundamental ground on which I would hold that
principle to be inapplicable. The maxim does not of course apply so
as to permit the renunciation of even a purely private privilege in the
face of express statutory provision (e.g. " This section shall have effect
notwithstanding any agreement to the contrary "). It follows that F
neither does it apply when there is a necessary implication that it shall
not. In my judgment there is such a necessary implication where the
application of the maxim would defeat the very object of the statutory
provision and reinstate the mischief which the statutory provision was
designed to remedy. That, in my view, would be the effect of applying
the maxim to section 24 (1).

In *Salford Guardians* v. *Dewhurst* [1926] A.C. 619 your Lordships' G
House was concerned with a statutory scheme providing superannuation
pensions for poor law officers and servants. It was held that it was not
open either to the guardians or to their officers or servants to contract
themselves out of the statutory obligations and rights respectively
imposed or conferred upon them by the Act. Viscount Cave L.C. said,
at p. 625: H

" But there is another way of putting the question, and that is, Can
the guardians by any action exclude the application of this statute
to any of their officers? If they can, then the guardians have a ready
way of relieving themselves from the burden imposed by the statute.
In that case they can either before appointing a particular officer or
servant, or before consenting to an increase of his remuneration,

Johnson v. Moreton (H.L.(E.))

A   require him to agree with them that this particular statute shall not
apply; indeed, they could make it their general practice before
appointing any officer to make it a condition that he shall not be
entitled to pension. I do not doubt that, if a board adopted that
practice, they would find persons who would accept employment on
those terms and would enter into an agreement that the Act shall
not apply. If that is so, then it is in the option of boards of
B   guardians to determine whether or not this statute shall apply, and
they can (as one of the learned Lords Justices said) make the statute
a dead letter."

In *Soho Square Syndicate Ltd.* v. *E. Pollard & Co.* [1940] Ch. 638
the court was concerned with the provisions of the Courts (Emergency
C   Powers) Act 1939 precluding a mortgagee from appointing a receiver of
the mortgaged property without the leave of the court. The mortgagor
had given his consent to the appointment. But Farwell J., refusing to
follow decisions on similar legislation for the 1914-18 war, held that this
provision was not the subject of contracting out. At p. 645 he said:

"If it be right to say that a mortgagee, by merely getting the
D   consent of the mortgagor, can avoid the necessity of applying to
the court, a large part of the protection which this Act was intended
to provide would virtually disappear. People in the position of such
persons as I have mentioned might easily be persuaded to give a
consent without really knowing what exactly was involved in such
consent, and an opportunity of expressing their reasons for their
inability to pay, whatever they may be, and of stating their diffi-
E   culties, which is now afforded to them by the necessity of an
application to the court would be entirely removed."

The decision and its reasoning were expressly approved unanimously by
a strong Court of Appeal in *Bowmaker Ltd.* v. *Tabor* [1941] 2 K.B. 1.
The principle which, in my view, emerges from this line of authority
is as follows. Where it appears that the mischief which Parliament is
F   seeking to remedy is that a situation exists in which the relations of
parties cannot properly be left to private contractual regulation, and
Parliament therefore provides for statutory regulation, a party cannot
contract out of such statutory regulation (albeit exclusively in his own
favour), because so to permit would be to reinstate the mischief which
the statute was designed to remedy and to render the statutory provision
G   a dead letter. I think that this principle applies to section 24 (1) of the
Act of 1948. It follows that, in my view, clause 27 of the lease is
invalidated by a necessary implication from the statute. (An alternative way of putting the same point is that the principle of law expressed
in the maxim Quilibet, etc., has no application to section 24 (1), the
plain words of which are therefore determinant). The appellants
H   accordingly fail on the first issue. It is thus unnecessary to consider
the second issue—namely, whether, if clause 27 had been valid, there
was a breach of it which fell within the meaning of section 24 (2) (*e*).
I would dismiss the appeal.

LORD EDMUND-DAVIES. My Lords, I have had the advantage of
reading in draft the speeches of my noble and learned friends, who
have expansively considered the issues involved in this appeal, and I

should like to pay respectful tribute in particular to the notable speech A
of my noble and learned friend Lord Simon of Glaisdale. I am in
complete agreement that, for the reasons they have given, the appeal
should be dismissed. It would therefore be mere supererogation for me
to furnish a speech of my own.

LORD RUSSELL OF KILLOWEN. My Lords, in the agricultural lease
for 10 years now in question clause 27 contains an agreement by the B
tenant (inter alia) that he would not in any event serve a counter-notice
under section 24 (1) of the Agricultural Holdings Act 1948. The
primary question is whether it is implicit in the structure and content
of the Act that such a bargain cannot be supported in law. In the
relevant legislative field Parliament has in two respects ever since 1920
interfered with the common law governing the duration of an agricultural C
tenancy: in the common case of a yearly tenancy it imposed a requirement of not less than a 12 month notice to quit in place of six months:
in the case of a term of two years or more it provided that the tenancy
should not end with the term but should continue after the date of
expiry as a yearly tenancy unless the landlord gave not more than two
years' nor less than one year's notice to quit on the expiry of the term. D
Those provisions are in sections 23 and 3 respectively of the Act of
1948, having been previously carried through into the 1923 consolidation.
Taken by themselves those provisions, while of benefit to the tenant,
did but little to protect the tenant in his occupancy of the farm. Part
III of the Agriculture Act 1947 (included in the 1948 consolidation)
introduced a radically different additional system for protection of
tenant farmers in the occupancy of their farms, which might truly be E
described as the conferring of an ability on such to obtain, in the
absence of particular circumstances, security of tenure. That system is
now found in sections 24 and 25 of the 1948 consolidation. Under that
system where the landlord has served a notice to quit (under section 23
or section 3) the tenant is given by section 24 (1) the right to serve a
counter-notice requiring that the notice to quit shall not have effect F
unless the Agricultural Land Tribunal (formerly the Minister) consents
to its operation: such counter-notice must be given within one month
of the giving of the notice to quit. There are in section 24 (2) a number
of circumstances in which the notice to quit cannot be so countered:
stated in very general terms they cover situations in which possession
of the land is required by the landlord for a different permitted use, or
the tenant has in some way misbehaved as such, and the relevant fact is G
asserted in the notice to quit. There is provision whereby the tenant
can challenge the validity of the fact so stated as excluding the right to
give a counter-notice.

In the instant case the landlords gave due notice to quit under section
3 to operate at the expiry of the 10 year term. The tenant in breach
of his contract under clause 27 of the lease purported within the month H
to serve a counter-notice. The landlords, faced with the possible, or
indeed probable, consequence that the procedure laid down by the Act
would result in a failure by the Agricultural Land Tribunal to consent
to the operation of their notice to quit, took avoiding action. They gave a
second notice to quit at the expiry of the 10 year term, this time relying
upon the allegation that by service of the counter-notice the tenant had
committed a breach of clause 27 which breach had materially prejudiced

A the interest of the landlords in the holding and was not capable of being
remedied, relying upon circumstances set out in section 24 (2) (e) as
excluding the right conferred by section 24 (1) on the tenant to serve
a counter-notice to that *second* notice to quit. The present proceedings
arise out of a challenge by the tenant to the validity of that second
notice under section 24 (2) (e). It will be at once perceived that if the
relevant contract by the tenant under clause 27 was one which by
B implication from the statute could not take effect the *second* notice to
quit based upon its breach cannot serve the landlords, and the consequences of the counter-notice to the first notice to quit remain to be
worked out.

    To revert to the system introduced in 1947. Once a counter-notice
is given it is for the Agricultural Land Tribunal to decide whether
C consent is to be given to the operation of the notice to quit, on an
application by the landlord for such consent. Section 25 provides that
consent is only to be given if the tribunal are satisfied of one or more
of certain grounds specified by the landlord. I need not specify those
grounds in detail: it suffices to say that it is for the landlord to produce
good reason why in the general interests of agriculture, or of other use
of the land, or on balance of hardships effect should be given to his
D notice to quit: and even if thus far satisfied the tribunal must withhold
consent to the operation of the notice to quit if it appears to them that
a fair and reasonable landlord would not insist on possession. So the
service of a counter-notice raises a formidable hurdle in the path of the
landlord seeking to support his notice to quit. (I have summarised in
broad outline section 25 of the Act of 1948 as amended in 1958: but
E the essence of the vast step forward in protection of the occupancy of
tenant farmers taken in 1947 is there). Is it implicit in the relevant
legislation that the tenant farmer cannot effectively bind himself in
advance not to serve a counter-notice? That is the question. In
considering this question I hope, my Lords, that I do not revert to
what proved to be heresy leading to my erroneous dissent in *Farrell* v.
F *Alexander* [1977] A.C. 59 if I say that it appeals to my mind to consider
the intention of Parliament in making this radical change in 1947. And
in this connection, lest it be thought that I seek to avoid the fact of the
presence in one statute in 1948 of sections 3, 23, 24 and 25, I comment
that by section 46 of the Act of 1947 Part III was to be read and construed
as one with the Act of 1923 which contained the predecessors of sections
3 and 23.

G   I have found two considerations compelling in favour of implying
from the subject matter and content of the statutory provision in 1947
that the intention of Parliament was that the tenant should not be able
to deprive himself by contract in advance of the right or power to serve
a counter-notice. It is in my opinion inconceivable that Parliament
should have intended that this tremendous advance in protection of
H tenant farmers from the ordinary impact of the law as to occupancy
should be one of which the tenant should be at liberty to deprive himself
by advance bargain when the lesser advantages conferred by sections 3
and 23 were conferred notwithstanding any agreement to the contrary.
The contrary would introduce a ludicrously lopsided operation of the
statute. Secondly, I find it inconceivable that it was the intention in
1947 of Parliament that the equivalent of sections 24 and 25 should bite
on all existing tenancies—in which of course there could be no equiva-

lent of the present clause 27—but not on future tenancies. I say not
on future tenancies, because would-be tenant farmers in need of a
tenancy, anxious to farm but unable to buy farming land, would be at
the mercy of landlords who could insist upon agreement to a clause 27.
I do not doubt that tenants would be forthcoming prepared to so agree,
and if the agreement were sustainable the protection afforded by the
counter-notice system would as farming tenancies fell in become a dead
letter.

The argument for the appellant landlord may be thus summarised.
Whether expressed in Latin or English you start with the principles
that prima facie contracts should be enforced, and that if a power or
right is conferred upon someone he is in general at liberty not only not
to exercise or enforce that power or right but also to bind himself in
advance not to do so. Section 24 (1) being silent upon the question
whether the right to serve a counter-notice can be dispensed with by
agreement those principles should hold the field. Moreover Parliament
could readily have made express provision against contracting out, as it
did in sections 3, 23 and 65 (compensation provisions) and did not do
so. These are of course forceful arguments, for otherwise the learned
county court judge would not have decided in favour of the landlords,
but I am not persuaded by them. So far as concerns the contrast
between the instances of express prohibition against contracting out
and the relevant silence of section 24, I venture to think that it is
legitimate to notice that they were born 27 years apart, with no doubt
different draftsmen, and as already mentioned the draftsmen in 1947
might well have thought that it went without saying that this novel and
much more extensive system of protection could not in effect be operated
in the case of future tenancies only as a concession by landlords.
Moreover there are other provisions, e.g., section 2 dealing with the
364 day tenancy dodge, whether there is comparable silence, but which
clearly cannot be avoided by agreement. Further there are instances
of express permission to contract out, which if the landlord's argument
has any force would point in the opposite direction. I find therefore no
pattern which lends force to the contrast between the sections expressly
forbidding contracting out and the relevant silence of section 24.

So far as concerns the starting point of principle I do not consider
that Parliament conferred this right upon tenant farmers exclusively
for their benefit as individual citizens. It was plainly conferred for the
public benefit. It is of immense importance to the economy that
agriculture should be properly and diligently pursued, that tenant
farmers who so pursue it by putting their energy and resources into the
land should be encouraged to continue to do so by the knowledge that
only in very special circumstances can they lose their occupancy. And
so I come back to the point that if the implication be not made in
favour of the tenant the protection afforded by the system would only
exist in the case of tenancies created after 1947 at the will of the landlord. I do not, my Lords, consider that we are obliged to treat that
as an oversight capable of correction only by Parliament, as was the
case of the 18 month tenancy which was neither a yearly tenancy
(within section 23 or its equivalent) nor a tenancy for a term of two
years or more (within section 3 or its equivalent).

I do not myself rely upon, as relevantly imperative, the provision in

3 W.L.R. Johnson v. Moreton (H.L.(E.)) Lord Russell
of Killowen

A section 24 (1) that if a counter-notice is served the notice to quit " shall not " have effect without the consent of the tribunal to its operation. That imperative seems to me to come later in sequence to the question now in issue. Nor am I satisfied to decide this case on the footing that clause 27 involves an impermissible exclusion of the exercise of a judicial function by the tribunal—a contention which I find not easy to extract from the case for the respondent, and which I think owed its

B origin to a suggestion of one of your Lordships to junior counsel for the respondent. I prefer to rest my opinion upon the wider grounds that I have sought to indicate.

I would add that the problems involved in a view that clause 27 is not implicitly forbidden themselves suggest that that view is erroneous. For if the second notice to quit may be relied upon by the landlords it

C means that the tenant by appealing to section 24 (1) has thereby invoked an exception to that very subsection: which to say the least would be a curious quirk of the law. I detect both in this (and the answer thereto) an unwholesome circularity.

I am not wholly in agreement with the reasons which led the Court of Appeal to their conclusion. I think that they relied too much upon a supposed transfer from sections 3 and 23 of the ban on contracting

D out to section 24, without noticing that historically sections 3 and 23 stood as relevant and important on their own feet, and purely limited to requiring a special notice to quit in point of time. But for the reasons I have sought to express I am of opinion that their decision was right, and I would dismiss the appeal.

Appeal dismissed with costs.

E

Solicitors: *Allen & Overy for Rotheram & Co., Coventry; Ellis & Fairbairn for Wright, Hassall & Co., Leamington Spa.*

T. J. M.

F

[FAMILY DIVISION]

NIXON v. FOX (FORMERLY NIXON)

1978 Feb. 27 Dunn J.

G

Husband and Wife—Divorce—Ancillary relief—Court's jurisdiction —Wife's application for ancillary relief for children—Wife's remarriage—Whether amendment of application to enable wife to apply for lump sum order permissible—Matrimonial Causes Act 1973 (c. 18), s. 28 (3)

H By her acknowledgment of service of the husband's petition for dissolution of the marriage, the wife indicated that she intended to apply on her own account for ancillary relief. She did not file an answer but made an application on Form 11 for an order for periodical payments and secured periodical payments on behalf of the children. The husband was granted a decree of divorce which was made absolute in January 1977. The wife remarried and, in February 1977, the registrar granted leave, on an ex parte application, to amend Form 11 to include an application for a lump sum and transfer of property order on behalf of the wife.

Nixon v. Fox (Fam.)   **[1978]**

On the husband's application for a declaration that the   A
wife was barred, under section 28 (3) of the Matrimonial
Causes Act 1973,[1] from making any application for financial
provision for herself by her failure to issue a notice of application before her remarriage: —

Held, granting the declaration, that the unamended Form
11 was an application for periodical payments on behalf of
the children of the family made by the wife in her capacity
as a mother having the care of those children; that such an   B
application was not an application for ancillary relief for the
wife's benefit and, since section 28 (3) of the Matrimonial
Causes Act 1973 permitted of no exceptions to the bar on a
party, who had remarried, bringing an application for ancillary
relief on their own behalf against a former spouse, the court
had no jurisdiction to entertain the wife's application for such
relief (post, pp. 572F—573A).

Wilson v. *Wilson* [1976] Fam. 142, C.A. considered.   C
Doherty v. *Doherty* [1976] Fam. 71, C.A. distinguished.

The following cases are referred to in the judgment:

Doherty v. *Doherty* [1976] Fam. 71; [1975] 3 W.L.R. 1; [1975] 2 All E.R.
    635, C.A.
Pace (formerly Doe) v. *Doe* [1977] Fam. 18; [1976] 3 W.L.R. 865; [1977]
    1 All E.R. 176.   D
Wilson v. *Wilson* [1976] Fam. 142; [1975] 3 W.L.R. 537; [1975] 3 All E.R.
    464, C.A.

No additional cases were cited in argument.

SUMMONS   E
On May 5, 1976, the husband presented a petition for the dissolution
of his marriage on the ground that the marriage had irretrievably broken
down because the wife had committed adultery and that he found it
intolerable to live with her. In her acknowledgment of service the wife
stated that she intended to apply in due course for ancillary relief. On
June 21, 1976, the wife gave notice to the husband that she intended to
apply for an order for periodical payments and secured periodical payments   F
for the four children of the family.

On September 23, 1976, in an undefended suit the husband was granted
a decree nisi of divorce. The decree nisi was made absolute on January 17,
1977. The wife remarried.

On February 25, 1977, by leave of the registrar the notice of application
made on Form 11 on behalf of the children was amended. The reamended   G
notice read: "Take notice that the respondent intends to apply to the
court for an order for periodical payments/secured periodical payments
for the respondent and for the children of the family, lump sum and transfer
of property order."

On January 25, 1978, the husband issued a summons seeking a declaration that the wife's claim for ancillary relief for herself was barred by her
failure to issue notice before her remarriage.   H

After a hearing in chambers, Dunn J. gave judgment in open court.
The facts are stated in the judgment.

Michael Horowitz for the husband.
David Sich for the wife.

[1] Matrimonial Causes Act 1973, s. 28 (3): see post, p. 568G.

A   DUNN J. This is an application by the husband for a declaration that
the wife's claim for ancillary relief for herself is barred by her failure to
issue a notice of application for ancillary relief before her remarriage. It
raises two questions: first, whether the court has jurisdiction in the events
which have occurred to consider such a claim, and secondly, if it has,
whether the court should exercise its discretion to allow the wife's application to be suitably amended so that she can proceed with the claim. I
B   would have liked to have dealt with both those questions at this hearing
but both counsel told me that they were not in a position to put before me
the full facts which were necessary for a consideration of the exercise of
discretion. The argument has therefore proceeded entirely on the first
question, as to whether or not the court has jurisdiction.

The background of the case is that the parties were married on
C   December 30, 1958, when the husband was 25 and the wife 24 years of age.
There are four children, varying in ages from 17 down to 13. On May 5,
1976, the husband filed a petition under section 1 (2) (a) of the Matrimonial
Causes Act 1973 alleging adultery by the wife with the second respondent.
The wife did not enter an appearance and on May 11, 1976, she filed an
acknowledgment of service in which she answered " Yes " to the question
whether she wished to make any application on her own account for
D   ancillary relief. But Mr. Sich has told me that he does not feel able to argue
that the acknowledgment of service in that form constitutes an application
for ancillary relief. On June 21, 1976, she made an application under the
rules on Form 11 stating that she intended to apply to the court for an
order for periodical payments and secured periodical payments for the
children of the family. The suit was undefended and the husband was
E   granted a decree nisi on September 23, 1976.

There had been negotiations between the parties as to financial matters.
It is alleged by the husband that there had been a concluded agreement
between them as to financial matters. On January 17, 1977, which was the
day that the decree was made absolute, the wife's solicitors wrote to the
husband's solicitors saying:

F   " We of course do not accept that there has been a concluded agreement and intend now to make formal application for property transfer
and a lump sum as well as formal orders for periodical payments."

At some time between the decree absolute and February 25, 1977, the
wife remarried, and on February 25, 1977, the notice of application on
Form 11 was amended by leave of the registrar, the words " lump sum and
G   transfer of property order " being added after the words " children of the
family." It does not appear from the correspondence that any notice was
given to the husband's solicitors of the proposed amendment, and so far as
I have been informed by counsel the husband was not represented at the
hearing before the registrar when the amendment was made. I put it in
that way because this is a case in which the parties were both represented
by London agents and there seems some little doubt as to precisely what
H   did happen. It is however not asserted by the wife that anything that was
done before the registrar on February 25, 1977, constituted an estoppel as
against the husband.

On March 3, 1977, the wife's solicitors forwarded to the husband's
solicitors a copy of an originating summons under section 17 of the
Married Women's Property Act 1882 which had been issued on March 1,
1977, with the affidavit in support. The wife is entitled to proceed
with that application, it having been made within the three-year period

after the dissolution of the marriage. On the same day they also enclosed A
a copy of the amended Form 11 to which I have referred.

On April 6, 1977, the wife's solicitors again wrote to the husband's
solicitors saying:

> " As we informed you on the hearing of the section 17 application
> yesterday we propose amending the application for financial provision
> by including the words ' for the respondent ' after the word ' payment ' B
> in the second line of the application, and we enclose a copy of the
> notice showing the proposed amendment. As reamended, therefore,
> the notice on Form 11 reads as follows: ' Take notice that the
> respondent intends to apply to the court for an order for periodical
> payments/secured periodical payments for the respondent and for the
> children of the family, lump sum and transfer of property order.' "
>   C

I have found that re-amended notice difficult to construe. I take it that
it means that the respondent intends to apply to the court for a lump sum
and transfer of property order for herself in addition to periodical payments and secured periodical payments for the children, because of course
after her remarriage she would be unable to make any application for
periodical payments for herself, and that is the only construction of the
notice of application which seems to me to make sense, although I am   D
bound to say that as a matter of grammar and the natural meaning of the
words it is not the construction that I would put upon it.

The response to that proposal to re-amend the notice of application was
contained in a letter from the husband's solicitors dated April 19, 1977, in
which they say:

> " The document by way of re-amended For 11 does not appear to E
> accord with the matters discussed before the registrar. Surely you
> conceded that the claim for periodical payments, secured periodical
> payments, transfer of property order and lump sum provision were
> barred by virtue of the fact that no claim in Form 11 had been
> presented prior to the respondent's remarriage."

It is the issue raised in that letter, which was repeated in another letter of F
the same date, which now comes before me for determination.

The relevant statutory provision is section 28 (3) of the Matrimonial
Causes Act 1973, which is in these terms:

> " If after the grant of a decree dissolving or annulling a marriage
> either party to that marriage remarries, that party shall not be entitled
> to apply, by reference to the grant of that decree, for a financial G
> provision order in his or her favour, or for a property adjustment
> order, against the other party to that marriage."

The procedure for making applications for ancillary relief is dealt with
by rules 68 and 69 of the Matrimonial Causes Rules 1977. Rule 68 (3)
provides: " An application by a petitioner or respondent for ancillary
relief, not being an application which is required to be made in the petition H
or answer, shall be made by notice in Form 11." It is common ground in
this case that, no answer having been filed, the only way in which the
respondent could make an application for ancillary relief was by notice
in Form 11. In the first note to Form 11 it is said: " set out the ancillary
relief claimed," and then there are other matters which do not seem to be
material to this application.

I was referred to two decisions of the Court of Appeal which deal with

A the question of applications for ancillary relief. The first was *Doherty* v. *Doherty* [1976] Fam. 71, that was also a case in which the wife had remarried. The application which she wished to make was an application for a lump sum payment. In fact she had never applied for a lump sum payment before her remarriage, although she had applied, first of all, for a transfer of property order and then for periodical payments. The Court of Appeal held that the original notice of application applying for the

B transfer of property order in respect of the matrimonial home was sufficient to include an order in respect of the proceeds of sale of the matrimonial home, out of which a lump sum could be paid. Ormrod L.J. said, at p. 80:

" There is no question in this case of the husband being lulled into a false sense of security, or of being in any way misled as to the wife's intention. From the beginning, everybody in the case knew perfectly

C well that what the wife was seeking was her share in the former matrimonial home in the form of a cash payment. All that has gone wrong is that nobody on the wife's side quite succeeded in expressing her claim correctly according to the rules."

He then held that R.S.C., Ord. 20, r. 5 gave the court power if it were necessary to amend the application in such a situation.

D   Buckley L.J. pointed out that orders for lump sum payments were made under section 23 of the Matrimonial Causes Act 1973 and orders for transfer of property under section 24 of that Act. He went on to say, at pp. 81–82:

" The powers conferred upon the court by those two sections are directed to enabling the court to achieve the single purpose which is

E expressed in the closing words of section 25 (1), which indicate the objective with which the court is to exercise the powers contained in the sections, that is to say, adjusting the rights of the parties, ' so far as it is practicable and, having regard to their conduct, just so to do,' and so on. The two sections, in my judgment, do in fact, as Ormrod L.J. said, incorporate one code indicating the extent of the powers of

F the court to give ancillary relief of this nature following upon the dissolution of a marriage. It is very important as a matter of practical expediency that the court should have the greatest measure of freedom in the choice of the kind of relief which it will grant under those sections upon any application that is made to it by either party to the marriage which has been dissolved. It may well be that where an application is made for a transfer of property the court, on considering

G all the matters which it is enjoined to take into consideration under section 25 (1), will come to the conclusion that the more just and the more convenient course is to make an order of a financial nature, an order for payment of either periodical payments or of a lump sum. But the court should not, in my judgment, be debarred from making that choice merely because the applicant has framed his or her appli-

H cation in a particular way."

   Mr. Horowitz has sought to distinguish the decision in *Doherty* v. *Doherty* [1976] Fam. 71 from the facts of the instant case by saying that, unlike the situation in *Doherty*, in this case there was no application by the wife on her own behalf at all until after her remarriage. The only application which had been made before the remarriage was an application on behalf of the children. There was no application by the wife, and the

wife, having failed to make an application for herself before her remarriage, A
falls squarely within the provisions of section 28 (3) of the Act of 1973
and is not entitled now to apply. He submitted that this was not a case
in which the wife had made an application for one form of ancillary
relief, and then, after her remarriage, had decided to apply for another
form of ancillary relief, as was the case in *Doherty* v. *Doherty* [1976]
Fam. 71; but that in the present case she had made no application for
ancillary relief at all. He went on to say that she was originally applying B
in a different capacity, as mother of the children, and not in her capacity
as a wife, and that she made no application on her own behalf until after
her remarriage.

In the other case in the Court of Appeal, *Wilson* v. *Wilson* [1976]
Fam. 142, there was no question of the wife having remarried. What had
happened was that the wife prayed for periodical payments for herself and C
the children in the petition and then, after decree nisi, she sought to claim
a lump sum and transfer of property without obtaining leave under rule
68 (2) of the Matrimonial Causes Rules 1973 and, in reliance on *Doherty*
v. *Doherty* [1976] Fam. 71, the circuit judge held that she could do so.
The Court of Appeal reversed that decision, saying that it was necessary
for her to obtain leave, and Cairns L.J. said, at p. 146:
D

> "It appears to me that this case differs from *Doherty* v. *Doherty*
> [1976] Fam. 71 in more than one respect. First of all, it by no means
> follows that, if when either a lump sum order or a property adjustment
> order is prayed the court is able to make whichever of those two orders
> it thinks fit, the same applies if a periodical payments order is all that
> is asked for in the petition and then at a later stage, without amend-
> ment and without getting leave, an attempt is made to get a lump sum E
> order. There is no such correspondence between periodical payments
> and a lump sum order as there is between a lump sum order and an
> adjustment of property order, though, of course, it is true that, if
> there is an application both for periodical payments and for a lump
> sum payment, then the order which is made under one part of that
> application will affect whether any order is made, and if so what order, F
> under the other. But I certainly do not regard *Doherty* v. *Doherty* as
> showing that the court should be free when the application is only for a
> periodical payments order to order a lump sum."

Mr. Horowitz relied on that passage as showing that where the only
application was an application for periodical payments the court would not
order a lump sum unless the application was amended and, said counsel, G
if in the meantime the wife had remarried there would be no jurisdiction
in the court to make the amendment, because of the provisions of section
28 (3) of the Matrimonial Causes Act 1973.

Scarman L.J., in *Wilson* v. *Wilson* [1976] Fam. 142, 147, said:

> "Mr. Lodge in his submissions on behalf of the wife relied strongly
> upon the situation that would arise if a wife, who had intended to H
> claim a lump sum payment in her petition but failed to do so, was
> faced with the difficulty arising from remarriage. It is certainly the law
> (see section 28 (3) of the Matrimonial Causes Act 1973) that a party
> shall not be entitled to apply for a financial provision order or for a
> property adjustment order after remarriage; and, although the facts of
> this case do not include the fact of remarriage, Mr. Lodge's argument
> was that, if we were to accede to the husband's argument, then we

A would have to face the fact that, had a mistake in pleading come to the knowledge of the former wife after remarriage, she would be unable then to claim a lump sum payment even though in justice she should have one. I think that that argument confuses a fresh application with an amendment to the petition. In the present case the wife did make an application in her petition for periodical payments. It is said now that she was mistaken in thus limiting her application, and

B wishes to make an application for a lump sum payment as well. If such a mistake should be made in future and not be discovered until after remarriage, then I would have thought that the court under its general jurisdiction to amend the petition would be able to amend the application in the petition so as to include a prayer for a lump sum payment. All a party cannot do is make a new or fresh application

C for ancillary relief after remarriage."

Mr. Horowitz made a number of submissions upon that judgment. He said, first, that it was not necessary for the decision of *Wilson* v. *Wilson* [1976] Fam. 142 and was therefore obiter dicta and, secondly, that in saying what he had said about the power of the court to amend the petition, or amend the application in the petition so as to include a prayer

D for a lump sum payment, Scarman L.J. was confusing the jurisdiction of the court after a remarriage with the discretion of the court to make amendment, and counsel submitted that after a remarriage the court had no jurisdiction to entertain an application for a lump sum payment if made after the remarriage, and consequently no question of discretion as to whether or not the petition should be amended arose. But, said Mr. Horowitz, the whole of the judgment of Scarman L.J. proceeds on the basis

E that there was already an application for periodical payments by the wife before remarriage. This, said Mr. Horowitz, is not the situation in this case, and he relied strongly on the last sentence of the paragraph of the judgment which I have read, namely: " All a party cannot do is make a new or fresh application for ancillary relief after remarriage." Counsel submitted that although on the face of it this appears to be an amendment, it is in

F fact a new or fresh application for ancillary relief.

I was also referred to *Pace (formerly Doe)* v. *Doe* [1977] Fam. 18, which is a decision of Sir George Baker P. In that case a wife, after remarriage, sought to apply to vary a maintenance agreement under section 35 of the Matrimonial Causes Act 1973 so as to include a lump sum payment for herself and the children. Sir George Baker P. refused the application, holding that the court had no jurisdiction under the section to

G vary it in that way in favour of a wife who had remarried, and it was submitted that although the application came before the court in a different way the principle was the same as in the instant case.

Mr. Sich for the wife pointed out that the power of the court to make orders for financial provisions and property adjustments is contained in sections 23 and 24 of the Matrimonial Causes Act 1973, and that under

H both sections the court is empowered to make orders either in favour of parties to the marriage or for the benefit of children of the family. He submitted, on the analogy of *Doherty* v. *Doherty* [1976] Fam. 71, that if an application in proper form was made under either of those sections, either for the wife or for the children, either for periodical payments, lump sum, or transfer of property, then the court had jurisdiction and in a proper case, in the exercise of its discretion, would amend the application so as to enable the wife to apply for a lump sum and transfer of property

order for herself, even if that amendment was made for the first time after   A
her remarriage, and even though she had never previously made any
application for ancillary relief for herself. He further submitted that *Wilson*
v. *Wilson* [1976] Fam. 142 was not concerned with jurisdiction but with
discretion, and he relied in particular on the judgment of Scarman L.J. when
he dealt with the position which might arise after a remarriage, and
submitted that the court had jurisdiction to give leave to amend an appli-   B
cation so as to apply for a lump sum payment, even if the wife had made
no such application before the marriage, provided that she had made some
application under either section 23 or section 24. Mr. Sich submitted that
R.S.C., Ord. 20, r. 5 gave the court wide powers of amendment, that the
situation of a wife who had remarried was analogous to the situation of a
party against whom time had run under the Limitation Acts 1939–1975,
and that in the matrimonial jurisdiction particularly there should be a wide   C
discretion to allow amendments in appropriate circumstances, and that the
rules should be applied flexibly rather than technically. He also submitted
that it was plain from a reading of sections 23 and 24 of the Act of 1973
that the claims for a wife and children are very often intermingled and that
relief for one may have to be considered in terms of the other, and so, he
said, application by a wife on behalf of children is sufficient application to
give the court jurisdiction to deal with any subsequent applications by the   D
wife herself.

I do not accept that the situation created by section 28 (3) of the
Matrimonial Causes Act 1973 is analogous to the situation created by the
Limitation Acts 1939–75. The court now has wide powers to grant leave
to plaintiffs to proceed with actions notwithstanding that the limitation
period has expired. The Limitation Acts 1939–75 are a shield, and a   E
voluntary shield at that, because they have to be expressly pleaded before
they can be raised as a defence. The situation under section 28 (3) is in
my judgment completely different. Mr. Sich complained that the effect of
section 28 (3) of the Act of 1973 was a drastic one. I accept that. It is
Parliament which has made it drastic. It would have been easy for Parliament to have provided in the section that after remarriage a party should
not be entitled to apply for ancillary relief without the leave of the court,   F
or save in exceptional circumstances, or to have qualified the words of the
section in some way, but there is no such qualification. I think the section
is unequivocal, in its terms. Nor do I accept that an application on behalf
of children can be said to be an application by a wife for her own benefit.
It seems to me that the two applications are made in different rights.
Whilst I, of course, accept and am bound by the judgment in *Doherty* v.   G
Doherty [1976] Fam. 71, it seems to me one thing to say that a wife who
has made an application under one section and then remarried may be
entitled, if there has been an oversight, to amend her application so as to
bring the application under another section of the Matrimonial Causes Act
1973, and quite another thing to say that a wife who had never made an
application on her own behalf at all can make an application simply   H
because she has previously made an application on behalf of the children.
It was suggested by Mr. Horowitz that if I were to allow this application
of the wife to proceed it would be, as he put it, driving a coach and horses
not only through the rules but also through the express provisions of
section 28 (3) of the Act of 1973, an Act of Parliament, and I agree with
that. In my judgment no application was made by this wife for ancillary
relief until after her remarriage, and by reason of the provisions of section

A 28 (3) of the Matrimonial Causes Act 1973 she is now barred from proceeding with it, and I declare accordingly.

> Declaration accordingly.
> Wife to pay husband's costs.
> Leave to appeal.

B Solicitors: *Wood, Nash & Winters* for *Ellison & Co.,* Colchester; *Howard, Kennedy & Rossi.*

[COURT OF APPEAL]

C

D. *v.* B. (ORSE. D.) (SURNAME: BIRTH REGISTRATION)

1978 May 24, 25   Stamp and Ormrod L.JJ.

Minor—Custody—Change of surname—Mother changing surname
D *by deed poll prior to birth—Mother registering birth in new*
surname without father's consent—Order to execute fresh deed
poll and to amend register—Principles applicable to use of
father's surname by child brought up in another household

The parties married in July 1970. A child was conceived early in 1975, but in September 1975, the mother left the father to live with another man. After her departure, she executed a deed poll by which she assumed the other man's surname for herself and any children. A son was born on
E November 23, 1975. The mother registered the birth in her assumed name but she declared that her husband was the father. The father's request to see the child was refused by the mother. The father then issued a summons seeking access to the child and an order that the deed poll and the Register of Births be altered to show the child's name as being that of the father. On December 13, 1976, Lane J. [1977] Fam. 145,
F granting the application on the ground that the mother could not unilaterally change the child's surname, gave access to the father and ordered that the mother should take all necessary steps to ensure that the deed poll and the Register of Births be amended. The judge further ordered that, until the child reached the age of 18, she should not let him be known by any other surname than that of the father, without the father's consent or order of the court. The mother failed to carry out
G the order so far as it related to the deed poll and the registration of the birth and the father applied to the judge for directions, the mother cross-applying for a variation. On April 10, 1978, Lane J., granting the father's application and dismissing the mother's, directed her to execute a statutory declaration and a fresh deed poll within 14 days, a penal notice being attached to the order.

On the mother's appeal: —
H *Held,* allowing the appeal, (1) that at common law a surname was the name by which a person was generally known and the effect of changing it by deed poll was merely evidential; that, in ordering the mother to execute a fresh deed poll, the judge was misled by the Enrolment of Deeds (Change of Names) Regulations 1949, as amended in 1974, which related to the enrolment of a deed poll and not to its

---

[Reported by MISS HENRIETTA STEINBERG, Barrister-at-Law]

execution; and that, therefore, since the deed poll had not   A
been vitiated by failure to comply with the requirements of
those regulations, the order could not be carried out and
would be set aside (post, p. 579C–D, F–H).

(2) That, with regard to the registration of a birth, under
regulation 18 (3) of the Registration of Births, Deaths and
Marriages Regulations 1968, the surname to be entered in the
register should be the surname by which it was intended that
the child should be known; that, since the mother intended   B
that the child should be known by her assumed surname, she
had made no error of fact which could be corrected under
section 29 (3) of the Births and Deaths Registration Act 1953
and, accordingly, the order requiring her to make a statutory
declaration could not be enforced and would be discharged
(post, pp. 580F–G, 582B–C).

(3) That the father having consented, that part of the order
of December 1976 requiring the mother not to allow the child   C
to be known by any other surname than that of the father
would be varied to enable the child to be known by the
mother's new surname.

Per curiam. That in the circumstances it was not in the
child's best interests to be generally known by his father's name
since a very young child might be confused if called by a
surname different from that of the other members of his family
and might later be embarrassed by it at school; that, further,   D
the important matter of substance was the relationship between
the father and the child, namely, that the child should identify
with the father in human terms and, in time, should recognise
him to be his natural father (post, p. 583C–E, H).

Order of Lane J. of April 10, 1978, discharged.
Order of Lane J. of December 13, 1976 [1977] Fam. 145
varied by consent.

E

No cases are referred to in the judgment.

The following cases were cited in argument:

D. (Minors) (Adoption by Parent), In re [1973] Fam. 209; [1973] 3 W.L.R.
595; [1973] 3 All E.R. 1001, D.C.

Practice Direction (Deed Poll: Minors) [1969] 1 W.L.R. 1330; [1969] 3   F
All E.R. 288.

T. (orse. H.) (An Infant), In re [1963] Ch. 238; [1962] 3 W.L.R. 1477;
[1962] 3 All E.R. 970.

WG 31/1975, *In re,* April 7, 1976; Court of Appeal (Civil Division)
Transcript No. 164 of 1976, C.A.

Y. v. *Y. (Child: Surname)* [1973] Fam. 147; [1973] 3 W.L.R. 80; [1973]
2 All E.R. 574.

G

APPEAL from Lane J.

The parties married on July 27, 1970. On September 13, 1975, the
mother executed a deed poll whereby she requested all persons to designate
and address her and her children and remoter issue by the assumed name
of B. A son, the only child of the mother and the father, was born on
November 23, 1975. On December 17, 1975, the mother registered the   H
birth under the new surname, which was that of the co-respondent.

On June 9, 1976, the father filed a petition for the grant of a decree
of divorce under section 1 (2) (a) of the Matrimonial Causes Act 1973
and prayed for the grant of a joint custody order and access to the only
child of the family. On June 10, 1976, the father issued a summons whereby
he asked that the child should assume his surname and that the mother
should concur in an application to make such an alteration in the Register

A   of Births to give effect to the change of name. The summons sought, in addition, reasonable access to the child.

On November 19, 1976, the father was granted a decree nisi of divorce in an undefended suit. No order was made relating to the child. On November 26, 1976, the summons was amended so as to enable the court to consider whether the arrangements for the child were satisfactory or the best possible in the circumstances under section 41 of the Matrimonial

B   Causes Act 1973, and that the father and the mother be granted joint custody. The summons was heard in chambers, judgment being delivered in open court on December 13, 1976. The judge granted the father reasonable access to the child and ordered, inter alia, that the mother should take all necessary steps to ensure that the deed poll and the Register of Births be amended to show the child's surname as being that of his father. The

C   judge further ordered that, until the child attained the age of 18 years, the mother should not cause or permit the child to be known by any other surname than that of the father without the father's written consent or further order of the court.

On the mother's failure to carry out the order, the father applied to the judge for directions as to the manner in which the child's surname might be registered, and the mother made a cross application for the judge's

D   order to be varied. On April 10, 1978, the judge, granting the father's application and dismissing the mother's cross application, ordered inter alia, that within 14 days the mother should execute the statutory declaration for the purpose of altering the register of births and should execute a fresh deed poll and that, if the mother neglected to obey the directions, she would become liable to committal proceedings.

E   The mother appealed on the grounds (1) that the judge was wrong in holding that it was not in the child's interests that he should be known by his mother's new surname: and (2) that the judge misdirected herself in that she (i) failed to have sufficient regard to the fact that the mother was expecting another child in June 1978 which would be known by her new surname, (ii) held that there was no advantage to the child in being known by the new surname, (iii) held that it was

F   important to all the strands between the father and the child that the father's surname be preserved, (iv) failed to have sufficient regard to the fact that the father was enjoying satisfactory access to the child, and (v) attached more weight to the father's wishes than to the paramount interest of the child.

The facts are stated in the judgment.

G
   Ian Davies for the mother.
   John Samuels for the father.
   Shirley Ritchie for the Official Solicitor as guardian ad litem.

STAMP L.J. I will ask Ormrod L.J. to deliver the first judgment.

H   ORMROD L.J. This is an appeal from an order which was made on April 10, 1978, by Lane J. in a case which has caused a great deal of difficulty and trouble. It is a singularly unfortunate case. The difficulties arise because an issue of substance, not in itself of any great complexity, has become entangled with formalistic considerations which have led to a great deal of litigation.

The human situation between these two parties, the father and the mother, is such as to lead inevitably to severe emotional reactions by each

side. That each should feel very strongly about the situation is all too easy   A
to understand. The tragedy is that these feelings have been exacerbated
to a point which is almost unbearable by, as I think, purely formalistic
considerations which have led to this litigation.

The substantive issue in the case was whether or not the father should
have access to a very young boy. The formalistic issues rotate round the
question as to the name by which this boy is to be known, and it is a
great pity that these issues have come to overshadow the real issue of   B
substance, which has been resolved by an earlier decision of the judge.

The judge's order which is under appeal should be read in full in so
far as the operative parts are concerned. The first paragraph of the order
is that the mother:

> " do within 14 days of today execute the statutory declaration in the
> unamended form " contained in a certain exhibit to the affidavit of the   C
> father. " (2) that the [mother] do within the said period execute
> a fresh deed poll in such terms as will be necessary to cancel a
> deed poll executed by her in September 1975."

Paragraph (3) reads:

> " [the mother] be on notice that if she neglects to obey the above   D
> directions by the time therein limited, she will be liable to process of
> execution for the purpose of compelling her to obey the same,"

and then there is a stay pending a possible appeal.

The inclusion of the third paragraph in the order is most unusual. It
was put in, I think it right to say, at the express direction of the judge
and it constitutes the plainest possible threat to the mother; a threat of   E
committal proceedings in the event that she does not obey the two directions. That, of course, inevitably provoked her to take every possible step
that is open to her to challenge those directions and, in the view that I have
formed, she was fully entitled to challenge them both. But it indicates the
relationship between these parties: that by April of this year it was
necessary, or thought to be necessary, for the father to adopt that sort of   F
attitude towards the mother with the result which, in my experience, always
follows. Committal proceedings in family disputes are almost always
disastrous and in this case, of course, they would be futile.

The facts of the case can be stated even more shortly than usual
because they have been dealt with in much more detail by the judge
in her judgment reported as D. v. B. (orse. D.) (Surname: Birth Registration) [1977] Fam. 145. These are the essential facts. The father and   G
the mother were married in July 1970. They were both aged 22 at the
time. The father is now a lawyer, and I do not specify any further
than that, and the mother is a school teacher. For almost the first
five years of the marriage there were no children, but a child was conceived early in 1975. Before that the marriage had run into difficulties, the
details of which are quite unknown to us and are irrelevant to any   H
question we have to consider. All that is relevant is that by the autumn
of 1974 the mother had formed an attachment to the man to whom she is
now married and it is common ground that that association had not reached
the sexual stage until the spring of 1975. Some attempt had been made
by the father to effect a reconciliation with the mother and those steps
may or may not have progressed. What is clear is that sexual intercourse
took place between the father and the mother early in 1975 as a result

The Weekly Law Reports, October 13, 1978

577

3 W.L.R.   D. v. B. (Surname: Birth Registration) (C.A.)   Ormrod L.J.

A of which a child was conceived, and the child is the subject of these present proceedings and he was born on November 23, 1975.

At a time when it is not clear whether or not the mother knew that she was pregnant, she resumed the association with the co-respondent, B., and for the first time had intercourse with him. Then her pregnancy became apparent and, of course, a situation of the most acute difficulty inevitably arose for all three adults. It was plainly an emotional situation of the

B utmost intensity for all. The mother made the decision in the course of the summer of 1975, that her marriage was at an end, that it was not capable of being repaired, and so she took the decision to set up house with the co-respondent. Steps were then taken to find accommodation and, when the accommodation was found, she left the father (by now, of course, she was six months or so pregnant) and thereafter she and the co-respondent

C have lived together.

Almost immediately after the mother left, which was in September, 1975, she executed a deed of deed poll changing her name from D. to B. The deed poll is, of course, in the usual form. By this time, as the correspondence between the mother and the father clearly indicates, both sides were under great stress and in a very confused state of mind as to

D what the future was to be. It is easy to understand the father's desperate anxiety that he was going to lose the child, his only child, who may have been conceived, perhaps, with considerable difficulty: one does not know. Equally it is extremely easy to understand the mother's feelings that this child was going to be born into a new family which she and the co-respondent were establishing; the father would have little or no contact with this child, and to her (as she mentioned in at least one letter) adoption by her

E and the co-respondent seemed to be a sensible solution. It is easy to understand that the father would take a very different view of it. So the situation became increasingly difficult.

When the child was born, the mother felt that it would be better if the father did not see the child or attempt to develop any relationship with him. The father, understandably, took exactly the opposite view. So the

F battle lines were drawn, and the only issue of substance, in my judgment, in this case is who is right in relation to the question of access.

The father, unfortunately (perhaps because he was a lawyer) took great exception to the fact that the mother intended the child to be known by the name of B. It is at this point that the first unusual fact arises in this case, because when the child was born the mother, who was the informant, registered the child in a very unusual way. It is necessary to look

G at the actual birth certificate. The birth was registered in the subdistrict of Cambridge and the date and place of birth of the child is given as " November 23, 1975. Maternity Hospital, Cambridge." In space 2, under the heading " Name and surname of child," the entry is " M. B. male." Then in space 4, under the heading " Father," appears " J. D." the name of the father, and his place of birth and occupation are given. In space 7,

H under the heading " Mother " appears " D. B. otherwise D. D." and her place and birth and her maiden name are given. Then she signs it as the informant mother in the name of D. B.

An enormous amount of effort has been expended in this case on the question as to whether or not that entry in the Register of Births first should, and secondly could, be amended. It is necessary at this point, I think, to say that the form of registration is wholly irrelevant to any real issue in this case, because the real issues are human issues and not legal ones. It is unfortunate that so much effort has been put into trying to A resolve the legal issues.

It will be necessary, unfortunately, in this case to look rather closely into these legal issues, and the reason for that, in my view, is this: that unless we can disentangle the formalistic aspects of this case from the substantive aspect, this family is never going to have any peace at all. Fortunately, as a result of some further instructions which Mr. Samuels for the father B received just before the court rose last night, the father felt able to make a constructive contribution to the solution of these problems that must have come as a very agreeable surprise to the mother. It is to be hoped that from now on the issues between these two parents can be resolved in real terms and not in formalistic ones. It is necessary, however, in view of the history of this litigation, to deal with the matter in some detail.

The matter began immediately after the parties were divorced. Just to C complete the record, the decree nisi was pronounced on November 19, 1976, and on December 13, 1976, the matter came first before Lane J. She had two main issues to resolve. The first, as I have already mentioned, was the substantive issue of access, which she resolved in favour of the father, the mother taking the line (which I can understand perfectly well, just as I can understand the father's line) that it would be better if the father did not attempt to play any role in this child's life. It was inevitable that the D co-respondent should be the father figure in this child's life; that was unavoidable; and the mother thought that it would only complicate the issue if there was another male adult involved in this child's life from an early age. Whether she was right about that or not is a matter of opinion. The father was clearly entitled to put his case, and put it as forcibly as he could to the court, to point out the advantages which he felt the child would E enjoy by establishing contact with him from an early stage. As I have already said, the judge resolved that issue in the father's favour.

But right in the forefront of the father's mind in 1976 was the issue of the registration of the child's birth. The first paragraph of the notice of application dated June 10, and amended on November 26, 1976, asked for an order that F

"the child of the family, now known as M. B., be henceforth known as M. D., and that the [mother] do concur in an application to the superintendent registrar of the registration district of Cambridge to make such alteration to the Register of Births as may give effect to the said change of name and/or that the [mother] do take such other steps to ensure that the said child is known as M. D. as the G court may direct. 2. The [father] be afforded reasonable access to the said child of the family, to be defined by the court. 3. The [mother] and/or the co-respondent may be ordered to pay the costs of this application. 4. That the court should consider whether the arrangements for the said child are satisfactory or the best that can be devised in the circumstances." H

Fifthly, the father asked for an order that custody of the child should be given jointly to the father and the mother, the intention being, of course, that care and control should be with the mother.

The first question is whether or not the order of the judge, made originally in December 1976, and reaffirmed in her recent order of April 1978, was an order which the court was competent to make, namely, the order

The Weekly Law Reports, October 13, 1978

579

3 W.L.R.   D. v. B. (Surname: Birth Registration) (C.A.)   Ormrod L.J.

A directing the mother to take all the necessary steps to alter the deed poll
and to effect a change in the Register of Births. The person who appears
to have appreciated the legal difficulties best, curiously enough, in this case
is the mother herself. So far as the deed poll is concerned, we asked
at an early stage in the hearing of this appeal what change it was
suggested the mother could make in the deed poll and how she was
supposed to do it. I emphasise that the order is a mandatory order on her,
B combined with the threat of enforcement proceedings, to execute a fresh
deed poll in such terms as would be necessary to cancel the deed poll executed in September 1975. What she was supposed to do under that term of
the order was quite unclear from the order itself; and Mr. Samuels for the
father was unable to suggest any answer to the question as to what the
mother was required to do. The answer is that she can do nothing. Her
C present name is B., but in order to keep one's mind clear it is, perhaps,
worth observing that the name B. is hers purely by convention; she has
married the co-respondent, Mr. B. and it is the normal convention in this
country but it is no more than that, that she takes the name B. and is
thereafter known as B. The deed poll had simply stated that that was
how she wished to be known before her marriage. It is common ground
that a surname in common law is simply the name by which a person is
D generally known, and the effect of a deed poll is merely evidential; it has
no more effect than that. This part of the order is unenforceable and,
therefore, should not have been made.

The judge may have been misled by certain matters which were
referred to in this respect at the earlier hearing. In the report of the
judgment in [1977] Fam. 145, 148, there is a reference by the judge to the
E Enrolment of Deeds (Change of Name) Regulations 1949, as amended
in 1974, from which she quoted extensively. The upshot of them is
that a woman cannot *enrol* a deed poll relating to change of name
unless she complies with the requirements of those regulations. Among
other requirements are that the deed should state whether she is single,
married, widowed or divorced; that she must produce her marriage certificate and show that notice of her intention to apply for enrolment of the
F deed has been given to her husband, and that she demonstrate either that
he has consented or that there is good reason why his consent should be
dispensed with. No doubt the judge felt that since the mother had complied
with none of those formalities, this deed poll could be amended or disposed
of, as being in some unspecified way contrary to the regulations.

But that, with respect, is a complete misunderstanding. There are no
G regulations governing the *execution* of deeds poll. The regulations only
apply to the enrolment of such deeds poll, and the purpose of enrolment
is only evidential and formal. A deed poll is just as effective or ineffective
whether it is enrolled or not; the only point of enrolment is that it will
provide unquestionable proof, if proof is required of the execution of the
deed and no more. So that the deed poll in this case is not vitiated in
H any way by failure to comply with those enrolment regulations. It simply
means that the deed cannot be enrolled. The regulations in fact go on
to provide that no deed poll which purports to change the name of a child
can be enrolled without the specific consent of the Master of the Rolls.
Quite clearly no attempt was made in this case, and no attempt was
required to be made, to enrol that deed poll and so there is no more to
be said about this aspect of the case. There is nothing that the mother
can do to comply with that part of the order.

The other part of the order relating to the registration of the child in the A
register of births and deaths is more complicated. There are only two
provisions in the Births and Deaths Registration Act 1953 relating to
effecting changes in the register. It is necessary to look, first of all, at
section 1 which simply provides that the birth of every child born in
England and Wales shall be registered in accordance with the Act. Section
2 provides that in the case of every birth it shall be the duty of the father
and mother of the child to give to the registrar information and particulars B
required to be registered concerning the birth, and to sign the register; but
that is subject to a proviso that the giving of information and the signing
of the register by any one qualified informant shall act as a discharge
of any duty under this section of every other qualified informant. So that
either parent can give the necessary information and sign the register.

Then there is a provision in section 13 relating to the alteration of the C
name of the child. Section 13 (1) provides:

> "Where, before the expiration of 12 months from the date of
> the registration of the birth of any child, the name by which it was
> registered is altered or, if it was registered without a name, a name is
> given to the child, the registrar," [upon delivery to him at any time of
> a certificate in the prescribed form, and upon the payment of the D
> appropriate fee shall] " . . . without any erasure of the original entry,
> forthwith enter in the register the name mentioned in the certificate as
> having been given to the child . . ."

It is not necessary to examine section 13 in detail because the period of
12 months had elapsed in any event before the judge's order was made.
Moreover, whether that section relates to changing the surname of the child E
is a matter which, in my opinion, might require further consideration. But
since it does not arise in this case I say no more about it.

The only other section which gives any power at all to correct an entry
in a register of births or deaths is section 29, and the form of this section
is important. Section 29 (1) reads: "No alteration shall be made in any
register of live births, still-births or deaths except as authorised by this or F
any other Act." Section 29 (2) deals with clerical errors. Section 29 (3)
deals with errors of fact and reads:

> "An error of fact or substance in any such register may be corrected
> by entry in the margin (without any alteration of the original entry) by
> the officer having the custody of the register, upon payment . . . and
> upon production to him by that person of a statutory declaration G
> setting forth the nature of the error and the true facts of the case made
> by two qualified informants of the birth or death with reference to
> which the error has been made, or in default of two qualified
> informants then by two credible persons having knowledge of the
> truth of the case."

It will be observed that it is essential to the operation of section 29 (3) H
that there should have been an error, and that the statutory declaration
should set forth the nature of the error and the true facts of the case. The
question then arises as to whether there was any error in the entry of this
child's birth in the register at Cambridge.

The only error that can be suggested is an error relating to the surname
of the child. But when one comes to look at the Registration of Births,

The Weekly Law Reports, October 13, 1978

581

3 W.L.R.   D. v. B. (Surname: Birth Registration) (C.A.)   Ormrod L.J.

A Deaths and Marriages Regulations 1968, one finds that the requirement is
that so far as the surname of the child is concerned, the entry shall
represent the " surname by which . . . it is intended that the child shall
be known." Regulation 18 (3) which is the relevant regulation reads:

> " With respect to space 2 (Name and surname) the surname to be
> entered shall be the surname by which at the date of the registration
B > of the birth it is intended that the child shall be known and, if a name
> is not given, the registrar shall enter the surname preceded by a
> horizontal line."

It may be surprising to some (certainly it was a surprise to me) to find
that definition of " surname " in the regulations. Here, of course, it is
perfectly plain that the mother, when she registered this child's birth,
C intended that the child should be known by the name of B. It seems,
therefore, clear to me that there was no " error " by her. She may have
acted in a way of which many people would disapprove and in a way
which may be, in moral terms, open to criticism, but so far as making an
error is concerned, it seems to me to be plain that she made no error at all.

It was suggested that the words " it is intended " should refer to the
intention of both parents, but, speaking for myself, I find it very difficult
D to extract that construction from the relevant provisions. So I think the
mother was entitled to take the point which she took herself, that there was
no error on her part and that, consequently, she was in extreme difficulty
in complying with the order of the court to make a statutory declaration
in the necessary terms. In fact when a statutory declaration was submitted
to her by the father's solicitors for her signature in compliance with the
E judge's order of December, 1976, she amended it. Paragraph 5 of the draft
statutory declaration reads:

> " At the date when the birth of the said child was so registered as
> aforesaid, I the said D. B. wrongly believed that I was entitled to
> register the surname of M. as B. I now know that the surname
> should have been registered as D."

F By paragraph 6:

> " In consequence of the above circumstances, the entry on the said
> register is wrong and the correct entry of the said child's name should
> be M. D. and we the said D. B. and the said J. D. make this
> solemn declaration conscientiously believing the same to be true and by
> virtue of the provisions of the Statutory Declarations Act 1835."

G The mother, receiving that draft, amended it by striking out in paragraph 5 the word " wrongly " before " believed," so that it now reads " I
the said D. B. believed that I was entitled to register the surname of M.
as B.," and then she struck out the words " have been " so that it now
reads " I now know that the surname should be registered as D.," and
in paragraph 6 she deleted the words " conscientiously believing the same
H to be true and " presumably because she did not conscientiously believe
the same to be true.

Of course, in its amended form the declaration was useless for effecting
the purpose of amending the register and that led to the second round of
this dispute. What then happened was that the father's solicitors took out
a summons asking for further directions as to the manner of effecting
the re-registration of the child, and the mother issued a cross summons

asking for a variation of the judge's order in relation to the certificate of   A
the register of births and the deed poll. Those were the two matters which
came on before Lane J. on April 10, 1978. It was agreed that the mother's
summons should be heard first asking for the variation, and it is right to
say that this point was not taken before the judge. Nor is it taken
in the notice of appeal. But since the threat of committal is overt in
this case, this court has felt bound to examine all aspects of this order, first   B
of all from the jurisdictional point of view and, secondly, to see whether it
was in fact possible for the mother to comply with it. She was thought to
be recalcitrant over the matter, but the view I have formed is that her
view was right that she could not properly execute or sign the necessary
statutory declaration. That, of course, reduces those two paragraphs of the
order of April 10, 1978, to nothing, so that in respect of those two parts   C
of the order, in my judgment, the mother is entitled to succeed on this
appeal.

The judge did not deal with the remainder of the mother's summons
in which she was seeking a variation of what one might call the substantive part of the earlier order of the judge, that is, in relation to the
practical questions relating to this child's name as opposed to the legal   D
ones. The original order had required that:

"until the child attains the age of 18 years the mother do not cause
or permit the said child to be known by any other surname than that
of the father, without the written consent of the father or further order
of the court."

E
This part of the order was also subject to the mother's application in
April 1978, for a variation. She was asking the judge to reconsider that
part of the order, in other words, what was she to do about this child's
name. The judge did not deal with that in her order because, having
made the order I have already recited, it followed that she was not prepared
to vary that part of the order of December 13, 1976, but we have to deal   F
with it because that issue is raised in the notice of appeal.

I am sure everyone understands that the question of the surname of a
child is a matter of great emotional significance, particularly to fathers.
If the name is lost, in a sense, the child is lost. That strong patrilineal
feeling we all to some extent share. But this has to be kept within the
bounds of common sense, in my judgment. It is not very realistic to be   G
litigating over how a child of 2½ years should be called, so far as its
surname is concerned. A child at that age is quite unaware of its surname,
even though it will acquire later on, fairly quickly perhaps, some idea of
what his or her name is. But what matters is whether the child identifies
with the father in human terms. I suspect that children are much better
at distinguishing between reality and formality than adults. If the child   H
knows that D. is his father, he may be confused later on if he is known by
the name B., but I would doubt it. When very young he is certain to be
confused if everybody insists on calling him D. when all the people he
lives with are called B. But this is, as one appreciates all too clearly, a
very sensitive issue. Fathers feel very sensitive about it. Mothers feel that
it is a plague on a day to day basis: they have to explain to schools,
people have to make special notes in records, and so on, about the name.

The Weekly Law Reports, October 13, 1978

583

3 W.L.R.   D. v. B. (Surname: Birth Registration) (C.A.)   Ormrod L.J.

A   The matter is one which, in my judgment, ought to be capable of being resolved by two sensible adults who bear in mind that they are dealing with a child, and a child who sooner or later (and probably sooner) will make some decisions for himself in the matter. Pressure, I would have thought, is more likely to produce unwanted results than anything else.

I cannot help reiterating the Official Solicitor's advice in this case at the
B   conclusion of his report which was prepared for the hearing in December. The Official Solicitor's report recommended that access between the child and the father should be started at the earliest moment, although at that time the child was very young indeed. The report concludes with these words:

C   "For [the child] to be known as D. when his mather and [the co-respondent] are called B. could cause him some embarrassment particularly when he attends school. The mother and [the co-respondent] might well have children of their own and this in itself could cause some distress in so far as [the child] will be the only one in the family unit with a different surname. In the circumstances, should the court decide that the father should have access to [the
D   child], and the Official Solicitor recommends that he should, the father might consider that it would be in [the child's] best interests for the future not to insist on his being known by his real surname of D."

If I may say so with great respect to the Official Solicitor, that passage
E   seems to me the best statement of good sense that I have read in this context for a long time. It seems to me human, sensible and practical. Any other solution seems to me inhuman, impracticable and bound to lead to trouble. The one thing that one should try to avoid in these cases is giving hostages to fortune, weapons to parties to quarrel with, when the real issue between them is something quite other.

F   Nothing is more depressing than to have a mother brought back to the court over some infringement of this requirement, such as registering the child in a particular play-group under the name B. when it ought to be D. Fortunately, at the end of the day, the father, I think, has realised that substantive issues are what matter to children and formal issues can be left to look after themselves. If they are forgotten about, nobody will
G   worry about them. I can understand the father, in the early stages of this case, taking steps about the registration and, indeed, steps about the deed poll, because it must have seemed, in the autumn of 1976, as if the mother had laid her plans pretty well. She had changed her own name to B. by deed poll so that she could say "Now I am properly known as B." and she had registered the child in the name of B. so that she could say
H   "But the child's real name is B.," and one can understand that the father's tactics should direct an attack on those two points. It is bad enough for him that both of them have proved abortive. But neither of them are real. What is real is that the father and the child should know one another, that the child should, in course of time, come to recognise the fact that D. is his natural father and, so long as that is understood, names are really of little importance and they only become important when they become a casus belli between the parents.

Having said that, I can only hope that from now on these young people **A** (and they are still quite young, under 30 years) will direct their attention to the issues about this child which matter and not about formalistic things that do not much matter. A vast amount of money has been spent on this case which is little short of a disaster and should have been avoided, and could have been avoided, by a little good sense.

I would, therefore, allow the appeal. Just what form the order should **B** take is not very easy. So far as the first two points are concerned, that is the deed poll point and the Register of Births point, all that will be necessary is to delete those two paragraphs of the order, which will in effect eliminate the order appealed against. But some order will have to be made, and it will be a question of deciding the appropriate form, to deal with the variation of the December 1976 order in relation to the practical use **C** of names. Perhaps that is a matter which can be left for discussion later. I would therefore allow the appeal and substitute an order in such form as proves to be appropriate.

STAMP L.J. I agree. Out of respect to the judge in the court below, because we are differing, I would have delivered a judgment of my own, **D** but having heard the way Ormrod L.J. has put it, I do not wish to do so. I entirely agree and would now invite submissions on the order as to which Ormrod L.J. spoke.

> *Appeal allowed.*
> *Order of April 10, 1978, discharged.*
> *Order of December 13, 1976, varied by* **E**
> *consent to enable child to be known*
> *under surname B.*
> *No order as to costs in Court of*
> *Appeal nor as to hearing of April*
> *10, 1978, below.*
> *Legal aid taxation for the mother.*

F

Solicitors: *Penningtons for Wild, Hewitson & Shaw, Cambridge; Jaques & Co.; Official Solicitor.*

G

H

A

[COURT OF APPEAL]

JONES v. WROTHAM PARK SETTLED ESTATES
AND ANOTHER

B 1977 Dec. 16, 19;   Stephenson, Orr and Goff L.JJ.
    1978 Jan. 26

Landlord and Tenant—Leasehold enfranchisement—Price of free-
hold—Long lease at low rent—Lease for 300 years subject to
existing lease—Provision for increase of rent on termination
of lease—Valuation of freehold depending on whether con-
current lease to be considered in determining price—Applica-
C *bility of statute to concurrent lease—Whether concurrent lease*
modifying right to acquire freehold—Leasehold Reform Act
1967 (c. 88), ss. 9 (1), 23 (1)

In 1962 the tenant who was the occupier of the house was
granted a lease of it from 1961 for 87 years at a yearly rent of
£15. By a leaseholder's notice dated October 5, 1973, and
served on October 8, the tenant gave notice to the freeholders
D of her intention to acquire the freehold in accordance with her
right under Part 1 of the Leasehold Reform Act 1967. Before
the notice was served, on October 6, the freeholders granted
a concurrent lease to a property company, the reversioner,
for 300 years, subject to the existing lease at a peppercorn
rent until the expiry of the tenant's lease and at a rack
rent thereafter. The reversioner was granted similar leases
in respect of other houses in the area. The concurrent
E lease provided by paragraph 5 of Schedule 4 that, if the
reversioner should grant a sublease to the tenant, then the
annual rent payable should be equal to the best yearly rent
for which the premises could be let in the open market. On
the tenant's application to the Lands Tribunal to determine
the price of the freehold under section 9 (1) of the Act, two
alternative valuations were agreed between the parties. The
valuations were that £50 was payable to the freeholders and
F £250 to the reversioner, when paragraph 5 of Schedule 4 was
left out of account, whereas, if that paragraph was taken into
consideration, the sum of £4,000 was to be paid to the freeholders, no sum at all being then payable to the reversioner.
It was conceded for the tenant that the reversioner was deemed
to have granted a sublease of the premises to the tenant
within the meaning of paragraph 5 for the purposes of the
assumption to be made under section 9 (1) (a) in determining
G the price of the freehold. But the tenant contended that
paragraph 5 should not be taken into consideration since it
was void by virtue of section 23 (1) of the Act as it purported
to modify the tenant's rights and provided for a penalty or
disability. After finding that the concurrent lease was a device
to increase the value of the freehold, the tribunal held that
section 23 (1) was not applicable to the concurrent agreement
as the tenant was not a party to it and that the agreement did
H not modify the tenant's rights nor impose any penalty or
disability. Therefore, the tribunal determined that the
tenant should pay £4,000 to the freeholders and need not pay
any sum to the reversioner on the basis that regard should be
had to paragraph 5 of Schedule 4 to the concurrent lease in
assessing the sum payable.
On the tenant's appeal: —

[Reported by MISS HENRIETTA STEINBERG, Barrister-at-Law.]

A   *Held*, allowing the appeal, that section 23 (1) of the Act was applicable to the concurrent agreement, since the words "any agreement relating to the tenancy" being very wide, should not be restricted to agreements between a landlord and tenant only and the concurrent agreement was an agreement "relating to" the tenancy by reason of the fact that paragraph 5 of Schedule 4 was capable of applying to the statutory right of enfranchisement and was intended by the parties to

B   apply to it, and that statutory right, being annexed to the tenancy by the statute, was an incident of the tenancy; and that, further, section 23 (1) operated to invalidate paragraph 5 in so far as the paragraph, coupled with the concession, by increasing the price of the freehold, purported to modify, in the sense of having the effect of modifying, the tenant's right to acquire the freehold under the Act (post, pp. 595c–d, f–g, 596a, 597g–h, 598c, e–f, 600f–g, h—601a). Accordingly, the

C   court, taking no account of paragraph 5, would substitute a determination that the price payable would be £50 to the freeholders and £250 to the reversioner.
          Dictum of Diplock L.J. in *Joseph* v. *Joseph* [1967] Ch. 78, 90, C.A. applied.
          Quaere. It may not be necessary in regard to the assumption which has to be made under section 9 (1) for the purpose of ascertaining the price of the freehold which requires the

D   concurrent lease and the estate in fee simple to be valued on the basis that the reversioner had actually granted a sublease to the tenant, to postulate the grant of a new tenancy the true effect of the subsection remains an open and arguable issue (post, pp. 593f–h, 596d–e, g–h, 597a, 599e–g).

The following case is referred to in the judgments:

Joseph v. *Joseph* [1967] Ch. 78; [1966] 3 W.L.R. 631; [1966] 3 All E.R. E
    486, C.A.

The following additional cases were cited in argument:

Elmdene Estates Ltd. v. *White* [1960] A.C. 528; [1960] 2 W.L.R. 359;
    [1960] 1 All E.R. 306, H.L.(E.).
Tedman v. *Wicker* [1944] K.B. 112; [1944] 1 All E.R. 26, C.A.
Wilkes v. *Goodwin* [1923] 2 K.B. 86, C.A.   F

Case stated by the Lands Tribunal.
    This was a reference by the tenants, William Selwyn Jones (now deceased) and Mrs. Lena Jones, in respect of the price payable for the freehold interest of 45 Wellesley Crescent, Potters Bar, Hertfordshire, under section 9 of the Leasehold Reform Act 1967. At the hearing G
before the Lands Tribunal (V. G. Wellings Q.C.) the proved facts formed part of the case.
    The tenants were granted a lease of the house, which they had occupied since October 1962, by Dugdale Hill Estate Co. Ltd., predecessors in title of the freeholders, Wentworth Securities Ltd. The lease was for a term of 87 years at a yearly rent of £15 from December 1961. On October 6, 1973, the freeholders interposed between the H
freehold and the lease a concurrent lease granting Wrotham Park Settled Estates, the reversioner, a term of 300 years from December 25, 1970, subject to the tenant's existing lease. The rent payable under the concurrent lease was a peppercorn until December 25, 2048, and thereafter rack rents were payable until the end of the term, the rack rents to vary from period to period. By paragraph 5 of Schedule 4 to the lease, it was provided that, if a sublease were granted by the reversioner,

A   then an amount equal to the best yearly rent for which the premises could be let in the open market would become payable.

The land certificates relating to the registered title showed that the freeholders had granted identical leases to the reversioner in respect of 106 properties in the district. The tribunal found that the concurrent lease was a device to increase the price of the freehold. The parties agreed that, if the provisions of paragraph 5 of Schedule 4 were not taken into consideration, then the price payable would be £50 to the freeholders and £250 to the reversioner, but that £4,000 should be paid to the freeholders and nothing to the reversioner if that paragraph were to be taken into consideration.

The tribunal was of the opinion that the reference in section 23 (1) of the Act of 1967 to " an agreement relating to a tenancy " meant an agreement to which the occupying tenant was a party to the exclusion of the concurrent lease. Further, the tribunal decided that, even if the concurrent lease could be regarded as falling within the subsection, it did not purport to exclude or modify the tenant's right to acquire the freehold which remained unqualified and absolute, nor could it be described as imposing a penalty or disability. The tribunal therefore held that the tenant should pay £4,000 to the freeholders and no sum at all to the reversioner. The question for the decision of the court was whether the tribunal was correct in law in holding that section 23 of the Leasehold Reform Act 1967 was not applicable.

The tenant appealed against the determination, seeking an order that the price payable to the freeholders for the freehold was £50 and to the reversioner for the leasehold was £250. The grounds of appeal were that the tribunal were wrong: (1) in holding that the reference in section 23 (1) to " an agreement relating to a tenancy " was confined to an agreement to which the tenant was a party; and that such reference in fact included the concurrent lease made between the freeholders and the reversioner; (2) in holding that the lease did not modify the tenant's right to acquire the freehold; and (3) in holding that the concurrent lease did not impose a penalty or disability on the tenant within section 23 (1); that the tribunal should have held that paragraph 5 of Schedule 4 to the concurrent lease, rightly described as a device to increase the value of the freehold, was rendered void by section 23 (1); and that, having regard to the facts and the valuations, the tribunal's decision was wrong.

G   N. T. Hague for the tenant.
T. M. E. B. Etherton for the reversioner on the matter of costs only.
E. G. Nugee Q.C. for the freeholders.

Cur. adv. vult.

H   January 26, 1978. The following judgments were read.

ORR L.J. This is an appeal by the tenant of a house, 45 Wellesley Crescent, Potters Bar, against a decision of the Lands Tribunal (Mr. V. G. Wellings Q.C.) on October 15, 1976, whereby it was determined, on a reference to the tribunal under section 21 of the Leasehold Reform Act 1967, that the price payable by the tenant on the exercise of her rights under the Act to acquire the ownership of the premises is, in respect of the freehold estate in the premises, £4,000, but that in respect

of a superior lease of the premises, which I shall call "the concurrent   A
lease," no sum is payable.

The facts of the case can be shortly stated.   On October 2, 1962, a
company named Dugdale Hill Estates Co. Ltd. leased the premises to
the tenant, Mrs. Jones, and her husband, who has since died, at a
yearly rent of £15 for a term of 87 years from December 25, 1961 (and
therefore expiring in December 2048).   By a leaseholder's notice under
the Act, dated October 5, 1973, but not served until October 8, notice   B
was given in the names of the tenant and her husband, Mr. and Mrs.
Jones, to the freeholders, the second respondents, Wentworth Securities
Co. Ltd., who had acquired the freehold title from Dugdale Hill Estates
Co. Ltd., of their desire to acquire the freehold.   It is common ground
that, had the matter rested on these facts, the sum payable for the
freehold would have been £300, but on October 6, 1973, between the   C
date of the tenant's notice and the date of its service, the freeholders,
Wentworth, interposed between their freehold and the lease to the
tenant and her husband the concurrent lease to which I have earlier
referred, being a lease of the premises to the reversioner Wrotham Park
Estate Co., since renamed Wrotham Park Settled Estates, the first
respondents in this appeal, for a term of 300 years from December 25,
1970, subject to and with the benefit of the lease to the tenant and her   D
husband.   We have been told, and it is not in dispute, that a large
number of similar leases were on or about the same date granted by
the freeholders to the reversioner in respect of some 100 other houses
in the same locality; that the tenants were informed of what was being
done; and that the freeholders and the reversioner are connected companies having at least one common director.   All these leases granted   E
to the reversioner a term of 300 years from December 25, 1970, subject
to and with the benefit of the pre-existing leases, the rents payable under
the concurrent leases being, by paragraph 1 of schedule 4 to each lease,
a peppercorn (if demanded) until December 25, 2048 (the date of expiry
of the tenant's lease and the other original leases), and thereafter, by
paragraphs 2 and 3 of the same schedule, rack rents to be determined
by an arbitrator for the periods from December 25, 2048, to December   F
25, 2098, and from the latter date until the end of the term; such rack
rents to be based on values at the commencement of each period.
Paragraph 5, which is the crucial provision for the purpose of the
present appeal, and paragraph 6 of the same schedule provided as
follows:

"(5) If and so often as a sub-lease (not being a tenancy from year   G
to year or any lesser interest) is granted by the tenant of the whole
of the premises the annual rent payable hereunder shall for the
period beginning with the commencement of the term granted by
the sub-lease and ending with the termination thereof (however the
same determines and if the term is extended by virtue of any
enactment then ending with the termination of the term so extended)
be (in lieu of the foregoing rents) an amount equal to the best   H
yearly rent for which the premises could be let in the open market
at the commencement of such terms with vacant possession free
from all incumbrances (including the existing lease) for a term
equal to the term granted by the sub-lease such amount to be ascertained (in default of agreement) by arbitration as aforesaid.
"(6) Provided always that if (whether by virtue of the provisions
of paragraph (5) of this schedule or otherwise) the yearly rent

A   which would (apart from this paragraph (6)) be for the time being
     payable hereunder shall be more than the yearly rent reserved by
     any sub-lease granted by the tenant (whether in pursuance of the
     provisions of the Leasehold Reform Act 1967 or any amendment
     or re-enactment thereof or otherwise howsoever) then the yearly
     rent payable hereunder under paragraphs (2) and (3) of this
     schedule shall be reduced to a peppercorn during a period (here-
B   after called ' a rent free period ') from the actual termination of
     the term of such sub-lease (howsoever the same shall determine and
     if the term shall be extended by statute then from the termination
     of the term as so extended) on December 25, 2048, or the expiration
     of any rent free period referably to any earlier sub-lease (whichever
     shall be the later date) until the expiration of the term hereby
C   granted (whichever shall last occur)."

     Before turning to the proceedings before the Lands Tribunal it
will be convenient to refer to the relevant provisions of the Leasehold
Reform Act 1967, which may be summarised as follows.
     Section 1 (1) of the Act provides that Part I of the Act shall have
the effect to confer on a tenant of a leasehold house, occupying the
D   house as his residence, a right to acquire on fair terms the freehold or
extended lease of the house and premises where (a) his tenancy is a
long tenancy at a low rent and the rateable value of the house and
premises is, if outside London, not more than £200, and (b) he has, at
the time when he gives notice of his desire to assert this right, occupied
the house under a long tenancy, at a low rent, and as his residence, for
E   a specified time. It is not in dispute that all these conditions were
satisfied in the present case and it is unnecessary to make any further
reference to them.
     Section 8 (1) provides:

     "Where a tenant of a house has under this Part of this Act a
     right to acquire the freehold, and gives to the landlord written
     notice of his desire to have the freehold, then except as provided
F   by this Part of this Act the landlord shall be bound to make to
     the tenant, and the tenant to accept, (at the price and on the con-
     ditions so provided) a grant of the house and premises for an estate
     in fee simple absolute, subject to the tenancy and to tenant's
     incumbrances, but otherwise free of incumbrances."

     Section 9 (1) provides:
G
     ". . . the price payable for a house and premises on a conveyance
     under section 8 above shall be the amount which at the relevant
     time the house and premises, if sold in the open market by a willing
     seller, might be expected to realise on the following assumptions: —
     (a) on the assumption that the vendor was selling for an estate in
     fee simple, subject to the tenancy but on the assumption that this
H   Part of this Act conferred no right to acquire the freehold, and
     if the tenancy has not been extended under this Part of this Act,
     on the assumption that (subject to the landlord's rights under
     section 17 below) it was to be so extended; . . ."

     Section 14 (1) provides:

     "Where a tenant of a house has under this Part of this Act a
     right to an extended lease, and gives to the landlord written

notice of his desire to have it, then except as provided by this A
Part of this Act the landlord shall be bound to grant to the
tenant, and the tenant to accept, in substitution for the existing
tenancy a new tenancy of the house and premises for a term
expiring 50 years after the term date of the existing tenancy."

Section 15 (2) provides that the rent payable under such a new
tenancy is to be a ground rent in the sense that it shall be the letting B
value of the site, without including anything for the value of buildings
on the site, for permitted uses to which the house and premises have
been put during the existing tenancy, and that such rent may, if
the landlord so requires, be adjusted on the expiry of 25 of the 50
years to accord with letting values then current.

Section 23 (1) provides: C

"Except as provided by this section, any agreement relating to a
tenancy (whether contained in the instrument creating the tenancy
or not and whether made before the creation of the tenancy or
not) shall be void in so far as it purports to exclude or modify any
right to acquire the freehold or an extended lease or right to compensation under this Part of this Act, or provides for the termination or surrender of the tenancy in the event of a tenant acquiring D
or claiming any such right or for the imposition of any penalty or
disability on the tenant in that event."

Schedule 1 to the Act, entitled " Enfranchisement or Extension by
Sub-Tenants " includes the following provisions relevant to the present
case:

"1. (1) Where a person (in this Schedule referred to as ' the E
claimant ') gives notice of his desire to have the freehold or an
extended lease of a house and premises under Part I of this Act,
and does so in respect of a sub-tenancy (in this Schedule referred
to as ' the tenancy in possession '), then except as otherwise
provided by this Schedule—(a) the rights and obligations of the
landlord under Part I of this Act shall, so far as their interests are F
affected, be rights and obligations respectively of the estate owner
in respect of the fee simple and of each of the persons in whom
is vested a concurrent tenancy superior to the tenancy in possession
(and references to the landlord shall apply accordingly); and
(b) the proceedings arising out of the notice, whether for resisting
or giving effect to the claim to acquire the freehold or extended G
lease, shall be conducted, on behalf of all the persons referred to in
(a) above, by and through that one of them who is identified by
this Schedule as ' the reversioner.' (2) Where there is a tenancy
reversionary on a tenancy in respect of which a person gives notice
as aforesaid, then (except in so far as special provision is made for
such a reversionary tenancy) this Schedule shall apply as if the
reversionary tenancy were a concurrent tenancy intermediate H
between the tenancy in possession and any interest superior to it.
(3) In the following provisions of this Schedule the persons for
whom the reversioner is by this paragraph authorised to act are
referred to as ' other landlords '; and in this Schedule references
to superior interests mean the estate in fee simple and any tenancy
superior (or treated by sub-paragraph (2) above as superior) to
the inferior interest in question.

A   " 2. Subject to paragraph 3 below, ' the reversioner ' shall be—
(a) if any person has a tenancy of the house carrying an expectation of possession of 30 years or more, that person or, if there is
more than one, that one of them to whose tenancy the other
tenancies are superior; . . ."

It is common ground that, by virtue of paragraph 2 (a), the first
B respondent is the reversioner for the purposes of Schedule 1 in the
present case.

Paragraph 4 provides:

" (1) Without prejudice to the generality of paragraph 1 above, the
reversioner may on behalf and in the name of the other landlords—
(a) execute any conveyance to give effect to section 8 of this Act,
C   or any lease to give effect to section 14; and (b) take or defend
any legal proceedings under Part I of this Act in respect of matters
arising out of the claimant's notice. (2) Subject to paragraphs 5
and 6 below, in relation to all matters within the authority given
to him by this Schedule the reversioner's acts shall be binding on
the other landlords and on their interests in the house and
premises or any other property; but in the event of dispute either
D   the reversioner or any of the other landlords may apply to the
court for directions as to the manner in which he should act on
the matter in dispute."

Paragraph 5 (1):

" Notwithstanding anything in paragraph 4 (2) above, any of the
E   other landlords shall be entitled, if he so desires, to be separately
represented in any legal proceedings in which his title to any
property comes in question, or in any legal proceedings relating to
the price payable for the house and premises under section 9 of
this Act. (2) For the purpose of deducing, evidencing or verifying
his title to any property, any of the other landlords, on giving
written notice to the reversioner and to the claimant, may deal
F   directly with the claimant, if he objects to disclosing his title to
the reversioner, and he shall deal directly with the claimant if
the claimant by written notice given to him and to the reversioner
so requires.   (3) For the purpose of agreeing the price payable for
his interest under section 9 of this Act, any of the other landlords,
on giving written notice to the reversioner and to the claimant,
G   may deal directly with the claimant; and whether he does that
or not, he may require the reversioner to apply to the Lands
Tribunal for the price to be determined by the Lands Tribunal."

It is common ground that the freeholders' locus standi in the present
proceedings is derived from paragraph 4 (1) and that they had also,
by virtue of a notice to that effect, obtained a right to deal directly with
H the tenant under paragraph 5 (3).   Paragraph 7 (1) provides:

" Where a conveyance is executed to give effect to section 8 of
this Act—(a) section 10 shall have effect in relation to rights and
restrictions arising by virtue of any tenancy superior to the tenancy
in possession (or by virtue of an agreement collateral to such a
tenancy), so far as they are directly or indirectly to the benefit
of or enforceable against the claimant during the tenancy in
possession, as if they arose by virtue of that tenancy; . . ."

592

Paragraph 10 (1) provides: A

> "Where a lease is executed to give effect to section 14 of this
> Act, then except as provided by paragraph 11 below the new
> tenancy shall be granted by the landlord having an interest suf-
> ficient in point of duration which is not superior to another such
> interest."

In consequence of the leaseholder's notice and in default of agree-   B
ment between the parties, an application was made to the Lands
Tribunal under section 21 of the Act to determine the price payable
for the house and premises, 45 Wellesley Crescent, under section 9 of
the Act, and on the hearing the tenant, the reversioner and the freeholders were all represented by counsel, but Mr. Etherton for the
reversioner took no part in the argument. There were before the   C
tribunal alternative agreed valuations, the first of which, relied on for
the tenant, was prepared on the basis that the valuers were required
to take account of the concurrent lease dated October 6, 1973, but to
ignore paragraph 5 of Schedule 4 thereto, and on that basis produced
agreed figures of £50 payable to the freeholders in respect of the
freehold estate and £250 payable to the reversioner in respect of the
concurrent lease, making a total of £300, and this basis of valuation   D
the tribunal referred to as assumption 1. The other valuation was
prepared on the basis, which the tribunal referred to as assumption 2,
that all the provisions of the concurrent lease, including paragraph 5
of Schedule 4, were to be taken into account, and produced an agreed
figure of £4,000 payable to the freeholders in respect of the freehold
estate but nothing payable to the reversioner in respect of the   E
concurrent lease.

On behalf of the freeholders it was argued before the tribunal that
the proper assumption to be applied in the valuation was assumption
2 because: (a) section 9 (1) of the Act required the price payable for
the freehold to be assessed on the double basis that the freehold was
subject to the tenant's lease of 1961 and that such lease was to be
extended for 50 years; (b) that for this reason, taken in conjunction   F
with paragraph 10 (1) of Schedule 1 to the Act, a new lease under
section 14 must be deemed to be granted by the reversioner; and (c) that
in the circumstances the deemed new lease under section 14 was a sub-
lease of the whole of the premises granted by the reversioner within
the meaning of paragraph 5 of Schedule 4 to the concurrent lease,
with the result that, for the purpose of assessing the compensation   G
payable to the freeholders in respect of the latter's freehold estate in
the premises, the rent must be taken to be the best yearly rent for
which the premises could be let in the open market as defined in
paragraph 5.

On behalf of the tenant it was conceded by Mr. Hague that the
concurrent lease was a valid lease and not a sham and that the submissions made by Mr. Nugee for the freeholders were correct subject   H
only to arguments which Mr. Hague for the tenant proceeded to
develop, based on section 23 (1) of the Act, to the effect, first, that
paragraph 5 of Schedule 4 to the concurrent lease was an agreement
relating to the tenant's tenancy within section 23 (1); that it purported
to modify the tenant's right to acquire the freehold by providing for a
greatly increased purchase price compared with the £300 which, but
for the execution of the concurrent lease, would have been payable

A under the Act; and that it also contravened section 23 (1) by providing for the imposition of a penalty or disability on the tenant in the event of her claiming the right to acquire the freehold.

In its decision the Lands Tribunal observed that there could be no doubt that the interposing of the concurrent lease between the freehold and the occupying tenant's lease was intended as a device to increase the
B value of the freehold under section 9 of the Act, and that the question at issue was whether this device had succeeded. Having said this, and having referred to the concessions made by Mr. Hague for the tenant, the tribunal proceeded to reject his submissions based on section 23 (1) of the Act of 1967 holding, first, that the reference in that subsection to " any agreement relating to a tenancy " applied only to an agreement to which the tenant was a party and could not therefore apply to the
C concurrent lease to which the tenant was not a party; and, secondly, that the concurrent lease did not purport to modify the tenant's rights, which remained intact and unqualified, nor did it provide for the imposition of any penalty or disability on the tenant in the event of her acquiring or claiming any right under the Act. Accordingly the tribunal held that assumption 2, whereby regard was to be had to all the terms
D of the concurrent lease, including paragraph 5 of Schedule 4, was the proper basis of valuation and determined that the price payable for the freehold estate was £4,000 and that no sum was payable in respect of the concurrent lease.

Against this determination the tenant now appeals and (the reversioner not being represented in this court) we have heard, on behalf of the tenant and of the freeholders, argument limited to the issues arising
E in relation to section 23 of the Act. In the course of the argument, however, questions were put by Goff L.J. to Mr. Hague for the tenant as to the concession made by him before the Lands Tribunal that, for the purpose of assessing the compensation payable to the freeholders, it was to be assumed that a sub-lease had actually been granted by the reversioner to the tenant within the meaning of paragraph 5 of Schedule
F 4 to the concurrent lease. One of the points put was that the apparent intention of section 9 is to secure to the tenant, when assessing the sum payable by him for the freehold, the benefit of his right, although not exercised, to have an extended lease at a ground rent and without paying a premium, and that all that is required for this purpose is to treat the tenancy as extended without postulating the grant of any
G actual sub-tenancy. Another point was that the assumption required to be made by section 9 (1) (a) of the Act is that the tenancy " was to be extended " which, as Mr. Nugee conceded for the freeholders, appears to recognise that there was not in fact going to be any new sub-tenancy. For these reasons Mr. Hague for the tenant was asked whether he wished to reconsider his concession, but he decided not to do so and in the result we heard no argument upon it. In these circum-
H stances I express no view on this matter save to say that it appears to me to be a very arguable one.

I turn to the issues in relation to section 23, and first to the broad arguments advanced on each side which may be summarised as follows. Mr. Hague for the tenant argued that it was the intention of Parliament that a qualified tenant should have the right given him by the statute; that the object of what was done by the freeholders in the present case was to defeat that right and that if in any doubt the court should resolve the matter in favour of the tenant. Mr. Nugee for the **A** freeholders submitted two broad arguments. The first was that it was a fallacy to suppose that there existed, independent of the provisions of the Act, any set of fair terms on which Parliament intended that the tenant should be entitled to obtain the freehold, the words " on fair terms " in section 1 being merely an introductory reference to the terms defined in subsequent sections of the Act, and it being common ground that the sum produced by those sections in the circumstances of this **B** case is £4,000. In the second place Mr. Nugee for the freeholders relied on the distinction drawn in decided cases in relation to the Rent Acts between, on the one hand, attempted exclusion of those Acts and, on the other, the parties' bona fide entering into a situation where those Acts have no application; a distinction which is clearly stated in the following passages in *Megarry, The Rent Acts,* 10th ed. (1967), vol. 1, **C** pp. 19–20:

> " (a) *Genuine Transactions.* There is nothing, however, to prevent the parties from so arranging matters that there is nothing to which the Acts can apply, provided the transaction in question is a genuine transaction and not a mere sham, such as a tenancy disguised as a contract for sale; ' real and lawful intentions cannot **D** be dismissed as shams merely because they are disliked.' The difference is between on the one hand a provision attempting to exclude the Acts from a transaction to which they apply, and on the other hand entering into a bona fide transaction to which the Acts have no application. (b) *Evasion and avoidance.* ' There is every difference between evasion and avoidance.' ' You do not evade an Act by doing something which is not forbidden by the Act, **E** but you do evade the Act by doing something which is prohibited under the guise of doing something else.' "

In relation to these passages Mr. Nugee relied strongly on the admission made by Mr. Hague for the tenant before the Lands Tribunal that the concurrent lease was not a sham, but I do not pause upon these passages because it is in my judgment clear that they cannot assist the **F** freeholders' case if the crucial provisions of the concurrent lease are rendered void by section 23 nor, in my judgment, can they assist the tenant if her case fails under that section.

The first issue under section 23 is whether the concurrent lease is " an agreement relating to the tenancy." It is claimed by Mr. Nugee for the freeholders that it is not, on the ground that the tenant is a necessary party to such an agreement and he sought to support this **G** argument by a passage from the judgment of Diplock L.J. in *Joseph* v. *Joseph* [1967] Ch. 78, 89, a case involving section 38 (1) of the Landlord and Tenant Act 1954, much of the language of which has been adopted in drafting section 23 of the Leasehold Reform Act 1967. It reads as follows:

> " Any agreement relating to a tenancy to which this Part of this **H** Act applies (whether contained in the instrument creating the tenancy or not) shall be void in so far as it purports to preclude the tenant from making an application or request under this Part of this Act or provides for the termination or the surrender of the tenancy in the event of his making such an application or request or for the imposition of any penalty or disability on the tenant in that event."

The Weekly Law Reports, October 20, 1978

595

3 W.L.R.   **Jones v. Wrotham Park Estates (C.A.)**   **Orr L.J.**

A   *Joseph* v. *Joseph* is authority for the proposition that in section 38 the words " in so far as it purports " denote " in so far as it has the effect of " and on that authority I have no doubt that the same meaning should be given to the same words in section 23 of the Leasehold Reform Act 1967. In addition, however, Diplock L.J. said at p. 90:

B   " In my judgment this subsection does render void any provision of an agreement between landlord and tenant whereby the tenant undertakes to do in the future any act which will have the effect under the statute of disqualifying him from applying for a new tenancy under sections 24 (1) and 29."

C   But the agreement in issue in that case was between landlords and tenants and it is clear in my judgment that Diplock L.J. who, at p. 89, had posed the question which he answered in the passage quoted above. " Can he [the tenant] . . . agree . . . with the landlord?" was not, in the passage quoted, putting any general construction on the words " agreement relating to a tenancy." For my part I can see no good reason in the context of section 23 of the Act of 1967 for adopting the narrow construction that the words " any agreement relating to a tenancy,"

D   which are in my judgment very wide words, are restricted to agreements between landlord and tenant. I would find it very surprising if they did not apply to an agreement between, for example, the landlord and a relative of the tenant, that on the tenant's obtaining enfranchisement the relative would pay to the landlord the amount by which the enfranchisement price fell short of a specified sum, and I would find it

E   equally surprising if such an agreement fell outside the section because the promise was made, not to the landlord, but to a company in which he was interested. It was not necessary for Mr. Nugee for the freeholders in the present case to argue that the landlords must be a party to " an agreement relating to a tenancy " under section 23 since the freeholders, the landlords in the present case, were a party to the concurrent lease, and he was content to argue no more than that the

F   landlords were probably a necessary party, but if the words " agreement relating to a tenancy " involve that the tenant must, but the landlord need not, be a party I would have expected the section to say so in terms. For these reasons, with great respect, I consider that the Lands Tribunal was wrong in the only reason which it gave for holding that the agreement in question was not " an agreement relating to the

G   tenancy." It remains, however, to consider whether the agreement in question was an agreement " relating to " the tenancy. In my judgment it was, because paragraph 5 in Schedule 4 to the concurrent lease was capable of applying to the statutory right of enfranchisement and was intended by both parties to do so, and such right, although not a term of the tenancy, was a right annexed to the tenancy by statute and therefore, in my judgment, an incident of the tenancy.

H   The next question is whether the agreement purports to " modify any right to acquire the freehold or an extended lease or right to compensation " under Part I of the Act. The Lands Tribunal held that it does not, on the ground that, while the effect of paragraph 5 of Schedule 4 is that the tenant has to pay £4,000 instead of £300 for enfranchisement, her right to obtain the freehold " remains absolute and unqualified "; in other words, although the value of the right has been drastically reduced, the right itself has remained unaffected. In my judgment, however, again with great respect to the Lands Tribunal, A this reasoning ignores the fact that until the act of enfranchisement £300 remained the proper price for the freehold, calculated in accordance with the Act and apart from paragraph 5 of Schedule 4 the exercise of the right of enfranchisement could not increase the price, but paragraph 5, coupled with the concession, makes it do so, and in that respect, in my judgment, modifies the right.

Having reached these conclusions I do not need to decide whether B paragraph 5 of Schedule 4 " provides for . . . the imposition of any penalty or disability " on the tenant in the event of her acquiring or claiming any right under Part I of the Act, but in my judgment this part of section 23 has no application in the present case since it is prefaced by the words " provides for " and paragraph 5 does not provide for the imposition of any penalty or disability.   C

For these reasons I would allow this appeal and, in lieu of the Lands Tribunal's determination that the price payable for the house and premises is £4,000, would substitute, subject to any observations that counsel may wish to make, a determination that the price is £300, being £50 payable to the freeholders and £250 payable to the reversioner.

GOFF L.J.   The facts which give rise to the question we have to determine are fully stated in the judgment of Orr L.J. and I need not take up time by repeating them.

I desire to stress, however, that I am not at all satisfied that the assumption which section 9 (1) (a) of the Leasehold Reform Act 1967 requires to be made for the purpose of ascertaining the price payable for the premises requires the two elements of the reversion, namely the E concurrent lease to the reversioner and the ultimate estate in fee simple remaining in the freeholders to be valued on the hypothesis that the reversioner had actually granted a subtenancy to the tenant.

It is true that where the tenant claims an extended lease, and not the freehold, the machinery provided by section 14 of the Act is to bind the reversioner to grant a new lease, and the existing lease is merged F or surrendered by operation of law, but where the freehold is claimed, although the valuation has, pursuant to section 9 (1) (a), to be made " if the tenancy has not been extended under this Part of this Act, on the assumption that . . . it was to be so extended," I think that that must be construed in the light of the context and clear intention of the section. That intention was to secure to the tenant, when assessing the price he has to pay for the freehold, the benefit of his right, albeit not in fact exercised, to have an extended lease at a ground rent only and without paying a premium. All that is required for that purpose is to treat his tenancy as if it were what it would be if it had been extended. It is not I think necessary to postulate the grant of a new tenancy. The words " was to be " are in my view significant, because as Mr. Nugee conceded for the freeholders they recognise that there is not H going to be any actual new tenancy.

It was common ground, however, that section 9 on its true construction does require the valuation to be made on the footing that the reversioner is to be deemed to have granted a sub-tenancy within the meaning of, and so as to bring into operation, the provisions of paragraph 5 of Schedule 4 to the lease of October 6, 1973, which I will call the concurrent lease, subject only to the effect, if any, of section 23

A   (1) of the Act, and Mr. Hague for the tenant, although offered the
opportunity to do so, refused to resile from that position.

　　We must therefore decide this case on that assumption, but without
deciding that it is correct, and should any case be brought upon any
of the other leases to which Orr L.J. has referred, the point as to the
true effect of section 9 will be open and, as I think, well arguable.

B   　　Having said this, I now turn to the argument on section 23 (1) on
which Mr. Hague for the tenant rested his case.

　　That subsection is qualified by opening words " Except as provided
by this section," but there is nothing relevant for present purposes in
that qualification.   The subsection continues as follows:

C
　　" . . . any agreement relating to a tenancy (whether contained in
　　the instrument creating the tenancy or not and whether made before
　　the creation of the tenancy or not) shall be void in so far as it
　　purports to exclude or modify any right to acquire the freehold or
　　an extended lease or right to compensation under this Part of this
　　Act, or provides for the termination or surrender of the tenancy in
　　the event of a tenant acquiring or claiming any such right or for
　　the imposition of any penalty or disability on the tenant in that
D 　　event."

　　Mr. Hague submits for the tenant that paragraph 5 of Schedule 4
to the concurrent lease is an agreement relating to the tenancy which
purports to exclude or modify the tenant's right to acquire the freehold,
or provides for the imposition of a penalty or disability on her in that
event. This raises several questions of which the first is whether the agree-
E ment embodied in paragraph 5 relates to the tenancy, and in my
judgment it does.

　　The Lands Tribunal held that it does not, because in their view
every such agreement must be one to which the tenant is a party.   It
is unnecessary to consider the position with regard to the freeholders,
because, of course, they were a party to the concurrent lease, but in
F my judgment it is not essential that the tenant should be a party.   In
common with Orr L.J. I cannot doubt that an agreement by a close
relative of the tenant, or anyone else for that matter, that if the tenant
should exercise his right to enfranchisement and, if the price payable
calculated in accordance with the Act should be less than £x, he would
pay the landlord the difference, would be an agreement relating to the
tenancy within the meaning of section 23 (1), notwithstanding that the
G tenant was not a party to the agreement.

　　So in my judgment the agreement contained in paragraph 5 of
Schedule 4 may fall within section 23 (1) of the Act, notwithstanding
that the tenant was not a party, but the question remains whether it
related to her tenancy and I agree with Orr L.J. that it did.

　　On the construction of section 9 on which this case proceeds, one of
H the events on which the operation of paragraph 5 is made to depend
is an assumed grant of a sub-tenancy by virtue of that section, and that
is not even a casual or fortuitous result.   It was intended that it should
be so, and the freeholders' whole case is that it is.   Therefore, as it
seems to me, the agreement in paragraph 5 clearly relates to the statutory right of enfranchisement.   Now that right, although not a term
of the tenancy, is an incident of it, and so the agreement in paragraph
5 relates also to the tenancy itself.

598

It is true that paragraph 5 would also have come into operation if the **A** tenant or her successors in title had forfeited her tenancy or allowed it to expire, and the reversioner, thus being entitled to grant a sub-tenancy, had actually done so, or if indeed she or they had in fact taken a sub-lease from the reversioner, but that seems to me to be an irrelevant consideration.

It was argued that the concurrent lease including, of course, para-graph 5 of Schedule 4, is a fair bargain between the reversioner and **B** the freeholder, and that if that clause were invalidated by section 23 of the Act it would become unfair. But in my judgment that is not so, because section 23 (1), if it applies, invalidates paragraph 5 only in so far as it purports to exclude or modify the statutory right, and therefore in any event leaves its operation untouched in the supposed case of an actual, as distinct from an assumed, sub-tenancy. **C**

But then does paragraph 5 purport to exclude or modify the right of enfranchisement? Again in my view it does. In this context, of course, " purport to " cannot bear the meaning it often has, which may very well be its primary meaning, that is to say " is expressed to but not effectively." It means " has the effect of ": see *per* Lord Denning M.R. and Diplock L.J. in *Joseph* v. *Joseph* [1967] Ch. 78, 87, 90. I ask myself, therefore, " does it have that effect?" And it seems to me **D** that there can be only one answer: " Yes, it does."

Immediately before the concurrent lease, the price for the freehold calculated in accordance with the Act was £300. Immediately after the execution of that lease, right down at least until the tenant had actually exercised the right of enfranchisement, that was still the proper price, because the freeholders could not get more than a nominal rent **E** from any concurrent lessee during the subsistence of the tenancy. Apart from paragraph 5 the exercise of the right of enfranchisement obviously could not increase that price. However, on the construction of section 9 adopted in this case, that exercise does have that result, and it does so solely because of the impact of paragraph 5. Therefore, that paragraph does " purport to " modify, that is, " has the effect of " modifying, the statutory right. **F**

In my judgment the freeholders' argument to the contrary on the ground that the increase in price is simply the result of making the valuation on the statutory hypothesis is unsound, since it assumes that paragraph 5 of Schedule 4 to the concurrent lease stands unaffected by section 23 (1) of the Act, and therefore begs the question. The alternative way in which this argument was presented, namely that the **G** valuation pursuant to and as directed by the Act is £4,000 and there is nothing on which section 23 can bite is in my judgment equally untenable for the same reason.

For these reasons I would allow this appeal and it is unnecessary to consider Mr. Hague's further argument on the tenant's behalf that paragraph 5 is invalidated in its application to the right of enfranchise-ment as being an agreement which **H**

" . . . provides for the termination or surrender of the tenancy in the event of a tenant acquiring or claiming any such right or for the imposition of any penalty or disability on the tenant in that event "

but were it necessary to decide this I would, I think, reject the sub-mission both because the verb governing this part of the section is " provides for " and not " purports to," and because it does not seem

A   to me that paragraph 5, or the effect of its coming into operation, can properly be described as a penalty or disability.

STEPHENSON L.J.   The question referred to the Lands Tribunal was as to:

B
"the prices payable on the acquisition of the intermediate leasehold and the freehold of the property described above under section 9 of the Act, . . ."

The member, giving the decision of the tribunal, said:

"There can be no doubt that the purpose of the interposition between the freehold and the occupying tenant's lease in each case was intended as a device to increase the value of the freehold under
C   section 9 of the Act of 1967. The question in the present case is whether it has succeeded."

He decided that it had succeeded on the ground that section 23 of the Act had no application. The question on which our decision is desired is stated in the case to be " whether the tribunal was correct in holding that section 23 of the Leasehold Reform Act 1967 had no application."
D   The notice of appeal asks us to set aside or vary that decision on the ground that the tribunal misdirected itself in holding that on its true construction section 23 had no application and did not render paragraph 5 of Schedule 4 to the intermediate or concurrent lease void.

Mr. Hague for the tenant conceded that, for the purpose of the assumption in section 9 (1) (a) that the tenancy was to be extended
E   under Part I of the Act, it was a sub-lease granted by the reversioner within the paragraph. That led Goff L.J. to question whether the concession was rightly made.

If the tenant had given notice of his claim to acquire an extended lease, not of his claim to acquire the freehold, the concurrent tenancy and paragraph 5 would be relevant in deciding the terms of the new tenancy under section 15. But I cannot see why, in making an
F   assumption required by section 9 to be made to determine the amount of the purchase price of the freehold, the tenancy should be treated as notionally extended in the actual circumstances of a concurrent tenancy. I would not feel compelled without further argument to make the further assumption that the notional new tenancy is a sub-lease granted by the intermediate tenant. I share the doubts expressed by Goff L.J. on the question whether this concession was rightly made, but I must
G   accept it as right when I consider the question whether section 23 applies to invalidate the concurrent lease or paragraph 5 of Schedule 4 to it.

The purpose of section 23 appears from its terms to be the preservation of the statutory rights, (1) to acquire the freehold or an extended lease and (2) to compensation, from being taken away, or restricted, or
H   made more difficult for the tenant to acquire or claim, by agreement. If a tenant qualifies under section 1 of the Act by the rent and the term of his tenancy, by the rateable value of the leasehold house and premises and by his occupation of the house as his residence, he is not to contract or be contracted out of the right to enfranchisement or extension conferred on him by that section, either completely or partly, or out of the right to compensation conferred on him by sections 17 (2) and 18 (4). He is not to be deterred from acquiring or claiming any of

those rights by being required to terminate or surrender the tenancy, A or by being penalised or disqualified, in the event of his acquiring or claiming the right.

The obvious method of contracting him out of that right or deterring him from acquiring or claiming it is by agreement between him and his landlord from whom he must acquire and claim the right to enfranchisement or extension, or by whom he must be paid compensation. So there can be little doubt that it is to agreements between landlord and tenant that section 23 is primarily addressed. The agreements excepted from subsection (1) by subsections (2) and (3) appear to be agreements between landlord and tenant. An agreement which "provides for the termination or surrender of the tenancy" within subsection (1) would seem also to be such an agreement. So it is not to be wondered at that Mr. Hague in his book on *Leasehold Enfranchisement* (1967), p. 199, C considers section 23 (1) as a subsection "which prevents the parties to a lease contracting out of Part 1 of the Act" and that Diplock L.J. considered the identical terms of section 38 (1) of the Landlord and Tenant Act 1954 as concerned with agreements between landlord and tenant: see *Joseph* v. *Joseph* [1967] Ch. 78, 90. But in neither Act does the subsection say "any agreement between landlord and tenant"; nor D does it say "any agreement" or "any agreement whatsoever." It says "Any agreement relating to the tenancy." Those are wide words, and the succeeding parenthesis indicates that they are wide and does not necessarily limit them to "any agreement between landlord and tenant," because, as was pointed out in argument, a guarantee by a third party might be "contained in the instrument creating the tenancy." I see no reason to exclude from section 23 (1) an agreement made between E one party to the lease and a third party if it relates to the tenancy and either purports to exclude or modify the statutory rights or provides for any of the matters specified in the subsection. I do not regard Mr. Hague the advocate as hoist with the petard of Mr. Hague the textbook writer. As the tenancy with which the whole Act, including this section, is concerned is a long tenancy at a low rent F from which a tenant with the other qualifications required by section 1 derives the rights conferred on him by the Act, any agreement which affects or bears upon any of those statutory rights of a tenant in my judgment relates to his tenancy.

I am therefore of the opinion, respectfully dissenting from the decision of the Lands Tribunal and concurring with Orr and Goff L.JJ. on this point, that an agreement between the landlord and a third G party which grants that party a lease of the leasehold house of which the qualified tenant has the necessary long tenancy at a low rent from the landlord, and indeed turns that tenant into a sub-tenant of the third party and his lease into a sub-lease, is an agreement relating to the tenancy. Is it also an agreement which purports to do or provides for the things which section 23 (1) declares void? H

I agree with the Lands Tribunal, for the reasons given by Orr and Goff L.JJ., that the concurrent lease does not provide for the imposition of any penalty or disability on the tenant in the event of his acquiring or claiming his right to acquire the freehold. It would be straining the language of the subsection to hold that paragraph 5 provides for a penalty of £3,700. But I am of the opinion, reached with some hesitation after the excellent arguments addressed to us by both counsel, but

The Weekly Law Reports, October 20, 1978

601

3 W.L.R.   Jones v. Wrotham Park Estates (C.A.)   Stephenson L.J.

A supported by both the judgments which have been delivered, that the concurrent lease by paragraph 5 of Schedule 4 " purports to modify " the tenant's right to acquire the freehold. It is, of course, true that section 1 confers on a qualified tenant a right to acquire on fair terms the freehold or an extended lease of the house and premises and that those terms include the purchase price payable for the freehold of the house and premises on the statutory assumptions, including the assump-

B tion under section 9 (1) (b) that the tenancy was to be extended under Part 1 of the Act, and the terms of the extended tenancy set out in section 15. There is therefore some force in Mr. Nugee's argument for the freeholders that the tenant's right to acquire the freehold is a right to acquire it for the purchase price payable under section 9, and *that* right is not modified by the interposition of the concurrent lease

C and the consequent purchase price of £4,000, because £4,000 is the purchase price payable by the tenant for the freehold at the time when he gives the freeholders notice.

The opening words of sections 8 (1) and 14 (1), " Where a tenant of a house *has* under this Part of this Act *a right . . . and gives* to the landlord written *notice* of his desire " (the emphasis is mine), may

D suggest that the right accrues before notice is given. The reference in section 5 (1) to " the rights and obligations of the landlord and tenant arising from the notice " perhaps indicates the contrary. But Mr. Nugee's argument for the freeholders appears to me to be met by the point which has been so clearly stated in both judgments just delivered that notwithstanding the execution of the concurrent lease the price payable in accordance with section 9 was £300, at least until the tenant

E exercised her right of enfranchisement.

We are bound by the decision of this court in *Joseph* v. *Joseph* [1967] Ch. 78 to construe " purports to exclude or modify " as " has the effect of excluding or modifying." There can be no doubt that paragraph 5 has the effect of increasing the price payable for the freehold by the tenant from £300 to £4,000. Mr. Nugee indeed con-

F cedes that that is the purpose of the clause. When I suggested to him that it was a barefaced attempt to increase the price, he admitted the attempt but objected to the epithet. The attempt can only succeed if the terms on which the freehold is acquired are not modified by increasing the purchase price from £300 to £4,000, because those terms and the amount payable as the purchase price are to be considered at or after the time when the right to acquire is exercised, and if the actual

G exercise of the right has the effect of introducing the price payable in accordance with the Act without regard to the price payable, or likely to be payable, until that time.

I cannot believe that the legislature intended to allow a landlord—I must not say an unscrupulous landlord, because he may be a trustee acting in the best interests of widowed or orphaned beneficiaries in need

H of every penny he can get for them—to reduce the apparent value of the tenant's right by ingenious devices of this kind. It was to defeat such devices or bargains that Parliament enacted section 23 in language wide enough to hit them. The freeholders' device does, in my opinion, purport to modify the right to acquire the freehold conferred on the tenant by section 1 by having the effect of increasing the purchase price.

I agree therefore that we should allow the appeal, set aside the order of the Lands Tribunal and declare that section 23 of the Leasehold

Reform Act 1967 does not apply to paragraph 5 of Schedule 4 to the A concurrent lease and that the prices payable under section 9 of the Act are £50 and £250. That is subject to what counsel may have to say on the form of our order.

> *Appeal allowed.*
>
> *Appellant's costs in Court of Appeal and half his costs below to be paid by respondents jointly.* B
>
> *Leave to appeal on condition that order as to costs be not disturbed and no application for costs be made in House of Lords.*

C

Solicitors: *Andrew Rowntree, Potters Bar; Farrer & Co.; Boodle, Hatfield & Co.*

D

[COURT OF APPEAL]

REGINA v. MENOCAL

| 1978 | May 22, 26; | Orr and Cumming-Bruce L.JJ. |
| | July 4 | and Wien J. |

E

Crime—Drugs—Importation—Offence of being knowingly concerned in fraudulent evasion of prohibition on importation of cocaine—Whether to be charged under Customs and Excise Act or Misuse of Drugs Act—Customs and Excise Act 1952 (15 & 16 Geo. 6 & 1 Eliz. 2, c. 44), s. 304 (as amended by Misuse of Drugs Act 1971, s. 26)—Misuse of Drugs Act 1971 (c. 38), ss. 3 (1), 26

Crime—Sentence—Deprivation of property—Money shown to relate F *to offence of illegal importation of drugs—Forfeiture order— Whether in nature of sentence—" Relate to the offence "— " Sentence imposed or other order made "—Courts Act 1971 (c. 23), s. 11 (2) (3)—Misuse of Drugs Act 1971, s. 27—Powers of Criminal Courts Act 1973 (c. 62), s. 42*

The appellant, who had money in her possession, was arrested on a charge of contravening section 304 of the G Customs and Excise Act 1952 by being knowingly concerned in the fraudulent evasion of the prohibition in section 3 (1) of the Misuse of Drugs Act 1971 against the importation of a controlled drug. She pleaded guilty to the charge and was sentenced to a term of imprisonment. More than three months after imposition of the sentence of imprisonment, on an application for an order forfeiting the money found in her possession on arrest, the court inferred that the whole of the money had H been provided to her to assist in the importation, and a forfeiture order was made, expressed to be under section 27 of the Act of 1971 [1] or, alternatively, under section 43 of the Powers of Criminal Courts Act 1973.[2] She appealed against the order of forfeiture on the grounds that it was made without jurisdiction since the charge was of contravention

[1] Misuse of Drugs Act 1971, s. 27: see post, p. 605c–d.
[2] Powers of Criminal Courts Act 1973, s. 43: see post, p. 605d–g.

A   of section 304 of the Act of 1952 and the power of forfeiture
under section 27 of the Act of 1971 was inapplicable in that
it was limited to offences under that Act, and that the time
limited for exercise of the power under section 43 of the Act
of 1973 was less than three months by virtue of section 11 (2)
(3) of the Courts Act 1971.[3]

    On the appeal: —

    Held, dismissing the appeal, that, since the offence arose
B   from a combination of the Customs and Excise Act 1952 and
the Misuse of Drugs Act 1971, it could be charged under
both Acts or either Act; and that, whereas the limitation as
to time in section 11 of the Courts Act 1971 applied to a
forfeiture order under section 43 of the Powers of Criminal
Courts Act 1973, which came within the words " or other
order made " in section 11 and was an order in the nature of
a sentence, the limitation as to time in section 11 did not
C   apply to an order made under section 27 of the Misuse of
Drugs Act 1971, which had protection of the public as its
object; accordingly, since the order of forfeiture of the money
found on the appellant on her arrest was expressed to be made
not only under section 43 but also alternatively under section
27, the forfeiture order was valid notwithstanding it was
made more than three months after the imposition of the
sentence of imprisonment on her.

D   *Rex* v. *Jones* (1928) 21 Cr.App.R. 27, C.C.A. and *Reg.* v.
Thayne [1970] 1 Q.B. 141, C.A. applied.
        Reg. v. *Lidster (Note)* [1976] R.T.R. 240, C.A. approved.

    The following cases are referred to in the judgment:

    Reg. v. *Lidster (Note)* [1976] R.T.R. 240, C.A.
    Reg. v. *Thayne* [1970] 1 Q.B. 141; [1969] 3 W.L.R. 480; [1969] 3 All E.R.
E   652, C.A.
    Rex v. *Jones* (1928) 21 Cr.App.R. 27, C.C.A.

    The following additional cases were cited in argument:

    Reg. v. *Attarde* [1975] R.T.R. 299, C.A.
    Reg. v. *Beard (Graham)* [1974] 1 W.L.R. 1549.
    Reg. v. *Grice* (unreported) July 26, 1977, C.A.

F

    APPEAL against order of forfeiture.

    On May 9, 1977, at Middlesex Crown Court (Judge Martin) the appel-
lant, Frances Kathleen Menocal, was ordered to forfeit £171, $7,053 and
6,200 pesetas, pursuant to powers in section 27 of the Misuse of Drugs Act
1971 or, alternatively, in section 43 of the Powers of Criminal Courts Act
G   1973. She applied for leave to appeal against the order of forfeiture on the
grounds that (1) the judge was wrong in law to assume jurisdiction to make
the order since (i) sentence of five year's imprisonment was imposed by him
on the appellant on January 31, 1977; (ii) forfeiture was in the nature of a
penalty and had to be exercised as part of sentence; (iii) by virtue of
section 11 of the Courts Act 1971 the power to vary the sentence imposed
on January 31, 1977, ceased on March 28, 1977; (2) the judge purported
H   to exercise the power of forfeiture under section 27 (1) of the Misuse of
Drugs Act 1971 notwithstanding the words of the section, which limited
the court's power to offences under that Act, and notwithstanding that the
appellant had pleaded guilty to an offence contrary to section 304 of
the Customs and Excise Act 1952 (as amended by section 26 of the Misuse
of Drugs Act 1971); (3) there was no, or no satisfactory evidence on which

    [3] Courts Act 1971, s. 11 (2) (3): see post, p. 606C–E.

the judge could conclude that the whole of the sum of money forfeited was A
related to the offence of which the appellant was convicted. The application
was, in the event, granted by the court, the hearing being treated as the
hearing of the appeal.

The facts are stated in the judgment.

Keith Knight for the appellant.
Sir Michael Havers Q.C. and *Michael Wilkinson* for the Crown. B

July 4. ORR L.J. read the following judgment of the court. On January
31, 1977, at the Middlesex Crown Court the applicant, Mrs. Menocal, of
previous good character, pleaded guilty to being knowingly concerned in
a fraudulent evasion of the prohibition on the importation of cocaine and
was sentenced to five years' imprisonment, and, on May 9, 1977, was C
ordered to forfeit sums of £171, 7,053 U.S. dollars and 1,200 pesetas found
upon her on her arrest. She now applies, after refusal by the single judge, for
leave to appeal against that forfeiture order but does not seek leave to
appeal against the sentence of imprisonment imposed upon her.

On April 1, 1977, two co-accused, Miss Gladys Henao and Miss Clara
Lopez, were on the same indictment convicted of conspiracy to contravene
section 304 of the Customs and Excise Act 1952, in relation to the same D
cocaine and were each sentenced to four years' imprisonment and recommended to be deported after serving such sentence. Miss Henao, after
refusal by the single judge, renewed her application for leave to appeal
against sentence, which came before this court as a non-counsel application
and was refused on May 26 last. Miss Lopez also applied for leave to
appeal against her sentence but did not renew the application after refusal E
by the single judge.

The facts of the offences may be summarised as follows. At about
midday on August 14, 1976, a customs officer on duty in the green channel
at Terminal 3 at Heathrow Airport intercepted Miss Henao on her
arrival from Bogota and her suitcase was found to have a false compart-
ment. She was allowed to leave and as she was walking through the public
concourse she was joined by Mrs. Menocal, and then by Miss Lopez who F
had travelled with her. They were detained by customs officers and the
suitcase was found to contain 2,646 grammes of cocaine. When interviewed
Miss Henao denied knowing about the cocaine and alleged that the suitcase
had been given to her by a man named Hans in Bogota, where she lived,
who had also given her 1,000 dollars for her ticket and a like sum for
expenses and had told her that someone would meet her at Heathrow and G
take her to a hotel. Mrs. Menocal had come to England on the same day
from her home in Ibiza and when her handbag was examined there were
found in it the sums in sterling, dollars and pesetas already referred to.
She eventually admitted having been involved with a drug ring since
January 1975, one of the organisers of which was a man named Gomez,
and that she had been the contact between Alfredo Lopez (the brother of
Clara Lopez) and a man named Keith in the U.S.A. and had visited Bogota H
and, in February and June 1976, had carried drugs from there to Madrid.
With regard to the offence charged she admitted having provided the suitcase and that her role had been to meet the co-accused at Heathrow, book
them into a hotel in London, and await instructions which were to be
given to her by telephone, and in respect of such services she was to receive
5,000 dollars. The prosecution case was that the cocaine was to have been
taken from England to Europe and possibly thence to the U.S.A.

A   In ordering, as he did after hearing legal arguments, the forfeiture of the money found upon Mrs. Menocal, the judge said that she was in England on the business of assisting in the importation and disposal of the drugs which arrived on August 14, 1976, and she must have been given substantial sums in order to pay for whatever outgoings arose. In the absence of any evidence from her, for she gave none, that part of the money was hers, he considered it proper to draw the inference that the whole of the
B   money found in her handbag had been provided by her employers to assist them in dealing with the importation, and he proceeded to make the forfeiture order under section 27 of the Misuse of Drugs Act 1971, or alternatively under section 43 of the Powers of Criminal Courts Act 1973.

Section 27 of the Misuse of Drugs Act 1971 provides:

C   " (1) Subject to subsection (2) below, the court by or before which a person is convicted of an offence under this Act may order anything shown to the satisfaction of the court to relate to the offence, to be forfeited and either destroyed or dealt with in such other manner as the court may order. (2) The court shall not order anything to be forfeited under this section, where a person claiming to be the owner of or otherwise interested in it applies to be heard by the court, unless
D   an opportunity has been given to him to show cause why the order should not be made."

Section 43 of the Powers of Criminal Courts Act 1973 provides:

" (1) Where a person is convicted of an offence punishable on indictment with imprisonment for a term of two years or more and the court by or before which he is convicted is satisfied that any property
E   which was in his possession or under his control at the time of his apprehension—(a) has been used for the purpose of committing, or facilitating the commission of, any offence; or (b) was intended by him to be used for that purpose; the court may make an order under this section in respect of that property. (2) Facilitating the commission of an offence shall be taken for the purposes of this section and section 44 of this Act to include the taking of any steps after it has
F   been committed for the purpose of disposing of any property to which it relates or of avoiding apprehension or detection, and references in this or that section to an offence punishable with imprisonment shall be construed without regard to any prohibition or restriction imposed by or under any enactment on the imprisonment of young offenders. (3) An order under this section shall operate to deprive the offender of
G   his rights, if any, in the property to which it relates, and the property shall (if not already in their possession) be taken into the possession of the police."

Against that order the applicant now seeks leave to appeal and it will be convenient to deal first with the last ground of appeal, which is the only ground of appeal involving questions of fact, that there was no, or no
H   sufficient, evidence on which the judge could conclude as he did that the whole of the sum forfeited related to the offence for the purposes of section 27 of the Misuse of Drugs Act 1971 or was intended to be used for the purpose of committing or facilitating the commission of the offence for the purposes of section 43 of the Powers of Criminal Courts Act 1973. On this issue counsel for the applicant sought to rely on a letter from the headmaster of a London school stating that the applicant had visited him on July 13, 1976, and paid him a registration fee for the admission of her

son to the school and also a sum of 1,000 dollars to cover the boy's first A
term, and claimed that the money found on the applicant at the airport
could have been intended, in whole or in part, for the payment of further
fees. In our judgment there is no substance in this ground of appeal and
in the absence of any evidence from the applicant, the judge was fully
justified in drawing the inference he did.

The other grounds of appeal, which raise questions of law, challenge
the jurisdiction of the judge to make the order he did on May 9, 1977, B
more than three months after the applicant was sentenced and more than
a month after April 1, 1977, when the co-accused Henao and Lopez were
convicted and sentenced.

Section 11 of the Courts Act 1971, so far as material, provides:

"(2) Subject to the following provisions of this section, a sentence
imposed, or other order made, by the Crown Court when dealing with C
an offender may be varied or rescinded by the Crown Court within
the period of 28 days beginning with the day on which the sentence
or other order was imposed or made, or where subsection (3) below
applies, within the time allowed by that subsection. (3) Where two or
more persons are jointly tried on an indictment, then, subject to the
following provisions of this section, a sentence imposed, or other order D
made, by the Crown Court on conviction of any of those persons on the
indictment may be varied or rescinded by the Crown Court not later
than the expiration of whichever is the shorter of the following periods,
that is—(a) the period of 28 days beginning with the date of conclusion
of the joint trial, (b) the period of 56 days beginning with the day on
which the sentence or other order was imposed or made. For the
purposes of this subsection the joint trial is concluded on the latest E
of the following dates, that is any date on which any of the persons
jointly tried is sentenced, or is acquitted, or on which a special verdict
is brought in. . . . "

It is common ground that in the present case, which involved a joint
trial, the period specified in (a) of subsection (3) (28 days beginning with
the date of conclusion of the joint trial) expired on April 28, 1977, and F
that specified in (b) expired on March 27, 1977, with the result that neither
the requirement under (a) nor that under (b) was satisfied, but the relevant
requirement was that under (b) since it provided the shorter of the two
periods. It follows that, if the forfeiture order which the judge made was
" a sentence imposed, or other order made by the Crown Court when dealing
with an offender " within the meaning of section 11 (2) of the Courts Act
1971, the time limit imposed by the Act was exceeded and the order is G
invalid. The judge, as already stated, purported to make the order under
section 27 of the Misuse of Drugs Act 1971, or alternatively under section
43 of the Powers of Criminal Courts Act 1973 and if he had power to do
so under both of those sections the question whether the order fell within
the words above quoted has to be considered in relation to each of them.

Mr. Knight, however, has argued that the judge was not entitled in the H
present case to make a forfeiture order under section 27 of the Misuse
of Drugs Act 1971, since the power of forfeiture conferred by that section
is expressly restricted to offences under that Act, whereas Mr. Knight
submits that the offence in the present case arose under section 304 of the
Customs and Excise Act 1952, which provides:

" Without prejudice to any other provision of this Act, if any person—
(a) knowingly and with intent to defraud Her Majesty of any duty

A   payable thereon, or to evade any prohibition or restriction for the time being in force under or by virtue of any enactment with respect thereto, acquires possession of, or is in any way concerned in carrying, removing, depositing, harbouring, keeping or concealing or in any manner dealing with any goods which have been unlawfully removed from a warehouse or Queen's warehouse, or which are chargeable with a duty which has not been paid, or with respect to the importation

B   or exportation of which any prohibition or restriction is for the time being in force as aforesaid; or (b) is, in relation to any goods, in any way knowingly concerned in any fraudulent evasion or attempt at evasion of any duty chargeable thereon or of any such prohibition or restriction as aforesaid or of any provision of this Act applicable to those goods, he may be detained and, save where, in the case of an

C   offence in connection with a prohibition or restriction, a penalty is expressly provided for that offence by the enactment or other instrument imposing the prohibition or restriction, shall be liable "—as amended by section 26 (2) of the Misuse of Drugs Act 1971—" (a) on summary conviction, to a penalty of three times the value of the goods or £400, whichever is the greater, or to imprisonment for a term not exceeding 12 months, or to both; (b) on conviction on indictment, to

D   a pecuniary penalty of such amount as the court may determine, or to imprisonment for a term not exceeding 14 years, or to both."

In support of this argument Mr. Knight pointed out that in the count of the indictment to which the applicant pleaded guilty the statement of the offence referred to section 304 of the Customs and Excise Act 1952 as amended (as to punishment) by section 26 of the Misuse of Drugs Act

E   1971, although the particulars of the offence referred to section 3 (1) of the Misuse of Drugs Act 1971, which provides that the importation of a controlled drug is prohibited. It is also relevant in our judgment that it is by virtue of section 22 of and Schedule 2 to the Misuse of Drugs Act 1971 that cocaine is classified as a Class A controlled drug. For these reasons, in our judgment, the offence in question arises from a combination of both

F   Acts and can properly be charged under both or either and can equally be said to be an offence arising under both or either, and we reject Mr. Knight's argument that the power of forfeiture conferred by section 27 of the Misuse of Drugs Act 1971 is inapplicable in the present case.

The remaining question in the appeal is whether the forfeiture order made alternatively under section 27 of the Misuse of Drugs Act 1971 and section 43 of the Powers of Criminal Courts Act 1973 was, within the

G   meaning of section 11 (2) of the Courts Act 1971, a " sentence imposed or other order made, by the Crown Court when dealing with an offender," and on this point there is no direct authority but we have derived some limited assistance from the judgment of the Court of Criminal Appeal in Rex v. Jones (1928) 21 Cr.App.R. 27, and that of the Court of Appeal (Criminal Division) in R. v. Thayne [1970] 1 Q.B. 141. In the first of these

H   cases it was held that an order that an accused person convicted of felony should pay a sum " by way of satisfaction or compensation " under section 4 of the Forfeiture Act 1870, such sum awarded being deemed to be a judgment debt due from the person so convicted, fell within the expression " sentence " which by section 21 of the Criminal Appeal Act 1907, included " any order of the court made on conviction with reference to the person convicted or his wife or children " and therefore in such a case an appeal lay against sentence. The power, however, conferred by the Forfeiture Act

1870 to order a payment "by way of satisfaction or compensation" and A
which would give rise to a judgment debt, seems to us to be very different
in character from that conferred by section 27 of the Misuse of Drugs Act
1971.

In the other case of *Reg.* v. *Thayne* [1970] 1 Q.B. 141, which involved
the Criminal Appeal Act 1968, it was held that, where a defendant had
failed to surrender to his bail and after his subsequent conviction the court
ordered an estreat of his recognisance and imprisonment in default of B
payment, such imprisonment was not a sentence "passed on him for the
offence" within section 9 of that Act and therefore the Court of Appeal had
no jurisdiction to review the order in question. In his judgment Lord
Parker C.J., after referring to the very wide definition of "sentence" contained in section 50 of the Act ("In this Act 'sentence' in relation to an
offence includes any order made by a court when dealing with an offender") C
pointed out that the limiting words "passed on him for the offence," contained in section 9 of the Act, remained and that accordingly the court had
no jurisdiction to interfere with the order.

In our judgment, in the light of these authorities, the words "or other
order made" in section 11 of the Courts Act 1971, should be construed as
denoting an order which, while not forming part of the sentence, is of the
nature of a sentence. On that basis Sir Michael Havers for the Crown D
argued that there is a clear difference in character between the power of
forfeiture contained in section 43 of the Powers of Criminal Courts Act 1973
and that contained in section 27 of the Misuse of Drugs Act 1971, the
former being limited to property which was in the possession or control of
the accused at the time of his arrest and operating only to deprive him
of his rights, if any, in the property, whereas section 27 of the Misuse of E
Drugs Act 1971 extends to anything shown to the satisfaction of the court
to "relate to the offence" and has the effect that the article may be forfeited or destroyed or otherwise dealt with. He claimed further that the
object of section 27 is not to punish the accused but to protect the public,
and as an example of the width of the provision claimed, and we think
rightly claimed, that it would apply where a pedlar of drugs is arrested
on the street and has upon him a telephone number which is found to be F
that of an illegal drug factory, so that in such circumstances an order could
be made under section 27 with reference to the equipment and materials in
the factory, whereas under section 43 of the Powers of Criminal Courts Act
1973 there would be no such power. In our judgment this argument is right
and there is a difference in character between the powers conferred by the
two sections, those under section 43 being in the nature of a sentence and G
those under section 27 having the different character and object of protection of the public.

It follows that in the recent case of *Reg.* v. *Lidster (Note)* [1976] R.T.R.
240 the power exercised under section 43 was rightly described in the
judgment of the Court of Appeal (Criminal Division) at p. 241, as "an
additional penalty over and above the term of imprisonment" but that
description, in our judgment, is not applicable to an order under section H
27 of the Misuse of Drugs Act 1971.

It was argued for the applicant that, if the time limit in relation to
section 43 does not apply to an order made under section 27, hardship
would be caused to defendants by an order being made long after the
event, but where, for example, moneys which are related to a drug offence,
or drugs themselves, have been hidden away we can see no injustice in
the order being made when they are found and this argument has not

A persuaded us that the construction we are otherwise disposed to put upon the section is wrong.

For these reasons, granting leave to appeal and by consent treating the hearing as that of the appeal, we dismiss the appeal.

Appeal dismissed.

B

Certificate under section 33 (2) of the Criminal Appeal Act 1968 that a point of law of general public importance was involved in the decision, namely, " whether in exercising its powers under section 27 of the Misuse of Drugs Act 1971

C

the Court is imposing a sentence or other order within the meaning of section 11 of the Courts Act 1971."

Leave to appeal refused.

Solicitors: *Amhurst, Brown, Martin & Nicholson; Solicitor, Customs and Excise.*

D

L. N. W.

July 27, 1978. The Appeal Committee of the House of Lords (Lord Wilberforce, Lord Salmon and Lord Keith of Kinkel) allowed a petition by the appellant for leave to appeal.

E

_____

[COURT OF APPEAL]

O'BRIEN (INSPECTOR OF TAXES) *v.* BENSON'S HOSIERY (HOLDINGS) LTD.

F

1978 April 17, 18, 19;   Buckley and Bridge L.JJ. and Sir David Cairns
       May 12

Revenue—Capital gains tax—Disposal of assets—Service contract —Payment to employer by employee to secure release from service contract—Whether employer's rights under service

G

contract " asset "—Whether capital sum giving rise to chargeable gain received by employer on disposal of assets— Finance Act 1965 (c. 25), s. 22 (1) (3)

In 1968 the taxpayer company, a holding company, acquired the whole of the issued share capital of B Ltd. Prior to the acquisition, the sales director of B Ltd. had a 25 per cent. shareholding in that company. Following the

H

acquisition that director became entitled to 245,000 shares in the taxpayer company and by a service agreement he was appointed sales and merchandise director of the taxpayer company for seven years at a salary of £4,000 per annum. For two years he carried out his duties as sales director with

_____

[Reported by MRS. HARRIET DUTTON, Barrister-at-Law.]

_____

[1] Finance Act 1965, s. 22: see post, pp. 417c–G.

O'Brien v. Benson's Hosiery Ltd. (C.A.)   [1978]

success but in 1970 at his request he was released from his   A
obligations under the service agreement on his paying £50,000
to the taxpayer company. The taxpayer company was
assessed to corporation tax for the accounting period ended
July 1971 on the basis that a chargeable gain accrued on the
receipt by the taxpayer company of the £50,000. The special
commissioners allowed an appeal by the taxpayer company
against the assessment holding that no chargeable gain
accrued on the receipt of the £50,000 because it was not a   B
sum derived from chargeable assets within section 22 of
the Finance Act 1965.[1] An appeal by the Crown was
allowed by Fox J. who held that an employer's rights under
a service contract fell within the meaning of " assets " so
that the £50,000 was a capital sum received in return for the
surrender of rights that constituted a " disposal of assets "
within the meaning of section 22 (3).
     On appeal by the taxpayer company: —   C
     Held, allowing the appeal, that although section 22 (1) of
the Act extended a wide definition to the meaning of " assets,"
the opening words of the subsection indicated that to fall
within the charge to tax they had to consist of some form of
property; that non-assignable contractual rights under a
service contract on which no market value was ascertainable
and which would be determined on the death of either party
to it were not property and thus did not constitute " assets "   D
within that definition with the result that no chargeable gain
accrued to the taxpayer company when they received £50,000
in return for surrendering their rights under the service
contract (post, pp. 618A–B, 619F, 621A–C, 622A, F–G).   ,
     Nokes v. Doncaster Amalgamated Collieries Ltd. [1940]
A.C. 1014, H.L.(E.) applied.
     Decision of Fox J. [1977] Ch. 348; [1977] 3 W.L.R. 206;
[1977] 3 All E.R. 352 reversed.   E

The following cases are referred to in the judgment of the court:

Inland Revenue Commissioners v. Crossman [1937] A.C. 26; [1936] 1
     All E.R. 762, H.L.(E.).
Inland Revenue Commissioners v. Montgomery [1975] Ch. 266; [1975]
     2 W.L.R. 326; [1975] 1 All E.R. 664; 49 T.C. 679.
Nokes v. Doncaster Amalgamated Collieries Ltd. [1940] A.C. 1014; [1940]   F
     3 All E.R. 549, H.L.(E.).

The following additional cases were cited in argument:

Aberdeen Construction Group Ltd. v. Inland Revenue Commissioners
     [1978] 2 W.L.R. 648; [1978] 1 All E.R. 962; H.L.(Sc.).
Davis v. Powell [1977] 1 W.L.R. 258; [1977] 1 All E.R. 471.   G
Floor v. Davis [1978] 3 W.L.R. 360; [1978] 2 All E.R. 1079, C.A.
Harrison v. Nairn Williamson Ltd. [1978] 1 W.L.R. 145; [1978] 1
     All E.R. 608, C.A.
London and Thames Haven Oil Wharves Ltd. v. Attwooll [1967] Ch. 772;
     [1967] 2 W.L.R. 743; [1967] 2 All E.R. 124; 43 T.C. 491, C.A.
Mangin v. Inland Revenue Commissioner [1971] A.C. 739; [1971] 2
     W.L.R. 39; [1971] 1 All E.R. 179, P.C.   H

APPEAL from Fox J.
     The taxpayer company, Benson's Hosiery (Holdings) Ltd., was a
holding company and in 1968 acquired the share capital of Benson's
Hosiery Ltd. in exchange for 7,850 ordinary shares of 2s. each. The
sales director of Benson's Hosiery Ltd., Robert Solomon Behar, entered
into a service agreement with the taxpayer company in 1968 to act as

A its sales and merchandise director for seven years. In 1970 he was released at his request from his obligations under the agreement on payment by him to the taxpayer company of £50,000. The taxpayer company was assessed to corporation tax for the accounting period ended July 31, 1970, in the sum of £5,000. The special commissioners, allowing an appeal by the taxpayer company, discharged the assessment on the ground that no chargeable gain arose on the receipt by the
B taxpayer company of the £50,000.

In paragraph 5 of the special case, the special commissioners set out the following facts which they found proved or admitted. (i) The tax-payer company was a holding company and did not itself trade. On September 25, 1968, the taxpayer company acquired the whole of the issued share capital of Benson's Hosiery Ltd. ("Hosiery") in exchange
C for 7,850 ordinary shares of 2s. each of the taxpayer company, credited as fully paid up. The share capital of Hosiery was taken into the taxpayer company's books at a value of £124,785. A figure of £49,851, being the excess of the value of £124,785 over £74,934 (which was taken to be the value of the net tangible assets of Hosiery) was included in the value of "goodwill" in the consolidated accounts of the taxpayer
D company and its subsidiaries. Goodwill was not, however, shown in the balance sheets of the taxpayer company or any of its separate subsidiary companies. Also on September 25, 1968, the taxpayer company, by way of capitalisation of the sum standing to the credit of share premium account, which arose from the acquisition of Hosiery, issued to its members 124 fully paid ordinary shares of 2s. each for each 2s. share already held. (ii) At about the same time as the taxpayer company
E acquired Hosiery, it also acquired for cash the whole of the issued share capital of South Coast Warehousemen Ltd. ("South Coast"). (iii) Hosiery and South Coast were the first two subsidiaries which the tax-payer company acquired. (iv) At the time of its acquisition by the taxpayer company, Hosiery carried on the business of marketing hosiery. One quarter of Hosiery's share capital was owned by Mr. Behar, who for
F some years had been Hosiery's sales and merchandise director and who had pioneered successful new methods of marketing. Following the taxpayer company's acquisition of Hosiery and the share issue referred to in (i) above, Mr. Behar became entitled to 245,250 ordinary shares of 2s. each in the taxpayer company. (v) By a service agreement dated September 23, 1968, Mr. Behar was appointed sales and merchandise director of the taxpayer company for 7 years at a salary of £4,000
G per annum. The material clauses of the agreement were:

"1. Mr. Behar shall be and he is hereby appointed sales and merchandise director of the [taxpayer company] upon the terms hereinafter appearing for the term of 7 years from September 23, 1968, and thereafter unless and until determined by not less than
H 3 months' notice in writing given by either party to the other and as such sales and merchandise director Mr. Behar will perform the duties and exercise the powers which may from time to time be assigned to or vested in him by the board of directors of the [taxpayer company] or any managing director of the company including rendering services to any subsidiary of the company.

"2. Mr. Behar shall devote the whole of his time attention and abilities to his duties hereunder (including the business of such of

O'Brien v. Benson's Hosiery Ltd. (C.A.)   [1978]

its subsidiary companies as the board may from time to time require) A
and shall comply with the directions from time to time given and
made by the board and shall well and faithfully serve the [taxpayer
company] and use his utmost endeavours to promote the interests
thereof . . .

"4. There shall be paid to Mr. Behar as such sales and
merchandise director (to include any remuneration payable to him
as a director of the [taxpayer company] or of any of its subsidiary or B
associated companies) a salary payable monthly in arrear on the
first of each month but to be deemed to accrue from day to day
from September 23, 1968, at the rate of £4,000 per annum such
salary to be the subject of review by agreement between the parties
from time to time . . .

"8. The board shall be at liberty from time to time to appoint C
any other person or persons to be a sales and merchandise director
of the company jointly with Mr. Behar and to appoint such assistant
sales and merchandise director . . . as they may think fit.

"9. The reconstruction or amalgamation of the [taxpayer
company] during the continuance of this agreement whereunder Mr.
Behar shall be offered comparable employment on terms not less D
favourable to him than those herein contained shall not give rise
to any claim by Mr. Behar for damages against the [taxpayer
company] . . ."

(vi) Mr. Behar acted as marketing director for both Hosiery and South
Coast. As such he was responsible for finding new outlets for marketing
(which were vital to replace those lost by wastage), for engaging and E
controlling the direct salesmen, overseeing the stocks held and for
formulating the purchasing policy of both companies. As far as his
responsibilities to the taxpayer company were concerned, he reported to
the main board of directors on the marketing activities of the taxpayer
company's subsidiaries. The duties of Mr. Behar's appointment required
special skills and energy and he carried out his duties with conspicuous
success. His remuneration from the taxpayer company and its sub- F
sidiaries, including his remuneration under the service agreement and
annual bonuses, was about £5,000 or £5,500 per annum. (vii) Early in
March 1970 Mr. Behar approached the directors of the taxpayer company
and asked to be released from his obligations under the service contract.
The taxpayer company agreed to Mr. Behar's release on the terms set
out in a supplemental agreement dated April 2, 1970, between the G
taxpayer company of the first part, Mr. Behar of the second part, two
directors of the taxpayer company (" the directors ") of the third part
and Mr. Norton, a director and shareholder in the taxpayer company, of
the fourth part. The material clauses of the agreement were:

"Now this agreement witnesseth as follows: 1. In consideration of
the sum of £50,000 to be paid by Mr. Behar to the [taxpayer H
company] in the manner hereinafter appearing the [taxpayer
company] hereby releases Mr. Behar from the agreement with effect
from May 1, 1970. 2. Mr. Behar hereby agrees with the [taxpayer
company] as follows: (a) to pay to the [taxpayer company] the said
sum of £50,000 on or before June 30, 1970. (b) (i) Not prior to
September 22, 1975 (hereinafter called ' the restricted period ')
without the consent of either of the directors to sell more than

A   100,000 ordinary shares or such larger number of shares as may represent 100,000 ordinary shares by reason of any bonus issues allotted by the company after the date hereof in the [taxpayer company] in any period of one year commencing on April 6, 1970, apart from any shares sold for the purpose of realising the said sum of £50,000. (ii) To sell in the manner provided by this deed not less than 50,000 ordinary shares in the [taxpayer company] in any

B one fiscal year during the restricted period. (c) To authorise the bank having custody of the share certificates relating to Mr. Behar's holding in the company to notify the [taxpayer company] of any direction by Mr. Behar to deliver share certificates to meet any sale of shares in the [taxpayer company] by Mr. Behar during the restricted period. (d) To give to either of the directors four weeks'

C notice of his intention to sell any shares in the [taxpayer company] during the restricted period specifying the number of shares he intends selling in order to give to either of the directors an opportunity of finding a purchaser through the London Stock Exchange at the middle market ruling on the day on which such notice is given at the opening of the London Stock Exchange after which

D period of four weeks in the event of the shares still remaining unsold then Mr. Behar may dispose of such shares in such manner as he thinks fit . . . 4. In the event of Mr. Norton or the directors collectively or individually selling more than 300,000 shares held by them in the [taxpayer company] varied in accordance with clause 2 (b) hereof in any one year during the restricted period then Mr. Behar shall be entitled to dispose in manner provided in this deed

E of one third of the excess numbers of shares sold by Mr. Norton or the directors over 300,000 shares. 5. Mr. Norton and the directors will on the date of any sale of shares by all *or* any of them in the [taxpayer company] in excess of 300,000 offered in any one year give immediate written notice of such sale to Mr. Behar. . . . "

F   (viii) The commissioners were not told what the taxpayer company did with the £50,000 which it received from Mr. Behar but the following adjustments were made in drawing up the taxpayer company's accounts as at July 31, 1970. (a) In the consolidated balance sheet for the taxpayer company and its subsidiaries, £50,000 was deducted in arriving at the value attributed to goodwill. A note on the accounts read:

" 6 GOODWILL

G   Goodwill consists of the excess cost of shares in subsidiaries over the book value of the net assets of those companies at the dates of acquisition, and is made up as follows:

	£
Balance July 31st, 1969	1,084,670
Add: In respect of the acquisition of subsidiaries completed during the year	222,733
	1,307,403
Less: Amount received from Mr. R. S. Behar, a director who resigned by agreement dated May 18th, 1970	50,000
	1,257,403 "

(b) In the taxpayer company's balance sheet £50,000 was deducted in A
arriving at the value of subsidiary companies. A note on the accounts
read: " 15 Subsidiary companies. This is made up of shares at cost
including expenses of acquisition less dividends received out of pre-
acquisition profits and amounts due on current account." (ix) After
Mr. Behar's resignation from the taxpayer company and its subsidiaries,
he was replaced as marketing director of Hosiery, his replacement being B
paid about £5,500 or £6,000 per annum. Mr. Behar was not replaced
on the taxpayer company's main board but his duties in relation to the
whole group were taken over by other directors.

By their written decision of October 24, 1974, the special commissioners held:

" 5 . . . An employers' right to the services of his employee is no doubt C
a form of property for certain purposes, so that, for example, an injury
to his employee may give the employer a right of action for damages.
But rights to an employee's services under a service contract are not
capable of being transferred nor do they affect an asset that is capable
of being transferred. In our view, and we so hold, an employer's
rights under a bona fide contract for personal services (such as we are
concerned with in these proceedings) are not ' property ' for the purposes D
of Part III of the Act.

" 6. If we are wrong in our decision on the construction of Part III
of the Act, it is necessary to consider the first alternative contention
advanced on behalf of the [taxpayer company], namely that the [tax-
payer company's] rights under the service contract were acquired
' partly for a consideration that cannot be valued ' within the meaning E
of section 22 (4) (b) of the Act. We have reviewed the circumstances
in which the service contract was entered into (paying particular regard
to the office which Mr. Behar held in Hosiery and the interest which he
formerly had in that company) and to the terms of the service contract
(in particular Mr. Behar's appointment for 7 years to a specific post
requiring his special skills and energy, which he appears to have
exercised with conspicuous success, and the [taxpayer company's] F
obligation under clause 9 in the event of its reconstruction or amalgamation to offer Mr. Behar 'comparable employment on terms not less
favourable to him '). In this connexion we have also considered the
application of the decision in Collier v. Sunday Referee Publishing Co.
Ltd. [1940] 2 K.B. 647. In our view Mr. Behar's contract with the
[taxpayer company] was founded on his appointment to perform G
specific duties, that the [taxpayer company] was under an obligation to
provide him with corresponding employment during the term of the
service contract and that this obligation formed part of the consideration
for the rights which the [taxpayer company] acquired under the service
contract. But we do not accept that the obligation cannot be valued.
While valuation is not an exact science and to assign a value to this H
obligation would no doubt be difficult and, more than with most valuations, open to subjective opinion ranging over a fairly broad band, we
think that the words ' cannot be valued ' apply only to something much
more nebulous than this. The inspector of taxes did not hazard any
opinion as to what the value was and asked only for a decision in
principle. If, therefore, the value is relevant (e.g. for the purposes of
paragraph 4 (1) (a) of Schedule 6 to the Act) and no agreement on it

A can be reached between the [taxpayer company] and the inspector of taxes, the matter will require to be argued before us.

" 7. It was also contended, in the further alternative, by the [taxpayer company] that the £50,000 was paid in part to compensate the [taxpayer company] for a possible diminution as a result of Mr. Behar's departure in the value of its shares in its two subsidiary companies,
B Hosiery and South Coast, and that the [taxpayer company's] shares in these subsidiaries were, therefore, the assets from which, for the purposes of section 22 (3) of the Act, the £50,000 was derived. While we would be prepared to infer from the evidence that this was the main factor which influenced the [taxpayer company] to exact such a large sum from Mr. Behar to release him from the service contract, we feel prohibited by the decision in *Inland Revenue Commissioners* v.
C *Montgomery* [1975] Ch. 266 from tracing the derivation of the £50,000 beyond the rights which the [taxpayer company] acquired under the service contract.

" 8. For the reasons given in paragraph 5 above the appeal succeeds and we discharge the corporation tax assessment in question."

On appeal by the Crown from the commissioners' decision, Fox J.
D held that the £50,000 was a capital sum received in return for the surrender of rights that constituted a " disposal of assets " within the meaning of section 22 (3) of the Finance Act 1965. He remitted the case to the commissioners for valuation of those rights.

The taxpayer company appealed on the grounds that (1) for the purposes of Part III of the Finance Act 1965 the right of an employer
E to the services of an employee under a contract of service did not constitute an asset within the meaning of section 22 (1) of the Act; (2) on the facts found by the special commissioners the sum of £50,000 received by the taxpayer company was derived within the meaning of section 22 (3) of the Finance Act 1965 from the taxpayer company's shares in its two subsidiaries, Benson's Hosiery Ltd., and South Coast Warehousemen Ltd., and that accordingly the receipt of the sum of
F £50,000 gave rise to a part disposal of the shares in the two companies; (3) the sum of £50,000 received by the taxpayer company was derived from the agreement entered into between the taxpayer company and Mr. Behar on April 2, 1970, and that the consideration given by the taxpayer company for the receipt of the sum of £50,000 was the release of Mr. Behar from the contract of service made between the taxpayer
G company and Mr. Behar on September 23, 1968.

Andrew Thornhill for the taxpayer company.
Brian Davenport for the Crown.

Cur. adv. vult.

H   May 12. BUCKLEY L.J. read the following judgment of the court. The taxpayer company, Benson's Hosiery (Holdings) Ltd. (" the taxpayer company ") appealed to the special commissioners for the purposes of the income tax against an assessment to corporation tax in a sum of £5,000. The commissioners allowed the appeal. The inspector of taxes appealed by way of case stated to the High Court and Fox J. on March 17, 1977, allowed that appeal. The taxpayer company now appeals from the decision of the judge. The facts are fully set out in

O'Brien v. Benson's Hosiery Ltd. (C.A.)   [1978]

the case stated and we need not recapitulate them in this judgment. **A**
We shall use the same names and descriptions as are used in the case.
The question which arose for the decision of the commissioners was
whether for the purposes of Part III of the Finance Act 1965 a chargeable gain arose on the receipt by the taxpayer company in the year
ended July 31, 1970, of £50,000 paid by Mr. Behar, an employee and
director of the taxpayer company, to secure his release from his service **B**
contract with the taxpayer company. The commissioners answered
that question in the negative and discharged the assessment appealed
against, holding that an employer's rights under a contract of service
are not " property " for the relevant purposes. Fox J., allowing the
appeal before him, held that the taxpayer company's rights under the
service agreement were assets for the purposes of section 22 of the Act
and that the £50,000 was derived from such assets.   **C**

In paragraph 6 of their decision the commissioners had held that
under the service agreement the taxpayer company was obliged to
provide Mr. Behar with employment during the term of the service
agreement, and that that obligation formed part of the consideration
for the rights acquired by the taxpayer company thereunder. They did
not accept the taxpayer company's submission that that obligation **D**
could not be valued and that accordingly the taxpayer company's rights
were acquired " partly for a consideration that cannot be valued "
within the meaning of section 22 (4) (b) of the Act. Fox J., having
decided that the £50,000 was derived from assets of the taxpayer
company, remitted the case to the commissioners for the determination
of the question whether the obligation to provide Mr. Behar with
employment can be valued and, if so, what the value is.   **E**

In paragraph 7 of their decision the commissioners rejected an
alternative argument presented by the taxpayer company that the
£50,000 was paid in part to compensate for a possible reduction in the
value of the shares in Hosiery and South Coast due to Mr. Behar's
departure, holding that they were prohibited from so doing by *Inland
Revenue Commissioners* v. *Montgomery* [1975] Ch. 266. Fox J. agreed **F**
with this view.

In this court the taxpayer company has contended that its rights
under the service agreement are not assets for the purposes of the
relevant sections. They have also contended that upon the facts of
the case their receipt of the £50,000 must be treated as derived not
merely from the supplemental agreement by which Mr. Behar was **G**
discharged from his obligations under the service agreement but rather
from the shares held by the taxpayer company in the two subsidiaries.

The tax to which the taxpayer company is liable, if at all, is
corporation tax under section 238 of the Income and Corporation Taxes
Act 1970, but under section 265 of that Act chargeable gains to be
included in the taxpayer company's profits for the purposes of the
corporation tax are to be computed in accordance with the principles **H**
applying to capital gains tax; so we have to apply the provisions of
Part III of the Finance Act 1965 as though this were a capital gains
tax case.

Section 19 (1) of the Finance Act 1965 provides:

" Tax shall be charged in accordance with this Act in respect of
capital gains, that is to say chargeable gains computed in accord-

A   ance with this Act and accruing to a person on the disposal of assets."

So there must be a chargeable gain which has accrued on a disposal of assets. Sections 22 to 26 of that Act deal with chargeable gains. Section 22 (1) provides:

B   " All forms of property shall be assets for the purposes of this Part of this Act, whether situated in the United Kingdom or not, including—(a) options, debts and incorporeal property generally, and (b) any currency other than sterling, and (c) any form of property created by the person disposing of it, or otherwise coming to be owned without being acquired."

C   The Act contains no other provision in the nature of a definition of " assets." It contains no definition of " disposal." Section 22 (2), (3) and (4), so far as relevant to the present case provide:

D   " (2) For the purposes of this Part of this Act—(a) references to a disposal of an asset include, except where the context otherwise requires, references to a part disposal of an asset, and (b) there is a part disposal of an asset where an interest or right in or over the asset is created by the disposal, as well as where it subsists before the disposal . . . (3) Subject to subsection (6) of this section, and to the exceptions in this Part of this Act, there is for the purposes of this Part of this Act a disposal of assets by their owner where any capital sum is derived from assets notwithstanding that no asset is acquired by the person paying the capital sum, and this subsection applies in particular to— . . . (c) capital sums received in return for forfeiture or surrender of rights, or for refraining from exercising rights . . . (4) Subject to the provisions of this Part of this Act, a person's acquisition of an asset and the disposal of it to him shall for the purposes of this Part of this Act be deemed to be for a consideration equal to the market value of the asset— (a) where he acquires the asset otherwise than by way of a bargain made at arm's length and in particular where he acquires it by way of gift or by way of distribution from a company in respect of shares in the company, or (b) where he acquires the asset wholly or partly for a consideration that cannot be valued, or in connection with his own or another's loss of office or employment or diminution of emoluments, or otherwise in consideration for or recognition of his or another's services or past services in any office or employment or of any other service rendered or to be rendered by him or another, or (c) where he acquires the asset as trustee for creditors of the person making the disposal."

There is no suggestion in this case that the supplemental agreement was not negotiated at arm's length.

H   The question to which we have to address our minds is whether a chargeable gain has in the circumstances accrued to the taxpayer company on the disposal, actual or notional, of any asset. So the case turns primarily upon the question whether the taxpayer company has, or must be treated as having, disposed of an asset. The taxpayer company said that their rights under the service agreement were not an assets or assets for the relevant purposes. The Crown contended that those rights fall within the term " incorporeal property generally " in

section 22 (1) (*a*) and that they are assets for the relevant purposes. **A**
At first impression one would not, we think, consider that an employer's
rights to personal services under a contract of employment were
appropriately described as " property." Counsel drew our attention to
Nokes v. *Doncaster Amalgamated Collieries Ltd.* [1940] A.C. 1014 in
which it was held in the House of Lords that, where an order was made
by the court under section 154 of the Companies Act 1929 for the
amalgamation of two companies, a contract of service existing at the **B**
date of the amalgamation between a workman and the transferor
company did not automatically become a contract of service between
the workman and the transferee company. Under that section of the
Companies Act 1929, when sanctioning a scheme for reconstruction or
amalgamation, the court had power to provide by order for the transfer
to a transferee company of the whole or any part of the undertaking **C**
and of the property or liabilities of the transferor company. Section
154 (4) provided:

> " In this section the expression ' property ' includes property, rights
> and powers of every description, and the expression ' liabilities '
> includes duties."

The question in that case was whether, where such an order was **D**
made transferring all the property of a transferor company to a transferee company, the effect was that a contract of service previously
existing between an individual and the transferor company became a
contract between that individual and the transferee company. Viscount
Simon L.C., after considering the practical results which might follow
from holding otherwise, reached the conclusion that contracts of service **E**
were not so affected. He said, at pp. 1023–1024:

> " At any rate, after examining section 154 with close attention and
> considering the consequences of its application in different cases, I
> can come to no other conclusion than that an order made under
> it does not automatically transfer contracts of personal service.
> The word ' contract ' does not appear in the section at all, and I **F**
> do not agree with the view expressed in the Court of Appeal that
> a right to the service of an employee is the property of the trans-
> feror company. Such a right cannot be the subject of gift or
> bequest; it cannot be bought or sold; it forms no part of the assets
> of the employer for the purpose of administering his estate. In
> short, section 154 when it provides for ' transfer ' is providing in **G**
> my opinion for the transfer of those rights which are not incapable
> of transfer and is not contemplating the transfer of rights which
> are in their nature incapable of being transferred. I must make
> it plain that my judgment is limited to contracts of personal service
> with which the present appeal is concerned."

Lord Atkin said, at p. 1033: **H**

> " My Lords, I should have thought that the principle that a man
> is not to be compelled to serve a master against his will is just as
> deep-seated in the common law of this country, as that which was
> under discussion in the case cited "—he was there referring to
> *Leach* v. *The King* [1912] A.C. 305 which he had cited on the previous
> page—" and that here there is no clear, definite, or positive enact-
> ment overturning it. But in truth the general words in this

A   section describing ' property' seem to me to add nothing to the word ' property' standing by itself which would be taken by any lawyer to include property, rights and powers of any description."

He said, at p. 1034:

    "I am satisfied that this in the main procedural section should not be construed so as to transfer rights which in their nature are by
B   law not transferable."

Lord Porter said, at p. 1051:

    "Having regard to these considerations I find myself thrown back upon a consideration of the meaning to be placed on the word ' property' in subsection (1) (a). Prima facie I should not expect it to include non-transferable contracts. In truth the word ' property'
C   is not a term of art but takes its meaning from its context and from its collocation in the document or Act of Parliament in which it is found and from the mischief with which that Act or document is intended to deal."

He said, at pp. 1053–1054:

D   "I may sum up my view by saying that the word ' property' in section 154, whether considered alone or in conjunction with the words ' rights and powers of every description' means property with which the original company has the right to deal without having to obtain the consent of some third party, and I cannot think that the addition of section 154, subsection (1) (f), empowering the court to make provision for incidental consequential and supple-
E   mentary matters is sufficient to widen the content of the section so as to include non-transferable contracts."

    In the light of those observations we ask ourselves whether there is here any ground for interpreting the word " property" as extending to non-assignable contractual rights such as arise under a contract of
F   personal service. The answer depends upon the proper construction of section 22. The opening words of section 22 (1) clearly indicate that an " asset " for the purposes of the charge to tax must consist of some form of property. The only word in the three following sub-paragraphs of that subsection which might possibly conflict with this view is the word " options," for incorporeal property is obviously a form of property, as also are debts and currency, and sub-paragraph (c) merely
G   refers to " any form of property." We are not in this case concerned with any kind of option, but we would construe " options " in this context as limited to options which are recognisable as having the character of property. We regard the sub-paragraphs as having been inserted in the subsection ex majori cautela in case anyone might possibly suggest that such things as are mentioned in them might not
H   have been intended to be caught by the opening general words of the subsection. As was said by Lord Atkin of the definition of the word " property " in Nokes's case at p. 1033, sub-paragraphs (a), (b) and (c) in the present case in our opinion add nothing to the effect of those general words.

    Mr. Davenport contended that incorporeal property here embraces all contractual rights. We think that section 22 (2) (b) may throw some light, although not very brilliant, upon whether this view is

correct. If incorporeal property for the present purpose embraces all A
contractual rights, it would seem that every distinct right under a
contract must constitute a separate asset, notwithstanding that all the
rights under a contract may also together constitute what one might
call a composite asset. If this were so, the creation of an interest or
right in or over that composite asset or any of the constituent rights
would, as it seems to us, itself constitute the disposal of an asset rather B
than a part disposal of a pre-existing asset as provided by section 22
(2) (b). Take for example a lease of property, which may comprise a
bundle of rights and liabilities. Any adjustment of those rights and
liabilities which is as a whole favourable to the lessor will result under
paragraph 15 (3) of Schedule 7 to the Act in a disposal by the lessee
of an interest in the property, that is to say, as we see it, a part disposal
under section 22 (2) (b) of the asset consisting of the leasehold interest C
which belongs to the lessee; not a disposal of an entire asset consisting
of any particular right previously belonging to the lessee under the
lease. This causes us to approach this submission of Mr. Davenport
with caution.

Section 22 (3) deals with what may be called notional disposals.
Mr. Davenport relied on section 22 (3) (c) for saying that such a D
notional disposal must be supposed to have occurred in this case because
the £50,000 was received by the taxpayer company in return for the
surrender by Mr. Behar of his rights under the service agreement.
Mr. Davenport said that such a disposal must be taken to have occurred
even if one cannot identify an asset which has been wholly or partly
disposed of either actually or notionally. In our opinion, however,
when sub-paragraph (c) is read with the opening words of section 22 E
(3), it is clear that it can only operate when it can be said that the
capital sum is derived from an asset or assets, for the sub-paragraphs
are particularisations of the general words in the opening part of the
subsection. So the rights surrendered, or which the recipient of the
capital sum refrains from exercising, must be rights forming part of or
appertaining to an asset, and section 22 (3) (c) cannot operate unless F
such an asset within the meaning of section 22 (1) can be identified.

Section 22 (4) introduces the important concept of a notional consideration for the disposal of an asset in certain cases, including where
the transaction is not a bargain at arm's length or the actual consideration cannot be valued. This takes one to section 44 (1) which
provides:
                                                                          G
    " Subject to the following subsections, in this Part of this Act
    ' market value ' in relation to any assets means the price which
    those assets might reasonably be expected to fetch on a sale in the
    open market."

So, to make these provisions workable, any asset to which they are
capable of applying must be one for which a market value can be H
ascertained in accordance with section 44 (1). A right to personal
services under a contract of service is, of course, unassignable. It
cannot be bought or sold. Moreover it cannot survive the demise of
either of the parties. It can have no actual marketable value, for there
can be no market for what is unsaleable. It would not, we think, be
practicable to suppose a notional market upon which the market value
for the right could be estimated such as was invoked in *Inland Revenue*

A *Commissioners* v. *Crossman* [1937] A.C. 26, for in the case of a contract of personal service the subject matter, which for the present purpose consists of the employer's rights under the contract, is inherently unsaleable; it is not merely subject to restrictions which can be taken into account in estimating a price on a hypothetical market. The rights of an employer under a contract of service could not even be sold and transferred with the consent and co-operation of the employee. All the
B employer could do would be to agree to discharge the employee from the existing contract so as to free him to enter into a new contract with a new employer. This could, no doubt, be achieved by a tripartite contract, but it would not be a contract of sale and there would, in our opinion, certainly be no actual disposal of any asset by the former employer to the new one. Moreover, we find it hard to see how a
C market value could be placed upon the right to services of an employee under a contract of personal service having regard to the fact that such a contract is always liable to be determined by the death of either party, that is, of either of the original parties to the contract.

If Mr. Behar had repudiated the service agreement, the taxpayer company could have recovered damages from him. These would pre-
D sumably have been quantified by estimating the cost of replacing Mr. Behar by another director with the same duties for the unexpired term of the service agreement and setting against that cost what it would have cost to continue to employ Mr. Behar under the service agreement for the same period. Loosely this might be said to involve making an estimate of the market value of Mr. Behar's services, but it would not, we think, in truth amount to this. In this type of employment no one
E man's skill can be reckoned to be the precise equivalent of another's. The commissioners found as a fact that Mr. Behar had been particularly successful. His skill and experience may have been of exceptional value to the taxpayer company. They might not be equally valuable to anyone else; and, even if they would be, the cost to the taxpayer company of an adequate replacement would not necessarily be a measure
F of the value of Mr. Behar's services either to the taxpayer company or to any new employer. In the light of these considerations it seems to us that the concept of a market value is entirely inappropriate to a contract of personal service. Section 22 (4) may not be applicable to this case, in which event market value may have no direct relevance, but this would not affect the validity of the preceding argument upon
G the construction of the section, for an asset must be something of a kind to which all the provisions of the section are capable of applying in suitable circumstances. It is, we think, worth noting that pension rights and analogous benefits are specially dealt with in section 22 (4) (*b*) where they are coupled with assets acquired for a consideration that cannot be valued. It is, of course, possible to put a market value on such a right or benefit, which is what the subsection requires to be done,
H but the significance of this sub-paragraph seems to us to be that it appears to assume that the services in consideration of which the right or benefit has been granted are incapable of valuation.

These considerations lead us to the conclusion that an employer's rights under the contract of service do not constitute an asset or assets within section 22.

Fox J. reached a contrary conclusion on this point. In so doing

O'Brien v. Benson's Hosiery Ltd. (C.A.)   [1978]

he was very much influenced by section 22 (3) (c). He said, we think A
rightly, that the concept of what are "assets" for the purposes of
section 22 is a very wide one. He considered two constructions of
section 22 (3) (c), viz. (i) that it defines certain events in which a
disposal of assets is to be deemed to have been made without any
necessity to identify an asset which has been disposed of or, we may
add, from which a capital sum has been derived; and (ii) using section B
22 (3) (c) as an aid to the construction of section 22 (1) to include in
the term "assets" a wide class of rights, so as to give to the word
"assets" a wholly unrestricted sense. He thus reached the conclusion
that it made no difference which construction was adopted, since on the
facts of the case one would reach the same conclusion by either route.
With deference to the judge, we do not think it legitimate to use or
construe section 22 (3) (c) in this way. In our opinion it is an over- C
riding requirement of section 22 (3) that for a chargeable gain to arise
a capital sum must have been "derived from assets," if there has not
been an actual disposal of an asset by the person paying the capital
sum. The four sub-paragraphs of the subsection are introduced by
the words "and this subsection applies in particular to." It is consequently, in our judgment, not admissible to use any of the sub-para- D
graphs to extend that overriding requirement, unless this is absolutely
necessary to give coherence to the provisions of the Act. The subsection must, of course, be read as a whole and in its context, but, in
our judgment, the considerations to which we have drawn attention do
not support an argument that to make sense of the statute section 22
(3) (c) must be read as controlling the interpretation of the overriding
requirement of the subsection. This, in our opinion, negatives both the E
alternative constructions envisaged by Fox J.

Fox J. placed some reliance on the reference in section 22 (1) (a)
to "options," which he said would, as a matter of language, include an
option to enter into a contract of service. If such an option were an
asset, he said, there seemed to be no reason why a contract of service
itself should not be an asset. We do not think, however, that upon the F
true construction of section 22 (1) "options" can there be understood
to extend to any form of option right which cannot be recognised as a
form of property. An option to acquire property can, we think,
appropriately be classified as itself a property right, but an option to
acquire or exercise some right or benefit which is not property (e.g. the
right to attend some public performance at a reduced price) cannot, we G
think, be appropriately classified as property. So if we are right in
thinking that the benefit of a contract of service is not property, neither
is an option for such a contract; and, if we are right in our construction
of "options" in section 22 (1), such an option would not fall within
the subsection.

Mr. Davenport urged that nowadays it is not unknown for anyone H
who can earn very large sums by the exploitation of his personal talents
to enter into a contract of service at a relatively low salary with a
company formed for the purpose of exploiting that person's talents for
profit. He contended that in such a case the right of exploitation would
be an asset of the company, and that, if a capital sum arising from the
exploitation of that asset were to be received by the company, it would
constitute a chargeable gain for the purposes of the Act. Perhaps this

A   may be correct (but we should not be taken so to decide), although it has not been made clear how any receipt arising from exploitation of the person's talents could have the character of a capital sum. It would seem to us more likely to have the character of the profit of carrying on a business. But, in any event, this is not such a case. It is true that under clause 1 of the service agreement Mr. Behar could be required by

B   the taxpayer company to render services to any subsidiary of the company, and that in pursuance of the service agreement he acted as managing director of both Hosiery and South Coast. The £50,000, however, was not received as consideration for any exploitation of the taxpayer company's right to require Mr. Behar to work for the subsidiaries, nor was it paid for the surrender of any right of Mr. Behar to be so employed. The service agreement seems to us to be more

C   analogous in this respect to a contract to act as a farm bailiff or a business manager. It is in terms a contract to act as the sales and merchandise director of the taxpayer company: any services to subsidiary companies are treated as part of his duties as such a director of the taxpayer company. Mr. Behar has no right under the agreement to insist upon his skills being employed in any business other than the taxpayer

D   company's. The £50,000 was paid for Mr. Behar's release from the service agreement, that is, from his obligation to serve as sales and merchandise director of the company, not as consideration for any exploitation of his talents.

   This brings us to the last point with which we need to deal. Mr. Thornhill contended as an alternative argument that on a true view of the facts the £50,000 was not paid for Mr. Behar's release but as com-

E   pensation for the loss in value of the taxpayer company's shares in the two subsidiaries resulting from Mr. Behar's ceasing to act as marketing director of each of those companies. The shares in the subsidiary companies were undoubtedly assets of the taxpayer company. The argument was that the sum paid " derived " from those assets. But in our judgment, it cannot be correct to say that the sum derived from those

F   assets within the meaning of the section. Such an anticipated loss in value may have had an important bearing on the negotiation of the amount of the sum paid. It was paid, however, as consideration for the taxpayer company's entering into the supplemental agreement whereby they released Mr. Behar from his obligations under the service agreement. The commissioners felt themselves to be prohibited by the

G   decision of Walton J. in Inland Revenue Commissioners v. Montgomery [1975] Ch. 266 from accepting this alternative argument, and Fox J. said that there was no more justification for going behind the service agreement than there was for going behind the policies of insurance in Montgomery. We agree with this view and would not have accepted the alternative argument, but, if we are right on construction, the point does not arise. Nor does the question which the judge remitted to the

H   commissioners arise.

   For these reasons we allow this appeal.

Appeal allowed with costs.
Leave to appeal on condition that
Crown does not ask for costs.

Solicitors: *Howard, Kennedy & Rossi; Solicitor of Inland Revenue.*

[1978]

A

[FAMILY DIVISION]

B. *v.* B. (MATRIMONIAL PROCEEDINGS: DISCOVERY)

1978 March 14, 15, 16, 17, 20, 21   Dunn J.

B

Company—Director—Action against—Matrimonial proceedings—
Husband director ordered to disclose company's documents
—Whether documents in possession or control of husband—
Validity of order—R.S.C., Ord. 24

The board of an "operating company" consisted of the
husband, who was chairman and managing director, and six
directors. A "holding company" owned 75 per cent. and a
"public company" owned the remaining 25 per cent. of the
operating company's issued shares. The husband owned 51   C
per cent. of the holding company's shares and the majority
of the remaining shares in that company were held by members
of his family.

The wife applied for an order for discovery in proceedings
concerning the occupation of the matrimonial home brought
by the husband under section 1 of the Matrimonial Homes
Act 1967. The registrar made the order under R.S.C., Ord. 24   D
and, by clauses 3, 4 and 11 of the order, the husband was to
disclose, inter alia, bills and receipts, whether paid by the
husband or by the operating company, for expenses incurred
by him relating to entertainment, travel, hotels and holidays
and also for the purchases of jewellery, furniture, pictures,
drink and food for himself, his wife and children. By
clause 17, he was to produce all books of accounts, private
ledgers, paid cheques, cheque stubs, documents and vouchers   E
relating to the operating company.

On appeal by the husband: —

Held, allowing the appeal in part, (1) that the court's
discretionary power to order disclosure and production of
relevant documents under R.S.C., Ord. 24 could only be
exercised against a party to the suit if the documents were in
his possession, custody or power; that, although the husband
had the right to inspect all the company's documents, that   F
right was a right as a director and unless it could be shown
either that the company's documents were or had been in his
custody or physical possession or that the company was in
reality the alter ego of the husband in the sense that he held
substantially all the shares and the minority shareholders
were not adverse to him so that he controlled the company,
then the documents were not under his control and he had
no power to disclose the documents in the legal possession   G
of the company (post, pp. 627H—628A, 629H—630A, G—631A,
632D).

Alfred Crompton Amusement Machines Ltd. v. *Customs*
and Excise Commissioners (No. 2) [1974] A.C. 405, H.L.(E.);
Williams v. *Ingram* (1900) 16 T.L.R. 451, C.A. and *Dallas*
v. *Dallas* (1906) 24 D.L.R. (2d) 746 applied.

(2) That the documents referred to in clauses 3, 4 and 11
were or had been in the husband's custody and, therefore,   H
they were to be disclosed and, if there was an objection to
the production of any of those documents in the operating
company's possession, the court in the exercise of its discretion
would decide whether to order production; that, although it
had not been shown to the court's satisfaction that the documents referred to in clause 17 were relevant, they were not
documents which were or had been in the custody of the
husband and, since the husband's control over the operating
company was not sufficient to make it his alter ego, there

A   was no power to order disclosure and production of those
documents in the possession of the company and clause 17
must be deleted from the order (post, pp. 634D–F, 635B–D,
D–F, 636A–E).

The following cases are referred to in the judgment:

Bovill v. *Cowan* (1870) L.R. 5 Ch.App. 495.
Carew v. *Carew* [1891] P. 360.
B   *Chantrey Martin* v. *Martin* [1953] 2 Q.B. 286; [1953] 3 W.L.R. 459;
    [1953] 2 All E.R. 691, C.A.
Crompton (Alfred) Amusement Machines Ltd. v. *Customs and Excise
    Commissioners (No. 2)* [1974] A.C. 405; [1973] 3 W.L.R. 268; [1973]
    2 All E.R. 1169, H.L.(E.).
Dallas v. *Dallas* (1960) 24 D.L.R. (2d) 746.
Hadley v. *McDougall* (1872) L.R. 7 Ch.App. 312.
C   *Kettlewell* v. *Barstow* (1872) L.R. 7 Ch.App. 686.
Nelson (James) & Sons Ltd. v. *Nelson Line (Liverpool) Ltd.* [1906]
    2 K.B. 217.
Norwich Pharmacal Co. v. *Customs and Excise Commissioners* [1974]
    A.C. 133; [1973] 3 W.L.R. 164; [1973] 2 All E.R. 943, H.L.(E.).
O'D. v. *O'D.* [1976] Fam. 83; [1975] 3 W.L.R. 308; [1975] 2 All E.R.
    993, C.A.
D   *Povey* v. *Povey* [1972] Fam. 40; [1971] 2 W.L.R. 381; [1970] 3 All E.R.
    612, D.C.
Rattenberry v. *Monro* (1910) 103 L.T. 560; 55 S.J. 76.
Reid v. *Langlois* (1849) 1 Mac. & G. 627.
Skoye v. *Bailey* (1971) 1 W.W.R. 144.
Swanston v. *Lishman* (1881) 45 L.T. 360, C.A.
Taylor v. *Rundell* (1841) Cr. & Ph. 104.
E   *Williams* v. *Ingram* (1900) 16 T.L.R. 451, C.A.

The following additional cases, supplied by the courtesy of counsel, were
    cited in argument:

Procter v. *Smiles* (1886) 2 T.L.R. 906; 55 L.J.Q.B. 527, C.A.
Salomon v. *Salomon & Co.* [1897] A.C. 22, H.L.(E.).
Ward v. *Marshall* (1887) 3 T.L.R. 578.
F
APPEAL from Mr. Registrar Kenworthy.

In proceedings under section 1 of the Matrimonial Homes Act 1967
initiated by the husband, Mr. Registrar Kenworthy made an order on
December 7, 1977, requiring the husband within 56 days to give discovery
of, inter alia, . . . (3) bills, invoices receipts, credit card accounts receipts and
G   other vouchers relating to entertainment, air fares, holidays, hotel, res-
taurants and night clubs and other places of entertainment and all other
activities including expenditure on the acquisition of horses and ponies and
livery charges in respect thereof and all other expenses incurred by the
husband in his own name or the name of the operating company for himself
and/or his wife and/or the children of the family and/or other persons
for the past two years and household and living expenses for the like
H   period other than those disclosed in the husband's list of documents;
(4) documents relating to the purchase and/or payment by the husband
for purchases by him and/or his wife for himself, his wife and/or the
children in respect of clothing, furs, jewellery, furniture, pictures, paintings,
objets d'art, and other household effects and household equipment and
whether the same were paid for by himself or the operating company;
(11) bills, invoices and receipts of suppliers of food and alcoholic liquor
delivered by such suppliers to or for the use of the family at the matri-

A monial home for the past two years whether paid for by the husband or the operating company; (17) all books of account, private ledgers paid cheques, cheque stubs, documents and vouchers of the operating company for three years from May 1, 1974, in relation to all bills and expenses incurred by the husband on his behalf and/or on behalf of the company and paid by and/or charged to the company and records of all receipts of moneys by that company in the course of its trading and the disposal thereof for the same period and to account for all documents B relating to any Swiss bank account or any bank account abroad either in the husband's name or in the name of any nominee, or nominees or over which the husband had the power to operate alone or jointly with any other person, firm, company, trust or trustee.

The husband appealed. The hearing of the appeal was in chambers. Dunn J. gave part of his judgment in open court. An extract from the C judgment given in chambers is published with the consent of the judge.

The facts are stated in the judgment.

J. H. Hames Q.C., Edward Cazalet and *David Ritchie* for the husband. Geoffrey M. Rutter, solicitor, for the wife.

D
DUNN J. This is an appeal by a husband against part of an order for discovery which was made by Mr. Registrar Kenworthy on December 9, 1977. The appeal raises important questions as to the law and practice relating to discovery in financial proceedings in the Family Division, and at the request of the parties I am giving judgment in open court.

The parts of the order against which the husband appeals are those E which refer to documents of a private company of which the husband is chairman and managing director. I shall call that company the " operating company." 75 per cent. of the shares of the operating company are held by another private company which I shall call the " holding company," of which the husband is the owner of 51 per cent. of the registered share capital. The majority of the remaining shares of the holding company are held by members of the husband's family. The remaining 25 per cent. of F the shares in the operating company are held by a public company which I shall call the " public company." The effect of the shareholdings is that the husband, through the holding company, has a controlling interest in the operating company. There are six other directors of the operating company in addition to the husband, of whom two are nominees of the public company. Three of the other four directors hold shares in the G holding company.

The husband, before the order was made, had already given discovery of certain documents relating to his own income tax returns and private bank accounts. The order made by the registrar ordered him to disclose and produce documents relating to his own personal expenditure and that of his family, whether made by himself or by the operating company, and also contained a clause, clause 17, requiring him to produce all the H books of account, private ledgers, paid cheques, cheque stubs, documents and vouchers of the operating company in relation to all bills and expenses incurred by the husband or the company, and paid by or charged to the company, and records of all receipts of moneys by the operating company in the course of its trading over the period from April 1, 1974. The effect of that clause is to enable the wife through accountants to carry out an audit of the books of the operating company from April 1, 1974.

A   It is said on her behalf that for reasons which were accepted by the registrar, such an audit is necessary to enable the court to dispose fairly of the issues between the parties. It is said on behalf of the husband that the registrar had no jurisdiction to make such an order, involving as it does not only discovery but also production of company documents, the operating company not being a party to the proceedings between the
B   husband and wife. Alternatively, it is said on behalf of the husband that in the exercise of his discretion the registrar should not have made the order.

Although the order for discovery was made in proceedings by the husband under section 1 of the Matrimonial Homes Act 1967, there are also before the court applications by the wife in the pending divorce suit for financial provision for herself and the two children of the family, and
C   for transfer of property. It is accepted by both parties before me that the order is applicable to those proceedings as well as to the proceedings under section 1 of the Matrimonial Homes Act 1967. It follows that all documents relating to the income, earning capacity, property, and other financial resources of the husband, are relevant documents, as are documents relating to his financial needs, obligations and responsibilities, to the
D   standard of living enjoyed by the family before the breakdown of the marriage, and to the contributions made by the husband to the welfare of the family, and, indeed, all matters referred to in section 25 of the Matrimonial Causes Act 1973.

By rule 77 (5) of the Matrimonial Causes Rules 1977, the registrar may at any stage of the proceedings order the discovery and production of any document and require any further affidavits. It was accepted on
E   behalf of the wife that that rule gives the registrar no greater powers in relation to discovery than those contained in R.S.C., Ord. 24 which, with modifications, is applicable to defended divorce suits by reason of rule 28 of the Matrimonial Causes Rules 1977. R.S.C., Ord. 24 is also applicable to proceedings under section 1 of the Matrimonial Homes Act 1967, since they are proceedings commenced by originating summons, and Order 24
F   applies to all such proceedings. Order 24, as is well known, places upon the parties to a suit the obligation to make discovery of all documents which are or have been in their possession, custody or power, relating to matters in question in the proceedings. In the first instance, discovery must be made without any order of the court. The court may make an order either for general discovery or discovery of specific documents or classes of documents. The court may also make an order for the production of
G   documents for inspection by the other party or by the court, but all these types of order are discretionary. The rules provide that the court shall refuse to make such an order if and in so far as it is of opinion that discovery is not necessary either for disposing fairly of the proceedings or for saving costs or is premature.

Although in practice it will often be convenient to deal with discovery
H   in one piece, it is important to remember that under the terms of the rule discovery proceeds by stages, and different considerations may apply at each stage. The order in this case was an order under Ord. 24, r. 7, for the discovery by the husband of specific classes of documents and for their production for inspection by the wife's solicitors. Before any question of discretion arises, however, the court has no jurisdiction to make an order for discovery or production unless, first, the person against whom discovery is sought is a party to the suit; secondly, the documents are in

his possession, custody or power; and thirdly, the documents relate to **A** matters in question in the proceedings. These requirements must be satisfied before discovery is ordered even if hardship is thereby caused to one party to the suit: see *James Nelson & Sons Ltd.* v. *Nelson Line (Liverpool) Ltd.* [1906] 2 K.B. 217 *per* Farwell L.J.

As to the first requirement, it is well established that, save in exceptional cases, and in cases falling within Ord. 24, r. 7 (*a*), which does not apply **B** to the Family Division, no discovery can be obtained against a person not party to the proceedings. A person cannot be made a party to proceedings solely for the purpose of obtaining discovery against him, except in exceptional circumstances. The exceptional circumstances are where a person without incurring any personal liability, has become involved in the tortious acts of another, so that he comes under a duty to assist one injured by those acts by giving him full information by way of discovery **C** and disclosing the identity of the wrongdoers: see *Norwich Pharmacal Co.* v. *Customs and Excise Commissioners* [1974] A.C. 133.

It is not suggested in this case that the wife could take proceedings against the operating company in reliance on that principle. In the course of his speech in *Norwich Pharmacal Co.* v. *Customs and Excise Commissioners* Lord Reid reaffirmed " the mere witness rule " and stated it in **D** these terms, at p. 174:

"It has been clear at least since the time of Lord Hardwicke that information cannot be obtained by discovery from a person who will in due course be compellable to give that information either by oral testimony as a witness or on a subpoena duces tecum."

If the wife cannot obtain the documents she requires on discovery, she may **E** be able to apply under R.S.C., Ord. 38 for leave, since these proceedings are in chambers, to issue a subpoena duces tecum against the secretary or other officers of the company to produce relevant documents.

The person to be considered is therefore the husband, the party to the suit; and the next and vital question in the case is are these documents which were ordered to be produced documents which are or have been **F** in the possession, custody or power of the husband? For this purpose " possession " means " the right to the possession of a document." " Custody " means " the actual, physical or corporeal holding of a document regardless of the right to its possession," for example, a holding of a document by a party as servant or agent of the true owner. " Power " means " an enforceable right to inspect the document or to obtain possession or control of the document from the person who ordinarily has it in fact." **G** The requirements of the Rules are disjunctive in their operation, so far as possession, custody and power are concerned.

Many authorities have been cited to me as to the application of the rule and of these definitions: most of them relate to the old Chancery practice before that was stated in Rules of Court, or to the Rules of Court before 1964 when the word " custody " was added to the words **H** " possession or power." Before 1964 the word " possession " was held to mean " corporeal possession pursuant to legal possession," but " corporeal possession " is now embraced by the word " custody."

In *The Supreme Court Practice* (1976) vol. 1, p. 399 there is a note, note 24/2/4, " Production and inspection." It is in the following terms:

"Until 1962, there was a distinction between the obligation to give discovery i.e. to disclose the existence of documents) and the

A   obligation to produce disclosed documents for inspection. A party was (and still is) obliged to disclose the existence of documents in his possession, etc., even though his possession may not be exclusive or may be only physical custody, e.g. as a servant; the obligation to produce documents was narrower and extended only to documents in the sole legal possession of the party giving discovery. . . . Under the present rules the obligation to give inspection extends prima facie

B   to all documents to which the obligation to give discovery extends. . . . But the court has a discretion whether to order inspection, and it may be that, in the exercise of such discretion, it will have regard to any prejudice to persons having a right to the documents in question. Moreover, the court will not make an order either for discovery or inspection which is premature or not necessary for disposing fairly

C   of the cause or matter or for saving costs."

The terms of that note were expressly approved by Lord Cross of Chelsea in *Alfred Crompton Amusement Machines Ltd.* v. *Customs and Excise Commissioners (No. 2)* [1974] A.C. 405, 429, and three others of their Lordships agreed with the speech of Lord Cross of Chelsea. It follows, therefore that a person has the obligation to disclose all relevant

D   documents which are or have been in his custody or power, even if he is not the owner or sole owner of them; and prima facie he is obliged to produce all such documents for the inspection of the other party. If he objects to production the court has a discretion whether or not to order production. In exercising its discretion the court will take into account all the circumstances of the case including any prejudice to persons having

E   any right or interest in the document in question. The party against whom an order for production is sought should state on affidavit the nature and the interest of any person not a party to the action: see *Bovill* v. *Cowan* (1870) L.R. 5 Ch.App. 495. He should also state whether or not he has tried to obtain consent to the production and why consent has been refused: see *Taylor* v. *Rundell* (1841) Cr. & Ph. 104. If the court should refuse production on the ground of joint possession, it may allow an inter-

F   rogatory as to the contents of the document: see *Rattenberry* v. *Monro* (1910) 103 L.T. 560 and *Swanston* v. *Lishman* (1881) 45 L.T. 360. Cases such as *Hadley* v. *McDougall* (1872) L.R. 7 Ch.App. 312; *Kettlewell* v. *Barstow* (1872) L.R. 7 Ch.App. 686; *Reid* v. *Langlois* (1849) 1 Mac. & G. 627 and *Chantrey Martin* v. *Martin* [1953] 2 Q.B. 286, on this point, are all examples of the old rule of Chancery practice incorporated

G   into the Rules of the Supreme Court before 1964, whereby production would not be ordered of documents of which a party was not the sole owner.

    As I have said, this is now a matter for discretion; though, in exercising that discretion, the court would no doubt have regard to the words of James L.J. in *Kettlewell* v. *Barstow,* L.R. 7 Ch.App. 686, 693:

H   " . . . the court will not order the defendants to do what they have no power to do; but it is no ground for resisting production that a person not before the court has an interest in the documents."

    How do these general principles apply to the director of a company in relation to company documents, that is, to documents which are in the possession of the company in the sense that the company has the sole legal right to their possession? If they are or have been in the custody or physical possession of the director, even if he only held them or holds

them as servant or agent of the company, or in his capacity as an officer   A
of the company, then they must be disclosed. Whether such documents
are or have been in his custody is a question of fact in each case. It is a
matter for the discretion of the court whether they should be produced: see
Skoye v. *Bailey* (1971) 1 W.W.R. 144 and *Williams* v. *Ingram* (1900)
16 T.L.R. 451.

   It is interesting to observe that as long ago as 1900, when *Williams* v.
Ingram was decided, Lord Alverstone M.R. said that it was well worth   B
consideration whether the power of the court was sufficient with regard
to the production before trial of documents in the possession of third
parties, but as matters then stood, Lord Alverstone M.R. was satisfied
that the decision of Byrne J., at first instance, was right. As the law and
practice then stood, said Lord Alverstone M.R., it was impossible to
compel production of the documents in question. If any alteration was   C
to be made in the practice, it could only be done by a new rule, if that
were possible, or by fresh legislation. In refusing production of books of a
company, in the absence of consent by the company to their production,
Byrne J. made it clear that the objection was a genuine one and that
he was not satisfied that there was any contrivance to defeat the powers
of the court such as would justify him in making an order of the kind   D
there asked for.

   It is plain from those cases that before 1964 it was not the practice of
the court to order production of such documents if the board of directors
objected to its production on affidavit, but the court must be satisfied that
the objection was not contrived. But what of relevant company documents
which are not and never have been in the custody of the director who is
a party to the proceedings to which the company is not a party? Are such   E
documents within the power of the director? Section 12 (1) of the
Companies Act 1976 provides that " Every company shall cause accounting
records to be kept . . ." and subsection (6) provides that such records

> " . . . shall be kept at the registered office of the company or at such
> other place as the directors of the company think fit and shall at all
> times be open to inspection by the officers of the company."   F

But the right to inspect, under the provisions of that section, is a right
vested in a director in his capacity as a director or officer of the company;
he is in a fiduciary relationship with the company; he owes duties to the
company and to its shareholders. Without the consent of the company
he has no right to inspect documents, much less to take copies of them
or remove them from the premises of the company for his own purposes   G
unconnected with the business of the company. Because, in his capacity
as a director, he has the right to inspect the company documents, it does not
follow that in his personal capacity he has an enforceable right to inspect
or to obtain possesssion or control of them so that the documents can be
said to be in his power. It is a question of fact in each case whether or
not a director has such an enforceable right; much will depend upon the   H
share structure of the company. In cases of a one man company, where
the director owns all or substantially all the shares and any minority shareholders are not adverse to him, then the inference may be drawn that the
company, although a separate legal entity, does not control him but he
controls the company in such manner as to make it his other person or
alter ego. In such a case, where the director controls the company and
nominates the other directors, all the documents of the company are

A within his power in the sense that in truth and in fact he is able to obtain control of them.

There is no English authority which has been cited to me to support this proposition but, as a result of the searches of the wife's solicitors, a Canadian case of *Dallas* v. *Dallas* (1960) 24 D.L.R. (2d) 746 was cited to me. *Dallas* v. *Dallas* is a decision of the Court of Appeal of British

B Columbia. It was an action between husband and wife for a declaration, the wife being the plaintiff, that they were joint owners of his shares in a limited company. The wife sought discovery of the documents of the company. She contended that the documents were in the husband's office and in his possession and that, therefore, he should be required to produce them. The husband contended that the documents, while in his possession, were nevertheless the property of the company and, therefore, the com-

C pany had the right to prevent his producing them, and he had no authority from the company to produce them. In giving the judgment of the court, Sheppard J.A. set out the shareholding of the company, which showed that of 1,200,003 shares the defendant, the husband, was the registered owner of 1,198,999, the wife, the plaintiff, of one share, and their 16 year-old-son 1,000 shares; and there were three qualifying shares issued to three

D directors. Sheppard J.A. said, at p. 747:

"It is therefore evident that the defendant controls the company, elects the directorate, and also has provided the qualifying shares for three of the four directors. The defendant and those three nominees are the board of directors. The company holds oil leases which were acquired from funds obtained by the defendant from a

E joint bank account of the plaintiff and defendant. The plaintiff in contending that she is entitled to one-half of whatever interest the defendant has in the company, seeks to make the defendant produce the company documents so that she may ascertain what is his interest, and possibly obtain evidence which will enable her to trace the funds for their joint bank account.

"The documents being in the defendant's office, and therefore in his

F possession, are prima facie within his control: *London & Yorkshire Bank Ltd.* v. *Cooper* (1885) 15 Q.B.D. 473 *per* Brett M.R. at p. 474: 'It has been argued that the documents are not in his control; but if they are in his possession, they are prima facie under his control.'

"The defendant contends, however, that he has the mere custody and that the company, which is not a party to the action, has control, and therefore he, the defendant, should not be required to produce

G those documents as he has no authority from the company to do so and as the company may prevent his so doing. The question is whether the defendant's control is such that his production of the documents should be excused. As a shareholder he controls the company subject to any restraint by the minority, but in this instance the minority interest is not important. One share is held by his wife

H who can offer no objection to her obtaining inspection by production of the documents; the remaining outstanding shares are not adverse to the defendant. The defendant's mind is the directing and controlling mind of the company and of the board of directors. Again, the defendant has provided funds whereby the company acquired oil leases and some of those moneys at least came from the joint bank account. It is evident that the company does not control him but that he controls the company in such manner as to make it his A 'other person'."

Then reference was made to certain English cases, which were distinguished. The judgment concludes, at p. 748:

"In the case at bar the defendant has possession and there are no minority shareholders in whose interest the company might assert control over the documents. On the appeal no argument was directed B to the question whether all the documents were relevant. Hence it should be understood that the defendant's obligation to produce should be limited to those documents relevant to issues in this action. . . ."

The appeal was allowed and the order for production of relevant docu- C ments was made. That case seems to be entirely in line with the various principles which have been followed by the English courts over the years, and I follow it and adopt it.

At the other end of the scale there is the case where the director who is involved in litigation cannot be said to control the company at all. The documents of such a company would not be in the power of the director without the consent of the board of directors. Then there are D cases, of which this case is an example, falling somewhere between the two. In such cases the court will consider the extent of the shareholding of the husband; whether it amounts to control of the company; whether the minority shareholders are adverse to him; how the board of directors is constituted; and whether there is any objection by the board to disclosure of any documents sought.   E

It was submitted on behalf of the wife that because the board in this case has consented to disclosure of certain company documents the court is entitled to draw the inference that other documents, to the disclosure of which the board has objected, are in the power of the husband. It was said that the board cannot pick and choose, and cannot approbate and reprobate. I do not accept that submission as a proposition of law. Every document or class of documents must be looked at separately, and because F disclosure of certain classes of documents is not objected to it does not follow that other classes of documents, the disclosure of which is objected to, are within the power of the husband. In any event it has been made clear that in this case the objection in point of law extends to all documents in the possession of the company, although an ex gratia offer to disclose certain documents has been made.   G

It was also submitted on behalf of the wife that the court was entitled to look at the way in which the husband had used the resources of the company for his private purposes over the years; and to the extent to which his business life and his personal life were intermingled, it was submitted that, if the evidence showed that the husband had lived off the company in the sense that the company had met all or substantially all H his private expenditure in cash and kind, that was an additional fact from which it could be inferred that the husband in truth and in fact controlled the company and that the documents of the company were in his power. I am not prepared to say that as a matter of law these factors are irrelevant, but the court will, however, consider them against the background of the share structure of the company, the constitution of the board, and other matters to which I have referred.

A   The third requirement before an order for discovery can be made is that the documents should be relevant to the matters in issue between the parties. It is a feature of financial proceedings in the Family Division that very wide ranging issues are involved. In *O'D.* v. *O'D.* [1976] Fam. 83, 90, Ormrod L.J. said:

B   " In approaching a case like the present, the first stage should be to make as reliable an estimate as possible of the husband's current financial position and future prospects. In making this assessment the court is concerned with the reality of the husband's resources, using that word in a broad sense to include not only what he is shown to have, but also what could reasonably be made available to him if he so wished. Much will depend upon the interpretation of accounts, balance sheets and so on, which will require in many cases the expert

C   guidance of accountants. It will rarely be possible to arrive at arithmetically exact figures. The court must penetrate through the balance sheets and profit and loss accounts to the underlying realities, bearing in mind that prudent financial management and skilled presentation of accounts are unlikely to overstate the husband's real resources and, on the other side, that there may be a great difference between wealth

D   on paper and true wealth. Valuations may overstate or understate the results of realisation of assets, many of which may not be realisable within the immediate or foreseeable future."

      It is another feature of such proceedings that one party, usually the wife, is in a situation quite different from that of ordinary litigants. In general terms, she may know more than anyone else about the husband's

E   financial position; she will know at first hand of the standard of living of the family during the marriage; she will know about the furnishings and equipment of the matrimonial home, and of the physical possessions of the husband, and perhaps the approximate amount of cash kept in the house. She may also know, from conversations with the husband in the privacy of the matrimonial home, the general sources of his wealth and how he is able to maintain the standard of living that he does. But she

F   is unlikely to know the details of such sources or precise figures, and it is for this reason that discovery now plays such an important part in financial proceedings in the Family Division.

      Applications for such discovery cannot be described as " fishing " for information, as they might be in other divisions. The wife is entitled to go " fishing " in the Family Division within the limits of the law and

G   practice.

      It is said on behalf of the husband, and this is indeed the fact, that if the court decided that the husband has not made a full disclosure of all relevant documents the court will accept the evidence of the wife and draw adverse inferences against the husband. It is said that that is the real sanction against non-disclosure by the husband. It is true that this

H   has been the practice ever since the days of the ecclesiastical courts, but it may result in injustice to one or both parties and it is no substitute for full discovery of all documents relating to the financial resources of the parties. The wife normally puts the husband to proof of his financial resources, and it is then for the husband to make full disclosure, including disclosure of all documents relating thereto. If his initial discovery is manifestly incomplete the wife may apply for further discovery. In many, perhaps most, cases audited accounts of companies of which the husband

is a shareholder will be sufficient, together with full disclosure of all the A
husband's personal financial records. But there are cases when the court
will go behind company accounts and order discovery of company books
and documents, if it has the power within the law and within the Rules to
do so. It is not usual, however, for the court to take this course unless
there is evidence before it from accountants or other experts that the
published accounts of the company cannot be relied upon.
          In cases in which it is alleged that the husband has the handling of B
very large sums of cash, the court should consider whether it is likely
that there would be records of such sums in the company's books, before
making any order against the company. It may be that in cases of that kind
the court will be more concerned with evidence as to the standard of living
of the husband, and of the expenditure actually made by him, than of
evidence of company records and books.   C
          I turn now to consider the question of the discretion of the court.
Assuming that the court has jurisdiction to order discovery and decides
to do so, then it is a matter for discretion whether or not to order
production. If there is no jurisdiction to order discovery no question
of discretion can arise. The various meanings of "discretion" are set out
by Sir Jocelyn Simon P. in *Povey* v. *Povey* [1972] Fam. 40, 48. So far   D
as the discretion to order production of company documents is concerned,
the court will have regard to all the circumstances. The discretion must be
exercised judicially, holding the balance evenly between the parties and
any third person affected by discovery. The court will not have discretion
to order production unless the documents are either in the custody of
the husband or in his power, in the sense which I have already described;
and, considering whether company documents are in the power of the E
husband, the court will already have considered any objections by the
board of directors to their production. In considering the exercise of
discretion the court will balance the relevance and importance of the
documents, and the hardship to the wife likely to be caused by non-
production, against any prejudice likely to be caused to the husband
and any other directors or shareholders of the company if an order for F
production is made; and the court will not order production unless it is of
opinion that the order is necessary either for fairly disposing of the matter
or for saving costs.
          The confidentiality of documents is of itself no ground for refusing
production. It may be relevant to the existence of one of the accepted
heads of privilege: see *Alfred Crompton Amusement Machines Ltd.* v.
Customs and Excise Commissioners (No. 2) [1974] A.C. 405, 429, *per* G
Lord Cross of Chelsea. In that context there is an implied undertaking
by a party who obtains production of documents against any improper
disclosure.
          Assuming that the court has no jurisdiction to make the order for
discovery sought, it is not powerless: it can give leave to issue a subpoena
duces tecum under Ord. 38, r. 14 against the secretary of the company H
for production of relevant documents: see *Carew* v. *Carew* [1891] P.
360; or the court can make an order for the production of documents
under R.S.C., Ord. 38, r. 13, which is incorporated into the Matrimonial
Causes Rules by rule 3 of the Matrimonial Causes Rules 1977. Although
Ord. 38, r. 13 is in quite general terms, it appears from the notes in
The Supreme Court Practice (1976) that the rule does not enable an order
to be made for the inspection of documents in the hands of persons not

A parties. On the other hand, it also appears from the notes that if it is proved
to the satisfaction of the court that a banking account nominally that
of a person not a party is really that of a party, or that the party is so
closely connected with it that items in it would be evidence against him
at the trial, then the court in its discretion may order inspection before
the trial.

B I will conclude this part of my judgment by summarising my conclusions as to the law. (1) A party to a suit must disclose all the documents
in his possession, custody or power which are relevant to the matters
in issue. The court has a discretion whether or not to order him to make
such disclosure, and also has a discretion whether or not to order
him to produce the documents for inspection by the other party or the
court. (2) The documents of a company are in the legal possession of
C the company. If they are or have been in the actual physical possession of
a director who is a party to litigation they must be disclosed by that
director, if relevant to the litigation, even though he holds them as servant
or agent of the company in his capacity as an officer of the company.
(3) Whether or not documents of a company are in the power of a
director who is a party to the litigation is a question of fact in each
case. " Power " in this context means " the enforceable right to inspect
D or obtain possession or control of the document." If the company is the
alter ego of such a director so that he has unfettered control of the
company's affairs, he must disclose and produce all relevant documents
in the possession of the company. (4) Where relevant documents in the
possession of a company are disclosed by a director as being in his
custody or power, the court has a discretion whether or not to order
E production of them. (5) The discretion is a judicial discretion, and in
exercising it the court will have regard to all the circumstances. The
court will balance the relevance and importance of the documents and
the hardship likely to be caused to the wife by non-production against
any prejudice to the husband and third parties likely to be caused by
production. It has not hitherto been the practice of the court to order
production of company documents to which the board of directors objects
F on affidavit, provided that the court is satisfied that the objection is not
contrived for the purpose of frustrating the powers of the court. The court
will not in the exercise of its discretion order parties to do that which
they have no power to do. The court will not order production unless it is
satisfied that production is necessary either for disposing fairly of the issues
between the parties or for saving costs.

G [His Lordship continued his judgment in chambers but the following
extract from that part of the judgment is published with his Lordship's
permission:] It is said that by reason of the discrepancies in the accounts
the wife does not accept the audited accounts of the company, and does
not trust the auditors to produce certified figures of the husband's expenditure. It is said, in these circumstances, that it is necessary for accountants
H on her behalf to see not only the receipts and any other documents
relating to the expenditure but also to see the company's books in order
to ascertain to whom the various items of expenditure were charged.
It is said on behalf of the husband that the books and documents of the
company would neither confirm nor deny the wife's allegations, especially
in regard to the large sums of cash; because, if they had been improperly
obtained, they would not have passed through the books.

I am not satisfied that at this stage the documents referred to in

clause 17 are relevant to the matters in dispute. I think that, having   A
regard to the allegations by the wife, the court at the hearing is likely
to be more interested in the actual standard of living and expenditure
of the husband over the years than in books and records of the company,
which may well not show cash expenditure. But I accept that the various
documents referred to in clauses 3, 4 and 11 are relevant to the matters in
issue. All those documents are in the possession of the company; they
are not in the possession of the husband in the sense that I have used it in   B
this judgment. The husband has, however, given some evidence as to
how those documents were dealt with. He said in his affidavit of April
22, 1977:

> " The mechanics of the financing of my expenditure is that the
> restaurant or night club will send the bill to the office, where it will be
> scrutinised by me, and I will give instructions to have it paid."   C

I take it that that procedure refers to all documents relating to the
expenditure and payments referred to in clauses 3, 4 and 11 of the order.
Those documents are documents, in my judgment, which are or have been
in the custody of the husband and, therefore, he must disclose them. The
company have offered limited disclosure of those documents, but they have
taken the position that they shall be the judges of which documents   D
are or are not relevant. The registrar refused to accept that position. I
deal with it in this way, which I believe to be the way that the law requires
it to be dealt with, namely, that the documents must be disclosed; and
if any objection is made to their production that objection can be made
on affidavit after the documents have been properly disclosed. The
registrar will then be able to consider the objections to production as they   E
are made in respect of the individual classes of documents, and will also
have the power to order their production, or the production of some
of them, to the court, so that he can make up his mind whether or not
they are documents which are relevant and which therefore should be
produced, or not. In deciding whether the document is to be produced
for inspection by the wife, he will of course have regard to the various
matters of discretion to which I have referred earlier in this judgment. If   F
that course is adopted, then production of the documents to the wife will
be regulated by the court and not by the company; but the documents
must be disclosed as being in the custody of the husband.

So far as clause 17 is concerned, I have already expressed the view
that at this stage I am not satisfied that those documents are relevant,
save in so far as they include documents under clauses 3, 4 and 11 which   G
I have already dealt with. I would add this: considering all the evidence
in the case and applying it to the principles which I have enunciated,
I cannot say that the operating company is the alter ego of the husband,
so that he can control it to the extent that he can require production of
those documents. Clause 17 must therefore be deleted from the order, save
for the provision relating to the Swiss bank accounts. So far as the Swiss
bank accounts are concerned, it seems to me that documents relating to   H
any Swiss bank account which the husband has a mandate to operate
alone or jointly with any other person or persons are documents which
are in his custody or power, and they must therefore be disclosed. If
there is any objection to production of any of those documents, then
that objection must be made on affidavit by any person who claims to
have a joint interest in the document. That also is a matter which will be
dealt with by the registrar in the discretion of the court.

A   The documents referred to in clause 12 of the order, namely, the documents in the action between the holding company and the public company, are not in my judgment documents within the custody or power of the husband; clause 12 must therefore be deleted from the order.

Finally, I deal with the second part of the order, which is an order requiring the husband to file an affidavit setting out particulars of visits abroad, and particulars of motor cars owned by the company. These
B   matters do not fall within the considerations affecting discovery, to which I have referred at some length, and I see no reason why the husband should not file a further affidavit in the terms ordered by the registrar. That affidavit must be filed within 21 days, and the affidavit will be in the form originally ordered by the registrar.

To the extent which I have stated, therefore, this appeal will be
C   allowed.

Order accordingly.
Leave to appeal.

Solicitors: *Theodore Goddard & Co.; S. Rutter & Co.*

D
                                                              M. B. D.

E   [CHANCERY DIVISION]

           COOK INDUSTRIES INCORPORATED *v.* GALLIHER
                            AND ANOTHER

                          [1978 C. No. 754]

F   1978   Feb. 20
                                                         Templeman J.

Practice—Discovery—Jurisdiction to order inspection abroad—
Action in England to enforce American judgment debt—Parties
all resident outside England and Wales—Plaintiffs seeking
declaration of title to property and chattels in France—
Whether jurisdiction to grant order for inspection—Whether
G   *action to be stayed*

        An American corporation, assignees of an unsatisfied judgment debt of U.S. $2,500,000 resulting from an action tried in New York in 1965 concerning fraud and manipulation of shares in an American company, suspected that the judgment debtor had transferred valuable works of art and furniture from his New York flat to a Paris flat. The lease of the flat was in the name of a friend of the debtor, but the rent was
H   paid by a company controlled by the debtor. The corporation issued a writ against the debtor and his friend, who were both American citizens, claiming a declaration that the lease of the flat and its contents were held on trust for the debtor; alternatively a declaration that the transfer of assets by the debtor to the friend was a conveyance made by the debtor with intent to defeat and delay his creditors and was void. The

              [Reported by MISS HILARY PEARSON, Barrister-at-Law]

corporation obtained an ex parte injunction restricting the friend **A**
from disposing of or removing any of the contents of the flat.
They also sought orders that the friend should disclose the
contents of the flat and should permit the flat to be inspected
by a French advocate who was also an English barrister. The
writ, notice of motion and injunction were served on the friend
some ten days later when he arrived from New York in
London, where he owned a flat.

On the preliminary questions whether the court had juris- **B**
diction to grant an order for inspection of premises outside
England and Wales and whether, even if the court had
jurisdiction, the action should be dismissed or stayed because
England was not the proper forum: —

Held, allowing the plaintiffs to proceed with their motion,
(1) that the court had jurisdiction to entertain an action for
the determination of the title or right to possession of any
immovable property situate out of England where there was **C**
an equity between the parties; that there was clearly an equity
between the corporation and the debtor, and if the evidence
showed that the friend had assisted the debtor in defeating his
creditors then there would be an equity between the corporation and the friend, giving the court jurisdiction to make the
order for inspection sought.

(2) That where an order in personam was sought and the
defendant, although a foreign citizen, was in the jurisdiction, **D**
it was not proper to order a stay on the ground that England
was not the natural forum, in particular when delay would
seriously prejudice the plaintiff.

The Atlantic Star [1974] A.C. 436, H.L.(E.) and *MacShannon*
v. *Rockware Glass Ltd.* [1978] 2 W.L.R. 362, H.L.(E.)
distinguished.

The following cases are referred to in the judgment: **E**

Anton Piller KG v. *Manufacturing Processes Ltd.* [1976] Ch. 55; [1976]
2 W.L.R. 162; [1976] 1 All E.R. 779, C.A.

Atlantic Star, The [1974] A.C. 436; [1973] 2 W.L.R. 795; [1973] 2 All
E.R. 175, H.L.(E.).

MacShannon v. *Rockware Glass Ltd.* [1978] 2 W.L.R. 362; [1978] 1 All
E.R. 625, H.L.(E.). **F**

The following additional cases were cited in argument:

Bennitt v. *Whitehouse* (1860) 28 Beav. 119.
Cranstown (Lord) v. *Johnston* (1796) 3 Ves.Jr. 170.
Portarlington (Lord) v. *Soulby* (1834) 3 My. & K. 104.

G
MOTION

On January 26, 1978, the plaintiffs, Cook Industries Inc., issued a writ
claiming a declaration (1) that the first defendant, John Galliher, held a
first floor flat at 44, Avenue Gabriel, Paris 8 and the contents thereof as
trustee for the second defendant, Jaques Sarlie, and that the plaintiffs were
entitled to execute a judgment obtained against the second defendant in
New York, or (2) that the transfer of assets by the second defendant to **H**
the first defendant was made by the second defendant with intent to defeat
and delay his creditors and was void against the plaintiffs, and claiming
damages for conspiracy to defeat and defraud the plaintiffs as creditors of
the second defendant. On the same date the plaintiffs obtained an ex
parte injunction restraining the first defendant from disposing of or removing
any of the contents of the flat at 44, Avenue Gabriel, Paris. The plaintiffs
also sought interlocutory orders that the first defendant should disclose

A full particulars of the contents of the flat, which he claimed to be beneficially entitled to, that he should verify that information by affidavit, and that he should permit a named French advocate to inspect the contents of the flat.

The first defendant was served with the writ, notice of motion and injunction when he visited London on February 6, 1978, and on February 9, 1978, he issued a notice of motion asking for the discharge of the interlocutory injunction and for an order dismissing or staying the action.

B The facts are stated in the judgment.

Andrew Morritt Q.C. and *Simon Mortimore* for the plaintiffs.
John Weeks for the first defendant.
The second defendant did not appear and was not represented.

C

TEMPLEMAN J. This is an interlocutory application for inspection which raises a preliminary question of jurisdiction. I must briefly set out some allegations made by the plaintiffs, without expressing any view as to whether they can be sustained.

It is the plaintiffs' case that the second defendant in these proceedings, Mr. Sarlie, was in 1965 involved in proceedings in which two American corporations sued him for fraud and manipulation of shares. It is further the plaintiffs' case that during those proceedings and before judgment Mr. Sarlie, who had been living in a New York apartment in a state of some ostentation and affluence, removed himself and his belongings from New York, and that those belongings included a collection of paintings—including 20 Picassos—and chattels which, according to one statement, might have been worth, in the aggregate, five million dollars. Judgment was given against Mr. Sarlie and I have before me the judgment in the case of one company, E. L. Bruce Co. Inc., where the judge began his judgment with this statement:

"The plaintiffs' former president, Edward M. Gilbert, arranged to fleece the plaintiffs to satisfy his personal indebtedness to Jacques Sarlie, the defendant. On the record herein the defendant could hardly be characterised as an innocent bona fide receiver of the plaintiffs' property. He shares with Gilbert the guilt of defrauding the plaintiffs."

Judgment was given for $387,650. A further judgment for another $500,000 was given, I think, in the Court of Appeal, and, with interest, that judgment debt is now said to amount to two and a half million dollars. There is another similar judgment debt in respect of a similar action brought by another American company against Mr. Sarlie, and there, too, Mr. Sarlie was condemned in a sum of an amount which now, with interest, amounts to two and a half million dollars.

As regards one of those judgments, $30,000 was recovered. As regards the other, nothing was ever recovered. Mr. Sarlie, having left New York, apparently carried on business in Europe. According to the plaintiffs, a flat in Paris was acquired by Mr. Galliher, the first defendant, in his own name, but really on behalf of Mr. Sarlie, and in that flat there is property belonging to Mr. Sarlie—in particular, pictures and objects d'art—which are either assets which Mr. Sarlie brought from America or, at any rate, represent those assets, and those assets, in turn, are derived from the fraud perpetrated by Mr. Sarlie on the two American companies. Apparently, according to the plaintiffs, it is not possible to make Mr. Sarlie bankrupt

by American law because there are only two creditors. But also, accord- A
ing to the plaintiffs, by New York law and, in particular, the New York
Debtor and Fraudulent Conveyances Act, a conveyance in fraud of
creditors, whether the debtor is bankrupt or not, gives the creditors a
right of action against anybody concerned in the fraud and it is the
plaintiffs' case in this action that Mr. Sarlie has conspired to defeat and
defraud the plaintiffs as creditors of himself, and that Mr. Galliher has
also been guilty of the same tort by lending his name to the lease of the B
flat and by sheltering Mr. Sarlie's possessions.

In New York Mr. Sarlie was found on a visit some time in 1976 or
1977. He was exposed to cross-examination and there is at the moment an
injunction—a New York injunction—restraining him from disposing of
any of his assets, because of the allegations made by the plaintiffs about the
contents of the flat in Paris.   C

The plaintiffs have brought these proceedings in England against both
Mr. Galliher and Mr. Sarlie and they seek an order for inspection of the
chattels which are in the Paris flat. If this application and this action
proceed, I shall have to determine whether it is right and proper to grant
that relief. But, on this preliminary point, Mr. Weeks, on behalf of Mr.
Galliher, says, first of all, that there is an absolute bar against the action
proceeding: there is no jurisdiction to continue with an action that relates D
to the ownership of foreign immovables. Secondly, he says if there is no
absolute bar, if there is jurisdiction, there is clearly a discretion in the court,
and on the principles enunciated by the authorities that discretion should
be exercised by staying the proceedings.

It is conceded that the court has no jurisdiction to entertain an action
for the determination of the title to or right to possession of any immov- E
able property situate out of England, with certain exceptions. One exception is where there is an equity between the parties, and it is Mr. Weeks's
submission that there is no equity as between the plaintiffs and Mr.
Galliher. First of all, the plaintiffs are not the original judgment creditors.
They are assignees of the judgment debt, but that does not seem to me
to make any difference. As assignees they have all the rights of the original F
creditor. Secondly, he says there is no equity, direct equity, between the
plaintiffs and Mr. Galliher, whatever the position may be between the
plaintiffs and Mr. Sarlie. There must be, he says, some personal equity
running from the plaintiffs to the defendant, citing for this purpose the
passage in *Dicey & Morris, Conflict of Laws,* 9th ed. (1973), p. 522.

It seems to me that, if the plaintiffs are right, there is a personal equity.
There is clearly a personal equity between the plaintiffs and Mr. Sarlie G
who, if the plaintiffs are right, has taken steps to defraud them of the
benefit of their judgment debt, and has taken steps to hide his property
which ought to be made available to the plaintiffs and ought to be there
for the plaintiffs to be able to impose a charging order and to get an
order for sale and satisfy their judgment debt. Similarly, it seems to
me that if—as I say, I make no finding on this: I cannot at the moment— H
Mr. Galliher has lent himself to assist Mr. Sarlie in a campaign ensuring
that Mr. Sarlie's assets do not become available to satisfy the judgment
debt, then it would be monstrous if equity turned its head and said
there is no relationship between the plaintiffs and Mr. Galliher. Accordingly, it seems to me that there is jurisdiction to bring this action as regards
the ownership of the flat.

In any event, the plaintiffs are more interested in the chattels than

A in the flat—or, at least, as interested. Indeed, if the plaintiffs are right, the chattels might even be sufficient to satisfy the judgment debt. Mr. Weeks says that, if there is no jurisdiction as regards the flat, there can be no jurisdiction as regards the contents. I take the view that there is jurisdiction to make an order about the flat for inspection, and that, if that were not right, there would be, in any event, jurisdiction to make an order as regards the chattels.

B
I now come to the question whether, pursuant to the authorities and, in particular, the two leading cases of *The Atlantic Star* [1974] A.C. 436 and *MacShannon* v. *Rockware Glass Ltd.* [1978] 2 W.L.R. 362, the action ought to be stayed. Mr. Weeks makes several factual submissions, which, for present purposes, I accept. He says England is not the natural forum. The plaintiffs are an American company; the debt is an American judgment

C debt; the defendants are United States citizens and, he says, Mr. Galliher resides in the United States; and the subject matter of the dispute is a flat in Paris. He says the action could be more conveniently tried in New York, where Mr. Sarlie has already been cross-examined and where, he says, Mr. Galliher lives. So far as Mr. Galliher's residence is concerned, the evidence shows that he has consistently in the the past few years spent

D roughly between November and April in New York and the rest of the time in a house in London which he has had for a number of years. Although he is a United States citizen, on the present evidence it looks as though he is as much or more in England as he is in the United States and, as far as he is concerned, it seems to me that it is just as easy to defend an action here as it is for him to defend an action in New York. But, more materially than that, there is in this present application a feature

E which is wholly absent from the authorities to which I have been referred. What the plaintiffs seek is an order against Mr. Galliher in personam that he should allow and authorise the plaintiffs to inspect the premises and chattels and that is an order which would operate on Mr. Galliher personally. He is here now. As I have said, he has a house in London, where he spends a good part of every year. The object is to see what is in the Paris flat—to open Pandora's box. As far as that application is

F concerned, it seems to me that, if I think there are sufficient grounds for it, I must bear this in mind: if I stay the action now, the flat will not be inspected in the near future. Mr. Weeks says, " Oh, that can be ordered by the New York court, if necessary, and undertakings could be given that nothing should be disposed of in the meantime." But I have to bear in mind that the plaintiffs' allegations are based on fraud. I do not, on

G this preliminary issue, determine whether the flat ought to be inspected. All I do determine is that, if it ought to be inspected, it ought to be inspected as quickly as possible, before anything else happens to the contents. It would defeat the whole object—or could well defeat the whole object— if the whole question was merely sent back to New York for action to be taken there.

H Accordingly, I have reached the conclusion that I have jurisdiction to hear the application and that the proper thing to do is to consider, on the evidence, whether a proper case has been made out and, in particular, a case which, on the authorities, is sufficient to justify the relief which is sought. On this preliminary matter I say nothing about the volume of evidence one way or the other or about what may transpire hereafter. I make no finding on that: I simply express my conviction that I have jurisdiction to allow the matter to go on for the present. Whether, if

inspection is refused, or if inspection is ordered and carried out, it would A
be proper at a later stage to stay proceedings, I know not. It may depend
entirely on what action is happening in New York; it may depend on a
good many circumstances and I do not wish it to be thought that my
decision, in the exercise of my discretion, that the action should not be
stayed at the moment, has necessarily any application at some future date.
It will be open to Mr. Galliher at some future date in different circumstances to renew his application for a stay on these proceedings. But, at the B
moment, I think it would be wrong to stay the action today, February 20,
1978.

[TEMPLEMAN J. then heard the application on behalf of the plaintiffs
for an order permitting the inspection of the flat at 44, Avenue Gabriel,
Paris 8 and continued:] This is an interlocutory application for inspection,
and I have already given my reasons for thinking that I have jurisdiction C
to entertain the application.

I now have to consider whether, in the exercise of my discretion, the
inspection should be allowed. The notice of motion seeks an order that
Mr. Galliher give his written permission and make arrangements to allow
Mr. Cordery, who is a solicitor in the firm of Clifford-Turner in Paris,
together with a valuer and photographer, to enter the first floor flat at 44,
Avenue Gabriel, Paris, between the hours of 9 a.m. and 6 p.m. for the D
purpose of inspecting the contents and photographing and taking an inventory thereof.

Mr. Weeks, who appeared for Mr. Galliher, conceded, subject to the
jurisdiction points I have dealt with already, that there is jurisdiction to
make such an order for inspection, but, as he rightly said, it is a power which
ought to be exercised very circumspectly. The power was exercised in E
Anton Piller KG v. *Manufacturing Processes Ltd.* [1976] Ch. 55 on an
ex parte application. Here, the application is now inter partes and Mr.
Galliher has not only put in affidavit evidence, but also has been cross-
examined and re-examined. But, nevertheless, an order for inspection of
the contents of a flat claimed by an individual is an order which, in my
judgment, should very sparingly be exercised in conditions which are only
the same—or, at any rate, not far short of those specified by Ormrod L.J., F
who said, at p. 62:

"First, there must be an extremely strong prima facie case. Secondly,
the damage, potential or actual, must be very serious for the applicant.
Thirdly, there must be clear evidence that the defendants have in
their possession incriminating documents or things, and that there is a
real possibility that they may destroy such material before any appli- G
cation inter partes can be made."

Ormrod L.J. was, of course, there dealing with infringement of copyright
and a case in which, as he said, it was clear that incriminating documents
were in the possession of the defendants.

With those warnings I now unfold the tale which has been told by this
affair, a tale based partly on the plaintiffs' evidence, partly on admissions H
made by Mr. Sarlie under examination in New York, and partly on Mr.
Galliher's affidavit and oral evidence. [His Lordship considered the
evidence, found that, if an order was made, the only possible injustice to Mr.
Galliher was that the contents of the flat at 44, Avenue Gabriel, Paris, which
he rarely used and was used by Mr. Sarlie and Osec, a Luxembourg
company under the control of Mr. Sarlie, would be photographed and an
inventory taken of the contents, which Mr. Galliher claimed belonged to

A   him. His Lordship continued:] Some argument was raised as to whether it was proper to exercise jurisdiction, having regard to the fact that Mr. Galliher, it was said, was a resident of the United States, and that the plaintiffs could take action against him in the United States. As to that, Mr. Galliher seems to be as much in London as he is in the United States and nothing I decide now will necessarily mean that litigation over here will be continued or will be expensive or will be oppressive. It seems to

B   me there are strong grounds for the action proceeding against Mr. Galliher in this country anyway, but if that is not right, once inspection has been carried out there is no reason why a renewed application should not be made to stay these proceedings, and I say nothing about whether such an application would have any chance of success. The important thing is that I am satisfied that if I stay these proceedings or if I take any course

C   other than ordering inspection now there is a very grave danger that the plaintiffs, if they are right, would be wholly frustrated and will never be able to prove that they are right. I think justice demands that they should not be deprived of their opportunity, having, as I said, reached the conclusion that no great harm can come to Mr. Galliher if inspection takes place—at any rate, no harm that could not be fully and adequately compensated by a sum of money—and, of course, I shall hear both counsel

D   now as to how they suggest the inspection ought to be carried out and what safeguards ought to be laid upon the plaintiffs and, if Mr. Weeks's client wishes it, I will hear argument as to whether there ought to be an inventory and no photographs, or photographs and no inventory. I do not want to cause any more disturbance than absolutely necessary, but the plaintiffs, in my judgment, are entitled to know what is in this flat, having

E   regard to the grave suspicion which hangs over both defendants at present.

> *Injunction granted on January 26, 1978, continued.*
> *Order for inspection of flat.*
> *Plaintiffs' costs in cause.*

F   Solicitors: *Clifford-Turner; Waterhouse & Co.*

G

[COURT OF APPEAL]

RANK XEROX LTD. *v.* LANE (INSPECTOR OF TAXES)

1978 April 24, 25, 26;   Buckley and Bridge L.JJ.
      May 12   and Sir David Cairns

H   *Revenue—Corporation tax—Allowance of charges on income—Company's rights to payments from overseas company pursuant to agreements executed under seal—Disposal by distribution to shareholders—Whether payments " due under a covenant "—Whether " annual payments "—Whether company relieved from liability on notional gain arising from distribution of its rights to payments—Finance Act 1965 (c. 25), Sch. 7, para. 12 (c)*

      Paragraph 12 of Schedule 7 to the Finance Act 1965 provides:

Rank Xerox Ltd. v. Lane (C.A.)   **[1978]**

A " No chargeable gain shall accrue to any person on the disposal of a right to . . . (c) annual payments which are due under a covenant made by any person and which are not secured on any property."

In 1956 an English company and one of its subsidiaries agreed with an American corporation, X, to engage in a joint venture for the world wide exploitation, outside the United States of America and Canada, of a reproduction process called xerography. Pursuant to the agreement the taxpayer company B was formed and X transferred to it all patents, patent applications and licence rights relating to the process. Following two further agreements under seal in 1964 and 1967, in consideration for payments by X of 5 per cent. of its net sales in Central and South America and the West Indies, the taxpayer company surrendered its rights to exploit xerography in those territories. In 1969 it was resolved that the taxpayer company's rights to receive payments under the 1964 and 1967 C agreements should be written up in the books at £8·4 million and that a dividend of £8·4 million should be declared and should be distributed among its shareholders in satisfaction of its rights to receive payments from X. That distribution was assessed to corporation tax for the accounting period to June 1970. On the taxpayer company's appeal against the assessment, the special commissioners held that the payments made by X to the taxpayer company were not trading receipts but D pure profit income; they rejected the taxpayer company's argument that paragraph 12 (c) of Schedule 7 to the Finance Act 1965 relieved the company of its liability to tax on the notional gain arising on the distribution of those rights on the ground that, although the rights were to annual payments, the payments were not due under a covenant within the sub-paragraph. Slade J. dismissed the taxpayer company's appeal E holding that, although the payments were due under a covenant, since they were payments in respect of the user of patents they were not " annual payments " within the meaning of sub-paragraph (c).

On appeal by the taxpayer company: —

Held, allowing the appeal, (1) that the effect of the 1964 and 1967 agreements was to transfer from the taxpayer company to X more than a mere right to the user of patents and, F since the patents became the absolute property of X and the payments were made on sales in the relevant countries whether or not the goods sold were protected by a patent, the payments were not made for the right to the user of patents; that, even if the payments were for such a right, the categories of annual payments and patent royalties were not mutually exclusive and providing the other characteristics of annual payments were present section 169 of the Income Tax Act G 1952, as applied by sections 52 and 53 of the Finance Act 1965, did not exclude payments " in respect of the user of a patent " from " annual payments " within the meaning of paragraph 12 (c) of Schedule 7 to the Act; and, accordingly, since the payments were pure profit income and not trading receipts, they were annual payments within the paragraph (post, pp. 651c, G—652F, 653F).

(2) That the words " due under a covenant " in paragraph H 12 (c) narrowed the class of annual payments to which the paragraph applied and that in the context of the paragraph the word " covenant " had its ordinary and primary meaning of a promise in a document executed by the promisor under seal and, accordingly, the payments by X were due under a covenant (post, pp. 653F–G, 654D–F).

Decision of Slade J. [1978] Ch. 1; [1977] 3 W.L.R. 410; [1977] 3 All E.R. 593 reversed.

3 W.L.R.   Rank Xerox Ltd. v. Lane (C.A.)

A   The following cases are referred to in the judgment of the court:

Abley v. *Dale* (1851) 20 L.J.C.P. 233.

Hanbury, In re (1939) 38 T.C. 588n., C.A.

Howe (Earl) v. *Inland Revenue Commissioners* [1919] 2 K.B. 336, C.A.

Inland Revenue Commissioners v. *Whitworth Park Coal Co. Ltd.* [1958] Ch. 792; [1958] 2 W.L.R. 815; [1958] 2 All E.R. 91; 38 T.C. 531, C.A.

Vickers, Sons & Maxim Ltd. v. *Evans* [1910] A.C. 444, H.L.(E.).

B

The following additional cases were cited in argument:

British Commonwealth International Newsfilm Agency Ltd. v. *Mahany* [1963] 1 W.L.R. 69; [1963] 1 All E.R. 88; 40 T.C. 550, H.L.(E.).

Carson v. *Cheyney's Executor* [1959] A.C. 412; [1958] 3 W.L.R. 740; [1958] 3 All E.R. 573; 38 T.C. 240, H.L.(E.).

Hayne v. *Cummings* (1864) 16 C.B.N.S. 421.

C   *Inland Revenue Commissioners* v. *British Salmson Aero Engines Ltd.* [1938] 2 K.B. 482; [1938] 3 All E.R. 283; 22 T.C. 29, C.A.

Jones v. *Inland Revenue Commissioners* [1920] 1 K.B. 711; (1919) 7 T.C. 310.

Stock v. *Frank Jones (Tipton) Ltd.* [1978] 1 W.L.R. 231; [1978] I.C.R. 347; [1978] 1 All E.R. 948, H.L.(E.).

Westminster Bank Executor and Trustee Co. (Channel Islands) Ltd. v.
D   *National Bank of Greece S.A.* [1971] A.C. 945; [1971] 2 W.L.R. 105; [1971] 1 All E.R. 233; 46 T.C. 472, H.L.(E.).

Wild v. *Ionides* (1925) 9 T.C. 392.

APPEAL from Slade J.

Pursuant to an agreement between Xerox Corporation of America
(" Xerox ") and Rank Organisation Ltd. and a subsidiary of that company
E   and made in 1956, the taxpayer company, Rank Xerox Ltd., was incorporated. Its main object was to exploit world wide, outside the United States
of America and Canada, the reproduction process known as xerography.
In 1964 and 1967, the taxpayer company entered into agreements under
seal with Xerox Corporation whereby it surrendered certain rights
relating to manufacturing and selling the process in Central and South
F   America and the West Indies in consideration for the payment by Xerox
of a royalty of 5 per cent. on net sales in those areas. In December
1969 the taxpayer company resolved to declare a dividend of £8·4
million which was to be satisfied by the distribution to shareholders in
specie of the right to receive payments from Xerox under the 1964 and
1967 agreements. The taxpayer company was assessed to corporation
tax for the accounting period of 12 months to June 30, 1970, in the sum
G   of £49·1 million. Its appeal was dismissed by the commissioners on
the ground that the rights in question were rights to " annual payments "
within paragraph 12 (c) of Schedule 7 to the Finance Act 1965 but the
payments were not " due under a covenant." The taxpayer company
appealed to the High Court. Slade J. held that the payments were " due
under a covenant " but were not " annual payments."

H   By a notice of appeal dated May 13, 1977, the taxpayer company
appealed against the decision of Slade J. on the grounds (1) that for the
purposes of paragraph 12 (c) of Schedule 7 to the Act of 1965 " annual
payments " meant those annual payments which were in the nature of
" pure income profit " in the hands of the recipient; (2) that the payments
due to the taxpayer company under the 1964 and 1967 agreements were
annual payments within the paragraph; (3) that, even if for the purposes
of the paragraph " annual payments " did not mean " pure income

Rank Xerox Ltd. v. Lane (C.A.)   **[1978]**

profit " in the hands of the recipient, the payments due to the taxpayer A
company were " annual payments " within sections 52 (3) (*a*) and 53 (5)
(*b*) of the Act of 1965 and were not " royalties or other sums paid in
respect of the user of a patent " within section 169 (3) of the Income
Tax Act 1952; (4) that, even if the payments were royalties or other sums
paid in respect of the user of a patent within the meaning of section
169 (3) of the Act of 1952 they were " annual payments " within the meaning of paragraph 12 (*c*) of Schedule 7 to the Act of 1965; and (5) that the B
judge in upholding the determination of the commissioners misdirected
himself and was wrong in law in holding that (a) for the purposes of
paragraph 12 (*c*) " annual payments " meant " annual payments " within
sections 52 (3) (*a*) and 53 (5) (*b*) of the Act of 1965 and so did not include
" royalties or other sums paid in respect of the user of a patent " within
section 169 (3) of the Act of 1952, (b) the payments due to the taxpayer C
company were royalties or other sums paid in respect of the user of a
patent within section 169 (3) of the Act of 1952 and (c) the payments due
to the taxpayer company were not annual payments within paragraph
12 (*c*) of Schedule 7 to the Act of 1965.

Michael Nolan Q.C. and *Andrew Thornhill* for the taxpayer company. D
D. C. Potter Q.C. and *Michael Dean* for the Crown.

Cur. adv. vult.

May 12. BRIDGE L.J. read the following judgment of the court.
The question at issue in this appeal is whether an amount was rightly E
included in the assessment to corporation tax on the appellant taxpayer
company, Rank Xerox Ltd., for the accounting period of 12 months
to June 30, 1970, as representing a chargeable gain accruing to the taxpayer company on the disposal of certain assets in December 1969. The
taxpayer company appealed against the assessment to the Commissioners
for the Special Purposes of the Income Tax Acts. The commissioners
dismissed the appeal. From this decision an appeal by case stated to F
the High Court was in turn dismissed by Slade J. [1978] Ch. 1. The
taxpayer company now appeals to this court. The question raised for
decision at all levels has been that of liability only. The amount of
the chargeable gain, if there was one, will depend on difficult questions
of valuation which happily are for another day.

By section 238 of the Income and Corporation Taxes Act 1970, the G
profits of companies on which corporation tax is charged include
chargeable gains as well as income and section 265 provides, so far as
relevant for present purposes, for the computation of chargeable gains
in accordance with the principles applying for capital gains tax, which
are to be found in Part III of the Finance Act 1965. It is common
ground both that the rights the subject of the present dispute are assets
to which section 22 of the Act of 1965 applies and that there was in H
December 1969 a disposal of those assets by the taxpayer company.
It follows from the application of the provisions of section 22 (9) and (10)
and section 23 (1) and (2) that, subject to the valuation question, there
was a chargeable gain (or an allowable loss) accruing to the taxpayer
company on that disposal unless the rights in question fall within the
provisions of paragraph 12 (*c*) of Schedule 7, which enacts:

A
" No chargeable gain shall accrue to any person on the disposal of a right to, or to any part of— . . . (c) annual payments which are due under a covenant made by any person and which are not secured on any property."

The special commissioners decided that the rights in question were to " annual payments," but that the payments were not " due under a
B covenant." Slade J. decided that the payments were " due under a covenant," but were not " annual payments." Thus both arrived at the same result by precisely contrary routes.

To do justice to the arguments it is necessary to examine the commercial history leading to the 1969 disposal of assets in some detail. In 1956 the Rank Organisation Ltd. and a subsidiary of that company
C agreed with the Xerox Corporation ("Xerox"), then known as the Haloid Co., to engage in a joint venture for the world wide exploitation, outside the United States of America and Canada, of the reproduction process known as xerography. The taxpayer company was the company which was to be, and was, formed to implement the agreement. Under the agreement Xerox were to transfer to the taxpayer company all patents, patent applications and licence rights relating to the process in
D those parts of the world to which the agreement related. The relevant patents granted, patent applications pending and licence rights subsisting at the date of the agreement were set out in a schedule to the agreement.

After the taxpayer company had been formed, an agreement was entered into on May 1, 1957, between Xerox and the taxpayer company
E which was called a licence agreement. This recited the 1956 agreement already referred to and provided that pursuant to that agreement Xerox granted to the taxpayer company an exclusive licence to use the inventions comprised in the letters patent and an exclusive sub-licence to use the inventions comprised in the licence rights set out in the schedule to the 1956 agreement. The licence agreement included a provision obliging
F Xerox to secure an assignment to the taxpayer company of the scheduled letters patent and patent applications on obtaining title thereto and the right to grant title. There is no finding in the case as to what, if any, assignments were ever made pursuant to this provision.

The combined effect of the 1956 and 1957 agreements, under provisions to which we need not refer in detail, was to impose upon the parties mutual obligations to exchange all information and know-how
G with respect to improvements and developments in the process of xerography and presumably, in so far as it was thought appropriate to protect such improvements and developments by patent applications, the necessary applications in countries outside the United States of America and Canada would have been made by the taxpayer company.

The 1957 licence agreement continued in force until 1964. During
H this period, in the commercial exploitation of the process of xerography, Xerox had the field to themselves in the United States of America and Canada; the taxpayer company had the field to themselves in the rest of the world. But in 1964 the parties agreed to a radical change in this state of affairs. In effect Xerox took over the entire business of the taxpayer company in Central and South America and thenceforth had the field to themselves in the whole of the Americas. In 1967 a further change was effected whereby Xerox similarly took over from

648

the taxpayer company the territory of the West Indies. The agreements A concluded in 1964 and 1967 whereby these changes were given effect are the crucial documents in the case, since it is the nature of the right to the payments due from Xerox to the taxpayer company under these agreements on which the appeal depends. For the purpose of deciding the questions in issue there is no material difference between the two agreements and it will suffice for the purposes of this judgment to B consider the first agreement dated February 20, 1964.

The 1964 agreement uses some rather complex geographical formulae to indicate its area of operation, but we shall for brevity substitute the simple, if not entirely accurate, term " Latin America." Clause 1 provides:

> " [Rank Xerox Ltd.] hereby sells, assigns and transfers to Xerox C its entire right, title and interest in all property, rights and assets in [Latin America] of whatsoever nature and description, excluding only its stock in Rank Xerox de Mexico, S.A. and including, without limitation, its goodwill, technical information, know-how, trade secrets, customer lists, patents, patent applications, rights to apply for patents, trade marks and trade mark applications."

D

The effect of clause 2 is to amend the 1957 licence agreement so as to exclude Latin America from its ambit.   Clause 3 provides:

> " All licences and sub-licences applicable to any place in [Latin America] heretofore granted by Xerox to [Rank Xerox Ltd.], and any right of [Rank Xerox] under paragraph one of the licence agreement to a licence or sub-licence applicable to any place in E [Latin America] are hereby cancelled and released."

Clause 4 provides: " In consideration of the premises, Xerox shall pay or cause to be paid to [Rank Xerox] a royalty of 5 per cent. of net sales in " Latin America.   " Net sales " are then defined by reference to " sales and rentals of xerographic machines, equipment, apparatus, paper and supplies."   And then, continuing the quotation from clause 4: F

> " Such royalty payments shall be made or caused to be made by Xerox quarter-annually in the currency of the country in which the xerographic machines, equipment, apparatus, paper and supplies are delivered, except where the existing laws of any country speci- fically authorise payment in pounds sterling, royalties with respect to such country may, at the option of Xerox, be paid in pounds G sterling in London."

Clause 6 provides: " This agreement is made in England and shall be construed in accordance with English law."   The agreement was executed under seal by Xerox.

To complete the story, in December 1969 the taxpayer company declared a dividend of £8·4 million to be satisfied by the distribution to H shareholders in specie, as it is put, of the right to receive payments from Xerox under the provisions of clause 4 of the 1964 and 1967 agreements (" the Xerox payments ").   Since there is, as we have already indicated, no dispute that this was a disposal of assets for capital gains tax purposes it is unnecessary to say more of the details of this transaction.

The two questions for decision, then, are whether the Xerox payments are " annual payments " and whether they are " due under a covenant "

A within the meaning of paragraph 12 (c) of Schedule 7 to the Finance
Act 1965. This paragraph is grouped with paragraphs 11 and 13 under
the heading " Debts and interests in settled property." In our judgment,
neither the group heading nor the provisions of the companion paragraphs in the group throw any conceivable light on the meaning of
paragraph 12 (c). Paragraph 12 as a whole reads:

B   " No chargeable gain shall accrue to any person on the disposal of
     a right to, or to any part of—(a) any allowance, annuity or capital
     sum payable out of any superannuation fund, or under any super-
     annuation scheme, established solely or mainly for persons employed
     in a profession, trade, undertaking or employment, and their
     dependants, (b) an annuity granted otherwise than under a contract
     for a deferred annuity by a company as part of its business of
C   granting annuities on human life, whether or not including instal-
     ments of capital, or an annuity granted or deemed to be granted
     under the Government Annuities Act 1929, or (c) annual payments
     which are due under a covenant made by any person and which are
     not secured on any property."

D   We do not find even this immediate context in the least illuminating.
It cannot in our judgment be legitimate, as was suggested by Mr. Potter
for the Crown, to look at the narrow and specific character of the
categories of payment under (a) and (b) and to treat this as a ground for
imposing some limitation on the language of (c) in order to confine it
within comparably narrow and specific limits. Certainly it is not possible
to apply the ejusdem generis rule. If the categories of payment in (a)
E and (b) can be fitted into a single genus, which we very much doubt, it
would be too narrow to accommodate the language of (c) at all. Finally,
to add one more negative observation, there is no help to be had in
construing any exempt category of right under paragraph 12 on the
supposition that in enacting the exemption Parliament's primary intention
was benevolently to excuse the taxpayer disposing of such a right from
F liability to a chargeable gain, for it may equally well have been the primary
intention, less benevolently, to deny him the benefit of any allowable loss.
Accordingly, we find ourselves in a singularly bleak and featureless stretch
of statutory territory, with nothing to help us choose the right direction
save the bare and cryptic words on the statutory signpost which fall to be
interpreted.
       The phrase " annual payments " has, of course, long been familiar
G in taxing statutes, albeit in a particular context. In current legislation
it is found, among charging provisions, in Case III of Schedule D in
section 109 of the Income and Corporation Taxes Act 1970, which
charges tax in respect of " any interest of money, whether yearly or
otherwise, or any annuity or other annual payment " and, among
machinery provisions, in section 52 (1) of the same Act which requires
H deduction of tax at source by the payer of " any annuity or other annual
payment." The origin of these provisions can be traced as far back as
section 102 of the Income Tax Act 1842, so it is not surprising to find
that the phrase " annual payments " has frequently been judicially
considered and has acquired, in what we shall call the Schedule D
context, a particular meaning. It is common ground in this appeal
that the basic characteristics which have been held necessary for the
identification of an " annual payment " in the Schedule D context must

also be taken to characterise an " annual payment " in the provision we   A
have to construe. What the relevant characteristics are may conveniently
be summarised by quoting extracts from the judgment of the Court of
Appeal delivered by Jenkins L.J. in *Inland Revenue Commissioners* v.
Whitworth Park Coal Co. Ltd. [1958] Ch. 792. He said, at pp. 815–817:

> " There have been many judicial pronouncements as to the scope of
> rule 1 (a) of Case III and the following propositions can be regarded   B
> as established: (1) To come within the rule as an ' other annual pay-
> ment ' the payment in question must be ejusdem generis with the
> specific instances given in the shape of interest of money and
> annuities: see *Hill* v. *Gregory* [1912] 2 K.B. 61, 70, 71, *per*
> Hamilton J.; *Howe (Earl)* v. *Inland Revenue Commissioners* [1919]
> 2 K.B. 336, 352, 353, *per* Scrutton L.J. . . . (2) The payment in
> question must fall to be made under some binding legal obligation   C
> as distinct from being a mere voluntary payment: see *Smith* v.
> *Smith* [1923] P. 191, 197, 202, *per* Lord Sterndale M.R. and
> Warrington L.J. . . . (3) The fact that the obligation to pay is
> imposed by an order of the court and does not arise by virtue of
> a contract does not exclude the payment from rule 1 (a) of Case
> III . . . (4) The payment in question must possess the essential   D
> quality of recurrence implied by the description ' annual.' But
> that description has been given a broad interpretation in the
> authorities. For example, in *Smith* v. *Smith*, Warrington L.J. said,
> at p. 202: ' Again the fact that the payment is to be made weekly
> does not prevent it being annual provided the weekly payments may
> continue beyond the year ' . . . (5) The payment in question must
> be in the nature of a ' pure income ' profit in the hands of the   E
> recipient."

The first and fifth factors mentioned in this enumeration are really
two sides of the same coin. The same principle underlies them both. It
is stated in a well-known passage from the judgment of Scrutton L.J.
in *Howe (Earl)* v. *Inland Revenue Commissioners* [1919] 2 K.B. 336,
352, who said: F

> " It is not all payments made every year from which income tax can
> be deducted. For instance, if a man agrees to pay a motor garage
> £500 a year for five years for the hire and upkeep of a car, no one
> suggests that the person paying can deduct income tax from each
> yearly payment. So if he contracted with a butcher for an annual
> sum to supply all his meat for a year. The annual instalment would   G
> not be subject to tax as a whole in the hands of the payee, but
> only that part of it which was profits."

Another statement of the principle is found in the judgment of Greene
M.R. in *In re Hanbury* (1939) 38 T.C. 588, 590, where he said:

> " There are two classes of annual payments which fall to be con-   H
> sidered for income tax purposes. There is, first of all, that class
> of annual payment which the Acts regard and treat as being pure
> income profit of the recipient undiminished by any deduction.
> Payment of interest, payment of annuities, to take the ordinary
> simple case, are payments which are regarded as part of the income
> of the recipient, and the payer is entitled in estimating his total
> income to treat those payments as payments which go out of his

A   income altogether. The class of annual payment which falls within that category is quite a limited one. In the other class there stand a number of payments, none the less annual, the very quality and nature of which makes it impossible to treat them as part of the pure profit income of the recipient, the proper way of treating them being to treat them as an element to be taken into account in discovering what the profits of the recipient are."

B

Before the special commissioners it was contended for the Crown that the Xerox payments were not pure profit income but were part of the trading receipts of the taxpayer company. In a supplemental case stated, confirming their finding in the original case that the Xerox payments were " annual payments " within the meaning of the relevant provision, the special commissioners rejected this contention and stated that " in reaching this determination we concluded that they were not trading receipts of [Rank Xerox] but could properly be called ' pure profit income.' " Before Slade J. the Crown did not pursue the contention that the Xerox payments were trading receipts and we must take the finding that they were pure profit income to be now beyond challenge.

C

D

The principal argument for the Crown now pursued, and that which persuaded Slade J. that the Xerox payments are not " annual payments " under paragraph 12 (c), is that one may use certain provisions found in Part IV of the Finance Act 1965 to construe the phrase " annual payments " in paragraph 12 (c) and by so doing find that " any royalty or other sum paid in respect of the user of a patent " cannot be an " annual payment." It is said that the Xerox payments were " paid in respect of the user of " patents, and therefore cannot be " annual payments." The provisions relied on are concerned with the machinery for the collection of tax and require or permit those liable to make certain classes of payment to deduct and to account to the Crown for the relevant tax. In relation to corporation tax, sections 52 and 53 of the Act of 1965 incorporate by reference section 169 of the Income Tax Act 1952, the statutory predecessor of section 52 of the Income and Corporation Taxes Act 1970. Both section 169 of the Act of 1952 and section 52 of the Act of 1970 provide in separate subsections for the deduction of tax by the payer from, on the one hand, " annual payments " within Case III of Schedule D, and on the other hand " any royalty or other sum paid in respect of the user of a patent."

E

F

G   Were the Xerox payments payable " in respect of the user of a patent "? Clearly they cannot have been so in their entirety because under the 1964 and 1967 agreements the taxpayer company transferred to Xerox a great deal more than the mere right to the user of patents. Some, but we know not what, fraction of the benefits conferred on Xerox for which the payments were the consideration may have taken the

H   form of the outright assignment of rights then vested in the taxpayer company or the surrender of licences then enjoyed by the taxpayer in respect of any patents which may then have been in force in any part of Latin America or the West Indies. After the agreements were concluded the taxpayer company no longer had any interest in any of these patents and the patents became the absolute property of Xerox. Moreover, the " royalties " payable under clause 4 were not confined to sales in the countries in which any relevant patents were in force, nor to

sales of apparatus protected by any such patents, nor to sales during the   A
life of any such patents. In these circumstances it would, in our judgment, be a misuse of language to describe the Xerox payments as being
made " in respect of the user of a patent."

This conclusion is sufficient to refute the main argument for the
Crown which Slade J. accepted. But suppose that, contrary to this view,
the Xerox payments were made " in respect of the user of a patent."
Does it then follow from a consideration of section 169 of the Income   B
Tax Act 1952 as applied by sections 52 and 53 of the Finance Act 1965,
that a payment " in respect of the user of a patent " cannot be an
" annual payment "?   Put in another way, are the categories of " annual
payments " within Case III of Schedule D and payments " in respect of
the user of a patent " to be regarded for all purposes as mutually
exclusive because they are the subject of separate provisions in the   C
machinery for the collection of tax?   In the great majority of cases
patent royalties will not fall within Case III of Schedule D because, being
trade or professional receipts taxable under Case I or Case II, they will
lack the quality of being pure profit income in the hands of the payee.
They have nevertheless been treated similarly to Case III payments under
the tax legislation by a provision originating in section 25 of the Finance   D
Act 1907, and now found in section 52 (2) of the Income and Corporation
Taxes Act 1970, authorising deduction of tax by the person liable to
make the payments.   This provision certainly applies to patent royalty
payments whether they are " annual payments " or not, but we find it
impossible to infer from the presence of this provision that payment of a
patent royalty is incapable of being an " annual payment " within Case
III if it otherwise exhibits the necessary characteristics to make it so.   E
We would therefore answer in the negative the two questions posed at
the beginning of this paragraph and on this ground also reject the
argument that the Xerox payments are excluded from the category of
" annual payments " under paragraph 12 (c) by an interpretation derived
from section 169 of the Income Tax Act 1952 as applied by sections 52
and 53 of the Finance Act 1965.   F

Independently of these particular statutory provisions Mr. Potter has
advanced a wider argument for the Crown to the effect that payments
which can properly be described as royalties, whether the term is used
strictly to describe receipts derived from patents or copyrights or in some
broader sense as in clause 4 of the 1964 and 1967 agreements, cannot
in their very nature qualify as " annual payments."   He submits that in   G
a case in which royalties, for any reason, were not taxable under Case I
or II of Schedule D, they would be taxed not as " annual payments "
under Case III but under the residual Case VI.   There is no authority
directly in point.   Counsel on both sides referred to authorities which,
it was suggested, bear upon this question indirectly, but we can derive so
little assistance from these that we excuse ourselves from discussing them   H
in this judgment.   The question must, we think, be decided as one of
principle.   The argument of principle by which Mr. Potter. seeks to
support his proposition is that royalties, in any sense of the term, must
represent payments for the exploitation of what he calls " intellectual
property " and they are thus, so he argues, analogous to payments of
hire for the use of chattels.   The answer to this argument lies, in our

A judgment, in the realisation that it is really an attempt to re-introduce by the back door the contention rejected by the special commissioners that the Xerox payments are not pure profit income but trade receipts. Mr. Potter submits that the nature of royalty payments cannot vary according to the particular circumstances in which they are payable. We cannot agree. We accept that in normal circumstances royalty

B payments will not be pure profit income because, in the language of Greene M.R. in *In re Hanbury*, 38 T.C. 588, the proper way to treat them will be " as an element to be taken into account in discovering what the profits of the recipient are." But this need not necessarily be so, and when the position of the payee is such that his absolute entitlement to receive the payments is wholly independent of any outgoings or expenses to which he may be liable, we can see no reason in principle

C why the payments should not be, as the special commissioners found that the Xerox payments in this case were, pure profit income and therefore " annual payments."

    The final argument for the Crown which needs to be considered in relation to the question of " annual payments " is the submission that the Xerox payments would be taxable under Case V of Schedule D as

D " income arising from possessions out of the United Kingdom " and on that account cannot fall within Case III as " annual payments." We do not find it necessary to decide the question, which does not appear to have been raised before the special commissioners, whether the Xerox payments are " income arising from possessions outside the United Kingdom," or if they are, whether in an issue arising directly under Schedule D the appropriate case under which they should be charged is

E Case III of Case V. For while we accept that " annual payments " under paragraph 12 (*c*) must exhibit the same general characteristics as in the Schedule D context, we do not think it at all follows that a payment having those characteristics cannot qualify as an " annual payment " under paragraph 12 (*c*) solely because it would fall to be charged under Schedule D under a different case from Case III for reasons unconnected

F with and not affecting its character as an " annual payment."

    Accordingly, on the first main point in the appeal we conclude, in agreement with the special commissioners, and respectfully differing from Slade J., that the Xerox payments were " annual payments."

    Were they " due under a covenant "? The category of " annual payments " being as wide as it is, it is difficult not to think that the

G words " due under a covenant " were introduced into paragraph 12 (*c*) with the object of narrowing the class of payments to which the exemption was to apply. It is tempting therefore immediately to speculate as to what may have been the rationale of the limitation intended to be imposed by these words. Mr. Potter's submission for the Crown is that the only reading which makes sense is to construe the phrase as

H applying to payments made without consideration which are enforceable only because covenanted by deed. We have been much impressed by this submission. Although, as Slade J. observed [1978] Ch. 1, 9:

      " there is no general principle of capital gains tax which exempts a disponer from tax on a chargeable gain arising on a disposition simply because he originally acquired the subject matter of the disposition through another's gift."

there is nothing fanciful in supposing that Parliament, in relation to the A
familiar category of gratuitous covenanted annual payments to relatives,
dependants and the like, may have thought it convenient to exclude any
chargeable gain or allowable loss which would otherwise accrue on the
disposal of the asset, particularly perhaps on the death of the covenantee
or the release of the covenant. On the other hand, if paragraph 12 (c)
is capable of embracing a whole range of "annual payments" of a
purely commercial character, as for instance the Xerox payments in this B
case, provided the obligation to pay is undertaken by deed, it is
impossible to conceive of any rational fiscal policy underlying the
statutory exemption. The essential character of such payments depends
on the commercial realities of the transaction. Whether the instrument
under which the payments are due was executed by the party liable under
hand or under seal is, one would have supposed, from the fiscal point of C
view wholly irrelevant. In the light of these considerations we have no
doubt at all that if the statutory language is reasonably capable of two
meanings, one being that for which the Crown contends, that is the
meaning we should prefer. We make no secret of the fact that we have
tried hard to discover just such an ambiguity, but in the end we find
ourselves defeated in the attempt. By itself the word "covenant" is D
admittedly ambiguous in that it is capable, in certain contexts, of
embracing promises not under seal, but that does not assist, since in the
context of paragraph 12 (c) "covenant" clearly bears its ordinary and
primary meaning of a promise in a document executed by the promisor
under seal. Mr. Potter has argued that there is ambiguity in the phrase
"payment due under a covenant" and that this is capable of meaning a
payment due by virtue of a covenant alone, i.e. a payment unsupported E
by consideration. The insuperable obstacle to this interpretation is
that once a promise to pay is embodied in a deed executed by the payer,
then, notwithstanding that there may have been valuable consideration
given for the promise, the debt arising on the promise is due as a
specialty debt and not as a simple contract debt; in other words it is a
"payment due under a covenant" and nothing else. As was said by F
Jervis C.J. in *Abley* v. *Dale* (1851) 20 L.J.C.P. 233, 235:

> "If the precise words used are plain and unambiguous, . . . we
> are bound to construe them in their ordinary sense, even though it
> do lead . . . to an absurdity or manifest injustice. Words may be
> modified or varied where their import is doubtful or obscure; but
> we assume the functions of legislators when we depart from the G
> ordinary meaning of the precise words used, merely because we
> see or fancy we see an absurdity or manifest injustice from an
> adherence to their literal meaning."

To give to the words "due under a covenant" the meaning for which
the Crown contends requires that other words be added, but "we are
not entitled to read words into an Act of Parliament unless clear reason H
for it is to be found within the four corners of the Act itself . . ."; *per*
Lord Loreburn L.C. in *Vickers, Sons & Maxim Ltd.* v. *Evans* [1910]
A.C. 444, 445. We can find no clear reason in the Finance Act 1965
for reading words into paragraph 12 (c). The words Parliament has
used are capable of only one meaning and according to that meaning
the Xerox payments are "due under a covenant."

A   We therefore allow the appeal and discharge so much of the assessment to corporation tax under appeal as related to the disposal by the taxpayer company of the right to receive the Xerox payments.

Appeal allowed with costs.
Case remitted to special commis-
sioners to determine amount of
B   *assessment.*
Leave to appeal.

Solicitors: *Linklater & Paines; Solicitor of Inland Revenue.*

A. R.

C

_____

[CHANCERY DIVISION]

D   *In re* DUKE OF NORFOLK'S SETTLEMENT TRUSTS

PERTH (EARL) AND ANOTHER *v.* FITZALAN-HOWARD
AND OTHERS

[1975 N. No. 84]

E   1978   Feb. 6, 8, 13;   Walton J.
March 9

Trusts—Trustee—Increase of remuneration—Settlement in 1958
creating discretionary trusts—Provision for professional trustees
to charge for professional services and for trustee company to
charge its normal fees as at date of settlement—Subsequent
addition of further properties to trust fund—Unforeseen work
F   *falling on trustees in respect of redevelopment of trust proper-*
ties and necessitated by fiscal changes—Trustees' claim to
increased remuneration—Court's inherent jurisdiction to award
increased remuneration

By a deed of settlement dated April 1, 1958, the 16th Duke of Norfolk assigned or conveyed certain properties including an interest in land in London forming part of the Strand G   estate on wholly discretionary trusts in favour of four separate classes of relatives, with an ultimate distribution date which might not occur until January 1, 2038, and subject thereto in trust for such of his four daughters as should attain the age of 21 years, and default for his sister. Clause 11 of the settlement contained a provision for any trustee who was an individual engaged in any profession or business to be entitled to " charge and be paid all professional or other H   reasonable and proper charges for any business done or time spent or services rendered by him in connection with the trusts . . . whether or not of a nature requiring the employment of a person so engaged," without any liability to account for " any benefits derived by him through the employment by the trustees of any firm or company of which he is a member or officer or in which he is otherwise interested." Clause 12 provided that the second plaintiffs, a trustee company, should be entitled to remuneration for its services as trustee in accordance with its usual scale of fees in force at the date of the settlement and empowered it to employ or concur in **A** employing an associated banking partnership to act as banker without such bank becoming accountable for profits. The clause also provided that the first plaintiff, who had been a salaried partner of the associated bank and a director of the second plaintiff from 1947 to 1957, should not be liable to account for any remuneration or other benefits received by him from the second plaintiff or from the bank. In 1962 the first plaintiff became a non-executive director of the **B** parent company of the second plaintiff and of a company formed to take over the former banking partnership. He retired from such directorship in 1976. It was agreed that the conditions of clause 11 never applied to him at any time.

In 1966 and 1969 the remaining parts of the Strand estate belonging to the settlor were added to the trust, thus paving the way for comprehensive redevelopment of the site. Such redevelopment involved the trustees in a considerable amount **C** of work falling wholly outside anything which could reasonably have been foreseen when they accepted office. Additional unforeseen work was also caused to them by reason of the introduction of capital transfer tax by the Finance Act 1975. By an originating summons dated January 10, 1975, the trustees asked that the court should, in the exercise of its inherent jurisdiction, authorise the plaintiffs to charge, be paid and retain remuneration for their services as trustees, in **D** accordance with certain draft minutes of order or as to the court should seem fit. The provision proposed for the first plaintiff was that from and after April 1, 1976, when he was to cease to be a director, he should be remunerated at the rate of £3,000 per annum. The increased remuneration proposed for the second defendant was claimed under different heads relating both to the past and future services. The 16th Duke **E** died on January 31, 1975.

On the question whether the court had jurisdiction to approve the increased remuneration sought: —

Held, (1) that the court's inherent jurisdiction to award remuneration to a trustee was a wholly exceptional one to be exercised sparingly, and, save where the circumstances were such as to raise an implied promise to pay on behalf of the beneficiaries, the court would only grant remuneration where **F** it was necessary to obtain a particular individual trustee whose services were of special value to the trust or to obtain the services of a particular kind of trustee, such as a trust corporation; would not that the court alter the general level of remuneration fixed by the trust instrument once the trust had been unconditionally accepted, unless there was no dispute and the general level was so derisory as to be de minimis and would be reluctant to award any remuneration unless the appli- **G** cation was made promptly on the assumption of office or there had since been a radical change of circumstances (post, pp. 670F–H, 674H—675C).

Dictum of Lord Simonds L.C. in *Chapman* v. *Chapman* [1954] A.C. 439, 443, 444, H.L.(E.); *Marshall* v. *Holloway* (1818) 2 Swan. 432; *In re Salmen* (1912) 107 L.T. 108, Eve J. and C.A. and *Forster* v. *Ridley* (1864) 4 De G.J. & S. 452 applied. **H**

In re Masters, decd. [1953] 1 W.L.R. 81 and *In re Codd's Will Trusts (Practice Note)* [1975] 1 W.L.R. 1139 considered.

(2) That the first and second plaintiffs were entitled on the basis of an implied promise to be remunerated by a proper allowance in respect of their services in connection with the assemblage and redevelopment of the Strand estate, which were wholly outside the scope of any duties which they, as trustees, could reasonably have been expected to perform, but that no remuneration could be ordered in respect of the

A   additional work involved as the result of the fiscal changes
(post, p. 675c–G).
      (3) That since there had been no fundamental change in
the nature or assets of the trust the court had no jurisdiction
to alter the general level of the second plaintiffs' fees specified
in the trust instrument despite the fact that those fees and
the fees now sought were lower than those currently charged
by similar institutions (post, p. 675G–H).

B   (4) That the second plaintiffs were, however, entitled to
retain the sum of £24,677, charged in the year 1971–72 to take
account of previous undercharges and that it was right that
there should be a revaluation of any freehold properties comprised in the trust, upon which the second plaintiffs' charges
allowed by the trust instrument were based, since the existing
valuation had become seriously out of date (post, pp. 677D—
678A).

C
      The following cases are referred to in the judgment:

Bainbrigge v. *Blair* (1845) 8 Beav. 588.
 . *Barbour's Settlement Trusts, In re* [1974] 1 W.L.R. 1198; [1974] 1 All
          E.R. 1188.
Brocksopp v. *Barnes* (1820) 5 Mad. 90.

D   *Campbell, decd., In the Estate of* [1954] 1 W.L.R. 516; [1954] 1 All
          E.R. 448.
Chapman v. *Chapman* [1954] A.C. 429; [1954] 2 W.L.R. 723; [1954] 1
          All E.R. 798, H.L.(E.).
Codd's Will Trusts, In re (Practice Note) [1975] 1 W.L.R. 1139; [1975]
          2 All E.R. 1051.
Cranstoun, decd., In re [1949] Ch. 523; [1949] 1 All E.R. 871.

E   *Dale* v. *Inland Revenue Commissioners* [1954] A.C. 11; [1953] 3 W.L.R.
          448; [1953] 2 All E.R. 671, H.L.(E.).
Forster v. *Ridley* (1864) 4 De G.J. & S. 452.
Freeman's Settlement Trusts, In re (1887) 37 Ch.D. 148.
Macadam, In re [1946] Ch. 73; [1945] 2 All E.R. 664.
Marshall v. *Holloway* (1818) 2 Swan. 432.
Masters, decd., In re [1953] 1 W.L.R. 81; [1953] 1 All E.R. 19.

F   *Pooley, In re* (1888) 40 Ch.D. 1, C.A.
Salmen, In re (1912) 107 L.T. 108, Eve J. and C.A.
Spedding, decd., In re [1966] N.Z.L.R. 447.
Thorley, In re [1891] 2 Ch. 613, C.A.
White, In re [1898] 1 Ch. 297; [1898] 2 Ch. 217, C.A.
Worthington, decd., In re [1954] 1 W.L.R. 526; [1954] 1 All E.R. 677.

G   No additional cases were cited in argument.

ORIGINATING SUMMONS
      By an originating summons dated January 10, 1975, the plaintiffs,
John David, Earl of Perth, and Schroder Executor & Trustee Co. Ltd., as
trustees of a settlement dated April 1, 1958, and made by Bernard
Marmaduke, Duke of Norfolk as settlor, sought the following relief,
H namely, that the court should in its inherent jurisdiction authorise the
plaintiffs to charge, be paid and retain remuneration for their services as
trustees of the settlement in accordance with certain draft minutes of order.
The first defendant was the settlor, who died on January 31, 1975, shortly
after the issue of the summons. The second to fifth defendants were,
respectively, Anne Elizabeth Fitzalan-Howard, now Lady Herries, Mary
Katherine Fitzalan-Howard, Sarah Margaret Fitzalan-Howard and Theresa
Jane Fitzalan-Howard, now Countess of Ancram, the four daughters of

In re Duke of Norfolk's Settlement (Ch.D.)   **[1978]**

the settlor. The sixth and seventh defendants were Edward William   A
Fitzalan-Howard and Gerald Bernard Fitzalan-Howard, the two sons of
Miles Francis, Baron Beaumont, who became the 17th Duke of Norfolk
on the death of the first defendant. The eighth to eleventh defendants
were, respectively, Miles Francis, Baron Beaumont, now the 17th Duke of
Norfolk, and his three brothers, Sir Michael Fitzalan-Howard, Martin
Fitzalan-Howard and Mark Fitzalan-Howard.

The summons was heard in chambers and judgment was delivered in   B
open court.

The facts are stated in the judgment.

Martin Nourse Q.C. and *Robert Walker* for the plaintiffs.
P. W. E. Taylor for the second, third, fourth and fifth defendants.
Maurice Price Q.C. and *Ian Romer* for the sixth and seventh   C
defendants.
P. W. E. Taylor for the eighth, ninth, tenth and eleventh defendants.

Cur. adv. vult.

March 3. Walton J. read the following judgment. On April 1,   D
1958, the late the 16th Duke of Norfolk executed a settlement as settlor,
the trustees whereof were the above named plaintiffs and one George
Bellord, a solicitor and a partner in the firm of Witham Weld & Co.,
since deceased. Subject to an overriding power of appointment in the
settlor which was never exercised and was finally released, the settlement
was a wholly discretionary settlement upon four separate classes of
persons, namely: (1) the descendants then living or thereafter to be born   E
before the distribution date of the settlor's late father, other than and
except the settlor himself; (2) the existing sons of the Rt. Hon. Bernard
Edward, Baron Howard of Glossop and the male descendants, tracing
their descent through males, of any of such existing sons born before
the distribution date; (3) the existing sons of Lord Perth and the descendants of either of such existing sons born before the distribution date;   F
(4) Lady Gillian Anderson, the sister of Lord Perth, and her daughter
Sarah Anderson. There was an ultimate distribution date which might
be as late as January 1, 2038, and, subject to any exercise of the discretionary powers, the trust funds would then be held upon trust for
such of the four daughters of the settlor as attain the age of 21, or in
default for the settlor's sister, Lady Rachel Davidson.

The provisions for the remuneration of the trustees is contained in   G
clauses 11 and 12 of the settlement, which read:

" 11. Any trustee hereof who shall be an individual engaged in any
profession or business shall be entitled to charge and be paid all
professional or other reasonable and proper charges for any business
done or time spent or services rendered by him in connection with
the trusts of this settlement or of the conveyance or of any con-   H
veyance on trust for sale of the property described in the third
schedule hereto whether or not of a nature requiring the employment of a person so engaged and no trustee shall be liable to account
for any benefits derived by him through the employment by the
trustees of any firm or company of which he is a member or officer
or in which he is otherwise interested.

" 12 (i) Schroder Executor and Trustee Co. Ltd. (hereinafter called

The Weekly Law Reports, October 27, 1978

659

3 W.L.R.   In re Duke of Norfolk's Settlement (Ch.D.)   Walton J.

A   ' the company ') shall be entitled to remuneration for its services
as trustee hereof or of the conveyance or of any conveyance on
trust for sale of the property described in the third schedule hereto in
accordance with its usual scale of fees in force at the date hereof.
(ii) The company may employ or concur in employing Messrs. J.
Henry Schroder & Co. (hereinafter called ' the bank ') to act as
banker to the trust and the bank may make advances to or otherwise
B   act as banker to the trust estate as fully and with the like protections
and rights including non-accountability for profits made as banker
as if the company were not a trustee hereof.   (iii) Lord Perth shall
not be liable to account for any remuneration or other benefits
received by him from the company or from the bank."

C   Then there is another sub-clause in that clause which is of no immediate
interest.

The property settled consisted of three main items: (a) 50,000 shares
of £1 each in Fitzalan Howard Estates Ltd. (the estates company).   This
was the entire issued share capital of the estates company, whose main
but not sole asset was the late Duke's life interest in certain freehold
property; (b) 3,000 acres of agricultural land in Yorkshire known as " the
D   Everingham estate "; (c) the south-east block of the late Duke's " Strand
estate."   This Strand estate, formerly part of settled Parliamentary estates,
consisted of four blocks of property lying between the Strand and the
river, bounded by Arundel Street and Surrey Street and intersected by
Norfolk Street and Howard Street.   The late Duke had sold off the north-
west block of this estate to subsidiary companies of Capital and Counties
E   Property Co. Ltd. in 1958.

As the combined result of (i) an order of Plowman J. dated March 22,
1966, varying the trusts of the 15th Duke's will; and (ii) the voluntary
winding up of the estates company, the trustees of the settlement became
entitled to the following assets in substitution for the shares in the
estates company, namely: (d) land in Sussex, mainly agricultural; (e) the
Clun estates in Shropshire; and (f) cash and proceeds of property con-
F   tracted to be sold—all subject to an annuity of £28,150 payable to Legal
and General Assurance Society Ltd. during the lifetime of the settlor.
On March 31, 1966, this annuity was purchased by the trustees, and
so became extinguished.

On April 4, 1966, the settlor added the north-east block of the Strand
estate to the settlement, subject to certain charges.   By a deed of
exchange dated February 25, 1969, the settlor added the south-west
G   block of the Strand estate to the settlement in exchange for the agricultural land in Sussex owned by the trustees.   This exchange in fact involved
a substantial element of bounty on his behalf.

This exchange paved the way for the comprehensive re-development
of the Strand estate in the manner with which we are all now familiar.
I am perfectly satisfied that this development involved the trustees in
H   work, as trustees, which was entirely outside anything which could
reasonably have been foreseen when they accepted office.   Details of the
work involved are set out in paragraphs 19 to 24 inclusive of Mr. Charles
Edmund Thomas Bellord's affidavit herein, sworn on December 6, 1977.
There is no point in rehearsing such work, but it was wholly exceptional.
This was not the only matter engaging the attention of the trustees.   The
introduction of capital transfer tax by the Finance Act 1975 caused them to
consider the form of the settlement very closely, and, having decided that

it was not in the best possible shape so far as that tax was concerned, they **A** executed, on March 30, 1976, an appointment designed, in general terms, either to produce an interest in possession within the meaning of that phrase as employed for capital transfer tax purposes, or else to produce maintenance and accumulation settlements. There is, however, one particular fund—about a tenth of the whole—which still retains its purely discretionary characteristics and is known as the reserve fund.

The originating summons, which is presently before me, was issued **B** on January 10, 1975. I have been informed that the main reason it has taken so long to come before the court is that the settlor died on January 31, 1975, and naturally this caused additional work for a number of the family's advisors. The summons claims the following relief:

> " (1) That this honourable court may in exercise of its inherent juris-
> diction authorise the plaintiffs to charge be paid and retain remuner- **C**
> ation for their services as trustees of the said settlement in accordance
> with the draft minutes of order intended to be exhibited to an
> affidavit of Alan William Lewis White intended to be sworn and
> filed therein, or in accordance with such other provisions as to this
> court shall seem fit."

Then there is the usual ancillary relief of costs and other relief. **D**

So far as Lord Perth is concerned, he is not a person to whom the provisions of clause 11 of the settlement apply or have ever applied. The evidence is that he joined the merchant banking firm of J. Henry Schroder & Co.—then an unincorporated partnership—in 1946, and was an associate or salaried partner from 1947 to 1957. In 1962 he became a non-executive director of Schroders Ltd. of which his co-plaintiff is a **E** wholly owned subsidiary. He was also a director of his co-plaintiff Schroder Executor and Trustee Co. Ltd. (" SETCO ") from 1947 to 1957, but is now no longer on the board of SETCO. He retired from his directorship of Schroders Ltd. on April 1, 1976.

I think it is only fair to Lord Perth to make it perfectly clear that the initiative for providing him with remuneration did not come from him. What is proposed in his case is set out in paragraph 8 of the draft minutes **F** of order, as follows:

> " From and after April 1, 1976, and so long as he remains a trustee
> of the settlement Lord Perth shall as remuneration for his services
> as a trustee of the settlement be entitled to an annual sum of £3,000
> payable out of the income of the trust fund such annual sum to
> accrue from day to day but to be paid by equal half-yearly instal- **G**
> ments in arrear the first instalment together with sums accrued to
> be payable on April 1, 1978."

April 1, 1976, is geared to coincide with Lord Perth's cessation of holding office as a director of Schroders Ltd. Whilst one can see that it might well be convenient for Lord Perth to obtain another source of remunera- tion when his fees as a director ceased, it can hardly be a matter of any **H** direct interest to any of the beneficiaries that this should happen.

I now turn to the remuneration of SETCO. It will be recalled that clause 12 of the settlement provides for their remuneration according to the terms of their then current booklet. This is in evidence before me, as an exhibit to the affidavit of Alan William Lewis White, sworn on December 6, 1977. I need not dwell on the acceptance fee. The three vital fees are: (i) Management fee. This is stated to be at the rate of

The Weekly Law Reports, October 27, 1978

661

3 W.L.R.   In re Duke of Norfolk's Settlement (Ch.D.)   Walton J.

A 2s. (now 10p) per £100 of capital held in the trust annually, payable out of capital, the capital values being " the book value as shown in the last audited accounts of the trust." (ii) Change of investment fee 2s. per £100 on the amount involved in any sale etc. of any security quoted on a recognised stock exchange in the United Kingdom. In the case of a security not so quoted, 5s. (25p) per £100 on the amount involved. (iii) Withdrawal fee 5s. per £100.

B   Now SETCO is claiming remuneration additional to this under a number of different heads: (i) Ratification of the charge of a sum of £24,677. This is a fee charged by SETCO for the year ending March 25, 1972, and was so charged in order to correct undercharging in every year from the inception of the trust until then. (ii) A sum of £25,000 in respect of its services to the trust, being services alleged to be outside the ordinary scope
C of a trustee's duties, performed prior to the issue of the originating summons. (iii) Two annual sums of £25,000 each in respect of its services to the trust during each of the two years ending on March 31, 1976, and March 31, 1977. (iv) A revised scale of charges to operate from March 31, 1977, as follows:

D
" (a) An annual management fee . . . at a rate not exceeding 40p per £100 of the aggregate amount or market value at that date of the capital of the trust fund; (b) A fee chargeable from time to time on the occasion of any change of investment (i) at the rate of 10p per £100 on the amount involved in any sale purchase redemption or conversion of any stocks shares or securities listed on a recognised stock exchange in the United Kingdom and (ii) at the rate of 25p per £100 on the amount involved in any sale purchase redemption
E or conversion of any stocks shares or securities not so listed; (c) A withdrawal fee chargeable on the occasion of the withdrawal of the whole or any part of the capital of the trust fund at the rate of 25p per £100 on the aggregate amount or market value at that time of the capital withdrawn."

Of course, it will be observed that those last two fees are very broadly
F in line with the original fee that they are entitled to charge. Then there were certain ancillary provisions, which are important, that for the purpose of the charging

" (a) the value of any property comprised in the trust fund shall be determined without deduction of any mortgage or charge affecting the same (b) in determining the market value as at April 1, 1978, of
G any freehold property then remaining comprised in the trust fund the trustees may if they think fit act on the memorandum as to current market values which forms exhibit ' CETB 12 ' to the affidavit of Charles Edmund Thomas Bellord sworn herein on December 20, 1977, and (c) without prejudice to any other right or duty of the trustees to make or cause to be made at the expense of the trust any valuation of the whole or any part of the trust fund the trustees may
H if they think fit act on any written certificate given by Messrs. Matthews & Goodman or other reputable surveyors nominated by the trustees (notwithstanding that such surveyors may be accustomed to act as the trustees' agents) to the effect that the market value as at the date of the certificate of any freehold or leasehold property then comprised in the trust fund is in the opinion of the surveyors not less than an amount specified in such certificate and may from time to time defray out of the capital or income of the trust fund

the costs and expenses of obtaining such a certificate at intervals of   A
not less than three years."

(v) Additional remuneration in respect of items alleged to be exceptional
or outside the ordinary scope of a trustee's duties as follows:

" (a) In addition to the fees hereinbefore provided for, SETCO shall
from and after the order date also be entitled to additional remuneration for any such services as are performed by SETCO after that   B
date and as are exceptional or outside the ordinary scope of a
trustee's duties including (without prejudice to the generality of the
foregoing) services involving—(i) dealing with a business; (ii) dealing
with assets situated outside the United Kingdom; (iii) supplying
information for the purpose of any proposed dealing with a
beneficial interest or for registering a notice of charge; (iv) supplying   C
copies of documents and additional copies of accounts; (v) an
administration following the cessation of a life or other interest in
property in circumstances in which no withdrawal fee is payable
and (vi) work incidental to an application to the court (other than
the application made by the originating summons herein).   (b) Such
additional fees shall be of such amounts as shall from time to time
be certified in writing by Messrs. Coopers & Lybrand (or some other   D
chartered accountants instructed by the trustees and being in the
opinion of the trustees of comparable standing) as reasonable and
proper having regard to the difficulty and responsibility of the matter
concerned and the time spent and acts done by SETCO and its
officers employees and agents in connection therewith."

However, before there is any question of considering any such applica-   E
tion on its merits, it appeared to me—although not, I think, prior to my
raising the point to any of the counsel engaged in the case—that a serious
question of jurisdiction arose.   That this is indeed so apparent from
a cursory reference to *Snell's Principles of Equity,* 27th ed. (1973),
pp. 243–244, where it is stated as follows:

" Remuneration of trustees.   As a result of the rule that a trustee   F
cannot make a profit from his trust, trustees and executors are
generally entitled to no allowance for their care and trouble.   This
rule is so strict that even if a trustee or executor has sacrificed much
time to carrying on a business as directed by the trust, he will usually
be allowed nothing as compensation for his personal trouble or loss
of time.   And a solicitor-trustee is not entitled to charge anything   G
except his out-of-pocket expenses for any business he does in relation
to the trust, whether contentious or non-contentious.   There are,
however, important exceptions to this rule."

Then, under (a) *Snell* deals with the question of agreement with
beneficiaries; then under (b) with " order of court ":

" Where the court appoints a corporation (other than the public   H
trustee) to be a trustee or administrator, the corporation may charge
such remuneration as the court authorities [sic].   Again, a judicial
trustee, whether an official of the court or not, may be paid out of
the trust property such remuneration as the court may assign
him.   There is also a general power for the court to authorise a
commission to be paid or allowed to the trustee for his trouble if
the execution of the trust is more than ordinarily burdensome.   The

The Weekly Law Reports, October 27, 1978

663

3 W.L.R.   In re Duke of Norfolk's Settlement (Ch.D.)   Walton J.

A   court cannot, however, review the remuneration which is given to
the trustees by the trust instrument or by statute or other authority."

Of course, it is always highly convenient to be able to find that the
court does indeed have an inherent jurisdiction to make some particular
order, rather than to discover that, after all, it does not. But one must
bear in mind the authoritative words of Lord Simonds L.C. in *Chapman*
B v. *Chapman* [1954] A.C. 429, 443–444:

"It was natural that the Lord Justice [Denning L.J.] should, upon
the basis of an unlimited inherent jurisdiction, proceed to the conclusion that, whenever the court had in the past asserted a want of
jurisdiction, it had of its own motion placed limitations on its own
jurisdiction and, giving as examples of this abnegation its declared
C   inability to remove a married woman's restraint on anticipation, to
permit a sale of heirlooms or to sanction an unauthorised transaction for the sake of expediency, should observe that in all these
cases the intervention of the legislature to vest these powers in the
court must not be read as delimiting the jurisdiction of the court, but
rather as removing limitations which the court had imposed on
itself. These statutory provisions, he said, 'show that the judges of
D   the late nineteenth century made a mistake in tying their own
hands in these matters. We ought not to make the same
mistake today' [see [1953] Ch. 276]. My Lords, I am unable to
accept as accurate this view of the origin, development and scope of
the jurisdiction of the Court of Chancery. . . . In my opinion, the true
view that emerges from a consideration of this jurisdiction through
E   the centuries is not that at some unknown date it appeared full-fledged
and that from time to time timid judges have pulled out some of its
feathers, but rather that it has been a creature of gradual growth,
though with many setbacks, and that the range of its authority can
only be determined by seeing what jurisdiction the great equity
judges of the past assumed and how they justified their assumption.
It is, in effect, in this way that the majority of the Court of Appeal in
F   the present case have approached the problem and, in my opinion,
it is the right way. It may well be that the result is not logical, and
it may be asked why, if the jurisdiction of the court extended to this
thing, it did not extend to that also. But, my Lords, that question is
as vain in the sphere of jurisdiction as it is in the sphere of substantive law. We are as little justified in saying that a court has a
G   certain jurisdiction, merely because we think it ought to have it, as
we should be in declaring that the substantive law is something
different from what it has always been declared to be, merely because
we think it ought to be so. It is even possible that we are not wiser
than our ancestors. It is for the legislature, which does not rest
under that disability, to determine whether there should be a change
in the law and what that change should be."

H
The scope of the inherent jurisdiction of the court must therefore
rest upon the usual twin pillars of principle and authority. Dealing first
with principle, what is the true nature of the trustees' right to remuneration where, as here, that right is conferred by the trust instrument? One
way of looking at the matter would be to say that it was based on contract: the original settlor made a contract with the trustee to the effect
that if the trustee accepted the trust, he should be entitled to the remunera-

664

tion, if any, provided by the trust instrument. The benefit of that contract **A** would then have to be regarded as settled by the trust instrument for the benefit of the beneficiaries thereunder. So far as subsequent trustees are concerned, the original settlor has conferred power upon whoever is entitled, under the trust instrument, to appoint such subsequent trustee to make a similar contract with such trustee, the benefit of which contract, like any other portion of the trust property, is once again held upon the trusts of the trust instrument. If one looks at the matter in this light, **B** then what conceivable inherent jurisdiction can this court have to interfere in the contractual position? Equity in general mends no man's bargains, and it would be an extremely odd kind of jurisdiction which could mend a bargain only where one party to it was a trustee, whom in general equity expects to work for nothing.

Mr. Price, however, who accepted gracefully a direction which I gave **C** him to argue the question of jurisdiction against Mr. Nourse, so that I might have the benefit of a full argument, did not accept this analysis of the position and put forward a much more subtle one. The right to remuneration, he submitted, was in the nature of a beneficial interest under the trust instrument. And in support of this proposition he cited: *In re Pooley* (1888) 40 Ch.D. 1; *In re Thorley* [1891] 2 Ch. 613; and *In* **D** *re White* [1898] 2 Ch. 217—all decisions of the Court of Appeal and all of which clearly establish that a benefit conferred upon a trustee in consideration of his executing the office—whether by way of profit costs in the case of a solicitor trustee or by way of an annuity whilst acting as trustee—is to be treated as a beneficial interest under the will, with such divers results as that the provision fails if the trustee witnesses the will, that whilst legacy duty remained with us the benefit was to be charged **E** with such duty, and that in the administration of an insolvent estate it had no priority as being an administration expense. To these three cases Mr. Price could have added *Dale* v. *Inland Revenue Commissioners* [1954] A.C. 11 in the House of Lords, where it was held that income which was the conditional gift of the testator might nevertheless also be earned by compliance with the testator's condition of serving as a trustee.

On the basis of these authorities, therefore, Mr. Price submitted that **F** as the remunerated trustee had a conditional beneficial interest under the trust instrument, since there can be no distinction in principle between the situation of a remunerated trustee under a will or any other trust instrument, the court had jurisdiction to vary that beneficial interest in precisely the same way and under the same conditions as it could vary any other beneficial interest; no more and no less. These were: (a) in the **G** exceptional cases pointed out in *Chapman* v. *Chapman* [1954] A.C. 429, so far as they could conceivably affect any trustee's position, namely compromise and salvage; and (b) more generally, by a scheme promoted under the Variation of Trusts Act 1958. Compromise could not possibly be in point here; the procedure under (b) has not been followed in the present case, and in any event every single beneficiary would have to be joined or represented in some fashion, and it would have to be shown **H** that the proposed variation of the trustees' remuneration was for their benefit. This might not, in some cases, prove an impossible task. So, says Mr. Price, the simple reason why the court has no power to alter the remuneration payable to trustees under a trust instrument is the same reason that it has no inherent jurisdiction to alter any other beneficial interest.

Mr. Nourse's counter to this submission was that when Lord Simonds

The Weekly Law Reports, October 27, 1978

665

3 W.L.R.   In re Duke of Norfolk's Settlement (Ch.D.)   Walton J.

A   L.C. in *Chapman* v. *Chapman* spoke of the necessity of grounding the inherent jurisdiction of the court upon principle and authority, he did not mean to imply that one must necessarily find a case in which the inherent jurisdiction had actually been exercised before finding that it did, indeed, exist. However, if this was required, he claimed that there was, first, no decision to the contrary; secondly, that in at least one reported case the jurisdiction was assumed and was actually exercised in another. He

B accepted Mr. Price's analysis of the remuneration as being a conditional gift, and submitted that the court could, as it had in other cases, make a conditional gift of this nature, which would then of course be a second conditional gift; that the House of Lords in *Chapman* v. *Chapman* had not considered the case of trustees' remuneration, and that the power of the court to award this was an exception additional to all others therein

C considered.

  I do not, however, think in this day and age that the court can assume a new inherent jurisdiction which has never before been exercised or, at the least, assumed clearly to exist by reported judgments in cases where the matter has been fully considered. On the other hand, there are undoubtedly cases where the court has, in the exercise of its inherent jurisdiction, awarded remuneration to trustees, and in order to discover

D the basis upon which it has done so it is, I think, necessary to consider them with some care.

  The first reported case of much materiality is *Marshall* v. *Holloway* (1818) 2 Swan. 432. There is no judgment on the present point, but the order in that case is extremely voluminous and makes the point decided very clear. It commences, for present purposes, at the bottom of p. 452:

E   "And his Lordship doth declare, that the said defendant Faithful Croft is entitled to the leasehold house and premises in Chancery Lane, given and bequeathed to him in and by the codicil of the said testator, bearing date the 20th day of January 1816, for the remainder of the term of years now to come therein, from the death of the said testator, for his own use and benefit; and it being alleged by the said

F   plaintiffs, the trustees, that the nature and circumstances of the estate of the said testator require the application of a great proportion of time, by and on the part of the said trustees, for the due execution of the trusts of his said will, in regard to his estate, and that they cannot undertake to continue the execution of the trusts without the aid and assistance of the said Faithful Croft, as a co-trustee, he having, during the life of the said testator, had the principal and

G   confidential management thereof, and being better acquainted therewith than any other person, and therefore it will be for the benefit of the said testator's estate that he should continue to be a trustee thereof; and the said Faithful Croft, alleging that due attention to the affairs and concerns of the said testator will require so much of his time and attention as will be greatly prejudicial to his other

H   pursuits and concerns in business, and therefore that he would not have undertaken to act therein, but under the assurance that an application would be made to this court to authorise the allowance and payment of a reasonable compensation out of the said testator's estate for such his labour and time, and that he cannot continue to act therein without such reasonable allowance being made to him, it is ordered, that it be referred to the said master to settle a reasonable allowance to be made to the said Faithful Croft out of the said

A

testator's estate for his time, pains and trouble, in the execution of the said trusts, for the time past, and, in settling such allowance, the said master is to have regard to the legacy of £200 given and bequeathed to the said Faithful Croft by the said will of the said testator, on the execution of the trust thereby reposed in him: and it is ordered, that the said master do inquire whether it will be for the benefit of the said testator's estate that the said Faithful Croft should continue to be a trustee under the said will, and to receive a compensation for the future employment of his time and trouble; and in case the said master shall be of opinion that it will be for the benefit of the said testator's estate that the said Faithful Croft should be continued a trustee, then the said master is to settle a reasonable allowance to be made to the said Faithful Croft therein; ..."

B

So in that case, although there was a certain element of " jumping the gun " in that Faithful Croft commenced his duties as a trustee at once, it is clearly a case where what he was saying was that he would not accept the trusteeship unless he was remunerated, and, on the basis that his services were of such importance that it would be for the benefit of the estate for him to continue as a trustee and be remunerated, the court authorised such remuneration.

C

D

Very shortly thereafter, at a time when *Marshall* v. *Holloway* must have been fresh in everybody's minds, *Brocksopp* v. *Barnes* (1820) 5 Mad. 90 was decided. I think I should read the whole of that case:

" John Brocksopp, by his will, October 11, 1812, directed certain businesses to be carried on by his trustees and executors, and directed several other onerous trusts to be performed by his trustees, but gave no legacies to them, or reward for their trouble. Barnes, the defendant, by petition stated, that he had devoted considerable time, and had travelled many hundred miles, in respect of the testator's concerns as trustee, and prayed that it might be referred to the master, to ascertain what would be proper to be allowed to the petitioner as a compensation or recompense for his loss of time, personal trouble, and expense in the management and settlement of the testator's affairs, and to certify out of what fund it ought to be paid. Mr. Bell for the petitioner. Mr. Maddock for the plaintiffs, who were infants, said he was instructed not to oppose the petition.

E

F

" Sir John Leach V.-C.: ' This trustee is of course entitled to all reasonable expenses which he may have incurred in the conduct of the trust, and requires no order for that purpose. But the general rule must be applied to him, that a trustee is not entitled to compensation for personal trouble and loss of time. If the nature of the trust be such that a trustee ought not to undertake it without compensation, a special case must be made in this court, before the trust is accepted.' "

G

H

So far as one can see, this was a case in which the application was a wholly meritorious one, and, as here, one which was not opposed. Yet Sir John Leach V.-C. made it perfectly clear that it was only where the trustee made a special case before the trust was accepted, that the court could allow him remuneration.

The next case is *Bainbrigge* v. *Blair* (1845) 8 Beav. 588. The sidenote reads:

The Weekly Law Reports, October 27, 1978

667

3 W.L.R.   In re Duke of Norfolk's Settlement (Ch.D.)   Walton J.

A   " A trustee acting as solicitor in the trust matters, is merely entitled
to costs out of pocket. The rule is not inflexible, and compensation
may, in special cases, be made him, under the authority of the court,
by a fixed allowance, but not by allowing him to make the usual
professional charges."

And I can pick up the judgment of Lord Langdale M.R., at p. 596:

B   " But assuming that all that was done here was highly beneficial, and
that a great benefit was acquired to the estate by the exertion of
the trustee, was he not bound to do his utmost for the benefit of his
trust? In every case a trustee might say, I have had a great deal
of trouble in these matters, and have spent a considerable portion of
my time about them: pay me for my time and trouble! Is that the
C   rule? I am not aware of the existence of any such rule, nor has any
authority been produced, which tends in the least to shew, that this
is the way in which trustees, who have strictly performed their duty
and thereby procured a benefit to the estate, are to be dealt with.
It is very different from the case, where a trust being in the course
of execution, and many things remaining to be done, which can be
done beneficially only by a particular trustee, who cannot, from
D   his situation, do it without grievous personal loss, and that party
comes to the court, and states, that he is in a situation and willing
to do these things, but that he cannot, consistently with his own
interest, proceed with such duties, and gratuitously devote his time
for the benefit of the trust. In such a case, it is competent for the
court, considering what is beneficial to the cestuis que trust, and is
E   calculated to promote their interest, to take the matter into consideration, and to give proper remuneration to that person who alone,
by his own exertion, can produce that benefit.
          " There are various ways in which provision might be made for such
a case; thus, a person appointed trustee with his own consent, might
say to the testator, ' there will be a great deal of law business in this
matter, is it reasonable that I should do it for nothing? If you so
F   intend, do not appoint me trustee.' A testator, though knowing
that if his trustee acted as solicitor, and were allowed to make his
professional charges, he would be enabled to make business for himself, might, nevertheless, insert an authority in the will permitting it,
and this is not unfrequently done; there would then be no question
about the matter. But here Mr. Blair, instead of guarding himself
G   in that way, took the legacy of £200, expressly as a compensation for
his trouble.
          " There is another way in which this matter might have been
brought forward. After the litigation and difficulty arose, Mr. Blair
might have applied to the court, stating the circumstances of the
suit, and how important it was that the legal business of this trust
should be carried on by him, that it would be a loss to him to carry
H   it on without remuneration, and asking the court permission to do
it. He did not so act; he put in his answer to the bill, without
claiming anything in respect of these matters; the cause comes to a
hearing; ' all just allowances ' are directed to be made to him, but
this point was not even mentioned. If Mr. Blair had stated the
matter in his answer or had presented a petition, to come on at the
hearing, to obtain any allowances of this sort, the circumstances
would then have been taken into consideration, and such directions

given by the court as the circumstances rendered proper; but here,   A
nothing of the sort was done, and the decree directed the accounts
to be taken and just allowances to be made.   Under these circumstances, I do not think there is any authority for me to make an
order on any part of this petition, and I must dismiss it with costs.

It is certainly presented contrary to the ordinary rule of this
court; and if it had succeeded, it could only have been an indulgence,
in allowing the petitioners something which they ought to have   B
secured to themselves, if they were intitled to it, by raising the points
at a proper period."

So in this case, the jurisdiction assumed to exist was put in rather wider
terms than previously.   It was assumed that if a trustee found himself in
a situation where he would be the best person to carry out some particular
piece of activity on behalf of the trust—say, conduct litigation—he could   C
come to the court, and ask to be allowed to carry it on and charge his
proper costs for so doing.   It is, I think, clear from the judgment that it
would have to be something wholly outside the ordinary course of the
administration of the trust, and that he would have to come before he
had actually carried out the work.   But if he came, in time, the court
would consider whether, in effect, it was more beneficial for the trust to   D
employ him to carry out the work than to employ an outside solicitor to
do so.

In 1887 *In re Freeman's Settlement Trusts* (1887) 37 Ch.D. 148 was
decided.   The relevant facts appear from the headnote:

"The cestuis que trust (some of whom were infants) under a settlement of freehold farms in Wales (dated in 1840), were all resident   E
out of the jurisdiction, either in Canada or the United States.   The
settlement contained a power of sale exercisable with the consent
of the equitable tenant for life, and a power of appointing new
trustees exercisable by the surviving or continuing trustee, or the
heirs or assignees of the last surviving or continuing trustee.   In
1874, when both the original trustees of the settlement were dead,
the executrix of the last surviving trustee, erroneously believing   F
herself empowered in that behalf, purported to appoint two persons
resident in Canada to be trustees of the settlement.   These two
persons, believing themselves to be duly appointed, had acted as
trustees since 1874, and had employed an English agent to receive
the rents of the farms, paying him a commission for so doing.   The
heir of the last surviving trustee could not be found, and there was no   G
one capable of exercising the power of appointing new trustees contained in the settlement.   Upon a petition by all the cestuis que trust
for the appointment by the court of the two Canadians and the
English agent as new trustees, and for authority to pay the English
trustee a commission on the rents while acting as manager and
receiver, the court appointed the two persons resident in Canada and
the English agent to be new trustees of the settlement, but required   H
an undertaking by the trustees out of the jurisdiction in case the
power of appointing new trustees should become exercisable by
them, or either of them, not to appoint any new trustee resident out
of the jurisdiction without the consent of the court.   The court also,
subject to the production of evidence as to the number of the holdings, the rents and dates of payment, the necessity of paying a commission for collecting the rents, and that the proposed remuneration

The Weekly Law Reports, October 27, 1978

669

3 W.L.R.   In re Duke of Norfolk's Settlement (Ch.D.)   Walton J.

A   was proper, sanctioned the payment of a commission to the English
       trustee."

It is, I think, important to note that the factual position was that the
beneficiaries had been wholly unable to find any person to act as a trustee
in England except Mr. Lloyd, and he would not become a trustee unless
his commission was continued: this appears from the summary of the
B facts at the bottom of p. 150 of the report.   Stirling J. obviously considered
the jurisdiction he was exercising to be a very narrow one.   He said, at
p. 152:

> " Upon being satisfied as to the propriety of Mr. Lloyd being paid a
> commission, I think I ought to appoint him to be a trustee together
> with the other two gentleman who are resident out of the jurisdiction.
C   > But I shall require an affidavit from Mr. Lloyd stating the number
> of the holdings into which the property is divided, and the amounts of
> the rents payable, the dates of payment; and if I am satisfied that it
> is necessary that Mr. Lloyd should receive a remuneration for collect-
> ing the rents, and that the proposed remuneration is a proper one, I
> shall be prepared under the peculiar circumstances of this case to
> allow him to continue to receive his commission."
D

The next case—a decision of great importance—is that of the Court
of Appeal in *In re Salmen* (1912) 107 L.T. 108.   Its importance lies in
this, that in this case for the first time, so far as I am aware, the basis
of the inherent jurisdiction of the court was stated by Eve J., whose
judgment was expressly approved by the Court of Appeal.   What
happened in that case was that at an early stage in the administration of
E the estate, after an order for administration of the estate had been made
by the court, a summons was in fact taken out for an order that the
executors and trustees might be at liberty to employ one of their number
to manage a business comprised in the estate, on the terms which the will
itself indicated he might be employed upon, at a salary of £300 per annum.
Since the estate was insolvent, he was clearly not entitled to take this
F bounty under the will as against the creditors.   No order was ever made
on the summons, but some time later, when the business had been sold,
the executors and trustees asked that they might be allowed a sum of
£703 16s. 10d. in their accounts in respect of such remuneration.   Eve J.
said, at p. 110:

> " I am not saying that the court has not jurisdiction in exceptional
G   > cases to provide for remuneration of executors and trustees even in
> the absence of special provision in the will.   And in the face of the
> decision in *Forster* v. *Ridley* (1864) 4 De G.J. & S. 452, to which
> Mr. Buckmaster has drawn my attention, it would be impossible for
> me to say that there is no such jurisdiction.   But I think that it is a
> jurisdiction which must be founded on some proposition of this sort:
> That the circumstances of the case raise an implied contract on the
H   > part of those persons against whom the claim for remuneration is
> made to remuneration for services which the person claiming to be
> remunerated has discharged, or must be presumed to have discharged,
> at the invitation of the person against whom the remuneration is
> sought to be recovered, and who must, therefore, be presumed to
> have agreed to pay such remuneration in consideration of services
> so rendered.   Apart from that, I cannot think that the court would
> ever impose upon creditors in the position of the creditors in the

670

present case an obligation to pay executors and trustees for work   A
which, in the absence of express contract, they are bound to do
without remuneration.

"In the circumstances I think that the sum has been properly
disallowed by the master on the footing that it is an insolvent estate.
And I do not see my way to direct any such inquiry as it was indicated
I might direct for the purpose of ascertaining whether or not any
remuneration is payable to these executors and trustees.   B

"I think that perhaps I ought to add this: A summons was issued
in the course of the action, in December 1908, two days after the
order for administration, asking that the executors and trustees might
be at liberty to continue on the business and to employ Mr. Bernstein,
one of their number, in the existing management to manage it.   If
an order to that effect had been made on the summons, a very different   C
state of things might have arisen.   But in fact no such order was
made, and the consideration of the summons stood over generally,
and when ultimately some direction was given on the summons in the
following May, it stopped short of any authorisation on the part of
the master or the judge in chambers to continue Mr. Bernstein as
manager on the then existing arrangement.   D

"In these circumstances I do not think that there is any order of
the court or any directions given in chambers which entitles the
executors and trustees to claim the remuneration on the footing that
it was remuneration which has been sanctioned or approved by the
court."

As I have indicated, the Court of Appeal, basing itself on *In re White*   E
[1898] 1 Ch. 297 approved Kekewich J.'s reasoning.   Cozens-Hardy M.R.
put it very bluntly, at p. 110:

"But really, when one gets simply and purely to the point to be
decided, I can feel no doubt whatever that we are bound to say that
this case comes within the principle that a trustee is not entitled to
make a profit out of his office in the absence of an express provision.
Further, an express provision in a will authorising a person in a   F
fiduciary position to make a profit out of his office against persons
benefiting under the will is of no force against creditors claiming
outside the will."

I now pass to the more modern cases to which my attention was called.
But before I do so, I would observe that, whilst undoubtedly when one   G
wishes to know what the up-to-date thinking of equity is upon any problem
one naturally turns to the later rather than the earlier cases, when
one is dealing with a question of inherent jurisdiction, it is to the older
rather than the later cases one must turn.   If such a jurisdiction did not
exist in 1912, it certainly did not spring into existence between 1912 and
1978.   With that word of caution, I turn to *In re Masters, decd.* [1953]
1 W.L.R. 81.   The headnote reads: H

"The court has jurisdiction under section 42 of the Trustee Act
1925, to authorize proper remuneration to be paid to a corporate
body which has been appointed by the court to be administrator and
trustee of the estate of an intestate.   There is also inherent jurisdiction in the court to authorize such remuneration, whether the
appointment has been made by the court or not."

The Weekly Law Reports, October 27, 1978

671

3 W.L.R.   In re Duke of Norfolk's Settlement (Ch.D.)   Walton J.

A   Danckwerts J. said, at p. 83:

"Apart from the statutory jurisdiction conferred by section 42 of the
Trustee Act 1925, it is also quite plain there is inherent jurisdiction
in the court to authorize remuneration of a trustee, whether appointed
by the court or not. Authority for that is to be found *In re Freeman's
Settlement Trusts* (1887) 37 Ch.D. 148 and *Marshall* v. *Holloway*
B   (1820) 2 Sw. 432. The same course was really adopted in *In re
Macadam* [1946] Ch. 73, reported on the question of the accountability of the trustee for certain directors' fees; but the report shows
that Cohen J. left to be decided the question whether in the circumstances of that case he should authorize the trustee in fact to retain
the directors' fees under the inherent jurisdiction of the court, and
that course was to my knowledge adopted and the remuneration was
C   in fact authorized. I also remember a case before Eve J., in which
I appeared as counsel, before the passing of the Act of 1925 in which,
though I do not remember the exact name of the trust, I do
remember that the very same bank, Coutts & Co., trustees of a
particular trust estate, were authorized by Eve J. to receive remuneration. There is, in my view, no doubt whatever about the inherent
D   jurisdiction of this court to authorize remuneration. That, therefore, decides the question of jurisdiction and I must now proceed
to consider on what scale I should allow remuneration in the present
case."

It is therefore quite plain that Danckwerts J. considered he was following *Marshall* v. *Holloway*, 2 Sw. 432 and *In re Freeman's Settlement
E   Trusts*, 37 Ch.D. 148. In this latter case, the authorisation of remuneration was effected, as we have already seen, at the same time as the appointment of the trustees was made by the court. I therefore do not think
that Danckwerts J. thought he was in any way enlarging the inherent
jurisdiction of the court. I would also comment that *In re Macadam*;
[1946] Ch. 73 is a case where a trustee was being asked to account to the
trust for an unauthorised profit he had made as a result of being a trustee,
F   but as the result of extra work—his activities as a director—which was not
strictly any part of the duties as a trustee. In these circumstances, Cohen J.
held that if he was satisfied that the trustee was the best person to be a
director, he would allow retention of some of the whole of the fees. This
seems plainly to be in a different category of cases. The trustees having
become accountable to the trust fund, the question is, for what sum are
G   they accountable? And that sum must, on plainest principles of equity,
be moulded so as to take account of any exceptional effort or skill shown
in acquiring the sum in respect of which they are accountable in the first
place.

The next case to which I was referred was *In the Estate of Campbell,
decd.* [1954] 1 W.L.R. 516, but I do not think that this adds anything to
the general picture, as the remuneration was there authorised from the
H   beginning in a case where it was quite obvious that the testator had
intended the bank to charge.

In the same volume is *In re Worthington, decd.* [1954] 1 W.L.R. 526.
The headnote reads:

"The general rule that a solicitor acting as trustee of an estate
cannot charge for his professional services is subject to the inherent
jurisdiction of the court to order a remuneration where it thinks fit,

but that jurisdiction should be exercised sparingly and only in excep- A
tional circumstances. A testator died in 1947 having appointed his
wife sole beneficiary and executrix under his will. The estate was
insolvent, the liabilities being greatly in excess of the assets, and the
widow on the advice of her solicitors did not take out a grant of
probate. During 1948, the first applicant, a partner in the firm of
solicitors who were conducting her affairs, negotiated with the
principal creditors with a view to a compromise of their claims in B
order to save something out of the estate for the widow. She
appointed him to act as her attorney, and he obtained a grant of
administration with the will annexed. It proved impossible to reach
a compromise and he decided that the estate ought to be administered
in bankruptcy. He prepared the bankruptcy petition, and carried
out the preparation and lodgment of accounts and receipts of the C
estate during administration under rule 304 of the Bankruptcy Rules,
1952. The solicitors asked for an order for payment of their profit
costs out of the estate in connexion with those matters, notwithstanding that the administrator was a solicitor and a partner in the firm of
solicitors acting for the widow : —
    " *Held,* that although the partner had acted properly and had done
work which had to be done, there were no exceptional circumstances D
to justify a departure from the rule that a solicitor trustee was not
entitled to remuneration."

It is perfectly true that in that case Upjohn J. assumed that there was
inherent jurisdiction to authorise the payment of remuneration at a time
later than that of his actual assumption of office. But that is not a
jurisdiction which he in fact exercised; and however he framed his under- E
standing of the jurisdiction, he thought it was extremely narrow, for
he said, at p. 529:

    " I must not be taken as laying down any rule that where trustees act
    as directors or refuse to undertake work in the future without
    remuneration, the court ought to treat them as exceptional cases and
    allow remuneration. I merely refer to those cases as examples of F
    what may in some circumstances be considered exceptional cases and
    where the court on a review of all the relevant facts may come to the
    conclusion that remuneration should be allowed."

Again, at p. 530:

    " It was said that the whole object of Mr. Leighton becoming attorney
    administrator was to keep the costs down to a minimum; the work G
    which he did in preparing the petition and the necessary accounts
    was work which had to be done by somebody, and the estate, there-
    fore, had suffered no loss; on the contrary it has benefited because
    Mr. Leighton was, of course, acquainted with the whole matter and
    could therefore prepare the petition and accounts more quickly
    and less expensively than anyone else. There is much force in that
    contention. But the rule seems to me to be a strict one, and if in H
    this case I granted the application it would be open to solicitors to
    say in almost every case that they had acted honestly and properly,
    and that there had been no loss to the estate, so that they were
    entitled to their costs; and the salutary rule that a solicitor trustee
    cannot charge for his services would be virtually destroyed."

The next case is *In re Spedding, decd.* [1966] N.Z.L.R. 447, a decision

The Weekly Law Reports, October 27, 1978

673

3 W.L.R.   In re Duke of Norfolk's Settlement (Ch.D.)   Walton J.

A of the Court of Appeal of New Zealand. The trustee in that case was entitled, under the terms of a statute, to fix its own remuneration by resolution of its board of directors, but not exceeding a certain figure. It had so fixed its remuneration generally, and the actual proceedings were designed to persuade the court to reduce its remuneration. This claim failed as a pure matter of construction of the statutory power, and the two judges in the Court of Appeal decided the matter purely on the true con-

B struction of the statute. McCarthy J., however, cast his net wider. He said, at p. 465:

"As Professor Hanbury says in his *Modern Equity* 7th ed. 234, the English trustee, unlike his American counterpart, must act without remuneration, contenting himself with reimbursement for his expenses out of pocket. The New Zealand trustee finds himself, as a general

C rule, in the same position, but here, as in England, there are excep- tions to this overall rule. First, the court may authorise payment of fees as part of its inherent jurisdiction. It also has statutory power to do that, see section 72 of the Trustee Act 1956, as substituted by section 10 of the Trustee Amendment Act 1960. Then payment may be obtained pursuant to the trust instrument, if that provides for it; but as Professor Hanbury again points out, the court will limit

D the charges in that instance strictly to those indicated by the creator of the trust. A right to payment may also arise out of a contract made upon acceptance of office. Such contracts may in some cases only be possible if the beneficiaries are sui juris. Finally, we have the exceptions created by the public trust office legislation and by the private Acts setting up the different trust companies operating

E in New Zealand.

"I have said earlier that when the trustee's charges are claimed pursuant to the terms of a trust instrument, the court will limit the charges strictly to the terms constituting deed or will. Mr. Spratt agrees that if a testator or settlor provides for payment of a fixed sum or for commission or other remuneration to be paid on an ascertain- able basis, that fixed or ascertainable remuneration cannot be

F questioned and the court has no jurisdiction to interfere."

It may very well be that McCarthy J.'s observations in relation to the quotation from Professor Hanbury's work on equity are based on a misreading of that work, but, that aside, it will be seen that his observa- tions are all fully in line with the cases to which I have so far referred.

G The next case to which I was referred was *In re Barbour's Settlement Trusts* [1974] 1 W.L.R. 1198, a decision of Megarry J. The point of that case is accurately stated in the headnote, the first paragraph whereof reads:

"Where a corporate trustee seeks an increase of the trustee's fees, it should do so by proceedings in which the court's approval is plainly sought as part of the substantive relief. When a genuine dispute

H between the beneficiaries is being resolved by the beneficiaries it is wrong for the trustee to include as one of the terms of compromise a provision which has nothing to do with the dispute and is directly for the trustee's benefit."

I really do not think that that case decides on this point anything further.

Finally, there is *In re Codd's Will Trusts (Practice Note)* [1975] 1 W.L.R. 1139 and I will read the whole of that case:

" The plaintiff, National Westminster Bank Ltd., sole trustee of the A
will of Arthur Mortimer Codd, deceased, by summons dated October
30, 1973, sought an order, inter alia, directing the bank to sell with
vacant possession, in execution of the trust for sale contained in the
will, freehold property . . . notwithstanding failure to obtain the
consent of the first defendant . . . The first and second defendant
. . . were beneficially interested in the income subject to the trusts
of the will. The third to fifth defendants . . . were beneficially B
interested in the capital subject to the trusts. In paragraph 9 of the
summons the bank sought an order authorising itself as trustee of the
will to charge remuneration as from the death of the testator's widow
(in addition to the customary share of brokerage) in accordance with
its scale of fees from time to time in force and so that its fees should
be paid out of capital but with power for the bank at its discretion to C
charge the whole or any part thereof against income. . . .

" Graham J. considered the application for an order directing the
bank to sell the properties and, having directed that the bank use its
best endeavours to sell the property, continued: ' The other matter
argued before me was the possibility of an increase in the remuneration for the bank, as asked for in the summons. I was referred to a
case before Megarry J. recently, In re Barbour's Settlement Trusts D
[1974] 1 W.L.R. 1198, where he refused to deal with the question of
the bank's remuneration on the basis that what he was really being
asked to do was to approve a compromise between the defendants
and therefore it was not right for the remuneration of the bank to
be brought in by a side wind. I think the case before me is quite
different. The bank is a party and its application is put forward in E
the summons. The bank has made it abundantly clear that it would
not ask for extra remuneration if there was any opposition. The
bank however, receives only £10 per annum and is obviously being
inadequately remunerated for the work it is doing, and will continue
to be inadequately remunerated in future if the figure remains
unchanged. In my judgment, it would be right and in the interest
of the trust as a whole for that remuneration to be increased. F
Fortunately, the parties have agreed to a formula which would only
apply after, but not before, the sale of the property. There will
then be cash assets out of which the remuneration can be paid, but it
will be confined within certain agreed limits to be set out in the
order. Subject to that, the proper course is to make the order I
have suggested with leave to the parties to apply if further directions G
are wanted.' "

There was no argument in that case, and the only case actually cited was
In re Barbour's Settlement Trusts, which was obviously cited on the
question of procedure. With all respect to Graham J., I do not consider
that that case adds to the law on this point at all. In any event, of course,
£10 per annum is so derisory a sum that in 1975 one would be quite H
justified in regarding it as de minimis.

These, then, being the main cases on the question of inherent jurisdiction to award remuneration to a trustee, if placed together with the
principles which govern the nature of such remuneration, they appear to
me to justify the following summary: (i) The jurisdiction is a wholly
exceptional one, to be exercised sparingly. (ii) Subject to (iii) below, the
only ground upon which the court has ever acted, so far as the reported

The Weekly Law Reports, October 27, 1978

675

3 W.L.R.   In re Duke of Norfolk's Settlement (Ch.D.)   Walton J.

A   cases go, has been the necessity for obtaining the services either of some
particular individual trustee, whose services were of special value to the
trust, or of obtaining the services of some particular kind of trustee, such,
for example, as a trust corporation. (iii) It was indicated by Eve J. in
In re Salmen (1912) 107 L.T. 108—and the Court of Appeal approved the
reasoning in his judgment—that remuneration might be awarded if the
circumstances of the case were such as to raise an implied promise to pay
B   it on behalf of the beneficiaries. *Forster* v. *Ridley* (1864) 4 De G.J. & S.
452 appears to have been such a case, though the facts are obscure. (iv)
There has never been a case in which the court has ever altered the general
level of remuneration fixed by the trust instrument, once the trust has been
unconditionally accepted, unless it be *In re Codd's Will Trusts* (*Practice
Note*) [1975] 1 W.L.R. 1139, where there was no argument and the general
C   level was so derisory as to be de minimis. (v) The court has always
shown marked reluctance to award any remuneration unless the application
has been made very promptly on assumption of office or where there has
been a radical change in the circumstances.

It appears to me that the only conceivable ground upon which I should
be justified in awarding the trustees in the present case any additional
remuneration is under head (iii). The situation appears to me to be that
D   in this particular case the trustees, quite exceptionally, in dealing with
the amalgamation, reclamation of part from subsidiaries of Capital and
Counties Property Co. Ltd. and general assemblage and development of
the Strand estate into Arundel Court, as it is now known, performed
services which can properly be regarded as wholly outside the scope of
any duties which could reasonably have been expected to be rendered by
E   any trustees in the normal course of their duties. There has undoubtedly
been financial gain to the trust as a whole; and I accordingly think that
any dispassionate observer, seeing the wholly exceptional nature of the
trustees' activities, would consider that such wholly exceptional services
were only being rendered on the basis that, if successful, they would be
remunerated by something over and above whatever the trustees would
otherwise have received out of the trust funds. I think the wholly excep-
F   tional nature of the services the trustees did indeed render in the present
case is emphasised by the fact that it would, I think, prove very difficult
to find specific powers in the trust instrument under which they could
claim, in strict law, to have acted.

Accordingly, I think that in respect of those services the trustees—
both Lord Perth and SETCO—are entitled to be remunerated by a proper
G   allowance. I shall discuss the amount of such allowance with counsel
later.

I do not, however, think that I have any inherent jurisdiction to alter
the general level of SETCO's fees whatsoever. I accept, of course, the
evidence that those fees now are, in comparison with the fees charged by
other similar institutions, low, and that the proposed fresh scale which
SETCO would like to charge would still be below the scales now normally
H   charged by other institutions, especially the public trustee. But I cannot
consider that there has been such a fundamental change in the nature or
assets of the trust such as to bring any facet of the inherent jurisdiction
into play.

Apart from what I may call the " special services " category of cases—
which I think dovetail neatly into those cases where the trustees are held
to be accountable for profits which they have made out of the trust, but
are in general allowed to keep that proportion of the profits so made—

doubtless, in many cases, the whole—which results from their own exer- **A** tions above and beyond those expected of a trustee—the cases in which the court acts to secure the services of a particular trustee are closely analagous to " salvage." If one has to have the services of Mr. Faithful Croft, as a matter of necessity, and one cannot get them in any other manner, well then, they will have to be paid for.

In the present case, the Strand estate having now been fully developed, and, indeed, proposed to be sold and the proceeds invested in **B** farm land in Sussex, it appears to me that the kind of property held in the trust is in no way radically different from that originally settled or subsequently added. It is, of course, true that there is now more property in the trust than there originally was, but since the scale is a proportionate scale, this does not appear to me to matter in any way. The fact that SETCO now say that they are losing money on admini- **C** stering the trust and that their charges are now too low appears to me to be nihil ad rem. It must be firmly borne in mind that a trusteeship is not an office of profit—quite the reverse. Trustees have always been expected to work for such remuneration only, if any, as the trust instrument provided. And if institutions now make a business out of trusteeships, I can see no inherent jurisdiction in the court to extricate **D** them from any bad bargains which they may have made. The trust here may well last until January 1, 2038, and they knew that when they accepted office.

I have not overlooked the fact that the beneficiaries are highly satisfied with the way SETCO have discharged their duties, and naturally wish to retain them as trustees, whilst SETCO have indicated that if they do not obtain the additional remuneration which they seek, they may **E** have to consider possibly retiring from their position as trustees. The question of retirement is, however, not in their own hands, but in the hands of the person who has the right to appoint new trustees, or, ultimately, in the hands of the court if such person will not appoint another trustee in their place. I am, however, unmoved by any such intimation on their behalf. If their services are thought of so highly **F** by the beneficiaries, there are undoubtedly ways in which the bene- ficiaries who are sui juris could remunerate them additionally to the remuneration for which provision has been made by the trust instrument. Otherwise, it might be necessary to appoint individual professional men in their place, since such persons could rely upon the provisions of clause 11 of the settlement. I see no reason whatsoever to think that **G** proper competent trustees could not be found to accept the trusteeship upon the terms set out in clause 11, or that trustees so appointed would be in any respect less efficient in any department of their duties than Lord Perth and SETCO have been.

I should here, I think, notice the arguments put forward by Mr. Taylor, appearing for certain adult beneficiaries. He submitted that **H** SETCO had by accident or mistake not put forward a claim for additional remuneration at two particular points in the history of the trust: (i) when the settlor added additional property, and (ii) when Plowman J.'s order and the winding up of the estates company took place. Had SETCO done so, the settlor would have made further provision for them when he added the additional property, and it is known that he was sympathetic to their claim for additional remune-

The Weekly Law Reports, November 3, 1978

677

3 W.L.R.   In re Duke of Norfolk's Settlement (Ch.D.)   Walton J.

A ration, and in the latter case, the court might have then sanctioned some additional remuneration.

As to the first point, I, of course, cannot say what the settlor might or might not have done. There is no claim for rectification of the settlement, however, and I for one certainly do not consider that the equitable jurisdiction to relieve against accident or mistake to which Mr. Taylor appealed is in point in the slightest. As regards the second

B matter, I have not held it against SETCO and Lord Perth that they have made their application for remuneration which I can allow at the conclusion, rather than at the inception, of the scheme for development of the Strand estate. Although doubtless there are passages in the relevant judgments which could be construed to indicate that the court will never grant special remuneration retrospectively, I cannot think

C that special services cease to be special if no claim for remuneration is made until completion. Indeed, where the basis is, as it is here, the enhancement of the value of the trust property, it is indeed even more appropriate that the application should be made when the scheme has been brought to a successful conclusion than that they should be made before embarking on the scheme. I therefore do not think that these

D arguments of Mr. Taylor should prevail.

However, this is far from the end of the matter. If I return now to SETCO's various claims for remuneration, the first, it will be recalled, was for a sum of £24,677 which they had charged in the year 1971–72, made up by taking into account previous undercharges. I see no reason why SETCO should not be allowed to retain this sum. It appears to me that the strict analysis is that they have apparently disclaimed,

E in earlier years, benefits under the trust instrument to which they were entitled. I see no reason why they should not later withdraw that disclaimer, provided that nobody's position has in the meantime been altered as a result of their acts: see *In re Cranstoun, decd.* [1949] Ch. 523. Accordingly, to the extent to which it is necessary, I think I should declare that SETCO are entitled to retain this sum.

F There is another point of some materiality upon which I think I am entitled to assist SETCO as a matter of administration of the trust. Under the terms governing their remuneration, such remuneration is calculated upon the " book value as shown in the last audited accounts of the trust." Now there can be really no argument but that the book value as at present shown in the last audited accounts of the trust is hopelessly out of date. At the same time, the trustees feel—and rightly

G —that it would be a breach of trust for them to have a revaluation of the assets of the trust solely for the purposes of increasing their own remuneration. It cannot, however, be right that the remuneration of the trustees should be left to depend upon the pure accident of whether or not the trust assets have in fact been recently revalued for reasons unconnected with their own remuneration or not. That they have

H express power to cause a valuation to be made, and to be made in such manner as they in their discretion think fit, appears from clause 9 (h) of the settlement, which reads:

> " power at any time or times to value or cause to be valued the trust fund or any part thereof for any of the purposes hereof in such manner as the trustees shall in their discretion think fit."

In my view, in order to hold the scales fairly as between the trustees

considered as beneficiaries under the trust instrument and other bene- A
ficiaries thereunder, there should be a revaluation of any freehold
property comprised in the trust funds as at April 1, 1978, on the basis
of the values contained in the memorandum as to current market values
which forms an exhibit to the affidavit of Charles Edmund Thomas
Bellord, sworn in these proceedings on December 20, 1977, and I so
direct accordingly.

I do not, however, consider that I have any jurisdiction, inherent or B
otherwise, to go beyond the matters which I have indicated. Perhaps
two of the matters I have felt unable to take into consideration deserve
some further mention. First, although I doubt not that the appointment
of March 30, 1976, was one which it was in every way proper for the
trustees to have made, and that it may well have involved them in the
greatest possible anxious care and consideration, it appears to me that C
the possibility of the necessity of making appointments from time to
time is, by its very nature, always inherent in the trusteeship of a
wholly discretionary trust. Fiscal complications as well have always—
certainly since the end of World War II—been with us. So I do not
consider that trustees of a discretionary trust who have to make the
kind of appointment which was made by the trustees in this case can D
properly claim non haec in foedera veni. Secondly, I do not think that
it would be proper at this stage to give any directions as to any further
revaluation of the trust property in future years. I certainly do not
intend to preclude the making of a further application along the lines
of the present one as I have interpreted it for the purposes of this
judgment in the future. But the matter would then have to be considered in the light of all the surrounding circumstances. E

I cannot part with this matter without making one or two general
reflections upon the inherent jurisdiction of the court. If, as I have
concluded, there are for practical purposes only two cases in which the
court has any inherent jurisdiction to remunerate trustees, namely
(a) as from the date of appointment of an otherwise unremunerated
trustee, or conceivably one whose remuneration as proposed by the F
settlor or testator was such that nobody of the category required would
accept office on those terms; and (b) in respect of special services
outside the line of strict duty, then it will be seen that the jurisdiction is
always one to award something more than, according to the position
apart from the court's intervention, could be awarded. But if the jurisdiction were any wider—that is to say, if the court has an inherent
jurisdiction to increase the rate of a trustee's remuneration because of G
the alteration of circumstances since the date when he first assumed
office—then, equally, the jurisdiction must exist to decrease such
remuneration. Trustees cannot be entitled always to the benefits of
the jurisdiction and never, in a proper case, to its burdens. There is
no trace in the books of such a jurisdiction ever having been invoked,
apart from the case in the Court of Appeal in New Zealand, where it H
failed on all counts.

In those cases in which the inherent jurisdiction is exercised, it
appears to me that any remuneration allowed ought to come out of
income, if it be remuneration for running the affairs of the trust pure and
simple—general remuneration. This, I have been informed by Chief
Master Ball, was the invariable practice in those cases decided by the
former Chancery judges whom he has served, and it accords with my

The Weekly Law Reports, November 3, 1978

679

3 W.L.R.   In re Duke of Norfolk's Settlement (Ch.D.)   Walton J.

A   own impressions. This would seem only logical. But in those cases such as the present where the special services rendered by the trustees have been, in substance, the development of the capital assets of their trust, it would be appropriate that any special remuneration should be paid out of capital.

B   The final reflection I would make is that it would be extremely odd if there were any such general inherent jurisdiction to raise the remuneration of trustees save in the most exceptional case, having regard to the oft repeated view of equity, that the office of a trustee is prima facie an unremunerated one, however diligent he may be in the performance of his duties. The fact that he is entitled to some benefit under the provisions of the trust instrument cannot alter the position in any way. Nor can the fact that a particular trustee has turned the

C   office of trustee into a business for himself, and, considered as a business, he has made a bad bargain. So has every unremunerated trustee. The jurisdiction is a wholly special one, to be confined to the special cases I have already mentioned.

Declaration accordingly.

D   Solicitors: *Witham Weld & Co.; Witham Weld & Co.; Fisher, Dowson & Wasbrough; Fisher, Dowson & Wasbrough.*

T. C. C. B.

E

[COURT OF APPEAL]

SECRETARY OF STATE FOR EMPLOYMENT *v.*
GLOBE ELASTIC THREAD CO. LTD.

F   1978   July 17, 18   Lord Denning M.R., Eveleigh L.J. and
Sir David Cairns

Employment—Redundancy—Rebate payment—Estoppel—Employee transferred to new employment—Dismissal for redundancy— New employers estopped from contending break in continuity of employment—Industrial tribunal finding that employers bound to make redundancy payment calculated on period
G   *covering old and new employment—Whether Secretary of State liable to make rebate calculated on total award— Redundancy Payments Act 1965 (c. 62), s. 30 (1)*[1]

From 1948 to 1970 an employee worked for H Ltd. In 1970 H Ltd. told him that there was no more work for him with them but that he could transfer to an associated company (" the employers "). The employee agreed to the transfer after
H   being given assurances both by H Ltd. and by the employers that he would not lose any of his accrued service benefits and that his employment would be treated as continuous since 1948. In 1975 the employers made him redundant and paid him a redundancy payment based only on his five years' work with them. He applied to an industrial tribunal for an additional payment calculated on the basis of continuous service since 1948. The tribunal found that although in law

[1] Redundancy Payments Act 1965, s. 30 (1): see post, p. 683E.

Employment Secretary v. Globe Elastic Ltd. (C.A.)   [1978]

his service was not continuous within the provisions of the   A
Redundancy Payments Act 1965 the employers were estopped
from denying the continuity of service by reason of the
assurances given to him in 1970 and that they were accordingly
liable under the Act of 1965 to make an additional payment.

The employers then applied under section 34 (2) of the
Act to another industrial tribunal for a declaration that they
were entitled under section 30 (1) to a rebate payable by the
Secretary of State for Employment out of the redundancy   B
fund on the full redundancy payment for which they had
been found liable. The tribunal held that the employers were
entitled to the rebate; and the Employment Appeal Tribunal
dismissed the Secretary of State's appeal.

On appeal by the Secretary of State:—

Held, dismissing the appeal, that the employee's claim
based on estoppel for a redundancy payment calculated on a
period of continuous employment since 1948 was a claim made   C
under the Redundancy Payments Act 1965; that the industrial
tribunal had jurisdiction to make the order under the Act
and the payment made by the employers in pursuance of
that order was a payment made under Part I of the Act and,
therefore, under section 30 (1), the Secretary of State was liable
to make a rebate on the full amount notwithstanding he was
not a party to the representation to the employee that his
employment would be treated as continuous with that of his   D
previous employment.

Evenden v. *Guildford City Association Football Club Ltd.*
[1975] Q.B. 917, C.A. applied.

Per Sir David Cairns. But for the *Evenden* decision, I
should have thought that if an employer has bound himself
by agreement to pay what he calls a redundancy payment
in excess of that for which the Act provides, he could not
cast liability for the excess on the redundancy fund; and the   E
same would apply if the employer was estopped against the
employee from contending that his payments were to be limited
to those prescribed by the Act: the agreement or estoppel
is res inter alios acta so far as the Secretary of State is
concerned (post, pp. 685H—686A).

Decision of the Employment Appeal Tribunal [1978] Q.B.
86; [1977] 3 W.L.R. 293; [1978] I.C.R. 473; [1978] 1 All E.R.
987 affirmed.   F

The following cases are referred to in the judgments:

Appleyard v. *Worthshire Ltd.* (unreported), May 7, 1975.
Crest Hotels Ltd. v. *Secretary of State for Employment* (1971) 6 I.T.R.
142.
Evenden v. *Guildford City Association Football Club Ltd.* [1975] Q.B. 917;
[1975] 3 W.L.R. 251; [1975] I.C.R. 367; [1975] 3 All E.R. 269, C.A.   G
Secretary of State for Employment v. *Atkins Auto Laundries Ltd.* [1972]
1 W.L.R. 507; [1972] I.C.R. 76; [1972] 1 All E.R. 987, N.I.R.C.
Robertshaw v. *Secretary of State for Employment* (unreported), July 29,
1974.

No additional cases were cited in argument.
     H

APPEAL from Employment Appeal Tribunal.

By an originating application to an industrial tribunal in London the
employers, Globe Elastic Thread Co. Ltd., Tiverton, Devon, asked for
declarations against the Secretary of State for Employment (1) that they
were entitled to a rebate under section 30 (1) of the Redundancy Payments
Act 1965, calculated by reference to the number of years of employment
in respect of which they had been found liable to make a redundancy

A   payment to Tadeusz Wijaszko, an employee, whose application for a redundancy payment was heard by an industrial tribunal sitting at Exeter on January 13, 1976; and (2) an order that the Secretary of State should pay such rebate (less any sum already paid by him in purported satisfaction of the rebate due) to the employers. The Secretary of State denied that the employers were entitled to payment of rebate on the further payment awarded by the tribunal at Exeter, on the ground, inter

B   alia, that the finding of the tribunal at Exeter was based on representations made to the employee which estopped the employers from denying continuity of employment; but that the Secretary of State was not a party to those representations and his liability under section 30 of the Act of 1965 was not affected thereby.

     The industrial tribunal on May 11, 1976, decided that the employers

C   were entitled to recover a rebate of 50 per cent. in respect of a redundancy payment of £1,086·98 for which they had been held liable to the employee; and the Employment Appeal Tribunal (Kilner Brown J. presiding) [1978] Q.B. 86, on April 25, 1977, affirmed that decision, holding that the Secretary of State for Employment had a duty under section 30 (1) (a) of the Act of 1965 to make a rebate whenever liability was established aginst an employer; that the employers were estopped from

D   denying that there was a break of continuity of employment because of assurances given to the employee and were therefore liable to make a redundancy payment calculated on the basis of the total period of employment; and that accordingly, since the liability of the Secretary of State was linked with that of the employers, he was bound to make a rebate to the employers irrespective of how the liability was incurred by them.

E   The Secretary of State appealed on the grounds that (1) the Employment Appeal Tribunal erred in law in holding that the employers were liable to pay Mr. Wijaszko a redundancy payment calculated on the basis of 20 years' continuous service when in fact (as the industrial tribunal expressly found) Mr. Wijaszko had been continuously employed for the purposes of the Act by the employers for a period of only five years; (2) it erred in law in holding that the payment in respect of 20 years'

F   continuous service was a redundancy payment under Part I of the Redundancy Payments Act 1965: the Act made no provision for such a payment; (3) it erred in law in holding that an employer was entitled to recover from the Secretary of State under section 30 (1) (a) of the Redundancy Payments Act 1965 50 per cent. of any payment which the employer was obliged to make to an employee, regardless of the fact that the

G   employers' liability arose from and depended upon a voluntary promise on the part of the employers and not the provisions of Part I of the Act; (4) it erred in law in holding that a finding that an employer was liable to make a redundancy payment to the employee was conclusive of the question of whether that employer was entitled to a rebate of 50 per cent. of the amount of the payment from the Secretary of State; (5) it erred in law in failing to give effect to, inter alia, the following principles of

H   estoppel: (a) an estoppel was binding only upon the party and the privies of the party who by words or conduct or both had made representations the effect of which he might not challenge; (b) an estoppel had no effect on the reality of the circumstances nor did it confer any title to the subject matter of the estoppel; (c) the jurisdiction of a tribunal could not be enlarged by an estoppel; (6) the Employment Appeal Tribunal failed to give effect to the provisions of 34 (2) (b) of the Act; and (7) if, contrary to the Secretary of State's contention, *Evenden* v. *Guildford City Associa-*

tion Football Club Ltd. [1975] Q.B. 917 was authority in support of the   A
employers' claim, the decision was wrong and/or ought not to be followed
in the present case.

T. H. *Bingham Q.C.* and *Peter Scott Q.C.* for the Secretary of State.
Alexander Irvine Q.C. and *Christopher Carr* for the employers.

LORD DENNING M.R.   Mr. Wijaszko (I expect he came from Poland   B
originally) started working as long ago as 1948 with an old-established
firm in Tiverton called John Heathcoat Ltd.   In 1962 a new factory was
established on the other side of the road.   Heathcoat Ltd. had an interest
in it.   They had 50 per cent. of the shares in the new company which was
running it.   An American company held the other 50 per cent.   The new
company was called Globe Elastic Thread Co. Ltd.   The new company   C
carried on its business on the other side of the road.   Heathcoat Ltd.
carried on as before.   Mr. Wijaszko was still employed by Heathcoat.
   In 1970, owing to the circumstances then prevailing, Heathcoat
suggested to Mr. Wijaszko that he should join Globe Elastic Thread Co.
Ltd.   He was quite willing to do that, as the new company was only across
the road and was so closely associated with Heathcoat.   The manager
saw Mr. Wijaszko and assured him that he would not lose any benefits   D
that he had acquired as a result of his service with Heathcoat.   So, in
1970, after 22 years with Heathcoat, Mr. Wijaszko was transferred to the
Globe Elastic Thread Co. Ltd.   From 1970 onwards he worked with the
Globe Elastic Thread Co. Ltd. for the next five years.
   Then in October 1975 he was given four weeks' notice terminating
his employment.   Thereupon he claimed redundancy payment.   He said   E
that he was dismissed by reason of redundancy because they did not need
him any more.   Globe Elastic agreed that he was entitled to redundancy
payment.   The only question was how much.   He claimed that he ought
to have redundancy payment for the whole of his service from 1948 until
1975—that is, 27 years.   (It had to be calculated on 20 years because
that is the maximum).   If he obtained redundancy payment for the 27
years, he would be entitled to £1,449·30.   But his employers, the Globe   F
Elastic Thread Co. Ltd., said that he was not entitled to redundancy
payment for 27 years.   They said that he was only entitled to it for the
five years that he had been with them.   They said that he was entitled
to only £362·32.   So they only paid him £362·32; whereupon he said that
there was a further sum due to him of £1,086·98.
   That matter went before an industrial tribunal at Exeter between Mr.   G
Wijaszko on the one side and the Globe Elastic Thread Co. Ltd. on the
other.   The industrial tribunal held that, by reason of the assurance that
he had been given on the change-over (that he would not lose any benefits)
he was to be treated as if his employment had been continuous with the
Globe Elastic Thread Co. Ltd. for the whole period of 27 years: and
the tribunal awarded him the extra sum of £1,086·98.
   In coming to that conclusion they were influenced by a decision of   H
this court in *Evenden* v. *Guildford City Association Football Club Ltd.*
[1975] Q.B. 917.   In that case it was held by this court that on a
change-over from one closely-related concern to another, if the man is told
that he will not lose any benefits by reason of the change-over—and
sometimes it goes further and the employee is told that his employment
will be treated as continuous—then the new employer cannot go back on
his word.   He has to pay redundancy payment for the full period as if

The Weekly Law Reports, November 3, 1978

683

3 W.L.R.   Employment Secretary v. Globe Elastic Ltd. (C.A.)   Lord Denning M.R.

A the employment had been continuous for the whole time. That is the substance of the *Evenden* case. That was why the industrial tribunal held that Mr. Wijaszko was entitled to the extra £1,086.

The company then turned to the Secretary of State. There are provisions in the Redundancy Payments Act 1965 which enable an employer who has made a redundancy payment to recover a proportion of the amount paid from the Secretary of State. It is called " a rebate." It

B has been varied from time to time. At one time it was 50 per cent. It is not quite so much now: it is only about 40 per cent. There it is. The employer is entitled to a rebate from the Secretary of State.

When the Globe Elastic Thread Co. Ltd. claimed a rebate for the sum that they had paid to Mr. Wijaszko, the Secretary of State objected. He said that he was not concerned with the *Evenden* case. It was the

C company's own doing that they gave the assurance to Mr. Wijaszko. Apart from that assurance, the only amount that Globe Elastic were liable to pay was for the period of five years during which Mr. Wijaszko had been with them and he was not entitled to anything else. The Secretary of State said that the rebate was limited to the statutory liability of Globe Elastic and not to their liability under the *Evenden* case. So the rebate should only have been on the £362·32 for the five years' service with the

D Globe Elastic Thread Co. Ltd.

That is the problem in this case. Who is right? Are the employers entitled to the full amount of rebate, or are they entitled to a rebate only in respect of a redundancy payment for five years' service?

It all turns on the provisions of the Redundancy Payments Act 1965. Section 30 says:

E   " (1) Subject to the provisions of this section, the Minister shall make a payment . . . out of the fund to any employer who—(*a*) is liable under Part I of this Act to pay, and has paid, a redundancy payment to an employee . . . (3) The amount of any rebate shall (subject to subjection (6) of this section) be calculated in accordance with Schedule 5 to this Act."

F Schedule 5 sets out how the amount of redundancy payment is to be calculated. It refers back again to Schedule 1 which deals with the period during which the employee has been " continuously employed." Section 34 (2) (*a*) says that when a claim is made for a rebate any question as to the liability of the employer to pay the employee's payment is to be referred to the industrial tribunal.

G   I may add that if an employer becomes insolvent or goes into liquidation, there is, so to speak, a guarantee given by the Minister that he will pay to the employee whatever should have been paid by the employer —that is section 32.

I need not go through all those sections now. It seems to me that the fundamental question is whether the employers were " liable under the Act " to pay redundancy payment calculated on the full 27 years or

H whether they were only liable to pay it on the last five years. It seems to me that that depends almost entirely upon the effect of the decision in the *Evenden* case. It has been suggested that that case was wrongly decided: that the only liability *under the Act* was to pay redundancy payment calculated on the last short period of years: and that any additional liability (based on a promise that they should treat his employment as continuous) was not a liability under the Act: but a liability on a promise for which he should have sued in the county court.

Lord Denning M.R.   Employment Secretary v. Globe Elastic Ltd. (C.A.)   [1978]

I can understand that suggestion; but I cannot accept it. The effect A of *Evenden* is that when an assurance or representation of that kind is given, the liability of the employer is a liability under the Redundancy Payments Act 1965. That is the only basis on which the tribunal could and did give the award.

Nor do I accept the suggestion that *Evenden* was wrongly decided. There is much to be said in its favour. It does no injustice whatever to the redundancy fund, because—(to take this very case)—if Mr. B Wijaszko had been regarded as being employed separately by two concerns, he would have been entitled from Heathcoat to redundancy payment for the first 22 years, and afterwards from Globe Elastic for the further five years. So the fund would have been liable in respect of the total period.

Not only does it do no injustice: but it might actually operate to C the benefit of the redundancy fund. For instance, if a man was 20 years with a first employer, and then went off to another employer (on an assurance of continuity) for 18 months, and then was dismissed, the fund would benefit. The man would be out of time to claim redundancy for the first 20 years and he would not have served long enough to claim it for the second period.

We were referred by Mr. Bingham to other cases, starting with *Crest* D *Hotels Ltd.* v. *Secretary of State for Employment* (1971) 6 I.T.R. 142, going on to *Secretary of State for Employment* v. *Atkins Auto Laundries Ltd.* [1971] 1 W.L.R. 507, 509, and two unreported cases, one of Miss Robertshaw on July 29, 1974 (*Robertshaw* v. *Secretary of State for Employment*, Leeds Industrial Tribunal) and the other of Mr. Appleyard on May 7, 1975 (*Appleyard* v. *Worthshire Ltd.*, Anlaby Industrial Tribunal). In E those cases it was pointed out very cogently that it would not be right in many cases for the Minister to be bound by the decisions of the industrial tribunal (as between the employee and the employer) because there might be private arrangements between them with regard to redundancy payments which could be used most unjustly against the redundancy fund. In such cases the Secretary of State ought to be able to reopen the matter and ought not to be bound by any such arrangements. I accept F those observations: but I do not think they should be applied to "continuity cases." The industrial tribunal has, and should have, jurisdiction to award the full sum. On this subject, I would read a few words of Brightman J. in the *Evenden* case [1975] Q.B. 917, 928. He said:

> "Very often where a business changes hands, the new employer is at pains to preserve the existing work force. So he assures them, G and they agree, that the continuity of their employment will not be affected by the change. That is a proper assurance to be given: an assurance that the work people can properly accept; an assurance which will in all ordinary circumstances lead to a valid agreement; and in my view an assurance that the courts should enforce when applying industrial legislation."

H

This is just this sort of assurance which was upheld in the *Evenden* case in which the employers were held liable for the full period of employment which they had promised to treat as continuous. It was certainly a just decision: a decision giving jurisdiction to the industrial tribunal. Having been so decided, it seems to me that it carries the day here. When an employer has made an agreement of that kind and has given an assurance in the interests of good industrial relations and has paid

The Weekly Law Reports, November 3, 1978

685

3 W.L.R.   Employment Secretary v. Globe Elastic Ltd. (C.A.)   Lord Denning M.R.

A redundancy payment as a result of it, it seems to me only right, viewing the statutory provisions broadly and sensibly as they should be viewed, that the employer should be able to get the appropriate sum (I believe it is about 40 per cent. now) by way of rebate from the Minister. I think the decision below was right, and I would dismiss the appeal.

B EVELEIGH L.J. I have found this case extremely difficult and would not wish to be thought that I regard the Minister as equivalent to an insurance company which has issued a liability policy. I can envisage cases where an employer, because of the way the case turns out, is held liable by an industrial tribunal when, if the matter had been properly presented, he would not have been held liable. There are many cases in which I could conceive that a decision of the industrial tribunal would C be arrived at on an unrealistic basis, and I would not wish anything I say to lead to the conclusion that the Minister will always be bound thereby.

On the other hand, it may well be that the Minister will be bound in many cases which have been tried by an industrial tribunal where he could have validly contended before such a decision was arrived at that he was not liable. Such are the complications which one can envisage D arising from this very difficult Redundancy Payments Act 1965.

However, in the present case, I have come to the conclusion that Evenden v. Guildford City Association Football Club Ltd. [1975] Q.B. 917 has decided that that which the employer had to pay was a redundancy payment under the Act. If, in the Evenden case the Minister had been called upon to pay the rebate, in my view he would have had to E do so, for a redundancy payment under the Act is that to which section 30 applies. Section 30 (1) reads:

" Subject to the provisions of this section, the Minister shall make a payment . . . out of the fund to any employer who—(a) is liable under Part I of this Act to pay, and has paid, a redundancy payment to an employee."

F I also think that the fact that it is by virtue of Evenden a redundancy payment under the Act that section 32 of the Act comes into play, or by virtue of section 36 (6) of the Act a redundancy payment would be an employer's payment under the Act. That being so, I can see no difference between the position of Evenden and the position of the employee in this case. The fact that the matter has not been litigated between master and servant in this case—where the facts are governed strictly by G Evenden—makes no difference.

I therefore agree with the judgment of Lord Denning M.R. that this appeal should be dismissed.

SIR DAVID CAIRNS. The effect of the Redundancy Payments Act 1965 is that the Secretary of State is liable to make payments of rebate H only when payments are made by an employer which are redundancy payments made in accordance with the provisions of the Act. If an employer has bound himself by agreement to make what he calls a redundancy payment in excess of that for which the Act provides, I should, apart from the decision in the Evenden case, be of the opinion that he cannot cast liability for the excess upon the redundancy fund. The same would apply if the employer is estopped against the employee from contending that his payments are to be limited to those prescribed by

the Act. The agreement or estoppel is res inter alios acta so far as the   A
Secretary of State is concerned.

I can see nothing in the provision for a presumption as to continuity
to prevent the Secretary of State from proving that the employment was
not in fact continuous. It was found necessary to enact expressly in
section 34 (3) that the presumption under section 9 (2) is to apply as
between the employer and the Secretary of State, but the presumption
applies there, as it does between employer and employee, subject to   B
evidence to the contrary.

It is true that in this case, if the Secretary of State were held liable
for the rebate, the fund would be no worse off than if the assurance given
on behalf of the employers had never been given and the employee had
claimed redundancy payment from his first employer as well as from
his latest employer. But if the Secretary of State is bound by the   C
employers' agreement or estoppel, I cannot see any reason in principle why
he should not be bound in cases where there would be a detriment
to the fund. For example, if the employee had had a series of employments, each for less than two years, and the last employer had agreed
to treat all those employments together with the employment by himself
as one continuous employment. Or, to take another case, if a man had
been dismissed from his earlier employment for reasons unconnected   D
with redundancy and the new employer had agreed to treat the two
employments as continuous.

The decision in *Evenden's* case [1975] Q.B. 917 does, however,
involve that the employee's claim against the employer is to be regarded
as a claim for a redundancy payment, a redundancy payment which the
employer was liable under Part I of the Act to pay, because it is only   E
on that basis that it could be held—as it was held by this court in that
case—to be within the jurisdiction of the industrial tribunal. Jurisdiction
cannot be conferred by agreement or estoppel. If then the employers'
payment is to be treated as a redundancy payment which the employers
were liable to pay under Part I of the Act and did pay, it follows from
section 30 (1) of the Act that the employers are entitled to the rebate.

I accordingly agree that the appeal should be dismissed but with the   F
same reluctance as the Employment Appeal Tribunal expressed about their
decision.

Appeal dismissed.
No order for costs.
Leave to appeal.

Solicitors: *Treasury Solicitor; Baker & McKenzie.*   G

M. M. H.

H

A

[QUEEN'S BENCH DIVISION: LIVERPOOL]

PATON *v.* BRITISH PREGNANCY ADVISORY SERVICE
TRUSTEES AND ANOTHER

B   1978   May 17, 24   Sir George Baker P.

Husband and Wife—Injunction—Injunction against abortion—
Paternal rights—Husband seeking to restrain wife from having
abortion—Whether husband having statutory or other right to
prevent abortion—Abortion Act 1967 (c. 87), s. 1

C
The wife, the second defendant, obtained a medical
certificate entitling her to a lawful abortion within the terms
of the Abortion Act 1967. On an application by the husband,
the plaintiff, seeking an injunction to restrain the wife and the
first defendants, a charitable organisation, from causing or
permitting an abortion to be carried out upon the wife without
the husband's consent: —

Held, that, since an unborn child had no rights of its own
and a father had no rights at common law over his illegitimate
D
child, the husband's right to apply for the injunction had to be
on the basis that he had the status of husband; that the courts
had never exercised jurisdiction to control personal relationships
in marriage and, in the absence of the right to be consulted
under the Abortion Act 1967, the husband had no rights
enforceable in law or in equity to prevent his wife from having
an abortion or to stop the doctors carrying out the abortion,
which was lawful under the Act of 1967.

E
Per curiam. It would be quite impossible for the courts
to supervise the operation of the Abortion Act 1967. The
great social responsibility is firmly placed by law upon the
shoulders of the medical profession (post, p. 691D).

The following cases are referred to in the judgment:

Elliot v. *Joicey* [1935] A.C. 209, H.L.(E.).
Forster v. *Forster* (1790) 1 Hag.Con. 144.
F
Gouriet v. *Union of Post Office Workers* [1978] A.C. 435; [1977] 3
W.L.R. 300; [1977] 3 All E.R. 70, H.L.(E.).
Jones v. *Smith* (1973) 278 So.Rep. 339.
Montgomery v. *Montgomery* [1965] P. 46; [1964] 2 W.L.R. 1036;
[1964] 2 All E.R. 22.
North London Railway Co. v. *Great Northern Railway Co.* (1883) 11
Q.B.D. 30, C.A.
G
Planned Parenthood of Central Missouri v. *Danforth A.G.* (1976)
S.Ct. 2831.
Reg. v. *Smith (John)* [1973] 1 W.L.R. 1510; [1974] 1 All E.R. 376, C.A.
Roe v. *Wade* (1973) 93 S.Ct. 705.
White v. *Yup* (1969) 458 P. 2d 617.

The following additional cases were cited in argument:

H
Bravery v. *Bravery* [1954] 1 W.L.R. 1169; [1954] 3 All E.R. 59, C.A.
D. (A Minor) (Wardship: Sterilisation), In re [1976] Fam. 185; [1976] 2
W.L.R. 279; [1976] 1 All E.R. 326.
Davies v. *Gaumont British Picture Corporation* (1939) 83 S.T. 185.
Davis v. *Johnson* [1978] 2 W.L.R. 553; [1978] 1 All E.R. 1132,
H.L.(E.).

[Reported by MISS MARILYN MORNINGTON, Barrister-at-Law]

Doe v. *Bolton* (1973) 93 S.Ct. 739.   A
Rex v. *Bourne* [1939] 1 K.B. 687; [1938] 3 All E.R. 615, C.C.A.
Walker v. *Great Northern Railway Co. of Ireland* (1891) 28 L.R.Ir. 69.

APPLICATION

The plaintiff, William Paton, was the husband of the second
defendant, Joan Mary Paton. On May 8, 1978, the wife's general
practitioner confirmed that she was pregnant. The wife thereafter applied B
for and obtained the necessary medical certificate entitling her to an
abortion within the terms of the Abortion Act 1967. On May 16, 1978,
the wife left the matrimonial home.

On May 17, 1978, the husband applied for an injunction to restrain
the first defendants, the trustees of the British Pregnancy Advisory
Service, and the wife from causing or permitting an abortion to be   C
carried out on the wife. Sir George Baker P. adjourned the case for
one week to May 24, 1978, to enable all the parties to be represented.
Also on May 17, the wife filed her petition for divorce.

The husband originally put his case on the basis that the wife had
no proper legal grounds for seeking the termination of her pregnancy
and that she was being spiteful, vindictive and utterly unreasonable in
so doing. At the resumed hearing on May 24, it was accepted by all   D
the parties that the provisions of the Abortion Act 1967 had been
correctly complied with. The husband contended that he had the right
to have a say in the destiny of the child he had conceived.

Andrew Rankin Q.C. and *S. J. Bedford* for the husband.
W. E. Denny Q.C. and *R. E. Rhodes* for the first defendant trustees.   E
T. F. Hatton for the wife.

SIR GEORGE BAKER P. By a specially endorsed writ the plaintiff,
who is the husband of the second defendant, seeks an injunction in effect
to restrain the first defendants, a charitable organisation, and particularly
his wife, the second defendant, from causing or permitting an abortion to   F
be carried out upon his wife without his consent.

Such action, of course, arouses great emotions, and vigorous opposing
views as was recently pointed out in 1972 in the Supreme Court of the
United States by Blackmun J. in *Roe* v. *Wade* (1973) 93 S.Ct. 705, 708–709.
In the discussion of human affairs and especially of abortion, controversy
can rage over the moral rights, duties, interests, standards and religious
views of the parties. Moral values are in issue. I am, in fact, con-   G
cerned with none of these matters. I am concerned, and concerned only,
with the law of England as it applies to this claim. My task is to apply
the law free of emotion or predilection.

Nobody suggests that there has ever been such a claim litigated
before the courts in this country. Indeed, the only case of which I have
ever heard was in Ontario. It was unreported because the husband's   H
claim for an injunction was never tried.

In considering the law the first and basic principle is that there must
be a legal right enforceable in law or in equity before the applicant can
obtain an injunction from the court to restrain an infringement of that
right. That has long been the law.

The leading case is *North London Railway Co.* v. *Great Northern
Railway Co.* (1883) 11 Q.B.D. 30. Mr. Rankin has helpfully read much

The Weekly Law Reports, November 3, 1978

689

3 W.L.R.   Paton v. B.P.A.S. Trustees (Q.B.D.)   Sir George Baker P.

A of the judgment of Cotton L.J. I will confine myself to the well known passage, where Cotton L.J. said, at p. 40:

"In my opinion the sole intention of the section" (that is section 25 (8) of the Judicature Act 1873) "is this: that where there is a legal right which was, independently of the Act, capable of being enforced either at law or in equity, then, whatever may have been the previous practice, the High Court may interfere by injunction in protection of that right."

B

In *Montgomery* v. *Montgomery* [1965] P. 46, a well known case in family law, Ormrod J., having cited the passage from the judgment of Cotton L.J., and reviewed the various authorities, concluded that the court could only grant an injunction to support a legal right, and since C the petitioner wife had no proprietary interest in the flat in which the parties were living, the court had no jurisdiction to make a mandatory order to exclude the husband from the flat. The words "husband and wife" were used, although the parties were no longer joined in matrimony, having been divorced.

The law relating to injunctions has been considered recently in the House of Lords, in *Gouriet* v. *Union of Post Office Workers* [1978] A.C. D 435. Many passages from their Lordships' speeches have been cited. I do not propose to go through them because it is now as clear as possible, that there must be, first, a legal right in an individual to found an injunction and second that the enforcement of the criminal law is a matter for the authorities and for the Attorney-General. As Mr. Rankin concedes, any process for the enforcement of the criminal law E in a civil suit must be used with great caution, if at all. The private individual may have the right only if his right is greater than the public right, that is to say, that he would suffer personally and more than the general public unless he could restrain this offence; that proposition is not accepted by Mr. Denny or by Mr. Hatton for the defendants, and in any event it is not now suggested that the proposed abortion upon Mrs. F Paton will be other than lawful. So, it is not necessary for me to decide that question or to consider *Gouriet* further.

The first question is whether this plaintiff has a right at all. The foetus cannot, in English law, in my view, have a right of its own at least until it is born and has a separate existence from its mother. That permeates the whole of the civil law of this country (I except the criminal law, which is now irrelevant), and is, indeed, the basis of the G decisions in those countries where law is founded on the common law, that is to say, in America, Canada, Australia and, I have no doubt, in others.

For a long time there was great controversy whether after birth a child could have a right of action in respect of pre-natal injury. The Law Commission considered that and produced a Working Paper H No. 47 in 1973, followed by a Final Report (Law Commission Report, No. 60 (Cmnd. 5709)), but it was universally accepted, and has since been accepted, that in order to have a right the foetus must be born and be a child. There was only one known possible exception which is referred to in the Working Paper at p. 3, an American case, *White* v. *Yup* (1969) 458 P. 2d 617—where a wrongful "death" of an 8-month-old viable foetus, stillborn as a consequence of injury, led an American court to allow a cause of action, but there can be no doubt, in my view, that in England and Wales the foetus has no right of action, A no right at all, until birth. The succession cases have been mentioned. There is no difference. From conception the child may have succession rights by what has been called a " fictional construction " but the child must be subsequently born alive: see *per* Lord Russell of Killowen in *Elliot* v. *Joicey* [1935] A.C. 209, 233.

The father's case must therefore depend upon a right which he has B himself. I would say a word about the illegitimate, usually called the putative, but I prefer myself to refer to the illegitimate father. Although American decisions to which I have been referred concern illegitimate fathers, and statutory provisions about them, it seems to me that in this country the illegitimate father can have no rights whatsoever except those given to him by statute. That was clearly the common law. One provision which makes an inroad into this is section 14 of the Guardian- C ship of Minors Act 1971 section 9 (1) and some other sections of that Act which applies to illegitimate children, giving the illegitimate father or mother the right to apply for the custody of or access to an illegitimate child. But the equality of parental rights provision in section 1 (1) of the Guardianship Act 1973 expressly does not apply in relation to a minor who is illegitimate: see section 1 (7). D

So this plaintiff must, in my opinion, bring his case, if he can, squarely within the framework of the fact that he is a husband. It is, of course, very common for spouses to seek injunctions for personal protection in the matrimonial courts during the pendency of or, indeed, after divorce actions, but the basic reason for the non-molestation injunction often granted in the family courts is to protect the other spouse or the living children, and to ensure that no undue pressure is E put upon one or other of the spouses during the pendency of the case and during the breaking-up of the marriage.

There was, of course, the action for restitution of conjugal rights, a proceeding which always belied its name and was abolished in 1970. It arose because in ecclesiastical law the parties could not end the consortium by agreement. In a sense the action for restitution was F something of a fiction. The court ordered the spouse to return to cohabitation. If the spouse did not return then that spouse was held to be in desertion. No more could happen. The court could not compel matrimonial intercourse: see *Forster* v. *Forster* (1790) 1 Hag.Con. 144. So matrimonial courts have never attempted the enforcement of matrimonial obligations by injunction. G

The law is that the court cannot and would not seek to enforce or restrain by injunction matrimonial obligations, if they be obligations, such as sexual intercourse or contraception (a non-molestation injunction given during the pendency of divorce proceedings could, of course, cover attempted intercourse). No court would ever grant an injunction to stop sterilisation or vasectomy. Personal family relationships in marriage cannot be enforced by the order of a court. An injunction in such H circumstances was described by Judge Mager in *Jones* v. *Smith* (1973) 278 So.Rep. 339 in the District Court of Appeal of Florida as " ludicrous."

I ask the question, " If an injunction were ordered, what could be the remedy?" and I do not think I need say any more than that no judge could even consider sending a husband or wife to prison for breaking such an order. That, of itself, seems to me to cover the

The Weekly Law Reports, November 3, 1978

691

3 W.L.R.   Paton v. B.P.A.S. Trustees (Q.B.D.)   Sir George Baker P.

A application here; this husband cannot by law stop his wife by injunction from having what is now accepted to be a lawful abortion within the terms of the Abortion Act 1967.

The case which was first put forward to me a week ago, and indeed is to be found in the writ, is that the wife had no proper legal grounds for seeking a termination of her pregnancy and that, indeed, not to mince words, she was being spiteful, vindictive and utterly unreasonable in
B seeking so to do. It now appears I need not go into the evidence in the affidavits because it is accepted and common ground that the provisions of the Act have been complied with, the necessary certificate has been given by two doctors and everything is lawfully set for the abortion.

The case put to me finally by Mr. Rankin (to whom I am most indebted
C for having set out very clearly and logically what the law is) is that while he cannot say here that there is any suggestion of a criminal abortion nevertheless if doctors did not hold their views, or come to their conclusions, in good faith which would be an issue triable by a jury (see *Reg.* v. *Smith (John)* [1973] 1 W.L.R. 1510) then this plaintiff might recover an injunction. That is not accepted by Mr. Denny. It is
D unnecessary for me to decide that academic question because it does not arise in this case. My own view is that it would be quite impossible for the courts in any event to supervise the operation of the Abortion Act 1967. The great social responsibility is firmly placed by the law upon the shoulders of the medical profession: see *per* Scarman L.J. in *Reg.* v. *Smith (John)* [1973] 1 W.L.R. 1510, 1512.

I will look at the Abortion Act 1967 very briefly. It provides by
E section 1:

"(1) . . . a person shall not be guilty of an offence under the law relating to abortion when a pregnancy is terminated by a registered medical practitioner if two registered medical practitioners are of the opinion, formed in good faith—(a) that the continuance of the
F pregnancy would involve risk . . . of injury to the physical or mental health of the pregnant woman. . . . (2) In determining whether the continuance of a pregnancy would involve such risk of injury to health as is mentioned in paragraph (a) of subsection (1) of this section, accounts may be taken of the pregnant woman's actual or reasonably foreseeable environment."

G That does not now arise in this case. The two doctors have given a certificate. It is not and cannot be suggested that the certificate was given in other than good faith and it seems to me that there is the end of the matter in English law. The Abortion Act 1967 gives no right to a father to be consulted in respect of a termination of a pregnancy. True, it gives no right to the mother either, but obviously the mother is
H going to be right at the heart of the matter consulting with the doctors if they are to arrive at a decision in good faith, unless, of course, she is mentally incapacitated or physically incapacitated (unable to make any decision or give any help) as, for example, in consequence of an accident. The husband, therefore, in my view, has no legal right enforceable in law or in equity to stop his wife having this abortion or to stop the doctors from carrying out the abortion.

Mr. Rankin made one point about a letter, which has now been   A
produced to the court, dated May 22, 1978, from Dr. Macrone, the family
doctor. I need only point out that Dr. Macrone says in his letter that
he had no objection to her seeking a termination of the pregnancy
whereas her affidavit seems to put it a little higher, in paragraph 8,
where she says she had the support of Dr. Macrone. But really that is
a matter of terminology. I do not think there is anything in the point
and I am sure Mr. Rankin was simply putting it forward as something   B
the court ought to look at, without any conviction that there was any
merit in the distinction.

This certificate is clear, and not only would it be a bold and brave
judge (I think Mr. Rankin used that expression) who would seek to
interfere with the discretion of doctors acting under the Abortion Act
1967, but I think he would really be a foolish judge who would try to   C
do any such thing, unless, possibly, where there is clear bad faith and an
obvious attempt to perpetrate a criminal offence. Even then, of
course, the question is whether that is a matter which should be left to
the Director of Public Prosecutions and the Attorney-General. I say
no more for I have stated my view of the law of England.

Very helpfully I have been referred to American authorities. The   D
U.S. Supreme Court has reached the same conclusion: that a husband,
or an illegitimate father, has no right to stop his wife, or the woman
who is pregnant by him, from having a legal abortion.

In *Planned Parenthood of Central Missouri* v. *Danforth A.G.* (1976)
96 S.Ct. 2831, the Supreme Court by a majority held, at p. 2841 *per*
Blackmun J., that the State of Missouri
                                                                        E
  " may not constitutionally require the consent of the spouse, as is
  specified under paragraph 3 (3) of the Missouri Act, as a condition
  for abortion during the first 12 weeks of pregnancy . . . Clearly,
  since the state cannot regulate or proscribe abortion during the first
  stage, when the physician and his patient make that decision, the
  state cannot delegate authority to any particular person, even the
  spouse, to prevent abortion during that same period."   F

A spousal consent provision in an English Act could not of course
be challenged as unconstitutional but there is no such provision in the
Abortion Act 1967 or in the Abortion Regulations 1968 (S.I. 1968 No.
390) to which a challenge of ultra vires could be made. There is no
provision even for consultation with the spouse and regulation 5
prohibits disclosure except in specified instances, of which disclosure to   G
the spouse is not one.

It is interesting to note that the Missouri spousal consent provision
would have required the husband's consent even if he was not the father.

Counsel have been unable to discover any extant decision in those
countries whose laws derive from the common law that the consent
of the husband is required before an otherwise legal abortion can be   H
performed on the wife. Mr. Rankin's researches show that in Roman
law, centuries ago, the father's consent was required otherwise abortion
was a crime, but today the only way he can put the case is that the
husband has a right to have a say in the destiny of the child he has
conceived. The law of England gives him no such right; the Abortion
Act 1967 contains no such provision. It follows, therefore, that in my

A opinion this claim for an injunction is completely misconceived and must be dismissed.

Order accordingly.

Solicitors: *Grey Lloyd & Co., Connahs Quay, Clwyd; Rigbey, Loose & Mills, Birmingham; Maxwell Cooke & Co., Birkenhead.*

B

―――――

[CHANCERY DIVISION]

VESTEY AND OTHERS *v.* INLAND REVENUE COMMISSIONERS
C   (No. 2)

1978   April 12, 13, 14;   Walton J.
       May 26

Revenue — Tax avoidance — Overseas settlement — Discretionary
beneficiaries resident in United Kingdom — Trust income
D *accumulated—Payments to beneficiaries—Whether " income "*
—Tax liability of beneficiaries—Income Tax Act 1952 (15 &
16 Geo. 6 & Eliz. 2, c. 10), s. 412 (1) (2) (5) (as amended by
Finance Act 1969 (c. 32), s. 33)

In 1942 two members of the taxpayers' family resident in
the United Kingdom settled on trustees resident abroad on
discretionary trusts certain overseas property, including an
E annual rent of £960,000 payable under a lease. The settlement directed the trustees to accumulate and invest the rent
so as to form a capital fund, the income on which was paid
into a bank in Northern Ireland and was divided into two
moieties corresponding with the two branches of the taxpayers'
family, each having a manager. The income from each
moiety was accumulated, added to the moiety and reinvested.
The trustees' investments included investments in securities and
F shareholdings in overseas companies. Under the powers contained in the settlement the trustees made appointments
between 1962 and 1966 of capital sums to the taxpayers
who were some of the discretionary beneficiaries, totalling
£2,608,000. At the time one of the taxpayers was a minor
and the sum appointed to him was paid to his mother as
trustee. For the years 1963 to 1967 inclusive the taxpayers
were assessed to income tax, totalling £3,185,000, and to surtax,
totalling, £1,995,472, under section 412 (1) and (2) of the
G Income Tax Act 1952 [1] on those capital payments. On the

―――――

[1] Income Tax Act 1952, s. 412: " For the purpose of preventing the avoiding
by individuals ordinarily resident in the United Kingdom of liability to income
tax by means of transfers of assets by virtue or in consequence whereof, either
alone or in conjunction with associated operations, income becomes payable to
persons resident or domiciled out of the United Kingdom, it is hereby enacted as
follows : —(1) Where such an individual has by means of any such transfer, either
H alone or in conjunction with associated operations, acquired any rights by virtue
of which he has, within the meaning of this section, power to enjoy, whether forthwith or in the future, any income of a person resident or domiciled out of the
United Kingdom which, if it were income of that individual received by him in
the United Kingdom, would be chargeable to income tax by deduction or otherwise,
that income shall, whether it would or would not have been chargeable to income
tax apart from the provisions of this section, be deemed to be income of that
individual for all the purposes of this Act. (2) Where, whether before or after
any such transfer, such an individual receives or is entitled to receive any capital
sum the payment whereof is in any way connected with the transfer or any associated operation, any income which, by virtue or in consequence of the transfer,

taxpayers' appeal the special commissioners, without dealing   A
with subsection (1), decided that section 412 (2) of the Act
applied to the capital payments so that the whole of the
income of the trustees and of the investments settlement in
the year of appointment and subsequently arising, while the
taxpayers were resident in the United Kingdom, was deemed
to be the income of each of the taxpayers and was chargeable
to income tax and the commissioners upheld the assessments.

The taxpayers appealed. Walton J. [1978] 2 W.L.R. 136   B
held that by section 412 (2) Parliament should be taken to
mean that the capital sums, to the extent to which they comprised income, ought to be treated as the income of each taxpayer for the year in which he received it and the trustees
income extended to what the taxpayer received and that, since
payment of a capital sum to the mother of the minor taxpayer did not entitle him to receive those moneys at the time
of payment, the taxpayer was to be assessed for tax on the   C
sum in the year he attained his majority and not in the year
the payment was made to his mother. He allowed the appeals
and remitted the cases to the commissioners for them to
consider the applicability of section 412 (1) and to receive
further evidence in case of the minor taxpayer, and to adjust
the assessments accordingly.

In the event the parties agreed matters relating to the   D
minor's assessments and no evidence was adduced. After
further hearing, the commissioners decided that under the
terms of the 1942 settlement each of the taxpayers, as potential
beneficiaries, had rights under which each of them had power
to enjoy the income of the trustees and the investment of the
capital fund under section 412 (5) (d) and that, as a result,
such income had to be separately deemed under section 412 (1)
to be the income of each of the taxpayers for all the purposes   E
of the Act of 1952, year by year as it arose, so long as each
of them remained a potential beneficiary of the settlement.

On further appeal by the taxpayers:—

Held, allowing the appeal, (1) that, since the trustee had
a mere power, as distinct from a trust power, to distribute
among a class of beneficiaries at his discretion, no beneficiary
had a right to enjoy income or any power over any part of
the trust income and, therefore, before section 412 was   F
amended by the Finance Act 1969, no beneficiary had the
necessary right to enjoy income within the meaning of subsection (1); that, after the amendment to the section including
the deletion of a " right " in subsection (1) under which a
beneficiary had power to enjoy income, the true construction
of " income " in subsection (5) and especially paragraph (d)
did not include accumulations of income which had been
capitalised and, therefore, the payments to the taxpayers had   G
to be treated as payments of capital chargeable under section
412 (2) and not as income chargeable under section 412 (1)
of the Act (post, pp. 701E–G, 702E–G, 703G).

(2) That, although the court was bound by authority to
construe " income " in section 412 as the income of the trustees and not merely the income that the taxpayer had power
to enjoy, " income " was the income actually paid to the
trustees from the trust investments and not the income of   H
those investments and, therefore, the power to enjoy income
of a foreign company was restricted to that of the dividends
paid by that company to the trustees as shareholders and did

either alone or in conjunction with associated operations, has become the income
of a person resident or domiciled out of the United Kingdom shall, whether it
would or would not have been chargeable to income tax apart from the provisions
of this section, be deemed to be the income of that individual for all the purposes
of this Act."

A   not include the whole of the company's income before profits
        were deducted (post, pp. 710B–G, 711C–D).
            Lord Howard de Walden v. Inland Revenue Commissioners
        [1942] 1 K.B. 389, C.A. applied.

        The following cases are referred to in the judgment:
        Absalom v. Talbot (1943) 26 T.C. 166; [1943] 1 All E.R. 589, C.A.
B   Bambridge v. Inland Revenue Commissioners [1955] 1 W.L.R. 1329;
            [1955] 3 All E.R. 812; 36 T.C. 313, H.L.(E.).
        Canadian Eagle Oil Co. Ltd. v. The King [1946] A.C. 119; 27 T.C. 205,
            H.L.(E.).
        Congreve v. Inland Revenue Commissioners [1948] 1 All E.R. 948; 30
            T.C. 163, H.L.(E.).
        Corbett's Executrices v. Inland Revenue Commissioners [1943] 2 All E.R.
C   218; 25 T.C. 305, C.A.
        Gartside v. Inland Revenue Commissioners [1968] A.C. 553; [1968] 2
            W.L.R. 277; [1968] 1 All E.R. 121, H.L.(E.).
        Howard de Walden (Lord) v. Inland Revenue Commissioners [1942] 1
            K.B. 389; [1942] 1 All E.R. 287, C.A.
        Inland Revenue Commissioners v. Bates [1968] A.C. 483; [1967] 2 W.L.R.
            60; [1967] 1 All E.R. 84; 44 T.C. 225, H.L.(E.).
D   Inland Revenue Commissioners v. Clifforia Investments Ltd. [1963] 1
            W.L.R. 396; [1963] 1 All E.R. 159; 40 T.C. 608.
        Inland Revenue Commissioners v. Frere [1965] A.C. 402; [1964] 3 W.L.R.
            1193; [1964] 3 All E.R. 796; 42 T.C. 125, H.L.(E.).
        Nelson, In re, (Note) [1928] Ch. 920, C.A.
        Reg. v. Catagas [1978] 1 W.W.R. 282.
        Smith, In re [1928] Ch. 915.
        Vestey v. Inland Revenue Commissioners [1978] 2 W.L.R. 136; [1977]
E   3 All E.R. 1073.
        Vestey's (Lord) Executors v. Inland Revenue Commissioners (1949) 31
            T.C. 1; [1949] 1 All E.R. 1108, H.L.(E.).

        The following additional cases were cited in argument:
        Baden's Deed Trusts, In re [1971] A.C. 424; [1970] 2 W.L.R. 1110; [1970]
F   2 All E.R. 228, H.L.(E.).
        Beatty's (Admiral Earl) Executors v. Inland Revenue Commissioners
            (1940) 23 T.C. 574.
        Gulbenkian's Settlements, In re [1970] A.C. 508; [1968] 3 W.L.R. 1127;
            [1968] 3 All E.R. 785, H.L.(E.).
        Herbert v. Inland Revenue Commissioners (1925) 9 T.C. 593.
        Inland Revenue Commissioners v. Transport Economy Ltd. (1955) 35
            T.C. 601.
G   Mangin v. Inland Revenue Commissioners [1971] A.C. 739; [1971] 2
            W.L.R. 39; [1971] 1 All E.R. 179, P.C.
        Norman v. Golder (1944) 26 T.C. 293.
        Perry v. Astor [1935] A.C. 398, H.L.(E.).
        Reg. v. Davison [1972] 1 W.L.R. 1540; [1972] 3 All E.R. 1121, C.A.
        Scott v. Russell (1948) 30 T.C. 394.
        Stock v. Frank Jones (Tipton) Ltd. [1978] 1 W.L.R. 231; [1978] 1 All
H   E.R. 948, H.L.(E.).

            CASES STATED by the Commissioners for the Special Purposes of the
        Income Tax Acts.
            By a settlement dated March 25, 1942, made between Sir Edmund
        Hoyle Vestey and Lord Vestey, as settlors, James Flynn and Reginald
        Beak, who were resident in Uruguay and in the Argentine respectively,
        as trustees, and Ulster Bank Ltd., the settlors settled, inter alia, specified

overseas property for certain discretionary trusts. The trustees were   A
directed to create a capital fund consisting of income from the trust
property and divide it into two moieties called Edmund's fund and
Samuel's fund, the names of the moieties corresponding with the two
branches of the Vestey family. Provisions were made to appoint a
manager for each moiety. The trustees were further given power to invest
the two moieties, accumulate their income, from time to time make such
appointments of the moneys as directed by the managers. Then there   B
were further directions. Subject to those trusts the trust property and
income thereof was held for Ronald Arthur Vestey and William Howarth
Vestey absolutely in equal shares. Additional trustees of the settlement,
none of whom were resident in the United Kingdom, were appointed from
time to time.

By a lease dated March 26, 1942, the trustees leased the property   C
comprised in the settlement to the Union Cold Storage Co. Ltd. for 21
years from April 10, 1942, in continuation or extension of an earlier demise
of 1921. In 1963 the 1942 lease came to an end and a new lease was
executed on April 10, 1963, the lessors being the then trustees of the
1942 settlement and the lessees the Union International Co. Ltd. (formerly
Union Cold Storage Co. Ltd.). That lease was expressed to be supple-   D
mental to the earlier demises of 1921 and 1942 and demised to the lessees
the property therein mentioned for a further term of 21 years from April
10, 1963, at the same rent and on the same terms and conditions as were
contained in the 1921 lease. By directions in writing of the trustees
dated July 27, 1950, and again dated June 30, 1967, and December 12,
1967, the rent payable by the lessees was paid to the Ulster Bank Ltd.
in Belfast and there placed to the credit of an account in the name of   E
the taxpayer, Ronald Arthur Vestey, and later to the credit of the account
of the then trustees. That income having been capitalised in two moieties,
the trustees accumulated the income of the moieties under the directions
of the managers of Edmund's and Samuel's funds.

The trustees of the 1942 settlement owned directly, or through
nominees, all the shares in the following companies: (i) Commercial   F
Insurance Corporation Ltd. which was incorporated in 1922 and its share
capital was purchased by the trustees in 1944. It had a wholly-owned
subsidiary company, New Holding & Finance Co. Ltd.; (ii) the Commercial Investment Co. Ltd., which was incorporated and managed and
controlled in Bermuda; (iii) the Salient Shipping Co. (Bermuda) Ltd.,
which was incorporated and managed and controlled in Bermuda. New
Holding & Finance Co. Ltd. was incorporated and managed and controlled   G
in England. All its share capital was owned by Commercial Insurance
Corporation to whom it paid substantial dividends.

Under the powers contained in the 1942 settlement the trustees made
appointments of capital sums to the taxpayers, Ronald Arthur Vestey,
Edmund Hoyle Vestey, Margaret Payne, Jane McLean Baddeley, Lord
Vestey and Mark Vestey, between 1962 and 1966, totalling £2,608,000.   H
Mark Vestey was a minor and the amount of the capital sum arising
from the appointment to him was paid to his mother as trustee. Consequent on those transfers the taxpayers were assessed to tax under section
412 (1) and (2) of the Income Tax Act 1952 for the years 1963–64 to
1966–67 in the sums totalling £3,185,000 and to surtax for the same years,
totalling £1,995,472.

The commissioners dismissed appeals against the assessments by all

A taxpayers on the grounds that they fell within the provisions of section 412 (2) of the Act of 1952, but did not give a decision on the effect of section 412 (1). They adjusted the assessments to amounts agreed by the parties, upholding the Crown's method of computing the taxpayers' income for tax purposes. The taxpayers appealed. Walton J. [1978] 2 W.L.R. 136 allowed the appeals holding that under section 412 (2) of the Act of 1952 such capital sums should to the extent to which they comprised income be treated for tax purposes as the income of each taxpayer and that the taxpayers should be assessed in respect of the sums appointed to them in the year in which they received them. As regards the minor taxpayer his Lordship held that he was to be assessed for tax on the capital sum in the year he attained his majority and not in the year the payment was made to his mother. The cases were remitted to the com-

C missioners for, inter alia, assessments to be adjusted and to consider the effect of section 412 (1).

The commissioners decided that although, bearing in mind the terms of the 1942 settlement, the taxpayers had no " right " to demand income from the trustees they acquired " rights " under which they had " power to enjoy " income, and that in view of the definition of the expression " power to enjoy " in section 412 (5) and its implification by section 412 (6),

D those rights fell to be assessed under section 412 (1). The commissioners decided further that under the settlement the taxpayers acquired the " right " to be considered as potential recipients of benefit and the " right " to have their interests protected by a court of equity. By section 412 (5) (d) an individual was deemed to have power to enjoy income if he might, in the event of the exercise of any power vested in any other

E person, become entitled to the beneficial enjoyment of the income. There was nothing to prevent the application of the Interpretation Act 1889 to that subsection and allow the word " power " to be construed as including separate exercises of separate fiduciary powers. Thus, the commissioners took the view that by the exercise of the powers vested in the managers of the settlement fund the taxpayers might become entitled to income of

F the trust property and that such income when received would be income to which the taxpayers had good title by virtue of their rights under the 1942 settlement. The taxpayers, accordingly, came within section 412 (1). A fortiori, after the section was amended by section 33 of the Finance Act 1969 the taxpayers had power to enjoy income of the 1942 settlement.

The taxpayers appealed.

G *D. C. Potter Q.C.* and *J. Holroyd Pearce* for the taxpayers.
Peter Archer Q.C. S.-G., Michael Nolan Q.C., Peter Gibson and *Brian Davenport* for the Crown.

Cur. adv. vult.

May 26. WALTON J. read the following judgment. This case is a

H sequel to the first *Vestey* v. *Inland Revenue Commissioners* [1978] 2 W.L.R. 136. It is concerned with the same settlement and the same payments made thereout to the taxpayers. But whereas the Crown's attack was previously mounted under section 412 (2) of the Income Tax Act 1952, it is now mounted under subsection (1) of that section. I need not, I think, rehearse the facts, which I set out in my previous judgment; nor the terms of the section, which I likewise set out therein. I think I can plunge straightaway into the Crown's claim.

It is that, given the terms of the settlement of March 25, 1942, each   A
of the taxpayers, as potential beneficiaries thereunder, has, within the
meaning of the preamble and the combined effect of section 412 (1), (4)
and (5), rights by virtue of which each of them has power to enjoy the
income of the trustees of that settlement, and that in consequence thereof
such income must be separately deemed to be the income of each of these
individuals for all the purposes of the Act of 1952, year by year as it
arises, at any rate so long as each of them remains a potential beneficiary   B
of the settlement.

So that once again, the Crown is claiming the right to recover multiple
tax from the unfortunate taxpayers, and to recover it year by year quite
irrespective of the question whether the taxpayers do or do not receive
anything further out of the settlement funds. If that is what the relevant
subsections, on their true construction, do provide, then, of course, so be   C
it. But this is a penal section, and accordingly falls to be construed
extremely strictly, although of course this does not mean that the court
is at liberty to distort its fair meaning, only that the person who is alleged
to have incurred the penalty must be given the benefit of any real doubt
or ambiguity. There can, however, be no possible burking the fact that
the consequences of the construction which the Crown seeks to place
upon the relevant subsections produce a monstrous injustice: an injustice   D
so monstrous that the Crown itself in the present case has resiled from
its logical consequence and, while claiming a wider right, has sought to
attribute to each of the taxpayers only a fraction of the income of the
trustees equivalent to the fraction of the total disbursements made to
them collectively which each individual has himself received.

Since at the moment I am dealing only with matters of principle and   E
not with precise figures (which, if required, remain to be agreed), I do
not think it is necessary to refer to the precise figures at all. It suffices
to say that, precisely as in *Vestey* v. *Inland Revenue Commissioners*
[1978] 2 W.L.R. 136, there are assessments to income tax and surtax upon
all the relevant recipients for the years 1963–64, 1964–65, 1965–66 and
1966–67, which were the years which were previously in issue, and also   F
for the year 1968–69. These last appeals were added by agreement
between the parties, and are designed to elicit a decision as regards an
amendment to section 412 which was effected by section 33 of the Finance
Act 1969, the year 1968–69 being the first year in which such amendment
took effect.

It is at this point that there arises what Mr. Potter, for the taxpayers,
has denominated as a serious constitutional question; namely, what rights   G
the Inland Revenue Commissioners have to pick and choose when recovering tax. The Solicitor-General says, and doubtless rightly says, that the
commissioners are under no duty to recover every halfpenny of tax
which may be due. One may say " Amen " to that very readily, because
the costs of recovery of extremely small amounts of tax would far outweigh the tax recovered. One expects the tax authorities to behave   H
sensibly. In this connection I was referred to section 1 of the Inland
Revenue Regulation Act 1890 and to section 1 of the Taxes Management
Act 1970, but I do not think that either of these provisions has any real
bearing on the matter. What the revenue authorities, through the Solicitor-
General, are here claiming is a general dispensing power, no more and
no less. He submitted that the system of extra-statutory concessions was
well known and well recognised, and that what was happening in the

A　present case was no more than the grant of an additional extra-statutory concession.

　　In the first place, I, in company with many other judges before me, am totally unable to understand upon what basis the Inland Revenue Commissioners are entitled to make extra-statutory concessions. To take a very simple example (since example is clearly called for), upon what basis have the commissioners taken it upon themselves to provide that B　income tax is not to be charged upon a miner's free coal and allowances in lieu thereof? That this should be the law is doubtless quite correct: I am not arguing the merits, or even suggesting that some other result, as a matter of equity, should be reached. But this, surely, ought to be a matter for Parliament, and not the commissioners. If this kind of concession can be made, where does it stop; and why are some groups C　favoured as against others?

　　As I have indicated, I am not alone in failing to understand how any such concessions can properly be made. I need refer only to Scott L.J. in *Absalom* v. *Talbot* (1943) 26 T.C. 166, 181, the second full paragraph (and may I here, in parenthesis, add that I fully concur in his tribute to the staff of the Inland Revenue); to Viscount Radcliffe in *Inland Revenue Commissioners* v. *Frere* [1965] A.C. 402, 429, and to Lord Upjohn in D　*Inland Revenue Commissioners* v. *Bates* [1968] A.C. 483, 516.

　　This is not a simple matter of tax law. What is happening is that, in effect, despite the words of *Maitland, The Constitutional History of England* (1909), p. 305, commenting on the Bill of Rights, " This is the last of the dispensing power," the Crown is now claiming just such a power. If I may, I would respectfully adopt the words of Freedman C.J.M. E　in the Court of Appeal in Manitoba in *Reg.* v. *Catagas* [1978] 1 W.W.R. 282, 287, a case which in terms decides that the Crown may not dispense with laws by executive action, where, after dealing with cases of prosecution for infraction of the criminal law in which in individual cases there was undoubtedly an element of discretion, he said:

F　　　" But in all these instances the prosecutorial discretion is exercised
　　　in relation to a specific case. It is the particular facts of a given
　　　case that call that discretion into play. But that is a far different
　　　thing from the granting of a blanket dispensation in favour of a
　　　particular group or race. Today the dispensing power may be
　　　exercised in favour of Indians. Tomorrow it may be exercised in
　　　favour of Protestants, and the next day in favour of Jews. Our laws
　　　cannot be so treated. The Crown may not by executive action
G　　　dispense with laws. The matter is as simple as that, and nearly
　　　three centuries of legal and constitutional history stand as the
　　　foundation for that principle."

　　But even if, contrary to my views, extra-statutory concessions are permissible and do form part of our tax code, nevertheless they do represent a published code, which applies indifferently to all those who H　fall, or who can bring themselves, within its scope. What is claimed by the Crown now is something radically different. There is no published code, and no necessity for the treatment of all those who are in consimili casu alike. In one case the Crown can remit one-third, in another one-half, and in yet another case the whole, of the tax properly payable, at its own sweet will and pleasure. If this is indeed so, we are back to the days of the Star Chamber. Again, I want to make it crystal clear that nobody is suggesting that the Crown has, or indeed ever would, so utilise

the powers which it claims to bring about unjust results; or really, of   A
course, which is not necessarily the same thing, results which it thought
to be unjust. The root of the evil is that it claims that it has, in fact,
the right to do so.

I turn next to the true construction of subsection (1) and associated
subsections of section 412. It would, I think, have been very much
easier to make rational sense of subsection (1) if the decision in *Lord
Howard de Walden* v. *Inland Revenue Commissioners* [1942] 1 K.B. 389   B
had been cast in another mould, as I think it could have been without
disturbing the actual result. For the effect of that case is to decide
that the income which is to be deemed the income of the taxpayer is
the whole of the income of the trustees, notwithstanding that (and at the
moment I am putting the matter very loosely) he has only a right to
enjoy a part of that income. Apart from that case (which received, of   C
course, approval in the House of Lords in *Congreve* v. *Inland Revenue
Commissioners* (1948) 30 T.C. 163) it would have been possible to make
better sense of subsection (1) by reading the words "any income . . .
that income" as being correlative to each other. So that, for example,
if the taxpayer had the right to receive one-quarter of the income he
would be taxable upon that one-quarter, and so forth. Indeed, I suspect
that this is so obviously the sensible and natural interpretation of the   D
subsection that it was adopted sub silentio in *Corbett's Executrices* v.
Inland Revenue Commissioners (1943) 25 T.C. 305. I am certainly not
prepared to regard this case as one in which the Crown simply exercised
its dispensing power, as claimed by the Solicitor-General. I accept that
the figures do appear odd, but I think the reason for the apparently low
assessment is as I have indicated, and not otherwise.   E

However, I am bound, it appears to me, to hold that if a taxpayer
has power to enjoy even a hundredth part of the income of the foreign
trustees, the whole of their income is to be deemed to be his. I shall
have to return to this point later in this judgment, but I see no escape
from this position as the law now stands. I at one time thought that
there might be an escape via the provisions of subsection (6), which it   F
will be convenient to recapitulate here:

> "In determining whether an individual has power to enjoy income
> within the meaning of this section, regard shall be had to the sub-
> stantial result and effect of the transfer and any associated operations,
> and all benefits which may at any time accrue to the individual as a
> result of the transfer and any associated operations shall be taken
> into account irrespective of the nature or form of the benefits."   G

But on reflection I have come to the conclusion that this is impossible,
for this subsection does not deal with anything more than whether a
person has power to enjoy income; there is nothing about quantum in
it at all. Supposing it was a millionth part of the income that a person
was clearly entitled to enjoy, subsection (6) could have no effect upon
the consequence that the enjoyment of that modest fraction might entail   H
—would entail—tax liability on a sum one million times as great. It
therefore appears to me that the only effect which subsection (6) could
possibly have as the law now stands is to enlarge—never to restrict—the
circumstances under which the individual has power to enjoy income.

I next turn to the requirements which must be satisfied before subsection (1) bites as regards the entitlement to income of the person sought
to be charged thereunder. That person must

A
"by means of any such transfer, either alone or in conjunction
with associated operations," have "acquired any rights by virtue of
which he has, within the meaning of this section, power to enjoy . . .
any income of a person resident or domiciled out of the United
Kingdom . . ."

Shortening it for present purposes, that person must have acquired rights
B by virtue of which he has power to enjoy any income of a person resident
or domiciled out of the United Kingdom. "Power to enjoy" is defined
in subsection (5), but for the moment I do not pause to consider what
that precisely means, for the first step is to see precisely what "rights"
have been acquired under the settlement (for it has not been suggested
on behalf of the Crown that there are any other relevant rights) by the
taxpayers.
C
Now the appointments here in question were made by the taxpayer
Ronald Arthur Vestey as Edmund's manager with the consent of Samuel's
manager in his own favour, and as Edmund's manager in favour of Edmund
Hoyle Vestey, Margaret Payne and Jane McLean Baddeley under the
provisions of clause 4 (D) of the settlement; and by Edward Brown as
Samuel's manager in favour of Lord Vestey and Mark William Vestey
D under clause 6(D) of the settlement. In each case the power—and as
matters stand they are the current relevant powers—is one to appoint
capital among a class "in such shares (if more than one) and in such
manner as" the appropriate "manager shall think proper." Ronald
Arthur Vestey could not, as Edmund's manager, appoint in his own
favour: the settlement required, in such an event, that the appointment
had to be made jointly with Samuel's manager or the trustees themselves.
E
The position therefore is that in each case we are dealing with a mere
power (as distinct from a trust power) in the appropriate person enabling
him to distribute among a class of beneficiaries as he thinks fit. What
"rights" are by such a provision conferred upon any individual potential
beneficiary? In my judgment, the only relevant rights which are conferred upon such a beneficiary are: (i) the right to be considered by
F the person exercising the power when he comes to exercise it; (ii) the
right to prevent certain kinds of conduct on the part of the person so
exercising the power—e.g., by distributing part of the assets to not within
the class—and (iii) the right to retain any sums properly paid to him by
the trustees in exercise of their discretionary powers. But beyond that
he has no relevant "right" of any description: and none of those
rights is a right under which he has power to enjoy the income. Indeed,
G no individual has any power over any part of the income whatsoever.
The most relevant right is, indeed, the third; but a right to retain what is
properly paid to you is simply the negative right of being afforded a
complete defence to any claim for repayment, and no more. Prior to
actual payment, to which there is no right whatsoever, the recipient has
no right to the money at all.

H
One may, indeed, contrast the situation in the present case with a
situation where trustees are obliged to distribute income year by year
under the terms of their trust deed among a certain class in such shares
and proportions as they may think fit—a case in which each potential
beneficiary is very much more likely in ordinary parlance to have power
to enjoy the income than the present case. Even in such a case no
individual potential beneficiary has any relevant right whatsoever, although,
collectively, they undoubtedly do have a right which, if they are all

sui juris, they may collectively enforce: see *In re Nelson* decided in 1918, A
reported as a note in [1928] Ch. 920; *In re Smith* [1928] Ch. 915; and
compare *per* Lord Reid in *Gartside* v. *Inland Revenue Commissioners*
[1968] A.C. 553, 606. But a collectively enforceable "right" is one
which does not fall within the ambit of the word "right" in subsection
(1). For this there is direct House of Lords authority in *Lord Vestey's
Executors* v. *Inland Revenue Commissioners* (1949) 31 T.C. 1: see *per*
Lord Simonds, at p. 85, Lord Morton of Henryton (with whose opinion B
Lord Normand expressly agreed: see p. 92), at p. 110, and Lord Reid,
at p. 119. The present case is clearly a fortiori to this case.

Therefore, it appears to me that none of these discretionary beneficiaries had any "right" to anything at all which could possibly bring the
subsection into play prior to the Finance Act 1969. Section 33 of that
Act effected two changes in section 412. First, in subsection (1) the C
words from "such an individual" to "he has" were deleted and replaced
by the words "by virtue or in consequence of any such transfer, either
alone or in conjunction with associated operations, such an individual
has." The second was that in subsection (6) there were added, after the
words "accrue to the individual," the words "(whether or not he has
rights at law or in equity in or to those benefits)." Dealing first with this
second amendment, no argument based on this addition has been advanced D
by counsel for the Crown. I need therefore only say that the addition
of these words merely serves to confirm me in my opinion that this subsection was not intended by Parliament as a restricting subsection.

Turning back again to subsection (1), I think it desirable to set out
the relevant wording as amended in full:

"Where by virtue or in consequence of any such transfer, either E
alone or in conjunction with associated operations, such an individual
has, within the meaning of this section, power to enjoy, whether
forthwith or in the future, any income of a person resident or
domiciled out of the United Kingdom. . . ."

The word "right" (upon which, in *Lord Vestey's Executors* v. *Inland
Revenue Commissioners*, 31 T.C. 1, Lord Simonds laid great emphasis, at F
p. 85, stating that it could not be disregarded) has vanished; and the
sole question is whether the individual in question has power to enjoy
the relevant income, as defined by subsection (5). It is no longer
necessary that he should have any right by virtue of which he has such
power. And one can well understand the removal of that word, because
in general no potential beneficiary has a right to income, having no G
entitlement beyond that of the usual discretionary beneficiary.

So I turn to consider the various paragraphs of subsection (5). The
argument has in fact exclusively raged around the second half of paragraph (d), which was not an original part of the subsection when enacted
for the first time in 1936, but was added by the Finance Act 1938. Now
it appears to me that, as submitted by Mr. Potter, throughout subsection
(5) "income" means income and nothing else. Thus one finds, in para- H
graph (a), the words "Income . . . so dealt with . . . as to be calculated . . .
whether in the form of income or not, to enure for the benefit of the
individual." There is no allotropic form of income known to me: the
antithesis of income is capital, and income can, indeed, become capital
by being accumulated. Hence it appears to me that the section is drawing
a deliberate contrast between income and accumulations of income which
have become capital, and is saying that it does not matter which enures

A for the benefit of the individual. The same argument is available as a result of paragraph (c). The words

> " out of . . . income or out of moneys which are or will be available for the purpose by reason of the effect or successive effects of the associated operations on that income and on any assets which directly or indirectly represent that income "

B once again show that the draftsman was perfectly well aware of the distinction between income and what income may, by direction of the trust instrument or by the exercise of powers conferred upon the trustees, become (for example, a policy of insurance).

Hence it appears to me that the inevitable conclusion is that in this subsection " income " means income and does not, save as expressly so provided, mean or include accumulations of income which have become C capitalised. Moreover, it appears to me that this is fully consistent with the structure of the section. I appreciate that subsection (2) comes from a different source, but obviously Parliament now considers that the provisions properly fall to be read as a whole, and one then has basically the simple dichotomy between the receipt of a capital sum, dealt with under subsection (2)—and, if I am correct in Vestey v. Inland Revenue D Commissioners [1978] 2 W.L.R. 136, dealt with to the extent to which it indeed represents income—and the receipt of income, dealt with under subsections (1) and (5).

As I have not had full argument on subsection (5) (a), (b) or (c), I do not propose to deal with them beyond saying that it was submitted to me that " calculated " in subsection (5) (a) meant " likely." This is, E of course, one of its possible meanings, although a glance at the Shorter Oxford English Dictionary makes it quite clear that this is not a precise translation of the word " calculated." On the other hand, its primary meaning is " reckoned, estimated, thought out," and I would think that this is the meaning which is intended here. I hardly think that Parliament would have intended the " likely " interpretation. If it had wanted to use that word it could so easily have done so. The question would then F be, how likely?—an almost insoluble problem. This being, as I have already noted, a penal section, I think a stricter interpretation than " likely " is undoubtedly called for.

I must here, however, note that the Solicitor-General expressly reserved the Crown's position with regard to paragraphs (a) and (b), which he outlined very briefly, although, as the special commissioners had not dealt with them, he otherwise, apart from such reservation, left alone. G He accepted, at any rate for the purposes of the present case, that the argument turned on paragraph (d). I turn therefore to that paragraph. Here, the meaning is quite clear: " income " means income, and as, on the facts of the present case, it was capital—capitalised income—which was paid out to each of the taxpayers, the second half of paragraph (d) is inapplicable to the actual situation here in question.

H My conclusion on construction in this matter would in fact be sufficient to decide the points at issue between the parties, but there are two more matters I must mention at this stage. That is the question of the possible operation of subsection (1) and subsection (2) together. One can imagine a case in which some paragraph of subsection (5) dealing with the receipt of a capital sum applies and in which subsection (2) also applies. It was, I think, the only point upon which the Crown and the taxpayers were both agreed: these subsections are, they both accept, concurrent

and not cumulative. A person cannot be taxed in any one year on A
the same sum under both subsection (1) and also subsection (2). Like
Warren Hastings, the Crown, in making this concession, doubtless stood
amazed at its own moderation in view of its other claims in the two
cases, but make it it did.

I now turn to the supplemental cases stated, in which the special
commissioners give their reasons for coming to different conclusions,
basically upon the construction of the section. I shall simply refer to B
that in the case of Ronald Arthur Vestey, since each of the other cases
simply refers to the reasoning in his case. The special commissioners
dealt first with what I may call the absence of any "rights" argument as
follows:

"We deal first with section 412 (1) before its amendment in 1969.
It was said on behalf of the [taxpayer] that his entitlement to income C
was subject to the exercise of divers powers and consents and he
acquired no 'rights' to income within section 412 (1). We accept
that according to the terms of the 1942 settlement he had no right
to demand income from the trustees but we prefer to pose the
question in a different form. What we have to decide is, not whether
he had 'rights,' but whether he acquired 'rights' by virtue of which D
he had within the meaning of section 412 'power to enjoy' income;
and the expression 'power to enjoy' (which is a component of the
sentence which we have to construe as a whole) is elaborately defined
in subsection (5) and amplified by subsection (6). Under the 1942
settlement the [taxpayer] acquired the 'right' to be considered as
a potential recipient of benefit and the 'right' to have his interest
protected by a court of equity. It is those 'rights' in the context E
cited above which we have to consider. By subsection (5) (d) an
individual is deemed to have power to enjoy income if he may, in
the event of the exercise of any power vested in any other person,
become entitled to the beneficial enjoyment of the income. Does the
Interpretation Act 1889 permit 'power'—in the singular—being
construed as including separate exercises of separate fiduciary powers?
We see nothing to prevent the application of the Interpretation Act F
to subsection (5) (d) and we take the view that by the exercise of
the powers vested in the managers the [taxpayer] may become
entitled to income of the trust property and that such income when
received would be income to which the [taxpayer] had a good title
by virtue of his rights under the 1942 settlement in the sense referred
to above. We do not think that directions to accumulate income . . . G
prevent income from being deemed to be income of the individual
concerned. We feel fortified in this conclusion first by the declared
purpose of section 412 as set out in the preamble thereto and,
secondly, by subsection (6) thereof by which we are enjoined to have
regard to the 'substantial result and effect' of the transfer and
associated operations."   H

It will be observed that the special commissioners correctly appreciated
that the rights which they had to consider were the rights acquired by
the taxpayer under the 1942 settlement; but, having firmly grasped that
point, they then allowed themselves to be diverted from the inevitable
conclusion that no relevant right was conferred in this manner, chiefly
because they posed an unreal question in relation to subsection (5) (d).
I would entirely agree with them that in that subsection "power" includes

A powers; but one cannot disregard the presence of the word "right" in the way they have done.

As regards the position after the Finance Act 1969, the special commissioners say simply: "A fortiori, after the section was amended by section 33 of the Finance Act 1969 the [taxpayer] had power to enjoy income of the 1942 settlement." The special commissioners do not appear to have considered the argument, which has appealed to me, concerning

B the precise meaning of "income" as "income" in subsection (5) (d).

They then dealt with what I may term the "bad for duplicity" argument, and came to the conclusion (which I think on authorities binding on them and this court cannot be refuted) that if a beneficiary is liable at all he is liable to be taxed on the whole of the income of the trustees, and not merely that part whereof he is the recipient, thus creating

C multiple liability.

Their treatment of the "discretion" point is more debatable. They say:

"Then it was said that by choosing to limit the total liability to the income of the trustees the Board of Inland Revenue are exercising a discretion. We do not think by so limiting the tax the board are

D exercising a discretion in a sense offensive to the law. There are many instances in the Taxes Acts where the board have express powers which affect the tax payable; for example, in section 115 (2) (b) of the Income and Corporation Taxes Act 1970. The existence of such powers is consistent with their duty under section 1 of the Inland Revenue Regulation Act 1890 and section 1 of the Taxes Management Act 1970 whereby they are to have all the necessary

E powers for carrying into execution every Act relating to Inland Revenue and the care and management of taxes. We can accept counsel's proposition that a person is not to be taxed by a discretion but by clear words charging him to tax, without construing section 412 (1) so as to avoid charging the individual at all. We do not think we can look at Hansard as an aid to construction. We must

F look at what was enacted."

The last observation is, of course, one which has since been forcibly made in the House of Lords, and is undeniably correct. But the suggestion that the discretions conferred upon the Crown by section 115 (2) (b) of the Act of 1970 are in any manner comparable with the discretions here in question is laughable. By that provision (and there

G are many other similar provisions in taxing statutes of this general nature) the board is entitled to choose which year is to be the relevant year for taxation purposes. A choice is the antithesis of a discretion. A provision that X is to be taxed on the profits of year 1 or year 2 results in X being taxed accordingly. What is here suggested is that the Crown may decide whether or not to tax X, and, if they do decide to tax him, upon what sum (not exceeding the income of the trustees) they choose.

H The one is reasoned and limited, the other is wholly arbitrary and despotic.

However, this is not in fact what the special commissioners thought was the result of their conclusion. They came to the conclusion that the manner in which the section worked was that the beneficiaries to be assessed in any one year could be assessed in total on the income of the trustees for that year, but no more. This conferred upon the board a discretion merely as to the distribution of the income among the beneficiaries, which they could do in any manner provided that the total

amount did not exceed the trustees' income. They expressed themselves A
as follows:

"The construction which we favour above need not result in double,
or multiple, taxation. If the income of A is deemed to be the income
of B, it cannot also be deemed to be the income of C unless the
enactment clearly so provides, which section 412 does not; nor, so
far as we are aware, does any other section of the Taxes Acts. In B
cases where income is deemed to be another individual's income there
are instances where the words 'and not the income of any other
person' appear; for example, in Part XVI of the Income and Corporation Taxes Act 1970 (Settlements). There are no such limiting
words in section 412. When section 412 was originally enacted in
1936 the maximum rate of income tax and surtax was 65 per cent.
Although the principle has been somewhat eroded in modern times C
Lord Macnaghten's dictum that income tax is a 'tax on income'
then held good. It seems to us highly improbable that (with the
caveat already mentioned) if income is deemed to be A's it can also
be deemed to be the income of B. In *Lord Herbert* v. *Inland
Revenue Commissioners* (1943) 25 T.C. 93 Macnaghten J. describes
such a proposition as extravagant. We take the view that the deem- D
ing process, whereby income of the non-resident person is deemed to
be income of an individual, operates once only and that such income
cannot be taxed more than once. Apportionment of the 'deemed'
income according to the quantum of the respective beneficial interests
has much to commend it, but (as we noticed in paragraph 12 of our
original decision) section 412 does not so provide. We recognise that
apportionment may be impossible in the case of some of the dis- E
cretionary beneficiaries whose expectancy may be insignificant.
Various methods of apportionment were canvassed before us, the
merits of each differing according to the circumstances. In our view,
in default of a method prescribed by the section, and we can find
none, it is for the board in exercise of their powers in the execution
of the Acts to decide on the appropriate apportionment."
F

I regret that I do not follow the logic of the second paragraph of this
reasoning; but, more importantly, it appears to contradict their own earlier
reasoning as to the amount for which each beneficiary was liable—i.e.,
the whole income—following *Lord Howard de Walden* v. *Inland Revenue
Commissioners* [1942] 1 K.B. 389. This is certainly not how the Crown
now seeks to interpret the section.

There are two remaining points in the special commissioners' decision, G
one of which is a point on section 413 which is not now, I understand,
pursued. I shall defer consideration of the other point (the position of
the income of a company in which the trust moneys are invested) until
later.

Finally, they pointed out, quite correctly, that there are no different
considerations which affected any of the other taxpayers, save for H
Mark Vestey [1978] 2 W.L.R. 136, 154, and so they dismissed the appeals
against all the assessments, including the 1968–69 assessments, and
adjourned them for the figures to be agreed. The matter has, however,
been brought before me as a matter of principle without waiting for the
figures to be agreed. I am not concerned with the precise figures.

This being the state of the matter when the case came on for hearing,
Mr. Potter, for the taxpayers, formally repeated some of the submissions

A which he made in *Vestey* v. *Inland Revenue Commissioners* [1978] 2 W.L.R. 136, 152–153, namely, Nos. I, IV and V, and then added the following new submissions: IX. That as regards the earlier four years prior to the year 1969, none of the taxpayers had any relevant " rights." X. That on the true construction of the words " power to enjoy " as defined for the purpose of section 5 (*d*), neither in fact nor in law did any of the taxpayers have power to enjoy any income of any part of the B trust property. XI. That the liability of any individual under subsections (1) and (2) was concurrent and not cumulative.

As regards Mr. Potter's first point, it is quite true, as he submitted, that there is no direct authority based on section 412 (1) as distinct from section 412 (2), and he therefore submitted that, notwithstanding the *Congreve*, 30 T.C. 163, and *Bambridge* [1955] 1 W.L.R. 1329, decisions, C the matter was still open. I do not, however, feel able to accept this submission. I cannot think that the section poses different tests in this regard according to whether the payments made are income or capital.

Still under this same head, he submitted that if the special commissioners were correct in their views—namely, that the Crown has a discretion as to apportionment of the total liability among the beneficiaries—the Crown could not have fulfilled its duty as it has all along been D arguing for a wider discretion than that of mere apportionment. If this submission had been accepted, then the assessments would, I suppose, have all been bad, notwithstanding that the Crown would have, if asked to start again in the light of the special commissioners' decision, arrived at precisely the same answer. The benefit to the taxpayers would be that it would by now be well out of time.

E I am, however, unimpressed by this argument. I am unable to see, in a case where the subsection clearly applies and an individual has any right by virtue of which he has power to enjoy the income in question, he is not liable to tax upon the whole of that income. I am, of course, equally unable to see by virtue of what right the Crown sees fit to remit a portion of that liability, but that is an entirely different matter of which no assessed—that is to say, otherwise properly assessed—taxpayer is F entitled to complain, whatever anguished howls his companions in misfortune, who do not have the luck to find the greater part of their tax bill remitted, may utter.

Mr. Potter's nos. IV and V were simply submitted to keep them open, since he could not properly (and of course did not) seek to persuade me to distinguish my own earlier decision against him on them.

G So far as his ninth point is concerned, he expanded this in the following form; namely, that the Crown must be able to point to a single individual who had, as respects any year of assessment, an individual right by virtue of which he had power to enjoy any income of the trustees. In other words, subsection (1) did not bite where the power was collectively that of a group of individuals. As I have already indicated, I see no answer to Mr. Potter's submission under this head, more particularly in view of the fantastic—and I use the word advisedly—results which a contrary conclusion would entail, and which I shall consider in more detail when analysing the contentions of the Solicitor-General.

It was under his tenth point that Mr. Potter dealt with the fact that the settlement and associated directions direct accumulations of income until the year 2030. Although these directions could be revoked, so long as the income was being accumulated it was all being accumulated in this manner, and there was just no income which could be enjoyed

by any potential beneficiary. Of course, if they lived to the year 2030 **A**
the taxpayers, as matters stood, did indeed stand to collect the accumulated
income. As, however, their ages would then range from 87 (in the case
of Mark Vestey) to 132 (in the case of Ronald Arthur Vestey) this would
be highly unlikely. And here Mr. Potter, like the Crown, sought to use
the provisions of subsection (6) restrictively, pointing out that the " substantial effect " of the settlement was to give the taxpayers very remote
interests indeed. I think the trouble with this submission is that, however **B**
theoretically remote their interests may be, these taxpayers have, each and
every one, received sums out of the settlement of a not insubstantial
amount.

I follow entirely Mr. Potter's analysis of the settlement, the division
of the settled funds and so forth, with the result that there are now
two funds with 16 (later 18) potential beneficiaries on the one side and **C**
13 (later 14) on the other. One may well ask why they, too, have not
been assessed if, as the Crown maintains, they are one and all theoretically
liable to be assessed on the whole of the income of the trustees (and,
indeed, more even than that, as I shall mention later), but this is no answer
to the problem. I prefer to place the matter securely upon the footing
that in subsection (5) (*d*) " income " means income, and the beneficiaries
have had capital sums paid to them which fall to be assessed under **D**
subsection (2) and not subsection (1).

Again, apart from the question of the income derived from certain
investments, consideration of which I once again postpone at this stage,
Mr. Potter's last point was, indeed, conceded by the Crown, and that is
that.

For the Crown, the Solicitor-General submitted, with evident enthusiasm, **E**
that if the conditions of the section were satisfied then the taxpayer was
chargeable in respect of the whole of the income of the non-resident—in
this case, of course, the trustees—and that none the less because there
might also be somebody else who was in precisely the same situation.
Moreover—and here he was able in part to cite the conclusions of the
special commissioners in his favour—the relevant income included not
only the income received by the trustees as the result of the transfer, but **F**
the whole of the income of the trustees. Thus, to take a simple example,
if the settlors in the present case had been unwise enough to select as
their foreign resident trustees, say, a New York bank which was trustee
of many other settlements as well, the whole of the income of that New
York bank, not only that derived from the actual settlement of which
they were trustees but the income of all other settlements of which they **G**
were trustees, and the whole of the bank's ordinary trading income (not
alone profits), was income upon which the beneficiary who fell within the
scope of subsection (1) could be assessed.

Nay, further: if the foreign trustees were unwise enough to invest
part of the trust assets in the shares of a foreign company, then, because
there is no correlation between the amount of income actually enjoyed
and the amount of the income of the foreign residents, the whole of that **H**
income also falls within the scope of the assessment. Thus, if the trustees
invest in one share of, say, Standard Oil, the whole of the income (again,
not even profits) of that company falls to be taken into consideration
when assessing the taxpayer, as Standard Oil would then become a foreign
resident part of whose income the taxpayer had power to enjoy.

But the cream of the jest is still to come. It was wholly unnecessary
for the purposes of *Vestey* v. *Inland Revenue Commissioners* [1978] 2

A W.L.R. 136 to set out the provisions of clause 14 of the settlement, but I must do so now. It provides:

"Lastly provided always that Edmund's manager and Samuel's
manager jointly may in their discretion at any time or times within
the specified period by deed revoke in respect of the whole or any part
or parts of the trust premises (then subject to the trusts hereof) all the
B trusts powers and provisions hereinbefore contained and transfer in
respect of the property concerned all or any of such trusts powers
and provisions to and constitute the same (with any desired modifications) as trusts powers and provisions operating in respect of
such property in and according to the law of any country or place
in the world. But this power shall be exercisable only as a power
of revocation and transfer combined (and not by way of mere
C revocation) and shall not be exercised so as to give to the settlors
or either of them (or any wife or widow of either of them) or to
enable them or either of them (or any wife or widow of either of
them) to take by resulting trust or otherwise howsoever any property
benefit right power or control whatsoever."

The Solicitor-General submitted or accepted that, having regard to the
D clear possibility envisaged of the settlor, or any wife or widow of the
settlor (if not, as of course they are, expressly excluded), being constituted
a beneficiary by any such re-settlement, this power must be in the widest
possible terms, not only so far as the trusts but also so far as the beneficiaries are concerned; so that anybody in the United Kingdom—anybody
whatsoever—might be included in the reconstituted settlement. I am not
E certain that I agree with this interpretation, and I must certainly not be
taken as having decided that it is indeed the correct meaning of clause
14. But, given the meaning accepted by the Solicitor-General, he solemnly
submitted that, unless subsection (6) came to the rescue, which he thought
it did (but which, as I have already indicated, I do not think is a correct
interpretation), anybody in the United Kingdom could be assessed for the
entire income of the trustees, together with the not significant enlarge-
F ments which I have already indicated, in every year that the settlement
continued and the funds were undistributed; because, by virtue of the
exercise of the powers conferred by clause 14, and possibly the exercise
by the trustees of the reconstituted settlement of powers of selection among
a group of discretionary beneficiaries, they might become entitled to the
beneficial enjoyment of a part of the trust income.

G   Of course, he also submitted that the whole of this was tempered
by the discretion of the Crown to select who was and who was not
assessed, and for what amount. However, to this submission in total
Mr. Potter made the acid but fully justified comment that, their powers
clearly being fiduciary, to whomsoever else the Inland Revenue Commissioners were entitled to show discretionary mercy, they were certainly
not so entitled to show it to themselves. Nor do I think that they would
H be entitled to show it to Her Majesty's Ministers of State, who, by their
inactivity in this regard, clearly show that they approve of the legislation
as it stands. We are therefore doubtless in for an interesting crop of
bankruptcies.

    The whole submission, however, is so far removed from reality, from
even the most rudimentary notions of justice and fair play, that one has
no more than to state it for it to be abundantly obvious that it cannot
be maintained. Yet here was the Solicitor-General, whom we all know

as one of the most amiable of men, voluntarily casting himself in the A
role of Count Dracula. What has gone wrong? Of course, if the
Solicitor-General's contentions are correct there is an even greater need
to read the whole section strictly than if they are wrong; and, reading it
strictly, I have already indicated that the appeals of the taxpayers fall
to be allowed. But it would not be right to leave the matter there and
to say that these submissions fall to be considered in a case where income
is actually in question.   B

In my view, what has gone wrong is the failure by the courts to
correlate the income upon which the taxpayer is to be taxed with the
income which he has power to enjoy. In other words, I have persuaded
myself that what is wrong is the decision of the Court of Appeal in
Lord Howard de Walden v. *Inland Revenue Commissioners* [1942] 1
K.B. 389. If this decision were to be out of the way and "that income" C
in subsection (1) be taken to be "the income which the taxpayer has
power to enjoy," then the whole section would be quite logical and
straightforward. Moreover, in this case subsection (6) would have a much
more logical place in the scheme of the section, and quantum would then
become a material factor. However, standing this decision, I can see no
answer to the Solicitor-General's main proposition that if a person receives
the income of the settlement to an insubstantial degree he is nevertheless D
taxable upon the whole income of the trustees. Sitting in this court, I
am bound to follow the decision of the Court of Appeal and give effect
thereto, monstrous as the result may be. I do not see how I can escape
the straitjacket.

However, the matter is otherwise in relation to two matters. The first
is as regards what I may call the "other income" of the trustees—income E
which has not arisen as the result of the transfer and associated operations.
I just refuse to believe that Parliament can ever have intended that
other income to be brought into charge to tax, the results being so
utterly unpredictable and unjust. So far as this submission is concerned,
at any rate, I have no contrary authority to bind me, and I simply hold
that the income with which section 412 is dealing throughout is the
income which becomes payable to the foreign trustees as a result of the F
transfer and associated operations, and none other. It is quite ridiculous
to think that the prevention of tax avoidance requires any operation
of any description upon any other income than that which has, in effect,
been transferred abroad.

Secondly, there is the income of any body in which the trustees have
invested any of the trust moneys. In the present case this arises directly, G
because one of the trust investments made by the trustees by means of a
purchase is shares in Commercial Insurance Co. Ltd. This is a company
incorporated and managed and controlled in Jersey. It carries on the
business of fire, fidelity and marine insurance. As regards this company.
the special commissioners said:

"The next matter is the income of Commercial Insurance Co. Ltd.
It was said that the purchase of its shares broke the chain of transfers H
and associated operations. For the purposes of subsection (1) we
can see no warrant for treating its income differently from that of the
other offshore companies. So to do would, in our view, create a
distinction between the subscribers' shares and purchased shares for
which we can see no justification. In each case the individual has
'power to enjoy' the income of the offshore companies by virtue
of the wide definition in subsection (3)."

A   And Mr. Nolan, for the Crown, said much the same thing in more felicitous language.

The answer to this fantastic suggestion—for, if those who subscribe to it will allow me to say so, it is utterly fantastic—is the very simple one that, as was pointed out by Mr. Potter in reply, the income of the company and the income derived from the company by the shareholders

B   are two quite different incomes. Indeed, I know of no manner in which a shareholder can under any circumstances enjoy the income of a company in which he is interested. He may hope, and frequently if not invariably does hope, that a distribution by way of dividend will be made to him out of its profits; but income and profits are, in the case of commercial undertakings, often two vastly different things.

Once again, the fact that the section is a penal section would fully

C   justify one in reading " income " as meaning income and not profits; but even were that solid rock to be swept away it would not avail the Crown in this instance, for in *Canadian Eagle Oil Co. Ltd.* v. *The King* (1945) 27 T.C. 205, 257, Lord Macmillan made it perfectly plain that

> " for the purposes of income tax, the income of a foreign company and the income received from it in dividends by its British share-
D > holders are not to any extent or effect one and the same income, but are two distinct incomes."

So here, the dividends received by the trustees from Commercial Insurance Co. Ltd. are part of the income of the trustees derived from the transfer of assets and associated operations, and it is upon that income, and no further component provided by that company, that section 412 fastens.

E   Accordingly, the more fantastic suggestions of the Solicitor-General fall to the ground. Enough remains, however, even when these excrescences are pared away, to be profoundly disturbing to anybody who cares about equity or equality in taxation, or, more importantly, the rule of law. I need not repeat what I said on this topic in *Vestey* v. *Inland Revenue Commissioners* [1978] 2 W.L.R. 136, especially since on this particular aspect of the Crown's alleged discretion Ungoed-Thomas J. put it far

F   better than I ever could when, in *Inland Revenue Commissioners* v. *Clifforia Investments Ltd.* [1963] 1 W.L.R. 396, 402, he said:

> " It would to my mind be intolerable that exception taken to the construction of a section on the ground that it leads to such a patently unjust result as double taxation should be overruled on the ground that the revenue would only apply it when it considered it
G > equitable to do so. Such a discretion in the revenue would go far beyond that degree of discretion which is inevitably involved in applying and administering the statutes. It would be a wide and arbitrary discretion applied without publicly established principles and, of course, without legislative authority. It would imply that the revenue could exempt from, and was therefore entitled to disregard
H > and overrule, the legislation. This offends our fundamental conception of the rule of law."

Standing *Lord Howard de Walden* v. *Inland Revenue Commissioners* [1942] 1 K.B. 389, my own fundamental conception of the rule of law is deeply offended. The only alternative is for the Crown to tax all who could possibly under any circumstances be recipients of any sliver of income upon the whole of that income—a suggestion equally as offensive. Being bound by that case I am, unhappily, in no position to right a

Walton J.   Vestey v. I.R.C. (No. 2) (Ch.D.)   [1978]

clearly perceived wrong. Fortunately, so far as the individual taxpayers A in the actual case before me are concerned, they, whether by accident or design, escape the charge under section 412 (1) as I have already explained, an escape well merited as they fall to be taxed, as I have already decided in *Vestey* v. *Inland Revenue Commissioners* [1978] 2 W.L.R. 136, under section 412 (2). The final result, therefore, is that all the assessments upon the taxpayers are left standing to the extent, but only to the extent, indicated in my judgment in *Vestey* v. *Inland Revenue Commissioners*; B any other assessments, and any assessments in excess of the figures thereby established, are discharged.

> *Appeals allowed with costs.*
> *Certificate under section* 12 *of the*
> *Administration of Justice Act* 1969
> *to appeal to the House of Lords* C
> *for both Vestey cases.*

Solicitors: *Speechly, Bircham; Solicitors of Inland Revenue.*

A. R.

D

[COURT OF APPEAL]

BELMONT FINANCE CORPORATION LTD. *v.*
WILLIAMS FURNITURE LTD. AND OTHERS

[1969 B. No. 5821]   E

1977 Feb. 14, 15, 16, 17   Buckley, Orr and Goff L.JJ.

> *Company—Psyche—Knowledge—Conspiracy for company to*
> *give financial aid to purchasers of its shares—Company*
> *victim of conspiracy—Directors' knowledge of illegal trans-*
> *action—Whether knowledge to be imputed to company—* F
> *Whether company conspirator—Companies Act* 1948 (11 &
> 12 *Geo.* 6, *c.* 38), *s.* 54
> *Practice—Pleadings—Constructive trust—Conspiracy pleaded*
> *between company directors and others—Company claiming*
> *damages—Plea that directors in breach of trust—Whether*
> *pleadings disclosing allegation that conspirators constructive*
> *trustees—Need to plead fraud and relief claimed—R.S.C.,*
> *Ord.* 18, *rr.* 12, 15 (1) (2) [1]; *Ord.* 20, *r.* 5 (5)   G

All the issued shares of the plaintiff company were held by the second defendant, a subsidiary company of the first defendant. The third to sixth defendants held all the issued shares in M and, on October 11, 1967, pursuant to a written agreement of October 3, they sold all their shares in M to the plaintiff company for £500,000 and, on the same day, purchased all the issued shares in the plaintiff company from H the second defendant for £489,000.

Subsequently the plaintiff company was in liquidation and through its receiver brought an action against the defendants, including two of its three directors, the seventh and eighth defendants, claiming that the value of M's shares was not

[1] R.S.C., Ord. 18, r. 15 (1) (2): see post, p. 727B.
Ord. 20, r. 5 (5): see post, p. 727D.
Ord. 18, r. 12: see post, pp. 730H—731B.

A   £500,000 but £60,038 and, therefore, to the extent that the
plaintiff company had purchased M's shares for an excessive
amount, it had given the third to sixth defendants financial
aid to purchase its shares in contravention of section 54 of the
Companies Act 1948. The statement of claim alleged that the
defendants were " at all material times aware or ought to
have been aware of the fact " that the third to sixth defendants
could not have purchased the shares without financial assistance
B   from the plaintiff company through the purchase of M's
shares at an excessive price and they had conspired together
to carry out the sale and purchase of the plaintiff's share
capital. It was further alleged that the defendant directors
were guilty of misfeasance and breach of trust. Foster J.,
at the close of the plaintiff company's case, held that on its
pleadings, it was a party to the agreement of October 3 and
therefore, it was a conspirator to an unlawful act and could
C   not sue its fellow conspirators in relation to that act and,
since the pleadings did not allege fraud or dishonesty, they
did not disclose a claim against the defendants of a breach
of constructive trust in that they had assisted a breach of
duty by the plaintiff company's directors, as trustees, in
misapplying the company's funds and also in a breach of
section 54. He refused leave for the plaintiff company to
amend its pleadings to specifically allege a breach of
D   constructive trust and dismissed the action.

On appeal by the plaintiff company: —

   Held, allowing the appeal, (1) that, if the defendant
directors knew at the board meeting on October 3, when
the agreement was entered into, that the sale of M's shares
was at an inflated price, then they had knowledge that
the agreement was illegal but, since the company was the
victim of the conspiracy, it was not to be treated on the basis
E   that the defendant directors had notionally transmitted their
knowledge to the plaintiff company to make it a conspirator;
that, even if the company had the knowledge that the agreement was illegal, the conspiracy alleged in the pleadings was
a conspiracy to enter into the agreement of October 3 and not
the agreement itself and, therefore, since the plaintiff company had not been shown to have had knowledge of the
transactions leading to the agreement, it was not a party to
F   the conspiracy (post, pp. 722G—723B, 725A–C, 730H).

   Reg. v. *Churchill* (*No. 2*) [1967] 2 A.C. 224, H.L.(E.);
Oram v. *Hutt* [1914] Ch. 98, C.A. and *Wallersteiner* v. *Moir*
[1974] 1 W.L.R. 991, C.A. considered.

   (2) That before the defendants could be held to be
liable as constructive trustees, they had to assist with
knowledge a dishonest and fraudulent design on the part of
G   the company's directors; that " dishonest " and " fraudulent "
in that context had the same meaning and, although neither
word needed to be specifically pleaded, the pleadings had to
disclose with particularity the allegation that the defendants
had knowledge of dishonesty; that the only knowledge
pleaded was that they were aware or ought to have been
aware of the facts that constituted a breach of section 54 of
the Companies Act 1948, and, in the absence of an unequivocal
H   plea that the defendants had been dishonest, the plaintiff
company could not rely on a breach of a constructive trust
without being granted leave to amend the pleadings (post,
pp. 726E, 728B, H—729F, 730E–F, H).

   Barnes v. *Addy* (1874) L.R. 9 Ch.App. 244; *Davy* v.
Garratt (1878) 7 Ch.D. 473, C.A. and *Selangor United Rubber
Estates Ltd.* v. *Cradock* [1965] Ch. 896 applied.

   Per Goff L.J. The statement of claim did disclose all
the facts necessary to constitute a fraudulent breach of
trust but it was necessary to plead fraud and the absence of

Belmont Finance v. Williams Furniture (C.A.)   [1978]

a specific pleading of fraud and of the relief claimed for A
breach of a constructive trust prevented the pleadings from
showing the defendants the case that they had to answer (post,
pp. 734F—735A, D).
Decision of Foster J. reversed in part.

The following cases are referred to in the judgments:

Alabaster v. Harness [1894] 2 Q.B. 897; [1895] 1 Q.B. 339, C.A.
Barnes v. Addy (1874) L.R. 9 Ch.App. 244.   B
Cargill v. Bower (1878) 10 Ch.D. 502.
Carl Zeiss Stiftung v. Herbert Smith & Co. (No. 2) [1969] 2 Ch. 276;
     [1969] 2 W.L.R. 427; [1969] 2 All E.R. 367, C.A.
Competitive Insurance Co. Ltd. v. Davies Investments Ltd. [1975] 1
     W.L.R. 1240; [1975] 3 All E.R. 254.
Crofter Hand Woven Harris Tweed Co. Ltd. v. Veitch [1942] A.C. 435;
     [1942] 1 All E.R. 142, H.L.(Sc.).   C
Davy v. Garratt (1878) 7 Ch.D. 473, C.A.
Karak Rubber Co. v. Burden (No. 2) [1972] 1 W.L.R. 602; [1972] 1
     All E.R. 1210.
Lawrance v. Lord Norreys (1890) 15 App.Cas. 210, H.L.(E.).
Oram v. Hutt [1914] 1 Ch. 98, C.A.
Reg. v. Churchill (No. 2) [1967] 2 A.C. 224; [1967] 2 W.L.R. 682;
     [1967] 1 All E.R. 497, H.L.(E.).   D
Selangor United Rubber Estates Ltd. v. Cradock [1965] Ch. 896;
     [1965] 2 W.L.R. 67; [1964] 3 All E.R. 709.
Selangor United Rubber Estates Ltd. v. Cradock (No. 3) [1968] 1 W.L.R.
     1555; [1968] 2 All E.R. 1073.
Sterman v. E. W. & W. J. Moore [1970] 1 Q.B. 596; [1970] 2 W.L.R.
     386; [1970] 1 All E.R. 581, C.A.
Wallersteiner v. Moir [1974] 1 W.L.R. 991; [1974] 3 All E.R. 217, C.A.   E

The following additional cases were cited in argument:

Letang v. Cooper [1964] 2 Q.B. 53; [1964] 2 W.L.R. 642; [1964] 1
     All E.R. 669; [1965] 1 Q.B. 232; [1964] 3 W.L.R. 573; [1964]
     2 All E.R. 929, C.A.
Vandervell's Trusts, In re (No. 2) [1974] Ch. 269; [1974] 3 W.L.R.
     256; [1974] 3 All E.R. 205, C.A.   F
Williams v. Williams (1881) 17 Ch.D. 437.

APPEAL from Foster J.
   The plaintiff company, Belmont Finance Corporation Ltd. of 1,
Fitzroy Square, London, W.1, was incorporated in March 1946 to carry
on business as a finance house. On September 2, 1954, it became a G
public company and in October 1954, its objects were amended to enable
it to carry on the business of general bankers. The nominal capital of
the plaintiff company was £1,250,000 and the amount of capital paid
up or credited as paid up was £1,080,000 consisting of 250,000 5 per
cent. cumulative redeemable participating shares of £1 each, 560,000
preferred ordinary shares of £1 each and 540,000 ordinary shares of 10s.
each.   H
   On October 3, 1963, the second defendant, City Industrial Finance
Ltd., which was the registered holder of the plaintiff company's entire
issued share capital consisting of 200,000 fully paid ordinary shares
of £1 each, entered into an agreement with the third defendant, James
Peter Grosscurth, of Maiden Hatch House, Pangbourne, Berkshire, the
plaintiff company, the first defendant Williams Furniture Ltd., which
held a majority of the issued share capital in the second defendant. The

A   agreement provided for the purchase by the third defendant of the entire issued share capital of the plaintiff company. On October 11, 1963, the third defendant, the fourth defendant, Andreas Demetri, of 17, Surrey Street, London, W.C.2, the fifth defendant, Kenneth Maund, of Maximum Finance Ltd., 65, Castle Street, Reading, Berkshire, and the sixth defendant, John Sinclair Copeland, of Russell Tillet & Co., 18, St. Swithin's Lane, London, E.C.4, sold all their shares in Maximum to the plaintiff com-
B   pany for £500,000 and bought all the issued shares of the plaintiff company for £489,000.

The value of the share capital of Maximum Finance Ltd. was not worth more than £60,038 as shown by the balance sheets and profit and loss accounts for 1963 and 1964. The plaintiff company was ordered to be compulsorily wound up on April 8, 1966, and by a further order
C   of the court dated May 10, 1966, John Peter Landau was appointed liquidator. The statement of affairs as at December 1966 disclosed a deficiency as regards creditors in the sum of £176,269.

By an amended statement of claim the plaintiff company alleged that the shares of Maximum were not worth more than £60,038, and that to the extent that the plaintiff company did not get value for money it gave the third, fourth, fifth and sixth defendants financial aid for the purchase of its
D   own shares in contravention of section 54 of the Companies Act 1948.

The plaintiff company claimed (1) a declaration that the transaction effected by the agreement of October 3, 1963, and made between the plain-tiff company and the first three defendants was unlawful and void under section 54 of the Companies Act 1948; (2) damages with interest thereon from October 11, 1963, to payment or judgment under the Law Reform
E   (Miscellaneous Provisions) Act 1934; (3) all necessary accounts and inquiries; (4) as against the seventh defendant, Archie Spector, and the eighth defendant, Frank Victor Smith, a declaration that they were guilty of misfeasance and breach of trust in relation to the plaintiff company as its directors in procuring the plaintiff company to enter into the unlawful agreement of October 3, 1963; (5) alternatively a declaration that the seventh and eighth defendants and each of them
F   were guilty of misfeasance and breach of trust in relation to the plaintiff company as directors in procuring the purchase by the plaintiff com-pany of the entire share capital in Maximum Finance Ltd. at a price of £500,000 which was to the knowledge of the defendants greatly in excess of the true value of such shares; (6) an order that all necessary accounts and inquiries be taken for ascertaining what sums the two defendants
G   were liable to contribute to the assets of the plaintiff company by way of compensation for such misfeasance and breach of trust in procuring the the plaintiff company to enter into the agreement of October 3, 1968, and/or for the purchase of the shares in Maximum Finance Ltd.; (7) an order that the seventh and eighth defendants should jointly and severally contribute to the assets of the plaintiff company and to pay all such sums as they might be found liable to contribute to such assets
H   on taking and making such accounts and inquiries with interest on such sums as from October 11, 1963, to payment or judgment under the Law Reform (Miscellaneous Provisions) Act 1934; as against all eight defendants for (8) costs (9) further and other relief.

Before the trial of the action and counterclaim before Foster J. the plaintiff company reached a compromise with the fifth defendant, Mr. Kenneth Maund and at the trial, the third defendant, who was adjudged bankrupt was in default of appearance. In 1970, the action was discon-

tinued against the eighth defendant, Frank Victor Smith, a man of little   A
substance on compassionate grounds but during the trial a claim in constructive trust was asserted against all the remaining defendants.

At the completion of the plaintiff company's case on October 4,
1976, Foster J. upheld the defendants' submission that there was no
case to answer, and held that, as against the first, second, fourth, sixth
and seventh defendants, the action should be dismissed on the ground
that the plaintiff company was a party to the agreement forming part of   B
the alleged conspiracy and the claim in conspiracy failed in limine
because a party to a conspiracy to do an unlawful act could not sue a
co-conspirator in relation to that act. He held further that on the
statement of claim as it stood it was not open to the plaintiff company to
claim relief against the defendants on a basis of constructive trust without
amendment of the pleadings and he refused leave to amend.   C

By a notice of appeal dated October 15, 1976, the plaintiff company
appealed on the grounds that the judge misdirected himself on the facts
and was wrong in law and in so far as he had discretion exercised the
same upon the wrong principles in holding (1) that the plaintiff company
as a party to the agreement of October 3, 1963, was ipso facto a party
to the conspiracy alleged in the statement of claim; (2) that the plaintiff
company could not succeed in its claim for damages for conspiracy   D
against any of the defendants; (3) that the plaintiff company could not
on the pleadings as they stood succeed in its claim for damages for conspiracy against any of the defendants; (4) that the plaintiff company could
not on the pleadings as they stood at the date of such order obtain any
relief against any of the defendants other than the eighth defendant on
the footing that they were liable as constructive trustees for the   E
plaintiff company; (5) refusing the plaintiff company leave to amend its
statement of claim in accordance with the proposed amendments.

The facts are stated in the judgment of Buckley L.J.

Michael Miller Q.C. and M. J. Roth for the plaintiff company.
N. C. H. Browne-Wilkinson Q.C. and Brian Parker for the first and
second defendants.   F
Nicholas Stewart for the fourth and sixth defendants.
Gerald Godfrey Q.C. and Ian McCulloch for the seventh defendant.

BUCKLEY L.J. On July 30, 1976, Foster J. dismissed this action at
the close of the plaintiff company's case upon the submission of the
defendants that there was no case to answer in relation to an alleged   G
conspiracy and that it was not open to the plaintiff company upon the
statement of claim to seek relief on the basis of constructive trust.

The facts are these: before the transaction out of which the action
arose took place, the second defendant, a wholly owned subsidiary of
the first defendant, owned all the issued shares of the plaintiff company;
the third, fourth, fifth and sixth defendants owned between them all the
shares in a company called Maximum Finance Ltd. (to which I shall   H
refer as "Maximum"); another company called Cityfields Properties Ltd.,
was a wholly owned subsidiary of Maximum; the seventh and eighth
defendants were at all relevant times directors of the plaintiff company.

The third, fourth, fifth and sixth defendants wished to acquire the
share capital of the plaintiff company; for this purpose they required
finance. The form which the transaction took was in essence this, that
under a written agreement of October 3, 1963, the third, fourth, fifth

The Weekly Law Reports, November 3, 1978

717

3 W.L.R.   Belmont Finance v. Williams Furniture (C.A.)   Buckley L.J.

A and sixth defendants sold all their shares in Maximum to the plaintiff company at the price of £500,000 and bought all the issued shares of the plaintiff company from the second defendant for £489,000. If the share capital of Maximum was worth £500,000, there would have been nothing wrong with this, but the plaintiff company asserts that the shares of Maximum were not worth more than about £60,000, and that to the extent that the plaintiff company did not get value for money it was
B giving the third, fourth, fifth and sixth defendants financial aid for the purchase of its own shares, in contravention of the Companies Act 1948, section 54.

The action is brought in the name of the plaintiff company by a receiver appointed out of court under debentures issued by the plaintiff company. The plaintiff company is now in compulsory liquidation and
C the receiver has prosecuted the action under the direction of the Companies Court.

On account of the way in which the case went, the judge has heard the evidence of the plaintiff company's side only; he has heard no evidence of, or on behalf of, any defendant. He made no findings of fact; in view of his judgment it was unnecessary for him to do so. He dealt with the case upon the plaintiff company's pleading, and on that
D alone he held that since the agreement is alleged to have formed part of the alleged conspiracy, and since the plaintiff company was a party to the agreement, the plaintiff company was a conspirator. So he held that the claim in conspiracy failed in limine on the ground that one party to a conspiracy to do an unlawful act cannot sue a co-conspirator in relation to that act. He also held that on the statement of claim
E it was not open to the plaintiff company to claim relief against the defendants on a basis of constructive trust.

It is common ground that for the purposes of this appeal we must assume that the plaintiff company will be able to establish all the allegations in its statement of claim. When considering the statement of claim, two questions have to be kept in mind. First, on the allegations contained in it, was the judge right in holding that the
F plaintiff company could not maintain its claim to relief on the basis that the defendants had conspired to the damage of the plaintiff company? Secondly, on those same allegations and having regard to the form of the endorsement on the writ and the prayer for relief in the statement of claim, is the plaintiff company entitled to any relief on the basis of constructive trust? The plaintiff company asks us to hold that the
G judge was wrong in holding that the plaintiff company could not succeed on the conspiracy point and that the constructive trust point was not open to the plaintiff company on the statement of claim. If he was right on the latter point, the plaintiff company says that the judge should have allowed an amendment of the statement of claim, which in fact he refused.

The endorsement on the writ is in precisely the same form as the
H claim to relief in the statement of claim, to which I shall come in due course. The statement of claim pleads the agreement which I have mentioned, the effect of which was as follows: by the agreement (a) the third defendant agreed to sell and the plaintiff agreed to buy all the issued share capital of Maximum for £500,000; that is clause 2. (b) Such sale to be completed on October 11, 1963; that is clause 3. (c) Subject to and upon the completion of that sale, the second defendant agreed to sell and the third defendant to buy all the share capital of the plaintiff

Buckley L.J.   **Belmont Finance v. Williams Furniture (C.A.)**   [1978]

company for £489,000 (clause 4) subject to adjustment as provided   A
by clause 5. (d) The last mentioned sale to be completed immediately
after the completion of the sale of the share capital of Maximum;
that is clause 6.

I pause there to say that it is important to notice the close relationship between the two transactions, the purchase of the plaintiff's share
capital being conditional upon the sale of the Maximum shares having
been completed, and itself to follow immediately after the completion   B
of the sale of the Maximum shares.

(e) Upon completion of the sale of the share capital to the
plaintiff company the second defendant agreed to subscribe at par for
230,000 5 per cent. redeemable preference shares of £1 each in the
plaintiff company, and to reconstitute the board of the plaintiff company in accordance with nominations by the third defendant; and the   C
third defendant agreed to subscribe at par for 20,000 5 per cent. redeemable preference shares and 50,000 ordinary shares, all of £1 each, of the
plaintiff company; that is clause 2.

There then follow some provisions of a subsidiary character, which I
need not read; then (f) by clause 13 the third defendant warranted the
correctness of the balance sheets of Maximum and Cityfield Properties
Ltd., and certain anciliary matters designed to ensure that those balance   D
sheets should substantially represent the state of those two companies at
the completion of the sale of the share capital to Maximum. (g) The
third defendant further warranted that the aggregate net profits before
tax of Maximum and its subsidiaries, for the period May 22, 1962, to
May 31, 1968, should not be less than £500,000; that is clause 13 (h) (i);
(h) such last-mentioned warranty being secured by a deposit of the   E
whole listed share capital of a company called Rentahome Ltd.: clause
13 (h) (ii). (i) The first and second defendants gave the third defendants
certain warranties relating to the plaintiff company and certain indemni-
ties: clause 14. (j) The first defendant guaranteed to the third
defendant the second defendant's due performance of the agreement.
That agreement is incorporated by reference into the statement of
claim.   F

The statement of claim proceeds to contain the following allegations: I do not read them in the language of the pleader, but in an
abbreviated form, with the exception of certain paragraphs towards
the end. It is alleged (a) that the fourth, fifth and sixth defendants
were associates of the first defendant and active participants in negotiating and procuring the agreement: paragraph 5. (b) That the seventh   G
and eighth defendants and another were at all material times until
October 11, 1963, directors of the plaintiff company: paragraph 6.
(c) That the terms of the agreement were approved at a board meeting
of the plaintiff company on October 3, 1963, which was attended by
the seventh defendant and one other director of the plaintiff; paragraph 8. (d) That at a board meeting of the plaintiff company held at
noon on October 11, 1963, at which the seventh and eighth defendants   H
and another director of the plaintiff company were present as directors,
it was resolved that the plaintiff company should purchase from the
third, fourth and fifth defendants the issued share capital of Maximum
for £500,000: paragraph 9. (e) That the purchase was completed at
that board meeting: paragraph 9 (A). (f) That the board meeting
was attended by the third, fourth, fifth and sixth defendants, by an
accountant employed by the first defendant and its secretary and by the

The Weekly Law Reports, November 3, 1978

719

3 W.L.R.   Belmont Finance v. Williams Furniture (C.A.)   Buckley L.J.

A third defendant's solicitor; paragraph 9 (B). (g) That on or about October 11, 1963, the second defendant resolved to sell the issued share capital of the plaintiff company to the third defendant or as he should direct and that that transaction was completed on October 11, 1963, the 200,000 issued shares in the plaintiff company being transferred as to 116,668 to the third defendant, as to 41,666 to the fourth defendant and as to 41,666 to the fifth defendant; that is paragraph 9 (A). (h) That

B at a further board meeting of the plaintiff company held in the afternoon of October 11, 1963, at which the same persons were present as were present at the board meeting held at noon on that day, the rest of the terms of the agreement were completed: paragraphs 10 and 10A. (i) That the initial negotiations for the third defendant's purchase of the shares of the plaintiff were conducted between the third defendant and one Lipert, then chairman of the second defendant, in the course

C of which the third defendant wrote to Mr. Lipert the letter which is set out in paragraph 12 of the statement of claim, from which I read this passage:

> ". . . my present intention is to arrange the consideration for the purchase of Belmont from Belmont's own resources and this I
D propose to accomplish by selling to Belmont the whole of the issued share capital of Rentahome Ltd."

(j) That later, in the course of negotiations the third defendant wrote to one James, who was by then the chairman of the first and second defendants, a letter set out in paragraph 15 of the statement of claim, from which I read this passage:

E > "I am sorry that it has taken me so long to write to you with firm proposals for the mechanics for the purchase of Belmont, following the news that I am unable to sell shares in Rentahome Ltd. because of the consequences of the Finance Act 1962. Following our recent meeting, I have given considerable thought to your very helpful suggestions, but I have come to the conclusion that it would be more convenient for the transaction to proceed as
F follows: (1) That you or your associates should lend me by way of bridging finance, the amount required for completion say £480,000. (2) That I personally should purchase from [the second defendant], the share capital of [the plaintiff company] for say £480,000. (3) That [the second defendant] should subscribe at par for £230,000 of redeemable preference shares in [the plaintiff company].
G (4) That [the plaintiff company] should purchase from me the whole of the share capital of Maximum Finance Ltd. for £500,000 (this will avoid me showing a large loan in [the plaintiff company's] accounts and deal with the section 54 difficulty). (5) That I will repay the bridging loan of £480,000 and my costs out of the proceeds of sale of Maximum Finance."

H I have of course described the various companies by their character in this action and not by the names by which they are described in the letter. (k) That in the event the transaction proceeded on the basis of the agreement without any bridging finance: paragraph 16. There then come four very important paragraphs, which I shall read in their entirety:

> "(17) The value of the entire share capital of Maximum Finance Ltd. was considerably less than the said sum of £500,000 as is

borne out by its balance sheets and profit and loss accounts as at   A
May 31, 1963, August 31, 1963 and August 31, 1964. The said
sum of £500,000 had been arrived at in order to enable the [third,
fourth and fifth defendants] to purchase the plaintiff company's
shares with money provided by it in contravention of section 54
of the Companies Act 1948. A receiver and manager of Maximum
Finance Ltd. was appointed on December 1, 1966. The statement
of affairs as at December 2, 1966, discloses a deficiency as regards   B
creditors in the sum of £176,269.   (18) The defendants and each of
them were at all material times aware or ought to have been aware
of the fact that the [third, fourth and fifth defendants] were unable
to purchase the share capital of the plaintiff company unless they
obtained financial assistance from the plaintiff company through the
purchase by it of their shares in Maximum Finance Ltd, at an inflated   C
price."

Then there is a reference to not being able to give particulars until after
discovery:

"(19) The defendants wrongfully conspired together to carry
into effect the said sale and purchase of the entire share capital
of the plaintiff company in contravention of the provisions of   D
section 54 of the Companies Act 1948 "

and then it states what is to be found in that section. Paragraph (20):

"Further and in the alternative the [seventh and eighth defendants]
are guilty of misfeasance and breach of trust in their capacities as
directors of the plaintiff company in procuring it to enter into the   E
agreement in contravention of section 54 of the said Act."

Paragraph 22 pleads damage and gives particulars from which it
appears that the value which is put by the pleader upon the entire share
capital of Maximum is £60,038; the damages claimed is the difference
between £500,000 and that sum of £60,038. The relief claimed was
in these terms: F

"The plaintiff company's claim is against all the defendants for (1)
a declaration that the transaction effected by the agreement dated
October 3, 1963, and made between the [third defendant] of the first
part, the plaintiff company of the second part, the [second defendant]
of the third part and the [first defendant] of the fourth part was
unlawful and void under the provisions of section 54 of the Companies   G
Act 1948.   (2) Damages with interest thereon from October 11, 1963,
to payment or judgment under the Law Reform (Miscellaneous
Provisions) Act 1934.   (3) All necessary accounts and inquiries. . . .
Further and in the alternative against the [seventh and eighth
defendants] for (4) A declaration that the said defendants and each
of them were guilty of misfeasance and breach of trust in relation
to the plaintiff company as directors in procuring the plaintiff com-   H
pany to enter into the said unlawful agreement dated October 3,
1963.   (5) Alternatively a declaration that the said defendants and
each of them were guilty of misfeasance and breach of trust in
relation to the plaintiff company as directors in procuring the
purchase by the plaintiff company of the entire share capital in Maximum Finance Ltd. at a price of £500,000 which was to the knowledge of the defendants greatly in excess of the true value of such

The Weekly Law Reports, November 3, 1978

721

3 W.L.R.   Belmont Finance v. Williams Furniture (C.A.)   Buckley L.J.

A shares. (6) An order that all necessary accounts and inquiries may be taken and made for ascertaining what sums the said [seventh and eighth defendants] are liable to contribute to the assets of the plaintiff company by way of compensation for such misfeasance and breach of trust in procuring the plaintiff company to enter into the said agreement dated October 3, 1963, and/or for the purchase of the said shares in Maximum Finance Ltd. (7)

B An order of the said [seventh and eighth defendants] do jointly and severally contribute to the assets of the plaintiff company and do pay to the plaintiff all such sums as they may be found liable to contribute to such assets on taking and making such accounts and inquiries as aforesaid with interest on such sums from October 11, 1963, to payment or judgment under the Law Reform

C (Miscellaneous Provisions) Act 1934. . . . Against all the defendants for: (8) Costs; (9) Further or other relief."

I shall deal first with the conspiracy claim. The plaintiff company's argument is to the following effect: on the allegations in the statement of claim, the agreement was illegal, and they say that an agreement between two or more persons to effect any unlawful purpose, with

D knowledge of all the facts which are necessary ingredients of illegality, in a conspiracy; and we were referred to *Crofter Hand Woven Harris Tweed Co. Ltd.* v. *Veitch* [1942] 435 and *Reg.* v. *Churchill (No. 2)* [1967] 2 A.C. 224. The agreement was carried out, and damaged the plaintiff company.

In the course of the argument in this court counsel for the first and second defendants conceded that the plaintiff company is entitled in this

E appeal to succeed on the conspiracy point, unless it is debarred from doing so on the ground that it was a party to the conspiracy, which was the ground that was relied upon by the judge.

The plaintiff company points out that the agreement was resolved on by a board of which the seventh and eighth defendants constituted the majority, and that they were the two directors who countersigned the

F plaintiff company's seal on the agreement, and that they are sued as two of the conspirators. It is conceded by Mr. Miller for the plaintiff company that a company may be held to be a participant in a criminal conspiracy, and that the illegality attending a conspiracy cannot relieve the company on the ground that such an agreement may be ultra vires; but he says that to establish a conspiracy to which the company was a party, having

G as its object the doing of an illegal act, it must be shown that the company must be treated as knowing all the facts relevant to the illegality; he relies on *Reg.* v. *Churchill.*

The plaintiff company in its reply denies being a party to the conspiracy and, says Mr. Miller, it would be for the defendants to allege the necessary knowledge on the part of the plaintiff company. But he further submits that even if the plaintiff company should be regarded

H as a party to the conspiracy, this would not debar it from relief; and he relies upon *Oram* v. *Hutt* [1914] 1 Ch. 98.

The defendants' argument on this part of the case was to the following effect: that no party to an illegal contract can sue any other party to it upon the contract. Here, Mr. Browne-Wilkinson, for the first and second defendants, says that the company relies on the agreement to establish the conspiracy; that the conspiracy involved the agreement, and he refers to paragraph 19 of the statement of claim,

which I have read, and to the particulars given under it. These were A
particulars given in response to a request for particulars of the allegation that the defendants wrongfully conspired together, specifying all
facts and matters relied on in support of this allegation, and the answer
to that request is in the following terms:

> " The best particulars which the plaintiff can give of overt acts
> of the parties to the said conspiracy are the negotiations which took B
> place between the defendants and/or their respective solicitors
> and/or their duly appointed agents both at meetings between two
> or more of them and through the correspondence disclosed in this
> action, and the entry by the parties into the agreement on October
> 3, 1963, the completion thereof on October 11, 1963, as alleged
> in the re-reamended statement of claim and the concurrence in
> the agreement by " the fourth, fifth and sixth defendants " as C
> evidenced in the correspondence."

So, submits Mr. Browne-Wilkinson, the plaintiff company cannot seek
relief in respect of the transactions there agreed upon—that is to say, agreed
upon in the agreement; one joint tortfeasor cannot sue another for
damages suffered by the plaintiff tortfeasor in consequence of the tort.
But I feel impelled to ask: can the plaintiff company sensibly be regarded D
as a party to the conspiracy, and in law ought it to be regarded as a party
to the conspiracy?

Section 54 of the Companies Act 1948 is designed for the protection of
the relevant company whose shares are dealt with in breach of the section;
that was so held in *Wallersteiner* v. *Moir* [1974] 1 W.L.R. 991.

In the present case the object of the alleged conspiracy was to E
deprive the plaintiff company of over £400,000-worth of its assets,
assuming always, of course, that it succeeds in establishing that allegation.
The plaintiff company was the party at which the conspiracy was aimed.
It seems to me that it would be very strange that it should also be one
of the conspirators. The majority of the board which committed the
company to carry out the project consisted of two of the alleged
conspirators. F

The judge said that the plaintiff company was a vital party to the
agreement, and it could not be said that the other parties were conspirators but not the plaintiff company. With deference to the judge,
who I think probably had very much less reference to authority in the
course of the argument before him than we have had in this court,
that view seems to me to be too simplistic a view, and not to probe far G
enough into the true circumstances of the case.

On the footing that the directors of the plaintiff company who were
present at the board meeting on October 11, 1963, knew that the sale
of the Maximum shares was at an inflated value, and that such value
was inflated for the purpose of enabling the third, fourth, fifth and
sixth defendants to buy the share capital of the plaintiff company,
those directors must be taken to have known that the transaction was H
illegal under section 54.

It may emerge at a trial that the facts are not as alleged in the
statement of claim, but if the allegations in the statement of claim
are made good, the directors of the plaintiff company must then have
known that the transaction was an illegal transaction.

But in my view such knowledge should not be imputed to the
company, for the essence of the arrangement was to deprive the company

The Weekly Law Reports, November 3, 1978

723

3 W.L.R.   Belmont Finance v. Williams Furniture (C.A.)   Buckley L.J.

A   improperly of a large part of its assets. As I have said, the company
was a victim of the conspiracy. I think it would be irrational to treat
the directors, who were allegedly parties to the conspiracy, notionally as
having transmitted this knowledge to the company; and indeed it is a
well-recognised exception from the general rule that a principal is
affected by notice received by his agent that, if the agent is acting in
fraud of his principal and the matter of which he has notice is relevant
B   to the fraud, that knowledge is not to be imputed to the principal.

So in my opinion the plaintiff company should not be regarded as
a party to the conspiracy, on the ground of lack of the necessary guilty
knowledge.

Even though the plaintiff company were to be supposed to be aware
of the illegality, would this disentitle it to relief against co-conspirators?
C   In *Oram* v. *Hutt* [1914] 1 Ch. 98, which I have already mentioned, the
plaintiff was a member of a trade union and he sued, as a member of
the trade union, to obtain relief for the union itself, which was an
unincorporated body. The union had passed a resolution that it would
indemnify any official of the union who took legal proceedings against
one of the members of the union, called McNicholas, for defamation,
D   and in reliance upon that indemnity Mr. Johnson, who was the general
secretary of the union, sued Mr. McNicholas for damages for defamation. He was successful and recovered damages. The union paid the
solicitor who acted for Mr. Johnson £775, I think it was, but the exact
figure does not matter. Mr. Oram, the plaintiff, sued for a declaration
that the payment was ultra vires and asked for an order for repayment
of the money to the union.

E   The matter came before Swinfen Eady J. at first instance, who held
that the union had no power to authorise its officers to take proceedings
for slander at the expense of the union and that the payment made in
respect of the costs of Mr. Johnson's action were invalid on the ground
that they offended against the law of maintenance. He took the further
subsidiary view that the acts of the union were ultra vires, inasmuch
F   as the rules of the union did not specifically provide for the step that
was taken; and he made a declaration and an order for the repayment
of the £775 paid to Mr. Johnson's solicitors.

In this court Lord Parker of Waddington dealt with the matter in this
way, at p. 104:

" The first question for decision, therefore, is whether the agree-
G   ment by the association to indemnify any of its officers who took
proceedings against McNicholas for libel was void on the ground
of maintenance. In my opinion Swinfen Eady J. was bound and
this court is bound to hold this agreement void unless this case can
be distinguished from the case of *Alabaster* v. *Harness* [1894] 2
Q.B. 897."

H   He then discussed *Alabaster* v. *Harness* and came to the conclusion that
the case then before the court could not be distinguished from that case,
and he went on to say at p. 105: " The question remains whether the payments in question were justified on any other ground." He discussed that
and he came to the conclusion that they were not, and in the result he
said: " I have come to the conclusion, therefore, that the appeal must be
dismissed."

Lord Sumner, who was also sitting in this court on that case, held

that the law of maintenance affected the case and that the transactions A
were illegal on that ground, and he also agreed with Swinfen Eady J.

Warrington J., who was the third member of the court said, at p. 109:

> "If the transaction amounted to maintenance on the part of the
> association, then the payment in question was made in pursuance
> of an illegal contract, and, in my opinion, it is impossible to hold
> that to make such a payment can be within the implied powers of B
> the association. I think, therefore, that the judgment of the learned
> judge was right and this appeal fails."

Mr. Miller put that case forward as authority for the proposition
that the illegality of the agreement did not debar the union from relief,
and he asked rhetorically: "Why should having been a party to the
agreement here debar the plaintiff from relief?"

Mr. Browne-Wilkinson has emphasised that in *Oram* v. *Hutt* the
court came to the conclusion that the payments by the union were
ultra vires payments; consequently no title to the property in the sum
of £775 passed when the payment was made, all parties to the agreement being aware of the circumstances, the solicitor being also the
solicitor to the union and Mr. Johnson being its general secretary, and
that accordingly the union did not have to rely upon the illegal contract D
in any way for the purpose of making a case for recovery of the money;
it relied upon its own legal ownership of the money, which had never
been determined as a result of the payment to Mr. Johnson or his
solicitors. He said that that case is unlike the present one because as he
contends, the claim in conspiracy in the instant case before us, is founded
upon the illegal agreement and the plaintiff was a party to that agreement and to its being carried into effect.

I think one must look with some care at what is alleged to have been
the conspiracy. I have read paragraph 19 of the statement of claim,
which asserts that the defendants wrongfully conspired to carry into
effect the sale and purchase of the share capital of the plaintiff company
The sale and purchase of the share capital of the plaintiff company is to
be found in the agreement—that is, the agreement for the sale and the F
agreement for the purchase—and as I read this paragraph, the allegation
is that antecedent to the agreement being entered into, the conspirators
conspired, the effect of the conspiracy being that they would enter into
the agreement; and when one comes to look at the particulars delivered
under paragraph 19, one finds that there are relied upon as overt acts
of the parties to the conspiracy the negotiations and the correspondence G
which took place before the agreement was entered into, the entry into
the agreement and its completion. I cannot understand how the
negotiations could be overt acts of the conspiracy unless the conspiracy
existed before those negotiations took place, because as I understand it,
an overt act establishing the existence of a conspiracy is an overt act
which shows that the agreement which is alleged to be conspiratorial has
already been made. The entering into of the agreement of October 3, H
1963, is referred to in these particulars, as I read them, as part of the
implementation of the conspiracy, not as itself constituting the conspiracy, and in the same way the completion of that agreement is part
of the implementation.

So for my part I do not feel able to accept Mr. Browne-Wilkinson's
contention that the conspiracy here is founded on the illegal agreement.
It is quite true that the illegal agreement was part and parcel of the

The Weekly Law Reports, November 3, 1978

725

3 W.L.R.   Belmont Finance v. Williams Furniture (C.A.)   Buckley L.J.

A implementation, but it seems to me that the allegation of a conspiracy relates to something different. The plaintiff company, not being shown to have knowledge of the facts relevant to the illegality of the agreement, is not in my judgment debarred from suing the defendants for damages for the conspiracy, because the plaintiff company is not shown to have been a party to the conspiracy or to guilty knowledge about the illegality of the transaction which was to be carried out under the

B agreement. On these grounds it seems to me that it is mistaken to regard the plaintiff company as being in law party to the conspiracy. I feel glad to be able to reach that decision because, for reasons that I indicated at the beginning of this section of my judgment, it seems to me to be completely unreal to regard the plaintiff company as party to the conspiracy. Accordingly, in my judgment, the judge was wrong

C in dismissing the action on that ground.

I come now to the subject of constructive trust. It should be realised that the claim in constructive trust came into the case only during the hearing before the judge. That arose in this way: the pleadings were framed in the way I have indicated and the case came before the judge with the statement of claim in that form. Shortly

D before the trial opened, the plaintiff had reached a compromise with the fifth defendant, Mr. Kenneth Maund, and the action was settled as far as he was concerned. The other defendants became aware of this when the trial opened and they asked to be allowed to know the terms of the settlement with Mr. Maund, which ultimately they received, I think on about the second or third day of the trial. There was then a request by all the defendants before the court for an adjournment so

E that they could amend their pleadings to plead that the settlement with Mr. Maund operated as a release of all the other alleged conspirators from any liability upon the alleged conspiracy. Those amendments will be found now incorporated in the pleadings.

We have not been concerned with that question at all; it has not yet been judicially considered in any way. The reason for that is that

F during the adjournment the plaintiff's advisers gave notice of the fact that they would raise a claim not only for damages for conspiracy, but also a claim asserting that the defendants are liable as constructive trustees. The settlement with Mr. Maund would not affect the viability of that claim in any way; so if the plaintiff company is allowed to bring in, or to pursue, the claim of constructive trust, there was no immediate purpose in pursuing the question of whether the settlement with Mr. Maund

G had released the other defendants from their liability under the alleged conspiracy, because the facts relied upon by the plaintiff company in support of the constructive trust claim are the same, or substantially the same, as the facts relied upon on the conspiracy claim.

But it is of some importance to realise that when the parties were preparing for trial, and indeed when the case came before the trial judge

H and for the first few days of the trial, the only claim before him was the claim in damages for conspiracy. Mr. Miller, for the plaintiff company, asserts that on the facts pleaded in the statement of claim, although there is no reference in it to constructive trusteeship, the plaintiff is entitled to relief on that footing against all the defendants before the court. I should perhaps have said that not all the original defendants were before the court; the third defendant is a bankrupt and is in default of appearance; Mr. Maund, as I say, has been disposed of by

compromise; and early in 1970 the action was discontinued against the A
eighth defendant, who I understand was a man of little substance and
we were told that the proceedings were discontinued against him on
compassionate grounds.   But the claim in constructive trust is asserted
against all the other defendants.

Mr. Miller contends that the statement of claim does not need any
amendment, accountability on the footing of a constructive trust flowing
as a legal result from the pleaded facts. He says that on those facts, B
particularly paragraphs 17, 18 and 19 of the statement of claim, if
proved, the court ought to find the plaintiff company entitled to damages
for conspiracy, and grant to the plaintiff company any other relief to which,
on those facts, it can show that it is entitled, particularly by way of account
against all the participants in the conspiracy, because, he says, the legal
consequences of the facts are to bring home to the participants in the C
conspiracy participation in a transaction which involved misapplying
the company's assets in breach of trust—that is to say, in breach of the
duties of the directors of the plaintiff company and in breach of section
54, and he emphasises that that section creates a criminal liability; he
does that to emphasise the undesirable nature of the transaction.

Distinguishing the decision of Pennycuick J. in *Selangor United* D
Rubber Estates Ltd. v. *Cradock* [1965] 1 Ch. 896, Mr. Miller says that
the plaintiff company does not in this case rely on any duty owed to
him by the first and second defendants in his claim against those
defendants as constructive trustees; but on the fact that in consequence of their conduct those two defendants are accountable on the
basis of constructive trusteeship and therefore, he says, an allegation of
the particular relationship giving rise to accountability is not necessary. E

The plaintiff company founds this part of its case on the statement
of principle of Lord Selborne L.C. in *Barnes* v. *Addy* (1874) L.R. 9
Ch.App. 244, 251–252, to the effect that anyone who assists with knowledge a dishonest or fraudulent design on the part of trustees is liable
to be treated as a constructive trustee. Mr. Miller says that there is
no need to plead fraud, and that knowing participation in a misfeasance F
or breach of trust ought to be held as a sufficient basis to claim liability
on the footing of constructive trusteeship particularly if, as in the
present case, the action complained of is of a criminal character directed
to depriving the plaintiff company of assets; he says that such an act must
be sufficiently dishonest for the purposes of the doctrine. He admits that
this is an extension of the rule as formulated by Lord Selborne L.C.;
but he says that it is an extension which this court ought to make. He G
says moreover that there are here in fact sufficient facts pleaded to
demonstrate that the transaction here in question was truly a dishonest
transaction. Moreover, he says that the statement of claim shows that
the second defendant and the third defendant received moneys of the
plaintiff, or money which for the present purpose sufficiently represents the plaintiff's money, in circumstances which would support a H
claim of constructive trusteeship under the other head mentioned by
Lord Selborne L.C., which relates to cases in which the defendant has
received and has become accountable for some part of the trust property.
That, shortly, and I hope not too inadequately, describes the nature
of the plaintiff company's argument.

The defendants have relied to a great extent upon the Rules of the
Supreme Court relating to pleadings.   They have referred us to R.S.C.,

A   Ord. 6, r. 2, which relates to the indorsement of the claim on the writ and statement of claim, which is required to contain a concise statement of the nature of the claim made or the relief or remedy required.

   Mr. Browne-Wilkinson also referred us to R.S.C., Ord. 18, r. 15 (1) and (2), which are in these terms:

B   "(1) A statement of claim must state specifically the relief or remedy which the plaintiff claims; but costs need not be specifically claimed. (2) A statement of claim must not contain any allegation or claim in respect of a cause of action unless that cause of action is mentioned in the writ or arises from facts which are the same as, or include or form part of, facts giving rise to the cause of action so mentioned; but, subject to that, a plaintiff may in his statement of claim alter, modify or extend any claim made by him in the
C   indorsement of the writ without amending the indorsement."

   Sub-rule (2) contemplates that, where two kinds of relief are sought arising out of common facts or facts which are to some extent common, those claims to relief may be combined in the statement of claim.

   We were referred by Mr. Godfrey to R.S.C., Ord. 20, r. 5 (5), which provides:
D
       "An amendment may be allowed under paragraph (2) notwithstanding that the effect of the amendment will be to add or substitute a new cause of action if the new cause of action arises out of the same facts or substantially the same facts as a cause of action in respect of which relief has already been claimed in the action by the party applying for leave to make the amend-
E   ment."

   It appears to me that in that sub-rule the Rules Committee must have been using the expression " cause of action " as referring to a type of relief claimed rather than to pleaded facts.

   The defendants argue that an account cannot be claimed, as the plaintiff company seeks to claim an account, on the basis of constructive
F   trusteeship, without pleading the circumstances which give rise to the accountability; and they say that if the plaintiff company relies upon alternative causes of action, or intends to claim alternative relief based upon facts which are to some extent, or even entirely, the same, each must be stated in the pleadings; and they say that the facts alleged in the present case in the statement of claim are insufficient to support a
G   claim to constructive trusteeship, because an agreement to do an illegal act may be entered into in circumstances which involve no dishonesty; the parties may not have recognised the illegality of the act, even though they may have known all the facts which in truth make the act illegal. For example the transaction may have been embarked upon and carried out under mistaken advice given in good faith by properly instructed advisers. Counsel drew our attention to the requirements of R.S.C.,
H   Ord. 18, r. 12 relating to the particularity with which misrepresentations, fraud, breach of trust, wilful default or undue influence should be pleaded, and to the notes in *The Supreme Court Practice* (1976) which relate to that subject; and also to note 18/12/2, which explains the functions of particulars in pleadings, and they have contended that if any fraud is intended to be pleaded by the statement of claim, this is only done by way of inference. They referred us to two authorities, *Davy* v. *Garratt* (1878) 7 Ch.D. 473, where Baggallay L.J. said at p. 489

Buckley L.J.   Belmont Finance v. Williams Furniture (C.A.)   [1978]

that fraud should not be inferred; and to *Lawrance* v. *Lord Norreys* A (1890) 15 App.Cas. 210, where Lord Watson made a rather similar observation at p. 221. They raised the question whether constructive knowledge that trust moneys were being wrongly applied was sufficient to render a defendant liable as a constructive trustee where he had not in fact received any of the trust moneys or any moneys sufficiently representing the trust moneys. I hope that gives a sufficient indication of the nature of the defendants' argument on this part of the case. B

I think two questions need to be considered: first, is it necessary when a person is sought to be charged as a constructive trustee that the design of which he is alleged to have had knowledge should be a fraudulent and dishonest design? For this purpose I do not myself see that any distinction is to be drawn between the words "fraudulent" and "dishonest"; I think they mean the same thing, and to use the C two of them together does not add to the extent of dishonesty required.

The second question is: if this is necessary, does the statement of claim here allege dishonesty with sufficient particularity? The plaintiff company has contended that in every case the court should consider whether the conduct in question was so unsatisfactory—whether it can be strictly described as fraudulent or dishonest in law—as to make D accountability on the footing of constructive trust equitably just. This, as I have said, is admitted to constitute an extension of the rule as formulated by Lord Selborne L.C. That formulation has stood for more than 100 years. To depart from it now would, I think, introduce an undesirable degree of uncertainty to the law, because if dishonesty is not to be the criterion, what degree of unethical conduct is to be sufficient? I think we should adhere to the formula used by Lord E Selborne L.C. So in my judgment the design must be shown to be a dishonest one—that is to say, a fraudulent one.

The knowledge of that design on the part of the parties sought to be made liable may be actual knowledge. If he wilfully shuts his eyes to dishonesty, or wilfully or recklessly fails to make such inquiries as an honest and reasonable man would make, he may be found to have F involved himself in the fraudulent character of the design, or at any rate to be disentitled to rely on lack of actual knowledge of the design as a defence. But otherwise, as it seems to me, he should not be held to be affected by constructive notice. It is not strictly necessary, I think, for us to decide that point on this appeal; I express that opinion merely as my view at the present stage without intending to lay it down as a final decision. G

In the present case, do the facts alleged in the statement of claim suffice to bring home to the defendants or any of them a charge that (a) the object of the alleged conspiracy was a dishonest one; and (b) that they actually knew, or must be taken to have known, that it was so?

An allegation of dishonesty must be pleaded clearly and with H particularity. That is laid down by the rules and it is a well-recognised rule of practice. This does not import that the word "fraud" or the word "dishonesty" must necessarily be used: see *Davy* v. *Garratt*, 7 Ch.D. 473, 489, *per* Thesiger L.J. The facts alleged may sufficiently demonstrate that dishonesty is allegedly involved, but where the facts are complicated this may not be so clear, and in such a case it is incumbent upon the pleader to make it clear when dishonesty is alleged.

The Weekly Law Reports, November 3, 1978

729

3 W.L.R.   Belmont Finance v. Williams Furniture (C.A.)   Buckley L.J.

A If he uses language which is equivocal, rendering it doubtful whether he is in fact relying on the alleged dishonesty of the transaction, this will be fatal; the allegation of its dishonest nature will not have been pleaded with sufficient clarity.

The facts that are asserted here are that the defendants and each of them were at all material times aware, or ought to have been aware, of the fact that the third, fourth and fifth defendants were unable to B purchase the share capital of the plaintiff company unless they obtained financial assistance from the plaintiff company through the purchase by it of their shares in Maximum at an inflated price. That must be read in conjunction with the allegation in paragraph 17, that the said sum of £500,000 had been arrived at in order to enable the third, fourth and fifth defendants to purchase the plaintiff's shares with money provided C by it in contravention of section 54. The allegation of the conspiracy is an allegation that the parties conspired to carry into effect the sale and purchase of the share capital of the plaintiff company in contravention of section 54, and all the defendants were, in one capacity or another, parties to the agreement of October 3. They were well aware of everything to be found in that agreement, and I drew attention earlier to the very intimate connection in that agreement between the sale of the D shares of Maximum and the sale of the plaintiff's shares.

The alleged design, namely, to procure that the plaintiff company should pay £500,000 for property worth about £60,000 in order to enable the third, fourth, fifth and sixth defendants to buy the share capital of the plaintiff company, which they could not otherwise do, was in my judgment clearly dishonest if the alleged inflation of the price was E actually known, but not otherwise. Paragraph 18 does not allege exclusively actual knowledge; it says that the defendants were aware, or ought to have been aware. It seems to me therefore that the plaintiff company does not unequivocally assert that the fact that the price was an inflated one was known to the defendants or any of them, although it is open to the plaintiff company on the pleadings to prove that this was so. The pleading does not demonstrate that the plaintiff relies on F dishonesty as an essential element of its cause of action. So in my opinion this statement of claim does not unequivocally and clearly indicate that the plaintiff is proposing to assert that the transaction was a dishonest one.

R.S.C., Ord. 18, r. 15 (1) requires that the statement of claim must state specifically the relief or remedy which the plaintiff claims. A G statement of claim must therefore specify at least one form of relief which the plaintiff claims, but on proof of the necessary facts the court is not I think confined to granting that particular or precise form of relief. We were referred to the Supreme Court of Judicature (Consolidation) Act 1925, sections 40 and 43, the first of which has the marginal note "Equities appearing incidentally." Section 40 says:

H "The court or judge shall take notice of all equitable estates, titles and rights, and all equitable duties and liabilities appearing incidentally in the course of any cause or matter, in the same manner in which the Court of Chancery would formerly have taken notice of those matters in any suit or proceeding duly instituted therein."

The marginal note to section 43 reads: "Determination of matter completely and finally." Section 43 says:

" The High Court and the Court of Appeal respectively, in the   A
exercise of the jurisdiction vested in them by this Act, shall, in
any cause or matter pending before the court, grant, either
absolutely or on such terms and conditions as the court thinks just,
all such remedies whatsoever as any of the parties thereto may
appear to be entitled to in respect of any legal or equitable claim
properly brought forward by them in the cause or matter, so that,
as far as possible, all matters in controversy between the parties   B
may be completely and finally determined, and all multiplicity of
legal proceedings concerning any of those matters avoided."

It is clear that a plaintiff cannot claim relief which is inconsistent with
the relief that he has explicitly claimed; the authority for that is *Cargill*
v. *Bower* (1878) 10 Ch.D. 502. But it appears to me that the court
must have jurisdiction to grant any relief that it thinks appropriate to   C
the facts as proved; but if a party seeks to raise a new claim, which
has not been adumbrated in his pleading, in the course of the trial, in
my opinion the court should not give relief of that kind, at any rate
without offering the opposing party an opportunity for an adjournment,
and giving them an opportunity to say whether they have been taken by
surprise, or have been prejudiced by the fact that that particular form   I
of relief had not been explicitly claimed earlier.

In the present case the absence of any claim in constructive trust,
which was introduced, as I have said, at a late stage, has greatly added,
it seems to me, to the likelihood of confusion about whether the statement of claim contains any sufficiently clear allegation of fraud and
dishonesty; and indeed whether the plaintiff company was intending to
rely on any allegations of fraud and dishonesty at all. Dishonesty was   E
not a necessary ingredient of the claim of conspiracy; all that would be
necessary to support that claim would be actual, or possibly imputed,
knowledge of the facts which rendered the transaction an illegal one.
" Crime " and " fraud " are not synonymous; a criminal act may well be
committed without any fraud or dishonesty.

In the present case, as it seems to me, there is no sufficiently clear   F
allegation of dishonesty to be found in this statement of claim; and if it
is to be raised it must be raised by amendment, and I understand that
an application for amendment is to be made later.

For these reasons I think the judge was justified in saying that a
claim in constructive trust was not one which was open to the plaintiff
company on the pleading as it stands. As I say, the judge refused   G
leave to amend; I have said nothing about that because we have to
hear argument about it later. For my part I think the judge was wrong
on the conspiracy point, but right, to the extent that I have indicated,
on the constructive trust point.

ORR L.J.　I entirely agree with the judgment that has just been
delivered by Buckley L.J. and only wish to add a few words. As to   H
the circumstances in which a person may be held liable as a constructive trustee, the statement of Lord Selborne L.C. in *Barnes* v.
Addy, L.R. 9 Ch.App. 244, has, as Buckley L.J. has pointed out, stood
for over 100 years. I agree with his view that it would be wrong to
extend the principle there stated and it might be productive of uncertainty
in the law to do so.

As to the obligation to plead fraud, the notes, in *The Supreme Court*

The Weekly Law Reports, November 3, 1978

731

3 W.L.R.   Belmont Finance v. Williams Furniture (C.A.)   Orr L.J.

A *Practice* (1976) to Ord. 18, r. 12, state: " Fraudulent conduct must be distinctly alleged and as distinctly proved, and it is not allowable to leave fraud to be inferred from the facts." That statement is fully justified by the passage to which Buckley L.J. has referred in the judgment of Thesiger L.J. in *Davy* v. *Garratt*, 7 Ch.D. 473, and in my judgment these requirements were plainly not satisfied in the present case.

B I would only add that where fraud has not been sufficiently pleaded, it is in my judgment no answer to say that if it had been sufficiently pleaded no further evidence would have been called for the defence. The presence or absence of a charge of fraud may, as it seems to me, affect the whole manner in which a defence is conducted.

I agree with the order proposed by Buckley L.J.

C

GOFF L.J. I would like to preface this judgment by pointing out that so far as the conspiracy question is concerned, we are dealing with a point of law on a particular pleading, and so far as the question of constructive trust is concerned we are dealing with a pleading point. It is, therefore, necessary that we should proceed on the footing that all D the facts alleged in the statement of claim have been, or will be, proved; but in fairness to the defendants I should state that they deny that they joined in any conspiracy and they deny that they were dishonest or party to any dishonesty. Whether that denial is well-founded or not is a matter which will have to be investigated at the trial.

On the question whether the plea that the plaintiff company cannot proceed on conspiracy because it became a party to the unlawful act, or E to the conspiracy, by becoming a party to the agreement of October 3, 1963, I entirely agree with the conclusion reached by Buckley L.J. and with his reasons. I would add only a few points of my own in amplification.

First, the agreement of October 3, 1963, was not per se unlawful. It was the other facts alleged concerning it, the fact that the purchase F by the plaintiff company was at an inflated price and that that price was arrived at, not for any purpose of the company, which indeed it injured, but to assist the third defendant, and to put him in a position to buy the shares in the plaintiff company which made the agreement illegal. In my judgment, therefore, the plaintiff company cannot on any showing be a party to that conspiracy and debarred from maintaining its action unless it knew those facts.

G This is shown by *Reg.* v. *Churchill* [1967] 2 A.C. 224 to which Buckley L.J. has referred, and I would read just two passages from the speech of Viscount Dilhorne in that case. He said, at p. 237:

"In answer to the question posed by the Court of Criminal Appeal in this case, I would say that mens rea is only an essential ingredient in conspiracy in so far as there must be an intention H to be a party to an agreement to do an unlawful act; that knowledge of the law on the part of the accused is immaterial and that knowledge of the facts is only material in so far as such knowledge throws a light on what was agreed."

Then Viscount Dilhorne said, at p. 237:

"The question is, 'What did they agree to do?' If what they agreed to do was, on the facts known to them, an unlawful act,

they are guilty of conspiracy and cannot excuse themselves by say- A
ing that, owing to their ignorance of the law, they did not realise
that such an act was a crime. If, on the facts known to them,
what they agreed to do was lawful, they are not rendered artificially
guilty by the existence of other facts, not known to them, giving a
different and criminal quality to the act agreed upon."

I agree with Buckley L.J. that it is not possible to impute to the B
company the knowledge of the sixth and seventh defendants. It was
suggested in reply that Mr. James was somehow in a different position,
but I cannot see myself how that affects the matter. If he was innocent,
it carries it no further; if he had knowledge of the improper purpose of
the conspirators, I do not see how his knowledge either could be imputed
to the plaintiff company, seeing that he was the chairman of the second
defendant, who was one of the conspirators.   C

Finally in support of what Buckley L.J. has said, I would wish to
cite two short passages from *Wallersteiner* v. *Moir* [1974] 1 W.L.R.
991; the first passage is in the judgment of Lord Denning M.R. where
he said, at p. 1014:

> "In *Essex Aero Ltd.* v. *Cross*, November 17, 1961; Bar Library
> Transcript No. 388 of 1961, Harman L.J. said: 'the section was   D
> not enacted for the company's protection, but for that of its
> creditors; . . . the company, . . . cannot enforce it.' I do not
> agree. I think the section was passed so as to protect the company
> from having its assets misused. If it is broken, there is a civil
> remedy by way of an action for damages."

Scarman L.J. spoke to the same effect and said, at pp. 1032–1033:   E

> "There was, on these facts, a breach of duty by Dr. Wallersteiner
> as a director. The companies were, also, in breach of the section.
> But the maxim 'potior est conditio defendentis' is of no avail to
> Dr. Wallersteiner, for the section must have been enacted to protect
> company funds and the interests of shareholders as well as creditors.
> I do not agree with the dictum of Harman L.J. in *Essex Aero Ltd.* v. F
> *Cross* . . . to the effect that the section was enacted not for the
> company's protection but for that of its creditors."

Turning to the other point, the question as to constructive trust,
the judge took many objections. We have heard argument upon them,
though in the end the matter came to be focused, rightly, on the
question of fraudulent breach of trust. I think I ought to refer to G
them and to say a few words about them. Foster J. said:

> "There is not one word in the statement of claim that the second
> defendant is a trustee, that it was in breach of trust, that it
> received the moneys knowing the moneys belonged to Belmont,
> or even that the moneys which it did receive did in fact belong to
> Belmont."   H

Foster J. cited a passage from Ungoed-Thomas J.'s judgment in *Selangor
United Rubber Estates Ltd.* v. *Cradock (No. 3)* [1968] 1 W.L.R. 1555,
1580, which includes these words:

> "There are thus three elements: (1), assistance by the stranger,
> (2) with knowledge, (3) in a dishonest and fraudulent design on
> the part of the trustees."

The Weekly Law Reports, November 3, 1978

733

3 W.L.R.   Belmont Finance v. Williams Furniture (C.A.)   Goff L.J.

A   And then Foster J. said:

"These passages show the various allegations which have to be made and proved. In the statement of claim none of these things are even alleged, let alone proved."

I am not able to agree with any of those objections, except the last, "(3) in a dishonest and fraudulent design on the part of the trustees."   In my judgment it was neither necessary nor proper to plead that the second defendants were trustees or that they had committed a breach of trust; that is not the basis on which it is sought to make them liable.   Further, this is not a tracing action, and therefore in my judgment it is enough to show that the moneys received by the second defendant sufficiently represented the plaintiff's money: see the *Selangor* case at p. 1614E.

As a matter of pleading, paragraphs 9A and 9B of the statement of claim, and the agreement of October 3, 1963, showing, as Buckley L.J. has pointed out, the direct and immediate connection between the purchase by the plaintiff company of the shares in the Maximum company and the purchase by the third defendant of the shares in the plaintiff company do, so far as the question is one of fact, in my judgment sufficiently allege that the moneys represented the moneys of the plaintiff company in the case of the second defendant; whilst so far as concerns the third defendant, he received payment direct from the plaintiff company.   It is not now alleged that actual receipt of moneys can be advanced on the pleadings as they stand, without amendment against any other of the defendants.

E   In my view the allegations in the statement of claim as a whole clearly plead participation in any breach of trust committed by the directors; and in my judgment paragraph 18 is a sufficient pleading of knowledge on the part of all the defendants, whether the true standard be actual knowledge or constructive notice.

It seems to me, therefore, that there are three questions which we have to decide: first, is it necessary to prove that the alleged breaches of trust by the directors were fraudulent or dishonest—and I agree with Buckley L.J. that the two things really mean one and the same; secondly, if so, is that sufficiently pleaded; and thirdly, was it necessary to specify, either in the body of the statement of claim or in the prayer, the claim for relief on the footing of constructive trusteeship?

On the first point Mr. Miller in support of his argument that it is permissible to extend the principle of *Barnes* v. *Addy*, L.R. 9 Ch.App. 244, relied on two passages in the *Selangor* case.   The first is where Ungoed-Thomas J. said, at p. 1582:

"It seems to me imperative to grasp and keep constantly in mind that the second category of constructive trusteeship (which is the only category with which we are concerned) is nothing more than a formula for equitable relief.   The court of equity says that the defendant shall be liable in equity, as though he were a trustee. He is made liable in equity as trustee by the imposition or construction of the court of equity.   This is done because in accordance with equitable principles applied by the court of equity it is equitable that he should be held liable as though he were a trustee. Trusteeship and constructive trusteeship are equitable conceptions."

The second passage was introduced by the judge saying, at p. 1590:   **A**
" I come to the third element, ' dishonest and fraudulent design on the
part of the trustees ' . . . ," and he said, at p. 1591 :

> " It seems to me unnecessary and, indeed, undesirable to attempt
> to define ' dishonest and fraudulent design,' since a definition in
> vacuo, without the advantage of all the circumstances that might
> occur in cases that might come before the court, might be to restrict   **B**
> their scope by definition without regard to, and in ignorance of,
> circumstances which would patently come within them. The words
> themselves are not terms of art and not taken from a statute or
> other document demanding construction. They are used in a
> judgment as the expression and indication of an equitable principle
> and not in a document as constituting or demanding verbal applica-
> tion and, therefore, definition. They are to be understood ' accord-   **C**
> ing to the plain principles of a court of equity ' to which Kindersley
> V.-C. referred in *Bodenham* v. *Hoskins* (1852) 21 L.J.Ch. 864,
> 873, and these principles, in this context at any rate, are just plain,
> ordinary common sense. I accept that ' dishonest and fraudulent,'
> so understood, is certainly conduct which is morally reprehensible.
> But what is morally reprehensible is best left open to identification   **D**
> and not to be confined by definition."

If and so far as Ungoed-Thomas J. intended, as I think he did, to
say that it is not necessary that the breach of trust in respect of which
it is sought to make the defendant liable as a constructive trustee should
be fraudulent or dishonest, I respectfully cannot accept that view. I
agree that it would be dangerous and wrong to depart from the safe   **E**
path of the principle as stated by Lord Selborne L.C. to the uncharted
sea of something not innocent (and Mr. Miller conceded that mere
innocence would not do) but still short of dishonesty. In my judgment,
therefore, it was necessary in this case to plead, and of course in due
course to prove, that the breach of trust by the directors was dishonest.

I turn then to the second question, which is whether fraud or
dishonesty has been sufficiently pleaded. I accept Mr. Miller's sub-   **F**
mission that the statement of claim, when carefully analysed, does plead
all the facts necessary to constitute a fraudulent breach of trust, namely,
a deliberate design to misapply the plaintiff company's money in buying
shares at an inflated price to place a third party in funds to buy the
shares in the plaintiff company, a design known to the directors and to
all the participants in it.
  G

However, in my judgment this pleading is defective so far as fraud
is concerned, because it does not make it clear that the pleader means
to charge fraud, because he says in paragraph 18 that the defendants
and each of them were at all material times aware, or ought to have
been aware; and the latter part is, as Mr. Miller was constrained to
admit, consistent with innocence.

I am unable to accept the submission that this should be construed   **H**
as a charge of fraud, with an alternative claim to relief in the event of
his failing to prove it; on the contrary, it seems to me to reflect what
has been his attitude throughout, namely, " I do not have to charge
fraud." This passage and the general tenor of the statement of claim
as a whole, taken in conjunction with the absence of any claim to relief
specifically on the basis of a constructive trust, even if that be not a
breach of the rules itself, in my judgment makes the pleading embarras-

The Weekly Law Reports, November 3, 1978

735

3 W.L.R.   Belmont Finance v. Williams Furniture (C.A.)   Goff L.J.

A sing and prevents it from showing the defendants what case they have to answer.

So far as the point on the relief claimed is concerned, it is said that the writ itself was defective under R.S.C., Ord. 6, r. 2, because it did not state the nature of the claim or the relief or remedy required, and reliance was placed on *Sterman* v. *E. W. & W. J. Moore* [1970] 1 Q.B. 596 as showing that a mere general claim for damages, accounts and inquiries is
B insufficient. However, in my judgment the writ was valid and regular, since it claimed a declaration that the transaction effected by the agreement of October 3, 1963, was unlawful and void. In my judgment that being so, it was competent under R.S.C., Ord. 18, r. 15 (2), for the plaintiff company to serve a statement of claim pending a case of conspiracy or constructive trust or both, because such cases depend upon,
C or include, the same facts as are required to support the cause of action for the declaration claimed in the writ. Indeed, apart from the special point that the plaintiff company, it was said, could not sue for conspiracy because it was itself a party, of which we have already disposed, it was not suggested that the statement of claim was bad so far as it alleged conspiracy.

D Nevertheless, in my judgment the pleading failed to comply with R.S.C., Ord. 18, r. 15 (1), in that it did not specify the remedy or relief claimed, so far as based on constructive trust.

Finally, whilst wilfully shutting one's eyes to the obvious, or wilfully refraining from inquiry because it may be embarassing is, I have no doubt, sufficient to make a person who participates in a fraudulent breach of trust without actually receiving the trust moneys, or moneys
E representing the same, liable as a constructive trustee, there remains the question whether constructive notice in what has been conveniently described as the " section 199 " sense, will suffice.

Ungoed-Thomas J. in the *Selangor* case held that it would, and Brightman J. in *Karak Rubber Co. Ltd.* v. *Burden* (*No. 2*) [1972] 2 Ch. W.L.R. 602, 639, followed that decision.

F But in *Carl Zeiss Stiftung* v. *Herbert Smith & Co.* (*No. 2*) [1969] 2 Ch. 276, Sachs L.J. at pp. 298 and 299, and Edmund Davies L.J., at p. 301, threw great doubt upon this. In *Competitive Insurance Co. Ltd.* v. *Davies Investment Ltd.* [1975] 1 W.L.R. 1240, which was in many respects a different case, but touched on similar ground, I took the view that constructive notice of the section 199 type would not be sufficient, and I adhere to that view. It is, however, as Buckley L.J. has said,
G unnecessary for us to decide that particular matter; it can be left to the trial judge, who may not in the end have to decide it, either because it may turn out that the defendants had actual knowledge, or because there may be insufficient proof to establish constructive notice.

For the reasons that both Buckley L.J. and Orr J.L. have given, which I entirely accept, and for those which I have sought to express
H myself, I agree that the judge was wrong in ruling that the plaintiff company could not maintain its claim in conspiracy, but that he was right in holding that they could not proceed on a claim based on constructive trust without amendment.

February 18. The Court of Appeal (Buckley, Orr and Goff L.JJ.) gave leave to the plaintiff company to further amend the statement of claim, on certain terms in order to formulate a plea of fraud, notwith-

Belmont Finance v. Williams Furniture (C.A.)   **[1978]**

standing the delay and the late stage at which the application was made,   A
on the ground of the exceptional facts of the case.

> *Appeal allowed in part.*
> *Leave to amend statement of claim.*
> *Costs of amendment to be borne by*
>   *plaintiff company but not to*   B
>   *include costs of application.*
> *Leave to appeal to all defendants.*

Solicitors: *Sidney Pearlman & Greene; Freshfields; Gentle Mathias*
& Co.; Arram, Fairfield & Co.

L. G. S.
                                                                          C

[COURT OF APPEAL]

PEARLMAN v. KEEPERS AND GOVERNORS OF

HARROW SCHOOL   D

1978 May 24, 25, 26;   Lord Denning M.R.,
      July 14   Geoffrey Lane and Eveleigh L.JJ.

> *Crown Practice—Certiorari—County court—Improvement to lease-*
>   *hold property—Whether " structural alteration . . . or addition "*
>   *—Determination " final and conclusive"—Whether certiorari*   E
>   *lies to quash order—County Courts Act* 1959 (7 & 8 Eliz. 2, c.
>   22), ss. 107, 115 (1) [1]*—Housing Act* 1974 (c. 44), *Sch.* 8,
>   *para.* 2 (2)
> *Landlord and Tenant—Leasehold enfranchisement—Improvement*
>   *—Rateable value reduction—Whether central heating installa-*
>   *tion " structural alteration . . . or addition "—Leasehold*
>   *Reform Act* 1967 (c. 88), s. 1 (4A) (*as amended by Housing Act*
>   1974, s. 118 (3))*—Housing Act* 1974, *Sch.* 8, *paras.* 1 (2), 2 (2)
>   F
> Section 1 (4A) of the Leasehold Reform Act 1967 provides:
> " At any time the tenant may take the action provided
> in Schedule 8 to the Housing Act 1974 for his rateable
> value to be adjusted and in all such cases the agreed
> rateable value or that determined by the court or district
> valuer shall be the rateable value for the purposes of that
> Act."
> Paragraph 1 (2) of Schedule 8 to the Housing Act 1974   G
> provides:
> " This Schedule applies to any improvement made by the
> execution of works amounting to structural alteration,
> extension or addition."
> Paragraph 2 (2) provides:
> " Where, . . . any of the following matters has not been
> agreed in writing between the landlord and the tenant,
> that is to say,—(a) whether the improvement specified in   H
> the notice is an improvement to which this Schedule
> applies; . . . the county court may on the application of
> the tenant determine that matter, and any such deter-
> mination shall be final and conclusive."
> A tenant held a long lease of a three-floored London house
> in which he had lived for over 30 years. He installed a

---
[1] County Courts Act 1959, s. 107: see post, pp. 742H—743A.
S. 115 (1): see post, p. 747C.

A   modern central heating system with a gas-fired boiler in the
     kitchen which was connected to some 20 radiators throughout
     the house.   Piping, which could not be removed, was laid from
     the boiler on the ground floor passing under floors and through
     specially made holes in the ceilings and walls up to a metal
     tank in the roof space.
          The tenant claimed that the rateable value of the house
     should be adjusted under section 1 (4A) of the Leasehold
B   Reform Act 1967 and applied to the county court for a
     determination that in consequence of the improvement which
     he had effected by the installation the rateable value for the
     purposes of the Act of 1967 should be reduced from £1,597
     to £1,487.
          Judge Curtis-Raleigh, differing from a previous decision
     in another county court, held that the installation was not
     " work . . . [of] structural alteration " and refused to make the
C   declaration sought.   The Divisional Court refused the tenant
     leave to apply for, inter alia, an order of certiorari to quash
     the judge's order.
          On appeal by the tenant: —
          Held, allowing the appeal, (1) that since the installation
     of the central heating involved substantial alteration or addi-
     tion to the fabric of the house it was an " improvement made
     by the execution of works amounting to structural alteration . . .
D   or addition " within the meaning of paragraph 1 (2) of
     Schedule 8 to the Housing Act 1974 (post, pp. 741E, 746F–H,
     752F).
          In re Gaskell's Settled Estates [1894] 1 Ch. 485 and In re
     Blagrave's Settled Estates [1903] 1 Ch. 560, C.A. distinguished.
          (2) (Geoffrey Lane L.J. dissenting) that since the judge
     had misconstrued the meaning of the words " structural
     alteration . . . or addition " in paragraph 1 (2) of Schedule 8
E   to the Housing Act 1974 he had erred in law and wrongly
     deprived himself of jurisdiction to determine the matters in
     respect of which jurisdiction was conferred on the county
     court by paragraph 2 (2) of Schedule 8, and, although his
     determination was made " final and conclusive " and notwith-
     standing the provisions of section 107 of the County Courts
     Act 1959, the remedy of certiorari was not excluded; and
     accordingly the appeal should be allowed and an order made
F   quashing the judge's decision with a declaration that the
     tenant's improvement fell within paragraph 1 (2) of Schedule 8
     to the Act of 1974 (post, pp. 743H—744A, 745C, 750F, 751G,
     753D, H).
          Reg. v. Hurst, Ex parte Smith [1960] 2 Q.B. 133, D.C. and
     Anisminic Ltd. v. Foreign Compensation Commission [1969]
     2 A.C. 147, H.L.(E.) applied.
          Per Geoffrey Lane L.J. The County Courts Act 1959
G   abolished certiorari for an error of law on the face of the
     record as a means of attacking a judgment or order of the
     county court, and, since the judge's determination was made
     " final and conclusive " by paragraph 2 (2) of Schedule 8 to
     the Housing Act 1974 and it could not be said to be outside
     his jurisdiction, certiorari was not available to the tenant
     (post, pp. 747F, 748B, 750A).
          Per Lord Denning M.R. Section 107 of the County
H   Courts Act 1959 applies only to proceedings in respect of
     which jurisdiction is given to the county court by that Act
     (post, p. 743B).
          Quaere. Whether the words " such determination shall
     be final and conclusive " in paragraph 2 (2) of Schedule 8
     to the Act of 1974 barred the tenant from appeal against the
     judge's determination on a question of law (post, pp. 745A, B,
     748B, 753C).
          Order of the Divisional Court the Queen's Bench Division
     reversed.

Pearlman v. Harrow School (C.A.)   **[1978]**

The following cases are referred to in the judgments: A

Anisminic Ltd. v. *Foreign Compensation Commission* [1968] 2 Q.B. 862; [1967] 3 W.L.R. 382; [1967] 2 All E.R. 986, C.A.; [1969] 2 A.C. 147; [1969] 2 W.L.R. 163; [1969] 1 All E.R. 208, H.L.(E.).

Blagrave's Settled Estates, In re [1903] 1 Ch. 560, C.A.

Bradlaugh, Ex parte (1878) 3 Q.B.D. 509, D.C.

British Launderers' Research Association v. *Borough of Hendon Rating Authority* [1949] 1 K.B. 462; [1949] 1 All E.R. 21, C.A.   B

Bunbury v. *Fuller* (1853) 9 Exch. 111.

Cardiff Rating Authority and Cardiff Assessment Committee v. *Guest Keen Baldwin's Iron and Steel Co. Ltd.* [1949] 1 K.B. 385; [1949] 1 All E.R. 27, C.A.

Challis v. *Watson* [1913] 1 K.B. 547, D.C.

Clarke's Settlement, In re [1902] 2 Ch. 327.

Cozens v. *Brutus* [1973] A.C. 854; [1972] 3 W.L.R. 521; [1972] 2 All   C
E.R. 1297, H.L.(E.).

Dyson Holdings Ltd. v. *Fox* [1976] Q.B. 503; [1975] 3 W.L.R. 744; [1975] 3 All E.R. 1030, C.A.

Gaskell's Settled Estates, In re [1894] 1 Ch. 485.

Hall v. *Arnold* [1950] 2 K.B. 543; [1950] 1 All E.R. 993, D.C.

Lee v. *Proprietors of Hay's Wharf Ltd.* [1940] 2 K.B. 306; [1940] 3 All E.R. 282, C.A.   D

Pickering v. *Phillimore,* Judge White, West London County Court, May 10, 1976.

Pyx Granite Co. Ltd. v. *Ministry of Housing and Local Government* [1960] A.C. 260; [1959] 3 W.L.R. 346; [1959] 3 All E.R. 1, H.L.(E.).

Reg. v. *Governor of Brixton Prison, Ex parte Armah* [1968] A.C. 192; [1966] 3 W.L.R. 828; [1966] 3 All E.R. 177, H.L.(E.).   E

Reg. v. *Hurst, Ex parte Smith* [1960] 2 Q.B. 133; [1960] 2 W.L.R. 961; [1960] 2 All E.R. 385, D.C.

Reg. v. *Medical Appeal Tribunal, Ex parte Gilmore* [1957] 1 Q.B. 574; [1957] 2 W.L.R. 498; [1957] 1 All E.R. 796, C.A.

Tehrani v. *Rostron* [1972] 1 Q.B. 182; [1971] 3 W.L.R. 612; [1971] 3 All E.R. 790, C.A.

Westminster Corporation v. *Gordon Hotels Ltd.* [1907] 1 K.B. 910, C.A.; [1908] A.C. 142, H.L.(E.).   F

Woodhouse v. *Peter Brotherhood Ltd.* [1972] 2 Q.B. 520; [1972] 3 W.L.R. 215; [1972] 3 All E.R. 91, C.A.

The following additional cases were cited in argument:

Bendles Motors Ltd. v. *Bristol Corporation* [1963] 1 W.L.R. 247; [1963] 1 All E.R. 578, D.C.   G

Giusti Patents & Engineering Works Ltd. v. *Maggs* [1923] 1 Ch. 515.

Kydd v. *Liverpool Watch Committee* [1908] A.C. 327, H.L.(E.).

Piper v. *St. Marylebone Licensing Justices* [1928] 2 K.B. 221, D.C.

Price v. *Bedbrook (Valuation Officer)* (1971) 18 R.R.C. 232.

Reg. v. *National Insurance Commissioner, Ex parte Hudson* [1972] A.C. 944; [1972] 2 W.L.R. 210; [1972] 1 All E.R. 145, H.L.(E.).

Rex v. *Nat. Bell Liquors Ltd.* [1922] 2 A.C. 128, P.C.

Rex v. *Northumberland Compensation Appeal Tribunal, Ex parte Shaw*   H
[1952] 1 K.B. 338; [1952] 1 All E.R. 122, C.A.

Rex v. *Paddington and St. Marylebone Furnished Houses Rent Tribunal, Ex parte Kendal Hotels Ltd.* [1947] 1 All E.R. 448, D.C.

APPEAL from Divisional Court.

On June 22, 1976, the tenant, Sidney Pearlman, applied to the Bloomsbury and Marylebone County Court under the Leasehold Reform

A Act 1967 and the Housing Act 1974 for a determination (1) that as a consequence of improvements carried out by him at 1 Vale Close, London, W.9, the rateable value for the purposes of the Act of 1967 should be reduced from £1,597 to £1,487; (2) that the improvements were improvements made by the execution of works amounting to the structural alteration or extension of the premises or a structural addition thereto; the works were involved in making the improvements; and the

B proportion of the cost born by the tenant was £2,440.54. The respondents to the application were the Keepers and Governors of Harrow School, the landlords. On December 10, 1976, Judge Curtis-Raleigh refused any declaration and dismissed the application.

On April 5, 1977, the Divisional Court dismissed the tenant's application for leave to apply for orders of certiorari and mandamus to

C remove into the court and quash the order made by Judge Curtis-Raleigh. The tenant appealed pursuant to leave of the Court of Appeal granted on April 25, 1977. The grounds of appeal were that (1) the judge's order disclosed an error on the face of the record; (2) the Divisional Court were wrong in law, or exercised their discretion wrongly in holding that it was not an appropriate case for an order of certiorari;

D (3) the tenant had no other means of redress to correct an error of law made by an inferior court or tribunal except by applying for an order of certiorari; (4) it was a matter of public disquiet that different courts of first instance could come to different conclusions on the same facts and that situation could only be put right by the intervention of the Court of Appeal.

E The facts are stated in the judgments of Lord Denning M.R. and Geoffrey Lane L.J.

Lionel Read Q.C. and *Matthew Horton* for the tenant.
Alistair Dawson Q.C. and *Joseph Harper* for the landlords.

Cur. adv. vult.

F July 14. The following judgments were read.

LORD DENNING M.R. The Leasehold Reform Act 1967 conferred a great benefit on some tenants. They were tenants who resided in houses which they held on long leases at a low rent. It gave them a

G right to acquire the freehold on very favourable terms. But it did not apply to large houses. In the London area it only applied to houses of a rateable value of not more that £400. Later on the valuation lists were reviewed, and all rateable values were much increased. By an amendment the Act was extended so as to apply in the London area to houses of a rateable value of not more than £1,500: see section 118 of the Housing Act 1974.

H Now there are many houses in the London area where the tenants have done improvements to the property at their own cost: and the rateable value has been increased on that account. The house might be assessed at over £1,500 just because of the tenant's improvements. Parliament realised that it was very unfair on a tenant that he should be deprived of the benefit of the Leasehold Reform Act 1967 simply by reason of improvements which he himself had made. So in the Housing Act 1974 Parliament inserted provisions enabling the tenant in such a

case to get the rateable value reduced for the purpose of the Act of A
1967.   These provisions are section 118 (3) (inserting subsection (4A)
after subsection (4) in section 1 of the Act of 1967) and Schedule 8 to
the Act of 1974.

The procedure is for the tenant to serve a notice on the landlord
saying that he made the improvements at his own cost and wants the
rateable value reduced.   The landlord may agree.   But if he disagrees, B
the matter is referred to the judge in the county court.   He has to
determine whether the tenant has a legitimate case for a reduction: but
he does not determine the quantum of it.   That is to be referred to the
valuation officer for him to certify the amount of the reduction.

The house and the improvements

The house is no. 1 Vale Close, Maida Vale, London, W.9.   It is a C
good-sized house with three floors.   It is owned by the Governors of
Harrow School.   They let it in 1933 on a long lease for 88 years.   So
that it is due to expire in 2021.   The leaseholder is Mr. Sidney Pearlman,
who has occupied it as his residence for over 30 years.   When he went
there it had an old-fashioned heating system.   There was a coal-fired
boiler in the kitchen.   It supplied hot water for the sinks and baths: D
and two radiators, one in the hall and the other on the first-floor landing.
The rooms in the house were heated by ordinary coal fires.

In 1960 Mr. Pearlman scrapped that system.   He installed a modern
full central-heating system.   It supplied 18 radiators and towel-rails all
over the house.   It supplied hot water to baths, sinks, and so forth.
The gas-fired boiler was in the kitchen.   It was connected with the flue E
and the chimney.   There was asbestos lining inserted right up the
chimney.   Pipes were laid from the boiler on the ground floor up to the
top floor, passing under floors and through ceilings and walls, some of
them load-bearing, from room to room right up to a metal tank in the
roof space.   Holes had to be made in the ceilings and walls and made
good afterwards.   Each radiator was connected to the walls with
brackets.   In 1971 Mr. Pearlman had two more radiators installed. F

That work undoubtedly was a great improvement to the house and
went to increase its rateable value.   In the latest revaluation the rateable
value of the house was £1,597.   This was over £1,500 and, as things
stood, Mr. Pearlman was unable to claim the benefit of the Leasehold
Reform Act 1967: because that was limited to houses in London of less
than £1,500 rateable value.   In the circumstances, Mr. Pearlman applied G
to his landlords asking them to agree to a reduction in the rateable value.
He proposed that the rateable value should be reduced to £1,487.   He said
that, by installing the full central heating system, he had himself made
improvements—increasing the rateable value—and that that increase
should not count against him for the purposes of the Leasehold Reform
Act 1967.
                                                                        H
The landlords did not agree.   So Mr. Pearlman applied to the county
court.   On December 10, 1976, the judge refused Mr. Pearlman's request.
Mr. Pearlman says that the determination of the judge was wrong in law.

The law

In order to qualify for a reduction, the improvement must be an
" improvement made by the execution of works amounting to structural

A alteration, extension or addition." Those are the words of the Housing Act 1974, Schedule 8, paragraph 1 (2). They are simple English words, but they have been interpreted by different judges differently. At any rate, when the judges have had to apply them to the installation of a full central heating system. In each house the primary facts have been exactly the same, or near enough the same, but one judge has found one way. Another the other way. One judge has held that the instal-
B lation is a " structural alteration." Another has found that it is not. It is said, nevertheless, that, being simple English words, we should not interfere. Neither decision can be said to be unreasonable. So let each decision stand. Reliance is placed for this purpose on the speech of Lord Reid in *Cozens* v. *Brutus* [1973] A.C. 854, 861.

I cannot accept this argument. As I pointed out in *Dyson Holdings*
C *Ltd.* v. *Fox* [1976] Q.B. 503, 510, when an ordinary word comes to be applied to similar facts, in one case after another, it would be intolerable if half of the judges gave one answer and the other half another. No one would know where he stood. No lawyer could advise his client what to do. In such circumstances, it is the duty of the Court of Appeal to give a definite ruling one way or the other. However simple
D the words, their interpretation is a matter of law. They have to be applied, in case after case, by lawyers: and it is necessary, in the interests of certainty, that they should always be given the same interpretation, and always applied in the same way: see two rating cases in 1949, *Cardiff Rating Authority and Cardiff Assessment Committee* v. *Guest Keen Baldwin's Iron and Steel Co. Ltd.* [1949] 1 K.B. 385, 396, and *British Launderers' Research Association* v. *Borough of Hendon*
E *Rating Authority* [1949] 1 K.B. 462, 471–472; and also *Woodhouse* v. *Peter Brotherhood Ltd.* [1972] 2 Q.B. 520, 536–537.

Applying the words of Schedule 8 to the house here, I am of opinion that the installation of full central heating to this house was an "improvement made by the execution of works amounting to structural alteration . . . or addition." It involved a good deal of tampering with the
F structure by making holes in walls and partitions, by lining the chimney with asbestos, and so forth. Much more than is involved in installing fitted cupboards instead of wardrobes, or a modern fireplace instead of old fire-dogs.

This is confirmed by the practice of rating authorities. They have always held that, when full central heating is installed, the rateable value of the house is increased. So much so that they have a formula for
G calculating the increase according to the number of rooms that are centrally heated: and the increase dates from the time when the central heating was installed, on the ground that it was a " structural alteration " within section 68 (4) (*b*) and section 79 (2) (*b*) of the General Rates Act 1967. Stronger still is the fact that when the installation was made after April 1, 1974, Parliament has expressly said that no increase was to be
H made in the rateable value by reason of the " structural alterations " involved in installing a central heating system: see section 21 (1) (*a*) of the Local Government Act 1974.

The contrary view was supported by some cases under the Settled Land Acts 1882 and 1890. The point there arose about the early form of heating houses by hot water through pipes. It was held that the tenant for life had to instal it himself out of his income: and that he could not require his trustees to pay it out of capital: see *In re Gaskell's*

Settled Estates [1894] 1 Ch. 485, because it was not a structural   **A**
alteration (see *In re Clarke's Settlement* [1902] 2 Ch. 327, 331, affirmed
in this court in *In re Blagrave's Settled Estates* [1903] 1 Ch. 560, 562-
563). I find no help in those cases, concerned as they were with a
different statute, worded differently, in a different context altogether.

My conclusion is, therefore, that in a previous case, *Pickering* v.
Phillimore, Judge White was right, and that in the present case Judge
Curtis-Raleigh was wrong. The installation of a full central heating   **B**
system is a "structural alteration . . . or addition" within Schedule 8 to
the Housing Act 1974. But is it possible for this court to correct the
decision of Judge Curtis-Raleigh? That brings me to the point of
jurisdiction.

Jurisdiction   **C**

There is an express provision in the Housing Act 1974 which makes
the decision of the judge in the county court "final and conclusive." It is
Schedule 8, paragraph 2 (2). It applies to the questions:

"(a) whether the improvement . . . is an improvement to which
this Schedule applies; (b) what works were involved . . . (c) whether
the tenant . . . has made it or contributed to its cost; and (d)   **D**
what proportion his contribution . . . bears to the whole cost; . . ."

If any such question is not agreed, then:

". . . . the county court may, on the application of the tenant
determine that matter, and any such determination shall be final
and conclusive."

  E

Those words "final and conclusive" have been considered by the
courts a hundred times. It has been uniformly held that they preclude
any appeal to a higher court—in the sense of an appeal proper where
the higher court reviews the decision of the lower tribunal and substitutes
its own decision for that of the lower tribunal: see *Westminster Corporation* v. *Gordon Hotels Ltd.* [1907] 1 K.B. 910; [1908] A.C. 142 and *Hall* v.
Arnold [1950] 2 K.B. 543. But those words do not preclude the High   **F**
Court from correcting the errors of the lower tribunal by means of
certiorari—now called judicial review. Notwithstanding that a decision
is by a statute made "final and conclusive," certiorari can still issue for
excess of jurisdiction, or for error of law on the face of the record (see
Reg. v. *Medical Appeal Tribunal, Ex parte Gilmore* [1957] 1 Q.B. 574,
583); or a declaration can be made by the High Court to determine the   **G**
rights of the parties. It can declare the law by which they are bound,
irrespective of what the lower tribunal has done: see *Pyx Granite Co.
Ltd.* v. *Ministry of Housing and Local Government* [1960] A.C. 260.
It can even consider the point of law by means of a case stated: see
Tehrani v. *Rostron* [1972] 1 Q.B. 182.

  H

The "No certiorari clause"—section 107

But it is said here that those decisions apply only to lower tribunals:
and that they do not apply to county courts. It is said that Parliament
has taken away certiorari to county courts. This argument is based on
section 107 of the County Courts Act 1959, which says:

"Subject to the provisions of any other Act relating to county
courts, no judgment or order of any judge of county courts, nor

A   any proceedings brought before him or pending in his court, shall
be removed by appeal, motion, certiorari or otherwise into any
other court whatever, except in the manner and according to the
provisions in this Act mentioned."

To my mind that provision has no application to the present case. It
applies only to proceedings under the Act of 1959, just as if the words
B   " under this Act " were written into it. Certiorari is taken away in
proceedings in which the Act of 1959 gives jurisdiction to county courts,
such as section 39 (actions of contract and tort); section 48 (recovery of
land); section 52 (Equity jurisdiction) and section 56 (Admiralty jurisdiction). In all such matters certiorari does not lie: but instead the
statute gives a right of appeal on points of law: see section 108. In so
C   interpreting section 107, I am following the lead of Cockburn C.J. in
Ex parte Bradlaugh (1873) 3 Q.B.D. 509, 512, where there was a " no
certiorari clause." He said:

     " I entertain very serious doubts whether that provision does not
     apply only to matters in respect of which jurisdiction is given by
     that statute, and not to matters in which jurisdiction is given by
D   subsequent statutes; . . ."

I am confirmed in this view by reference to section 108 of the Act, which
gives an appeal to the Court of Appeal on points of law. It seems to
me to be dealing with matters in respect of which the Act of 1959 gives
jurisdiction to the county court: and not to matters in respect of which
jurisdiction is given by subsequent statutes.

E   Moreover, in subsequent Acts giving fresh jurisdiction to the county
court (additional to that in the Act of 1959), Parliament has expressly
said whether there is to be an appeal (as in the Building Societies Act
1962, section 72 (5)), or no appeal (as in the Industrial and Provident
Societies Act 1965, section 42 (3) (b)). In both those cases it uses the
words " final and conclusive " leaving the remedy by certiorari or
F   declaration unimpaired.
     So I would hold that certiorari lies in the case of a decision by the
county court judge under Schedule 8 to the Housing Act 1974 when
he goes outside his jurisdiction or there is an error of law on the face of
the record.

Jurisdictional error
G
     But even if section 107 does apply to this case, it only excludes
certiorari for error of law on the face of the record. It does not
exclude the power of the High Court to issue certiorari for absence of
jurisdiction. It has been held that certiorari will issue to a county court
judge if he acts without jurisdiction in the matter: see *Reg.* v. *Hurst,
Ex parte Smith* [1960] 2 Q.B. 133. If he makes a wrong finding on a
H   matter on which his jurisdiction depends, he makes a jurisdictional error;
and certiorari will lie to quash his decision: see *Anisminic Ltd.* v.
Foreign Compensation Commission [1969] 2 A.C. 147, 208, *per* Lord
Wilberforce. But the distinction between an error which entails absence
of jurisdiction—and an error made within the jurisdiction—is very fine.
So fine indeed that it is rapidly being eroded. Take this very case.
When the judge held that the installation of a full central heating system
was not a " structural alteration . . . or addition " we all think—all three of

us—that he went wrong in point of law. He misconstrued those words. **A**
That error can be described on the one hand as an error which went to
his jurisdiction. In this way: if he had held that it was a " structural
alteration . . . or addition " he would have had jurisdiction to go on and
determine the various matters set out in paragraph 2 (2) (*b*) (*c*) and
(*d*) of Schedule 8. By holding that it was not a " structural alteration . . . or
addition " he deprived himself of jurisdiction to determine those matters.
On the other hand, his error can equally well be described as an error **B**
made by him within his jurisdiction. It can plausibly be said that he
had jurisdiction to inquire into the meaning of the words " structural
alteration . . . or addition "; and that his wrong interpretation of them was
only an error within his jurisdiction, and not an error taking him outside
it.

    That illustration could be repeated in nearly all these cases. So fine **C**
is the distinction that in truth the High Court has a choice before it
whether to interfere with an inferior court on a point of law. If it
chooses to interfere, it can formulate its decision in the words: " The
court below had no jurisdiction to decide this point wrongly as it did."
If it does not choose to interfere, it can say: " The court had jurisdiction
to decide it wrongly, and did so." Softly be it stated, but that is the **D**
reason for the difference between the decision of the Court of Appeal
in *Anisminic Ltd.* v. *Foreign Compensation Commission* [1968] 2 Q.B.
862 and the House of Lords [1969] 2 A.C. 147.

    I would suggest that this distinction should now be discarded. The
High Court has, and should have, jurisdiction to control the proceedings
of inferior courts and tribunals by way of judicial review. When they
go wrong in law, the High Court should have power to put them right. **E**
Not only in the instant case to do justice to the complainant. But also
so as to secure that all courts and tribunals, when faced with the same
point of law, should decide it in the same way. It is intolerable that a
citizen's rights in point of law should depend on which judge tries his case,
or in which court it is heard. The way to get things right is to hold thus: no
court or tribunal has any jurisdiction to make an error of law on which the **F**
decision of the case depends. If it makes such an error, it goes outside
its jurisdiction and certiorari will lie to correct it. In this case the
finding—that the installation of a central heating system was not a
" structural alteration "—was an error on which the jurisdiction of the
county court depended: and, because of that error, the judge was quite
wrong to dismiss the application outright. He ought to have found that
the installation was an " improvement " within Schedule 8, paragraph 2 **G**
(2) (*a*), and gone on to determine the other matters referred to in
Schedule 8, paragraph 2 (2) (*b*) (*c*) and (*d*).

    On these grounds I am of opinion that certiorari lies to quash the
determination of the judge, even though it was made by statute " final
and conclusive."

H

Appeal

    In case certiorari does not lie, the tenant submitted that he had a
remedy by way of appeal: and he asked to be given leave out of time.
He submitted that the words " final and conclusive " meant that the
determination of the judge was final and conclusive on the facts, but
not on the law: see *Tehrani* v. *Rostron* [1972] 1 Q.B. 182, 187.

A Accordingly, he submitted that he could appeal under section 108 of the County Courts Act 1959.

I must say that, if I had been of opinion that certiorari did not lie, I would have held that the tenant could have appealed under section 108: because I would never accept a situation where different judges on the same set of facts could come to different conclusions on points of law. I B would have held that " final and conclusive " excluded appeal on the facts but not on the law. But, as I have already said, I think that section 108, like section 107, is confined to the jurisdiction conferred on judges in the county court by the Act of 1959 itself. Neither section applies to new jurisdiction created under new statutes, such as the Housing Act 1974, Schedule 8. And it is because neither section applies that I am of opinion that certiorari does lie.

C

Conclusion

In my opinion the judge made an error of law when he determined that the installation of a full central heating system was not a " structural alteration . . . or addition " to the house. His decision was made by the statute " final and conclusive." Those words do not exclude remedy D by certiorari, that is, by judicial review. I would, therefore, allow the appeal and make an order quashing his decision and declaring that the improvement made by Mr. Pearlman fell within Schedule 8, paragraph 2 (2) (*a*), to the Housing Act 1974: and remitting the matter to the county court to determine the remaining matters.

E   GEOFFREY LANE L.J. The tenant, Mr. Pearlman, holds from the landlords no. 1 Vale Close, Maida Vale, W.9, under an 88-year lease due to expire in the year 2021. He is anxious to take advantage of the provisions of the Leasehold Reform Act 1967 to acquire the freehold of the house on advantageous terms. The landlords are equally anxious that he should not. By virtue of section 118 of the Housing Act 1974 F where the rateable value of houses in the London area is more than £1,500 the Act of 1967 has no application. The rateable value of this house is £1,597. Therefore at first sight it seems that the landlords are safe. However, the Housing Act 1974, Schedule 8, provides machinery whereby the rateable value of a house may for the purposes of the Act of 1967 be notionally reduced in circumstances where a tenant has made improvements to the premises " by the execution of works amounting to structural G alteration, extension or addition."

It is not disputed that Mr. Pearlman carried out extensive works in the house between 1960 and 1971. They consisted of removing the old central heating system which had been fired by a solid fuel boiler serving the hot water system and a couple of radiators and replacing it with a modern small-bore gas-burning system to heat the domestic water and no less than 20 radiators. He proposed to the landlords that these H improvements had resulted in an increase in the rateable value and that without them the value would be reduced to £1,487. The landlords did not agree that this was a relevant improvement, and the matter accordingly went to the county court for decision under the terms of Schedule 8, paragraph 2 (2):

" Where . . . any of the following matters has not been agreed in writing between the landlord and the tenant, that is to say,—(*a*)

whether the improvement . . . is an improvement to which this   A
Schedule applies . . . the county court may on the application of
the tenant determine that matter, and any such determination shall
be final and conclusive."

The judge determined that the improvements were not "by the
execution of works amounting to structural alteration, extension or
addition," and Mr. Pearlman now seeks an order from this court that   B
the judge was wrong.   He is particularly aggrieved because it seems that
in other county courts on basically similar facts the decision has gone in
favour of the tenant.   There is a lot to be said for the view that the
outcome of litigation should not depend upon which particular judge
is sitting in the county court on the day of the trial, but that cannot be
an overriding consideration.   C

There are two issues.   First, what is the meaning of the words
"works amounting to structural alteration, extension or addition"?
Secondly, to what extent do the words of Schedule 8, paragraph 2 (2)
(a) "such determination shall be final and conclusive" inhibit Mr.
Pearlman from obtaining redress from this court?

" Structural alteration "   D

The new central heating system entailed the usual work being carried
out.   The gas-fired boiler is a substantial affair.   It is connected not
only to the various radiators and towel-rails, but also, of course, to
the cold water supply.   It must also be connected to the electrical
system (to provide power for the circulating pump and the programming
mechanism) and the gas supply.   It is also connected to the flue and   E
chimney.   The chimney has been lined to prevent damage through
condensation.   The pipes from the boiler have been run under the
ground floor coming up at skirting levels to most of the rooms. They pass
through holes which have been made specially in the walls, loadbearing
and otherwise, and in the floors and ceilings.   The piping eventually rises
to the roof space where it is connected to the metal header-tank and over-   F
flow pipe.   It would be impossible to remove the piping.   It would be
possible to remove the boiler, but only by dismantling it.

"Structural" in this context means, I believe, something which
involves the fabric of the house as opposed to the provision merely of a
piece of equipment.   It matters not whether the fabric in question is
load-bearing or otherwise, if there is any substantial alteration, extension
or addition to the fabric of the house the words of the schedule are   G
satisfied.   I have no doubt that the works done here "amount to"
such alteration or addition.   The system is connected in permanent
fashion to the gas, water and electrical installations which are part of the
fabric of the house.   The walls, floors and ceilings have been drilled
with holes to accommodate the piping.   The flue is connected in
permanent fashion to the chimney (part of the fabric) which has itself   H
been altered by lining.   This is not merely the provision of equipment,
it amounts to alteration and addition to the structure.

I do not derive assistance from decisions such as *In re Gaskell's
Settled Estates* [1894] 1 Ch. 485 which was made upon different facts
and upon the words of the Settled Land Acts 1882 and 1890 which were
not the same as the words under consideration here.   The judge in the

The Weekly Law Reports, November 3, 1978

747

3 W.L.R.   Pearlman v. Harrow School (C.A.)   Geoffrey Lane L.J.

A present case was, I think, wrong in the conclusion which he reached on this aspect of the case.

Has this court any power to intervene?

By section 107 of the County Courts Act 1959:

B ". . . no judgment or order of any judge of county courts, nor any proceedings brought before him or pending in his court, shall be removed by appeal, motion, certiorari or otherwise into any other court whatever, except . . . according to the provisions in this Act mentioned."

These words are designed to deal with two separate situations. First, a C judgment or order which has already been given or made by the court, and, secondly, any proceedings which have not yet reached the stage of judgment or order. The section removes the remedy of certiorari in either case. Section 115 (1) of the Act provides:

" The High Court . . . may order the removal into the High Court, by order of certiorari or otherwise, of any proceedings commenced D in a county court, if the High Court . . . thinks it desirable that the proceedings should be heard and determined in the High Court."

It is clear from the words themselves that that section applies only to the second type of situation, namely, where the proceedings have not yet reached judgment or order. Otherwise the matter would already have been " determined " by the county court. This conclusion is confirmed E by section 117 (1):

" The grant by the High Court . . . of leave to make an application for an order of certiorari . . . to a county court shall, if the High Court . . . so directs, operate as a stay of the proceedings in question. . . ."

F If completed proceedings were contemplated this section would be meaningless.

Thus what the Act of 1959 has done is to abolish certiorari for error of law on the face of the record as a method of attacking a judgment or order of the county court. It has retained certiorari as a method of removing a pending or uncompleted action from the county court to G the High Court: see *Challis* v. *Watson* [1913] 1 K.B. 547, 549, *per* Lush J. (a decision on section 26 of the Act of 1888 which was in similar terms to section 115) and *Lee* v. *Proprietors of Hay's Wharf Ltd.* [1940] 2 K.B. 306 (a decision under section 111 of the Act of 1934). The action in the present case is not uncompleted. The judgment has been delivered. Therefore neither of those two forms of certiorari are H available to the tenant.

Mr Dawson on behalf of the landlords has conceded however that the Act of 1959 has not affected the power of the High Court in a proper case to remove and quash a decision of the county court which was made in excess of that court's jurisdiction. It must follow that the only basis for an order of certiorari would be if the judge had acted in excess of his jurisdiction.

Geoffrey Lane L.J.   Pearlman v. Harrow School (C.A.)   [1978]

Is there an appeal on a point of law?

A

Section 108 of the County Courts Act 1959 gives a general right of appeal to the Court of Appeal on a point of law to any party who is dissatisfied with the judge's determination. Section 109 specifies the circumstances in which there may be an appeal on a question of fact. None of them is applicable here.

What then is the effect of the words of Schedule 8, paragraph 2 (2), of the Housing Act—" such determination shall be final and conclusive "? Since there is in any event no appeal on fact, the words of the Schedule can only apply to questions of law and one must therefore conclude that they are effective to bar an appeal on a point of law. There is nothing else to which they can apply.

B

It follows from that reasoning that the only circumstances in which this court can correct what is to my mind the error of the judge is if he was acting in excess of his jurisdiction as opposed to merely making an error of law in his judgment by misinterpreting the meaning of " structural alteration . . . or addition."

C

In order to determine the ambit of the words " excess of jurisdiction " one must turn to the decision of the House of Lords in *Anisminic Ltd.* v. *Foreign Compensation Commission* [1969] 2 A.C. 147. The effect of the majority speeches in that case may perhaps be expressed as follows: where words in a statute purport to oust the jurisdiction of the High Court to review the decision of an inferior tribunal they must be construed strictly. That is to say, if there is more than one way in which they can reasonably be construed the construction which impairs the power of the High Court the least should be selected. A provision to the effect that the determination of a tribunal " shall not be called in question in any court of law " does not exclude the power of the High Court to quash a decision which has been reached by the tribunal acting in excess of its jurisdiction. Jurisdiction in this sense has a wide meaning. It includes any case where the apparent determination of the tribunal turns out on examination to be a nullity, because it cannot properly be called a determination at all. Lord Reid said, at p. 171:

D

E

F

> " But there are many cases where, although the tribunal had jurisdiction to enter on the inquiry, it has done or failed to do something in the course of the inquiry which is of such a nature that its decision is a nullity. It may have given its decision in bad faith. It may have made a decision which it had no power to make. It may have failed in the course of the inquiry to comply with the requirements of natural justice. It may in perfect good faith have misconstrued the provisions giving it power to act so that it failed to deal with the question remitted to it and decided some question which was not remitted to it. It may have refused to take into account something which it was required to take into account. Or it may have based its decision on some matter which, under the provisions setting it up, it had no right to take into account. I do not intend this list to be exhaustive. But if it decides a question remitted to it for decision without committing any of these errors it is as much entitled to decide that question wrongly as it is to decide it rightly."

G

H

In that case the Foreign Compensation Commission in adjudicating upon the appellants' claim to compensation considered that they were

The Weekly Law Reports, November 3, 1978

749

3 W.L.R.   Pearlman v. Harrow School (C.A.)   Geoffrey Lane L.J.

A bound by the relevant order to determine whether the appellants had a
" successor in title " and if so whether that successor was a British
national. Having decided that there was such a successor and that he
was not a British national they considered themselves obliged to reject
the claim. In fact the order did not require them to make any determination at all about " successors in title " or their nationality and the
commission was basing its decision " on some matter which, under the
B provisions setting it up, it had no right to take into account." Therefore
the apparent or purported determination was a nullity and no determination at all and was not protected by the words of ouster. Lord
Wilberforce, expressing similar views in somewhat different terms said,
at p. 210:

C   " . . . the cases in which a tribunal has been held to have passed
       outside its proper limits are not limited to those in which it had no
       power to enter upon its inquiry or its jurisdiction, or has not
       satisfied a condition precedent. Certainly such cases exist (for
       example Ex parte Bradlaugh (1878) 3 Q.B.D. 509) but they do not
       exhaust the principle. A tribunal may quite properly validly enter
       upon its task and in the course of carrying it out may make a
D   decision which is invalid—not merely erroneous. This may be
       described as ' asking the wrong question ' or ' applying the wrong
       test '—expressions not wholly satisfactory since they do not, in
       themselves, distinguish between doing something which is not in the
       tribunal's area and doing something wrong within that area—a
       crucial distinction which the court has to make."

E It is plain that this decision makes the ambit of excess of jurisdiction very
wide, but does it embrace what the judge did in the present case?
    For my part I am unable to see what the judge did which went outside
the proper area of his inquiry. He seems to have taken the view that
the word " structural " qualifies the following words, " alteration, extension
or addition " and does not qualify the part of the house to which the
F alterations etc. are made. That is to say the words do not mean " non-
structural alterations " or " additions to a structure ". Assuming he was
wrong in that method of interpreting the words of the Schedule, it does
not seem to me to be going outside his terms of reference in any way
at all, nor does it contravene any of the precepts suggested by Lord
Reid and Lord Wilberforce which I have already cited. The question
is not whether he made a wrong decision, but whether he inquired into
G and decided a matter which he had no right to consider: see Lord Reid
at p. 174E.
    The judge summarised matters in the final passage of his judgment
as follows:

       " I think in the final analysis it is a matter of first impression
       tested by argument, analogy and illustration and finally it is a
H   question of fact. There can be little doubt. I do not intend to
       give any definition at all."

In short what he is saying is that in his view the works executed by Mr.
Pearlman did not amount to structural alteration or addition, within the
ordinary meaning of those words. I am, I fear, unable to see how that
determination, assuming it to be an erroneous determination, can
properly be said to be a determination which he was not entitled to

750

make. The judge is considering the words in the Schedule which he A ought to consider. He is not embarking on some unauthorised or extraneous or irrelevant exercise. All he has done is to come to what appears to this court to be a wrong conclusion upon a difficult question. It seems to me that, if this judge is acting outside his jurisdiction, so then is every judge who comes to a wrong decision on a point of law. Accordingly, I take the view that no form of certiorari is available to the B tenant. I am fortified in this view of the matter by the fact that Mr. Read on behalf of the tenant accepted that the judge was acting within his jurisdiction, and added that " the nature of the judge's error was within his jurisdiction and was in relation to his interpretation and construction of the Schedule." Consequently Mr. Dawson did not feel himself obliged to address us on the *Anisminic* [1969] 2 A.C. 147 line of argument. Indeed for that reason alone I would have been C reluctant to allow the appeal.

I would accordingly dismiss this appeal.

EVELEIGH L.J.   By Schedule 8, paragraph 2 (2), the judge in the county court is given a trenchant power. His determination on certain matters is made final and conclusive. That finality will affect not only the D immediate parties but also their successors. His determination will be virtually decisive in many cases of the wider question, namely, whether or not the tenant has the right to buy the freehold and, should that question come before the High Court in an action by the tenant claiming that right, the determination of the county court judge affecting as it does the vital factor of rateable value will be binding upon that court. Apart from paragraph 2 (2) of Schedule 8, the judge would E have no say in the matter at all. The simple determination could not come within the exercise of his general jurisdiction as a judge of the county court. By Schedule 8 he is given arbitral power. Parliament would look upon it in another light also. It has imposed upon him a duty. That duty is to answer certain questions which the law is asking. In so far as he answers them his determination is binding. F If he answers some other question he is wasting everybody's time. He is not performing his duty. He is not exercising any power granted to him by Parliament. His decision is ultra vires. It is a nullity. Because his jurisdiction extends to answering a different question only, the determination which he has made will be outside his jurisdiction.

I believe that this is the approach to the question indicated by G *Anisminic Ltd.* v. *Foreign Compensation Commission* [1969] 2 A.C. 147, 234. I do not regard that decision as being in any way revolutionary. It has been said that the power of the court by certiorari to control errors of law has lain dormant for over a hundred years. This assertion is more pertinent in relation to an error on the face of the record made within the jurisdiction or intra vires. It is not true of certiorari used H to ensure that the tribunal does not exceed its jurisdictional power.

In *Administrative Law, Wade,* 4th ed. (1977), p. 232, we read:

" . . . the rule that a determination which is ultra vires may always be challenged in the High Court. This is no more than a corollary of the main principle of jurisdictional control, which ordains that no tribunal can give itself jurisdiction which it does not possess."

A   In other words a tribunal cannot give itself power to decide a question that Parliament has not empowered it to answer. The absurdity of allowing the tribunal so to do is all the more apparent when Parliament has made the answer of the tribunal binding upon other courts. That the answer to a question which has not been asked should be binding upon a court as the answer to a totally different question which Parliament requires to be asked is utterly absurd.

B   In *Bunbury* v. *Fuller* (1853) 9 Exch. 111, 140, Coleridge J. said:

"Now it is a general rule, that no court of limited jurisdiction can give itself jurisdiction by a wrong decision on a point collateral to the merits of the case upon which the limit to its jurisdiction depends; and however its decision may be final on all particulars, making up together that subject matter which, if true, is within its
C   jurisdiction, and, however necessary in many cases it may be for it to make a preliminary inquiry, whether some collateral matter be or be not within the limits, yet, upon this preliminary question, its decision must always be open to inquiry in the superior court."

In the present case, before the tribunal could embark upon its inquiry, it was necessary for it to decide the meaning of the question it was required
D   to answer. This was a collateral matter. It had nothing to do with the merits of the case. It was indeed "a point collateral to the merits of the case upon which the limit to its jurisdiction depends; . . ."

    It is not for the judge of the county court to decide, i.e., to lay down, what structural alteration, etc. means, although of course he has to comprehend what it means before he can answer the question he is
E   empowered to decide under Schedule 8, paragraph 2 (2) (*a*). Parliament determines what structural alteration means. If the judge proceeds to answer the question having wrongly comprehended its meaning his decision is a nullity.

    Fundamentally it is necessary to ask if the ". . . tribunal has jurisdiction to enter on the inquiry and to decide a particular issue . . .":
F   see *per* Lord Reid in *Reg.* v. *Governor of Brixton Prison, Ex parte Armah* [1968] A.C. 192, 234. The fundamental question which the court is entitled to and must decide is whether the judge was entitled to enter on the inquiry he in fact made. He had to ask whether the work was "works amounting to structural alteration, extension or addition." If in his mind those words meant X and by using those words Parliament meant Y the judge was answering a question he was not asked.

G   It is clear to my mind that the reason why two judges on identical facts gave different answers to the question was because one understood it to mean one thing and the other understood it to mean another. The facts of the cases permitted of no other explanation. In the case before this court we can discover how the judge understood the question. He has delivered a judgment in which he explains his approach to the words
H   "works amounting to structural alteration, extension or addition." In my opinion he wrongly understood the meaning of those words. He therefore did not answer the question he was asked. In *Anisminic* [1969] 2 A.C. 147, 194, Lord Pearce said:

"It would lead to an absurd situation if a tribunal, having been given a circumscribed area of inquiry, carved out from the general jurisdiction of the courts, were entitled of its own motion to extend that area by misconstruing the limits of its mandate to inquire and

decide as set out in the Act of Parliament. If, for instance, A
Parliament were to carve out an area of inquiry within which an
inferior domestic tribunal could give certain relief to wives against
their husbands, it would not lie within the power of that tribunal
to extend the area of inquiry and decision, that is, jurisdiction, thus
committed to it by construing ' wives ' as including all women who
have, without marriage, cohabited with a man for a substantial
period, . . ." B

By the use of certiorari the courts ensure that the right question is
answered and that the answer to the wrong question is not accepted.
The courts thus ensure that a decision is arrived at in accordance with
Parliament's intention. Lord Pearce said, at p. 195:

" It is simply an enforcement of Parliament's mandate to the C
tribunal. If the tribunal is intended on a true construction of the
Act to inquire into and finally decide questions within a certain
area, the courts' supervisory duty is to see that it makes the authorised inquiry according to natural justice and arrives at a decision
whether right or wrong. They will intervene if the tribunal asks
itself the wrong questions (that is, questions other than those which
Parliament directed it to ask itself)." D

There are several passages in the speeches of their Lordships to the same
effect namely that if the tribunal answers the wrong question its determination is a nullity.

One must therefore seek to determine what was the question which
the judge was required to ask. The judge had to ask himself whether E
the improvement specified in the notice was " an improvement to which
this Schedule applies." He could only answer that question if he knew
what it was to which the Schedule applied. Paragraph 1 (2) of Schedule
8 reads: " This Schedule applies to any improvement made by the
execution of works amounting to structural alteration, extension or
addition." In my opinion structural means appertaining to the fabric
of a building so as to be a part of the complex whole. In *Pickering* v. F
Phillimore, West London County Court, May 10, 1976, Judge White
said:

" A house is a ' complex unity,' particularly a modern house.
' Structural ' implies concern with the ' constituent or material '
parts of that unity. What are the ' constituent ' or ' material '
parts? In my judgment in any ordinary sense they involve more G
than simply the load bearing elements for example the four walls
the roof and the foundations. The constituent parts are more
complex than that."

He then suggested a definition of structural as being " Appertaining to
the basic fabric and parts of the house as distinguished from its decor-
ations and fittings." The judge said that it would be wrong to describe H
the central heating system as mainly fittings for throughout the house
the system became built into it and became part of it in a layman's sense.

In my opinion Judge White has the right conception of what Parliament meant by structural. In the case before this court the judge
perhaps wisely did not attempt a definition. There is much to be said
for that approach. Alternative definitions often take the matter no

A further. However when a word has more than one meaning the court has to make up its mind which meaning it will adopt and it is helpful if it says so not as an alternative definition but as an explanation of what Parliament meant by the words in question. However the judge did reject the meaning adopted by Judge White. From this it follows that he was proceeding upon some other meaning of the word and consequently asked himself the wrong question.

B
I agree with the judgments just delivered that the central heating in this case comes within the wording of the Schedule. In the course of argument there was some conjecture as to why the expression used was "works amounting to . . ." In my opinion it is because we have to look at the final result. That which is achieved must amount to a structural alteration extension or addition. Work that simply involves

C structural alteration will not necessarily come within the definition.

I have had some difficulty in persuading myself that there is no appeal on a point of law from the decision of the judge in the county court. I have been inclined to treat his determination as final and conclusive only on questions of fact. Paragraph 2 (2) of Schedule 8 lists matters for the judge's determination which is made final and conclusive but I regard them

D all as questions of fact. It may well be, however, that as the decision was a nullity the court must say that there is nothing to appeal against. Therefore, I regard the remedy of certiorari as more appropriate to the present situation. I agree with the judgments just delivered that the County Court Act 1959 does not exclude certiorari in the kind of case which goes to jurisdiction. I would also add that for myself I did not understand counsel for the tenant to say that the judge was acting within his jurisdiction in the

E sense with which the *Anisminic* case [1969] 2 A.C. 147 deals. He seemed to be taking the view that, because this was a judge and not a tribunal, different considerations applied. He was wrong in that, and I think he realised this when he came to reply when he developed the argument more fully. In any event, certiorari is a matter for the court to decide where necessary, and I therefore agree with Lord Denning M.R. that certiorari

F should go in this case.

> *Appeal allowed with costs in Court*
> *of Appeal and county court.*
> *Leave to appeal.*

Solicitors: *Enever, Freeman & Co., Ruislip; Fladgate & Co.*

G
                                                                    A. H. B.

H

A

[COURT OF APPEAL]

SCIENCE RESEARCH COUNCIL *v.* NASSE

LEYLAND CARS LTD. *v.* VYAS

1978   June 21, 22, 23, 26, 29, 30;   Lord Denning M.R., Lawton and   B
        July 3, 26   Browne L.JJ.

Industrial   Relations—Industrial   tribunals—Procedure—Discovery
and inspection of documents—Complaint of discrimination on
grounds of sex and trade unionism—Complaint of racial
discrimination—Discovery of documents concerning other
employees requested in both cases—Discretion of tribunal   C
chairman or judges in county court to inspect documents and
rule on disclosure—County Court Rules, Ord. 14, rr. 1, 2—
Industrial Tribunals (Labour Relations) Regulations 1974 (S.I.
1974 No. 1386), Sch., r. 4 (2) (a) (b)
Practice—Discovery—Privilege—Confidentiality—Complaints   by
employees of discrimination—Whether employers obliged to
disclose documents relating to other employees

D

A married woman clerical officer employed by a research
council run on civil service lines was passed over for interview for promotion to executive officer grade when two
colleagues, a man and a single woman, were selected. She
filed complaints with an industrial tribunal alleging discrimination on grounds of sex and married status, contrary
to the Sex Discrimination Act 1975, and on the ground of
her active trade unionism, contrary to section 53 (1) of the   E
Employment Protection Act 1975. Before the hearing she
applied under rule 4 (1) of the Rules of Procedure scheduled
to the Industrial Tribunal (Labour Relations) Regulations 1974
for discovery and inspection, inter alia, of recent annual confidential reports, not only on herself but also on the two
colleagues selected for interview. The council, whose routine
system of operation included annual detailed confidential assessments on every employee, while ready to produce the con-   F
fidential reports on the applicant herself, objected to produce
those relating to the two selected colleagues. The tribunal
ordered their disclosure, and on the council's appeal the
Employment Appeal Tribunal (Bristow J. presiding) confirmed
the order as clearly necessary to do justice to both parties at
the hearing. One of the two candidates at once objected that
a personal report which he had not seen himself and whose
contents he had had no opportunity to challenge should be   G
made available to a third party; and his objection was supported
by the staff side of the Whitley Council as contrary to the
policy agreed between the council and the staff side. On the
council's appeal a fresh affidavit on its behalf was admitted,
stating that the council's system of confidential reports on
every employee was used throughout the civil service, by many
local and educational authorities, and by businesses throughout
the country, and that in the sphere of employment real harm   H
could be caused by such disclosure.

A methods analyst of Asian origin employed by a large
industrial concern applied for a level transfer at the works; he
and three white candidates were interviewed for the post.
Two of them were successful; he was not. He sought
help from the Commission for Racial Equality under the
provisions of the Race Relations Act 1976 to claim discrimination on the grounds of race, colour, ethnic or national origins,
and asked for preliminary discovery of, inter alia, records

A   kept by the company on the other persons interviewed and
the interview panel's completed forms relating to all the
persons interviewed for the post. The employers were ready
to disclose some information and documents on all the
candidates and explained their system on considering promotion, but objected to produce confidential reports on the
other persons interviewed and the interview panel's forms.
The chairman of the industrial tribunal upheld the objection;
B   but on the applicant's appeal the Employment Appeal
Tribunal (Phillips J. presiding) followed its own previous decision and ordered discovery, though with some reservations.
On the employers' appeal, a fresh affidavit was admitted,
stating, inter alia, that if the particular documents were disclosed it would be in gross breach of faith and could lead to
industrial trouble; and it was argued for them that " public
interest privilege " should attach to all such confidential
C   records kept by all industrial concerns.
    On the appeals by the council and the employers: —
    Held, allowing the appeals, that orders for general dis-
covery should not normally be made on complaints of discrimination, either by industrial tribunals or in the county
court; but that in each case the procedure should be the
same, and where disclosure of information given, received or
compiled as confidential was sought, the chairman of the
D   tribunal or the judge in the county court should exercise the
discretion conferred by the tribunal's rules of procedure and
the County Court Rules by himself inspecting each particular
document in each specific case to satisfy himself whether it
was essential, in order to do justice between the parties, that
the confidence should be overridden, and even then should
impose such conditions as he thought fit by restricting the
scope of the disclosure; and that, in the present cases, the
E   orders made should be set aside as unnecessary or premature.
    D. v. *National Society for the Prevention of Cruelty to
Children* [1978] A.C. 171, H.L.(E.) applied.
    Per Lawton and Browne L.JJ. " Public interest privilege "
should not be extended to the classes of documents here in
question. If so great an extension of immunity were permitted
it would not only prevent the statutory commissions appointed
F   under the relevant Acts from obtaining information which the
Acts required them to obtain, but it could also apply in
ordinary litigation and might operate not only against a
plaintiff but also to deprive a defendant of an established
defence (post, pp. 771D—772A, 774H, 775B–C).
    Per Lord Denning M.R. The court in face of an entirely
new piece of social legislation is free to balance the public
interests involved, having regard to the immense powers
G   granted by Parliament to the statutory commissions to compel
disclosure of confidential information on the one hand and
on the other the importance to the public services and
industrial concerns of preserving from public disclosure
information given and received in confidence (post, p.
767C–E, H).
    Decisions of the Employment Appeal Tribunal in *Science
Research Council* v. *Nassé* [1978] I.C.R. 777 and *Leyland Cars
H   Ltd.* v. *Vyas* (unreported), April 28, 1978 reversed.

The following cases are referred to in the judgments:

Alterskye v. *Scott* [1948] 1 All E.R. 469, C.A.
Attorney-General v. *Clough* [1963] 1 Q.B. 773; [1963] 2 W.L.R. 343;
    [1963] 1 All E.R. 420.
Beswick v. *Beswick* [1968] A.C. 58; [1967] 3 W.L.R. 932; [1967] 2 All
    E.R. 1197, H.L.(E.).

Science Research Council v. Nassé (C.A.) [1978]

Crompton (Alfred) Amusement Machines Ltd. v. Customs and Excise A
Commissioners (No. 2) [1974] A.C. 405; [1973] 3 W.L.R. 268;
[1973] 2 All E.R. 1169, H.L.(E.).

D. v. National Society for the Prevention of Cruelty to Children [1978]
A.C. 171; [1976] 3 W.L.R. 124; [1976] 2 All E.R. 993; [1977] 2 W.L.R.
201; [1977] 1 All E.R. 589, C.A. and H.L.(E.).

Ehrmann v. Ehrmann [1896] 2 Ch. 826.

McIlraith v. Grady [1968] 1 Q.B. 468; [1967] 3 W.L.R. 1331; [1967] B
3 All E.R. 625, C.A.

Norwich Pharmacal Co. v. Customs and Excise Commissioners [1974]
A.C. 133; [1973] 3 W.L.R. 164; [1973] 2 All E.R. 943, H.L.(E.).

Rasul v. Commission for Racial Equality [1978] I.R.L.R. 203, E.A.T.

Rex v. Davies [1906] 1 K.B. 32.

Rex v. Edwards, Ex parte Welsh Church Temporalities Commissioners
(1933) 49 T.L.R. 383, D.C.
C
Reg. v. Lewes Justices, Ex parte Secretary of State for the Home Department [1973] A.C. 388; [1972] 3 W.L.R. 279; [1972] 2 All E.R.
1057, H.L.(E.).

Riddick v. Thames Board Mills Ltd. [1977] Q.B. 881; [1977] 3 W.L.R.
63; [1977] 3 All E.R. 677, C.A.

Wheeler v. Le Marchant (1881) 17 Ch.D. 675, C.A.

D
The following additional cases were cited in argument:

Attorney-General v. British Broadcasting Corporation [1978] 1 W.L.R.
477; [1978] 2 All E.R. 731, D.C.

Burns v. Thiokol Chemical Corporation (1973) 483 F. 2d 300.

Carr v. Monroe Manufacturing Co. (1970) 431 F. 2d 384.

Chantrey Martin v. Martin [1953] 2 Q.B. 286; [1953] 3 W.L.R. 459.

Conway v. Rimmer [1968] A.C. 910; [1968] 2 W.L.R. 998; [1968] E
1 All E.R. 874, H.L.(E.).

Fears v. Burris Manufacturing Co. (1971) 436 F. 2d 1357.

Georgia Power Co. v. Equal Employment Opportunity Commission
(1969) 412 F. 2d 462.

Green (A Bankrupt), In re, Ex parte The Trustee [1958] 1 W.L.R. 405;
[1958] 2 All E.R. 57n, C.A.
F
Greenlaw v. King (1838) 1 Beav. 137.

Hope v. Brash [1897] 2 Q.B. 188, C.A.

Humphreys v. Board of Managers of St. George's Church of England
(Aided) Primary School [1978] I.C.R. 546, E.A.T.

K (Infants) In re [1965] A.C. 201; [1963] 3 W.L.R. 408; [1963] 3 All
E.R. 191, H.L.(E.).

McDonnell Douglas Corporation v. Green (1973) 411 U.S. 792. G

McIvor v. Southern Health and Social Services Board [1978] 1 W.L.R.
757; [1978] 2 All E.R. 625, H.L.(N.I.).

Oxford v. Department of Health and Social Security [1977] I.C.R. 884,
E.A.T.

Peruvian Guano Co., In re, Ex parte Kemp [1894] 3 Ch. 690.

Rex v. Daily Mail, Ex parte Farnsworth [1921] 2 K.B. 733, D.C.

Stone (L.P.) v. Charrington & Co. Ltd. [1977] I.C.R. 248, E.A.T. H

Warner-Lambert Co. v. Glaxo Laboratories Ltd. [1975] R.P.C. 354,
C.A.

Whyte v. University of Manchester [1976] I.R.L.R. 218.

Woodworth v. Conroy [1976] 1 Q.B. 884; [1976] 2 W.L.R. 338; [1976]
1 All E.R. 107, C.A.

INTERLOCUTORY APPEALS from Employment Appeal Tribunal.

A   SCIENCE RESEARCH COUNCIL *v.* NASSÉ

The Science Research Council, a body incorporated by Royal
Charter and conducted on civil service lines, appealed with leave of the
Court of Appeal from the decision of the Employment Appeal Tribunal
(Bristow J. presiding) given on March 20, 1978, confirming an order of an
industrial tribunal sitting in London on November 23, 1977, on the
B application of Joan Marguerite Nassé, a married clerical officer, that
certain documents should be disclosed to her prior to the hearing of her
complaints of discrimination against her, contrary to section 53 (1) of
the Employment Protection Act 1975 on account of her trade union
activities and contrary to section 6 of the Sex Discrimination Act 1975
because she was a married woman, which she alleged had blocked her
promotion to the grade of executive officer.   The documents ordered to
C be disclosed to her were (1) the confidential reports for 1975 and 1976 on
two clerical officers, who were selected for interview for promotion when
she herself was not so selected; and (2) the minutes of the council's local
review board relating to the decision to select those two officers for
interview with a view to recommendation for promotion and to the
decision not to select her; and it was further ordered that those documents should be inspected at the office of the council's solicitor with
D liberty to the applicant to take copies of them at her expense.   The
council appealed, asking that the order to disclose documents relating to
officers other than the applicant herself might be set aside or varied.
The grounds of the appeal were (1) that the Employment Appeal Tribunal
erred in law in that they (a) wrongly held that the discretionary power
of an industrial tribunal to order discovery and/or inspection of docu-
E ments pursuant to rule 4 (1) (*b*) of the Industrial Tribunal Rules of
Procedure should be exercised in the same manner as in civil proceedings in a county court; (b) failed to have sufficient regard to the confidential nature of the documents and the need to balance the interests
of the applicant and that of the two clerical officers and of the
employers in the maintenance of the confidentiality and privacy of the
documents relating to the two clerical officers; (c) failed to have sufficient
F regard to the purpose of making and keeping reports confidential,
namely, to protect the privacy of the officer on whom the report had
been made and to encourage those making reports (who would have
to continue to work alongside the persons who were the subjects of
their reports) to be frank and uninhibited; (d) failed to adjourn the
application and/or to give sufficient consideration as to the extent
G to which the disclosure of the documents relating to the two clerical
officers mentioned above was necessary, or necessary at that stage and in
particular ordered that there be disclosure of such documents without
(i) having first inspected the documents themselves; (ii) and/or without
giving the two clerical officers any opportunity to object to such disclosure; (iii) and/or before the applicant had shown that there was any
substance in her complaint and when such material as was before the
H tribunal indicated that her complaints were without substance; (e) wrongly
regarded the consideration that justice should be done between the
applicant and the employers as paramount over all other considerations.
(2) In the alternative, if the Employment Appeal Tribunal were right to
order disclosure of the documents, they were wrong in law in not limiting
the order to protect the confidential nature of the documents as far as
the circumstances permitted.   (3) The Employment Appeal Tribunal
further erred in law in holding, in relation to the applicant's application for

compensation under sections 53 to 56 of the Employment Protection Act
1975, that the burden of proof rested on the employers, whereas, by virtue
of section 55 of that Act the burden was placed on the applicant.

LEYLAND CARS LTD. v. VYAS

The employers, Leyland Cars Ld., appealed from the decision of the
Employment Appeal Tribunal (Phillips J. presiding) on April 28, 1978,
allowing an appeal by the applicant, Nat Vinu Vyas, from the refusal
of the chairman of an industrial tribunal sitting at Reading on March
4, 1978, prior to the hearing of the applicant's complaint of discrimination
against him, in relation to his unsuccessful application for a level transfer
at the works where he was a methods analyst, on the grounds of his race,
colour, ethnic or national origin, contrary to the Race Relations Act 1976,
to make an order for further and better particulars of the following
matters. (1) Details of the employment record of the persons apart from
the applicant who were interviewed for the position of Methods Analyst
Grade 9 in the service division; their service records while in the employment of the respondent employers—namely, length of service, position held,
promotions, job classification according to grades, personal history forms,
personal assessment records and details of commendations (if any) etc.
together with their application forms for the post advertised and applied
for by the applicant. (2) The completed interview report forms returned
by each and every member of the interview panel in relation to every person,
including the applicant, interviewed for the post in the service division,
and ordering that any documents of the kind referred to in items 3 and 6
be listed, that the lists be sent to the Central Office of the Industrial
Tribunal, and that the applicant be entitled to inspect them.

The Employment Appeal Tribunal, following its own decision in the
Nassé case made the order. The employers appealed on the grounds
(1) that the Employment Appeal Tribunal erred in law in that they
(a) wrongly held that the discretionary power of an industrial tribunal
to order further and better particulars pursuant to rule 4 (1) of the Rules
of Procedure set out in the Industrial Tribunals (Labour Relations) Regulations 1974 should be exercised in the same manner as in civil proceedings
in a county court; (b) failed to have sufficient regard to the confidential
nature of the information and documents; (c) failed to have sufficient
regard to the public interest in the preservation of the confidentiality of the
information and documents; (d) failed to balance the interests of the applicant against the interests of the other applicants for the post and of the
employers and the public in the preservation of the confidentiality of
the information and documents; (e) failed to have sufficient regard to the
purpose of making and keeping personal assessment records confidential,
namely, to protect the privacy of the employee to whom the assessment
related and to encourage those making the assessment (who would have
to continue to work alongside the persons who were the subjects of their
assessment) to be frank and uninhibited and to the public interest in the
advancement of that purpose; (f) failed to have sufficient regard to the
purpose of making and keeping commendations confidential, namely, to
protect the privacy of the employee to whom the commendation related
and to encourage those making such commendations to be frank and
uninhibited and to the public interest in the advancement of that purpose;
(g) failed to have sufficient regard to the purpose of making and keeping
interview report forms confidential, namely, to protect the privacy of the
employee to whom the report form related and to encourage those making

A such reports to be frank and uninhibited and to the public interest in the advancement of that purpose; (h) failed to give any sufficient consideration to the extent to which the provision of the information and documents was necessary and in particular in ordering that the information and documents be provided without (i) directing that the chairman of the industrial tribunal should first consider the information and documents himself; (ii) directing that the other applicants for the post

B be given an opportunity to object to the provision of the information and documents; (iii) having ascertained that there was any substance in the applicant's complaint; (j) failed to give any sufficient consideration to the provisions of section 65 of the Race Relations Act 1976 which assisted persons who considered that they might have been discriminated against in contravention of the Act to obtain certain information; and

C (k) wrongly regarded the consideration that justice might be done between the applicant and the employers as being paramount over all other considerations.   (2) In the alternative, if the Employment Appeal Tribunal were right to order the provision of the information and documents it was wrong in law in not limiting the order to protect the confidential nature of the information and documents so far as the circumstances permitted.

D

H. K. Woolf and *David Blunt* for the Science Research Council.
Michael Howard for Leyland Cars Ltd.
Frederic Reynold for the applicants, Mrs. Nassé and Mr. Vyas.
Anthony Lester Q.C. for the Equal Opportunities Commission and the Commission for Racial Equality.

E   *Cur. adv. vult.*

July 26.   The following judgments were read.

LORD DENNING M.R.   Joan Marguerite Nassé is a married woman, aged 45.   She has been employed since 1971 by the Science Research Council at the Appleton Laboratory at Ditton Park, near Slough.   She

F was graded as a clerical officer.   She was a member of a trade union called the Civil and Public Service Association (C.P.S.A.) and took an active part in its affairs.   She was chairman of the Appleton Laboratory sub-branch.

Early in 1977 she was keen to be promoted to the grade of executive officer.   But she was dismayed to find that she was not one of those selected for interview.   Two others were asked to go to the interview

G panel.   They were a Mr. Roberts and a Miss Richardson.   Mrs. Nassé was convinced that she was better qualified for promotion than those two: and that she was being discriminated against because of her trade union activities.   So she wrote this letter on February 7, 1977, to the Director of the Appleton Laboratory:

H "I have looked at the selection procedure at Appleton and considered, as impartially as one is able to under the circumstances, the merits of the two selected candidates.   They are both able officers, but I find that I have more experience and have covered a wider range of work and responsibilities.   On many occasions my supervisors have made very favourable comments on my work and ability.   I feel convinced therefore that my exclusion is attributable solely to my union activities on behalf of the members of the C.P.S.A., and propose to take the matter to the industrial tribunal."

On the same day the director replied: A

"While your performance during the period under review as a
clerical officer has been very good, you were not considered to have
the potential for the executive officer grade and you were therefore
not recommended for promotion.   Your C.P.S.A. activities did not
influence this decision."

The director suggested that she should appeal by an internal procedure, B
but she did not take advantage of it.   Instead she determined to complain
to the industrial tribunal.   Meanwhile, before she lodged her complaint,
she had heard it said by someone that, as married women were not mobile,
they would not normally be considered to have potential for promotion.
So on May 8, 1977, she applied to the tribunal on the grounds: "(a)
Discrimination against me for carrying out trade union activities. (b)   C
Discrimination against me because I am a married person."   On June 9,
1977, the Treasury Solicitor, on behalf of the council, resisted her claim
on the ground: "It is denied that there was any discrimination against
the applicant."   Mrs. Nassé then made application to the tribunal for
discovery of documents.

The Science Research Council were quite willing to produce, and did
produce, a great number of documents.   To understand them it is   D
necessary for me to describe the way in which staff are selected for
promotion.

Every year there is an annual confidential report on every person
employed.   It is made by his or her immediate superior.   It is countersigned by the next senior, with his remarks, and then the one senior to
him.   It is very detailed with an assessment of his or her performance E
during the year and suitability for promotion.   All these confidential
reports are studied by a local review board.   This board goes through
them, makes an analysis of them in writing and makes comments in
writing on each one.   They do not interview anybody but deliberate
upon them and then put forward the names of those whom they recommend for promotion.   Their recommendations go forward to a central
review board in London: and that board decides which clerical officers F
shall be called for interview.

In the present case the persons called for interview were a Mr.
Roberts and a Miss Richardson.   Mr. Roberts was an active member of
the committee of the union (the C.P.S.A.).   He was secretary of the local
staff side.   Miss Richardson was also a member of the C.P.S.A.

The Science Research Council were quite willing to produce, and did   G
produce, all the annual confidential reports on Mrs. Nassé herself: and
also all the summaries and minutes of the local review board relating to
all other persons.   But they declined to produce the confidential reports
on the two clerical officers (Mr. Roberts and Miss Richardson) who were
selected for interview.   The industrial tribunal ordered the production of
the confidential reports of those two persons, and their decision was
affirmed by the Employment Appeal Tribunal.   Bristow J. said [1978] H
I.C.R. 777, 780:

"... disclosure of the documents which are in question here is ...
clearly necessary in order that the industrial tribunal may be in a
position to do justice not only to her, but to [the council], at the
hearing."

When those concerned heard of this ruling, they themselves took

The Weekly Law Reports, November 10, 1978

761

3 W.L.R.   Science Research Council v. Nassé (C.A.)   Lord Denning M.R.

A strong objection.   Mr. Roberts wrote this letter of protest to the Treasury
Solicitor:

"I have always considered the report a personal one, only to be
seen by a restricted number of senior S.R.C. officers, and I consider
it most unfair that this report, which I myself have not seen and
whose contents I have not had the opportunity to challenge, should
B be made available to a third party.   Accordingly I object most
strongly to this action."

His objection was supported by the Whitley Council—Staff Side,
whose chairman wrote:

"The staff side wishes to point out that the system of annual
confidential reporting . . . which includes the principle that con-
C fidential personal reports on individuals should not be disclosed to
other members of staff who might have a personal interest, has been
agreed between SRC and its staff side.   The staff side must therefore object to the supply of confidential personal reports on individual
members of staff to other members (or ex-members) of staff."

These objections have been reinforced by an affidavit on behalf of
D the Treasury Solicitor.   He says that the system adopted by the Science
Research Council is used throughout the whole of the Civil Service, by
many local authorities, by education authorities, and by innumerable
businesses throughout the country.   He says that "in the sphere of
employment very real harm could . . . be caused by disclosure."

The question in Mrs. Nassé's case is whether the court should overrule those objections and compel the Science Research Council to disclose
E to the tribunal and to Mrs. Nassé the confidential reports on Mr. Roberts
and Miss Richardson.

Mr. Vyas's case

Mr. Nat Vinyu Vyas is employed by Leyland Cars at their Cowley
Works.   He is 40 years of age.   He is a methods analyst.   He applied
F for a transfer from one division of the works to another.   Two others
besides him were interviewed.   They were white.   He was coloured.   He
failed.   He considered that he was discriminated against because of his
race.   He went to the Commission for Racial Equality.   The commission
helped him by putting a series of interrogatories to Leyland Cars.   This
is authorised by section 65 of the Race Relations Act 1976.   It is a
printed form in which he questioned Leyland Cars on various matters.
G Leyland Cars answered them to the best of their ability.   But I do not
stop to set out the questions and answers.   It would take too long.   I
only say that the Commission for Racial Equality were not satisfied with
those answers.   They helped him to make a complaint to an industrial
tribunal.   His grounds were inserted by the commission as follows:

"I applied for a level transfer to methods analyst grade 9 and was
H interviewed for the position.   Of the *two other* interviewed applicants, one was already graded 9 and the other was a lower grade 7.
As far as I am aware no particular qualifications were necessary for
the position.   Both the other applicants were appointed although
the person graded 7 had less service than myself and had previously
left the company twice.   I have questioned the respondents on form
RR.65 but I consider their response to be unsatisfactory in that they
have simply stated that the other (white) applicants were **more**

acceptable. I therefore conclude that I was rejected on the grounds   A
of my race, colour, ethnic or national origin."

In reply the company resisted the claim on the ground:

"There was no discrimination by the respondents against the applicant within the meaning of the Race Relations Act 1976, Part II,
section 4 (2) (*b*)."

B

The commission pressed on with the case. In the name of Mr. Vyas
they applied to the industrial tribunal for an order for further particulars.
Leyland Cars gave them, as follows: 1. the persons interviewed for the
job were Mr. A. E. J. Bedford, Mr. M. A. J. W. Hamblin, Mr. J. Jarvis
and Mr. Vyas. The successful candidates were Mr. Jarvis and Mr.
Hamblin.

Leyland Cars were ready to give the employment records of all those   C
four persons with Leyland Cars, such as their length of service, their
performance during service, the positions held by them, the promotion
they had obtained, and their job classification according to grades. *But*
Leyland Cars declined to produce information which they had received in
confidence about the four men, such as their personal history and the
reports on their personal qualities as to their fitness for promotion.   D

2. Leyland Cars described their procedure in relation to interviews.
It was as follows: vacancies were advertised by internal notices. The
candidates filled in the application forms and their personal history
forms. They were then interviewed at a first interview and, if necessary,
short-listed candidates were interviewed again. All the candidates then
received either an offer of the position applied for or a letter of rejection.

3. Leyland Cars gave the names of the members of the interviewing   E
panel. They were Mr. A. D. Tyler, the systems development manager;
Mr. J. McGarry, the operations and procedures supervisor; and Mr. R.
Adams, the recruitment officer. *But* Leyland Cars refused to produce the
forms on which the interviewing panel had recorded their opinions on
the person interviewed. They regarded them as strictly confidential.

4. Leyland Cars gave the reasons why the successful candidates   F
were preferred to Mr. Vyas in these words:

"All applications are assessed against the standard factors, i.e.
personal, health, qualifications, training, experience, intelligence,
social abilities, leadership, self-reliance, stability, motivation,
interests. Taking all factors into consideration, the interviewers
considered that other applicants were more suitable for these vacan-   G
cies."

The Commission for Racial Equality were still not satisfied. They
asked the industrial tribunal to order Leyland Cars to give discovery of
the documents which they had withheld. The chairman refused to make
the order. The commission appealed to the Employment Appeal Tribunal.
They relied on the cases of *Rasul* v. *Commission for Racial Equality*   H
[1978] I.R.L.R. 203, and of Mrs. Nassé, where Bristow J. had made an
order for similar documents to be disclosed. Phillips J. felt that the
Employment Appeal Tribunal should follow those cases, but he made
these pertinent observations:

"It seems to us plain that all the documents sought in this case are
relevant and therefore in principle are discoverable and disclosable,
unless the interests of public policy based on confidentiality lead to a

The Weekly Law Reports, November 10, 1978

763

3 W.L.R.   Science Research Council v. Nassé (C.A.)   Lord Denning M.R.

A contrary conclusion. In many ways we would have been very happy, had we not had the previous decisions of the appeal tribunal, to come to a decision in accordance with Mr. Howard's submissions; and we have, it is fair to say and should be said, some reservations about the decisions in the previous cases, and some sympathy with the need for a measure of protection for the documents of third parties who have no interest in these proceedings at all. But . . .

B it would only cause confusion were we at this stage to take a different line from that which has been taken previously."

On the appeal before us Leyland Cars sought leave to put in an affidavit, and we gave leave. Mr. McCulloch (the staff director specially charged with employees) explained the concern felt by Leyland Cars if they were compelled to disclose confidential information about employees

C or applicants. He said that Leyland Cars have a system of appraisals compiled by heads of department on employees. They are split up under two headings: (1) performance, (2) promotional prospects. The reports concerning performance are shown to the individual concerned. But the report on promotional prospects is confidential to the employers and is used by interviewers to decide between candidates. He said that

D Leyland Cars objected to produce them because, by disclosing them, Leyland Cars "would in effect be committing a gross breach of faith." He said:

"Such a breach may cause industrial unrest and even dispute, which in this day and age and in particular in British Leyland has proved to have disastrous effects on our industry. Such a consequence I can-

E not see being confined to British Leyland. It would have far-reaching consequences."

The issues

The issues arising in these cases are of the first importance. On the one side stand the new statutory commissions. These seek to stamp out discrimination on the ground of race or sex: and, to do so, they wish to

F see all the documents relating to it, no matter how confidential. On the other side stand the great concerns which employ men and women in the public service and in industry. These seek to keep faith with those who work for them—to preserve confidence—and to avoid the unrest which they feel would inevitably flow from a breach of it. The issue concerns equally the universities and colleges which educate young people. Are

G they to be compelled to disclose reports from headmasters about other candidates which are given to them in confidence? It also concerns the traders who give credit, or the landlords, including local councils, who let houses. Are they to be compelled to disclose the reports about the other applicants because of an allegation that they are guilty of discrimination?

Such is the scale of the problem before us today. We have looked

H through all the statutes which Parliament has passed to see if they offer a solution to the problem. But it is not to be found in the statutes nor in the regulations made under them. We are left with the sobering reflection that Parliament never thought of it at all: or, if they did, they were afraid to tackle it and left it to the judges to decide. At any rate, we must do it. It is no good asking Parliament to do it. That would take far too long. The issue does not brook of any delay. We must decide it, and decide it now.

Lord Denning M.R.   **Science Research Council v. Nassé (C.A.)**   [1978]

The statutes   A

There are three statutes to consider: the Sex Discrimination Act
1975; the Race Relations Act 1976; and the Employment Protection Act
1975 (sections 53 to 56).   The Equal Opportunities Commission is under
a duty to work towards the elimination of discrimination on the ground
of sex.   The Commission for Racial Equality is under a like duty in
respect of race.   There is no special commission in relation to trade   B
union activities: it being thought, no doubt, that the trade unions can
look after their side.

Complaints of discrimination go to different tribunals.   It depends on
whether the complaint is about discrimination in the *employment* field,
on the one hand, or discrimination in other fields, such as *education* or
housing or *credit,* on the other.   When there is discrimination in the
employment field in respect of race or sex, it goes before an industrial   C
tribunal: see section 54 of the Race Relations Act 1976 and section 63
of the Sex Discrimination Act 1975; but when there is discrimination in
the other fields, such as education or housing or credit on the grounds of
race or sex, it goes before the county court: see section 57 of the Race
Relations Act 1976 and section 66 of the Sex Discrimination Act 1975.

That difference between tribunals led to a suggestion that discovery
of documents might be different according to whether the complaint was   D
heard by an industrial tribunal or by a county court.   The industrial
tribunals are regulated by rule 4 (1) (*b*) of the Industrial Tribunal (Labour
Relations) Regulations 1974. The county courts are regulated by Ord. 14,
rr. 2 and 3 of the County Court Rules.   But I must say that, in my opinion,
in discrimination cases, the practice of both should be the same in regard
to discovery.   The governing principle is the same as in the High Court: E
R.S.C., Ord. 24, r. 2 (5):

" Discovery shall not be ordered if and in so far as the court is of
opinion that it is not necessary either for disposing fairly of the
proceedings or for saving costs."   (C.C.R., Ord. 14, r. 2 (2)).

Although this is the governing principle, its application may vary
according to the nature of the proceedings and of the tribunal.   In these   F
discrimination cases the complainant may often be unrepresented.   No
costs are awarded by the industrial tribunal.   They should be tried
simply and speedily without any undue burden on either side.   There
should not be oppressive discovery nor lengthy trials.

There is a difference between the tribunals in another respect.   There
are statutory provisions which enable industrial tribunals to sit in private   G
in cases where the evidence may consist of confidential information: see
the Trade Union and Labour Relations Act 1974, Schedule 1, paragraph
21 (5) (*c*), and the Employment Protection Act 1975, Schedule 6, paragraph 16 (1) (*c*): whereas there is no corresponding provision for county
courts.   Further, if a person fails to comply with an order for discovery
made by an industrial tribunal, he may be taken before the justices and
liable on summary conviction to a fine of £100: see paragraph 21 (6) of   H
Schedule 1 to the Act of 1974; whereas, if he disobeys an order of the
county court he is guilty of a contempt punishable by the High Court:
see *Rex* v. *Davies* [1906] 1 K.B. 32; *Rex* v. *Edwards, Ex parte Welsh
Church Temporalities Commissioners* (1933) 49 T.L.R. 383; and R.S.C.,
Ord. 52, r. 1 (2) (*a*) (iii): and by the county court itself: see Ord. 25, rr. 67
and 68 of the County Court Rules and *McIlraith* v. *Grady* [1968] 1 Q.B.
468.

A   *The inquisitorial powers of the commissions*

Each of the two commissions is given by statute large powers to obtain information. These are inquisitorial powers of a kind never before known to the law. They are given so as to enable the commissioners to see if any employer or anyone else has broken the law against discrimination. The commission is empowered to conduct what is called a " formal

B   investigation: " and for that purpose the commission may require any person to give oral information and produce all documents in his possession or control relating to any particular matter. If he fails, he can be taken before a county court and fined: see section 50 of the Race Relations Act 1976 and section 59 of the Sex Discrimination Act 1975. But the person concerned cannot be compelled to produce any documents which he could not be compelled to produce in civil proceedings before the High

C   Court. This leaves open an important question to which I will revert hereafter. What documents could the employers be compelled to produce in civil proceedings before the High Court ?

The statutes do contain safeguarding provisions designed to protect the person who is thus compelled by inquisition to give information or produce documents. None of it is to be disclosed except on order of a

D   court: or with the consent of the informant: or for the purposes of proceedings under the Act to which the commission is a party. And in making any report for publication, the commissions are to exclude matters which might prejudicially affect an individual: see section 52 of the Race Relations Act 1976 and section 61 of the Sex Discrimination Act 1975.

E   If the commissions, as a result of their inquisition, believe that the employer has been guilty of discrimination, they can take proceedings against him—using the information which they have obtained as a result of their formal investigation.

The litigious powers of the commissions

F   In addition to those inquisitorial powers the commission is given power to assist any claimant, actual or prospective, who asserts that he has been discriminated against. It can assist him in his proceedings before the industrial tribunal or the county court. It can give him advice. It can arrange for him to be represented by solicitors and counsel. It can pay his costs. It can give him whatever assistance it considers appropriate. In short, it can take proceedings against the

G   employer, using the name of the complainant so as to stop discrimination on the employer's part, and make him pay compensation: see sections 65 and 66 of the Race Relations Act 1976 and sections 74 and 75 of the Sex Discrimination Act 1975. These sections do not consider at all the question of discovery of documents. But I cannot believe that the commissions, by conducting litigation on behalf of a claimant, can do

H   away with all the restrictions placed on them by statute in the exercise of their inquisitorial powers.

The ultimate issue

So at last we get to the issue to be decided. It is of general interest in all the cases under the statutes which seek to eliminate discrimination. The issue arises in all cases where someone applies for a job or seeks promotion in the employment field: or where he seeks entry into a university or college in the educational field, or sits for an examination: or where **A** he seeks to rent a house or to obtain credit in the general field. Very often some applicant or candidate is disappointed with the result. He does not get the job or the promotion: he does not get the place in the university or get a pass in the examination: he is not allocated a house, or he is denied credit.

Thinking it over in his disappointment, he compares himself favourably with the others. He puts a high value on his own abilities. In his own **B** reckoning he puts himself in such a good light that he persuades himself that his failure is due to his race or sex or his trade union activities. So he lodges a complaint with the industrial tribunal or the county court. Often enough he is helped by the Equal Opportunities Commission, or the Commission for Racial Equality: because they see his point of view and think it warrants investigation.   **C**

The burden of proof is on the applicant in cases of discrimination on the ground of sex and race. But it is on the employer in the case of discrimination on the ground of trade union activities: see section 55 of the Employment Protection Act 1975. Discovery, however, comes before burden of proof. The applicant, often enough, says that he needs discovery in order to make out his case. The documents will **D** prove it, he says.

The law

On several occasions in recent years attempts have been made to formulate a general principle in regard to confidential information. In *Norwich Pharmacal Co.* v. *Customs and Excise Commissioners* [1974] **E** A.C. 133, 140, I ventured to suggest:

"The law about confidential information has developed much of recent years. The cases show that the public interest has two sides to it. On the one hand it is usually in the public interest that when information is received in confidence—for a limited and restricted purpose, as it always is—it should not be used for other purposes. In such cases confidences will be held sacrosanct . . . On the **F** other hand, confidences will sometimes be overcome by a higher public interest, such as the interest of justice itself, the prevention of wrongdoing, or the security of the state."

Next from *D.* v. *National Society for the Prevention of Cruelty to Children* [1978] A.C. 171 I said, at p. 190:   **G**

"To my mind it is all a question of balancing the competing interests. 'Confidentiality,' as Lord Cross of Chelsea said . . . 'is not a separate head of privilege.' But it is a very material consideration when deciding whether to compel disclosure. In holding the scales of justice, the courts should not allow confidences to be lightly broken. When information has been imparted in confidence, and particularly where there is a pledge to keep it confidential, the courts should **H** respect that confidence. They should in no way compel a breach of it, save where the public interest clearly demands it, and then only to the extent that the public interest requires."

When the *N.S.P.C.C.* case reached the House of Lords they seem to have been a little shy of accepting that principle. Lord Diplock said, at p. 220, it was "broader than necessary," but did not contradict it. Lord

A Hailsham of St. Marylebone said, at p. 225, it propounded a "lucid and coherent system," but he said that "in the breadth and generality" of it, he did not find it acceptable. But Lord Edmund-Davies, at p. 245, put forward a principle which is virtually the same. He said:

> ". . . where (i) a confidential relationship exists (other than that of lawyer and client) *and* (ii) disclosure would be in breach of some ethical or social value involving the public interest, the court has a discretion to uphold a refusal to disclose relevant evidence provided it considers that, on balance, the public interest would be better served by excluding such evidence."

B

Lastly, in the *N.S.P.C.C.* case Lord Hailsham of St. Marylebone said significantly at p. 230:

C
> "The categories of public interest are not closed, and must alter from time to time whether by restriction or extension as social conditions and social legislation develop."

In our present case we have an entirely new piece of social legislation. We are, therefore, free to balance the public interest involved: and that is what I now propose to do.

D

Holding the balance

Before even considering the confidential documents I would draw attention to the immense powers already granted by Parliament to the statutory commissions. They can conduct "formal investigations" by which they can interrogate employers and educational authorities up to E the hilt and compel disclosure of documents on a massive scale. They can take up the cause of any complainant who has a grievance and, in his name, issue a questionnaire to his employers or educational authorities. They can use his name to sue them, and demand full particulars in the course of it. They can compel discovery of documents from them to the same extent as in the High Court. No plea is available to the accused F that they are not bound to incriminate themselves. You might think that we were back in the days of the Inquisition. Now we come to the most presumptuous claim of all. They demand to see documents made in confidence, and to compel breaches of good faith—which is owed to persons who are not parties to the proceedings at all. You might think we were back in the days of the General Warrants.

G It is suggested that the confidence can be respected by holding hearings in private or by reason of the decision in *Riddick* v. *Thames Board Mills Ltd.* [1977] Q.B. 881. But this is very illusory. Mankind—and womankind—without discrimination—are tale-bearers by nature. Once confidences are broken, the story spreads like wildfire.

In holding the balance I have been much impressed by the evidence adduced before us—which was not before the Employment Appeal Tri-H bunal. This shows that it is very important in the public interest that confidential reports should not be disclosed. Not only would their disclosure be a gross breach of faith with the makers of them, but once the subjects of the reports got to know of the disclosures, it might lead to much disturbance and unrest. Furthermore, in the long run, if the tribunals made a practice of ordering discovery (as they have done in the two cases before us) the likely result would be that the makers of the reports would make them in future by word of mouth: or write the

Lord Denning M.R.   **Science Research Council v. Nassé (C.A.)**   **[1978]**

reports in a colourless and neutral fashion, rendering them useless for the   A
purpose in hand.   So great is it in the public interest that these reports
should be kept confidential that I do not think the tribunals should ever
make an order at large or in general terms for the disclosure of confidential reports.   They should not order the disclosure of all the
references on applicants for employment, or of all the reports on candidates for entry to universities, or anything of that kind.   The very
furthest they should go is to order disclosure of specific documents in   B
respect of specific individuals, where that is shown to be essential in
the interests of justice: and so essential that it warrants overriding the
confidence in which they were made.

Such cases must be rare.   So rare, indeed, that the chairman of the
tribunal should not make such an order unless and until he has seen
the documents himself: and considered any objection that may be made   C
by the maker or subject of the document: and decided to override those
objections on the ground that disclosure is essential in the interests of
justice.   I may add, it is not only the claimant who may seek an order
for production.   Justice is not only for him.   It is for the employer also.
If there are cases where confidences may be overruled in favour of the
complainant, there are also cases where they may be overruled in favour   D
of the employers.   So this is how I would state the principle: The industrial tribunals should not order or permit the disclosure of reports or
references that have been given and received in confidence except in
the very rare cases where, after inspection of a particular document, the
chairman decides that it is essential in the interests of justice that the
confidence should be overriden: and then only subject to such conditions
as to the divulging of it as he shall think fit to impose—both for the   E
protection of the maker of the document and the subject of it.   He might,
for instance, limit the sight of it to counsel and solicitors on their undertaking that it should go no further.

Applied to these cases
                                                                            F
First, it must be noticed that the Science Research Council and
Leyland Cars have answered many questions and given many particulars
already.   They have given the names of the other applicants—both those
who were successful and those who were unsuccessful.   They have given
their qualifications, and all sorts of details about them.   They have only
drawn the line at information which was given and received in confidence,
and which they feel that it would be a breach of faith to disclose.   For   G
myself, I think that the information already given is all that is " necessary
for fairly disposing " of the matter.   To disclose these confidential reports
would be going beyond what is necessary.   Fairness means fairness not
only to the complainant but also to the many people who make these
reports and receive them.   It means fairness, too, to the public services
and industrial concerns of this country.   They have to cope with these   H
problems of discrimination, and should be trusted to deal with them
fairly.   The statutory commissions should not treat them as if they were
miscreants seeking to evade the law—seeking to keep back incriminating
documents.   If the statutory commissions seek to pull the rope too tight,
they will find that it will lash back against them.

I would, therefore, allow the appeals, and set aside the order made
by the tribunals.

A   LAWTON L.J.   The main issue in this case is this: when Parliament
made discrimination because of trade union activities (sections 53 to 55 of
the Employment Protection Act 1975), sex (sections 62 to 66 of the Sex
Discrimination Act 1975) and race (section 56 of the Race Relations Act
1976) a cause of action, did it intend to give aggrieved parties the right,
through discovery and before the hearing, to have inspection of all
relevant documents in the possession of or under the control of the other
B   party, even though such documents had come into existence under a
promise, whether expressed or implied, that they would be treated as
confidential?   Mr. Lester on behalf of the statutory commissions says
" yes " because without full discovery applicants would be deprived of
access to what may be the only source of evidence touching on their
complaints.   Mr. Howard on behalf of Leyland Cars says " no " because
C   such discovery would be in breach of confidence and would be likely to
damage industrial relations and impair the efficient working of the kind of
promotion procedures which his clients and many other industrial concerns
have established.   Mr. Woolf on behalf of the Science Research Council,
which is run on Civil Service lines, says " yes " but subject to restrictions.

This court must look at the words used in the relevant legislation to
D   find out what Parliament did intend: Beswick v. Beswick [1968] A.C. 58,
73-74 per Lord Reid.   If the words used can only bear one construction
and that is one which may cause unexpected upset to many or may
damage the body politic, this court, in my judgment, must adjudge that
those unfortunate consequences follow.   If the upset is big enough or
the damage is clear it is for Parliament to repeal or amend the harmful
legislation, not for this court to twist the meaning of the statutory words.
E   If Mr. Lester's submission is right there are likely to be disturbing
consequences if, in discrimination cases, orders for discovery are made
in the sort of terms set out in the cases now under appeal.   I doubt,
however, whether they would be as common as Mr. Howard submitted
they would be.   Three examples, each from a different standpoint,
illustrate the mischief likely to be caused by an order for the discovery
F   of all relevant documents.   A, a skilled worker in a large industrial
undertaking, applies for a supervisory job in another department.   His
foreman, when asked to report upon him, says, and for good reason, " He
is a trouble maker, who is forever invoking union rules over the smallest
trivialities."   If on failing to get the job A made a complaint that he had
been discriminated against because of his trade union activities, that
report would be relevant.   If he could show that it was a prejudiced
G   one it might help him to prove his complaint.   But it might cause a
strike; and for a certainty it would cause difficulties for the foreman if
A went on working under him.   B is a female clerk in a large commercial organisation.   She wants promotion to a higher grade.   Three
of her male colleagues are promoted but she is not.   She alleges sex
discrimination and asks for, and gets, discovery of all the documents
H   relating to their qualifications and their work records for the purposes
of comparison.   The " curriculum vitae " of one reveals that he was
a foundling who was brought up in care by a local authority.   This man
might bitterly resent having this fact disclosed among those with whom
he works.   The areas in which the consequences of general discovery are
likely to be the most disturbing are in relation to education, housing and
the supply of services.   Although none of these areas have to be considered specifically in these appeals, it would, I think, be helpful to look at

Lawton L.J.   **Science Research Council v. Nassé (C.A.)**   **[1978]**

one of them, education. C, an Asian, has applied unsuccessfully, for   A
admission to a popular faculty in a popular university. There were
over a thousand applications for a hundred places. He suspects that he
was the victim of racial discrimination and starts proceedings against the
university in a county court pursuant to section 57 of the Race Relations
Act 1976. A general order for discovery could necessitate the disclosure
of the files of all the successful candidates. They would be likely to
have in them references given by headmasters; and these might contain   B
information which by any reasonable standards of behaviour ought never
to be disclosed (for example, " This girl's examination results did not
reflect her true potential. During the past six months she has been
upset by the fact that her stupid autocratic father, who disapproves of
higher education for girls, has made study difficult for her by imposing
on her many domestic duties "). If on the true construction of the relevant   C
legislation these results follow, so be it.

All three relevant statutes give an aggrieved party a right to compensation. In cases of alleged sex or racial discrimination the burden of
proof is on the applicant; but when there is a complaint based on discrimination because of trade union activities, the employer has to show
" the purpose for which action was taken against the complainant ": see   D
section 55 (1) (a) of the Employment Protection Act 1975. All complaints
under this Act have to be made to an industrial tribunal, as do complaints
arising out of employment under the other two Acts; but all other complaints relating to sex or racial discrimination are made to a county court
and when made are to be " the subject of civil proceedings in like manner
as any other claim in tort ": see section 66 (1) of the Sex Discrimination
Act 1975 and section 57 (1) of the Race Relations Act 1976. It follows,   E
in my judgment, that in the county court discrimination cases are to be
treated like any other claim in tort. If discovery is necessary for disposing
fairly of the proceedings or for saving costs then there must be discovery:
see the County Court Rules, Ord. 14, r. 2 (2).

The complaints, however, which have led to these appeals were made
to industrial tribunals because they both arose out of employment. The   F
Industrial Tribunal (Labour Relations) Regulations 1974 set out the
procedure to be followed. Rule 4 (1) (a) of the Schedule to the Regulations provides that a tribunal may grant a party to proceedings " such
discovery or inspection of documents as might be granted by a county
court." It follows, so it seems to me, that industrial tribunals should apply
the County Court Rules and the county court practice when asked to
make orders for discovery and inspection.   G

Both Mr. Woolf and Mr. Howard accepted that this is so; but they
differed from each other and from Mr. Lester as to what the consequences
of doing so are likely to be. Mr. Woolf submitted that the County Court
Rules give the court a discretion. There is to be no discovery if it is not
necessary for disposing fairly of the proceedings or for saving costs. This
entitles the judge, or the chairman of an industrial tribunal, to call upon   H
the party asking for discovery to show why he wants it. In many cases,
submitted Mr. Woolf, general discovery is unnecessary; as, for example,
when the qualifications, or lack of them, of the other workers under
comparison are known or admitted; or when the applicant's case is based
upon the fact that persons of his race or sex are never, or very seldom,
chosen, appointed or promoted; or when, as in Mrs. Nassé's case to which
I will refer in detail later, the known facts and issues make it unlikely

The Weekly Law Reports, November 10, 1978

771

3 W.L.R.   Science Research Council v. Nassé (C.A.)   Lawton L.J.

A that discovery would help the party asking for it. Mr. Woolf pointed out that under section 74 of the Sex Discrimination Act 1975 and section 65 of the Race Relations Act 1975 there is a statutory procedure available to those who think they have been discriminated against for getting information; and when proceedings have started the court or tribunal can order further particulars to be given: see rule 4 (1) (a) of the Tribunal Rules of Procedure. Applicants should use their statutory and procedural rights

B before asking for discovery. If after considering all the known facts the judge or chairman thought that discovery of documents said to be confidential might be helpful for the disposing of the proceedings he should order the party who was reluctant to make discovery to bring them to the hearing when he could look at them and decide which of them should and which should not be made available to the other side.

C The general principle, submitted Mr. Woolf, should be that there should be no order for the discovery of confidential documents unless the court or tribunal was satisfied that their disclosure was necessary.

Mr. Lester came very near to accepting Mr. Woolf's approach. He pointed out, however, that denying a party inspection until the hearing might prove inconvenient because on seeing the documents the party who had asked for them might want, and be entitled to have, an adjournment

D to call further evidence.

Mr. Howard's submission was much more fundamental. He said that whenever a party was in possession of confidential documents a claim of public interest privilege should be put forward unless the person supplying the information in such documents was willing to allow dis-

E closure. In industry, and probably in other areas where discrimination could be alleged, the disclosure of confidential documents would cause such upsets that the public weal could be damaged. He compared this class of case to that of D. v. National Society for the Prevention of Cruelty to Children [1978] A.C. 171. In my judgment the comparison is not apt. His submission must be rejected. In the N.S.P.C.C. case the party claiming public interest privilege was performing a public duty pursuant

F to an Act of Parliament for the protection of children. Although, as was said in that case, the categories of public interest privilege are not closed, it is difficult to see how everyone who writes a confidential reference or makes a confidential appraisal of ability can be said to be performing a public function. Confidentiality by itself is not a separate head of immunity: see Alfred Crompton Amusement Machines Ltd. v. Customs

G and Excise Commissioners (No. 2) [1974] A.C. 405, 433 per Lord Cross and the N.S.P.C.C. case per Lord Hailsham [1978] A.C. 171, 230. Further if confidentiality brings with it the immunity from discovery which Mr. Howard submitted it did, confidential documents could never be admitted in evidence. This could deprive litigants of defences which were open to them. In a libel action, for example, a defendant in support of a plea of qualified privilege might want to say that he wrote

H what he did out of a sense of duty because of information sent to him in confidence by someone whom he trusted. If Mr. Howard's submission were right, he could not put the letter in evidence. In discrimination cases the operation of this immunity would operate unfairly on defendants. Not all who allege discrimination have suffered it. Some of them are paranoid. For many defendants the best way of disproving discrimination is likely to be through disclosure of all their documents. Finally, to grant immunity from discovery to such a large class of relevant

Lawton L.J.   **Science Research Council v. Nassé (C.A.)**   **[1978]**

documents would come near to frustrating the intention of Parliament A
as expressed in the three statutes under consideration in these appeals.

As Lord Denning M.R. has said, what has to be done is a balancing
act. The interest of the party seeking discovery, which is to prove
or disprove his case, has to be put against those of the party trying to
safeguard confidentiality and of the public generally in the maintenance
of efficient and fair procedures for taking on and promoting employees, B
allotting places in universities and for the granting of housing accommodation and services. I am satisfied that general orders for discovery such
as are commonly made in the High Court are not necessary.

Lord Denning M.R. has stated the principle to be followed. I agree
with the general effect of what he has said. I differ from him only on
what perhaps may be described as emphasis. In my judgment, when
balancing the interest of the applicant against the desirability of preserving C
confidentiality, the judge or chairman must remember that Parliament
has created new causes of action which it has enacted are to be tried like
actions in tort. If among the defendants' documents there are some
(albeit confidential ones) which will help the applicant to prove his case,
he is entitled to see them—the statutory Rules of Procedure and the
County Court Rules say so.
                                                                          D
I turn now to the facts of these two cases. Mrs. Nassé founded her
complaint on two allegations of discrimination; the first was on the
ground of her trade union activities and the second was on the ground
that she was a married woman. The Science Research Council have
disclosed her own confidential reports. She will get such help from
them as she can in support of her allegations. The confidential reports
on the two clerical officers who were selected for interview, and which E
the Employment Appeal Tribunal ordered to be disclosed are most unlikely
to contain any references to Mrs. Nassé's trade union activities. Her
allegation of discrimination against her because she was a married woman
is based, so we are told by Mr. Lester, not on what the local review board
did specifically but on a policy decision made by someone in authority.
She claims that she can prove the making of this policy decision by F
calling a witness who was told there was such a policy. This being her
case, there is no need for her to see the minutes of the local review
board. In my judgment Mrs. Nassé has not shown that the documents
for which she has asked and which were ordered to be disclosed are
necessary for disposing fairly of her complaint. I would allow the
Science Research Council's appeal.
                                                                          G
Mr. Vyas, as an unsuccessful applicant for a transfer from one department to another in Leyland Cars, persuaded the Employment Appeal
Tribunal that he should be allowed to inspect all the documents listed in
paragraphs 3 and 6 of a letter dated February 15, 1978, and written on
his behalf by the Commission for Racial Equality. They relate to other
persons who also applied. Leyland Cars are willing to disclose some
of these documents, such as service records, but they do not want to dis- H
close either the " personal history forms, personal assessment records and
details of commendation (if any), etc., of the other applicants together
with their application forms for the post " or " the completed interview
report forms returned by each and every member of the interview
panel in relation to every person, including the applicant, interviewed "
for the post. As the basis of Mr. Vyas's claim is that applicants with
inferior qualifications to his were chosen in preference to him, the tribunal

The Weekly Law Reports, November 10, 1978

773

3 W.L.R.   Science Research Council v. Nassé (C.A.)   Lawton L.J.

A will have to compare his work record and qualifications with those of the successful applicants. Any documents containing relevant information will be necessary for disposing fairly of his complaint and he will be entitled to have sight of them. The documents relating to the other unsuccessful application, a Mr. Bedford, are probably not relevant to the issues at all and in my judgment are not necessary for disposing fairly of Mr. Vyas's complaint. Those of the successful candidates may be.

B I do not know whether they will be. The chairman of the industrial tribunal can decide this when he looks at them.

I would quash the order for discovery made by the Employment Appeal Tribunal. If Mr. Vyas still thinks that the documents which Leyland Cars have refused to disclose will help him he can take the appropriate steps to ensure that they are available before the tribunal

C at the hearing for the chairman to look at and decide which of them, if any, are necessary for disposing fairly of the proceedings and order inspection accordingly. I would allow Leyland Cars' appeal.

BROWNE L.J. I agree that both these appeals should be allowed. As Lord Denning M.R. has said, the questions which arise in them are

D of the first importance. We are faced with a conflict between the need not to frustrate or hamper the working of the legislation intended to eliminate discrimination and to do justice to applicants for redress under those Acts, and the need, so far as possible, to protect the secrecy of information or opinions given under an express or implied promise that they will be treated as confidential and not to frustrate or hamper the working of the system of confidential reporting on staff

E which is described in the affidavits of Mr. Sandal and Mr. McCulloch; this system is used throughout the Civil Service, by many local authorities, by education authorities and many businesses and other organisations, including the appellants in both these appeals. This is not, I think, merely a problem of discovery, but also affects the admissibility and compellability of evidence at the hearing before an industrial tribunal or a

F county court: see D. v. *National Society for the Prevention of Cruelty to Children* [1978] A.C. 171, *per* Lord Hailsham at p. 225E, Lord Simon of Glaisdale at pp. 231–233, and compare *Attorney-General* v. *Clough* [1963] 1 Q.B. 773.

It is well established that the mere fact that information or opinions have been given in confidence does not *in itself* confer any privilege or immunity from disclosure if such disclosure is necessary in the interests

G of justice: see, for example, *Wheeler* v. *Le Marchant* (1881) 17 Ch.D. 675, 681, *per* Sir George Jessel M.R. *Reg.* v. *Lewes Justices* [1973] A.C. 388, *per* Lord Salmon at pp. 411–412; *Alfred Crompton Amusement Machines Ltd.* v. *Customs and Excise Commissioners* [1974] A.C. 405, 433–434, *per* Lord Cross of Chelsea, with whom all the other members of the House agreed on this point; and *D.* v. *N.S.P.C.C.* [1978] A.C. 171,

H *per* Lord Diplock at p. 218A–C, Lord Hailsham at p. 230C–E, Lord Edmund-Davies at p. 245 (Proposition I). But confidentiality may be relevant in deciding whether there exists some wider public interest which should give protection from disclosure: see Lord Diplock and Lord Hailsham in the *N.S.P.C.C.* case. Also, I have no doubt that the courts should and will do all they can to uphold the moral and social duty not to break confidences: see *per* Lord Denning M.R. in the Court of Appeal in *D.* v. *N.S.P.C.C.* [1978] A.C. 171, 190; Lord Hailsham at p. 227,

Browne L.J. **Science Research Council v. Nassé (C.A.)** **[1978]**

quoting the Sixteenth Report of the Law Reform Committee (1967) **A** (Cmnd. 3472); and Lord Edmund-Davies at p. 245, Proposition II.

Conflicts between the need to disclose all documents and information relevant to the issues in some litigation and the wish to protect the secrecy of information given in confidence have of course arisen from time to time in the past. But I think the result of the anti-discrimination legislation will be that such conflicts will arise much more often and more sharply in the future. Where, as in these appeals, a person alleges that **B** he or she has been discriminated against by not being given a promotion or an interview or a transfer, the decision of the issue may well involve a comparison between what was called in another discrimination case a few weeks ago the "personal equation" of the applicant and those of the other candidates, successful or even perhaps unsuccessful. And one of the factors in the "personal equation" of the applicant and **C** the other candidates may well be the confidential reports and confidential references in respect of them. If the reports disclose that the other candidates were less suitable than an applicant this might well support an inference of discrimination. Although both these appeals relate to proceedings in industrial tribunals, our decision must also affect proceedings in county courts under Part III of the Race Relations Act **D** and of the Sex Discrimination Act relating to education, goods, facilities (including banking and insurance), services and premises. General discovery of confidential documents would be even more oppressive and damaging in these fields than in the employment field. Lawton L.J. has given some examples in education. The prospect that an applicant who alleged discrimination by a bank by the refusal of an overdraft might be able to compel the bank to disclose the confidential documents relating **E** to every customer who had been granted an overdraft is appalling.

Mr. Howard, for Leylands, submits that what is conveniently (though misleadingly) called "public interest privilege" should be extended to protect from disclosure, either by discovery or in evidence, the following categories of confidential information in the possession of Leylands: (i) confidential reports on the applicant himself or herself, including any **F** confidential references from people outside Leylands; (ii) confidential reports on the other candidates, again including any confidential references; (iii) confidential information provided by the other candidates about themselves. He suggests eight reasons why it was in the public interest that such information should not be disclosed, which are supported by Mr. McCulloch's affidavit. "Public interest privilege" is **G** not a privilege in the sense that it is an immunity which can be waived by the person entitled to it—it is a duty not to disclose—see for example, *Reg.* v. *Lewes Justices, Ex parte Secretary of State for the Home Department* [1973] A.C. 388, *per* Lord Reid at p. 400, Lord Pearson at p. 406, Lord Simon of Glaisdale at p. 407 and Lord Salmon at p. 412. I am most impressed by the disadvantages of the disclosure of such information shown by the affidavit of Mr. McCulloch and by the affidavit of Mr. Sandal **H** and the letters from Mr. Roberts and from the Whitley Council Staff Side exhibited to it. But I have come to the conclusion that I cannot hold that the disclosure of this information is prohibited by "public interest privilege." It is now established that this "privilege" is not confined to government departments or other organs of the central government, but it has so far been confined to bodies exercising statutory duties or functions. Further, it has so far been confined to cases analogous

The Weekly Law Reports, November 10, 1978

775

3 W.L.R.   Science Research Council v. Nassé (C.A.)   Browne L.J.

A   to the " police informer " immunity: *Reg.* v. *Lewes Justices* [1973] A.C. 388 and *D.* v. *N.S.P.C.C.* [1978] A.C. 171. If it extends to the present cases, it would mean that an employer who wished to rely on some such confidential report (presumably with the consent of the author) would not be able to do so: Mr. Howard said that Leylands would accept this, and would rather lose a case than disclose confidential information; but other employers, who are not represented before us, might take a different

B   view. Further, if such a " public interest privilege " applies, the commission would not be entitled to require such information in their inquisitorial role: see Sex Discrimination Act 1975, section 59 (3) and the Race Relations Act 1976, section 50 (3). And if there was a duty not to disclose such documents in discrimination proceedings it would also apply in ordinary litigation.

C   Mr. Woolf did not support Mr. Howard in his submission as to " public interest privilege "; he based his submissions on the discretion of the county courts and the industrial tribunals and suggested " guide-lines " for its exercise. Although I do not feel able to hold that " public interest privilege " should be extended to cover the confidential documents in question in these cases, I entirely agree with Mr. Woolf that their dis-

D   closure is most undesirable and should only be ordered in the last resort, when it is absolutely essential in the interests of justice and after all other methods of getting the information necessary to do justice to an applicant have been exhausted. In my view, it would very seldom, if ever, be right to make a general order for their discovery, especially at an early stage. Such an order should never be made automatically, but always as an

E   exercise of discretion in the particular case.

It is clear that in the county court discovery is not automatic, and that the court has a discretion whether or not to order it. A party requiring discovery must make an application to the court (Ord. 14, r. 2 (1) and (1A), and by Ord. 14, r. 2 (2)):

F   " On the hearing of an application the court *may* order such discovery to be made . . . either generally or limited to certain classes of documents *as the court thinks fit,* but discovery *shall not* be ordered if and in so far as the court is of opinion that it is *not necessary* either for disposing fairly of the proceedings or for saving costs " (my italics).

By section 103 of the County Courts Act 1959:

G   " In any case not expressly provided for by or in pursuance of this Act, the general principles of practice in the High Court may be adopted and applied to proceedings in a county court."

In my view, therefore, a county court can exercise the general discretions which the High Court exercises in discovery, for example, to prevent oppresive discovery or to impose conditions: see *Alterskye* v. *Scott*

H   [1948] 1 All E.R. 469, and the power to inspect documents which a party objects to produce: see R.S.C., Ord. 24, r. 13 (2) and *Ehrmann* v. *Erhmann* [1896] 2 Ch. 826, since when the rule has been amended to confirm that decision. It is also clear that industrial tribunals have at least the same discretion whether or not to order discovery as county courts. Rule 4 (1) of their Rules of Procedure provides:

" . . . a tribunal *may* on the application of a party to the proceedings . . . made either by notice . . . or at the hearing . . . (*b*) grant to the

person . . . making the application such discovery or inspection A
of documents as might be granted by a county court " (my italics).

In many cases, it will be completely unnecessary for confidential documents to be disclosed, for example when the allegation is of a
discriminatory *policy,* as Mrs. Nassé alleges in respect of married women.
A great deal of information about other candidates can be disclosed
without any breach of confidence, which these appellants have disclosed B
or offered to disclose. An applicant has other powers of obtaining
information, by means of the questionnaire procedure under section 74
of the Sex Discrimination Act and the Sex Discrimination (Questions
and Replies) Order 1975 (S.I. 1975 No. 2048) and under section 65 of
the Race Relations Act 1976; sections 74 (2) (*b*) and 65 (2) (*b*) give a
court or tribunal a draconian power to draw from " evasive or C
equivocal " answers inferences of unlawful conduct. An industrial
tribunal has wide powers under rule 4 (1) (*a*) to order particulars of
" the grounds on which [a party] relies and of any facts and contentions relevant thereto." As Mr. Woolf pointed out, a respondent
can make admissions or give information voluntarily or offer edited
versions of the documents; and, as Mr. Lester pointed out, the more
co-operative a respondent is in these ways the less likely it is that D
disclosure of confidential documents will be necessary. If after all this
an applicant still makes an application for discovery of confidential documents, the tribunal should deal with it in its discretion. On such an
application, I think the tribunal (or the county court) should consider the
documents individually; it should normally inspect the documents itself,
and should consider whether to impose any protective conditions (for E
example, as to covering up parts of the documents and as to persons to
whom disclosure is to be limited). If it decides that disclosure is essential
in the interests of justice, they must be disclosed.

In substance, I agree with the " guide-lines " suggested by Mr. Woolf,
the effect of which I have tried to set out in this judgment. No one
suggests that the results are perfectly satisfactory, but I think they are
the best which can be done in a very difficult situation. F

Although Mr. Lester began by saying that if either Mr. Woolf or Mr.
Howard was right the result would be gravely to impair the ability of
alleged victims of discrimination to get redress and the ability of
the commissions to perform their duties, I understood him in the end
very nearly to agree with Mr. Woolf. These " guide-lines " seem to be
consistent with the practice of the United States courts in discrimination G
cases; those courts do not recognise a " public interest privilege " in respect
of confidential documents, but impose protective conditions when they
think it appropriate.

I entirely agree with the principle stated by Lord Denning M.R. at
the end of his judgment:

    " The industrial tribunals should not order or permit the disclosure H
    of reports or references that have been given and received in con-
    fidence except in the very rare cases where, after inspection of a
    particular document, the chairman decides that it is essential in the
    interests of justice that the confidence should be overridden: and
    then only subject to such conditions as to the divulging of it as he
    shall think fit to impose—both for the protection of the maker of the
    document and the subject of it."

3 W.L.R.   **Science Research Council v. Nassé (C.A.)**   **Browne L.J.**

A   The result is that I would allow both appeals. If either applicant renews the application for discovery at the hearing, the tribunal should deal with it as suggested in our judgments.

> *Appeals allowed.*
> *Orders set aside with costs in V yas* v.
> *Leyland Cars only.*
> *Leave to appeal refused.*

B

Solicitors: *Treasury Solicitor; Barlow, Lyde & Gilbert; Lawford & Co; Bindman & Partners.*

M. M. H.

C   October 19, 1978. The Appeal Committee of the House of Lords (Lord Wilberforce, Lord Fraser of Tullybelton and Lord Scarman) allowed a petition by the applicants for leave to appeal.

———————

D

[COURT OF APPEAL]

SPINDLOW *v.* SPINDLOW

1978   May 16   Stamp, Lawton and Ormrod L.JJ.

E   *Injunction—Domestic violence—Exclusion from " matrimonial" home—Man and woman living together—Joint tenants of council house—Breakdown of relationship—No serious physical violence—Need to provide home for children—Whether county court having jurisdiction to order man's exclusion from house —Domestic Violence and Matrimonial Proceedings Act 1976 (c. 50), ss. 1 (1) (a) (b) (c), 2 (1)*

F   The applicant, the mother of two young children, was living with the respondent, who was the father of her younger child, in a council house. They were joint tenants of the house, which had been allocated to them by the council because they were living together as a family unit with children. The applicant left the respondent and with the two children went to live with neighbours in overcrowded conditions. She applied to the county court for injunctions under section 1 (1) (a) (b) and (c) of the Domestic Violence and Matrimonial Proceedings Act 1976 [1] to restrain the respondent from molesting her or the children and to exclude him from the home. The judge found that the

G

———————

[Reported by MISS HENRIETTA STEINBERG, Barrister-at-Law.]

H   [1] Domestic Violence and Matrimonial Proceedings Act 1976, s. 1: " (1) Without prejudice to the jurisdiction of the High Court, on an application by a party to a marriage a county court shall have jurisdiction to grant an injunction containing one or more of the following provisions, namely,—(a) a provision restraining the other party to the marriage from molesting the applicant; (b) a provision restraining the other party from molesting a child living with the applicant; (c) a provision excluding the other party from the matrimonial home or a part of the matrimonial home or from a specified area in which the matrimonial home is included; . . . . (2) Subsection (1) above shall apply to a man and a woman who are living with each other in the same household as husband and wife as it applies to the parties to a marriage and any reference to the matrimonial home shall be construed accordingly."

Spindlow v. Spindlow (C.A.) [1978]

respondent was not guilty of any serious physical violence but   A
took the view that the parties' relationship was at an end and
that the children would be adversely affected if the parties
continued to live in the same house. He therefore granted
the injunctions sought.

On the respondent's appeal: —

Held, dismissing the appeal, but discharging the injunction
against molestation, that, under section 1 (1) (c) of the Act,
the county court's discretion to grant an injunction excluding   B
one of the parties, who were living together, from the home
they shared was unfettered and was not subject to the
qualification that the party excluded had been violent or that
his conduct had adversely affected the other party or their
children; that, since the relationship between the applicant
and the respondent had broken down, the principal need was
to provide a home for the children and, therefore, since
neither party had substantial property rights in the house   C
belonging to the council and the applicant was best able to
look after the children, the judge had rightly ordered the
respondent to leave the house even though he had not been
violent to the applicant or the children.

Davis v. *Johnson* [1978] 2 W.L.R. 553, H.L.(E.) and
Bassett v. *Bassett* [1975] Fam. 76, C.A. applied.

Per Stamp and Lawton L.JJ. The injunction restraining the
respondent from molesting the applicant or the children should   D
be discharged because there was no real evidence of molestation
(post, pp. 783H, 784H—785A).

The following cases are referred to in the judgments:

Bassett v. *Bassett* [1975] Fam. 76; [1975] 2 W.L.R. 270; [1975] 1
    All E.R. 513, C.A.
Davis v. *Johnson* [1978] 2 W.L.R. 553; [1978] 1 All E.R. 1132, H.L.(E.).   E

No additional cases were cited in argument.

APPEAL from Judge Stock sitting at Basingstoke County Court.

The applicant applied on April 10, 1978, to the Basingstoke County
Court under section 1 of the Domestic Violence and Matrimonial Pro-   F
ceedings Act 1976 for orders to restrain the respondent with whom she
had been living (i) from molesting the applicant or her two children
living with her and (ii) from remaining in 1 Renoir Close, Basingstoke,
Hampshire, a council house of which they were the joint tenants. By
her affidavit, she claimed that the respondent had become aggressive
towards her, frequently threatening and on occasion using violence
towards her, and had been guilty of threatening conduct towards the   G
applicant's elder child.

Judge Stock found that it was not a case where there had been serious
violence but he granted the injunctions sought, ordering the respondent
to vacate the house by April 28, 1978, on the ground that that course
would be in the best interests of the children. The respondent's
application for a stay of execution of the order was refused by the judge   H
on April 26, at Southampton County Court.

The respondent appealed for the order to be set aside on the ground
that the judge erred in granting the injunctions for the reasons that
(i) in view of the applicant's evidence that the respondent had shown no
violence towards her or the children save once to have pushed her onto
a settee; (ii) in view of there being no evidence that the respondent had
evicted or threatened to evict the applicant or the children and the

A   judge's finding that the respondent had asked the applicant to return
to the house; and (iii) the injunction excluding the respondent from the
house deprived him of his right to possession without any finding of
physical violence, threat of violence or eviction of the applicant and
children; and (iv) the judge refused to adjourn the application for
evidence as to what alternative accommodation the local authority would
provide for the applicant and the children if the respondent were not
B   excluded from the house.

The facts are stated in the judgment of Ormrod L.J.

Richard Crabb for the applicant.
Richard Gordon for the respondent.

C   STAMP L.J.   I will ask Ormrod L.J. to deliver the first judgment.

ORMROD L.J.   This is an appeal from an order which was made by
Judge Stock on April 14, 1978, at Basingstoke County Court under the
Domestic Violence and Matrimonial Proceedings Act 1976.   Under the
order, he ordered the appellant, Mr. Spindlow, to leave what had been
D   the joint home of himself and a lady known as Mrs. Spindlow and two
children at 1 Renoir Close, Basingstoke.   The judge had an affidavit
before him of Mrs. Spindlow and heard evidence from Mr. Spindlow
and Mrs. Spindlow, and he gave a fairly detailed judgment.   He concluded, first, that it was a difficult case; and he noted it was a case in
which there had not been any considerable physical violence.   There
E   was one occasion when Mr. Spindlow pushed Mrs. Spindlow on to a
settee.   The judge also said it was alleged that he shouted at her and
said he would smack the elder child, who was a child of Mrs. Spindlow,
aged 3, and not of Mr. Spindlow.   The judge did not think he had shown
any violence or ill will to that child. It was said, also, that he was an
extremely jealous man.   The judge thought that that allegation had been
exaggerated to some extent, but Mr. Spindlow himself agreed that he was
F   a jealous character.

On March 18 Mrs. Spindlow left, with the children, to live with
friends in very congested conditions, which could not possibly continue
for any length of time.   She and her two children were sharing one
room in a friend's house, and the house obviously was overcrowded in
those circumstances.   It is true that Mr. Spindlow himself had no
G   immediate alternative accommodation.   It is possible he might have
been able to stay with his mother for a time, or find other temporary
accommodation.

Mrs. Spindlow took the line that she was not on any account prepared
to return to live with Mr. Spindlow again, nor was she prepared to go
back to the house if he were in it.   She said that rather than that she
would go to the local authority and put the children into care.   The
H   judge thought that she meant it.   He said:

"I have to consider the effect if I do not make the order.   Either
the children will be put in care or she will go back to 1 Renoir Close
in spite of what is said.   Although the respondent is in my view not
guilty of any great violence, I think, if she did go back, the pressures
of life are extremely serious and make a severe impact on these
children.   I do not think it is practicable for these four to live

under one roof.   They agree the relationship is at an end.   She says **A**
he shouts at the children; I think that is exaggerated.   If the
children lived under these conditions tension would immediately
build up and do them harm.   A very difficult case—if the respondent
is not excluded either the children would be put in care—not in
their interest—or alternatively an attempt would be made to resume
cohabitation with a separate existence.   I do not think that in **B**
practice living separate lives that is, in the same house, would work.
It would only do the children harm.   Mr. Spindlow suggests that
they should come back and live separately.   This would not be
permitted physically and Mrs. Spindlow is not prepared to try."

He then pointed out again that this was not a case of a battered wife or
battered children.   In the circumstances he regarded it as in the interests **C**
of the children that he should make an order excluding Mr. Spindlow
from the house, and he thought that the most fair, just, reasonable and
practicable solution he could come to.

The short facts are these.   These parties started to live together in
October 1976.   Mrs. Spindlow has one child by her former marriage, a
daughter who was born in October 1974; she has another child, by
Mr. Spindlow, born on January 5, 1977.   As a result of their form- **D**
ing a family consisting of themselves and the elder child they were
allotted, by the local authority, the house at 1 Renoir Close.   It is
perfectly obvious that the basis on which the local authority allotted
them this accommodation was that they had one child, and another was
on the way.   For whatever reason, in March 1978 the relationship
between them came to an end.   Therefore the problem arises as to **E**
what is to be done so far as living arrangements are concerned in the
new situation.   Mr. Gordon, who has said everything that could be said
on behalf of Mr. Spindlow has argued that this is not the class of case
which was contemplated by Parliament when it passed section 1 of
the Domestic Violence and Matrimonial Proceedings Act 1976.   That
section has been the subject of a great deal of litigation, which finally **F**
reached the House of Lords in *Davis* v. *Johnson* [1978] 2 W.L.R. 553.
But before going to the report of that case in the House of Lords it is
as well to look at the Act itself.   In the first place Mr. Gordon relies on
the short title of the Act, where the word " violence " appears, but as
was pointed out by Lawton L.J. in argument, in the long title the reference
to violence relates only to police powers.   When one comes to look at
the two sections, sections 1 and 2, one finds that section 1 (1) gives the **G**
county court an unfettered discretion to grant an injunction containing
one or more of the following provisions:

" (*a*) a provision restraining the other party to the marriage from
molesting the applicant; (*b*) a provision restraining the other party
from molesting a child living with the applicant; (*c*) a provision
excluding the other party from the matrimonial home or a part of **H**
the matrimonial home or from a specified area in which the
matrimonial home is included;"

It is paragraph (*c*) that is relevant to this case.   Then section 1 (2)
provides:

" Subsection (1) above shall apply to a man and a woman who are
living with each other in the same household as husband and wife

A   as it applies to the parties to a marriage and any reference to the matrimonial home shall be construed accordingly."

But when one looks at section 2, which deals with the attachment to an injunction of a power of arrest, one finds, at the end of subsection (1), that that subsection is qualified by the words:

B   " if [the judge] is satisfied that the other party has caused actual bodily harm to the applicant or, as the case may be, to the child concerned and considers that he is likely to do so again . . ."

So that section 2 is expressly qualified by a reference to violence. Section 1 is not so qualified. So that it would be, on ordinary principles, surprising if it were right to construe section 1 as if it, too, were C subject to a similar qualification in relation to violence. That is the substantial point on which Mr. Gordon has to rely in support of this appeal: he has to say that section 1 should be read as though it were subject to some qualifying words importing violence, or some adverse conduct of that kind.

He supports his argument by reference to the speeches in *Davis* v. *Johnson* [1978] 2 W.L.R. 553. It is true that there are passages D particularly in Lord Salmon's speech, which indicate that in Lord Salmon's view violence is an essential factor in the jurisdiction under this Act; but the other speeches contain very little to support that, and it is essential to bear in mind that their Lordships were not considering the limits of the jurisdiction of the county court to make an order excluding one party from the home. They were concerned with quite E other things, and the fact that various observations were made by way of illustration of the sort of things that might or might not lead to an order under section 1 does not conclude the matter at all. This is the first time since *Davis* v. *Johnson* that this court has had to interpret the section in the light of that decision of the House of Lords, but without, of course, being bound by the dicta that appear there.

F   One thing that is plain, in my judgment, as a result of *Davis* v. *Johnson* is that the court must apply section 1 of the Domestic Violence and Matrimonial Proceedings Act 1976 to persons who are living together, although unmarried, in exactly the same way as the section would be applied to married persons. There is no doubt—as Mr. Gordon rightly concedes—that had these two parties been married, and had there been a divorce petition on the file, the court would have had G jurisdiction, in the circumstances of this case, to make an order excluding Mr. Spindlow from the home. That is clear from *Bassett* v. *Bassett* [1975] Fam. 76, which dealt with the position as between husband and wife. This court has stressed many times that the court is primarily concerned in husband and wife cases of this kind with the welfare of the children. The High Court itself could make such an order under its H powers in wardship proceedings if the interests of the children required it.

There is, therefore, no difficulty at all about jurisdiction, so far as the High Court is concerned, whether the parties are married or unmarried. There is no difficulty, as I see it, in the county court if a petition for divorce is on the file. Section 1 of the Domestic Violence and Matrimonial Proceedings Act 1976 fills in the gap which arises in the county court where there are no divorce proceedings on the file and therefore no suit which is pending to which an injunction can be attached.

It gives the court power to grant an injunction without there being any   A
other proceedings on foot. It is true that it can be said to be intended
primarily as an emergency type of proceeding, and so it is; but, then,
so are ex parte and interim injunction proceedings. So, as I see it, the
discretion under section 1 is completely general and unfettered except by
the application of common sense to the circumstances before the court.

What is the position here? All the facts are relevant. The first is   B
that these parties became joint tenants of the council accommodation
only because they were living together as man and wife and there was
one child and another child on the way. So that the allocation to these
two adults of this house was directly dependent on the fact that there were
children to be considered; and so it was clearly intended by the local
authority to be a home for children. If the adults' relationship breaks   C
down, as it has in this case, it is not very profitable to consider why.
The fact of the matter is that it has broken down to the extent, as in
Bassett v. *Bassett* [1975] Fam. 76, when a young woman takes her two
children and goes off and lives, not just for a night or two but for quite
a time, in thoroughly difficult and uncomfortable conditions and says
that nothing will induce her to return to live with the man. In those
circumstances the court has to deal with the situation as it finds it, that   D
is, that the relationship between the adults has wholly broken down and
suitable arrangements have to be made primarily for housing the children.
If there were no children here, if they were two independent adults, they
could be left to get on with it, and the court might very well say, " It is
up to her. If she chooses to walk out and put herself into an uncomfortable position that is her affair." But where there are two small   E
children, that is not the position. Somebody has got to provide a home
for these small children. Clearly the only person who can do it is Mrs.
Spindlow in the circumstances of this case. So she and the two children
must be provided with a home. If it is clear, as it was clear to the
judge, that she is not prepared to go back and share her home with
Mr. Spindlow there is only one solution, namely, that she must go back   F
to the house and he must leave. It is all the more striking in this case
that, if any other order were made, the absurd situation would arise that
the local authority would have a single man living in a three-bedroom
house on his own, with a woman and two children to house in other
accommodation, all at public expense. The position is the more absurd
because the local authority is in a position to terminate Mr. Spindlow's
tenancy of this house at a month's notice. They are not in any legal   G
difficulty about the Rent Act or anything of that kind, though it is
true that they are inhibited by general feelings of not wishing to be
unkind or rough or tough on their tenants. One can understand that
the housing department may well feel some reluctance to act against
Mr. Spindlow unless they have support from the court.

If this case is looked at rationally it is essentially a housing matter,   H
housing for the children, and it should be looked at, in my judgment,
mainly in that light. Parliament has, as it were, put on to the court
the responsibility for making the decision, which was previously left with
the housing authority. Now that the court has jurisdiction it may be
more convenient and better that the court should adjudicate rather than
that some administrative adjudication should be made. However, I am
not to be taken as saying that exactly the same considerations would

A apply where the house, perhaps, is owned by one of the unmarried pair or one of the unmarried pair is a protected tenant of the property and has really substantial property rights in his house. It is clear from *Davis* v. *Johnson* [1978] 2 W.L.R. 553 that in such cases the right way to operate section 1 of the Act of 1976 may be to use it on a temporary basis, not interfering unduly with the property rights but making temporary adjustments pending alternative arrangements being made.
B But in the present context, where it is a council house and the council are going to have to house these people, that kind of consideration does not apply.

So I come back to my conclusion that the effect of the Act, combined with the decision of the House of Lords in *Davis* v. *Johnson*, is for all practical purposes to equate the position of a couple living together, with
C children, either their own or children of either of them, with the position of a married couple with children; and the court, in my view, should approach these cases with common sense in exactly the same way. It is said, of course—and it always is—that if this view is right a malicious girl with a child or children could oust her man friend from the house by merely walking out and putting up a bogus case. That may be the
D logical conclusion. But it is no good taking up a great deal of time talking in terms of blame or conduct. What we have to deal with is the reality of the situation, which is that two children are in need of a home and are without one. That is the basis of my judgment and I think the judge arrived at the same conclusion in this case, and I would dismiss this appeal.

E   LAWTON L.J. I agree with the judgment delivered by Ormrod L.J. I have only a few comments to add. In my opinion, in the words of Viscount Dilhorne in *Davis* v. *Johnson* [1978] 2 W.L.R. 553, 568:

"Our task is to give effect to the intention of Parliament if that can be seen from the language of the [Domestic Violence and Matrimonial Proceedings Act 1976]. Here the language is clear and
F   unambiguous and Parliament's intention apparent. Unmarried persons living together in the same household as husband and wife are for the purposes of section 1 (1) to be treated as if they were married."

I turn now to the wording of section 1 of that Act. In my judgment it is clear what was intended by subsection (1): the jurisdiction of the county
G court to grant injunctions was to be extended in specified ways with the object of bringing it into line with the jurisdiction of the High Court. The subsection provided in paragraph (*a*) that a county court could grant an injunction containing a provision restraining the other party to the marriage from molesting the applicant; and in paragraph (*b*) a provision restraining the other party from molesting a child living with
H the applicant. It is clear from the wording of those two paragraphs that before an injunction could be granted there would have to be some evidence of molestation. There was no saisfactory evidence that Mr. Spindlow had molested Mrs. Spindlow. It follows that no injunction in this respect should have been granted. It is interesting, however, to note that in paragraph (*c*) there is no reference to molestation. There is to be a power in the county court, akin to the jurisdiction of the High Court, to insert into an injunction a provision excluding the other

784

party from the matrimonial home, or a part of the matrimonial home, **A**
or from a specified area in which the matrimonial home is included.
The question in this case is whether the High Court would have had
power, in the circumstances of this case, to make an injunction in the
terms of section 1 (1) (c). In the course of argument Mr. Gordon
accepted that, in the High Court, in the case of spouses with children,
there would have been power for the court, without any evidence of **B**
violence or molestation, to make an order of a kind akin to paragraph
(c) if it was in the interests of the children. That power was considered
by this court in *Bassett* v. *Bassett* [1975] Fam. 76. I refer to the
judgment of Ormrod L.J. in that case. He said, at p. 84:

> " My conclusion is that the court, when it is dealing with [cases
> involving children], particularly where it is clear that the marriage **C**
> has already broken down, should think essentially in terms of homes,
> especially for the children, and then consider the balance of hard-
> ships as I have indicated, being careful not to underestimate the
> difficulties which even single men have these days in finding some-
> where to live, bearing in mind that the break will have to be made
> in the relatively near future and that property rights as between
> the spouses are of comparatively minor importance." **D**

Once it is accepted, as it now has to be, having regard to the judgment of the House of Lords in *Davis* v. *Johnson* [1978] 2 W.L.R. 553,
that unmarried couples are to be treated in the same way as married
couples for the purposes of section 1 of the Act of 1976, it seems to me
clear that the judge did have the jurisdiction which he purported to **E**
exercise. There was evidence before him that the relationship had
broken down; and once again, if I may rely on what Ormrod L.J. said
in *Bassett* v. *Bassett* [1975] Fam. 76, the woman in this case walked
out taking the two young children with her. There was no evidence that
she was going off with another man; there was no evidence that she was
immature and running back to her mother. She must have had some
reason for leaving, albeit, as the judge found, it was not based upon **F**
any violence shown to her by the man. But as the relationship has
broken down, something has got to be done about finding a home for
the children.

For the reasons that Ormrod L.J. has already given it seems to me
right that the judge should have made the order which he did.

G

STAMP L.J. I, too, agree with all that Ormrod L.J. has said in the
instant case. We should, I think, do a great disservice to the administration of the law if we concluded that a judge in the county court,
in relation to section 1 (1) (c) of the Domestic Violence and Matrimonial
Proceedings Act 1976, ought to exercise the jurisdiction as between man
and mistress in a different way from a case between husband and wife **H**
on precisely the same facts.

As a matter of construction of the section I can see no reason for
drawing any such distinction. It would be anomalous if, on precisely
the same facts, the interests of the children in the former case were less
well protected than they would be if the parents were married. I, too,
would dismiss the appeal as regards so much of the order as excluded
Mr. Spindlow from the matrimonial home, but would discharge so much

A of the order as related to molestation, because there was, as I understand
it, no real evidence of molestation.

> *Appeal dismissed.*
> *Order varied by discharging injunc-*
> *tion against molestation.*
>
B > *No order as to costs save legal aid*
> *taxation.*

Solicitors: *Lamb, Brooks & Bullock, Basingstoke; Morris & Hodges,*
Basingstoke.

C

[CHANCERY DIVISION]

SINGH (SUDAGAR) *v.* NAZEER

[1973 S. No. 2973]

D 1978 March 15; 22

Megarry V.-C.

Vendor and Purchaser—Specific performance—Contractual condi-
tions—Order against vendor in purchaser's action—Purchaser's
non-compliance with order and delay—Vendor giving notice
to complete under contract—Effect of decree of specific
performance on contract—Whether completion notice valid

E
By an agreement in writing governed by The Law Society's
Contract for Sale, 1970 edition, the defendant vendor agreed to
sell his house to the plaintiff purchaser. June 23, 1972, was
fixed as the date for completion. General condition 19 provided for giving a notice in writing to complete by either party
in case of the other's default so as to make time of the essence
of the contract. The condition further provided that if the
F purchaser did not comply with an effective notice served
under that condition the vendor might, inter alia, forfeit the
deposit and resell the property. On the vendor's failure to
complete the purchaser issued a writ seeking specific performance of the contract by the vendor and other relief. That
decree was made by the court. The vendor's appeal against
that order was dismissed on June 3, 1977, and leave to
appeal was refused. He then became ready to comply with
G the court's order, but the purchaser became dilatory. Due to
lack of progress the vendor gave a 28 days' completion notice
on December 9, 1977, under general condition 19. The
purchaser failed to complete.
On the vendor's motion for, inter alia, an order forfeiting
the deposit, liberty for the vendor to resell and damages: —
Held, dismissing the motion, that the contract, although
not merged in the decree, was materially affected by it since
H the carrying out of the contract had become essentially a
matter for the court and not the parties; that as a matter of
construction general condition 19 did not apply when a decree
of specific performance had been made; that even if it was
intended to apply, it would not operate unless the decree had
contained some provision which preserved its effect, which was
not the case; and that the completion notice was accordingly
bad (post, pp. 790c, G—791A, G—792A).
Austins of East Ham Ltd. v. *Macey* [1941] Ch. 338, C.A.
applied.

Singh (Sudagar) v. Nazeer (Ch.D.) [1978]

The following cases are referred to in the judgment:

Austins of East Ham Ltd. v. *Macey* [1941] Ch. 338, C.A.

Capital and Suburban Properties Ltd. v. *Swycher* [1976] Ch. 319; [1976] 2 W.L.R. 822; [1976] 1 All E.R. 881, C.A.

Griffiths v. *Vezey* [1906] 1 Ch. 796.

Hasham v. *Zenab* [1960] A.C. 316; [1960] 2 W.L.R. 374; [1958] 1 W.L.R. 1214; [1958] 3 All E.R. 719, P.C.

No additional case was cited in argument.

MOTION

By a contract in writing dated June 5, 1972, on The Law Society's form of the Contract for Sale, 1970 edition, the vendor, Ahmed Nazeer, agreed to sell his house known as 355 London Road, Reading, to the purchaser, Sudagar Singh. The vendor did not complete on the date fixed for completion. The purchaser brought an action for specific performance of the contract. The order sought was made in the High Court. The vendor appealed. The Court of Appeal dismissed the appeal and refused leave to appeal to the House of Lords. The vendor thereupon was willing to sell but the purchaser became dilatory.

On December 9, 1977, under general condition 19 of the contract the vendor gave the purchaser a notice to complete within 28 days. The purchaser failed to complete. On February 29, 1978, the vendor gave notice of motion seeking an order that the deposit paid to him by the purchaser should be forfeited; that he should be at liberty to resell the property and that he was entitled to damages in case the property was sold for less than the contract price.

D. J. Ritchie for the vendor.
Vivian Chapman for the purchaser.

Cur. adv. vult.

March 22. MEGARRY V.-C. read the following judgment. This motion raises a point that is curious and, so far as I know, novel. By an agreement dated June 5, 1972, in the form of the 1970 edition of The Law Society's Contract for Sale, the defendant (whom I shall call the vendor) agreed to sell no. 355 London Road, Reading, to the plaintiff (whom I shall call the purchaser) for £6,400. The date fixed by the contract for completion was June 23, 1972. Nearly six years have passed, but the contract still has not been completed. As the purchaser could not get the vendor to complete, on February 8, 1973, he issued a writ against him claiming specific performance and other relief. On May 6, 1976, the purchaser obtained judgment in this division for the specific performance of the contract. The vendor gave notice of appeal, and on June 3, 1977, the Court of Appeal dismissed the appeal and refused the vendor leave to appeal to the House of Lords. Up to that point the general position had been that a willing and anxious purchaser had been proceeding against a firmly resisting vendor.

The next eight months or so were to exhibit a very different picture; for the purchaser became dilatory and the vendor became willing and anxious. The purchaser's solicitors seem to have left matters for some five weeks after the decision of the Court of Appeal, and then, on July

A   12, 1977, they wrote to the vendor's solicitors to say that they understood that the vendor had vacated the property, and asking for confirmation that the vendor was prepared to implement the contract. The next day the vendor's solicitors replied, stating that subject to a point on the legal aid certificate the vendor had instructed them that the order of the court should be complied with. Thereafter there was further correspondence between the solicitors, with the vendor's solicitors
B   pressing the purchaser's solicitors, until on October 13, 1977, the purchaser's solicitors brought their London agents into the correspondence. On October 26, 1977, the vendor's solicitors wrote to them, threatening a motion for rescission and forfeiture of the deposit unless they confirmed within seven days that they had lodged a bill of costs for taxation. As will be seen, this bill was directly relevant to the
C   order for specific performance. The London agents replied, not very satisfactorily, on October 31, and then on November 21 the vendor's solicitors again wrote to them threatening proceedings. Finally, on December 9 the vendor's solicitors wrote to the purchaser's solicitors complaining of their unreasonable delay, and enclosed a 28 days' completion notice given under general condition 19 of the contract of sale. It is from this notice that the point of novelty arises.
D   The matter comes before me under a notice of motion issued by the vendor on February 27, 1978. On behalf of the vendor, Mr. Ritchie moves for an order forfeiting the deposit, liberty for the vendor to resell the property, and an order that the purchaser pay the vendor the difference between £6,400 and the price at which the property is resold (if that is less than £6,400), together with the expenses of the sale. His
E   claim to this order is founded upon the purchaser's failure to comply with the completion notice, which by virtue of general condition 19 (4) made it an express term of the contract that the purchaser should complete within 28 days after service of the notice, time being of the essence. He made no claim under general condition 19 (4) (c), since that relates only to resale within a year from the date fixed for completion, and that, of course, has long gone by. On behalf of the purchaser
F   Mr. Chapman contended that the motion was misconceived.
        There is nothing very remarkable about the order for specific performance. It was made on May 6, 1976, and entered on June 18, 1976. It contained the usual declaration that the contract should be specifically performed and carried into execution, and then ordered an inquiry whether a good title could be made, and when this was first shown, an
G   account of what was due to the vendor for the balance of the purchase money, and an account of the fair rent allowable to the purchaser under general condition 16 (4) of the contract. I pause there to say that under this condition, where due to the vendor's default completion is delayed after the date fixed for completion and the vendor retains physical possession of the property (as was the case), the purchaser can require the vendor to pay or allow him on actual completion the equivalent of
H   a fair rent, calculated at two-and-a-half times the gross annual value of the property for rating purposes at the date of the contract. The order then continued by ordering the purchaser's costs to be taxed unless agreed, and ordering what was due for the fair rent and the costs to be deducted from the balance of the purchase price, and the balance certified. The order then provided for the vendor to execute a proper transfer of the property (which was registered with an absolute title), and for completion at a time and place to be appointed by the court,

with the vendor thereupon delivering vacant possession to the purchaser. A
There was also to be a legal aid taxation of the vendor's costs. The
only material change made by the Court of Appeal was to order that
the costs of the appeal should be deducted from the purchase price payable to the vendor under the order. I have not seen the order of the
Court of Appeal, but this appears from a note of the judgment that is
before me.

Nothing much turns on the fair rent, I think. There seems to be B
no dispute that the relevant gross annual value was £115, as alleged in
the statement of claim, and so the total amount is a mere matter of
calculation. This seems to have been dealt with by the master's
principal clerk in October 1976. The costs are another matter. Not
until November 22, 1976, over five months after the decision at first
instance, did the London agents of the purchaser's solicitors even give C
instructions to an agency for the purchaser's bill of costs to be drawn
up; and nearly two months later they lodged the bill for taxation. On
March 1, 1977, nearly six weeks later, the papers were understandably
withdrawn so that a brief could be drawn up for counsel for the purchaser on the impending appeal by the vendor. As I have said, the
appeal was dismissed on June 3, 1977, and leave to appeal to the House
of Lords was refused. However, not until October 11, over four D
months later, did the London agents even bespeak the order of the
Court of Appeal; and when on October 31 they wrote in answer to complaints of delay, they calmly said that the order " has not yet come
through," and then added a comment about the registrar who was
dealing with the matter. The truth of the matter is, of course, that
of the nearly five months that had elapsed since the Court of Appeal E
had decided the case, over four months had been due not to any
difficulty about the registrar but to the London agents failing for over
four months even to bespeak the order. The vendor's solicitors' complaint on October 26 coincided with the London agents at last lodging
with the taxing office the bill of costs at first instance which had been
withdrawn in March to prepare a brief for the Court of Appeal; and
this activity seems to have moved the London agents to give instructions F
a few days later to costs draftsmen to prepare a bill of costs for the
hearing in the Court of Appeal, by then nearly five months past. The
draft bill was received by the London agents on November 25, but
neither the complaints made by the vendor's solicitors nor the arrival
of the completion notice dated December 9 sufficed to curtail the seven
weeks or so that were to elapse between the London agents receiving the G
draft bill and their lodging the bill for taxation, which they did on
January 16, 1978. The completion notice was sent, of course, not to
them but to the purchaser's solicitors whose agents they were; but one
assumes that some degree of communication exists between solicitors
and their London agents, not least when the other side has been
vigorously complaining.

The upshot of all this was that the purchaser's costs have at last H
been taxed; those at first instance were taxed on December 5, 1977, and
those on appeal on February 7, 1978. Three weeks then went by, and
then the purchaser (presumably by his solicitors) attended the master's
principal clerk for an appointment to proceed. There was a brief delay
while the master's file was being found, but then the appointment was
given for March 9; and there was an appointment for finally settling the
certificate for March 16, the day after I heard the motion. The taxing

A master's certificate for the costs of the Court of Appeal has also been issued. All is at last ready for the order of specific performance to be carried out and a date fixed for completion. But that, of course, is subject to the vendor's completion notice and the motion now before me.

Now whatever the result of the motion, it seems to me plain that the vendor's solicitors have very real grounds of complaint about the wholly unexplained delays on the purchaser's side. For over four months after the decision of the Court of Appeal, and for some three months after the vendor's solicitors had written to say that the vendor had given instructions that the order of the court should be complied with, not even preparatory work seems to have been done on the purchaser's side. The order of the Court of Appeal had not been

C bespoken, instructions to draw the bill of costs in the Court of Appeal had not been given, and the bill of costs at first instance, with its supporting papers, had not been returned to the taxing office. It is not in the least surprising that the vendor's solicitors should have felt impelled into action. In saying that, I do not forget the long vacation and all that it entails for solicitors who are engaged in litigation: but there are limits to what can be imputed to the long vacation in relation

D to a judgment given nearly two months before it began.

There is, however, another factor that has to be borne in mind, and that is the time-scale created by the vendor while he was resisting specific performance. His resistance was on the ground that the contract was not a binding agreement, but was preliminary, or conditional on his finding another home. As I have mentioned, the purchaser issued his writ

E on February 8, 1973. He then applied for summary judgment under R.S.C., Ord. 86. At the first hearing before the master the vendor sought and obtained an adjournment to put in evidence. At the second hearing he did not appear, and judgment was given against him. He then applied for the summons to be restored, but at the restored hearing he tendered no evidence and sought a further adjournment. The master refused this and adjourned the proceedings into court as a procedure

F summons. The case was listed for hearing on February 20, 1974, but the vendor somehow managed to have it taken out of the list, and it then came before Plowman J. on March 11. The vendor produced an affidavit that he had sworn that morning, and the purchaser was then given an adjournment to consider it, with the costs of the day. On March 18 the vendor produced another affidavit sworn that day, but the

G application was heard and the judge gave the vendor leave to defend on the footing that he had an arguable defence. After a dispute about the probable length of the trial which came before Foster J., the case was put in Part II of the Witness List, and ultimately came before Judge Rubin, sitting as a Deputy High Court judge, on May 4, 1976. The vendor once more sought an adjournment, saying that he was not

H ready for trial; but this was refused, and, as I have said, judgment for specific performance was given on May 6, 1976. The judge said that he did not believe the vendor was a man capable of telling the truth except when it happened to suit his case.

The appeal came on for hearing on May 17, 1977, when once more the vendor sought an adjournment, this time because he had not received the transcript of Judge Rubin's judgment. He was given a 14 days adjournment, but had to pay the costs of the day. As I have

mentioned, on June 3, 1977, the Court of Appeal dismissed the appeal. A
A note of the judgment makes it clear that the appeal was hopeless.

That is the background. The vendor is a man who on June 5, 1972,
contracted to convey the property to the purchaser on June 23, 1972,
and who for nearly five years strenuously and with many attempts at
delay sought to resist carrying out his contract on grounds which have
no substance. Then, within five months of his first professing himself
to be willing to carry out the contract, he rounds on the purchaser and B
serves on him a notice requiring completion of the contract within 28
days; and he is now seeking, among other things, to forfeit the purchaser's deposit. Without for a moment condoning the purchaser's
delays after the decision of the Court of Appeal, I think that the
vendor's contentions require to be closely scrutinised With that, I turn
at last to the substantive point before me. When an order for specific C
performance has been made, is a completion notice subsequently
served under the contract valid and effective?

First, it seems clear that when an order for the specific performance
of a contract for the sale of land is made, the contract continues to
exist and is not merged in the order. This, I think, sufficiently appears
from *Austins of East Ham Ltd.* v. *Macey* [1941] Ch. 338. That was
a case in which a vendor had obtained an order for specific perform- D
ance, and when the purchaser failed to complete on the date fixed for
completion under the order, the vendor moved for rescission of the
contract. The Court of Appeal held that such a motion was not a
means of enforcing an order of the court for which leave was required
under the Courts (Emergency Powers) Act 1939, but was a means of
putting an end to the still subsisting contract, and also the order for E
specific performance, as an alternative to enforcing it: see also *Capital
and Suburban Properties Ltd.* v. *Swycher* [1976] Ch. 319. That, however, does not conclude the point before me. To say that a contract
still exists does not necessarily mean that the exercise of the rights that
it confers remains unaffected by an order for specific performance of
that contract.

Second, it also seems clear that once an order for specific perform- F
ance has been made, there are adequate remedies available to either
party if the other does not appear to be proceeding under the order with
due dispatch. Thus an application may be made for a time and place for
completion to be fixed, or for an order rescinding the contract, either
forthwith, if the other party is refusing to complete, or else in default
of completion within a limited time. I need not set out all the G
possibilities in detail: they appear in *Fry on Specific Performance,* 6th
ed. (1921), pp. 546–553; and see *Capital and Surburban Properties Ltd.*
v. *Swycher* [1976] Ch. 319, especially at pp. 330, 331. By applying
to the court for an order of specific performance, and obtaining it, I
think that the applicant has put it into the hands of the court how the
contract is to be carried out. As the court has become seised of the
matter, and has made an order, it seems to me that subject to anything H
that the parties may then agree, the working out, variation or cancellation of that order is essentially a matter for the court. The continued
existence of the contract is one thing, its working out is another.

Third, it seems plain that in ordinary circumstances the machinery
provisions of a contract for the sale of land are intended to govern the
carrying out of the contract between the parties out of court, and
are not directed to carrying it out when an order for specific

A performance has been made. That order is made, of course, by reference to the rights of the parties under the contract; but, when made, it is the provisions of the order and not of the contract which regulate how the contract is to be carried out. Provisions in the contract as to the deduction of title, the preparation and delivery of the conveyance, the mode and date of completion and many other matters must all, it seems to me, yield to any directions on these matters which are given in

B or under the order for specific performance. Mr. Ritchie attempted to drive a wedge between compliance with contractual obligations and compliance with the order for specific performance, emphasising that a failure to comply with the order was not a breach of contract but was a contempt of court, and so on. I think that this approach is ill-founded. It gives little or no weight to the consideration that the order

C of the court is not independent of the contract, but is the court's order as to how that contract is to be carried out, replacing the mode in which it should have been carried out had no order been made. In my judgment, where, as in this case, an order for specific performance contains not only the declaratory part but also the consequential directions (I adopt the terminology of *Hasham* v. *Zenab* [1960] A.C. 316), those consequential directions regulate the performance of the contract

D so long as they stand and are not varied by the court. If those consequential directions are not complied with, then the court may make an appropriate order in respect of the default, that default being a breach not so much of the still subsisting contract as of the order of the court as to how that contract is to be carried out: see *Griffiths* v. *Vezey* [1906] 1 Ch. 796.

E That brings me to the fourth point, namely, whether a completion notice served under the contract after the order for specific performance has been made is valid and effective; and that, of course, is the point that I have to decide on this motion. Mr. Ritchie was constrained to admit that if his contention that the notice was valid and effective was sound, it would have been open to either party to serve a completion notice the day after the order for specific performance had

F been made, and that this notice would have been equally valid and effective. If the vendor had served the notice, it would have been effective unless within the stipulated 28 days the purchaser had achieved the virtual impossibility of producing a bill of costs, having it taxed, and carrying through (however dilatory the vendor) all the stages of the consequential directions in the order. If emphasis is needed,

G let it be supposed that an order for specific performance in this form had been made on July 31 or December 21 in any year.

I do not think that this contention can possibly be right. First, as a matter of construction I do not consider that general condition 19 can be intended to operate in any case where a full decree of specific performance has been made. I can see nothing in it which suggests that the parties intend to contract that a notice under that condition is to

H supersede or transcend or vary or interfere with an order of the court for specific performance. The condition seems to me to be a useful and beneficial provision which is to apply in all normal cases where the parties are carrying out the contract out of court, but it is not intended to apply where the contract is being carried out under the directions of the court, and those directions are not compatible with the operation of the condition.

Second, quite apart from the construction to be put upon the con-

Megarry V.-C.   **Singh (Sudagar) v. Nazeer (Ch.D.)**   [1978]

dition, and even if the condition were to be intended to apply despite an   A
order for specific performance, I do not think it would be operative
unless the order of the court contained some saving provision which
preserved its effect. The applicability of the condition is something
that could and should be argued out when the court decides what order
to make, and it may or may not help to shape the order that is made.
Just as other provisions of the contract were superseded by the consequential directions given by the court, so I think that this condition   B
will be superseded by these directions. I hold that the completion
notice is bad.

It follows that on the only basis on which the motion has been put
forward (namely, that of non-compliance with the completion notice)
the motion must fail. If instead of giving that notice the vendor (preferably at an earlier date, when his complaints of delay were being   C
made) had applied to the court to fix a day for completion, I do not
doubt that the court could and would have induced a greater sense of
urgency in the purchaser, and could, if need be, have provided assistance
in any steps which had to be taken by the court. But that was not
done. In my judgment, once an order for specific performance has
been made, the remedy for a party who complains of delay is to come
to the court and not to attempt the extra-curial remedy of serving a   D
completion notice. [His Lordship then dealt with the question of making
an order under R.S.C., Ord. 62, r. 8, based on undue delay on the part of
the London agents of the purchaser's solicitors, which is not relevant to
the present report.]

Motion dismissed.

E

Solicitors: *Rowberry, Morris & Co., Reading; Sharpe, Pritchard &
Co. for Francis & Parkes, Reading.*

A. R.

F

[COURT OF APPEAL]

JOHNS v. JONES

1978 June 15, 16   Stamp and Orr L.JJ. and Sir David Cairns

Children and Young Persons—Care of—Child received into care   G
by local authority—Mother's request for return of child—
Authority's resolution assuming parental rights—Mother's
objection—Decision by juvenile court that resolution to stand
—Whether child in care when resolution passed—Whether
resolution effective—Children Act 1948[1] *(11 & 12 Geo. 6,*
c. 43), ss. 1 (3), 2 (1) (as amended and substituted by Children
Act 1975 (c. 72), s. 57)

H

In September 1976 the mother voluntarily placed her
two-month-old child in the care of the local authority. On
April 18, 1977, she telephoned the local authority asking for

[Reported by MISS HENRIETTA STEINBERG, Barrister-at-Law.]

[1] Children Act 1948, s. 1 (3): post, p. 796C–D.
S. 2 (1): see post, p. 796F–H.

A   the child to be returned to her. On May 25, the social
services committee of the local authority passed a resolution
under section 2 of the Children Act 1948, as substituted by
section 57 of the Children Act 1975, assuming the parental
rights over the child on the basis that the mother had so
consistently failed to discharge the obligations of a parent as
to be unfit to have the care of the child. The mother was
informed of the resolution and of her right to object to it. She
B   then served on the local authority a counter-notice, setting out
her objections to the resolution. On the local authority's
application, the juvenile court considered the facts and
decided that the resolution should stand. The mother
appealed to the Divisional Court of the Queen's Bench
Division on the ground that the resolution was invalid. The
Divisional Court dismissed the appeal and held that the
resolution was effective since the child remained in the care
C   of the local authority for as long as she was de facto being
cared for by the authority.
On the mother's appeal: —
Held, allowing the appeal, that on its true construction
section 2 (1) of the Act only conferred power on a local
authority to make a resolution assuming parental rights and
duties in respect of a child who was in its care under section
D   1; that the authority's right to keep a child in care under
section 1 ceased, by virtue of section 1 (3), as soon as a parent
or guardian advised the authority that he or she desired to
take over the care of that child, and therefore the local
authority had no power to make a resolution under section 2
after the mother had telephoned requesting the return of her
child and, accordingly, the resolution was invalid.
Bawden v. *Bawden,* post, p. 798, C.A. followed.
Decision of the Divisional Court reversed.
E

The following cases are referred to in the judgment:

Bawden v. *Bawden* [1978] 3 W.L.R. 798, C.A.
Halvorsen v. *Hertfordshire County Council* (1975) 5 Fam. Law 79, D.C.

No additional cases were cited in argument.
F
APPEAL from the Divisional Court of the Queen's Bench Division.
On June 30, 1977, a complaint was preferred on behalf of the
Wirral Borough Council against the mother, stating that on May 25, 1977,
the local authority's social services committee, in the exercise of its
delegated powers, passed a resolution pursuant to section 2 of the
Children Act 1948, as substituted by section 57 of the Children Act
G   1975, assuming the mother's parental rights in respect of the child,
since it appeared to the committee that the mother had so consistently
failed without reasonable cause to discharge the obligations of a parent
as to be unfit to have the care of the child, and that the resolution should
not lapse. On June 15, 1977, the mother was notified of her right to
object to the resolution. On June 17, the mother informed the local
H   authority of her objection.

On July 27 and August 8, 1977, the juvenile court heard the complaint
and found the following facts. The child was received into care on
September 28, 1976, having been voluntarily placed in care by the mother.
On April 18, 1977, the mother made a request by telephone for the return
of the child. On May 25, the local authority by resolution assumed the
parental rights and duties in relation to the child. The juvenile court had
to consider the evidence and decide whether the resolution should continue

or lapse. To allow the child to return to the mother would place an A
intolerable burden on her as she had three other young children and was
expecting a fifth child. Although the mother had told the court that a
united family was possible, the court was doubtful as to the attitude
of the mother's husband. The mother's telephone call for the return of
the child did not amount to a notice within section 1 (3A) (b) of the Act
of 1948 and was not followed by any positive action by her. There had B
been very little contact between the mother and the child. The relationship
between the child and the foster parents was happy and, in view of the
expert evidence, it would be hazardous to transfer the child from the
foster parents to another adult. The appropriate time for transferring the
child to its mother was not the present.

It was contended for the mother, inter alia, (i) that there was a failure
by the local authority to return the child after the mother's telephone C
request which constituted notice under section 1 (3A) (b) of the Act; (ii)
that the local authority having received the notice, was obliged in law
to return the child forthwith or at least after the expiry of 28 days;
(iii) that, on the expiry of 28 days after such notice, the child had
ceased to be in the care of the local authority so that the local authority
had no power to pass a resolution assuming parental rights; and that D
thereafter the child's detention was illegal and (v) that the local authority,
if they wished to assume parental rights, had to pass a resolution within
28 days of the receipt of the notice.

It was contended for the local authority, inter alia, (i) that the local
authority was right in passing the resolution, there being sufficient
evidence to justify it; (ii) that, even if the notice was valid, the local
authority was not bound to hand over the child, when requested by the E
mother, if it was not in the interests of the child to do so in the circumstances; (iii) that the local authority was entitled to pass the resolution
even after the expiry of 28 days from the date of the notice and that
(iv) section 59 of the Children Act 1975 placed a burden on the local
authority to safeguard and promote the welfare of a child in its care.
The juvenile court upheld the complaint and confirmed the resolution. F

The questions stated for the opinion of the High Court were: (1)
whether it was the court's duty to consider whether there was sufficient
evidence before the local authority to justify the resolution or to consider the evidence before the court on the day of the hearing; (2)
whether the telephone call was sufficient notice under section 1 (3A) (b)
and (3) whether the court was right in holding that the local authority
was not bound to hand over the child, if in its opinion, it was in the G
child's interests not to do so, and might in fact proceed to pass a valid
resolution after the expiry of 28 days.

The Divisional Court on February 21, 1978, held that section 1 (3A) (b),
which created a criminal offence, in no way affected the time when the
child ceased to be in care and that the resolution was valid on the ground
that the child remained in the care of the local authority so long as she H
was being physically cared for by the authority so that she was actually
in care at the time when the resolution was passed.

The mother appealed, by leave of the Divisional Court, on the grounds
that (1) at the time when the local authority purported to pass the resolution under section 2 of the Children Act 1948, the child was no longer in
care under section 1 of the Act and that, accordingly, the local authority
had no power to pass the resolution which was ultra vires; and that (2)

A the child had ceased to be lawfully in the local authority's care under section 1 after the expiry of 28 days from the mother's request for her return on April 18, 1977.

David Marshall Evans for the mother.
Nicholas Lyell for the local authority.

B
STAMP L.J. I will ask Orr L.J. to deliver the first judgment.

ORR L.J. This is an appeal by a mother, against an order made by a Divisional Court of the Queen's Bench Division on February 21, 1978, whereby her appeal to that court by case stated against a decision of the Wirral justices sitting as a juvenile court was dismissed, and the decision
C of those justices that the social services committee of the Wirral Borough Council had power to pass, as they did, on May 25, 1977, a resolution under section 2 of the Children Act 1948, as amended by section 57 of the Children Act 1975, assuming parental rights in respect of the appellant's daughter, was upheld, but leave was granted to appeal against that decision to this court.

D   The facts of the case, which are not in dispute, are that the girl, born on July 16, 1976, and now just under two years of age, whose parents are the appellant and her husband, was on September 28, 1976, received into the care of the Wirral Borough Council, having been voluntarily placed into such care by the mother, but on April 18, 1977, the mother made a request by telephone to the local authority for the return of the child to her. On May 25, 1977, the social services committee of the
E local authority passed a resolution assuming the parental rights and duties as respects the child on the ground that it appeared to the committee that the mother had so consistently failed, without reasonable cause, to discharge the obligation of a parent as to be unfit to have the care of the child, and on June 15, 1976, notice was served by post, by recorded delivery, on the mother informing her of her right to object to the
F resolution and as to the effect of any such objection. Two days later, on June 17, a notice of objection to the resolution was served by the mother on the respondent, the authorised representative of the local authority, and proceedings instituted by the local authority followed before the juvenile court in which that court found as a fact that on April 18, 1977, some five weeks before the passing of the resolution, the mother had, by telephone, requested the return of the child.
G   The justices at the hearing made certain findings adverse to the mother on which it is unnecessary to pause since the sole ground of the appeal to the Divisional Court was that, in the circumstances to which I have referred, the local authority's resolution to assume the parental rights was in law invalid. The question, on this appeal, is whether that decision was correct in law, the mother's case before the
H Divisional Court being that, by reason of the mother's telephone call to the local authority on April 18, 1977, requesting the return of the child to her, the child had ceased, before the date of the resolution, to be in the care of the local authority, with the result that the resolution was invalid.

For the present purposes the relevant provisions of the Children Act 1948, as amended by the Children Act 1975, are as follows. Section 1 provides:

"(1) Where it appears to a local authority with respect to a child A
in their area appearing to them to be under the age of 17—
(a) that he has neither parent nor guardian or has been and remains
abandoned by his parents or guardian or is lost; or (b) that his
parents or guardian are, for the time being or permanently, prevented
by reason of mental or bodily disease or infirmity or other incapacity
or any other circumstances from providing for his proper accom- B
modation, maintenance and upbringing; and (c) in either case, that
the intervention of the local authority under this section is necessary
in the interests of the welfare of the child, it shall be the duty of
the local authority to receive the child into their care under this
section. "(2) Where a local authority have received a child into their
care under this section, it shall, subject to the provisions of this Part
of this Act, be their duty to keep the child in their care so long as C
the welfare of the child appears to them to require it and the child
has not attained the age of 18. "(3) Nothing in this section shall
authorise a local authority to keep a child in their care under this
section if any parent or guardian desires to take over the care of the
child, and the local authority shall, in all cases where it appears to
them consistent with the welfare of the child so to do, endeavour to D
secure that the care of the child is taken over either—(a) by a parent
or guardian of his, or (b) by a relative or friend of his, . . ."

Subsection (3A), inserted by the Act of 1975, provides:

"Except in relation to an act done—(a) with the consent of the local
authority, or (b) by a parent or guardian of the child who has given
the local authority not less than 28 days' notice of his intention to do E
it, subsection (8) (penalty for taking away a child in care) of section 3
of this Act shall apply to a child in the care of a local authority
under this section (notwithstanding that no resolution is in force
under section 2 of this Act with respect to the child) if he has been
in the care of that local authority throughout the preceding six
months; and for the purposes of the application of paragraph (b) F
of that subsection in such a case a parent or guardian of the child
shall not be taken to have lawful authority to take him away."

Section 2, as amended by the Act of 1975, provides:

"(1) Subject to the provisions of this Part of this Act, if it appears
to a local authority in relation to any child who is in their care
under the foregoing section—. . . . (b) that a parent of his—. . . . (v) has G
so consistently failed without reasonable cause to discharge the
obligations of a parent as to be unfit to have the care of the child
. . . the local authority may resolve that there shall vest in them
the parental rights and duties with respect to that child, and, if the
rights and duties were vested in the parent on whose account the
resolution was passed jointly with another person, they shall also be H
vested in the local authority jointly with that other person."

Before the Divisional Court, and on this appeal, the argument for the
mother has been that by virtue of the mother's telephone request on
April 18, 1977, for the return of the child to her the local authority were
not thereafter, in the terms of section 1 (3) of the Act, authorised to
keep the child in their care under section 1 of the Act and, accordingly,
the child was not, for the purposes of section 2 of the Act, in their care

A   under section 1 on May 25, 1977, when they made the resolution under
that section, with the result that the resolution was invalid. This
argument was rejected by the Divisional Court without reference to any
authorities and on the basis that the child remained, for the purposes
of the Act, in the care of the local authority so long as the authority
continued de facto to care for him. Before this court Mr. Lyell, for the
B   local authority, has renewed this argument and claims that, so long as
the local authority continue de facto to care for the child, they are
entitled to pass a resolution under section 2. But with great respect to
the conclusion reached by the Divisional Court I am unable to accept
this construction of the Act, since the opening words of section 2 (1),
which confer the power to make a resolution, do not refer to any child
who is in their care but to any child " who is in their care under the
C   foregoing section. . . . " For this reason I do not find it possible to construe those words as applying to a mere de facto care and in my judgment
they are too strong to accommodate the local authority's argument.

    Moreover, there is, in my judgment, authority of this court on the
point at issue. In *Halvorsen* v. *Hertfordshire County Council* (1975)
5 Fam. Law 79 the Divisional Court took the same view as they have
D   adopted in the present case, but it was rejected by another division of this
court in *Bawden* v. *Bawden*, post, p. 798.

    For these reasons I would allow this appeal, and I would reverse the
decision of the Divisional Court.

    SIR DAVID CAIRNS. In my judgment the words: " Nothing in this
section shall authorise a local authority to keep a child in their care
E   under this section if any parent or guardian desires to take over the care
of the child," in section 1 (3) of the Children Act 1948, have the effect
that, if a parent informs the local authority of his or her desire to take
over the care of the child, the child is thereafter not in the care of the
local authority under the section. I should have formed that opinion
without the assistance of any authority, That view is fortified by the
F   judgment of this court in *Bawden* v. *Bawden*, post, p. 798.

    Accordingly I, too, would allow the appeal, entirely agreeing with
the fuller reasons given by Orr L.J.

    STAMP L.J. I agree. As I read the judgment in the Divisional Court
it appears that Mr. Evans for the mother had there relied primarily on
the submission, rejected by the Divisional Court, that the local authority's
G   right to retain the child in care ceased 28 days after the telephone
conversation to which Orr L.J. has referred. This submission rested on
the argument that section 1 (3A) of the Children Act 1948 was applicable.
I would accept Mr. Lyell's submission on behalf of the local authority
which was accepted by the Divisional Court, that that subsection is not
relevant. Nevertheless, before ever that subsection came into force
H   this court, in *Bawden* v. *Bawden*, post, p. 798 had decided that, by the
effect of section 1 (3) once a parent had manifested a desire to take
over the care of the child, the local authority's right to keep the child
in their care under section 1 (1) of the Act came to an end; and if the
right of the local authority to keep the child, which was conferred by
section 1 (1), has come to an end then, as a matter of language, the
local authority must, as I see it, cease to have the child " in their care
under the foregoing section "—I quote from section 2 of the Act, and

Stamp L.J.   **Johns v. Jones (C.A.)**   **[1978]**

I emphasise the words "under the foregoing section." No doubt in A
the sense that a person with no legal right to have the care of a child,
but is looking after the child, may be said to have the care of the child
the local authority, following the request of his parent, continues to have
the care of the child; but until a physical transfer of the child, the child is
not, as I see it, under the care of the local authority under section 1 of
the Act. As I have, I think, indicated, the reference to the new subsection (3A) of section 1 introduced confusion into the case before the B
Divisional Court. That subsection prevents a parent resorting to self-
help, and to the extent that the submissions of the mother in this court
and in the Divisional Court rested on that subsection I agree with the
Divisional Court that that submission is not well founded. But in my
judgment nevertheless the mother's contention in this case is right.

    I, too, would allow the appeal.   C

> *Appeal allowed with costs in Court*
> *of Appeal and below.*
> *Legal aid taxation of mother's costs*
> *to take place in Birkenhead District*
> *Registry.*
> *Leave to appeal refused.*

    Solicitors: *Oliver & Co. Ellesmere Port; Sharpe, Pritchard & Co. for
P. J. Mills, Director of Administrative and Legal Services, Wirral Borough
Council.*

    July 27, 1978. The Appeal Committee of the House of Lords (Lord E
Wilberforce, Lord Salmon and Lord Keith of Kinkel) dismissed a
petition by the Director of Social Services for the local authority for
leave to appeal.

NOTE

[COURT OF APPEAL]

BAWDEN v. BAWDEN

1975   Dec. 12   Stamp, Orr and Goff L.JJ.

> *Children and Young Persons—Care of—Child received into care
> by local authority — Divorce proceedings — Order granting
> custody care and control to father — Local authority not
> parties—Appeal by local authority—Whether residual discre-
> tion remaining in local authority—Children Act 1948 (11, 12
> & 13 Geo. 6, c. 43), s. 1 (3)—Matrimonial Causes Act 1973
> (c. 18), s. 42 (5)*

    APPEAL from Judge Sellers sitting as an additional judge of the Family
Division.

    The facts are set out in the judgment of Goff L.J.

[Reported by EVERARD CORBALLY, ESQ., Barrister-at-Law]

3 W.L.R.   Bawden v. Bawden (Note) (C.A.)

A   The following cases are referred to in the judgments:

Halvorsen v. Hertfordshire County Council (1975) 5 Fam.Law 79, D.C.
Krishnan v. Sutton London Borough Council [1970] Ch. 181; [1969] 3
    W.L.R. 683; [1969] 3 All E.R. 1367, Goff J. and C.A.
R. (K.) (An Infant), In re [1964] Ch. 455; [1963] 3 W.L.R. 991; [1963]
    3 All E.R. 337.
S. (An Infant), In re [1965] 1 W.L.R. 483; [1965] 1 All E.R. 865, C.A.

B

Ian McCulloch and Susan Burridge for the local authority.
Rupert Evans for the official solicitor as guardian ad litem.
John Bull for the father.
John Ungley for the mother.

STAMP L.J.   We propose to give a judgment on the local authority's appeal
C and we will then go on to deal with the question of access.
I will ask Goff L.J. to give the first judgment.

GOFF L.J.   This is an appeal by the Hampshire County Council from an
order made by Judge Sellers on November 7, 1975, when he was sitting as
a judge of the Family Division.   The order concerns twins, one a boy and
the other a girl, who were born on August 5, 1968.   They were two of the
children of a Mr. and Mrs. Bawden.   There was also a further child of the
D family, but no question arises as to that child.   He is an elder brother, born
in 1964 and in the care of the mother.   In the divorce proceedings in which
the order of November 7, 1975, was made, the father was the petitioner, and
the mother was the respondent.
The marriage broke down and the parties separated on April 10, 1973.
On April 24, 1970, when the parents were living together the twins were
removed under a place of safety order but when the matter came before the
E magistrates, the case was not proved; however, the boy only was placed in
voluntary care, or under voluntary supervision, for a few days in November
1970, and then went back to the family.   When the parties separated in April
1973, all three children were, for a while, in the care of the mother.   The
local authority in fact looked after them for three days a week, but that was
not a taking into care under the Children Act 1948, it was a private arrangement.
F   On July 7 or 8, 1973, the father made an urgent call to the social worker
and to the doctor, saying that the mother had left the twins with him and
a lady with whom he was then living (and whom he has since married); that
he had found weal marks upon them and considered that they were being
ill-treated.   He wanted them taken out of the care of the mother altogether,
and she agreed to the twins being taken into care.   Accordingly, on July 9,
1973, they were received into care by the Hampshire County Council, under
G section 1 of the Children Act 1948, where they so remained until the
commencement of these proceedings.
In the divorce proceedings, the father and mother both now wishing to
have the children, application was made for an order for custody and care
and control, and the matter was heard by the judge, who made the order
from which there is now an appeal.   The local authority not only had notice
of proceedings, but they were actually present thereat by their solicitor.   By
H the order, custody and care and control were given to the father until
further order.   There were directions about the children remaining within the
jurisdiction and about their surname, and then the order provided:

"It is directed that the said children be handed over to the petitioner
by the Hampshire County Council on December 18, 1975, or at the end
of the present school term if the term ends before December 18, 1975,
to the petitioner's home."

Then followed directions about access.

There is a respondent's notice by the wife concerning those directions, A
on which we have not yet heard argument, and this judgment deals solely with
the appeal by the local authority.

They claim that that order was one which ought not to have been made,
and they have sought, I think, in the argument to say that they are entitled
to have it reviewed at large, and to challenge custody, care and control—and
everything else. Alternatively, they say that it should not have included an
order on them, or direction to them to hand over the children. The argument B
ranged at length, but in the end it really came down to three questions—
and indeed, finally, there was not much, if anything, between the parties on
at least one, if not two, of those questions.

The first question is this: Is the Hampshire County Council bound by the
order from which they have appealed? It now seems to be common ground
that they are not. At all events it is quite clear that they are not. The
order was made in the exercise of the statutory jurisdiction under the Matrimonial Causes Act 1973, section 42 (5) of which provides: C

"Where an order in respect of a child is made under this section, the
order shall not affect the rights over or with respect to the child of
any person, other than a party to the marriage in question, unless the
child is the child of one or both of the parties to that marriage and that
person was a party to the proceedings on the application for an order
under this section."

D

Though the local authority was present it was not a party, and therefore,
quite clearly, is not bound by the order, having regard to the terms of the
subsection which I have just read. That does not mean that if the local
authority were to refuse to comply with it, and particularly if they were to
obstruct compliance with it, they would not be amenable to proceedings
for contempt, but I do not think I need pursue that any further. As a matter
of law, the order is not binding upon them; but that, of course, does not E
give them any ground for appealing against it. Nevertheless, in my judgment,
they have a locus standi to appeal because they are persons interested, or
claiming to be aggrieved by the order. Therefore we have heard them at
length upon the appeal.

The second question which has been raised is this: was it possible for
them to have been parties, and to have brought the question of the welfare
of the children before the court? Again, it seems to me perfectly plain that F
it was. I turn to the Matrimonial Causes Rules 1973 (S.I. 1973 No. 2016),
rule 92 (7), which is in these terms: "The court may at any stage of the
proceedings give directions as to the filing and service of pleadings and as to
the further conduct of the proceedings."

For my part, I have no doubt that the words "the further conduct of the
proceedings" cover the question of parties, and authorise the court in any
proceedings under section 42 to cause additional parties to be added. It may
do that of its own motion, or upon the application of any of the parties, G
or upon the application of a person not already a party; and in such cases,
any local authority may apply to the court to have itself added under that
rule, although of course it is a matter for the court to decide whether it
will make such an order.

But if that be not right, the Matrimonial Causes Rules contain a further
rule, rule 3 (1):

H

"Subject to the provisions of these Rules and of any enactment, the
County Court Rules 1936 and the Rules of the Supreme Court 1965
shall apply, with the necessary modifications, to the commencement of
matrimonial proceedings in, and to the practice and procedure in matrimonial proceedings pending in, a divorce county court and the High
Court respectively."

Whatever else the effect of rule 92 (7) may be, it is certainly not a
provision excluding the Rules of the Supreme Court relating to the joinder

A of parties. Therefore, if rule 92 (7) does not go far enough, then rule 3 brings into play R.S.C., Ord. 15, r. 6, which does give the court the necessary power if it thinks fit to join a local authority in such matters.

Quite apart from that, of course, it was open to the local authority to have commenced wardship proceedings and to have taken steps to have the divorce application and the wardship proceedings considered together.

I come then to the third of the questions, which Mr. Evans, in his very
B able and helpful argument, expressed thus: are the children still in the care of the local authority under section 1, having regard to the order? And he said: " My answer is No." Mr. McCulloch, who appeared for the local authority, would wish to add to that question: If not, has the local authority any residual discretion? It appears now to be conceded that the answer to the question as formulated by Mr. Evans is indeed as he said, " No." But it is contended that even so, there remains in the local authority some residual
C discretion.

Well, the answer appears to me to be well established by a line of some five or six cases. I need not cite them all, but I would mention two. The first is *In re R. (K.) (An Infant)* [1964] Ch. 455, a decision of Pennycuick J. I would cite from the judgment of Pennycuick J. this passage, at pp. 461–2:

D
> " This is a cogent argument, but it seems to me to encounter difficulty when one considers the position which arises immediately on the notice by a parent which brings to an end the right of the county council under section 1 (3) of the Act. Once the notice has been given, it is I think clear not only that the common law rights of the mother revive but also that the jurisdiction of this court in relation to the infant becomes fully effective."

And again, at pp. 462–3:

E
> " It would, of course, be right to accept Mr. Rattee's contention if it were clear beyond doubt that this was indeed the intention underlying the Act. Section 1 (3), however, imposes no mandatory obligation to return the infant to its parent. The first limb of subsection (3) merely puts an end to the right of the local authority to keep the child, and the second limb of the subsection is applicable only where it appears to the local authority consistent with the welfare of the child to secure that the child's care is taken over by others."

F
That is a clear statement in both the passages that when the parent requires the return of the child, the right of the local authority to keep it ceases, and, moreover, that there is no residual discretion left in the local authority because, as the judge pointed out (and as I respectfully think perfectly rightly) the common law rights of the mother revive and also (and this is the significant point) the jurisdiction of this court in relation to the
G infant becomes fully effective. As soon as the parent desires to have the child returned, the discretion of the local authority ceases, as does its care, and the jurisdiction of the court revives in toto.

The other case which I would cite is a decision of the Court of Appeal in *In re S. (An Infant)* [1965] 1 W.L.R. 483. There Lord Denning M.R. and Danckwerts L.J. made the same position absolutely clear. Lord Denning M.R. said, at pp. 487–8:

H
> " It seems to me to be very important that the jurisdiction of the Court of Chancery over its wards should be maintained, even when a local authority has taken a child into its care under section 1 of the Act of 1948. The reason is because the statute gives to a natural parent the right to demand that the local authority give the child up to him or her if he or she desires to take over the care of the child. The imminence of such a demand is a very relevant consideration. Their care may be terminated at any moment. That puts the welfare of the child at peril. It may be taken away from a good home with foster parents and

Goff L.J.   **Bawden v. Bawden (Note) (C.A.)**   **[1978]**

A

removed to a very undesirable home with its natural parents whom it does not know in the least. In order to avoid this peril and secure the welfare of the child, the jurisdiction of the Court of Chancery must be maintained."

Danckwerts L.J. said, at p. 489:

"It is clear that the court's jurisdiction is not entirely ousted by the Act of 1948, and in appropriate circumstances it may be right for the court to exercise its jurisdiction. In [*In re G. (Infants)* [1963] 1 W.L.R. 1169] before Ungoed-Thomas J. there was an example in which it was right for the court to interfere and it did in fact interfere for the assistance of the London County Council and the mother of the children. There are other cases which one can think of, for instance, where the parents make a demand under section 1 (3) of the Act of 1948 requiring the infant to be handed over and, therefore, the powers of the London County Council are abruptly brought to an end. It might be that the parents' house was one of ill-repute or it might be that the parents wished to cut short the education of the child in order to take advantage of the earning power which the child might have acquired according to its age. In those circumstances it seems to me that the court might rightly interfere in order to protect the interests of the child."

B

C

Pausing there, it would appear to me clear that there is no residual authority left in the local authority, and no grounds upon which they could successfully maintain an appeal.

D

They seek to escape that difficulty, first, in reliance on a decision of the Divisional Court in *Halvorsen* v. *Hertfordshire County Council* (1975) 5 Fam.Law 79. It does not appear whether or not *In re S. (An Infant)* [1965] 1 W.L.R. 483 was cited to the Divisional Court, but I would imagine that it was not. That authority does hold that it is only a "suitable" parent who can make an effective demand under section 1 (3), from which it would seem to follow—and in fact would be right—that the local authority might have a residual discretion to determine whether the parent asking for its child was a "suitable" parent. But in my judgment that case cannot stand with *In re S.;* it is inconsistent with it. *In re S.* is of course binding on this court, and the local authority can, in my judgment, obtain no assistance from the *Halvorsen* case, 5 Fam.Law 79.

E

F

Secondly, they said that there is no absolute statutory duty to deliver up the child, and they place great reliance on *Krishnan* v. *Sutton London Borough Council* [1970] Ch. 181, a decision of my own which was upheld by the Court of Appeal. But in my judgment there is nothing there to show any residual discretion residing in the local authority, or to suggest that the local authority may refuse to deliver up the child. The circumstances there were that the child was in the hands of foster parents who refused to deliver it up. The local authority could not compel them to do so, if at all, save by litigation, the result of which would be uncertain, and it was held that they could not be obliged to embark upon that—particularly as the child was, in fact, only one month short of her 18th birthday. In my judgment that case does not in any way cut across or present any inconsistency with the line of cases to which I have been referring.

G

The last point which the local authority suggested might show some residual discretion in themselves was that in certain circumstances they have power to pass a resolution divesting the parent of parental control and vesting it in themselves under section 2 of the Children Act 1948. In this case no such resolution has been passed. Indeed, Mr. McCulloch conceded there were no grounds on which it could be passed, and I think, therefore, it is unnecessary for me to say anything further about that.

H

It is possible that it was technically wrong to include a "direction" that the children be handed over to the petitioner. That would be purely a

A technicality and a matter of form, since in substance the order of the judge was one he was entirely entitled to make. He prescribed a fixed date for the handing over; it was desirable that he should do so, and he did so with welfare officers' reports before him—and indeed, in the presence of the solicitors for the local authority.

In my judgment, the local authority have wholly failed to make out any ground which would enable them to succeed in this appeal, which I would
B dismiss, though if requested to do so, I would delete the direction to which I have referred.

ORR L.J. I agree.

STAMP L.J. I entirely agree. The recent decision in *Halvorsen* v. *Hertfordshire County Council*, 5 Fam.Law 79 runs completely contrary to the decision
C of this court in *In re S. (An Infant)* [1965] 1 W.L.R. 483, and must be taken to have been wrongly decided. I would only wish to add, in regard to that case, that I cannot think that any of the authorities, to which we have been referred in this case, were brought to the attention of the Divisional Court.

It is equally clear, from the decision of this court in *Krishnan* v. *Sutton London Borough Council* [1970] Ch. 181 that the court will not order the local authority to hand over a child to a parent where this would involve, or may involve, the local authority in taking proceedings against a third party,
D such as a foster parent, who has actual control of the child at the time of the request. That, in my judgment, is what Megaw L.J. meant when he said in that case that section 1 (3) imposed no mandatory obligation to return the child to its parents.

Once the first limb of subsection (3) is brought into play, the local authority simply has no right to keep the child. If the child is not handed over to the parent—at any rate I hope it will not happen in this case—as
E it seems to me then the parent may go and fetch it.

It is convenient that a judge, in a case such as this when he is determining the question of custody, should make a suitable arrangement for the handing over of the child. But it may I think (and I agree with Goff L.J.) be wrong to do so when the local authority is not before the court because a local authority may have some reason why it cannot effectively hand the child over. If in this case the local authority still objects to that part of the order, then
F we can no doubt delete it.

I too would dismiss the appeal.

Appeal dismissed.

Solicitors: *Theodore Goddard & Co.; Official Solicitor; Emerson, Mott, Basingstoke; Lamb, Brooks & Bullock, Basingstoke.*

G

H

[1978]

A

[HOUSE OF LORDS]

OWNERS OF M.V. ELEFTHEROTRIA . . . RESPONDENTS

AND

OWNERS OF M.V. DESPINA R . . . . APPELLANTS

THE DESPINA R

B

SERVICES EUROPE ATLANTIQUE SUD (SEAS)
OF PARIS . . . . RESPONDENTS

AND

STOCKHOLMS REDERIAKTIEBOLAG SVEA OF
STOCKHOLM . . . . APPELLANTS

C

1978 July 17, 18, 19, 20;   Lord Wilberforce, Lord Diplock,
    Oct. 19   Lord Salmon, Lord Russell of Killowen,
                                         Lord Keith of Kinkel

Currency—Tort—Damages for negligence—Collision between ships D
—Plaintiffs' ship damaged—Dollars currency of plaintiffs' busi-
ness—Loss and expense incurred in other currencies—Agree-
ment on liability—Currency of judgment
Currency—Contract—Damages for breach—Charterparty—Cargo
damaged owing to owners' breach of warranty of seaworthiness
—Charterers settling cargo receivers' claim in local currency—
Currency of charterers' business used to acquire local currency
—Owners admitting liability—Currency of award E
Ships' Names—Despina R—Eleftherotria—Folias

    The first appeal arose out of a collision between two Greek
ships, the *Despina R* and the *Eleftherotria,* in which the latter
was damaged. The *Eleftherotria* was owned by a Liberian
company which had its head office in Piraeus. The managing
agents had their principal place of business in New York and
the bank account used for moneys received and payments made F
on behalf of the owners was a U.S. dollar account in New
York.
    An agreement was reached under the terms of which the
owners of the *Despina R* were to pay to the owners of the
Eleftherotria 85 per cent. of the loss and damage suffered as a
result of the collision. The expenses of repair had been incurred
in various currencies. The question whether the damages were
to be paid in sterling or some other currency was referred to G
the Admiralty judge. Brandon J. held that he had jurisdiction
to award damages in a foreign currency, but that he was bound
by authority to award them in the currency of expenditure.
The Court of Appeal, dismissing an appeal by the owners of the
Despina R and allowing a cross-appeal, held that there was
jurisdiction to award damages in tort in sterling or in a foreign
currency, and that, in the circumstances, the appropriate H
currency was the plaintiffs' currency rather than the currency
of the expenditure.
    The second appeal was in respect of a cargo of onions shipped
to Brazil by the French charterers of a Swedish-owned motor
vessel, the *Folias.* The cargo arrived damaged, and the cargo
receivers' claim for damages was settled by the charterers in

[Reported by ROBERT WILLIAMS, ESQ., Barrister-at-Law]

A

Brazilian cruzeiros, which they purchased with French francs, their normal business currency. The hire under the charter-party was payable in U.S. dollars, and the proper law of the contract was English law. In arbitration proceedings the owners admitted their liability to the charterers, but contended that payment should be made in cruzeiros. By then the value of the cruzeiro against the French franc was half what it had been when the charterers had paid the cargo receivers. The

B

arbitrators made their award in French francs. On a special case stated Robert Goff J. held that the award should have been made in cruzeiros as being the currency of the loss. On appeal by the charterers the Court of Appeal restored the award of the arbitrators.

On appeals by the owners of the *Despina R* and the Swedish shipowners: —

C

Held, dismissing both appeals, (1) that, in a claim based on tort, it was fairer to give judgment in the currency in which the loss was sustained than in the sterling equivalent at the date of the breach or loss; that the principles to be applied in ascertaining the currency of the loss were those of restitatio in integrum and reasonable foreseeability and, therefore, where a plaintiff proved that he conducted his business in a specific currency and it was reasonably foreseeable that he would use that currency to purchase the necessary currency to meet the

D

immediate and direct expenditure caused by the defendant's tort, then judgment should be expressed in the plaintiff's currency and, accordingly, the Court of Appeal had properly varied the order from a judgment expressed in the currencies of expenditure to the currency of the business conducted on behalf of the ownes of the *Eleftherotria*, namely, U.S. dollars (post, pp. 808H—809A, F–H, 814H—815A, H, 816H).

E

Miliangos v. *George Frank (Textiles) Ltd.* [1976] A.C. 443, H.L.(E.) applied.

S.S. Celia (Owners) v. *S.S. Volturno (Owners) (The Volturno)* [1921] 2 A.C. 544, H.L.(E.) and *The Canadian Transport* (1932) 43 Ll.L.Rep. 409, C.A. distinguished.

(2) That where the terms of a contract governed by English law did not expressly or by implication show that the parties had intended that payments arising from a breach of contract

F

were to be paid in the currency of account or other named currency, the court should give judgment in the currency that best expressed the party's loss; that, although the second appeal concerned a charterparty which expressly stated that certain contractual payments should be made in U.S. dollars, the terms of the charterparty did not show that payment for damage arising out of a breach of contract was to be made in that currency; that, arising from the owners' breach, the charterers

G

had used French francs to purchase the necessary cruzeiros to settle the receivers' claim and, in those circumstances, the Court of Appeal had correctly affirmed the arbitrators' decision that the currency that best expressed the charterers' loss was the currency of their business, namely, French francs (post, pp. 812C–E, G—813A, 814C–D, H—815A, 816E–F, H).

Di Ferdinando v. *Simon, Smits & Co. Ltd.* [1920] 3 K.B.

H

409, C.A. overruled.

Jugoslavenska Oceanska Plovidba v. *Castle Investment Co. Inc.* [1974] Q.B. 292, C.A. and *Jean Kraut A.G.* v. *Albany Fabrics Ltd.* [1977] Q.B. 182 approved.

Decisions of the Court of Appeal in *The Despina R* [1978] Q.B. 396; [1977] 3 W.L.R. 597; [1977] 3 All E.R. 874, Brandon J. and C.A. and *Services Europe Atlantique Sud (SEAS)* v. *Stockholms Rederiaktiebolag Svea* [1978] 2 W.L.R. 887; [1978] 2 All E.R. 764, C.A. affirmed.

The Despina R (H.L.(E.))   **[1978]**

The following cases are referred to in their Lordships' opinions: A

Canadian Transport, The (1932) 43 Ll.L.Rep. 409, C.A.

Celia (S.S.) (Owners) v. *S.S. Volturno (Owners) (The Volturno)* [1921] 2 A.C. 544, H.L.(E.).

Di Ferdinando v. *Simon, Smits & Co. Ltd.* [1920] 3 K.B. 409, C.A.

Federal Commerce and Navigation Co. Ltd. v. *Tradax Export S.A.* [1977] Q.B. 324; [1977] 2 W.L.R. 122; [1977] 2 All E.R. 41, C.A.

Jugoslavenska Oceanska Plovidba v. *Castle Investment Co. Inc.* [1974] Q.B. 292; [1973] 3 W.L.R. 847; [1973] 3 All E.R. 498, C.A.

Kraut (Jean) A.G. v. *Albany Fabrics Ltd.* [1977] Q.B. 182; [1976] 3 W.L.R. 872; [1977] 2 All E.R. 116.

Miliangos v. *George Frank (Textiles) Ltd.* [1976] A.C. 443; [1975] 3 W.L.R. 758; [1975] 3 All E.R. 801, H.L.(E.).

United Railways of Havana and Regla Warehouses Ltd., In re [1961] A.C.   C
1007; [1960] 2 W.L.R. 969; [1960] 2 All E.R. 332, H.L.(E.).

The following additional cases were cited in argument:

Applegate v. *Moss* [1971] 1 Q.B. 406; [1971] 2 W.L.R. 541; [1971] 1 All E.R. 747, C.A.

Argentino, The (1888) 13 P.D. 191; sub. nom. *S.S. Gracie (Owners)* v. *S.S. Argentino (Owners)* (1889) 14 App.Cas. 519, H.L.(E.).   D

Baarn, The [1933] P. 251, C.A.

Barclays Bank International Ltd. v. *Levin Brothers (Bradford) Ltd.* [1977] Q.B. 270; [1976] 3 W.L.R. 852; [1976] 3 All E.R. 900.

Bishop v. *Cunard White Star Co. Ltd.* [1950] P. 240; [1950] 2 All E.R. 22.

Bradburn v. *Great Western Railway Co.* (1874) L.R. 1 Ex. 1.

Bunclark v. *Hertfordshire County Council* (1977) 243 E.G. 381.   E

Cookson v. *Knowles* [1978] 2 W.L.R. 978; [1978] 2 All E.R. 604, H.L.(E.).

Federal Commerce & Navigation Co. Ltd. v. *Molena Alpha Inc.* [1978] 3 W.L.R. 309, Kerr J. and C.A.

Helmsing Schiffdhrts G.m.b.H. & Co. K.G. v. *Malta Drydocks Corpn.* [1977] 2 Lloyd's Rep. 444.

Henriksens Rederi A/S v. *T.H.Z. Rolimpex* [1974] Q.B. 233; [1973] 3 W.L.R. 556; [1973] 3 All E.R. 589, C.A.   F

Liesbosch (Dredger) (Owners) v. *S.S. Edison (Owners)* [1933] A.C. 449, H.L.(E.).

Radford v. *De Froberville* [1977] 1 W.L.R. 1262.

Stoomvaart Maatschappy Nederland, The v. *The Peninsular and Oriental Steam Navigation Co.* (1882) 7 App.Cas. 795, H.L.(E.).

Taylor v. *O'Connor* [1971] A.C. 115; [1970] 2 W.L.R. 472; [1970] 1 All E.R. 365, H.L.(E.).   G

Yorkshire Insurance Co. Ltd. v. *Nisbet Shipping Co. Ltd.* [1962] 2 Q.B. 330; [1961] 2 W.L.R. 1043; [1961] 2 All E.R. 487.

APPEALS from the Court of Appeal.

The first appeal to be heard was by the appellants, the owners of the motor vessel *Despina R,* from an order of the Court of Appeal (Stephen- H son, Orr and Cumming-Bruce L.JJ.) dated June 17, 1977, dismissing an appeal by them from an order of Brandon J. dated January 28, 1977, and perfected on February 16, 1977, and allowing a cross-appeal by the respondents, the owners of the motor vessel *Eleftherotria.*

The second appeal was by the appellants, Stockholms Rederiaktiebolag Svea of Stockholm, from an order of the Court of Appeal (Lord Denning M.R., Ormrod and Geoffrey Lane L.JJ.) dated February 22, 1978, allowing

A an appeal by the respondents, Services Europe Atlantique Sud (SEAS) of
Paris, from an order of Robert Goff J. dated July 9, 1976.
   The facts are stated in their Lordships' opinions.

   Nicholas Phillips Q.C. and *John Reeder* for the appellants in the first
appeal.

B *Christopher Staughton Q.C., M. N. Howard* and *Sarah Miller* for the
respondents in the first appeal.
   N. F. Merriman and *Timothy Young* for the appellants in the second
appeal.
   Gordon Pollock for the respondents in the second appeal.

   Their Lordships took time for consideration.

C
   October 19. LORD WILBERFORCE. My Lords, in *Miliangos* v. *George
Frank (Textiles) Ltd.* [1976] A.C. 443, this House decided that a plaintiff
suing for a debt payable in Swiss francs under a contract governed by Swiss
law could claim and recover judgment in this country in Swiss francs.
Whether the same, or a similar, rule could be applied to cases where (i) a
D plaintiff sues for damages in tort, or (ii) a plaintiff sues for damages for
breach of contract, were questions expressly left open for later decision.
These questions were regulated before *Miliangos* as to tort by the *S.S.
Celia (Owners)* v. *S.S. Volturno (Owners) (The Volturno)* [1921] 2 A.C.
544 and as to contract by *Di Ferdinando* v. *Simon, Smits & Co. Ltd.*
[1920] 3 K.B. 409, which decided that judgment in an English court could
only be given in sterling converted from any foreign currency as at the
E date of the wrong.   Now these questions are directly raised in the present
appeals in each of which your Lordships have the advantage of judgments
of the Court of Appeal and of judgments of high quality at first instance.
These enable the House, as it could not have done in *Miliangos*, to consider some of the problems which may exist in the varied cases of torts and
breaches of contract.

F
   OWNERS OF M.V. ELEFTHEROTRIA *v.* OWNERS OF M.V. DESPINA R

   These are two Greek vessels which collided in April 1974 off Shanghai.
On July 7, 1976, a settlement was arrived at under which it was agreed
that the appellants should pay to the respondents 85 per cent. of the loss
and damage caused to the respondents by the collision.   This is therefore
G a tort case based upon negligence.
   After the collision *Eleftherotria* was taken to Shanghai where temporary repairs were carried out. She then went to Yokohama for
permanent repairs, but it turned out that these could not be carried out
for some time. She was therefore ordered to Los Angeles, California,
U.S.A., for permanent repairs. Expenses were incurred under various
H headings (particularised in the judgment of Brandon J. [1978] Q.B. 396,
399) in foreign currencies, namely, renmimbi yuan (" R.M.B."), Japanese
yen, U.S. dollars, and as to a small amount in sterling. The owners of
the ship are a Liberian company with head office in Piraeus (Greece).
She was managed by managing agents with their principal place of business in the State of New York, U.S.A. The bank account used for all
payments in and out on behalf of the respondents in respect of the ship
was a U.S. dollar account in New York—so all the expenses incurred in

the foreign currencies other than U.S. dollars were met by transferring A
U.S. dollars from this account. The expenses incurred in U.S. dollars
were met directly by payment in that currency from New York.

The judge ordered that the following questions be tried separately,
namely: (a) whether, where the plaintiffs have suffered damage or
sustained loss in a currency other than sterling, they are entitled to recover
damages in respect of such damage or loss expressed in such other currency,
(b) if, in such a case, the plaintiffs are only entitled to recover damages B
expressed in sterling, at what date the conversion into sterling should be
made. Under question (a) there are two alternatives. The first is to
take the currency in which the expense or loss was immediately sustained.
This I shall call " the expenditure currency." The second is to take the
currency in which the loss was effectively felt or borne by the plaintiff,
having regard to the currency in which he generally operates or with C
which he has the closest connection—this I shall call " the plaintiff's
currency." These two solutions have to be considered side by side with
the third possible solution, namely, the sterling solution, taken at the
date when the loss occurred (applying *The Volturno*) or at some other date.

I consider first *The Volturno* [1921] 2 A.C. 544. Although, as in this
case, there had been expenses for repairs incurred in foreign currency, D
these were not in issue on the appeal. That was only concerned with a
claim for damages in respect of detention which was assessed in Italian
lire. It was thought to be clear at that time that an English court could
only give judgment for a sum in sterling, and it is this which formed
the basis of the decision arrived at, namely, that conversion must be
made at the date of the breach and not at the date of judgment. This
most clearly appears in the speech of Lord Sumner. He states, at p. 558, E
the argument in favour of conversion at the date of judgment—the creditor
in that event would get the exact sum to which he was entitled. This
would inevitably, he says, introduce a speculative element into all transactions—waiting to convert the currency until the date of judgment only
adds the uncertainty of exchange to the uncertainty of the law's delays.
There is no answer to this, he continues, except that the claimant's right F
is exclusively a right to lire and would result in a judgment for lire, if
only an English court was, so to speak, competent to express itself in
Italian. Earlier he had described the agreed numbers of lire as only
part of the foreign language in which the court is informed of the damage
sustained, which, like the rest of the foreign evidence, must be translated
into English as at the date when the damage accrues.

The whole of this process of argument flows from the accepted inability G
of the court to receive a claim in lire and to give judgment in lire. The
same point underlies just as clearly the opinion of Lord Parmoor, at p.
560:

> " The necessity for transferring into English money damages ascer-
> tained in a foreign currency arises in the fact that the courts of this
> country have no jurisdiction to order payment of money except in H
> English currency."

The contrary view—based firmly on the principle of restitutio in integrum
—is clearly stated by Lord Carson at pp. 566–567.

My Lords, I do not think that there can now be any doubt that, given
the ability of an English court (and of arbitrators sitting in this country)
to give judgment or to make an award in a foreign currency, to give a

A   judgment in the currency in which the loss was sustained produces a juster result than one which fixes the plaintiff with a sum in sterling taken at the date of the breach or of the loss. I need not expand upon this because the point has been clearly made both in *Miliangos* v. *George Frank (Textiles) Ltd.* [1976] A.C. 443, and in cases which have followed it, as well as in commentators who, prior to *Miliangos,* advocated abandon-
B   ment of the breach-date-sterling rule. To fix such a plaintiff with sterling commits him to the risk of changes in the value of a currency with which he has no connection: to award him a sum in the currency of the expendi-ture or loss, or that in which he bears the expenditure or loss, gives him exactly what he has lost and commits him only to the risk of changes in the value of that currency, or those currencies, which are either his currency or those which he has chosen to use.

C   I shall consider the objections against the use of that currency or those currencies, but first it is necessary to decide between the expenditure currency and the plaintiff's currency—a matter which gave the judges below some difficulty. Brandon J. would have preferred adoption of the plaintiff's currency but he considered himself prevented from doing so by *The Canadian Transport* (1932) 43 Ll.L.Rep. 409, a collision case decided
D   by a strong Court of Appeal. There the loss was originally suffered in Argentinian pesos but a claim was made which involved converting pesos into sterling, sterling into francs at one rate and francs into sterling at another rate, thus producing an exchange profit for the cargo owners. The decision of the Court of Appeal, against the cargo owners, was based in part on their rejection of the treble exchange manoeuvre and in part on their acceptance of the necessity of giving judgment in sterling. They
E   could not have given judgment in either sterling or francs. In my opinion—and I agree with the Court of Appeal in the present case on this —this case, like *The Volturno* [1921] 2 A.C. 544, does not preclude a decision in favour of the plaintiff's currency or the currency of the loss (there it would have been francs or pesos) once the possibility of giving judgment in a foreign currency exists.

F   I return to consider the alternatives.

My Lords, in my opinion, this question can be solved by applying the normal principles, which govern the assessment of damages in cases of tort (I shall deal with contract cases in the second appeal). These are the principles of restitutio in integrum and that of the reasonable fore-seeability of the damage sustained. It appears to me that a plaintiff, who normally conducts his business through a particular currency, and who,
G   when other currencies are immediately involved, uses his own currency to obtain those currencies, can reasonably say that the loss he sustains is to be measured not by the immediate currencies in which the loss first emerges but by the amount of his own currency, which in the normal course of operation, he uses to obtain those currencies. This is the currency in which his loss is felt, and is the currency which it is reasonably
H   foreseeable he will have to spend.

There are some objections to this, but I think they can be answered. First, it is said that to use the method of finding the loss in the plaintiff's currency would involve the court or arbitrators in complicated inquiries. I am not convinced of this. The plaintiff has to prove his loss: if he wishes to present his claim in his own currency, the burden is on him to show to the satisfaction of the tribunal that his operations are conducted in that currency and that in fact it was his currency that was used, in a

normal manner, to meet the expenditure for which he claims or that his   A
loss can only be appropriately measured in that currency (this would
apply in the case of a total loss of a vessel which cannot be dealt with by
the " expenditure " method).   The same answer can be given to the
objection that some companies, particularly large multi-national companies, maintain accounts and operate in several currencies.   Here again
it is for the plaintiff to satisfy the court or arbitrators that the use of the   B
particular currency was in the course of normal operations of that company and was reasonably foreseeable.   Then it is said that this method
produces inequality between plaintiffs.   Two claimants who suffer a
similar loss may come out with different sums according to the currency
in which they trade.   But if the losses of both plaintiffs are suffered at
the same time, the amounts awarded to each of them should be equivalent
even if awarded in different currencies: if at different times, this might   C
justify difference in treatment.   If it happened that the currencies of
the two plaintiffs relatively changed in value before the date of judgment,
that would be a risk which each plaintiff would have to accept.   Each
would still receive, for himself, compensation for *his* loss.

    Finally it is said (and this argument would apply equally if the expendi-
ture currency were taken) that uncertainty will take the place of certainty   D
under the present rule.   Undoubtedly the present (sterling-breach-date)
rule produces certainty—but it is often simpler to produce an unjust rule
than a just one.   The question is whether, in order to produce a just,
or juster, rule, too high a price has to be paid in terms of certainty.

    I do not think so.   I do not see any reason why legal advisers, or
insurers, should not be able, from their knowledge of the circumstances,
to assess the extent of probable liability.   The most difficult step is to   E
assess the quantum of each head of damage.   Once this is done, it should
not be difficult, on the basis of information which the plaintiff must
provide, to agree or disagree with his claim for the relevant currency.
I wish to make it clear that I would not approve of a hard and fast rule that
in all cases where a plaintiff suffers a loss or damage in a foreign currency
the right currency to take for the purpose of his claim is " the plaintiff's   F
currency."   I should refer to the definition I have used of this expression
and emphasise that it does not suggest the use of a personal currency
attached, like nationality, to a plaintiff, but a currency which he is able
to show is that in which he normally conducts trading operations.   Use
of this currency for assessment of damage may and probably will be
appropriate in cases of international commerce.   But even in that field,
and still more outside it, cases may arise in which a plaintiff will not be   G
able to show that in the normal course of events he would use, and be
expected to use, the currency, or one of several currencies, in which he
normally conducts his operations (the burden being on him to show this)
and consequently the conclusion will be that the loss is felt in the currency
in which it immediately arose.   To say that this produces a measure of
uncertainty may be true, but this is an uncertainty which arises in the   H
nature of things from the variety of human experience.   To resolve it is
part of the normal process of adjudication. To attempt to confine this
within a rigid formula would be likely to produce injustices which the
courts and arbitrators would have to put themselves to much trouble to
avoid.

    Apart from these general considerations there are certain special
problems which may arise in Admiralty cases to which attention was

A rightly drawn by Brandon J. I do not think it necessary, or wise, to comment on them in detail for I am satisfied that they do not in themselves create insuperable, or great, difficulties in the way of adopting the plaintiff's currency, where to do so is appropriate. Brandon J. expressed upon them provisional views which must clearly command respect and which demonstrate that the problems are soluble. I think it best to leave such cases to be decided as they arise in the light of full argument.

B Lastly there are some difficulties foreseen by the Court of Appeal [1978] Q.B. 396, 436–437. I appreciate these but I think that the answer to them lies in the necessity for a plaintiff—claiming a judgment in the plaintiff's currency—to prove his case—that his loss was naturally and foreseeably borne in that currency. There should be no automatic and invariable rule to this effect: if, in the circumstances, he fails to satisfy

C the court or arbitrators, they may give judgment or award in whatever other currency represents his loss.

In my opinion the Court of Appeal reached a right conclusion on this case and I would dismiss the appeal.

SERVICES EUROPE ATLANTIQUE SUD (SEAS) OF PARIS *v.* STOCKHOLMS

D   REDERIAKTIEBOLAG SVEA OF STOCKHOLM

This case arises out of a charterparty under which the appellants chartered the *Folias* to the respondents for a round voyage from the Mediterranean to the East Coast, South America. The hire was expressed to be payable in U.S. dollars, but there was a provision that in any general average adjustment disbursements in foreign currencies were to be

E exchanged in a European convertible currency or in sterling or in dollars (U.S.). The appellants are Swedish shipowners, the respondents are a French company which operates shipping services. The proper law of the contract was English law.

In July 1971 the respondents shipped a cargo of onions at Valencia (Spain) for carriage to Brazilian ports. They issued bills of lading in their

F own name. There was a failure of the vessel's refrigeration as a result of which the cargo was found to be damaged on discharge. The cargo receivers claimed against the respondents and, with the concurrence of the appellants as to quantum, this claim was settled in August 1972 by a payment in Brazilian currency of cruzeiros 456,250. In addition, the respondents incurred legal and other expenses.

G The respondents discharged the receivers' claim by purchasing the necessary amount of cruzeiros with French francs. The arbitrators found that French francs were the currency in which the respondents accounted and that it was reasonable to contemplate that, being a French corporation and having their place of business in Paris, they would have to use French francs to purchase other currencies to meet cargo claims.

The respondents then claimed against the appellants for the French

H francs which they had expended and for the amount of their expenses. In the alternative they claimed the equivalent in U.S. dollars, that being said to be the currency of the contract (viz. the charterparty). The basis of their claim was for damages for breach of the contract of affreightment.

The claim was referred to arbitration in London, and the arbitrators held that they had jurisdiction to make an award in a foreign currency: in this they followed the decision of the Court of Appeal in *Jugoslavenska Oceanska Plovidba* v. *Castle Investment Co. Inc.* [1974] Q.B. 292. They

recorded that, along with other City of London arbitrators, they had A
frequently since that case made awards in a currency which was not
the currency of the contract.   They awarded the sum claimed in French
francs for the reason that this seemed to them to be the most appropriate
and just result.   On the hearing of the special case, Robert Goff J. set
aside the arbitrators' award and held that damages should have been
awarded in Brazilian cruzeiros.   This judgment was in turn reversed by B
the Court of Appeal which restored the award of the arbitrators.

My Lords, the effect of the decision of this House in *Miliangos* v.
George Frank (*Textiles*) *Ltd.* [1976] A.C. 443 is that, in contractual as
in other cases a judgment (in which for convenience I include an award)
can be given in a currency other than sterling.   Whether it should be,
and, in a case where there is more than one eligible currency, in which
currency, must depend on general principles of the law of contract and on C
rules of conflict of laws.   The former require application, as nearly as
possible, of the principle of restitutio in integrum, regard being had to
what was in the reasonable contemplation of the parties.   The latter
involve ascertainment of the proper law of the contract, and application
of that law.   If the proper law is English, the first step must be to see
whether, expressly or by implication, the contract provides an answer to D
the currency question.   This may lead to selection of the " currency of
the contract."   If from the terms of the contract it appears that the parties
have accepted a currency as the currency of account and payment in
respect of all transactions arising under the contract, then it would be
proper to give a judgment for damages in that currency—this is, I think,
the case which Lord Denning M.R. had in mind when he said in *Jugo-*
slavenska Oceanska Plovidba v. *Castle Investment Co. Inc.* [1974] Q.B. E
292, 298:

> " [arbitrators] should make their award in that currency because it
> is the proper currency of the contract.   By that I mean that it is
> the currency with which the payments under the contract have the
> closest and most real connection."

F

But there may be cases in which, although obligations under the contract are to be met in a specified currency, or currencies, the right
conclusion may be that there is no intention shown that damages for
breach of the contract should be given in that currency or currencies.
I do not think that Lord Denning M.R. was intending to exclude such
cases.   Indeed in the present case he said [1978] 2 W.L.R. 887, 892, in
words which I would adopt " the plaintiff should be compensated for the G
expense or loss in the currency which most truly expresses his loss."   In
the present case the fact that U.S. dollars have been named as the
currency in which payments in respect of hire and other contractual
payments are to be made, provides no necessary or indeed plausible reason
why damages for breach of the contract should be paid in that currency.
The terms of other contracts may lead to a similar conclusion. H

If then the contract fails to provide a decisive interpretation, the
damage should be calculated in the currency in which the loss was felt
by the plaintiff or " which most truly expresses his loss."   This is not
limited to that in which it first and immediately arose.   In ascertaining
which this currency is, the court must ask what is the currency, payment in which will as nearly as possible compensate the plaintiff in
accordance with the principle of restitution, and whether the parties must

A be taken reasonably to have had this in contemplation. It would be impossible to devise a simple rule, other than the general principles I have mentioned, to cover cases on the sale of goods, on contracts of employment, on international carriage by sea or air: in any of these types of contract the terms of the individual agreement will be important.

My Lords, it is obvious that this analysis, involving as it does a reversion to the ordinary law governing damages for breach of contract,
B necessitates a departure from older cases decided upon the " breach-date-sterling " rule. I should comment upon some of the latter.

Di Ferdinando v. *Simon, Smits & Co. Ltd.* [1920] 3 K.B. 409 was clearly decided on the sterling-breach-date principle so that the foundations of it have been impaired. It is possible, as suggested by Lord Denning M.R. [1978] 2 W.L.R. 887, 894, that the same result could have
C been reached if judgment had been given so as truly to express the plaintiff's loss, but the case itself can no longer be regarded as authoritative. The decision of Eveleigh J. in *Jean Kraut A.G.* v. *Albany Fabrics Ltd.* [1977] Q.B. 182 is in line with the principles I have endeavoured to state. The learned judge in effect applied to a claim in damages the same rule as the *Miliangos* case applied to debt, thus applying, in reverse, the
D principles which led Viscount Simonds in *In re United Railways of Havana and Regla Warehouses Ltd.* [1961] A.C. 1007 to apply the same rule to debt as he held to apply to damages. *Federal Commerce and Navigation Co. Ltd.* v. *Tradax Export S.A.* [1977] Q.B. 324 I would regard as a decision on the " currency of the contract " and correct on that basis. *The Canadian Transport*, 43 Ll.L.Rep. 409 I have already mentioned when dealing with the appeal in the *Despina R.* I
E regard the decision as depending on the sterling-breach-date rule which was thought to prevent a choice between the currency of expenditure and the currency of the plaintiff. Finally I would regard rule 172 of *Dicey & Morris, Conflict of Laws,* 9th ed. (1933), based as it is upon existing authorities, as requiring revision, or reinterpretation, so as, at least, to reflect the principle that, subject to the terms of the contract, damages should be
F recoverable in the currency which most truly expresses the plaintiff's loss.

The present case is concerned with a charterparty for carriage by sea, the parties to which are Swedish and French. It was in the contemplation of the parties that delivery of the goods carried might be made in any of a number of countries with a currency different from that of either of the parties. Loss might be suffered, through non-delivery or incomplete delivery, or delivery of damaged or unsuitable goods, in any of those
G countries, and if any such loss were to fall upon the charterer, he in turn might have a claim against the shipowners. Although the proper law of the contract was accepted to be English by virtue of a London arbitration clause, neither of the parties to the contract, nor the contract itself, nor the claim which arose against the charterers, nor that by his charterers against the owners, had any connection with sterling, so that prima facie
H this would be a case for giving judgment in a foreign currency. This is not disputed in the present appeal, and the only question is which is the appropriate currency in which to measure the loss.

Prima facie, there is much to be said in favour of measuring the loss in cruzeiros: the argument for this was powerfully stated by Robert Goff J. The initial liability of the charterers was measured in that currency by the difference between the value of sound goods arrived at the port of discharge and the damaged value at that port. To require or admit a

further conversion can be said to introduce an unnecessary complication **A**
brought about by an act of the charterers' choice. I am unable in the end
to accept this argument. The essential question is what was the loss
suffered by the respondents. I do not find this to be identical with that
suffered by the cargo receivers: the charterers' claim against the owners
is not one for indemnity in respect of expenditure sustained but is one for
damages for breach of contract. Robert Goff J. makes this plain in his
judgment [1977] 3 W.L.R. 176, 179:   **B**

> " ... the charterers' claim [as formulated] was a claim for damages,
> on the basis that [they] incurred a personal liability to the receivers
> under the bills of lading which they were compelled to discharge; ... "

I think it must follow from this that their loss, which they claim as
damages, was the discharge of the receivers' claim, together with the legal **C**
and other expenses they incurred. They discharged all these by providing
francs—until they provided the francs to meet the receivers' claim they
suffered no loss. Then secondly was this loss the kind of loss which, under
the contract, they were entitled to recover against the owners? The
answer to this is provided by the arbitrators' finding that it was reasonable to contemplate that the charterers, being a French corporation and
having their place of business in Paris, would have to use French francs **D**
to purchase other currencies to settle cargo claims arising under the bills
of lading. So in my opinion the charterers' recoverable loss was, according to normal principle, the sum of French francs which they paid.

My Lords, there may be many variants of situations, *The Canadian
Transport*, 43 Ll.L.Rep. 409 is one, in which a loss arises immediately in the
form of expenditure or indebtedness in one currency, but is ultimately felt **E**
in another, which other may be the normal trading currency of the plaintiff.
In my opinion a decision in what currency the loss was borne or felt can
be expressed as equivalent to finding which currency sum appropriately or
justly reflects the recoverable loss. This is essentially a matter for arbitrators to determine. A rule that arbitrators may make their award in the
currency best suited to achieve an appropriate and just result should be a **F**
flexible rule in which account must be taken of the circumstances in
which the loss arose, in which the loss was converted into a money sum,
and in which it was felt by the plaintiff. In some cases the " immediate
loss " currency may be appropriate, in others the currency in which it
was borne by the plaintiff. There will be still others in which the appropriate currency is the currency of the contract. Awards of arbitrators **G**
based upon their appreciation of the circumstances in which the foreign
currency came to be provided should not be set aside for, as such, they
involve no error of law.

The arbitrators' decision in the present case was both within the
permissible area of decision, and further was in my opinion right.

I agree with the Court of Appeal that the award ought not to have **H**
been set aside and with the judgments in that court. I would dismiss
the appeal.

LORD DIPLOCK. My Lords, in each of these appeals I have had the
advantage of reading in advance the speech of my noble and learned
friend, Lord Wilberforce. I agree with what he says and, for the reasons
that he gives, would dismiss both these appeals.

A   LORD SALMON.   My Lords, I agree with my noble and learned friend,
Lord Wilberforce, that, for the reasons stated in his written speech, both
these appeals should be dismissed.

LORD RUSSELL OF KILLOWEN.

OWNERS OF M.V. ELEFTHEROTRIA v. OWNERS OF M.V. DESPINA R
B

My Lords, this appeal, heard immediately before that in *The Folias*,
concerned a collision in the China seas between the *Despina R* (the
appellant) and the *Eleftherotria* (the respondent), the negligent responsibility
of the appellant being agreed at 85 per cent.   As a result of the damage
the respondent incurred repair and other costs in various currencies.   The
C   first question is whether having regard to the decision in this House in the
Miliangos case [1976] A.C. 443 the approach in *The Volturno* [1921] 2
A.C. 544 should still be adhered to.   In *The Volturno* decision there were
two salient features which together led to the one conclusion that judgment
should be given in the amount of sterling resulting from conversion of the
foreign currency expended at the breach date, a factor which might well
result in hardship to a claimant in this country from a decline in the
D   exchange rate of sterling.   One salient feature was the theory that a claim
could only be made here in sterling: the other was that damages had to be
assessed at the breach date.
The first question is whether it flows, or should flow, from the
Miliangos case that in a case such as the present of damages for tort a
claim may be made and judgment given here in a foreign currency.
E   The *Miliangos* case was one of debt in a foreign currency, and it may
rightly be said that the parties were in agreement that the payment should
be made in that currency, whereas in the case of damages for tort it is at
least highly unlikely that there should be such agreement, and it was not so
here.   But the rule that a claim here must be made only in sterling and
judgment given only in sterling is basically a rule of procedure, and in my
opinion it is undesirable that the rule of procedure should be retained
F   for a claim for damages (whether in tort or for breach of contract) while
departed from in a case of debt.   I observe in this connection that
Viscount Simonds in particular in the *Havana* case [1961] A.C. 1007
considered that damages and debt should follow the same procedural
rule.
If this be right the second feature of *The Volturno* is no longer of
G   relevance, since there would be no question of conversion of the relevant
foreign currency into sterling at the breach date, with the concomitant
hardship to a plaintiff of a weakening of the exchange rate of sterling in
what might be a long delay between damage done and judgment.
There remains in this appeal the question in what foreign currency the
respondent is to be entitled to claim: is it to be a mixed bag of Chinese
R.M.B., yen, and U.S. dollars, or is it to be U.S. dollars?   (I doubt if it
H   makes a great deal of difference in this case because the bulk of the direct
expenditure and loss to the respondent was in U.S. dollars).   In this case
the respondent's business was conducted in U.S. dollars, it being managed
in New York.   The other foreign currency was necessarily acquired in
exchange for U.S. dollars.   The true loss of the respondent was a loss of
U.S. dollars, and in pursuit of the remedy of restitutio in integrum, or full
and proper compensation, I conclude that the claim and judgment should
be for the U.S. dollars lost.   It may be said that there is in any given case

support in simplicity for a system by which you take as the relevant foreign **A**
currency the currency of direct disbursement: but that simplicity may
lead away from a true and fair assessment of the damage sustained by the
claimant.

I have not overlooked the arguments advanced based upon complications involved in departure from *The Volturno* in fields such as set off,
counterclaim, limitation of liability, insolvency. They do not arise in
this case, and should not be incapable of just solutions when they do **B**
arise. I do not propose to advance hypothetical solutions.

I would dismiss this appeal.

SERVICES EUROPE ATLANTIQUE SUD (SEAS) OF PARIS *v.* STOCKHOLMS
REDERIAKTIEBOLAG SVEA OF STOCKHOLM

C

This appeal raises the question of a claim for damages by the respondent charterer for breach by the owners of a warranty of seaworthiness.
The refrigeration plant in the *Folias* which the respondent had chartered
to carry onions from Spain to Brazil was defective: the onions were
damaged: the respondent having issued the bills of lading was liable to
the receivers in Brazil and paid them a substantial sum in cruzeiros.

It was common ground between the parties that this claim for breach **D**
of contract was properly advanced in arbitration here in terms of a
currency other than sterling; and that, as I have indicated in my speech
in *The Despina R.* appeal, is correct.

The respondent is a French company which conducts its business
basically in French francs. In order to pay the receivers of the onions
in cruzeiros the respondent had to dip into its assets to produce the francs **E**
required to acquire those cruzeiros. In what foreign currency was the
respondent entitled to make its claim here? Should it be in cruzeiros, as
the appellant claims? Or should it be in French francs as the respondent
claimed and the arbitrators awarded?

My Lords, in this case also the goal of restitutio in integrum is the aim.
In cases such as this for damages for breach of contract—subject of
course to questions of remoteness—the question is what is truly the **F**
claimant's loss resulting from the breach of contract? True, the direct
disbursement was in cruzeiros: but in order to make that disbursement
the respondent had perforce to expend francs, against which by the time
of the award cruzeiros had steeply (and indeed predictably) declined.
The arbitrators found:

" It was reasonable to contemplate that the charterers, being a French **G**
corporation and having their place of business in Paris, would have
to use French francs to purchase other currencies to settle cargo
claims arising under the bills of lading."

In my opinion the award was properly made in French francs, and I
would dismiss this appeal.

H

LORD KEITH OF KINKEL. My Lords, I agree that each of these appeals
should be dismissed for the reasons stated by my noble and learned friend
Lord Wilberforce.

Appeals dismissed.

Solicitors: *Holman, Fenwick & Willan; Hill, Dickinson & Co.;
William A. Crump & Son; Holman, Fenwick & Willan.*

A

[PRIVY COUNCIL]

DUDLEY HOLDER . . . . PETITIONER

AND

THE QUEEN . . . . RESPONDENT

B

1978 July 10, 11;   Viscount Dilhorne, Lord Edmund-Davies,
    Sept. 5   Lord Fraser of Tullybelton, Lord Scarman
                                                    and Sir Robin Cooke

[PETITION FOR SPECIAL LEAVE TO APPEAL FROM THE COURT OF APPEAL
OF BARBADOS]

C

*Barbados—Court of Appeal—Jurisdiction—Conviction for murder
— Conviction quashed and new trial ordered — Court of
Appeal's power to grant leave to appeal to Privy Council in
criminal matter — Whether discretion to order new trial
affected by lapse of time between trial and hearing of appeal
or by weakness of prosecution case — British Caribbean
(Appeals to Privy Council) Order in Council 1962 (S.I. 1962*

D
*No. 1087), s. 3 b—Federal Supreme Court Regulations 1958
(Laws of West Indies), reg. 22 (2)*

The defendant was charged with the murder of his wife
at " some time between September 1 and September 4, 1974."
At his trial the evidence was that the wife had last been seen
alive at 10 p.m. on September 1 and one L. testified that at
about 11.20 p.m. he had heard the wife shout: " Murder,

E
murder, I beg you Dudley [the defendant] don't kill me,
Lord have mercy." The defence made no objection to the
admission of L.'s evidence. Later on during the trial the
expert medical witness for the Crown, who had conducted a
post-mortem examination of the wife, put the earliest time of
death at 3 p.m. on September 2. The defendant was convicted on February 6, 1975. On February 19, he gave notice
of appeal. The Court of Appeal of Barbados heard the

F
appeal on September 30 and October 1 and 8, 1976, and gave
judgment on December 17, 1976. The court decided that
L.'s evidence was admissible and that the jury was not bound
to accept the medical expert's limit as to the time of death,
and it also upheld the judge's admission of evidence of a
confession by the defendant, but allowed the appeal, quashed
the conviction and ordered a new trial under regulation 22 (2)
of the Federal Supreme Court Regulations 1958.[1] On March

G
25, 1977, the Court of Appeal gave leave to appeal to the
Privy Council against the order for a new trial purporting to
act under section 3 b of the British Caribbean (Appeal to the
Privy Council) Order in Council 1962.[2] In addition on June
22, 1978, the defendant lodged a petition to the Privy Council
for special leave to appeal on the grounds that the interests
of justice did not require a new trial having regard to the
lapse of time between the trial and the hearing of the appeal

H
and to the fact that L.'s evidence was not admissible at the
trial as part of the res gestae and had it not been wrongly
admitted there would have been no case for the defendant to
answer.
    Held, (1) that section 3 b of the British Caribbean (Appeal
to Privy Council) Order in Council 1962 gave the Court of

---

[1] Federal Supreme Court Regulations 1958, reg. 22 (2): see post, p. 820A.
[2] British Caribbean (Appeal to Privy Council) Order in Council 1962, s. 3 b: see
post, p. 819C.

Appeal no power to grant leave to appeal to the Judicial **A**
Committee of the Privy Council in a criminal matter and
accordingly the Court of Appeal's order purporting to do so
was a nullity (post, p. 819F).

    Chung Chuck v. *The King* [1930] A.C. 244, P.C. followed.

    (2) That regulation 22 (2) of the Federal Supreme Court
Regulations 1958 did not impose any fetter on the court's
discretion and although a court in exercising its discretion
would consider various matters such as the gravity of the **B**
charge and the lapse of time since the commission of the
offence, passage of time itself was not a ground for deciding
that the Court of Appeal had erred in exercising its discretion
to order a new trial nor was the fact that certain evidence
might have been inadmissible because on the facts of a
particular case there might still be a case for the defendant
to answer; accordingly, there was no reason to grant special
leave to appeal and it would be for the trial judge to rule **C**
both on whether L.'s evidence and evidence of the confession
were admissible (post, pp. 820C–E, 823E, F, 824C, D).

    Reg. v. *Saunders* (1973) 58 Cr.App.R. 248, C.A. considered.

The following cases are referred to in the reasons for the report of their
    Lordships:

Chung Chuck v. *The King* [1930] A.C. 244, P.C.   **D**
Nirmal v. *The Queen* [1972] Crim.L.R. 226, P.C.
Oteri v. *The Queen* [1976] 1 W.L.R. 1272, P.C.
Ratten v. *The Queen* [1972] A.C. 378; [1971] 3 W.L.R. 930; [1971]
    3 All E.R. 801, P.C.
Reg. v. *Saunders* (1973) 58 Cr.App.R. 248, C.A.
Reg. v. *Turner (Bryan)* (1975) 61 Cr.App.R. 67, C.A.
Subramaniam v. *Public Prosecutor* [1956] 1 W.L.R. 965, P.C.   **E**

The following additional cases were cited in argument:

Director of Public Prosecutions v. *Ping Lin* [1976] A.C. 574; [1975]
    3 W.L.R. 419; [1975] 3 All E.R. 175, C.A. and H.L.(E.).
Peacock v. *The King* (1911) 13 C.L.R. 619.
Reg. v. *Isequilla* [1975] 1 W.L.R. 716; [1975] 1 All E.R. 77, C.A.
                                           F

PETITION for special leave to appeal from part of a judgment
(December 17, 1976) of the Court of Appeal of Barbados (Williams
C.J.(Ag.), Johnson and Tulloch JJ.(Ag.)) ordering a new trial of the
petitioner, Dudley Holder, on a charge of murder having quashed his
conviction (February 6, 1975) before Hanschell J. and a jury and set
aside the sentence of death passed upon him. On March 25, 1977, the **G**
Court of Appeal granted leave to appeal to Her Majesty in Council. On
June 22, 1978, the petitioner lodged a petition for special leave to appeal
to Her Majesty in Council.

The facts are stated in the reasons for the report of their Lordships.

Louis Blom-Cooper Q.C. and *Richard Plender* for the petitioner.
Stuart McKinnon for the Crown.   **H**

July 11. VISCOUNT DILHORNE said that their Lordships would
advise Her Majesty that special leave to appeal should be refused and
would give their reasons later.

September 5. The reasons for the report of their Lordships were
delivered by VISCOUNT DILHORNE.

A   On February 6, 1975, the petitioner was convicted of the murder of his wife Geraldine Holder and sentenced to death. On February 19, he gave notice of appeal and his appeal was heard by the Court of Appeal of Barbados on September 30, October 1 and 8, 1976, the judgment of that court being delivered on December 17, 1976. The court allowed the appeal, quashed the conviction, set aside the sentence and ordered a new trial. Their Lordships were not told why it was B that so long a period elapsed between the giving of the notice of appeal and its determination two years and four months after the murder was alleged to have been committed.

On January 7, 1977, the petitioner lodged a petition with the Court of Appeal asking their leave to appeal to the Judicial Committee of the Privy Council. On March 25, 1977, the Court of Appeal granted leave C by virtue of the British Caribbean (Appeal to Privy Council) Order in Council 1962 (S.I. 1962 No. 1087). That court may grant leave to appeal from a

"judgment . . . if, in the opinion of the court, the question involved in the appeal is one which, by reason of its great or general import-ance or otherwise, ought to be submitted to Her Majesty in Council D   for decision."

"Judgment" is defined in section 2 (1) of the order as including "a decree, order, ruling, sentence or decision of the court." This Order in Council has remained in force since Barbados became independent.

A similar Order in Council was considered in *Chung Chuck* v. *The King* [1930] A.C. 244 where it was held that it did not confer a new E right on the Court of Appeal to grant leave to appeal to the Privy Council in a criminal matter. In *Oteri* v. *The Queen* [1976] 1 W.L.R. 1272, the Full Court of Western Australia purported to grant leave to appeal to the Privy Council in a criminal matter and Lord Diplock, delivering the judgment of the Board, pointed out, at p. 1275, that an appeal to the Privy Council in a criminal matter lay only with the special F leave of Her Majesty granted upon the advice of the Judicial Committee. Just as in that case so here, the Court of Appeal has no power by virtue of the Order in Council to grant leave in a criminal matter and their deci-sion to do so is consequently a nullity. On June 22, 1978, the petitioner lodged a petition for special leave to appeal to Her Majesty in Council, and the matter came before their Lordships as an application for such G leave.

The Federal Supreme Court Regulations 1958, by regulation 22 (1), provided that the Supreme Court should on an appeal against conviction allow the appeal if they thought that the verdict of the jury should be set aside on the ground that it was unreasonable or could not be supported having regard to the evidence or that the judgment of the court before H whom the appellant was convicted should be set aside on the ground of a wrong decision of any question of law or that on any ground there was a miscarriage of justice and that in any other case the court should dismiss the appeal. This regulation contained the proviso that the court might, notwithstanding that they were of opinion that the point raised in the appeal might be decided in favour of the appellant, dismiss the appeal if they considered that no substantial miscarriage of justice had actually occurred. Regulation 22 (2) reads as follows:

Holder v. The Queen (P.C.)　　　　　　　　　　　**[1978]**

" Subject to the special provisions of this part of these regulations A
the Federal Supreme Court shall, if it allows an appeal against
conviction, quash the conviction and direct a judgment and verdict
of acquittal to be entered, or if the interests of justice so require,
order a new trial."

These regulations were made applicable to the British Caribbean Court
of Appeal by section 12 of the British Caribbean Court of Appeal Order B
in Council 1962 (S.I. 1962 No. 1086) and to the Barbados Court of
Appeal by the Supreme Court of Judicature Act 1966 (Act 39 of 1966).
　　The petitioner sought special leave to appeal from the order of the
Court of Appeal on the ground that in view of the passage of time since
the killing of his wife, the interests of justice did not require a new trial.
It was also contended on his behalf that the Court of Appeal was wrong C
in its conclusion that certain evidence given by a witness for the prosecution at the trial, Mr. Everton Licorish, and evidence of an alleged confession made by the petitioner was admissible. It was contended that
without such evidence there was no case for the petitioner to answer and
that therefore the new trial should not have been ordered. Regulation
22 (2) does not impose any fetter on the exercise by the court of its
discretion to order a new trial or lay down any guidelines as to the D
exercise of that power. Their Lordships do not intend to attempt to lay
down any guidelines or desire to impose any fetter on its exercise. No
doubt the court entrusted with the power to order a new trial will, when
considering the exercise of its discretion, have regard to many matters,
including the gravity of the charge, the time that has elapsed since the
alleged commission of the offence and whether it is possible to hold a E
proper new trial were one ordered. As Lawton L.J. said in *Reg.* v.
Turner (Bryan) (1975) 61 Cr.App.R. 67, 79:

" It is in the interests of the public that criminals should be brought
to justice; and the more serious the crimes the greater is the need
for justice to be done."
　　　　　　　　　　　　　　　　　　　　　　　　　　　　F
In *Nirmal* v. *The Queen* [1972] Crim.L.R. 226 the Judicial Committee
did not uphold an order for a new trial made by the Fiji Court of Appeal
when the only object of the new trial would have been to have given
the prosecution an opportunity to make out a new case or to fill gaps
in the evidence. In *Reg.* v. *Saunders* (1973) 58 Cr.App.R. 248, Lord
Widgery C.J. said, at p. 255:　　　　　　　　　　　　　　　G

" . . . it is not in the court's knowledge that it has ever before been
contemplated that a retrial should take place some three and a half
years after the original offence was committed. A delay of one
year, perhaps two years, is not uncommon, but none of us can
remember a case in which it has been thought right to order a
retrial after such a long period, when regard is had to the fact that H
this appellant has already stood his trial once, and has been in
prison for a number of years and would, if a new trial is ordered,
have to run the gauntlet and the hazards and prejudice of being
tried yet again."

Lord Widgery's observations were related to England. In some other
territories the process of justice may operate more slowly. Their

A Lordships would not be prepared to hold that the decision of the Court of Appeal was wrong on account of the time that had elapsed when that decision was given. They would not think it right to interfere with the exercise of discretion by that court unless it was clear that that court had erred by taking into account matters to which it ought not to have had regard or by not taking into account matters to which it should have paid attention. To order a new trial merely to enable the prosecu-

B tion to present a new case would not in their Lordships' view be a proper exercise of discretion. Their Lordships do not know to what matters the Court of Appeal in this case had regard when making its decision, but they see no reason to conclude that that court either failed to have regard to matters to which it should have had regard, or erred in taking into account matters which it should not have done.

C Unfortunately, neither counsel for the petitioner nor counsel for the prosecution was able to give any information as to the causes of the delay in the determination of the appeal. When one of the grounds of appeal is delay, it is desirable that counsel should be provided with information as to the reasons for it. A petitioner cannot rely on the passage of time that has occurred which has been brought about by

D dilatoriness on his part. An undue length of time has passed since the determination of the appeal due in part to the application for leave to appeal being made to the Court of Appeal and to the delay until June 1978 in lodging the petition for special leave to appeal. Mr. Blom-Cooper did not seek to rely on such delay as a ground for reversing the order for a new trial.

E The case for the prosecution at the trial can be summarised as follows: the petitioner was charged with the murder of his wife " some-time between September 1, 1974, and September 4, 1974." Mrs. Holder was last seen alive on September 1. Her dead body was discovered on September 4. Mr. Licorish testified that he had seen Mrs. Holder

F enter her house a little after 10 p.m. on the night of September 1. He lived on the opposite side of the road to her. That was the last time she was seen alive. A little later Mr. Licorish saw the petitioner lurking behind the fence to his, Mr. Licorish's, house and saw him go into his wife's house through the front door. The petitioner was not living there then. At about 11.20 p.m. Mr. Licorish said he heard Mrs. Holder

G shout, " Murder, murder I beg you Dudley don't kill me, Lord have mercy." In cross-examination Mr. Licorish said that he did not take this shouting seriously because he was accustomed to " hearing her holler-ing for murder at night. Sometimes she inside hollering for murder and sometimes she outside by the gate." On the evening of September 4 the body of Mrs. Holder was found in the bedroom of her house. She had

H been stabbed four times in the chest. At the time no objection was taken to Mr. Licorish testifying as to what he heard Mrs. Holder shout, but on appeal to the Court of Appeal it was contended that this evidence should not have been admitted. This contention was based on evidence later given by Dr. Brathwaite. He first saw the body of Mrs. Holder at 9 p.m. on September 4. The next day at 9 a.m. he performed a post-mortem. The body was in a state of decomposition. In his evidence in chief he said she had been dead for more than 48 hours. In cross-

examination he said the probable number of hours which had elapsed A
since her death was 36 to 48 and that he was prepared to put the upper
limit at 54 hours, i.e. 3 p.m. on Monday, September 2. He was not
prepared to say that she had died at the earliest that Monday night or
at the latest the Tuesday morning. He was not asked whether in his
opinion the state of her body was consistent with her having been killed
on the Sunday night. In the course of his evidence he drew a distinction
between what was probable and what was possible. B

If Mrs. Holder could only have been killed after 3 p.m. on September
2, then the evidence of Mr. Licorish as to what he had heard Mrs.
Holder say on the night of September 1 was not admissible as evidence,
for it was not evidence relevant to murder after that time on September
2 having been committed by the petitioner. If, on the other hand, the
state of her body on September 5 was consistent with her having been C
killed on the night of September 1, Mr. Licorish's evidence as to the
shouts he had heard and what he had heard said was clearly relevant.

In *Ratten* v. *The Queen* [1972] A.C. 378, 387 Lord Wilberforce
delivering the judgment of the Board said:

"The mere fact that evidence of a witness includes evidence as to
words spoken by another person who is not called, is no objection to D
its admissibility. Words spoken are facts just as much as any
other action by a human being. If the speaking of the words is a
relevant fact, a witness may give evidence that they were spoken.
A question of hearsay only arises when the words spoken are relied
on 'testimonially,' i.e., as establishing some fact narrated by the
words."

E

He cited the following passage from the judgment of the Board in
Subramaniam v. *Public Prosecutor* [1956] 1 W.L.R. 965, 970:

"Evidence of a statement made to a witness by a person who is not
himself called as a witness may or may not be hearsay. It is hearsay
and inadmissible when the object of the evidence is to establish the
truth of what is contained in the statement. It is not hearsay and F
is admissible when it is proposed to establish by the evidence, not
the truth of the statement, but the fact that it was made."

In *Ratten* v. *The Queen* [1972] A.C. 378 it was held that evidence that
the deceased had a few minutes before her death sought to speak to the
police on the telephone and that her voice was hysterical and that she
sobbed was admissible. Lord Wilberforce referred to a statement made G
by a victim of an attack or by a bystander indicating directly or indirectly
the identity of an attacker and said, at p. 379:

"The test [as to admissibility] should be not the uncertain one,
whether the making of the statement should be regarded as part of
the event or transaction. This may often be difficult to show. But
if the drama, leading up to the climax, has commenced and assumed H
such intensity and pressure that the utterance can safely be regarded
as a true reflection of what was unrolling or actually happening, it
ought to be received."

Later he said, at p. 391:

"On principle it would not appear right that the necessary
association should be shown only by the statement itself . . . Facts

A   differ so greatly that it is impossible to lay down any precise general rule: it is difficult to imagine a case where there is no evidence at all of connection between the statement and principal event other than the statement itself, but whether this is sufficiently shown must be a matter for the trial judge. Their Lordships would be disposed to agree that, amongst other things, he may take the
B   statement itself into account."

In the present case, as has been said, Mr. Licorish heard Mrs. Holder shouting, " Murder, murder I beg you Dudley don't kill me, Lord have mercy," and the case is complicated by the fact that he was accustomed to "hearing her hollering for murder at night." In the light of that evidence, even if the evidence of what she said was admissible and
C   admitted in the exercise of judical discretion, it is clear that the jury should have been warned that it might not be safe to conclude that at the time her husband was in the process of killing her or about to kill her and that if they accepted evidence as to what she shouted, it might be safe only to conclude that there was a row between her and her husband. They might, if they accepted the evidence as to what she shouted, hold
D   that it was her husband who was in the house with her. The naming of her husband supported Mr. Licorish's evidence that he had seen the petitioner, who was not then living there, enter the house. The Court of Appeal held that Mr. Licorish's evidence as to the shouts was rightly admitted by the trial judge. They said that the jury was not bound to accept Dr. Brathwaite's upper limit as the time within which the
E   murder took place and that the shouts were in essence part of something that was going on. That they were part of something going on does not of itself render them admissible as evidence. To be admitted it had to be shown that what was going on was the drama which culminated in Mrs. Holder's death, and in the light of Dr. Brathwaite's evidence that was not shown. It is indeed unfortunate that Dr. Brathwaite was
F   not asked whether it was possible or probable that she might have been killed on the night of September 1. That not having been asked, their Lordships are inclined to the view that the evidence as to what Mrs. Holder shouted was not rightly admitted. If inadmissible, that does not of itself show that the order for a new trial should not have been made.

On September 10 Mrs. Pierce saw the petitioner lying in the bush.
G   He had one hand in a sock. It was later found that he had a badly infected wound in his left arm. He asked her to call an ambulance for him and said that he had had nothing to eat for six days and had six black-outs. He was taken to hospital where he was seen between 4.30 and 5 p.m. by Dr. Sears. Dr. Sears said he was conscious and well orientated but could have been delirious before he examined him. At
H   11.20 that morning Inspector Whittaker saw the petitioner in the hospital. He had taken a long statement from the petitioner at the mortuary on September 5. On September 10 Inspector Whittaker asked the petitioner if he knew him. The answer was, " Yes Inspector. I glad you come. I killed my wife and I feel I should dead too." Inspector Whittaker said the petitioner appeared fully conscious and Corporal Trotman, who was present, said that he appeared to be quite normal. Admission in

evidence of this confession was objected to on the ground that it was A
not the product of a conscious and deliberate will, evidence having been
given that in view of his condition the petitioner had " almost definitely "
been delirious at times. After a trial within the trial the judge admitted
the confession, observing that there was no medical evidence that he
was delirious when he made it. The Court of Appeal upheld his
conclusion. In their Lordships' view on the evidence given at the trial,
it is not possible to conclude that they were wrong in doing so.   B

The petitioner did not give evidence but made a statement from the
dock.

In their Lordships' view the passage of time that occurred between
the murder and the decision of the Court of Appeal is not such as to
show any error on the part of the Court of Appeal in the exercise of
their discretion to order a new trial. It was not suggested that a proper C
trial cannot now take place. Even if Mr. Licorish's evidence as to what
he heard Mrs. Holder shouting is excluded, there would appear to be a
case for the petitioner to answer. He was seen to go into her house
late on September 1 after she had entered it. That was the last time
she was seen alive. She was stabbed in the chest and on September 10
the petitioner confessed to having killed her.   D

In these circumstances their Lordships saw no reason to grant special
leave to appeal from the order of the Court of Appeal. They regard
it as important that the trial should take place without delay. At
that trial it will be for the trial judge to rule on the admissibility both
of the evidence as to what Mrs. Holder shouted and as to the confession
in the light of the evidence as it then emerges. In reaching his conclusions on those questions he should not allow himself to be influenced E
in any degree by the conclusions reached on them at the earlier trial or
by the Court of Appeal. If he should decide that the evidence of what
the deceased woman said is admissible he should then, of course, go on
to consider whether in the exercise of his discretion he should exclude it
on the ground that its admission would be unduly prejudicial to the
petitioner. Their Lordships, however, would not wish anything that they
have said to be taken as an indication as to the manner in which his F
discretion should be exercised. For these reason their Lordships humbly
advised Her Majesty to refuse the application for special leave.

Solicitors: *Philip Conway Thomas & Co.; Charles Russell & Co.*

                                                        T. J. M.   G

A

[COURT OF APPEAL]

MALHOTRA v. CHOUDHURY

[1973 M No. 54]

B 1977 Oct. 18, 19, 20, 21   Stephenson and Cumming-Bruce L.JJ.

*Damages—Sale of land—Damages in lieu of specific performance
—Option to purchase house on dissolution of medical partnership—House belonging to junior partner and wife—Senior
partner exercising option—Junior partners' failure to obtain
wife's consent to sale—No evidence of attempt to persuade
wife to sell property—Measure of damages—Date for assessing
damages—Chancery Amendment Act 1858 (Lord Cairns' Act)
(21 & 22 Vict. c. 27), s. 2*

C

In 1969 the plaintiff, on becoming a junior partner in a
medical practice, was granted an option to purchase a house
and surgery known as Novar, the senior partner's residence,
on the latter's retirement. The plaintiff preferred to buy a
house in a neighbouring village and did not take up the
D option. In May 1972, the defendant became the plaintiff's
junior partner and bought Novar from the senior partner
(who had retired), the conveyance being in the joint names of
the defendant and his wife and containing an express trust
for sale. Two weeks later, the plaintiff and the defendant
entered into a partnership deed, providing, inter alia, that if
the defendant should cease to be a partner, he would offer
to sell Novar to the plaintiff, the market price to be fixed
E by a valuer in the absence of agreement.

Within a short period, the partnership proved to be
unworkable. In March 1973, the plaintiff gave the defendant
notice of the dissolution of the partnership and required the
defendant to sell Novar to him under the option clause. The
defendant refused to sell, claiming that the notice was invalid.
In June, the plaintiff, after failing to obtain the title deeds,
sought the appointment of a valuer. In August, the defendant
F informed his patients that, the partnership having ceased, he
would continue practising on his own. By his writ, the
plaintiff claimed specific performance of the contract of sale
and an injunction restraining the defendant from denying
him the use of the surgery. In his defence, the defendant
contended that, by his notice, the plaintiff had either exercised
his right to retire or had repudiated the partnership. In his
affidavit, he stated that Novar was the home of his wife and
G himself, the surgery being integral to it.

On October 28, 1973, the judge granted specific performance and ordered, inter alia, access for the valuer, inquiry as
to title, delivery of the title deeds and a continuation of an
undertaking to permit the plaintiff access to the surgery. The
order was confirmed by the Court of Appeal, save that the
court substituted for specific performance a declaration that
the option clause was valid. The plaintiff's demands for an
H abstract of title and inspection by the valuer received no
reply. Access to the surgery was denied on the basis of the
wife's refusal to permit it. By a summons, the plaintiff then
sought access and a valuation of the defendant's beneficial
interest. In an affidavit, the defendant's wife confirmed that
she would not agree to a sale or give access.

[Reported by MISS HENRIETTA STEINBERG, Barrister-at-Law]

Malhotra v. Choudhury (C.A.) [1978]

In January 1977, the plaintiff claimed damages for breach A
of contract constituted by the option, the defendant contest-
ing the issue of damages only. After finding that the
defendant had shown a marked lack of enthusiasm in carrying out his contractual duties and that the defendant's wife
would not agree to a sale of Novar, the judge decided that
the plaintiff could only recover damages limited to his costs
under the rule in *Bain* v. *Fothergill.*

On the plaintiff's appeal for substantial damages: — B

Held, allowing the appeal, (1) that where a vendor of real
property sought to limit his liability for breach of contract
under the rule in *Bain* v. *Fothergill,* he had a duty to show
that he had used his best endeavours to fulfil his contractual
obligations, the onus being on him, both in the case of a defect
of title and of conveyance; that, in the absence of fraud, mere
unwillingness to carry out the duty could constitute bad faith
sufficient to exclude the rule and to entitle the purchaser to C
substantial damages; and that, since the defendant had shown
no enthusiasm for carrying out his duty and had given no
evidence of an attempt by himself to obtain his wife's consent to the sale, he had not discharged the burden of proof
that he was unable to convey the property to the plaintiff
and, in those circumstances, the plaintiff was entitled to
substantial damages (post, pp. 839C–E, 840G–H, 843F–G, 844C–D,
G). D

Bain v. *Fothergill* (1874) L.R. 7 H.L. 158, H.L.(E.)
distinguished.

Day v. *Singleton* [1899] 2 Ch. 320, C.A.; *Keen* v. *Mear*
[1920] 2 Ch. 574 and dictum of Salter J. in *Braybrooks* v.
Whaley [1919] 1 K.B. 435, 441, D.C. applied.

(2) That, in assessing damages, the value of the realty
should be assessed at the date of the judgment and not at the
date of the breach of contract; but that the date for valuing E
Novar should be moved back by one year to October 21,
1976, to take account of the plaintiff's delay in pursuing his
claim; and that, in addition, the plaintiff should recover
damages for any loss in his medical practice, past and present,
that could be shown to flow from his inability to use the
surgery rather than from competition by the defendant (post,
pp. 844F, 846H, 847G—848A, G—849A).

General and Finance Facilities Ltd. v. *Cooks Cars (Rom-* F
ford) Ltd. [1963] 1 W.L.R. 644, C.A.; *Grant* v. *Dawkins*
[1973] 1 W.L.R. 1406 and *Wroth* v. *Tyler* [1974] Ch. 30
applied.

Decision of Blackett-Ord V.-C. reversed.

The following cases are referred to in the judgments:

Bain v. *Fothergill* (1874) L.R. 7 H.L. 158, H.L.(E.).
Braybrooks v. *Whaley* [1919] 1 K.B. 435, D.C. G
Day v. *Singleton* [1899] 2 Ch. 320, C.A.
Engel v. *Fitch* (1868) L.R. 3 Q.B. 314; (1869) L.R. 4 Q.B. 659.
Flureau v. *Thornhill* (1776) 2 Wm.Bl. 1078.
General and Finance Facilities Ltd. v. *Cooks Cars (Romford) Ltd.* [1963]
    1 W.L.R. 644; [1963] 2 All E.R. 314, C.A.
Grant v. *Dawkins* [1973] 1 W.L.R. 1406; [1973] 3 All E.R. 897.
Hopkins v. *Grazebrook* (1826) 6 B. & C. 31. H
Keen v. *Mear* [1920] 2 Ch. 574.
Leeds Industrial Co-operative Society Ltd. v. *Slack* [1924] A.C. 851,
    H.L.(E.).
Rosenthal v. *Alderton & Sons Ltd.* [1946] K.B. 374; [1946] 1 All E.R.
    583, C.A.
Sachs v. *Miklos* [1948] 2 K.B. 23; [1948] 1 All E.R. 67, C.A.
Watts v. *Spence* [1976] Ch. 165; [1975] 2 W.L.R. 1039; [1975] 2 All
    E.R. 528.

A   *Wroth* v. *Tyler* [1974] Ch. 30; [1973] 2 W.L.R. 405; [1973] 1 All E.R.
897.

No additional cases were cited in argument.

APPEAL from Blackett-Ord V.-C.

On May 30, 1973, the plaintiff, Dr. Prem Krishan Malhotra, gave to
B his junior partner, the defendant, Dr. Jagodindra Kumar Choudhury,
notice of dissolution of their partnership and, under clause 22 of the
deed of partnership dated May 19, 1972, exercised his option to purchase
a house and surgery, Novar, 37 Butt Hill, Kippax, West Yorkshire, which
had been conveyed to the defendant and his wife on August 1, 1972, by
the then senior partner of the medical practice, Dr. Mathieson. The
C defendant denied that on the true construction of clause 22 and the
events that had happened the plaintiff could exercise his option to
purchase Novar. The plaintiff issued a writ on September 21, 1973
(1973 M No. 54) seeking, inter alia, a declaration that the affairs of the
medical partnership should be wound up and an order for specific
performance of the agreement whereby the defendant had agreed to sell
and the plaintiff agreed to purchase Novar.

D   On October 28, 1973, Blackett-Ord V.-C., holding that the option
was exercisable, directed that the agreement of May 19, 1972, should be
specifically performed and ordered access for the valuer, inquiry as to
title, delivery of the deeds, vacant possession and a continuation of the
defendant's undertaking to allow the plaintiff use of the surgery. The
order was perfected on November 6. On June 4, 1974, the Court of
E Appeal confirmed the judge's order, except that, after striking out the
order for specific performance, the court declared that the option clause
had been validly exercised by the plaintiff. That course was taken due
to the possibility that the defendant's wife might resist an order of sale.

The defendant did not comply with the order and in subsequent
proceedings to enforce the order, the defendant's wife filed an affidavit
F stating that she had refused to agree to the sale of Novar. By a notice
of motion of January 21, 1977, the plaintiff moved (1) for damages for
breach of contract constituted by the option as referred to in the order
of November 6, 1973, and varied on appeal on June 4, 1974, and (2) that
the measure of damages should be ascertained in accordance with the
attached schedule.

The schedule provided for (a) an inquiry as to the value of Novar
G on June 4, 1974; (b) an inquiry as to its value on January 31, 1977; (c) a
direction that, if the valuer could obtain access, the estimate of values
should be received as evidence; (d) an inquiry as to any loss in the medical
practice suffered by the plaintiff; (e) which was abandoned; (f) a direction
that the damages should be certified as the aggregate of the following,
namely, (i) the difference between the value found on inquiry (b) less the
H value on inquiry (a), if the former were greater than the latter, and (ii)
the sum found under (d). The defendant did not dispute (a) and (c), in
the event of the appeal succeeding.

On March 29, 1977, Blackett-Ord V.-C. held that the plaintiff was
entitled to damages limited to the costs of investigating title and of
obtaining a valuation of the property under the rule in *Bain* v. *Fothergill*
(1874) L.R. 7 H.L. 158.

The plaintiff appealed on the grounds, inter alia, that the judge

was wrong in holding that the rule in *Bain* v. *Fothergill* was applicable **A**
and that the defendant's failure to make title was due to a defect of title
and not of conveyancing; that the judge should have held that the
defendant's want of enthusiasm in making the title disentitled him from
benefiting under the rule; and that the judge wrongly inferred that the
defendant's want of enthusiasm had no effect on the attitude of the
defendant's wife in making good title.

By a respondent's notice the defendant sought to uphold the judg- **B**
ment on the grounds, inter alia, that the plaintiff's writ and statement
of claim contained no claim for damages for breach of contract, or for
damages in lieu of specific performance, and no allegation of wilful
default, the plaintiff electing not to apply for leave to amend; that the
evidence being on affidavit and in the absence of direct allegations, the
judge should have held that no findings of fact adverse to the defendant **C**
should be made without giving him the opportunity of giving evidence;
that the judge should have held that the plaintiff's delay in issuing the
motion disentitled him from damages in lieu of specific performance;
and, if the judge was wrong in applying *Bain* v. *Fothergill,* the measure
of damages should be the difference between the value of Novar at the
date of the breach of contract in January 1975 and its value at the date **D**
of the Court of Appeal hearing in June 1974; and that *Wroth* v. *Tyler*
[1974] Ch. 30 wrongly held that the measure of damages was the
difference in value at the date of the present hearing and at the date of
the contract.

By consent the appeal was heard by two Lords Justices.

The facts are stated in the judgment of Stephenson L.J. **E**

Matthew Caswell for the plaintiff.
Clive Behrens for the defendant.

STEPHENSON L.J. This is an appeal from a decision of Blackett-Ord
V.-C. dated March 29, 1977. The appeal is concerned with a dispute
between two doctors practising in Kippax, Swillington, West Yorkshire. **F**

In 1972 Dr. Choudhury, the defendant, gave Dr. Malhotra, the
plaintiff, an option to purchase the house and surgery called Novar,
37 Butt Hill, Kippax; but he has not conveyed that house and surgery to
the plaintiff and still lives in it himself, practises from it and will not
even allow the plaintiff to use it.

The house was built for a Dr. Mathieson in 1933. In 1969 Dr.
Mathieson took into his medical practice as junior partner the plaintiff **G**
and he gave him an option to purchase Novar at the market price if and
when he retired. We are not concerned with the terms of that option.
Thereafter the plaintiff bought himself a house in the neighbouring
village of Swillington, where the partners in this practice had, with others,
a surgery, at a National Health Service clinic. So the plaintiff did not
need Novar and did not exercise his option to purchase it from Dr. **H**
Mathieson when Dr. Mathieson retired in 1972.

In that year the plaintiff took the defendant into the practice and
into partnership as junior partner. It is not disputed that at that time
Dr. Mathieson and the plaintiff saw both the defendant and his wife,
but there is a dispute as to what was said when they met.

It is not disputed that in 1972 three legal documents were executed.
First of all on May 5 contracts for the sale of Novar by Dr. Mathieson

A   to the defendant and his wife for £9,000 were exchanged—" exchanged "
by the same solicitor acting for both vendor and purchaser. A fortnight
later, on May 19, the plaintiff and defendant entered into a deed of
partnership containing, among more common form provisions, in clause
22 an option in favour of the plaintiff to purchase Novar in certain
circumstances. Finally on August 1 a conveyance of the property to
B   the defendant and his wife was executed for the price of £9,000 raised
entirely on a mortgage from the Halifax Building Society.

     Unfortunately the partnership did not work. On May 30, 1973,
the plaintiff, through his solicitors, gave the defendant a written notice.
The relevant parts of it are in these terms:

C   " . . . we do hereby give you formal notice of the dissolution of
the partnership to take effect on the expiry of six months from the
day of your receipt of this letter. We would add that if you wish
to have the termination take effect at an earlier date Dr. Malhotra
would be prepared to agree to this."

Later in the letter comes this notice:

D   " *House and Surgery at Novar Kippax.* We refer you to clause 22
of the deed of partnership whereby upon dissolution of your partnership with Dr. Malhotra you are required to offer to sell the house and
surgery to Dr. Malhotra. We hereby give you notice that Dr.
Malhotra does require you to offer the same to him for sale. We hope
that a figure for fair market price will be agreed; otherwise Dr.
Malhotra will rely on the provisions contained in this clause for fixing
E   the same."

     The partnership deed was made between the plaintiff giving his
address in Swillington and the defendant giving an address in Amersham,
Buckinghamshire, from which he came with his wife and children to
live in Novar. By clause 1:

F   " The partners hereby mutually agree to become partners in the
medical practice hitherto carried on by Dr. Malhotra with Dr.
Mathieson in Kippax Swillington and district in the West Riding
of the County of York as from July 17, 1972, until determination
as hereinafter provided and upon the terms hereinafter expressed."

By clause 3:

G   " Each partner shall provide and maintain himself in a dwelling
house suitable for his share of the practice and pay the whole costs
thereof, including surgeries, consulting rooms and waiting rooms at
such dwelling house . . ."

By clause 18:

H   " Either partner may retire from the partnership upon giving to the
other six months previous notice in writing of his intention so to
do. Upon such retirement the partner so retiring shall be entitled to
receive his share of the profits up to the time of such retirement."

There follows clause 19 which provides for what shall happen if the
partnership is determined apart from retirement under clause 18; and
it may be determined by, among other things, either partner giving
notice to the other with the intention so to do, if such other partner be

guilty of gross neglect or any breach of these articles and so on. The
notice to which I have referred, purported to be given not under clause
19 but under clause 18 which I have just read. By clause 20:

> "The partners hereby mutually agree that if one partner ceases
> to be bound by this agreement the party so ceasing to be bound
> shall not for a period of three years from the date on which he so
> ceases to be bound practise within a distance of five miles from any
> premises at which the times [sic] of such cesser the partnership
> practice is being carried on."

Then I come to clause 22:

> "If Dr. Choudhury shall cease to be a partner under any of the
> provisions hereof, or while remaining a partner cease to reside at
> Novar, Kippax he will further offer to sell such house, surgeries and
> grounds to Dr. Malhotra at a fair market price (to be fixed in
> the absence of agreement by a valuer) (to be appointed by Hartley
> & Worstenholme Solicitors Castleford) and Dr. Malhotra shall have
> one month from the date of such offer in which to accept and if he
> does not so accept shall be deemed to have refused."

That partnership deed containing clause 22 was signed, sealed and
delivered by both parties in the presence of the same Castleford solicitors.

There followed the conveyance of August 1, and it is only necessary
to refer to the fact that in clause 2 (a) there is an express trust to sell:

> "The purchasers shall hold the said property upon trust to sell the
> same with power to postpone the sale thereof and shall stand
> possessed of the net proceeds of sale and of other money applicable
> as capital and the net rents and profits thereof until sale upon trust
> for themselves as joint tenants."

The break-up of the partnership and the service of the notice of
March 30, 1973, led to the first dispute which has brought these two
doctors to court. It was a dispute as to whether the option was
exercisable against the defendant on the true construction of clause 22,
in the events which had happened. The defendant said it was not.
But on November 6, 1973, Blackett-Ord V.-C. decided against him and
held that the option was exercisable, and that decision was affirmed by
this court on June 4, 1974, with one variation to which I shall refer
later.

The defendant's attitude to this purported exercise of the option is
relevant to the present dispute which divides the parties and which came
before Blackett-Ord V.-C. much later. So I must go into the history
of the matter between March 30, 1973, and the present dispute in 1977.

The plaintiff's solicitors naturally wished to go ahead with the exercise
of the option, the valuation of the property and so on. But the defendant
refused from the start and, as the judge rightly found, showed a marked
lack of enthusiasm in carrying out the order of the court after it was
made; indeed it is not too much to say that he obstructed it at every
turn. On May 3, 1973, his solicitors wrote to the plaintiff's solicitors
as follows:

> "With regard to the house and surgery at Novar Kippax as your
> client is aware our client has spent considerable sums of money in
> renovating and making the property suitable for his own and his

A families [sic] personal occupation and it is felt that your client has terminated the partnership to enable him to endeavour to get hold of this property."

That shows his attitude before the matter was taken to court and in that attitude he persisted. On May 24 his solicitors wrote:

B "Our client is not bound by the option conferred by clause 22 as he has not ceased to be a partner under any of the provisions of the agreement. As we have considered the notice you have given is an effective notice under clause 18 of the partnership deed."

On May 30 the defendant's solicitors wrote to the plaintiff's solicitors:

C "With regard to the house 'Novar' the question of negotiations for the sale of this property to your client does not arise as our client has not given notice of retirement. We contend that as your client has exercised his right to resign your client is not entitled to invoke clause 22 of the partnership deeds [sic].

  "We observe that you intend writing to Messrs. Hartley & Worstenholme asking them to appoint a valuer to fix a fair market price. As Messrs. Hartley & Worstenholme prepared the partner-
D ship deed no doubt they will consider the notice served by your client prior to appointing a valuer on your behalf."

The next month the plaintiff's solicitors tried to get hold of the title deeds of the property and they wrote on June 15:

  "We have, as promised, asked Messrs. Hartley & Worstenholme
E to appoint a valuer and they have today written us and we enclose a copy of their letter for your information. We are today writing Mr. Dickinson and hope to receive a copy of his valuation shortly. Perhaps in the meantime you could be obtaining your client's title deeds in order to deliver a full abstract of title to us so that we may draft the conveyance."

F It was in consequence of that letter that the defendant's solicitors wrote two letters on June 18. In the first they referred the plaintiff's solicitors to their own letter of May 30, which I have read, as having "set out our views quite clearly and in view of this cannot understand your further action in the matter." On the same day they also wrote to Mr. Dickinson saying:

G "We understand from A. Maurice Smith & Co. that they have written to ask you to make a valuation of the above property. We act for Dr. Choudhury the owner of the property and he has no intention of selling to A. Maurice Smith's client."

On July 13 the plaintiff's solicitors, presumably because they had had brought to their attention, or remembered, that Mrs. Choudhury was a
H party to the contract and to the conveyance, wrote to her: "Re: 'Novar' 37 Butt Hill, Kippax, Yorkshire," they said they were acting for the plaintiff and they drew her attention to clause 22. They enclosed a copy of the notice of March 30, 1973, and said:

  "Please take notice that it is Dr. Malhotra's intention to exercise this option in conformity with the terms set out in the said clause 22. As we understand that 'Novar' is held in the joint names of Dr. Choudhury and yourself we are sending you this letter on behalf

of our client Dr. Malhotra so that you may be fully appraised of A
the position and take note thereof."

They were, of course, not the solicitors who had been acting for the
parties in the making of the contract and the executing of the conveyance.
To that letter the plaintiff's solicitors received no reply. Two months
later, on September 13, 1973, they wrote to the defendant's solicitors
again: B

"We and our client are even more disturbed by the recent circular
that your client has been distributing to the patients on his panel
in the Kippax and Swillington areas. The circular appears to us
to be gravely misleading as to Dr. Malhotra's plans and seems to us
to prejudice the outcome of the legal action for possession of
'Novar' which will presumably commence at the very beginning C
of October next.

"Our position at the present time is as follows: — (a) There
is a legally enforceable option to purchase 'Novar' embodied in
the partnership deed which is binding upon your client. The option
has been registered against your client and his wife at H.M. Land
Charges Registry. Our client has given due notice in the dissolution
of the partnership of his intention to exercise such option on the D
1st October next. Accordingly there is a legally binding contract
of sale of 'Novar' between your client and ours. (b) As from the
1st October we have precise instructions to proceed to acquire
'Novar' if necessary by an action for specific performance in the
Chancery Division of the High Court as early in October as the
legal process will allow. (c) We cannot tolerate the position set E
out in your client's circular which in our opinion clearly prejudices
the subject matter of the option."

The circular was in these terms, apparently circulated in the
preceding month, August, while the plaintiff's solicitors were waiting
for a reply from Mrs. Choudhury: F

"The above members of your family are my patients and I am
writing to advise you that as from September 30, 1973, the partnership of Malhotra and Choudhury will cease and I will continue to
practise alone from the surgery at my home 37 Butt Hill, Kippax
and also from Swillington at the Hill Crest Close, daily. . . ."

On September 18, the defendant's solicitors replied to that letter of G
complaint with a warning:

"With regard to the third paragraph of your letter, in our opinion,
our client has no legal obligation in respect of the house and the
option contained in the partnership deed will not become operative."

The letter goes on:

"With regard to the points raised we reply as follows: — (a) We H
do not agree that there is a legally binding contract for the sale of
'Novar.' (b) As stated above you must take such action as you
feel is necessary. (c) Our client's circular was quite clear to the
effect that he was to continue in practice as there appear to be
rumours circulating that he was retiring from the practice."

That defence, if it can be so called, led to the writ in the action

A which is the subject of the order under appeal. On September 21, 1973, the plaintiff issued his writ against the defendant, claiming:

"1. A declaration that the affairs of a medical partnership between the plaintiff and the defendant constituted by a deed of partnership dated May 19, 1972, between the plaintiff of the one part and the defendant of the other part may be wound up; 2. For the purposes
B aforesaid all necessary accounts and inquiries to be taken and made; 3. A receiver. 4. An injunction to restrain the defendant from denying the plaintiff the use and access to the partnership surgery at the house known as 'Novar,' 37 Butt Hill Kippax in the County of York until the affairs of the said partnership shall have been fully wound up; 5. Specific performance of an agreement whereby the defendant agreed to sell and the plaintiff agreed to purchase the
C said house 'Novar.' 6. For the purposes aforesaid all necessary orders and directions. 7. Costs. 8. Such further or other relief as to the court may seem fit."

Contemporaneous with that writ, the plaintiff issued a notice of motion on September 21, moving the court for an order that Dr. Mathieson:
D

"or some other fit and proper person may be appointed to collect get in and receive the debts now due and owing and other assets property or effects belonging to the partnership of medical practice carried on between the plaintiff and defendant in Swillington and in Kippax in the County of York. (2) An injunction to restrain the defendant by himself servants agents or otherwise from pre-
E venting the plaintiff from having access to or the use of the surgery at 'Novar' . . ."

In support of that notice of motion was filed the first of the plaintiff's affidavits [His Lordship read the affidavits and continued:] It will be clear from what I have read from the correspondence, the pleadings,
F and the evidence, that in none of them is there on the defendant's side a mention of the wife's position, except in the sub-paragraph of the affidavit which I have just read, a statement that Novar is the home of his wife and himself vested in them both. He is saying that it is the plaintiff and not he who has repudiated the partnership. He admits refusing to sell and refusing to allow the plaintiff to use the surgery: but his defence to the claims in the action, including the claim for specific
G performance of the option, is based on his construction of clause 22 and his view that he was not legally bound to offer Novar to the plaintiff for sale at all. His wife has only been brought into the matter at all by a letter written to her by the plaintiff's solicitors, a letter which, as I have pointed out, she did not answer and nobody answered on her behalf.

H As I have said the defendant's view of his legal obligation, namely, that it did not exist, was rejected by Blackett-Ord V.-C. and the Court of Appeal agreed. The Vice-Chancellor had ordered, on October 28, 1973 (his order was perfected on November 6) first that the defendant should give Mr. Dickinson, the valuer, access to the property for the purpose of valuing it, then an inquiry whether a good title could be made to the said property, then that the defendant deliver to the plaintiff all the deeds in writing and give to the plaintiff vacant possession;

and he continued the defendant's undertaking to allow the plaintiff to use A
the surgery. The order directed that the agreement dated May 19, 1972,
ought to be specifically performed and carried into execution.

When the matter came before the Court of Appeal in 1974, it was
appreciated that although the case was one in which, in the ordinary way,
specific performance would be ordered, there was a bar to specific
performance being in fact ordered, namely, the possibility that the
defendant's joint tenant of the property might resist any order for sale B
and might refuse to concur in any conveyance of Novar to the plaintiff.
So that part of Blackett-Ord V.-C.'s order was struck out and the court
declared that the option contained in clause 22 of the deed of partnership dated May 15, 1972, had been validly exercised by the plaintiff.
Otherwise the order and directions which the Vice-Chancellor had given
were affirmed and repeated by the Court of Appeal.   C

Naturally the first thing the plaintiff's solicitors did after the decision
of the Court of Appeal was to ask the defendant's solicitors for an
abstract of title and for inspection of the property by Mr. Dickinson,
the valuer. They did that by a letter dated June 5, 1974. To that they
got no reply. This is the beginning of the period in which Blackett-Ord
V.-C. noted the defendant's lack of enthusiasm to carry out the terms D
of the Court of Appeal's order.

So the plaintiff's solicitors wrote again on July 16. They said:

"Our client is hoping to take an annual fortnight's holiday away
from the practice in early August next. Would you please confirm
that you agree with us that the mutual undertakings given by our
respective clients to the court will enable Dr. Malhotra to have his E
new junior partner, Dr. Smith, practice in Dr. Malhotra's place as
normal at the Kippax surgery."

They pointed out that, if the defendant did not agree to that, they would
have to go back to the court for fresh directions to cover not merely Dr.
Malhotra's use of the surgery on the defendant's undertaking, but that
of his locum tenens as well.   F

On July 19 the defendant's solicitors replied to that letter in these
terms:

"Dr. Choudhury states that from an ethics point of view he has
no objection to Dr. Smith carrying on in Dr. Malhotra's absence
but has discussed this matter with his wife and his wife is quite
adamant that she is not prepared to allow Dr. Smith into the G
precincts of the property. She states she has been very patient in
this matter and has allowed Dr. Malhotra to continue practising
there even though relationships have been very very strained over
the past year. Mrs. Choudhury feels she must now insist on her
rights. We have discussed the matter with Dr. Choudhury and
he states that obviously his wife is quite adamant in her views on
this matter and she will not agree to Dr. Smith taking the surgery." H

That led the plaintiff's solicitors to take out a summons to proceed
under Order 44. They wanted the title deeds to the property, they
wanted access to the surgery for Dr. Smith, the locum tenens, and they
wanted inquiry as to the title and a valuation of the defendant's interest
which was obviously an undivided half share of the equitable beneficial
interest in the property.

A   The plaintiff's solicitors after taking out that summons wrote to the defendant's solicitors on October 11 asking for these things and complaining of needless delays and prevarications and on October 28 the defendant's solicitors replied:

"We have been unable to deal with the question of the abstract of title as we have not been able to obtain Mrs. Choudhury's authority
B   to forward this to you . . ."

and they indicated that it might be necessary for Mrs. Choudhury to be separately represented.

By the time that summons to proceed came on, Mrs. Choudhury had sworn an affidavit, on November 8, and that is of course a document of considerable importance. It was a short affidavit. Like many of the
C   documents copied in this case it is not easy to read. It simply said:

"1. I am the wife of the defendant herein. 2. I have read the affidavit sworn herein by my husband. I do refuse to agree or concur to any sale of the property to the plaintiff. 3. I object to the plaintiff or any locum tenens having any access to or use of the property most strongly as a disturbing influence on my home and
D   want it stopped."

The summons was supported by an affidavit of a Mr. Smith, exhibiting correspondence, some of which I have read, and the result was an order of January 3, 1975, made it is to be noted in this partner-ship action, 1973 M No. 54, that inquiry as to title may proceed, that for the purposes aforesaid such directions are made, namely (a) that the
E   defendant produce all deeds and documents of title, (b) that the defendant and his wife do attend for cross-examination on the adjourned hearing before the district registrar, (c) that inquiry be made as to the value of the defendant's interest in Novar and (d) that notice of the judgment and order be served on the defendant's wife. So there was an order in these proceedings that the defendant and his wife should attend for cross-examination and as the defendant's wife had sworn an affidavit in these
F   proceedings, there can be no doubt that there was power to order her to attend for cross-examination. But that order was never carried out: neither the defendant nor his wife, to say nothing of any other witness, was ever cross-examined on affidavit nor was any oral evidence ever given in this or any other litigation between the parties. [His Lordship read letters between the parties' solicitors concerned with an offer by the
G   plaintiff that the defendant either convey his undivided share in Novar to the plaintiff or that the plaintiff purchase the surgery in Novar; referred to a notice of motion which led to an order by consent on April 28, 1975, permitting the plaintiff's junior partner to use the surgery at Novar while the plaintiff was on holiday; the plaintiff's summons dated January 22, 1976, against both Dr. and Mrs. Choudhury,
H   seeking under sections 30 and 203 (5) of the Law of Property Act 1925 an order for the execution of the trust for sale and the immediate sale of Novar and, after reading affidavits filed in those proceedings and the action, 1973 M No. 54, his Lordship stated that the plaintiff had not pursued the section 30 proceedings and continued:]

On January 21, 1977, the plaintiff went back to move the court in his original action against the defendant Dr. Choudhury alone, and in this action asked for damages at common law for breach of the contract

constituted by the option. That is the plain effect of the notice of   A
motion. He asks:

> " the defendant may be ordered to pay to the plaintiff damages for
> breach of the contract constituted by the option secured by the
> plaintiff as the same is referred to in the order of this court made
> on November 6, 1973, as varied by the order of the Court of Appeal
> made on June 4, 1974. (2) for the purpose of ascertaining the   B
> measure of damages as aforesaid inquiries be made as the same are
> set out and directed in the schedule hereto."

Then he asks for costs. [His Lordship read the schedule to the
motion, an affidavit filed in support of the motion and an affidavit by
the defendant and continued:] The motion came on for hearing
before Blackett-Ord V.-C. on that material on February 7, February 21   C
and March 28; and on March 29, 1977, he gave his judgment and made
the order under appeal. His order declared:

> " the plaintiff is entitled to damages, such damages to be limited
> to the costs incurred investigating title of the property known as
> ' Novar ' and the costs (if any) in connection with attempts to value
> the said property in accordance with the order of the Court of   D
> Appeal dated June 4, 1974.
> "And it is directed that the district registrar do determine
> the amount of damages (if any) to be paid by the defendant to
> the plaintiff."

No order for costs was made except taxation of the defendant's costs
under the Legal Aid Act,   E

> "And it is ordered that the undertaking given by the defendant
> through his counsel on September 26, 1973, do continue until June
> 29, 1977, after which date the said undertaking be discharged."

That order was not satisfactory to the plaintiff because it limits the
amount of damages to those recoverable under what is known as the   F
rule in *Bain* v. *Fothergill* (1874) L.R. 7 H.L. 158 and deprives him, he
says, of the substantial damages to which, if the case does not come
within that rule, he would be entitled. The defendant seeks to support
the judgment of Blackett-Ord V.-C. on the ground set out in the
respondent's notice.

The judgment of Blackett-Ord V.-C. applied this exceptional and
anomalous rule. He set out the history of the matter in his judgment.   G
He pointed out that the defendant had refused to admit that the option
had been validly exercised, and not on the ground that his wife was
concerned. He pointed out that the defendant had been less than
enthusiastic in carrying out the order of the court made in 1973 and
affirmed in 1974. He read from the defendant's short affidavit of June
29, 1976, and he referred to Mrs. Choudhury's shorter affidavit simply   H
saying that she refused to sell and stated that that was sworn, like the
defendant's affidavit, in subsequent proceedings brought by the plaintiff
under section 30 of the Law of Property Act 1925. If by shorter he
means the shorter of her two affidavits and not shorter than her husband's
affidavit, he would appear to be in error because he would then be
referring to an affidavit which was sworn not in the proceedings under
section 30 but in the 1973 proceedings.

A   However that error does not seem to matter, because it is perfectly
plain that by consent of everybody the affidavits of the parties in both
sets of proceedings were treated as evidence in these proceedings.
Blackett-Ord V.-C. goes on to say, quite rightly, that the breach of the
contract to offer Novar to the plaintiff was not denied but the contest of
the present motion had been as to the measure of damages.   He then
gave a correct exposition, as one would expect, of the principle laid
B   down in *Bain* v. *Fothergill* and applied to this case:

> " that the damages recoverable by Dr. Malhotra are substantially
> limited to the costs he has been put to in connection with the
> contract and the investigation of the title, and he cannot claim
> general damages "

C   and he went on to cite the observations of Lord Chelmsford in *Bain* v.
Fothergill, where he said, at p. 207:

> " I think the rule as to the limits within which damages may be
> recovered upon the breach of a contract for the sale of real estate
> must be taken to be without exception.   If a person enters into a
> contract for the sale of a real estate knowing that he has no title
> to it, nor any means of acquiring it, the purchaser cannot recover
> D   damages beyond the expenses he has incurred by an action for the
> breach of the contract; he can only obtain other damages by an action
> for deceit."

He cites that passage of Lord Chelmsford's speech in which Lord
Chelmsford referred to the rule being without exception and invited,
as Blackett-Ord V.-C. put it, a party who seeks to get round and out of
E   the rule to obtain his damages by an action for deceit.   He points out
that that invitation is not one which has been taken up on this occasion,
and he goes on to say:

> " But the rule is an anomalous one and is not to be extended.   It
> is limited to defects of title, the original reason for it having been,
> it is said, the complications involved in showing title to land under
> F   English law.   There is many a slip, the vendor can enter into a
> contract and then the purchaser's researches into the title may
> show that unknown to himself the vendor cannot sell what he has
> contracted to sell.   So the rule is limited to defect of title and it
> does not excuse a vendor from doing his best to show title."

He then distinguished the decision of Megarry J. in *Wroth* v. *Tyler*
G   [1974] Ch. 30 because of the different chronological order of the contract
broken and the contract to convey in the two cases, and proceeded:

> " Now as regards the second point that I mentioned, the duty of the
> vendor to use his best endeavours to carry out his contractual
> obligations, Dr. Choudhury says on oath that his wife refuses to
> consent and Mrs. Choudhury says the same.   They have not been
> H   cross-examined on their affidavits and I must, I think, accept that
> Mrs. Choudhury will not consent whatever within reason Dr.
> Choudhury may do to try to compel her to.   There is no suggestion
> anywhere in the evidence that Dr. Choudhury has tried to persuade
> his wife not to consent and the case is therefore different from *Day*
> v. *Singleton* [1899] 2 Ch. 320 where the property for sale was
> leasehold, the consent of the lessors to the assignment was required
> and the vendor induced the lessors to withhold their consent.   So

although, as I have said, Dr. Choudhury has not shown any enthu- A
siasm for accepting the judgment of the court, the position in my
judgment on the evidence is that he cannot show title and prima
facie therefore the damages for which he is liable are limited by
the rule in *Bain* v. *Fothergill.*"

Having distinguished *Day* v. *Singleton* in that way, Blackett-Ord V.-C.
then went on to consider an allegation of representation and held that   B
there had been no representation by the defendant that he had or could
make a good title.   He said of the solicitor acting for both partners:

" his left hand did not know what his right hand was doing on
what it seems are the facts as they have come out, but I acquit
Dr. Choudhury of any intention at any time of seeking to defeat
the option in the partnership deed by the ingenious expedient of   C
vesting half the property in his wife, and the option itself cannot
I think be treated as a representation, otherwise every contract would
imply a representation and every vendor would be warranting his
title."

So he distinguished the decision of Graham J. in *Watts* v. *Spence* [1976]
Ch. 165.   D

Then he went on to deal with the equitable interest of the defendant
in this property and held that he was not entitled on an authority cited
in *Watts* v. *Spence* and followed by Graham J. in that case, to grant
part specific performance.   So he held that the rule in *Bain* v. *Fothergill*
applied.   Hence this appeal.

Mr. Caswell for the plaintiff has abandoned his appeal against the   E
finding of Blackett-Ord V.-C. that there was no misrepresentation.   On
the evidence such a finding seems to have been plainly right and I say
no more about it.   Nor do I find it necessary, on the view I take of
this case, to consider whether the Vice-Chancellor was right in rejecting
part specific performance.   Nor again do I consider the other interesting
submissions which Mr. Caswell has put before us.   I have to consider
whether this rule, laid down in *Flureau* v. *Thornhill* (1776) 2 Wm.Bl.   F
1078 in 1775—that is when Lord Chelmsford said it was laid down—and
affirmed by the House of Lords in 1874 in *Bain* v. *Fothergill*, L.R. 7
H.L. 158, applies in 1977 to a case as different as possible from those
two cases.

It follows from the excerpts which I have read from the judgment
of Blackett-Ord V.-C., that this is not a case where the owner's difficulties   G
in discovering whether he had a perfectly good title could excuse him.
The defendant knew all along what his title was to Novar and that he
shared it with his wife.   Yet a fortnight after entering into a contract
binding his wife, he granted an option which he clearly knew could not
be enforced against him without her concurrence.   As I have tried to
point out, there is not a word in any of his affidavits to explain how he   H
came to do that.

Blackett-Ord V.-C. decided this case I think on the ground that, no
fraud being alleged or proved, he had to accept that the uncontradicted
evidence—as there had in fact been none of the ordered cross-examination
upon the affidavits of the defendant and his wife—went so far as to
prove that the defendant had tried to make good his title by asking his
wife to concur in selling but had failed or perhaps—but it is not clear

A which view the Vice-Chancellor held—that if he had tried, his wife would nonetheless have refused her concurrence.

This seems to me, with all respect to Blackett-Ord V.-C., to ignore first of all the duty of the vendor to which he refers, to use his best endeavours to carry out his contractual obligations, in this case by obtaining his wife's consent; and, secondly, the absence of any evidence that he did use those endeavours. Further it seems to me to ignore the

B inevitable inference from the evidence which was given, that the failure of the defendant to convey Novar to the plaintiff was due not to his inability to do so but to his unwillingness to do so by obtaining his wife's consent. I do not find it necessary to consider whether he should have gone as far as to convey his half share or to try to get his wife's consent to conveying the surgery alone, or whether he should have himself

C applied to the court under section 30 of the Law of Property Act 1925 to execute the trust for sale and enforce an immediate sale against the wishes of his co-tenant.

But I conclude from my study of the authorities to which we have been referred, that to come within this anomalous exception a vendor must prove his inability to carry out his contractual obligations. And if the evidence leaves the court in the position where the right inference is that

D inability is not proved, then, even where there is no allegation of the duty to use his best endeavours to carry out his contractual obligations and of a breach of that duty, as in this case, it is open to the court to hold that the ordinary principle of damages, putting a victim of a breach of contract in the position in which he would have been if the contract had been performed, applies to the exclusion of the anomalous exception

E created in *Flureau* v. *Thornhill*, 2 Wm. Bl. 1078 and *Bain* v. *Fothergill*, L.R. 7 H.L. 158.

I am not saying that this matter should not be pleaded or that there may not be cases in which, the duty and the breach of it not being pleaded, the court would be bound to reach the same conclusion as Blackett-Ord V.-C. reached in this case. What I do say is that in the

F circumstances of this case, the affidavits standing as pleadings and all the material that was before the Vice-Chancellor being taken into account, the fact that in a partnership action followed by a notice of motion as to damages there was no pleaded allegation to this effect does not prevent the court from considering whether the duty has been discharged.

If I am right, want of enthusiasm in carrying out the order of the

G Court of Appeal, if it extended to inhibiting the defendant from trying to obtain his wife's consent to something which obviously he himself would not lightly, wish to come about, would be passivity, not a wilful act but an omission, fatal to a claim to rely on the exceptional rule in *Bain* v. *Fothergill*, because what is required by the rule is proof of activity. Blackett-Ord V.-C. seems to me, if I may respectfully say so,

H first of all to have attached too much importance to the language of Lord Chelmsford in *Bain* v. *Fothergill*, L.R. 7 H.L. 158, 207, and too little to other matters which appear from the report of that case and in particular the speech of Lord Hatherley, at pp. 208 et seq., and also to have been misled by the headnote to the decision of this court in *Day* v. *Singleton* [1899] 2 Ch. 320.

It is quite true that in *Flureau* v. *Thornhill*, 2 Wm. Bl. 1078 the rule laid down by De Grey C.J. was:

"Upon a contract for a purchase, if the title proves bad, and the A vendor is (without fraud) incapable of making a good one, I do not think, that the purchaser can be entitled to any damages for the fancied goodness of the bargain, which he supposes he has lost."

Those words are referred to in the speech of Lord Chelmsford in *Bain* v. *Fothergill*, L.R. 7 H.L. 158, 201; the speech ends, at p. 208, with a reference to "any fraud or wilful act" on the part of vendors preventing B them from performing their contract.

But, as Mr. Caswell pointed out, the question which the judges were summoned by their Lordships to answer and which was proposed for their consideration was:

"Whether, upon a contract for the sale of real estate, where the vendor, *without his default,* is unable to make a good title, the C purchaser is by law entitled to recover damages for the loss of his bargain?" (See L.R. 7 H.L. 158, 170.)

That is the question (see p. 170) which was answered in the judgment of Pollock B., which was also the judgment of Kelly C.B., Keating and Brett JJ., as appears from pp. 170 and 176 of the report, and the question as it was stated by both Denman J., at p. 176 and Pigott B. at p. 193. D I note this is the way in which the rule is stated in *Williams, The Contract of Sale of Land* (1930), p. 128 cited by Megarry J. in *Wroth* v. *Tyler* [1974] Ch. 30, 53:

"Where the breach of contract is occasioned by the vendor's inability, *without his own fault,* to show a good title, the purchaser is entitled to recover as damages his deposit, if any, with interest, E and his expenses incurred in connection with the agreement, but not more than nominal damages for the loss of his bargain."

It is not necessary to decide how far the words "without his own fault" go, if I am right in thinking that inability without default is what one has to consider as attracting the rule in *Bain* v. *Fothergill.*

There may be cases in which there has been no lack of bona fides, F yet the rule in *Bain* v. *Fothergill* has been excluded. I would not, however, venture to suggest that anything less than lack of good faith could exclude the rule. But it seems from later decisions that fraud, in the full sense of that word such as would found an action for deceit, may not be necessary to exclude the rule. No doubt Blackett-Ord V.-C. had in mind that fraud must be strictly alleged and proved in all ordinary circumstances. But in my judgment, unwillingness to use best endea- G vours to carry out a contractual promise is bad faith and for there to be bad faith which takes the case out of this exceptional rule, it is not necessary that there should be either a deliberate attempt to prevent title being made good or anything more than the unwillingness which I find it inevitable to infer in this case. If a man makes a promise and does not use his best endeavours to keep it, it cannot take much and, in my judg- H ment, may not need more to make him guilty of bad faith and to entitle the victim of his bad faith to his full share of damages to compensate him for what he has lost by reason of that breach of contract and bad faith.

Apart from the nature of the question which was proposed to the judges in *Bain* v. *Fothergill,* L.R. 7 H.L. 158 I would also call attention to the speech of Lord Hatherley, at p. 209, in which he said, after refer-

A ring to *Engel* v. *Fitch* (1868) L.R. 3 Q.B. 314; (1869) L.R. 4 Q.B. 659
to which we were also referred:

"The vendor in that case was bound by his contract, as every
vendor is bound by his contract, to do all that he could to
complete the conveyance.   Whenever it is a matter of conveyancing,
and not a matter of title, it is the duty of the vendor to do everything
B that he is enabled to do by force of his own interest, and also by
force of the interest of others whom he can compel to concur in
the conveyance."

I confess that I have not found it easy—perhaps as a common
lawyer I may be forgiven—to define or apply a distinction between
matters of title and matters of conveyance which comes easily to minds
C better versed in equity; but I venture to think that, whether the defect
is a real defect of title or a mere matter of conveyance, a vendor is
equally bound to use his best efforts either to cure the defect in title or
to remedy the matter of the impediment which is a matter of conveyance.
I hope I may be forgiven also for referring in that connection to a case
which was not cited to us: *Keen* v. *Mear* [1920] 2 Ch. 574, 581, where
Russell J. seems to have treated it as plain law that one of two co-owners
D must have been acting perfectly bona fide in selling property, which
belonged to him and the co-owner, to another without the consent of
the co-owner and must satisfy the court not only of his perfect good
faith but also that he has done his best to get his co-owner's consent to
the sale to which he has without his authority agreed for his case to fall
within the rule in *Flureau* v. *Thornhill* and *Bain* v. *Fothergill*.

E But as it seems to me, if I am right in this, the authority of this
court which Mr. Caswell relied on is really conclusive of this case.   I
refer to *Day* v. *Singleton* [1899] 2 Ch. 320.   The headnote is in these
terms:

"A purchaser of leasehold property, which the vendor cannot assign
without a licence from his lessor is entitled to damages (beyond
F return of the deposit, with interest and expenses) for loss of his
bargain by reason of the vendor's omission to do his best to procure such licence.

"A vendor agreed with a purchaser for the sale of a leasehold
hotel, subject to the consent of the lessor being obtained to the
assignment of the lease, and the purchaser paid a deposit on his
G purchase-money.   The vendor died without having completed his
contract, and the purchaser then brought an action against his legal
personal representative for specific performance.   The defendant,
being desirous of freeing the vendor's estate from the action, induced
the lessor to refuse his consent to the assignment, which the lessor
accordingly did, and the purchaser thus lost his bargain.   Thereupon
the purchaser amended his action by claiming damages and return
H of the deposit:—

"*Held*, that the plaintiff was entitled, not only to the return of
his deposit, with interest and costs of investigating title, but also
to the damages he had sustained by the loss of his bargain through
the omission of the defendant to obtain the lessor's consent."

That case turned on a letter written by the solicitors for the vendor's
personal representative, of which Romer J. the trial judge, had taken

what Sir Nathaniel Lindley M.R., giving the judgment of himself and   A
Rigby L.J. in the Court of Appeal, described as a very charitable view.
Romer J. had thought that the letter was not an inducement to the
lessors to withhold their consent to the assignment to the plaintiff Day.

In the Court of Appeal [1899] 2 Ch. 320 Sir Francis Jeune took
the view that the letter was an inducement, and that view is embodied
in the headnote which I have just read and which I respectfully suggest   B
may have misled Blackett-Ord V.-C. But a reading of the majority
judgment of Sir Nathaniel Lindley M.R. indicates, I think, that the
headnote does not accurately represent the decision of the Court of
Appeal, because as I understand that majority judgment, it was a decision
that even on the charitable view which Romer J. took of the letter,
Bain v. *Fothergill* did not apply.

It is plain from the bottom of p. 322 of the report that there was in   C
that case (unlike this) an amendment to allege that Singleton, the
personal representative of Dunn the vendor:

"instead of doing his best to obtain the consent of the lessors to
the assignment to him, the plaintiff, and in breach of his duty
towards him, the plaintiff, endeavoured to induce and did induce
the lessors to refuse to consent to an assignment to him, the   D
plaintiff."

But in giving the majority judgment, Sir Nathaniel Lindley M.R. said,
at p. 327:

"The question raised by this appeal is whether a purchaser of
leasehold property which the vendor cannot assign without a licence
from his lessor is entitled to damages (beyond the return of the   E
deposit with interest, and expenses) by reason of the vendor's
omission to do his best to procure such licence."

That was the question. It is *not* stated to be whether the purchaser
was entitled to those damages by reason of the vendor's inducing the
lessor not to give his consent to give the licence. He stated: F

"It was Singleton's business, as Dunn's representative, to obtain
that consent if he could," and that "Singleton never asked the
lessors to accept Day as their tenant without a bar, and consequently
it would be for him, Singleton, to show that if he had asked them
they would have refused."

Sir Nathaniel Lindley M.R., at p. 328 also pointed out that the first   G
question submitted to the judges in *Bain* v. *Fothergill*, as I have said,
used the words "without his default, is unable to make a good title,"
and added, at p. 329:

"Lord Chelmsford's speech is addressed to that question; and his
observations on fraud are part of his comment on *Hopkins* v. *Grazebrook* (1826) 6 B. & C. 31, which had decided that the exceptional   H
rule laid down in *Flureau* v. *Thornhill,* 2 Wm. Bl. 1078 did not
apply where the vendor knew that he had not a good title, although
he believed he could get one, and had in fact an equitable title.
Neither Lord Chelmsford's speech nor Lord Hatherley's is an
authority for the application of that exceptional rule to the case
of a vendor who can make good title but will not, or will not do
what he can do and ought to do in order to obtain one. Such a

A   case is, however, covered by *Engel* v. *Fitch*, L.R. 3 Q.B. 314; L.R. 4 Q.B. 659, which was to a certain extent based on *Hopkins* v. *Grazebrook*, and was much commented on in, but not overruled by, *Bain* v. *Fothergill*."

Now I need not refer further to Sir Francis Jeune's judgment in *Day* v. *Singleton* [1899] 2 Ch. 320, which, as I have said, appears
B responsible for the form of the headnote, except to say that he did agree, as I read his judgment, with the statement of the duty contained in the judgment of Sir Nathaniel Lindley M.R. and he agreed that *Bain* v. *Fothergill* did not conflict with this view of the duty of the vendor. He stated, at pp. 332–333:

    " it is the duty of a vendor to make a good title for his purchaser
C   if he can, and certainly not to do anything to impair or spoil such title."

That decision of this court is, of course, binding on us both as a decision and in what it says that *Bain* v. *Fothergill* did or did not decide. It was followed by a Divisional Court in *Braybrooks* v. *Whaley* [1919] 1 K.B. 435, where the facts were very different, but I think it is relevant
D to read what Salter J. said. That was a case in which the mortgagor in possession called attention to the fact that the mortgagee seeking to convey the premises to another had not taken the statutory steps required by the Courts (Emergency Powers) Act 1914 to eject him, and in following the decision in *Day* v. *Singleton*, Salter J. giving the second judgment of the court said, at p. 441:

E   "With regard to the suggestion that the application" for leave under the Act "would have failed on the merits I think that where it is alleged that damage has been caused to a person by reason of the wrongful omission of another to take some step which it was his duty to take, the onus rests upon the person in default, if he alleges that the step must have failed, to prove it. That, I think, is supported by the observations of Lindley M.R. in *Day* v. *Singleton*
F   [1899] 2 Ch. 320, 328, where he said: ' Singleton never asked the lessors to accept Day as their tenant without a bar, and consequently it would be for him, Singleton, to show that if he had asked them they would have refused.' "

In my judgment those authorities show that it is for the vendor seeking to excuse his admitted breach of contract to show that it was
G inability and not unwillingness that has prevented him from carrying out his contract if he wishes to limit the purchaser's damages to those obtainable under *Bain* v. *Fothergill*: compare the observations of Cockburn C.J. in *Engel* v. *Fitch*, L.R. 3 Q.B. 314, 333.

If that is right, what is the effect of the evidence, the uncontradicted evidence, of the defendant and his wife in this case? Accepting all his
H and her denials, rejecting in so far as they conflict with these denials the evidence of the plaintiff and Dr. Mathieson, where is there any evidence that the defendant tried to persuade his wife to consent to conveying Novar to the plaintiff? The striking thing is that the defendant never says so. In one letter his solicitors say that he discussed with his wife admitting Dr. Smith to the surgery but that she was adamant, and in another that she was preventing Mr. Dickinson from entering and was adamant in refusing to convey. But nowhere is there

on affidavit any statement to assert that the defendant tried to obtain   A
his wife's consent to sell Novar.   There is simply his statement and her
statement that she refused to give it, which might mean that she refused
the request from her husband or might simply mean that she refused the
request from the plaintiff or his solicitors.

I would go on to add that it may well be that the reason why he
never swears in any affidavit that he did ask his wife to consent is the
excellent reason that, if he had sworn so, it would have been perjury   B
because in fact he never did ask her.   His inclination, as Mr. Caswell
has pointed out, is obviously in line with his denial so long maintained,
that he was under any legal liability to honour this option, namely, to
agree with her that they should remain with their children in the home
which they had got so cheap and on which they had spent so much in
improvements together with this convenient surgery.   There is, on the   C
authorities, a plain duty, in my judgment, to try for consent in a case
like this, whether it is a matter of conveyancing or a defect of title which
you seek to remove.   There is evidence that the wife refused, from
which, in other circumstances, a request by the defendant might be
assumed.   But on the evidence in this case and on consideration of the
matters to which I have referred, it would be impossible to presume such   D
a request, still less any persistent or persuasive requests.   So prima facie
there is a failure by him in his duty to the plaintiff and he was in
default.   It is his unwillingness and not his inability which caused the
failure to convey and the plaintiff is entitled to the damages caused by
that failure, even though in the circumstances of this case that is not
a matter of any positive pleading or allegation.

There is no evidence in this case that the defendant was mistakenly   E
expecting his wife to sign when he signed the partnership deed, including
clause 22.   Blackett-Ord V.-C., in my judgment, had to be satisfied on
the evidence that the defendant did act in good faith and did his best
to induce his wife to concur in the sale of Novar to the plaintiff.   In
my judgment, it would be wrong to be so satisfied and to apply *Bain* v.
Fothergill.   F

I accordingly regard the plaintiff as entitled to substantial damages.
I understand that Cumming-Bruce L.J. agrees with me.   I agree with
what he is going to say, both as to how those damages should be
measured and how the registrar should be directed to assess them.
We are much obliged to counsel for the assistance they have given us.
I would allow the appeal.   G

CUMMING-BRUCE L.J.   I agree with all that has fallen from Stephenson
L.J.   In particular it appears to me that Blackett-Ord V.-C. manifestly
was misled by the headnote to *Day* v. *Singleton* [1899] 2 Ch. 320 when
one considers the terms of his judgment, where he relies upon the fact
that Mrs. Choudhury will not consent, whatever Dr. Choudhury may do
to try and compel her.   There is no suggestion anywhere in the evidence   H
that Dr. Choudhury had tried to persuade his wife not to consent.   So
the case is different from *Day* v. *Singleton.*   That ratio of the Vice-
Chancellor is not consistent with the ratio of Sir Nathaniel Lindley M.R.
and Rigby L.J. in *Day* v. *Singleton.*   Indeed a scrutiny of the observations of Sir Nathaniel Lindley at p. 329 shows that it was present to
the minds of the majority that their decision had the effect that the
measure of damages was going to vary according to whether the

A   defendant had tried and failed as compared to whether the third party
had been resolutely recalcitrant without any attempt to change his mind.
For the reasons stated by Stephenson L.J., it is quite clear that on the
ratio of *Day* v. *Singleton* the vendor who seeks to avail himself of the
protection afforded by what is described as the rule in *Bain* v. *Fothergill*,
L.R. 7 H.L. 158 must go to the length of satisfying the court that he
has done all that he reasonably can to mitigate the effects of his breach
B   of contract by trying to remove such fault on the title as appears.

I turn to damages. The plaintiff is entitled to such damages as are
properly to be assessed without the restriction placed by the application
of the *Bain* v. *Fothergill* rule. Though at one stage Mr. Behrens was
presenting submissions covering a wider field in relation to damages,
the issues between the parties are now accepted on both sides to be the
C   following: (1) Are the damages awarded in substitution for a decree of
specific performance to be assessed by reference to the value of the
house at the date of the declaration and order of the Court of Appeal on
June 4, 1974, or by reference to its value at the date of judgment of
this court on October 21, 1977? (2) Are the damages to include such
loss in the plaintiff's medical practice as the plaintiff may prove to flow
D   in the past or in the future from the failure of the defendant to deliver
up the house and surgery? (3) Is the assessment of damages to be
reduced by reason of the failure of the plaintiff to mitigate his damage,
in particular by reason of the plaintiff's delay in the conduct of his legal
proceedings during a period when the price of real property was rising
such that the plaintiff increased the damages by his own delay?

E   Mr. Caswell submits that, when the court holds that where on the
facts the contractual right of the plaintiff is such that specific performance
may be ordered, if having regard to equitable principles it is appropriate
to do so, but damages are awarded in substitution for specific performance, the value of the res will be assessed at date of judgment, and the
plaintiff is entitled to the difference between the value at the date of
contract— in this case by concession advanced to June 1974—and date
F   of judgment. He relies on the decision of Megarry J. in *Wroth* v. *Tyler*
[1974] Ch. 30 and of Goff J. in *Grant* v. *Dawkins* [1973] 1 W.L.R. 1406.

Mr Behrens seeks to distinguish *Wroth* v. *Tyler* on the facts and
further submits that the decision was wrong and should not be followed.
Though there are many differences between the facts in *Wroth* v. *Tyler*
and the instant case, there is, in my view, no distinction relevant to the
G   problem common to this case and *Wroth* v. *Tyler,* that is, are damages
awarded in substitution for an order of specific performance to be
assessed at date of breach of contract or at the date of judgment?

There is no authority binding on this court directly on the point.
It is therefore necessary to consider the question in the light of general
principles, having regard to the words of section 2 of the Chancery
Amendment Act 1858, the substance of which remains in force in
H   spite of repeal of parts of that Act by the Statute Law Revision Act
1898: see *Leeds Industrial Co-operative Society Ltd.* v. *Slack* [1924]
A.C. 851.

Mr. Behrens submits that if the approach of Blackett-Ord V.-C. is
right, it will produce the anomaly that damages in substitution for an
order for specific performance could be, and in a period of rising price
level will be, higher than damages at common law. He submits that at

common law the underlying principle has always been to restore the   A
injured party to the position he would have been in had the contract been
performed, but that the courts have evolved rules which are now binding
and which determine the way in which the general principle of restitutio
in integrum should be applied.   One such rule is that damages fall to be
assessed at date of breach and that rule applies even though by the date
of judgment changes in price levels may have rendered such assessment   B
no guide to the plaintiff's true loss.

So when the court comes to the task of assessing damages in substitution for an order of specific performance, a court of equity, he
submits, should follow the law and address itself to finding the proper
substitute, having regard to those rules which the common law has
evolved in order to restore the plaintiff to the position in which he would
have been had the contract not been broken.   Mr. Behrens distinguishes   C
the decision in *Leeds Industrial Co-operative Society Ltd.* v. *Slack* on the
ground that that was a case for damages in substitution for a quia timet
injunction and so damages were awarded once for all to compensate for
the future loss.

I cannot accept that these criticisms are valid.   I would be content
to adopt with respect the reasoning and conclusions of Megarry J. in   D
Wroth v. *Tyler* [1974] Ch. 30.   The equitable remedy of specific performance has features markedly different from damages at common law
for breach of contract.   But there is an analogy at common law to the
equitable remedy of specific performance.   This is to be found in the
action in detinue.   The remedies in that action available are well
summarised in the note in *The Supreme Court Practice* (1976), to R.S.C.,
Ord. 13, r. 3 and are explained by Diplock L.J. in *General and Finance*   E
Facilities Ltd. v. *Cooks Cars (Romford) Ltd.* [1963] 1 W.L.R. 644, 648,
649.

As Diplock L.J. explained, the action in detinue partakes of the
nature of an action in rem in which the plaintiff seeks specific restitution
of his chattel.   In this action where an order for a writ of specific
delivery can be made, the plaintiff has always been entitled instead to   F
claim its value in money assessed at date of judgment.

That distinguishes the remedy of damages in detinue from damages
for conversion and the dictum to the contrary in the judgment of Lord
Goddard C.J. in *Sachs* v. *Miklos* [1948] 2 K.B. 23, 38 is unnecessary,
is too wide, and is based on the headnote in *Rosenthal* v. *Alderton &*
Sons Ltd. [1946] K.B. 374, which is not in accordance with the last   G
paragraph of the judgment in that case.

Thus where the common law is concerned with the remedy of
specific restitution of a chattel, it does seek to restore the plaintiff as
completely as money can to the position he would have been in if he
had the chattel delivered up on the date of judgment.   To this end the
value of the chattel is assessed at the date of the judgment and not at
the date of breach.   H

So I am satisfied that equity is following the law if in relation to an
award of damages in substitution for an order for specific performance
of a contract of sale of real property, it awards damages assessing the
value of the realty at date of judgment and not at the date of breach.
Had Blackett-Ord V.-C. been referred to the cases of the common law
remedy of specific restitution in detinue, he would not have had to

A contrast obedience to section 2 of Lord Cairns' Act with the principle that equity follows the law.

The plaintiff seeks as an element in his damages in substitution for specific performance, compensation for the loss sustained to his medical practice by reason of the breach of contract in failing to sell him the house with the surgery. Mr. Behrens submits that that damage is too remote. He submits that, on a proper construction of the option clause,

B the parties did not contemplate such a type of loss flowing from a failure to sell the house. He points to clause 3 of the partnership deed whereby each party covenanted to provide and maintain himself in a dwelling house suitable for his share of the practice and to pay the whole costs thereof, including surgeries and consulting rooms and waiting rooms at such dwelling house. And in clause 20 of the partnership deed it

C is provided that if one partner ceases to be bound by the agreement, the party so ceasing to be bound shall not, for a period of three years from the date on which he so ceases, practise within a distance of five miles from any premises at which, at the time of such cesser the partnership practice is being carried on, but there is no reference to the particular premises specified in the option clause.

D By clause 22, which imposes the obligation upon the defendant to sell the house, it is provided that he will offer to sell such house, surgeries and grounds at a fair market price.

Accepting that no finding of fact should be made inconsistent with the evidence of the defendant in respect of any matter on which the defendant has given unchallenged evidence, there still remains the clear background accepted by both sides to the effect that when the defendant

E entered into the partnership deed and became a partner to the plaintiff, the plaintiff was at the time practising from the surgery at Novar, that from the time when the partnership came into existence the two partners practised from that surgery although they also practised from a health service clinic in another village. Further the option clause appears as one clause in a partnership agreement which is wholly concerned in

F setting out the terms by which the two partners shall carry on medical practice. The option clause dealing with the sale of Novar is one of the clauses which provides for the practice and opportunities of practice to each of the partners after cessation of the partnership or dissolution thereof.

In that context it appears to me that the parties must have con-

G templated that if the plaintiff decided to exercise his option, he would exercise his option with the intent to use the surgery for the purpose for which it had been built and for which it had been used from the date of the partnership deed.

Thus if and in so far as the plaintiff is able to prove, upon inquiry, that he has sustained loss in his professional practice, which has a sufficient nexus to the inability of the plaintiff to practise from the

H surgery at Novar, such loss is a proper ingredient of the damages and should be added to such figure as is arrived at by taking the value of the house at the date of judgment and assessing the difference between that value and the value on June 4, 1974, which by concession is accepted as the starting date.

It is perhaps unnecessary for me to emphasise that there is a distinction between loss of practice sustained by the plaintiff caused by

his inability to practice from the surgery at Novar and loss sustained A
by the plaintiff in his practice as a consequence of the competition of
the defendant. In so far as the plaintiff has sustained damage by
reason of the competition of the defendant, that is a matter which,
unless covered by restrictive covenant, is not an element for which the
plaintiff can claim. He is entitled to such loss as can reasonably be
inferred to have flowed from the fact that for such period as may be
proved he was unable to practise from Novar. I use the past tense. B
If the plaintiff could prove on the balance of probabilities that as a
result of being kept out of Novar in the future there was likely to be
a quantifiable diminution in his practice income, damages awarded in
substitution for specific performance would include such figure as
appeared right to capitalise that future loss. But again as the loss will
flow from the lack of use of the surgery, as compared to the competition C
of the defendant or other doctors, it is a matter of common sense that
every month that passes, assuming that the plaintiff is practising at
Kippax, it is likely that such goodwill, if that is the right phrase, as is
adherent to the Novar surgery, will progressively diminish as patients
gradually get used to following the plaintiff to whatever lair he may have
established for himself. We are told he has established himself in a lair D
25 yards from the defendant's premises.

So I come to the third issue in dispute which is the question of delay.
Counsel have agreed that they would prefer this court to determine
whether the plaintiff's delay in bringing these proceedings to a conclusion should be taken into account by way of reducing the damages to
which he is entitled on the ground that during the time the plaintiff has
been dragging his heels through the law courts, if he has been dragging E
them, the price level of real property has been steadily moving upwards;
and so if, for example, 12 months passed by, which could have been
avoided by greater exertion on the part of the plaintiff or his legal
advisers, the damages have been enhanced by that very delay.

I do not think at this juncture it is necessary for me—I certainly
would be very reluctant to do it—to begin a careful examination of F
every step in the proceedings stating the dates of every affidavit or
summons and exhibiting expressly the intervals of time that have passed
before the next step in the action. Suffice it to say, the plaintiff
undoubtedly was engulfed in tactical and legal problems of substantial
difficulty, as is evidenced by the fact that the unfortunate plaintiff is
now having the privilege of paying for a second appearance of his legal G
advisers in the Court of Appeal.

Nonetheless, when all is said and done, it is unfair to the defendant
that the deliberation with which the plaintiff moved from the middle
of 1975 until he issued the present proceedings in January 1977 should
be allowed to enhance the damage which the defendant has to pay the
plaintiff if the price level of real property has risen during that period.
For my part I would think that justice is done between them by holding H
that the plaintiff did not sufficiently mitigate his damage by proceeding
with greater celerity in the various and difficult legal convolutions that
he has been forced to undergo. The right order is that, for purposes of
valuation of Novar and the loss sustained by the plaintiff by the failure of
the defendant to honour the contract for sale, the terminal date by reason
of delay should be moved back from October 20, 1977, to October 21,

A 1976. Therefore the task of the assessment of damages is to arrive at the value on June 4, 1974, and the value on October 21, 1976, and to award the plaintiff as one of the items in his damages the difference between those two sums.

Appeal allowed.

Legal aid taxation of defendant's costs.

B *Plaintiff's costs to be taxed and paid out of legal aid funds, provided no objection by Law Society within 28 days; in case of objection, costs to be adjourned.*

C Solicitors: *Maurice Smith & Co., Castleford; Willey, Hargrave & Co., Leeds.*

D

[HOUSE OF LORDS]

SAIF ALI AND ANOTHER . . . . RESPONDENTS

AND

SIDNEY MITCHELL & CO. (A FIRM) AND OTHERS . APPELLANTS

E

1978 July 10, 11, 12;   Lord Wilberforce, Lord Diplock, Lord Salmon,
      Nov. 2   Lord Russell of Killowen and Lord Keith of Kinkel

Barrister—Negligence—Immunity from suit—Extent—Advice as to parties to litigation and pleadings—Whether action for negligence will lie at suit of client

F *Barrister—Duty to court—Nature of—Need for independence and immunity*

The plaintiff was injured in a motor accident in March 1966 when there was a collision between a van in which he was travelling as a passenger and a car driven by a wife and owned by her husband. The wife subsequently pleaded guilty to driving without due care and attention. In 1967 both the plaintiff and the driver of the van consulted the defendant solicitors regarding a claim in respect of the accident. In October 1968 the solicitors instructed a barrister, the third party, to settle proceedings on behalf of the plaintiff and the driver of the van in respect of the accident and to advise. The barrister settled a draft writ and statement of claim claiming damages against the husband on the basis that he was the owner of the car and his wife had been driving as his agent. The writ was issued in November 1968 and served in August 1969. Before the three-year limitation period expired in March 1969 the solicitors consulted the barrister about allegations by the husband's insurers that there was contributory negligence by the driver of the van and that the wife was not driving as her husband's agent. The barrister did not advise any change in the writ or the statement of claim. The husband's defence to the action of October 1969 alleged that the accident was caused wholly or in part by the van driver's negligence; an amended defence admitted the wife's agency

G

H

but that was denied by a re-amended defence. In April 1974 A
the plaintiff's action against the husband was discontinued.
Any claim by the plaintiff against the wife or the van driver
was by then time-barred.

In September 1974 the plaintiff issued a writ claiming
damages for professional negligence against the defendant
solicitors in their conduct of his claim in respect of the accident
of March 1966 in that they failed to advise him to take proceedings against either or both of the drivers concerned. In B
May 1975 the solicitors issued a third party notice against
the barrister claiming an indemnity from him. The district
registrar struck out the third party proceedings as disclosing no
reasonable cause of action. Kerr J. allowed the solicitors'
appeal.

On appeal, the Court of Appeal reversed that decision holding that the advice tendered fell within the ambit of the
immunity from an action for negligence granted to a barrister C
in respect of his conduct and management of a cause in court.

On appeal by the solicitors: —

Held, allowing the appeal (Lord Russell of Killowen and
Lord Keith of Kinkel dissenting), (1) that in principle those
who undertook to give skilled advice were under a duty to take
reasonable care and skill, and that a barrister's immunity
from suit for negligence in respect of his conduct of litigation
on the ground of public policy was an exception and applied D
only in the area to which it extended; that the immunity was
not confined to what was done in court but included some pre-
trial work but that the protection should not be given any wider
application than was absolutely necessary in the interests of the
administration of justice and each piece of pre-trial work had
to be tested against the one rule, namely, that the protection
existed only where the particular work was so intimately
connected with the conduct of the cause in court that it could E
fairly be said to be a preliminary decision affecting the way that
cause was to be conducted when it came to a hearing (post, pp.
856D—857A, 864F—865A, 871A–B, H—872A).

(2) That on the assumption that the factual basis of the
allegations of negligence was correct the acts complained of
did not come within the above rule, and that, accordingly,
there was no justification for striking out the third party claim
(post, pp. 853E, 857B–D, 865C–D, 867G–H, 872E–F). F

Dictum of McCarthy P. in *Rees* v. *Sinclair* [1974] 1
N.Z.L.R. 180, 187 applied.

Rondel v. *Worsley* [1969] 1 A.C. 191, H.L.(E.) considered.

Per Lord Wilberforce, Lord Diplock and Lord Salmon. The
same immunity attaches to a solicitor acting as an advocate in
court as attaches to a barrister (post, pp. 857A, 864E–F, 868B).

Per Lord Wilberforce and Lord Salmon. The rule of G
immunity is quite distinct from the question what defences
may be available to a barrister when he is sued. It by no
means follows that if an error takes place outside this immunity
area, a liability in negligence arises (post, pp. 857A–B, 871C–E).

Decision of the Court of Appeal [1978] Q.B. 95; [1977]
3 W.L.R. 421; [1977] 3 All E.R. 744 reversed.

The following cases are referred to in their Lordships' opinions: H

Anns v. *Merton London Borough Council* [1977] 2 W.L.R. 1024; [1977]
2 All E.R. 492, H.L.(E.).

Arenson v. *Arenson* [1977] A.C. 405; [1975] 3 W.L.R. 815; [1975] 3
All E.R. 901, H.L.(E.).

Cabassi v. *Vila* (1940) 64 C.L.R. 130.

Candler v. *Crane, Christmas & Co.* [1951] 2 K.B. 164; [1951] 1 All E.R.
426, C.A.

A   *Chambers* v. *Goldthorpe* [1901] 1 Q.B. 624, C.A.
Dorset Yacht Co. Ltd. v. *Home Office* [1970] A.C. 1004; [1970] 2 W.L.R.
    1140; [1970] 2 All E.R. 294, H.L.(E.).
Finnegan v. *Allen* [1943] K.B. 425; [1943] 1 All E.R. 493, C.A.
Hedley Byrne & Co. Ltd. v. *Heller & Partners Ltd.* [1964] A.C. 465;
    [1963] 3 W.L.R. 101; [1963] 2 All E.R. 575, H.L.(E.).
Herrington v. *British Railways Board* [1972] A.C. 877; [1972] 2 W.L.R.
    537; [1972] 1 All E.R. 749, H.L.(E.).
B   *Kennedy* v. *Broun* (1863) 13 C.B.N.S. 677.
Launchbury v. *Morgans* [1973] A.C. 127; [1972] 2 W.L.R. 1217; [1972]
    2 All E.R. 605, H.L.(E.).
Marrinan v. *Vibart* [1963] 1 Q.B. 234; [1962] 2 W.L.R. 1224; [1962] 1
    All E.R. 869; [1963] 1 Q.B. 528; [1962] 3 W.L.R. 912; [1962] 3 All
    E.R. 380, C.A.
C   *Practice Statement (Judicial Precedent)* [1966] 1 W.L.R. 1234; [1966]
    3 All E.R. 77, H.L.(E.).
Rees v. *Sinclair* [1973] 1 N.Z.L.R. 236; [1974] 1 N.Z.L.R. 180.
Rondel v. *Worsley* [1967] 1 Q.B. 443; [1966] 3 W.L.R. 950; [1966] 3
    All E.R. 657, C.A.; [1969] 1 A.C. 191; [1967] 3 W.L.R. 1666; [1967]
    3 All E.R. 993, H.L.(E.).
Sutcliffe v. *Thackrah* [1974] A.C. 727; [1974] 2 W.L.R. 295; [1974] 1
    All E.R. 859, H.L.(E.).
D   *Swinfen* v. *Lord Chelmsford* (1860) 5 H. & N. 890.
Tojo Maru, The [1972] A.C. 242; [1971] 2 W.L.R. 970; [1971] 1 All
    E.R. 1110, H.L.(E.).
Watson v. *M'Ewan* [1905] A.C. 480, H.L.(Sc.).

The following additional cases were cited in argument:

E   *Anderson (W. B.) & Sons Ltd.* v. *Rhodes (Liverpool) Ltd.* [1967] 2 All
    E.R. 850.
Attorney-General v. *Jonathan Cape Ltd.* [1976] Q.B. 752; [1975] 3
    W.L.R. 606; [1975] 3 All E.R. 484.
Biggar v. *McLeod* [1977] 1 N.Z.L.R. 321.
Esso Petroleum Co. Ltd. v. *Mardon* [1976] Q.B. 801; [1976] 2 W.L.R.
    583; [1976] 2 All E.R. 5, C.A.
F   *Hinds* v. *Sparks* [1964] Crim.L.R. 717.
Hollington v. *F. Hewthorn & Co. Ltd.* [1943] K.B. 587; [1943] 2 All
    E.R. 35, C.A.
Leslie v. *Ball* (1863) 22 U.C.R. 512.
Liversidge v. *Anderson* [1942] A.C. 206; [1941] 3 All E.R. 338, H.L.(E.).
Losner v. *Michael Cohen & Co.*, April 29, 1975; Court of Appeal (Civil
    Division) Transcript No. 179B of 1975, C.A.
G   *Majid* v. *Muthuswamy* [1968] 2 M.L.J. 89.
Midland Bank Trust Co. Ltd. v. *Hett, Stubbs & Kemp* [1978] 3 W.L.R.
    167; [1978] 3 All E.R. 571.
Miliangos v. *George Frank (Textiles) Ltd.* [1976] A.C. 443; [1975] 3
    W.L.R. 758; [1975] 3 All E.R. 801, H.L.(E.).
Miranda v. *Khoo Yew Boon* [1968] 1 M.L.J. 161.
Roy v. *Prior* [1971] A.C. 470; [1970] 3 W.L.R. 202; [1970] 2 All E.R.
    729, H.L.(E.).
H   *Scudder* v. *Prothero & Prothero*, The Times, March 16, 1966.
Sirros v. *Moore* [1975] Q.B. 118; [1974] 3 W.L.R. 459; [1974] 3 All
    E.R. 776, C.A.
Stokes v. *Trumper* (1855) 2 K. & J. 232.

APPEAL from the Court of Appeal.
This was an appeal by leave of the House of Lords from an order of
the Court of Appeal (Lord Denning M.R., Lawton and Bridge L.JJ.)

dated May 13, 1977, allowing an appeal by the respondent, a barrister, A
from an order of Kerr J. made on February 24, 1977, allowing an appeal
by the appellants' solicitors, in third party proceedings from an order
made on July 26, 1976, by Mr. District Registrar Barrington-Ward striking
out the third party notice and statement of claim and dismissing the third
party proceedings on the grounds that the third party notice and statement of claim disclosed no reasonable cause of action against the third
party.   B

The issue arising in this appeal concerned the immunity of barristers
from suit for damages for negligence at the instance of their clients or
for an indemnity or contribution at the instance of solicitors instructing
them. The particular question in the appeal was whether a claim might
be maintained against a barrister in respect of the advice given by him
to his client and to his instructing solicitors as to the party to be sued C
by the client.

The facts are set out in the opinions of Lord Wilberforce and Lord
Salmon.

Richard Yorke Q.C., Gavin Lightman and *Stuart Isaacs* for the
appellants, the solicitors.
                                                                          D
John Peppitt Q.C., Colin Smith and *Ian Geering* for the respondent,
the barrister.

Their Lordships took time for consideration.

November 2. LORD WILBERFORCE. My Lords, in *Rondel* v.
Worsley [1969] 1 A.C. 191, this House decided that a barrister was E
immune from any action for professional negligence in respect of acts
or omissions during the trial of criminal proceedings against his lay
client. Now in this case it is necessary to decide whether the barrister's
immunity covers pre-trial acts or omissions in connection with civil proceedings brought by his lay client.

The plaintiff, Mr. Saif Ali, a passenger in a van driven by his F
friend, Mr. Akram, was injured on March 26, 1966, in a collision with
a car driven by Mrs. Sugden, to whose husband the car belonged.
There is no doubt that Mrs. Sugden was to blame, and possibly wholly
to blame. On the instructions of solicitors the barrister settled proceedings and drafted a pleading on behalf of Mr. Ali and Mr. Akram
against Mr. Sugden. This was on the basis that as Mrs. Sugden was
using the car to drive their children to school, Mr. Sugden was respons- G
ible for her negligence. Though, with hindsight, it might have been
wise to sue Mrs. Sugden as well as her husband, the course adopted, to
sue Mr. Sugden who was the insured party, was correct in law. Indeed
it appeared at first that Mr. Sugden would not deny responsibility.
However, when his insurers took charge of the matter, they suggested
(a) that Mrs. Sugden's agency for Mr. Sugden might be disputed H
and (b) that a case of contributory negligence might be raised against
Mr. Akram. The barrister was informed of this and instructions were
sent to him to consider amendment of the pleading. By this time,
February 24, 1969, such was the leisurely pace of proceeding, there
was little time left before the three-year period of limitation from the
date of the accident (on March 26, 1969) would expire. The barrister,
however, so it is said in the third party notice, orally confirmed his

A   advice that no amendment was necessary, on what date is not stated, and later, on April 1, 1969, advised in writing. When he did this the three-year period had elapsed, and the advice was that it was too late for the plaintiff to sue Mr. Akram. It was also, of course, too late to sue Mrs. Sugden. Mr. Sugden in his first defence dated October 16, 1969, denied Mrs. Sugden's agency, but by an amendment in June 1971 admitted it. Later still (apparently in June 1972) he asked leave to

B   re-amend so as to deny the agency. This seems to have been agreed to unconditionally by the plaintiff's solicitors, and leave was given. Later, on the advice, it is said, of leading counsel, proceedings against Mr. Sugden were dropped, so the plaintiff, who started with an impregnable claim for damages, found after five years that he had nobody he could sue. He therefore brought proceedings against his solicitors for

C   negligence, and the solicitors brought third party proceedings against the barrister. Later, the plaintiff also brought direct proceedings against the barrister. This appeal is concerned with the third party proceedings only. The Court of Appeal has struck them out on the ground that the barrister is immune from suit.

It is important to see what is the precise negligence alleged. According to the amended third party notice the negligence consisted of: (i)

D   delaying until after the expiry of the limitation period to advise whether the proceedings should be resettled in view of the non-admission by Mr. Sugden that Mrs. Sugden was driving as his agent and the possible negligence of Mr. Akram. (ii) Failing to advise until a late stage that there might be a conflict of interest between the plaintiff and Mr. Akram. (iii) Failing to advise the plaintiff that he should take proceed-

E   ings against Mr. Sugden and/or Mrs. Sugden and/or Mr. Akram and advising that proceedings should be issued against Mr. Sugden only.

For the purposes of this appeal it has to be assumed that the factual basis for these allegations (as set out above) is correct, that there was some degree of negligence on the barrister's part as regards one at least of the three matters, that such negligence resulted in damage and that the solicitors are entitled to indemnity or contribution from the

F   barrister. All of these assumptions may turn out to be incorrect if the matter goes to trial, but cannot be challenged at this stage.

The question now for this House is whether on the assumptions stated the claim by the solicitors against the barrister is so clearly unfounded that it ought to be struck out. This involves a reconsideration of *Rondel* v. *Worsley* [1969] 1 A.C. 191 in order to see what rule of law is to be extracted from it.

G   *Rondel* v. *Worsley* gave rise to a restatement of the traditional principle of barristers' immunity in the light particularly of the decision of this House in *Hedley Byrne & Co. Ltd.* v. *Heller & Partners Ltd.* [1964] A.C. 465. Previously an important if not the main reason for the immunity was supposed to lie in the fact that a barrister could not sue for his fees: this reason, if valid, would of course have thrown a

H   blanket of immunity over all barristers' actions, in or out of court, whatever their nature. This House, however, in 1967 took the inevitable view that this reason no longer applied: liability for negligence might exist in the absence of a contract for reward. Nevertheless the immunity was held to exist on grounds, essentially, of public policy; mainly upon the ground that a barrister owes a duty to the court as well as to his client and should not be inhibited, through fear of an action by his client, from performing it; partly upon the undesirability

Lord Wilberforce   **Saif Ali v. Sidney Mitchell & Co. (H.L.(E.))**   [1978]

of relitigation as between barrister and client of what was litigated   A
between the client and his opponent. This necessarily involved a
removal of the total blanket immunity and a restriction of it to such
cases as might fall within the area of public policy.

   Rondel v. *Worsley* [1969] 1 A.C. 191 was concerned and only concerned with matters taking place in court which resulted in an outcome
unfavourable to the client. But the speeches contain considered observations as to the extent of barristers' immunity for matters taking place   B
outside court and in barristers' chambers. Since the case was not concerned with such matters, these observations have the status of obiter
dicta. However, not all obiter dicta have the same weight, or lack of
weight, in later cases. Of those then made in the House two things
may be said. First, they were considered and deliberate observations
after discussion of the same matters had taken place in the Court of
Appeal and in the light of judgments in the Court of Appeal. It may   C
be true that the counsel in the case did not present detailed arguments
as to the position outside the court room—they had no interest in doing
so—but I cannot agree that this invalidates or weakens judicial pro-
nouncements. Judges are more than mere selectors between rival views
—they are entitled to and do think for themselves. Secondly, it would
have been impossible for their Lordships to have dealt with the extent   D
of barristers' immunity for acts in court without relating this to their
immunity for other acts. As I shall shortly show, their Lordships
attached the immunity to the conduct of litigation. But litigation takes
some time to arrive in court for trial, so unless they were prepared to
confine the immunity to that part of litigation which occurs in the
court room, it was not only appropriate but necessary to deal with
such acts—in relation to litigation—as occur outside the court room.   E
A statement of principle which stopped at the door of the court would
have been truncated and irrational. These factors, in my opinion, tell
in favour of giving considerably more weight to their Lordships' expressions of opinion than obiter dicta normally receive. We may clarify
them, but we should hesitate before disregarding them.

   This leads to another point. The general principle that barristers   F
are entitled to some immunity was established, or re-established, by
unanimous decision of all their Lordships. It was argued that barristers
should enjoy no greater immunity than other professional men. But
that argument was rejected: barristers, it was firmly held, have a special
status, just as a trial has a special character: some immunity is necessary
in the public interest, even if, in some rare cases, an individual may   G
suffer loss. Now I would accept that the existence of a duty of care,
and correspondingly of liability in negligence for failure to exercise that
duty, continues in the natural course of legal evolution to expand as new
situations come before the courts. But I do not think that this natural
process which bears upon the existence of a duty of care should lead
us to sweep away after so short a time an immunity from suit on special
grounds of principle, which after many centuries of existence has been   H
restated by this House. No ground was suggested why we should
reopen the decision in *Rondel* v. *Worsley* [1969] 1 A.C. 191 and I do
not think we should do so. What is required of us is a decision on the
limits of an immunity held by this House to exist—a fringe decision
rather than a new pattern. I will now consider the opinions.

   Lord Reid considered that there was no doubt about the position of
barristers appearing in court (p. 227). There he introduced the phrase

A   " their work in conducting litigation" (p. 231D). He made this more explicit when he said, " The same public duty applies when drawing pleadings or conducting subsequent stages in a case as applies to counsel's conduct during the trial" and "the same will apply at a stage when litigation is impending" (pp. 231–232). It is clear from this that his Lordship was not seeking with any precision to define the limit of immunity but that his thinking was in terms of litigation—more

B   broadly than of work in court.

Lord Morris of Borth-y-Gest's expressions were more restrictive: " what is said or done in the . . . management of a case in court" (p. 247D; "relating only to the limited field of the conduct and management of a case in court" (p. 248F). But his Lordship quotes, at p. 243B, from the leading case of *Swinfen* v. *Lord Chelmsford* (1860) 5

C   H. & N. 890, 923 (a case not limited to action in court) the sentence " no action will lie against counsel for any act honestly done in the conduct or management of the cause," and he expressed agreement with the judgment of Salmon L.J. in the Court of Appeal which I think it fair to say drew the line between litigation and paper work. Lord Pearce's expressions were wider: there is no distinction " between the liability of a barrister in litigation and in his other non-litigious work

D   as a barrister" (p. 265B). He held that a counsel in giving opinions " not only those on which an action is to be started or not started" owes a duty to the court (p. 276F). Lord Upjohn held that the immunity covers litigation " at all events in matters pertaining to litigation" (p. 281D) and that it must " start before counsel enters the doors of the court to conduct the case " (p. 285F). He continued, at pp. 285–286 :

E   " He will have had to give fearlessly to his client advice on the prospects of success; he will have settled the pleadings; and on discovery and in his advice on evidence and on many other matters he may have had to refuse to adopt his client's wishes. As a practical matter, I do no more than suggest that the immunity of counsel in relation to litigation should start at [the] letter before action . . ."

F

Finally Lord Pearson used words of exclusion. He asked, " Does the barrister's immunity extend to ' pure paper work,' that is to say, drafting and advisory work unconnected with litigation? " (p. 293F).

My Lords, none of these expressions is precise, in the nature of things they could not be, but they show a consensus that what the immunity covers is not only litigation in court but some things which

G   occur at an earlier stage, broadly classified as related to conduct and management of litigation. The spectrum of the opinions is a wide one: we are now concerned to narrow it.

In considering how far a barrister's immunity extends, it is necessary to disentangle three separate strands.

The first is that of privilege. This attaches to proceedings in court

H   and protects equally the judge, counsel, witnesses, jurors and parties. It has nothing to do with a barrister's duty to his client. It is worth noting that the courts will not allow this privilege to be outflanked by basing a claim on statements made or agreed to be made out of court if these were clearly and directly made in relation to the proceedings in court: *Watson* v. *M'Ewan* [1905] A.C. 480 and *Marrinan* v. *Vibart* [1963] 1 Q.B. 528.

The second is that of the defences available to barristers. Much if

not most of a barrister's work involves exercise of judgment—it is in the   A
realm of art not science.   Indeed the solicitor normally goes to counsel
precisely at the point where, as between possible courses, a choice can
only be made on the basis of a judgment, which is fallible and may turn
out to be wrong.   Thus in the nature of things, an action against a
barrister who acts honestly and carefully is very unlikely to succeed.
But this is not an argument for giving him total immunity from proceedings.   B

The third is that of immunity from an action, which depends upon
public policy.   In fixing its boundary, account must be taken of the
counter policy that a wrong ought not to be without a remedy.
Furthermore, if the principle is invoked that it is against public policy
to allow issues previously tried (between the client and his adversary)
to be relitigated between client and barrister, it may be relevant to ask   C
why this principle should extend to a case in which by the barrister's
(assumed) fault, the case never came to trial at all.   These two considerations show that the area of immunity must be cautiously defined.

How can this be done? " Conduct and management " is the expression which has emerged and no doubt this is not a sharp definition.   I
think that something more precise is required if immunity in respect
of acts out of court is to be properly related to the immunity for acts in   D
court.   A helpful expansion of the phrase was suggested by McCarthy
P. in the New Zealand Court of Appeal in *Rees* v. *Sinclair* [1974] 1
N.Z.L.R. 180.   I quote his words, at p. 187:

> "I cannot narrow the protection to what is done in court: it must
> be wider than that and include some pre-trial work.   Each piece of
> before-trial work should, however, be tested against the one rule;   E
> that the protection exists only where the particular work is so
> intimately connected with the conduct of the cause in court that it
> can fairly be said to be a preliminary decision affecting the way
> that cause is to be conducted when it comes to a hearing.   The
> protection should not be given any wider application than is
> absolutely necessary in the interests of the administration of justice,
> and that is why I would not be prepared to include anything which   F
> does not come within the test I have stated."

I do not understand this formulation as suggesting an entirely new
test, i.e. a double test requiring (a) intimate connection with the conduct
of the cause in court and (b) necessity in the interests of the administration of justice.   The latter words state the justification for the test but
the test lies in the former words.   If these words involve a narrowing of   G
the test as compared with the more general words " conduct and
management " I think that this is right and for that reason I suggest
that the passage, if sensibly, and not pedantically, construed, provides a
sound foundation for individual decisions by the courts, whether
immunity exists in any given case.   I should make three observations.
First, I think that the formulation takes proper account, as it should,   H
of the fact that many trials, civil and criminal, take place only after
interlocutory or pre-trial proceedings.   At these proceedings decisions
may often fall to be made of the same nature as decisions at the trial
itself: it would be illogical and unfair if they were protected in the one
case but not in the other.   Secondly, a decision that a barrister's liability
extends so far as I have suggested necessarily involves that it does not
extend beyond that point.   In principle, those who undertake to give

A skilled advice are under a duty to use reasonable care and skill. The immunity as regards litigation is an exception from this and applies only in the area to which it extends. Outside that area, the normal rule must apply. Thirdly, I would hold that the same immunity attaches to a solicitor acting as an advocate in court as attaches to a barrister. Fourthly, it is necessary to repeat that the rule of immunity is quite distinct from the question what defences may be available to a barrister

B when he is sued. It by no means follows that if an error takes place outside this immunity area, a liability in negligence arises.

Finally, as to the present case. The question is whether the third party claim should be allowed to go to trial, or whether it should be held that it falls within the area of immunity so as to justify striking out at this stage. In the Court of Appeal Lord Denning M.R. and Lawton

C L.J. held that the acts and omissions complained of came within the general words " conduct and management of litigation." Bridge L.J. held that they came within the narrower test of *Rees* v. *Sinclair.*

My Lords, I think that the narrower test is the correct one, and I do not consider that the acts complained of come within it so as to justify striking out. An oversight, or failure to consider the consequences of not adding Mrs. Sugden as a defendant before the limitation

D period expired, if such took place, may have been defensible, but in my opinion falls well outside the immunity area. I would allow the appeal.

LORD DIPLOCK. My Lords, the decision of this House in *Hedley Byrne & Co. Ltd.* v. *Heller & Partners Ltd.* [1964] A.C. 465 cast doubt upon the facile explanation, which had been current for 100 years, that a barrister's immunity from liability for economic loss sustained

E by a client in consequence of his incompetent advice or conduct, was due to his incapacity as counsel to enter into a contractual relationship with his client. In 1967 these doubts were tested in your Lordships' House in *Rondel* v. *Worsley* [1969] 1 A.C. 191 and the explanation, which would have covered all work undertaken as a barrister, however remote from litigation it might be, was rejected as legal folklore. If

F the immunity in respect of any part of his professional work was to be maintained, some other legal justification would be needed for it.

In *Rondel* v. *Worsley* the barrister, Mr. Worsley, had accepted a dock brief at the Old Bailey on behalf of Mr. Rondel, as he was bound to do. So there was no solicitor instructing counsel and no allegations of negligence save in the actual conduct of the case in court. The absence of any substance or merit in the charges of negligence made by

G Mr. Rondel and the fact that the " cab rank " principle had actually operated in his case lent point to the argument that unless counsel remained immune from liability for his conduct of a case in court, he would be exposed to the risk of baseless and vexatious actions for negligence on the part of disappointed clients, to whom he had no option to deny his professional services.

H *Rondel* v. *Worsley* came before this House upon a summons to strike out the statement of claim as disclosing no reasonable cause of action. The only matter for decision was whether a barrister could be liable in negligence to his lay client for the way in which he had conducted the client's defence in court at his trial upon a criminal prosecution. The argument, however, ranged widely and the opinions expressed in the majority of the speeches were not confined to criminal cases nor to the actual conduct of a case in court. They referred also to civil cases and

to work done out of court.   Although expressed in somewhat different   A
terms in individual speeches the highest common factor to be discerned
in them is in my view accurately stated in the headnote as follows:

> ". . . a barrister was immune from an action for negligence at the
> suit of a client in respect of his conduct and management of a cause
> in court *and the preliminary work connected therewith such as the
> drawing of pleadings."*
                                                                        B

In the instant case the negligence alleged against the barrister has
been stated by my noble and learned friend Lord Wilberforce.   In
substance what it amounts to is that in a very common kind of running
down action he gave negligent advice as to who should be joined as
defendant to his client's claim for damages and settled the pleadings in
conformity with that erroneous advice.   It thus falls within the words   C
that I have italicised in the headnote to *Rondel* v. *Worsley* [1969] 1
A.C. 191.   The statement of law expressed in them was not necessary
to the actual decision in that case.

In deciding whether propositions of law expressed in speeches of
members of this House on the determination of an appeal are binding
upon lower courts the question whether they form part of the ratio
decidendi of the majority or are mere obiter dicta is crucial.   Proposi-   D
tions that fall into the former class are binding: those in the latter are
persuasive only.   In this House, however, since the Practice Direction
of 1966 [*Practice Statement (Judicial Precedent)* [1966] 1 W.L.R.
1234], all propositions of law laid down in the speeches in previous
appeals are persuasive only, whether they constituted an essential logical
step in the author's reasons for disposing of the appeal in the way that   E
he proposed, and so formed part of his ratio decidendi or, though not
regarded by him as necessary for that purpose, were included as a
helpful guide to judges in the disposition of future cases and so were
obiter dicta.   Leaving aside all such invidious distinctions as depend
upon the reputations which individual former members of the Appellate
Committee may have gained as jurists, the persuasive value of propositions of both classes depends to a considerable extent upon the   F
course followed in the arguments presented to the court in the particular
case in which they were laid down.

In *Rondel* v. *Worsley* [1969] 1 A.C. 191 it was to the interest of
neither party to the case to argue that any distinction was to be drawn
between the liability of a barrister for negligence in that part of his
work that is done in the court itself and work that he does out of court.   G
In the dialectic between counsel this played no active part.

It was the majority of the members of this House who, in seeking
a new rationale that would justify retention of a barrister's immunity
from liability for negligence in doing the kind of thing that Mr. Worsley
had been charged with doing negligently in a criminal trial, themselves
suggested a distinction between what a barrister does in the conduct and
management of litigation and his non-litigious work.   In respect of the   H
former all five members of this House were of opinion that notwithstanding that a barrister's immunity could no longer be based upon his
incapacity to enter into a contract for the provision of his professional
services, nevertheless the policy of the law required that the immunity
should be maintained on other grounds.   In respect of work not directly
connected with the conduct of a case in court four members (Lord
Pearce dissenting) expressed opinions that he would be liable: but they

A were not of one mind as to where the dividing line lay between what work attracted immunity from liability for negligence and what work did not. At the one extreme Lord Pearson limited himself to the expression of a doubt as to whether the barrister's immunity extended to " pure paper work," which he explained as drafting and advisory work unconnected with litigation. At the other extreme Lord Morris of Borth-y-Gest appears to have regarded the immunity as confined to the actual conduct of a cause in court. He suggests no extension beyond this. Between these two extremes Lord Reid, in a passage clearly intended to be obiter, expressed the view that the immunity would extend to drawing pleadings or conducting subsequent stages in a case, as it applies to counsel's conduct during the trial; while Lord Upjohn, also obiter, suggested that the immunity of counsel, which he regarded as confined to the conduct of litigation in and out of court should start in a civil case at the moment when the letter before action was sent.

My Lords, in recognising a barrister's immunity from liability for negligence in the conduct of his professional work of a particular kind this House was granting to the Bar a privileged status which the common law does not accord to members of any other profession or skilled craft. Those who hold themselves out as qualified to practise other professions, although they are not liable for damage caused by what in the event turns out to have been an error of judgment on some matter upon which the opinions of reasonably informed and competent members of the profession might have differed, are nevertheless liable for damage caused by their advice, acts or omissions in the course of their professional work which no member of the profession who was reasonably well-informed and competent would have given or done or omitted to do.

This exceptional immunity of the barrister and its extension to various kinds of professional work that he does outside the court room can no longer be justified as the automatic corollary of the rule that a barrister cannot contract to render professional services. In my view, it must be justified, if at all, as a matter of policy of the law and by the special characteristics of the kind of work to which the immunity applies that distinguish it from professional work undertaken by members of other professions.

The general trend in the policy of the law as developed by your Lordships' House in recent years has been to extend to new areas of activity the notion that a man is liable for loss or damage to others resulting from his failure to take care. *Hedley Byrne & Co. Ltd.* v. *Heller & Partners Ltd.* [1964] A.C. 465 itself marked an important milestone in this development; and the indication of their view by the majority of this House in *Rondel* v. *Worsley* [1969] 1 A.C. 191 that at any rate some kinds of work done by a barrister would no longer attract immunity from liability for negligence was another, if hesitant, step along the same road. During the years that have passed since *Rondel* v. *Worsley* was decided, the extension of liability for negligence in doing things that were not previously regarded as giving rise to any legal duty of care has gone on apace. A few examples serve to show how broad this trend has been. Architects have been held liable for negligence in valuing work for the purposes of certificates of interim payments under building contracts: *Sutcliffe* v. *Thackrah* [1974] A.C. 727; accountants for negligence when acting as valuers for the purpose of a contract

between other parties: *Arenson* v. *Arenson* [1977] A.C. 405; building A
inspectors employed by local authorities for negligence in inspecting the
foundations of a building in course of erection: *Anns* v. *Merton
London Borough Council* [1977] 2 W.L.R. 1024; Borstal officers, for
negligent failure to control their charges: *Dorset Yacht Co. Ltd.* v.
Home Office [1970] A.C. 1004; and professional salvors have been held
liable for negligence in carrying out salvage operations: *The Tojo Maru*
[1972] A.C. 242.   The extension to the duty of care to trespassers to   B
land that was made in *Herrington* v. *British Railways Board* [1972]
A.C. 877 illustrates the existence of a similar general trend extending
beyond the limited field of professional work.

In the face of this trend it would in my view be hard to justify
founding the decision of the instant appeal upon an uncritical acceptance of the highest common factor in the observations of the majority C
of the members of this House who spoke upon the subject in *Rondel* v
Worsley [1969] 1 A.C. 191 as defining the kind of work done by a
barrister outside the courtroom door in respect of which he is immune
from liability for negligence.   What is needed is to identify those reasons
based on public policy which were held to justify a barrister's immunity
from liability for negligence for what he did in court during the trial of
a criminal case and, having done so, to decide whether they suffice to   D
justify a like immunity when advising a client, through his solicitor, as
to who should be made a party to a proposed civil action and when
settling pleadings in the action in conformity with that advice.

There were several reasons given in *Rondel* v. *Worsley* for distinguishing between the work done by a barrister in the conduct of a
criminal trial in court and work done by members of any other pro-   E
fession, so as to entitle the former to an exemption from liability for
negligence which no other type of professional work enjoyed.

The special characteristic of a barrister's work upon which the
greatest stress is laid by their Lordships was that he does not owe a
duty only to his client; he owes a duty also to the court.   This is an
overriding duty which he must observe even though to do so in the   F
particular case may appear to be contrary to the interests of his client.
Furthermore a barrister has to exercise his judgment as to where the
balance lies between these competing duties immediately and without
opportunity for calm reflection as the trial inexorably proceeds.   His
ability to give his best service to the court and to his client, it is said,
would be diminished if he were compelled continually to give consideration to the possible effects that the way in which he exercised that   G
judgment might have upon his own liability to his client for negligence.

To say of a barrister that he owes a duty to the court, or to justice as
an abstraction, to act in a particular way in particular circumstances
may seem to be no more than a pretentious way of saying that when a
barrister is taking part in litigation he must observe the rules; and this
is true of all who practise any profession.   The rules which may appear H
to conflict with the interests of the client are simple to state, although
their application in borderline cases may call for a degree of sophistry
not readily appreciated by the lay client, particularly one who is defendant in a criminal trial.   A barrister must not wilfully mislead the court
as to the law nor may he actively mislead the court as to the facts;
although, consistently with the rule that the prosecution must prove its
case, he may passively stand by and watch the court being misled by

A reason of its failure to ascertain facts that are within the barrister's knowledge. Again, although he must not abuse the privilege which the law accords to him as counsel in rendering him immune from liability for aspersions which he makes against anyone in the course of litigation, however unfounded, irrelevant or malicious they may be, questions of considerable nicety may arise as to what constitutes sufficient foundation or relevance to justify the particular aspersion which his client wants him to make.

B The fact that application of the rules that a barrister must observe may in particular cases call for the exercise of finely balanced judgments upon matters about which different members of the profession might take different views, does not in my view provide sufficient reason for granting absolute immunity from liability at common law. No matter

C what profession it may be, the common law does not impose on those who practise it any liability for damage resulting from what in the result turn out to have been errors of judgment, unless the error was such as no reasonably well-informed and competent member of that profession could have made. So too the common law makes allowance for the difficulties in the circumstances in which professional judgments have to be made and acted upon. The salvor and the surgeon, like the barrister,

D may be called upon to make immediate decisions which, if in the result they turn out to have been wrong, may have disastrous consequences. Yet neither salvors nor surgeons are immune from liability for negligent conduct of a salvage or surgical operation; nor does it seem that the absence of absolute immunity from negligence has disabled members of professions other than the law from giving their best services to those to

E whom they are rendered.

My Lords, the argument founded upon the barrister's competing duties to court and client, upon which this House so strongly relied in *Rondel* v. *Worsley* [1969] 1 A.C. 191, loses much of its cogency when the scene of the exercise of the barrister's judgment as to where the balance lies between these duties is shifted from the hurly-burly of the

F trial to the relative tranquillity of the barrister's chambers. The kind of judgment which a barrister has to exercise in advising a client as to who should be made defendant to a proposed action and how the claim against him should be pleaded, if made with opportunity for reflection, does not seem to me to differ in any relevant respect from the kind of judgment which has to be made in other fields of human activity, in which prognosis by professional advisers plays a part. If subsequently

G a barrister is sued by his own client for negligence on what he advised or did in the particular case, he has the protection that the judge before whom the action for negligence against him will be tried is well qualified, without any need of expert evidence, to make allowance for the circumstances in which the impugned decision fell to be made and to differentiate between an error that was so blatant as to amount to negligence

H and an exercise of judgment which, though in the event it turned out to have been mistaken, was not outside the range of possible courses of action that in the circumstances reasonably competent members of the profession might have chosen to take.

In *Rondel* v. *Worsley* some reliance was also placed upon the " cabrank " principle as distinguishing the Bar from all other professions. A barrister is not allowed by the rules of his profession to pick and choose between clients on whose behalf he will accept instructions. If he is

disengaged and a proper fee is tendered to him, he is bound to accept **A**
instructions to act on behalf of any client desirous of his services in a
field of law in which he holds himself out as practising. The " cab-
rank " principle was a reality in *Rondel* v. *Worsley.* Mr. Worsley was
instructed directly by the lay client; he was the recipient of a dock brief.
But with the virtual disappearance of the dock brief the effect of the
cab-rank principle is limited to preventing a barrister from refusing
from a solicitor instructions in a field of law within which he practises **B**
simply because he does not like the solicitor or the solicitor's client or
the nature of a lawful claim or ground of defence of which that client
wishes to avail himself. I doubt whether in reality, in the field of civil
litigation at any rate, this results often in counsel having to accept work
which he would not otherwise be willing to undertake. But even if
there are rare cases where it does, this does not seem to me to affect **C**
the character of the decisions that the barrister has to make in carrying
out instructions that he receives through the client's solicitor. True it is
that he may be obliged to accept instructions on behalf of an obstinate
and cantankerous client who is more likely than more rational beings to
bring proceedings for negligence against his counsel if disappointed in
the result of his litigation; but the existence of this risk does not, in my
view, justify depriving all clients of any possibility of a remedy for **D**
negligence of counsel, however elementary and obvious the mistake he
has made may be. There are other and more specific means of disposing summarily of vexatious actions.

In the light of the developments of the law of negligence which have
taken place since 1967, I could not readily find today in the reasons that
I have so far discussed convincing ground for holding that a barrister **E**
ought to be completely immune from liability for negligence for what
he does in court in conducting criminal or civil proceedings—let alone
for anything that he does outside court in advising about litigation
whether contemplated or pending or in settling documents for use in
litigations.

There are, however, two additional grounds referred to in some of
the speeches in *Rondel* v. *Worsley* [1969] 1 A.C. 191 which can be used **F**
to supplement those reasons so far as they protect a barrister from
liability in respect of the way in which he has conducted proceedings in
court, including in this expression interlocutory proceedings before the
master or in chambers; save to a very limited extent, however, neither
of them would apply to work done out of court.

The first is that the barrister's immunity from liability for what he **G**
says and does in court is part of the general immunity from civil liability
which attaches to all persons in respect of their participation in proceedings before a court of justice; judges, court officials, witnesses, parties,
counsel and solicitors alike. The immunity is based on public policy,
designed, as was said by Lord Morris of Borth-y-Gest (p. 251), to
ensure that trials are conducted without avoidable stress and tensions
of alarm and fear in those who have a part to play in them. As was **H**
pointed out by Starke J. in *Cabassi* v. *Vila* (1940) 64 C.L.R. 130, 141, a
case in the High Court of Australia, " The law protects witnesses and
others, not for their benefit, but for a higher interest, namely, the
advancement of public justice." The courts have been vigilant to
prevent this immunity from indirect as well as direct attack—for
instance by suing witnesses for damages for giving perjured evidence or
for conspiracy to give false evidence; *Marrinan* v. *Vibart* [1963] 1 Q.B.

A 528. In *Watson* v. *M'Ewan* [1905] A.C. 480, this House held that in the case of witnesses the protection extended not only to the evidence that they give in court but to statements made by the witness to the client and to the solicitor in preparing the witness's proof for the trial; since, unless these statements were protected, the protection to which the witness would be entitled at the trial could be circumvented.

B The second reason is also based upon the need to maintain the integrity of public justice. An action for negligence against a barrister for the way in which he has conducted a case in court is founded upon the supposition that his lack of skill or care has resulted in the court having reached a decision that was not merely adverse to his client as to liability or quantum of damages but was wrong in being adverse and in consequence was unjust, for otherwise no damage could be shown to

C have resulted from the barrister's act or omission of which complaint is made. The client cannot be heard to complain that the barrister's lack of skill or care prevented him from obtaining a wrong decision in his favour from a court of justice. So he must prove that if the action had been conducted competently by his counsel he would have succeeded instead of failed.

D Under the English system of administration of justice, the appropriate method of correcting a wrong decision of a court of justice reached after a contested hearing is by appeal against the judgment to a superior court. This is not based solely on technical doctrines of res judicata but upon principles of public policy, which also discourage collateral attack on the correctness of a subsisting judgment of a court of trial upon a contested issue by re-trial of the same issue, either

E directly or indirectly in a court of co-ordinate jurisdiction. Yet a re-trial of any issue decided against a barrister's client in favour of an adverse party in the action in respect of which allegations of negligent conduct by the barrister are made would be an indirect consequence of entertaining such an action.

The re-trial of the issue in the previous action, if it depended on oral evidence, would have to be undertaken de novo. This would involve

F calling anew after a lapse of time witnesses who had been called at the previous trial and eliciting their evidence before a different judge by questions in examination and cross-examination that were not the same as those that had been put to them at the previous trial. The circumstances in which the barrister had made decisions as to the way in which he would conduct the previous trial, and the material on which

G those decisions were based, could not be reproduced in the re-trial; and the initial question in the action for negligence: whether it has been established that the decision adverse to the client reached by the court in the previous trial was wrong, would become hopelessly entangled with the second question: whether it has been established that notwithstanding the differences in the circumstances in which the previous trial was conducted, it was the negligent act or omission of the barrister in

H the conduct of his client's case that caused the wrong decision by the court and not any other of those differences.

My Lords, it seems to me that to require a court of co-ordinate jurisdiction to try the question whether another court reached a wrong decision and, if so, to inquire into the causes of its doing so, is calculated to bring the administration of justice into disrepute. Parliament indeed itself stepped in to prevent a similar abuse of the system of justice by convicted criminals in bringing civil actions for libel against

Lord Diplock   **Saif Ali v. Sidney Mitchell & Co. (H.L.(E.))**   [1978]

those who described them as having been guilty of the crimes of which **A** they had been convicted: see Civil Evidence Act 1968, section 13. A consequence of the decision of this House in *Rondel* v. *Worsley* [1969] 1 A.C. 191 was to prevent its happening in actions for negligence against barristers.

A similar objection, it may be mentioned, would not apply in cases where an action has been dismissed or judgment entered without a contested hearing, and there is no possibility of restoring the action and **B** proceeding to a trial. If the dismissal or the entry of judgment was a consequence of the negligence of the legal advisers of a party to the action, a claim in negligence against the legal advisers at fault does not involve any allegation that the order of the court which dismissed the action or entered judgment was wrong.

I find it an unsatisfactory feature of the instant appeal, which has **C** called for a re-examination of the speeches in *Rondel* v. *Worsley* in the light of the subsequent development of the law of negligence by later decisions of this House, that your Lordships have not had the benefit of any argument from counsel in support of a more radical submission that the immunity of the advocate, whether barrister or solicitor, for liability for negligence even for what he says or does in court ought no longer to be upheld. Counsel cannot be blamed for this. The parties **D** whom they represent are solicitors and a barrister respectively. It is not to their interest as members of either branch of the legal profession to argue that this immunity no longer exists. Nevertheless, despite this handicap, I have reached the clear conclusion that these two additional grounds of public interest which I have just discussed, when taken with those reasons upon which greater stress had been placed in most of **E** the speeches in *Rondel* v. *Worsley,* suffice to justify your Lordships in accepting as a premise for the purpose of deciding the instant appeal that the decision of this House in *Rondel* v. *Worsley* upholding such immunity is still good law.

The two additional grounds of public policy for granting a barrister immunity for what he does in court apply with equal force to what a solicitor does when acting as advocate in those courts in which solici- **F** tors have rights of audience; but subject to what is said below neither of them applies to what a barrister does outside court in advising about litigation or settling documents for use in litigation. Without the support of those additional grounds of public interest, as I have already indicated, I can find no sufficient reason for extending the immunity to anything that a barrister does out of court; save for a limited exception **G** analogous to the extension of a witness's protection in respect of evidence which he gives in court to statements made by him to the client and his solicitor for the purpose of preparing the witness's proof for trial. The extent of this exception was in my view well expressed by McCarthy P. in the Court of Appeal of New Zealand (where the profession is a fused one) in *Rees* v. *Sinclair* [1974] 1 N.Z.L.R. 180, **H** 187:

  " Each piece of before-trial work should . . . be tested against the one rule; that the protection exists only where the particular work is so intimately connected with the conduct of the cause in court that it can fairly be said to be a preliminary decision affecting the way that cause is to be conducted when it comes to a hearing. The protection should not be given any wider application than is

A   absolutely necessary in the interests of the administration of
justice. . . ."

So for instance in the English system of a divided profession where the
practice is for the barrister to advise on evidence at some stage before
the trial his protection from liability for negligence in the conduct of
the case at trial is not to be circumvented by charging him with
B   negligence in having previously advised the course of conduct at the
hearing that was subsequently carried out.

It would not be wise to attempt a catalogue of before-trial work
which would fall within this limited extension of the immunity of an
advocate from liability for the way in which he conducts a case in
court.

C   The work which the barrister in the instant case is charged with
having done negligently, viz. in advising as to who was to be a party to
an action and settling pleadings in accordance with that advice, was
all done out of court. In my view, it manifestly falls outside the limited
extension of the immunity which I have just referred to.

It follows that in my view the third party proceedings ought not to
have been struck out upon the grounds stated in the judgments in the
D   Court of Appeal. Whatever other grounds there might have been for
doing so have not been relied upon by the respondents. So, the consequence must be that the order of the Court of Appeal should be
reversed, and the appeal allowed.

It should not be thought, however, that I am assenting to the proposition that the facts stated in the claim in the third party proceedings
disclose a reasonable cause of action by the solicitors against the
E   barrister. That is a matter that will fall to be decided at the trial—if
there is one.

I would accordingly allow this appeal.

LORD SALMON. My Lords, this appeal raises a point of law of great
public importance, namely—what is the extent of a barrister's immunity
F   (if any) against a claim for damages for negligence in the performance
of his professional duties out of court. It is a pity that such an
important point falls to be decided in a case such as the present since
its facts are somewhat tenuous and unsatisfactory.

On March 26, 1966, Mr. Saif Ali was travelling as a passenger in a
van being driven by his friend Mr. Akram. The van collided with a
motor car which belonged to Mr. Sugden and was being driven by his
G   wife; she was taking their children to school. As a result of the
accident (a) Mrs. Sugden was prosecuted in October 1966 for driving
without due care and attention, and she pleaded guilty to that offence,
and (b) Mr. Ali and Mr. Akram suffered serious injuries and were away
from work for many months. Mr. Ali had an unanswerable claim for
substantial damages, certainly against Mrs. Sugden, probably against
H   Mr. Sugden and possibly against Mr. Akram.

Soon after the accident, Mr. Ali and Mr. Akram consulted a firm
of solicitors. In October 1968 those solicitors laid the facts which I
have recited before a barrister and instructed him to settle proceedings
and to advise. The barrister promptly settled a writ and a statement
of claim making Mr. Ali and Mr. Akram joint plaintiffs and Mr.
Sugden the sole defendant. The solicitors issued the writ on November
14, 1968, but did not serve the writ or the statement of claim until

August 29, 1969. In the meantime, but well before March 26, 1969 **A** (when the period of limitation expired), the solicitors informed the barrister, amongst other things, that the solicitor acting for Mr. Sugden's insurers apparently in the course of negotiation had stated that Mr. Akram should be joined as a defendant and that the allegation in the statement of claim that Mrs. Sugden had been driving as her husband's agent might be put in issue. The solicitors asked the barrister for his advice. The barrister then advised that there was no **B** foundation for any challenge of the allegation that Mrs. Sugden was driving as her husband's agent; and that accordingly no amendment to the statement of claim would be worthwhile. In accordance with that advice, the statement of claim was not amended by adding either Mrs. Sugden or Mr. Akram as defendants.

The barrister's advice not to join Mrs. Sugden and Mr. Akram as **C** defendants and his failure to do so is the negligence which is alleged against him in circumstances to which I shall presently refer.

In November 1969 the barrister advised Mr. Ali that he should be separately represented; and Mr. Ali instructed new solicitors and a new barrister to act for him.

Mr. Sugden's original defence, served on October 16, 1969, denied **D** that his wife had been driving as his agent at the time of the accident. On June 24, 1971, an amended defence was served, withdrawing the denial and admitting that Mrs. Sugden had been driving as her husband's agent.

On January 21, 1972, a consent order was made giving leave to Mr. Sugden to re-amend his defence by withdrawing the admission made in the amended defence and reverting to the stance he had taken in the **E** original defence. The re-amended defence was duly served on January 24, 1972. It seems strange to me that Mr. Ali's then solicitors should have consented to the order allowing the amended defence admitting Mrs. Sugden's agency to be re-amended by denying her agency. With her agency admitted, and Mrs. Sugden having pleaded guilty to driving without due care and attention, Mr. Ali must have succeeded in his **F** action against Mr. Sugden. It was particularly important for him that he should do so as it was then years too late for Mrs. Sugden or Mr. Akram to be joined as defendants.

On April 22, 1974, Mr. Ali's then solicitors served notice of the discontinuance of Mr. Ali's action against Mr. Sugden. We have been told from the Bar that the notice of discontinuance was served on the advice of leading counsel. It is possible that this advice was founded **G** on the decision of your Lordships' House in *Launchbury* v. *Morgans* [1973] A.C. 127. In that case Mr. Morgans had left his wife at home for the evening and at 10.40 p.m., when the accident occurred, he was in her car on what has been described as a " pub crawl " which had then been going on for about four hours. This House decided that, in these circumstances, it was impossible that he was using the car on **H** behalf of his wife or for any purpose of hers; and that accordingly his wife was not responsible for the negligent driving of her car. The crucial difference between the relevant facts in that case and those in Mr. Ali's case is surely obvious.

The present appeal concerns a simple running down action in which Mr. Ali, if properly advised, must have recovered judgment, or settled his claim, for substantial damages against Mr. Sugden, Mrs. Sugden

A and Mr. Akram or one or more of them. As it is, after inordinate delays, whilst he had left himself in the hands of his lawyers and followed their advice for about eight years, he now finds himself barred in law from taking his case to court against any of the defendants whose negligence caused him damage, and accordingly he is deprived of any of the damages to which he was clearly entitled.

B It would, in my opinion, be a shocking reflection on the common law if, in the melancholy circumstances I have recited, Mr. Ali has no remedy against any of his advisers who are responsible for his present situation. It may be that the solicitors, having accurately instructed counsel about the facts, cannot be held to be negligent for having acted in accordance with counsel's advice. I cannot, however, find any reason or principle or sound authority to justify counsel's immunity

C from being sued for damages by clients who have suffered loss as a result of counsel's negligent advice. I have no doubt that, for the reasons I shall presently explain, the common law does give Mr. Ali a remedy against his advisers—whether solicitors or counsel—whose advice negligently caused his loss.

In September 1974 Mr. Ali brought an action against his original solicitors for damages for negligently advising him that neither Mrs.

D Sugden nor Mr. Akram ought to be added as defendants, and for negligently failing to make either of them defendants. No claim for damages for negligence was made against the solicitor who consented to the order giving leave to Mr. Sugden to re-amend his defence and who later discontinued the action against Mr. Sugden; nor was any claim made against leading counsel who advised that the action should be

E discontinued.

The original solicitors entered a defence denying negligence to the claim against them and issued third party proceedings claiming an indemnity against the barrister who advised them in 1968 mainly on the ground that he had negligently advised that neither Mrs. Sugden nor Mr. Akram should be joined as defendants. Mr. Ali then joined the barrister as a defendant and claimed damages for negligence against

F him. The barrister applied to have the third party claim against him struck out on the grounds that as a barrister he was immune from the claim in negligence made against him in the third party proceedings. The district registrar struck out the third party claim but Kerr J. restored it. The Court of Appeal allowed the appeal from Kerr J.'s order and ordered that the third party proceedings should be struck out on the ground that the barrister was immune from any such claim.

G The present appellants now appeal from that decision to your Lordships' House.

I hope that nothing in this speech will leave an impression that I hold a view, one way or another, as to whether the barrister who advised in 1968 was negligent. I have certainly formed no view on this issue; it is an issue which, if this appeal is allowed and the action is fought, will have

H to be decided by the judge who hears the evidence. It has, in my opinion, been rightly conceded at the Bar that, as the facts alleged in the third party claim are capable of constituting negligence, the only issue before this House is whether or not the barrister is immune from the claim made against him.

A great deal of reliance has been placed by both sides on *Rondel* v. *Worsley* [1969] 1 A.C. 191. It is, I think, important to remember that this authority decided only one point, albeit a point of great importance,

Lord Salmon   **Saif Ali v. Sidney Mitchell & Co. (H.L.(E.))**   **[1978]**

namely that a barrister, like a judge, juryman and witness, is immune from A
being sued in respect of anything he says or does or omits to say or do in
the course of performing his role in court.   This was the first occasion
when this point had come before your Lordships' house for decision but
there was much long-established and powerful authority to support the
decision at which this House arrived: see for example *Swinfen* v. *Lord
Chelmsford*, 5 H. & N. 890 and *Kennedy* v. *Broun* (1863) 13 C.B.N.S. 677.
Each of their Lordships fully explained why public policy required the B
immunity which they proclaimed in respect of anything said or done in
court.   With respect, I entirely agree with all that was said on that point
in this House; and it is unnecessary for me to repeat anything I said when
Rondel v. *Worsley* was heard in the Court of Appeal [1967] 1 Q.B. 443,
516–520.   I would only add that, in my view, a solicitor acting as an
advocate in court enjoys exactly the same immunity as a barrister. C

The decision in *Rondel* v. *Worsley* is, however, almost as irrelevant to
the present appeal as the question which this appeal raises was irrelevant
in *Rondel* v. *Worsley*.   In that case, Mr. Rondel brought an action for
damages for negligence against a barrister, Mr. Worsley, who had
defended him, on a dock brief, for causing bodily harm with intent to do
so.   Mr. Worsley applied to have the claim struck out.   When this
application came before the judge in chambers, the plaintiff admitted D
inflicting the shocking injuries in respect of which he had been convicted.
His claim was that he had inflicted them in self-defence.   His only real
complaint against his counsel was that he had not cross-examined the
Crown witnesses to show that the plaintiff had inflicted those injuries with
his teeth and bare hands rather than with a knife.   The plaintiff also
admitted to the judge in chambers that he was not alleging that had E
counsel cross-examined the witnesses as he had wished, he would have
had any chance of being acquitted.   It followed from that admission
that the plaintiff had suffered no damage from the line of cross-examination which counsel had pursued.   Since the claim by Mr. Rondel against
his counsel was based on negligence and not on contract, and proof of
damage is an essential ingredient of the tort of negligence, Mr. Rondel's
claim was clearly unmaintainable.   The learned judge might well have F
dismissed it, briefly, as disclosing no cause of action and as an abuse of the
process of the court.   He, however, took the view that the case involved
an important point of law; and he delivered a long and learned judgment
in open court reviewing all the authorities back to the Year Books and
explaining why public policy demanded that counsel and also solicitors
should enjoy complete immunity from an action alleging negligence in G
respect of their conduct of a case in court.   A conclusion with which I
agree.   I would point out that the learned judge, in my view, quite rightly
confined himself to immunity in respect of what was said or done by
advocates in court: he did not express any views as to whether such
immunity could extend to paper work done by counsel out of court—and
for the very good reason that this issue was irrelevant to the case he was
deciding. H

When *Rondel* v. *Worsley* [1967] 1 Q.B. 443 reached the Court of
Appeal, that court unanimously decided that a barrister was in law
immune against any claim in negligence relating to what he had said or
done in court.   The majority, however, considered that the court should
express its views on the issue which seemed to the judge in chambers and
to the minority in the Court of Appeal to be irrelevant.   The majority
expressed the view clearly, that a barrister enjoyed a blanket immunity

A in respect of any work which he did out of court: see Lord Denning M.R., at p. 506 and Danckwerts L.J., at pp. 512–513. I entirely disagreed and still disagree on that point. I need not repeat any of the reasons which I gave for dissenting, which are fully set out at pp. 521–526.

I recognise that it is most unpleasant for a barrister to have to fight an allegation that he has been negligent, but such an experience is no more unpleasant for a barrister than it is for a physician or a surgeon, an B architect or an accountant. I cannot understand how there can be any justification for the law affording a blanket immunity to a barrister in respect of all work done out of court when it affords none to the members of any other profession; nor do I believe that the Bar would wish to claim such an immunity.

When *Rondel* v. *Worsley* [1969] 1 A.C. 191, came to this House, this C House faced a dilemma. The Law Lords did not agree with the majority of the Court of Appeal which had decided, obiter, that a barrister enjoyed a blanket immunity against any claim in negligence in respect of all paper work. It was indubitably plain to this House that the obiter dictum of the majority of the Court of Appeal, although not binding, would carry great weight. Indeed it was extremely doubtful that any judge of first instance or any division of the Court of Appeal would D depart from that obiter dictum unless this House disagreed with it. Accordingly, this House had no real choice but to deal with it. And this they did. By a majority of four to one the Law Lords rejected the proposition that the Bar enjoyed the blanket immunity proclaimed by the majority of the Court of Appeal in respect of all paper work done by a barrister. They all considered that some paper work should be covered E by immunity, but they differed from each other as to where the line ought to be drawn.

In the present case, the question for decision is—on what side of the line does the advice fall which was given by the barrister against whom the third party proceedings have been brought?

It must be remembered that although all the four differing opinions in *Rondel* v. *Worsley* carry great weight and command profound respect, F each of them is obiter. It should also be remembered that, during the period of almost 11 years since *Rondel* v. *Worsley* was decided, there has been a strong tendency for your Lordships' House to extend the ambit of the duty of care in negligence cases and to cut down the immunity enjoyed by professional men from being sued in actions for negligence. I shall refer only to the latter class of case.

G It used to be thought that an architect employed by a building owner to supervise the erection of a building and to certify the sums due to the contractor, enjoyed an immunity against being sued for negligence however negligent he may have been in issuing his certificates; this immunity strangely enough was based on the fact that he owed a duty to the building owner and to the contractor to act impartially: see *Chambers* v. *Goldthorpe* [1901] 1 Q.B. 624. That authority was however H overruled and the immunity of architects was abolished by the unanimous decision of your Lordships' House in *Sutcliffe* v. *Thackrah* [1974] A.C. 727.

Similarly, it was formerly held that if an accountant was called in to assess the value of shares knowing that the price which A might pay B, or B might accept for them, was to be the price at which the accountant valued them, then however negligently he may have conducted his valuation, he was immune from being sued either by A or B in respect

of his negligence: *Finnegan* v. *Allen* [1943] K.B. 425. That supposed A
immunity accorded to accountants was swept away by the unanimous
decision of your Lordships' House in *Arenson* v. *Arenson* [1977] A.C.
405.

There are several excellent reasons to which I have already referred
and each of which is cogently set out by this House in *Rondel* v. *Worsley*
[1969] 1 A.C. 191 explaining why public policy demands that a barrister,
in common with a judge, juryman, or witness, shall be immune against   B
being sued in respect of anything he does or says in court. I entirely
agree with that immunity for the reasons I gave when *Rondel* v. *Worsley*
[1967] 1 Q.B. 443 was before the Court of Appeal, and I shall not repeat
any of them. I cannot, however, understand how any aspect of public
policy could possibly confer immunity on a barrister in a case such as
the present should he negligently fail to join the correct persons or to   C
advise that they should be joined as defendants; or for that matter should
he negligently advise that the action must be discontinued. It seems
plain to me that there could be no possibility of a conflict between his duty
to advise his client with reasonable care and skill and his duty to the
public and to the courts. I do not see how public policy can come into
this picture. This is certainly not a case where it could possibly be
regarded as oppressive to join Mrs. Sugden as a defendant. After all,   D
she had pleaded guilty to driving without due care and attention at the
material time. Nor do I understand how any aspect of public policy
could have required counsel to advise that the action against Mr. Sugden
should be discontinued. Once it is clear that the circumstances are such
that no question of public policy is involved, the prospects of immunity
for a barrister against being sued for negligently advising his client   E
vanish into thin air, together with the ghosts of all the excuses for such
immunity which were thought to exist in the past.

The theory that because the barrister had no contractual relationship
with his client he could not be liable for negligent advice causing financial
loss, vanished with *Hedley Byrne & Co. Ltd.* v. *Heller & Partners Ltd.*
[1964] A.C. 465 which overruled *Candler* v. *Crane, Christmas & Co.*
[1951] 2 K.B. 164.   F

The other theories supporting a barrister's supposed blanket immunity
from liability for negligence in respect of any paper work cannot survive in
the realistic atmosphere of the late 20th century. These were based on
the fact that (a) a barrister cannot sue his client for his fees and (b) he
is obliged to accept briefs relating to a field of law in which he normally
practices, providing he is offered a proper fee.   G

Although a barrister cannot sue for his fees, he can demand that his
fees be paid before he appears in court. If the barrister does not demand
his fees in advance and the lay client does not pay them after the barrister's
services have been rendered, the solicitor can sue the lay client for the
barrister's fees. It is true that if the solicitor recovers the fees from the
lay client and does not pay them over to the barrister, the barrister cannot   H
sue the solicitor; but he can report him to the Law Society, and this as
every lawyer knows would be likely to cost the solicitor far more than
the fees he retains. There is no reason to suppose that the Bar incurs
more bad debts than any other profession.

The rule that a barrister must accept a brief in the circumstances
which I have described was made to ensure that every accused person or
litigant could be represented in court by counsel. I do not, however,

A know of any firm rule which obliges counsel to accept instructions to advise or to draft pleadings.

Unless what seems to me to be an untenable proposition is accepted, namely that public policy always requires that a barrister should be immune from liability for his neglect or incompetence in respect of all paper work, he is rightly in no better position than any other professional man who is sued for negligence. The normal rule applied by the law is
B that if anyone holding himself out as possessing reasonable competence in his avocation undertakes to advise or to settle a document, he owes a duty to advise or settle the document with reasonable competence and care. This duty is owed to anyone he should foresee may suffer loss if the duty is breached.

If in breach of that duty, he fails to exercise reasonable competence
C or care and as a result the person to whom the duty was owed suffers damage he is liable to compensate that person for the damage he has suffered. The law requires the damage to be borne by the person whose breach of duty has caused it, rather than by the innocent person who has suffered it.

I am far from saying that if the advice or document turns out to be wrong, it necessarily follows that he who gave or drew it is liable for the
D loss caused by its imperfection. The barrister is under no duty to be right; he is only under a duty to exercise reasonable care and competence. Lawyers are often faced with finely balanced problems. Diametrically opposite views may and not infrequently are taken by barristers and indeed by judges, each of whom has exercised reasonable, and sometimes far more than reasonable, care and competence. The fact that one of
E them turns out to be wrong certainly does not mean that he has been negligent. In my opinion, however, it can only be in the rarest of cases that the law confers any immunity upon a barrister against a claim for negligence in respect of any work he has done out of court; and this case is certainly not amongst them.

I ought to add that when *Rondel* v. *Worsley* [1967] 1 Q.B. 443 came to the Court of Appeal, I felt bound for the reasons I have given to deal
F with points which I considered to be wholly irrelevant to anything we had to decide. I may have put the case too high if I used words which might give the impression that counsel's immunity always extended to the drafting of pleadings and to advising on evidence. I should have said that the immunity might *sometimes* extend to drafting pleadings and advising on evidence. If in an advice on evidence counsel states that
G he will not call Y as a witness whom he believes his client wishes to call solely to prejudice his opponent, counsel is immune on grounds of public policy from being sued in negligence by his client for advising that Y must not be called or for refusing to call him. In such a case the advice would be so closely connected with the conduct of the case in court that it should be covered by the same immunity. It would be absurd if counsel who is immune from an action in negligence for refusing in
H court to call a witness could be sued in negligence for advising out of court that the witness should not be called. If he could be sued for giving such advice it would make a travesty of the general immunity from suit for anything said or done in court and it is well settled that any device to circumvent this immunity cannot succeed: see e.g. *Marrinan* v. *Vibart* [1963] 1 Q.B. 234; [1963] 1 Q.B. 528.

I think that the passage from the judgment of McCarthy P. in *Rees* v. *Sinclair* [1974] 1 N.Z.L.R. 180, 187, cited in the Court of Appeal, relates to facts similar to those I have just postulated. I think that McCarthy P. would be astonished to hear his judgment cited in support of the decision made by the Court of Appeal in the circumstances of the present case. The facts in *Rees* v. *Sinclair* do not emerge from the report of that case in the New Zealand Court of Appeal. The report, however, at first instance [1973] 1 N.Z.L.R. 236, throws light on those facts. It appears that the plaintiff living apart from his wife under a deed of separation had paid her maintenance since 1962 and had entered into an agreement in 1964 to pay her future maintenance; he also abandoned his divorce petition. The defendant who was a solicitor and barrister acted for the plaintiff in proceedings in which the plaintiff claimed a variation of the agreed maintenance and his wife asked for an order of permanent maintenance. The plaintiff wished to support his case by alleging wrongful conduct by his wife prior to 1962. The defendant apparently considered that there was no justification for making these allegations and no evidence to support them. He accordingly advised that they should not be made and he refused to put them forward on the plaintiff's behalf. The defendant acting in his capacity as counsel, or indeed as solicitor, clearly owed a duty to the court on grounds of public policy not to put those allegations forward, taking the view that he did about them. The plaintiff sued him for negligence and the court held rightly that the defendant was immune from such proceedings. There is all the difference in the world between *Rees* v. *Sinclair* [1974] 1 N.Z.L.R. 180 and the present case. I respectfully agree with McCarthy P. when he says, at p. 187:

"... the protection exists only where the particular [paper] work is so intimately connected with the conduct of the cause in court that it can fairly be said to be a preliminary decision affecting the way that cause is to be conducted when it comes to a hearing."

The "intimate connection" to which McCarthy P. referred, undoubtedly existed in *Rees* v. *Sinclair* and in the case I have just postulated. In my opinion there is no such connection between the advice given in the present case and conduct of a case in court. The advice given made it impossible for the plaintiff's unanswerable case to be heard in court. It was not even remotely connected with counsel's duty to the court nor with public policy.

My Lords, for the reasons I have stated I would allow the appeal.

LORD RUSSELL OF KILLOWEN. My Lords, in arriving at a conclusion in this appeal I have striven, I hope successfully, to avoid being influenced by the fact that I find it difficult to see where the barrister erred in selecting as defendant the owner of the car, whose wife was driving it (negligently) for the purpose of taking their children to school. However unsatisfactory it may be, we are obliged to assume for the purposes of this appeal that the barrister was negligent in the respects summarised by my noble and learned friend on the Woolsack. Should, on that assumption, the third party notice be struck out as disclosing no cause of action against the barrister recognised by the law?

The history relating to claims for negligence by professional people, and barristers in particular, has been very fully canvassed in your Lordships' speeches, as has also the tendency of recent years for decisions of the courts to stress responsibility in all fields of those guilty of errors of

A commission or omission towards others to whom harm has been caused
by such errors.

For myself, my Lords, I accept without qualification the decision of
this House in *Rondel* v. *Worsley* [1969] 1 A.C. 191. The negligence
there alleged was the method of conduct of a criminal defence in court.
I cannot find that there is any sound distinction between that and the
conduct of civil proceedings in court.

B It is to be observed that nowhere, so far as I am aware, has it been
suggested that a barrister in respect of his conduct of a case in court
should have a special immunity from suit for negligence because what
he does in court is (so to speak) in the heat of battle, when he must make
a decision in the obscurity of dust and smoke. Nor do I consider that
such immunity is rightly connected with a quite different (as it seems to
C me) immunity of judges, witnesses, and jurors.

What then is the justification for immunity from *claims* for negligence
that has so far been established? It lies in my opinion in the public duty
that rests upon the Bar in particular to participate in and contribute to
the orderly proper and expeditious trial of causes in our courts. In the
exercise of such a duty it appears to me that it is highly undesirable and
against public policy that a barrister in deciding in court upon a particular
D course of action, or attitude, should be in a position of having to wonder
whether a different course of action, or attitude, would not be more likely
to avoid a *claim* that he was negligent. I take a simple illustration. It is
desirable in a civil case to prove a fact. Five people say that they can
testify to it. Counsel decides to call two, saving the time of the court.
Those two turn out to be not good witnesses, or are not in the end
E accepted to be such by the judge. Is the barrister to be subjected to a
claim in negligence by his disappointed client for his attempt to facilitate
the administration of justice? I consistently stress the word *claim*. He
may or may not have been negligent in not calling the other three
witnesses. It his vulnerability to a *claim* that may interfere with his duty.

The example which I have given is of something done (or rather not
done) in the course of the trial of a civil action inside the court. I cannot
F accept that there is a universally acceptable distinction between what is
done (or omitted) in the court in the presence of the judge and what is
done (or omitted) outside court or before trial. Preliminary hearings
before a master may be regarded as upon the same basis as the trial.
But what of actions (or omissions) of counsel in the course of steps taken
upon which the trial (if any) is to be based? I do not accept the suggestion
G that the calm atmosphere of chambers in the Temple (or even Lincoln's
Inn) marks a distinction: I have already remarked that the heat, dust
and smoke of the battle has never been urged as a special ground of
immunity from suit for negligence. In my opinion if a decision by
counsel is arrived at—albeit negligently—before trial which might well
have been arrived at at trial, or before a master, it should not be open to
a claim for negligence. In particular, as here, a decision as to the proper
H party to be joined as defendant.

I can find no justifiable line to be drawn at the door of the court, so
that a claim in negligence will lie against a barrister for what he does or
omits negligently short of the threshold though not if his negligent
omission or commission is over the threshold. His immunity from claims
of negligence should (granted that it is to exist at all) extend to areas
which affect or may affect the course of conduct of litigation, in which
areas are to be found the public duty and obligation of the barrister to

participate in the administration of justice. And this should be so even A
if the result of the alleged negligence is that litigation does not in fact
come about. A decision which shapes, or may shape, the course of a
trial should be within the umbrella (or blanket) of freedom from claims
whether it is arrived at before trial or during it. This must include advice
on settlement: advice on evidence: advice on parties: to list only
examples. A barrister is offered an opportunity in the course of a
trial to add a party: he misunderstands the case and allegedly negligently B
declines the opportunity: as I understand *Rondel* v. *Worsley* [1969] 1
A.C. 191 he is immune from the claim. Is there any reason for not
holding him also immune from a claim for not originally adding that
party? I think not.

My Lords, there may be much to be said for denying immunity from
claims for negligence by a barrister in the conduct of civil litigation in C
court. But while that immunity stands, as I think it does as involved in
the decision of this House in *Rondel* v. *Worsley,* I see no escape from
the extension to pre-trial alleged negligence so strongly supported (obiter)
in that case.

I find myself in agreement with the views expressed in his speech
(which I have had the advantage of seeing in draft) of my noble and
learned friend Lord Keith of Kinkel and, finding myself in concurrence D
with them, I would dismiss this appeal.

LORD KEITH OF KINKEL. My Lords, the facts of this case and the
circumstances under which it comes before your Lordships' House have
been narrated in the speech of my noble and learned friend Lord
Wilberforce, whose account I gratefully adopt. E

According to the headnote in the report of *Rondel* v. *Worsley* [1969]
1 A.C. 191 this House held in that case that a barrister was immune from
an action for negligence at the suit of a client in respect of his conduct and
management of a case in court and the preliminary work connected therewith such as the drawing of pleadings. A majority of the House expressed
the view that the immunity does not extend to matters unconnected with
cases in court. F

Rondel v. *Worsley* was on its facts concerned only with alleged
negligence in connection with a barrister's work in court in the course of
a criminal trial, so all that was said in their Lordships' speeches about
other aspects of a barrister's work may strictly be described as obiter
dicta. But their Lordships were clearly concerned to review, in the light
of the authorities, the law as to the scope of a barrister's immunity from G
suits for negligence in connection with all aspects of his work, and what
they said about those activities which are carried on elsewhere than in
the actual court-room in the course of a trial was carefully considered.
Accordingly the views so expressed should not, in my opinion, lightly be
departed from.

In the present appeal it was not argued that no aspect of a barrister's
work attracted immunity, but it was contended that the immunity was H
strictly limited to work done actually in court in the conduct of a cause.

It is apparent that in the opinion of at least four of their Lordships in
Rondel v. *Worsley* [1969] 1 A.C. 191 the scope of the immunity is not
so limited. The position of Lord Morris of Borth-y-Gest in this respect
is not entirely clear. The relevant passages from the speeches have been
quoted by my noble and learned friend Lord Wilberforce, and I need not
repeat them.

A   The principle upon which the decision in *Rondel* v. *Worsley* proceeded
was that of public interest. The principal aspect was the consideration
that the proper administration of justice had better prospects of being
achieved if barristers, in their conduct of litigation, were not inhibited
in any decision they might make by the fear of being sued for negligence
by a disappointed client. Such fear, so it was considered, might detract
from the degree of attention given by the barrister to his duty to the
B   court and to the administration of justice generally in situations where
that duty conflicted with the personal interests of his client. In my view
that consideration is valid and has a sound basis. Further, I have no
doubt that its application extends further than the actual conduct of a
case in court. A barrister's duty to the court and the due administration
of justice has to be kept firmly in view when he directs his mind to
C   whether an action should be brought and against what parties, to whether
an action should be settled or abandoned and to advising on evidence
and on the discovery of documents. It is true that decisions on such
matters normally are taken in situations offering more opportunity for
reflection than is present in face of the court in the course of a trial.
But that might well mean that the decision is less instinctively correct
in the light of the barrister's duty to the court and more likely to be
D   influenced by thoughts of the action which the client, in the absence of
an immunity, might take.

     I am therefore of opinion that the grounds of this aspect of public
interest extend beyond the actual conduct of a case in court and are
applicable to all stages of a barrister's work in connection with litigation,
whether pending or only in contemplation.

E   The second aspect of public interest considered relevant in *Rondel* v.
Worsley [1969] 1 A.C. 191 was the undesirability of re-litigating between
barrister and client issues which had ex hypothesi been decided adversely
to the client in previous litigation. Here again I regard as convincing
the reasons which led their Lordships to rely upon this ground for
affirming the existence of immunity. It was argued that this ground
could not apply where as a result of a barrister's negligence the client's
F   claim had never been litigated at all. The answer to the argument is,
in my view, that the purpose of the indemnity is to exclude in the public
interest the bringing of actions of a certain category. The matter must
rest upon principle, and it is not critical that the relevant factors of
public interest may apply less strongly upon the facts to certain cases in
the category covered by the principle than they do to others.

G   In *Rondel* v. *Worsley* there also entered to some extent into the
grounds of decision stated by certain of their Lordships the rule that a
barrister may not decline to act for a particular client in a field in which
he normally practises, if he is disengaged and is tendered a reasonable
fee. I do not myself regard this aspect as having much importance from
the point of view of public interest, as I do not consider that if barristers
H   were liable to be sued for negligence this would, having regard to the
standards of the profession, be likely to result in any person being
deprived of competent representation in any litigation.

     In *Rees* v. *Sinclair* [1974] 1 N.Z.L.R. 180 the New Zealand Court of
Appeal accepted that a limit should be placed upon a barrister's immunity
from actions for negligence in respect of work done in connection with
litigation. The nature of the limitation was thus expressed by McCarthy
P., at p. 187:

A   " But I cannot narrow the protection to what is done in court: it must be wider than that and include some pre-trial work. Each piece of before-trial work should, however, be tested against the one rule; that the protection exists only where the particular work is so intimately connected with the conduct of the cause in court that it can fairly be said to be a preliminary decision affecting the way that cause is to be conducted when it comes to a hearing. The protection should not be given any wider application than is B absolutely necessary in the interests of the administration of justice, and that is why I would not be prepared to include anything which does not come within the test I have stated."

In my opinion the restriction thus expressed is not consistent with the principal ground of the decision in *Rondel* v. *Worsley* [1969] 1 A.C. 191, namely that immunity should apply to all situations where there is the C possibility of conflict between the barrister's duty to the court and to the proper administration of justice and the personal interests of his client. That possibility was considered by the majority at least in *Rondel* v. *Worsley* to exist in relation to all aspects of a barrister's work in connection with litigation, and I respectfully agree with them. I am unable to perceive any distinction valid for the purposes of the relevant D principle between work in connection with litigation which affects the way the case is conducted when it comes to a hearing and that which does not. Further, I consider that it would be undesirable, and of marginal utility to disappointed litigants, to open the door to inquiry in individual cases whether or not the distinction is established. To do so would go some length towards defeating the purpose of the immunity, which is to enable barristers to apply their minds to litigation work undistracted by E consideration of whether or not they might be sued for negligence. If the considerations of public interest held valid in *Rondel* v. *Worsley* [1969] 1 A.C. 191 are to be accepted as being so, as in my opinion they should be, then they should in my view be applied so as to achieve their purpose as effectively as possible. Further, I think there is merit in the maintenance of a rule which is relatively simple and easy to apply. F That immunity extends to all of a barrister's work in connection with litigation is such a rule. The suggested restriction of the immunity would presumably exclude from its scope all cases relating to contemplated litigation which did not actually reach the stage of a hearing in court, and all litigation settled, compromised or abandoned. In other cases the suggested restriction would, in my opinion, prove difficult to apply in practice and would almost inevitably require inquiry into the facts. It G would seldom, if ever, be possible to decide the issue of immunity upon an application for striking out. So the objective of relieving the barrister of any apprehension of contentious litigation regarding the conduct of his cases would not be achieved.

In the present case the negligence alleged against the third party took place in connection with his conduct of litigation. I am of opinion that the immunity therefore applies to it.   H

My Lords, for these reasons I would dismiss the appeal.

Appeal allowed.

Solicitors: *The Law Society; Hewitt, Woollacott & Chown.*

J. A. G.

A

[COURT OF APPEAL]

INTERNATIONAL FACTORS LTD. *v.* RODRIGUEZ

[1975 I. No. 9135]

B 1978 May 9

Buckley and Bridge L.JJ.
and Sir David Cairns

*Conversion—Right to sue—Factoring agreement—Debts owed to
company assigned to factor—Any payment by debtor direct
to company to be held in trust for and immediately handed
to factor—Debtors' cheques paid into company's bank
C account by director—Whether right to sue director in conversion—Whether measure of damages face value of cheques*

By a standard factoring agreement the plaintiffs purchased
the book debts of a company of which the defendant was a
director. It was a term of the agreement that if, contrary to
the machinery of the agreement, any payment in respect of
an assigned debt was made direct to the company, it was to
D be held in trust for the plaintiffs and immediately handed to
them. In breach of that term four cheques sent to the
company in respect of debts assigned to the plaintiffs were
paid into the company's bank account on the instructions of
the defendant. The plaintiffs sued the defendant for conversion and obtained judgment for the face value of the cheques.

On appeal by the defendant: —

Held, dismissing the appeal, that the trust in favour of the
E plaintiffs, which arose as soon as the cheques came into the
possession of the company, along with the company's obligation to hand over the cheques immediately to the plaintiffs,
gave the latter a sufficient proprietary right to sue in conversion (post, p. 881A–B); that the disposition of the cheques
amounted to a conversion by the defendant (post, p. 881F–G);
and that the plaintiffs were entitled to damages measured by
the face value of the cheques regardless of whether they had
F any right to recover the amount of the debts from the original
debtors (post, p. 882E).

Healey v. *Healey* [1915] 1 K.B. 938 and *Marquess of
Bute* v. *Barclays Bank Ltd.* [1955] 1 Q.B. 202 approved.

Jarvis v. *Williams* [1955] 1 W.L.R. 71, C.A. distinguished.

Per Buckley L.J. Whether or not an immediate trust
would attach to a cheque in payment of a debt direct to
the company, there is a contractual right for the plaintiffs
G to demand immediate delivery of the cheque to them, and
that is a sufficient right to possession to give them a status to
sue in conversion (post, p. 883D–E).

The following cases are referred to in the judgment of Sir David Cairns:

Bute (Marquess) v. *Barclays Bank Ltd.* [1955] 1 Q.B. 202; [1954] 3
W.L.R. 741; [1954] 3 All E.R. 365.
H *Fairline Shipping Corporation* v. *Adamson* [1975] Q.B. 180; [1974] 2
W.L.R. 824; [1974] 2 All E.R. 967.
Healey v. *Healey* [1915] 1 K.B. 938.
Jarvis v. *Williams* [1955] 1 W.L.R. 71; [1955] 1 All E.R. 108, C.A.
Performing Right Society Ltd. v. *Ciryl Theatrical Syndicate Ltd.* [1924]
1 K.B. 1, C.A.

No additional cases were cited in argument.

APPEAL from Mr. John Newey Q.C. sitting as a deputy judge of the A
Queen's Bench Division.

The plaintiffs, International Factors Ltd., by writ in November 1975,
alleged that the defendant, Roy A. Rodriguez, managing director of
Sound Components Ltd., "the company," in breach of an agreement,
dated April 27, 1973, made between the plaintiffs and the company,
paid or caused to be paid into the company's bank account four cheques
drawn by debtors whose debts had been assigned to the plaintiffs and B
thereby wrongfully converted the cheques and/or acted in or caused a
breach of trust imposed under clause 11 (e) of the agreement, and
claimed damages of £11,370·69 together with interest. On May 20,
1977, Mr. John Newey Q.C., sitting as a deputy judge of the Queen's
Bench Division, gave judgment for the plaintiffs in the full amount of
their claim.
 C
The defendant by notice of appeal dated June 3, 1977, appealed on
the grounds that the judge was wrong in law in holding that (1) the
plaintiffs had a good cause of action in conversion against the defendant
since the plaintiffs at no material time had any proprietary interest
in the cheques sufficient to sustain a claim in conversion, their only
entitlement being a mere contractual right vested in them under the
terms of the agreement and (2) the plaintiffs had suffered any damage D
by reason of the alleged conversion in that each of the assignments
being complete at law the plaintiffs' cause of action as against the
original debtors was in no way impaired by reason of the cheques having
been paid into the company's bank account instead of being handed
over to the plaintiffs.

The facts are stated in the judgment of Sir David Cairns.
 E

Alan Steinfeld for the defendant.
Neil Butter Q.C. and *G. D. Conlin* for the plaintiffs.

BUCKLEY L.J. I have asked Sir David Cairns to deliver the first
judgment.
 F

SIR DAVID CAIRNS. This is an appeal from a judgment of Mr. John
Newey Q.C., sitting as a deputy judge of the Queen's Bench Division.
He gave judgment for the plaintiffs in the action for the sum of
£11,370·69 plus interest, a total of something over £14,000.

There are two issues on the appeal, both of them issues of law. The
defendant adduced no evidence at the trial and the judge found all the G
facts to be as deposed to by the plaintiffs' witnesses.

The defendant was a director of a company called Sound Components Ltd., now in liquidation; I shall refer to it simply as "the
company." Its business was the manufacture of loudspeakers and other
components for hi-fi equipment. The defendant was also a guarantor
of the company's bank account.

On April 7, 1973, an agreement under seal was entered into between H
the plaintiffs and the company. The plaintiffs carry on the business of
discounting debts, and the agreement was in a standard form of what
is called a factoring agreement. By it the plaintiffs agreed to purchase
from the company all the book debts of the company and the company
agreed to sell them to the plaintiffs for the sum of 98½ per cent. of the
full amount of the debts. The detailed machinery is of course set out
in the agreement. It was contended in the court below that that

A   machinery had not been complied with, but that argument has not been pursued in this court.

The machinery involved that in order to ensure that the plaintiffs received the amount of the debts, all the company's invoices were to be indorsed with a statement indicating that the debt flowing from the invoice was assigned to the plaintiffs, and then the practice was for the company in the case of each debt to execute an assignment to B   the plaintiffs and to give express notice to every debtor as soon as the assignment had been completed. There was an express provision in the agreement that if any debtor paid the company by cheque the company was to hand over that cheque immediately to the plaintiffs.

In June and July of 1974, four cheques were sent by debtors to the company, the total amount of the four cheques being the sum which C   I have mentioned, £11,370·69. Those payments were made in purported discharge of debts for goods supplied, but it is now accepted that those were debts which had been assigned to the plaintiffs and the judge found that all the machinery laid down in the agreement had been duly complied with. As I have already indicated, there is now no issue about that. But what happened was that, instead of the cheques being handed straight to the plaintiffs as they should have been, they were D   all paid into the company's bank account and, as the judge found and as is now no longer in issue, this was done on the instructions of the defendant himself, who was largely responsible for the running of the company, which at that time was in considerable financial difficulties, and he knew perfectly well that what he was doing was contrary to the agreement with the plaintiffs.

E   That this was a breach of contract by the company is obvious. It is also obvious that a cause of action in contract would not lie by the plaintiffs against the defendant, who as an individual was not a party to the contract. The judge, however, found that a cause of action in tort, in conversion, was established against the defendant, and he based his judgment on three propositions. First, that a director is liable for torts committed by him in connection with the affairs of a company. He F   cited, as authority for that proposition, *Performing Right Society Ltd. v. Ciryl Theatrical Syndicate Ltd.* [1924] 1 K.B. 1 and *Fairline Shipping Corporation v. Adamson* [1975] Q.B. 180. It is not now in dispute that the judge was right up to that point.

Mr. Steinfeld, on behalf of the defendant in this court, has interpreted the judge's judgment as meaning that the tort was primarily G   a tort of the company and that the defendant became liable as the person who was instrumental in committing the tort on behalf of the company. I do not so read the judgment. I read it as meaning that the defendant himself was here the primary tortfeasor, and the fact that he was acting on behalf of the company is no defence to him.

There now come two propositions which are challenged. The first H   is that the judge held that payment of the cheques into the company's bank account was a conversion of the cheques. The second is that, having so found and having held that the defendant was liable for that conversion, the judge went on to hold that the measure of damages was the face value of the cheques.

As to whether this was a conversion, counsel for the defendant says that the plaintiffs here had no more than a contractual right to receive these cheques; they had no proprietary right so as to enable them to

sue in conversion. On the issue of damages, Mr. Steinfeld's proposition A
is that in this case, because the debts had been assigned, because notice
of the assignment had been given to the debtors, their payment of the
debts to the company did not discharge them from liability; that
accordingly the plaintiffs are in a position to recover the full amount of
those debts from the original debtors and that their damages should be
limited to any trouble, inconvenience and expense to which they might
be put in recovering the debts from the debtors and, no doubt, to any B
amount that proved to be irrecoverable if it so happened that any of
the debtors were not able to pay.

I do not find it necessary to go any further into the provisions of
the agreement of April 7, 1973, except to refer to one vital clause; that
is clause 11 (e) which provides as follows:

" If any payment in respect of an assigned debt is paid direct to the C
supplier "—the supplier being the company—" then the supplier
shall hold the same in trust for the factor "—the factor being the
plaintiffs. " The supplier shall in that event immediately after
receipt of any such payment hand to the factor the identical cash
cheque or bill of exchange and if it be necessary for such cheque
or bill of exchange to be endorsed to the factor to enable the
factor to receive payment the supplier shall endorse the same D
over to the factor."

In support of his contention that the plaintiffs were not entitled to
sue in conversion, counsel relies, first, on a passage in *Clerk & Lindsell
on Torts*, 14th ed. (1975), para. 1108, indicating that to have a right to
sue in conversion, a plaintiff must have a right to possession; that a
mere contractual right is not sufficient, but that a cestui qui trust E
would have a right to sue for conversion of property the legal ownership
of which was in a bare trustee.

It is clear law that a contractual right to have goods handed to him
by another person is not in itself sufficient to clothe the person who
has that right with power to sue in conversion. That was the decision
of this court in *Jarvis* v. *Williams* [1955] 1 W.L.R. 71. The headnote F
reads:

" In January, 1948, J. delivered bathroom fittings to W. at P.'s
request. P. did not pay for them and in September, 1949, it was
agreed, between J. and P., that J. should take back the goods,
collecting them from W. at P.'s expense. W., however, refused to
deliver up the goods to J. J. claimed in detinue against W. for G
the return of the the goods: — *Held*, that J. could not maintain
an action in detinue against W. since the property in the goods,
which had passed to P. on delivery to W. at P.'s request, had
remained vested in P., notwithstanding the agreement that J. should
recover the goods."

Sir Raymond Evershed M.R., giving the leading judgment, after citing H
passages from the judgment in the court below, said, at p. 74:

" I take that to mean that the contractual right which the plaintiff
had vis-à-vis Paterson to go and collect these good from Paterson's
agent was a right of a sufficient character to enable the plaintiff
to bring an action in detinue against the agent of the owner of the
property in these goods. But, with all respect to the county court
judge, I am unable to accept that as a good proposition of law."

A So a contractual right is not sufficient.

In my view, however, there was here something more than a contractual right. Clause 11 (e) of the agreement provided both that the company was to hold any debt paid direct to the company in trust for the plaintiffs and immediately after receipt of a cheque, in the case of payment by cheque, to hand over that cheque to the plaintiffs.

B Taking together the trust which was thereby set up and the obligation immediately on receipt to hand over the cheque to the plaintiffs, I am satisfied that the plaintiffs had here a sufficient proprietary right to sue in conversion.

For the proposition that a person with an equitable title to goods can sue in conversion assistance is derived from the decision of Shearman J. in *Healey* v. *Healey* [1915] 1 K.B. 938. That was a case where by a

C marriage settlement a husband assigned to trustees certain chattels upon trust to allow them to be used by the wife during her life; the wife brought an action against the husband for wrongful detention of the chattels and it was held that the action could be maintained by the wife without joining the trustees of the settlement as parties. It is perhaps curious that that is the only decision that counsel has been able to discover of a cestui qui trust being entitled to sue in conversion, but

D it seems to me that since the fusion of law and equity that is sound law.

It was contended on behalf of the defendant that no trust arose here until some further act had been done by the company after receipt of the money. In my view that is wrong. The effect of clause 11 (e) was that as soon as one of these cheques came into the possession of the company there arose a trust for the plaintiffs along with the obligation

E of immediately handing over the cheque itself to the plaintiffs. It is further contended that *Healey* v. *Healey* is no authority for the proposition that the trustee himself can be sued in conversion. It would be surprising to me if the trustee could not be sued in conversion; certainly before the Theft Act 1968 there was a specific crime of conversion by trustee; probably under the Theft Act a disposal for his own purposes of goods held in trust by the trustee would constitute theft, and I find it

F difficult to suppose that a trustee making away for his own benefit with trust property, or for the benefit of some person other than the equitable owner of it, would not be liable in conversion. But however that may be, the defendant himself was not the trustee; the defendant himself disposed of the cheques in such a way as to take them away from the plaintiffs, who were entitled to have them, and put them into the com-

G pany's bank account; that was a disposition which I am quite satisfied amounted to a conversion.

The judge in the court below derived assistance in reaching his decision from the judgment of McNair J. in *Marquess of Bute* v. *Barclays Bank Ltd.* [1955] 1 Q.B. 202. That was a case of conversion of certain warrants by a farm manager, who had received the warrants

H in connection with his occupation as farm manager with the intention that the money should go to his employer, the Marquess of Bute; the defendant used the warrants for his own purposes and it was held that notwithstanding the fact that the warrants were made out in the name of the defendant his act constituted a conversion of them. That decision is of some assistance to the plaintiffs in this case, inasmuch as it shows that the fact that the cheques were made out in favour of the company is no sufficient answer to the claim of the plaintiffs that they were the persons who owned the cheques in equity and were entitled to have them handed directly to them. I am accordingly satisfied that conversion was established here.

So far as damages are concerned, in my view, the general position in relation to the conversion of a cheque is that the conversion gives the person entitled to the cheque a right to damages measured by the face value of the cheque. That, as the judge stated, has been established by a whole series of cases in some of which the defendants were banks. The damages may, of course, be mitigated by special circumstances; for example, to take the case which Mr. Steinfeld suggested to us, if the cheque were stopped before payment into his bank by the wrongdoer and a fresh cheque given in substitution for it which was duly met. But it would be for the defendant to establish that there were circumstances of that kind which relieved him of his full liability in damages.

It is said here that the plaintiffs are not shown to have suffered any damage and certainly not the amount of damages which they claim, because they still have a right of action against the debtors. That seems to me to be no ground upon which the defendant can escape from paying damages in full. The position simply is that, assuming, as I will, that there is a right of action against the debtors, a plaintiff who has two causes of action cannot be met when he makes a claim against one defendant by the answer: " Oh, no; you've suffered nothing by my tort because you have a cause of action against somebody else." That clearly cannot be right. To take an example, if X wrongfully converted Y's motor car and handed it to Z, an auctioneer, who innocently sold it, Y could recover full damages from Z and it would be no answer to his claim to say that, he had an equal claim against X. This is an a fortiori case, because here it is the defendant who is the wrongdoer, and, in my judgment, he cannot set up against the plaintiffs' claim to the full value of the cheques the contention that the plaintiffs could call upon the debtors to pay over again for goods that they have already paid for, though unfortunately they made the mistake of paying them to the wrong person at the time.

I am quite satisfied that the judge was right both as to liability and as to damages and I would dismiss the appeal.

BRIDGE L.J. I agree.

BUCKLEY L.J. I agree. On the first point, the question of the status of the plaintiff to sue the defendant in conversion, it seems to me to be inescapable that under clause 11 (e) of the agreement the plaintiffs had a right to immediate possession of any cheque which might come into the possession of the company as the result of a debt which had been assigned to the plaintiffs being mistakenly paid to the company. Clause 11 (e) not only provides that if any payment in respect of an assigned debt is paid directly to the company, then the company shall hold the same in trust for the plaintiffs, but it goes on to provide specifically that the company shall in that event, immediately after receipt of any such payment, hand to the plaintiffs the identical cash, cheque or bill of exchange, and that, if it is necessary for such cheque, bill or bill of exchange to be endorsed to the plaintiffs to enable the plaintiffs to receive payment, the company shall endorse the same over to the plaintiffs.

The Weekly Law Reports, December 1, 1978

883

3 W.L.R.   International Factors v. Rodriguez (C.A.)   Buckley L.J.

A   It is manifest on the terms of clause 11 (e) of the agreement that the intention of the parties was that the cheque itself, if payment was by cheque, should be handed on, endorsed if necessary, to the plaintiffs, and that confers upon the plaintiffs, as it seems to me, an immediate right to possession of any such cheque quite sufficient to support a cause of action in conversion against anyone who wrongfully deals with the cheque in any other manner. The payment of the cheque into the

B   company's bank account was a wrongful application of the cheque in direct conflict with the requirements of clause 11 (e) of the contract, and the fact that the company would have been accountable to the plaintiffs for the proceeds of the cheque does not, in my judgment, make that application any less wrong.

Mr. Steinfeld, in a well-presented argument, has urged that it
C   cannot be a conversion to pay the cheque into the company's account, the company being, under the terms of this clause of the agreement, a trustee of the proceeds of the cheque for the benefit of the plaintiffs; but, in my judgment, that cannot be an answer to a claim in conversion when the clearest possible indication is contained in the contract between the parties that the cheque shall not be paid into the company's own account but shall be handed over in specie to the plaintiffs in order that

D   they may have the benefit of it and be able to negotiate it or deal with it in any way they choose, at their own discretion.

Accordingly, whether or not an enforceable trust would attach immediately on the payment of any debt direct to the company by cheque; whether or not an immediate trust would attach to such a cheque, I think that there is a contractual right here for the plaintiffs

E   to demand immediate delivery of the cheque to them, and that that is a sufficient right to possession to give them a status to sue in conversion.

On the findings of the judge the defendant was personally responsible for the payment of each of the four cheques to which this case relates into the company's account, and in those circumstances the right conclusion appears to me to be that it was the defendant who misapplied

F   the cheque and who is liable for conversion. Mr. Steinfeld has suggested that he could only be made liable in conversion if the company itself was guilty of conversion and so he, as an officer of the company, could be made vicariously responsible for conversion. In my view, that is the wrong approach; the cheque was physically in the possession or under the control of the defendant; it was he who applied

G   it wrongly in a manner in conflict with the rights of the plaintiffs and, in my judgment, it was he who was guilty of conversion as a primary participant and not merely as a secondary participant in the transaction.

Accordingly, I fully agree with the view expressed in the judgment delivered that in this case the plaintiffs are entitled to recover against the defendant for conversion. I also agree with what Sir David Cairns has said about the measure of damages, and I consequently agree that

H   this appeal should be dismissed.

Appeal dismissed with costs.

Solicitors: *Raymond Dobson & Co., Chichester; Sidney Pearlman & Greene.*

C. N.

[1978]

A

[QUEEN'S BENCH DIVISION]

In re SHAHID IQBAL

1978 April 24;   Lord Widgery C.J., Boreham
    May 23   and Drake JJ.

B

*Habeas Corpus—Commonwealth immigrant—Validity of return—
Detention order erroneously stating detention for further
examination of immigrant—Examination completed—Whether
order valid—Court's jurisdiction—Immigration Act* 1971
(c. 77), Sch. 2, para. 16 (1) (2) [1]—Habeas Corpus Act 1816
(56 Geo. 3, c. 100), ss. 3, 4 [2]

C

The applicant claimed that he had entered the United
Kingdom in October 1964 travelling with K, who he said was
his father, and on K's passport, that he had then been given
unconditional leave to remain and that except for two visits
to Pakistan on his own passport he had remained and worked
in the United Kingdom ever since. After investigations by
immigration officers, which disclosed a number of flaws in the
applicant's story, the Home Secretary concluded that the
applicant was not the son of K and that he had entered
the United Kingdom as an illegal immigrant in 1969 or 1970.
The applicant was taken into custody pursuant to a detention
order from an immigration officer to a prison governor which
read: " The above named is a person whose detention I have
authorised under paragraph 16 of Schedule 2 to the Immigration Act 1971. I accordingly request you to receive the
said person * pending his further examination under the Act
* pending the completion of arrangements for dealing with
him under the Act." The grounds indicated by asterisks, which
were references respectively to sub-paragraphs (1) and (2) of
paragraph 16 of Schedule 2, were in the alternative. The
immigration officer deleted the second alternative. It was not
in dispute that that was an error, as that was the ground
which was appropriate for the applicant's detention.

D

E

On an application for a writ of habeas corpus on the
grounds that on the facts the applicant had the right to enter
and remain in the United Kingdom, and that the detention was
invalidated by the error in the order: —

F

Held, (1) that the court's function was not to try the facts
on which the Home Secretary's conclusion was based, but was
limited to satisfying itself that he had acted in good faith
and on adequate evidence; and that there was ample evidence
to justify his conclusions and no suggestion of bad faith (post,
pp. 886H—887c, 891E–G).

G

Reg. v. *Secretary of State for the Home Department, Ex
parte Hussain* [1978] 1 W.L.R. 700, D.C. and C.A. followed.

(2) That, the immigration officer having particularized the
reference to the fact that the authority for the detention was
the Act of 1971, with a specific ground, that ground could not

---

[Reported by MICHAEL HAWKINGS, ESQ., Barrister-at-Law]

H

[1] Immigration Act 1971, Sch. 2, para. 16: " (1) A person who may be required
to submit to examination under paragraph 2 above may be detained under the
authority of an immigration officer pending his examination and pending a decision
to give or refuse him leave to enter. (2) A person in respect of whom directions
may be given under any of paragraphs 8 to 14 above may be detained under the
authority of an immigration officer pending the giving of directions and pending his
removal in pursuance of any directions given."
[2] Habeas Corpus Act 1816, ss. 3, 4: see post, p. 887G–H.

A   be disregarded by the court as superfluous, and the court
should examine its validity (post, pp. 888F–G, 889E, 893F—894B).
      Per curiam. It was doubtful whether a detention order,
which merely specified that the applicant was detained under
paragraph 16 of Schedule 2 to the Act, was sufficient especially
as R.S.C., Ord. 54, r. 7, required the return to state " all
causes of the detainer of the person restrained " (post, pp.
888E–F, 893D–E).

B   (3) Dismissing the application (Boreham J. dissenting),
that the court, being empowered by sections 3 and 4 of the
Habeas Corpus Act 1816 to inquire into the true state of
the facts on a habeas corpus application, was entitled in the
interests of justice to determine whether good grounds for
detention did in fact exist notwithstanding defects in the
detention document; that the applicant's detention was amply
justified on the facts and he had not been prejudiced by the
C   error and, accordingly, the application should be dismissed
(post, pp. 894D–F, H—895A, B–C).
      Per Boreham J. The detention of an individual was not
permissible unless the true reason for it was stated in the
detention order and the proper procedure had been followed
(post, p. 890D–E).

D   The following cases are referred to in the judgments:

Christie v. *Leachinsky* [1947] A.C. 573; [1947] 1 All E.R. 567, H.L.(E.).
Greene v. *Secretary of State for Home Affairs* [1942] A.C. 284; [1941]
      3 All E.R. 388, H.L.(E.).
Reg. v. *Secretary of State for the Home Department, Ex parte Hussain*
      [1978] 1 W.L.R. 700; [1978] 2 All E.R. 423, D.C. and C.A.
Sheriff of Middlesex's Case (1840) 11 Ad. & El. 273.

E   No additional cases were cited in argument.

APPLICATION for writ of habeas corpus.
      The applicant, Shahid Iqbal, applied for a writ of habeas corpus directed
to the Governor of H.M. Prison, Winson Green, Birmingham, to secure
his release from the prison, where he had been detained as an illegal
F   immigrant on January 28, 1978, pursuant to a detention order from an
immigration officer. The order was made under the authority of Schedule 2,
paragraph 16 of the Immigration Act 1971.
      The facts are stated in the judgments of Boreham J. and Drake J.

      Sibghatullah Kadri for the applicant.
      Michael Kennedy for the Secretary of State.
G
                                                            Cur. adv. vult.

      May 23. The following judgments were read.

      LORD WIDGERY C.J. I will ask Boreham J. to give the first judgment.

H   BOREHAM J. Mr. Kadri moves on behalf of the applicant, Shahid Iqbal,
for a writ of habeas corpus directed to the Governor of H.M. Prison,
Winson Green, to secure the applicant's release.
      The matter arises in this way. On January 28, 1978, the applicant was
taken into custody as an illegal immigrant pursuant to the written authority
of one of H.M. immigration officers. The applicant's case is that he was
born in Pakistan on September 20, 1950, the son of Ghulam Sarwar Khan,
that he arrived with his father at Heathrow on October 1, 1964, having

travelled from Pakistan on his father's passport, that he and his father A
were then granted unconditional leave to enter the United Kingdom and
that, save for two visits to Pakistan, when he travelled on his own passport
and on his return from which he was given leave to enter for an indefinite
period, he has lived and worked in this country ever since. Entries in the
passports confirm the granting of leave on three occasions. He contends
that he is a lawful entrant.

For the Secretary of State it is contended that the applicant is not the B
person he pretends to be, that he is not the son of Ghulam Khan, that he
did not enter the United Kingdom before 1969 or 1970 and that the documents produced by Ghulam Khan on October 1, 1964, do not relate to the
applicant. He is therefore an illegal immigrant. The central issue therefore
is one of identity and, therefore, one of fact.

Mr. Kadri has taken two points on the applicant's behalf: (1) that, C
although the written authority for the applicant's detention is valid in law
on its face, it is invalid in fact; (2) that the applicant is the son of Ghulam
Khan, that he entered the country lawfully in 1964, and was given
unconditional leave to stay and is therefore entitled to remain. In either
event it is said that the applicant's detention is unlawful. It is convenient
to deal with the second point first.

The applicant's evidence of his own identity and of the circumstances D
of his arrival in this country in 1964 is supported by the affidavits of
Ghulam Khan (his alleged father) and of Arshad Mahmood and Shahid
Mahmood Aktar, two of Ghulam Khan's sons. There is evidence by three
other deponents, each of whom say that they recognise the photograph of
the applicant as that of a youth who was resident in Birmingham prior to
1970. Prima facie this appears to constitute a powerful body of evidence. E

The immigration authorities have made inquiries. They have interviewed, amongst others, the applicant and the deponents referred to above
and the persons in whose house the applicant alleges that he lived for most
of the period from December 1964 until 1969. These interviews have
revealed discrepancies and lacunae which together suggest that the applicant is not the person he says he is and that he was not where he says he F
was prior to 1970. For instance, when first interviewed in November 1977
the applicant failed to include Arshad Mahmood as a member of Ghulam
Khan's family; when this omission was pointed out to him he said that he
had never heard of Arshad Mahmood. The applicant has been unable to
produce any documentary evidence of his presence in the United Kingdom
prior to 1970 and he lacked knowledge of the pre-decimal currency.
When the persons with whom the applicant says he lived between 1964 and G
1969 were interviewed, they were sure that no one by the name of Shahid
Iqbal had lived at the address during that period. At a later interview one
of them said that he had seen the applicant on two or three occasions
between 1964 and 1969 and blamed his prior failure to recall the applicant
on a faulty memory and the fact that he had been sleepy when interviewed.

The evidence of the three witnesses who purported to recognise the H
applicant's photo as that of a youth resident in Birmingham prior to 1970
was considered by the Secretary of State, who concluded that they were
mistaken.

Mr. Kadri concedes that we cannot re-try the questions of fact. He
accepts that we must be guided by the principles laid down by the Court
of Appeal in *Reg.* v. *Secretary of State for the Home Department, Ex parte
Hussain* [1978] 1 W.L.R. 700. Those principles are to be found in a short

A   extract from the judgment of Geoffrey Lane L.J., at pp. 706–707, quoting with approval the approach laid down by Lord Widgery C.J. in the Divisional Court, at p. 703:

> "Questions of fact in these matters are ultimately questions of fact for the Secretary of State. There are limits to the extent to which this court can go, and, as I see it, our obligation at the moment is to be
B   satisfied that the Home Office approach to the problem is one taken in good faith. Further we have to decide whether there is or is not adequate evidence here to justify the sort of conclusion which the Secretary of State has reached."

In the present case there is nothing to impugn the good faith of the Secretary of State. As to the merits, there was evidence both for and
C   against the applicant. It was for the Secretary of State to weigh that evidence. He has done so. He has concluded that the applicant is not the son of Ghulam Khan and that he entered the country illegally. I think there was ample evidence to justify those conclusions. Mr. Kadri's second point fails.

His first point has more substance; it is that the written authority by virtue of which the applicant is detained is invalid. The document in
D   question is in standard form. It is headed "Immigration Act 1971" and stamped thereunder "Detention Order." It purports to have been issued —as doubtless it was—from H.M. Immigration Office, Birmingham Airport. Below this, in the space provided for the purpose, is entered the applicant's name. It continues: "The above-named is a person whose detention I have authorised under paragraph 16 of Schedule 2 to the Immigration Act
E   1971. I accordingly request you to receive the said person," and then follow two alternatives. The first: "pending his further examination under the Act"; both counsel accept that this would be appropriate for detention ordered under paragraph 16 (1). The second: "pending the completion of arrangements for dealing with him under the Act"; it is agreed that this would be appropriate for detention under paragraph 16 (2).

Each alternative is marked with an asterisk denoting that it should be
F   deleted as appropriate. On the order in question the immigration officer has deleted the second alternative. There are other matters in the order which are irrelevant for present purposes. After signature by the immigration officer the order is addressed to the Governor of H.M. Prison at Winson Green.

Mr. Kadri conceded that the order is apparently complete and valid in law on its face. At one time this would have been conclusive against him.
G   By the Habeas Corpus Act 1816, the court was given specific power in a civil matter to inquire into the facts. The material part of section 3 provides:

> "... in all cases provided for by this Act, although the return to any writ of habeas corpus shall be good and sufficient in law, it shall be lawful for the justice or baron before whom such writ may be return-
H   able, to proceed to examine into the truth of the facts set forth *in such return*, by affidavit or by affirmation . . ." (My italics).

Section 4 further provides:

> "... the like proceeding may be had in the court for controverting the truth of the return to any such writ of habeas corpus, awarded as aforesaid, although such writ shall be awarded by the said court itself, or be returnable therein."

Our duty therefore is to inquire into the truth of the facts set out in the A return of which the important part is the detention order.

In this case the inquiry has been brief, for Mr. Kennedy, who appears for the Home Secretary, concedes that at the time the detention order was made the examination of the applicant was complete and it was no longer lawful to detain him " pending his further examination under the Act." It would, however, have been lawful to detain him " pending the completion of arrangements to deal with him under the Act." In other words the B immigration officer had deleted what were the appropriate words and had allowed the inappropriate to remain.

Mr. Kadri contends that that concludes the matter in the applicant's favour. He says, look at it how you will, there are two alternatives: either (a) the immigration officer had no power to make the order he did and therefore the order was invalid and the detention unlawful, or (b) in C any event, the examination having been completed, there cannot be any right now to detain " pending further examination under the Act."

Mr. Kennedy's reply is that (i) the detention order was and is valid. It is expressed to be made under the provisions of paragraph 16 of Schedule 2 to the Act of 1971. So it is. The contention is that this is sufficient to validate the order that no complaint could have been made if the order D had stopped with the words " I accordingly request you to receive the said person " and that what follows in the order is unnecessary and should be disregarded; (ii) if the first argument is unacceptable, nevertheless the detention is lawful, notwithstanding the defective order, because the true and valid reason for the detention is to be found in the affidavit showing cause.

Neither counsel has referred the court to any authority on what is an E interesting, but not easy, problem. Nor am I aware of any authority.

I doubt whether there is any real basis for the Home Secretary's argument as to the validity of the detention order. R.S.C., Ord. 54, r. 7 requires the return to state all the causes of the detainer of the person restrained. The detention order is the essential part of the return and I doubt if an order, which simply states that detention was authorised under F paragraph 16 of Schedule 2 to the Immigration Act 1971, without giving further particulars justifying such detention, could be said to comply with the rule.

But even assuming that a detention order in such general terms would suffice, the question remains whether, if particulars are given which fail to justify the detention, they can now be disregarded as unnecessary. I think not, and for a number of reasons. First, in accordance with the G provisions of section 3 of the Habeas Corpus Act 1816, the court may, and I think should, examine the facts set out in the return. Secondly, and apart from the statute, there is authority for the proposition that in habeas corpus proceedings the court may examine any grounds given for the detention, notwithstanding that it was unnecessary to give them. In *Sheriff of Middlesex's* case (1840) 11 Ad. & El. 273 the important question was H whether in habeas corpus proceedings a warrant directed by the Speaker of the House of Commons to the Serjeant at Arms committing the sheriff for contempt of the House was bad because it omitted to state the grounds on which contempt had been found. In his judgment Littledale J. in a passage quoted with approval by Lord Maugham in *Greene* v. *Secretary of State for Home Affairs* [1942] A.C. 284 said, at p. 295:

A   " If the warrant declares the grounds of adjudication, this court, in
         many cases, will examine into their validity; but, if it does not, we
         cannot go into such an inquiry."

         Finally, I find helpful and adopt the approach stated by Professor de
Smith in *Judicial Review of Administrative Action*, 3rd ed. (1973),
p. 525 (5):

B   " A further distinction is drawn between superior and inferior courts.
         A superior court, and a body such as the House of Commons which
         is analogous to a superior court, can validly commit under a warrant
         which does not set out the facts giving it jurisdiction; though if it does
         set out the facts and they disclose lack of any legal justification for
         commitment, habeas corpus may properly issue. Inferior courts ought
C   to recite the facts giving them jurisdiction to commit."

I would add that what applies to inferior courts should apply a fortiori to
executive officers.
         Professor de Smith compares the approach in habeas corpus proceedings
with the approach of this court in proceedings for certiorari to quash a
speaking order. If the order states no ground or justification and is complete
D and valid on its face it may not be impugned. If, however, a ground or
justification is given—albeit unnecessarily—which fails to justify the order,
then the order may be quashed. I find this an acceptable and helpful
analogy.
         Applying these principles to the present case it seems to me clear that
the words in the detention order " pending his further examination under
E the Act " were intended to justify the applicant's detention under paragraph 16 of Schedule 2. Even if the argument that they were unnecessary
is correct, their validity should be and has been examined. It is admitted
that they did not justify the detention. They purported to be the sole
justification. Thus it follows that the applicant's detention was not justified
by the terms of the order which purported to authorise it. This is no mere
technicality. The order is one which has deprived the applicant of his
F liberty. It is the authority under which he has been detained. It is the
prison governor's sole authority for detaining him. It appears to be valid
on its face, but when the facts are examined it is shown that what purports
to be the sole justification for the detention cannot be sustained. I think
this is a fundamental error which invalidates the detention order.
         It remains to consider Mr. Kennedy's second point, namely, that not-
G withstanding the defective or invalid detention order, the applicant's
detention is lawful because there was in fact a valid justification for it as
is shown by the affidavit showing cause. That there was in fact a valid
justification is not disputed. Nevertheless, I find the argument unattractive.
If it is correct it reduces the detention order to the level of a " mere scrap
of paper." That, however, does not necessarily dispose of the argument.
         The question is this: can an admittedly valid justification now be
H relied upon in substitution for the invalid justification in the detention
order?
         In the absence of direct authority there comes to mind the analogous
situation of the constable exercising his powers of arrest without warrant.
It is now well settled that a constable must not only act within his legal
powers, he must also make known to the person detained the reason or
justification for the arrest. If he gives a reason which is invalid he cannot

justify the arrest by the fact that he had a valid reason which he kept to **A** himself: *Christie* v. *Leachinsky* [1947] A.C. 573.

I find this sort of approach acceptable in the case of an executive officer ordering the detention of an individual—perhaps even more acceptable because he, unlike the constable, may order detention for a substantial period without the intervention of any judicial authority. Moreover, I can think of no good reason for allowing an executive officer to order the detention of an individual unless the true and lawful justification for the **B** detention is stated in the detention order. It seems no more reasonable to allow one, who has given an invalid justification in the detention order, to justify the detention by asserting—albeit that he asserts truly—that he had a valid justification which was not disclosed. So far as I am aware, there is no authority which impels or even encourages such an approach. Indeed such authority as I have discovered tends to the contrary. In **C** *Christie* v. *Leachinsky* [1947] A.C. 573, 595, Lord Simonds expressed himself thus:

"... the liberty of the subject and the convenience of the police or any other executive authority are not to be weighed in the scales against each other. This case will have served a useful purpose if it enables your Lordships once more to proclaim that a man is not to be **D** deprived of his liberty except in due course and process of law."

Bearing in mind the facts and issues in that case, I take those final words to mean that not only must the detention be justified in law but the proper procedures must be followed. One of the proper procedures in that case was for the constable to inform the detainee of the true and valid reason for his arrest. It had not been done. In my view one of the proper proce- **E** dures in the present case was the making of a true and valid detention order. This has not been done.

I have come to the conclusion that the Home Secretary should not now be allowed to rely upon a justification for the applicant's detention which is different from that which was relied upon in the detention order and in the return. It is said that the true justification for the applicant's detention now appears from the affidavit showing cause and so it does. No doubt **F** the affidavit proves the foundation or basis on which the detention order rests. It certainly explains the circumstances in which the detention order came to be made. But to allow it to be used as Mr. Kennedy now suggests is to substitute it for the detention order. This, in my judgment, goes too far. It is the detention order which is the prison governor's authority to detain the applicant and which is his sole justification for that detention **G** in his return in these proceedings. It seems to me that a true and valid detention order is essential if the detention is to be justified.

I am encouraged in this strict approach by the provisions made by the Rules of the Supreme Court for the amendment and substitution of the return. Ord. 54, r. 7 (2) provides:

"The return may be amended, or another return substituted therefor, **H** by leave of the court or judge before whom the writ is returnable."

I see no reason why a fresh and valid detention order should not have been served on the prison governor and application then made to substitute a fresh return. In fact no fresh order has been served and no application has been made to amend the return or substitute another. The proper procedures have not been followed and no attempt has been made to put right that which it is admitted is wrong.

A   In these circumstances it ought not to avail the Home Secretary to say that a valid detention order could have been drawn up, that there is a valid justification for such an order and thus no injustice has been done. If the detention order could have been put right it should have been put right. The applicant should not remain in custody unless it be under the authority of a valid detention order. In my judgment, for the reasons I have attempted to give, the detention order is not valid.

B   Accordingly I would grant the relief which the applicant now seeks.

DRAKE J. This is a motion on behalf of one Shahid Iqbal for a writ of habeas corpus to release from H.M. Prison at Winson Green the applicant who is at present detained there. The authority for the applicant's detention there is said to be paragraph 16 of Schedule 2 to the Immigration C Act 1971; but a complication arises, as I shall explain later, because the authority was originally stated to arise under sub-paragraph (1) of paragraph 16, whereas it should have been claimed that it arises under sub-paragraph (2) of paragraph 16 of Schedule 2.

Mr. Kadri, who moves on behalf of the applicant, relies on two separate grounds in support of the application. The first ground relates to the complication I have just referred to, in that there was an error in the D document issued by an immigration officer under the authority of which the applicant was detained by the Governor of H.M. Prison at Winson Green. The second ground alleges that the applicant was not validly detained because an examination of the facts shows that the applicant is entitled to enter and remain in the United Kingdom.

I think it convenient to deal first with this second ground, which E requires a review of the facts of this particular case, and which is a ground very commonly relied on by applicants in proceedings similar to these.

The principles on which this court deals with applications such as this, when it is alleged that the facts do not support the conclusion reached by the Secretary of State for the Home Office, are clearly laid down in *Reg.* v. *Secretary of State for the Home Department, Ex parte Hussain* [1978] 1 W.L.R. 700. In that case the Court of Appeal approved as correct the F approach which had been formulated by Lord Widgery C.J. in the same case when it was before this court, when his Lordship said, at p. 703:

"Questions of fact in these matters are ultimately questions of fact for the Secretary of State. There are limits to the extent to which this court can go, and, as I see it, our obligation at the moment is to be satisfied that the Home Office approach to the problem is one taken G in good faith. Further we have to decide whether there is or is not adequate evidence here to justify the sort of conclusion which the Secretary of State has reached."

In the present case I am quite satisfied that there was ample evidence on which the Secretary of State could properly reach the decision he came to, and no suggestion has been made that he acted other than in good faith.

H   The applicant contends that he is the son of one Ghulam Sarwar Khan (who I shall refer to as Mr. Khan) and that he is entitled to enter and remain in the United Kingdom as a member of Mr. Khan's family. The Secretary of State has refused the applicant permission to stay here and has denied his right to stay here on the ground that he has been guilty of deception and is not in fact the son of Mr. Khan. The applicant relies on a number of affidavits filed on his behalf and sworn by various people who in one way or another support his case. But inquiries carried out on behalf

of the Home Office, including oral examination of the applicant and of Mr.   A
Khan and others by immigration officers, have revealed important flaws
in the applicant's case.

He says he was born in Pakistan and first came to this country, accompanying his father, Ghulam Sarwar Khan, in October 1964. He says that
he lived and had casual employment in this country from 1964 until 1973
when he returned to Pakistan on holiday and became engaged to be
married. He says he returned to England in November 1973 and remained   B
here until November 1974 when he went back to Pakistan and was married;
and that he finally came back here on May 1, 1975 and thereafter lived
and worked in the Birmingham area until January 1978 when he was
detained by immigration officers.

When he was first interviewed by an immigration officer he failed to
mention the existence of one Arshad Mahmood, a son of Mr. Khan, and   C
therefore, if his own story is correct, one of his brothers. Furthermore
when the immigration officer asked him if he knew Arshad Mahmood the
applicant denied all knowledge of his existence.

The applicant told the immigration officer that he had no children,
whereas Mr. Khan had told the officer that the applicant did have one
child. The applicant was unable to produce any documentary evidence
whatsoever to support his claim that he had been in England prior to   D
1970, and he had no knowledge at all of the pre-decimal pre-1971 English
currency. When an immigration officer interviewed the man and wife
with whom the applicant said he had lived for a period of about four years
from 1966 until 1970, both of these people emphatically denied any
knowledge of the applicant. They later explained that this denial was due
to a misunderstanding, but this explanation did not convince the immigration   E
officer.

For these and for other subsidiary reasons set out in an affidavit filed
on behalf of the Home Secretary, I think there was ample evidence on
which the Home Secretary could properly reach the decision he came to,
namely, that the applicant Shahid Iqbal is not in truth the son of Mr. Khan.
Accordingly, in so far as the application is based on this ground, in my   F
judgment it fails.

The remaining ground relied on by the applicant raises an interesting
point of law and one which, so far as I am aware, is not directly covered
by any decision of the court. We were not referred to any authorities by
counsel on either side. As I have said, it relates to an error in the document
under which the applicant has been detained in prison.

The document in question is a standard Home Office form used by   G
immigration officers to authorise the detention of persons under the Immigration Act 1971. It is headed " H.O. Form IS 91, Immigration Act 1971 "
and is stamped " Detention Order." There is a space for the insertion of
the name of the person to be detained in which, in this case, has been
written the name of the applicant, and then follows the printed part of the
form which reads: " The above-named is a person whose detention I have   H
authorised under paragraph 16 of Schedule 2 to the Immigration Act 1971."
Then follow the words: " I accordingly request you to receive the said
person," and then underneath are set out on separate lines what are clearly
alternatives, first, " pending his further examination under the Act," and,
secondly " pending the completion of arrangements for dealing with him
under the Act." There is a further reference to the possible charging for
the cost of detention and any escort, which is irrelevant to the present case,

A and then a space for a signature by and above the printed words "Immigration Officer." The form ends with the wording: "To the Chief Constable of," and a blank to be filled in, if appropriate, and the alternative "To the Governor H.M. Prison," and a space, filled in, in this case "Winson Green."

The alternative wording requesting the person to whom the form is sent to receive the detainee, either: "pending his further examination
B under the Act" (which would be a detention under paragraph 16 (1) of Schedule 2 to the Act) or "pending the completion of arrangements dealing with him under the Act," which would be a detention under paragraph 16 (2), are each accompanied by a request that they be deleted as appropriate.

In the present case the immigration officer deleted the second of these alternatives and left in the first one "pending his further examination under
C the Act." We do not know why he did this, but it was conceded at the outset of this hearing that the deletion was in error. The examination of the applicant had in fact been completed, and the immigration officer intended to request his detention "pending the completion of arrangements for dealing with him under the Act," that is to say under the provisions of paragraph 16 (2).

D It is certainly arguable that the alternative wording on the Home Office Form is surplusage, in that it would suffice for the immigration officer to authorise detention simply "under paragraph 16 of Schedule 2" to the Act, without condescending to the particulars of whether such detention is authorised under sub-paragraph (1) or (2) of paragraph 16. I am not wholly convinced that this is correct having regard to the requirement under R.S.C., Ord. 54, r. 7 that the return to a writ of habeas corpus ad
E subjiciendum ". . . must state all the causes of the detainer of the person restrained." If in fact the return would be valid if it merely stated that the detention was authorised under paragraph 16 of Schedule 2, it would lend some weight to the further argument that an error in the further particulars, unnecessarily given, cannot be regarded as being as serious as a failure to state the *main* provision under which the applicant was detained.

F Be that as it may, the document with which we are concerned did state the particular sub-paragraph under which the applicant was detained and it has been argued on his behalf that that error in the document vitiates it to the extent that the detention, whilst it could have been justified "pending the completion of arrangements for dealing with" the applicant, is unlawful and that habeas corpus should therefore be granted to the applicant as of right.

G For the Home Secretary it is said, as I understand the argument of counsel appearing on his behalf, that the document does properly state the reason for the applicant's detention, as being under paragraph 16 of Schedule 2 to the Act; and that the error of the immigration officer in deleting the wrong wording which in effect gives further particulars of the reason for detention, does not render the whole document a nullity; and
H that provided the court is satisfied that the applicant was in fact detained on good grounds the detailed wording of the document is not material.

If I have properly understood the argument of counsel on behalf of the Home Secretary, then I am far from happy with such an approach. The document, which is relied on as the return to this application, is the authority under which a man has been deprived of his liberty; and it ought to be regarded as of very great importance and should be completed with care. If, as may be inevitable, some mistake is at some time made in the

completion of such a document, then when the error is discovered it   A
should be rectified immediately, or a fresh document, properly compiled,
issued in its stead. That has not been done in this case and I think the
omission unfortunate and wrong.

But it does not in my view conclude the matter against the Home
Secretary; and leaves open the question which may be stated thus: " When
the person having custody of an applicant produces, as the justification
for his detention, a document which, though valid on its face, is sub-   B
sequently found to contain some material error, is the court entitled to
inquire further to determine whether there were in fact good grounds on
which the applicant was detained? Or is the applicant entitled as of right
to be released on the ground of the defect in the document which authorised
his detention? "

Long ago the return to the writ of habeas corpus was all important. It   C
was the beginning and the ending of the matter, and the court acted solely
on the reasons for detention stated on the face of the return. If the reason
shown was bad the person detained was entitled to be released; if the
reason was good he was not entitled to habeas corpus, although it may have
been open to him to pursue some other remedy, such as certiorari, under
which the court would go behind the return and inquire into the evidence
on which the detention was said to be justified.   D

But since the Habeas Corpus Act 1816 the court is empowered to inquire
into the truth of the facts stated in the return. Indeed that is precisely
the procedure relied on by applicants in the majority of applications
which come before this court; and it is under that procedure that the
applicant in the present case has sought to persuade this court to hold
that, irrespective of what is stated on the return, there was in fact no   E
sufficient evidence on which the Home Secretary should have reached
his conclusion as to the true identity of the applicant.

Since the court is empowered to go behind the mere wording on the
face of the return and inquire into the true facts, why should it not do so
if and when, as in the present case, it is discovered that some mistake
has been made in the wording of the document? In my judgment, the
overriding function of the court is to see that no injustice is done to the   F
person detained; and in order to see that justice is done the court should
inquire into the true facts and not be hampered by the wording of the
return.

I think it can be said that this is a situation in which the court should
look to the substance rather than to the form, subject always to the overriding consideration that justice should be done.   G

I am strengthened in this view by the provisions of R.S.C. Ord. 54, r. 7
which expressly provides:

> " (1) The return to a writ of habeas corpus ad subjiciendum must
> be indorsed on or annexed to the writ and must state all the causes
> of the detainer of the person restrained. (2) The return may be
> amended, or another return substituted therefor, by leave of the
> court or judge before whom the writ is returnable."   H

Since the return may be amended, or another return substituted by leave
of the court, it does not seem to me to be right to hold that the court is
bound to regard a return as bad when, as in the present case, the inquiry
into the facts has shown, as in my judgment is the case, that the immigration officer did have valid grounds on which to authorise the detention
of the applicant. Had the error been in some way prejudicial to the

A applicant, for example, by misleading him and causing him to take some step or omit to take some step by which his position or the presentation of his case to remain in this country had been harmed, then I think different considerations would arise. In the present case no such prejudice to the applicant has been suggested, and in my judgment no injustice is done to him by this court declining to grant his application on the ground of the error made when the immigration officer signed the authorisation
B for his detention.

I would therefore dismiss this application.

LORD WIDGERY C.J. I also would dismiss this application for the reasons just given by Drake J. The court has been required to examine the facts behind the return and this discloses a lawful power of detention under
C paragraph 16 of Schedule 2 to the Immigration Act 1971. I cannot see any difference in the nature and effect of the detention, according to whether it occurs after the completion of immigration inquiries or before such inquiries are concluded. Even where the liberty of the subject is involved, the court should strive not to be hamstrung by pointless technicalities.

Application dismissed.

D

Solicitors: *Sharpe, Pritchard & Co. for Taylor, Hall-Wright & Co., Birmingham; Treasury Solicitor.*

E   [COURT OF APPEAL]

LIM POH CHOO v. CAMDEN AND ISLINGTON AREA
HEALTH AUTHORITY

[1974 C. No. 7783]

F 1977   Nov. 22, 23, 24, 25;
           Dec. 7   Bristow J.
   1978   June 6, 7, 8, 9, 10;
           July 7   Lord Denning M.R., Lawton and Browne L.JJ.

*Damages—Personal injuries—Assessment—Severe brain injuries
   —Doctor aged 36 with good prospects as consultant—Hospital
G   negligence—Prognosis of long expectation of life under maxi-
     mum care—Doctor having no dependants—Whether assessment
     under conventional heads excessive—Extent to which inflation
     and high taxation to be considered—Whether reappraisal of
     principles governing awards of damages for personal injuries
     desirable
Law Reform—Whether necessary—Damages—Personal injuries—
     Excessive damages injurious to body politic*
H
        In 1973 a woman doctor, aged 36, working as a senior
     psychiatric registrar in a London mental hospital and with
     almost certain prospects of becoming a consultant within a few
     years, suffered irreparable brain damage following cardiac arrest
     after a minor operation in one of the area health authority's
     hospitals. Liability was admitted. At the date of the trial in
     1977 on the issue of damages, when the plaintiff was 41, her
     condition, though not wholly insentient, was such that she
     would require total care for the rest of her estimated span of

Lim v. Camden Health Authority (C.A.)   [1978]

life, about 37 years—for a further seven years at her home in   A
Penang, Malaysia, where she had been taken in 1974, in the
care of her elderly mother with paid assistance, and thereafter at a nursing home in England, where she had a sister, for
the rest of her life.

Bristow J. awarded the plaintiff £243,309 damages plus permitted interest, a total of £254,765.   Treating her future care
as the first priority the judge found cost of care at home in
Penang for seven years, disregarding any purely domestic   B
element " to avoid overlap with loss of future earnings," to be
£2,600 a year—£18,200, which he discounted to £17,500 because
part would earn interest before being spent, and cost of care
on 1977 figures at an appropriate English institution at £8,000
a year, to which he applied as the appropriate multiplier 11
(making " some increase for prospective inflation "), viz. £88,000
—a total of £105,500; (2) special damages to date of trial £25,809
plus interest; (3) loss of future earnings as a National Health   C
Service consultant with some private practice in England
£6,000 a year with a multiplier of 14 (to include " a small
increase to build in some anti-inflation protection ")—£84,000—
and £8,000 for loss of pension—total £92,000; and (4) a " conventional " award of £20,000 for pain, suffering and loss of
amenities of life increased to £25,930 for the interest it would
have carried before the Court of Appeal decision in Cookson v.
Knowles [1977] Q.B. 913, that damages under that head should   D
be assessed at the date of trial.   The judge then considered the
total awarded for elements relating to future loss on the assumed
annuity basis and held that the total award, though high, was
appropriate.

On an appeal by the health authority and a cross-notice by
the plaintiff on the amount of the pain and suffering award,
fresh evidence was admitted showing that the plaintiff's return
to England would probably be sooner than seven years owing to   E
her mother's deteriorating health: —

Held, dismissing the appeal (Lord Denning M.R. dissenting),
(1) that as the judge had assessed the heads of damage in
accordance with authorities binding on the court, had taken
care to ensure that there was no overlapping and that the sum
looked at in the round was fair and reasonable, his award should
stand, having regard to the plaintiff's long expectation of life,
the probability that she would have earned a substantial income,   F
and the fact that the case fell within the recently established
limited exception to the rule against making allowance for
inflation, namely, where the assumed annuity which the sum
awarded for future loss would buy was large enough to attract
tax at a high rate so that some method such as increasing
the multiplier could be applied to allow for future inflation.

Dictum of Lord Fraser of Tullybelton in Cookson v.
Knowles [1978] 2 W.L.R. 978, 991, H.L.(E.) applied.   G

(2) That although the plaintiff's condition was such that
she could not benefit by compensation for future economic
loss and had no dependants, compensation for future economic
loss, namely, loss of future earnings and pension rights, must be
awarded as a separate item of damage in its own right, for it
was a benefit of which she had been deprived by negligence
for which the defendants were responsible.   H

(3) That, as on the evidence the plaintiff was not wholly
insentient and her appreciation of her loss might not be so
minimal as the judge had thought, there was no justification
for awarding a modest conventional figure for pain, suffering
and loss of amenities such as was awarded in the case of death;
and that the judge's award under that head was amply supported
by comparable awards in cases of complete unconsciousness
and was less than had been awarded in comparable cases in
the last few years.

A   *Phillips* v. *London and South Western Railway Co.* (1879)
5 C.P.D. 280, C.A. and *H. West & Son Ltd.* v. *Shephard*
[1964] A.C. 326, H.L.(E.) applied.
     Fletcher v. *Autocar and Transporters Ltd.* [1968] 2 Q.B.
322, C.A. considered.
     Benham v. *Gambling* [1941] A.C. 157, H.L.(E.)
distinguished.
     Per Lord Denning M.R. Where a plaintiff is rendered
B unconscious or insensible, fair compensation should not include
an item for loss of earnings as such, but instead it should
include an item for pecuniary loss suffered by the dependants
of the injured person by reason of the injury, so long as full
compensation is given for every expense incurred on his or
her behalf and every service rendered him by relatives and friends
sufficient to care for the injured person in comfort for the rest
of life. It is not fair to make the defendants pay both; and it
C may endanger the body politic if awards of damages become
too large (post, pp. 908D–E, 909E, 910G—911A).
     Per Lord Denning M.R. and Browne L.J. The principles
on which damages are awarded in personal injury cases need
radical reappraisal (post, pp. 908C–D, 926E–F).
     Decision of Bristow J., post p. 899C et seq., affirmed.

D   The following cases are referred to in the judgments of the Court of
         Appeal:

Armsworth v. *South-Eastern Railway Co.* (1847) 11 Jur. 758.
Benham v. *Gambling* [1941] A.C. 157; [1941] 1 All E.R. 7, H.L.(E.).
Bolton v. *Essex Area Health Authority*, The Times, November 8, 1977.
Cavanagh v. *Ulster Weaving Co. Ltd.* [1960] A.C. 145; [1959] 3 W.L.R.
     262; [1959] 2 All E.R. 745. H.L.(N.I.).
Cookson v. *Knowles* [1977] Q.B. 913; [1977] 3 W.L.R. 279; [1977] 2
E   All E.R. 820, C.A.; [1978] 2 W.L.R. 978; [1978] 2 All E.R. 604,
     H.L.(E.).
Fletcher v. *Autocar and Transporters Ltd.* [1968] 2 Q.B. 322; [1968] 2
     W.L.R. 743; [1968] 1 All E.R. 726, C.A.
McCarty v. *Derby and Leeds Health Authority* (unreported), Jupp J.,
     Sheffield Crown Court, July 29, 1977.
Mitchell v. *Mulholland* (*No. 2*) [1972] 1 Q.B. 65; [1971] 2 W.L.R. 1271;
F   [1971] 2 All E.R. 1205, C.A.
Oliver v. *Ashman* [1962] 2 Q.B. 210; [1961] 3 W.L.R. 669; [1961] 3
     All E.R. 323, C.A.
Phillips v. *London and South Western Railway Co.* (1879) 4 Q.B.D. 406
     D.C.; 5 Q.B.D. 78; 5 C.P.D. 280, C.A.
Roach v. *Yates* [1938] 1 K.B. 256; [1937] 3 All E.R. 442, C.A.
Rowley v. *London and North Western Railway Co.* (1873) L.R. 8 Ex. 221.
G *Shearman* v. *Folland* [1950] 2 K.B. 43; [1950] 1 All E.R. 976, C.A.
Sinclair v. *O'Byrne* (unreported) Kilner Brown J., Leeds Crown Court,
     April 8, 1976.
Skelton v. *Collins* (1966) 115 C.L.R. 94.
Smith v. *Central Asbestos Co. Ltd.* [1972] 1 Q.B. 244; [1971] 3 W.L.R.
     206; [1971] 3 All E.R. 204, C.A.; [1973] A.C. 518; [1972] 3 W.L.R.
     333; [1972] 2 All E.R. 1135, H.L.(E.).
H *Taylor* v. *Bristol Omnibus Co. Ltd.* [1975] 1 W.L.R. 1054; [1975] 2 All
     E.R. 1107, C.A.
Taylor v. *O'Connor* [1971] A.C. 115; [1970] 2 W.L.R. 472; [1970] 1
     All E.R. 365, H.L.(E.).
West (*H.*) *& Son Ltd.* v. *Shephard* [1964] A.C. 326; [1963] 2 W.L.R.
     1359; [1963] 2 All E.R. 625, H.L.(E.).
Wise v. *Kaye* [1962] 1 Q.B. 638; [1962] 2 W.L.R. 96; [1962] 1 All E.R.
     257, C.A.
Young v. *Percival* [1975] 1 W.L.R. 17; [1974] 3 All E.R. 677, C.A.

Lim v. Camden Health Authority (C.A.)   [1978]

The following additional cases were cited in argument in the Court of A
Appeal:

Jefford v. *Gee* [1970] 2 Q.B. 130; [1970] 2 W.L.R. 702; [1970] 1 All
E.R. 1202, C.A.

Mallett v. *McMonagle* [1970] A.C. 166; [1969] 2 W.L.R. 767; [1969]
2 All E.R. 178, H.L.(N.I.).

The following cases are referred to in the judgment of Bristow J.:   B

Cookson v. *Knowles* [1977] Q.B. 913; [1977] 3 W.L.R. 279; [1977] 2
All E.R. 820, C.A.

Fletcher v. *Autocar and Transporters Ltd.* [1968] 2 Q.B. 322; [1968] 2
W.L.R. 743; [1968] 1 All E.R. 726, C.A.

Taylor v. *O'Connor* [1971] A.C. 115; [1970] 2 W.L.R. 472; [1970] 1
All E.R. 365, H.L.(E.).
                                                                        C

The following additional cases were cited in argument before Bristow J.:

Bolton v. *Essex Area Health Authority,* The Times, November 8, 1977.

Grace v. *Lamoureux* [1977] C.L.Y. 751.

Harris v. *Harris* [1973] 1 Lloyd's Rep. 445, C.A.

Jefford v. *Gee* [1970] 2 Q.B. 130; [1970] 2 W.L.R. 702; [1970] 1 All
E.R. 1202, C.A.   D

Taylor v. *Bristol Omnibus Co. Ltd.* [1975] 1 W.L.R. 1054; [1975] 2 All
E.R. 1107, C.A.

West (H.) & Son Ltd. v. *Shephard* [1964] A.C. 326; [1963] 2 W.L.R.
1359; [1963] 2 All E.R. 625, H.L.(E.).

Wise v. *Kaye* [1962] 1 Q.B. 638; [1962] 2 W.L.R. 96; [1962] 1 All E.R.
257, C.A.

                                                                        E
ACTION

The plaintiff, Dr. Lim Poh Choo, suing by her mother and next
friend, Lim Gim Hoe, residing in Penang, West Malaysia, issued a writ
on September 19, 1974, claiming damages for personal injury, loss and
damage and expenses sustained by reason of the negligence of the
defendants, Camden and Islington Area Health Authority, their servants F
or agents on or about March 1, 1973, in the course of the provision of
medical treatment. By her statement of claim served on October 15,
1974, she claimed that the defendant authority were responsible for the
administration of the Elizabeth Garrett Anderson Hospital, London,
N.W.1; that on or about February 28, 1973, she was admitted to the
hospital for a minor gynaecological operation and after a thorough
clinical examination she was found to be in good health and free from   G
any respiratory and cardiovascular disease and was not anaemic; that
on March 1 a dilatation and curettage operation was carried out under
general anaesthetic; that on completion of the operation she was
transferred to a recovery room where she suffered a cardiac arrest
and sustained in consequence thereof extremely serious permanent and
irreversible brain damage and had since suffered loss and damage; and   H
that the injury and brain damage were caused by the negligence of the
defendant authority, the anaesthetists and/or the nursing staff engaged
in treating her. Particulars were given of the negligence which indicated that it consisted in failure to take adequate steps to deal with the
cyanosed condition of the plaintiff while still in the operating room or
at any stage prior to arrival in the recovery room and failure to take
adequate steps in the recovery room. She claimed that by reason of

A the particularised negligence she had been rendered permanently and severely physically and mentally handicapped.

The defendant authority delivered a defence dated November 1, 1974, denying the allegations of negligence and liability; but shortly before the trial in November 1977, liability was admitted and the issue at the trial was limited to the quantum of damages.

B   *Christopher French Q.C.* and *George Newman* for the plaintiff.
    John Davies Q.C. and *Peter Scott* for the health authority.

                                        Cur. adv. vult.

December 7, 1977. BRISTOW J. read the following judgment. On
C February 28, 1973, Dr. Lim Poh Choo, a 36-year-old senior psychiatric registrar working for the Southgate Group of Hospitals and the Royal Free Hospital, was admitted to the Elizabeth Garrett Anderson Hospital for minor gynaecological surgery. Following upon the operation, which took place next morning, she suffered a cardiac arrest as the result of the failure by someone, for whom the area health authority are vicariously responsible, to take reasonable care for her safety.

D   The consequences have been disastrous. Before March 1, 1973, she was in mid-career practising in her chosen field of medicine. She had qualified in Singapore in 1963 at the age of 26. In the next few years she served in junior house appointments in Singapore and worked for a short time as a general practitioner in Hong Kong. Then her lawyer father fell ill and she returned to Malaysia and in 1967 started
E training in psychiatric medicine at University Hospital, Kuala Lumpur. In 1971 she came to England. She worked first as a full time clinical assistant at the Halliwick Hospital, and gained her diploma in psychiatric medicine. In 1972 she was appointed senior registrar at the hospital complex for which she was working at the time of the accident. Although she failed the examination for membership of the Royal
F College of Psychiatrists, a necessary qualification for consultant status in England, in autumn 1972 her performance and quality were such that she was confidently expected to pass, probably at the April 1973 sitting. The career structure in the National Health Service is such that barring accidents or a decision to move into another field she would have become a consultant psychiatrist by 1978, if not earlier.

As a result of what happened on March 1, 1973, she was in a coma
G for two weeks, and on regaining consciousness she did not talk, had two epileptic fits, and could not walk. In the Wolfson Rehabilitation Unit she recovered the ability to walk a little with help and to speak a few words. On September 25, 1973, six months after the disaster, she was assessed by the consultant neurologist at the Royal Free Hospital as suffering from diffuse brain damage producing a lack of coordination in
H all four limbs, and to be depressed and withdrawn and to have difficulty in speaking. Tests at the Maudsley Hospital showed that her disabilities were purely organic in origin, due to the extensive brain damage caused by the cardiac arrest.

Dr. Lim's mother, a retired teacher, now a widow living in Penang, decided that the right place for her to be cared for was at home, so she was flown home on February 2, 1974. She spent from February 28 to June 7, 1975, in the Department of Rehabilitation Medicine, Tan

Tock Sing Hospital, Singapore, under the care of Dr. Don and Dr.   A
Loong. She was found to be depressed, occasionally aggressive, and
totally dependent on others in all self-care activities including feeding,
toileting and grooming, and her speech was impaired. This condition
was the result of gross neurological deficit arising from the brain damage.
She could not walk without help or propel her wheel chair. Their
conclusion was that she would require maximum personal assistance for
the rest of her life and would not be able to function as a doctor.   B

The picture which emerges from the agreed medical reports is that
of a helpless invalid who will require nursing for the rest of her life, and
is only intermittently sentient. When she is sentient it looks as if it is at
a comparatively low level, and though she sometimes remembers that
she was a doctor in England, she is so intellectually impaired that she
does not appreciate what has happened to her. This picture was borne   C
out by the evidence of Dr. MacQuaide of St. Andrews Hospital,
Northampton, who examined Dr. Lim at her mother's home in Penang in
July 1976. He found her emotional state to be blank and she was
completely lacking in volition and spontaneity. Her powers of reasoning were impossible to test. Dr. MacQuaide's conclusion was that she
showed evidence of dementia and gross physical disability due to severe   D
cerebral damage. She would always need total care at home or in an
institution and would never get better. If she continues to be cared
for as she is by her mother at present, her expectation of continued
existence, for you cannot call it life, will not be shortened. Otherwise it
will almost certainly be less than average.

That a doctor who had so much to offer the mentally ill should be
subjected by want of care in hospital to the appalling disability from   E
which Dr. Lim is condemned to suffer for the rest of her existence is a
very great tragedy. Her mother, who has been in court throughout the
trial, in which counsel on both sides have given me the greatest possible
help, will realise that the law cannot pretend to compensate her daughter
for the destruction of her life. The court can only award a sum of
money, and in justice to the defendants as well as to Dr. Lim that sum   F
must be in proportion to awards in other cases of those who have suffered
injuries of comparable severity.

I have been helpfully referred by counsel to the relevant authorities,
and especially *Fletcher* v. *Autocar and Transporters Ltd.* [1968] 2 Q.B.
322 and *Taylor* v. *O'Connor* [1971] A.C. 115. I bear in mind the
warnings against awarding damages which might overlap from one into   G
another of the categories into which the authorities require me to divide
the problem in order to reach a fair result. I also bear in mind what is
said in the authorities about the question of protecting plaintiffs against
the consequences of future inflation, because damages have to awarded
once for all here and now. In *Taylor* v. *O'Connor* [1971] A.C. 115
the accident which caused the death of the plaintiff's husband took   H
place in June 1965. The award of damages by Lyell J. at first instance
was on May 8, 1968. The House of Lords gave judgment on
January 21, 1970. Lord Pearson dealt with this aspect of the matter
at pp. 142–143, where he commented on the fact that Lyell J. had
increased the multiplier to a modest extent to shield the plaintiff to some
extent against the effects of inflation. He said:

A   " Certainly it is right to have regard to the prospect of continuing
inflation as an important factor in the situation, but I do not think
a mere increase in the multiplier is a suitable method for protecting
against inflation, though it achieves something. I think protection
against inflation is to be sought by investment policy, and the lump
sum of damages should be assessed on the basis that it will be
investied with the aim of obtaining some capital appreciation to
B   offset the probable rise in the cost of living."

In 1970 the rise in oil prices and the acceleration in wage demands
to figures with which we are now familiar were still in the future, and
relatively stable money was the context in which these words of Lord
Pearson were uttered. But since 1970 our world has dramatically
changed. We have experienced inflation at rates approaching 30 per
C   cent. in a single year. We see the Government doing its best to reduce
inflation to single figures, with success said to be dependent on trade
unions being content with wage settlements of the order of 10 per cent.
We have passed through three years in which investment advisers could
hardly do more than to say: " If you take our advice you might, if all
goes well, reduce the impact on you of the certain rise in the cost of
D   living."

In these circumstances I take the view that the court must do what
it reasonably can to protect a plaintiff against inflation, and that what
the House of Lords thought it wrong for Lyell J. to do in the conditions
of 1968 it is right to do in 1977 when we can see more clearly where the
world is going.

E   I will now consider the assessment of the appropriate damages under
the various heads.

1.   *Future care of Dr. Lim*

This is clearly the first priority. For her there is nothing the law
can do other than to try to provide enough for her to be reasonably
looked after for the rest of her days. It is clear on the evidence that
F   her mother, now aged 71, will look after Dr. Lim at home in Penang for
as long as she is able. But the time will come when she can do so no
longer. What then?

Dr. Lim has a sister, Mrs. Plowright, herself a doctor of philosophy
of London University, married to a member of the B.B.C. staff, living in
Hampstead with her husband and two small children. She has a
G   brother, who is an architect, married to a German girl, living and
working in Kuala Lumpur with three boys, twins aged 12 and a six-year-
old. The brother's wife finds living in Malaya difficult, and Mr. Lim
has contemplated emigration and work somewhere else in the world
for that reason.

I have to put myself in the position of the officious bystander at the
H   family conference which in my judgment is going to take place, probably in
seven years time, about what is to be done with Dr. Lim when her
mother can no longer look after her. In my judgment the probable
situation then will be: Mr. and Mrs. Plowright in London, Mr. and Mrs.
Lim, if still based in Kuala Lumpur, anxious to emigrate. Neither
branch of the family would contemplate leaving Dr. Lim alone in
Malaya, where the evidence is that there are no institutions which could
cope satisfactorily with her as a long-term patient. In my judgment the

joint family answer will be that Dr. Lim should go to England and be   A
cared for in an institution within range of Mrs. Plowright. Neither
family, as it seems to me, can reasonably be expected to care for her at
home.

The cost of caring for Dr. Lim at home in Penang, disregarding any
purely domestic element and so avoiding any overlap with the loss of
future earnings problem, I find to be approximately £2,600 per year. The
straight £2,600 × 7 = £18,200 must be discounted to some extent because   B
part of the award will earn interest before it is expended. In my
judgment £17,500 is the appropriate figure for seven years of future care
of Dr. Lim in Penang.

On this basis, when Dr. Lim is expected to be brought to London she
will be 47 years old. What is the proper multiplier for the remaining
care element? Her expectation of life, according to the tables, will be   C
in the order of a further 37 years. In this case I must make a substantial discount because of the accelerated payment, some reduction for
the contingency that she will not reach the average age, some reduction
to allow for the purely domestic element, and some increase for prospective inflation. Balancing these elements as best I can, I find the
appropriate multiplier for the period of future care in England to be 11.   D

On the evidence the present cost of looking after Dr. Lim in an
appropriate institution in England is in the order of £8,000 per year. So
£88,000 is the appropriate figure to allow for future care in London,
making a total for the cost of future care, the top priority, of £105,500.

2. *Cost of care of Dr. Lim to date*

On the evidence the cost of care of Dr. Lim at home in Penang to   E
date is the cost of one full-time and two part-time servants, plus a physiotherapist five times a week and visits from the family doctor and
medicines, amounting to $850 a month. It is agreed that the rate of
exchange should be taken at $4.25 to the pound, making a monthly
figure of £200. Dr. Lim has been looked after on this basis for approximately 40 months, so the total under this head is £8,000.   F

3. *" Out of pockets " to date*

These are agreed to a large extent. The accepted items amount to
£3,296. I find the approximate figure for the disputed item as follows:
telephone £300. So the total here is £3,596.

                                                                          G
4. *Loss of earnings to date*

Dr. Lim received her salary for some time after the accident. Taking
that into account, her net loss of earnings to date is £14,213, an average
of £3,158 per annum.

5. *Loss of future earnings*   H

I have no evidence other than the history of Dr. Lim's plans for a
career as a consultant. There are more opportunities in England though
the rewards in Malaysia are greater. Her sister is fixed in England. Her
brother is not fixed in Malaysia. On the probabilities I conclude that
she would have practised as a consultant in England.

Assuming the present National Health Service salary rates, and allowing for a small amount of earnings from private practice, in my judgment

A the fair multiplicand to take is £6,000. Including a small increase to build in some anti-inflation protection, 14 looks like an appropriate multiplier. On this basis the figure for loss of future earnings is £84,000.

6. *Loss of pension rights*

B Had Dr. Lim reached pensionable age and lived her life-table span of 12 years thereafter, she would have received £49,866 pension. Discounting that amount by the appropriate percentage if she received it now, the figure is £18,500. But I must make a further discount for the contingency that Dr. Lim would never have reached pensionable age at all, or if she did, would not have survived the 12 tabular years, though she might have survived far longer. There are even more imponderables under this head, and I think the appropriate award would be £8,000.

C

7. *General damages for pain and suffering and loss of the amenities of life*

Under this head we pass from the wholly or partly calculable into the field of convention. Dr. Lim's loss of the amenities of her good and useful life is total. On the evidence, her appreciation of that loss,
D and so the agony which knowing what you have lost must cause, is nil, or very small. In the light of the authorities, in my judgment, the right conventional award would be £20,000.

When we add up the total of the individual sums reached by the above approach, the total is £243,309. It is then necessary to look at the total and ask ourselves whether it does justice to both parties. Dr.
E Lim's situation is terrible. £243,309 is a very large sum for a hospital authority to have to pay by way of damages. The most that can be done for Dr. Lim herself is to look after her. She has no dependants, so that when she dies it is likely, though I have no evidence about it, that her estate will pass to her brother and sister and inure for the benefit of her nephews and nieces.

F As a rough cross check of the appropriateness of such an award it is interesting to see what net income Dr. Lim would receive by buying an annuity with an amount equal to those elements which relate only to the future and to the pain and suffering element: that is £217,500. A payment of £200,000 would produce a net income of £12,896 per annum with no inflation hedge. With the cost of care in England in what seems an appropriate but in no way luxurious or extravagant institution
G presently £8,000 per year, and the present inflationary trends, does £217,500 to look after the future and compensate for being condemned to a living death look too much?

If we were to approach the problem on the basis considered by Diplock L.J. in *Fletcher* v. *Autocar and Transporters Ltd.* [1968] 2 Q.B. 322, but not held to be right by the court, we would have to take
H into account only the cost of care to date and the cost of future care, being those elements which go to Dr. Lim's "happiness," with a "pain and suffering" figure, in her case nominal, plus out of pockets. Loss of earnings and pension rights, as Dr. Lim now is, makes no difference whatever to her. That loss simply affects the benefits that would pass on to others on her death. The total award on that basis would be, say, £117,500. Using the same rough cross check, £100,000 would produce

an annuity of £7,540 net, not enough to cover the present annual cost of care in England.   £150,000 would produce an annuity of £10,131.

In my judgment the authorities require me to take into account the loss of earnings amounts and to award a pain and suffering and loss of amenity sum proportionate to other awards in cases of injury of the maximum severity.   Going by this road the total award is high, but not, in my judgment, disproportionately high when I remember that Dr. Lim is only 41, there is no reason to suppose that her expectation of existence has been reduced, and she will need total care for the rest of her days.

There will be judgment for the sum of £243,309 plus interest of the appropriate amount on the appropriate elements, liberty to apply if the amount of interest cannot be agreed.

The award of £20,000 for the general damages for pain and suffering and loss of the amenities of life is assessed on the pre-*Cookson* v. *Knowles* [1977] Q.B. 913 basis, so as to be comparable with other awards and assuming that it carries interest. Since it is the *Cookson* v. *Knowles* basis that should be applied now, that must be increased by the amount of interest it would have carried, and so the total damages must be increased by the amount which, before that decision, would have been awarded by way of interest.

> *Judgment for Plaintiff for £243,309.*
> *Payment of £111,590 to plaintiff's*
> *solicitors within 14 days.*
> *Stay of execution as to balance pend-*
> *ing appeal.*

Solicitors: *Coward Chance; J. Tickle & Co.*

[Reported by BERNARD O. AGYEMAN, ESQ., Barrister-at-Law]

APPEAL from Bristow J.

The area health authority appealed, on the grounds 1. the judge's award was apportioned as follows:

(1)	Pain, suffering, loss of amenities	£20,000	
	Interest from the date of writ	5,930	£25,930
(2)	Out-of-pocket expenses, including £680, cost of stay at Tang Tock Seng Hospital and Singapore Nursing Home	3,596	
(3)	Cost of care to date of judgment; 40 months at £200 per month—£2,400 per annum	8,000	
(4)	Interest on (2) and (3) from date of accident, 1.3.73, to judgment	2,482	14,078
(5)	Loss of earnings to date of judgment	14,213	
(6)	Interest on (5) from date of accident to judgment	3,044	17,257

A   (7)   Cost of future care:
             Malaysia 7 × £2,600 p.a., discounted to   17,500
             England 11 × £8,000 p.a.   88,000   105,500

       (8)   Loss of future earnings:
             14 × £6,000   84,000
             Loss of pension   8,000   92,000
B

                                                                        £254,765

2. The judge misdirected himself in the respects set out below: 3. The
C   sums awarded were excessive both in total and in respect of each of
the heads of damage specified at 1 (1), (5), (7) and (8) above. The
amount of the award was out of line with current awards in cases of
comparable injury and contrary to public policy. 4. The judge was
wrong in law in the way he purported to apply the principle in *Cookson*
v. *Knowles* [1977] Q.B. 913. Moreover his award for pain, suffering
and loss of amenities failed sufficiently to take into account that there
D   was no evidence that the plaintiff was suffering any pain, that she was
only intermittently sentient and even then at a low level and so intellectually impaired as not to be able to appreciate what had happened to
her. 5. The judge wrongly treated the several items of loss specified in
paragraph 1 above as independent and substantive heads of damage
which fell to be aggregated for the purposes of arriving at the amount
E   of the total award. He was wrong in regarding such itemisation other
than as a mere working aid in the process of arriving at a composite
award of damages which would be fair and reasonable to both plaintiff
and defendants. 6. He wrongly failed to have due regard to the duplication (or overlap) in the separate sums he assigned to the following items
of damage: (a) loss of amenities under 1 (1) above, (b) loss of earnings
and pension under 1 (8); and (c) cost of care under 1 (3) and 1 (7), and in
F   respect of £680 being part of 1 (2) above. In particular he was wrong
in giving damages for loss of earnings and pension (£106,213) in addition
to the sum he awarded for cost of care (£114,180), (that is to say, £680
plus £8,000 plus £105,500), and whatever sum he allocated to loss of
amenities; a fortiori, where the damages for cost of care exceeded the
loss of earnings and where there was no evidence that but for the
G   accident the plaintiff's earnings would have been more than sufficient
for her own maintenance. 7. The judge proceeded on the basis that the
award should be such as to enable the plaintiff to be cared for out
of income without resort to capital. He was wrong in so doing. 8. The
judge was wrong in law in that, contrary to the decision of the House of
Lords in *Taylor* v. *O'Connor* [1971] A.C. 115, and of the Court of
Appeal in *Young* v. *Percival* [1975] 1 W.L.R. 17, he inflated the
H   damages awarded professedly to offset the effect of future inflation.
9. The judge's finding that on the probabilities the plaintiff would be
brought to England to be cared for in seven years' time was against the
weight of evidence and contrary to the probabilities, especially having
regard to her condition and to the fact that by then she would be 48
years of age, and would have been cared for in her native Malaysia for
11 years. The judge's assessment of damages on that basis was wrong

in law in that it ignored the duty of reasonable mitigation, especially A
having regard to the estimated relative cost of care in Malaysia and
England. 10. The multipliers of 14 in the case of loss of earnings and 18
in the case of future care were excessive in the case of a woman of 41
years.

By a respondent's notice the plaintiff gave notice that she intended
on the hearing of the defendant's appeal to contend that the judgment should be varied or affirmed on the additional grounds (1) that B
while the award of £20,000 damages for pain, suffering and loss of
amenities was a proper sum had the trial been in 1973, it was an
insufficient sum to award in 1977 and (2) the plaintiff was entitled to
interest pursuant to section 3 of the Law Reform (Miscellaneous Provisions) Act 1934, as amended by section 22 of the Administration of
Justice Act 1969 on a proper award in 1977.   C

During the hearing of the appeal the court granted leave to admit
fresh evidence on behalf of the plaintiff, consisting in letters written by
or on behalf of her mother in Penang to charitable organisations in
England inquiring as to the cost of English nursing homes to which
her daughter (the plaintiff) might be admitted in the near future, owing
to deterioration in the mother's health.   D

John Davies Q.C. and *Peter Scott Q.C.* for the health authority.
Christopher French Q.C. and *George Newman* for the plaintiff.

Cur. adv. vult.

                                                                      E
July 7. The following judgments were read.

LORD DENNING M.R. It happened on March 1, 1973. A lady doctor,
Dr. Lim Poh Choo, had gone into hospital for a minor gynaecological
operation. It was for dilatation and curettage. She was quite a healthy
woman. She was put under a general anaesthetic. The operation was
performed. She was moved from the operating theatre to the recovery F
room. Whilst she was still unconscious she began to go blue. The
doctors call it cyanosis. This was a sign of trouble. It showed that her
breathing had been affected. The recovery sister sent for help. They
gave her oxygen, but nevertheless the cyanosis increased. Five minutes
later her breathing stopped. This affected her heart. The blood
stopped flowing to her brain. She suffered what the doctors call G
" cardiac arrest." The heart was massaged. After 25 minutes her
breathing was restored to normal. She was brought back to life. The
more's the pity of it! For it was to a living death. Her brain was
severely damaged beyond repair. She was in a deep coma for two weeks.
At length she recovered consciousness but could not talk. She had
two epileptic fits. After four months she could speak a few words and
could walk a little with help. Now five years later she is still helpless. H
Her mind is gone. She can speak a few words, but without meaning or
sense. She cannot dress, bath herself or attend to her toilet. In the
words of the specialist, she

     " shows evidence of dementia and gross physical disability due to
     severe cerebral damage. She will always need total care either at
     home or in an institution."

A   Now by her mother (who is her next friend) she has brought an action for damages against the area health authority. At first they denied liability: as indeed they well might. Accidents such as this do happen in operations through sheer misadventure—some allergy or sensitivity in the patient to a particular drug—without negligence at all. But, after consideration, the health authority accepted liability: and the only issue is the amount of damages. The judge has awarded nearly £250,000. It

B is a staggering figure. It is the highest sum ever yet awarded in these courts. The health authority appeal to this court on this amount.

In considering damages in personal injury cases, it is often said "The defendants are wrongdoers. So make them pay up in full. They do not deserve any consideration." That is a tendentious way of putting the case. The accident, like this one, may have been due to a pardonable

C error such as may befall any one of us. I stress this so as to remove the misapprehension—so often repeated—that the plaintiff is entitled to be *fully* compensated for all the loss and detriment she has suffered. That is not the law. She is only entitled to what is, in all the circumstances, a *fair* compensation—fair both to her and to the defendants. The defendants are not wrongdoers. They are simply the people who

D have to foot the bill. They are, as the lawyers say, only vicariously liable. In this case it is in the long run the taxpayers who have to pay. It is worth recording the wise words of Parke B. over a century ago:

"Scarcely any sum could compensate a labouring man for the loss of a limb, yet you don't in such a case give him enough to maintain him for life . . . you are not to consider the value of his existence as if you were bargaining with an annuity office . . . I therefore advise

E you to take a reasonable view of the case and give what you consider a fair compensation": see *Armsworth* v. *South-Eastern Railway Co.* (1847) 11 Jurist 758, 760, quoted in *Rowley* v. *London and North Western Railway Co.* (1873) L.R. 8 Ex. 221, 230.

The lady here was born on October 18, 1936. So at the operation in

F 1973 she was 36. She is now 41. She was educated in Malaysia. In 1963 at the age of 26 she qualified as a doctor and specialised in psychiatry. She was for eight years working in hospitals out there. She came to England in 1971, when she was 34. She passed her Diploma in Psychiatry and was appointed a senior registrar at the Friern Hospital. She was due in April 1973 to take her examination for membership of the Royal College of Psychiatrists. Two distinguished doctors describe

G Dr. Lim as "a remarkably good doctor, intelligent, conscientious, reliable, able to make good contact with patients, supportive to and popular with the nursing staff." Each doctor regarded it as almost certain that she would have passed her membership examination and obtained a post as a consultant psychiatrist within four or five years.

The disaster happened on March 1, 1973. She lay stricken in hos-

H pitals in England for several months. Then, on February 2, 1974, she was flown back to Malaysia. She was then taken to her mother's home in Penang where she has been ever since, save for a month or two in a nursing home in Singapore. Her mother looks after her, together with the help of one full-time servant and two part-time servants. It is doubtful, however, how long her mother will be able to look after her. It has been suggested that the best thing would be for her to be moved

back to England and put in an institution here where she could be cared A
for. Especially as she has a married sister living here in London.

If this lady had died under the operation—as in former times she
would probably have done—then, even though it was due to the fault
of the hospital, the damages would have been minimal. She had no
relatives dependent on her. So there would be no payment under the
Fatal Accident Acts. The only sum to be awarded to her estate would be
the conventional sum of £750 for loss of expectation of life.   B

But now, by reason of the advances of medical science, she was
snatched back from death under the operation and has been brought back
to a life which is not worth living. The body has been kept alive, but
the mind is gone. The doctors and nurses, with the aids available today,
say that they can keep the body going for the normal expectation of life.
In her case 37 years. But every moment of it distressing to her and those C
about her. Sadness and happiness are all alike to her. Many might say:
" 'Twere better she had died."

Such cases, we are told, are not uncommon: and we are faced with
the problem: on what principles should compensation be awarded to
her? As I said in *Taylor* v. *Bristol Omnibus Co. Ltd.* [1975] 1 W.L.R.
1054, 1060, the subject needs radical reappraisal. This case gives the D
opportunity for it.

On principle

One thing is beyond doubt: fair compensation must mean that she
is to be kept in as much comfort and tended with as much care as
compassion for her so rightfully demands: and that she should not want E
for anything that money can buy. But I see no justification in law or
in morals in awarding to her large sums of money in addition to those
needed to keep her in comfort. Such extra sums will avail her nothing.
She herself can make no use of them. All that will happen to them is
that they will be accumulated during her lifetime at high interest rates
of which 80 per cent. or more will go to the revenue. Invested well the
capital will be worth more and more. She will be unable to dispose of any F
of it by will, since she has not the mental capacity to make a will. On her
death, all will go to her nearest relatives, or if she then has none, I
suppose to the Crown as bona vacantia: and the Crown will not know
what to do with the money. If she should not last the 37 years, but die
within five years—as a layman may think very probable—this huge sum
will do no one any good. It was for reasons such as these that Lord G
Pearson's Commission, the Royal Commission on Civil Liability and Compensation for Personal Injury (1978) Cmnd. 7054–I, recommended that
non-pecuniary damages should no longer be recoverable for permanent
unconsciousness: see paragraphs 393 and 398. Similar reasoning seems
to me to apply to permanent insensibility.

One cannot forget, also, that in these days after such an accident as H
this, the relatives—and the doctors—are faced with an agonising
decision: is she to be kept alive? Or is she to be allowed to die? Is the
thread of life to be maintained to the utmost reach of science? Or
should it be let fall and nature take its inevitable course? Such a
decision should not be influenced in the least by a law which whispers in
the ear: " If she is kept alive, there will be large sums of compensation
payable—for the benefit of the relatives; whereas, if she dies, there will

The Weekly Law Reports, December 1, 1978

909

3 W.L.R.   Lim v. Camden Health Authority (C.A.)   Lord Denning M.R.

A be nothing." Rather those about her should say: " For mercy's sake, let the end come now."

To be fair to her relatives in this case—to be fair to her mother, her sister and her brother—they do not ask for anything more than fair compensation on the grounds that I have stated. They want nothing for themselves. They seek to uphold this large award of £250,000 solely to ensure that the expenses of nursing and attendance shall be met, whatever the future may bring in the way of inflation. Their fears on this score can, I believe, be met in other ways, as I will show.

B

It is a modern problem—the impact of modern science—in prolonging life in a body destitute of mind. To my mind on principle fair compensation requires that there should be ample provision in terms of money for comfort and care during the lifetime of the sufferer such as to safeguard her in all foreseeable contingencies, including the effect of inflation: that, if he or she has any dependants, they should be compensated for any pecuniary loss which they suffer by reason of his or her incapacity and inability to earn—just as if he or she had died and compensation was being awarded under the Fatal Accident Acts. Beyond that there can be conventional sums for pain and suffering and loss of amenities, but these should not be too large—seeing that they will do her no good—and can only accumulate during her lifetime to benefit others who survive after her death. This is reinforced by the views of Lord Pearson's Commission. Half of them thought there should be a statutory maximum of £20,000. The other half thought that there should not be a statutory maximum but that the Court of Appeal should exercise a restraining hand: see paragraphs 391-392.

C

D

E

I may add, too, that if these sums get too large, we are in danger of injuring the body politic: just as medical malpractice cases have done in the United States of America. As large sums are awarded, premiums for insurance rise higher and higher, and these are passed to the public in the shape of higher and higher fees for medical attention. By contrast, we have here a National Health Service. But the health authorities cannot stand huge sums without impeding their service to the community. The funds available come out of the pockets of the taxpayers. They have to be carefully husbanded and spent on essential services. They should not be dissipated in paying more than fair compensation. In many of these cases the National Health Service willingly provides full care, nursing and attention without charging anything for it. Surely this, too, should go to reduce the amount awarded against them. The damages should not be inflated so as to cover the cost of being kept in the most expensive nursing home. It has been known—I am not saying in this case—that when such damages have been awarded, the relatives have afterwards arranged to take advantage of the facilities afforded by the National Health Service—see Lord Pearson's Report, paragraph 341—and thus save money for themselves.

F

G

H

The authorities

Such being the position in principle, I turn to see whether there is any authority which prevents it. The practice is now established and cannot be gainsaid that, in personal injury cases, the award of damages is assessed under four main heads. First, special damages in the shape of money actually expended. Second, cost of future nursing and atten-

Lord Denning M.R.   **Lim v. Camden Health Authority (C.A.)**   **[1978]**

dance and medical expenses. Third, pain and suffering and loss of   **A**
amenities. Fourth, loss of future earnings.

I need not comment on the first two items except to say that the sum
is to include compensation for the services of wife or husband, mother
or father, given voluntarily and gratuitously. So far as the third item is
concerned, we have the authority of the House of Lords for giving an
award in a substantial sum for pain and suffering and loss of amenities   **B**
(see *H. West & Son Ltd.* v. *Shephard* [1964] A.C. 326) but we have the
suggestion of Lord Pearson's Commission that it should be a modest sum,
with a maximum, some suggest, of £20,000. So far as inflation is
concerned, we have it established by the House of Lords that it is not to
be taken into account in the ordinary run of cases, but there are
exceptional cases (where the sum awarded attracts high tax) where
allowance may be made for future inflation: see *Young* v. *Percival*   **C**
[1975] 1 W.L.R. 17, as qualified in *Cookson* v. *Knowles* [1978] 2
W.L.R. 978.

The real problem is the fourth item, the loss of future earnings. It
is often assumed that these are to be calculated on an annuity basis and
given as an additional award over and above the other items. The
courts take an appropriate sum for his annual earnings and an appro-   **D**
priate multiplier, and add the result on to the other items. That method
may be good enough when the injured man was a married man with a
family, who was in work at the time of the accident—and would have
continued to work until his retirement but for the accident—and lives
at home after the accident with little extra expense. His loss of
earnings, calculated in that way, is a fair compensation for the depen-   **E**
dency of his family on him, as in the asbestosis cases: see *Smith* v.
Central Asbestos Co. Ltd. [1972] 1 Q.B. 244, 255-265. But in cases like
the present, that method gives more than fair compensation. Much
more. Whilst unconscious or insensible, he gets his full salary without
doing any work for it and no expenses out of it: and at the same time
he gets his full board and keep at a very expensive nursing home. In
Fletcher v. *Autocar and Transporters Ltd.* [1968] 2 Q.B. 322, I tried   **F**
to modify it by invoking a doctrine of " overlapping." In *Taylor* v.
Bristol Omnibus Co. Ltd. [1975] 1 W.L.R. 1054, I sought to reduce the
sum for loss of future earnings, but my brethren persuaded me otherwise.
And I know of several good judges of first instance who have expressed
their unease at the high figures in these cases of severe brain damage,
notably Kilner Brown J. in *Sinclair* v. *O'Byrne* (unreported), April 8,   **G**
1976, Leeds Crown Court, and Jupp J. in *McCarty* v. *Derby and Leeds
Health Authority* (unreported), July 29, 1977, Sheffield Crown Court.

As this case will, I hope, go to the House of Lords, I take my stand
on principle. In my opinion when a plaintiff is rendered unconscious
or insensible, fair compensation should not include an item for loss of
earnings as such, but instead it should include an item for pecuniary loss
suffered by the dependants of the injured man by reason of his accident.   **H**
After all, if that is the compensation regarded as fair by the legislature in
case of his natural death, it may justly be regarded as fair in case of his
living death—provided also that full compensation is also given for
every expense that may be incurred on his behalf and every service that
may be rendered to him by relatives and friends. The cost of keeping
the plaintiff for the rest of his days will exceed by far the salary or

The Weekly Law Reports, December 1, 1978

911

3 W.L.R.   Lim v. Camden Health Authority (C.A.)   Lord Denning M.R.

A wages that he would have earned if he never had been injured. It is not fair to the defendants to make them pay both.

Similarly, if *Oliver* v. *Ashman* [1962] 2 Q.B. 210 is overruled by the House of Lords and a man is given compensation for his loss of earnings during his " lost years," there again these should be calculated, not for loss of earnings as such, but for the pecuniary loss suffered by his dependants during those lost years. In *Skelton* v. *Collins* (1966)
B 115 C.L.R. 94 the High Court of Australia only awarded £2,000, which was far less than any actuarial calculation.

Application to this case

The first item is the cost of nursing and keep of the plaintiff for the rest of her days.
C This lady was unmarried with no one dependent on her, nor likely to be. Beyond doubt the damages must provide for the cost of nursing and attendance and keep for the rest of her days. If she is looked after by her mother and the servants at their home in Penang, the sum must include not only the outgoings on doctors, nurses, medicines, and the like: but also a sum for food and nourishment: and to recompense the
D mother and staff: and a proportion of the outgoings on the house: and so forth. If she is moved over to England, the sum must include the cost of any nursing home or institution, and any other expenses that may have to be incurred.

The difficulty in this item is to know how long she is likely to stay in Penang: and whether she is likely to come over to England, or not.
E This is most uncertain. The judge thought that she would probably stay in Penang for another seven years at an expense of £2,600 a year, and then come to England for a further 30 years at £8,000 a year—at present-day costs. But additional evidence was tendered before us to show that her mother was frail and could not look after her in Penang very much longer: and in that case Dr. Lim might be brought to England very soon.
F Apart from these uncertainties, there are these other matters to be taken into account: the fact that the payment will be a lump sum which will be paid immediately and can be invested to produce income, which will be subject to tax: the possibility that she may not live the expected span of 37 years: and that the costs in Penang or in England will go up with inflation: and the possibility (as has happened in other cases) that
G after expenses have been awarded on the basis of an expensive nursing home, it is afterwards saved by taking advantage of the facilities of the National Health Service: see Lord Pearson's Report, paragraphs 340-341.

So many are the uncertainties and contingencies that I do not think it can be solved by actuarial evidence. Nor do I think it desirable. There should be a simple method which is available to all the many
H people who have to consider the amount. Sometimes in negotiations for a settlement. Sometimes by decision in a court. Experience shows that, in order to ascertain nursing expenses (over the rest of expected life) or loss of earnings or dependency (over the rest of working life) the best way is to take an appropriate multiplicand and multiply it by an appropriate multiplier. The practitioners in this field have become very expert in it, once the courts have shown the way.

A

In the result, I assess the damages in this case as follows:

Cost of nursing and care to date of trial (as found by the judge)	£8,000
Out-of-pockets to date (as found by the judge)	£3,596
Cost of future nursing, care and keep (allowing for possibility of early return to England) £7,000 a year.	
Number of years purchase (increased for inflation) 15	
Total (same as found by the judge)	£105,000
Pain and suffering and loss of amenities	£20,000
	£136,596

B

C

The fears of the relatives

The relatives fear that a sum of this magnitude may not be sufficient. They need not fear. If the usual course is adopted, the sum will be put under the control of the Court of Protection. If the lady should die in a few years' time—as may well be the case—the greater part of it will still be intact and will go to the relatives themselves.

D

She may, however, live a very long time. I cannot think that she will live so long as to outlive this large sum of money. The Court of Protection, with its expert advice, will be able to see that it will suffice. But, in the remote contingency that she should live to a great age, there is nowadays machinery in the Rules of the Supreme Court by which this sum of £136,596 can be regarded as an interim award. It needs some ingenuity to adapt the Rules, but I think it could be done. If it is regarded as an interim award, it will be open to her, by her next friend, in that remote contingency, to come back for an additional award to last out the rest of her days. Alternatively, and more simply—without adapting the Rules—the health service can be asked to give an undertaking to pay whatever extra is necessary or to look after her in comfort in that very remote contingency. I have no doubt they would give such an undertaking. Such a solution would be much more fair than awarding an immense sum now: and it would offer a satisfactory middle course between the rival views on periodic payments expressed in the report of Lord Pearson's Commission, paragraphs 555–630.

E

F

I would add that the Master of the Court of Protection has provided for us a most interesting analysis of 46 cases where large sums have been awarded in cases of severe brain damage. They show how well these sums are administered by the court. But they also show that, in no case, even in the more recent times, has the figure exceeded £130,000. If it be right to have some regard to the scale of awards in these cases, the present award is far, far above the current scale. It is just about double.

G

I would, therefore, allow this appeal and reduce the award to £136,596·00, with the appropriate interest.

H

LAWTON L.J. The award in this case of just over a quarter of a million pounds is startling, Mr. Davies on behalf of the defendants described it as absurd. In a full and careful judgment Bristow J. set out how he had reached this sum: £105,000 for future care; £8,000 for care to date; £3,596 for out of pocket expenses to date; £84,000 for loss of future

A   earnings; £8,000 for loss of pension rights; £20,000 for pain and suffering and the loss of the amenities of life; and a sum for interest calculated in accordance with the guidelines set out by this court in *Cookson* v. *Knowles* [1977] Q.B. 913.

The conventional method of assessing damages

B   Nearly all who are concerned with personal injury claims, whether as judges, barristers, solicitors or insurance company claims managers would have made their own assessments of damages in the same kind of way; and the experienced among them would have taken care, as Bristow J. said he did, to ensure first that there was no overlapping between the heads of damage, as they are called, and secondly that the sum to be awarded, when looked at in the round, was fair and reasonable.
C   All my professional life claims have been settled and awards fixed in this sort of way; and it is pertinent to remember that the great majority of claims are settled without the issue of a writ. In *H. West & Son Ltd.* v. *Shephard* [1964] A.C. 326, all the members of the House of Lords seem to have approached the assessment of damages in the conventional way to which I have referred although two, Lord Reid and Lord Devlin,
D   differed from their brethren as to the sum to be assessed for the physical injury and loss of the amenities of life sustained by the plaintiff.

Departure from the conventional method

          Lord Denning M.R. in his judgment has said that in cases in which the injuries are as grave as in this case and there are no dependants, compensation should not include an item for loss of earnings. As is
E   usual with him, what he has said has a compelling attraction; but in this case I have had to remind myself that, like the centurion at Capernaum, I am a man under authority—that of the decided cases binding on this court. There may be, as Lord Denning M.R. has said, sound reasons for thinking that awards of this size, which have been assessed in the conventional way, will injure the body politic. Parliament may
F   decide to take action against such danger as there may be. I cannot see how we can do so without departing from the principles enunciated by this court nearly a hundred years ago in the much litigated case of *Phillips* v. *London and South Western Railway Co.* (1879) 4 Q.B.D. 406; 5 Q.B.D. 78 and 5 C.P.D. 280 and followed ever since.

G   The authorities

          The plaintiff, D. Phillips, before the accident out of which his claim arose, had practised as a physician and as such had earned a substantial income. The reports do not say what his injuries were; but Cockburn C.J. said this about them, at 4 Q.B.D. 406, 408:

          " The plaintiff was a man of middle age and of robust health. His
H   health had been irreparably injured to such a degree as to render life a burden and source of the utmost misery. He has undergone a great amount of pain and suffering. The probability is that he will never recover. His condition is at once helpless and hopeless ... Medical attendance still is and is likely to be for a long time necessary."

          At first instance the trial judge, Field J., directed the jury as to the heads of damage in respect of which the plaintiff was entitled to com-

pensation. The details of his direction are set out in 5 Q.B.D. 78, 80–82. **A**
He told the jury to consider what sum should be given for the plaintiff's
loss of future earnings and directed them to take account of the contingencies of life. The jury awarded a sum which showed that they
could not have made any, or any proper, provision for loss of future
earnings. The plaintiff asked for a new trial. The Divisional Court
ordered one: 4 Q.B.D. 406, 408. The defendants appealed. This court
confirmed the order for a new trial and did not accept a submission that **B**
Field J. had misdirected the jury as to the assessment of damages: see 5
Q.B.D. 78. There was a new trial before Lord Coleridge C.J. By this
time it seems likely that the prognosis was better than when the case was
before Field J.: see 5 C.P.D. 280, 281. The jury awarded the plaintiff
£16,000, a figure which at the present value of the pound sterling would
be the equivalent of well over £100,000 and might be about £200,000. **C**
The chief justice had directed them to take into account loss of future
earnings.

This time the defendants applied to the Divisional Court for a new
trial. They were unsuccessful. They then appealed to this court: see
5 C.P.D. 280. One of the arguments put by the defendants' counsel,
the redoubtable Serjeant Ballantine, was that the plaintiff's loss of pro- **D**
fessional income was too remote and ought not to have been taken into
account. This court (Bramwell, Brett and Cotton L.JJ.) would have
none of this. Each member of this court thought that loss of future
earnings had to be taken into account when assessing damages. At no
time during this protracted litigation was the precise method of calculating prospective pecuniary loss in issue; but during argument on the
occasion of the first appeal to this court, James L.J. said, 5 Q.B.D. 78, **E**
p. 84:

> "The proper direction to the jury, as it seems to me, would have
> been to tell them to calculate the value of the income as a life
> annuity, and then make an allowance for its being subject to the
> contingencies of the plaintiff retiring, failing in his practice, and so
> forth."   **F**

This direction was adopted by this court in *Roach* v. *Yates* [1938] 1 K.B.
256, a case not unlike the present one: see Greer L.J. at p. 266, and
Slesser L.J. at p. 269.

The calculation of loss of earnings

Since then, and probably for decades before, the loss of future **G**
earnings in cases where on the evidence the plaintiff was likely to be
unable to earn anything for the rest of his life has been calculated on
what Lord Fraser of Tullybelton in *Cookson* v. *Knowles* [1978] 2
W.L.R. 978, referred to as the assumed annuity basis. As far as I know
Phillips v. *London and South Western Railway Co.* has never been
questioned by the House of Lords. In *H. West & Son Ltd.* v. *Shephard* **H**
[1964] A.C. 326, it was cited with obvious approval by Lord Morris of
Borth-y-Gest at p. 346, by Lord Devlin at p. 356 and by Lord Pearce at
p. 365. I consider myself bound to follow and apply *Phillips* v. *London
and South Western Railway Co.* This means that when reviewing
Bristow J.'s award I must take into account the plaintiff's pecuniary loss
arising from her loss of future earnings and pension rights. Perhaps it
would be more accurate, as Mr. Davies submitted, to describe this loss

A   as that of her earning capacity. However it is described, what Bristow J. had to do was to consider all the factors, save one, mentioned by Lord Tucker in *Cavanagh* v. *Ulster Weaving Co. Ltd.* [1960] A.C. 145, 163-164. In that case, Lord Tucker said in respect of a labourer, aged 20, who had lost a leg:

B
> ". . . the jury had, of *course*, [my italics] to consider what he might reasonably have been expected to earn during a working life of perhaps 45 or 50 years, taking account of the fall in the value of money, the tendency for wages to rise and the possibility of his improving his status in the labour market contrasted with his present position and future prospects in the event of an increase in the number of unemployed."

C   The reference to the factor of inflation must now be understood and applied in the limited way explained by Lord Diplock and Lord Fraser of Tullybelton in *Cookson* v. *Knowles* [1978] 2 W.L.R. 978, 985, 990-991. Bristow J. heard evidence about the plaintiff's expectation of life, which was only slightly less than the normal for a woman of her age, about what her chances of becoming a consultant psychiatrist would have been and what she would have been likely to earn as such in the
D National Health Service with some private practice after the deduction of tax. In addition he had expert evidence as to what the incidence of taxation would be if he calculated her loss under this head on an assumed annuity basis, as in my judgment he was entitled to do. On the figures produced there would have been a substantial tax element. This would bring into operation the exception to the general rule against
E making allowance for inflation to which Lord Fraser of Tullybelton referred in his speech in *Cookson* v. *Knowles* [1978] 2 W.L.R. 978, 991. Bristow J. made an allowance for inflation by increasing the multiplier. This is what Lord Fraser said could be done when there is a high tax element in the calculation. In my judgment the calculation he made was right. The sums which he awarded for loss of future earnings (£84,000) and pension rights (£8,000) must be added to the other heads
F of damage. As I agree with Lord Denning M.R. what the sums for those other heads should be, it follows that I would confirm the trial judge's award.

Outstanding points

G   For the sake of completeness, however, I shall deal shortly with three of Mr. Davies' submissions: first, that Bristow J. should not have found on the evidence that there was a probability that the plaintiff would be brought to England when her mother died or became too frail to look after her in Penang; secondly, that the sum awarded for pain and suffering and the loss of the amenities of life was too high and should have been a conventional one of the *Benham* v. *Gambling* [1941] A.C.
H 157, kind, albeit much greater; and thirdly, that no allowance of any kind should have been made for future inflation.

England or Penang

  The evidence about what was likely to happen to the plaintiff when her mother could no longer look after her was vague; and some of it was tainted with hearsay: see the sentence in Dr. MacQuaide's report about there being no suitable institutions in Malaysia for patients such as the

plaintiff. In my judgment the trial judge was entitled to find on such A
evidence as there was that the plaintiff one day would have to be cared
for in England. The defendants as a subordinate body of the Department of Health and Social Security retained Dr. MacQuaide to find
out what were the plaintiff's circumstances in Penang. If they had
any reason to think that he was wrong about there being no suitable
institutions in Malaysia, with the resources of the state behind them,
they could easily have shown that he was wrong.   B

The loss of the amenities of life

I do not accept that the plaintiff was in such an insensitive condition
that it can be assumed that she does not appreciate what her condition is.
Her mother told Dr. MacQuaide that sometimes she laughs and cries.
The plaintiff has not been reduced to the condition of a zombie. She   C
retains some memory of what she learned whilst in training for her
profession as a doctor. The fact that she cannot express what she
feels does not mean she does not feel at all. Far from £20,000 being too
high a sum for this head of damage, it may be too low. But as the trial
judge may not have allowed enough for overlap between future loss of
earnings and the cost of future care I would not alter his final figure. D

The factor of inflation

As to inflation I have read the speech of Lord Fraser of Tullybelton,
with which Viscount Dilhorne, Lord Salmon and Lord Scarman agreed,
in the same sense as Lord Denning M.R. has done and as meaning that
in exceptional cases where there is a high tax factor, inflation can be   E
taken into account when calculating the heads of damage for which the
assumed annuity method is appropriate.

Conclusions

I end as I began. This is a startling award; but it is not an absurd
one. A number of factors have gone to make it as high as it is. There   F
is the long expectation of life—some 30 years, during most of which,
but for this appalling accident, the plaintiff would probably have been
earning a substantial income. Above all there is the fact of inflation in
recent years. As I have already pointed out, the present day equivalent
in purchasing power of the £16,000 which Mr. Phillips was awarded in
1879 would probably be nearly £200,000; and as Mr. French pointed out G
the present day equivalent of the £51,447 awarded by this court in
Fletcher v. *Autocar and Transporters Ltd.* [1968] 2 Q.B. 322 to the
plaintiff, a quantity surveyor, who was 56 at the time of the accident
and had an expectation of life of 16 years, would be about £150,000 when
account is taken of the inflation factors set out in *Kemp and Kemp,
The Quantum of Damages*, 4th ed. (1975), vol. 2, p. 601. Lord
Denning M.R. has commented that any sum over that necessary for the   H
plaintiff's care will avail her nothing and will accumulate at high interest
rates for the benefit of her relatives who have told us through Mr. French
that they want none of it. This may be so; but with respect, it is optimistic speculation. My concern for the plaintiff is that the award may
not be enough for her care during her life time. If inflation goes on
during the next decade as it has done in the past one, those having charge
of the plaintiff may have difficulty in paying her maintenance costs.

A Anyway on the authorities the courts should not concern themselves with
what happens to any damages awarded: see *H. West & Son Ltd.* v.
Shephard [1964] A.C. 326, 341–342 *per* Lord Reid, at p. 349 *per* Lord
Morris of Borth-y-Gest, at p. 363 *per* Lord Devlin, and at p. 364 *per*
Lord Pearce.

I would dismiss the appeal.

B
BROWNE L.J. I agree with Lawton L.J. that this appeal should be dismissed. On February 28, 1973, the plaintiff, at the age of 36, could
look forward to a successful life in her chosen branch of her chosen
profession, a life which would no doubt have given satisfaction to herself
and been of great value to her patients. She is said to have been " a
remarkably good doctor, intelligent, conscientious, reliable, able to make
C good contact with patients, supportive to and popular with the nursing
staff and a loyal member of my team" and to have shown "great
promise" (see the letter of February 11, 1975, from the Royal Free
Hospital, confirmed by Professor Russell in evidence). She had come
to England in 1971, and was already senior registrar at Friern Hospital,
working between the New Southgate Group of Hospitals and the Royal
D Free Hospital. In all probability she would have reached the status of
consultant psychiatrist within four or five years.

On March 1, 1973, as a result of negligence for which the defendants
admitted liability (though Mr. French told us only on the day before
the trial), she lost everything, except her life. I cannot do better than
adopt what the judge said, ante, p. 900E–F:

E
"That a doctor who had so much to offer the mentally ill
should be subjected by want of care in hospital to the appalling
disability from which Dr. Lim is condemned to suffer for the rest
of her existence is a very great tragedy. Her mother, who has
been in court throughout the trial, in which counsel on both
sides have given me the greatest possible help, will realise that the
law cannot pretend to compensate her daughter for the destruction
F   of her life. The court can only award a sum of money, and in
justice to the defendants as well as to Dr. Lim that sum must be in
proportion to awards in other cases of those who have suffered
injuries of comparable severity."

As I understand it, the defendants at the trial did not put forward
any constructive suggestions for dealing with the disastrous situation
G which had been created by the negligence for which they are responsible,
although I suppose that as an area health authority they ought to be in a
good position to make such suggestions. Now on this appeal they
challenge all the major items in the total damages and interest of
£254,765 awarded by the judge. It is convenient to divide these
damages, as Mr. Davies did, into two main heads. Physical damage (or
H non-economic loss) and economic loss, though of course in the end one
must look at the total.

Physical damage or non-economic loss

Under this head the judge awarded £25,930. In form, he split this
item into £20,000 damages and £5,930 interest. As I understand it, the
reason why he did it in this form was this. In *Cookson* v. *Knowles*
[1977] Q.B. 913, 921, this court said, obiter, that damages under this

head should be assessed as at the date of the trial and that therefore no A
interest should be awarded.   When the present case was before Bristow J.,
Cookson v. *Knowles* had been decided by this court and was under
appeal to the House of Lords but the House had not given its decision.
Bristow J. assessed the damages on the " pre-*Cookson* v. *Knowles* basis
so as to be comparable with other awards."   He increased that amount
to the " *Cookson* v. *Knowles* basis " by adding the amount which would
have been awarded as interest before that decision.   The House of B
Lords left this point open: see the last paragraph of Lord Diplock's
speech [1978] 2 W.L.R. 978, 987-988, and I think we must follow
what was said by this court.   I treat the judge's award as an award of
£26,000 as at the date of the trial.

Mr. Davies would have wished to argue that in a case like this,
where there was, he said, no appreciation by the plaintiff of her loss and C
she had been reduced to " living death," the damages ought to be a
conventional figure analogous to the conventional figures which are
given for loss of expectation of life when the victim has been killed:
Benham v. *Gambling* [1941] A.C. 157.   But he rightly recognised and
accepted that this argument was not open to him in face of the decisions
of this court in *Wise* v. *Kaye* [1962] 1 Q.B. 638 and of the House of D
Lords in *H. West & Son Ltd.* v. *Shephard* [1964] A.C. 326.   He submitted, however, that this head of damages in cases like this should be
limited to a " conventional " figure of £10,000 to £15,000.

Mr. French disputed Mr. Davies' suggestion that the plaintiff had no
appreciation of her loss.   He referred us to the medical evidence, and
submitted that this is by no means what is sometimes called a " cabbage "
case; he described it as a " twilight case, with the twilight sometimes E
getting lighter and sometimes darker."

I think Mr. French is right about this.   I do not think I need refer
in detail to the agreed medical reports.   Their effect is that the plaintiff's moods vary widely.   On good days she has some memory of the
past (including, it seems, some memory of having been a doctor), can
understand a little, can read a little, can speak a little.   At other times F
" she would lapse into a depressed, withdrawn, non-responsive, non-
communicative and even non-co-operative behaviour not unlike a child
of a few years old."   At times, she appears to be deeply miserable.
One doctor says that " her intellectual functions were probably better
than what could be drawn out of her."   As to her physical condition,
the medical reports fully support the judge's findings that " the picture G
which emerges from the agreed medical reports is that of a helpless
invalid who will require nursing for the rest of her life, and is only
intermittently sentient."   The report of Dr. MacQuaide, who went
out to Penang in July 1976 to examine the plaintiff on behalf of the
defendants, was that " She will always need total care either at home H
or in an institution.   I do not consider that significant improvement is
likely to occur in the future and certainly not to a degree that would
enable her to look after herself."   He reported that if the plaintiff
continues to get the personal attention she has had since she went
home to Penang he could see no reason why her life expectancy should
be shortened, though if the standard of care should deteriorate significantly her life expectancy would almost certainly be less than average.

A Her normal expectation of life at the date of the trial would have been about 37 years. The judge said, ante, p. 903c–d:

"Dr. Lim's loss of the amenities of her good and useful life is total. On the evidence, her appreciation of that loss, and so the agony which knowing what you have lost must cause, is nil, or very small."

B As I understand the medical reports, I think the judge rather under-rated the plaintiff's appreciation.

Any award of damages under this head can only be "conventional," in the sense that there can be no money equivalent for losses of this kind. But I can see no justification for Mr. Davies' suggestion of a "conventional" figure of £10,000 or £15,000 in this type of case; each case must depend on its own facts, as is illustrated by the comparable C cases to which we were referred. In my view, the judge's award is amply supported by the damages awarded in those cases. In *Wise* v. *Kaye* [1962] 1 Q.B. 638, where the accident was in 1958 and the trial in 1961, the damages under this head were £15,000. In that case the plaintiff had been unconscious ever since the accident and there was no prospect that she would ever recover consciousness; she was aged 20 at the time of the accident:

D

"No doctor could say how long the plaintiff will live but it was accepted that she cannot be expected to endure for anything approaching a normal span of life": p. 646.

The majority of this court, Sellers and Upjohn L.JJ. (Diplock L.J. dissenting) held (a) that *Benham* v. *Gambling* [1941] A.C. 157 had no E application; (b) that it was irrelevant that the plaintiff herself could not use or enjoy the damages, and that in the end they would probably pass to her next-of-kin; (c) that the plaintiff was entitled to damages for the physical injury and loss of amenities which she sustained (though not for pain and suffering) even though she had no realisation of what had happened to her. In *H. West & Son Ltd.* v. *Shephard* [1964] A.C. 326 F the plaintiff was aged 41 at the time of the accident in 1959; she probably had some realisation of what had happened to her (certainly more than the plaintiff in *Wise* v. *Kaye* [1962] 1 Q.B. 638); her expectation of life had been reduced to five years from about the date of the trial. The judge in 1962 awarded £17,500 for physical injuries and loss of amenities, holding (see *H. West & Son Ltd.* v. *Shephard* [1964] A.C. 326, 329) that because she had some appreciation of her G condition she was in a worse position than the plaintiff in *Wise* v. *Kaye,* but that the damages were limited by the limitation of her expectation of life to five years. He gave nothing for pain and suffering. This award was upheld by this court and by the majority of the House of Lords. The plaintiff in that case was about the same age as the plaintiff in this case; she had perhaps rather more appreciation of her condition (though I am not sure of this); on the other hand, she had an expectation H of life of only five years, as against something like 30 years in this case. All the members of the House, except Lord Devlin but including Lord Reid, who dissented as to the result, held that *Benham* v. *Gambling* [1941] A.C. 157 did not apply; that the way in which a plaintiff spends the damages is irrelevant and that therefore the fact that a plaintiff can get no personal benefit from them is irrelevant; and that the expected period of life was relevant. The majority (Lord Morris of Borth-y-

Gest, with whom Lord Tucker agreed, and Lord Pearce) in dismissing A
the appeal approved the decision of the majority of this court in *Wise*
v. *Kaye* [1962] 1 Q.B. 638, and, as I understand it, the judge's view
that Mrs. Shephard was entitled to rather more damages than Miss
Wise because she had some realisation of her condition. In *Fletcher*
v. *Autocar and Transporters Ltd.* [1968] 2 Q.B. 322, the plaintiff was
aged 56 at the time of the accident in 1964; his expectation of life was B
about 16 years; he had little if any appreciation of what had happened
to him but suffered some pain (see pp. 332, 351 and 354); his physical
injuries were less than those in *Wise* v. *Kaye* and *West's* case. The
judge in 1967 awarded £10,000 for pain and suffering and loss of
amenities. Diplock L.J. thought that if there had been no overlap with
loss of earnings a figure of £15,000 would not have been wrong: p. 353,
and Salmon L.J. would have awarded £17,000: p. 366.   C
    In *Taylor* v. *Bristol Omnibus Co. Ltd.* [1975] 1 W.L.R. 1054 the
accident was in 1968 and the trial in 1974. The plaintiff was in 1968
aged 3½. He was completely helpless but was aware of his condition;
his expectation of life was not reduced to any great extent. This court
upheld £27,500 damages for pain, suffering and loss of amenities.
    Mr. French put before us an advance copy of a table which is to D
appear in the new edition of *Kemp and Kemp, The Quantum of
Damages*, 4th ed. showing the value of the pound at various dates. Without going into detailed figures, it is clear that if the awards in the four cases
to which I have referred are translated into their 1977 equivalents they
would be far more than the £20,000 or £26,000 awarded by the judge in
the present case—something like £40,000 or £50,000 or even more.
Finally, in *Bolton* v. *Essex Area Health Authority*, The Times, Novem- E
ber 8, 1977, decided a month before Bristow J.'s decision in the present
case, Thompson J. awarded £40,000 under this head (we were provided
with a copy of the judgment). The accident was in 1975. The plaintiff
was aged 53. His expectation of life was about 10 years. He was
paralysed and unable to speak, but his intellect appeared to have escaped
damage, and he could understand and communicate, although not F
properly or easily. By comparison with the present case, his faculties
were less completely affected, and I should suppose that he therefore
had more realisation of the loss he had suffered, but his expectation of
life was much less.
    In my judgment, Bristow J. made no mistake in principle on this
head of damages and his award was not excessive in comparison with
the other cases to which I have referred. It is enough at this stage to G
say that £20,000 or £26,000 was in my view not excessive, but by her
respondent's notice the plaintiff alleges that it was insufficient.

Economic loss

    Leaving interest out of account, the sums awarded by the judge
under this general head were: H

    Special damages
        Cost of care to date of trial   £8,000
        Out-of-pocket expenses to date of trial   £3,596
        Loss of earnings to date of trial   £14,213
                                                        ————————
                                                         £25,809

A   *Loss of future earnings*
        £6,000 a year multiplied by 14   £84,000
        Loss of pension rights   £8,000

        £92,000

B   *Cost of future care*
        7 years in Malaysia at £2,600 a year
        £18,200 discounted to £17,500   £17,500
        Thereafter in England at £8,000 a year
        multiplied by 11   £88,000

C   £105,500

Mr. Davies attacked these awards on two matters of principle, and also made various detailed criticisms. The matters of principle were: (a) duplication between future loss of earnings and cost of care and (b) the way in which the judge dealt with inflation.

D   As to (a), Mr. Davies' submission in its primary form was, as I understand it, that nothing should be awarded for loss of future earnings in the circumstances of this case. He said that what he called the "basic fallacy" was to regard loss of future earnings as an item of damages "in its own right." He said—and I quote from his written submissions which he helpfully put before us—that "the plaintiff's loss is not a loss of earnings, but the material loss he suffers
E   by not being able to live and to keep his family (if he has one) in the lifestyle which his rate of earning, and his earning prospects, enable him to do." This may well be right, but it seems to me only a matter of words. I agree of course that the earnings to be considered are the net earnings, after deducting the expenses of earning them (for example, fares going to work), but I am afraid that I simply cannot understand the rest of the argument set out in another paragraph of Mr. Davies'
F   written submissions. The effect seems to be that if the labourer is worthy of his hire, and the value of his work is equal to what he is paid for it, he gets nothing for loss of earnings. However, Mr. Davies' concluding submission was that: "The true question is, what is the cost of keeping the plaintiff in reasonable comfort for the rest of her life, and of keeping the plaintiff's dependants (if any) in a style and comfort
G   commensurate with the plaintiff's earnings, past and prospective, for the estimated duration of her working life?" In the written submissions it is said that: "Her loss, therefore, is not a loss of earnings, but consists of the inability to use her earnings for the purposes for which she would have used them, but for the accident. The enjoyment she would have got from that alternative use is already compensated in
H   the figure for loss of amenities. What then has she lost? Since (i) there was, and there could be, no evidence that she would have saved anything from her earnings, and (ii) her maintenance is wholly covered by an additional award of £6,000, she cannot be said to have suffered a greater loss than the sum required for her care."

In my judgment, Mr. Davies' submissions are wrong, both on principle and authority. At least since *Phillips* v. *London and South Western Railway Co.,* 4 Q.B.D. 406; 5 Q.B.D. 78; 5 C.P.D. 280, to

which Lawton L.J. has referred in detail, loss of future earnings has   A
been treated as a separate item of damages "in its own right" in
personal injury cases.   In several of the cases to which I have referred
under the heading of physical injury or non-economic loss damages
were awarded under the separate heads of future loss of earnings and
future care.   The exceptions were *Wise* v. *Kaye* [1962] 1 Q.B. 638
where the plaintiff was being cared for free of charge by the National
Health Service, but an award was made for future loss of earnings,   B
and *H. West & Son Ltd.* v. *Shephard* [1964] A.C. 326, where I understand the position was the same.   In my judgment this court cannot
and should not depart from this well settled practice.   I am confirmed
in this view by what Lord Pearce said in *H. West & Son Ltd.* v. *Shephard* [1964] A.C. 326, 369 and what Orr L.J. (with whom Stamp L.J.
agreed) said in *Taylor* v. *Bristol Omnibus Co. Ltd.* [1975] 1 W.L.R.   C
1054, 1061E–F.   In that case, the majority of this court, with whom
Lord Denning M.R. rather reluctantly agreed, rejected what seems to
have been the same argument as to that put forward by Mr. Davies
(see p. 1061), and Lord Denning M.R. said, at p. 1059G: "This suggestion is, however, contrary to present practice."

The only authority which gives any support to Mr. Davies' argument   D
is *Fletcher* v. *Autocar and Transporters Ltd.* [1968] 2 Q.B. 322, in
which Lord Denning M.R. and Diplock L.J. held that the damages in
respect of future loss of earnings and future care should be reduced;
Salmon L.J. dissented.   Neither of the majority held that *nothing*
should be given for future loss of earnings.   Lord Denning M.R., at
p. 337, thought that the plaintiff should only

> "be compensated for his loss of future earnings to the extent that   E
> he would have used them for supporting his wife in comfort for
> the rest of her life, including any savings that he would have made
> out of his earnings if uninjured."

He also pointed out the danger of overlapping between sums awarded
for loss of future earnings and those awarded for loss of amenities and   F
for future care.   Diplock L.J. reduced the sums awarded by the
judge for loss of future earnings and for future care.   He too pointed
out the danger of overlapping between damages for loss of future earnings
and for loss of amenities (pp. 342–345); but as I understand it the actual
ground of his decision that the damages under these heads should be
reduced was that as a result of a detailed criticism of the judge's figures
for loss of future earnings (which he reduced from £32,000 to £22,000)   G
and the cost of future care (pp. 345–350) he thought the figures were too
high, and not because of overlapping.   He did think there was some
overlapping between loss of future earnings and general damages for loss
of amenity.   It is true that at p. 352 he referred to a method of assessing
damages on the lines of Mr. Davies' submission in the present case, but
he introduced this part of his judgment by saying: H

> "Although . . . it is not a conventional way of assessing damages,
> it is I think possible to check very roughly whether a total award of
> the order of £51,000 accords with what, in agreement with the Master
> of the Rolls, I think that social justice requires in [this] case . . ."

Salmon L.J. would have dismissed the appeal.   In my judgment *Fletcher*
v. *Autocar and Transporters Ltd.* [1968] 2 Q.B. 322, does not, as a

A   matter of decision, support Mr. Davies' primary submission, and we are
bound by *Taylor v. Bristol Omnibus Co. Ltd.* [1975] 1 W.L.R. 1054 to
reject it; in that case Lord Denning M.R. referred at p. 1060 to *Fletcher*
and cannot have thought it was inconsistent with the decision in *Taylor,*
with which he agreed.

       I think that Mr. Davies' argument is also wrong in principle.
B   Whether you call this head of damages loss of future earnings or
whether you call it loss of the standard of living which those earnings
would have enabled the plaintiff to enjoy, she has been deprived of it
by negligence for which the defendants are responsible. I can see no
reason why she should be debarred from recovering this loss because she
is also entitled to recover the expenses of a different standard of living
C   imposed on her by the defendants; the two are not connected. Further,
it seems to me that it would be quite impossible for a court to investigate
how a plaintiff would have spent or saved his or her earnings if he or
she had not been injured. I think that the most which can and should
be done is to see that as far as possible there is no overlapping between
the sums awarded for loss of future earnings and the cost of future care
D   in respect of the " domestic element " (food, rent, electricity etc.), as
was done in *Shearman* v. *Folland* [1950] 2 K.B. 43 and *Mitchell* v.
Mulholland (No. 2) [1972] 1 Q.B. 65; see Sir Gordon Willmer at p. 88.
Bristow J. did this.

       Mr. Davies also made some subsidiary criticisms of the judge's award
under this head: (a) the way in which the judge dealt with inflation;
E   I will come to this later; (b) overlapping; I will deal with this under costs
of future care; (c) expenses to be deducted from earnings.

       Mr. French rightly accepts that the plaintiff's expenses of earning
her salary must be deducted in calculating her future loss of earnings.
Mr. Davies submits that the judge did not make any or any sufficient
deduction. Mr. Eccleshall, the accountant who gave evidence on behalf
F   of the plaintiff, calculated the plaintiff's future earnings on the alternative assumptions that she would have gone on working in the United
Kingdom or that she would have gone back to Malaysia and worked
there. His estimate of her average future earnings (after deduction of
tax and national insurance contributions) if she had stayed in the United
Kingdom was £6,700 a year. If she had gone back to Malaysia, her
G   net earnings would have been substantially higher, I gather mainly
because of lower taxation. Bristow J. found that on the probabilities
she would have practised in England, and found that a fair multiplicand
would be £6,000. Mr. Davies accepts the judge's figure of £6,000, but
submits that £3,000 should be deducted for expenses. I understand
this submission to be based on two answers given by Mr. Eccleshall in
H   cross-examination:

          " Q. As an accountant who deals with people's affairs do you
       think you can help us on this? Would I be very far out if I were
       to suggest to you that it would cost a professional person like a
       consultant about £3,000 a year to live in this country today? A.
       I think that would be a pretty low figure. I only have my own
       expenses to go by and I know they are more than that. Q. Of

course when we are dealing with a consultant, a consultant would A
have to have rooms to practise from if he or she were carrying on
private practice?   A.   Yes."

The first question and answer seem to relate to the whole cost of
living, not to the plaintiff's expenses of earning her salary and fees.   As
to the consulting room, the assumption was that the plaintiff would have B
worked as a consultant in the National Health Service, for which she
would not have had to provide a consulting room.   Mr. Eccleshall's
figures do include some fees for private practice, but they are comparatively small and seem unlikely to involve much expense.   The
judge reduced Mr. Eccleshall's estimate of £6,700 a year to £6,000,
which I think is ample.   In my view there is nothing in this point.   C

Inflation

Bristow J. referred to *Taylor* v. *O'Connor* [1971] A.C. 115 and the
changes in circumstances since then and said, ante, p. 901D:

"In these circumstances I take the view that the court must do
what it reasonably can to protect a plaintiff against inflation, and D
that what the House of Lords thought it wrong for Lyell J. to do
in the conditions of 1968 it is right to do in 1977 when we can see
more clearly where the world is going."

He took future inflation into account at two points.   In the multiplier
for cost of future care he made " some increase for prospective inflation " E
and in the multiplier for loss of future earnings he included " a small
increase to build in some anti-inflation protection."   Mr. Davies submits that he should not have taken it into account at all.

In *Taylor* v. *O'Connor* [1971] A.C. 115, 130 Lord Reid said that
" it would, I think, be quite unrealistic to refuse to take [future
inflation] into account at all," though he thought that it would not F
make much difference in that case because of high rates of interest and
capital appreciation.   He also held that taxation must be taken into
account: pp. 128 and 129.   It is even more unrealistic to refuse today
to take future inflation into account.   But until the decision of the
House of Lords in *Cookson* v. *Knowles* [1978] 2 W.L.R. 978 there were
decisions binding on this court that future inflation must not be taken G
into account: *Young* v. *Percival* [1975] 1 W.L.R. 17 and *Cookson* v.
Knowles [1977] Q.B. 913.   In my judgment, however, the House of
Lords has held in *Cookson* v. *Knowles* [1978] 2 W.L.R. 978—(a) that
future inflation " is taken care of in a rough and ready way " by the fact
that damages are normally awarded on the basis of the conventional
multipliers which assume a rate of interest of 4 per cent. or 5 per cent., H
whereas the actual rates of interest today are very much higher (see Lord
Diplock at pp. 984–986, especially 986, and Lord Fraser of Tullybelton
at pp. 990–991, with whom Viscount Dilhorne, Lord Salmon and Lord
Scarman agreed); but (b) that in

" exceptional cases, where the annuity is large enough to attract
income tax at a high rate . . . it might be appropriate to increase

A   the multiplier, or to allow for future inflation in some other way . . ."

according to the evidence in the case: (Lord Fraser at p. 991; see also Lord Diplock at p. 985—inflation can be largely offset by investment policy " at any rate if the rate of the tax on the dependant's gross income is low "). The present case seems to me to be one of the exceptional
B cases referred to by Lord Fraser of Tullybelton; the high incidence of tax on the assumed annuity in this case is shown on Mr. Eccleshall's exhibit XII. In my view, the judge (who seems to have had a premonition of what the House of Lords was going to say in *Cookson*) made no mistake in principle on this point and I am not satisfied that he made any excessive allowance.
C

Cost of future care

     Mr. Davies challenged the judge's finding that the probability was that the plaintiff would have to come to England about seven years after the trial to be looked after here. He also submitted that the
D judge had not made enough allowance for overlap between loss of future earnings (if his primary submission on that point was rejected) and cost of future care.

     As to the first point, I agree with Lawton L.J. that the evidence was vague, but in my view the judge was entitled to find as he did. The additional evidence which was put before us supports the view that she
E may have to come here sooner than the judge thought.

     The information that there were no satisfactory institutions in Malaysia which could cope satisfactorily with the plaintiff came from Dr. MacQuaide's report of August 4, 1976. At that stage he was advising the defendants. At the trial he was called as a witness for the plaintiff. The defendants had ample time and opportunity to find
F out whether this information was correct, but no questions were put to Dr. MacQuaide in cross-examination to suggest that it was not. The plaintiff's mother is over 70 and is not in good health. Dr. MacQuaide said in evidence that at the time of the trial (November 1977) she was not as well as when he had seen her a year before; she suffered from osteo-arthritis of the knees and was very much more crippled than she
G had been. No one suggested any possibility except that the plaintiff should be looked after either in her mother's house in Penang or in an institution in England. I have no hesitation in drawing the inference that fairly soon (probably sooner than the judge's finding of seven years) the plaintiff will have to come to England to be looked after here.

     As to overlap, the judge had this problem in mind. In his figure for
H care in her mother's house at Penang he allowed nothing for the " domestic element," in order to avoid overlap. He allowed nothing for the value of the mother's services, which he could have done. On this part of the award I think he made an ample allowance for overlap. On the figure for care in England, he allowed for the " domestic element " by a reduction in the multiplier. It is not clear how much he allowed, and this seems to be an unorthodox way of dealing with this

problem. But, without going into details of the figures, I agree with A
Mr. French that the judge pared the figures of the cost of care in
England to the bone and beyond, and so made a further provision for
overlap. Mr. Eccleshall's figure (at 1977 prices) was £8,500 a year on
a modest basis and the judge reduced this to £8,000. There was no
question of her " being kept in the most expensive nursing home." Dr.
MacQuaide's figure for care at St. Andrew's Hospital, Northampton, was B
about £13,000 a year initially, though it would be less if she was later
put in a long-term ward. In my view, the judge made ample allowance
for overlapping.

Conclusion

The paramount consideration in this case must be that the plaintiff C
should be looked after for the rest of her life. I entirely accept that
this is the only consideration of her family. If the figure of £8,000 a
year as the cost in 1977 of her care in England is right, I think there
is a real risk that the damages awarded may not enable this sum to be
provided if she survives for anything like her expectation of life: see
Mr. Eccleshall's Exhibit XII. At least, I am not satisfied that they D
are excessive for this purpose. We are not entitled to tinker with the
judge's award, and I have no wish to do so. If (which I do not accept)
the judge made insufficient allowance in favour of the defendants under
some heads, I think that the award under the head of non-economic loss
might well have been higher, and he might well have held that the
probabilities were that the plaintiff might have to come to this country E
sooner than in seven years' time.

I have had the advantage of reading the judgments which Lord
Denning M.R. and Lawton L.J. have delivered. I agree with the
Master of the Rolls that the principles on which damages are awarded
in personal injury cases need re-appraisal—not only in cases like this
but in all cases. High inflation and high taxation have completely F
distorted the traditional methods of assessment. Mr. Eccleshall's
Appendix XII illustrates that in a case where heavy damages are
awarded a large part of the damages which a defendant has to pay is
paid for the benefit of the revenue and not of the plaintiff; it is a matter
of chance that in this particular case it is merely a transfer from one
pocket of the State to another. But I agree with Lawton L.J. that we G
are bound by the authorities to which he refers to hold that we cannot
do what Lord Denning M.R. would do: see also Stamp L.J. and Orr
L.J. in *Taylor* v. *Bristol Omnibus Co. Ltd.* [1975] 1 W.L.R. 1054,
1060, 1061. Nor am I satisfied that his figure of £136,596 would
produce a just result in this case. According to Mr. Eccleshall's
Appendix XII a capital sum of £100,000 would produce a spendable H
income of £7,540 a year and of £150,000 a spendable income of £10,131.
The figure of £8,000 a year for future care in England was based on
1977 prices, and I cannot believe that an income of this sort would be
enough to provide for the plaintiff's needs if she lives for the expected
30 years, or even if she only lives for 10 or 15 or 20 years. I know of
no authority which would enable this court at this stage (or a trial

A judge) to make an interim award as suggested by Lord Denning M.R.; R.S.C., Ord. 29, rr. 9–16 would not authorise such an order.   As I have said, I would dismiss this appeal.

> *Appeal dismissed with costs on common fund basis.*
>
> *Leave to appeal with condition that appellants will not seek to disturb order in Court of Appeal as to costs.*
>
> *Costs in House of Lords to be dealt with by House of Lords itself.*
>
> *Stay of execution as to balance of money on same terms as in court below pending decision of House of Lords.*

Solicitors: *J. Tickle & Co.; Coward Chance.*

M. M. H.

_____

[PRIVY COUNCIL]

E **ARTHUR ALLAN THOMAS** . . . . . . Petitioner

AND

THE QUEEN . . . . Respondent

1978 July 4;   Lord Wilberforce, Lord Hailsham of St. Marylebone,
      Oct. 5   Lord Edmund-Davies, Lord Fraser of Tullybelton
F   and Lord Scarman

[PETITION FOR LEAVE TO APPEAL FROM THE COURT OF APPEAL OF NEW ZEALAND]

Privy Council—Jurisdiction—Governor-General's reference—Prerogative of mercy—Reference to Court of Appeal of New Zealand — Whether appeal lying from opinion of Court of Appeal on Governor-General's reference—Crimes Act 1961 (No. 43 of 1961), s. 406 (b)—Judicial Committee Act 1833 (3 & 4 Wm. 4, c. 41), s. 3 [1]

Section 406 of the Crimes Act 1961 provides:

" Prerogative of mercy—Nothing in this Act shall affect the prerogative of mercy, but the Governor-General in Council on the consideration of any application for the exercise of the mercy of the Crown having reference to the conviction of any person by any court or to the sentence (other than a sentence fixed by law) passed on any person, may at any time if he thinks fit, whether or not that person has appealed or had the right to appeal against the conviction or sentence, . . . (b) If he desires the assistance of the Court of Appeal on any point arising

_____

[1] Judicial Committee Act 1833, s. 3: see post, p. 932B–C.

Thomas v. The Queen (P.C.) [1978]

A

in the case with a view to the determination of the application, refer that point to the Court of Appeal for its opinion thereon and the court shall consider the point so referred and furnish the Governor-General with its opinion thereon accordingly."

The defendant was convicted of two murders. The Court of Appeal dismissed his application for leave to appeal. He applied to the Governor-General to quash the convictions. The Governor-General referred the application to the Court of Appeal under section 406 (*b*) of the Crimes Act 1961. The Court of Appeal furnished an opinion to the Governor-General adverse to the defendant.

B

On the defendant's petition to the Judicial Committee for special leave to appeal from the opinion of the Court of Appeal: —

Held, dismissing the petition, that the wording of section 406 (*b*) showed that the legislature had not intended that an opinion of the Court of Appeal furnished on a reference to it under paragraph (*b*) should be appealable to the Judicial Committee and further that since such an opinion did not bind the Governor-General or impinge on any legal right of the defendant it was not a " decision " within the ambit of section 3 of the Judicial Committee Act 1833 and that, accordingly, the Judicial Committee had no jurisdiction to entertain the appeal.

C

D

Théberge v. *Laudry* (1876) 2 App.Cas. 102, P.C. applied.
Oteri v. *The Queen* [1976] 1 W.L.R. 1272, P.C. distinguished.

The following cases are referred to in the reasons for the report of their Lordships:

E

Arzu v. *Arthurs* [1965] 1 W.L.R. 675, P.C.
Commonwealth of Australia v. *Bank of New South Wales* [1950] A.C. 235, P.C.
Moses v. *Parker* [1896] A.C. 245, P.C.
Oteri v. *The Queen* [1976] 1 W.L.R. 1272, P.C.
Patterson v. *Solomon* [1960] A.C. 579; [1960] 2 W.L.R. 685; [1960] 2 All E.R. 20, P.C.

F

Tata Iron and Steel Co. Ltd. v. *Bombay Chief Revenue Authority* (1923) 39 T.L.R. 288, P.C.
Théberge v. *Laudry* (1876) 2 App.Cas. 102, P.C.

The following additional cases were cited in argument:

Australian Consolidated Press Ltd. v. *Uren* [1969] 1 A.C. 590; [1967] 3 W.L.R. 1338; [1967] 3 All E.R. 523, P.C.

G

Knight and Tabernacle Permanent Building Society, In re [1892] 2 Q.B. 613, C.A.
Lloyds Bank Ltd. v. *Jones* [1955] 2 Q.B. 298; [1955] 3 W.L.R. 5; [1955] 2 All E.R. 409, C.A.
Reg. v. *Podola* [1960] 1 Q.B. 325; [1959] 3 W.L.R. 718; [1959] 3 All E.R. 418, C.C.A.
Shell Co. of Australia Ltd. v. *Federal Commissioner of Taxation* [1931] A.C. 275, P.C.

H

Wi Matua's Will, In re [1908] A.C. 448, P.C.

PETITION by Arthur Allan Thomas for special leave to appeal from an opinion of the Court of Appeal of New Zealand (Wild C.J., McCarthy P., Richmond, Macarthur and McMullin JJ.) furnished on January 29, 1975, in response to a reference to it by the Governor-General (Order-in-Council

A   November 4, 1974) under section 406 (b) of the Crimes Act 1961 of the defendants' convictions of the murder of David Harvey Crewe and Jeannette Lenore Crewe. The respondent disputed the jurisdiction of the Judicial Committee.

The facts are stated in the reasons for the report of their Lordships.

B   *Louis Blom-Cooper* Q.C. and *Jonathan Caplan* for the defendant.
R. C. Savage Q.C., Solicitor-General for New Zealand, and *D. S. Morris* (of the New Zealand Bar) for the Crown.

LORD WILBERFORCE said that their Lordships considered that they had no jurisdiction to grant special leave to appeal and would give their reasons later.

C

October 5. The reasons for the report of their Lordships were delivered by LORD EDMUND-DAVIES.

Arthur Allan Thomas (the defendant) petitions for special leave to appeal to Her Majesty in Council from an "opinion" of the Court of Appeal of New Zealand expressed in response to a reference to it by His Excellency the Governor-General. The reference, which was made under

D   section 406 of the Crimes Act 1961, followed an application to the Governor-General to quash the defendant's convictions of murder. Their Lordships defer for later consideration the terms of the reference and the defendant's complaints of misdirection by the Court of Appeal. Something must first be said regarding the nature of the case itself.

The history is long and complicated, but it is sufficient to relate it only

E   in outline. In June 1970 Harvey and Jeanette Crewe were missing from their farmhouse at Pukekawa. In mid-August Mrs. Crewe's body was discovered in Waikato River, wrapped in a blanket and tied with wire. There was a bullet wound in her head. In mid-September Mr. Crewe's body was also found in the river, again tied with wire, and underneath it was the axle of a trailer. He too had been shot in the head. Late in

F   October, Detective Senior Sergeant Charles allegedly discovered a spent brass cartridge case ("exhibit 350") in the Crewes' garden. In November the defendant was arrested and charged with the murder of Mr. and Mrs. Crewe. During 1971 he was tried and convicted on both charges and received the statutory sentence of life imprisonment, and his appeal against conviction was dismissed. In February 1972, in response to several petitions for a new trial, the Governor-General referred the matter to

G   Sir George McGregor (a retired judge of the Supreme Court) who in his report advised against granting the petitions. Thereafter, further representations were made to the Governor-General and, by Order in Council, in August 1972 he referred the whole case to the Court of Appeal so that they could consider certain fresh evidence. This reference was made pursuant to section 406 (a) of the Crimes Act 1961, the text of which must

H   be considered later. Having considered the fresh material, in February 1973 the Court of Appeal ordered a new trial. This was concluded in April, and the defendant was again convicted of both murders. The defendant then applied for leave to appeal against these fresh convictions, but in July 1973 the Court of Appeal dismissed the application. A year later, in response to an application (supported by affidavits and fresh evidence) to quash the convictions, the Governor-General, this time pursuant to section 406 (b) of the Crimes Act 1961, by Order in Council referred the application to the Court of Appeal, "with a request that the A court consider it and hear such submissions on it as it thinks fit and answer the following questions. . . ." The text of the two questions posed will be considered later. On January 29, 1975, the "opinion of the court" was furnished, answering the first question in a manner adverse to the defendant and reporting that, in the circumstances, no answer was required to the second question. It is in respect of this opinion that the defendant now seeks special leave to appeal to this Board. B

Although it is not necessary for present purposes to consider the whole body of evidence called, it is essential to say something about one important feature of the Crown's case. Their Lordships have already said that both Mr. and Mrs. Crewe had been shot. Fragments of the bullets which killed them were recovered from their heads and there was forensic evidence that certain markings on these fragments indicated that both C bullets *could* have been fired by a Browning pump-action 0·22 rifle which the defendant owned. There was also evidence that this rifle *did* fire the cartridge case (exhibit 350). The Crown relied upon this as indicating that the defendant had been present in the Crewes' garden and had shot them with his rifle through an open window. Other evidence called need not now be gone into, for in its opinion the Court of Appeal observed that it refrained D

"from any discussion of the considerable body of evidence against [the defendant], other than that relating to exhibit 350, which was before the jury for their consideration in reaching their verdict."

Having regard to the conclusion which their Lordships have come to regarding the competency of this Board to deal with the petition, it is E sufficient to say that a fierce contest was waged regarding the important issue as to whether or not the cartridge case (exhibit 350) could have been loaded with pattern 8 bullets, corresponding to those which undoubtedly killed both Mr. and Mrs. Crewe. In his petition to the Governor-General (which the Court of Appeal described in its opinion as ". . . in effect an appeal to the royal prerogative of mercy, and not an appeal to this court"), the defendant sought the quashing of his convictions on the ground that F that issue should have been resolved in his favour.

Section 406 of the Crimes Act 1961 must now be considered in its entirety. It reads as follows:

"Prerogative of mercy—Nothing in this Act shall affect the prerogative of mercy, but the Governor-General in Council, on the consideration of any application for the exercise of the mercy of the Crown having G reference to the conviction of any person by any court or to the sentence (other than a sentence fixed by law) passed on any person, may at any time if he thinks fit, whether or not that person has appealed or had the right to appeal against the conviction or sentence, either—

(a) Refer the question of the conviction or sentence to the Court H of Appeal or, where the person was convicted or sentenced by a magistrate's court, to the Supreme Court, and the question so referred shall then be heard and determined by the court to which it is referred as in the case of appeal by that person against conviction or sentence or both, as the case may require; or

(b) If he desires the assistance of the Court of Appeal on any

A   point arising in the case with a view to the determination of
         the application, refer that point to the Court of Appeal for
         its opinion thereon, and the court shall consider the point
         so referred and furnish the Governor-General with its opinion
         thereon accordingly."

B   It is not unimportant to see how the Court of Appeal regarded its functions
    under the Governor-General's reference. After quoting paragraph (b) of
    section 406 they continued:

         "It is in pursuance of this particular statutory provision that the
         case has been referred to us. We have been asked to express our
         opinion on certain questions only, to assist His Excellency in Council
         in arriving at a decision upon the matters raised by the petition.
C   There is no question of our ordering a new trial, nor is this a case
         of the usual kind, of an appeal against conviction. His Excellency in
         Council has asked for our opinion on two questions which are as
         follows: 1. Has it been established by the [defendant] that neither of
         the bullets of which fragments were found in the bodies of David
         Harvey Crewe and Jeannette Lenore Crewe could have been assembled
         with the cartridge case identified as exhibit No. 350 in the course of
D   the manufacture of an 0·22 rimfire round of I.C.I. ammunition?
         2. If it is so established in such a finding inconsistent with the verdict
         of guilty, on both counts of murder, returned by the jury on April 16,
         1973, at the trial of [the defendant]?"

    Having considered the available material in detail, the Court of Appeal
    concluded their opinion by saying:
E
         "In those circumstances our opinion is that Question 1 must be 'No.'
         Conclusion: The court's answers to the questions are as follows:
         Question 1: No; Question 2: In view of the answer to Question 1, no
         answer to Question 2 is required. For that reason, and also because
         a determination on the [defendant's] petition is a matter for the
         Governor-General in Council, the court refrains from any discussion
F   of the considerable body of evidence against [the defendant], other
         than that relating to exhibit 350, which was before the jury for their
         consideration in reaching their verdict."

    In the petition to this Board for special leave, the principal grounds of
    complaints are these:

G   "i. that the said 'opinion' of the Court of Appeal is reviewable
         and properly the subject of a petition to Her Majesty in Council and
         further, having regard to the grounds below, ought to be so reviewed;
         ii. that the Court of Appeal misdirected itself and/or otherwise erred
         in law in its interpretation of the onus, if any, resting on [the
         defendant] in relation to the said Question 1 posed in the reference
         of July 1, 1974. The Court of Appeal wrongly found that the onus
H   required that [the defendant] 'must exclude a reasonable possibility
         that either of the bullets was assembled with exhibit 350' whereas,
         if an onus did rest on [the defendant], the proper onus was that he
         need only do so 'on the balance of probabilities' as was accepted by
         the crown; iii. that the Court of Appeal erred in law in answering
         Question 1 in the negative and in not furnishing an answer to Question
         2 since the court accepted [the defendant's] submission, and his
         evidence in support thereof, on Question 1 'on the probabilities' and

A

was only ' unable to exclude the reasonable possibility ' that the bullets could not have been assembled with the cartridge case identified as exhibit 350; iv. that [the defendant's] case has become the subject of persistent national debate in New Zealand and there is widespread public concern as to the propriety of his convictions."

B

In support of the first submission, viz. that the " opinion " is properly the subject of a petition to Her Majesty in Council, counsel for the defendant relied upon section 3 of the Judicial Committee Act 1833, which provides as follows:

" *Appeals to King in Council from sentence of any judge, etc., shall be referred to the committee, to report thereon.* III . . . all appeals or complaints in the nature of appeals whatever, which, either by virtue of this Act, or of any law, statute, or custom, may be brought before His Majesty or His Majesty in Council from or in respect of the determination, sentence, rule, or order of any court, judge, or judicial officer . . . shall from and after the passing of this Act be referred by His Majesty to the said Judicial Committee of His Privy Council. . . ."

C

Mr. Blom-Cooper submitted that the opinion rendered by the Court of Appeal was a " determination," within section 3, and that it is accordingly appealable to this Board, subject to the granting of the special leave which, in his submission, is shown by *Oteri* v. *The Queen* [1976] 1 W.L.R. 1272 to be capable of being granted in such cases as the present.

D

Reliance was likewise placed upon the New Zealand Order in Council (S.R. & O. 1910 No. 70, (L.3)) regulating all appeals to Her Majesty in Council from the Dominion of New Zealand, in respect of judgments of the Court of Appeal. The submission is that the opinion of the Court of Appeal was a " judgment " within rule 1, which provided that:

E

" ' *Judgment* ' includes decree, order, sentence, or decision, whether in the exercise of the appellate or original jurisdiction of the court, and whether in a proceeding removed into the court from any other court or on a case stated for the opinion of the court or otherwise howsoever."

F

Turning to section 406 of the Crimes Act 1961, Mr. Blom-Cooper relied upon the power thereby conferred upon the Governor-General in Council, " on the consideration of any application for the exercise of the mercy of the Crown " to

G

(*a*) Refer the question of the conviction or sentence to the Court of Appeal . . . and the question so referred shall then be heard and determined by the court to which it is referred as in the case of an appeal. . . ."

The submission was that the instant reference had resulted in a determination by the Court of Appeal, and that determination was appealable. Regarding that submission the following comments are called for:

H

1. The present reference was expressly made pursuant to section 406 (*b*), and not to section 406 (*a*), and there are important differences in the wording of the two paragraphs. 2. Paragraph (*a*) requires the question referred to " be heard and *determined* by the court . . . *as in the case of an appeal*," and it will be recalled that, when the case was first referred by the Governor-General back in August 1972 to the Court of Appeal, that is

A precisely what happened, the court itself ordering a new trial in February 1973, and that new trial promptly taking place in the following month. 3. The wording of paragraph (*b*) makes clear that the reference to the Court of Appeal is simply to obtain its " assistance . . . with a view to the *determination* of the application." The application in question relates to the exercise of the prerogative of mercy, and no-one but the Governor-General himself has the ultimate power to deal with such an application.

B Its exercise by any other person or body being unconstitutional, the reference of " any point in the case " to the Court of Appeal is merely in order to obtain its " opinion " thereon. When its labours are over the Court of Appeal is required to furnish that opinion to the Governor-General so that he, and he alone, may determine whether the application for the exercise of the prerogative of mercy is to be granted or refused.

C 4. Finally, the wording of the reference itself (earlier quoted, ante, p. 931c) makes clear that the Court of Appeal were free to conduct their " inquiry " in such a manner and in accordance with such procedure as they thought fit and were not obliged to conform to the rules governing criminal appeals.

Pausing there, it has accordingly to be said that the language of section 406 (*b*) itself seemed, in the judgment of their Lordships, wholly inconsistent with the notion that the " opinion " formed by the New Zealand Court of

D Appeal in a reference thereunder is appealable to this Board. But, had their Lordships entertained any doubts on the matter, they would have been finally dispersed by the reply of the Solicitor-General in a speech the effectiveness of which, if their Lordships may say so, was in direct ratio to its admirable brevity. He made two submissions, and these must be considered in turn.

E A. *The Court of Appeal were called upon by the Governor-General to perform statutory functions in relation to which no appeal was intended to lie.* In *Théberge* v. *Laudry* (1876) 2 App.Cas. 102 this Board was called upon to consider the Quebec Controverted Elections Act 1875, which contained a provision (section 90) that a judgment of the Supreme Court " shall not be susceptible of appeal." The petitioner whose election had

F been declared null and void by the Superior Court, sought special leave to appeal to this Board from that declaration. Dismissing the petition, Lord Cairns L.C. said, at pp. 106, 108:

"Now, upon that 90th section it is contended on behalf of the petitioner that it does not take away any prerogative right of the Crown; that the Crown and the prerogative of the Crown are not

G specially or particularly mentioned; and that the general rule is, that the prerogative of the Crown cannot be taken away except by a specific enactment. It is said that this section may be satisfied by holding that the intention of the legislature was, that there should be no appeal from a superior court to the Court of Queen's Bench in the colony, which was the kind of appeal that existed in civil

H cases in the colony, and that the prerogative of the Crown is not in any way affected . . . In the opinion of their Lordships . . . the 90th section . . . is an enactment which indicates clearly the intention of the legislature under this Act . . . to create this tribunal for the purpose of trying election petitions in a manner which should make its decision final to all purposes, and should not annex to it the incident of its judgment being reviewed by the Crown under its prerogative."

Commenting on that decision, Lord Hobhouse said in *Moses* v. *Parker* A [1896] A.C. 245, 248:

> " The statute provided that the judgment of the court should not be susceptible of appeal. Though that provision would destroy the right of a suitor to an appeal, it did not taken by itself destroy the prerogative of the Crown to allow one. But this Board held that they must have regard to the special nature of the subject; to the B circumstance that election disputes were not mere ordinary civil rights; and that the statute was creating a new and unknown jurisdiction for the purpose of vesting in a particular court the very peculiar jurisdiction which up to that time had existed in the assembly. And they came to the conclusion that the intention of the legislature was to create a tribunal in a manner which should make its decision final to all purposes, and should not annex to it the incident of being C reviewed by the Crown under its prerogative."

Those decisions have been consistently followed in a series of cases arising out of election petitions—see, for example *Patterson* v. *Solomon* [1960] A.C. 579 and *Arzu* v. *Arthurs* [1965] 1 W.L.R. 675. But of far wider application is the underlying principle that regard must be had to the precise wording of the legislation upon which appeals to this Board are D sought to be based, in order to determine whether it was ever intended that an appeal should lie. In the instant case, the Solicitor-General relied strongly upon the wording of paragraph (*b*) of section 406, which he contrasted with that of paragraph (*a*), submitting that, whereas an issue referred under the latter is *determined* by the Court of Appeal as if it were dealing with an appeal, the markedly different wording of paragraph (*b*) E clearly indicated that the " opinion " (a word which nowhere appears in paragraph (*a*)) could not be the subject matter of an appeal. It was determinative of no issue and in no sense bound the Governor-General in relation to his exercise of the royal prerogative, which was exclusively his concern and wholly outside the functions of any court.

It may here be added that, were it even remotely conceivable that the Governor-General was intended to be fettered in any way by the opinion F of the Court of Appeal, one would have expected to find in the Crimes Act 1961 some express wording to that effect, such as was employed, for example, in the District Court of Western Australia Act 1969, section 49, viz. :

> " A District Court judge may reserve any point of law arising in any trial of a person on indictment for the opinion of the Full Court G sitting as a court of criminal appeal, and defer passing judgment therein until that opinion has been given, and in such case shall pass judgment in conformity with that opinion."

This wording shows that the case of *Oteri* v. *The Queen* [1976] 1 W.L.R. 1272 is no authority for the granting of special leave in the present case, since the opinion of the Full Court was given for a different purpose and H had a different effect from the " opinion " of the Court of Appeal of New Zealand.

B. *The opinion of the Court of Appeal is not appealable under the relevant statutes.* The Solicitor-General secondly submitted that this petition for special leave does not lie unless it falls within the provisions of the Judicial Committee Act 1833, section 3 (which their Lordships have earlier quoted) or the succeeding statutory provisions in that regard, and that the

A petition does not come within the ambit of any of them. For any of the
Acts to apply (so the submission went) there must have been in the lower
court from which the appeal is brought, a judicial decision binding on the
parties. The decision in *Commonwealth of Australia* v. *Bank of New South
Wales* [1950] A.C. 235 was cited in support. Dealing with section 74 of
the Commonwealth of Australia Constitution 1900, Lord Porter said, at
p. 294:

B

> " It deals with the royal prerogative to grant special leave to appeal
> and imposes certain limitations on . . . that right. But the appeal by
> special leave is what it always has been, an appeal from an order or
> other judicial act which affects adversely the rights claimed by the
> appellant party. It is in the light of this consideration that the section
> must, if possible, be construed. To give effect to the appellants'
C
> submission would appear to involve the admission of an appeal not
> from a judicial act but from the pronouncement of an opinion on a
> question of law . . .
>
>   " As its opening words show, the section deals with ' appeals ' to
> His Majesty in Council and, as already observed, an appeal is the
> formal proceeding by which an unsuccessful party seeks to have the
D
> formal order of a court set aside or varied in his favour by an
> appellate court. It is only from such an order that an appeal can be
> brought. In section 74 the appeal is described as an appeal ' from a
> decision of the High Court ' and so far no difficulty arises. ' Decision '
> is an apt compendious word to cover ' judgments, decrees, orders, and
> sentences,' an expression that occurs in section 73. It was used in the
> comparable context of the Judicial Committee Acts of 1833 and 1844
E
> as a generic term to cover ' determination, sentence, rule or order ' and
> ' order, sentence or decree.' Further, though it is not necessarily a
> word of art, there is high authority for saying that even without such
> a context the ' natural, obvious, and prima facie meaning of the word
> " decision " is decision of the suit by the court ': see *Rajah Tasadduq
> Rasul Khan* v. *Manik Chand* ((1902), L.R. 30 I.A. 35, 39)."

F Of the several other cases to a like effect cited by the Solicitor-General,
their Lordships need mention only *Tata Iron and Steel Co. Ltd.* v. *Bombay
Chief Revenue Authority* (1923) 39 T.L.R. 288. There this Board held, on
a preliminary objection, that a " decision, judgment or order " of the High
Court of Bombay upon a reference made to them by the Chief Revenue
Authority pursuant to the provisions of an Income Tax Act were merely
advisory and not final, and that an appeal to His Majesty in Council was
G therefore incompetent.
    Their Lordships have not found it necessary to refer to further authori-
ties, for in their judgment this second submission of the Solicitor-General,
like the first, was well-founded. The wording of section 406 (*b*) of the
Crimes Act 1961 is such that no power or duty of determination binding
upon the Governor-General was entrusted to the Court of Appeal. The
H opinion they expressed impinged upon no legal right of the defendant, nor
did it place any fetter upon the exercise by the Governor-General of the
royal prerogative of mercy. For these reasons, their Lordships were of the
opinion that they had no jurisdiction to entertain the petition and humbly
advised Her Majesty that it should be dismissed.

    Solicitors: *Simons, Muirhead & Allan; Allen & Overy.*

                                                           T. J. M.

[1978]

A

[COURT OF APPEAL]

MALONE v. METROPOLITAN POLICE COMMISSIONER

[1978 M. No. 839]

1978   May 19, 22, 23; 26   Stephenson and Roskill L.JJ.

B

*Police—Powers—Retention of money—Search warrant to search
for suspected stolen property—Large sum partly in foreign
currency seized from house—Owner committed for trial on
charges of conspiracy to handle and handling stolen goods—
No specific charges made in respect of money—Whether police
entitled to retain money as material evidence until conclusion
of trial—Whether police entitled to retain money for purpose*
of satisfying restitution, compensation or forfeiture orders— C
*Theft Act 1968 (c. 60), s. 28 (1) (c) (as amended by Criminal
Justice Act 1972, Sch. 5)—Powers of Criminal Courts Act
1973 (c. 62), ss. 35 (1) (4), 43 (1) (3)*

Acting under a search warrant the police entered the
plaintiff's house and seized from a concealed wall cupboard in
the basement over £7,000 in Bank of England notes and the
equivalent of about £3,000 in United States dollar and Italian   D
lira notes and the movement of a grandfather clock, which
was subsequently identified as having been stolen, and from
other parts of the house other items of suspected stolen
property. The plaintiff and eight other persons were committed for trial on charges of conspiracy and of handling
stolen property but no specific charge was made in respect of
the money. On the refusal of the police to return the bulk
of the money before the criminal trial the plaintiff commenced   E
an action in detinue against the Metropolitan Police Commissioner and by an amended statement of claim added a
claim for a mandatory injunction ordering the commissioner
to deliver up to him the banknotes and the foreign currency
notes. Wien J. granted the injunction.

On appeal by the commissioner on the ground that he was
entitled to retain the money until the conclusion of the
criminal trial either as being material evidence in that trial or   F
in order to make it available in the event of a conviction
for the purpose of satisfying a restitution order under section
28 (1) (c) of the Theft Act 1968 (as amended) [1] or a compensation or forfeiture order under section 35 or section 43 of the
Powers of Criminal Courts Act 1973 [2]: —

Held, allowing the appeal, that, although there was no
general power in the police to retain property lawfully seized
which was not the subject of any charge and the police must   G
justify such retention upon some ascertainable ground and
although the money had not been exhibited in the committal
proceedings, circumstances could arise under which it would
form material evidence at the trial so that it would become
necessary for it to be produced and it would gravely hamper
the administration of justice if it had been handed back and
spent; and that accordingly the commissioner was entitled to
retain the money until the conclusion of the criminal trial   H
(post, pp. 941B–C, 943G–H, 944B–G, 953H—954B).

Ghani v. *Jones* [1970] 1 Q.B. 693, C.A. distinguished.

Held, further, that if the money could not have been

[Reported by EVERARD CORBALLY ESQ., Barrister-at-Law]

[1] Theft Act 1968 (as amended), s. 28 (1) (c): see post, p. 951A.
[2] Powers of Criminal Courts Act 1973, s. 35: see post, p. 946F–G.
S. 43: see post, p. 947A–B.

The Weekly Law Reports, December 8, 1978

937

3 W.L.R.   Malone v. Metropolitan Police Comr. (C.A.)

A   retained as material evidence in the criminal trial the commissioner would not have been entitled to retain it for the purpose
of making it available in the event of a conviction to satisfy an
order under section 28 (1) (c) of the Theft Act 1968 or under
section 35 or section 43 of the Powers of Criminal Courts
Act 1973 because none of those sections conferred power on
the police to retain money not the subject of any charge
which had been found in the possession of an accused at the
B   time of his arrest (post, pp. 944H—945A, 946A–E, 948A, 950H,
952F—953A).
     Dictum of Scrutton L.J. in *Jagger* v. *Jagger* [1926] P. 93,
102, C.A. applied.
     Per curiam. It would not be right to grant a mandatory
injunction for the return of the foreign currency which the
plaintiff appeared to have been holding contrary to the
provisions of the Exchange Control Act 1947 (post, pp. 948C–D,
C   955A–B).

The following cases are referred to in the judgments:

American Cyanamid Co. v. *Ethicon Ltd.* [1975] A.C. 396; [1975] 2
     W.L.R. 316; [1975] 1 All E.R. 504, H.L.(E.).
Dillon v. *O'Brien and Davis* (1887) 16 Cox C.C. 245.
Ghani v. *Jones* [1970] 1 Q.B. 693; [1969] 3 W.L.R. 1158; [1969] 3 All
D   E.R. 720; [1969] 3 All E.R. 1700, Talbot J. and C.A.
Gordon v. *Chief Commissioner of Metropolitan Police* [1910] 2 K.B.
         1080.
Jagger v. *Jagger* [1926] P. 93, C.A.
Reg. v. *Bunce* (1977) 66 Cr.App.R. 109, C.A.
Reg. v. *Hinde* (1977) 64 Cr.App.R. 213, C.A.
Reg. v. *Lushington, Ex parte Otto* [1894] 1 Q.B. 420.
Reg. v. *Thompson (Graham)* (1977) 66 Cr.App.R. 130, C.A.
E   *Rex* v. *Barnett* (1829) 3 C. & P. 600.
Rex v. *O'Donnell* (1835) 7 C. & P. 138.
Rex v. *Rooney* (1836) 7 C. & P. 515.
Truman (Frank) Export Ltd. v. *Metropolitan Police Commissioner*
     [1977] Q.B. 952; [1977] 3 W.L.R. 257; [1977] 3 All E.R. 431.
Siskina (Owners of cargo lately laden on board) v. *Distos Compania
     Naviera S.A.* [1977] 3 W.L.R. 532, Kerr J. and C.A.; [1977] 3
F   W.L.R. 818; [1977] 3 All E.R. 803, H.L.(E.).

The following additional cases were cited in argument:

Bowmakers Ltd. v. *Barnet Instruments Ltd.* [1945] K.B. 65.
Chic Fashions (West Wales) Ltd. v. *Jones* [1968] 2 Q.B. 299; [1968] 2
     W.L.R. 201; [1968] 1 All E.R. 229, C.A.
Garfinkel v. *Metropolitan Police Commissioner* [1972] Crim.L.R. 44.
G   *Rex* v. *Leigh* (1764) 1 Leach 52.

INTERLOCUTORY APPEAL from Wien J.
     The Metropolitan Police Commissioner, the defendant, appealed from
the judgment of Wien J. in chambers granting to the plaintiff, James
Malone, a mandatory injunction ordering the return to the plaintiff by the
H   commissioner of Bank of England notes, United States dollar notes and
Italian lira notes seized from him by the police at the time of his arrest.
The grounds of appeal were that (1) the judge having rightly found that the
commissioner was entitled in law to seize the money misdirected himself
in holding that the commissioner was not entitled to retain it until the
criminal proceedings pending against the plaintiff had been concluded;
(2) the money was evidence in the criminal proceedings pending against the
plaintiff and in seeking to retain it the commissioner was acting reasonably

938

The Weekly Law Reports, December 8, 1978

Malone v. Metropolitan Police Comr. (C.A.)   [1978]

and not detaining it longer than was necessary within the principles set A
out in *Ghani* v. *Jones* [1970] 1 Q.B. 693; (3) the judge misdirected himself in holding that the contention that the money should be retained by
the commissioner until the conclusion of the criminal proceedings so that
the court of trial could upon conviction consider making an order under
section 35 or section 43 of the Powers of Criminal Courts Act 1973 was not
justified and speculative; (4) it would be against public policy for the
commissioner to be ordered to return the large amount of foreign currency B
in American dollars and Italian lire to the plaintiff even though no criminal
charge had been brought against the plaintiff in respect of his possession
of that currency.

The facts are stated in the judgment of Stephenson L.J.

John Hazan Q.C. and *Leonard Gerber* for the defendant commissioner. C
Daniel Serota and *Charles Gordon* for the plaintiff.

Cur. adv. vult.

May 26. The following judgments were read.

STEPHENSON L.J. This case concerns a large amount of money in D
English and foreign currency seized and retained by the police on behalf
of the appellant commissioner (the defendant) but claimed as his property
by the respondent Malone (the plaintiff).

In March 1978, by specially indorsed writ, the plaintiff claimed
delivery up of 514 Bank of England notes to the value of over £6,000 and
United States dollar notes and Italian lira notes to the value, at present
exchange rates, of about £3,000. He alleged that they had been wrong- E
fully in the defendant's possession for a year (since March 22, 1977)
and the defendant had refused to deliver them up on demand. He also
claimed damages for their detention. The circumstances in which the
police had taken the notes and by which the defendant claimed to be
authorised by law to take and detain them are set out in paragraph 3 of
his defence served on April 10, 1978: F

"(a) From the beginning of 1977 police officers commenced an
observation on the activities of the plaintiff and various of his associates."

I will not read out paragraphs (b) to (e), but I start at (f):

"(f) Immediately thereafter the search warrant was executed and G
police officers took possession of a large number of items from the
said house which were subsequently identified by witnesses to be
goods stolen from them by means of burglary.

"(g) On March 22, 1977, after the arrest of the plaintiff Detective
Sergeant Ware in possession of a search warrant in respect of 15
Aldebert Terrace went to the said address with other officers and
together with the wife of the plaintiff who had been arrested on a H
charge of dishonestly handling stolen goods knowing or believing the
same to be stolen.

"(h) The search warrant was then executed and amongst property
seized by Detective Sergeant Branchflower were the various bank
notes the subject of the proceedings herein which together with a
grandfather clock movement were found in a concealed wall cupboard in the basement kitchen of the aforesaid premises.

The Weekly Law Reports, December 8, 1978

939

3 W.L.R.   Malone v. Metropolitan Police Comr. (C.A.)   Stephenson L.J.

A
" (i) The grandfather clock movement has been identified as stolen by means of a burglary, and other property seized has been identified subsequently by witnesses to be goods stolen from them by means of burglary.

" (j) On September 26, 1977, the plaintiff and eight other persons were committed for trial from the Horseferry Road Magistrates' Court to the Inner London Crown Court.

B
" (k) The indictment against the plaintiff and his co-accused charges the plaintiff with conspiracy to dishonestly handle stolen goods between January 1, 1976, and March 23, 1977, and also with four substantive counts of handling stolen goods."

C
On March 29, 1978, the plaintiff's advisers took the remarkable step of issuing a summons for judgment under R.S.C., Ord. 14. That summons was supported by an affidavit from an articled clerk in the firm of the plaintiff's solicitors swearing that he verily believed that there was no defence to the action.

At the hearing of the summons Master Elton had before him four further affidavits. The plaintiff himself swore that, in addition to the sum of money claimed, police officers had seized the sum of £1,419 in Bank of England notes which had been returned to him through his solicitors on March 29, 1977. The senior partner in the firm of his solicitors set out two requests in 1977 for the return of the sum of about £11,000 and swore:

D

E
" . . . Detective Sergeant Ware refused to release the said money, giving the reason on each occasion that if the plaintiff were to be found guilty at his trial he, Detective Sergeant Ware, might be criticised by the trial judge in the event that a compensation order or an order for costs were made against the plaintiff and it transpired that such orders could not be satisfied without the aid of the sum of about £11,000."

F
It was not disputed before us that the £1,419 was found on the plaintiff's person when arrested and was returned to him a week later, and that Detective Sergeant Ware had said substantially what he was alleged to have said in the paragraph I have just read.

In opposition to that summons the defendant filed affidavits by Detective Sergeant Branchflower and Detective Sergeant Ware. The former corrected the number found of two denominations of English bank notes, which increased the total value of those to over £7,000, and swore to their discovery as subsequently particularised in the defence. The latter was the officer in charge of the case against the plaintiff, deposed to the plaintiff's committal, produced schedules of stolen property including that found at the plaintiff's two addresses, and concluded with these paragraphs:

G

H
" (6) With regard to the various bank notes seized by Detective Sergeant Branchflower on March 22, 1977, from the concealed wall cupboard at 15 Aldebert Terrace consisting of notes of English, American and Italian denominations I have reason to believe on the available evidence that this was money used by the plaintiff to pay burglars, thieves and other dishonest handlers for stolen property he was purchasing and accordingly the bank notes will be valuable and the best evidence in the plaintiff's forthcoming trial.

The Weekly Law Reports, December 8, 1978

940

Stephenson L.J.   Malone v. Metropolitan Police Comr. (C.A.)   [1978]

"(7) Accordingly I am advised and verily believe that there is a   A
proper defence to the plaintiff's claim and ask this honourable court
to dismiss the application for leave to sign judgment and grant the
defendant unconditional leave to defend."

It is not disputed, notwithstanding this affidavit and the return of the
£1,419, that the plaintiff has been granted legal aid to defend himself on
these charges.   Instead of dismissing the application and ordering the   B
plaintiff to pay the costs forthwith under R.S.C., Ord. 14, r. 7 (1), the
master gave the defendant unconditional leave to defend, and the defendant served the defence from which I have already read.   That led the
plaintiff's legal advisers to take two further steps in the action: to appeal
against the master's order and to amend the statement of claim on April
27, 1978, by adding a claim for an injunction (in terms unspecified).

On May 2, 1978, the plaintiff's appeal and his application for a man-   C
datory injunction ordering the defendant forthwith to deliver up to the
plaintiff the bank notes referred to in the statement of claim came together
before Wien J.   In the approved note which we have of his judgment the
judge stated that "the matter can be disposed of by my deciding the
application for an injunction."   He read the affidavits I have already
mentioned and a further affidavit from another member of the firm of the   D
plaintiff's solicitors in these terms.   I read from Mr. Klahn's affidavit:

"(1) I have perused the committal documents in my possession
regarding the plaintiff's trial at the Inner London Crown Court on
June 6, 1978, and the banknotes referred to in the plaintiff's statement of claim are not exhibits in the trial.   I produce list of exhibits ...

"(2) I have been informed by the plaintiff and verily believe that   E
although he has substantial assets in his two properties in London
and Dorking, he has at present very limited liquid assets and requires
the money he is claiming in his action in order to pay his solicitors
fees at his trial on June 6, 1978."

No argument was addressed to him on the application of *American
Cyanamid Co.* v. *Ethicon Ltd.* [1975] A.C. 396, but the argument was   F
confined to two points, to which I must come in due course.   At the end
of the argument the judge made no order on the appeal except that the
costs of the appeal were to be costs in the cause; but he granted the
injunction, ordered the costs of the application for it to be the plaintiff's
in any event and stayed execution for seven days pending an appeal.

I at first found this a surprising result of the hearing of the appeal
and application.   If the judge thought, as he clearly did, that the   G
defendant's detention of the notes was unlawful, why did he not allow the
appeal, for there was nothing left of his action except a possible but unreal
claim for nominal damages?   Yet he left the master's unconditional leave
to defend and ordered costs to be costs in a cause which his injunction had
brought to an end.   If, on the other hand, he thought that there was an
arguable defence and an issue to be tried, why did he grant the injunction?   H

The answer appears to be that both parties agreed to his disposing of the
whole action in this way, as was done by Talbot J. in *Ghani* v. *Jones*
[1970] 1 Q.B. 693, 698; so that the judge cannot be criticised for making
two apparently inconsistent orders.   It was important that the fate of the
bank notes should be decided before the criminal trial came on.   Accordingly no point was raised in the defendant's notice of appeal that an
injunction was not an appropriate remedy on the ground that there is a

The Weekly Law Reports, December 8, 1978

941

3 W.L.R.   Malone v. Metropolitan Police Comr. (C.A.)   Stephenson L.J.

A   serious issue to be tried; damages would be an adequate remedy and the balance of convenience tips against the injunction granted.   And though at one time Mr. Hazan was disposed to argue the point on behalf of the defendant, he agrees with Mr. Serota, for the plaintiff, that we should dispose of the action by deciding the issues between them on the grounds raised in the notice of appeal.   I feel bound to express my opinion that, had we been asked to consider that other ground, Mr Serota would have had the greatest difficulty in persuading me that this injunction should have been granted, whether the defendant's claim to these notes is or is not well founded.   I doubt whether we ought not to allow the appeal on that ground.   But I yield to the wish of both parties to have this appeal decided on the important points which have been argued here and below.

B

It is not disputed in these proceedings that the police officers acted
C   lawfully in seizing the English bank notes and foreign currency, although Mr. Serota reserved the right to argue the contrary elsewhere.   The only question is whether it is necessary for the defendant to detain them until the trial of the plaintiff is concluded.   If it is necessary, the judge was wrong to grant the injunction ordering their release and the appeal should be allowed.   If it is not necessary, he was right and the appeal should be dismissed.

D

The defendant rested his case before the judge that retention of these notes was necessary on two grounds: (1) that the notes were material evidence in connection with the offences for which the plaintiff had been committed for trial; (2) that they might be the subject of a forfeiture order under section 43 of the Powers of Criminal Courts Act 1973.

On the first point the judge held that the production of the money
E   proved nothing that the witness who discovered it in the cupboard could not prove without producing it.   He said:

"The applicant's contentions are that there is no question of the notes being produced to prove any material fact.   The police rely on the fact that a large amount of money in notes was found at the applicant's premises at the time the search warrant was executed.
F   The relevant evidence can be given by the police officer who conducted the search.   I have no doubt that this evidence will not be disputed.   The evidence of the police officer is the best evidence of the money seized, not the money itself.   The production of the money is of no benefit to anyone else; so the first ground on which the police claim the right to retain the money fails."

G   On the second point he thought that it would be difficult to prove the conditions necessary to satisfy this section.   He said:

"The applicant contends that the police should not retain the money for an event that may never occur and which is highly improbable. In Ghani v. Jones [1970] 1 Q.B. 693, 708, Lord Denning M.R. sets out certain requisites where a person has not been arrested or
H   charged, which is not the case here.   These requirements are not intended to be all-embracing—but it seems to me beyond any doubt that police must not keep money, not alleged to be stolen, longer than necessary for the purpose of evidence.   I see no justification at all for the police to retain the money for no other purpose than to invite the court which may or may not make an order under section 43.   On the evidence before me it is not the duty of the police to retain property purely for that speculative purpose."

The Weekly Law Reports, December 8, 1978

942

Stephenson L.J.   Malone v. Metropolitan Police Comr. (C.A.)   [1978]

His conclusion on both points he stated thus:

> " While the police were initially entitled to seize the money counsel for
> the applicant is, in my opinion, correct in submitting that they are
> no longer entitled to retain it.   What is the best evidence is the fact
> that it was seized and there is no justification for the police keeping it
> for the speculative purpose of an application under section 43.   I
> do not see how or on what grounds the Crown Court could ever be
> satisfied that the money was intended to be used to pay thieves or
> receivers."

The first point is not, to my mind, easy to decide.   The notes are
not alleged to be stolen nor to be the proceeds of selling stolen property,
but to be for use in paying for the purchase of stolen property.   They were
not made an exhibit, so may not have been literally " produced in court "
by a witness so as to make it right and necessary for the court or the
police to preserve and retain them until the trial is concluded: *Reg.* v.
Lushington, Ex parte Otto [1894] 1 Q.B. 420, 423, *per* Wright J.   But I
suspect that it was for reasons of administrative convenience that they were
not made an exhibit, certainly not, as Mr. Serota suggested, because the
prosecution does not intend to produce them at the trial: and they
were referred to in detail, including some of them being wrapped in
Midland Bank plastic bags, by Detective Sergeant Branchflower in his
statement produced to the committing magistrates' court under section 2
of the Criminal Justice Act 1967.   I can see no material difference
between the two procedures for the purpose of deciding whether it was
necessary for the police to detain them, except that if they had been
produced and exhibited, and it were necessary to detain them, they could
not be safely returned to the plaintiff without leave of the Crown Court.
So the question is whether they were required, in addition to the officers'
evidence about them, to prove the offences charged in the indictment
against the plaintiff.

Mr. Serota is instructed that the evidence as to them, their number and
denominations, their hiding place and their discovery, is accepted by the
plaintiff as given in Detective Sergeant Branchflower's statement and will
not be disputed at the trial.   Nor will that evidence be objected to as inadmissible.   In other words, it is not disputed that the officer's evidence is
material, and reasonably believed to be so, as tending to prove the charges
on which the plaintiff is being prosecuted, within the law as declared by
Lord Denning M.R. in *Ghani* v. *Jones* [1970] 1 Q.B. 693, 706.   There
Lord Denning said:

> " I take it to be settled law, without citing cases, that the officers are
> entitled to take any goods which they find in his possession or in his
> house which they reasonably believe to be material evidence in relation
> to the crime for which he is arrested or for which they enter.   If in the
> course of their search they come upon any other goods which show
> him to be implicated in some other crime, they may take them
> provided they act reasonably and detain them no longer than is neces-
> sary."

Compare what he went on to say at p. 709A; and the judgment of
Swanwick J. in *Frank Truman Export Ltd.* v. *Metropolitan Police Commissioner* [1977] Q.B. 952.   I accept the second part of the statement of
the law as to seizure of property in *Halsbury's Laws of England*, 4th ed., vol.
11 (1976), paras. 126–135.   These paragraphs are very much cut down

A from what they must have originally contained. They simply read in this way:

> " A constable effecting a search should not take property which is in no way connected with the offence alleged to have been committed by the person arrested; but if, in the course of the search, he comes upon other property which shows a person to be implicated in some
> B other offence, he may take that property also, provided he acts reasonably and retains it no longer than is necessary. The police are entitled to retain property relevant to the offence charged for the purpose of its production in court but may not retain it for longer than the period required for the trial or any appeal."

The first sentence would be relevant if the plaintiff were being prose-
C cuted for an offence against the Exchange Control Act 1947, but it is only the second sentence which is directly relevant to this appeal, and it compels us to allow it unless Mr. Serota is right in his submission to us, as to the judge, that the production at the trial of the actual notes is not necessary in this case. He relies on *Gordon* v. *Chief Commissioner of Metropolitan Police* [1910] 2 K.B. 1080, 1094, *per* Fletcher Moulton L.J., and the observation of Lord Denning M.R. in *Ghani* v. *Jones* [1970] 1
D Q.B. 693, 709: " If a copy "—of an article such as a passport or letter— " will suffice, it should be made and the original returned."

I find it impossible to assume that the plaintiff will continue to admit the police officers' evidence about the notes or to be sure that the actual notes will not help the prosecution to prove to the jury the offences charged in the indictment. Juries may be irrational, but I do not regard it as
E unreasonable to believe that circumstances difficult to predict may arise at the trial in which the police witnesses may be discredited or handicapped in their evidence by being unable to produce the actual notes to the court and jury. It is not necessary to suppose that the plaintiff may, at the trial, go back on the admission made on his instructions by counsel appearing for him before us, although nothing could stop him from doing so, and
F accuse the police officers of " planting " the notes on him. It is only necessary to remind oneself how unpredictable is the course of a criminal trial and how important it is for the prosecution to prove every link in the chain of evidence leading to proof of the offences charged. These notes seem to me to differ from the money found on the plaintiff in much more than their value. They are also wholly different from the passports, note-book and letters released in *Ghani* v. *Jones* [1970] 1 Q.B. 693. There
G there was no charge preferred against the owners or possessors of the documents and I am by no means sure that if they had been charged Lord Denning M.R. would have considered that copies of those documents would have sufficed and the originals could be released. Had these notes been made exhibits, their release before the conclusion of the plaintiff's trial would have been more difficult, as Mr. Serota concedes. If I had then
H been asked to release them to the plaintiff, I would have refused to do so, and I would refuse to do so, although they are not exhibits because they will, in my opinion, " form material evidence in his prosecution " for the offences of conspiracy and receiving on which he has been committed for trial: *Dillon* v. *O'Brien and Davis* (1887) 16 Cox C.C. 245, 249, *per* Palles C.B.

Mr. Serota has called our attention to three old decisions at nisi prius in which (before the days of legal aid) judges ordered sums of money found

The Weekly Law Reports, December 8, 1978

944

Stephenson L.J.   Malone v. Metropolitan Police Comr. (C.A.)   [1978]

on prisoners to be restored to them in order to enable them to make their   A
defence, where the money was in no way material to the charges on which
they were to be tried: *Rex* v. *Barnett* (1829) 3 C. & P. 600; *Rex* v.
O'Donnell (1835) 7 C. & P. 138 and *Rex* v. *Rooney* (1836) 7 C. & P. 515.   If
I could say that these notes were in no way material to the charges against
the plaintiff, I would follow those decisions and let the injunction stand.
But I cannot say that, knowing the circumstances disclosed in the evidence
of the police officers and set out in the defence, including the discovery   B
of the notes hidden with stolen clock parts in a concealed wall cupboard,
but not knowing what the plaintiff's evidence about these notes and his
dealings in antiques may be.

If the officers can give their evidence about them, that evidence is
material to the charges and the only question is the narrow one: Are the
actual notes a reasonably necessary, and valuable, part of that evidence?   C
I am not sure that that is the same question as the question: What is
the best evidence?   The judge called the fact that the notes were seized
the best evidence but I doubt if the officers' evidence of seizure is " better "
than the evidence of the notes themselves.   If the two questions differ, I
would ask the first and give it an affirmative answer.

I was unfavourably impressed, as I think was the judge, by the reliance   D
of the police officers on reasons other than the importance of these notes
as evidence for the prosecution.   But police officers are naturally concerned
with criticisms which the court may make; the value of the notes as
evidence is stressed in Detective Sergeant Ware's affidavit, though not so
prominently as in the defence; and it is for the court to give proper weight
to the views of the police but to make up its own mind and decide for itself
whether justice requires that the original notes should be available as   E
evidence.

I hesitate to give effect to what may appear speculative in balancing the
public interest in the conviction of the guilty against the right of the
individual, presumed innocent, not to be deprived of his own property,
even for a time, unless public policy requires the deprivation and makes it
lawful.   Where a man is charged with conspiracy and the scope of relevant   F
evidence is thereby enlarged, the court must be even more careful not to
confiscate his property without justification.   In all the circumstances of
this case, however, I conclude that the balance tips on the side of the
public interest and I differ, with hesitation, from the judge's opinion that
the notes are not the best evidence and, therefore, of benefit to no one,
judge, jury or prosecution, in tending to prove the offences charged.   I
would accordingly allow the appeal on this ground.   G

The second point has had a chequered career in this court and undergone more than one metamorphosis.   Mr. Hazan first asked us to consider
the power of the court of trial to make a restitution order under section 28
(1) (c) of the Theft Act 1968, as amended by the Criminal Justice Act 1972,
in place of its power to make a forfeiture order under section 43 of the
Powers of Criminal Courts Act 1973.   Mr. Serota did not object to the   H
substitution, although the earlier section was not pleaded in the defence,
or argued before the judge, or raised in the notice of appeal.   Then Mr.
Hazan asked us to consider the powers given by both sections and a third,
again relied on for the first time in this court, the power to make a
compensation order given by section 35 of the Powers of Criminal Courts
Act 1973.   Mr. Serota continued to be accommodating and we have
considered all three powers.   But at an early stage of our consideration

The Weekly Law Reports, December 8, 1978

945

3 W.L.R.   Malone v. Metropolitan Police Comr. (C.A.)   Stephenson L.J.

A Mr. Hazan abandoned section 28 (1) (c) as inapplicable to this case and I
say no more about that enactment except that in its amended form, conveniently set out in Schedule 5 to the Criminal Justice Act 1972, it is
clearly confined to cases in which stolen goods are no longer in the possession of the person convicted but can be specified and valued, whereas in
this case the defendant concedes that all the stolen goods referred to in
the indictment were either in the possession of the plaintiff and therefore
B recoverable themselves or unspecified and therefore incapable of valuation.

We were therefore left to consider whether the defendant was justified
in retaining these notes until the trial was concluded because their retention
would enable the court of trial to consider making an order on conviction
under section 35 or section 43 of the Act of 1973. But once more the
point for our consideration took on a new shape, this time at the request
C of Mr. Serota and without objection from Mr. Hazan. Whereas the
point, as stated and decided by the judge, was whether the possibility of
the court of trial making an order was too speculative to make the retention of the notes lawful, Mr. Serota challenged the court's power to
make any order under either section if the evidence was not material and
the judge was right on his first ground. He assured us that he had taken
this point, fundamental to his case and of general importance, before the
D judge, but there is no trace of it in the note of his judgment, and it took
Mr. Hazan and the court by surprise. It is nevertheless an important point
on which we have heard full argument because both parties wish us to
decide it, and I think we should decide it, raising, as it does, an issue
of interest alike to the police and to persons subjected to arrest and search
by the police.

E Mr. Serota submits on behalf of the plaintiff that the defendant has no
right to detain any property for any purpose, including compensation,
restitution or forfeiture, unless it is reasonably required as material
evidence or it is goods alleged to be stolen or the fruits of goods alleged to
be stolen. If these sums of money are not so required, contrary to what
I have decided, admittedly not being goods, or the fruits of goods, alleged
F to be stolen, they must be returned. Mr. Hazan submits, on behalf of the
defendant, that on the contrary the defendant has a right to detain for
those particular purposes any property reasonably suspected of being
connected with the crimes charged—or I think he must logically and did
ultimately submit, with any crime. Even if these sums of money are not
so required, they must be detained for those purposes.

It is the plaintiff's case that the authorities establish a right at common
G law to seize and detain as long as reasonably necessary money like other
property; but no one, not even a police officer, has a right at common
law or under any statute to detain money or other property belonging to
a person being prosecuted or sued simply to provide security or compensation or punishment or satisfaction of a judgment. In *Jagger* v. *Jagger*
[1926] P. 73, 102 Scrutton L.J. said:

H   " I am not aware of any statutory or other power in the court to
      restrain a person from dealing with his property at a time when no
      order against him has been made."

Matrimonial legislation has made inroads on that since then. The
courts have qualified it recently by granting *Mareva* injunctions. But the
courts will not permit any general encroachment upon a defendant's
right to do what he likes with his own property by freezing his assets in

the hands of the police or anybody else: see the comments of Lord Hail-   A
sham of St. Marylebone in *Siskina* (*Owners of cargo lately laden on board*)
v. *Distos Compania Naviera S.A.* [1977] 3 W.L.R. 818, 829–830, with
which Lord Simon of Glaisdale and Lord Russell of Killowen agreed.

The common law can develop in many ways, but I would accept it as
clear law that, generally speaking, the right or power to deprive a defendant
of his property even for a time, whether in criminal or in civil proceed-   B
ings, for the purpose of punishing him by forfeiture or compensating the
victim of his wrongdoing by any form of restitution can only be conferred
by express and unambiguous statutory provisions.   There is admittedly
no such provision in the three enactments on which the plaintiff here
relies, even if they are not construed as strictly as a criminal statute should
be: see, e.g., *Reg.* v. *Hinde* (1977) 64 Cr.App.R. 213, 216.

Mr. Hazan answers this point not by challenging that statement of what   C
the common law right to detain property *was* but by asking us to develop
or expand the common law by asserting that there *is* now a power to
detain it for the exercise of the new powers conferred on criminal courts
by those three enactments.   His submission in its final form was that two
of these powers, those conferred by section 28 of the Act of 1968 and
section 35 of the Act of 1973, give speedy relief to losers of property or   D
other victims of crime by restitution or compensation, an object which
would be to a considerable extent defeated without the extended power he
asks us to assert; and one of those powers, the power of forfeiture conferred by section 43 of the Act of 1973, is conferred in language which
envisages or assumes or implies that extended power.   And that extended
power is necessary, and clearly regarded by Parliament as necessary, to
defeat the sophisticated crime which threatens society in this country   E
today.

I find no warrant for that expansion or assumption in these enactments,
their object or the language in which that object has been expressed.

I need not read section 28.   It certainly gives the court wide powers to
order restitution, but it certainly cannot apply to these notes, and Mr.
Hazan admits that it does not by itself support the extension of police   F
powers for which he contends.   Section 35 provides:

"(1) Subject to the provisions of this Part of this Act, a court by
or before which a person is convicted of an offence, in addition to
dealing with him in any other way, may, on application or otherwise,
make an order (in this Act referred to as ' a compensation order ')
requiring him to pay compensation for any personal injury, loss or   G
damage resulting from that offence or any other offence which is
taken into consideration by the court in determining sentence. . . .
(4) In determining whether to make a compensation order against any
person, and in determining the amount to be paid by any person under
such an order, the court shall have regard to his means so far as they
appear or are known to the court."   H

As Mr. Serota points out, nowhere in the section is there any
reference to the source from which compensation is to be paid for loss or
damage resulting from an offence.   The section itself confers no power
to seize or retain anything, and again Mr. Hazan can find in it, by itself,
no support for this contention of his.   But he does claim support for it
in the remaining enactment, to which I now turn.   Section 43 provides:

The Weekly Law Reports, December 8, 1978

947

3 W.L.R.   Malone v. Metropolitan Police Comr. (C.A.)   Stephenson L.J.

A   " (1) Where a person is convicted of an offence punishable on indictment with imprisonment for a term of two years or more and the
court by or before which he is convicted is satisfied that any property
which was in his possession or under his control at the time of his
apprehension—(a) has been used for the purpose of committing, or
facilitating the commission of, any offence; or (b) was intended by
him to be used for that purpose; the court may make an order under
B   this section in respect of that property . . . (3) An order under
this section shall operate to deprive the offender of his rights, if any,
in the property to which it relates, and the property shall (if not already
in their possession) be taken into the possession of the police.   (4)
The Police (Property) Act 1897 shall apply, with the following modifications, to property which is in the possession of the police by
C   virtue of this section— . . ."

and then the subsection goes on to state the modifications.

This section, too, confers no power to seize or retain anything.   Mr.
Serota conceded that it applies to money (compare the definition of
" property " in section 4 (1) of the Act of 1968); and it covers property
which was in a convicted person's possession at the time of his appre-
D   hension but is, at the date of conviction, already in the possession of the
police.   It also covers property which is not then in their possession.

Now it may be that the powers conferred by these three sections could
be more extensively used if the police had their powers of detaining
property extended as Mr. Hazen submits that they have been or should be.
But it cannot be said that there is not considerable scope for the exercise
of the court's powers under all three sections without any extension of
E   the powers of the police.   There is nothing to prevent a court taking
into account money seized and returned to a convicted thief or receiver
before conviction as part of his means and requiring him to pay compensation accordingly.   There is nothing to prevent a court from depriving
him of property used, or intended for use, for purposes of crime, whether
that property is money or the more usual motor car and whether it is in
F   the possession of the convicted thief or receiver or of the police or some
other person.   Indeed, Mr. Hazan conceded that he got no help from
section 35—or from the Theft Act—but he argued that the language of
section 43 did presuppose that the police had the power to take into
possession and keep in their possession property used, or intended for
use, for the purposes of committing any offence.   He relied particularly
on the words in parenthesis in subsection (3), contending that they postu-
G   lated that property so used, or intended to be so used, could lawfully be in
the possession of the police before an order was made under the section.
But the words in parenthesis could, in my judgment, apply to property
used, for example, for the purpose of committing the particular offence
with which the convicted person had been charged, and they do not begin
to suggest, let alone require, the existence or addition of an extended
H   police power to detain his property.

If such a power or powers as Mr. Hazan wants the police to have, or
the courts to assert that they have, are now required for the protection
of the public against the increase of crime, it is for Parliament, not the
courts, to grant them.   Until I listened to this argument, I never heard
that the statute book was a source of the common law.   The argument
has nothing to commend it but its audacity.   Even Mr. Hazan could not
make it viable.   I reject it.

Stephenson L.J.   Malone v. Metropolitan Police Comr. (C.A.)   **[1978]**

I therefore conclude that the defendant has no right to detain these   A
notes for the purpose of enabling the court of trial to consider making
an order under section 43 or any other statutory provision which we
have been asked to consider.   I would uphold the plaintiff's objection in
the form which it has now taken and would not allow the appeal on this
ground.

It is therefore unnecessary to consider the plaintiff's objection in its
first form to the defendant's argument on this point and to decide whether   B
the judge was right in holding that the court of trial was so unlikely to
exercise its statutory power over these notes that their detention for that
purpose could not be justified.

There remains the fourth ground in the notice of appeal:

" (4) It would be against public policy for the defendant to be ordered   C
to return the large amount of foreign currency in American dollars
and Italian lire to the plaintiff even though no criminal charges have
been brought against the plaintiff in respect of his possession of the
said currency."

This would appear to allege in support of the appeal what has not yet
been pleaded in the defence or alleged in any prosecution, that the plain-   D
tiff, in possessing the foreign currency seized, was committing an offence
against section 2 of the Exchange Control Act 1947.

On this topic, as on other points in the case, I agree with all that will
be said by Roskill L.J. in the judgment which I have had the benefit of
reading in draft.   I would allow the appeal and discharge the injunction on
the ground that the production of all the notes retained by the defendant
may be relevant and necessary to the case for the prosecution at the   E
plaintiff's trial the week after next.

ROSKILL L.J.   This appeal raises an important point of principle in
relation to police powers.   It is the duty of the courts to protect the
freedom and property of the individual against arbitrary action by the
executive, whatever the form which the particular action may take.   But   F
the courts, when performing that duty, must always have in mind that
the administration of justice must not be hampered and that from time
to time the rights of individuals have to yield to a wider public interest
which requires the abridgement of individual rights.   The appellant, the
defendant, in this action, the Commissioner of the Metropolitan Police,
claims that the present is a case in which that wider interest must prevail
over the private interest of the plaintiff, which is immediately to receive   G
back a substantial sum which by concession is his but of the possession
of which he was lawfully deprived at the time of his arrest in March
1977.   The plaintiff, on the other hand, asserts the paramountcy of his
personal right of property.   Wien J. decided this matter in favour of
the plaintiff.   Hence this appeal by the defendant.

The facts admit of no dispute and have been fully stated by   H
Stephenson L.J.   Both the sterling and the foreign currency, possession
of which the plaintiff seeks to recover from the defendant, are admitted
to be the plaintiff's property.   For brevity I shall call these " the money,"
and I shall ignore, in this part of the judgment, the question raised by the
court itself—it was not raised before Wien J., and indicated in the notice
of appeal of the defendant, whether, all else apart, the provisions of
the Exchange Control Act 1947 in any event operate to bar the plaintiff's

The Weekly Law Reports, December 8, 1978

949

3 W.L.R.   Malone v. Metropolitan Police Comr. (C.A.)   Roskill L.J.

A claim to recover possession of the foreign currency, the plaintiff having no Treasury permission to hold that foreign currency or to refrain from disposing of it otherwise than in accordance with that Act.

It was not disputed before us that the search which led to the discovery of this money was lawful and that the seizure of the money following the search was also lawful. Mr. Serota, for the plaintiff, did, however,
B reserve the right to argue the contrary elsewhere, if necessary. The sole question for decision is whether the continued retention of the money by the defendant is lawful. As already stated, the judge held that it was not.

Before dealing with the substantial issues in this appeal I would say something of the procedure which has been adopted in this case, no doubt with the best intentions, to secure a speedy decision but with what I would regard as somewhat irregular results. In the first instance, the plaintiff,
C after issuing his writ, sought judgment against the defendant under R.S.C., Ord. 14. I am afraid I do not begin to follow how it could seriously have been thought that the defendant did not have at least an arguable defence to this claim. Yet an articled clerk in the employment of the plaintiff's solicitors permitted himself to swear he believed that there was no defence to the action. Not surprisingly, in those circumstances, Master Elton gave unconditional leave to the defendant to defend. For
D my part I regard it as quite wrong that Order 14 proceedings should have been started. The plaintiff then appealed to the judge in chambers still somewhat surprisingly seeking judgment under R.S.C., Ord. 14. But he also, by a fresh summons, added a claim against the defendant for a mandatory injunction for the delivery up of the money. The master, of course, had had no power to grant such a mandatory injunction had it initially
E been sought, but the judge in chambers had such power. Conveniently the appeal in the Order 14 proceedings and the summons for the mandatory injunction were heard by Wien J. together. The judge dealt with the matter, seemingly without objection from either party, by making no order on appeal in the Order 14 proceedings, but, considering that the plaintiff's contentions were correct by granting a mandatory injunction
F against the defendant. Since such a mandatory injunction must dispose of the action if this money were handed over to the plaintiff, in my view it ought only to have been granted if there were, in all the circumstances, clearly no defence to this action, as was the position in *Ghani* v. *Jones* [1970] 1 Q.B. 693. Yet if there were no defence to the action, judgment should have been entered under Order 14 for the plaintiff. It seems to me, with all respect to the judge, that his two orders were mutually incon-
G sistent, though this appears to have been almost by consent.

Before us the appeal has been argued on a far wider basis than it was before Wien J. Indeed, by the time the argument was concluded the case might well have been unrecognisable by him or by anyone present before him. Both sides sought our decision irrespective of the matters which had been pleaded or argued before the judge, and we were pressed
H to deal with this appeal in effect as if it were an appeal from a decision on the trial of an action determined on an agreed statement of facts or on a preliminary point of law. In order to help the parties on a matter which we were told required urgent decision before the plaintiff's trial begins early next month we agreed to proceed upon this basis, but in my view our consent so to do must not be taken as approval by this court of the course which was adopted below, which strikes me as not only irregular and not complying with the principles upon which mandatory

injunctions are granted, but as resulting in two mutually inconsistent   A
orders. The factual position in *Ghani* v. *Jones* [1970] 1 Q.B. 693, where
a mandatory injunction was granted notwithstanding that it in effect
disposed of the action, was very different: see the final passage of the
judgment of Talbot J. at p. 698—a decision subsequently approved in this
court. But in that case there were no Order 14 proceedings.

The defendant sought to defend his continued retention of the money
upon two main grounds. Whilst he accepted that it could not be justified   B
on the ground that the money itself was the subject of a criminal charge,
he claimed that it was material evidence in relation to both the conspiracy and substantive charges which the plaintiff had to face at his
forthcoming trial, or at the least was, in the circumstances in which the
money had been found in close physical proximity to certain stolen parts
of a grandfather clock, sufficiently closely connected with the subject   C
matter of those charges as to be liable to be lawfully retained by him
until the conclusion of the relevant criminal proceedings.

Alternatively he argued that he was entitled to retain the money until
the conclusion of these criminal proceedings in order that the money
might then be available in the event of the plaintiff's conviction so that
the court of trial might, if it thought fit thereupon avail itself of the   D
money for the purpose of making a restitution order under section 28 of
the Theft Act 1968 (as amended), or one or more compensation orders
under section 35 of the Powers of Criminal Courts Act 1973, or a forfeiture order under section 43 of that last-mentioned Act. Of those three
relevant statutory provisions only section 43 had been pleaded in the
defendant's defence, but no objection was raised before us on behalf of the
plaintiff to the defendant's reliance on those two other statutory provisions.   E
These last-mentioned contentions are, we are told, of general importance
to police forces throughout the country.

It seems apparent from an affidavit of one of the police officers
involved in the case that that officer feared that if the money were not
retained so as to facilitate the making of one or more of these orders in
the event of the plaintiff's conviction there might be sharp judicial criticism   F
of the police for releasing the money to the plaintiff so that it was no
longer available for this purpose—a point of view of an experienced
police officer which I can readily understand.

In the further alternative, Mr. Hazan, on behalf of the defendant,
argued that if, as the plaintiff contended, none of these statutory provisions
justified the continued retention of the money, this court ought—and I
quote Mr. Hazan's words—" to develop the common law to assert that   G
power " which the defendant claimed to exist in order to justify that
retention which ex hypothesi those three recent statutory provisions did
not of themselves justify—a proposition which Mr. Serota for the plaintiff
at once roundly condemned as offending against all the ordinary canons
of statutory construction.

Though the various questions were argued before us in the order in   H
which I have just indicated, I propose to deal with the three statutory provisions first, for, as will shortly emerge, I find myself unable to find in any
of them any justification for the continued retention of the money. I
will deal first with section 28 of the Theft Act 1968 (as amended).
Reliance was placed, on behalf of the defendant, upon the provisions of
section 28 (1) (c) which, as amended, reads:

The Weekly Law Reports, December 8, 1978

951

3 W.L.R.   Malone v. Metropolitan Police Comr. (C.A.)   Roskill L.J.

A

"The court may order that a sum not exceeding the value of the first-mentioned goods shall be paid, out of any money of the person convicted which was taken out of his possession on his apprehension, to any person who, if those goods were in the possession of the person convicted, would be entitled to recover them from him."

B

It was argued at first that it was enough to justify the making of an order under section 28 (1) (c) if the money so taken could be shown to have some connection with reference to theft. It seems to me that the argument for the defendant overlooks the importance of the opening words of paragraph (c). There is there a reference back to "the first-mentioned goods." That, in the context, must mean the goods referred to in the opening of subsection (1), namely, goods which have been stolen. That is the first pre-requisite for making an order. The second is that some-

C

one—in this case the plaintiff—has been convicted of some offence with reference to the theft—it does not matter whether or not stealing is the gist of that offence. Then the court may, under paragraph (a), order anyone—not necessarily the convicted person—having possession or control of those stolen goods, to restore them to anyone entitled to recover them from him, or, under paragraph (b) where those goods have, as it

D

were, been converted in whole or in part into other goods, order those other goods to be similarly delivered up, or under paragraph (c) in a case where, if those stolen goods were still in the possession of the convicted person, the person claiming the money could have recovered possession of those goods from him, order a sum not exceeding the value of those goods to be paid out of any money of the convicted person which was taken out of his possession on his apprehension. When faced with

E

this difficulty—that is, the absence of any relevant stolen goods—I did not understand Mr. Hazan seriously further to press his argument under this section.

I turn next to section 35 of the Act of 1973. I would observe that whereas both section 28 of the Theft Act 1968 (as amended) and section 43 of the Act of 1973 refer to money in the former case and to property in

F

the latter case as the possible source or subject matter of any order which the court may make under those sections, section 35 makes no similar reference. It simply empowers the making of a compensation order. The section is wholly silent as to the source of funds whence any order made by the court is to be satisfied. Other statutory provisions constitute an elaborate code whereby compensation orders may be enforced by the court, by imprisonment in appropriate cases: see the discussion of these

G

powers in Reg. v. Bunce (1977) 66 Cr.App.R. 109. Further, the court is required—as has frequently been emphasised in the Criminal Division of this court—to have regard to the means of the offender against whom such an order is sought following conviction. Mr. Serota drew our attention to the principle stated in Jagger v. Jagger [1926] P. 93 that in the absence of any statutory power to the contrary a person is not to be

H

restrained by the court from dealing with his own property as he wishes at a time when no order of a court of competent jurisdiction has been made against him: see especially the judgment of Scrutton L.J. at p. 102. He also drew our attention to the statement of the law by Lord Hailsham of St. Marylebone in The Siskina [1977] 3 W.L.R. 818, 829, that generally speaking an unsecured creditor cannot convert himself into a partially secured creditor merely by bringing an action against an alleged debtor and then seeking to freeze his assets by injunction, a principle now

admittedly somewhat eroded, at least in the case of foreign based defen- A
dants with assets in this country, by the so-called *Mareva* injunction. But
if the defendant is entitled legitimately to claim to retain moneys found in
an accused person's possession—admittedly his own and not the subject of
any charge—against the contingency of a court, upon that accused person's
conviction (if any) at some future and maybe distant date, making one or
more compensation orders against him, the defendant is almost constituting himself and other police authorities similarly placed a stakeholder B
or perhaps a trustee for a class of possible future beneficiaries who would
or might thereby become almost partially secured creditors at the expense
of others perhaps less fortunate. I cannot think that Parliament intended
this result, nor can I read section 35 as authorising the police to retain
money—not the subject of a charge and not required as evidence—found
in the possession of an accused person and that person's property, against C
any such contingency. In truth section 35 was designed to afford a cheap
and convenient form of relief to persons dishonestly deprived of the property or otherwise injured or afflicted. It was not concerned with anything
else.

Finally as to section 43, although from the terms of the note which
we have of the judge's judgment this matter appears to have been argued
before him on the basis that, though section 43 did give the requisite power, D
the present was not a suitable case for the exercise of that power, Mr.
Serota, before us, contended that the section gave no such power, saying
that he had advanced this argument before the judge. Section 43 differs
from section 35 in that subsection (3) of the section does contemplate that
property will or may have remained in police possession from arrest until
the conclusion of the trial. But the section is contained in a criminal E
statute and it must be strictly construed: see *Reg.* v. *Hinde,* 64 Cr.App.R.
213 and, more recently, *Reg.* v. *Thompson* (*Graham*) (1978) 66 Cr.App.R.
130. The original purpose of this section is well known. It may be that the
language of the section is wide enough to justify the making of orders for
the forfeiture of money as being " property " within this section provided
that the other prerequisites set out in the section for the making of the F
order are satisfied. But I can find nothing in the section to justify the
police retaining moneys belonging to an accused person which have
been found upon him at the time of his arrest merely against the possible
contingency that an order may thereafter be made under section 43.

Ultimately Mr. Hazan found himself constrained to admit that in
none of the three statutory provisions could he point to any specific power
conferred upon the police to retain money admittedly lawfully seized in G
the first instance solely in anticipation of the possibility of orders being
made under one or more of those sections in the event of conviction. But
he argued that the common law should now be developed and extended by
the court to justify such retention which the language of the relevant
statutory provisions does not justify. With respect, this is an impossible
argument. Compensation orders, restitution orders and forfeiture orders H
are, in their modern form, the creation of recent statutes. Before those
creations the common law could not and did not justify the retention of
such moneys for use for the purposes which did not then exist. When
the power to make the orders was given, the statutes were silent on this
crucial question. To extend the common law to justify what Parliament
has not empowered is to write into the statutes that which has not been
included in them. I know of no warrant for such construction. If the

The Weekly Law Reports, December 8, 1978

953

3 W.L.R.   Malone v. Metropolitan Police Comr. (C.A.)   Roskill L.J.

A   police require such powers for this purpose—and one can appreciate that in this day and age it might be convenient for them to have them—the police must seek the requisite powers from Parliament—if they can obtain them.   This further argument therefore fails.

If, therefore, this appeal is to succeed it must be upon other grounds. I agree with Mr. Serota when he says that if the defendant is to succeed he must show that there is a common law power which justifies that which

B   he claims to be entitled to do.   Mr. Serota relied upon the five propositions stated by Lord Denning M.R. in his judgment in *Ghani* v. *Jones* [1970] 1 Q.B. 693, 708–709.   As already stated, Mr. Serota did not seek to challenge the legality of the seizure of this money.   But he argued that this money was not required as material evidence against the plaintiff, either on the conspiracy charge or on the substantitve charges of dishonestly

C   handling stolen property, and that therefore the police had no right to retain it further.   He accepted that if this money could be shown to be material evidence either on the conspiracy charge or on the substantive charges, there would be a right to retain it as such evidence until the conclusion of the trial.   Mr. Serota relied upon the statement of the police officer who made the search and found the money, which was put in evidence at the magistrates' court at the time of the commital pro-

D   ceedings against the plaintiff and his co-accused.   This statement related how and where the money was found.   The money itself was not made an exhibit at the magistrates' court.   Mr. Serota said that the plaintiff would be willing at the trial to admit the whole of the contents of that officer's statement without his being called.   The material fact was, he contended—and Wien J. accepted this—that the money had been found

E   in the circumstances related in the statement, but proof of that fact did not require the production of the money itself in evidence and this was, he argued, why the money itself had not been exhibited in the magistrates' court.

For my part I do not attach great importance to the failure formally to exhibit the money though, had it been so exhibited, Mr. Serota's argu-

F   ment might—as he frankly accepted—have been more difficult for him to advance.   There may well have been administrative reasons for not exhibiting it.

It seems to me that the line of authorities to which Mr. Serota referred, and to which I do not find find it necessary to refer in detail, show that there is no general power in the police, when they have lawfully seized property which is thereafter not the subject of any charge and

G   is clearly shown not to have been stolen, to retain that property as against the person entitled to possession of it against some uncertain future contingency.   The police must be able to justify the retention of such property in such circumstances upon some clearly ascertainable ground. To my mind the only question in this case is whether it can be predicted with sufficient certainty that under no circumstances irres-

H   spective of the fact that that money was not exhibited in the committal proceedings, will it become necessary to adduce that money in evidence at the trial which starts next month, so that it can now, without risk to the administration of justice, be safely returned to the plaintiff.   If it became necessary for the prosecution to adduce that money in evidence, it would obviously gravely hamper the administration of justice if that money had been handed back and spent, so that it was no longer available to be put in evidence whenever required.   Whatever

Mr. Serota's present instructions are (and, of course, I unreservedly A
accept that he has received those instructions I have mentioned) as to the
course which the plaintiff at present intends to take at the trial, this will
be a long trial and it seems to me quite impossible to predict, at this
juncture, every turn which that long trial may ultimately take. It is not
difficult to envisage circumstances in which it might become highly
material for that money to be produced, either on behalf of the prosecution or of the defence, even though the prosecution do not seek to say B
that the money itself was stolen and have not so far exhibited it as part
of the police officer's evidence. I think, therefore, on this narrow ground
the defendant is entitled to retain this money until the conclusion of the
criminal proceedings against the plaintiff, and in this respect I venture to
disagree with the judge. On this ground I would allow the appeal and
discharge the injunction.   C

So far I have said nothing about the position under the Exchange
Control Act 1947. This Act, of course, does not touch the sterling which
was found in the plaintiff's possession. But I am quite unable to see how it
can be said that the plaintiff's possession of the dollars and the lire in
question was otherwise than unlawful, having regard to the clear statutory
obligation upon him under section 2 of the Act of 1947 to sell that foreign
currency to the Treasury or to an authorised dealer unless, of course, he D
could obtain authority to retain that foreign currency in his own possession. There was no suggestion in evidence that he had any such authority.
Although no point was taken before the judge under the Act, the point is
now taken, albeit without specific reference to the Act, in the notice of
appeal. If the court were of the opinion that the plaintiff's possession
of any part of the money was unlawful, whether under the Act or other- E
wise, it would be the court's duty to take the point of its own motion
irrespective of whether it had been raised by the defendant, and this the
court has done. Ultimately I did not understand Mr. Serota to contend
that the plaintiff's original possession of the foreign currency had been
lawful. But he strenuously argued that he, the plaintiff, had not been
prosecuted for any offence under the Act of 1947 though the police had
known of his possession and apparent breach of the statute for a long F
time. As to this point, I do not think it impossible that he may still be
prosecuted for such an offence.

Principally, however, Mr. Serota relied upon the decision of this court
in *Gordon* v. *Chief Commissioner of Metropolitan Police* [1910] 2 K.B.
1080, where a predecessor of the defendant sought to justify his refusal to
return moneys to the plaintiff which were the proceeds of street book- G
making on the ground of their supposed unlawful origin. Particular
reliance was placed on passages in the judgment of Vaughan Williams L.J.
at pp. 1090-1091, Fletcher Moulton L.J. at pp. 1094 and 1096, and
Buckley L.J. at pp. 1098-1099. But the facts of *Gordon's* case are
clearly distinguishable from those in the present case. There was nothing
unlawful about the plaintiff's possession of the proceeds of street book- H
making. He was entitled to retain those whatever their origin, even though
he might not have been able to sue to recover for the bets from those who
owed them. But his right to immediate possession of that money was
undoubted. In the present case the plaintiff's initial possession was
unlawful, for he ought to have sold the foreign currency to the Treasury
or to an authorised dealer. Here the seizure of the foreign currency by
the police was perfectly lawful. Ought the court, then, to lend its aid

The Weekly Law Reports, December 8, 1978

955

3 W.L.R.   Malone v. Metropolitan Police Comr. (C.A.)   Roskill L.J.

A to grant an equitable remedy to a plaintiff who, in relation to the foreign currency, had no lawful right to immediate possession, to enable him to regain immediate possession from the defendant whose taking of the foreign currency from the plaintiff under the search warrant was lawful? In my view, whether or not the maxim ex turpi causa non oritur actio strictly applies, it would not be right, in those circumstances, to grant a mandatory injunction for the return of the foreign currency, even if,

B contrary to my view, the plaintiff were entitled to recover on other grounds. And if it were wrong for those reasons to grant equitable relief in relation to the foreign currency, I would not think it right, in those circumstances, for the court in its discretion to grant the like relief in relation to the sterling.

I do not wish to rest my decision, in a case which raises wider issues,

C on this last-mentioned ground, but even had I come to the opposite conclusion in the plaintiff's favour upon the matters upon which I have decided in favour of the defendant I would have thought that this last-mentioned ground operated as a complete bar to the grant of a mandatory injunction for the recovery of the dollars and the lire, and that the court, in its discretion, should, in those circumstances, refuse the like relief in relation to the sterling.

D Since writing this judgment I have had the advantage of reading in draft the judgment just delivered by Stephenson L.J.   I find myself in complete agreement with him on all points.

In the result I would allow the appeal and discharge the injunction.

Appeal allowed, with costs in Court of
Appeal and below.
E   *Injunction discharged.*
Leave to appeal refused.

Solicitors: *Solicitor, Metropolitan Police; Davis Hanson & Co.*

F   [HOUSE OF LORDS]

PICKETT (ADMINISTRATRIX OF THE ESTATE OF
RALPH HENRY PICKETT DECD.)   .   .   .   .   .   APPELLANT

AND

G BRITISH RAIL ENGINEERING LTD. .   .   .   . RESPONDENT

1978   June 12, 13, 14, 15;   Lord Wilberforce, Lord Salmon,
       Nov. 2   Lord Edmund-Davies, Lord Russell
                                              of Killowen and Lord Scarman

Damages — Earnings, loss of — Loss of expectation of life — Man
*   expecting to work another 10 years — Injury reducing life*
H *   expectancy to less than year — Whether prospective earnings*
*   during lost years recoverable as separate head of damage*
Interest—Award of damages—Personal injury cases—Sum for pain
*   and suffering and loss of amenities—Interest on sum compen-*
*   sation for being kept out of award*

The defendant employed the plaintiff from 1949 to 1974 as a railway vehicle builder. The work involved contact with asbestos dust and in 1974 when he was 51 the plaintiff contracted mesothelioma. In July 1975 he brought an action against the

Pickett v. British Rail Engineering Ltd. (H.L.(E.))   **[1978]**

defendant claiming damages for personal injuries. The defendant admitted liability but contested the issue of quantum of
damages. At the trial in October 1976 the evidence was that
had the plaintiff not contracted the disease he could have continued to work until he was 65 and that his expectation of life
had been reduced to one year. The judge awarded him £7,000
general damages for pain, suffering and loss of amenities plus
interest at 9 per cent. from the service of the writ; £1,508·88
as a net sum in respect of loss of earnings and £500 for loss of
expectation of life. The plaintiff appealed but died before the
hearing of the appeal. His widow as administratrix of his estate
carried on the proceedings. The Court of Appeal decided that
the plaintiff was not entitled to be compensated for any loss
of earnings during the period he would have been likely to
survive had he not contracted the disease (the lost years) but
increased the general damages to £10,000 without interest and
the damages for loss of expectation of life to £750.

On the administratrix's appeal and the defendant's cross-
appeal: —

Held, allowing the appeal and the cross-appeal, (1) (Lord
Russell of Killowen dissenting) that an injured plaintiff was
entitled to recover damages for loss of earnings during the
lost years but that those damages should be computed after
deduction of his probable living expenses during that period and,
therefore, the case should be remitted to the Queen's Bench
Division for damages to be assessed accordingly (post, pp.
962G–H, 963D–E, 964C–D, 965D–G, 966D–E, 973H—974A, 981H—
982A).

Pope v. *D. Murphy & Son Ltd.* [1961] 1 Q.B. 222 and
Skelton v. *Collins* (1966) 115 C.L.R. 94 applied.

Harris v. *Brights Asphalt Contractors Ltd.* [1953] 1 Q.B.
617 and *Oliver* v. *Ashman* [1962] 2 Q.B. 210, C.A. overruled.

Benham v. *Gambling* [1941] A.C. 157, H.L.(E.); *Phillips* v.
London and South Western Railway Co. (1879) 5 Q.B.D. 78,
C.A. and *Roach* v. *Yates* [1938] 1 K.B. 256, C.A. considered.

(2) That interest on general damages was awarded for the
purpose of compensating a plaintiff for being kept out of the
capital sum between the date of the service of the writ and
judgment and that therefore the Court of Appeal erred in not
awarding such interest and the order of the trial judge should
be restored (post, pp. 963G–H, 970F–G, 975H—976A, B, 984C–E).

Dictum of Lord Denning M.R. in *Cookson* v. *Knowles*
[1977] Q.B. 913, 921, C.A. disapproved.

(3) That the judge, in assessing the appropriate sum to be
awarded for pain, suffering and loss of amenities, had not erred
in principle or misunderstood the facts and, in those circumstances, the Court of Appeal could not substitute its view on
the amount to be awarded for that of the judge and the sum
assessed by the judge at £7,000 would be restored (post, pp.
963H—964A, 970F–G, 974E–H, 976B, 983B–C).

Davies v. *Powell Duffryn Associated Collieries Ltd.* [1942]
A.C. 601, H.L.(E.) applied.

Decision of the Court of Appeal reversed.

The following cases are referred to in their Lordships' opinions:

Admiralty Commissioners v. *S.S. Amerika (Owners)* [1917] A.C. 38,
    H.L.(E.).
Benham v. *Gambling* [1941] A.C. 157; [1941] 1 All E.R. 7, H.L.(E.).
Chaplin v. *Hicks* [1911] 2 K.B. 786, C.A.
Cookson v. *Knowles* [1977] Q.B. 913; [1977] 3 W.L.R. 279; [1977] 2
    All E.R. 820, C.A.; [1978] 2 W.L.R. 978; [1978] 2 All E.R. 604,
    H.L.(E.).
Davies v. *Powell Duffryn Associated Collieries Ltd.* [1942] A.C. 601;
    [1942] 1 All E.R. 657, H.L.(E.).

A

Flint v. *Lovell* [1935] 1 K.B. 354, C.A.

Griffiths v. *Kerkemeyer* (1977) 51 A.L.J.R. 792.

Harris v. *Brights Asphalt Contractors Ltd.* [1953] 1 Q.B. 617; [1953] 1 W.L.R. 341; [1953] 1 All E.R. 395.

Jefford v. *Gee* [1970] 2 Q.B. 130; [1970] 2 W.L.R. 702; [1970] 1 All E.R. 1202, C.A.

Livingstone v. *Rawyards Coal Co.* (1880) 5 App.Cas. 25, H.L.(Sc.).

B

McCann v. *Sheppard* [1973] 1 W.L.R. 540; [1973] 2 All E.R. 881, C.A.

Murray v. *Shuter* [1972] 1 Lloyd's Rep. 6, C.A.

Murray v. *Shuter* [1976] Q.B. 972; [1975] 3 W.L.R. 597; [1975] 3 All E.R. 375, C.A.

Oliver v. *Ashman* [1962] 2 Q.B. 210; [1961] 3 W.L.R. 669; [1961] 3 All E.R. 323, C.A.

Phillips v. *London and South Western Railway Co.* (1879) 4 Q.B.D. 406, D.C., 5 Q.B.D. 78; 5 C.P.D. 280, C.A.

C

Pope v. *D. Murphy & Son Ltd.* [1961] 1 Q.B. 222; [1960] 2 W.L.R. 861; [1960] 2 All E.R. 873.

Read v. *Great Eastern Railway Co.* (1868) L.R. 3 Q.B. 555.

Reid v. *Lanarkshire Traction Co.*, 1934 S.C. 79.

Roach v. *Yates* [1938] 1 K.B. 256; [1937] 3 All E.R. 442, C.A.

Rose v. *Ford* [1936] 1 K.B. 90, C.A.; [1937] A.C. 826; [1937] 3 All E.R. 359, H.L.(E.).

D

Skelton v. *Collins* (1966) 115 C.L.R. 94.

West (H.) & Son Ltd. v. *Shephard* [1964] A.C. 326; [1963] 2 W.L.R. 1359; [1963] 2 All E.R. 625, H.L.(E.).

Williams v. *Mersey Docks & Harbour Board* [1905] 1 K.B. 804, C.A.

Wise v. *Kaye* [1962] 1 Q.B. 638; [1962] 2 W.L.R. 96; [1962] 1 All E.R. 257, C.A.

E

The following additional cases were cited in argument:

Daish v. *Wauton* [1972] 2 Q.B. 262; [1972] 2 W.L.R. 29; [1972] 1 All E.R. 25, C.A.

Davies v. *Smith* (unreported), January 30, 1958 Court of Appeal (Civil Division) Transcript No. 34A of 1958, C.A. but see *Kemp & Kemp, The Quantum of Damages*, 2nd ed., vol. 1 (1961), p. 353.

F

Naylor v. *Yorkshire Electricity Board* [1968] A.C. 529; [1967] 2 W.L.R. 1114; [1967] 2 All E.R. 1, H.L.(E.).

Richards v. *Highway Ironfounders (West Bromwich) Ltd.* [1955] 1 W.L.R. 1049; [1955] 3 All E.R. 205, C.A.

Slater v. *Spreag* [1936] 1 K.B. 83.

Smith v. *Central Asbestos Co. Ltd.* [1972] 1 Q.B. 244; [1971] 3 W.L.R. 206; [1971] 3 All E.R. 204, C.A.

G

APPEAL from the Court of Appeal.

This was an appeal by Joan Kathleen Pickett in her capacity as administratrix of the estate of the plaintiff, Ralph Henry Pickett, deceased and a cross-appeal by British Rail Engineering Ltd. (the defendant) from a judgment (November 14, 1977) and order of the Court of Appeal (Lord Denning M.R., Lawton and Goff L.JJ.) allowing an
H appeal by the administratrix from a judgment (October 12, 1976) and order of Stephen Brown J. whereby he awarded the plaintiff £7,000 general damages for pain, suffering and loss of amenities; £787·50 interest on the general damages at 9 per cent. from the service of the writ; £1,508·88 for loss of earnings and £500 for loss of expectation of life. The Court of Appeal varied that order by increasing the award of general damages to £10,000 without interest and that for loss of expectation of life to £750. The issues raised in this appeal were (1) whether, where a plaintiff's

expectation of working life has been reduced as a consequence of injuries   A
caused by the defendant, the damages awarded for loss of future earnings
should be limited to the period of reduced life expectancy or whether the
plaintiff should also be compensated for loss of earnings during the
period for which, but for the injuries, he would have survived (the lost
years); (2) whether the award of general damages made by the Court of
Appeal should have carried interest.

B

Peter Weitzman Q.C. and Alistair McDuff for the administratrix.
Michael Lewis Q.C. and Geoffrey Nice for the defendant.

Their Lordships took time for consideration.

November 2. LORD WILBERFORCE. My Lords, this appeal raises   C
three questions as to the amount of damages which ought to have been
awarded to Mr. Ralph Henry Pickett (" the deceased ") against his
employer, the respondent, for negligence and/or breach of statutory duty.
From 1949 to 1974 Mr. Pickett was working for the respondent in the
construction of the bodies of railway coaches, which work involved contact
with asbestos dust. In 1974 he developed symptoms which proved to be   D
of mesothelioma of the lung, of which he later died. On July 14, 1975,
he issued a writ against the respondent claiming damages for personal
injuries or physical harm. The respondent admitted liability but contested the issue of quantum of damages. The case came for trial before
Stephen Brown J. who on October 12, 1976, awarded damages under
various heads. Those in issue in this appeal were three: (1) £7,000 by
way of general damages in respect of pain, suffering and loss of amenities;   E
(2) £787·50 as interest on the £7,000 at 9 per cent. from the service of the
writ; (3) £1,508·88 as a net sum in respect of loss of earnings. This sum
was based on a finding that the deceased's expectation of life had been
reduced to one year from the date of trial, and the loss of earnings related
to that period, i.e. the period of likely survival. The judge also awarded
£500 for loss of expectation of life, and the total for which he gave judg-   F
ment was £14,947·64. Mr. Pickett appealed to the Court of Appeal
against this judgment, but before the appeal was heard he died. An order
to carry on the proceedings was made in favour of his widow as administratrix of his estate. The appeal was heard in November 1977. The
Court of Appeal did not award any sum for loss of earnings beyond the
survival period but increased the general damages award to £10,000, without interest. The administratrix now appeals to this House contending   G
that a much larger amount ought to have been awarded in respect of loss
of future earnings. She also claims that interest should be awarded on
the general damages. The respondent appeals against the award of
£10,000 general damages.

In 1974, when his symptoms became acute, the deceased was a man of
51 with an excellent physical record. He was a champion cyclist of   H
Olympic standard, he kept himself very fit and was a non-smoker. He
was leading an active life and cycled to work every day. He had a wife
and two children. There was medical evidence at the trial as to his
condition and prospects, which put his then expectation of life at one
year: this the judge accepted. There can be no doubt that but for his
exposure to asbestos dust in his employment he could have looked forward
to a normal period of continued employment up to retiring age. That

A   exposure, for which the respondent accepts liability, has resulted in this
period being shortened to one year. It seems, therefore, strange and
unjust that his claim for loss of earnings should be limited to that one year
(the survival period) and that he should recover nothing in respect of the
years of which he has been deprived (the lost years). But this is the
result of authority binding on the judge and the Court of Appeal: *Oliver
v. Ashman* [1962] 2 Q.B. 210. The present is, in effect, an appeal against
B   that decision.

Oliver v. Ashman* is part of a complex of law which has developed
piecemeal and which is neither logical nor consistent. Judges do their
best to make do with it but from time to time cases appear, like the
present, which do not appeal to a sense of justice. I shall not review in
any detail the state of the authorities for this was admirably done by
C   Holroyd Pearce L.J. in *Oliver v. Ashman.* The main strands in the law
as it then stood were (1) the Law Reform (Miscellaneous Provisions) Act
1934 abolished the old rule actio personalis moritur cum persona and
provided for the survival of causes of action in tort for the benefit of the
victim's estate. (2) The decision of this House in *Rose v. Ford* [1937]
A.C. 826 that a claim for loss of expectation of life survived under the Act
of 1934, and was not a claim for damages based on the death of a person
D   and so barred at common law: see *Admiralty Commissioners v. S.S.
Amerika (Owners)* [1917] A.C. 38. (3) The decision of this House in
Benham v. Gambling [1941] A.C. 157 that damages for loss of expectation of life could only be given up to a conventional figure, then fixed at
£200. (4) The Fatal Accidents Acts under which proceedings may be
brought for the benefit of dependants to recover the loss caused to those
E   dependants by the death of the breadwinner. The amount of this loss
is related to the probable future earnings which would have been
made by the deceased during " lost years." This creates a difficulty.
It is assumed in the present case, and the assumption is supported by
authority, that if an action for damages is brought by the victim during his
lifetime, and either proceeds to judgment or is settled, further proceedings
F   cannot be brought after his death under the Fatal Accidents Acts. If this
assumption is correct, it provides a basis, in logic and justice, for allowing
the victim to recover for earnings lost during his lost years. This assumption is based upon the wording of section 1 of the Act of 1846 (now section
1 of the Act of 1976) and is not supported by any decision of this House.
It cannot however be challenged in this appeal, since there is before us no
claim under the Fatal Accident Acts. I think, therefore, that we must for
G   present purposes act upon the basis that it is well founded, and that if the
present claim, in respect of earnings during the lost years, fails, it will not
be possible for a fresh action to be brought by the deceased's dependants in
relation to them.

With this background, *Oliver v. Ashman* [1962] 2 Q.B. 210 may now
be considered. I shall deal with it on authority and on principle. It is
H   clear from the judgment of Holroyd Pearce L.J. that he considered that,
apart from the decision in *Benham v. Gambling* [1941] A.C. 157, there
was, at the least, a case for giving damages in respect of the lost years.
Thus he says, at p. 228:

" On one view of the matter there is no loss of earnings when a man
dies prematurely. He is no longer there to earn them, since he has
died before they could be earned. He has merely lost the prospect
of some years of life which is a complex of pleasure and pain, of

good and ill, of profits and losses.   On the other view, he has, in   A
addition to losing a prospect of the years of life, lost the income he
would have earned, and the profits that would have been his had he
lived."

He then proceeded to examine *Benham* v. *Gambling* and reached the
conclusion that it was a binding authority in favour of the first view.

The critical passage in the speech of Viscount Simon L.C. was that   B
containing these words, at p. 167:

" Of course, no regard must be had to financial losses or gains during
the period of which the victim has been deprived.   The damages are
in respect of loss of life, not of loss of future pecuniary prospects."

My Lords, if more recent periods in the House exemplify excessive   C
multiplication of speeches, there are instances, of which this must certainly
be one, where a single speech may generate uncertainty.   How far was
Viscount Simon intending to go?   Was he intending to lay down a principle " in clear and careful terms " of general application?   Or are his
words to be related to the case then before this House?   These and other
perplexities might well have been resolved if any of the five (sic) other
learned Lords had expressed his views in his own words.   It is, of course,   D
the function of this House to lay down general rules, to reduce the partiali-
ties of previous decisions to some simple universal, but even after the most
comprehensive of arguments there remain aspects of a legal problem
which were not in view when the decision is reached.   *Benham* v. *Gambling*
[1941] A.C. 157 was a case of a small child (2½ years old) almost
instantly killed: the claim was for loss of expectation of life: there was   E
no claim for loss of future earnings.   Claims for loss of expectation of
life, validated by *Flint* v. *Lovell* [1935] 1 K.B. 354, and held to survive
in *Rose* v. *Ford* [1937] A.C. 826, had begun to proliferate, and sums of
differing amounts, some quite large, had begun to be awarded.   The judge
in *Benham* v. *Gambling* had awarded £1,200.   There was a clear need to
bring order into this situation and the solution, to fix a conventional sum,
was adapted to this need.   The quoted words of Viscount Simon can well   F
be understood as expressing no more than a principle for assessing
damages under this particular heading of life expectation and as saying no
more than that there was not inherent in a claim for such damages any
claim for pecuniary loss arising from the loss of earnings.

Apart from these general considerations, such references as can be
made to the argument point both ways.   There was a reference to the   G
speech of Lord Roche in *Rose* v. *Ford* [1937] A.C. 826 and to the judgment of Lord Blackburn in the Inner House in *Reid* v. *Lanarkshire
Traction Co.*, 1934 S.C. 79.   It was said that in each of these cases passages
can be found to support the proposition that loss of earnings can only be
recovered as an element in the loss of expectation of life.   But these
passages—in particular the judgment of Lord Wark as Lord Ordinary in   H
Reid's case—were neither reported as relied on in argument nor taken up
in the speech of Viscount Simon.   So I do not find here any support for
the argument that his Lordship was dealing with loss of earnings in any
way.   Secondly, as the reporter mentions in a parenthesis ([1941] A.C.
159), mention was made in argument of the recent Court of Appeal case
of *Roach* v. *Yates* [1938] 1 K.B. 256.   The headnote in that case describes
it as deciding that damages for earnings during the lost years *can* be

A recovered. Whether that headnote is wholly accurate or not, it is inconceivable that Viscount Simon would have made no mention of the case if, as is contended, he was laying down a rule to govern the assessment of damages for loss of earnings in the future. If he was, he must have expressed disagreement with it.

The conclusion must be (and to my mind it is clear) that *Benham* v. *Gambling* [1941] A.C. 157 was no authority compelling the decision in *Oliver* v. *Ashman* [1962] 2 Q.B. 210. It was not dealing with, and Viscount Simon did not have in mind, a claim by a living person for earnings during the lost years. Once this is established, the two views stated by Holroyd Pearce L.J. remain open, and on them the existing balance of authority was slightly the other way: see *Phillips* v. *London and South Western Railway Co.* (1879) 4 Q.B.D. 406; 5 Q.B.D. 78; *Roach* v. *Yates*
C [1938] 1 K.B. 256; *Pope* v. *D. Murphy & Son Ltd.* [1961] 1 Q.B. 222 and *Harris* v. *Brights Asphalt Contractors Ltd.* [1953] 1 Q.B. 617; contra.

As to principle, the passage which best summarises the underlying reasons for the decision in *Oliver* v. *Ashman* [1962] 2 Q.B. 210 is the following *per* Willmer L.J. at p. 240:

"... what has been lost by the person assumed to be dead is the
D   opportunity to enjoy what he would have earned, whether by spending it or saving it. Earnings themselves strike me as being of no significance without reference to the way in which they are used. To inquire what would have been the value to a person in the position of this plaintiff of any earnings which he might have made after the date when ex hypothesi he will be dead strikes me as a hopeless task."

E Or as Holroyd Pearce L.J. put it, at p. 230: "... what is lost is an expectation, not the thing itself."

My Lords, I think that these are instinctual sentences, not logical propositions or syllogisms—none the worse for that because we are not in the field of pure logic. It may not be unfair to paraphrase them as saying: "Nothing is of value except to a man who is there to spend or save it.
F The plaintiff will not be there when these earnings hypothetically accrue: so they have no value to him." Perhaps there are additional strands, one which indeed Willmer L.J. had earlier made explicit, that the whole process of assessment is too speculative for the courts to undertake: another that the only loss is a subjective one—an emotion of distress: but if so I would disagree with them. Assumptions, chances, hypotheses enter into most assessments, and juries had, we must suppose, no difficulties with
G them: the judicial approach however less robust can manage too. And to say that what calls for compensation is injured feelings does not provide an answer to the vital question which is whether, in addition to this subjective element, there is something objective which has been lost.

But is the main line of reasoning acceptable? Does it not ignore the fact that a particular man, in good health, and sound earning, has in these
H two things an asset of present value quite separate and distinct from the expectation of life which every man possesses? Compare him with a man in poor health and out of a job, is he not, and not only in the immediate present, a richer man? Is he not entitled to say, at one moment I am a man with existing capability to earn well for 14 years: the next moment I can only earn less well for one year? And why should he be compensated only for the immediate reduction in his earnings and not for the loss of the whole period for which he has been deprived of his ability to

earn them?   To the argument that " they are of no value because you will A
not be there to enjoy them " can he not reply, " yes they are: what is of
value to me is not only my opportunity to spend them enjoyably, but to
use such part of them as I do not need for my dependants, or for other
persons or causes which I wish to support.   If I cannot do this, I have
been deprived of something on which a value—a present value—can be
placed "?

I do not think that the problem can be solved by describing what has B
been lost as an " opportunity " or a " prospect " or an " expectation."
Indeed these words are invoked both ways—by the Lords Justices as denying a right to recover (on grounds of remoteness, intangibility or speculation), by those supporting the appellant's argument as demonstrating the
loss of some real asset of true value.   The fact is that the law sometimes
allows damages to be given for the loss of things so described (e.g. *Chaplin* C
v. *Hicks* [1911] 2 K.B. 786), sometimes it does not.   It always has to
answer a question which in the end can hardly be more accurately framed
than as asking, " Is the loss of this something for which the claimant
should and reasonably can be compensated? "

The respondent, in an impressive argument, urged upon us that the real
loss in such cases as the present was to the victim's dependants and that D
the right way in which to compensate them was to change the law (by
statute, judicially it would be impossible) so as to enable the dependants
to recover their loss independently of any action by the victim.   There is
much force in this, and no doubt the law could be changed in this way.
But I think that the argument fails because it does not take account, as in
an action for damages account must be taken, of the interest of the victim.
Future earnings are of value to him in order that he may satisfy legitimate E
desires, but these may not correspond with the allocation which the law
makes of money recovered by dependants on account of his loss.   He may
wish to benefit some dependants more than, or to the exclusion of, others
—this (subject to family inheritance legislation) he is entitled to do.   He
may not have dependants, but he may have others, or causes, whom he
would wish to benefit, for whom he might even regard himself as working. F
One cannot make a distinction, for the purposes of assessing damages,
between men in different family situations.

There is another argument, in the opposite sense—that which appealed
to Streatfeild J. in *Pope* v. *D. Murphy & Son Ltd.* [1961] 1 Q.B. 222.
Why, he asked, should the tortfeasor benefit from the fact that as well as
reducing his victim's earnings capacity he has shortened his victim's life?
Good advocacy but unsound principle, for damages are to compensate G
the victim not to reflect what the wrongdoer ought to pay.

My Lords, in the case of the adult wage earner with or without
dependants who sues for damages during his lifetime, I am convinced
that a rule which enables the " lost years " to be taken account of comes
closer to the ordinary man's expectations than one which limits his interest
to his shortened span of life.   The interest which such a man has in the H
earnings he might hope to make over a normal life, if not saleable in a
market, has a value which can be assessed.   A man who receives that
assessed value would surely consider himself and be considered compensated—a man denied it would not.   And I do not think that to act in
this way creates insoluble problems of assessment in other cases.   In that
of a young child (cf. *Benham* v. *Gambling* [1941] A.C. 157, neither present
nor future earnings could enter into the matter: in the more difficult case

A of adolescents just embarking upon the process of earning (cf. *Skelton* v. *Collins* (1966) 115 C.L.R. 94) the value of " lost " earnings might be real but would probably be assessable as small.

There will remain some difficulties. In cases, probably the normal, where a man's actual dependants coincide with those for whom he provides out of the damages he receives, whatever they obtain by inheritance will simply be set off against their own claim. If on the other hand this

B coincidence is lacking, there might be duplication of recovery. To that extent injustice may be caused to the wrongdoer. But if there is a choice between taking a view of the law which mitigates a clear and recognised injustice in cases of normal occurrence, at the cost of the possibility in fewer cases of excess payments being made, or leaving the law as it is, I think that our duty is clear. We should carry the judicial process of

C seeking a just principle as far as we can, confident that a wise legislator will correct resultant anomalies.

My Lords, I have reached the conclusion which I would recommend so far without reference to *Skelton* v. *Collins*, 115 C.L.R. 94 in which the High Court of Australia, refusing to follow *Oliver* v. *Ashman* [1962] 2 Q.B. 210 achieved the same result. The value of this authority is twofold:

D first in recommending by reference to authority (*per* Taylor J.) and in principle (*per* Windeyer J.) the preferable solution, and, secondly, in demonstrating that this can properly be reached by judicial process. The judgments, further, bring out an important ingredient, which I would accept, namely that the amount to be recovered in respect of earnings in the " lost " years should be after deduction of an estimated sum to represent the victim's probable living expenses during those years. I

E think that this is right because the basis, in principle, for recovery lies in the interest which he has in making provsiion for dependants and others, and this he would do out of his surplus. There is the additional merit of bringing awards under this head into line with what could be recovered under the Fatal Accidents Acts. *Skelton* v. *Collins* has been followed and applied recently by the High Court in *Griffiths* v. *Kerkemeyer* (1977) 51

F A.L.J.R. 792.

I would allow the appeal on this point and remit the action to the Queen's Bench Division for damages to be assessed accordingly. We are not called upon in this appeal to lay down any rules as to the manner in which such damages should be calculated—this must be left to the courts to work out conformably with established principles.

I shall deal briefly with the other issues. As to interest on damages, I

G would restore the decision of the judge. This was varied by the Court of Appeal on the theory that as damages are now normally subject to increase to take account of inflation, there is no occasion to award interest as well. I find this argument, with respect, fallacious. Increase for inflation is designed to preserve the " real " value of money: interest to compensate for being kept out of that " real " value. The one has no relation to the

H other. If the damages claimed remained, nominally, the same, because there was no inflation, interest would normally be given. The same should follow if the damages remain in real terms the same. Apart from the inflation argument no reason was suggested for interfering with the exercise of the judge's discretion.

As to the general damages, I would also restore the judgment of the trial judge. He gave this matter most careful attention and the Court of Appeal were unable to find that he erred in principle in any way. It is important that judges' assessments should not be disturbed unless such **A** error can be shown, or unless the amount is so grossly excessive or insufficient as to lead to the conclusion that some such error must have taken place.

If the appeal and cross-appeal are disposed of as I have suggested, the appellant should have the costs of the appeal in this House and the respondent the costs of the cross-appeal.

B

LORD SALMON. My Lords, the relevant facts have been fully and lucidly set out by my noble and learned friend Lord Wilberforce. They raise only one point of law which is of great public importance; I shall confine myself to examining that point alone. I propose to do so first by considering the principles involved and then the authorities.

Suppose a plaintiff who is 50 years old and earning a good living with **C** a reasonable expectation of continuing to do so until he reaches 65 years of age. As a result of the defendant's negligence, he has contracted a disease or suffered injuries which cut down his expectation of life to, say, five years and prevent him from earning any remuneration during that period. Are the damages to which he is entitled confined to compensation for the loss of the remuneration he would probably have earned during **D** those five years, or do they include compensation for the loss of the remuneration which, but for the defendant's negligence, he would probably have earned for a further 10 years, i.e., for the rest of what would have been his working life? In my opinion, there is no reason based either on justice or logic for supporting the view that he, and therefore his estate, is entitled to no damages in respect of the money he has been deprived from earning during these 10 years.

E

Suppose that, in the case I have postulated, the plaintiff's action for damages for negligence came to trial two years after he first became incapacitated. He would obviously be entitled to compensation for the remuneration he had lost in those two years. He would also, in my opinion, be entitled to a lump sum to compensate him for the undoubted loss of remuneration which, but for the defendant's negligence, he would **F** probably have earned in the next 13 years, i.e., up to the date when he would have reached retiring age. I do not accept that there can be any justification for limiting this compensation to compensation for the earnings he would have lost in the three years immediately following the trial, and awarding him nothing in respect of the remuneration he would, but for the defendant's negligence, have lost during the next 10 years— commonly known in cases such as these as the "lost years." In most **G** cases of this kind, the plaintiff, whether or not he knows he is likely to die as a result of the defendant's negligence, will bring his case to court or settle it as soon as possible because he is in urgent need of that part of the damages to which he is entitled, so that he may support himself and his family during his life. There can be no sensible reason why by doing so, he should forfeit the balance of the damages attributable to the loss of **H** remuneration caused by the defendant's negligence.

Although the point has never been considered by your Lordships' House, it is generally assumed that should the plaintiff accept a sum in settlement of his claim or obtain judgment for damages in respect of the defendant's negligence, his dependants will have no cause of action under the Fatal Accidents Acts after his death. This assumption is supported by strong authority: see *Read* v. *Great Eastern Railway Co.* (1868) L.R.

A 3 Q.B. 555; *Williams* v. *Mersey Docks & Harbour Board* [1905] 1 K.B. 804 and *Murray* v. *Shuter* [1972] 1 Lloyd's Rep. 6, 7. No point about the correctness of this assumption arises for decision in this appeal and therefore I express no concluded opinion about it. I think, however, that the assumption which has held the field for upwards of 100 years is probably correct and that, for present purposes, it must be accepted. In the overwhelming majority of cases a man works not only for his personal

B enjoyment but also to provide for the present and future needs of his dependants. It follows that it would be grossly unjust to the plaintiff and his dependants were the law to deprive him from recovering any damages for the loss of remuneration which the defendant's negligence has prevented him from earning during the " lost years." There is, in my view, no principle of the common law that requires such an injustice to be

C perpetrated.

When the Fatal Accidents Acts 1846 to 1908 were passed, it is, in my view, difficult to believe that it could have occurred to Parliament that the common law could possibly be as stated, many years later, by the Court of Appeal in *Oliver* v. *Ashman* [1962] 2 Q.B. 210. The clear intention of Parliament in passing those Acts appears to have been to deal with the all too frequent cases in which, as a result of someone else's negligence, a

D man suffered injuries which incapacitated him from earning and caused his death before he could obtain any damages from the tortfeasor to compensate him for the loss of the money he would have earned but for the tort. The policy of the Acts was, in my opinion, clearly to put that man's dependants, as far as possible, in the same financial position as they would have been in if the bread-winner had lived long enough to obtain

E judgment against the tortfeasor. In my opinion, Parliament correctly assumed that had the deceased lived, he would have recovered judgment for a lump sum by way of damages as compensation for the money he would have earned but for the tortfeasor's negligence; and that these damages would have included the money which the deceased would have earned during " the lost years." Otherwise, Parliament would, surely, have made it plain that no judgment in favour of the deceased or settle-

F ment of his claim could bar a claim by his dependants under the Fatal Accidents Acts; I certainly do not think that Parliament would have used the language which it did use in section 1 of those Acts.

The common law does not award a plaintiff annual payments in respect of the money he would have earned during the rest of his life had it not been for the defendant's negligence. It awards him a lump sum by way of

G damages to compensate him for all the money he has probably been prevented from earning because of the defendant's negligence. The common law takes many factors into account in assessing those damages, e.g., that the lump sum awarded will yield interest in the future; that the plaintiff might have lost his job in any event; that he might have been incapacitated or killed in some other way, so that the defendant's negligence may not

H necessarily have been the cause of his loss of earnings.

One of the factors which, however, the common law does not, in my view, take into account for the purpose of reducing damages is that some of the earnings, lost as a result of the defendant's negligence, would have been earned in the " lost years." Damages for the loss of earnings during the " lost years " should be assessed justly and with moderation. There can be no question of these damages being fixed at any conventional figure because damages for pecuniary loss, unlike damages for pain and suffering,

can be naturally measured in money. The amount awarded will depend A
upon the facts of each particular case. They may vary greatly from case
to case. At one end of the scale, the claim may be made on behalf of a
young child or his estate. In such a case, the lost earnings are so unpredictable and speculative that only a minimal sum could properly be
awarded. At the other end of the scale, the claim may be made by a
man in the prime of life or, if he dies, on behalf of his estate; if he has been
in good employment for years with every prospect of continuing to earn a B
good living until he reaches the age of retirement, after all the relevant
factors have been taken into account, the damages recoverable from the
defendant are likely to be substantial. The amount will, of course, vary,
sometimes greatly, according to the particular facts of the case under
consideration.

I recognise that there is a comparatively small minority of cases in C
which a man whose life, and therefore his capacity to earn, is cut short,
dies intestate with no dependants or has made a will excluding dependants,
leaving all his money to others or to charity. Subject to the family inheritance legislation, a man may do what he likes with his own. Certainly, the
law can make no distinction between the plaintiff who looks after dependants and the plaintiff who does not, in assessing the damages recoverable D
to compensate the plaintiff for the money he would have earned during the
" lost years " but for the defendant's negligence. On his death those
damages will pass to whomsoever benefits under his will or upon an
intestacy.

I think that in assessing those damages, there should be deducted the
plaintiff's own living expenses which he would have expended during the
" lost years " because these clearly can never constitute any part of his E
estate. The assessment of these living expenses may, no doubt, sometimes
present difficulties, but certainly no difficulties which would be insuperable
for the courts to resolve—as they always have done in assessing dependency
under the Fatal Accidents Acts.

I now turn to the authorities. The first reported case in which the
assessment of damages for loss of future earnings was discussed in relation F
to a plaintiff (a consultant physician) who faced a speedy death as a result
of the defendant's negligence was *Phillips* v. *London and South Western
Railway Co.*, 5 Q.B.D. 78. After reciting a passage from the trial judge's
summing up, James L.J. said, at p. 87:

"That comes to this, you are to consider what his income would
probably have been, how long that income would probably have G
lasted, and you are to take into consideration all the other contingencies to which a practice is liable. I do not know how otherwise
the case could be put."

Brett and Cotton L.JJ. agreed with that judgment. I am not at all surprised that it never occurred to that distinguished court that the " lost
years " should be ignored in assessing damages for loss of earnings: nor H
that it did not occur to Serjeant Ballantine, who appeared for the defendants. In my opinion, to ignore the " lost years " would be to ignore the
long established principles of the common law in relation to the assessment
of damages.

The next relevant case was *Roach* v. *Yates* [1938] 1 K.B. 256. The
judgments in that case were given extempore. I confess that I find it
difficult to discover anything from the judgment of Greer L.J. except that

A he and his brethren had agreed that the damages of £2,742 awarded by the
trial judge were far too low and should be increased to £6,542. The
reasons upon which Greer L.J. based that conclusion are obscure. He
did, however, refer to the judgment in *Phillips* v. *London and South
Western Railway Co.*, 5 Q.B.D. 78 without disagreeing with it. On the
other hand, Slesser L.J. did make plain the grounds on which he based his
conclusions. He said, at p. 268:

B
"Speaking for myself . . . I think the proper way of approaching the
problem is that which was followed in *Phillips* v. *London and South
Western Railway Co.*, the leading case on this matter—namely, first
to consider what sum he [the plaintiff] would have been likely to
make during his normal life if he had not met with the accident."

C MacKinnon L.J.'s judgment consists only of the enigmatic words "I
agree." It is by no means plain whether he agreed with the reasons given
by Slesser L.J. who had indicated, in giving those reasons, that he was
speaking for himself, or whether MacKinnon L.J. was agreeing only that
the damages should be raised to £6,542. Although I agree with the
reasons given by Slesser L.J., I think that it is doubtful whether the headnote was correct in saying that those reasons were the reasons upon which
D the whole court based its judgment.

I now turn to *Harris* v. *Brights Asphalt Contractors Ltd.* [1953] 1 Q.B.
617. This is the first case in this country in which it was argued and
indeed decided that (a) damages for the loss of earnings for the "lost
years" is nil, and (b), at p. 634:

E
"the only relevance of earnings which would have been earned after
death is that they are an element for consideration in assessing
damages for loss of expectation of life, in the sense that a person earning a reasonable livelihood is more likely to have an enjoyable life."

Slade J. who gave that judgment attempted, I think unsuccessfully, to
explain away what had been said in *Phillips* v. *London and South Western
Railway Co.*, 5 Q.B.D. 78 and *Roach* v. *Yates* [1938] 1 K.B. 256. It is
F interesting to note that although counsel for the defendants and third
parties had relied at pp. 624 and 625 upon *Benham* v. *Gambling* [1941]
A.C. 157, Slade J. apparently considered, correctly in my view, that
Benham v. *Gambling* had so little to do with the point in issue that it was
not worth even mentioning in his judgment. Nor was he able to cite any
other authority in support of his decision.

G
In *Pope* v. *D. Murphy & Son Ltd.* [1961] 1 Q.B. 222, Streatfeild J.
refused to follow Slade J.'s judgment in *Harris* v. *Brights Asphalt Contractors Ltd.* and decided the issue on damages in favour of the plaintiff,
relying upon what had been said in the Court of Appeal in the earlier cases
to which I have referred.

Then came *Oliver* v. *Ashman* [1962] 2 Q.B. 210. The plaintiff was a
young boy who, when 20 months old, had suffered injuries as a result of
H the defendant's negligence which turned him into a low-grade mental
defective and reduced his expectation of life from 60 years to 30 years.
He claimed damages not only for loss of expectation of life, pain, suffering, loss of amenities and the expenses incurred in taking care of him, but
also for the loss of what he might have earned but for the accident. Lord
Parker C.J., who tried the case at first instance, followed the decision in
Pope v. *D. Murphy & Son Ltd.* [1961] 1 Q.B. 222 and awarded him a
lump sum of £11,000. The plaintiff appealed on the ground that that

award was too low.   The defendant cross-appealed on the ground that the   A
award was too high.   The Court of Appeal overruled *Pope* v. *D. Murphy
& Son Ltd.* and held that *Harris* v. *Brights Asphalt Contractors Ltd.*
[1953] 1 Q.B. 617 had been correctly decided.   Nevertheless they did not
reduce the award because they concluded, quite rightly in my view, that
in the case of a child of such tender years, the amount of the earnings
which he might have lost was so speculative and unpredictable that the
sum in the award attributable to that element must have been minimal and   B
could therefore be disregarded.

In considering whether loss of earnings during the " lost years " could
ever be taken into account in assessing damages, Holroyd Pearce L.J. said,
at p. 228:

"On one view of the matter there is no loss of earnings when a man   C
dies prematurely.   He is no longer there to earn them, since he has
died before they could be earned.   He has merely lost the prospect
of some years of life which is a complex of pleasure and pain, of good
and ill, of profits and losses.   On the other view, he has, in addition
to losing a prospect of the years of life, lost the income that he
would have earned, and the profits that would have been his had he
lived."   D

Holroyd Pearce L.J. came down in favour of the first view because he
concluded that he was bound to do so by the decision of your Lordships'
House in *Benham* v. *Gambling* [1941] A.C. 157.   So did Willmer and
Pearson L.JJ.   I cannot agree with that conclusion.   In *Benham* v.
Gambling the plaintiff was the father and administrator of the estate of his
infant child who was 2½ years old and who was so badly injured by the   E
negligent driving of the defendant that he died on the day of the accident.
Not surprisingly, no claim was made for damages in respect of the earnings
that this infant might have lost because such damages could only have
been minimal; and accordingly no argument was addressed to this House
on the issue raised on the present appeal.   The claim was confined solely
to damages for the loss of expectation of life.   The trial judge assessed   F
those damages at £1,200.   The Court of Appeal, by a majority, refused to
reduce that amount on the defendants' appeal.   The defendants then
successfully appealed to your Lordships' House.   Accordingly, the decision in *Benham* v. *Gambling* does not touch the issue now before this
House.   Indeed, Viscount Simon L.C. who made the only speech in
Benham v. *Gambling* (with whom all the other noble and learned Lords   G
agreed) said, at p. 162:

". . . . The present appeal raises the problem of the assessment of
damage for ' loss of expectation of life ' before this House for the first
time, and it is indeed the only issue with which we are now concerned."

H
He then went on, carefully, to explain all the factors to be taken into
account in assessing those damages and to stress the necessity for moderation, which he perhaps emphasised by reducing the damages, in the circumstances of that case, to £200.   Two sentences which concluded a paragraph
from p. 167, towards the end of that speech, were fastened on by the Court
of Appeal in *Oliver* v. *Ashman* [1962] 2 Q.B. 210, 229, and indeed constituted the cornerstone of their judgment.   The sentences read as follows:

A   " Of course, no regard must be had to financial losses or gains during
the period of which the victim has been deprived.   The damages are
in respect of loss of life, not of loss of future pecuniary prospects."

Those sentences exactly fitted the facts of that case because no claim in
respect of pecuniary loss was being made.   As Viscount Simon himself
acknowledged, the only issue with which the House was then concerned
B was the assessment of damages for loss of expectation of life.

Holroyd Pearce and Willmer L.JJ. considered that what I call the two
excised sentences in Viscount Simon's speech must have been intended to
apply to cases in which damages for loss of earnings during the " lost
years" are being claimed, because the speech by Lord Roche in *Rose* v.
Ford [1937] A.C. 826 and the judgment in *Reid* v. *Lanarkshire Traction
Co.*, 1934 S.C. 79, had been cited in the argument in *Benham* v. *Gambling*
C [1941] A.C. 157.   I would point out that *Rose* v. *Ford* was itself a case
solely concerned with a claim for damages for loss of expectation of life.
No damages for pecuniary loss were claimed on behalf of the deceased's
estate.   Lord Roche alone did, however, make some obiter observations
which might have been of some help to the defendant in *Oliver* v. *Ashman*.   According to the report of the argument in *Benham* v. *Gambling*
D at p. 159, that, however, was not the passage in Lord Roche's speech which
was cited to this House.   Similarly, it is true that in *Reid* v. *Lanarkshire
Traction Co.*, Lord Wark, the Lord Ordinary, made some observations
which would also have helped the defendant in *Oliver* v. *Ashman*; but
again, according to the report of *Benham* v. *Gambling*, that judgment was
not cited in argument.   What was cited was a passage from Lord Blackburn's judgment in the Inner House which had nothing to do with claims
E for pecuniary loss.

I hardly think that the excised sentences were intended to apply to
cases in which there was a claim for damages in respect of loss of earnings
during the " lost years."   If they had been, it seems as incredible to me as
it does to my noble and learned friend Lord Wilberforce that Viscount
Simon would not have disapproved *Roach* v. *Yates* [1938] 1 K.B. 256,
F and I think also *Phillips* v. *London and South Western Railway Co.*, 4
Q.B.D. 406; 5 Q.B.D. 78.

My Lords, in my opinion, *Benham* v. *Gambling* [1941] A.C. 157
illustrates how unfortunate it may sometimes be to have only one speech,
however excellent, to explain the decision of the Appellate Committee.   I
have little doubt that if any other of the noble and learned Lords concerned in that case had also delivered a speech, there would have been no
G misunderstanding about the meaning of what I have described as the two
excised sentences in Viscount Simon's speech.   I agree with the view often
expressed by Lord Reid, that if there is only one speech it is apt to be
construed as a statute, which is not how a speech ought to be treated.   If,
however, there is a number of speeches, the general principles which it is
the function of this House to lay down will be distilled from them.   I am
H not, of course, suggesting that there are not sometimes circumstances in
which, for instance, one section in a statute has to be construed, and one
speech may accordingly be appropriate.

Before leaving *Oliver* v. *Ashman* [1962] 2 Q.B. 210, I should like to
refer to the passage in the judgment of my noble and learned friend Lord
Pearson at p. 245 which reads as follows:

" In my view the conclusion, shortly stated, is that the conventional
sum in the region of £200 which is to be awarded for loss of expecta-

tion of life should be regarded as covering all the elements of it— A
e.g., joys and sorrows, work and leisure, earning and spending or
saving money, marriage and parenthood and providing for dependants
—and should be regarded as excluding any additional assessment for
any of those elements."

I say nothing about the exiguous amount of the damages with which the
present appeal is not concerned.   I do not, however, agree with the rest of B
that passage unless one excludes from it the words " earning and spending
or saving money . . . and providing for dependants . . ."   These words
seem to me to conflict with the two sentences in Viscount Simon's speech
in *Benham* v. *Gambling* [1941] A.C. 157 to which I have already referred
and with which I agree.

I am reinforced in the opinion I have formed by the judgments of
Kitto, Taylor, Menzies, Windeyer and Owen JJ. in *Skelton* v. *Collins*, C
115 C.L.R. 94.   I will cite only the judgment of Windeyer J., at p. 129:

" The next rule that, as I see the matter, flows from the principle of
compensation is that anything having a money value which the plaintiff has lost should be made good in money.   This applies to that
element in damages for personal injuries which is commonly called
' loss of earnings.'   The destruction or diminution of a man's capacity D
to earn money can be made good in money.   It can be measured by
having regard to the money that he might have been able to earn had
the capacity not been destroyed or diminished.   . . . what is to be
compensated for is the destruction or diminution of something having
a monetary equivalent . . . I cannot see that damages that flow from
the destruction or diminution of his capacity to [earn money] are any E
the less when the period during which the capacity might have been
exercised is curtailed because the tort cut short his expected span of
life.   We should not, I think, follow the English decisions in which in
assessing the loss of earnings the ' lost years ' are not taken into
account."

The only English decisions to which the High Court of Australia can have F
been referring in relation to the " lost years " were the decisions of Slade
J. in *Harris* v. *Brights Asphalt Contractors Ltd.* [1953] 1 Q.B. 617 and of
the Court of Appeal in *Oliver* v. *Ashman* [1962] 2 Q.B. 210.   My Lords,
I have already stated my reasons for holding that both those decisions were
wrong and should be overruled.

I entirely agree with what my noble and learned friend Lord Wilberforce has said about the issues relating to (a) the interest on the general G
damages and (b) the amount of the general damages for pain and suffering
and the like to which I cannot usefully add anything.   I would, therefore,
allow the appeal and cross appeal and remit the action to the Queen's
Bench Division to access the damages in relation to the plaintiff's loss of
earnings during the " lost years."

H

LORD EDMUND-DAVIES.   My Lords, in the autumn of 1976 Stephen
Brown J. had before him a claim for damages for negligence brought by a
workman against his employers.   For many years Mr. Pickett had worked
in contact with asbestos dust and, as a result, he developed mesothelioma
of the lung, a condition which first exhibited symptoms in 1974.   In the
following year he instituted these proceedings and, at the time of the hearing, he was a married man of 53 with a wife and two children.   Until 51

A years of age he had been very fit, and was leading a most active life. Liability was admitted by the employers, and the one issue arising in this appeal relates to the award of general damages. This was compounded for the greater part by the sum of £7,000 for pain, suffering and loss of amenities. The learned judge also awarded interest at 9 per cent. on the £7,000, calculated from the date of service of the writ to the date of trial. Mr. Pickett died on March 15, 1977, less than four months after he

B had obtained judgment, and his widow and administratrix was substituted as plaintiff for the purpose of appealing from that decision. The Court of Appeal increased the award for pain and suffering from £7,000 to £10,000, and the compensation for shortened expectation of life (as to which no question arises) from £500 to £750, but ordered that no interest should be awarded on the general damages.

C   Three questions now arise for determination. These are: (1) Is it right that in calculating an award for loss of future earnings, it should be restricted to the sum which the injured plaintiff would have earned (but for the accident) during what remains of his shortened life, or should he be further compensated by reference to what he could reasonably have been expected to earn during such working life as would in all probability been left to him had it not been cut down by the defendant's negligence? In

D short, is he also entitled to be compensated for what have conveniently been called the "lost years"? (2) Should the Court of Appeal have increased the general damages? (3) Was the Court of Appeal right in depriving the plaintiff of interest on the general damages? I proceed to deal with these questions in turn.

E (1) *Damages for the lost years*
      The question has long been debated—indeed, ever since *Oliver* v. *Ashman* [1962] 2 Q.B. 210. Before considering that case in any detail, it should be stressed that the decision proceeded upon the basis that the Court of Appeal was there bound by what Viscount Simon L.C. had said in the House of Lords in *Benham* v. *Gambling* [1941] A.C. 157; see for example, the judgment of Holroyd Pearce L.J., from p. 228 onwards, and

F that of Willmer L.J. at p. 238. But, my Lords, in reality that was not so. It is true that in *Benham* v. *Gambling* the Lord Chancellor did say at one stage, at p. 167:

    "Of course, no regard must be had to financial losses or gains during the period of which the victim has been deprived. The damages are in respect of loss of life, not of loss of future pecuniary

G   prospects."

But the claim there being considered was what sum should be awarded to the estate of a child of 2½ years who died the day he was injured. Ever since the decision in *Rose* v. *Ford* [1937] A.C. 826, the awards for shortened expectation of life had varied enormously, and it is clear from the submissions of learned counsel in *Benham* v. *Gambling* that

H guidance only on that matter was there being sought. This was stated in terms by the Lord Chancellor, who added, at p. 162, ". . . and it is indeed the only issue with which we are now concerned." Notwithstanding its citation by Upjohn L.J. in *Wise* v. *Kaye* [1962] 1 Q.B. 638, 659 as authority for the contrary proposition that ". . . a dead man's estate . . . cannot . . . claim for loss of future pecuniary prospects," in my judgment the proper conclusion is that, as Lord Morris of Borth-y-Gest said in *H. West & Son Ltd.* v. *Shephard* [1964] A.C. 326, 348:

"The guidance given in *Benham* v. *Gambling* was, I consider, A
solely designed and intended to apply to the assessment of damages
in respect of the rather special 'head' of damages for loss of
expectation of life."

There being thus no decision compelling the Court of Appeal in *Oliver*
v. *Ashman* [1962] 2 Q.B. 210 to reject a claim for damages for the
"lost years," what guidance was to be found in the earlier cases? B
James L.J. said in *Phillips* v. *London and South Western Railway Co.*,
5 Q.B.D. 78, 87, of a physician injured in railway accident:

". . . you are to consider what his income would probably have
been, *how long that income would probably have lasted,* and you
are to take into consideration all the other contingencies to which
a practice is liable." (The italics are mine).   C

In *Roach* v. *Yates* [1938] 1 K.B. 256, Slesser L.J. took a similar view
regarding a claim made by a plaintiff of 33. He said, at p. 268:

"Criticism has been made of the suggestion that one method of
estimating his loss [of wages] . . . is to consider what he would have
earned during his life. Speaking for myself, I see no justification for D
approaching that problem by starting with the assumption that he
would only have lived so long as the accident has now allowed him
to live. I think the proper way of approaching the problem is that
which was followed in *Phillips* v. *London and South Western Railway
Co.*, 5 Q.B.D. 78, the leading case on this matter—namely, first
to consider what sum he would have been likely to make during his
normal life if he had not met with the accident."   E

It is said that it is not clear whether Greer L.J. was of the same view,
but MacKinnon L.J. agreed with both judgments, and it is difficult to
regard as other than accurate the headnote which attributes to all three
members of the court the view expressed by Slesser L.J. But in *Harris*
v. *Brights Asphalt Contractors Ltd.* [1953] 1 Q.B. 617 Slade J. doubted F
that this was so, and held that no compensation could be awarded for
earnings during the "lost years" to a plaintiff of 37 whose expectation
of life had been reduced to two years. He said, at pp. 633–634:

". . . I cannot think it right that I should give damages for loss
of earnings for a period during which ex hypothesi he is not alive to
earn them. . . . In my judgment, therefore, the only relevance of
earnings which would have been earned after death is that they are G
an element for consideration in assessing damages for loss of
expectation of life, in the sense that a person earning a reasonable
livelihood is more likely to have an enjoyable life."

The whole field of decisions was again surveyed by Streatfeild J. in
Pope v. *D. Murphy & Son Ltd.* [1961] 1 Q.B. 222 and led him to say, in H
arriving at the opposite conclusion, at p. 231:

"In my view the proper approach to this question of loss of earning
capacity is to compensate the plaintiff, who is alive now, for what he
has in fact lost. What he has lost is the prospect of earning whatever it was he did earn from his business over the period of time that
he might otherwise, apart from the accident, have reasonably
expected to earn it."

A   And so we come to *Oliver* v. *Ashman* [1962] 2 Q.B. 210, where a boy aged 20 months was injured by an accident which it was estimated had halved his reasonable expectation of living another 60 years. Lord Parker C.J. followed *Pope* v. *D. Murphy & Son Ltd.* [1961] 1 Q.B. 222 by taking as a separate head of damage the earnings which would have accrued to the plaintiff during the period by which life had been shortened. But this was reversed in the Court of Appeal, although
B Holroyd Pearce L.J. accepted that the earlier authorities were in accord with *Pope's* case. He summarised the nature of the conflict between that case and *Harris* v. *Brights Asphalt Contractors Ltd.* [1953] 1 Q.B. 617 in this way, at p. 228:

C   " On one view of the matter there is no loss of earnings when a man dies prematurely. He is no longer there to earn them, since he has died before they could be earned. He has merely lost the prospect of some years of life which is a complex of pleasure and pain, of good and ill, profits and losses. On the other view, he has, in addition to losing a prospect of the years of life, lost the income that he would have earned, and the profits that would have been his had he lived."

D
Holroyd Pearce L.J. then examined *Benham* v. *Gambling* [1941] A.C. 157 in detail, and concluded, at p. 230:

    " In my judgment, therefore, the matter is concluded in this court by *Benham* v. *Gambling,* and the decision of Slade J. in *Harris* v. *Brights Asphalt Contractors Ltd.* was correct."

E But, as I have already sought to show, the House of Lords had *not* concluded the matter, and it would have been sounder to say that the point had been disposed of in *Roach* v. *Yates* [1938] 1 K.B. 256 by the Court of Appeal itself in favour of the plaintiff. Willmer L.J. was, with respect, similarly mistaken about the effect of *Benham* v. *Gambling*: see p. 238. Pearson L.J. after a wider citation of authorities, said, at
F p. 245:

    " In my view the conclusion, shortly stated, is that the conventional sum in the region of £200 which is to be awarded for loss of expectation of life should be regarded as covering all the elements of it— e.g., joys and sorrows, work and leisure, earnings and spending or saving money, marriage and parenthood and providing for depen-
G   dants—and should be regarded as excluding any additional assessment for any of those elements."

My Lords, I am unable to accept that conclusion. I prefer not to complicate the problem by considering the impact upon dependants of an award to a living plaintiff whose life has been shortened, as to which see section 1 (1) of the Fatal Accidents Act 1976; *Murray* v. *Shuter*
H [1976] Q.B. 972 and *McCann* v. *Sheppard* [1973] 1 W.L.R. 540. For our present consideration relates solely to the personal entitlement of an injured party to recover damages for the " lost years," regardless both of whether he has dependants and of whether or not he would (if he has any) make provision for them out of any compensation awarded to him or his estate. With respect, it appears to me simply not right to say that, when a man's working life and his natural life are each shortened by the wrongful act of another, he must be regarded as having lost nothing by

the deprivation of the prospect of future earnings for some period A
extending beyond the anticipated date of his premature death. In the
Australian case of *Skelton* v. *Collins*, 115 C.L.R. 94, Taylor J. referred
to " the anomaly that would arise if *Oliver* v. *Ashman* [1962] 2 Q.B.
210 is taken to have been correctly decided," adding, at p. 121:

> " An incapacitated plaintiff whose life expectation has not been
> diminished would be entitled to the full measure of the economic B
> loss arising from his lost or diminished capacity. But an incapaci-
> tated plaintiff whose life expectancy has been diminished would not."

And Windeyer J. speaking of " the principle of compensation . . . that
anything having a money value which the plaintiff has lost should be
made good in money," continued, at p. 129:

> " This applies to that element in damages for personal injuries C
> which is commonly called ' loss of earnings ' . . . . The plaintiff
> could, if he had not been injured, have sold his labour and his
> skill or the fruits of his labour and his skill. I cannot see that
> damages that flow from the destruction or diminution of his capacity
> to do so are any the less when the period during which the capacity
> might have been exercised is curtailed because the tort cut short his D
> expected span of life."

My Lords, neither can I see why this should be so. In my judgment,
Holroyd Pearce L.J. was in error in saying in *Oliver* v. *Ashman* [1962]
2 Q.B. 210, 230:

> " When the [variegated] tapestry [of life] is severed there is but one
> sum recoverable in respect of that severance. And what is lost is an E
> expectation, not the thing itself. The House of Lords have laid
> down that on an objective and artificial valuation, the sum at which
> the loss of expectation is to be assessed must be a moderate one
> on the scale indicated in *Benham* v. *Gambling*."

In the present case Goff L.J. expressed the view that *Oliver* v. *Ashman*
" does seem . . . to work a grave injustice," and I regard it as wrongly F
decided. It follows that the judgment of the trial judge and the Court of
Appeal on this first question, based as they were on that case, should
now be reversed.

   This House lacks the material to enable it to estimate what would be
proper compensation for the " lost years," and the task will have to be
remitted to the Queen's Bench Division for determination. It is likely to G
prove a task of some difficulty, though (contrary to the view expressed
by Willmer L.J. in *Oliver* v. *Ashman* [1962] 2 Q.B. 210, 240) the lost
earnings are not " far too speculative to be capable of assesment by any
court of law." The only guidance I can proffer is that, in reaching their
final figure, the court should make what it regards as a suitable deduction
for the total sum which Mr. Pickett would have been likely to expend H
upon himself during the " lost years." This calculation, too, is by no
means free from difficulty, but a similar task has to be performed
regularly in cases brought under the Fatal Accidents Act. And in
Scotland the court is required, in such cases as the present, to " have
regard to any diminution . . . by virtue of expenses which in the
opinion of the court the pursuer . . . would reasonably have incurred
. . . by way of living expenses ": Damages (Scotland) Act 1976, section

A   9 (2) (c). For, macabre though it be to say so, it does not seem right that, in respect of those years when ex hypothesi the injured plaintiff's personal expenses will be nil, he should recover more than that which would have remained at his disposal after such expenses had been discharged.

B   (2) *General damages*

My Lords, I am unable to adopt the view of the Court of Appeal that the experienced trial judge erred in any way in assessing the general damages at £7,000. They do not criticise his general approach; indeed, Lawton L.J. said expressly, ". . . it is manifest that he approached the matter of the assessment of damages on the right lines." What is suggested is that he committed errors (a) by failing to take sufficiently C   into account the distress caused to Mr. Pickett by the realisation "that his dependants would be left without him to care for them"; and (b) by starting at too low a figure and then failing to allow sufficiently for inflation. I have to say that I see no signs of the trial judge having failed in these or any other respects. It may be that £7,000 would be regarded by some judges as on the low side, but even so, in my judgment it did D   not merit interference. I would therefore allow the defendant's cross-appeal against the decision of the Court of Appeal to increase this head of damages to £10,000 and restore the £7,000 awarded.

(3) *Interest on general damages*

Although it was seemingly agreed by both sides before the learned E   trial judge that the sum of £7,000 was to carry interest at 9 per cent. from the date of service of the writ (amounting to £787·50), the Court of Appeal ordered that no interest was to be payable upon the increased sum of £10,000. We have no record of what led to this variation in the trial judge's order, but we were told that it sprang from the Court of Appeal decision in *Cookson* v. *Knowles* [1977] Q.B. 913, 921, where Lord Denning M.R. said:

F   "In *Jefford* v. *Gee* [1970] 2 Q.B. 130, 151, we said that, in personal injury cases, when a lump sum is awarded for pain and suffering and loss of amenities, interest should run 'from the date of service of the writ to the date of trial.' At that time inflation did not stare us in the face. We had not in mind continuing inflation and its effect on awards. It is obvious now that that guide-line should be G   changed. The courts invariably assess the lump sum on the 'scale' for figures current at the date of trial—which is much higher than the figure current at the date of the injury or at the date of the writ. The plaintiff thus stands to gain by the delay in bringing the case to trial. He ought not to gain still more by having interest from the date of service of the writ."

H   My Lords, I have to say with great respect that the fallacy inherent in the passage quoted is in thinking that a plaintiff who, owing to inflation, gets a bigger award than he would have secured had the case been disposed of earlier is better off in real terms. But in fact the bigger award is made simply to put the plaintiff in the same financial position as he would have been had judgment followed immediately upon service of the writ. The reality is that the plaintiff in this case has been kept out of £7,000 until the date of judgment, and there is no reason why he

should be deprived of the £787 interest awarded by the trial judge for the A
15-month period between writ and judgment simply because a lesser
sum than £7,000 might or would have been awarded had the case come
on earlier. Furthermore, the suggestion that the defendant is prejudiced
overlooks the fact that he has meanwhile had the use of the money.

My Lords, in the result, I would allow the plaintiff's appeal in respect
of points (1) and (3) and the defendant's cross appeal in respect of point
(2). I am in agreement regarding the proposed order as to costs. B

LORD RUSSELL OF KILLOWEN. My Lords, on two of the three
questions in this case, those touching interest and the increase in damages
by the Court of Appeal from £7,000 to £10,000 I am in agreement, and
need not repeat the reasons given for what is proposed.

The third question, touching the "lost years" I have found very C
difficult. We are not directly concerned on that question with either
the Law Reform (Miscellaneous Provisions) Act 1934 or the Fatal Accidents Acts. The deceased plaintiff survived to trial and judgment: the
appeal is by his personal representative as representing his estate and
does not need the Act of 1934 to support it, the cause of action having
merged in the judgment.
D
The problem is this. Was the plaintiff at the time of judgment
entitled to damages on the ground that as a result of the wrong done to
him his life has been shortened and that he will not in consequence
receive financial benefits which would in the ordinary course of events
have come to him during those lost years.

I may say at once that I do not regard what was said in Benham v.
Gambling [1941] A.C. 157 in this House as throwing any light on this E
problem. That case was dealing only with a head of damages for loss
of expectation of life which, as was there stressed, is not a question of
deprivation of financial benefits at all. The problem has, as your Lordships have pointed out, been touched upon in a number of cases, but its
solution is at large for this House.

I have stated the problem without confining it to earnings in the F
lost years. Suppose a plaintiff injured tortiously in a motoring accident,
aged 25 at trial, with a resultant life expectation then of only one year.
Suppose him to be life tenant of substantial settled funds. If the lost
years are to be brought into assessment of damages presumably allowance
must be made for that part of the life interest which he would have
received but will not receive. So also if he had a reversionary interest
contingent upon surviving a life in being then aged 60: he will have G
been deprived of the probability of the funds coming to him during the
lost years. Again he might at the trial be shown to be the sole beneficiary under the will of a rich relation whose age made it probable
that the testator would die during the lost years, and whose testimony at
the trial was that he had no intention of altering his will: in such cases
presumably an allowance in damages would require to be made for the H
lost, and may be valuable, spes successionis: unless the testator was an
ancestor of the plaintiff and the plaintiff was likely to have children
surviving him. (Section 32, Wills Act 1837).

I refer to these possible situations in order to suggest that the problems which exist even in the field of earnings in the lost years may in a
given case be far more difficult of solution, once there is introduced into
the field of damages allowance for financial "loss" of that which

A   death ex hypothesi forestalls.   Damages are compensatory not punitive: so that it is no valid argument that a wrongdoer should not benefit by inducing early death rather than a full lifetime of pain and suffering: that must happen anyway, e.g. when an infant is killed outright.

It has been said that if in a case such as this damages are not to be awarded in respect of benefits that would have accrued to the plaintiff in the lost years it introduces an anomaly, since if the claim were under the
B   Fatal Accidents Act by dependants their claim would extend into the lost years.   But this so called anomaly arises from the particular nature of such a claim, which is by living people in respect of their living periods, which is expressly based upon what they have lost by a death.   It is not a claim by a dead person.   I do not accept the suggestion that Parliament in enacting the Fatal Accidents Acts must have assumed a live plaintiff's
C   claim for the lost years.

It has, my Lords, correctly been remarked that though in the instant case the plaintiff had dependants who (it was assumed) were barred from a Fatal Accidents Act claim by the judgment, the question of the lost years must be answered in the same way in a case of a plaintiff without dependants.   But the solution proposed, involving as it does deduction
D   from lost years' earnings of the plaintiff's living expenses, appears to me to attempt to splice two quite separate types of claim: a claim by dependants for dependency and a claim by the plaintiff himself.   If a plaintiff is to be entitled to claim in respect of lost years' earnings, why should his claim be reduced by what, no doubt enjoyably, he would have spent on himself?   Why should he be limited to that which he would have given away either inter vivos or by will or intestacy?   The answer is I suppose
E   that being dead he has no living expenses.   But this, in the current phrase, is where we came in.   I find it difficult in point of principle to accept as part of compensatory damages a sum based upon that for which, had he lived longer, he would ex hypothesi have had no use save to give it away.   The comment that the law is not concerned with what a plaintiff does with the damages to which he is entitled is of course
F   sound: but it assumes entitlement to the damages, which is the very question.   My Lords, these problems have been debated by the Law Commission.   An attempt to solve them has been made for Scotland by the Damages (Scotland) Act 1976.   My own opinion is that the solution is a matter whose complications are more suited for legislation than judicial decision by this House in the manner proposed.   Your Lordships being unanimously of opinion on this problem to the contrary,
G   I have not felt it necessary to argue the point in great detail.

In the result I would allow the appeals on the questions of interest and quantum of damages (£7,000 or £10,000) and dismiss the appeal on the lost years point.   In the circumstances of your Lordships' decision I agree with the order for remission proposed and for costs.

H   LORD SCARMAN.   My Lords, I agree with the speeches of my noble and learned friends, Lord Wilberforce, Lord Salmon and Lord Edmund-Davies.   My excuse for burdening your Lordships with a speech must be that, as my Lord, Lord Wilberforce, has remarked, in some cases a single speech may generate uncertainty.   I would add a comment: one justification (there are others) for several speeches in your Lordships' House supporting the same conclusion is that they can show that there

are more ways than one of journeying to the same end. They can shed **A**
light, and diminish the possibility of misunderstanding.

Mr. Pickett, who was the plaintiff in the action, claimed damages
from the defendant, British Rail Engineering Ltd., his employer, for
serious personal injury sustained in the course of his employment.
The defendant admits liability. The issue between the parties is as to the
amount of damages which the judge at trial ought to have awarded
Mr. Pickett, a living plaintiff.   **B**

Mr. Pickett, a married man with two children, was aged 53 at the
time of trial, which was on October 11 and 12, 1976. His wife was
then 47 years old. He first realised he was ill when he became short
of breath in the spring of 1974. In the words of the trial judge:

> "He was then 51 years of age, a very fit man who was a non-
> smoker, a cyclist of great accomplishment, for he had been a **C**
> champion cyclist of apparently Olympic standard, and he was still
> leading a most active life in March 1974, cycling to work each day."

Medical treatment and investigations culminating in an operation in
January 1975 revealed a malignant tumour which covered the whole of
his right lung and could not be wholly removed. It was caused by
asbestos dust inhaled over the years while he was working in the   **D**
defendant's workshops. Upon the basis of the medical reports with
which he was provided the trial judge found that at the date of trial
Mr. Pickett's expectation of life was one year. In fact, he died five
months later, on March 15, 1977. But for his injury, Mr. Pickett could
have expected to work until normal retiring age (i.e. 65) and to enjoy
thereafter a period of retirement.   **E**

The judge's task was to assess the damages to be paid to a living
plaintiff, aged 53, whose life expectancy had been shortened to one
year. He awarded a total of £14,947·64 damages. This total included
(1) £7,000, general damages for pain, suffering, and loss of amenities;
(2) £787·50, interest upon the award of these general damages from
date of service of writ (July 18, 1975) to date of trial; (3) £1,508·88 **F**
damages for loss of the earnings which he could have expected to earn
during his shortened life expectancy; (4) £500 damages for loss of
expectation of life.

Mr. Pickett appealed but before the appeal could be heard he had died.
His widow, as administratrix of his estate, obtained an order to carry
on the proceedings, and the appeal was heard in November 1977. The
Court of Appeal increased the award of general damages to £10,000; **G**
but refused to allow interest upon this award. Following *Oliver* v.
Ashman [1962] 2 Q.B. 210, the court left undisturbed the award for loss
of future earnings. It increased to £750 the award for loss of expectation
of life. The administratrix now appeals against the refusal of interest
upon the general damages and against the sum awarded for loss of
future earnings. The defendant appeals against the increase by the **H**
Court of Appeal in the award of general damages.

First, some general observations. The recent development of the
judicial practice of "itemising damages," though as a matter of history
closely linked with the need to differentiate between heads of damage for
the purpose of calculating interest upon damages, has, my Lords, helped
towards a juster assessment of the capital element in damages for personal injuries. For it ensures that pecuniary loss and non-pecuniary loss

A will be assessed separately. As the Law Commission has shown in its
report Law Commission Report on Personal Injury Litigation—Assessment of Damages, July 24, 1973 (Law Com. No. 56), the assessment of
damages for non-pecuniary loss is a very different matter from assessment
of damages for pecuniary loss. There is no way of measuring in money
pain, suffering, loss of amenities, loss of expectation of life. All that the
court can do is to make an award of fair compensation. Inevitably this
B means a flexible judicial tariff, which judges will use as a starting-point
in each individual case, but never in itself as decisive of any case. The
judge, inheriting the function of the jury, must make an assessment which
in the particular case he thinks fair: and, if his assessment be based on
correct principle and a correct understanding of the facts, it is not to be
challenged unless it can be demonstrated to be wholly erroneous: *Davies* v.
C *Powell Duffryn Associated Collieries Ltd.* [1942] A.C. 601.

But, when a judge is assessing damages for pecuniary loss, the
principle of full compensation can properly be applied. Indeed, anything
else would be inconsistent with the general rule which Lord Blackburn
has formulated in these words:

D "... that, where any injury is to be compensated by damages, in
settling the sum of money to be given ... you should as nearly as
possible get at that sum of money which will put the party who has
been injured, or who has suffered, in the same position as he would
have been in if he had not sustained the wrong ...": *Livingstone*
v. *Rawyards Coal Co.* (1880) 5 App.Cas. 25, 39.

Though arithmetical precision is not always possible, though in
E estimating future pecuniary loss a judge must make certain assumptions
(based upon the evidence) and certain adjustments, he is seeking to
estimate a financial compensation for a financial loss. It makes sense in
this context to speak of full compensation as the object of the law. It
is on this basis, my Lords, that I approach the three questions raised in
this appeal, with which I propose to deal in this order: (1) damages for
loss of future earnings; (2) damages for pain, suffering, and loss of
F amenities; (3) interest on the damages for pain and suffering.

(1) *Damages for loss of future earnings*

In *Oliver* v. *Ashman* [1962] 2 Q.B. 210, the Court of Appeal decided
that in an action for damages for personal injuries, whether brought by
a living plaintiff or on behalf of the estate of a dead plaintiff, damages
G for loss of earnings are limited in the first case to the period of shortened
expectation of life, and, in the second, to the shortened period of life.
Under the *Oliver* v. *Ashman* rule no claim for loss of earnings can be
made in respect of the period the plaintiff could have expected to live,
had his life expectation not been shortened by the accident giving rise
to his claim. He cannot recover in respect of the earnings he could
H have expected during the " lost years."

My noble and learned friends Lord Wilberforce, Lord Salmon and
Lord Edmund-Davies have analysed the case law which lies behind this
decision. I agree with them in thinking that the decision was based
upon a misconception of what this House had decided in *Benham* v.
Gambling [1941] A.C. 157. The relevant line of authority is not that
which culminated in *Benham* v. *Gambling* but that which had begun with
Phillips v. *London and South Western Railway Co.,* 5 Q.B.D. 78 and

culminated in *Roach* v. *Yates* [1938] 1 K.B. 256. If, therefore, attention   A
be directed only to the authorities, I think it may be said that *Oliver* v.
Ashman was wrongly decided, and that the court in that case should
have followed its own decision in *Roach* v. *Yates.*

Your Lordships' House is, however, concerned with the principle of
the matter. The principle has been exhaustively discussed in the
Australian case of *Skelton* v. *Collins,* 115 C.L.R. 94. Windeyer J., at p.
129 found it in " The general principle that damages are compensatory."   B
He thought it flowed from that principle " that anything having a money
value which the plaintiff has lost should be made good in money." He
went on: " The destruction or diminution of a man's capacity to earn
money can be made good in money." And he concluded by saying:

> " I cannot see that damages that flow from the destruction or
> diminution of his capacity to [earn] are any the less when the   C
> period during which the capacity might have been exercised is
> curtailed because the tort cut short his expected span of life."

The same point was made by Streatfeild J. in *Pope* v. *D. Murphy & Son
Ltd.* [1961] 1 Q.B. 222, 231:

> " What he has lost is the prospect of earning whatever it was he did   D
> earn from his business over the period of time that he might other-
> wise, apart from the accident, have reasonably expected to earn it."

I would add that this line of reasoning is consistent with Lord Blackburn's formulation of the general principle of the law, to which I have
already referred: *Livingstone* v. *Rawyards Coal Co.,* 5 App.Cas. 25.

Principle would appear, therefore, to suggest that a plaintiff ought to   E
be entitled to damages for the loss of earnings he could have reasonably
expected to have earned during the " lost years." But it has been
submitted by the defendant that such a rule, if it be thought socially
desirable, requires to be implemented by legislation. It is argued that a
judicial graft would entail objectionable consequences—consequences
which legislation alone can obviate. There is force in this submission.   F
The major objections are these. First, the plaintiff may have no dependants. Secondly, even if he has dependants, he may have chosen to
make a will depriving them of support from his estate. In either event,
there would be a windfall for strangers at the expense of the defendant.
Thirdly, the plaintiff may be so young (in *Oliver* v. *Ashman* [1962] 2
Q.B. 210 he was a boy aged 20 months at the time of the accident) that it
is absurd that he should be compensated for future loss of earnings.   G
Fourthly—a point which has weighed with my noble and learned friend,
Lord Russell of Killowen—if damages are recoverable for the loss of the
prospect of earnings during the lost years, must it not follow that they are
also recoverable for loss of other reasonable expectations, e.g. a life
interest or an inheritance? Fifthly, what does compensation mean
when it is assessed in respect of a period after death? Sixthly, as my   H
noble and learned friend Lord Wilberforce has pointed out, there is a
risk of double recovery in some cases, i.e. of both the estate and the
dependants recovering damages for the expected earnings of the lost
years.

The law is not concerned with how a plaintiff spends the damages
awarded to him. The first two objections can, therefore, be said to be
irrelevant. The second objection is, however, really too serious to be

A thus summarily rejected. The social justification for reversing the rule in *Oliver* v. *Ashman* [1962] 2 Q.B. 210 is that it imposes hardship on dependants. But this justification is undermined if a plaintiff, having recovered damages for his lost future earnings, can thereafter exclude by will his dependants from any share of his estate. To this objection the law provides an answer: his estate will be subject to the right of dependants for whom no or no sufficient provision has been made to

B apply for provision under the Inheritance (Provisions of Family and Dependants) Act 1975. The third objection will be taken care of in the ordinary course of litigation: a measurable and not too remote loss has to be proved before it can enter into the assessment of damages. The fourth " objectionable consequence " does not seem to me objectionable. I agree with the Law Commission, where in paragraph 90 of Law Com.

C No. 56 they say:

"There seems to be no justification in principle for discrimination between deprivation of earning capacity and deprivation of the capacity otherwise to receive economic benefits. The loss must be regarded as a loss of the plaintiff; and it is a loss caused by the tort even though it relates to moneys which the injured person will

D not receive because of his premature death. No question of the remoteness of damage arises other than the application of the ordinary foreseeability test."

For myself, as at present advised (for the point does not arise for decision and has not been argued), I would allow a plaintiff to recover damages for the loss of his financial expectations during the lost years provided

E always the loss was not too remote.

There is, it has to be confessed, no completely satisfying answer to the fifth objection. But it does not, I suggest, make it unjust that such damages should be awarded. The plaintiff has lost the earnings and the opportunity, which, while he was living, he valued, of employing them as he would have thought best. Whether a man's ambition be to build up a

F fortune, to provide for his family, or to spend his money upon good causes or merely a pleasurable existence, loss of the means to do so is a genuine financial loss. The logical and philosophical difficulties of compensating a man for a loss arising after his death emerge only if one treats the loss as a non-pecuniary loss—which to some extent it is. But it is also a pecuniary loss—the money would have been his to deal with as he chose, had he lived. The sixth objection appears to me unavoid-

G able, though further argument and analysis in a case in which the point arose for decision might lead to a judicial solution which was satisfactory. But I suspect that the point will need legislation. However, if one must choose between a law which in some cases will deprive dependants of their dependency through the chances of life and litigation and a law which, in avoiding such a deprival, will entail in some cases both the

H estate and the dependants recovering damages in respect of the lost years, I find the latter to be the lesser evil.

I conclude, therefore, that damages for loss of future earnings (and future expectations) during the lost years are recoverable, where the facts are such that the loss is not too remote to be measurable. But I think, for the reasons given by Lord Wilberforce, Lord Salmon and Lord Edmund-Davies, that a plaintiff (or his estate) should not recover more

than that which would have remained at his disposal after meeting his own **A**
living expenses.

(2) Damages for pain, suffering, and loss of amenities

The Court of Appeal thought that the sum (£7,000) awarded by the
judge was too low, and substituted a figure of £10,000. Lord Denning
M.R. said: **B**

> " Although I well appreciate the care which the judge gave to this
> case, it seems to me that there is one feature which the judge did
> not take into account sufficiently, and that is the distress which Mr.
> Pickett must have suffered knowing that his widow and dependants
> would be left without him to care for them. I think we ought to take
> this distress into account. Taking it into account, it seems to me that **C**
> we can properly increase the figure given by the judge to the sum of
> £10,000. This seems itself all too little; but, as I have said, with the
> law as it now stands, I do not think it is open to the court to increase
> it further because no compensation is at the moment available for loss
> of earnings during the ' lost years.' " (See Court of Appeal (Civil
> Division) Transcript No. 428A of 1977.)

D

My Lords, I have to say that I think that in this passage the Master of the
Rolls was influenced—understandably, if I may respectfully say so—by
the pitifully small sum available to the plaintiff as damages for loss of
future earnings under the law which bound the judge and the Court of
Appeal. The distress suffered by Mr. Pickett knowing that his widow and
children would be left without him to care for them was an element in his
suffering for which I agree Mr. Pickett was entitled to fair compensation. **E**
But it would be bad law if this element of non-pecuniary damage should be
used to make good in whole or in part the loss of earnings during the " lost
years," which under the law as it stood when this case was before the
Court of Appeal were not recoverable as damages. I am far from being
persuaded that the judge failed to take into account this element of Mr.
Pickett's suffering. The Master of the Rolls in the passage which I have **F**
quoted paid his tribute to the care which the judge gave the case. Lawton
L.J. hesitated before differing from the judge. He said: " My reason for
having some hesitation is that it is manifest that he approached the matter
of the assessment of damages on the right lines." I respectfully agree.
In the course of an eloquent passage in his judgment describing Mr.
Pickett's pain and suffering, the trial judge said: **G**

> " He has, according to his evidence, no precise knowledge of what the
> future holds for him, but he must be aware—I am certain that he is
> aware—that it is a very limited future. It may be that he will become
> aware of the position so far as the future is concerned. Although he
> has been kept out of court, it is unfortunately impossible to guarantee
> that that fact will not be communicated to him in some way. I am
> satisfied that it is right that the court should bear in mind the **H**
> possibility; indeed, I would rate it as a probability."

And he summed it all up when he said that he had endeavoured to take
into account " all the features of the tragic situation in which Mr. Pickett
finds himself." It is not possible, therefore, to fault the judge's approach
to the assessment of general damages.

It is not the function of an appellate court to substitute its opinion for

A   that of the trial judge.   Lord Wright stated the general principle in a
well-known passage in his speech in *Davies* v. *Powell Duffryn Associated
Colleries Ltd.* [1942] A.C. 601, 617 :

> " In effect the court, before it interferes with an award of damages,
> should be satisfied that the judge has acted on a wrong principle of
> law, or has misapprehended the facts, or has for these or other reasons
B > made a wholly erroneous estimate of the damage suffered.   It is not
> enough that there is a balance of opinion or preference.   The scale
> must go down heavily against the figure attacked if the appellate court
> is to interfere, whether on the ground of excess or insufficiency."

The trial judge correctly apprehended the facts, and adopted the correct
approach in law.   Though to some the award of £7,000 may seem low, it
C is not so low as to support the inference that the judge's estimate was
wholly erroneous.   In a task as imprecise and immeasurable as the award
of damages for non-pecuniary loss, a preference for £10,000 over £7,000
is a matter of opinion, but not by itself evidence of error.   I would, therefore, allow the cross appeal and restore the judge's award of £7,000 general
damages.

D   (3) *Interest*

In *Cookson* v. *Knowles* [1978] 2 W.L.R. 978 your Lordships' House
has recently reviewed the guidelines for the exercise of the court's discretion in awarding interest upon damages in fatal accident cases.   The
House expressly left open the question of interest upon damages for non-
pecuniary loss in a personal injury action.   My noble and learned friend,
E Lord Diplock, concluded his speech with these words, at pp. 987–988 :

> " The question of damages for non-economic loss which bulks large
> in personal injury actions, however, does not arise in the instant case.
> It has not been argued before your Lordships and I refrain from
> expressing any view about it."

F   When, however, that case was in the Court of Appeal [1977] Q.B. 913,
the court did deal, obiter, with interest upon damages for non-pecuniary
loss awarded to a living plaintiff in a personal injury case.   Lord Denning
M.R., delivering the judgment of the court, said at p. 921:

> " In *Jefford* v. *Gee* [1970] 2 Q.B. 130, 151, we said that, in personal
> injury cases, when a lump sum is awarded for pain and suffering and
> loss of amenities, interest should run ' from the date of service of the
G > writ to the date of trial.'   At that time inflation did not stare us in
> the face.   We had not in mind continuing inflation and its effect on
> awards.   It is obvious now that that guide-line should be changed.
> The courts invariably assess the lump sum on the ' scale ' for figures
> current at the date of the trial—which is much higher than the figure
> current at the date of the injury or at the date of the writ.   The
H > plaintiff thus stands to gain by the delay in bringing the case to trial.
> He ought not to gain still more by having interest from the date of
> service of the writ.   We would alter the guide-line, therefore, by
> suggesting that no interest should be awarded on the lump sum
> awarded at the trial for pain and suffering and loss of amenities."

In the instant case the Court of Appeal has followed its dictum, disallow-
ing the interest granted by the judge on the damages for pain and suffering.

Lord Scarman   Pickett v. British Rail Engineering Ltd. (H.L.(E.))   [1978]

My Lords, I believe the reasoning of the Court of Appeal to be unsound on **A** this point.   It is based upon a fallacy; and is inconsistent with the statute.

First, the fallacy.   It is assumed that because the award of damages made at trial is greater, in monetary terms, than it would have been, had damages been assessed at date of service of writ, the award is greater in terms of real value.   There is here a complete non sequitur.   The cash awarded is more, because the value of cash, i.e. its purchasing power, has diminished.   In theory the higher award at trial has the same purchasing **B** power as the lower award which would have been made at the date of the service of the writ: in truth, of course, judicial awards of damages follow, but rarely keep pace with, inflation so that in all probability the sum awarded at trial is less, in terms of real value, than would have been awarded at the earlier date.   In theory, therefore, and to some extent in practice, inflation is taken care of by increasing the number of money units **C** in the award so that the real value of the loss is met.   The loss, for which interest is given, is quite distinct, and not covered by this increase.   It is the loss which is suffered by being kept out of money to which one is entitled.

Secondly, the statute.   Section 22, Administration of Justice Act 1969, amending section 3, Law Reform (Miscellaneous Provision) Act 1934, pro- vides that the court *shall* (my emphasis) exercise its power to award **D** interest on damages, or on such part of the damages as the court considers appropriate, " unless the court is satisfied that there are special reasons why no interest should be given in respect of those damages."   Such is the general rule laid down by the statute, which does, however, confer upon the court a discretion as to the period for which interest is given and also permits differing rates. Nothing can be clearer than the duty place **E** upon the court to give interest in the absence of special reasons for giving none. Inflation is an economic and financial condition of general application in our society. Its impact upon this plaintiff has been neither more nor less than upon everybody else: there is nothing special about it.

For these reasons I think the Court of Appeal erred in refusing to allow interest on the award of damages for non-pecuniary loss. I would reinstate the judge's award. **F**

In conclusion, I agree that the appeal and cross-appeal should both be allowed and that the order proposed by my noble and learned friend, Lord Wilberforce should be made.   I also agree with the order as to costs which he has proposed.

Appeal allowed with costs.
Cross-appeal allowed with costs.   **G**

Solicitors: *John L. Williams; Evan Harding.*

T. J. M.

H

A

[PRIVY COUNCIL]

AMERICAN LEAF BLENDING CO. SDN. BHD. . APPELLANT

AND

DIRECTOR-GENERAL OF INLAND REVENUE . RESPONDENT

B

[ON APPEAL FROM THE FEDERAL COURT OF MALAYSIA]

1978 June 6, 7;   Lord Diplock, Viscount Dilhorne,
     July 18   Lord Edmund-Davies, Lord Russell
                               of Killowen and Sir Robin Cooke

C *Malaysia—Revenue—Income tax—Accumulated losses—Company
   abandoning tobacco business after incurring losses — Letting
   of company's business premises—Assessment of tax on income
   from lettings — Claim to deduct accumulated losses from
   assessment — Whether rents derived from business source —
   Income Tax Act 1967 (No. 47 of 1967), ss. 4 (a) (d), 43 (1) (a)*

      In 1964, after abandoning a tobacco business in which it
D had incurred losses, the company let a warehouse which was
   a part of its business premises. In 1967, the remainder of the
   premises, a factory, became empty and was also let. By 1968,
   five successive lettings of the premises had been made. The
   company was assessed to income tax, under section 4 (d) of
   the Income Tax Act 1967,[1] in respect of rents received for the
   lettings. It claimed that it was entitled, under section 43 (1)
   (a) and (2) of the Act, to set off the losses against the assess-
E ments as the income from the rents was derived from a source
   consisting of a business. The claim was disallowed by the
   Director-General of Inland Revenue on the ground that the
   lettings did not amount to the carrying on of a business. On
   appeal, the Special Commissioners of Income Tax, who were
   of the opinion that the lettings were made in the course of a
   business because the letting of its property was one of the
   objects stated in the company's memorandum of association,
F allowed the claim and stated a case for the opinion of the
   High Court. The claim to be able to deduct the losses was
   upheld by the High Court; but that decision was reversed by
   the Federal Court. Both courts, however, rejected a contention
   by the Director-General that since rents were included in
   paragraph (d) of section 4, they were incapable of being income
   derived from a business source which fell under paragraph (a)
   of the section.
G   On appeal by the company to the Judicial Committee: —
      Held, allowing the appeal, (1) that the five paragraphs in
   section 4 of the Income Tax Act 1967 specifying the five
   classes of income in respect of which tax was chargeable under

──────────────

[Reported by BERNARD O. AGYEMAN, ESQ., Barrister-at-Law]

H

[1] Income Tax Act 1967, s. 4 (1): see post, pp. 988H—989A.
   S. 43. " (1) The aggregate income of a person for a year of assessment (that person
and year of assessment being . . . referred to as the relevant person and the relevant
year respectively) shall consist of (a) the aggregate of his statutory income, if any,
for the relevant year from each of his sources consisting of a business, reduced by
any deduction falling to be made for the relevant year pursuant to subsection (2); . . .
(2) . . . there shall be deducted under subsection (1) (a) pursuant to this subsection
from the aggregate of the relevant person's statutory income from each of his sources
consisting of a business for the relevant year the amount ascertained . . . for any
particular year of assessment preceding the relevant year. . . . "

the Act were not mutually exclusive, so that "rents," despite **A**
being referred to in paragraph (*d*), could constitute income
from a business source under paragraph (*a*); that where
premises were let in the course of carrying on the business
of putting them to a profitable use, section 43 (1) gave primacy
to the classification of the rents receivable as income from a
source consisting of a business notwithstanding that they might
also be classified as "rents" (post, p. 989F–H).

    Commissioner of Income Tax v. *Hanover Agencies Ltd.* **B**
[1967] 1 A.C., P.C. applied.

    Fry v. *Salisbury House Estate Ltd.* [1930] A.C. 432,
H.L.(E.) distinguished.   (2) That where a company had
been incorporated for the purpose of making profits, any
gainful use to which it put its assets prima facie amounted
to the carrying on of a business; that, although the fact that
the letting of its premises was included in the objects of the
company was not conclusive in deciding that the company **C**
was carrying on a business, since the only conclusion of fact
which any reasonable commissioners could have reached on
the evidence was that the company was carrying on a business
of letting its premises for rent, it was unnecessary to remit
the case for further consideration and the order of the High
Court should be restored (post, pp. 990A–D, F, 991A–C).

    Dicta of Pollock M.R. in *Inland Revenue Commissioners*
v. *Westleigh Estates Co. Ltd.* [1924] 1 K.B. 390, 409, C.A. **D**
and of Lord Warrington of Clyffe and Lord Macmillan in *Fry*
v. *Salisbury House Estate Ltd.* [1930] A.C. 432, 451, 470,
H.L.(E.) considered.

    Per curiam. In the case of a private individual it may well
be that the mere receipt of rents from property that he owns
raises no presumption that he is carrying on a business (post,
p. 990F).

    Decision of the Federal Court of Malaysia reversed. **E**

The following cases are referred to in the judgment:

Commissioner of Income Tax v. *Hanover Agencies Ltd.* [1967] 1 A.C.
    681; [1967] 2 W.L.R. 565; [1967] 1 All E.R. 954, P.C.
Fry v. *Salisbury House Estate Ltd.* [1930] A.C. 432, H.L.(E.)
Inland Revenue Commissioners v. *Westleigh Estates Co. Ltd.* [1924]
    1 K.B. 390, C.A. **F**

The following additional cases were cited in argument:

Inland Revenue Commissioners v. *Korean Syndicate Ltd.* [1921] 3 K.B.
    258, C.A.
Liverpool and London and Globe Insurance Co. v. *Bennett* [1912] 2 K.B.
    41, C.A.; [1913] A.C. 610, H.L.(E.).
Murphy v. *Australian Machinery and Investment Co. Ltd.* (1948) 30 T.C. **G**
    244, Atkinson J. and C.A.
Scottish Mortgage Co. of New Mexico v. *McKelvie* (1886) 2 T.C. 165.
South Behar Railway Co. Ltd. v. *Inland Revenue Commissioners* [1925]
    A.C. 476, H.L.(E.).
Town Investments Ltd. v. *Department of the Environment* [1978] A.C.
    359; [1977] 2 W.L.R. 450; [1977] 1 All E.R. 813, H.L.(E.).

H

APPEAL (No. 12 of 1976) by American Leaf Blending Co. Sdn. Bhd.
from a judgment (March 1, 1975) of the Federal Court of Malaysia
(Gill C.J., Ong and Suleiman F.JJ.) allowing an appeal by the Director-
General of Inland Revenue, from a judgment (May 30, 1974) of Sani J.
whereby he upheld a decision of the Special Commissioners of Income Tax
made on February 13, 1973, that the company was entitled, under section
43 (1) (*a*) and (2) of the Income Tax Act 1967, to set off unabsorbed losses

A of its business against assessments of income tax in respect of rents received
for letting the company's business premises.

The facts are stated in the judgment of their Lordships.

Donald Rattee Q.C. for the company.
Patrick Medd Q.C. and *Christopher Bathurst Q.C.* for the Director-
B General.

Cur. adv. vult.

July 18. The judgment of their Lordships was delivered by LORD
DIPLOCK.

The appellant taxpayer (" the company ") was incorporated in 1960.
The principal object for which it was established was to cut and blend
C tobacco and to manufacture cigarettes; but, as is usual, its memorandum
of association incorporated a wide variety of objects including granting
licences over and generally dealing with the land rights and other property
of the company.

The company purchased land in Petaling Jaya whereon it erected a
building, which contained a factory in which cigarette-making machinery
D was installed and a bonded warehouse for storing tobacco and cigarettes.
The company started to manufacture cigarettes there in February 1961;
but this proved so unprofitable that the manufacturing business was
abandoned in November of the same year and thereafter until 1964 its
activities were confined to trading in tobacco. This likewise proved
unprofitable and was in turn abandoned in 1964, by which time the
company had accumulated adjusted losses for income tax purposes
E amounting to $399,303·00.

With the abandonment of trading in tobacco the company no longer
needed to make use itself of the storage space provided by the bonded
warehouse. So, in April 1964, it licensed Caxton Press (1957) Ltd. to
occupy and use the warehouse for storing paper on what was in effect a
monthly tenancy. It is convenient to refer to this and subsequent licences
F as " lettings " and payments made thereunder as " rents " since they fall
within the definition of " rent " in the Income Tax Act 1967. It does
not appear when this first letting ended; but on January 18, 1965, there
was a fresh letting of the warehouse to a new licensee, Zuellig Feedmills
(Malaya) Ltd., for storing maize. This was a letting until May 31, 1965,
terminable then or at any time thereafter on one month's notice. This
second letting of the warehouse was followed by a third on October 1,
G 1966, to Dunlop Malayan Industries Ltd. to store its own goods. This was
a three months' letting; it does not appear whether this licensee in fact
held over after the expiry of the three months.

In the course of 1967 the cigarette-making machinery which had
remained in situ in the factory was sold and removed, thus making the
factory as well as the warehouse available for letting for storage purposes.
H On January 30, 1967, the company let the factory area to Tien Wah
Press (Malaya) Ltd. for three months terminable on April 30, 1967, or at
any time thereafter on one month's notice.

Finally on October 1, 1968, factory and warehouse were let to Gammon
South East Asia Berhad for storage purposes for 12 months terminable
on September 30, 1969, or at the end of any subsequent month on six
months' notice.

In the years of assessment 1968 and 1970 the company was assessed to income tax under section 4 (*d*) of the Income Tax Act 1967, in respect of **A** rents from these lettings. There is no dispute about the figures which amount to $7,040·00 in 1968 and $33,234·00 in 1970. The company, however, claims to be entitled under section 43 (1) (*a*) and (2) to set off against these, and any subsequent assessments, the accumulated adjusted losses of $399,303·00 until they are exhausted.

The claim was disallowed by the Director-General of Inland Revenue. On appeal, it was allowed by the special commissioners who, at the request **B** of the Director-General, stated a case for the opinion of the High Court. The High Court (Sani J.) upheld the company's claim to be entitled to deduction of the unabsorbed adjusted losses; but Sani J.'s decision on this matter was reversed by the Federal Court (Gill C.J., Ong F.J., Suleiman F.J.). It is from the judgment of the Federal Court that this appeal is brought.   **C**

Before the special commissioners and in both courts below the company claimed that it was entitled to set off against its income from the letting of its property the balance of unabsorbed capital allowances in respect of its tobacco-manufacturing business. This claim was rejected by the High Court and the Federal Court. It has been abandoned before their Lordships, who are accordingly concerned only with the appellant's **D** claim under section 43, to have deducted from the assessments on the company to income tax for 1968 and 1970 the unexhausted balance of adjusted losses incurred in carrying on its tobacco business between 1961 and 1964.

Section 43, under which adjusted losses from a business of the taxpayer for previous years of assessment (as ascertained under section 40) are to be deducted from the aggregrate of the taxpayer's statutory income for any **E** year for the purpose of ascertaining his chargeable income for that year, draws a distinction between income from a "source consisting of a business " and income from any other source. It is only against income from a source consisting of a business that adjusted losses from a business for previous years of assessment can be set off. The taxpayer's business from which the previous loss was incurred, however, need not be the same **F** business as that from which his statutory income for the year of assessment is derived. So the only question in this appeal is : were the rents received by the company for letting its premises or parts thereof to other persons for use for storage, income from a "source consisting of a business " for the purposes of section 43 (1) (*a*) and (2) of the Act?

In support of the contention that they were not, two arguments have been advanced on behalf of the Inland Revenue. The first is general : that, **G** as a matter of construction of the Income Tax Act 1967, income derived from the receipt of rents of premises is incapable of constituting income from a source consisting of a business. The second is special to the instant case : that on the facts found by the special commissioners the company in the years of assessment 1968 and 1970 was not carrying on a business of letting out its premises or, it would seem, any other business at all. **H**

The first and general argument on the construction of the Act failed in both courts below. It can be dealt with shortly by their Lordships. It is based upon the charging section, section 4, which reads as follows:

> " 4. Subject to this Act, the income upon which tax is chargeable under this Act is income in respect of—(*a*) gains or profits from a business, for whatever period of time carried on; (*b*) gains or profits from an employment; (*c*) dividends, interest or discounts; (*d*) rents,

A   royalties or premiums; (e) pensions, annuities or other periodical payments not falling under any of the foregoing paragraphs; (f) gains or profits not falling under any of the foregoing paragraphs."

The contention is that paragraphs (a) to (e) refer to five separate classes of income that are mutually exclusive, in the same way as the various Schedules of the United Kingdom Income Tax Act 1918 were held to be

B mutually exclusive by the House of Lords in *Fry* v. *Salisbury House Estate Ltd.* [1930] A.C. 432. As was pointed out by the Judicial Committee in the Jamaican appeal *Commissioner of Income Tax* v. *Hanover Agencies Ltd.* [1967] 1 A.C. 681, the *Salisbury House* case turned on the peculiar structure and provisions of the United Kingdom Act, and threw no light upon the construction of other taxing statutes such as those of Jamaica or Malaysia whose structure and provisions are quite different.

C   If the words in the various paragraphs of section 4 of the Malaysian Act are given their ordinary meaning, and their Lordships see no reason why they should not be, there is plainly room for overlapping between one paragraph and another. A company may carry on business as an investment or holding company deriving its gains or profits from dividends and interest from the securities it owns. The gains or profit from the business of a bank

D or moneylender are largely derived from interest received on money lent. A property company or an individual may be carrying on the business of letting premises for rents from which the gains or profits of that business are derived.

That there is potential overlapping between paragraph (a) and paragraphs (c) and (d) is, in their Lordships' view, put beyond doubt by the provisions

E of section 24. The general rule laid down in sections 27 and 28 is that income other than income from a business does not become chargeable until it has actually been received. By section 27 (1) this is applied specifically to "rent." The purpose of section 24 is to provide, as an exception to the general rule, that on computing chargeable income from a business book debts arising in the period of assessment shall be brought into account although not actually received. Subsections (4) and (5) apply this

F exception to dividends and interest on securities held by investment companies and interest receivable in the course of carrying on a business of lending money; while subsection (1) applies the same exception inter alia to debts arising "in respect of . . . (c) the use or enjoyment of any property dealt with at any time in the course of carrying on a business."

So it is clear that "rents," despite the fact that they are referred to in

G paragraph (d) of section 4, may nevertheless constitute income from a source consisting of a business if they are receivable in the course of carrying on a business of putting the taxpayer's property to profitable use by letting it out for rent.

Where premises are let in the course of carrying on the business of putting them to profitable use, section 43 (1) in their Lordships' view gives primacy to the classification of the rents receivable as income from a

H source consisting of a business, notwithstanding that they may also be classified under section 4 (d) as "rents." What section 43 (1) requires is that one should first determine whether the rents are income from a business. If they are, no further inquiry is necessary; adjusted losses from a business of the taxpayer for previous years of assessment are deductible in ascertaining the taxpayer's aggregate income. Thus on the question of construction of the Act their Lordships are in agreement with the High Court and the Federal Court.

American Leaf Co. v. Director-General (P.C.)   [1978]

On the question special to the instant case, viz. whether the company **A** in 1968 and 1970 was carrying on a business of letting out its premises for rents, the special commissioners were of opinion that it was. The question is one of fact, and in the High Court Sani J. treated this expression of opinion as a finding of fact by the commissioners which he should not disturb. Closer analysis of the stated case, however, discloses that the opinion expressed by the special commissioners was not a finding of fact but a conclusion of law. They accepted the company's **B** submission that because the letting of its property was one of the objects set out in its memorandum of association this was in law conclusive that in making any letting of its premises it was carrying on a business.

So stated this is, in their Lordships' view, too broad a proposition. It derives apparent support from an observation of Pollock M.R. in *Inland Revenue Commissioners* v. *Westleigh Estates Co.* [1924] 1 K.B. 390, where **C** he said, at p. 409: " . . . if [a company's] objects are business objects and are in fact carried out, . . . the company carries on business . . ." This, however, was said in the context of a company which was carrying out one of the principal objects stated in its memorandum. Their Lordships would not endorse the view that every isolated act of a kind that is authorised by its memorandum if done by a company necessarily constitutes the carrying **D** on of a business.

On the other hand their Lordships do not think that the dicta to be found in some of the speeches in the *Salisbury House* case [1930] A.C. 432 and in particular those of Lord Warrington of Clyffe and Lord Macmillan upon which the Federal Court relied and which suggest that the letting of land does not constitute a " trade," have any relevance to the question whether the letting of land by the company in the instant case amounted **E** to the carrying on of a " business " within the meaning of the Malaysian Income Tax Act 1967. " Business " is a wider concept than " trade "; and in the *Hanover Agencies* case [1967] 1 A.C. 681 the Board uttered a warning against seeking to apply these dicta outside the narrow context of British income tax law and in particular that of Schedule D.

In the case of a private individual it may well be that the mere receipt **F** of rents from property that he owns raises no presumption that he is carrying on a business. In contrast, in their Lordships' view, in the case of a company incorporated for the purpose of making profits for its shareholders any gainful use to which it puts any of its assets prima facie amounts to the carrying on of a business. Where the gainful use to which a company's property is put is letting it out for rent, their Lordships do **G** not find it easy to envisage circumstances that are likely to arise in practice which would displace the prima facie inference that in doing so it was carrying on a business.

The carrying on of " business," no doubt, usually calls for some activity on the part of whoever carries it on, though, depending on the nature of the business, the activity may be intermittent with long intervals **H** of quiescence in between. In the instant case, however, there was evidence before the special commissioners of activity in and about the letting of its premises by the company during each of the five years that had elapsed since it closed down its former tobacco business. There were three successive lettings of the warehouse negotiated with different tenants; there was the removal of the machinery from the factory area which made it available for use for storage and a separate letting of that area to a fresh

A tenant; and as recently as October 1968 there was the negotiation of a letting to a single tenant of both the factory area and the warehouse.

As has been mentioned, the question whether the company was carrying on a business of letting out its premises for rent was one of fact for the special commissioners: but it is one to which they did not apply their minds because of their mistake of law as to the effect of the presence in the company's memorandum of power to let its premises or

B any part thereof. Nevertheless their Lordships do not find it necessary to require the case to be remitted to the special commissioners for further consideration; for, in their Lordships' view, upon the evidence to which they have referred there is only one conclusion of fact that any reasonable commissioners could reach, viz. that there is nothing in the evidence capable of rebutting the prima facie inference that in the relevant periods

C of assessment the company was carrying on a business of letting out its premises for rent. On the contrary the evidence serves only to reinforce that prima facie inference.

Their Lordships will advise His Majesty the Yang di-Pertuan Agong that the appeal be allowed, the order of the Federal Court set aside and the order of the High Court restored. They will further advise that the respondent pay the costs of this appeal but that there be no order as to

D the costs in the Federal Court or the High Court.

Appeal allowed.

Solicitors: *Freshfields; Stephenson Harwood.*

E

[HOUSE OF LORDS]

FEDERAL COMMERCE & NAVIGATION CO. LTD. . Respondents

F   AND

MOLENA ALPHA INC. and Others .   .   .   . Appellants

1978 Oct. 3, 4, 5, 9, 10, 11;   Lord Wilberforce, Viscount Dilhorne,
       Nov. 23   Lord Fraser of Tullybelton, Lord Russell of
                                          Killowen and Lord Scarman

G

Shipping—Charterparty—Time charter—Owners' instructions to masters—Directions not to sign freight pre-paid bills of lading —Whether repudiatory breach of contract
Ships' Names—Lorfri—Nanfri—Benfri

By time charters of November 1974 the owners let three ships to the charterers for periods of six years to carry grain from the Great Lakes to Europe and, on the return

H voyage, steel. Most of the cargoes were carried on c.i.f. terms, the shippers paying the freight in advance and receiving " freight pre-paid " bills of lading. Clause 6 of the charters provided for the payment of hire twice monthly in advance; in default of payment the owners to have the right of withdrawing the vessel, but before invoking any right or remedy the owners had to notify the charterers of the non-receipt of the hire payment when due. Clauses 11 and 14 of the charters provided for permissible deductions from hire. By clause 9 the masters were

Federal Commerce v. Molena Alpha (H.L.(E.)) **[1978]**

to be under the orders of the charterers as regarded employ- A
ment, agency or other arrangements; and accordingly the bills
of lading were issued and signed by the charterers on behalf of
the master and freight was paid to the charterers or their agents.
Clause 18 gave the owners a lien on all cargoes, sub-freights
belonging to the time charterers and any bill of lading freight.

After a dispute had arisen regarding deduction from hire
made by the charterers under clauses 11 and 14 the owners by
telex on October 4, 1977, informed the charterers that the B
masters of all three ships were being instructed " to withdraw all
direct or implied authority to charterer or its agents to sign bills
of lading "; and that the masters would not sign any bill of
lading indorsed " freight pre-paid " or not bearing an indorsement incorporating the lien under clause 18 on bill of lading
freight. Instructions in those terms were given by the owners
to the masters.

On October 5, 1977, a series of telex exchanges took place. C
The charterers maintained that they had been put in " an
impossible position commercially " and demanded a withdrawal
of the owners' instructions to the masters. The owners
insisted that the instructions to the masters would stand. Finally
the charterers accepted the totality of the owners' conduct as a
repudiation of the charters which was accepted.

The question whether the charters had been determined by
repudiation and acceptance was referred to arbitration. In the D
interim, by a " without prejudice " agreement, the ships
remained in service as before October 1977 and the charterers
paid disputed deductions and agreed to make no more deductions without the owners' approval.

The two arbitrators disagreed. The umpire held in favour
of the charterers that the owners' conduct amounted to a
repudiation of the charterparties and that the charterers had
validly terminated them on October 5, 1977. A special case in E
respect of each ship was stated under section 21 (1) (b) of the
Arbitration Act 1950, the questions for the court (to which the
umpire gave the answers " yes ") being: (1) whether on the true
construction of the charterparty the charterers were entitled to
deduct from hire without the consent of the owners valid
claims which (a) arose under clause 11 of the charterparty or
(b) constituted an equitable set off; (2) whether the charterers F
validly terminated the charterparty on October 5, 1977. Kerr J.
held that the answer to question (2) was " No " and the answers
to question 1 (a) and (b) " Yes."

On appeal by the charterers and cross appeal by the owners
the Court of Appeal allowed the appeal and dismissed the cross-
appeal.

On appeal: —

Held, that the signing of freight pre-paid bills of lading was G
not inconsistent with the owners' right of lien and that, since
the issue of such bills was essential to the maintenance of the
charterers' trade, the instruction of the owners to the masters
constituted an anticipatory breach of contract and, though that
was not a breach of a condition automatically giving the charterers the right to put an end to the contract, it was, when
examined on its individual demerits in the light of the
immediate need to issue the bills promptly, repudiatory of the H
contract as going to the root of it as substantially depriving
the charterers of virtually the whole benefit of it (post, pp.
998F—999A, F–G, 1000C, 1001C–D, 1002A–F, 1003E–H, 1004F—
1005B, E, 1006H—1007A).

James Shaffer Ltd. v. *Findlay Durham & Brodie* [1953] 1
W.L.R. 106, C.A. and *Sweet & Maxwell Ltd.* v. *Universal News
Service Ltd.* [1964] 2 Q.B. 699, C.A. distinguished.

Per Viscount Dilhorne and Lord Russell of Killowen. The
giving by the owners of instructions to the masters to refuse

3 W.L.R.   **Federal Commerce v. Molena Alpha (H.L.(E.))**

A to sign bills of lading marked " freight pre-paid " and to insist that all bills of lading should be claused was an actual and not anticipatory breach of contract (post, pp. 1001c, 1004H).

Decision of the Court of Appeal [1978] 3 W.L.R. 309; [1978] 3 All E.R. 1066 affirmed.

The following cases are referred to in their Lordships' opinions:

B *Aries Tanker Corporation* v. *Total Transport Ltd.* (*The Aries*) [1977] 1 W.L.R. 185; [1977] 1 All E.R. 398, H.L.(E.).

Decro-Wall International S.A. v. *Practitioners in Marketing Ltd.* [1971] 1 W.L.R. 361; [1971] 2 All E.R. 216, C.A.

Freeth v. *Burr* (1874) L.R. 9 C.P. 208.

Hongkong Fir Shipping Co. Ltd. v. *Kawasaki Kisen Kaisha Ltd.* [1962] 2 Q.B. 26; [1962] 2 W.L.R. 474; [1962] 1 All E.R. 474, C.A.

C *Shaffer (James) Ltd.* v. *Findlay, Durham & Brodie* [1953] 1 W.L.R. 106, C.A.

Shillito, The (1897) 3 Com.Cas. 44.

Smyth (Ross T.) & Co. Ltd. v. *T. D. Bailey, Son & Co.* [1940] 3 All E.R. 60, H.L.(E.).

Sweet & Maxwell Ltd. v. *Universal News Services Ltd.* [1964] 2 Q.B. 699; [1964] 3 W.L.R. 356; [1964] 3 All E.R. 30, C.A.

Turner v. *Haji Goolam Mahomed Azam* [1904] A.C. 826, P.C.

D
The following additional cases were cited in argument:

Aegnoussiotis Shipping Corporation of Monrovia v. *A/S Kristian Jebsens Rederi of Bergen* (*The Aegnoussiotis*) [1977] 1 Lloyd's Rep. 268.

Aktieselskabet Pinewood v. *J. W. Baird & Co. Ltd.* (1926) 24 Ll.L.R. 282, C.A.

E *Annefield, The* [1971] P. 184; [1971] 2 W.L.R. 320; [1971] 1 All E.R. 394, Brandon J. and C.A.

Arrospe v. *Barr* (1881) 8 R. 602.

Brankelow Steamship Co. Ltd. v. *Canton Insurance Office Ltd.* [1899] 2 Q.B. 178, C.A.; [1901] A.C. 462, H.L.(E.).

Bremer Handelsgessellschaft m.b.H. v. *Vanden Avenne-Izegem P.V.B.A.* [1978] 2 Lloyd's Rep. 109, H.L.(E.).

Canada, The (1897) 13 T.L.R. 328.

F *Cehave N.V.* v. *Bremer Handelgesselschaft m.b.H.* [1976] Q.B. 44; [1975] 3 W.L.R. 447; [1975] 3 All E.R. 739, C.A.

Consorzio Veneziano di Armamento e Navigazione v. *Northumberland Shipbuilding Co. Ltd.* (1919) 98 L.J.K.B. 1194.

Danube & Black Sea Railway & Kustenjie Harbour Co. Ltd. v. *Xenos* (1863) 13 C.B.N.S. 825.

Davidson v. *Gwynne* (1810) 12 East 381.

G *Dumenil (Peter) & Co. Ltd.* v. *James Ruddin Ltd.* [1953] 1 W.L.R. 815; [1953] 2 All E.R. 294, C.A.

Forslind v. *Bechely-Crundall*, 1922 S.C.(H.L.) 173, H.L.(Sc.).

Hain Steamship Co. Ltd. v. *Tate & Lyle Ltd.* [1936] 2 All E.R. 597, H.L.(E.).

Hochster v. *de la Tour* (1853) 2 E. & B. 678.

Jonassohn v. *Young* (1863) 4 B. & S. 296.

H *Krüger & Co. Ltd.* v. *Moel Tryvan Ship Co. Ltd.* [1907] A.C. 272, H.L.(E.).

Mareva Compania Naviera S.A. v. *International Bulkcarriers Ltd.* [1975] 2 Lloyd's Rep. 509, C.A.

Mersey Steel and Iron Co. Ltd. v. *Naylor, Benzon & Co.* (1884) 9 App. Cas. 434, H.L.(E.).

Mihalis Angelos, The, [1971] 1 Q.B. 164; [1970] 3 W.L.R. 601; [1970] 3 All E.R. 125, C.A.

Molthes Rederi Aktieselskabet v. *Ellerman's Wilson Line Ltd.* [1927] 1 K.B. 710.

Federal Commerce v. Molena Alpha (H.L.(E.)) [1978]

Simmons v. *Hoover Ltd.* [1977] Q.B. 284; [1976] 3 W.L.R. 901; [1977]   A
  1 All E.R. 775, E.A.T.
Steelwood Carriers Ltd. of Monrovia, Liberia, v. *Evymeria Compania
  Naviera S.A. of Panama* [1976] 2 Lloyd's Rep. 192.
Stewart (C. A.) & Co. v. *Phs. Van Ommeren (London) Ltd.* [1918] 2 K.B.
  560, C.A.
Strathlorne Steamship Co. Ltd. v. *Andrew Weir & Co.* (1934) 50 Ll.L.R.
  185, C.A.
Sunbeam Shipping Co. Ltd. v. *President of India* [1973] 1 Lloyd's Rep.
  482.   B
Tagart, Beaton & Co. v. *James Fisher & Sons* [1903] 1 K.B. 391, C.A.
Wehner v. *Dene Steam Shipping Co.* [1905] 2 K.B. 92.
Wickman Machine Tool Sales Ltd. v. *L. Schuler A.G.* [1974] A.C. 235;
  [1973] 2 W.L.R. 683; [1973] 2 All E.R. 39, H.L.(E.).
Universal Cargo Carriers Corporation v. *Citati* [1957] 2 Q.B. 401; [1957]   C
  2 W.L.R. 713; [1957] 2 All E.R. 70.

APPEALS from the Court of Appeal.

These were three consolidated appeals from a judgment of the Court
of Appeal (Lord Denning M.R., Goff and Cumming-Bruce L.JJ.) dated
April 18, 1978, allowing three appeals from a judgment of Kerr J. dated
February 23, 1978. By that judgment Kerr J. had, on cases stated,   D
ordered that three awards made by Mr. Clifford Clark as umpire on
January 12, 1978, be remitted to him with directions to answer a crucial
question of law in favour of the appellants, Molena Alpha Inc., Molena
Beta Inc. and Molena Gamma Inc. (the owners) rather than the
respondents, Federal Commerce & Navigation Co. Ltd. (the charterers).

The facts are summarised in the opinion of Lord Wilberforce. They
were fully stated in the judgment of Kerr J. [1978] 3 W.L.R. 309, 314–322.   E

Robert Alexander Q.C., Nicholas Phillips Q.C. and *Adrian Ginsberg* for
the appellants.

A. G. S. Pollock and *Peter Gross* for the respondents.

Their Lordships took time for consideration.   F

November 23. LORD WILBERFORCE. My Lords, this litigation
arises from three charterparties in identical form dated November 1,
1974, and amended by addenda dated June 12, 1975, by which the
appellants chartered three vessels called the *Nanfri,* the *Benfri* and the
Lorfri to the respondents for six years. Because of the world recession   G
in shipping the charters were, at the time when the relevant events
occurred, advantageous to the owners and disadvantageous to the
charterers. It is therefore in the charterers' interest to contend that
the charters are at an end. Their contention is that the owners have
committed a repudiatory breach of contract so that they were entitled,
as they did in October 1977, to determine the charters. Separate
litigation has arisen regarding each of the three ships, but this has been   H
consolidated, and I shall deal with the dispute as a single identical issue
which equally affects each contract.

The relevant facts are fully given in the award in the form of a
special case made by the umpire (the matter having gone to arbitration)
and these, with the relevant clauses in the charterparties, appear in the
judgments of Kerr J. and of the Court of Appeal. No doubt they will
be restated in the report of this appeal. I shall not set them out at

A length. The relevant points which, as it appears to me are necessary for the decision of these appeals, are the following.

1. The charters, being time charters on Baltime form 1939, provided for the payment of hire in advance on the 1st and 16th of each month. There was a clause (11) allowing deductions to be made from hire in specified events, one of which was the event of time being lost, or

B expense incurred, through slow steaming. It appears that in the initial years of the charters certain deductions from hire were made by charterers under clause 11, some of which were agreed with owners in advance; others were the subject of discussion and subsequent agreement. In 1975 charterers put forward a claim in respect of slow steaming of the Nanfri. Owners did not agree with this claim and suggested that it be taken to arbitration, but this suggestion was not taken up by

C charterers, and the claim remained dormant until September 1977. In July and September 1977 charterers made deductions in respect of each of the three vessels which owners did not agree: they contended that charterers had over-deducted some $46,000. On September 19, 1977, charterers resurrected the 1975 slow steaming claim and said that in respect of it they intended to deduct some $47,000 from the Nanfri hire

D due on October 1. Owners rejected this claim. On September 21 they gave notice of arbitration in respect of the validity of the deductions of $46,000 and also on the question of principle whether the charterers had any right unilaterally to deduct sums not agreed as valid. Charterers proceeded to make the threatened deductions from the October 1 hire.

2. Early in October 1977, owners, having consulted lawyers in London and in New York, gave instructions to their masters to refuse

E to sign bills of lading marked " freight pre-paid " and to insist that all bills of lading should be " claused " so as to incorporate the terms of the charters. On October 4 owners, by telex of their managers, informed charterers of this action. Charterers protested against these instructions and insisted that they be withdrawn. Owners replied that they would withdraw the instructions if all unilateral deductions were

F immediately paid. On October 5 charterers telexed that they treated owners' conduct as repudiation of the charters and that they terminated the charters.

3. A " without prejudice " agreement was immediately entered into by which the three vessels remained in service, all disputed deductions were paid, the charterers agreed to make no more deductions without owners' approval, and freight prepaid bills of lading were issued without

G any reference therein to the charterparties.

4. Findings made by the umpire include the following: (a) The owners and their managers knew at all material times that charterers wished to use the vessels for Great Lakes trade, involving outward carriage of grain and inward carriage of steel. They also knew that each of these types of shipment was usually made on c.i.f. terms in which

H it would be usual for freight pre-paid bills of lading to be issued clean of any reference to a time charter. (b) The owners and their managers knew that refusal to issue freight pre-paid bills was likely to cause the charterers severe commercial embarrassment and possibly substantial liability to third parties. (c) Owners intended that the effect of their action (as communicated in October telexes) would be that charterers would pay the disputed deductions under protest and that all issues would shortly be resolved by arbitration. (d) The consequences for

charterers of the orders issued by owners on October 4 were extremely A
serious since, unless charterers could ensure the issue of freight pre-paid
bills of lading not claused by reference to a time charterparty, the vessels
would be largely debarred from the grain and steel trade; charterers
would be unable to comply with existing obligations to sub-charterers;
charterers were likely to be blacklisted by Continental Grain (their sub-
charterers and one of the world's largest shippers of grain) and likely to
incur substantial liabilities to that company if cargoes currently being B
loaded or about to be loaded did not have promptly issued freight pre-
paid bills of lading.

My Lords, before attacking the real question in these appeals—which
is whether the owners' actions were repudiatory—it is necessary to clarify
the situation as regards the right of the charterers to make deductions.
There are two separate questions: the first concerns the scope of the C
contractual right to make deductions, under clause 11 of the charterparties; the second the right, apart from clause 11, to make deductions
by way of equitable set-off. The nature of the latter was discussed to
some extent, in relation to voyage charters, in *Aries Tanker Corporation* v. *Total Transport Ltd.* (*The Aries*) [1977] 1 W.L.R. 185, and
in earlier cases there referred to, but there is room for argument, at
least in this House, how far what was there laid down applies to time D
charters.

As regards the contractual claims, the umpire made only provisional
findings. These were that part of the slow steaming deduction made
from the *Nanfri* hire in October was probably justified but not all; that
owners believed all the July and September deductions to be invalid; and
that owners knew that part of the deductions (presumably of that made E
in respect of the slow steaming claim) was valid. In these circumstances the issue between the parties would be whether, in order to
entitle the charterers under clause 11 to make a deduction, their claim
must be (a) previously established as valid, or (b) bona fide believed to
be valid and calculated on a reasonable basis, or whether (c) a deduction
may be made of any sum claimed whether ultimately found to be valid F
or not.

Kerr J. and the Court of Appeal were able to deal with the main issue
of repudiation independently of whatever answer should be given to the
questions regarding deductions. Kerr J. held that the owners' conduct
did not amount to repudiation of the contract, but, formally, also held
that the charterers were entitled to deduct under clause 11 and also
by way of equitable set-off claims believed to be valid and calculated on G
a reasonable basis. In other words, he held the owners' conduct not to
be repudiatory although they were substantially wrong on the deduction
issue.

The Court of Appeal unanimously held the owners' conduct to be
repudiatory but they differed on the deduction questions. All three
members held in favour of the charterers that all the deductions in dis- H
pute could be made under clause 11 as held by Kerr J. As regards
equitable set-off, Lord Denning M.R. and Goff L.J. held that such a
right existed in relation to time charters (so distinguishing *The Aries*),
Cumming-Bruce L.J. to the contrary thought that it did not. From
this analysis it appears clear that the answer to the main issue as regards
repudiation does not depend on the answers to be given on the deduction
issues. Counsel at the Bar agreed that this was so, and in view of this,

A and there being no definite findings of fact on the deduction issues
themselves, did not address arguments upon them. While therefore I
recognise the interest which the commercial community may have in
decision of them, whether as they arise under a contractual right to
deduct or under a general doctrine of equitable set-off, I must reluctantly agree to decline this task on the present occasion.

B   I come then to the issue of repudiation. It is first necessary to see
whether the owners' conduct on October 4, 1977, was a breach of contract
at all: Mr. Alexander for the owners contended that it was not. His argument was that the owners, while giving the charterers very wide powers
under clause 9 of the charterparties (" the master to be under the orders of
the charterers as regards employment, agency, or other arrangements ")
which would include in general the power to require the master to issue
C bills of lading, nevertheless always retained the right to insist that any
action required to be taken by the master, or taken by the charterers
themselves, should be in accordance with the terms and provisions
of the charterparties as a whole. This, it was said, would lead to two
results: first the owners would be within their rights in insisting that
bills of lading should be " claused " by a reference to the time charters,
D secondly that the owners would be entitled to object to (and to instruct
their masters to refuse) bills of lading which derogated from their right
of lien on cargoes, sub-freights and bill of lading freight, as expressly
conferred by clause 18.

        There can be no exception taken to a general proposition that a
charterparty, as any other contract, must be taken as a whole; the
obligations and rights created by one clause must be read in the light
E of the fact that it forms part of a complex of contractual provisions.
Some charters in fact contain in clauses corresponding to clause 9 such
words as " without prejudice to the charter " which no doubt emphasise
this point. But it may well be that a particular clause is so clearly
worded, and its purpose so clear, as to resist any suggestion that it
should be limited, or written down, on account of some supposed inconsistency with the general purpose of the contract or by some other clause
F in the contract.

        It is important in this connection to have in mind that the present
charters are time charters, the nature and purpose of which is to enable
the charterers to use the vessels during the period of the charters for
trading in whatever manner they think fit. The issue of bills of lading
in a particular form may be vital for the charterers' trade, and indeed
G in relation to this trade, which involves c.i.f. or c. & f. contracts, the
issue of freight pre-paid bills of lading is essential if the trade is to be
maintained. Furthermore, clause 9, as is usual in time charters, contains an indemnity clause against all consequences or liabilities arising
from the master signing bills of lading. This underlines the power of
the charterers, in the course of exploiting the vessel, to decide what bills
H of lading are appropriate for their trade and to instruct the masters
to issue such bills, the owners being protected by the indemnity clause.

        Then what limitations are there upon this power? It must be clear
that the owners cannot require bills of lading to be claused so as to
incorporate the terms of the time charter: such a requirement would be
contrary to the whole commercial purpose of the charterers. But the
appellants contend that at any rate the charterers have no right to
require the master to issue bills of lading which would defeat the owners'

right of lien: this under clause 18 extends to " all cargoes and sub- A
freights belonging to the time-charterers and any bill of lading freight."
A freight pre-paid bill of lading might prejudice this lien, since, if the
freight had been paid before the lien was sought to be exercised, there
would be nothing on which it could operate.

In my opinion this argument attributes too much force to the lien
clause. This clause, just as much as clause 9, must be read in the context of the whole contract, and must be related to the commercial B
situation which exists under time charters. The lien clause must be
read as giving the owners a lien upon such freights or subfreights as, in
the event, come to be payable, and which in fact are payable, under any
subcharter or bill of lading, but it cannot be read as interfering with
the time charterers' primary right to use the ship and to direct the
master as to its use. Such authority as there is in relation to time C
charters supports this view. In *The Shillito* (1897) 3 Com.Cas. 44, an
action between the master and the owners, the judgment of Barnes J.
contains this passage, at p. 49:

> " The charterer [in fact a time charterer] has a right to present any
> bills he chooses, and although there is a lien clause, it is inoperative,
> because the bills of lading contain no reference to the charterparty, D
> and there is no freight on which a lien can be exercised."

The master was held not to be negligent in signing bills showing freight
paid in advance, and the inference is that he was bound to do so. In
Turner v. *Haji Goolam Mahomed Azam* [1904] A.C. 826, the time
charter contained the words " without prejudice to this charter." In
the judgment of the Privy Council it is said, at pp. 836–837: E

> " These words introduce a difficulty. It is said that they limit the
> authority of the captain to sign bills of lading which do not preserve
> to the owners . . . their lien on all goods under condition 22. This
> construction is a possible construction, but it has long ago been rejected
> both by commercial men and by judicial decision."

It is true that these decisions bear upon the authority of the master to sign F
bills of lading rather than directly upon the powers of the time charterers,
but I think it must follow from their reasoning that to require the master
to sign freight pre-paid bills of lading is not to require him to act inconsist-
ently with the charter, that to do so is within the powers of the time
charterers and that for the owners to prevent their masters from acting on
any such requirement is a breach of the time charter—specifically a breach G
of clause 9. If the masters had in the present case, acted upon the owners'
instructions, an actual breach would, in my view, have been committed:
they did not in fact do so because the " without prejudice " agreement was
immediately made. But the owners' instructions (communicated to the
charterers) clearly constituted a threat of a breach, or an anticipatory breach
of the contract.

Was this then such a threatened, or anticipatory breach as to entitle H
the charterers to put an end to the charters? It was argued for the charterers that clause 9 of the charters amounted to a condition of the contract,
so that any breach of it automatically gave the charterers the right to put
an end to it. I do not agree with this. The clause is not drafted as a
condition, and on its face it admits of being breached in a number of ways
some of which might be far from serious and would certainly not go to
the root of the contract. I regard the clause as one, breaches of which

A   charterers at once to terminate the contract. I do not agree. It is
clearly not expressed as a condition. Nor in my opinion is it converted
into a condition, or strengthened in any way, by the third sentence of
clause 43 of the charterparty which was relied on by the respondents.
That sentence provides:

B   " Owner hereby expressly undertakes and agrees that it will at no
time use or employ the vessel in any manner inconsistent with the
terms of this charter or with the owner's obligations hereunder,
or with the legitimate orders for the employment of the vessel given
from time to time by the charterer. . . ."

The owner's instructions as to the form of bills of lading to be signed by
the master cannot be regarded as " employing " the vessel in a manner
inconsistent with the charter and the sentence appears to me to have
C   no bearing upon the construction of clause 9.

It is easy to imagine minor breaches of the charterers' orders that
would be of no consequence in the performance of the contract as a
whole. The argument for the respondents was that the second sentence
in clause 9 contained hidden within itself two obligations—first an obligation on the owners to place the master under the orders to the charterers
D   and second an obligation on the master to obey those orders. Only the
first of these was said to be a condition, on the ground that it went to
the root of the contract. So failure by the master to carry out an order
from the charterers in any respect, however trivial, would be a breach of
a condition (and therefore repudiatory) if caused by the owner's failure
to place him under the charterers' orders, but would only be a breach of
contract (giving rise to a claim for perhaps minimal damages) if caused
E   by the master's personal fault. Everything would depend on the cause
of disobedience. That seems to me to be unacceptable.

Treating the second sentence of clause 9 then as an innominate or
intermediate term, I proceed to consider whether the threatened breach
of it here was so fundamental as to amount to repudiation of the contract. The test of repudiation has been formulated in various ways by
F   different judges. I shall adopt the formulation by Buckley L.J. in *Decro-
Wall International S.A.* v. *Practitioners in Marketing Ltd.* [1971] 1
W.L.R. 361, 380c as follows:

" Will the consequences of the breach be such that it would be
unfair to the injured party to hold him to the contract and leave
him to his remedy in damages as and when a breach or breaches
G   may occur? If this would be so, then a repudiation has taken
place."

Judged by that test I have no doubt that the breach here was repudiatory.
The whole purpose of the contract from the charterers' point of view was
that they should have the use of the ship for carrying on their trade
from the Great Lakes, but if the owner's threat had been carried out it
would have been ruinous to that trade. I need not repeat the umpire's
H   finding as to the consequences in full but I attach particular importance
to his finding in paragraph 28 (iii):

" The charterers were likely to be blacklisted as grain carriers by
Continental Grain, which is one of the world's largest shippers of grain.
In consequence the charterers' reputation would be very seriously
damaged and they would probably have been unable to obtain business
for the vessels from other major shippers of grain."

Such damage to their reputation might well have been lasting and A
not limited to the duration of actual interruption of the trade. In
face of that finding, I am, with all respect to Kerr J., unable to agree
with his view that the owners were only creating a "temporary
impasse." It was said that the breach was not repudiatory because the
owners were merely reacting against the charterers' unilateral deductions
from the hire, and particularly against their revival of a stale claim for
deductions. This is really a plea in mitigation but it does not affect the B
result. If the owners' reaction involved committing a breach that went
to the root of the contract, they cannot in my opinion escape the legal
consequences by pleading that they had been provoked. I would therefore hold that the breach was repudiatory

For these reasons I would dismiss the appeal.

C

LORD RUSSELL OF KILLOWEN. My Lords, as these three cases have
progressed there fall for decision in each of them only two questions,
the same in each case. The first question is whether the owner committed a breach of contract in instructing the master to refuse to sign
bills of lading marked "freight pre-paid" and threatening to adhere to
those instructions.

It is quite clear that clause 9 prima facie confers on the time charterer D
the right to require bills of lading to be so marked. The contention of
the owner is that—at least when hire is allegedly in arrear by unjustified
deductions—the instructions to the master were justified because that
marking of bills of lading detracted from the owner's lien rights (so
labelled) under clause 18. This, and this only, was the justification
advanced by the owner for its actions. But this attempted justification E
involves a fallacy. That marking of bills of lading could not possibly
detract from the clause 18 "lien" rights.

The fact that clause 18 refers expressly to bill of lading freights
appears to me to add nothing to the lien conferred by that clause on
sub-freights belonging to the charterer, and serves only to distract the
mind from the true scope of the lien. The lien operates as an equitable F
charge upon what is due from the shipper to the charterer, and in order to
be effective requires an ability to intercept the sub-freight (by notice of
claim) before it is paid by shipper to charterer. The simple question is
whether the marking of bills of lading "freight pre-paid" interferes with
that ability to intercept. It cannot. If freight is in fact pre-paid before
issue of the bill of lading, cadit quaestio. If not, how does the marking
"freight pre-paid" interfere with such ability to intercept as may be G
available to the other? For these reasons I say that the justification
suggested by the owners for its action is fallacious.

For the owner the only answer put forward was that it would be
strange that, if the master for the owner signed a bill of lading "freight
pre-paid," the owner should demand of the shipper that freight *not* paid
should be paid to the owner. I see nothing impossible in this. The H
shipper would if necessary interplead. He could not, not having paid the
freight, assert that he *had* paid: nor could he assert an estoppel against
the owner: he would be simply faced with rival claims, not caring which
was right, and knowing only that he owed someone the sub-freight.

For those reasons I have no doubt that the owner was in its actions
guilty of a breach of contract.

I would have been prepared also to arrive at the same conclusion on a

A different ground: that is that in the particular circumstances of the trade for which these vessels were time chartered it was preponderantly essential, as concerned with c.i.f. or c. & f. contracts, that bills of lading should be marked " freight pre-paid." In such circumstances I cannot conclude that the actions and proposed actions of the owner were a sensibly justifiable intervention with the charter's clause 9 requirements as to the marking of bills of lading: in other words in the circumstances

B of the charter clause 18 must relevantly yield to clause 9 to make sense.

Having reached that conclusion upon the first question, the second question is whether the breach of contract by the owner was such as entitled the charterer to treat it as repudiation of the charter contract by the owner.

For the charterer it was contended that clause 9 involved either

C expressly or by implication a strict *condition* that the charterer's rights thereunder would not be breached by the owner, so that any breach by the owner would entitle the charterer to assert repudiation. I do not favour that approach. In recent cases it has not found favour. It was argued that if the master disobeyed an order by the charterer it would (or could) be a mere breach of warranty: it might be a minor matter.

D But if the owner countermanded an order by the charterer under clause 9 it must be breach of a condition. I am not content with this division, attractive as it was at first submission. I would be unwilling to hold that every contradiction by the owner of an order by the charterer to the master was necessarily repudiatory of the charter contract.

But the question remains whether this particular contradiction could properly be regarded as repudiatory, as it was considered by the umpire

E and all members of the Court of Appeal, though not by Kerr J.

The question is whether, objectively regarded and in all the circumstances of the case, the conduct of the owners can properly be said to strike at the root or essence of this contract. In my opinion it can. As I have said the ability to have bills of lading issued marked " freight prepaid " was essential to the time charterer's exploitation of the vessels in

F trading therewith: and this was of course known to the owners. Counsel for the owners frankly admitted in argument that the instructions to the masters would have been fatal to the charterer's trade. Indeed on the crucial date of October 5 bills of lading in respect of two of the three vessels were due to be called for that very day. The special case made the following findings in paragraph 28:

G   " The consequences for the charterers of the orders issued by the owners on October 4, 1977, were extremely serious, in that (i) Unless the charterers could ensure the issue of freight prepaid bills of lading which were not claused with any reference to a time charterparty the vessels were largely debarred from use by the charterers in the grain and steel trades, since nearly all of the shippers of grain and

H   steel would not agree to accept bills of lading if they were either non-freight prepaid or claused with a reference to a time charter. (ii) The charterers would be unable to comply with their existing obligations to sub-charterers. (iii) The charterers were likely to be blacklisted as grain carriers by Continental Grain, which is one of the world's largest shippers of grain. In consequence the charterers reputation would be very seriously damaged and they would probably have been unable to obtain business for the vessels from other major

shippers of grain. (iv) The charterers were likely to incur very A
substantial liabilities to Continental Grain if the cargoes which were
being loaded or which were about to be loaded on October 5 were
not completed and if freight prepaid unclaused bills of lading
were not issued promptly."

And in paragraph 26 it was found that the owners knew that the
charterers were likely to suffer those consequences.   B

It was contended for the owners that their breach should not be
regarded as striking at the root or essence of the contract because they
had already set on foot arbitration proceedings designed to decide the
disputed questions of deductions from hire: that such arbitration could
produce a decision within a reasonably short time: that the question
whether the owner's instructions to the masters were or were not C
breaches of contract could be raised and solved in that arbitration: and
that thereafter a considerable period of the time charters would remain to
the charterers. Accordingly, it was contended, in those circumstances it
could not be said that the action of the owners (if persisted in) would
deprive the charterers of more than some part of the benefit of their
contract, and so should not be regarded as striking at the root or essence
of the contract. I do not accept that contention. Having regard to the D
findings in the special case I cannot regard the conduct of the owners
as something which, if persisted in, would lead merely to a temporary
suspension of the charterer's benefits under the charter.

It was further contended for the owners that, insofar as they made it
plain that the instructions to the masters would be withdrawn if the
charterers paid at once to the owners the total of the unpaid hire the E
deduction of which was disputed, the breach or threatened breach, however grave, being in a sense conditional, could not be regarded as repudiation. And, it was added, since the charterers were anyway prepared to
place the disputed amount " in escrow " it was reasonable to insist on
that condition, inasmuch as if in arbitration it proved that the deductions
were justifiable there would be plenty of scope under the charter there- F
after for the charterers to recoup themselves by deduction from future
hire obligations.

I am not able to accept this contention that a breach or threatened
breach of the character now in question escapes the quality of being
repudiatory because it is indicated that it will not be pursued if the other
party to the contract gives way in a field of dispute thereunder: and I G
do not think that it matters whether the indication is phrased thus, or
whether it is indicated that the breach will be pursued unless the other
party gives way.

A further contention for the owners was that their action or threat
could not seriously and objectively be regarded as repudiation, because
the hire rates under this time charter were greater than the current going H
rates, and termination of the charters could only harm the owners.
That the owners would be so harmed is true, but that does not appear to
me to detract from the essential gravity of the breach and threatened
breach so as to reduce it to the level of a mere tactical exercise of
" muscle," or even bluff.

I am accordingly of opinion that there was here repudiation by the
owners accepted by the charterers, and would dismiss these appeals.

A must be examined on their individual demerits. Was this breach, or threatened breach, repudiatory or not? I shall not set out at any length the numerous authorities on anticipatory breach: this is one of the more perspicuous branches of the law of contract and the modern position is clear. The form of the critical question may differ slightly as it is put in relation to varying situations: ". . . an intimation of an intention to abandon and altogether to refuse performance of the contract . . ." or

B " evince an intention no longer to be bound by the contract . . ." (*Freeth* v. *Burr* (1874) L.R. 9 C.P. 208, 213, *per* Lord Coleridge C.J.)

> " I do not say that it is necessary to show that the party alleged to have repudiated should have an actual intention not to fulfil the contract. He may intend in fact to fulfil it, but may be determined to do so only in a manner substantially inconsistent with his obli-
C gations, and not in any other way." (*Ross T. Smyth & Co. Ltd.* v. *T. D. Bailey, Son & Co.* [1940] 3 All E.R. 60, 72, *per* Lord Wright).

Such as to deprive:

> " the charterers of substantially the whole benefit which it was the intention of the parties. . . that the charterers should obtain from
D the further performance of their own contractual undertakings." (*Hongkong Fir Shipping Co. Ltd.* v. *Kawasaki Kisen Kaisha Ltd.* [1962] 2 Q.B. 26, 72, *per* Diplock L.J.).
> " To constitute repudiation, the threatened breach must be such as to deprive the injured party of a substantial part of the benefit to which he is entitled under the contract. . . . Will the consequences of the breach be such that it would be unfair to the injured party to hold
E him to the contract and leave him to his remedy in damages . . . ? " (*Decro-Wall International S.A.* v. *Practitioners in Marketing Ltd.* [1971] 1 W.L.R. 361, 380, *per* Buckley L.J.).

The difference in expression between these two last formulations does not, in my opinion, reflect a divergence of principle, but arises from and is related to the particular contract under consideration: they represent,
F in other words, applications to different contracts, of the common principle that, to amount to repudiation a breach must go to the root of the contract.

My Lords, I do not think that there can be any doubt that the owners' breach or threatened breach in the present case, consisting in their announcement that their masters would refuse to issue bills of lading freight pre-paid and not " claused " so as to refer to the charters, prima
G facie went to the root of the contract as depriving the charterers of substantially the whole benefit of the contract. This is clear from the findings of the umpire to which I have already referred. It was in fact the owners' intention to put irresistible pressure upon the charterers (" to compel the charterers to pay over all sums deducted from hire by the charterers which the owners disputed, irrespective of whether such deductions should ultimately be determined to be valid or invalid "
H (Award, paragraph 27), through the action they threatened to take. If the charterers had not given way, the charters would have become useless for the purpose for which they were granted. I do not think that this was disputed by the owners—in any event it was not disputable. What was said was that the action of the owners, in the circumstances in which it was taken, should not be taken to be repudiatory. They had, on September 21, 1977, referred the whole question of deductions to arbitration: in a short time the whole issue would be cleared up one way

Lord Wilberforce   Federal Commerce v. Molena Alpha (H.L.(E.))   [1978]

or another, after which the charters would continue to be operated in   A
accordance with the arbitrators' decision. The owners' action was of an
interim character designed to have effect only until the position as to
deductions could be clarified. The owners' interest was strongly in the
direction of maintaining the charters: their move was simply a tactical
one designed to resolve a doubtful situation. The sums which they
were forcing the charterers to pay were inconsiderable. The charterers
had already offered to pay them in " escrow."   B

My Lords, with genuine respect for the judgment of Kerr J. who in
substance agreed with this argument, I find myself obliged to reject it.
Even if I were prepared to accept the assumption that arbitration proceedings set in motion on September 21, 1977, would be rapidly concluded
through an early and speedy hearing, without a case being stated and
without appeals in the courts (all of which must in fact be speculative),   C
even so the owners' action must be regarded as going to the root of the
contract. The issue of freight pre-paid bills of lading in respect of each
of the three vessels was an urgent, indeed an immediate, requirement.
Nanfri completed loading a cargo, shipped by Continental Grain for
Europe, on October 5, 1977; *Benfri*, on passage to Chicago, was to load a
cargo in Duluth for Europe; *Lorfri* had loaded one parcel of grain for
Continental Grain on October 3 in respect of which a separate bill of   D
lading was to be issued: thereafter she was scheduled to load the balance
of her capacity from Continental Grain at other Great Lakes ports.

These were pending transactions, and " the charterers were likely to
incur very substantial liabilities to Continental Grain if the cargoes which
were being loaded or which were about to be loaded on October 5 were
not completed and if freight pre-paid unclaused bills of lading were not   E
issued promptly" (award, paragraph 28). Black-listing by Continental
Grain was likely to follow. Thus the resolution of the deductions
issue by arbitration, however soon this might be achieved, would still have
left the charterers in a position where they might have lost the whole
benefit of the time charters. That a " without prejudice " agreement
was in fact entered into which averted these consequences is of course
irrelevant though the fact that it was made does underline the extent of the   F
pressure on the charterers. It is also irrelevant that the steps the charterers were being compelled, under threat of a breach of contract, to
take were not very serious for them. A threat to commit a breach, having
radical consequences, is nonetheless serious because it is disproportionate
to the intended effect. It is thirdly irrelevant that it was in the owners'
real interest to continue the charters rather than to put an end to them.   G
If a party's conduct is such as to amount to a threatened repudiatory
breach, his subjective desire to maintain the contract cannot prevent the
other party from drawing the consequences of his actions. The two cases
relied on by the appellants (*James Shaffer Ltd.* v. *Findlay Durham &*
Brodie [1953] 1 W.L.R. 106 and *Sweet & Maxwell Ltd.* v. *Universal News*
Services Ltd. [1964] 2 Q.B. 699) do not support a contrary proposition,   H
and would only be relevant here if the owners' action had been confined
to asserting their own view—possibly erroneous—as to the effect of the
contract. They went, in fact, far beyond this when they threatened a
breach of the contract with serious consequences.

For these reasons I agree with the decision of the Court of Appeal that
the charterers were entitled to determine the contracts. The appeals
must accordingly be dismissed with costs.

A   VISCOUNT DILHORNE.   My Lords, now that I have had the advantage
of reading the speech of my noble and learned friend, Lord Wilberforce,
I do not think any useful purpose would be served by my delivering the
speech I had prepared.

It is indeed unfortunate that determination of the question whether
deductions can lawfully be made by way of equitable set-off from the hire
payable under a time charter and the question whether, if deductions can
B   be made either by way of equitable set-off or by virtue of provisions in
the charterparty, the charterers are entitled to deduct (a) only amounts
which they have established their right to deduct or which they have
agreed with the owners or (b) sums to which they bona fide believe they
are entitled calculated on a reasonable basis or (c) any sum they claim
to be due to them whether or not it is must be left to another occasion.

C   Save in one minor respect I entirely agree with the reasoning and the
conclusions reached by my noble and learned friend.

The point on which I differ from him is that I think the giving by the
owners of instructions to the masters to refuse to sign bills of lading
marked " freight pre-paid " and to insist that all bills of lading should be
" claused " was an actual and not anticipatory breach of contract as it
amounted to a breach of clause 9 of the charterparty whereby it was
D   agreed that the masters should be under the orders of the charterers.

However it makes no difference whether the conduct of the owners
amounted to an actual breach, or anticipatory breach for, as my noble
and learned friend has so clearly demonstrated, their conduct was
repudiatory.

I agree that the appeals should be dismissed.

E
LORD FRASER OF TULLYBELTON.   My Lords, the only question now
remaining in this appeal is whether the charterers (respondents) validly
terminated the charterparty on October 5, 1977.   It raises two issues:
(1) whether the owners (appellants), by asserting a right to control the
form of bill of lading, had acted or threatened to act in breach of the
charterparty, a time charter on the Baltime form, and (2) if so, whether
F   their breach amounted to repudiation of the contract, entitling the
charterers to terminate it.

On the former of these issues the umpire and all the judges who have
considered it have been against the owners.   As I agree with that view,
I shall summarise my reasons briefly.   Clause 9 of the charterparty
provides in the second and third sentences as follows:

G   " The master to be under the orders of the charterers as regards
employment, agency, or other arrangements.   The charterers to
indemnify the owners against all consequences or liabilities arising
from the master, officers or agents signing bills of lading or other
documents or otherwise complying with such orders. . . ."

The latter sentence shows beyond possibility of doubt that the signing of
H   bills of lading was included among the respects in which the master was
to be under the charterers' orders.   Accordingly when the owners on
October 4, 1977, instructed the master to refuse to sign any bill of
lading indorsed " freight pre-paid " and which did not bear an indorsement referring to the conditions of the charterparty, they were in breach
of their obligation under clause 9 unless that obligation is to be read as
qualified by some other provision of the charterparty.   The argument
was that it was qualified by clause 18.   But in my opinion there is no

conflict or inconsistency between clause 9 and clause 18 and no need   A
to regard the former as being qualified by the latter. Clause 18 does
not give to the owners any right to require that the charterers shall
procure that cargoes (not belonging to the charterers) shall be carried
on terms that give the owners a lien over them or that there shall be in
existence sub-freights over which the owners can exercise their lien.
The effect of clause 18 was simply that, if and when there were cargoes
belonging to the charterers or sub-freights due to them, the owners were   B
to have a lien over them, whatever the exact meaning of a " lien " on
sub-freights may be.

That is the effect of reading the clauses according to their ordinary
meaning. It is powerfully reinforced by the consideration that, if the
instructions issued by the owners to masters on October 4 had been
carried out, the consequences for the charterers would, as found by the   C
umpire in paragraph 28 of his award, have been " extremely serious,"
and they would have been largely debarred from using the ships for the
trade for which they had hired them under these time charters. It is
therefore difficult to suppose, as a matter of commercial sense, that the
contract can have entitled the owners to give such instructions; if it did,
the owners could at any time have held a pistol to the charterers' head
and demanded that the charterparty be amended in any way that seemed   D
good to them.

Further, the main reason why the owners contended that they were
entitled to instruct the master to refuse to sign clean bills of lading was
that, if he did sign, they would lose their so-called " lien " on any sub-
freights that might be due from the shippers to the charterers. I very
much doubt whether the contention is well-founded. The bills of lading   E
are a contract between the shipper and the shipowner—see *Turner* v.
Haji Goolam Mahomed Azam [1904] A.C. 826 and they would not affect
the rights and obligations of the shipowners and charterers inter se
including such rights as the owners have under clause 18. No doubt the
shipper or his consignee, holding clean bills of lading, would be entitled
to have the cargo unloaded free from lien, but if in fact the shipper had
not paid the freight due to the charterers I do not think he could rely   F
on the clean bill of lading in defence to a claim for payment. The only
question for him would be to whom was the payment due.

We heard some argument as to whether, if the result of carrying out
the owner's instructions would have been a breach of their contract, a
breach had been actually committed or merely threatened. In the
circumstances of this case it would not make any difference, but my view   G
is that the breach was only threatened. True, the instructions were
actually given to the masters and the charterers were so informed, but
the issue of instructions was merely a preparatory step, useful in making
the threat realistic and necessary to enable it to be carried out
quickly. The instructions given by the owners to their own servants
could be cancelled at any time and the umpire found that the charterers   H
knew that if they paid the disputed deductions the instructions to the
masters would be withdrawn. That is what happened; the threat to the
charterers was enough and it did not have to be put into action.

The second issue is whether the threat, if it had been carried out,
would have been repudiatory. It was argued that the second sentence in
clause 9 under which the master was to be under the orders of the
charterer contained a " condition," the breach of which entitled the

A charterers at once to terminate the contract. I do not agree. It is clearly not expressed as a condition. Nor in my opinion is it converted into a condition, or strengthened in any way, by the third sentence of clause 43 of the charterparty which was relied on by the respondents. That sentence provides:

> B " Owner hereby expressly undertakes and agrees that it will at no time use or employ the vessel in any manner inconsistent with the terms of this charter or with the owner's obligations hereunder, or with the legitimate orders for the employment of the vessel given from time to time by the charterer. . . ."

The owner's instructions as to the form of bills of lading to be signed by the master cannot be regarded as " employing " the vessel in a manner inconsistent with the charter and the sentence appears to me to have

C no bearing upon the construction of clause 9.

It is easy to imagine minor breaches of the charterers' orders that would be of no consequence in the performance of the contract as a whole. The argument for the respondents was that the second sentence in clause 9 contained hidden within itself two obligations—first an obligation on the owners to place the master under the orders to the charterers

D and second an obligation on the master to obey those orders. Only the first of these was said to be a condition, on the ground that it went to the root of the contract. So failure by the master to carry out an order from the charterers in any respect, however trivial, would be a breach of a condition (and therefore repudiatory) if caused by the owner's failure to place him under the charterers' orders, but would only be a breach of contract (giving rise to a claim for perhaps minimal damages) if caused

E by the master's personal fault. Everything would depend on the cause of disobedience. That seems to me to be unacceptable.

Treating the second sentence of clause 9 then as an innominate or intermediate term, I proceed to consider whether the threatened breach of it here was so fundamental as to amount to repudiation of the contract. The test of repudiation has been formulated in various ways by

F different judges. I shall adopt the formulation by Buckley L.J. in *Decro-Wall International S.A.* v. *Practitioners in Marketing Ltd.* [1971] 1 W.L.R. 361, 380c as follows:

> "Will the consequences of the breach be such that it would be unfair to the injured party to hold him to the contract and leave him to his remedy in damages as and when a breach or breaches
> G may occur? If this would be so, then a repudiation has taken place."

Judged by that test I have no doubt that the breach here was repudiatory. The whole purpose of the contract from the charterers' point of view was that they should have the use of the ship for carrying on their trade from the Great Lakes, but if the owner's threat had been carried out it would have been ruinous to that trade. I need not repeat the umpire's

H finding as to the consequences in full but I attach particular importance to his finding in paragraph 28 (iii):

> " The charterers were likely to be blacklisted as grain carriers by Continental Grain, which is one of the world's largest shippers of grain. In consequence the charterers' reputation would be very seriously damaged and they would probably have been unable to obtain business for the vessels from other major shippers of grain."

Such damage to their reputation might well have been lasting and A
not limited to the duration of actual interruption of the trade. In
face of that finding, I am, with all respect to Kerr J., unable to agree
with his view that the owners were only creating a " temporary
impasse." It was said that the breach was not repudiatory because the
owners were merely reacting against the charterers' unilateral deductions
from the hire, and particularly against their revival of a stale claim for
deductions. This is really a plea in mitigation but it does not affect the B
result. If the owners' reaction involved committing a breach that went
to the root of the contract, they cannot in my opinion escape the legal
consequences by pleading that they had been provoked. I would therefore hold that the breach was repudiatory

For these reasons I would dismiss the appeal.

C

LORD RUSSELL OF KILLOWEN. My Lords, as these three cases have
progressed there fall for decision in each of them only two questions,
the same in each case. The first question is whether the owner committed a breach of contract in instructing the master to refuse to sign
bills of lading marked " freight pre-paid " and threatening to adhere to
those instructions.

It is quite clear that clause 9 prima facie confers on the time charterer D
the right to require bills of lading to be so marked. The contention of
the owner is that—at least when hire is allegedly in arrear by unjustified
deductions—the instructions to the master were justified because that
marking of bills of lading detracted from the owner's lien rights (so
labelled) under clause 18. This, and this only, was the justification
advanced by the owner for its actions. But this attempted justification E
involves a fallacy. That marking of bills of lading could not possibly
detract from the clause 18 " lien " rights.

The fact that clause 18 refers expressly to bill of lading freights
appears to me to add nothing to the lien conferred by that clause on
sub-freights belonging to the charterer, and serves only to distract the
mind from the true scope of the lien. The lien operates as an equitable F
charge upon what is due from the shipper to the charterer, and in order to
be effective requires an ability to intercept the sub-freight (by notice of
claim) before it is paid by shipper to charterer. The simple question is
whether the marking of bills of lading " freight pre-paid " interferes with
that ability to intercept. It cannot. If freight is in fact pre-paid before
issue of the bill of lading, cadit quaestio. If not, how does the marking
" freight pre-paid " interfere with such ability to intercept as may be G
available to the other? For these reasons I say that the justification
suggested by the owners for its action is fallacious.

For the owner the only answer put forward was that it would be
strange that, if the master for the owner signed a bill of lading " freight
pre-paid," the owner should demand of the shipper that freight *not* paid
should be paid to the owner. I see nothing impossible in this. The H
shipper would if necessary interplead. He could not, not having paid the
freight, assert that he *had* paid: nor could he assert an estoppel against
the owner: he would be simply faced with rival claims, not caring which
was right, and knowing only that he owed someone the sub-freight.

For those reasons I have no doubt that the owner was in its actions
guilty of a breach of contract.

I would have been prepared also to arrive at the same conclusion on a

A different ground: that is that in the particular circumstances of the trade for which these vessels were time chartered it was preponderantly essential, as concerned with c.i.f. or c. & f. contracts, that bills of lading should be marked " freight pre-paid." In such circumstances I cannot conclude that the actions and proposed actions of the owner were a sensibly justifiable intervention with the charter's clause 9 requirements as to the marking of bills of lading: in other words in the circumstances of the charter clause 18 must relevantly yield to clause 9 to make sense.

B

Having reached that conclusion upon the first question, the second question is whether the breach of contract by the owner was such as entitled the charterer to treat it as repudiation of the charter contract by the owner.

For the charterer it was contended that clause 9 involved either C expressly or by implication a strict *condition* that the charterer's rights thereunder would not be breached by the owner, so that any breach by the owner would entitle the charterer to assert repudiation. I do not favour that approach. In recent cases it has not found favour. It was argued that if the master disobeyed an order by the charterer it would (or could) be a mere breach of warranty: it might be a minor matter. D But if the owner countermanded an order by the charterer under clause 9 it must be breach of a condition. I am not content with this division, attractive as it was at first submission. I would be unwilling to hold that every contradiction by the owner of an order by the charterer to the master was necessarily repudiatory of the charter contract.

But the question remains whether this particular contradiction could properly be regarded as repudiatory, as it was considered by the umpire E and all members of the Court of Appeal, though not by Kerr J.

The question is whether, objectively regarded and in all the circumstances of the case, the conduct of the owners can properly be said to strike at the root or essence of this contract. In my opinion it can. As I have said the ability to have bills of lading issued marked " freight prepaid " was essential to the time charterer's exploitation of the vessels in F trading therewith: and this was of course known to the owners. Counsel for the owners frankly admitted in argument that the instructions to the masters would have been fatal to the charterer's trade. Indeed on the crucial date of October 5 bills of lading in respect of two of the three vessels were due to be called for that very day. The special case made the following findings in paragraph 28:

G   " The consequences for the charterers of the orders issued by the owners on October 4, 1977, were extremely serious, in that (i) Unless the charterers could ensure the issue of freight prepaid bills of lading which were not claused with any reference to a time charterparty the vessels were largely debarred from use by the charterers in the grain and steel trades, since nearly all of the shippers of grain and steel would not agree to accept bills of lading if they were either H   non-freight prepaid or claused with a reference to a time charter. (ii) The charterers would be unable to comply with their existing obligations to sub-charterers. (iii) The charterers were likely to be blacklisted as grain carriers by Continental Grain, which is one of the world's largest shippers of grain. In consequence the charterers reputation would be very seriously damaged and they would probably have been unable to obtain business for the vessels from other major

shippers of grain. (iv) The charterers were likely to incur very A
substantial liabilities to Continental Grain if the cargoes which were
being loaded or which were about to be loaded on October 5 were
not completed and if freight prepaid unclaused bills of lading
were not issued promptly."

And in paragraph 26 it was found that the owners knew that the
charterers were likely to suffer those consequences.   B

It was contended for the owners that their breach should not be
regarded as striking at the root or essence of the contract because they
had already set on foot arbitration proceedings designed to decide the
disputed questions of deductions from hire: that such arbitration could
produce a decision within a reasonably short time: that the question
whether the owner's instructions to the masters were or were not C
breaches of contract could be raised and solved in that arbitration: and
that thereafter a considerable period of the time charters would remain to
the charterers. Accordingly, it was contended, in those circumstances it
could not be said that the action of the owners (if persisted in) would
deprive the charterers of more than some part of the benefit of their
contract, and so should not be regarded as striking at the root or essence
of the contract. I do not accept that contention. Having regard to the D
findings in the special case I cannot regard the conduct of the owners
as something which, if persisted in, would lead merely to a temporary
suspension of the charterer's benefits under the charter.

It was further contended for the owners that, insofar as they made it
plain that the instructions to the masters would be withdrawn if the
charterers paid at once to the owners the total of the unpaid hire the E
deduction of which was disputed, the breach or threatened breach, however grave, being in a sense conditional, could not be regarded as repudiation. And, it was added, since the charterers were anyway prepared to
place the disputed amount " in escrow " it was reasonable to insist on
that condition, inasmuch as if in arbitration it proved that the deductions
were justifiable there would be plenty of scope under the charter thereafter for the charterers to recoup themselves by deduction from future F
hire obligations.

I am not able to accept this contention that a breach or threatened
breach of the character now in question escapes the quality of being
repudiatory because it is indicated that it will not be pursued if the other
party to the contract gives way in a field of dispute thereunder: and I
do not think that it matters whether the indication is phrased thus, or G
whether it is indicated that the breach will be pursued unless the other
party gives way.

A further contention for the owners was that their action or threat
could not seriously and objectively be regarded as repudiation, because
the hire rates under this time charter were greater than the current going
rates, and termination of the charters could only harm the owners. H
That the owners would be so harmed is true, but that does not appear to
me to detract from the essential gravity of the breach and threatened
breach so as to reduce it to the level of a mere tactical exercise of
" muscle," or even bluff.

I am accordingly of opinion that there was here repudiation by the
owners accepted by the charterers, and would dismiss these appeals.

3 W.L.R. **Federal Commerce v. Molena Alpha (H.L.(E.))**

A   LORD SCARMAN. My Lords, I have had the advantage of reading in draft the speech delivered by my noble and learned friend, Lord Wilberforce. I agree with it: and for the reasons which he gives I would dismiss the appeal with costs.

Appeal dismissed.

B   Solicitors: *Richards, Butler & Co.; Ince & Co.*

F. C.

C

D

END OF VOLUME 3

E

F

G

H